# THE ENCYCLOPEDIA OF
# AMERICAN
# COMICS

Edited by Ron Goulart

A Promised Land Production

Facts On File
*New York • Oxford*

**THE ENCYCLOPEDIA OF AMERICAN COMICS**

Facts On File, Inc.        Facts On File Limited
460 Park Avenue South      Collins Street
New York NY 10016          Oxford OX4 1XJ
USA                        United Kingdom

**Library of Congress Cataloging-in-Publication Data**

Encyclopedia of American Comics / edited by Ron Goulart.
    p.  cm.
  ISBN 0-8160-1852-9  (hardcover)
  ISBN 0-8160-2582-7  (paperback)
    1. Comic books, strips, etc.—United States—Dictionaries.
  2. Cartoon characters—United States—Dictionaries.  3. Cartoonists—
  United States—Biography.  I. Goulart, Ron, 1933-
741.5' 0973—dc20                          90-2974

A British CIP catalogue record for this book is available from the
British Library.

Facts On File books are available at special discounts when purchased in
bulk quantities for businesses, associations, institutions or sales
promotions. Please call our Special Sales Department in New York at
212/683-2244 (dial 800/322-8755 except in NY, AK or HI) or in Oxford at
865/728399.

Jacket design by Catherine Hyman
Composition by Facts On File, Inc.
Manufactured by the Maple-Vail Book Manufacturing Group
Printed in the United States of America

10 9 8 7 6 5 4 3 2 1

This book is printed on acid-free paper.

# CONTENTS

# PREFACE

I had hoped to use this prefatory note chiefly to convey a wealth of interesting material about myself, about how I became habituated to the funnies back in the 1930s and gradually developed into a respected savant in the field of panelology. All of it illuminated with well chosen, pithy anecdotes. My publishers, however, suggested that a little something about the book itself might be more appropriate.

Let me explain, therefore, that *The Encyclopedia of American Comics* is the first of its kind. There have been histories of comics before, even an encyclopedia or two. But ours is the first encyclopedia devoted exclusively to the native product, solely to American strips and comic books.

It is the purpose of this book to provide you with a great deal of information about the comics of the United States in a relatively compact form. We cover the entire 20th century to date as well as the tail end of the 19th. There are entries on every major American comic strip and comic strip artist, plus a good many minor ones. We've also included entries on the important comic book heroes and heroines, artists and writers. Each entry has been made as accurate as possible, even when that has meant contradicting the long-held, though wrong, beliefs of some previous comics historians.

This encyclopedia has been over two years in the making—or over 50, if you count from the day back around 1936 when I first discovered comics. About half the entries were written by me and the rest by people who share my enthusiasm for comics and my respect for clarity. We hope that you find it was worth waiting for and that you enjoy reading it and using it as much as we enjoyed putting it together.

—**Ron Goulart**

# ACKNOWLEDGMENTS

In addition to the contributors and the assorted artists and writers who were interviewed for this project, we'd like to thank the following for help of various kinds: Mike Barson, Jim Ivey, Doug Kendig, Paul Leiffer, Richard Marschall, Will Murray, Don Thompson, and Brian Walker.

While many of the entries are based on primary source research, we also consulted the standard works in the field, including Bill Blackbeard and Martin Williams's *The Smithsonian Collection of Newspaper Comics*, Maurice Horn's *The World Encyclopedia of Comics*, Robert M. Overstreet's *Official Overstreet Comic Book Price Guide*, Martin Sheridan's *Comics and Their Creators*, and Coulton Waugh's *The Comics*.

The Packagers would like to thank all those who helped us through the labyrinths of copyright information. Among them, we especially thank Belynda Feaster, Jim Cavett, Mark Johnson, Dennis Kitchen, Andrea Neuman, and Kay Shadley. The Packagers have endeavored to acknowledge all copyright holders of the images reproduced in this book. However, in view of the complexity of securing copyright information, should any image not be correctly attributed, then the Packagers shall undertake to make any appropriate changes in future editions of this book.

# HOW TO USE THIS BOOK

The articles in this book are arranged alphabetically and fall into two basic categories: biographical entries on the people of the comics field (artists, creators, packagers, writers) and entries on the comic strips or books themselves. The exceptions to this rule are the article on the Reuben Award and the essay on Romance Comics. In many instances, there are articles on both the artist and his or her comic strips or books; when a specific artist or book or strip is not covered in an individual entry, you will find a cross-reference with the word "see" referring you to the article in which the subject is covered. This encyclopedia is also fully indexed; please see page 401 and following.

Throughout this book, the subjects of the biographical entries are listed under the names by which they are best known. When this name differs from the full name, the full name is given in the body of the article.

Each entry is signed with the contributor's initials, a key to which can be found on page viii.

**BIOGRAPHICAL DATA**   When exact beginning and end dates for a comic strip or book are known, they are given as such in the body of the entry. In many cases, it is difficult, if not impossible, to assign precise day and month dates; in these cases, only the year is given.

Every effort has been made to supply birth and death dates for the biographical entries; when a date is unavailable, the omission is indicated by a question mark.

**TECHNICAL TERMS**   Although many of the terms used in this volume can be understood in context, a brief glossary follows.

*Anti-Comics Crusade*: While certainly comic books had been criticized from the beginning, the 1950s were marked by mass media attacks, which charged that the comics' influence was detrimental to American youth. In 1954, this trend was capped with the publication of Dr. Fredric Wertham's *Seduction of the Innocent* (see the article on Dr. Wertham for more), a Senate hearing on the comics and their influence, and the establishment of the comics industry's own regulatory group, the Comics Magazine Association of America, and its own Comics Code. The effect of the crusade was to end the comic book boom.

*Inker*: The secondary artist  who renders the penciller's sketch in ink in a comic strip or book (see *penciller* below).

*Packager*: An inventor of concepts for comic strips and books who, having engaged the services of a writer and an artist, sells the strip or book to a syndicate or a publisher.

*Penciller*: The primary artist of a comic strip or book who does the layout and the drawing. Depending on the penciller's style, these renderings can be either sketchy or detailed. The inker then renders the sketch in ink. This division of labor was invented to speed the production of comic strips and books; a letterer often did all the lettering. While in the modern comic the various hands are credited, in decades past usually only the penciller's name was credited.

*Splash panel*: The first panel of a comic book story, larger (sometimes a full page) than the other panels; it acts as a "hook" or "teaser" for the reader. Joe Shuster started the splash panel in the 1930s, but Joe Simon and Jack Kirby were its champions. The splash panel is now a standard  component of the comic book.

*Syndicate*: A distribution system in which newspaper features (including comic strips) owned by one newspaper are sold to and printed in other newspapers across the country.

*Topper*: In the mid 1920s, syndicates began to offer an extra comic feature with the regular feature being distributed. Run above the regular strip, it was called a "top strip" or a "topper."

# CONTRIBUTORS

**K.B.** Ken Barker has written for the now-defunct *Strip Scene* and for comics fandom for years. His speciality is newspaper comics, from the 1890s to the end of World War I.

**J.B.** John Benson, an expert on romance comics, was the editor and publisher of two comics fanzines, *Squa Tront* (devoted exclusively to the EC comics line) and *Panels* (a general magazine). He has edited and contributed introductions to many of the EC reprints. He also staged, in 1966, one of the first comics conventions.

**W.D.** William Dunn is a national correspondent for *USA Today* and the Gannett News Service. His articles have appeared in numerous publications, including *Cartoonist Profiles*, *Us*, and *Writer's Digest*. A cartoon buff and collector, he is the son of the late Bob Dunn, the cartoonist of *They'll Do It Every Time* and *Little Iodine*.

**R.G.** Ron Goulart, both the general editor and a contributor to this volume, has written over 140 books. Recognized as one of the United States' leading historians of the comics, he has written *The Great Comic Book Artists* and the *Great History of Comic Books*, as well as many articles on comics, which have appeared in *The Comics Buyer's Guide*, *Comics Feature*, *Comics Collector*, and *Amazing Heroes*, among others. He was the winner of an Ink Pot award in 1989, given for distinguished contributions to the comics field.

**S.L.H.** Stephen L. Harris is a former newspaper and television news editor, who is currently the editor of *GE Monogram*. A contributor to *Cartoonist Profiles*, *American Spectator*, and *Yankee*, he is the grandnephew of cartoonist Raeburn Van Buren.

**R.C.H.** Robert C. Harvey holds a Ph.D. in English literature and is a former cartoonist. He is a contributor to *The Comics Journal*, where he has a regular column of reprints; his articles have also appeared in *Rocket's Blast/Comic Collector* and the *Menomonee Falls Gazette*. He is at work on an authorized biography of Milton Caniff.

**M.J.** Mark Johnson is a frequent contributor to *Nemo*, *Strip-Scene*, and *The Funnies Paper*. His articles on early strips have been on a range of subjects, from children's fantasy strips like *Bobby Make-Believe* to the rough and ready burlesques like *Barney Google*. He and his brother Cole have been active in promoting the fame of *Hairbreadth Harry* and its creator, C.W. Kahles.

**G.J.** Gerard Jones is coauthor of *The Beaver Papers* and *The Comic Book Heroes* and author of *The Scare*. His comic books include *The Trouble with Girls*, *Tommy and the Monsters*, and *El Diablo*.

**J.L.** Jim Lowe, former editor and publisher of *The Videophile*, is now the staff director of the Florida House of Representatives Bill Drafting Service. He also writes and publishes a fanzine, *Vot Der Dumboozle*, which is devoted exclusively to the life, work, and times of H.H. Knerr.

**J.M.** Jay Maeder is the editor of *The New York Daily News Magazine*. He is the author of *Dick Tracy: The Official Biography*.

**J.R.** John Reiner was the assistant to the late Bill Hoest, and has taken over production of *The Lockhorns*, *Agatha Crumm*, and *What A Guy!* daily and Sunday comics for King Features Syndicate, as well as *Bumper Snickers* for *The National Enquirer* and *Howard Huge* and *Laugh Parade* for *Parade* Magazine.

**B.S.** Bhob Stewart has contributed to comic books as a scripter, inker and colorist; to magazines, among them *Heavy Metal*, *Nemo* and *The Comics Journal*; and to books, *Bare Bones* and *Conversations on Terror with Stephen King*. He has written on EC for both *The Complete EC Library* and *Focus on Wallace Wood*, and his cartoons were reprinted in *Best of the Realist*.

**M.T.** Maggie Thompson is coeditor of *The Comics Buyer's Guide*, the weekly trade journal of the comics industry. She is also coauthor, with Don Thompson, of *The Official Price Guide to Science Fiction and Fantasy Collectibles*. She has been actively involved with comics fandom for over 30 years.

**J.V.** Jim Vadeboncoeur Jr. is the senior editor of *Who's Who in American Comics*. A contributor to Eclipse Comics' "Seduction of the Innocent," he has written on Al Williamson, Alex Toth, and Doug Wildey.

**D.W.** Dennis Wepman is the author of 10 books, nine of them biographies. He is the associate editor of *Manhattan Arts*, a contributor to *Contemporary Graphic Artists*, and is a regular art reviewer for *SunStorm*.

# A

**ABE MARTIN** One of the earliest and most successful examples of what was once a fairly popular type of comic page feature, *Abe Martin* started in 1904 and was first syndicated in 1910. Written and drawn by Kin Hubbard, it consisted of a small, one-column cartoon with a few lines of copy beneath it. Abe Martin was a bewhiskered old gent, a small-town loafer and philosopher who offered his opinions on life, love and politics each day.

Frank McKinney Hubbard first went to work for the *Indianapolis News* in 1891. "I took a place as a caricaturist," he said, "developing a little natural ability along that line after accepting the place." He first drew *Abe Martin* for the *News*, where it began on December 17, 1904. Readers took at once to the deadpan, cracker-barrel humor: "When Lem Moon was acquited fer the murder of his wife and Judge Pusey asked him if he had anything t' say, he replied: 'I never would have shot her if I'd knowed I'd have t' go thru so much red tape.'"—"Some fellers git credit fer bein' conservative when ther only stupid."—"It seems like th' less a statesman amounts to th' more he loves th' flag."—"Women are jest like elephants t' me. I like t' look at 'em, but I wouldn't want one." Hubbard usually ran two unrelated remarks under each drawing of Abe Martin. The old philosopher could loaf just about anyplace, by the way—against a lamp post, on a porch, even sitting on a barbed wire fence.

Hubbard had him residing in Brown County, Indiana—"a wild, hilly county without telegraph or railroad"—and created a large cast of locals for him to quote, among them Lafe Bud, Uncle Ez Pash, Bentley Gap, Judge Pusey, Ludlow Mapes, Tell Binkley, Miss Tawney Apple, Miss Germ Williams, Pony Mopps, and Miss Fawn Lippincut.

George Mathew Adams began syndicating *Abe Martin* in 1910 and John F. Dille took over about six years later. At the height of its popularity the feature was appearing in nearly 200 newspapers across the country and in Canada, and there were annual book compilations, usually issued under the title *Abe Martin's Sayings*. When anyone accused Hubbard of being an artist and an author, he'd respond, "I'm neither...If anyone asks what I do, just say I'm a newspaper writer." He continued with the panel until his death in 1930 at the age of 62. *Abe Martin* kept running for years thereafter, relying on reprints.

The format was used for dozens of other features, ranging from *Aunt Het* to *Flapper Fanny*. *Ching Chow*, who still dispenses his fortune cookie philosophy six times a week, is just about the only survivor of the genre. **R.G.**

**ABIE THE AGENT** The first nationally syndicated comic strip to star a Jewish character, Harry Hershfield's *Abie the Agent* began in 1914. Distributed initially by Hearst's International News Service, it started as a daily and dealt with the middle-class life of Abe Kabibble, a small, pudgy, mustachioed businessman, and his circle of friends, rivals, and associates.

Abe wasn't a theatrical agent, but rather an agent—that is, a dealer—for an automobile company. The strip, which later added a Sunday page, lasted until 1940, with a gap of four years in the early 1930s during which time Hershfield and Hearst were on the outs because of contract problems. Like Milt Gross' *Nize Baby*, it was always considered a big-town strip: one that, because of its relative sophistication, its Jewish cast of characters and its use of Yiddish expressions, didn't play well in the heartland.

A roughcut fellow, Abe was something of a grouch—he was continually calling somebody or other "A dirty crook!"—and a champion complainer. He loved to argue and even when he agreed with someone he did it at the top of his voice. Although Hershfield eventually became known as one of the great joke tellers of his day, *Abie* didn't usually go in for jokes with socko punchlines. Hershfield was more interested in kidding the ambitions and pretensions of his upwardly mobile characters. In one early daily Abe is bragging about his family. His sister Gussie "owns a big millinereh hat store on Halstead Street." His brother Irving "is doing elegant. He owns two swell butcher shops." His other brother, however, is still working for a salary—"He's the black sheep of the family!" Reba was a pretty, plump young woman who was engaged to Abe; she devoted considerable time to improving his manners, his outlook and his character and eventually she married him.

Not a great draftsman, Hershfield drew in a simple, direct cartoon style, but he was fond of using cross-hatching and other pen techniques to embellish his work. He was also an expert on the props and paraphernalia of his characters, devoting considerable attention to the furnishings of their homes, apartments and offices, as well as the clothes of his men and the fashionable attire of his women.

In an essay reprinted in *Nemo* John J. Appel said of *Abie the Agent*, "The strip kidded rather than satirized aspects of American Jewish middle class life: Abie's all-Jewish circle of friends, Cohen, Mandelbaum, Jake and Meyer; his eagerness to purchase at discount; his tortuous attempts to make a better living and be a responsible family man. Above all, his accent, syntax and vocabulary placed him squarely into an American-Jewish first generation immigrant, bourgeois, urban and commercial mileau."                                    **R.G.**

**ACE DRUMMOND**  Yet another aviation strip about a daring young pilot of the Charles Lindbergh sort, this Sunday page was introduced by King Features early in 1935. Though it was credited to two men who'd actually been air aces during World War I, *Ace Drummond* proved to be far from successful. Clayton Knight, who'd flown with the Lafayette Escadrille and later become a top aviation illustrator, was the original artist. Eddie Rickenbacker, who'd flown with the 94th Aero Squadron, downed 26 German planes and been awarded the Congressional Medal of Honor, the Legion of Honor and the Croix de Guerre, was listed as writer. A business executive at the time, it's unlikely that Rickenbacker did more than approve the continuities.

Ace was a lanky young fellow who wore the accepted outfit of riding breeches, boots and windbreaker; sometimes he added a goggled pilot's helmet. Accompanied by a gang of stalwart sidekicks, including his copilot Dinny Doyle and a teenager named Bill, Ace flew to various trouble spots around the world. He won an air race to China, undertook a rescue mission to Alaska, and thwarted a South American gang of air pirates. He was especially good when it came to routing what the copy liked to call "a desperate band of unprincipled ruffians."

Although Knight was an expert at drawing airplanes, his people tended to be bland and uninteresting. His pages were unimaginatively laid out, looking usually like a series of similar illustrations strung together. Late in 1937 he ceased drawing *Ace*, but kept on with its accompanying topper, a non-fiction effort titled *Hall of Fame of the Air*. Royal King Cole, who drew in a straightforward, cartoony style, took over depicting Ace's airborne adventures, but the closest Cole had come to aircraft previously was his drawing of Santa Claus' sled

in King's annual Christmas strips. *Ace Drummond* was last listed among the syndicate's features in 1940.
                                    **R.G.**

**ADAM AMES**  This daily strip began in 1959, drawn by Lou Fine in a tight, slick style that was closer to his advertising strips than to his work on such early comic book superheroes as the Ray and the Black Condor. *Adam Ames* was in the soap opera category and written, anonymously, by Elliott Caplin, who also scripted *Abbie an' Slats*, *The Heart of Juliet Jones* and *Big Ben Bolt*. He had considerable experience in turning out continuities that could compete with the best that *Mary Worth* had to offer.

Ames, the handsome, graying protagonist, had an unusual occupation for a comic strip hero. He was an artist, a painter who was reluctant to tackle any subject that didn't interest him aesthetically. Readers first met the widowed Ames as he and his three children—teenage son, preteen daughter, small son—arrived in a commuter town and took up residence in a large, old Victorian house. They hire a no-nonsense housekeeper named Bessie and proceed to get into one emotional mess after another.

If Adam Ames got a commission to do a wealthy and beautiful matron's portrait, you could be sure she'd be throwing herself at him before the paint was dry. If his son met an older woman—someone, say, in her late twenties—he'd soon be lured into a potentially dangerous relationship. Like all towns in soap opera country, the one where the Ames family lived seethed, and untold trouble was always ready to erupt.

Lou Fine did an excellent, though slightly cold, job of illuminating all this angst. Despite that, the strip expired in the early 1960s.                                    **R.G.**

**ADAMS, NEAL** (1941–  )  Although he has worked on newspaper strips and in advertising, Adams' greatest impact as an artist has been in comic books. After drawing the *Ben Casey* strip from 1962 to 1966, he moved into comic books. His work on such notable heroes as Batman, Deadman, X-Men, the Avengers, and the team of Green Lantern and Green Arrow brought him considerable attention—and awards—and he was an important influence on many of the younger artists who followed him.

Adams has said that he was influenced not only by comic book artists like Joe Kubert and Russ Heath, but also by such illustrators and commercial artists as Bob Peak, Bernie Fuchs, and Austin Briggs. Adams, who studied at the School of Industrial Arts in New York, went to work for the Johnstone & Cushing art service when he was 19 and turned out advertising comic books and strips. At 21 he got the job of doing the *Ben Casey* newspaper strip, which was based on the then popular nighttime television soap opera. After that he assisted and/or ghosted on such strips as Lou Fine's *Peter Scratch*, John Prentice's *Rip Kirby* and Stan Drake's *Juliet Jones.*

When Adams moved into comic books in 1967, he brought the slick illustrational style he had developed on strips and advertising with him, giving a sophisticated gloss to the work. While his drawing showed traces of the influence of Fine and, especially, Drake, Adams' layouts were entirely his own. "His panels sliced up pages in unexpected ways, his long and medium shots favored unusual angles," notes *The Great Comic Book Artists*, "and his closeups rarely showed his heroes striking a handsome pose. The work was both slick and gritty, sort of soap opera with warts."

Adams drew *Deadman* in DC's *Strange Adventures* in 1967, doing *The Spectre* and then *Batman* next. His work on the caped crusader, which many fans felt finally rescued the character from the camp phase induced by the television show, attempted to bring back the mysterious, brooding, nocturnal feeling of earlier days. When Adams teamed with writer Denny O'Neil, they made a team of the Green Lantern and the Green Arrow. The veteran heroes became relevant, using their combined powers and knacks to combat such contemporary problems as drugs, prejudice and pollution. The work in *Green Lantern/Green Arrow* won awards, but the magazine failed to sell especially well.

Adams also did work for Marvel during this period, beefing up the look of such titles as *X-Men* and *The Avengers*. He has kept doing commercial art and in recent years became a packager and publisher of comic books. His most recent venture is his Continuity Associates, which has tried such titles as *Crazyman* and *Urth 4*.
**R.G.**

**ADVENTURES OF PATSY**  Reality had a way of catching up with the Associated Press syndicate's kid characters of the 1930s. Dickie Dare began life having fantasy encounters with such fictional characters as Robin Hood and Robinson Crusoe but then switched abruptly to realistic adventures involving spies and pirates. Patsy, who came along in March of 1935, underwent a similar transition.

Mel Graff, who was already working in the AP art bullpen, was the original artist on the strip. "She was my own idea," he once explained, "and was supposed to be an *Alice in Wonderland* strip. But it didn't jell, so I worked Patsy into a Temple movie moppet." It took him a couple of years to move Patsy from one wonderland to the other. In the opening sequence, drawn in a very stylized cartoon fashion, Patsy is carried away to the kingdom of Ods Bodkins by her new kite, where she encounters a colony of small-sized folks, ruled by King Silhouette, and an assortment of giants, witches, and, for good measure, robots. To pull Patsy and her little boy sidekick Thimble out of various scrapes, Graff introduced the Phantom Magician. Decked out in tights, boots, domino mask, and cape, the Phantom was able to fly, perform an impressive array of magic feats, and when necessary, become invisible. What Graff had introduced here, a year before Lee Falk's Phantom and three years before Superman, seems to be the first costumed superhero in the comics.

After a few months of fairy tales, Graff and his editor decided that the Depression-era public was not in the mood for magic and whimsy, and the strip returned to reality. The Phantom Magician was last seen in August of 1935. Trading in his costume for a business suit, he became Patsy's uncle and never again showed any superhero tendencies; his new name was Phil Cardigan.

For Patsy's adventures in the real, world, Graff began changing his style. Obviously influenced by his AP coworkers, Noel Sickles and Milton Caniff, he started to use heavily brushed-in shadows and intricate, realistic backgrounds. His middle- and late-thirties *Patsy* strips contain the best work he ever did.

In December of 1936 Patsy and Uncle Phil arrived in Hollywood. Graff didn't try to make her play the sort of cute, dimpled roles Shirley Temple was then undertaking in her films; instead he made Patsy an actress, embroiling her in the relatively real side of Temple's life. Graff had never been to Hollywood, and his movie capital has that larger-than-life fantasy feel of all imagined locales: There are palm trees sprouting everywhere, and almost everybody lives in a ranch-style house, while inside the studios you couldn't take a step without bumping into a huge movie camera, a bank of lights, or a flock of extras.

The Hollywood adventures were balanced among behind-the-scenes stories of old actors trying to make comebacks, headstrong directors being reconciled with their wives and families, and kidnapping and highjacking interludes with gangsters and escaped cons. Graff took Patsy on location, too, using the South Seas, the Frozen North, and other remote spots. There was also some kidding of the movie business, especially when Patsy's Goldwynesque producer, J. P. Panberg of Paragon Pictures, was on the scene. (Phil, by the way, became a successful screenwriter while Patsy was rising in the Hollywood firmament.)

Graff stayed with the strip until 1940, when he was lured away to the seemingly greener pastures of King Features to take over *Secret Agent X-9*. Replacing him was Charles Raab, a former assistant to both Milton Caniff and Alfred Andriola, who had a style that was a somewhat bolder, less graceful version of Caniff's. His

*Adventures of Patsy*, Mel Graff,
© 1935, The A.P.

first *Patsy* dailies, which look as though Caniff may have helped out on them, began appearing in June 1940. Raab sent Phil Cardigan off to Manhattan to see his play through production. He then created a new mentor for the little movie star in the person of a lanky, dark-haired, out-of-work agent named Skidd Higgins. Judging from photos, Skidd looked and dressed—right down to his flamboyant neckties—something like Raab himself.

His continuities kept up the mixture as before, alternating studio intrigues with encounters with crooks and other lowlifes. Raab stuck with the strip until the end of 1942, for part of the time getting help from just about the best ghost he could have had—Noel Sickles. Sickles once said he couldn't afford to devote much time to the ghosting job, so he worked on *Patsy* with an alarm clock close by, giving just one hour to each strip. But even this hurried work by Sickles was fairly impressive.

George Storm was the next artist on the strip. He, too, kept Patsy in Hollywood, but soon introduced a long fantasy sequence involving witches, warlocks, and talking animals. All these elements were supposed to be in the movie the little actress was making. After that Patsy, like many a full-grown star, is told she's been working too hard and must take a vacation. This device allowed Storm to get Patsy into the rural milieu he was so fond of returning to in his work and in his life. Restless, as he often was, Storm left *Patsy* after less than a year and a half and returned to comic books. Al McClean, one of several artists to work on Fawcett's Captain Marvel, next had a turn, and then came the rather bland Richard Hall. A Sunday page, titled *Patsy in Hollywood*, had been

added in the early forties and the lackluster artist remained, wisely, anonymous.

Bill Dyer, originally a sports cartoonist, took over the daily and Sunday in 1946 and produced a more cartoony version of Patsy's adventures in show business until the strip retired in the middle 1950s. All in all, Patsy had had roughly 15 years as a Hollywood child star. **R.G.**

**AFONSKY, NICHOLAS** (1892–1943) A Russian-born artist, Afonsky worked on newspaper comics from the 1920s to the 1940s. He ghosted sequences of *Minute Movies*, drew the *Little Orphan Annie* Sunday page for nearly a decade, drew the *Ming Foo* page, did *Heroes of American History*, and turned out advertising strips for a popular vitamin tonic.

Prior to coming to the United States in the early 1920s, he'd led a life rivaling that of any adventure strip hero. He served in the Russian army during World War I and, according to *The New York Times*, "was wounded five times and received eleven decorations." Besides training in the fine arts, Afonsky studied law and was practicing as a criminal attorney at the time of the Russian Revolution. "He stood six feet five and had been a member of Czar Nicholas' court," his former King Features colleague Bob Dunn has recalled. "After escaping from a prison train on his way to his execution at the hands of the Reds, Afonsky got to America." First, though, he worked as an artist for newspapers in Greece, Turkey, Armenia, and France.

Ed Wheelan hired him as an assistant in 1929. It was Afonsky who ghosted many of the *Minute Movies* adaptations of such classics as *Treasure Island, Ivanhoe,* and *Hamlet.* His work was stiffer, more sentimental and less comics-oriented than that of his boss. Before signing on with Wheelan, he had worked on more serious newspaper strips, such as *Famous Love Romances.*

Early in 1934 he was hired away by William Randolph Hearst's King Features Syndicate. Wheelan always maintained that Hearst, with whom he'd had a falling out years earlier, lured the Russian away only in order to sabotage *Minute Movies.* Once at King, Afonsky was given the *Little Annie Rooney* Sunday page. He did a competent job, working in a style that mixed illustrative techniques with broader cartoon approaches learned from Wheelan.

On March 17, 1935, a *Ming Foo* Sunday page began appearing as a companion to *Annie.* The title character was an epigrammatic Oriental who'd appeared earlier in the other strip and bore a strong resemblance to *The Gumps'* Ching Chow. Accompanied by a plucky lad named Joey, Ming Foo suffered through a series of slambang adventures around the world and never failed to come up with an apt aphorism. In the middle 1930s Afonsky also found time to draw *Heroes of American History,* a nonfiction Sunday page no doubt inspired by Hearst's belief that the funnies could be used as a teaching medium. From April to November of 1938 Afonsky drew the daily *Secret Agent X-9* as well, but his lush style didn't quite fit the hardboiled doings and he didn't stay long. Afonsky drew advertising strips, too, notably *Old Scottie,* a New England seaport saga in which a crusty old seadog, much given to expressions like "Jumpin' codfish!" touted the virtues of a tonic called Scott's Emulsion. Its chief ingredient was cod liver oil.

At the time of his death Afonsky was drawing *Little Annie Rooney* and *Ming Foo.* The latter died with him.

**R.G.**

**AHERN, GENE** (1895–1960) An artist and a writer, he was one of the leading exponents of what has been called the screwball school of cartooning, a school that boasts such alumni as Rube Goldberg, Bill Holman, Milt Gross, and Dr. Seuss. Ahern is best remembered as the creator of *Our Boarding House,* the panel that introduced Major Hoople. He also invented the surreal Nut Bros. and coined the immortal phrase "Nov shmoz ka pop?"

After attending the Chicago Art Institute for three years, Ahern joined the NEA syndicate in Cleveland during its 1914–1915 bullpen expansion. At first he was called upon to do odd-space fillers, in panels and half-size strips. These included *Fathead Fritz, Sporty Sid and his Pals,* and *Squirrel Food.* During this early period Ahern openly aped Rube Goldberg, yet despite a certain crudeness his gift for a zany, freewheeling sort of

humor was already apparent. Prolific, he would often draw multiple cartoons daily and write his own column of slang patter as well.

He soon developed a personal art style and began working on standard-sized strips. The first was *Balmy Benny,* followed by *Otto Auto.* Otto began as a man who loved his car and driving it so much that he never stopped. The strip depicted him each day in motion on the road, and even the numerous suggestions sent in by readers didn't succeed in getting him to pull over and stop. Ahern himself finally halted Otto and used him in a short-lived series about a garage.

In 1921 Ahern created *The Crazy Quilt,* a topical gag strip that introduced the Nut Bros., Ches & Wal. In September of that year he began his panel, *Our Boarding House.* The landlady's windbag husband, Major Hoople, made his entrance into the menage in January 1922 and assured the feature's success. His inventive and endless bragging soon made *Our Boarding House* a hit with readers. The Nut Bros. came to star in the topper that accompanied the Major's Sunday page. Their surreal settings, bewhiskered jokes, shameless puns ("If you chop suey what will it be?") and audacious riddles (Q. "What has horns, gold teeth and web feet?" A. "A brass band, a dental parlor and a duck.") endeared them to nonsense fans.

Ahern left NEA in March 1936, having been lured over to Hearst's King Features. There he began *Room and Board,* whose boarding house was dominated by the very Hoople-like Judge Puffle. As a top page Ahern created *The Squirrel Cage,* whose recurring character was a small, bearded hitchhiker in tam and black overcoat. His favorite, and often repeated, roadside remark was "Nov shmoz ka pop?," the meaning of which was never revealed. Both features ended with Ahern's death.

**M.J.**

**AIRBOY** A flying boy wonder, the blond Airboy was originally seen in the second issue of *Air Fighters Comics* (November 1942).

The first issue of the magazine, which had come out a full year earlier, hadn't been a hit, and the title was shelved while the publisher, Hillman Periodicals, went about recruiting a new lineup of characters. One of the people they turned to for help was editor-writer-artist Charles Biro, who believed that boy readers would naturally dote on boy heroes. Called upon to create a new star for the revamped *Air Fighters,* he came up with Airboy, just a few months after he'd come up with the teenaged Crimebuster for *Boy Comics.*

Kids were excited by flying in those early years of World War II and the adolescent air ace proved successful. Late in 1945 the comic book even changed its name to *Airboy Comics.* He stayed aloft initially until 1953.

Biro, one of the best packagers in comics, designed and drew the early covers. The cover that introduced Airboy showed a dying Japanese fighter pilot in the foreground, blood gushing from his mouth, while the young hero in his eccentric plane, which was nicknamed Birdie and could flap its wings, stood in the background. Various blocks of copy were spotted on this scene of aerial combat: "Greatest Comic Book Yet!!" "Only 10¢ Nothing Like It!!" and "Who Is AIRBOY? He's What You've Waited For...See Inside!!" Inside readers learned how a lad named Davy, raised in a monastery, inherited the birdplane invented by one of the monks and used the wing-flapping craft to avenge the old fellow's death. Donning blue riding breeches, a crimson tunic with a yellow V across its chest, and blue scarf and aviator's goggles—usually worn on his forehead and not over his eyes—Airboy took off to combat his country's foes. He and Birdie flew to all corners of the world, dogfighting with the Japanese and the Nazis. Each bright cover promised more and more: "Mad Sky Action!! The Greatest Air Show Yet!! Latest War Thrills!"

A bizarre array of other exotic flyers filled up *Air Fighters'* remaining 64 pages. These included Skywolf, the Iron Ace—who wore armor in the cockpit—and a hairless aviator named the Bald Eagle. There was also the Black Angel, a *zoftig* lady who combated Nazis, werewolves, vampires, and similar antagonists.

Because of his prior commitments to *Boy* and *Daredevil*, Biro never signed his covers and he never drew the young flyboy inside the magazine. A succession of young hotshots handled that job, including Dan Barry and Fred Kida. It was Kida who illustrated the majority of adventures involving Airboy with his most formidable opponent, the lady airfighter known as Valkyrie. Though captions sometimes described the sexy, dark-haired young woman as having a heart "as black as the devil's," she was actually one of those good-bad girls so popular in the movies of the Thirties and Forties. She and Airboy were strongly attracted to each other—the first time they kiss he exclaims, "Whew!"—and eventually, despite ideological differences, they team up in a somewhat uneasy way. Valkyrie commanded a gang of ruthless lady flyers called the Airmaidens.

Airboy was somewhat subdued after the end of World War II, yet managed to stay in business until the spring of 1953. The independent Eclipse Comics outfit revived him in 1986, giving him a magazine of his own. He did all right on the stands and several of his old wartime associates, most notably Valkyrie, returned from limbo to join him. **R.G.**

**ALEXANDER, F.O.** (1897– )  The successor to C.W. Kahles on *Hairbreadth Harry* and a noted editorial car-

toonist, Franklin Osborne Alexander began his long career after a stint with the AEF Camouflage Engineers in France during World War I. He attended Northwestern University and studied cartooning at the Chicago Academy of Fine Arts under Billy DeBeck.

His first effort as a professional penman was in 1921, running a short-lived advertising cut service, providing ready-made art to advertisers. After this, in about 1923, he launched two unsuccessful strips—*Billy Stiff* for the Art Crafts Guild and *The College Widow's Son* for the John F. Dille Company. In 1926 Alexander joined the Western Newspaper Union, a small syndicate that distributed daily comic strips, mainly to rural newspapers. For them he took over *The Featherheads*, a typical family comedy strip, from L.F. Van Zelm; he signed it with his middle name, Osborne. In 1927 he created *Finney of the Force* about a neighborhood cop.

His break came when he was selected to take over *Hairbreadth Harry* upon Kahles' death in 1931. Alexander moved from Oklahoma City to Philadelphia to take on this new assignment for the Ledger Syndicate. His first entries appeared in April, but he didn't sign the page until June. While Alexander drew in a slightly more realistic style than his predecessor, he wrote perfectly acceptable satires on all the contemporary forms of melodrama and action yarns, from Wild West to science fiction, maintaining the strip's long-standing tradition of fantasy and satire, although he occasionally added new characters.

At the end of 1931, all the Sunday Ledger pages added a second, smaller strip; Alexander's was *High Gear Homer*, about a hardselling door-to-door salesman, which debuted on November 8, 1931.

Eventually uncomfortable with the Ledger Syndicate, Alexander left in 1939 to pursue a free-lance career, mostly in advertising. In 1941 he began a 26-year stint as a political cartoonist for the *Philadelphia Evening Bulletin*. Though the paper was conservative, some of Alexander's most memorable panels expressed his early condemnation of Senator Joseph McCarthy. **M.J.**

**ALICE IN WONDERLAND**  Lewis Carroll's pragmatic underground wayfarer has had several incarnations in both funny papers and comic books. She had her own Sunday page in the middle 1930s and again, by way of the Disney organization, in the early 1950s. Alice has also been an occasional visitor to the newsstand.

United Features introduced a Sunday tabloid version of *Alice in Wonderland* in 1934. The adaption was credited to Alice Ray Scott, and the drawing was by Ed Kuekes, who had been on the art staff of the *Cleveland Plain Dealer* since 1922. Although he would win the Pulitzer Prize in 1953 for one of his political cartoons, his work on *Alice* is unimpressive. Alice is depicted as a scrawny, bland-faced child, and Wonderland itself is a dull, hurriedly drawn place. Kuekes quite evidently didn't enjoy this chore, though the page lasted long enough to get through adaptations of both *Alice in Wonderland* and *Through The Looking Glass*.

A much better looking version came along in 1942, though it lasted only a few weeks: Chad Grothkopf, a cartoonist with an affinity for fantasy, drew a short adaptation for the *Famous Fiction* Sunday page. And in 1951 the Disney version, handsomely drawn and closer to the animated cartoon than to the book, was offered in a 16-Sunday sequence.

The lackluster Kuekes pages were reprinted, a few at a time, in early issues of *Tip Top Comics* in 1936, and a whole book appeared on the stands in 1940. There have been various other Alices over the years, including a *Classics Illustrated* adaptation in 1948 and two Dell comic books based on the movie in 1951. *Mad's* Dave Berg tried some new adventures of Alice in a short-lived 1952 comic book, and a few other adaptations followed. Most recently an artist named Lela Dowling has drawn an interesting and continuing adaptation of *Alice in Wonderland* for Eclipse Comics' *The Dreamery*. **R.G**

**ALLEY OOP** The first continuity strip to feature prehistoric characters, *Alley Oop* was born in the daily papers on August 7, 1933, and began its Sunday run on September 9 of the following year. The brainchild of V.T. Hamlin, who wrote and drew it for almost four decades, it was and continues to be syndicated by Newspaper Enterprise Association. *Alley Oop* was an immediate success and, though fallen off in readership, remains a relatively healthy survivor of its era, appearing in about 300 papers.

An engaging combination of humor, fantasy, and adventure, *Alley Oop* was originally set in the imaginary prehistoric land of Moo, although it was soon to range far beyond that kingdom's borders. Its titular hero,

*Alley Oop*, V.T. Hamlin, © 1939, NEA Service, Inc. Reprinted by permission, NEA Service, Inc.

named for the French tumblers' call, is a virtuous if somewhat dimwitted caveman who fights himself into and out of adventures with unflagging energy and unswerving rectitude. Forever at odds with the Moovian monarch King Guzzle and his formidable wife Queen Umpateedle, Oop is a valiant champion of social justice. His companions include his shapely girlfriend Oola, whose romantic yearning for him seems perennially to be frustrated; his shifty sidekick Foozy, who speaks in doggerel; and, perhaps first in his affections, his faithful mount Dinny, a loving and lovable stegosaurus.

Hamlin varied his Stone Age setting with a new and ingenious plot device on April 5, 1939, when Oop and Oola were rescued from capture by the intervention of a new character—the 20th-century scientist Dr. Wonmug (his name a bilingual pun on that of physicist Albert Einstein—*ein stein* = "one mug"). The good doctor had perfected a time machine just in time to snatch the Neanderthal couple from their foes and into the present age. Since then, Oop and his pals have galloped freely through time and space, involved in adventures and misadventures among American cowboys and medieval crusaders, Roman legionaries and World War I soldiers. Oop has wielded his stone axe alongside King Arthur and Queen Cleopatra, accompanied Ulysses on his odyssey, and rocketed to the moon.

The sturdy Oop, who dresses in a fur breechclout in his own country but accommodates to the sartorial standards of other places and times, tends toward the simian, although the considerably more evolved Oola might be a modern pin-up girl. The men of the stone age all have limbs like Popeye's, reed-like upper arms and thighs tapering to hugely inflated forearms and calves. The anatomy of the local fauna, however, is invariably very accurate. For a time in the 1930s, paleontology-buff Hamlin included a topper panel, "Dinny's Family Album," with precise views and descriptions of the very real beasts romping through the primeval forests of the main strip.

The action is fluid and continuous. Drawn with great feeling for movement, it sweeps across the page at such a lively pace that the droll improbability of the story and the anachronism of the slang are accepted without question.

Written and drawn since Hamlin's retirement in 1971 by his former assistant Dave Graue, *Alley Oop* has expanded its element of fantasy and occasionally includes a little gentle satire, but the strip remains essentially true to the simple, good-natured spirit of its creator. **D.W.**

**ALPHONSE AND GASTON** See OPPER, F.

**AMAZING-MAN** When *Amazing-Man Comics* first hit the stands in the summer of 1939, it probably seemed

*Amazing Man*, Paul Gustavson, © 1941, Comics Corporation of America.

to many readers an old, established title, especially since the initial issue was numbered "5." The magazine also sported a rather unusual cover, showing Amazing-Man, chained hand and foot, taking a healthy bite out of the neck of an impressively large cobra—something you certainly weren't likely to see Superman or Batman doing. But then Aman the Amazing-Man wasn't your average superhero. A perusal of his origin story soon convinced you of that, and you found that snakebiting was but one of his unusual talents.

Bill Everett was in his early twenties, and a veteran newspaper and commercial artist, when he created the Amazing-Man character. Years later he recalled Aman as "the first *successful* one." Amazing-Man shared his comic book with an assortment of odd and eccentric heroes—including an android and a team of doll-size crimebusters.

One of the amazing things about Amazing-Man was that he was in business for over six months before he got a costume. His origin was amazing as well. It happened like this: "25 years ago, in the mountains of Tibet, the Council of Seven selected an orphan of superb physical structure, and each did his part to develop in the child all the qualities of one who would dominate the world of men by his great strength, knowledge and courage...His friend Nika, the young chemist, endowed him with the power to make himself disappear in a cloud of green vapor, and extracted from him the promise to always be good and kind and generous."

Before graduating and being sent to America to combat evil, Aman had to undergo a series of tests that make the average college midterm look like a snap. Among the hurdles he overcame were a tug-o-war with a bull elephant and a tussle with a cobra, hands manacled behind his back.

In issue #11 Aman finally got a costume, having worked mostly in a business suit before. A caption described the new togs as "his Tibetan uniform." Why anyone in the snowcapped vastness of Tibet would have gone around wearing nothing but a pair of blue shorts and a small shield, with an "A" engraved on it and strapped to his chest, is never explained.

Having given his hero a costume, Everett moved on to other things. Sam Glanzman, using the pen name of Sam Decker, took over and stayed with the feature until its demise. Just as Aman was slow to get a super-suit, he took quite a while to acquire a boy sidekick. He finally got around to that in #23 (August 1941), and his youthful companion was named nothing more dynamic than Tommy. The magazine folded a few issues later. **R.G.**

**THE AMERICAN ADVENTURE** A nonfiction strip, whose purpose was to educate as well as entertain, *Adventure* began in January 1949 and ran daily and Sunday, offering colorful continuities based on American history.

In the 1940s the funny papers had again started paying attention to real-life heroes, historical figures, and famous characters from fiction. The increased amount of true stories and adaptations of classics was probably a side effect of the early criticism of comic books, since this sort of material allowed newspaper comic sections to be touted as more uplifting and soberminded than the average violence-packed comic magazine.

Written by historian Bradford Smith, *The American Adventure* jumped around in United States history, devoting stories to John Smith, the Liberty Bell, Lafayette, Fulton's Folly, Wild Bill Hickok, and so on. Uncle Sam himself appeared as narrator, recounting the historical tales to a pair of zealously attentive teenagers named Betty and John. To enhance the educational value, each day's strip ended with a quiz question—"How many Indians were there east of the Mississippi in 1607?"—and the answer to yesterday's query: "Captain John Smith landed in Virginia on April 26, 1607, but the Jamestown site was not chosen until May 13th."

What made the strip considerably more lively than might have been suspected was the artwork of Dan Heilman. In his middle twenties at the time and a veteran of four and a half years in the Air Force, Heilman was a dedicated disciple of Milton Caniff. He worked diligently to emulate Caniff and to draw and stage his strip as his mentor would have—a practice that sometimes led to a bit of swiping and helped to explain why Robert Fulton looked a good deal like Steve Canyon and Jean Lafitte resembled Pat Ryan. Heilman left the strip in 1950, and it expired soon thereafter. He did better with his next one, *Judge Parker*.                **R.G.**

## ANDERSON, CARL (1865–1948)

Already long-established as an illustrator and cartoonist, though not particularly successful, Anderson, whose full name was Carl Thomas Anderson, created his only enduring strip, *Henry*, when he was nearly 70.

Born in Madison, Wisconsin, Anderson worked at his father's trade of cabinetmaking until he was 27, when a taste for drawing led him to spend a year in art school in Philadelphia. For the next dozen years he worked as a fashion illustrator, art editor, and strip cartoonist with papers in Pennsylvania and New York. Hired alternately by Hearst and Pulitzer in their battle for supremacy in the comics, Anderson created several broadly humorous strips during the first years of this century; between these short-lived efforts he kept afloat by teaching art in night school and contributing gag cartoons to such magazines as *Judge, Life, Puck*, and *Collier's*.

A skillful juvenile-illustrator, Anderson had a flair for expressive detail, but it was with the minimal style of the expressionless, silent Henry, who appeared in a *Saturday Evening Post* single-panel feature from 1932 to 1934, that he reached a wide audience. Rehired by Hearst (who had last fired him 19 years before) to do *Henry* as a strip in 1934, Anderson drew it daily and Sunday until illness forced his retirement in 1942.

Although Anderson never married and had little contact with children, he became well-known because of the oddly appealing little boy he created in his old age.                **D.W.**

## ANDERSON, MURPHY (1926– )

A cartoonist with a fondness for fantasy and science fiction, Anderson has drawn in both the comic book and comic strip fields. For comic books, as an artist and/or inker, he worked on such characters as Hawkman, the Green Lantern, and Adam Strange. During the late 1940s and again in the late 1950s he drew the *Buck Rogers* newspaper strip.

Anderson was born in North Carolina and briefly studied art at the state university. *Buck Rogers* had been his favorite strip in his youth—"I was simply fascinated by the concept of *Buck Rogers*, and I made a great effort to get an out-of-town newspaper every week just to get Buck." While still in his teens, he began traveling to New York and making the rounds of comic book publishers. The science-fiction-minded young artist finally found work with *Planet Comics*, drawing *Star Pirate*, a blend of space opera and comedy. "His pages had a professional look," comments *The Great Comic Book Artists*, "and he made up in enthusiasm for what he lacked in technical skill."

After serving in the Navy, which he entered in 1944, Anderson settled in Chicago. In 1947 he was hired to replace the departing Dick Calkins on the daily *Buck Rogers* strip. Despite the fact that he was now drawing the strip he'd doted on as a boy, Anderson was not overly pleased. The pay was low and he found he could make more money from the comic book stories he was doing on the side. He abandoned Buck in 1949.

Resettling in New York, Anderson devoted most of the 1950s to comic books, contributing to *Amazing Adventures*, drawing one of his own titled *Lars of Mars*, and doing a wide range of DC features—*Hawkman, Atomic Knights, Captain Comet, The Spectre* etc. With Carmine Infantino as penciller and Anderson as inker, they did *Adam Strange* for *Mystery in Space* and it proved highly successful. He was persuaded to return to the *Buck Rogers* daily in 1958, remaining with it just a year this time. In the 1960s he and Infantino worked on *Batman*, and Anderson also inked for Gil Kane on *The Atom* and *The Green Lantern*.

Gradually Anderson moved out of comics and into commercial art. For the past several years he's run Murphy Anderson Visual Concepts.                **R.G**

## AND HER NAME WAS MAUD   See OPPER, F.B.

## ANDRIOLA, ALFRED (1912–1983)

As much a promoter as he was an artist or writer, Andriola was associated with five newspaper strips in his lifetime. The most successful was *Kerry Drake*, and he also created a comic book superhero in the early 1940s.

A protégé and disciple of Milton Caniff and Noel Sickles, he was the first to utilize their sophisticated style for detective and crime material, initially on *Charlie Chan* and then on *Kerry Drake*. Small and personable, a lifelong bachelor, Andriola was an articulate champion of the comic strip medium. He also devoted his public relations skills to hiding the fact that he neither drew nor wrote much of the work that he signed his name to throughout his career.

Andriola was born in New York City and raised in New Jersey. Interested in both drawing and writing, he studied at Cooper Union and Columbia. In 1935 he wrote a fan letter to Caniff to express his admiration for the drawing and writing of *Terry and the Pirates* and included a sketch he'd made of Pat Ryan. Caniff invited the young man up to the studio he was sharing with Sickles in the Tudor City apartment complex in Manhattan. The three hit it off, with the result that Andriola

FAINTLY, LANCE HEARS BIFF AND WITH GREAT EFFORT PULLS HIS RIGHT HAND OVER HIS LEFT WRIST... WITH A MIGHTY CRASH, THE ALL-POWERFUL **CAPTAIN TRIUMPH** STANDS WHERE LANCE HAD LAIN UNCONSCIOUS!

CRASH!

*Captain Triumph*, Alfred Andriola, © 1943, Comics Magazines.

was hired to help out around the studio. Although he's sometimes referred to as having been Caniff's assistant, he did no actual drawing; instead, he took care of cleanup and handled all the secretarial chores. When Caniff moved out to New City, Andriola went along. He was still working for Caniff in 1938 when he heard that the McNaught Syndicate was looking for an artist/writer to handle their proposed Charlie Chan newspaper strip. With some help from Caniff and Sickles, he prepared two weeks of samples and won the assignment. At the age of 26 he had his first newspaper strip.

The style used on *Charlie Chan*, based on that of Sickles and Caniff, eventually became one of the better varia-

tions. Andriola had considerable assistance, initially from Charles Raab, a friend and onetime helper of Caniff's. After the Chan strip folded in 1942, Andriola put together a six-week run of *Yankee Rangers*, an overseas wartime adventure strip syndicated by King Features. In later years he was never able to recall why the strip had lived so short a time, but did feel he'd known at the start that it was to have only a limited run. Next he began negotiating with Publishers Syndicate, who wanted him to take over *Dan Dunn*.

During the months between strips Andriola also found time to invent a new comic book superhero. This was Captain Triumph, who made his debut in the January 1943 issue of *Crack Comics*. Altogether Andriola turned out six unsigned episodes. Triumph was actually two people, twin brothers named Michael and Lance Gallant. After Michael was killed in an explosion rigged by saboteurs, his spirit came back and offered the surviving twin the opportunity of becoming a superman. All Lance had to do was rub a birthmark on his wrist and his brother's spirit would enter into him and together they'd be Captain Triumph. The captain was, incidentally, one of the few blond superheroes to be found in comic books at the time.

Andriola did the venerable *Dan Dunn* strip from January to October 1943. He took sole credit for it, but the scripts were actually written by Allen Saunders. And it was Saunders who created and scripted the new detective strip, *Kerry Drake*, that replaced the Dunn opus. Again Andriola insisted on taking all credit and was fond of giving out interviews discussing how he plotted and thought up his continuities. After Saunders quit in the 1970s, William Overgard did the writing. Andriola relied heavily on assistants and ghosts for the artwork as well. Sururi Gumen served the longest stretch, starting in 1955 and sticking until the strip ended in 1983. Gumen also ghosted *It's Me, Dilly!*, a comedy strip about a blond model that ran in 1958 and 1959. Andriola signed the pen name Alfred James to *Dilly*.  **R.G.**

**THE ANGEL**  One of the few costumed heroes to sport a mustache, the Angel began operations in *Marvel Comics* #1 (November 1939) and hung on until #79 (December 1946). He also backed up Prince Namor in the first 21 issues of the *Sub-Mariner* quarterly. He was written and drawn by Paul Gustavson, who later maintained that what he had in mind was an imitation of the Saint. The average case handled by the blue-clad, red-caped Angel, however, would have given the urbane Simon Templar the heebie jeebies.

The Angel had no civilian identity, although he did now and then show up in a business suit. In his earliest adventures, he satisfied himself with combating crooks and gangsters. By the fourth issue of *Marvel Mystery* (as the magazine had started calling itself from the second issue on) hoodlums are still present but they have a monster working with them. During his second year in business things picked up, and the Angel started encountering such problems as a werewolf ("a hideous half-animal and half-human form") a green, slavering chap known as the Python ("contortionist and tool of the Gestapo") and the Armless Tiger Man who gnaws his victims to death ("the vicious flash of white you see is the flash of teeth, TEETH! TEETH!").

The 24th issue of *Marvel* introduced one of the most unsettling villains, a white-smocked fellow calling himself Dr. Hyde. His specialty, as a breathless caption explained, was a somewhat unusual one—"Some men held up banks and others kidnapped children, but the terrible loot of Dr. Hyde was eyes…HUMAN EYES!" Sure enough, readers saw the insidious doctor climbing into an unsuspected victim's bedroom and plucking his eyeballs right out of their sockets. What Hyde then does, after carrying off the eyes in the palm of his hand,

*The Angel*, Jimmy Thompson, ™ & © 1943, Marvel Entertainment Group, Inc. All rights reserved.

is offer to put them back for a flat fee of $100,000. Despite the far from antiseptic way he works, the doctor actually could restore sight. And he had quite a good racket going until the shadow of the Angel fell across his path.

The World War II years were a particularly fruitful period for the Angel. During that time he met an impressive array of zombies, monsters, living skeletons, and simple, everyday madmen. While Gustavson was doing the feature, the Angel often got involved in a case by way of protecting a pretty young woman, usually a blond, from some dire peril. Since he had an instinct for this sort of thing, the lady didn't even have to solicit his aid; he simply appeared to keep an eye on her, like "an unseen guardian."

Gustavson relinquished the feature after #21 (July 1941), and just prior to that he pitted his angelic avenger against a formidable villainess who dressed up in a black pantherskin, committed a series of vicious murders, and called herself the Cat's Paw. It took the Angel three issues to bring her finally to justice. Despite the gloom and doom that was his lot, the Angel was always ready with a quip or a snappy rejoinder. On incapacitating a voodoo drummer, for example, he remarked, "This is the end of your musical career, bud!"

A variety of artists carried on after Gustavson. George Mandel, Eddie Robbins and Jimmy Thompson were among them.

Marvel created a new Angel in 1963, as a member of its "mutant" superhero group, the X-Men. This Angel was wealthy, amorous teenager who was both cursed and blessed by having wings growing out of his back. He continued in *X-Men* until its cancellation in 1970, then popped up here and there in the Marvel Universe until joining a similar group, X-Factor, in 1985. The character was killed in 1987.                    **R.G./G.J.**

**APARTMENT 3-G**  The three girls in 3-G have been sharing an address and endless troubles for close to three decades now. Created by writer Nick Dallis and artist Alex Kotzky, the hardy soap opera strip began appearing in May of 1961 and is still going.

When he undertook *Apartment 3-G*, Dallis, a former psychiatrist, already had two successful soapers to his credit—*Rex Morgan, M.D.* and *Judge Parker*. Kotzky had long been active in comic books and commercial art, having been one of the early artists on *Blackhawk* and later on *Plastic Man*. In the middle-1950s he had collaborated with writer Allen Saunders on an advertising strip called *Duke Handy* for Philip Morris cigarettes. Kotzky had also ghosted *Steve Canyon*.

The three perennially young women who share the Manhattan apartment are Margo Magee, a brunette, Tommie Thompson, a redhead, and LuAnn Powers, a blond. Syndicate publicity described them: "Tommie, dedicated, big-hearted nurse; Margo, smart, stylish ad agency secretary; LuAnn, wealthy young widow with a weakness for underdogs." The other regular character also lives in the building, Professor Papagoras, a bearded mentor to the girls, who offers "fatherly advice and protection."

With this quartet of regulars and innumerable second leads Dallis has spun out dozens of soap opera plots over the years, involving his heroines with romance, mystery, intrigue, heartbreak and all the other staples of this sort of thing. Kotzky is a fairly slick and very thoughtful artist, and his staging of *3-G* has given it a look that possibly upgrades the content.          **R.G.**

**A. PIKER CLERK**   Quite possibly the first regular daily comic strip, *A. Piker Clerk* began in 1903 and lasted, with lapses, until June of 1904. Drawn by Clare Briggs, it originated in Hearst's *Chicago American*. Mr. Clerk was devoted to playing the horses, passing on tips about real races to his readers. It's likely that his life, short though it was, inspired Bud Fisher to come up with *A. Mutt* in 1907.

The pioneering daily was the invention of Moses Koenigsberg, then the editor of the *American* and in the following decade the founder of King Features Syndicate—the King of which was translated from the Koenig of his name. Like many an editor to come, Koenigsberg had the notion a comic strip would help his paper's circulation grow, especially one "linked to the paddock or the track." It was assumed that, while Sunday funnies were read by kids almost exclusively, the daily newspaper was the province of grownups only. Hence a daily strip would have to deal with more adult themes, such as horse betting.

Koenigsberg brought in Briggs, a longtime friend and colleague, instructing him to come up with a character "equally as irrepresible as a scalawag or boob." The concept drawing he picked showed A. Piker Clerk as "a lanky fellow with a receding chin, pompadour hair, a bushy mustache generally affected in those days, scrawny neck, eyes always popping with astonishment." A fitting description, with a few slight modifications, not only of A. Mutt but also of Andy Gump and countless other chinless, mustachioed heads of households-to-come in domestic funnies.

According to Koenigsberg, in his autobiography *King News* (1941), soon after the turf strip started running on the sports page the circulation of the *Chicago American* started to climb, eventually exceeding that of the rival *Daily News*. The strip was discontinued because a minion of Hearst's passed on the news that "I'm afraid he thinks it's vulgar." That a feature could be too vulgar for William Randolph Hearst seems unlikely, but nevertheless Clerk ended his run in June 1904.     **R.G.**

**AQUAMAN**   This long-lived but rarely very popular superhero of the DC comic book stable was created by editor-writer Mort Weisinger and artist Paul Norris for *More Fun Comics* in 1941. A better-natured variant of Timely Comics' popular Sub-Mariner, this "Sea-King" could swim at tremendous speeds and communicate telepathically with aquatic creatures; while serving as monarch of the underwater realm of Atlantis, he also battled monsters, super villains, and criminals in the sea and, occasionally, on the land (although he was hampered by the fact that he would die without hourly contact with water).

From 1946 to 1961, Aquaman and his boy sidekick Aqualad battled evil as a backup feature in *Adventure Comics;* the stories (by many hands) were rarely remarkable, until the lively, decorative art of Ramona Fradon made it an attractive series. Aquaman was also a founding member of the Justice League of America in 1959, although he was rarely a prominent figure (DC was short on heroes at the time, and Aquaman's presence often seemed perfunctory).

In 1962 he finally earned his own comic book; his Atlantean universe was developed in stories beautifully rendered by artist Nick Cardy, and be became the first superhero to get married and sire a child in the course of a series. Steve Skeates and Jim Aparo took over the writing and drawing in 1968 (under editor Dick Giordano), pushing it to new heights of emotional force and complexity with a long story about Aquaman's frenzied quest for his abducted wife. *Aquaman* failed to click with readers, however, and was cancelled in 1971.

After a long period of flopping around the DC Universe like a fish out of water, he returned in a popular series in 1989, in which his personality was revamped and his origin overhauled.          **G.J.**

**ARCHIE**   The best-known citizen of Riverdale, the ageless Archie Andrews has been a teenager for close to half a century. Created by cartoonist Bob Montana, with a possible nudge from his publisher, he began life in comic books. That was in 1941 and over the years he branched out into a radio show, a newspaper strip, an animated television show, and all sorts of other merchandising areas. Archie is undoubtedly the most successful non-superhero comic book character ever invented.

The rise of swing and the advent of jitterbugs had made teenage characters into popular entertainment stereotypes by the late 1930s, and they were frequently to be found in movies, on the radio, in the funny papers, and even in Broadway plays. Among the fictional adolescents who influenced the creation of Archie were Andy Hardy, as portrayed by Mickey Rooney in a successful series of MGM programmers, and Henry

Aldrich, who first showed up in Clifford Goldsmith's Broadway play *What a Life* in 1938 and quickly moved into radio and movies.

The MLJ company had been featuring mostly super-heroes and the usual assortment of detectives, magicians, and other heroic types in *Pep Comics, Zip Comics* etc. But in 1941 it decided to add some teenagers. A blond young man named Wilbur was the first; he made his debut in *Zip* #18 (September 1941). A bit later in 1941 the redheaded Archie showed up just about simultaneously in both *Pep* #22 and *Jackpot* #4. The wholesome, blond Betty and the somewhat dense Jughead were there from the start. The slinky, dark-haired Veronica appeared a few months later. Montana drew in an attractive, lively style, and most of the plots were pure situation comedy with considerable slapstick thrown in; this Archie version of teen life was one a great many readers apparently enjoyed. The first issue of Archie's own magazine came out in the fall of 1942 and by late 1947 he'd nudged all the serious heroes out of *Pep* and was the star of that title, too.

New Archie titles proliferated over the following years, including *Archie's Pal, Jughead; Archie's Girls, Betty and Veronica; Archie's Rival, Reggie; Archie's Joke Book;* and a variety of digests as well. Eventually MLJ changed its name to Archie Comics Inc.

The *Archie* newspaper strip started in 1946 and Montana, just back from four years in the Army Signal Corps, drew it from its inception until his death in 1975. His immediate successor on the comic book *Archie* had been Harry Sahle, and a string of other cartoonists followed—Bill Vigoda, Tom Moore, George Frese, among them. Dan DeCarlo, who joined the team in 1961, has been the chief illustrator of the adventures of the Riverdale High gang for many years and is also responsible for the newspaper strip.                    **R.G.**

**ARRIOLA, GUS** (1917–  )  Arriola established himself as a pioneer in "ethnic" comics when he created *Gordo* in 1941, and for over four decades he amused Mexicans and gringos alike with the gracefully drawn and affectionately scripted series.

Arriola's Mexican-born family moved from his birthplace, Florence, Arizona, to Los Angeles when he was a boy, and the young artist went straight from high school to a job as an animator with MGM. After six or seven years of working on such features as "Tom and Jerry," Arriola felt ready to develop something from his own experience, and he hit on the natural idea of drawing on the warmth, color, and easy-going humor of his Mexican heritage. United Features Syndicate bought *Gordo*, a gag strip about a corpulent, life-loving Mexican tourist guide, in November 1941.

In 1942 Arriola enlisted in the Air Force, where he served as a film animator, and discontinued his young strip; but in 1943 he began a Sunday *Gordo* and soon after his discharge in 1946 resumed the dailies.

The droll word play, gentle whimsy, and above all the elegant and often innovative visual imagination of *Gordo* earned Arriola the National Cartoonists Society's Best Humor Strip awards in 1957 and 1965 and kept it a paper strip until Arriola retired it and himself in 1985. A retrospective collection of Sunday strips featuring animals, *Gordo's Critters*, appeared in 1989.      **D.W.**

**THE ARROW**  The first costumed hero to appear in comic books after the advent of Superman was the Arrow, who made his debut in *Funny Pages* #21 (September 1938), just about three months after the Man of Steel burst onto the scene.

A very mysterious character, the Arrow had absolutely no superpowers or superweapons but was content to fight crime with a bow and arrow. His costume consisted of a rumpled red suit and a face-concealing cowl, all of which tended to make him look like a sort of sinister Santa Claus. He starred in 21 issues of *Funny Pages* and was there to the end (October 1940). He also showed up in *The Arrow* and was last seen in the third and final issue (October 1941).

For most of his career the Arrow had no civilian identity and readers never even got a look at his face. He operated in the best pulp mystery man fashion, simply showing up when he was needed. In a midnight mansion, in a mad scientist's lair, in a gangsters' hideout, he was there to save distressed innocents—a goodly portion of them pretty blond young women—with his capable archery. It wasn't until 1941 that the crimson bowman was identified as a handsome, blond U.S. intelligence agent named Ralph Payne.

The chief artist on the feature was Paul Gustavson. Bob Lubbers came in to draw some of the last adventures.                    **R.G.**

**THE ATOM (I)**  The original Atom began in *All-American Comics* #19 (October 1940). The creation of writer Bill O'Connor and artist Ben Flinton, he had no superpowers whatsoever, and in his first adventure he worked in a business suit rather than a hero costume.

Redheaded college boy Al Pratt was short and therefore "the object of much ridicule." He couldn't get dates and was picked on by his larger classmates. Finally, like the bullied 97-pound weaklings of contemporary Charles Atlas musclebuilding ads, he vowed to do something about it. Working with a down-and-out trainer he'd befriended, he developed "a perfect body. He now has a tremendous strength that is unbelievable in one so small." After turning himself into a muscleman, Pratt's first job as a hero was saving a pretty coed, who'd turned him down for a date, from kidnappers. In the next issue he acquired a costume, consisting of tightfitting leather shorts, a yellow tunic, and a blue cape and cowl.

Like the troubled superheroes that Stan Lee invented for Marvel in the 1960s, Al Pratt didn't live a smooth, trouble-free life. Since he did not want to reveal his Atom identity to the world, he found himself still considered a shrimp, shunned by girls, and razzed by his fellow students. But he suffered through, and dedicated himself to fighting crime, although the Atom didn't go up against criminal masterminds or colorful villains of the Joker and Penguin sort. Instead, he limited himself to crooks, grafters, and racketeers.

When Flinton and O'Connor went into the service in 1942, Joe Gallagher took over as artist. He had a distinctive style that mixed cartoon and illustration elements and the Atom's looks improved during the several years he was on the job.

The Atom left comic books initially in 1949. He had been a member of the Justice Society of America, appearing in *All Star Comics*. In the final two years of his career, he switched to *Flash Comics* and toward the end updated his costume so that he looked more like his superhero buddies. The character has reappeared over the years, notably in the 1960s in the annual teamups between the Justice Society and the Justice League in the latter's magazine. It must have cheered Al Pratt to meet the new Atom, someone even smaller than he. **R.G.**

**THE ATOM (II)**    Launched in 1961, this was the last of National (DC) Comics editor Julius Schwartz's major Golden Age superhero revivals. It was written by Gardner F. Fox and drawn mainly by Gil Kane.

This Atom shared only a name with his antecedent: He was a research scientist named Ray Palmer whose contact with matter from a white dwarf star gave him unlimited shrinking powers. At six inches in height he could also alter his mass, becoming feather-light or packing 180 pounds behind one tiny fist. Most of Fox's plots were clever mysteries involving strange robberies, culminating in fistfights in which the "six-inch savage" bounced off erasers or other objects to hurl himself dramatically at his foes; Kane's muscular art made such scenes especially effective.

Fox also took some flights into science fiction (such as visits to subatomic worlds), and created an amusing group of regular villains, including Oscar D. Dollar (to whom only the oddest, unlikeliest events occur) and Chronos, "The Time-Wise Guy," obsessed with clocks. He also wrote a series of stories about a "Time Pool" in which Atom journeyed to the past to meet Edgar Allan Poe, Ben Franklin, and others.

Although consistently well-crafted and charming. *Atom* was never one of DC's greater successes. Later, as the writing grew rather stale and Kane left as artist, it was unable to sustain itself. In 1968 it became half of *Atom and Hawkman*, which lasted only six issues. Atom thereafter became just a minor supporting character in the DC pantheon.

In 1983 Kane and writer Jan Strnad brought him back in the *Sword of the Atom* miniseries, in which he got stuck at his six-inch height and ended up as a sword-wielding swashbuckler in a hidden civilization of other six-inch people. The series was popular enough to inspire a couple of follow-ups, but never became a regular feature. In 1988 DC restored the hero to his earlier form in a new series, *Power of the Atom*, only to cancel it the following year.    **G.J.**

**AUTRY, GENE** (1907–  )    One of the most successful singing cowboys ever to ride across the silver screen, the Texas-born Autry entered the movies in the middle 1930s and went on to star on radio and television as well. His movie image, that of an amiable, clean-living, two-fisted cowpoke, served as the inspiration for comic books, Big Little Books, and two separate newspaper strips.

A former radio singer, Autry began starring in his hit Republic westerns in 1935 with *Tumblin' Tumbleweeds*. Dozens of films followed, including *Boots and Saddles*, *Springtime in the Rockies*, and *South of the Border*. Autry as a character first came to comic books in the late 1930s, when *Popular Comics* now and then included short adaptations of some of his movies among their features. Fawcett, up to then content with superheroes like Captain Marvel and Bulletman, launched *Gene Autry Comics* on the very last day of 1941. It was drawn by authentic cowboy artist Till Goodan, who worked in a simple, folksy illustrational style and who continued on when Dell took over the title in 1943. The magazine lasted until 1959. Much of the later drawing was done by the versatile Jesse Marsh, who was as much at home on the range as he was in the jungles he was drawing in the *Tarzan* comic book. Russ Manning also took a turn drawing Autry.

*The Gene Autry Show* aired on CBS television from 1950 to 1956, helping the sales of the comic book and inspiring a second title devoted to the cowboy's horse. *Gene Autry's Champion* made it through 19 issues from 1951 to 1955, expiring at about the same time that the TV spinoff *The Adventures of Champion* began its short run.

The first Autry Big Little Book, *Gene Autry in Public Cowboy No. 1*, was published by Whitman in 1938 and was illustrated with photos from the movie. The next year came *Gene Autry in Law of the Range*, an original. Between 1938 and 1950 a dozen Autry BLBs were issued.

Among the writers and artists were Gaylord DuBois, Russ Winterbotham, Erwin Hess, Henry Vallely, and Goodan.

The singing cowboy first showed up in the funnies in 1940, the same year *Gene Autry's Melody Ranch* took to the air by way of CBS radio. He appeared in a Sunday page with the exclamatory title *Gene Autry Rides!* The artwork was by Goodan and the script by Gerald Geraghty, a screenwriter who also went on to write several of the Falcon B-mysteries in the 1940s. Geraghty and his brother Maurice had written Autry's 1935 serial *The Phantom Empire*, one of the few cowboy- science fiction epics ever attempted; they also went on to write numerous Westerns for Autry and for both the Three Mesquiteers and the Hopalong Cassidy series. Initially the Autry Sunday, available in both half-page and—surprisingly—full-page format, offered a loose adaptation of the SF serial. It then moved on to more traditional horse opera fare. Autry actually sang in the strip, usually around the campfire with his wrangler buddies, but it didn't have the force of his movie warbling. The page didn't last long.

In 1952, during the run of the television show, a strip titled simply *Gene Autry* was syndicated, daily and Sunday, by General Features. Credited to Bert Laws and Bob Stevens, it was the work of various hands, including artist Tom Cooke. Autry had almost always appeared in adventures set in the contemporary West, and the strip also showed him in up-to-date settings: He spent as much time with airplanes and fast cars as he did with horses. The strip ended in 1955.            **R.G.**

**THE AVENGERS** Marvel's most changeable and most popular superhero team comic book debuted in the summer of 1963, written by Stan Lee and drawn by Jack Kirby. Its original roster included, in the manner of DC's *Justice League*, most of the company prominent heroes: Thor, Iron Man, the Hulk, Ant Man (later Giant Man), and the Wasp, soon to be joined by Captain America.

In 1964 Kirby was replaced by journeyman Don Heck, and the original heroes (except Captain America) were replaced by an odd bunch of former villains who had crossed to the right side of the law: Hawkeye the marksman (from *Iron Man*) and the sibling mutants Quicksilver and the Scarlet Witch (from *X-Men*). Thus *The Avengers* broke from the conventional super-team pattern and became a vehicle for showcasing minor heroes. Its roster changes have been so many over the past 20 years as to be virtually unchartable, and it seems as though nearly every character in the Marvel pantheon has passed through it. At its best this has made it one of Marvel's liveliest and most unpredictable series; at its worst, a dumping ground for heroes the company wants to keep around but can't find a good use for.

The team has also introduced some interesting new characters, among them the Vision (created by Roy Thomas), an agonized android with a human-like soul who became a fan favorite in the late 1960s; and Steve Englehart's Mantis, a mystical Vietnamese heroine of the early 1970s who ascended spiritually to become a "cosmic Madonna."

Nearly as many artists as characters have passed through its pages, most notably John Buscema, who replaced Heck in 1966 and has popped up frequently ever since, and Neal Adams, whose brief but stunning tenure in 1971–72 is still widely remembered.

The writing has been more consistent. Thomas inherited the series from Lee in 1966, and for four years used it as a forum for ambitious writing and intense emotionality; his work developed a strong fan following and pushed modern superhero comics further in the direction of complex melodrama. Englehart followed, also becoming a fan favorite with long and intricate storylines that united various aspects of the Marvel universe and tied up old continuities. Subsequent writers (especially Jim Shooter and Roger Stern) have generally built upon the Thomas and Englehart approaches and kept *The Avengers* a popular title. More recently it has sired two spin-offs, *West Coast Avengers* and *Solo Avengers*.            **G.J.**

# B

**BAILEY, RAY** (1913–1975) A master of the Caniff style, Bailey drew three comic strips of his own, *Vesta West*, *Bruce Gentry*, and *Tom Corbett, Space Cadet*, and assisted Caniff on *Terry and the Pirates, Male Call*, and *Steve Canyon*. He also did sports cartoons and editorials and put in time drawing for comic books.

Born in New York, he was the son of Ray Bailey Sr., a longtime sportswriter and columnist for the *New York Sun*. He was a self-taught artist and his first professional job was with the Fleischer animation studios in Manhattan during its *Betty Boop* and *Popeye* days. Subsequently Bailey drew sports cartoons and editorials for newspapers and magazines. By the late 1930s he was assisting Gus Edson on *The Gumps*, and in the early 1940s he became Milton Caniff's assistant, working on both *Terry* and *Male Call*. It was in these years that Bailey became proficient at emulating not only Caniff's approach to drawing but his lush inking style as well.

His first solo effort was *Vesta West*, a cowgirl Sunday strip that ran in the *Chicago Tribune*'s *Comic Book Magazine* during the early years of World War II. Next came Bailey's best shot at the big time, *Bruce Gentry*, a handsome, slickly done adventure strip dealing with a daredevil aviator in South America, which was syndicated by the *New York Post*. Caniff was one of the most popular strip artists in the country at the time and many newspapers that couldn't get *Terry* were happy to settle for the seemingly similar *Bruce Gentry*. The strip did well at first, but while Bailey could almost match his mentor's brushwork and approach to staging, he was never able to match him in writing and characterization. The competition from Caniff's new *Steve Canyon* in 1947 probably didn't help much either. Bailey's strip ended in the early 1950s.

He returned to newspaper comic pages soon after with the *Space Cadet* strip, based on the then-popular television show. Bailey took a realistic, somewhat gritty approach to science fiction, in contrast to the more idealistic, heroic look made popular by Alex Raymond and Mac Raboy on *Flash Gordon*. Tom Corbett and his Space Academy cronies did not last long in the funnies.

From the middle 1950s to late 1960s Bailey worked chiefly in comic books, drawing a variety of TV adaptations such as *The Gray Ghost* and *Ripcord*, and doing occasional jobs for publishers like Tower and Charlton. During these same years he now and then assisted on *Steve Canyon* and also drew some of the comic books based on the strip. Personal problems curtailed his career, and when he died in San Francisco in 1975, he had been long inactive. **R.G.**

**BAILY, BERNARD** (1920– ) He started working in comic books in 1936 and in 1940 became the first artist to draw the Spectre, the ghostly superhero who's managed to survive, with a layoff now and then, right up to the present. Baily also packaged and published comic books in the Forties and hired oldtimers like C.A. Voight and newcomers like Frank Frazetta.

Baily was born in New York and had no formal art training. He did his first professional drawing for *Wow Comics* in 1936, then served with the Eisner-Iger shop. In 1938 he went over to DC, doing *The Buccaneer* for *More Fun Comics* and *Tex Thomson* for *Action Comics*. Originally Tex was a world-roaming soldier of fortune, but early in 1941 he donned a star-spangled costume to fight spies and subversives as Mr. America. The next year he changed his name to the snappier Americommando. For *Adventure Comics*, starting early in 1940, Baily wrote and drew a superhero named Hourman.

His best known character was the Spectre, which began in *More Fun* #52 (February 1940). On that he collaborated with Jerry Siegel. "Siegel came up with the feature," Baily once explained. "The look of the character I created, the script he wrote." Baily's early work had been shaky and derivative, but by the time he got to the grim Spectre he was drawing well, in a straightforward brush style that seems to have been inspired equally by newspaper adventure strips and pulp illustrations. The Spectre's first go-round lasted until 1945 and Baily drew him the whole time.

In the middle-1940s Baily started a shop and provided artwork for such magazines as *Prize Comics, Headline Comics*, and *Treasure Comics*. He also dabbled in publishing with such shortlived titles as *Spook Comics* and *Cisco Kid Comics*. He returned to DC in the early 1950s, specializing in horror and science fiction for various titles. He left the comic book field in the early 1970s. **R.G.**

**BAKER, GEORGE** (1915–1975)  Baker owed his success as a cartoonist to World War II. Prior to entering the Army in the summer of 1941 he was just one of many Disney animators, but, after less than a year in the service, he created *Sad Sack*. Fame and fortune followed.

George Baker was born in Lowell, Massachusetts. He attended high school in Chicago and went on to study art in the Windy City's Academy of Fine Arts for exactly one month. He moved westward in 1937 to take a job with the Walt Disney studio. While Baker was employed there he worked on such full-length animated features as *Pinocchio, Dumbo,* and *Bambi.* He credited what he learned as an animator and in Disney art classes with providing a strong foundation for his work and helping him get rid of the clichés of cartooning. "Disney's of course had a great deal to do with my sense of depth," he once explained. "In animation, the third dimension is demanded of one's work to give the illusion of space *around* a character."

Baker first drew his hapless, sausage-nosed GI as an entry in a contest for servicemen cartoonists. It won and was widely reprinted in camp newspapers. *Sad Sack* started appearing in *Yank,* the weekly soldiers' magazine, in 1942 and quickly became a favorite of enlisted men and civilians. Baker drew his feature in the form of a two-tier comic strip, but never used borders to separate his panels. The strip was pantomime, drawn in a sketchy bigfoot style and making good use of Baker's mastery of perspective and camera angles. The weekly strips looked something like storyboards for silent sequences in animated cartoons and almost never showed the hapless Sack triumphing. "To me he was the pictorial representation of the humility and resignation to abuse the civilian feels," Baker said, "on entrance to the gigantic machine, the Army."

By 1944 Baker's *Yank* strips were being offered to American newspapers by the Bell Syndicate. In May of 1946, when Sad Sack and George Baker were both civilians again, Bell launched a Sunday page. The Sack was as much a loser as ever, but Baker's postwar gags and situations were nowhere near as raunchy as they'd been during his Army days. The page hung on for only a few years. Harvey Publications started *Sad Sack Comics* in the summer of 1949. Initially the hero was a civilian, but Harvey wisely put him back in uniform in the 22nd issue. The magazine became a hit and there were several spinoff titles—*Sad Sack's Army Life, Sad Sack's Funny Friends* etc. The character remained a comic book favorite into the 1980s. Baker didn't draw any of the interior stories, which used dialogue, but he did contribute covers to the various Sad Sack titles. Baker owned his character and he was active in merchandising him and selling Sad Sack to radio and the movies.                                    **R.G.**

**BANANA OIL**  See GROSS, MILT.

**BARKS, CARL** (1901–  )  He has long been ranked as one of the great comic book artists. The work that eventually won Barks an international reputation and following was done anonymously from 1942 to 1966 when he drew and wrote the first original *Donald Duck* comic book stories and along the way created such characters as Gyro Gearloose, Gladstone Gander, the Beagle Boys, and Uncle Scrooge. In the days before his identity became known, fans referred to him simply as "the Good Artist."

Barks was born in Oregon and "by the time I was sixteen, I had become pretty well assured that I wanted to be an artist or a cartoonist." It took him some time to realize his ambition. "I had to go out and be a cowhand and a farmer, a muleskinner, lumberjack, anything that happened to come along that would furnish me with a living," Barks once said. "I'd worked in a printing shop, been a cowboy and a whole bunch of other things, with practically no success whatever."

Finally in the late 1920s he started to sell his cartoons to magazines such as *College Humor* and *Judge.* His more risque gags, featuring sexy ladies wearing a minimum of clothing, found a home in a Minneapolis-based magazine called *The Calgary Eye-Opener,* and in 1931 they offered him a staff job. In 1935 Barks decided he wasn't earning enough and applied for a job with the Walt Disney outfit. He sent samples and was hired at the salary of $20 a week to be an in-betweener in the Southern California animation studios.

He didn't exactly shine as an apprentice animator, but "I turned in so many gags to the comic strip department and the story department…that I got put in the story department on a permanent basis." After working nearly seven years, Barks made up his mind to quit and relocate in the desert country. Just before he left Disney he worked on a one-shot comic book titled *Donald Duck Finds Pirate Gold.* Based on an abandoned movie, it was the first original Donald Duck comic book. Later in 1942 Barks was hired by Dell-Western to do original, 10-page Duck stories in *Walt Disney's Comics & Stories.* His first job appeared in #31 (April 1943), and soon he was writing as well as drawing the stories.

The character of Donald changed as Barks began to think of him as his own. "Instead of making just a quarrelsome little guy out of him, I made him a sympathetic character," he once explained. "He was sometimes a villain, and he was often a real good guy and at all times he was just a blundering person like the average human being." The three nephews were modified as well. "I broadened them like I did Donald, started out with mischievous little guys and ended up with little scientists."

Barks started doing full-length Duck books in 1943 as well. It was in these—*The Mummy's Ring, Frozen Gold, Volcano Valley* etc.—that he really began to shine. He started doing graphic novels filled with adventure, comedy, satire, and some of the best cartooning to be found in comics. In 1947 came *Christmas on Bear Mountain*, which introduced Barks' major creation, Uncle Scrooge.

Barks' forte was the mock adventure tale and he put his ducks into handsomely rendered locales where they could experience every sort of action, intrigue, fantasy, and mystery situation. He built his settings carefully, often using such reference sources as *The National Geographic* magazine. He drew his characters so well in every kind of situation that they became close to real. And the Barks dialogue was just about the best to be found in a kids' comic book—equaled only by that of Walt Kelly. He was especially good at the invective spouted by the avaricious and short-tempered Uncle Scrooge. The current, successful animated television show *Duck Tales* owes much to ideas and approaches done much earlier, and usually much better, by Barks.

Barks retired at the age of 65 to devote himself to painting. As his identity became known, he became the object of increasing attention in both fan circles and in mainstream publications. His entire output on the Ducks, as well as his work on other characters such as Mickey Mouse and Barney Bear, has been reprinted. Since Barks did all of it as a worker-for-hire, he hasn't become rich, but he's most certainly grown famous.

R.G.

**BARNABY** In the spring of 1942, just a few months after the United States entered World War II, *Barnaby* began appearing in the liberal New York tabloid *PM*. One of the best-drawn and best-written strips of the decade, it had been cooked up by a man who had little interest in or liking for comics. Crockett Johnson, who'd begun life 36 years earlier as David Johnson Leisk, was the creator of the new strip. He explained that his prime motivation was a desire to find something that would guarantee him a steady living.

Before Johnson sold *Barnaby*, a task that took him two years, he'd earned a modest living doing department store art and then cartoons for magazines such as *Collier's*. In a little more than a year after its modest debut, the strip was in syndication with a growing list of major newspapers. It had been reprinted in a handsome hardcover book and was being raved about by such mainstream periodicals as *Time, Newsweek,* and *Life,* which called it "a breath of cool, sweet air."

The strip that generated all this excited response was unlike anything that had ever popped up on comic pages. Johnson's drawing style, inspired by the simple and effective work of men like Gluyas Williams, accom-

*Barnaby*, Crockett Johnson, © 1944, Field Enterprises.

plished a great deal with just outline and flat blacks. There was no noodling, feathering or shading to be seen, and Johnson relied almost entirely on medium and long shots. Everything—people, animals, trees, buildings, automobiles—was drawn flat and dimensionless. He achieved a feeling of perspective the way a paper cutout diorama does.

Although a few historians have characterized his drawing as static and lacking in action, it was not. He often used chases, slapstick struggles, and other devices assimilated from the movie comedies he was fond of. Johnson was also very good at suggesting character and attitude, conveying anguish, frustration, self-importance etc. with a few deft lines. A typographer on the side, he set his dialogue in a distinctive, lower-case, sans-serif type. This may have saved a little time, but his main reason was a desire to fit more copy into his balloons—he often used a hundred or more words in a daily. The average wordage in most of today's humor strips is around 25.

The costars of the strip were Barnaby, a bright and articulate preschooler, and Mr. O'Malley, his windy and not completely effectual Fairy Godfather. O'Malley, a child-size, pudgy fellow in an overcoat that allowed his pink wings to flap freely, used a Havana cigar as a magic wand and never encountered a problem, large or small, he wasn't ready to tackle or at least—sometimes at great length—to discuss tackling. O'Malley, saving his magical powers for a last resort, was a great one for drawing up complicated plans and intricate charts. He was also fond of polls and telephone surveys. In other words, he was a pixie who believed in blending ancient sorceries with the latest public relations techniques.

Mr. O'Malley showed up on the strip's second day, after Barnaby, inspired by a fairy tale his mother had read him, wished for a fairy godmother. Instead he got Jackeen J. O'Malley, who came flying in the open bedroom window, made a less than perfect landing and bent his stogie. "Cushlamochree! Broke my magic wand!…Lucky Boy! Your wish is granted! I'm your Fairy Godfather!" Johnson made it perfectly clear from the start that O'Malley wasn't an imaginary playmate. Barnaby's parents never managed to see him and, in fact, waged an unsuccessful campaign for the life of the strip to persuade Barnaby—once enlisting the help of a child psychologist—that O'Malley didn't exist. Barnaby, and the reader, knew better.

While Barnaby avoided some of the more common physical hazards of childhood—he was rarely sick, there were no kid bullies in his venue, neither parent took a hairbrush to him—he suffered most of the psychological ones. His folks often didn't listen to him in anything but a critical way and they nearly always assumed his perceptions and assumptions were not only hopelessly naive but also dead wrong. One of the boy's most frequent emotions was frustration. When he knew the truth or the answer to a question, he was rarely paid attention to.

The supporting players in the strip were a rich and varied lot. There was Barnaby's dog, Gorgon, who could, when in the mood, talk. Gorgon was inclined toward puns and never tired of remarking he was dog tired or led a dog's life. Once, when Gorgon was recruited to play a dog on a radio show O'Malley put together, the critics dismissed his performance as unconvincing.

The sprawling suburban neighborhood the Baxters lived in came complete with a haunted house. The resident ghost was a timid wraith named Gus. An extremely literate spook—he even wore glasses—Gus was continually being conned into performing tasks for O'Malley. Writing his political speeches, helping him stage his version of *Hamlet* etc. The surrounding woods contained a variety of pixies, ogres, elves, and other so-called mythical creatures.

Mr. O'Malley was a member, not always in good standing, of the Elves, Leprechauns, Gnomes and Little Men's Chowder and Marching Society. When he was not hanging around with Barnaby, concocting a new scheme or availing himself of the leftover roast lamb always to be found in the Baxter refrigerator, he could be found at the group's headquarters. Or at Paddy's Bar & Grill, a convivial establishment that didn't discriminate against pixies. Readers never went with O'Malley to these spots and had only his accounts of what went on there to go by.

After 1945 Johnson stopped signing the strip for awhile. In the autumn of 1946 Ted Ferro and Jack Morley's names appeared on it, although Johnson still kept an eye on things. Morely did an exceptional job of imitating the drawing style. Within a little more than a year Ferro dropped out as writer and from then on the credit read "Jack Morely & C.J." *Barnaby* ended on February 2, 1952.

And a poignant finish it was. As Barnaby approached his sixth birthday his father pointed out that "big boys don't have Fairy Godfathers." O'Malley looked that up in his *Fairy Godfather's Handy Pocket Guide* and it turned out to be true. Barnaby's fairy godfather and Gus the Ghost attended his sixth birthday party and then took their leave. That night Barnaby saw a shooting star out his bedroom window and, remembering he saw one when O'Malley first appeared, wondered if that was he going away. The final panel of the final strip showed O'Malley flying away across a starry sky.

In 1962 Johnson was persuaded by the Hall Syndicate to resurrect the strip. He updated the scripts of some of the old continuities and Warren Sattler redrew them. *Barnaby* didn't attract an audience the second time around and was soon gone.                    **R.G.**

**BARNEY BAXTER**  One of the best-looking of the aviation strips that began in the 1930s, especially when it came to the meticulous and accurate rendering of planes, was *Barney Baxter in the Air*. Written and drawn by Frank Miller, it ran from the middle 1930s to 1950.

An Iowan by Birth, Miller (1898–1949) shifted from job to job—bookkeeper, grocer, cattle rancher—and by the late 1920s was a staff cartoonist with the *Rocky Mountain News*. It was for that Denver newspaper that he started doing *Barney Baxter* late in 1935. The *News* had a Junior Aviator section each week and was running a series of model airplane contests; apparently the strip was originally intended to promote these activities. In that initial version Barney was much younger than in the later version of the strip: He was an apple-cheeked, freckle-faced kid of about 12, and a Junior Aviator and model builder. After aiding a renowned aviator named Cyclone Smith, he was invited to accompany him on a flight to Alaska in his "trim little hydroplane." After getting his mom's permission, Barney takes off and is soon encountering plane crashes, blizzards and the first of a long line of bestial villains.

When Miller's Rocky Mountain editor was hired away by Hearst to come East and work for the *New York Mirror*, he brought Miller along. Miller started drawing *Barney Baxter* for the paper and for King Features as of December 1936. Upon joining the Hearst organization, Barney aged several years and turned into an apple-cheeked, freckle-faced kid of about 20. Like most of the

*Barney Baxter*, Frank Miller, © 1942, King Features. Reprinted with special permission of King Features Syndicate, Inc.

funny paper flyers of that period, Barney was something of a mercenary. When he wasn't outwitting spies and saboteurs on his home ground, he was involved in some kind of South American air war. Miller was a patient, dedicated artist who loved all the time-consuming pen techniques that had been handed down from artists like Winsor McCay. If his scriptwriting had matched his drawing *Barney Baxter* would have been an impressive strip indeed.

Besides Barney, who loved planes, his mom, and, originally, a girl named Patricia, there were two flying sidekicks, Hap Walters and a onetime desert rat named Gopher Gus. America's entry into World War II opened up new horizons for Miller. Instead of machine-gunning and bombing only Latins, Barney and his flying pals could now devote their attention to the Nazis and the Japanese. Working several weeks ahead of publication, Miller managed to second guess General Jimmy Doolittle and have Barney bombing Tokyo on the same day as the April 1942 raid actually took place. By this time Miller was living on a ranch he'd bought in the Colorado Rockies. It was there late in 1942 that he suffered a heart attack. Bob Naylor, a King bullpen veteran, took over the drawing and writing of the feature.

Miller recooperated and, after putting in some time in the Coast Guard, returned to see his creation through the postwar years. Barney mellowed considerably after leaving the service. Out in the South Pacific he met a sarong-wearing young woman named Maura. He fell in love and eventually married her. Although he continued to fly and to get involved with odd villains and secret weapons—such as the B-Bomb—he was a subdued man. On Sundays, which were given over to separate continuities, Barney was a bit more flamboyant and even got involved in science fictional doings. Miller died at the end of 1949 and when the strips he'd drawn in advance ran out in January 1950, *Barney Baxter* came to an end.                                                      **R.G.**

**BARNEY GOOGLE**  One of the most popular strips ever devoted to the sporting life, *Barney Google* began in 1919. It was the creation of Billy DeBeck, a gifted cartoonist and writer. Among the byproducts of the strip were a racehorse named Spark Plug and a grouchy mountaineer called Snuffy Smith.

On the Fourth of July, 1919, Jess Willard was due to defend his heavyweight title against Jack Dempsey in Toledo, Ohio. Reporters and sports cartoonists started flocking to Toledo about the middle of June, where they visited the fighters' training camps, interviewed them and their managers and turned out assorted columns, sketches, and predictions. One of the cartoonists on the scene was 29-year-old Billy DeBeck of the *Chicago Herald-Examiner*, who'd been in the business for over a decade. What DeBeck produced while in Toledo was not sports panels but a new comic strip, initially about a henpecked husband who's obsessed with the Dempsey-Willard bout. It was originally titled *Take Barney Google, For Instance* and first appeared on the sports pages of various Hearst papers around the country on Tuesday, June 17, 1919.

Up until July of 1922 the *Google* strip had merely dabbled in sports while concentrating on domestic and office situations. Just before launching this one, DeBeck had been doing a strip called *Married Life* and for a while it looked as though readers were going to get more of the same. Barney, who kept getting smaller as the strip progressed, played the perennial loser who is browbeaten by a succession of sourfaced bosses and nagged by his enormous wife. But then, in a July 17th strip, Barney happened to stroll by the Pastime Jockey Club at the moment a silkhatted gent was heaved out the window by some irate cronies. He landed on Barney rather than the hard concrete and in gratitude gave him a two-year-old racehorse. In the final panel Barney phoned his wife to announce, "All our troubles are over now, sweet woman. I gotta race hoss!"

The horse is named Spark Plug and his meager frame is covered, down to the ankles, with a tacky horse blanket. Seeing Barney and his new horse, you might conclude that here were a pair of losers. But, when Barney entered the nag in his first race, the famed Abadaba Handicap, he won and made his new owner $50,000 richer.

From then on, for the next several years, the strip was devoted to the career of Barney and Spark Plug. It wasn't all ease and luxury, though. Barney took to wearing a silk hat and smoking a better grade of cigar, but there were times when he was too broke to come up with the entry fee for a race. And there were times when Sparky lost a race. On such occasions Barney was not above booting his horse in the backside. Theirs was a complex relationship, mixing exasperation and affection, much like that between parent and child.

When DeBeck introduced Spark Plug, he also discovered the power of the words "to be continued." A surefire gag wasn't needed every day if you got your readers hooked on the continuity. He built suspense, stretching a race across several weeks, sometimes making daily followers wait from Saturday to the following Monday to see if Sparky won a particular race. Barney's wife had dropped from the strip, and DeBeck got many subplots out of Barney's courting of various pretty young ladies. Like many comedians of the silent screen, Barney never got the girl. Throughout the 1920s, he and his horse and his loyal black jockey, Sunshine, made a picaresque journey across America and even into foreign climes, racing, gambling, romancing. The plots got trickier as DeBeck involved his cast with all the fads and foibles of the Roaring Twenties. At one point Sparky even swam the English Channel.

DeBeck's drawing had a scratchy vitality and his dialogue made good use of slang and vernacular. He coined, or at least promoted, several catchphrases that just about everybody was saying in the Twenties— "Osky wow wow," "Sweet mama," and "Heebie jeebies." Louis Armstrong even made a record called *Heebie Jeebies*, his very first real hit. Like many another chronicler of the Jazz Age, DeBeck was both cynical and sentimental. His Barney Google was a hardboiled softie too, suspicious that almost everything was a con and yet always willing to take in waifs and strays.

The public became fascinated with the strip, especially with Barney's woebegone horse. The title was changed to *Barney Google and Spark Plug* and Sparky became the Snoopy of his day. DeBeck was able to announce in an introduction to an early collection of strips that "All over the United States you find stuffed Spark Plugs and Spark Plug games and Spark Plug drums and Spark Plug balloons and Spark Plug tin pails. And there is a Spark Plug play on the road." There was a hit song, too, written by Billy Rose and Con Conrad and celebrating Spark Plug and "Barney Google with his goo-goo-googly eyes." DeBeck saw to it that characters sang the song in the strip.

In the late 1920s he started incorporating mystery and melodrama into the strip. After several such continuities, including one involving a secret society and one wherein Barney substitutes for a millionaire and is nearly railroaded into the boobyhatch, he concocted a full-length murder mystery burlesque. That daily adventure commenced in September 1930 and ran on until April 1931. It's possible that all this was too heady and quirky for an audience used to more straightforward humor in the funnies. At any rate, DeBeck brought back Spark Plug later that year and Barney returned to the turf. The next year found him managing the Sultan of Sulu, who wrestled under the name Sully.

For Barney Google 1934 was a fateful year. He started it off, decked out in a suitable uniform, being supreme dictator of a Caribbean island. Then he was suddenly summoned to the states by a law firm and informed he was the sole heir of an estate in North Carolina. Barney headed South and arrived on June 16th to find himself owner of a ramshackle cabin in the heart of hillbilly country. Al Capp, by the way, would be setting up shop on similar terrain two months later with *Li'l Abner*.

There was, in fact, considerable interest in that hillbilly life style at the time. Just the year before, *Tobacco Road*, the hit play based on the Erskine Caldwell novel, had caused a sensation on Broadway, and DeBeck himself had long been interested in the folklore of the mountain people. Barney's first adventure in the rural milieu got him tangled in a feud, and then he played an uncle role in a romantic triangle featuring a virtuous country girl, a virtuous country boy, and a rich and handsome young "furriner." The country girl and boy decided to get married and a huge wedding was planned. Among the guests invited are Snuffy Smith and his wife Lowizie. Snuffy, who was the same size and shape as Barney, was a cantankerous, short-tempered, and meanminded fellow. Initially he thought little of Barney and his citified ways, suspecting he was probably "tetched in the haid."

Snuffy began, from his first day on the job, to steal the limelight; he made the formerly feisty and outspoken Barney seem sedate and conservative. His advent perked up the strip, just as Spark Plug had a decade earlier. By the end of the 1930s the strip was titled *Barney Google and Snuffy Smith*.

Although their subsequent joint ventures were usually of an earthy nature, DeBeck managed occasionally to introduce mystery and fantasy. There was a Sunday continuity about a flying horse and one about a magical tribe of little flying hillbillies called the Feather Merchants. By this time Barney was making only token appearances.

DeBeck died in November of 1942. His longtime assistant, Fred Lasswell, eventually took over the strip. Barney faded out of the picture, making only rare reappearances. The feature, now known as *Snuffy Smith*, has long been devoted to delivering a simple hillbilly gag each and every day.                                    **R.G.**

**BARRY, DAN** (1923– )  Barry, who's produced the *Flash Gordon* comic strip for nearly four decades, began his career in the early 1940s in comic books. Over the next several years he drew such characters as Airboy, Johnny Quick, and the Vigilante and also did very influential work in true crime comics like *Gang Busters*. He crossed over into newspapers in 1947, when he became the artist on the *Tarzan* daily.

Barry had entered comic books in 1940, as a teenager fresh from New Jersey. Initially he assisted artist George Mandel (who went on to become a novelist) on such features as *Doc Strange*. Later on he worked with George's brother Alan on a string of second banana heroes—Young Robin Hood, Blue Bolt, Thirteen, and the like. After three years in the Air Force, Barry came back to comic books and for the next several years was one of the most successful artists in the field. His style had improved, too, and now, as *The Great Comic Book Artists* points out, "blended the figure work of Alex Raymond with the lush inking and realistic backgrounds of Milton Caniff with considerable input of his own. Barry brought a slickness to comic books that would have been out of place a few years earlier."

In the immediate postwar years Barry drew for a variety of publishers. For Gleason he did *Crimebuster* and *Daredevil*, for Hillman it was *Gunmaster*, *Airboy*, and that walking compost pile known as *The Heap*. He was

also associated with an outfit called General Comics, which turned out advertising and educational comics for clients such as International Harvester and Blue Cross. Barry's work appeared as well in the comic books being given away by the Buster Brown shoestore chain. In 1947 he added DC to his client list, going to work on their *Gang Busters* title. He was the star of the early issues, providing covers and the leadoff story. He'd already illustrated this type of material—albeit with more violence and realism—in Gleason's *Crime Does Not Pay*. Equally at home with plainclothes heroes and costumed supermen, Barry drew *Johnny Quick* and *The Vigilante* for DC, along with the first issue of *The Adventures of Alan Ladd* and the first few issues of *Big Town*, based on the radio show about newspaper life. By this time he had help on his work, using his brother Sy and others as inkers. His style, one of the most distinctive of the years after World War II, spread through comic books, carried on by those who'd worked with him or merely been influenced by him.

In 1947, when Rex Maxon was at last dumped from the *Tarzan* daily, Barry assumed the job. The task didn't pay well and Barry, not certain he'd stay with it, never bothered to sign his name to the jungleman strip. He quit after less than two years. The *Flash Gordon* daily was revived in 1951 and, after some soul searching, Barry decided to accept King Features' offer to do it. In 1967 he also assumed responsibility for the Sunday page. He did his most impressive work on the first few years of *Flash* dailies in the early 1950s—with a little help from Frank Frazetta, Jack Davis, and Harvey Kurtzman, to name a few. Eventually his increasing interest in painting led him to hire others to do much of the work. Now and then, though, he'll try his hand at a batch of strips, and they'll be nearly as good as those of the 1950s.                                    **R.G.**

**BARRY, SEYMOUR**  See THE PHANTOM.

**BATIUK, TOM** (1947– )  A job as a junior high school art teacher provided Tom Batiuk with a natural source of material for his daily and Sunday gag strip *Funky Winkerbean*, and if that strip is different from most teen strips, it is because its characters derive from the real experience of its author. Batiuk was born in Akron, and grew up in Elyria, Ohio. He switched his major at Kent State University from fine arts to education because he had no confidence in being able to make a living in art, and for a time combined the two disciplines by teaching art in his hometown junior high school.

In 1972, however, the deadly tedium of the study hall (he says that the way he ran study hall, he was "one of the few teachers that would get detentions from the *kids*") drove him to the sketchpad "to kill time." The resulting doodles turned into the strip that provided an escape from the classroom when *Funky Winkerbean* was taken by Publishers-Hall Syndicate. The credible, and even sometimes touching, problems of a typical high school kid trying to cope with the demands of the classroom, a less-than-satisfactory love life, and the demands of a world he never made provide the easily recognizable material of *Funky* and have given it a broad middle-class and middle-brow audience. Despite his name, there is little funk in Funky, or in any of his friends.

A recurring character in *Funky*, a television personality described as "the master of the no-depth interview," provided the subject for a second strip for Batiuk when he created *John Darling*, originally drawn by Tom Armstrong and currently by Gerry Shamray. Rich in topical reference and caricatures of real people, *John Darling* has little interaction with the strip that spawned it, deriving its humor from media parody rather than from character. It made its debut on March 25, 1979, distributed by Field Newspaper Syndicate to about 150 papers.

Batiuk's imagination brought forth a third strip, *Crankshaft*, in 1987. Balancing the youth-oriented humor of *Funky*, it deals with a crusty old man who drives a school bus and lives in a constant state of friction with the world. When a pleasant drugstore clerk hands Crankshaft his prescription and says, "Have a nice day," he typically responds, "Make me!" Drawn by Chuck Ayers, *Crankshaft* is distributed by Creators Syndicate to over 200 papers.

Batiuk (whose name is pronounced BAT-ick) seems to have an inexhaustible fund of genial humor and a keen eye for the small ironies and absurdities of everyday life. He makes his home where he grew up, in Elyria, Ohio, and returns periodically to his old high school to draw the students and teachers and stay in touch with the world of Funky Winkerbean. **D.W.**

**BATMAN** The joint creation of artist Bob Kane and writer Bill Finger, Batman made his debut in *Detective Comics* #27 (May 1939). He very soon became the most popular DC hero after Superman. Batman, who celebrated 50 years on the job in 1989, also proved to be a very successful merchandising property and has earned millions by way of toys, costumes, television shows, and movies.

One of the things the new, original-material comic books of the 1930s did was deliver pulp magazine and movie elements in a funny paper format. The popular entertainments enjoyed by the artists and writers of this burgeoning new industry while growing up, now got recycled and turned into comic book stories. Batman was one of the most successful examples—inspired by movie melodramas and pulpwood yarns but becoming a distinctive character in his own right. When Kane and

his writer-friend Finger invented Batman, they were only a few years out of their teens themselves and still very much in touch with the kind of adventure material that had excited them as kids.

Though pulp fiction magazines had been around for most of the century, it was in the Thirties that the single-hero magazines really blossomed. *The Shadow* began in 1931, followed by *Doc Savage, The Spider*, and *The Phantom Detective* in 1933, *The Whisperer* in 1936, and *The Avenger* in 1939. The 1930s was definitely the decade of the mystery men, and they were to be found in just about every other popular entertainment medium as well. Radio offered the Lone Ranger and the Green Hornet, movies provided Zorro, the Scarlet Pimpernel, and the Lone Wolf, newspaper strips had the Phantom.

Bill Finger once said, "My first script was a take-off on a Shadow story...I patterned my style of writing Batman after the Shadow. Also after Warner Bros. movies, the gangster movies." Kane has mentioned that another source of inspiration was the 1931 movie *The Bat Whispers*. Basically an old dark house story, it had to do with stolen money, secret rooms and passages, and a crazed killer who dressed up like a bat. The nightstalking Bat, especially when prowling the rooftops or casting his weird shadow on a wall, was certainly an ancestor of Batman.

In civilian life Batman was Bruce Wayne, "a bored young socialite." When night fell, however, playboy Wayne became "powerful and awesome" and a "weird menace of crime." Batman's origin didn't appear until *Detective* #33 (November 1939). In a terse two-page account readers were told that 15 years before Bruce Wayne's parents were gunned down on the street by a stickup man and that the boy had vowed to dedicate his life to "warring on criminals." Having no supernatural powers, Wayne had to work at becoming a hero. He devoted years to preparing for his crimefighting career, turning himself into both a master scientist and a top athlete. Determining that he'd need a disguise capable of striking terror into the hearts of criminals, he was inspired by the intrusion of a bat into his den—"It's an omen...I shall become a BAT!"

Another major event in Batman's life was recounted in *Detective* #38 (April 1940). He acquired a sidekick. "An exciting figure whose incredible gymnastic and athletic feats will astound you...A laughing, fighting young daredevil who scoffs at danger like the legendary Robin Hood whose name and spirit he has adopted...Robin the Boy Wonder." The fact that both Batman and Robin were vulnerable, that they could be hurt or killed, added to their appeal. Though readers knew, rationally, that DC, Inc. wasn't going to let Kane and crew kill off either member of its hottest team, they suspended disbelief and anguished over Batman's reaching the diving bell before Robin suffocated and hoped against hope they'd find a way out of that subterranean room before the spiked ceiling minced them.

Also appealing were the gimmicks and props. The batplane and the batmobile, in their various incarnations. The utility belts, which seemed to contain an endless supply of lifesaving gadgets. The Batcave, which first showed up in the early 1940s, was also fascinating and something most kids wouldn't have minded having under their own house, in place of a damp, musty basement. The cave kept expanding, growing from simple garage to garage-laboratory-trophy room. The subsidiary characters, too, were interesting. Commissioner Gordon, who was in the saga from the very first episode, was on the dull side. But any policeman who was imaginative enough to use the bat signal had to be okay. Alfred, a very Wodehousian butler, signed on in 1943. He was a likable fellow, whether in his original fat mode or in his later slim state.

One of the best ways to judge a comic book hero is by the villainous company he keeps. Batman and Robin did combat with quite an array of colorful and entertaining foes. Their leading opponent was unquestionably that "harlequin of hate," the Joker. A man who combined the mastermind qualities of Professor Moriarty, the fiendishness of Fu Manchu, and the audacity of Groucho Marx, the Joker first struck in *Batman* #1 (Spring 1940). In fact, he struck twice, in the first and last of the magazine's four tales. The most appealing thing about the white-faced Joker was his inventiveness. While his main goal in life remained loot—jewels, cash, objects of art—he was continually varying his methods. On one caper he and his gang would rely on costumes and uniforms, next he'd base a series of murders on the punchlines of old jokes. On another occasion he undertook to commit a crime a day, daring Batman to stop him. The purple-clad clown quickly became the team's most frequently fought foe. In 1940 they met him five times in *Detective* and *Batman*. The number of clashes dropped to three in 1941, then climbed to an impressive eight in 1942.

Another of Batman's favorite enemies was the polite and dapper little scoundrel known as the Penguin. Dressed in tails and top hat, with one of his dangerous umbrellas clutched in his gloved hand, he first waddled onto the scene in *Detective* #58 (December 1941). Among the other early antagonists were the complex Two-Face, the Scarecrow, the Cavalier, Mr. Baffle, and the Catwoman, who was long *the* woman in Batman's life.

In the late 1960s Kane ended his association with the character, and new writers and artists began working with Batman. These included Denny O'Neil, Frank Robbins, Irv Novick, and Neal Adams. The most successful Batman project of recent years was *Dark Knight*, a special-format series of four issues by writer-artist Frank Miller that appeared in 1986. *Dark Knight* featured an aging Batman and a Gotham City that was tottering on the brink of collapse. It earned a number of fan awards and considerable attention outside comics fandom.

In the half-century plus of his career Batman has worked with more than one Robin. The original was Dick Grayson, orphaned son of circus acrobats; he eventually grew too old and was replaced by a lad named Jason Todd. In Frank Miller's Dark Knight version a 13-year-old girl gymnast named Carrie Kelly played the part. in 1988, after a reader telephone poll that earned nationwide publicity for DC, the Robin that was Jason Todd was allowed to die, beaten to death by the Joker. In 1989 a new Robin was brought onto the scene.

The *Batman* motion picture released in 1989 and starring Michael Keaton as the caped crusader and Jack Nicholson as the Joker was a tremendous hit at the box office. Batman merchandise flourished as it hadn't since the camp television show of the 1960s and retail sales of licensed merchandise estimated at $650 million were run up.                                                    **R.G.**

**B.C.**  Modern in language and style despite its prehistoric setting, *B.C.* has been a popular gag strip since its appearance in 1958. Written and drawn by then-27-year-old Johnny Hart, who had never worked on a comic strip before, it was an immediate success, with some of its Neanderthal characters acquiring their own fan clubs.

The slapdash drawing and irreverent humor of the strip were not immediately acceptable to the industry, however, and Hart was turned down by five major syndicates before the *New York Herald Tribune* took it on. The daily *B.C.* first appeared on February 17, 1958, and the Sunday strip on October 19. The strip later went with Publishers Syndicate and has since gone to Creators Syndicate. Despite the vicissitudes of its syndication, however, the strip's circulation has remained stable at about 400 papers.

By turns caustically satiric and broadly farcical, *B.C.* features a well-defined cast of cave men, women and animals (no children ever appear, as sex has apparently not been discovered yet). The eponymous hero would be the typical caveman on the street if there were streets; he is a *naif*, without pretension, and profoundly impressed by the accomplishments of his autochthonous compeers. (When Peter, the resident philosopher, comes to the "profound conclusion about the sun"— that "it only appears during the day"—B.C. proclaims him a genius.) The anachronistically bespectacled Clumsy Carp is awkward but still the only one around who can make waterballs. The ingenious Thor, having invented the wheel, improves it by inventing a square version that can't roll away, and then tops that achievement with a triangular wheel that eliminates one of the bumps. The male cast is completed by the peg-legged proto-poet Wiley, who is terrified of water; Grog, a primitive even among primitives; and the sardonic Curls. The distaff side is dominated by the aggressive Fat Broad, whose efforts at snaring a man are doomed. The only romance that develops in *B.C.* is the star-crossed relationship between an anteater and his coy mistress, an armadillo.

Anachronism is a key element of the humor in *B.C.* No subject is excluded for reasons of chronology. B.C., sitting among drifting leaves, rejoices that "nobody's invented the rake yet." On a cave wall he paints a bison—by numbers. Traffic congestion, air pollution, war, psychiatry, golf, and baseball all provide rich sources of material. Hart has mined every convention of vaudeville for jokes, some as primeval as his characters. Running gags include a newspaper advice column, written by Fat Broad; Peter's Insult Exchange; and Wiley's Dictionary ("after-math" is defined as "algebra").

One of the most admired features of *B.C.* is its truly innovative use of onomatopoeia. "Zot," the sound of an anteater's tongue striking its prey, has become the school cheer of the University of California at Irvine, which has adopted *B.C.*'s ruminative anteater as its mascot. GRONK! is now the accepted transcription of the cry of a dinosaur.

As befits a strip that draws its humor from the contrast between the primitive and the sophisticated, Hart's deceptively simple graphic style succeeds in conveying a look of casual spontaneity while remaining tightly controlled. Political cartoonist Bill Mauldin observed of *B.C.* in 1964 that although it was regarded as a brilliant example of the "new school" of comic strips, it was graphically in the grand tradition of *Krazy Kat* and *Toonerville Folks:* a simple, cartoony style that masks a rigid discipline.

Many collections of *B.C.* have been published since the first one appeared in 1958, and the strip has been adapted several times to television. Its popularity has not been limited to the United States, and the strip appears in many countries and languages around the world.          **D.W.**

**BECK, C.C.** (1910–1989). The co-creator of the original Captain Marvel, Beck drew the red-suited comic book superhero from the captain's advent in 1940 to his

C.C. Beck, Self Portrait, 1974.

cancellation in 1953. When the character was revived in 1973, Beck drew him briefly again. And his remains the definitive version.

An outspoken man of strong opinions, Charles Clarence Beck never thought highly of the comic book field or most of his contemporaries. He listed among his influences newspaper strip cartoonists such as Chester Gould, Billy DeBeck and Harold Gray. Of himself he said, "I'm really just a commercial artist and always have been." He was born in Minnesota and studied at the Chicago Academy of Fine Arts. After a variety of art jobs, he joined Fawcett Publications in 1934. The publishers were then based in Minnesota and Beck drew cartoons and spots for several of their humor magazines, including *Captain Billy's Whiz Bang*. When Fawcett relocated in New York, Beck went along. In 1939 it was decided to try comic books and he was the artist selected to draw a competitor for the fast-rising new Superman. Working with editor/writer Bill Parker, Beck came up with Captain Marvel.

In addition to the Captain, he had a hand in drawing the early episodes of *Spy Smasher* and *Ibis*, features that shared *Whiz Comics* with the superhero. He drew as well the majority of *Whiz Covers*, displaying a strong sense of design. Beck's handsome, uncluttered covers also graced such subsequent Fawcett titles as *Captain Marvel Adventures*, *Wow Comics*, *Nickel Comics* and *Master Comics*.

His best work is on display in the first twenty or so issues of *Whiz*, in pages drawn before the growing popularity of Captain Marvel required more material than one man could produce. In these adventures of the World's Mightiest Mortal Beck ably demonstrates his theories on how to tell a graphic story with verve and clarity. His style was ideally suited to the fantastic and not quite serious exploits of his hero. On some of the earlier escapades he had a little help from Pete Costanza, his long time partner. From the middle 1940s to the early 1950s Beck, usually assisted by Costanza, also produced the Captain Tootsie advertising strip. This ran in Sunday funnies sections and comic books and featured a blond version of the *Whiz* hero, although this captain got his abilities chiefly from eating Tootsie Rolls.

Beck remained the chief artist on Captain Marvel until 1953, the year Fawcett suspended its comic book line. Twenty years later, when DC revived the character under the new title *Shazam!*, Beck came back to draw it. He worked on ten issues, then got into a disagreement over the quality of the scripts—"Dull, boring and childish," Beck thought they were—and quit.

Semi-retired in recent years, he resided in Florida. He wrote a lively and opinionated column, appropriately entitled *Crusty Curmudgeon*, that appeared fairly regularly in *The Comics Journal* until his death.   **R.G.**

**BEETLE BAILEY** A daily and Sunday gag strip set on an army base, Mort Walker's *Beetle Bailey* has performed the remarkable feat of amusing a wide audience with military humor through two increasingly unpopular wars. From a seemingly inexhaustible fund of genial wit, it has rung innumerable changes on the absurdity of army life, the pomposity of rank, the sexual yearnings of the aged, and the droll interaction of an assortment of well-defined humorous types for almost four decades.

Modestly launched by King Features Syndicate on September 4, 1950, Beetle made his first appearance in 12 newspapers as a college student. In its first six months, the strip's sales progressed only to 25, and it was slated for cancellation at the end of its first year. But the growing national preoccupation with the Korean War suggested a change of setting, and Beetle dropped out of college to enlist in the army on March 13, 1951. The decision proved a shrewd one. With many of the same basic gag themes derived from the confrontation of the individual with the establishment, and some of the same characters carried over from Rockville U. to Camp Swampy, *Beetle Bailey* added 100 papers almost immediately and has grown steadily since. A Sunday strip was added on September 14, 1952. In 1965, the strip became the second in history to pass the 1,000-paper mark (after *Blondie*) and now appears in about 1,800 papers worldwide.

The strip stars the eternal goof-off Beetle in an unusually large cast of fellow-soldiers, including the crude but lovable bully Sgt. Snorkle, the ineffectual General Halftrack, the callow Lt. Fuzz, the hip black Lt. Flap, the innocent farmboy Zero, the lecherous Killer, the intellectual Plato (based on Walker's friend and colleague Dik Browne), and numerous others.

When the Korean War ended, Beetle was scheduled to return home on furlough and join his sister, brother-in-law, and their kids, but the shift did not prove popular, and he returned to camp, never to leave again. The relatives evolved into a strip of their own in 1954 as *Hi & Lois*, scripted by Walker and drawn by Dik Browne.

Its crisp, clean lines, simple compositions, and concise dialogue make *Beetle Bailey* easy to read, and its broad slapstick humor has kept it an unfailing source of merriment. The strip has won many awards and generated numerous paperback books, games, and toys, as well as animated cartoons.   **D.W.**

**BELIEVE IT OR NOT** A cartoon panel devoted to dispensing three or four odd and incredible facts each day, *Believe It Or Not* has been running in newspapers for over 70 years. Its title phrase has become part of the American language, and its creator, Robert L. Ripley, earned millions of dollars for himself with nothing more than pen, paper and an insatiable curiosity about strange and unusual bits of information.

Leroy Ripley—he added the Robert later in life—was born in Santa Rosa, California, in 1893. His two major ambitions were to be a professional ballplayer and an artist. While still in his teens he became a sports cartoonist in San Francisco, first on the *Bulletin* and later on the *Chronicle*. At the age of 19, and at the urging of cartoonist Jimmy Swinnerton, Ripley headed for New York City. He was hired to do sports cartoons for the *Globe*, and one day in December 1918, when at a loss for an idea, he put together a panel of sports oddities—"J. Darby of England jumped backwards 12 ft. 11 in. (with weights)…H. Hillman and Lawson Robertson did 100 yds. in 11 secs. in a three-legged race" etc.,—and titled it *Champs and Chumps.* After some consultation with his editor the title was changed to *Believe It Or Not.*

Before too long Ripley was drawing *Believe It Or Not* six days a week and giving out not only sports oddities but also strange and debatable facts about everything. And he was generating an impressive reader response. In 1927 Lindbergh made his solo flight across the Atlantic and Ripley had an item about that. "When I asserted that Lindbergh was the sixty-seventh man to make a non-stop flight across the Atlantic Ocean, you should have seen the deluge of mail that poured in," he once said. "Five thousand people indignantly wrote me to demand why I had made such a statement. They were all sure they were right." What that mass of indignant readers had missed was that Ripley hadn't said anything about *solo* flights. To get his total of 67 he had to count the crews of two dirigibles that had made the transatlantic flight.

Ripley drew in a straightforward sports cartoonist style and was good at figures, portraits, landscapes, and assorted unusual props. He added puzzlers, palindromes, riddles, and braintwisters to his fare as well as odd items about unusual pets, people, and, fairly often, potatoes that resembled presidents or turnips that looked like movie stars. Ripley always maintained that he could document any and all of the facts drawn up in *Believe It Or Not,* even though his idea of documentation often involved the acceptance of dubious printed accounts and some slurred math. He never retracted a "fact" and printed explanations went out with every panel. Some newspapers printed those as well, while others kept them on hand to refute angry readers.

Ripley's panel was taken on by King Features in 1929 and he was earning $100,000 a year by 1930, a figure that kept growing, aided by increased newspaper clients, radio shows, *Believe It Or Not* museums, and lectures. A compulsive world traveler once he struck it rich, Ripley employed a large staff to research the panel and help

with the artwork. One longtime ghost was Clemens Gretter.

Several imitations of the panel were attempted, especially during the 1930s. The most successful and longest-running was John Hix' *Strange As It Seems.*

Ripley died in 1949, but *Believe It Or Not* kept right on. Paul Frehm drew it for many years and, after his death, his brother Walter Frehm took over. United Features took over the feature in 1990, giving it a new artist and a more humorous appearance. **R.G.**

**BEN WEBSTER** He was an honest, clean-cut, blond young man, and he remained one throughout the 15 or so years he was a funny paper hero. He first appeared in 1926, when he took over as the star of the *Bound to Win* strip. Jay Jerome Williams, under the pen name Edwin Alger, wrote his adventures and a succession of anonymous artists drew them.

The feature, which comics historian Bill Blackbeard has aptly summed up as "forcefully dull," appeared under a variety of names. The daily ran as *Bound to Win* (which had begun as *Phil Hardy* in 1925), *Ben Webster's Career,* and *Ben Webster.* (Depending on which newspaper the strip was running in, there was some overlap in these titles.) The Sunday was originally known as *Ben Webster's Page* and later simply as *Ben Webster.* Under this last title some of the Sunday sequences were reprinted in *All-American Comics* from 1939 to 1941.

Williams was a firm believer in the Horatio Alger Jr. trappings, and his decent young hero showed a good deal of pluck and luck as he journeyed through life. Ben encountered plenty of ruthless bankers, an abundance of innocent young women, and lots of widows in need of aid. The mortgage was one of Williams' favorite props and it figured in his strip almost as much as the tommygun did in *Dick Tracy.* The daily alternated foreclosure continuities with standard boys' book fare—lost treasures, bandit lairs, old dark houses, shipwrecks etc. Ben had a mutt dog named Briar, who served as companion and sounding board for many a long year and, like Orphan Annie's Sandy, had to listen to an awful lot of monologues.

The Sunday dealt originally with nonfiction accounts of the lives of famous men, then converted to adventure; many of these stories had fantasy and science fiction elements. The artist on the final years of *Ben Webster* Sunday pages seems to have been a Florida newspaper cartoonist named Calvin Fader, who was the best of the lot. Ben's career came to an end in the early 1940s. **R.G.**

**BERG, DAVID** (1920– ) Berg's career as a cartoonist can be divided into two distinct phases—before and after he joined *Mad.* In the years from 1940 to the mid-

1950s, except for three years service in the Air Force during World War II, Berg worked in comic books. While he drew superheroes, soldiers, and monsters, his strong suit was humorous fantasy. After becoming a *Mad* regular in the mid-Fifties, he was still funny but the fantasy was gone, and he concentrated on examining the lighter side of every day, middle-class suburban life.

He was born in the Brownsville section of Brooklyn and studied art at several schools, including Pratt and Cooper Union. His first professional cartooning job was working in Will Eisner's shop. He assisted on *The Spirit* and also drew an occasional episode of *Uncle Sam* in that patriotic hero's own magazine. Berg's Uncle Sam stories, which he wrote himself, were quite different from the ones rendered by such artists as Reed Crandall, Lou Fine, and Eisner himself; a typical one, for example, dealt with comic book villains going on strike.

The earliest feature he got to sign was *Death Patrol*. It appeared in Quality's *Military Comics*, where Blackhawk was the star and Eisner the editor. The patrol was made of a group of high-risk free-lance fliers, who wore uniforms that were striped like those of convicts and who fought the Nazis. The gifted Jack Cole had created the feature, and Berg was able to carry on pretty well, achieving a blend of violence, humor, and unorthodox layouts that came close to matching Cole's.

Moving next to Fawcett, Berg wrote and drew some adventures of Captain Marvel. He produced a very unorthodox version of the already somewhat unorthodox superhero. For Fawcett Berg also did several fantasy fillers—*Spooks* in *Wow Comics*, and *Sir Butch*, which popped up in various titles. Butch was a tough Brooklyn kid who, by falling down a manhole, ended up in a fantasy realm where he tangled with dragons and sorcerers. This mix of *Alice in Wonderland* and the Dead End Kids was one of Berg's most ambitious efforts, and he put an impressive amount of first-rate fantasy drawing into the six pages he was allowed for each episode, which he obviously enjoyed.

Returning to comics after World War II, Berg again worked for a while with Eisner. He got a chance for fantasy again in 1952 and did a short-lived *Alice in Wonderland* comic for Ziff-Davis. He also worked on straight war stories, editing several war comics for Marvel and drawing *Combat Kelly*.

In 1957 Berg found his way to *Mad* and he's been there ever since. His mildly satirical looks at various aspects of life in Middle America, under the title *The Lighter Side of...*, became one of the magazine's most popular features. He's done over a dozen paperbacks as well.

**R.G.**

**BEROTH, LEON** See DON WINSLOW.

**BERNDT, WALTER** (1899–1979) The creator of the long-running strip *Smitty* began his newspaper and cartooning career as an office boy at the *New York Journal*, "sweeping floors, running errands, [and] drawing strips, sports cartoons, and what have you." The 16-year-old Brooklyn boy, with six months of high school ("That was too slow for me," he explained years later) and two nights at Pratt Institute ("They had me drawing girls' dresses," he recalled. "I said, 'This is not cartooning, this isn't for me!'"), got his first job in journalism, for $5 a week, "but a million dollars worth of experience," in 1916. Working around such notables as Thomas A. "Tad" Dorgan, Harry Hershfield, Milt Gross, E.C. Segar, and Winsor McCay, the ambitious young Berndt quickly began to involve himself in production, lettering and reworking their old strips with new gags when any of them didn't come in to work. Dorgan was so impressed with his energy and talent that he began to teach him some of the tricks of the trade—Berndt copied the initial "T" in Tad's signature as the last letter in his own by way of acknowledgment—and in time let Berndt do his Monday sports panels, for an extra $10. When Milt Gross was promoted, Berndt took over his humor panel, *Then the Fun Began*, published six times a week, and rose to $10 a week. Berndt quit the *Journal* in 1920 to do his own strip, *That's Different*, for the Bell Syndicate, but was so dissatisfied with his work that he abandoned it. "I couldn't draw it and the syndicate couldn't sell it," he explained, "so after a year we tore up the contract."

Turning to his own experience at the *Journal* for material for another feature, he came up with a gag strip called *Bill the Office Boy* and sold it to the *New York World* in 1922. That affiliation lasted an even shorter time; in two weeks Berndt was fired—"because of the way I addressed my boss," he recalled. At the suggestion of Segar, the undismayed young cartoonist offered the strip to the *Chicago Tribune*, where publisher Joseph M. Patterson accepted it for his *New York Daily News*, after changing the name to *Smitty*.

Berndt became a close friend and confidant of Patterson and was responsible, over the long course of their association, for the recruitment to the *News* of many important cartoonists, among them Bill Holman, Zack Mosley, Gus Edson, and Al Posen. His own creation, *Smitty*, was distributed to a wide reading public by the Tribune-News Syndicate for over half a century, earning him many honors. In 1969 the National Cartoonists Society selected him to represent American cartoonists at the World's Fair in Montreal and awarded him its Reuben as the Outstanding Cartoonist of the Year.

Drawn with a pleasantly loose, sketchy line, *Smitty* retained the affection of its large public more for the warmth of its characterization and the geniality of its humor than for any graphic distinction. In 1930 Smitty's kid brother Herby became the titular hero of his own appropriately shorter strip, a four-panel topper appearing on Sundays. Berndt employed an assistant, Charles Mueller, for the first 30 years of *Smitty* but took over the full work of the strip when Mueller became eligible for social security and retired in 1952; he wrote and drew every panel of *Smitty* and *Herby* until he retired them both, with himself, in 1973. **D.W.**

**BETTY** One of many features dedicated to glorifying the American girl, *Betty* began in 1920 and lasted until 1943. It was written and drawn by Charles A. Voight, whose gags usually fell far short of his impressive artwork.

A Sunday page, *Betty* first appeared in the *New York Tribune* on April 4, 1920, and was syndicated by the newspaper, which became the *Herald Tribune* in 1924. Voight was a veteran cartoonist and illustrator who also drew a daily strip titled *Petey*. He had a forceful, highly individual pen and ink style that put him in the same league with Frank Godwin and Russell Patterson. His Sunday page dealt chiefly with the social life of a pretty young blond named Betty Thompson, who was a member of the idle class. Voight's comic situations were most often built around parties, dances, dinner parties, and similar events; during the warm months his characters spent a good deal of time at the beach, allowing Voight to depict large quantities of young ladies in the latest swimwear.

Like many of the pretty girls of the funnies—among them, Fritzi Ritz and Tillie the Toiler—Betty dated a wide variety of conventionally handsome men but had as her steadiest date a diminutive and inept suitor. In Betty's case the steady beau was Lester DePester, a singularly unappealing fellow without any visible chin.

In the *Betty* page's final years Voight experimented with continuity, constructing rambling stories that dealt with mystery, fantasy, and science fiction. It ended in June of 1943 and was replaced by a more up-to-date young woman—Harry Haenigsen's *Penny*. In the few remaining years of his life Voight drew for comic books. **K.S.B.**

**BETTY BOOP** The undisputed queen of merchandising, Betty Boop broke into show business in the early 1930s by way of animated cartoons. A popular and appealing character from the start, she soon branched out into other areas and in 1934 started appearing in a King Features newspaper strip. Like many movie stars, she's had her ups and downs. In the 1980s, however, Betty Boop made a distinct comeback, one of the results of which was a return to the funny papers.

Betty was born in New York in the Fleischer Brothers animation studios in 1930. Her initial appearance, in a Talkartoon entitled *Dizzy Dishes*, wasn't particularly auspicious and she was, according to film historian Leonard Maltin, "a hybrid of a dog and a sexy girl, with a voluptuous feminine body but dog ears and a canine nose." Betty was originally going to be the ladyfriend of Bimbo, a dog character who was a star at Fleischer. But Betty gradually changed into the sexy shortskirted human she was to remain. Bimbo, an example of the fleetingness of stardom, later became her pet pooch.

The actual creator of Betty Boop was an animator named Grim Natwick. He has said that he based the character, on orders from Dave Fleischer, on the then popular singer Helen Kane. Kane, who'd become famous in the late 1920s for inserting the scat phrase "boop-boop-a-doop" into her rendition of the hit tune *I Wanna Be Loved By You*, starred in several movies in the early 1930s. "The girl on the cover of the sheet music had spit curls," Natwick once recalled, "so I swiped that idea and went to work." Kane's piping, little girl voice was imitated in the Fleischer cartoons by Mae Questal.

The merchandising of Betty followed close on the heels of her screen success. "Her popularity was instantaneous and Max Fleischer…pushed her profitably into toys, games, dolls and related merchandise," reports Robert Lesser in *A Celebration of Comic Art and Memorabilia*. In addition to Betty Boop dolls, watches, windup toys, radios, and necklaces, there was a *Betty Boop* Big Little Book issued in 1934. That same year, on July 23, King Features introduced a newspaper strip. Although Max Fleischer took credit for it, the strip was actually drawn by Bud Counihan, a veteran cartoonist and sometime assistant to Chic Young on *Blondie*. As on the screen, Betty was wide-eyed and large-headed in the strip and wore a skimpy dress—or less. Her garter, as specified in the studio model sheets, always appeared on her left leg. In the strip Betty worked as a movie star and the gags, which were rarely very strong, were based on her career. A Sunday page was added in 1935, but the whole project ended in 1938.

Betty's popularity waxed and waned over the next few decades. By the early 1980s, however, she was a popular icon again. There were new toys, books, dolls, watches, clothes, even a TV special, and her old cartoons became available on videocassette. In 1984 King Features decided to take another chance on her. For good measure she was teamed with another oldtime animated cartoon character, and the new strip was called *Betty Boop and Felix*. It began on November 19, 1984, and was credited to the Walker Brothers. They were Mort Walker's four sons—one pencilled, one inked, and the other two came up with gags. Betty was an actress and a model this time around, and there were references to real celebrities such as Burt Reynolds, Raquel Welch, and Cher. Felix, living "the life of a retired superstar," shared Betty's penthouse with her and pretty much acted as a standin for Bimbo. The strip lasted until the last day of January, 1988.      **R.G.**

**BEYOND MARS**  This science-fiction strip ran only on Sunday and only in the *New York Daily News;* nevertheless, its circulation could be considered national since the Sunday edition was sold on newsstands across the country. Scripted by longtime SF author Jack Williamson and drawn by Lee Elias, the page ran from February 17, 1952, to May 13, 1955.

"That was when TV had just begun to hurt the circulation of Sunday papers," Williamson once explained. "Somebody at the *News* noticed that all the competing papers had the same comics and that the *News* might gain a competitive edge by developing some original strips of its own." Using the novels he'd written about Seetee (CT stood for contraterrene, better known these days as antimatter) as a basis, Williamson invented a tabloid page about Mike Flint, a "licensed spatial engineer" who lived some 200 years in the future on Brooklyn Rock in the asteroid belt. It was a time when, as a caption told the reader, "a new force—paragravity— has enabled men to live and breathe on the asteroids." According to Williamson, "the plot pattern of the strip was taken more or less from *Dick Tracy*…Each episode involved a conflict with a new villain, with a new group of colorful characters."

Williamson got the job of writing and creating *Beyond Mars* somewhat by chance when his novel *Seetee Ship* received a somewhat patronizing review in the *New York Times*. "It is a pity that the quality of the writing is such that this 'space opera' ranks only slightly above that of a comic strip adventure," the reviewer remarked. Reading that, editors at the rival *New York Daily News* decided that Williamson was just the man they needed to write their new science fiction adventure strip for them.

He recalled that his copy was frequently altered to fit "the *News'* notion of which ideas and assumptions the readers could understand and accept." Despite these handicaps, Williamson managed to construct a fast-moving space opera with touches of both real science fiction and genuine humor. The artist, Lee Elias, was a comic book graduate and a disciple of Milton Caniff. He did an attractive job, but after three years the paper lost interest in the idea of having its own exclusive features and *Beyond Mars* was dropped.      **R.G.**

**BIFF BAKER**  Credited to Henry Lee, this Sunday page was actually written by NEA syndicate comics editor Ernest "East" Lynn and drawn by Henry Schlensker. It was launched on September 7, 1941.

Biff Baker was a "college senior, football star and amateur aviator," but two months before the bombing of Pearl Harbor proved to be an inopportune time to introduce a college football star who dabbled in flying. Some changes were made, and by early 1942 Biff was capturing a Nazi spy ring that was attempting to flourish on campus. In June he graduated from Midwestern University and, through the intercession of an influential uncle, went into the Air Corps. When Biff heard the news that he'd been accepted, he exclaimed, "Oh, boy, that's great! Uncle Jim, you're a wonder!"

By shifting focus between Biff and some of his chums, the Sunday page managed to cover the war in both the Pacific and Europe. The Japanese were an especially cunning and fiendish lot and delighted in delivering lines like, "I will take gun! I insist on pleasure of shooting American and hearing him beg for mercy!" As the Forties progressed, Schlensker left the feature to enter the service himself, and Walt Scott took over the artwork. *Biff Baker* ended in 1945.

Schlensker became Roy Crane's assistant on *Buz Sawyer* after the war, exhibiting no trace of the straight illustrative style he used on *Biff*. He went on to ghost the *Buz Sawyer* daily and eventually got a credit on the strip when Crane retired.      **R.G.**

**BIG BEN BOLT**  Pugilism had had a fair representation in the comics ever since Ham Fisher's *Joe Palooka* first appeared in 1930. But when Elliot Caplin proposed a boxing strip to King Features Syndicate in 1949, the selection of noted sports cartoonist and illustrator John Cullen Murphy assured that the new strip would be graphically superior to most of its predecessors. *Big Ben Bolt* proved to be more than usually literate, and stylish as well.

Big Ben Bolt (a name probably taken from the hero of the popular 1843 poem *Ben Bolt* by Thomas Dunn English, still a standard song and recitation piece in the 1950s) began its run as a daily continuity strip on February 20, 1950, and added a Sunday version on May 25, 1952. Unlike most strips about the ring, it featured a boxer neither simpleminded nor inarticulate, and treated the professional milieu with reasonable respect. Bolt is intelligent, well-educated (he has a college degree), and honorable, without being a prig. Of course he is big—big enough, and a good enough boxer, to win the world's heavyweight championship early in the strip's career. In 1955, however, he suffered an eye injury that forced him out of the ring for a time. He became a sports writer, and for the next 20-some years he engaged in a variety of adventures as a journalist, a detective, and an all-around good model for youth.

Plausible characterization, accurate dialogue, and well-paced stories, along with some sophisticated realistic art, kept the strip going until long after continuity features had begun to disappear. The last Sunday *Big Ben Bolt* strip was dated April 13, 1975, and the last daily April 10, 1978. It shared the National Cartoonists Society's award as the Best Story Strip of the year with Murphy's *Prince Valiant* in 1971.

Murphy was assisted with the drawing of *Big Ben Bolt* from the early 1950s, notably by Carlos Garzón, who produced the dailies for several years. As Murphy became increasingly involved with Hal Foster's strip *Prince Valiant*, which he took over in 1971, he relinquished more and more of the production to others. From August 1, 1977, until its demise eight months later, the daily feature was signed by Gray Morrow.

**D.W.**

**BIG CHIEF WAHOO**   When it began in November of 1936, it was a comedy strip about a diminutive English-mangling Indian and a windy conman. *Big Chief Wahoo*, however, gradually transformed itself into a straight adventure feature. Eventually the strip, created by writer Allen Saunders and artist Elmer Woggon, dropped the chief entirely and changed its name. Finally even Woggon was dropped.

*Big Chief Wahoo*, Elmer Woggon.

The initial continuity had Wahoo, newly rich from the oil discovered on his land, leaving his home in Tepee Town to journey eastward to New York. His true love Minnie-ha-cha was there, singing in a night spot. En route the little Indian, who spoke standard movie redman patois ("Ugh. Gotta watch um wampum" etc.), fell in with an itinerant medicine show huckster named J. Mortimer Gusto. Wahoo got conned into traveling with the medicine show and helping to sell Ka-zowie Kure-all. The Great Gusto, who looked and behaved like W.C. Fields, had been the titular head of their strip when Saunders and Woggon originally tried to sell it. Since editors proved fonder of Wahoo, the Indian was made the star. Along the way to Manhattan Wahoo and Gusto befriended a runaway little girl named Pigtails, and she became part of the cast.

The early stories went in for puns, gags, and fairly broad kidding of New York's cafe society set and, later, the similar types in Hollywood. Saunders, though, came to believe that what they ought to be doing was something closer to an adventure strip, and throughout the late 1930s his continuities grew more serious, with suspense and melodrama easing out slapstick and burlesque. Since Woggon's simple cartoon style didn't suit the new approach, ghost artists were brought in, first his brother, Bill Woggon, and then Don Dean. Late in 1940 a new character arrived in Tepee Town, a handsome, blond, pipesmoking fellow wearing the jodphurs and boots that were one of the accepted costumes of funny paper adventurers. This was Steve Roper, globetrotting magazine photographer. From that point on Wahoo became the second banana in his own strip.

For a while Roper even romanced Minnie-ha-cha and, had not an important secret mission intervened, he would have married her. During the early 1940s Steve Roper, with Wahoo tagging along in a loyal sidekick capacity, fought spies and secret agents around the globe, from Egypt to Brazil. Saunders was now using storylines that included the sort of soap opera events to be found in his *Mary Worth* and the bizarre villains he utilized in *Kerry Drake*. After Don Dean left in 1944, Pete Hoffman took over as ghost. The feature had long since changed its title to *Steve Roper and Wahoo*. By 1947 Wahoo was hardly taking part in the action at all and one fine day he simply stopped showing up for work. The strip then became *Steve Roper*.

**R.G.**

**BIG GEORGE**   Virgil Franklin Partch, who signed his cartoons "Vip," had already established himself as one of America's most prolific and stylistically distinctive cartoonists when, in 1958, his friend Hank Ketcham suggested that he try a syndicated feature. Partch offered Hall Syndicate, which distributed Ketcham's *Dennis the Menace*, a series called simply *Vip*, consisting of unrelated gag-cartoons in his familiar style, but Hall was not interested. The cartoonist tried again at Publishers Syndicate, and after two years of discussion and revision, won them over with a panel series called *Big George*, a relatively bland feature with little of the bizarre and sometimes raunchy style for which Partch had long been famous.

Partch, who was born in 1916, began publishing gag cartoons in a wide variety of magazines—his total count was to exceed 150, ranging from the rawest men's monthlies to sophisticated European periodicals like *Paris-Match*—in the late 1930s, and had developed a large and loyal following for his peculiar blend of outre fantasy and slapstick. Rendered in an easily recognizable style, devoid of background, his line-drawings featured his trademark of faces whose foreheads sloped down in an unbroken line to the end of the nose. His humor was similarly *sui generis*, relying on zany exaggeration and literal interpretation of slang. With syndication, however, Partch was forced to tone down the outlandishness and occasional earthiness of his humor, and *Big George* was something of a disappointment to his fans. The barroom and the desert island—two cartoon settings whose conventions Partch had made peculiarly his own—were abandoned for the suburban town; and the voluptuous girls, heavy drinkers, and soldiers of his magazine cartoons had to make way for a middle-class married couple. George, his patient wife Helen, and their nondescript dog Ajax (loosely based on Partch's own Great Dane of the same name) experience situations not much stranger or more farcical than those of Dagwood, Blondie, and Daisy, or Hi, Lois, and Dawg.

Beginning hopefully with more than 300 newspapers in the United States and Canada, *Big George* soon declined in popularity because, as Partch admitted in 1967, "Alas, George wasn't as good as the advance billing." By the mid- 1960s it stabilized and has remained a modest success, adding a comic-strip version on Sundays.

Partch was always an immensely productive cartoonist, and he produced several other strips as well as advertising art and a huge output of gag cartoons. At his death in August 1984, he left enough of the daily panels and Sunday strips of *Big George* to carry the strip through December 1990.                    **D.W.**

**BIG LITTLE BOOKS**  Between 1932 and 1950 the Whitman Publishing Company issued well over 500 small, thick novels in their Big Little Book and Better Little Book series. The majority of them were adapted from comic strips, including *Dick Tracy, Mickey Mouse, Flash Gordon*, and *Blondie*.

The fat little hardcovers sold for 10 cents and were approximately 3.75 inches wide, 4.5 inches high and usually more than 400 pages thick. Profusely illustrated, a page of text alternated with a full-page illustration. In the adaptations from strips these illustrations came from the panels and had the dialogue balloons whited out and the backgrounds enhanced to make the art fit the page. A caption ran under each picture—"Jack Landed the Autoplane," "Mandrake Accepted Her Invitation," "Easy Grabs His Foot," for example. The text presented the plot and dialogue of the strip sequence in the form of a novel. In the process of conversion from strip to book the artwork, and sometimes the dialogue, was butchered, but kid readers of the 1930s didn't seem to mind. According to BLB authority Larry Lowery, Whitman was "selling a million books per month at its peak." The bright-covered books were sold not on newsstands but chiefly in five-and-dime stores.

Samuel E. Lowe, an executive with Whitman's Racine, Wisconsin, office, is credited with inventing the Big Little Book and launching the dime novel series during the Christmas season of 1932. The very first title was *The Adventures of Dick Tracy*, and that was followed by *Mickey Mouse* and *Little Orphan Annie*. Lowe, by the way, was a man who continued to think small. In the early 1940s, when he had a company of his own, he introduced a series of Mighty Midget Comics.

Strips of the larger syndicates, especially King and the Chicago Tribune-New York News, were the most frequently used by Whitman. *Mickey Mouse* holds the record for most appearances between 1932 and 1950, having been featured in 29 different titles; *Dick Tracy* is next with 27, followed by *Donald Duck, Tarzan*, and *Little Orphan Annie*. Other popular strips were *Blondie, Flash Gordon, Terry and the Pirates, Buck Rogers, Dan Dunn*, and *Smilin' Jack*. In the early 1940s Whitman introduced an All Pictures series and produced some very fat black and white comic books in the BLB format, including *Smokey Stover, Smitty*, and *Felix the Cat*.

Although the books got increasing competition from comic books throughout the 1930s, the two formats managed to coexist peacefully. In the first six years over 250 Big Little Books were published, and several other publishers tried similar packages, most notably Saalfield with its Little Big Books. Whitman changed the name of its line to Better Little Books in 1938.

In addition to strips Whitman published nearly 50 movie novelizations. These included the MGM version of *David Copperfield* with W.C. Fields, DeMille's *The Buccaneer*, and two of the *Tarzan* movies. Western films were popular, too, and those of Tim McCoy, Ken Maynard, and Tom Mix were among those adapted. All were illustrated with movie stills.

There were also over 60 original titles done. Among these were novels based on popular radio shows, such as *The Lone Ranger, The Green Hornet, Jack Armstrong, Captain Midnight, Mr. District Attorney,* and *Gang Busters.* Ellery Queen appeared in two BLBs, the Shadow in three. Whitman even tried superheroes of its own, with three books about Maximo the Amazing Superman in 1941 and one about the Ghost Avenger in 1943. Among the teenage heroes and heroines were Kay Darcy, Frank Merriwell, Peggy Brown, and Bob Stone, Young Detective. Several real-life movie cowboys showed up in fictional adventures, among them Gene Autry and Roy Rogers. One of the rarest originals is *The Laughing Dragon of Oz,* an unauthorized 1934 addition to the Oz canon. Illustrations for many of the original titles were provided by two Whitman regulars, Irwin Hess and Henry Vallely. Ken Ernst, Fred Guardineer, and Alden McWilliams were also among the illustrators.

In the early 1940s Whitman tried an added attraction. They put an extra little picture in the corner of each illustration and turned each book into an animation flipbook—"flip the pages and see 'em move." Alas, this innovation further fouled up the artwork.

The BLB operation shut down in 1950. Whitman has attempted to revive the format several times over the years, but never with the success of the 1930s and 1940s.

**R.G.**

**BIG TOP** This strip about the circus ran for a little more than half a year and was Ed Wheelan's last go-round as a newspaper cartoonist. Distributed by the small Frank Jay Markey Syndicate, *Big Top* began in April 1937 and ended in November. There was a short-lived Sunday page as well, but the strip spent more than half of its life as a daily only.

As he'd done in the final years of *Minute Movies,* Wheelan curtailed his sense of humor and strove to produce a straight adventure strip. The melodramatic continuities dealt with the trials and tribulations of the Bangs Bros. Circus as it toured small-town America. Its regular cast included kindly old circus owner Jeff Bangs, lovely aerialist Myra Labelle, and handsome foursquare trick rider Hal Thompson, as well as clowns, chimps, elephants, and all the other props and personages of circus life. Wheelan drew everything with affection and attention to detail, but his stories hearkened back to the material he'd kidded a decade earlier in *Minute Movies.*

All the Sundays and then the dailies were reprinted in *Feature Funnies/Feature Comics* from #1 (October 1937) through #26 (November 1939). Markey, who owned a piece of the magazine, also resyndicated *Big Top* to weekly newspapers in the early 1940s. When the re-

prints ceased in *Feature,* the strip continued with new pages drawn by Johnny Devlin and then Bernard Dibble.

**R.G.**

**BILL AND DAVEY** A seagoing adventure strip, *Bill and Davey* was written and drawn by James P. McCague. Daily only, it began in the *Brooklyn Eagle* on September 16, 1935, and was distributed by the newspaper's Watkins Syndicate.

Something of an oddity, the strip told serious tales of mystery, melodrama, and mutiny on the high seas, but the drawing was cartoony and primitive. McCague's people were rough-hewn and many of them looked like sketches for hand-carved wooden puppets.

The title characters were Bill Bilson, a husky seaman given to expressions like "Aw, bilge," and Davey, a blond orphan lad whom Bill befriended on the strip's first day. They were continually helping young women in distress, hunting for lost treasure, and signing on with evil-hearted captains. McCague favored names that telegraphed character, and the strip was full of such people as Captain Lash, Captain Stabb, and Miss Trew. McCague modified his style, moving a bit closer toward realism, as the strip progressed, and he allowed Davey to grow into a teenager. *Bill and Davey* continued until 1940.

Though never widely circulated, the strip was reprinted in two comic books: Dell's shortlived *The Comics* offered it in the lineup in 1938 and Eastern Color's *Heroic Comics* ran a few pages of dailies in its first 11 issues, commencing in 1940.

**R.G.**

**BILLY MAKE BELIEVE** A Sunday kid page that originally mixed fantasy with a *Popular Mechanics* sort of practicality. It was introduced by United Features in 1935 and was drawn by Harry Homan.

Like Frank King's *Bobby Make-Believe* of two decades earlier, *Billy Make Believe* initially had a fondness for embarking on imaginary adventures. His accomplices on these early undertakings were his pudgy pal Bub and his equally pudgy girlfriend Dolly. In these stories Billy imagined himself into a protracted war in toyland, an encounter with a will-o-the-wisp in an enchanted forest, and similar fairy tale setups.

Homan, who had worked as an architectural design artist, an advertising art director, and a political cartoonist, drew the page in a cozy cartoon style that echoed both children's book illustrations and animated cartoons of the cuter sort. His middle name was Elmer and he always signed his work "He Homan."

The bottom strip that accompanied the page was titled *How to Make It* and therein Homan offered young craftsmen practical step-by-step plans for constructing a wide range of useful objects—an airplane kite, a tin can tractor, a tiny piano constructed from cigar boxes and pins, a rubber band peashooter, a magnetic compass, and the like.

This practical side eventually took over, and Billy moved away from fantasy lands into the real world; from then on he had more conventional encounters, with a mysterious band of outlaws, a hidden treasure, an avalanche, a heroic pilot—in sum, the standard fare of action yarns.

*Billy Make Believe* ended in 1938 but could still be seen as late as 1940 among the reprints in UFS' *Comics on Parade*. Homan next ghosted the daily *Joe Jinks* strip and worked as United Features' political cartoonist. He died in 1940 at the age of 51.                                           **R.G.**

**BINDER, OTTO** (1911–1974) An impressively prolific writer, Binder turned out comic-book scripts for 30 years, from 1939 to 1969. He wrote the majority of scripts about the original Captain Marvel and also provided material for dozens of other characters, including the Shadow, Captain America, Blackhawk, Superman, and Hoppy the Marvel Bunny. Nearly all of his comic book work was uncredited.

He started writing professionally in 1932, when he and his brother Earl collaborated on pulp magazine science fiction under the pen name Eando Binder. The Eando byline appeared in such magazines as *Amazing Stories, Startling Stories, Thrilling Wonder,* among others. Eando Binder's best-remembered character was the robot Adam Link, who starred in a series in *Amazing* from 1939 to 1942.

Otto got into comic books through another brother, artist Jack Binder. Jack was managing the Chesler shop, and Otto wrote his first scripts for comic books the outfit was packaging. Among the characters he was assigned was a science fiction hero named Dan Hastings, one of the earliest such characters in the comics. He found his way to Fawcett in 1941 and from then until 1953 was the chief writer on Captain Marvel as well as the other members of the Marvel Family, also scripting Spy Smasher, Ibis, Bulletman, and even the Marvel Bunny in Fawcett's *Funny Animals.*

"My first *Captain Marvel Adventures* script was written in December 1941," he once recalled. "The end result of this, some 12 years later in 1953, was a total of 529 stories about the Big Red Cheese alone." Binder took care of nearly all the adventures dealing with time travel, space travel, and other SF themes. He also invented Mr. Tawny, the talking tiger who shared many a story with Billy Batson and the captain. When asked to name the favorite character of all those he had written about, Binder replied, "Without a doubt Captain Marvel."

During the 1940s he managed to produce scripts for a dozen other publishers and handled such characters as Captain Battle, Hangman, the Shield, Dollman, the Young Allies, Doc Strange, Captain America, the Shining Knight, and Robotman. After Captain Marvel was retired, Binder went over to DC and wrote scripts for Superman as well as Supergirl, in whose creation he had a hand. He contributed to EC, and in 1957 he created the character Mighty Samson for Gold Key with Frank Thorne as the artist. In 1967 he teamed once again with Captain Marvel artist C.C. Beck on the ill-fated *Fatman.* Two years later he retired from comic books.

He devoted the years after comics to writing nonfiction books and articles, mostly in the field of science.                                            **R.G.**

**BIRO, CHARLES** (1911–1972) A highly influential figure in the comic book field, Biro worked as an artist, writer, and editor. His heyday decade was the 1940s, during which he created such heroes as Steel Sterling, Crimebuster, and Airboy. He also revitalized the original Daredevil and helped create *Crime Does Not Pay,* one of the bestselling comic books ever. The packaging and promotion tricks Biro developed for the titles he was editing set a style that numerous publishers and editors, notably Stan Lee, have followed.

Biro was born in New York, and in 1936 he went to work for the enterprising Harry "A" Chesler, who owned the very first sweat shop devoted to producing art and editorial material for comic books. The equally enterprising Biro was soon the supervisor of the operation. After departing Chesler in the late 1930s, he moved over to MLJ and took charge of *Pep Comics, Zip Comics, Blue Ribbon,* and the rest of the company's pre-Archie titles. It was at this point that he abandoned his interest in cute bigfoot cartooning and switched to tough, determinedly sleazy, straight adventure stuff.

His most successful creation at MLJ was the superhero Steel Sterling for *Zip Comics.* His early pages were badly drawn, yet had a strong sense of action, movement, and life. Biro next went to work for the Lev Gleason company. When Daredevil got his own magazine in 1941, Biro was one of its editors and drew the costumed crimefighter. Besides exploiting the blend of sex and violence he had developed at MLJ, Biro now added some packaging tricks. From its first issue *Daredevil* carried the line "The Greatest Name in Comics" emblazoned on its cover. There were also colored headlines and boxes of copy promising all sorts of things within—"$100 CASH PRIZES You May WIN!" Biro got into the habit of addressing his readers directly: "None can rival the wild fantasy that will unfold within these pages!…So dim the lights and lock your doors well for this monster might strike at even YOU!"—"THIS war above all must not be lost! You may not be a DARE-

DEVIL, but no person is too insignificant to help! DO YOUR PART!!!" etc.

In the spring of 1942 Biro added *Boy Comics* to the Gleason list. The new magazine offered "a boy hero in every strip!!" It was coedited by Bob Wood and was introduced with typical Biro flair: "Ready at last! Two years in the making! Produced behind closed doors in utmost secrecy!" The leading boy hero was Crimebuster, drawn and written by Biro. One of the recurrent villains was a fellow named Iron Jaw, a Nazi who'd had the lower half of his face replaced by a metal contrivance that resembled a bear trap. Biro again came up with surefire slogans to be spread across the covers: "First Torture, Then DEATH! With 130,000,000 Lives At Stake! Can CRIMEBUSTER Squelch This Foul Jap Treachery?"

Right after *Boy*, Biro, Gleason, and associates brought forth *Crime Does Not Pay*. This was the first successful true crime comic book, and it helped pave the way for the near collapse of the comic book business in the middle 1950s because of the anti-comics crusade. The World War II years constituted Biro's peak creative period. It was a time when many publishers came to realize that not only kids but also adolescents and a great many GIs were potential customers. A typical Biro story of those years would include considerable bloodshed and violence—probably at least one stabbing and maybe even an impaling. There'd be sex, usually symbolized by tight sweaters and hiked skirts. Now and then Biro even tossed in a few anti-gay jokes. The usual Biro villain, as typified by Iron Jaw, had the temperament of the Tasmanian Devil and the social attitudes of the Marquis de Sade. Biro never drew anything but the covers for *Crime Does Not Pay*. These contained some of his most provocative work and went in for bright colors, complex violence, and plenty of hardselling copy.

By the time the 1950s arrived Biro had toned down. He dropped the wild villains from both *Daredevil* and *Boy* and was taking stands against juvenile delinquency and other social ills of the day. Like many another entrepreneur, he took credit for most of the scripts in these two magazines, though the majority were actually written by a lady named Virginia Hubbell. Biro even went so far as to try a comic book titled *Uncle Charlie's Fables*. This sort of gentleness was not his strong suit and the magazine failed. He left comics to join NBC as a graphic artist in 1962. **R.G.**

**THE BLACK CAT** One of the first of the costumed lady crimefighters, Black Cat beat Wonder Woman into print by several months and tied with Phantom Lady. Apparently the creation of artist Al Gabrielle, she made her debut in Harvey's *Pocket Comics* #1 (August 1941). This odd-format digest lasted for only four issues. After

that the Black Cat transfered to *Speed Comics*, starting with #17.

In the summer of 1941, red-haired Linda Turner, "Hollywood movie star and America's sweetheart," had begun to suspect that her movie director was a Nazi agent. Learning that he was also afraid of black cats, Linda, who'd become increasingly bored with the empty life of a glamorous actress, decided to design herself a black cat costume and fight subversion: "If this works I'll kill two birds with one stone…I'll have my thrills and I'll do my duty to my country." The costume Linda ran up was a scanty one, and if it didn't scare spies, it at least distracted them.

While tracking down her first spy ring, Black Cat met Rick Horne, a handsome reporter on the *Los Angeles Globe*. Horne was quite taken with her—"What a gal!"—and immediately started addressing her as "Beautiful." But when Linda was in her Black Cat mode she was feisty and independent. Her pet name for Horne was "Stupid." Teaming up, they thwarted the spies and edited all the Nazi propaganda and secret code messages out of Linda's latest film.

She continued to fight spies in Hollywood, usually with an assist from reporter Horne. Though she professed to be annoyed by him—"Must I be plagued by you again?"—it was obvious she was fond of the guy. At the end of an early adventure, which wound up on a tramp steamer, she tripped him, tackled him, planted a resounding kiss on his lips, and then dived overboard—a formidable lady indeed.

After Gabrielle, the team of Pierce Rice and Arturo Cazeneuve took over and her looks improved considerably. Bob Powell, one of whose specialties was pretty ladies, served a stint, as did a young Joe Kubert. By 1946 Black Cat was popular enough to rate her own magazine. In the first issue she was drawn by Jill Elgin, the only woman ever to handle the feature. For the final phase of her 10-year career, Black Cat's adventures were drawn by the capable Lee Elias. A disciple of Milton Caniff, Elias gave the strip a more sophisticated look and slipped real Hollywood stars into the stories. He couldn't do much for Rick Horne, however, and the reporter never did tumble to the fact that the redheaded Linda Turner and the redheaded Black Cat were one and the same.

The character has returned occasionally over the years, always in reprints, most recently in 1989. **R.G.**

**BLACKHAWK** The most successful soldier in comic books, Blackhawk began his combative career almost a half century ago in *Military Comics*. One of the Quality Comic Group's original quartet of titles, *Military* was launched during the summer of 1941, just a few months before the United States entered the Second

World War. The magazine was edited by Will Eisner and offered its prospective readers "Stories of the Army and Navy." This cover slogan was rather loosely interpreted, and some fairly unconventional warriors were to be found doing battle in *Military*'s bright four-color pages. The undisputed star of the new magazine, however, was Blackhawk.

He was created by Eisner, who wrote the scripts and laid out the pages; Charles Cuidera provided the finished art. The first issue explained that Blackhawk was a Polish aviator whose brother and sister had been killed by the Nazis. Escaping his occupied homeland, he acquired a mysterious island to use as a base and recruited a band of freedom-minded international outcasts and fugitives to wage aerial guerilla warfare against Nazi Germany.

What Eisner had come up with was a World War II version of King Arthur and his Round Table, with bits of the Foreign Legion, the Flying Tigers, and possibly Captain Midnight and his Secret Squadron tossed in for good measure. It was an appealing concept. As the saga unfolded from issue to issue readers got to know the rest of the Blackhawks—Olaf, Andre, Hendrickson, the later-controversial Chop Chop, and others. The distinctive Blackhawk planes, described as "revamped Grumman skyrockets," were first seen in issue #2.

With issue #12 the appearance of the Blackhawks, as well as that of their planes and all the artillery, improved greatly as Reed Crandall, with an assist from Alex Kotzky in that issue, took over the drawing of the feature. Crandall, one of the best illustrators of the period, seemed more at home with the Blackhawk crew than he had with any of the superheroes Quality had stuck him with. He remained with Blackhawk, off and on, for the next several years.

A separate *Blackhawk* magazine was added in 1944. When Quality gave it up in 1956, DC took over the title. The Blackhawks hung on until the late 1960s, combating a wide range of postwar villains and even putting in a spell as costumed superheroes. In 1976, returned to their WWII turf, they came back with George Evans illustrating their adventures; later, writer Mark Evanier and artist Dan Speigle took over. After another hiatus Howard Chaykin produced a three-part miniseries, aimed at a more mature audience, in 1988. *Blackhawk* next showed up in the short-lived *Action Comics Weekly*, and was then given a book of his own. It was, however, cancelled in 1990.  **R.G.**

**THE BLACK HOOD**  A fine early example of the costumed hero as vigilante, the Black Hood made his debut in MLJ's *Top-Notch Comics* #9 (October 1940). The superhero began life as Kip Burland. While a uniformed cop, Burland was framed by a greenfaced villain aptly

named the Skull. Worse still, in the same issue he was taken for a ride and left to die in the woods. But he was found by a helpful old hermit who converted him into a costumed crimefighter who would defeat the Skull and then use his "abilities against all crime and criminals!"

It took the Hood several issues, but eventually he sent the Skull to the hot seat. He was one of several impatient comic-book policemen who donned hoods and masks to avoid the law's delays in eliminating criminals. As his career progressed he battled a succession of bizarre foes, including the Panther Man, the Mist, and the Mad Killer of the Opera. In 1946, with interest in his type of hero waning, Burland put his costume in mothballs and became a private eye, doing business at the Black Hood Detective Agency. The following year he was gone from comics, although he returned briefly, hooded once again, in the middle 1960s and in the early 1980s.

Writer-editor Harry Shorten and artist Al Camy created the Black Hood, and Irv Novick saw him through his transition to PI. His most recent return was illuminated by Gray Morrow and Alex Toth.  **R.G.**

**BLACK WIDOW (I)**  The first costumed superheroine in comic books beat Wonder Woman into print by well over a year. The Black Widow, drawn by Harry Sahle and chronicled by writer George Kapitan, debuted in *Mystic Comics* #4 (August 1940) in a skintight black costume, gold-trimmed boots, and a blue and green cape. Her impressive list of superpowers included the ability to fly, to materialize at will, and to strike her opponents dead. An unfortunate aspect of the lady was that all her powers came from Satan himself.

She began her comic book life as a spirit medium named Claire Voyant. Murdered by an irate client, she was carried down to Hell where the Devil performed a mystic rite that transformed her into the Black Widow. She then returned to Earth, "endowed with supreme powers," to track and kill evildoers, and see that their souls got safely below. She could, when sufficiently annoyed, turn the pupils of her eyes into images of skulls—an ability that helped her a good deal in her work.

Perhaps not surprisingly she didn't catch on and appeared only twice more in *Mystic* and two more times elsewhere.  **R.G.**

**BLACK WIDOW (II)**  This durable supporting character of the Marvel Comics Group was introduced by writer Stan Lee and artist Don Heck, as a kind of Soviet Mata Hari, in *Iron Man* in 1964. Later she renounced communism, defected to the Americans, and aided Marvel's superhero team, the Avengers (one member of whom, the archer Hawkeye, was also her lover).

In a *Spider-Man* story in 1969 Lee and artist John Romita revamped her as a "liberated," acrobatic crime-fighter, garbed in skin-tight black leather, with stinging gadgets on her wrists. She had her own backup series briefly in *Amazing Adventures* (1970), then joined Daredevil as partner and lover, sharing the title with him for a while (*Daredevil and Black Widow*, 1972). Since then she has floated around the periphery of the Marvel universe, most often as Daredevil's friendly ex-lover.

**G.J.**

**BLAKE, BUD** (1918– ) The creator of the popular kid-strip *Tiger*, Bud Blake was born and educated in Nutley, New Jersey. An early talent for wood carving brought him a job in his teens touring state fairs, carnivals, and seaside boardwalks as a demonstrator for a penknife company, doing quick portraits of spectators in balsa wood. Encouraged by such a promising beginning in the arts, he studied at several art schools, including the National Academy of Design, after graduating from high school.

Blake began working in advertising in 1937, reaching the position of executive art director with the Kudner Advertising Agency, but he became so tired of the two-hour commute and the administrative details of his work that he was determined to try his luck as a freelance cartoonist. In the spring of 1954 King Features Syndicate accepted his feature *Ever Happen to You?*, which reported life's little ironies and irritations. For the next dozen years Blake carried on this daily panel while free-lancing advertising art to such national magazines as *Business Week*, *Family Circle*, *Pictorial Review*, and *American Weekly*. A little strip called *Junior* that he ran at the bottom of a St. Joseph's Aspirin calendar inspired him to propose doing a strip for King Features, and in May 1965 he came up with *Tiger* for them. A gracefully-drawn daily and Sunday strip, neither sentimental nor

arch, about a gang of believable kids, *Tiger* is rendered in clean, sure lines and solid patches of black. It has maintained a loyal audience for two decades and earned the applause of many of Blake's colleagues, twice being named Best Humor Strip of the Year by the National Cartoonists Society.

**D.W.**

**BLONDIE** One of the most popular comic strips in the history of cartooning, and a feature that has enjoyed the greatest circulation over the longest time, *Blondie* was created by Chic Young and began its long run in the summer of 1930.

The title character, Blondie Boopadoop, had to be dragged into public view on September 8, 1930, by her latest beau, Dagwood Bumstead, who insisted on introducing her to his millionaire father. At that point Blondie was just another flighty dumb blond looking for a good time on funny pages still flush with dizzy flappers left over from the fading Jazz Age. For a while the daily strips focused on the comic turmoil this socially unacceptable nobody caused in the Bumstead clan, but then other suitors began to crowd Dagwood offstage. When circulation began to slip, Young brought Dagwood back to declare his intention of marrying Blondie. The Bumsteads finally agree to the marriage, but Dagwood's father nonetheless disinherits his son. When Dagwood and Blondie are wed on February 17, 1933, one of the most famous marriages of our time begins on as impoverished a footing as Everyman's.

For a year Young concentrated on the comedy of newlyweds, and when that began to wear thin, he gave the Bumsteads a son. With the arrival of Baby Dumpling on April 15, 1934, the strip became a family strip. Much of the humor for quite a while revolved around the baby—or, more exactly, around Dagwood's bungling attempts at performing his assorted fatherly duties, such as changing diapers. And the strip's circulation began to climb sharply.

*Blondie*, Chic Young, © 1941, King Features Syndicate, Inc. Reprinted with special permission of King Features Syndicate, Inc.

By the 1940s Young had evolved an approach to domestic comedy that would keep his strip at the top of worldwide circulation for decades to come. He distilled daily living to its basic, and therefore universal, elements, and his strip dealt with them almost exclusively: eating, sleeping, making a living, and managing a household and family. Dagwood works for Julius C. Dithers and Company, and at least one strip a week finds him at his desk in the office being either browbeaten or actually beaten by Mr. Dithers. Understandably reluctant to leave a warm bed for this kind of abuse, Dagwood regularly oversleeps on workdays, and then runs down the postman, Mr. Beasly, as he races out the front door to catch the bus downtown. At home, Dagwood squabbles with his neighbor, Herb Woodley, whose wife Tootsie is Blondie's best friend. And as often as he can Dagwood takes a nap—or a bath, which is always interrupted, not to say invaded, usually by an impertinent neighbor boy named Elmo. Dagwood also carries on a never-ending battle with door-to-door salesmen.

Dagwood developed into the bumbling husband stereotype that became a national institution. Good-intentioned and faithful, but otherwise lazy and fairly inept, Dagwood over the years emerged as the star of the strip—its most reliable figure of fun—while Blondie became a model of wifely patience and tolerance, the principal stabilizing element in their family. Blondie, though, does have weak moments when she falls under the spell of a new hat or dress, and at times, in discussions with her husband, her logic can take on a distinctly scatterbrained quality.

In April 1941 the Bumsteads had a baby girl, named Cookie by one of the 431,275 readers who entered the naming contest. *Blondie*'s enduring appeal stems in part from the fact that Dagwood and his family are ordinary folks, or so it first appears. Most of Dagwood's adventures commence normally enough, but before a strip reaches its punchline a manic inventiveness inspires a zany deviation from the norm and Dagwood manages to achieve the implausible. The famous Dagwood sandwich is a symbol of the fact that even a humble sandwich can attain heroic, if lunatic, proportions.

Young employed several assistants, including Alex Raymond and Ray McGill. Starting in 1935 Young's chief helper was Jim Raymond, who took over all the drawing in 1950 when Young's eyesight began to fail. Raymond continued in the Young tradition—meticulous renderings, uncluttered compositions accented by strategically placed solid blacks and, even more remarkable in a time of shrinking formats, characters drawn full-figure. After Young died in 1973, Raymond shared a byline on the strip with Young's son Dean, who had helped his father with the writing since 1963. After

Raymond's death in 1981, the drawing chores fell to his assistant for 17 years, Michael Gersher. But Gersher was shortly replaced by Stan Drake, who quickly mastered the Young-Raymond style, even though it was a far cry from the illustrative technique he used on his continuity strip *The Heart of Juliet Jones.* By the middle 1980s *Blondie* had attained an international circulation of over 1,900 papers, all through judicious application of Chic Young's proven formula.                          **R.C.H.**

**BLOOM COUNTY**   One of the sharpest and most provocative gag strips of the 1980s, Berke Breathed's *Bloom County* originated as *Academia Waltz* in the University of Texas *Daily Texan*, where it ran from 1978 to 1979. Widely read in the area and published in two collections, it came to the attention of the *Washington Post*, which was looking for something to replace Garry Trudeau's *Doonesbury*, recently lost to a rival paper. The Washington Post Writers Group took a chance on it as their first comic strip and launched it, pruned of its more sophomoric elements and renamed *Bloom County*, on December 8, 1980. It ran until August 6, 1989, when the artist voluntarily brought it to an end.

Set in an imaginary middle-American town, *Bloom County* is populated by an assortment of precocious youngsters, broadly caricatured adult-types, and engagingly verbal fauna. The children at the heart of the strip are Milo Bloom, a perceptive lad terrified of catching puberty; his timorous pal Michael "Mad Dog" Binkley, who has a private anxiety closet containing, among other nocturnal visitors, a giant spotted snorklewacker; and Oliver Wendell Jones, a black computer pirate. The two regular adult characters carried over from *Academia Waltz* are Steve Dallas, a smug sexist lawyer (originally the archetypal fratrat), and Cutter John, a cool paraplegic Vietnam vet. The most distinctive, and probably the most popular, member of the strip's dramatis personae is neither child nor adult but a beguiling, bow-tied penguin named Opus, whose wistful fantasies and shrewd observations have captivated a wide audience and created an industry of Opus-dolls, T-shirts, and other merchandise.

Charged with being derivative of Garry Trudeau's 10-years-older satire strip *Doonesbury*, whose obvious influence Breathed acknowledges, *Bloom County* shares with the older strip a simple, sketchy style, a preference for profiles, an absence of balloons around its dialogue, and a liberal concern for contemporary social issues. But Breathed had a markedly gentler and more whimsical comedic approach and relied for much of his humor on such fantasy elements as talking animals (including an antlered basset hound called a basselope). Often trenchant, *Bloom County* was seldom caustic, leaning rather to good-natured raillery than to mordant satire. During its nearly nine years, it deftly poked fun at television, the press, British royalty, and the comics themselves, as well as at politics.

The strip's sensitive treatment of the handicapped earned it a Disability Awareness Award from the Paralyzed Veterans of America in 1982, and in 1987 it was the second comic strip (after *Doonesbury*, 12 years earlier) to win a Pulitzer Prize for editorial cartooning. At the end of its run, it was carried by over 1,000 newspapers, including more college papers than any other strip, and its collections, published by Little, Brown, consistently reached the best-seller lists.          **D.W.**

**BLOSSER, MERRILL** (1892–1983) Essentially a one-strip cartoonist, Blosser was the creator of *Freckles and His Friends*, which began, initially as a daily, in 1915. He signed his name to it for over a half century.

While growing up in Nappanee, Indiana, Blosser took the Landon School correspondence course in cartooning. After a year in college and then some courses at the Chicago Academy of Fine Arts, he moved through a succession of art jobs with magazines and newspapers. The year 1915 found him in Cleveland, drawing political cartoons for the *Plain Dealer*. C.N. Landon, who was also an editor at the Cleveland-based NEA syndicate, hired him, and later that year *Freckles and His Friends* was launched. As part of the NEA package, the strip eventually boasted 700 newspapers. In the 1920s Blosser was one of the graduates the Landon School bragged about in its publications—"Blosser makes more each day than many men earn in a week."

Originally, in the days when Freckles was a diminutive gag-a-day grade school kid, Blosser drew in a simple, correspondence-school style. Gradually, as Freckles grew a bit older and began indulging in continuity, Blosser's style changed and showed the strong influence of Walter Hoban, who drew *Jerry on the Job*. Blosser's style grew even more realistic as the 1920s progressed, and adventure sequences became frequent. In the middle 1930s he relinquished the drawing of the daily strip to Henry Formhals, although he continued to sign it. Blosser continued to draw the Sunday page, which had begun in the 1920s, for several more years.

Blosser migrated to Southern California in 1926, living his last years in a large, comfortable home in Pasadena.          **R.G.**

**THE BLUE BEETLE** A seemingly unsinkable comic book superhero, the Blue Beetle first appeared in Fox's *Mystery Men Comics* #1 (August 1939); in that initial incarnation he lasted until 1950. He has managed to return, somewhat like an aging diva making one more farewell tour, in every decade since.

The Beetle's parentage is somewhat clouded. Will Eisner has admitted that he may have had a hand in the invention of the blueclad crimebuster, since his shop provided all the features for Victor Fox's line of comic books. Charles Wojtkowski, who adopted the pen name Charles Nicholas, was the first artist to draw the feature, and he also contributed to the creation. When asked in later years how the character came about, he supposedly replied tersely, "Green Hornet, Blue Beetle." While the Blue Beetle's name was obviously inspired by that of the then popular radio hero, he had little else in common with him.

The Blue Beetle wasn't originally intended to be the leading character in the magazine and had a mere four pages near the back of the first issue in which to get his act together. Thrown onto the stage without benefit of origin, he didn't even get his costume worked out for several issues. Finally abandoning short sleeves and the little bug antennae on his cowl, he settled for a suit of blue chain mail—apparently lightweight stuff.

Early readers knew only that he was in reality a rookie cop named Dan Garret, who "dons the clothes of the Blue Beetle to rid the city of the worst criminals it has ever seen." He apparently had not a single superpower when he started, although he did have beetle props. For a time he drove a high-powered car with his insignia emblazoned on the side, a sort of Beetlemobile. He had scarabs of various sizes that he'd lower into crooks' lairs, causing them to exclaim, "It's the sign of the BLUE BEETLE!!" and a beetle projector that flashed the symbol on walls to produce similar fearful reactions. He passed out little beetle whistles to kids, instructing them, "When you're in any danger, blow it!"

Like his more successful colleague, Superman, the Beetle had a pretty lady reporter to save from innumerable perils. She was blond Joan Mason, and the various chroniclers seem never to have given a name to the sheet she wrote for. While a cop the Beetle was partnered with a plump, not too bright fellow named Mike Mannigan. He never tumbled to the true identity of the Blue Beetle, firmly believed he was a hardened criminal, and continually vowed to bring him to justice. The other important character was Dr. Franz, who was not a highfaluting medical man but simply a humble pharmacist.

In 1940, thanks to Dr. Franz, the Blue Beetle acquired new powers. The druggist started providing him with doses of Vitamin 2X, a little invention of his own that imbued the Beetle with "super-energy," and he was now to be seen leaping off rooftops and tossing automobiles around. His chain mail outfit was improved, too, making him "almost invulnerable." Apparently it never occurred to him to stock up on 2X, and every time he wanted to become super, he dropped in at the drugstore and stepped into the backroom. Equipped with a slug of the super vitamin, he went forth to enjoy some rather prosaic adventures, now up to 13 pages, hunting down villains such as the Wart, Scrag, the Eel, Mr. Downhill, and a crazed scientist called Doc.

The Blue Beetle became Fox's most popular character: He moved to the front of *Mystery Men* and was showcased on every cover. He got a second magazine all his own before a year had passed and for a while appeared in a newspaper strip drawn by Jack Kirby. There was even a short-lived radio show—"Thrilling Drama of the Avenging Gang Smasher...Twice-a-week"—in which Frank Lovejoy starred.

Although Charles Nicholas continued to get a byline, a small army of other artists drew the feature, among them Al Carreño, Sam Cooper, and Louis Cazeneuve. Edd Ashe and Ramona Patenaude took care of most of the Beetle's flamboyant cover appearances. In 1942 Fox left the comic book business, suspending most of his titles, but *The Blue Beetle* magazine continued, taken over by a printing firm whom Fox owed money. Fox made a comeback in 1944 and kept the Blue Beetle going until 1950.

The Beetle was briefly seen in a series of mostly reprints from Charlton in 1955. Charlton brought him back again in the middle 1960s, starring in brand-new adventures and wearing a new costume in place of the azure chain mail. Steve Ditko provided much of the artwork. Charlton reprinted some of the new Beetle material in 1977. In 1986 DC took over the character and introduced a revised and redesigned version. Once again the character didn't exactly thrive, but it seems safe to assume that he'll be back again eventually.

**R.G.**

**BLUE BOLT** Not a major comic book superhero, yet noteworthy as the first collaborative effort of the formidable 1940s team of Joe Simon and Jack Kirby, Blue Bolt flashed into view in the first issue of *Blue Bolt* (January 1940), a magazine he shared with Sub-Zero Man, Sergeant Spook, Dick Cole the Wonder Boy, and several others. Simon had created the character and drew the origin story himself, and Kirby came aboard as penciller with the second issue. Even then Kirby's work was energetic, hyperactive, and unlike anything else in comics.

Fred Parrish, a Harvard football star, became the Blue Bolt by way of a complex and painful initiation that involved being struck by lightning, crashing his airplane, abduction to a secret underground kingdom, and zapping by artificial lightning bolts. Once he was established as a superhero, he devoted his time to combating an emerald-hued Dragon Lady–type known as the Green Sorceress.

When Simon and Kirby moved on, George Mandel took over, and during his tenure Blue Bolt returned topside. In the fall of 1942, less than a year after the United States entered the Second World War, Blue Bolt quit being a superman and joined the Army Air Corps. He soon forgot he ever had a single superpower, and after the war he worked as a roving adventurer. He made his final original comic book appearance in 1949.

Other artists who drew the feature included Dan Barry, John Giunta, Tom Gill, and Wayne Boring under the pen name Jack Harmon.

**R.G.**

**BOBBY MAKE-BELIEVE** Over the years there have been many strips that explored a boy's imagination and fantasies, from *Little Nemo* to *Calvin and Hobbes*. Frank King's *Bobby Make-Believe* ran from early in 1915 to late in 1919 and was one of the more interesting examples of the genre.

Bobby was a daydreamer, a boy-sized Walter Mitty who could segue from everyday life into fantasy. His real-life world contained the usual problems and perplexities of an imaginative boy. He had a pal named Spud, a girlfriend named Virginia, and a mother. A bullying delivery boy named Adolph was the chief threat in his world, and a spoiled rich kid named Sissy Bly the chief annoyance.

In his reveries Bobby moved into a variety of alternate realities, becoming a baseball star, a World War I pilot, a giant, a spycatcher, a fireman, a big game hunter, or a noble prince. The vision always faded in the penultimate panel and Bobby came home to reality. Since he seemed to be able to get along fairly well in his own home world, these returns were not especially jarring.

This wasn't a gag page and King rarely built up to a punchline. He drew it in the inventive, posterlike style that he'd later perfect in his *Gasoline Alley* Sunday pages, obviously enjoying himself experimenting with layout and color. He resigned from the feature in November 1919, and it did not survive long without him.

After a layoff of over 20 years Bobby returned in 1940, and one of his old pages was reprinted each week for several months in the *Chicago Tribune's Comic Book Magazine*.

**R.G.**

**BOBBY THATCHER** A pioneering daily adventure strip, *Bobby Thatcher* got going in 1927 and lasted for over 10 years.

After leaving *Phil Hardy* and before setting up in business with a boy adventurer of his own, George Storm did some short-run strips for the McClure Syndicate, the most notable of which was a 22-week adaptation of *Swiss Family Robinson*. Adaptations of the classics were common on the comics pages of the 1920s, but most of them were done in a stodgy, reverent way and

Bobby Thatcher, George Storm,
© 1928, McClure Newspaper
Syndicate.

looked like book illustrations strung together. Storm's handsomely drawn version of the Johann Wyss novel, however, was a true comic strip, with action, blood and thunder, and cliffhangers. The adaptation ended in March of 1927, with a shot of the rescued family sailing away across a moonlit sea, and was replaced by Storm's brand-new *Bobby Thatcher*.

"Bobby Thatcher, a bright lad of fourteen, lives on a farm near the village of Lakeview. He is the ward of Jed Flint and lives with Flint and his housekeeper," Storm told his readers by way of introduction. "Since the death of Mrs. Flint, who was kind to him, Bobby no longer attends school and his life is one of increasing hardship." Bobby's chief hardship was old Flint, as hard as his name implied. Flint overworked the boy, scorned his ambitions, appropriated any outside money he earned, and in general behaved in the accepted fashion of stepfather/guardians. Bobby, of course, ran away before the strip was two weeks old.

Storm then added some contemporary touches: The boy hitched a ride from a stranger in a powerful touring car, but the helpful stranger, it turned out, was wanted by the sheriff and the state troopers. A chase, including a race to beat a screaming locomotive to a grade crossing, ensued. Storm continued to mix this sort of movie excitement with the Alger story line throughout the strip's run, alternating babies left in wicker baskets on doorsteps with surly rumrunners blasting away with tommy guns. Bobby's picaresque wanderings through the 1920s and 1930s exposed him to almost every kind of adventure format, including aviation, detective, cowboy, seafaring and more. Like many early adventure strips, the continuities contained a fair share of hokum, but Storm drew everything with such a forceful, enthusiastic style that they were most often compelling.

The strip ended in the midst of a sequence late in 1937, with a notice stating that Storm "has announced his abandonment of the strip to take up other work." Actually the last few weeks of *Bobby Thatcher* had been ghosted by young Sheldon Mayer, who was working at the syndicate as an all-around editorial assistant. "I think by that time it had become drudgery to him," Mayer recalled. The strip, tame by then in comparison to the new adventure strips that had gotten going in the Thirties, was now earning Storm only about $100 a week. Not a bad salary for the time, but a long way from the $1,000 and more per month Bobby had brought in during his heyday, when the strip ran in nearly 60 newspapers—including the *New York World*, the *Washington Post*, and the *Philadelphia Ledger*.

Apparently there was some thought given to continuing the feature with Mayer, but that didn't happen. Mayer recalled being told *Bobby Thatcher* had been canceled while he still had two weeks of penciled dailies to ink. Selling his Long Island home, Storm returned to Enid, Oklahoma, where he and his wife took up farming. Storm had gone back to his boyhood hometown, a place he couldn't seem to stay away from, and would be absent from cartooning for nearly two years until his return to the field by way of comic books.　　**R.G.**

**BODYGUARD**  Initially a Sunday-only feature, it began appearing on May 2, 1948. *Bodyguard* should've been a hit. It was well written by Lawrence Lariar, gag cartoonist, editor, and sometime mystery novelist, whose *The Man With the Lumpty Nose* (1944), about murder in the comics world, had won Dutton's Red Badge prize. The artwork was by John Spranger, who had some pretty fair credits himself: A graduate of comic books, he'd worked in the Binder shop and then gone on to Quality where he drew Plastic Man and Dollman. When Will Eisner returned to the weekly *Spirit* in 1946, Spranger went to work for him and did quite a bit of drawing. By the time he took on *Bodyguard*, he'd blended the Eisner inking and inventive breakdowns, the Jack Cole approach to action, and his own natural ability into a highly effective style.

The page's star, Ben Friday, was, like many comic strip heroes of the period, a returning serviceman. In the first sequence his old OSS commanding officer helped Friday set up as a free-lance bodyguard-private investigator by arranging for him to protect an eccentric millionaire named Hyram Tucker. Tucker had a lovely red-haired granddaughter named Linda and a rare One Cent Guiana postage stamp that rival collectors were willing to kill for. This initial caper took Friday to an assortment of dangerous locales and concluded on a mysterious island ruled by an ex-Nazi who was a dead ringer for his client. There was plenty of action, intrigue, and romance plus some comedy and a dandy explosion.

Later assignments involved him in shipboard dangers, treks through the jungles of India, and the like. On one of his adventures Friday aided a pudgy and highly intelligent little boy known as the Bantam Prince, little realizing that the ingratiating tyke would eventually oust him from his own strip. A daily was added in 1949, and in the summer of that year *Bodyguard* became *Ben Friday*. Then, in October of 1950, the title changed to *The Bantam Prince*. Early the following month Friday sailed out of the strip, in the company of a pretty blond, and was seen no more. Spranger stayed with it for another year and then moved on. The artwork for the strip's final two years was by Carl Pfeufer.　　**R.G.**

**BOLLE, FRANK** (1924– )  Before taking over *Winnie Winkle* in the middle 1980s, Bolle had a long career drawing for both comic books and comic strips. In over 40 years as a professional cartoonist he's drawn everything from superheroes to soap operas.

New York born, Bolle attended the High School of Music and Art and Pratt Institute. He worked briefly in the Jacquet comic book shop before entering the Air Force in 1943. A civilian again in 1946, he returned to comic books. He teamed up with Leonard Starr, another alum of HSMA, Pratt and Jacquet, and the two of them drew adventure features for a variety of publishers— with Starr penciling and Bolle inking. Their best-known character was the walking compost pile, the Heap, in *Airboy*.

Soloing from the late 1940s on, Bolle drew, among others, *Tim Holt*, *Dr. Solar*, and *Big Valley*. He worked initially in a loose, Caniff-inspired style, but has tightened up and become more traditionally illustrative over the years. Bolle drew several strips, including *Alexander Gate*, *Debbie Deere*, a *Children's Tales* Sunday page and *Encyclopedia Brown*, before settling down with the long-running *Winnie Winkle*.　　**R.G.**

**BOLTINOFF, HENRY** (1914– )  A cartoonist for over 50 years, Boltinoff has worked in sundry branches of the field. His simple, lively style has been seen in comic books, comic strips, and magazine gags.

He was born in New York City and attended New York University and the Art Students League. After an assortment of jobs that included working for Hearst's *New York American*, Boltinoff entered comic books in 1939. DC was his major market and he turned out hundreds of humorous filler pages for the company— among them, *Clancy the Cop*, *Private Pete*, *Jerry the Jitterbug*, and *Chief Hotfoot*. He even tried a straight adventure feature, *Young Doc Davis*, for DC's *World's Finest Comics*.

Simultaneously Boltinoff was selling gag cartoons to such magazines as *Collier's* and *The Saturday Evening*

*Post.* His one-column panel *Stoker the Broker* started appearing in 1960 and continued in newspapers for 27 years. He also drew the *Nubbin* strip for 17 years and most recently was drawing a tiny comic strip called *Tiny* for King Features. Boltinoff has won two awards from the National Cartoonists Society over the years, one for his comic book work and one for his panel.     **R.G.**

**BONER'S ARK** Mort Walker was already a star cartoonist in the firmament of King Features Syndicate with *Beetle Bailey, Hi & Lois,* and *Mrs. Fitz's Flats* and had borne and buried *Sam's Strip* when he and his staff originated a fourth strip in 1968. King syndicated *Boner's Ark* on March 11 of that year, with an advance sale of 85 newspapers and signed with Walker's first name, Addison.

Looking for a vehicle for satire and fantasy, Walker and his associates decided on an animal strip but wanted a self-contained community in which the animals could interact. They hit on an ark, "so the animals could mix freely without cages," Walker has written, "[and] put a bumbling captain in charge....The characters are animals acting out human roles in a ship that represents capsulized civilization." Among the bestiary on board are Aarnie, an aardvark who cries "Land Ho!" every time he weeds the ark's flowerpot; Cubcake, a koala bear whose name was selected in a competition that generated over 50,000 letters; Priscilla Pig, a vain Miss Piggy-type; a penguin whose tuxedo-like coloring fits him for the role of man (or penguin) about town; and other assorted creatures, identifiable and unidentifiable, under the blundering human Captain Boner, who built the ship out of knotty pine and who carries his soap and scrub brush and demands his rubber duck when forced to walk the plank by mutineers.

Since early in 1982 *Boner's Ark* has been drawn and signed by Frank Johnson but continues to be scripted by Walker, along with Ralston "Bud" Jones and Jerry Dumas. Its broad, cartoony style, as simple and unsophisticated as its gags, has remained unchanged through more than two decades and at the hands of two artists.

The circulation of *Boner's Ark* quickly rose from its initial number to about 100 papers, but then began to fall off. Analyzing the situation, the team producing it concluded that it had too many characters. "Readers can absorb only so much," Walker observes. "So we reduced the cast." Apparently that solved the problem, because the readership began to grow again until the circulation reached a level of about 145, at which it has remained constant ever since. A solid, traditional, slapstick gag-strip, *Boner's Ark* maintains that comfortable balance of perceptive irony and good-natured nonsense that appeals to all ages equally.     **D.W.**

**BOOB McNUTT** A lunatic picaresque, Rube Goldberg's Sunday page about a zealously naive, red-headed young wanderer began in 1915 and lasted until 1934. It was an eclectic jumble of satire, burlesque, fantasy, and cockeyed technology. While it was not consistently hilarious, *Boob McNutt* was certainly more representative of Goldberg's various talents and interests than many of his other features.

Boob was a plump, boyish young man whose tiny hat, ill-fitting and too-tight coat, and spotted pants—the spots of which changed from polka dots to asterisks to bullseyes etc. from week to week—gave him a certain affinity to the oddly dressed fellows who starred in silent movie comedies. Kindhearted and perennially innocent, Boob's journey through life was a manic version of that of the typical waif of melodrama. His simplest effort to do good or help out would lead to a complex catastrophe—quite often involving the smashing of valuable objects, ranging from rare vases to palatial mansions—that further inspired those around Boob to try to eliminate him in drastic and inventive ways.

In 1922 Goldberg introduced an attractive young woman named Pearl to the page, and Boob was immediately smitten. "Pearl became his romantic quest," comics historian Jim Ivey has said, "the balance of the strip's run was largely devoted to Boob's comic adventures in search of Pearl." The couple was separated, reunited, married, divorced, remarried. Goldberg was using continuity by then, building up a sort of screwball suspense, and the pursuits of Pearl were intertwined with encounters with mad scientists, nasty rivals, and weird creatures. In addition to utilizing the complex and inefficient inventions that put his name in the dictionary, Goldberg also practiced his own form of zoology in the Sunday page. Strange birds, mammals, and fish got tangled up in the cliffhanging plots—the snazzum, the bibbim, the goppledong, the ploff, and Bertha the Siberian Cheesehound, to name but a few. Bertha became Boob's constant companion and was to him what Sandy was to Little Orphan Annie. Two of Goldberg's earlier creations were also added to the cast, the diminutive twins known as Mike and Ike. Throughout the 1920s and into the 1930s they tagged along with Boob and Pearl on assorted expeditions and excursions. There were even space explorations, though most of those aborted.

Syndicated by Hearst for most of its life, *Boob McNutt* was Goldberg's longest-running Sunday page. He abandoned it in the autumn of 1934 to move on to other, not necessarily better, things.     **R.G.**

**BOOMER** Among the comic strips that reflected the changing sexual mores of the 1960s and 1970s was *Boomer* by Bill Brown and Mel Casson, which began its life as *Mixed Singles* on November 13, 1972, under the aegis of United Features Syndicate. Its gentle and relatively wholesome treatment of the dating game was good-natured, and its handling of such potentially offensive clichés as male insecurity (or lechery) and female insincerity (or cupidity) never violated the canons of good taste or threatened the readers' sensitivity. Without any clearly defined characters or point of view at first, *Mixed Singles* began to crystallize some stock types in the singles scene during its early years, finally focusing on a handsome stud named Boomer. The popular macho figure increasingly took over, and on March 10, 1975, the strip was renamed for him.

Gracefully drawn in a simple, linear style with minimal detail, *Boomer* and its parent strip *Mixed Singles* captured the stylish spirit and fluid movement of the discos at which its characters were most often to be found. The strip's creators shared both scripting and the drawing. William F. Brown is the author of numerous television shows and cabaret revues and has scripted three Broadway productions (including *The Wiz* ) in addition to his work on *Boomer;* Mel Casson has been a regular contributor of cartoons to national magazines, with five collections published, and has done advertising art for such corporations as ITT, Kodak, IBM, and General Electric as well as several other strips. Together the two kept the strip booming for nearly a decade, and in 1973, the year after its inception, it brought them the Philips Award from the Festival of International Humor.

*Boomer* ended its Sunday run on April 29, 1979, and the daily strip was retired a little more than two years later, on August 1, 1981.                                   **D.W.**

**BOOTS AND HER BUDDIES**  The success of Cliff Sterrett's *Polly and her Pals* (1912) and Russ Westover's *Tillie the Toiler* (1921) for King Features Syndicate and of Martin Branner's *Winnie Winkle* (1920) for the Tribune-News Syndicate prompted Newspaper Enterprise Association to enter the lists with a fourth alliteratively-titled flapper strip in 1924. Edgar Everett (Abe) Martin's daily *Boots and Her Buddies* began on February 18 of that year and quickly established itself as a distinctive entry, which, although its title was a clear echo of *Polly and Her Pals*, had a personality and a graphic style of its own.

The thoroughly respectable Boots was one of the emancipated girls of the 1920s but was never either a rebel or a flirt. Chastely sexy, she was pursued as ardently as any of the sophisticated young things in the medium but did nothing to encourage it and always protected her virtue with delicacy and charm. Boots underwent more changes of situation in her 40-some years than most characters in the comics. She began as

a college student, with the usual problems and pleasures of the collegiate crowd: She studied for exams, played the ukulele, dated boys, and gossiped with her classmates. As the image of the flapper faded from the national scene, she became an efficient working girl and, in the fullness of time (on September 2, 1945, to be exact) duly married. She and her amiable, bespectacled husband Rod became parents on July 4th of the next year, and Boots was as warm and sympathetic a middle-class suburban housewife and mother as she had been a coed and wage earner. Never an extraordinary personality, she was an intelligent, composed, responsible figure and an attractive model for the young ladies of four decades.

The character changed in other ways, too. Always gracefully drawn, she dressed in the height of the current style throughout her career, though Martin's delineation of her body seemed to fluctuate from time to time; she was randomly slim or chubby, flat-chested or buxom. The styling of her short, blond hair never changed, however, but somehow managed to appear smartly coiffed through all changing tonsorial fashions, and she remained as young-looking as ever from schoolgirl to matron.

Abe Martin was born in Illinois in 1898 and studied at the Chicago Academy of Fine Arts. He created several other strips for NEA, including *Babe and Horace*, a spin-off of *Boots* that ran as a topper to his main feature and focused on a young couple from *Boots* along with Boots herself. Girls from both strips were presented as cutouts on Sundays with a choice of fashionable outfits for their readers to try on them.

In 1933 Boots appeared as a character in Martin's Sunday strip *Girls*, begun in 1931, and on September 9, 1934, she became its title character. Martin continued drawing and writing the daily *Boots and Her Buddies* and the Sunday *Boots* till his death in 1960, when the daily strip was retired and the Sunday passed into the hands of his assistant Les Carroll. Drawn with no perceptible change in style or tone, the Sunday feature lasted another nine years, making its final appearance on March 30, 1969.                                   **D.W.**

**BORING, WAYNE** (1916–1986)  His major achievement as a cartoonist was drawing *Superman* for over 30 years. Boring contributed to the saga of the Man of Steel from just about the beginning, eventually inheriting the character in both comic books and the newspaper strip. He fared even less well than Superman's creators and never reaped great financial rewards or a secure old age from his long association with the enormously successful superhero.

Boring studied at the Chicago Art Institute, then put in time as assistant on the *Big Chief Wahoo* newspaper strip. After a stint in the advertising department of a Virginia newspaper he got hired by Jerry Siegel and Joe Shuster. Moving to Cleveland, where the young partners had a studio, he started ghosting *Slam Bradley*, *Federal Men*, and then their new hit *Superman*. The work Boring did then was drawn in a variation of Shuster's diagrammatic, cartoony style. He was allowed early on to sign such features as *Federal Men*, but never *Superman*. He drew several of the man from Krypton's comic book adventures and by the early 1940s was doing sequences of the newspaper strip as well.

Starting in the middle 1940s Boring was responsible for most of the newspaper strip, daily and Sunday. Gradually he came to work in his own slicker, more muscular style. He beefed up Superman's looks and even glamorized Lois Lane.

During this same period, to boost his income, Boring did some comic book work for an outfit called the Novelty Press, drawing the title character in *Blue Bolt* and a lady detective named Tony Gayle for *Young King Cole*. Not wanting DC to know what he was up to, he signed the work Jack Harmon—using the first and middle names of his father.

Siegel and Shuster were put out to pasture by DC in the late 1940s, but Boring stayed on. He remained the chief artist on *Superman* and, by the 1950s, was getting a credit on the feature. He stayed with the superhero until the late 1960s, working with editor Mort Weisinger until one day Weisinger simply called him in and fired him. He did a little work for Marvel in the early 1970s, mostly on their Captain Marvel character. He concentrated on assisting and/or ghosting on such newspaper strips as *Prince Valiant*, *Davy Jones*, and *Rip Kirby*. He and his wife finally settled in Florida. He pretty much gave up comics in favor of painting, although he did a few *Superman* jobs in the 1980s. He made his living, though, working as a security guard. "This is a mild job I've got," he explained, "and they pay me well." **R.G.**

**THE BORN LOSER**  After 20 years as an illustrator, drawing other people's strips for the Newspaper Enterprise Association's comic art department, Art Sansom created the engaging victim/hero of *The Born Loser*, Brutus P. Thornapple. Carried by NEA daily since May 10, 1965 (with Sundays beginning on the 27th of the next month), the strip touches a universal chord as its hapless hero confronts the myriad minor defeats of everyday life with bland equanimity and resignation. Consistently voted among the most popular comic strips in newspaper polls, *The Born Loser* appears in more than 1,000 papers in 26 countries, including England, Greece, Hong Kong, Malaysia, Sri Lanka, Australia, and Mexico.

Thornapple maintains a delicate balance of power with his sharp-tongued wife Gladys (who, when he tells her he has been put in charge of a dummy corporation, observes, "It figures."). More often than not she outwits him with no trouble and there is little doubt who has the upper hand in their marriage. "What'd ever happen if you agreed with me on anything?" he asks her in one strip. Her reply is inevitable: "I'd be wrong."

Other characters before whom Brutus is more or less helpless include his formidable mother-in-law, his five-year-old son Wilberforce, their self-assured six-year-old neighbor Hurricane Hattie O'Hara, his boss Rancid W. Veeblefester (who, when Brutus asks for a raise, lifts him off the floor), and an endless succession of drunks, panhandlers, and hold-up men.

Educated as an engineering draftsman, Sansom draws *The Born Loser* in a minimal style, usually without backgrounds, but his economical line achieves considerable expression. With a simple stroke, he conveys a smirk or a befuddled look—Thornapple's usual response, which Sansom acknowledges that he got from watching Jack Benny on television.

Sansom's son Chip collaborates on gags for *The Born Loser*, and since the mid-1980s his name has been included in the strip's signature. Together Art and Chip Sansom manage to keep the image of modern man as victim remarkably fresh. **D.W.**

**BORTH, FRANK**  See KEN STUART.

**BOSTWICK, SALS** (1902–1930)  In his brief life Bostwick accomplished a great deal as a newspaper cartoonist, but up until now he has never managed to earn himself a place in the history of comics. He was one of Frank King's first assistants on *Gasoline Alley*, going on from there to do a half-dozen syndicated strips and panels of his own for the *Chicago Tribune* and King Features. His best-known feature was probably *Room and Board*.

Salisbury Bostwick learned cartooning by way of a correspondence course from the Federal Schools, and before he reached 20 he was working with Frank King on his strip. Bostwick moved from there to doing features for the *Tribune*, which included a kid strip called *One Round Teddy*. In the middle 1920s he was lured over to Hearst's *Chicago American* for a reported salary of $15,000 a year. He drew *Main Street Jed*, a daily about a small-town young man who was something of a go-getter, and followed that with *Hello, Hattie*, an office life strip centering on the pretty young switchboard operator.

Late in 1928 Bostwick came up with a daily panel titled *Room and Board*, which was apparently intended as King Features' answer to NEA's *Our Boarding House*.

Bostwick's large cast resided in the Fizzbeak Inn, which was presided over by the plump Mrs. Fizzbeak herself. His characters were mostly younger than those who inhabited Gene Ahern's rival establishment and many of the gag situations grew out of dating and courtship. There was no one in residence who resembled Major Hoople. When Ahern came over to King Features in the middle 1930s, the *Room and Board* title was revived and a Major Hoople surrogate installed.

Bostwick drew in an appealing style, closer to that of such *Tribune* colleagues as Walter Berndt and Frank Willard than to that of his former mentor Frank King. Hearst obviously considered him a contender, but Bostwick didn't live to achieve a major comic strip success. He died at the age of 27 of the complications of appendicitis.                              **R.G.**

## THE BOY COMMANDOS

One of several successful kid gangs created by the team of Joe Simon and Jack Kirby, the Boy Commandos first appeared in *Detective Comics* #64 (June 1942). Unlike many of the boy heroes of World War II comic books, they were directly involved in combat overseas and fought against Axis forces in both Europe and the Pacific.

Originally numbering four teenagers, the group was international in makeup and consisted of Alfy from England, Jan from Holland, Andre from France, and Brooklyn from America. They were regular kids, not superheroes, who wore paramilitary uniforms—with the exception of the flamboyant Brooklyn, who decked himself out in a green turtleneck and a bright red derby. In the early stories Brooklyn also carried around a violin case containing his own personal tommygun. "We're out ta get Hitler and his mob cuz dere ain't room fer both of us, see?" is how he introduced himself to readers in the premier episode. The gang's mentor was Captain Rip Carter, the leader of "an outfit of tough commandos," and the boys were described as "company mascots." While Rip tried to see that the lads kept up with their schooling as best they could, he usually had no objection to their coming along on commando raids in Nazi-held areas and engaging in hand to hand combat. They were most often found in the thick of the action, shouting their battle cry: "The commandos are coming!"

Carrying on with the lively and audacious layouts and storytelling techniques they had developed over at Marvel on *Captain America* and were now using at DC, Simon and Kirby did a vigorous job on *The Boy Commandos*. They mixed action, some humor and even a touch of fantasy now and then—managing to toss into their war yarns such elements as the predictions of Nostradamus, Egyptian mummies, and ghosts. The boys

quickly proved popular enough for a book of their own, which began in late 1942.

Both the partners went into the service, abandoning their feature late in 1943. Their names continued to appear on it but artist Louis Cazeneuve fell far short of carrying on in the style they had established. After the war Simon and Kirby resumed doing *The Boy Commandos*, while the lads, all in civvies now, stayed teamed with Rip Carter and worked as international troubleshooters. Jan was the first to leave the group and Alfy followed in 1947, to be replaced by a Stetson-wearing youth named Tex. Simon and Kirby added a bit more fantasy, even sending the lads to Atlantis.

When they gave up the feature, Curt Swan was one of the artists who took over. The group went out of business at the end of 1949, but just before they did, a revised team—consisting of Andre, a boy detective named Percy, and a redesigned Brooklyn—had operated as the Boy Commandos. The original gang reappeared very briefly in 1973 in two issues of reprints.
                              **R.G.**

## BRANNER, MARTIN

(1888–1970) The New York-born creator of the long-running *Winnie Winkle* set his cap for a career in art early in his life. He applied for a job in the art department of the *New York World* while he was still in high school; although he was turned down, he would continue to do free-lance advertising art for nearly a decade before he became established as a strip-cartoonist. At 18, however, he saw no way to support himself with his pencil, and his career took a sharp and romantic turn when he eloped with the 15-year-old Edith Fabrini and formed a vaudeville act. As Martin and Fabrini the duo danced their way to considerable success, which Branner supplemented by drawing occasional ads for *Variety* and for fellow-vaudevillian and later radio star Fred Allen.

The Martin and Fabrini Continental Dance Act played the Palace and had reached $400 a week when World War I broke out, just as they were preparing for a European tour. Branner enlisted in the Army, where he served in the Chemical Warfare Division until he returned in 1918 to resume his career on the vaudeville stage. The dream of becoming a cartoonist had not faded, however, and he began submitting ideas to the syndicates. In 1919, Bell accepted a Sunday feature about a bald little attorney from him, and *Looie the Lawyer* was soon followed by a second Sunday strip, *Pete and Pinto*, which he sold to the *New York Sun* and the *New York Herald*. In the spring of 1920, the Chicago Tribune-New York News Syndicate gave him a contract for the daily strip that was to make his name and occupy the rest of his professional life, *Winnie Winkle the Bread-*

*winner*, which debuted on September 20, with a Sunday feature following in 1923.

Branner kept all three strips running for a time, but soon dropped *Looie* and *Pete and Pinto* to devote his full time to Winnie Winkle. The first of the major working-girl strips, *Winnie Winkle* began as a humor feature with a daily gag but evolved into a continuity strip with realistic stories about the life of a stenographer and her family. He revived Looie, who for many years had a strip of his own beneath the *Winnie* Sunday. Branner, with help, wrote and drew the strip until his retirement, following a stroke, in 1962. He died in 1970, four months short of the 50th anniversary of his creation's appearance. His legacy, *Winnie Winkle*, remains alive and well, one of the few survivors of the continuity strips of its period.                                         **D.W.**

**BREATHED, BERKE** (1957– )   Creator of the Pulitzer Prize-winning daily and Sunday humor strip *Bloom County*, Berke Breathed (rhymes with "work method") began his newspaper career while still in college. As a University of Texas undergraduate majoring in photojournalism, he doodled a one-panel political cartoon for the student paper in 1978 "on a lark, to see if [he] could draw as well as the ones [he] was seeing professionally." The *Daily Texan* panel soon developed into a gag strip called *Academia Waltz*, which acquired such a readership in the Austin area that collections published in 1979 and 1980 sold about 10,000 copies.

Born Guy Berkely Breathed in the Los Angeles suburb of Encino, California, he was in his early teens when his family moved to Houston, Texas. His first ambition was to work for the *National Geographic* as a photographer or to become a filmmaker, but when *Academia Waltz* attracted the attention of the Washington Post Writers Group syndicate, he agreed to adapt the campus-oriented strip for them. As *Bloom County*, the new feature debuted on December 8, 1980, and went on to become one of the most popular sophisticated-humor strips in the country, reaching over 1,000 papers while maintaining a wide collegiate audience.

*Bloom County*, with its spare graphic line, its idiomatic dialogue without speech balloons, and its keen contemporary satire, was at first accused of looking like Garry Trudeau's *Doonesbury* (of which Breathed is a big fan), and indeed in its early days the similarities were obvious. But Breathed was soon to develop a distinctive voice, and the two strips soon shared a large readership with relatively little conflict.

Breathed has been one of the industry's most articulate spokesmen for newspaper reproduction in a larger format. "The Incredible Shrinking Comics Page," he protests, puts pressure on cartoonists to print larger and use fewer words, and "the only reason I like being in the comics [is] because I can write." The trenchancy of his social and political satire prove that Berke Breathed can indeed write. The first collection of *Bloom County*, published by Little, Brown in 1983, was on the *New York Times* best-seller list for 32 weeks, and the strip was awarded the Pulitzer Prize in 1987.

On May 1, 1989, Breathed announced that he planned to retire *Bloom County* on August 6, explaining, "A good comic strip is no more eternal than a ripe melon. The ugly truth is that, in most cases, comics age less gracefully than their creators. *Bloom County* is retiring before the stretch marks show." A new strip, entitled *Outland*, appeared on September 3, to the general bewilderment of Breathed's large public, which found its bizarre fantasy incomprehensible. Set in a dream world combining features of Herriman's Coconino County and the Land of Oz, *Outland* appears on Sunday only. At first without any of the characters of *Bloom County*, it gradually restored some of them to life, bringing Opus back in installment number 5 on October 1. The strip has begun to crystallize as a socio-political commentary, taking repeated jabs at environmental pollution and Vice President Quayle. Breathed, who has declined to comment on his intentions regarding his new strip, has since October 1989 served as an associate editor of *Boating* magazine, to which he contributes a monthly column called "Overboard," illustrated with drawings of Opus.
                                         **D.W.**

**BREGER, DAVE** (1908–1970)   One of the few cartoonists ever to do an autobiographical panel, Breger was also the man who created the term G.I. Joe. His *Private Breger* began in the *Saturday Evening Post* shortly after he was drafted early in 1941 and soon became a daily King Features offering. Starting in 1942, the character also appeared in *Yank*, the enlisted man's weekly magazine, and it was for his appearances there that Breger renamed him G.I. Joe, the initials standing for Government Issue.

Born in Chicago, Breger was a self-taught cartoonist, and his work never lost its primitive, homemade look. He studied architecture at the University of Illinois, but eventually ended up with a degree in psychology from Northwestern. The Depression forced him into working in a sausage factory, and in 1937 he fled to New York City to try his luck as a gag cartoonist. He was moderately successful, selling to *Liberty, Collier's*, and the *Saturday Evening Post*. Finally, using himself as the central character, he began doing the Private Breger panels.

Although Breger rose to the rank of lieutenant and served as an overseas correspondent for both *Yank* and *Stars and Stripes*, his cartoon counterpart remained a private and a foot soldier. Pvt. Breger was another of the hapless GIs of comics, a civilian at heart. He never lost the hope that Army life would eventually make sense and he approached war's discomforts, indignities, and dangers with low-grade hope and a very tentative optimism. Cartoonist Breger drew him as a condensed, woebegone caricature of himself.

Like many of his warborn pen and ink contemporaries—such as Sad Sack, Hubert, and the Wolf—Pvt. Breger carried on as a newspaper character in the postwar world. His creator renamed him Mister Breger and early in 1946 added a Sunday page. While the bespectacled cartoon Breger did not fare especially well in the civilian world, the feature managed to last until Dave Breger's death in January 1970.                    **R.G.**

**BRENDA STARR**    Perhaps the first among the new generation of liberated women in the comics of the 1940s was Dale Messick's Brenda Starr, a dashing descendant of Winnie Winkle the Breadwinner who earned her bread as an ace reporter rather than as a stenographer. *Brenda Starr* made its first appearance as a Sunday strip on June 30, 1940, in the *Chicago Tribune* and so appealed to the growing sense of independence among American women that it was joined by a daily feature in October of 1945.

*Brenda Starr*, Dale Messick, © 1980. Reprinted by permission: Tribune Media Services.

Dale Messick (who had shortened and obscured the gender of her first name, Dalia, because of the prejudice against women in the comics field) created the character as an even more emancipated type originally: Brenda began as a girl bandit. The strip was promptly turned down by Joseph Medill Patterson of the *Tribune*, who is said to have told Messick that he would never hire a woman artist. But Patterson's editorial assistant Mollie Slott saw possibilities in the strip and advised Messick to change the heroine into a reporter. Together the two women christened the character Brenda, for Brenda Frazier, a newsworthy debutante of the time, and gave her the surname Starr because she was a star reporter. In this relatively demure and respectable form the character was acceptable, and the *Tribune* agreed to take the strip. Patterson never really liked it, though, and it did not appear in the *New York News* until after his death in 1946.

A mixture of adventure and romance, *Brenda Starr* was never a realistic strip. (Messick has been quoted as saying, "Authenticity is something I always try to avoid.") and has been attacked as an implausible soap opera; but its balance of love and peril has satisfied over four decades of readers, and Messick won the National Cartoonists Society silver plaque for Best Story Strip in 1975. Its plucky and glamorous heroine divided her time between breaking sensational news stories and pursuing a seemingly doomed love affair with her "mystery man." Her impeded romance with the handsome Basil St. John, who spent much of his time raising the black orchids necessary to his survival from a "secret malady," finally reached fruition, after a 36-year series of interruptions, in 1976, when the two married and immediately went about their separate ways on their respective, daring missions.

Among the other regular characters who surround Brenda are her apoplectic managing editor Mr. Livewright, her androgynous colleague Hank O'Hair, and her plump country cousin Abretha Breeze, all adding a nice note of humor to the strip's mix of sighs and thrills.

Messick, who admitted "I don't consider myself a really good artist," employed John Oleson from the early 1950s to draw the action scenes and the backgrounds and do the lettering, and Jim Mackey contributed the cars and the architecture for many years, but the women's fashions were always Messick's own work. The attention to such feminine details—always an important feature of the strip—is one of the things that have marked it as essentially directed to women. The strip has continued to have a wide general audience, however. In 1945, Columbia Pictures produced a movie serial, *Brenda Starr, Reporter*, starring Joan Woodward and Kane Richmond.

One of the few women to achieve a major success in comics, despite Patterson's unrelenting opposition, Dale Messick wrote and drew *Brenda Starr* for over three decades, and when she retired both tasks remained in female hands. The strip has kept current with the tastes of the times and now deals with such contemporary themes as an international drug ring, which Brenda and her still mysterious husband helped in their separate ways to destroy in 1988. *Brenda Starr* is currently drawn in an elegantly realistic, illustrative style by Ramona Fradon, and written by Mary Schmick. **D.W.**

**BRICK BRADFORD** Customarily grouped with *Flash Gordon* and *Buck Rogers* as the third of the 1930s' leading science fiction strips, *Brick Bradford* more correctly belonged to the Sinbad school of heroic high adventure—a romance of sky gods and flaming chariots, mad dragons and wrathful queens, howling storms and ruined empires. The feature's creator, a Cleveland newsman of encyclopedic knowledge named William Ritt, was a devotee of the period's pulp genres as well as of classical mythology and anthropology, and Brick Bradford was successively an aviator, explorer, soldier, costumed avenger, confidante of physicists, gentleman sleuth, and sometimes even a cowboy. He was also a space knight who spent some of his time many thousands of years in the intergalactic future, and eventually the strip acquired an enduring hallmark motif—time travel.

While best known in its 1930s prime as a florid Sunday page set against the likes of Ancient Atlantis and the Middle of the Earth, *Brick Bradford* had first appeared, daily only, on Aug. 21, 1933, in a relative handful of rural newspapers serviced by the Central Press Association, a heartland branch office of King Features. It was just another of the day's many airplane adventure strips. But this one fast proved to be considerably more literate and attractively drawn than the rest. In fact, artist Clarence Gray's stately formalism was at the time quite unknown in comics outside of Harold Foster's *Tarzan*. Through the 1930s and into the early 1940s, Ritt and Gray were extraordinary collaborators: Ritt's penchant for bewilderingly labyrinthine plotting and Gray's taste for distance shots and silent panels made the strip notable.

The strip's hero, a resourceful young American who was a troubleshooter for the day's leading scientists and who journeyed with them into the unknown, was subordinate to the ingenious construction of his adventures. The first 10 years' daily stories saw the valiant Brick discovering a forgotten city of Incan ancients, saving the civilized world from a bloodthirsty gang of submarine pirates, meeting a tribe of Vikings in the Arctic, preventing a Mongol warlord from conquering North America, shrinking himself to subatomic size and battling bacterial horrors, fighting desert brigands with the Foreign Legion, thwarting a madman's plan to rule the Earth with monster robots, battling diamond thieves out West, and test-piloting an experimental airplane into a lost world of dinosaur-riding warriors at the South Pole.

The *Brick Bradford* Sunday page was actually a Saturday page at first, introduced Nov. 24, 1934, as an element of a weekend strip package prepared by King Features for smaller client papers. It employed a separate set of conventions. Here were the fantastic worlds stories, and ultimately the time travel stories, that made the feature's reputation, particularly once comic book reprints were established as a popular newsstand mainstay in the David McKay Co.'s monthly King Comics. The strip's primary device, a wonderful, top-shaped time-traveling machine (first seen in 1935 in a short-lived *Bradford* companion strip titled *The Time Top*) appeared in August 1937, shooting Brick into a treasure-hunting excursion across the 17th-century globe. Concluding that assignment in late 1941, Brick miss-set the Top's controls and flung himself far into the future, where he remained for most of the rest of the decade, derring-doing through many an intergalactic incident; it was mostly these 1940s rocketeering adventures that firmed up his popular credentials as a *Flash Gordon* contemporary. (The daily strip never once did a Time Top story, always preferring to cast the hero as Charles Lindbergh/Frank Buck/Rip Kirby instead, though there was in the 1940s an intricate cross-dimensional story that dispatched Brick to the moon.)

The strip's wild variousness was both its strength and its drawback. Devotees rejoiced in its freedoms; but more linear minds found it increasingly digressive and desultory. Indeed, Bill Ritt, a busy working editor who had less and less time to devote to a side job that had never paid him much more than chump change in any case, was discernibly tiring of his masterwork. The best of the Ritt-Gray *Bradford* was gone by 1945, and the collaboration fell apart. Ritt was finally severed by King Features for missing deadlines, and he surrendered the solo byline to Clarence Gray (the daily strip in October 1948, the Sunday page in June 1949).

Gray elected to drop the epic literary traditions in favor of standard postwar space opera starring the Time Top, and he pursued a popular if not particularly remarkable course. His strip was still a widely circulated one when, as of Oct. 1, 1952, illness forced him to relinquish the daily to King Features stablehorse Paul Norris (who continued to produce his entirely competent, Sunday *Jungle Jim* at the same time). Gray kept the Sunday until he died in January 1957, whereafter Norris assumed that job as well.

Paul Norris subsequently proceeded to make the feature his own, successfully maintaining a readable storyline through the 1950s and 1960s while faithfully preserving Bill Ritt's old Time Top motif and continuing *Brick Bradford* at the frontiers of time and space. The venerable feature ended its days as one of the final survivors of King Features' grand old B-strip lineup, finally expiring in May 1987.                    **J.M.**

**BRIEFER, DICK** (1915– ? )  Briefer entered comic books in 1936, when the industry was just getting started, and remained until 1954. While his major achievement was drawing the Frankenstein monster in both serious and humorous versions, he also drew science fiction, true crime, and even an unusual series about an American Indian crimefighter, as well as an adventure strip for *The Daily Worker*.

While he had originally intended to be a doctor, Richard Briefer eventually decided he would rather be an artist and, after studying at the Art Students League in Manhattan, he got a job with the Eisner-Iger shop. He did a serialized adaptation of *The Hunchback of Notre Dame* that appeared in *Jumbo Comics*, and drew *Flint Baker* for *Planet Comics* and *Rex Dexter of Mars* for *Mystery Men Comics*. He also contributed *The Human Top* to Marvel's one-shot *Red Raven Comics*, giving the world a superhero who possessed the dubious ability of being able to spin around and around at great speed. Perhaps this feature was actually an example of the sense of humor Briefer would later display in his work.

The first version of *Frankenstein* that he drew and wrote started in *Prize Comics* in 1939. In the middle 1940s he converted the monster, whom—like many a movie-goer—he called Frankenstein, into a comedy character. Since Briefer always worked in a loose, somewhat cartoony style, he made the transition from real horror to burlesque horror quite easily. The funny Frankie lasted until the late 1940s, even branching out into a magazine of his own. Then in the early 1950s, with straight horror very popular in comic books, Briefer revived the monster in a serious, grimmer than before, version.

During the 1940s he also drew a character called Real American #1 for *Daredevil*. Also known as the Bronze Terror, his hero was an Indian who doubled as a crimefighter, one of the very few ever to appear in comic books. For *Silver Streak Comics*, Briefer did *The Pirate Prince*, starring a liberal buccaneer who specialized in raiding slave traders and setting their captives free. Briefer did considerable work for *Crime Does Not Pay*, and, under the penname Dick Floyd, he contributed an adventure strip titled *Pinky Rankin* to the American Communist Party newspaper *The Daily Worker* during the World War II years.

He left comics in the middle 1950s to go into commercial art. He was working as a portrait painter at the time of his death in the early 1980s.                    **R.G.**

**BRIGGS, AUSTIN** (1909–1973)  He was one of the most successful illustrators and commercial artists of his generation, and, as one of the founders of the Famous Artists School, he died a millionaire. In the 1930s and 1940s, before he achieved fame and fortune, he drew two popular comic strips—*Secret Agent X-9* and *Flash Gordon*.

Briggs was born in Michigan and grew up in Detroit, and while barely out of his teens, he went to New York with his portfolio. He was then drawing very much like the exceptional pen and ink artist, Joseph Clement Coll, and he quickly got assignments from such slicks as *Collier's* and *McClure's*. "This auspicious beginning was blighted by the Depression," art historian Walt Reed has pointed out, "as the magazines retrenched. Briggs, who had not yet developed his own individual style, was expendable." A period of scuffling and self-doubt followed.

The magazine that helped Briggs to survive was *Blue Book*, for its editor Donald Kennicott saw to it that his adventure fiction pulp was better illustrated than any of its newsstand competitors. While he couldn't pay Briggs slick magazine fees, he did encourage him to experiment and expand. Briggs turned out a great number of illustrations for *Blue Book* throughout the 1930s and developed from a gifted imitator of Coll to a powerful and inventive illustrator with an approach all his own.

To add to his income Briggs also took a job assisting Alex Raymond, whom he had met at a cocktail party sometime around 1935. He went to work helping out on, and sometimes ghosting, *Secret Agent X-9*, *Flash Gordon*, and *Jungle Jim*.

From the late 1930s on Briggs began working toward a more naturalistic and relaxed approach to drawing. He officially took over *X-9* in 1938 and even signed it. His new approach could be seen on the G-Man strip, too. In 1940 he gave up *X-9* to take on the new *Flash Gordon* daily that King Features was launching. Briggs used his newer style there, too, taking his version away from the stiff, posed look Raymond was still favoring on the Sunday *Flash Gordon*. But a certain amount of sloppiness was evident in Briggs' newspaper work now; increasingly unhappy as a comic artist, and not especially proud of the profession, he decided not even to sign the new strip.

By the time he took over the *Flash Gordon* Sunday in 1944, the daily had ceased, and Briggs worked in an even looser style than before. The page looked like the rough sketches of a very gifted artist who was short of time. He refused to sign the Sunday page, and finally in 1948 he balked at renewing his contract. Later, he admitted that when he left the syndicate that day he felt sick, worried that maybe he'd made the wrong decision. But he went on to do years of impressive and award-winning illustrations for such magazines as *Cosmopolitan*, *Redbook*, and *The Saturday Evening Post*, as well as numerous advertising illustrations including a much-admired series for *TV Guide*.

He lived in Paris at the time of his death.      **R.G.**

**BRIGGS, CLARE A.** (1875–1930)    A cartoonist whose abundant body of work provides a social history of his time, Clare Briggs created a memorable panorama of middle-class, middle-brow, middle-America at the turn of the century. Born in Reedsburg, Wisconsin, Briggs lived in a succession of small midwestern towns before his family settled in Lincoln, Nebraska, where the artist went to college. His first regular job was as a newspaper sketch artist in St. Louis, and during the Spanish-American War he served that city's *Chronicle* as an editorial cartoonist. Efforts at finding a job in New York City were unavailing until a former professor of his gave him a letter of introduction to an editor of the *New York Journal*, where his work so impressed owner William Randolph Hearst that he sent Briggs to Chicago to work with the *Examiner* and the *American* there. For the *Chicago American* the artist created one of the first daily continuity comic strips, *A. Piker Clerk*, in 1904.

It was in Chicago, with the inspiration and support of noted *Chicago Tribune* cartoonist John T. McCutcheon, that Briggs developed the particular brand of warm, nostalgic humor for which he became famous. During his 17 years in Chicago and the remaining 13 of his short life, spent with the *New York Tribune*, Briggs created several other strips and dozens of single-panel series. Titles like *When a Feller Needs a Friend*, *The Days of Real Sport*, and *Ain't It a Grand and Glorious Feelin'?* were to enter the nation's vocabulary, encapsulating, like the cartoons they named, elements of universal emotional experience. Briggs' simple, seemingly casual graphic style, its sketchy stroke rendering a multitude of telling details, was perfectly suited to the warm, affectionate character of the mini-dramas it presented.

A popular figure as personally sympathetic as his perceptive cartoons, Briggs was much in demand as a public speaker and earned $100 an evening delivering chalk talks. In 1914 he accepted a five-week contract for $500 a week to appear on the vaudeville circuit. His cartoons were collected in many volumes, and one of his strips, *Mr. and Mrs.*, was continued in syndication for many years after his death in 1930.      **D.W.**

**BRINCKERHOFF, ROBERT**    See LITTLE MARY MIX-UP.

**BRINGING UP FATHER**    The comic strip that everyone called *Jiggs* or *Jiggs and Maggie* began running under its true title in the *New York American* and other Hearst papers on January 12, 1913. But, according to its creator George McManus, the characters had been appearing off and on under other McManus strip headings since November of 1911. Still going, *Bringing Up Father* is one of the longest-running strips in history.

The inspiration for the strip was a play McManus had seen in 1895 as a youth in St. Louis, *The Rising Generation*, which concerned the trials and tribulations of an Irish laborer who'd struck it rich and moved to Fifth Avenue. In the Irishman's "uninhibited naturalness," and his socially ambitious wife and daughter's feelings of shame about him, and in his consequent desire to escape from the pretensions of his new social world, McManus found the themes for his strip.

Jiggs, too, was newly rich when the feature began and in Maggie he had a critical and social-climbing spouse. Jiggs' abiding affection for a game of cards, a drink, the fellowship of his old cronies at Dinty Moore's corner saloon, and for corn beef and cabbage indicated how uneasy he was in his new world. The comedy arose from the extremes to which Jiggs went to escape from Maggie's world to that of Dinty Moore. When she locked him in his room, he'd slip out the window, creep along a cornice 20 stories above the ground and then make his way to the skyscraper next door by means of balancing along a telephone wire, descending to the

*Bringing Up Father*, George McManus, © 1948, King Features Syndicate.

street at last on a swinging steel girder. In one of the often repeated reversals of the strip, Maggie invariably found that Jiggs was already the intimate companion of some social lion she'd been striving to meet. And Jiggs had done it by being himself.

When they first appeared, Jiggs and Maggie were the same size, and Jiggs had the build of the hodcarrier he had formerly been. But during their first decade McManus shrunk his hero for comic contrast with his wife and to enhance the humor of the strip's most frequent refrain at the punchline—the hail of crockery around Jiggs' ears that proclaimed Maggie's discovery of his latest departure from the path of propriety. After that modification, the strip changed very little, its simple formula repeated with infinite variations throughout the remaining years of McManus' 41-year tenure. Through much of that run, *Bringing Up Father* was among the most popular strips in the world, appearing in about 500 newspapers.

McManus had been assisted from the middle 1930s by Zeke Zekely. In McManus' last years Zekely ghosted the strip, but he was not invited to carry it on. Instead Vernon Greene was brought in to do the daily, while Frank Fletcher drew the Sunday (borrowing heavily on what had gone before). Hal Camp took over in the middle 1960s and currently Frank Johnson and Warren Sattler do the strip.                    **R.C.H**

**BRONC PEELER** Fred Harman's first redheaded cowboy started appearing in daily newspaper comic sections late in 1933. Initially Harman syndicated *Bronc Peeler* himself, and the cowpoke and his creator had some rough times in those lean Depression years, but gradually things improved, an attractive Sunday page was added, and the number of client papers increased. By 1938, syndicated now by the John F. Dille organization and accompanied by an Indian lad named Little Beaver, Bronc was doing okay. Harman then converted him to Red Ryder.

Harman, a one-time animation partner of Walt Disney, was ranching in Colorado when he got the urge to return to cartooning by way of a cowboy comic strip. In the early 1930s, according to a *Collier's* article in 1948, "he went to Hollywood, borrowed money and set out to syndicate his own cartoon strip." One of those he most likely borrowed from was his brother Hugh, a very successful animator who, with his partner Rudolf Ising, had created the *Looney Tunes* and *Merrie Melodies* series for Warner Brothers.

Bronc, who originally hung around with a mustachioed galoot named Coyote Pete, was a gangling redheaded youth. As the strip progressed Harman added a few years to Bronc's age and some inches to his shoulders. Bronc was a hard-riding, fast-shooting hom-

bre, good with his fists and attractive to the ladies; he also dropped final G's as often as he could and called his horse a "hoss." Harman drew in a gruff, forceful style, having no fears about his ability to depict horses, cattle, and other cowboy objects that often defeated dude cartoonists. His stories, though, came not out of the real West but from the pages of pulp fiction magazines and off the movie screen. Bronc tangled with rustlers, Mexican bandits, crooked lawyers, and tinhorn gamblers. At the suggestion of his wife, Harman gave Bronc a boy sidekick in hopes of winning a larger juvenile audience, naming him Little Beaver, after his late father Chief Beaver.

In the Sunday page, under the spell of Will James, Harman gave his readers not only 12 panels of adventure but a scenic view of the West as well. The extra panel, called *On the Range*, ran beneath the Peeler half page and was always accompanied by a few paragraphs of Harman's best aw-shucks prose: "History books tell us about wild Injuns an' how they killed white people. When they weren't killin' cowboys an' soldiers, they were fightin' other Injun tribes. But shucks, ya can't blame them fer all the massacres. They were pikers compared to us folks," etc.

Sometime around 1938 Harman's work came to the attention of agent-packager-entrepreneur Stephen Slesinger, possibly by way of Whitman's 1937 *Bronc Peeler* Big Little Book. Slesinger invited Harman East and converted the strip to *Red Ryder*. Thanks to the enterprising Slesinger, Bronc remained alive after the advent of Red. The earlier strip was reprinted until the early 1940s in *Popular Comics*.                    **R.G.**

**BRONCHO BILL** One of the earliest Western adventure strips, it began life in 1928 under the title *Young Buffalo Bill*. For awhile in the early 1930s it was called *Buckaroo Bill* and finally in 1932 it became *Broncho Bill*. The strip lasted until 1950 and the writer-artist for the entire run was Harry O'Neill.

A former professional acrobat, O'Neill got his art training through the mail by way of the Landon correspondence school. He drew in a quirky illustrational style and his perspective and anatomy—especially when it came to drawing horses—were always slightly askew. Bill was a clean-cut blond young man, given to expressions like "Gee willikers!" His cowboy outfit included chaps and a Stetson with the front brim turned up. Bill, often accompanied by his hard-riding girlfriend Nell, operated in a timeless Old West and dealt with the same problems as most movie cowboys: bank robbers, claim jumpers, rustlers—including at least one gang of pig rustlers—crooked gamblers, and wild Indians. Outlaws frequently behaved badly toward women, prompting Bill to call them scoundrels and thrash them. After working for a time as a sheriff in a typical false-front Western town, Bill formed a vigilante group with some of his friends; they called themselves the Boy Rangers and behaved somewhat like bloodthirsty Boy Scouts.

O'Neill added a Sunday page in 1933. As a companion feature he drew *Bumps*, a much lighter effort that dealt with a boy whose father was an acrobat with a traveling circus. When *Broncho Bill* stopped in 1950, it was replaced by a strip about Buffalo Bill, with Fred Meagher in charge. **R.G.**

**BROOKS, DICK** See THE JACKSON TWINS.

**BROOM-HILDA** A wild and anarchic humor strip that respects neither the unities of time and place nor the laws of logic, *Broom-Hilda* has been exploring the humorous possibilities of its limited cast of characters since the Chicago Tribune-New York News Syndicate (now Tribune Media Services) began syndicating it on April 19, 1970. The strip is scripted and drawn by Russell Myers, who employs a bold, slapdash penstroke with a whimsical originality that sometimes suggests the settings of Herriman's *Krazy Kat*. It is a sturdy survivor of its vigorous generation of comic strips, reflecting something of the acidulous tone of *The Wizard of Id*, to whose creator, Johnny Hart, Myers acknowledges a debt.

Broom-Hilda (a witch whose name, a pun on Brunhilde, includes an allusion to her favored vehicle) was born in 474 A.D. and seems to have the power to pass through time at will. The setting, like the period, is unidentified and varies with the exigencies of the daily gag, giving Myers an infinite range of props and situations to draw on. Broom-Hilda may reminisce with Attila the Hun (her last husband) one day and get her big nose caught in a closing bus door the next. Green-hued and warted, she has been sex-starved for a century and puts her name on restroom walls to advertise for obscene phone calls, but she has none of the malevolence we might expect of a witch and is, ultimately , a rather touching figure.

Her companion, Gaylord Buzzard, is no less benign; a fastidious vegetarian, he is repelled by the sight of carrion. Irwin the Troll, the third member of the regular cast, is the soul of gentle sweetness and simplicity, a naive hairball easily bullied or deceived; in 1971 a clump of flowers stole his wallet. His nephew Nerwin, a miniature version of himself with a beanie, pays the strip an occasional visit, but generally the three stars handle the gags without the need of outside help.

Against the background of the genteel Gaylord and the timorous, sweet-tempered Irwin, the heroine's cheerfully vulgar spirit, and her inveterate gluttony, lust, peevishness, and mendacity, have kept *Broom-Hilda* popular with a wide audience since its inception. It is carried by some 300 newspapers daily and Sunday. **D.W.**

**BROWNE, DIK** (1917-1989) The cartoonist who drew *Hi and Lois* and created the lovable Viking *Hagar the Horrible* was born Richard Arthur Allan Browne in Manhattan and spent a year at the Cooper Union Art School before taking his first job with a newspaper in 1936. As a copy boy with the *New York Journal-American* he tried to become a reporter but discovered, as he recalls, that he "had no talent for it" and accepted a transfer to the art department because his office doodles impressed his employers more than his news reporting. In the art department he drew maps and charts, and went on to do the same for more money with *Newsweek*. In 1942 he joined the army where he rose to staff sergeant, drawing more maps and charts for an engineering unit; he also got his first taste of the life of a strip-cartoonist drawing *Ginny Jeep*, a strip about a WAC, for army and air force newspapers.

After the war, Browne went into advertising illustration at the Johnstone & Cushing art service and became well known in the field for such creations as the Birdseye bird, Chiquita Banana, and a revitalized version of the Campbell Soup kids. From 1950 to 1960 he also drew *The Tracy Twins*, a humorous adventure strip, for *Boy's Life*. His work for this strip and for a candy ad brought him to the attention of King Features Syndicate, which asked him to collaborate with Mort Walker on a projected domestic strip called *Hi and Lois*. His art for *Hi and Lois* was to earn him the National Cartoonists Society's Best Humor Strip plaque in 1959, 1960, and 1972, and its Reuben as Outstanding Cartoonist of the Year in 1962.

In 1973, Browne created *Hagar the Horrible*, a daily and Sunday gag strip about a robust, childlike barbarian with all the problems of a henpecked suburbanite. *Hagar*, also distributed by King, experienced one of the fastest increases in readership in comics history, selling to over 600 papers in its first two years and currently reaching more than 1,800 in 58 countries, including 100 papers in Scandinavia. For Hagar the NCS voted him a second Reuben in 1973, and three more Best Humor Strip awards in 1977, 1984, and 1986.

Browne's art—delicate and graceful in *Hi and Lois*, vigorous and bold in *Hagar*, but always expressive and economical—has been collected in numerous volumes. He also illustrated several inspirational works by Bishop Fulton J. Sheen and children's books by Mort Walker.

Browne's sons Robert and Chris, the latter a cartoonist who has appeared frequently in *Playboy* and other national magazines, assisted with *Hagar* for a number of years before Browne's death in 1989 and have continued the strip since.                                       **D.W.**

**BRUCE GENTRY**  It was an adventure strip very much in the Caniff vein, with a handsome aviator as its hero, and the action unfolded against such colorful backgrounds as South America, Alaska, and what was then called IndoChina. Drawn by Ray Bailey, *Bruce Gentry* started in 1945 and ended in 1951.

Syndicated by the *New York Post*, the strip got going in March 1945. Bailey had spent the World War II years as assistant on *Terry and the Pirates*. He was a crackerjack inker, having assimilated most of Caniff's tricks and techniques. Anticipating the end of World War II, Bailey commenced with a hero who was already out of the service. A former captain in the Air Force intelligence, Gentry arrived in the imaginary South American country of Cordillera to go to work as a pilot and troubleshooter for Southern Cross Airlines. His first partner was a Latin named Ricardo, who spoke movie Spanish—"We weel be a great team!" There was a hep Indian named Jive, a beautiful and mysterious brunette called Eden Cortez, and considerable action and intrigue. Gentry tracked down smugglers, escaped killers, and criminal masterminds.

Like his former boss, Bailey kept the strip populated with unconventional and strikingly-named women, who included Tango, Bandy Muffet, Yukon, Mandalay, and Cleo Patric. Since the daily and Sunday continuities were separate, Gentry could romance two different ladies, at least, each week. As the strip progressed, Gentry teamed up with various sidekicks (a couple of whom looked to be related to *Terry*'s Hotshot Charlie), moved beyond South America for adventures in Alaska, Manhattan and Vietnam. Bailey staged all his stories well, and nobody could beat him when it came to drawing planes and all the other mechanical props or the sweeping landscapes that were a trademark of the strip. His people, though, were somewhat on the dull, stock character side.

*Bruce Gentry* was an adventure strip that never quite lived up to its potential, and its chances for long-term success weren't helped by the arrival of Milton Caniff's *Steve Canyon* in January of 1947. Both strips were quite close in basic formula at the start, right down to the South American locale. But at that point in time nobody could do that sort of material better than Caniff. *Bruce Gentry* held on until the first week of January 1951. The final story ended with Gentry marrying longtime ladyfriend Cleo Patric and carrying her across the threshold, a sure sign in those days that his adventuring was over.                                       **R.G.**

*Bruce Gentry*, Ray Bailey, © 1946,
New York Post Corp.

**BUCK ROGERS** It was the first serious science fiction comic strip, one that influenced a wide range of subsequent strips and comic books. *Buck Rogers* began in 1929, less than a year before the Depression would strike. Philip Nowlan was the author, Dick Calkins the artist.

"When I began my long sleep, man had just begun his real conquest of the air in a sudden series of transoceanic flights in airplanes driven by internal combustion motors. He had barely begun to speculate on the possibilities of harnessing sub-atomic forces…The United States of America was the most powerful in the world…I awoke to find the America I knew a total wreck." Thus spoke Anthony Rogers when he woke up in the pages of the August 1928 issue of *Amazing Stories* after a 500-year nap. He repeated his Rip Van Winkle act a few months later, this time in the new newspaper strip called *Buck Rogers.*

Syndicator John F. Dille had noticed Nowlan's novelette and asked him to convert his story into a comic strip. Dille felt the hero needed a snappier first name and borrowed one from the then popular movie cowboy, Buck Jones. The artist chosen to launch Buck was Dick Calkins (1895–1962). In his middle thirties at the time and a graduate of the Chicago Art Institute, Calkins had been a newspaper cartoonist since before World War I and had worked on the *Detroit Free Press* and the *Chicago Examiner.* Just as the war was ending, he entered the United States Air Service and got his commission as a pursuit pilot. He never went overseas, but his brief stint as an aviator made a lasting impression on him and well into the 1930s he was still signing himself Lt. Dick Calkins. *Buck Rogers*, at first a daily only, made its debut on Monday, January 7, 1929. That was, purely by chance, the day the first *Tarzan* strip appeared.

Unlike earlier fantasy and science fiction strips, *Buck Rogers* took a completely straight approach to comic strip storytelling. More importantly, it introduced many science fiction notions to a general public that had little interest in or knowledge of either book or pulp magazine SF. The strip popularized the props and paraphernalia—ray guns, rocket ships, robots etc.—that heretofore had been the property of the pulps.

The strip wasted no time. On the very first day readers saw Buck wake up 500 years in the future and meet Wilma Deering, who seemed to be capable of flying through the air, and they also got a hint that some sort of conflict was going on. Before the week was out, it was revealed that many years earlier the Mongol Reds from the Gobi Desert attacked America and that "the country's industrial, transportation, and credit structures crumbled. Government ceased to exist." Furthermore, "on the ruins of New York, San Francisco, Detroit, and a dozen others, the Mongols reared cities of super-scientific magnificence." Gradually the Americans, who now lived mostly in the wilds and woodlands, were rebuilding, and they had created organizations, known as Orgs, to carry on a guerilla war against the ruthless invaders. Wilma is a member of one of these and is quickly established as feisty, independent, and somewhat taken with Buck.

As an artist, Lt. Calkins was barely adequate. Anatomy, perspective, inking techniques and other basics of his chosen profession were beyond his mastery. Even much of his staging was clumsy, but he had a considerable enthusiasm and an almost boyish fondness for the gimmicks and gadgets that were so important to the strip. Scriptwriter Nowlan seems to have been a bit restless, and he ignored the Asian invaders now and then to introduce other SF elements. Early in the strip's second year, Martians visit Earth and readers got their first look at the Tiger Men—who were the Red Planet equivalent of the Mongols. Like many a flying saucer visitor to come, the Martians are interested in collecting and examining human specimens. Wilma is one of the specimens they pick and this starts Buck on a new adventure. In this particular sequence he is inspired to design the world's very first interplanetary rocket ship so that he can rescue other kidnap victims who have

*Buck Rogers*, Phil Nowlan and Dick Calkins, © 1934, John F. Dille Co. Used by permission of The Dille Family Trust.

been taken back to Mars—"Roaring rockets! We'll show these Martians who's who in this solar system!" Calkins dutifully provides a diagram of the ship, complete with Inertron lift-ballast, electroformers, and liquid Ultronium ballast.

The strip soon developed a cast of regulars, most of whom stuck around. There was Dr. Huer, brilliant scientist and egghead (although in his earliest appearances he had a handsome head of curly locks), who served as Buck's friend and mentor and seemed to begin just about every sentence with the word "Heh!"; Killer Kane, traitor and all-around scoundrel, who was Buck's archrival; Black Barney, who started out as a villainous air pirate and then became Buck and Wilma's staunchest sidekick.

A Sunday page was added early in 1930, introducing more new characters. In fact, Buck Rogers himself didn't appear at all in the early Sunday continuities and was only an occasional visitor throughout the 1930s. The star was a teenager named Buddy Deering, a hitherto unheralded younger brother of Wilma. Buddy, obviously intended for the youthful readers who were supposed to make up a large part of the audience for Sunday funnies, was a bright and inventive lad, and he got himself involved with a Martian princess and journeyed to her planet in his very first adventure. Her name was Alura and she was of the Golden People, a different race than the nasty Tiger folk. Astute readers may have noticed that the Sunday pages were considerably better looking than the daily strips. This was because a talented young man named Russell Keaton was ghosting the Sundays. Keaton stayed with the feature for several years before moving on. He was replaced by another young ghost artist, Rick Yager.

By 1939 the atomic bomb was appearing in the strip. Again, Nowlan was introducing something that had been written about in science fiction magazines—as well as, obviously, scientific journals—for quite some time. With the advent of World War II most of the villains again became Orientals. In the dailies a new order of Martians appeared, looking quite Japanese. On Sundays descendants of the Japanese responsible for the attack on Pearl Harbor gave Buddy, Barney, Doc, and the others trouble out in space.

The strip began to undergo a variety of changes in the 1940s. According to cartoonist Murphy Anderson, "Phil Nowlan was fired from the strip before he died. He was fired for getting too 'far out.'"—Calkins apparently wrote as well as drew the daily from that point and Yager scripted and drew the Sunday. Calkins left the feature in 1947, and Anderson, who'd begun his career drawing for *Planet Comics*, took over the drawing of the daily until 1949 and came back again for a short spell in 1958. By the late 1950s, after several comings and goings by

Yager, Anderson and Leonard Dworkins, George Tuska became the artist on both the daily and the Sunday. The syndicate brought in real science fiction writers again, among them Fritz Leiber and Judith Merril, and Buck's adventures became somewhat more sophisticated. The Sunday ended in 1965 and the daily two years later.

Buck returned in 1979 and was seen in a feature film starring Gil Gerard. That was followed by a television series. The revived interest prompted the New York Times Syndicate to try another comic strip version. Written by Jim Lawrence and drawn by Gray Morrow, *Buck Rogers in the 25th Century* began anew on Sunday, September 9, 1979, in a small list of newspapers. It was not a conspicuous success. Cary Bates replaced Lawrence as writer early in 1981. In the autumn of 1982 Jack Sparling, with over a half-dozen other syndicated strips to his credit, became the artist and stayed with the strip until it ended the next year.                    **R.G.**

**BUELL, MARJORIE HENDERSON** (1904– )  Born Marjorie Lyman Henderson in Philadelphia, the cartoonist signed herself "Marge" and in 1935 created *Little Lulu*, originally as a panel in *The Saturday Evening Post*.

In the February 13, 1937, issue of the *Post* she wrote, "My artistic career began in a big way at the age of eight, when I painted a calf red. Then, at about ten, I discovered that I could keep myself in Irish potatoes by drawing paper dolls and selling them to friends for a penny a sheet. That financial success, plus a brisk Christmas-card business the next year, convinced me that an artistic career was just the thing for a young girl. Easy money and something you could do in your spare time. Have since found out I was wrong on both counts."

On graduating from high school, she had begun drawing professionally and had sold large numbers of cartoons by the mid-1930s to such markets as *Life, Judge, Collier's,* and *The Saturday Evening Post*. She lived in Pennsylvania with her husband, C. Addison Buell, and their two sons, Fred and Larry. And it was there that she created *Little Lulu*. When the *Post* looked for a replacement for Carl Anderson's *Henry* panel in 1934, she had been selling the magazine gag cartoons for nine years. A *Post* editor asked her to try to come up with a panel to replace the Anderson feature.

The character she developed had the same corkscrew curls she had worn as a child—in fact, she once wrote that Lulu looked "a lot like me"—and editors supplied the character's name. *Little Lulu* first appeared in the February 23, 1935, issue. Marge drew the panel in the style she'd developed years earlier. It was simple and uncluttered, something of a warmer, softer version of the kind of work being done by such artists as John Held Jr., Ethel Hays, and Gladys Parker.

Her work on the printed character continued—including Lulu's stint as spokesperson for Kleenex in magazine and newspaper ad strips—while Paramount adapted the character for animated cartoons. When Lulu was licensed to comic books in 1945, the job of creating stories and art was turned over to the company, but Marge retained creative control until Western Publishing bought all rights some years later. Even at that point, she continued to provide the company with her thoughts on the handling of her character.

Marge's own artwork appeared in comic books in the late 1930s and the early 1940s. She provided illustrations for the poems and children's stories of Ruth Plumly Thompson, which ran in *King Comics*.

**M.C.T.**

**BUGS BUNNY** Despite occasional competition, Bugs Bunny remains the best-known rabbit in the world. A star of the silver screen since 1938, an Academy Award winner and a television favorite for the past several decades, he has also had a fruitful career in comic books and comic strips.

Bugs' comic book debut was made late in 1941 in the first issue of Dell's *Looney Tunes and Merrie Melodies*. He shared the magazine with several other members of the Warner Brothers animated cartoon stable, including Porky Pig, Elmer Fudd, and Sniffles. The magazine was packaged and printed by Whitman Publishing out of its Southern California offices. The first solo story about the rabbit was drawn by Win Smith, who had drawn the *Mickey Mouse* newspaper strip in its early weeks. Newspaper veteran George Storm took over in the second issue.

After a few more issues, Chase Craig assumed the drawing of Bugs. His version was much closer to the zany hare of the screen, though not quite as rowdy and vulgar. At Warners, directors such as Bob Clampett, Chuck Jones, and Tex Avery were not aiming their audacious animated cartoons just at a kid audience. And, of course, no word balloon could recreate Mel Blanc's incomparable vocal characterization. The phrase "What's up, doc?" did frequently appear, however.

The first solo *Bugs Bunny* comic book, a black-and-white effort, appeared in 1942 with artwork by Carl Buettner. The LT&MM comic lasted until 1962 on its first go-round. Revived by Whitman/Gold Key in 1975, the second series continued until 1984. After a couple dozen one-shots, a regular *Bugs Bunny* comic book got going in late 1952, and lasted until 1983. DC brought Bugs back in 1990.

Bugs branched out into newspaper comic sections in 1943. At first there was just a Sunday page, also produced by Whitman's Southern Cal offices, which began on January 10, 1943, and was syndicated by NEA. Even though the strip was in Bugs' name, the syndicate specified that the other well-known Warners cartoon characters also appear. And Porky, Elmer, and several others shared the page with the rabbit.

The first six Sundays were written and drawn by Chase Craig. When he went into the Navy, Roger Armstrong got the job: "I did the writing, penciling, lettering, inking and mailing out." He was paid $25 a week for the job. He handled the Sunday for the next two years and then was replaced by Buettner. In 1946 a daily *Bugs Bunny* strip was added. Ralph Heimdahl, who'd been drawing the Sunday since 1946, drew the daily as well. He worked with several different writers. After two and a half decades, Heimdahl left because of illness. The current artist is Shawn Keller.

**R.G.**

**BULLETMAN** He was first seen in 1940 in the cheapest comic book ever published in America: Fawcett's *Nickel Comics* came out twice a month, offering 32 pages of assorted heroes for just 5 cents. But *Nickel Comics* failed to thrive and expired with the eighth issue, whereupon Bulletman rocketed over to the already established *Master Comics*. He was pretty much the star of the magazine until the arrival of Captain Marvel Jr., late in 1941.

Jim Barr was one of those who became a superhero through his own efforts. A mild-mannered civilian employee in a metropolitan police lab, he invented a serum that "makes him the most powerful man on Earth" and for good measure created a gravity-regulator helmet. The bullet-shaped hat made him look somewhat like a pinhead, but it enabled him to "fly by making the force of gravity work in any direction."

In the spring of 1941 he took on a partner, in the person of Bulletgirl, in reality Susan Kent, daughter of a police sergeant and girlfriend of Jim Barr. Her flying helmet was identical to his, but her costume considerably abbreviated. The team also appeared in 16 issues of *Bulletman* and in *America's Greatest Comics* and was last seen in *Master* #106 (September 1949). While nowhere near as successful as Captain Marvel and the rest of the Marvel Family, they did rank among Fawcett's most popular characters.

A goodly portion of the adventures of the human projectiles was written by the prolific Otto Binder. Among the many artists were Jack Binder, Jon Small, and Mac Raboy.

**R.G.**

**THE BUNGLE FAMILY** Misanthropic, mean-minded, and highly amusing, *The Bungle Family* started in 1918 and lasted, with a few lapses, until 1945. The strip was created, written, and drawn by Harry J.

Tuthill, a man who looked upon domestic life in urban America with, at best, amused disdain.

After working on midwestern newspapers as a political cartoonist, Tuthill got a job in New York City with the *Evening Mail*. In 1918 he came up with a daily strip he called *Home, Sweet Home*, which introduced George and Josie, who eventually became, with the addition of a daughter, the Bungle Family.

At its commencement the strip wasn't that different from the chronicles of domestic life being drawn by Clare Briggs, Tad, and others. Gradually, though, Tuthill began ignoring most of the conventional situations and started poking into areas that interested him. George and his wife, for the life of the feature, resided in a succession of furnished, walkup flats, and the petty annoyances and the daily challenges of that life style became one of his preoccupations. George's complex feuds with his neighbors and his run-ins with the landlord took on an almost surreal quality. The bleak halls and stairways of the apartment buildings, where other tenants—or their vicious pets—lay in wait to ambush George, and the spectral cellars where anything from rats to a homicidal neighbor might lurk, became frequent settings for Tuthill's gags.

George Bungle's face was a variation on the basic funny paper husband doodle of the day—complete with sausage nose, scraggly mustache, and minimal chin. He was petty, argumentative, ill-informed, and brimful of grandiose schemes for getting rich quick. Though not especially likable, he was a loser on such an impressive, almost cosmic, scale that he was fascinating to follow. His wife, Jo, had somewhat more common sense, but was quite adept at nagging and, when the occasion arose, was capable of monumental obtuseness. Her marathon quarrels with her husband were famous in whatever lower-middle-class neighborhood they happened to be dwelling in and could be triggered by anything from a serious household problem to a disagreement over the correct pronunciation of a word neither of them knew the meaning of. Unlike many comic strip wives, she was moderately attractive and no larger than her husband.

In 1923 Tuthill's strip was picked up for syndication by McNaught. Two years later the title was changed to *The Bungle Family* and about that same time a Sunday page was added. Fairly early in the strip he'd introduced continuity; some of the stories were built around various domestic crises, a favorite recurrent one being an extended visit from unwanted relatives: "Ike R. Bungle! My word! Think of a baby who has won four or five pie- and egg-eating contests so cold-bloodedly arranging to come here." There were also extended sequences dealing with George's intricate feuding with his strange and vindictive fellow tenants, as well as frequent conti-

nuities devoted to his many schemes for acquiring sudden wealth. Tuthill grew increasingly fond of mock melodramas, many of which involved the Bungles' attractive young daughter Peggy. She was often courted by the rather stodgy millionaire Montgomery El Dorado and by the dashing ne'er-do-well Hartford Oakdale. Another recurrent character was the attractive Sybil Dardanella, a lady who intruded in George's life and schemes in sundry ways. Although Jo considered Sybil a hussy, George was quite taken with her.

By the middle 1930s, in the daily, Tuthill was moving further from the problems of urban life, and he turned to stories involving political intrigue in Latin America, lost civilizations in the jungle, and even time travel. He returned now and then to domestic scenes, but would then toss in an alien from another dimension. These fantasy sequences were funny, but very unlike what he'd been doing a decade earlier.

Tuthill seemed to grow restless as the 1930s ended. He announced he was ending the strip and actually did shut down operations for awhile. He returned to it, quit again, and then started up again. Finally in 1945 he quit for good and all.                                          **R.G.**

**BUNKY** Bunker Hill Jr., better known as Bunky, was the hero of an epic mock-melodrama that took decades to unfold. He was the creation of Billy DeBeck and, from the late 1920s on, could be found upstairs from the *Barney Google* Sunday page. His topper strip, originally entitled *Parlor, Bedroom & Sink*, was at once satirical, lowbrow, erudite, meanminded, and sentimental and surely one of the wackiest soap operas ever concocted. Bunky, who sprang out of a literary tradition that includes Candide, Oliver Twist, and Little Orphan Annie, was a precocious tyke who roamed the world in the baby clothes and bonnet he was christened in. He possessed a nose that rivaled that of Jimmy Durante and a vocabulary that many a pundit would envy.

When *Parlor, Bedroom & Sink* began on May 16, 1926, Bunky was nowhere in evidence—which, in terms of propriety, was probably just as well, since the first Sunday dealt with the wedding of his parents. DeBeck soon shifted from domestic gags to continuity and increasingly wild burlesque melodrama that kidded all the clichés and conventions of the success-has-its-price sort of movies, plays, and novels. Initially it was Bunky Sr., who had the dire adventures and reversals of fortune. On the fateful day of November 13, 1927, Bibsy succeeded in tracking down her wayward husband and showed him their new baby. This is Bunky, but he has neither the beezer nor the vocabulary he'll soon acquire. His nose is button-small and all he says is "Yaw."

Within a few weeks, however, little Bunky's nose had blossomed and he'd begun to speak in a worldly-wise manner. "We must prove to the world that we are capable of overcoming the great obstacles that my poor misguided father has thrown in our paths," he advised his mother. "Don't worry, mother of mine! Together we will work out our salvation without assistance from anyone" This sort of discourse in a Mary Pickford pluck-and-luck movie wouldn't have caused much in the way of chuckles, but delivered deadpan by the bonneted Bunky it took on a somewhat different coloration.

Early in 1928, during a period when Bunky was wandering the cruel world on his own, DeBeck introduced a new character. Fagan, who dressed like a bum, robbed widows and orphans, kicked stray dogs, beat children, and wasn't above stealing the pennies from a blind man's cup, was a total lowlife, without any redeeming social value, and yet he was somehow an attractive character. On Fagan's second appearance DeBeck told his readers that poor little Bunky had "unwittingly committed himself into the hands of a vicious, unscrupulous 'Fagan' (famous Dickens character)." A case for DeBeck's devotion to Dickens would be easier to make if he'd spelled Fagin correctly. It wasn't until the middle 1930s that his loutish villain got around to substituting an I for the A in his monicker.

Another of Fagan's crimes was the murder of the English language. One of his favorite locutions was "youse" and this became a trademark. His usage was infectious, and soon sundry other characters of all stations took to inserting "youse" into their conversations. In fact, Bunky himself started addressing Fagan with the immortal phrase, "Youse is a viper!"

Throughout the Thirties the Bunky story unfolded like a Victorian picaresque novel. There were separations and reunions, wanderings, ups and downs of fortune, changes of identity. Bunky became a reluctant star of talking pictures, the mascot of a big league baseball team, a flyweight boxer, a performer in a rather sinister circus. DeBeck also indulged quite a bit in pure fantasy in the 1930s: One sequence dealt with a gorilla who went around, at Bunky's suggestion, dressed in a suit and top hat, another with a shapechanging witch who turned Fagan into a bullpup and Bunky into a duck. The longest fantasy yarn, which ran for well over a year of Sundays, got rolling early in 1937 when Bunky teamed up with a talking dog named John Thomas and eventually returned to the dog's homeland, Poochadina.

The strip underwent several format changes, growing from two tiers to three and then stretching from a third- to a half-page. In September of 1932 the official title became *Parlor, Bedroom & Sink starring BUNKY.* By the spring of 1935 that was shortened to just plain *Bunky.* When DeBeck died in 1942, his features were continued by Joe Musial and Fred Lasswell. Bunky, never quite the same after his creator's death, survived until 1948.  **R.G.**

**BURGOS, CARL** (1917–1984)  By his own admission he was not a great artist, yet Carl Burgos managed to create one of the most successful comic book heroes—the Human Torch. By the time he introduced the Torch in 1939, he'd already been working in comics for over a year, making him almost a veteran in a business that was only a few years old itself.

He studied at the National Academy of Design in Manhattan and went on to work in an engraving plant and then to write and draw for the comic shop run by Harry "A" Chesler. The next year he moved up to Lloyd Jacquet's Funnies, Inc. shop, and in 1942 he was drafted into the service. During his first four or so years in comics he created a batch of characters, including the Iron Skull and the White Streak, both of whom were androids. His most famous creation was also, despite his name, an android: The Human Torch debuted in *Marvel Comics* #1 (November 1939).

Burgos was the kind of artist who could have flourished only in the early days of comic books. He wasn't slick or especially accurate, but he had a raw energy and he conveyed action well. His people, with the possible exception of some of his heroes, were unhandsome and squatty and given to wrinkled clothes. (For beautiful women, *Marvel* readers had to look to the work of such colleagues as Bill Everett and Jack Kirby.) "I enjoyed everybody's strips, but if they wanted Raymond or Caniff, they could look at Raymond or Caniff," Burgos once said. "The miserable drawing was all mine, but I was having fun."

He returned to the field after World War II, but, if the dullness of the strip is any indication, he didn't appear to be having fun anymore. Burgos drew the Torch again, in the middle 1940s and again in the middle 1960s. He also drew and edited some black-and-white comics and worked up an android named Captain Marvel—a name that didn't happen to be in use at the time. He eventually gave up drawing and moved into other areas of the magazine business for most of the rest of his life.  **R.G.**

**BURNLEY, JACK** (1911– )  Christened Hardin Burnley, he was something of a prodigy and started working as a professional newspaper sports cartoonist while in his teens. From 1939 to 1947 he drew for comic books, doing both *Superman* and *Batman,* as well as ghosting sequences of both their newspaper strips.

A self-taught artist, Burnley got a job as an office boy in the art department of King Features Syndicate in Manhattan in the late 1920s. In 1929 he was given a sports panel of his own, one that he drew for the next nine years, which featured portraits of athletes as well as drawings of figures in action. When that job ended, Burnley took his portfolio to DC where he was hired. In 1940 he ghosted several *Superman* stories in *Action Comics*.

He drew in a patient, realistic style. His training as a sports cartoonist served him well and his heroes were always muscular, athletic types who knew how to run, jump, and punch properly. He made no effort to imitate Joe Shuster's simpler, more cartoony approach to drawing the Man of Steel and readers didn't seem to mind. Burnley, of course, never signed any of this work. He stayed with Superman into 1941 and worked on the newspaper Sunday page in 1943 and 1944. He moved over to *Batman* in 1942, drawing some of the dark knight's adventures in *Detective Comics* and *Batman*. From 1944 to 1946 he penciled the *Batman* newspaper strip as well. Again he worked in his own style and anonymously.

Burnley had been given a superhero of his own in 1941 when *Starman* started appearing in *Adventure Comics*, the only DC work he was allowed to sign. Written by Gardner Fox, the feature dealt with yet another languid playboy who doubled as a costumed crimefighter—in this case with the aid of a gravity rod of his own invention that enabled him to fly. For a time the redclad Starman was the leading character in *Adventure*, but his popularity soon waned and Burnley left him in 1942. He also contributed to *All Star Comics* and did a number of covers for various DC titles. In the early 1940s he did sports pages for some of the McKay comic books, such as *Magic Comics*.

Leaving comics in the late 1940s, Burnley returned to sports cartooning. He then worked in the art departments of various West Coast newspapers until he retired.                                                                         **R.G.**

**BUSHMILLER, ERNIE** (1905–1982)  A master gagman who worked in a quintessential cartoon style, Bushmiller was the creator of the highly successful *Nancy* strip. He started drawing professionally while still in his teens and was involved with cartoons and comic strips for over 60 years. In addition to the fuzzyhaired little Nancy and her tough beau Sluggo, he created *Phil Fumble* and drew *Fritzi Ritz* from 1925 onward.

Bushmiller was born in the Bronx. After six months of high school, the redheaded youth quit to take a job as a copy boy with the *New York World:* "I was the personal office boy for Alexander Woolcott, Heywood Broun, Walter Lippmann and many other immortals." Eventually he worked his way into the art department, becoming a colleague and friend of Rudolph Dirks, H.T. Webster, Milt Gross, and Herb Roth. His own drawing style, first developed on the sidewalks and brick walls of the Bronx, was simple and direct and obviously influenced by those around him. Bushmiller also studied nights at the National Academy of Design.

In 1925, after handling an assortment of cartoon jobs on the *World*, Bushmiller was given the opportunity of taking over *Fritzi Ritz*. Begun in 1922 by Larry Whittington, the strip dealt with a pretty flapper who got a job in the movie business, which still had flourishing studios in the East at the time. In most later autobiographical accounts Bushmiller went in for some revising of history, usually claiming he had created Fritzi and not mentioning poor Whittington at all.

Although he used simple continuities in the strip, Bushmiller's prime concern was with building a strong gag each and every day. Unlike most of the other artists doing pretty girl features at the time—C.A. Voight with *Betty*, Russ Westover with *Tillie the Toiler*, among them—Bushmiller rarely relied on cute dialogue and wisecracks for his payoffs. He was always more fascinated with props and pantomime, and many of his punchlines were visual as well as verbal. Quite probably, by the 1930s, he was one of the best builders of gags in the business. It wasn't until much later that the mechanisms became too obvious and the striving for simplicity and clarity in his drawing gave way to a rubber stamp look.

A *Fritzi Ritz* Sunday page was started in 1929 and the following year a topper starring Phil Fumble was added. Phil, like his creator, was a redheaded fellow; in fact, Bushmiller often caricatured himself as looking like a taller, plumper Fumble. Early in 1933, shortly before Ritzi went West to try to crash the movies in Hollywood, Bushmiller introduced a small, spongyhaired niece to the daily. This was Nancy and by 1938 she was so popular that the strip was rechristened in her name. Bushmiller, who'd been moving away from gags about Fritzi's social life, now concentrated almost entirely on the kid world of Nancy and Sluggo. On Sunday he began doing a *Nancy* half-page and a *Fritzi Ritz* half-page, sending the now homeless Phil Fumble in to become Fritzi's perennial boyfriend. By the 1940s *Nancy* was one of the most popular strips in America, appearing in several hundred papers.

Bushmiller and his wife, who had no children, settled in Connecticut in the 1950s. He led a relatively quiet life there, contrasting with the period some years earlier when he shared studio space in New York City with Milt Gross, H.T. Webster, and Dow Walling. Never especially vain about himself, he once said, "I look like a honeydew melon in all my pictures." A fellow artist, Charlie Plumb, described him as "redhaired and babyfaced...you might mistake him for the butcher's boy minus the meat."

Bushmiller had help on his strips, employing both assistants and ghosts. Bernard Dibble worked with him and eventually ghosted the *Fritzi Ritz* Sunday page in the 1950s. Al Plastino drew the Sunday *Nancy* for many years, and Will Johnson drew the daily during Bushmiller's final years of association with the strip. "Although he was proud of his accomplishments, Ernie was uncomfortable with fame," Brian Walker has written in his book on Nancy and her creator. "He loved to put himself down and viewed himself as the champion of the underdog. To him, children were the ultimate underdogs." **R.G.**

**BUSTER BROWN** Richard Outcault's Buster Brown, who dressed like a sissy but was a rough and tumble kid at heart, first appeared in the *New York Herald* on May 4, 1902. He eventually became Outcault's most enduring, and lucrative, character.

Although Buster Brown and his girlfriend Mary Jane (named after the artist's wife) lived in respectable wealth as opposed to the slum violence of Outcault's earlier work, notably *The Yellow Kid*, Buster was an incorrigible scamp. Each Sunday page ended with a promise to mend his mischievous manners. Also included in the regular cast was Tige, his pet dog and one of the earliest talking animals in newspaper funnies.

At the beginning of 1906 Outcault was once again persuaded to return to the Hearst fold, which he'd left late in the last century. His final *Buster Brown* page for the *Herald* appeared on December 31, 1905 and his first for the *New York Journal* on January 14, 1906. It's difficult to document Outcault's later *Buster Brown* efforts, since the series didn't always appear in major Hearst papers; however, it continued to be syndicated by the Hearst organization as late as December 11, 1921. The non-Outcault version, carried on by various hands, is also difficult to catalogue. It was carried in the *Herald* until July 15, 1906 and thereafter sold to other papers as late as January 22, 1911.

*Buster* was not, of course, the first comic series featuring the antics of a mischievous boy, but Outcault's page added a touch of superficial respectability. Outcault was one of the first newspaper comic artists to exploit the full commercial value of his characters. The Yellow Kid had been used to sell buttons, cigarettes, ladies' fans, and kitchen stoves. Buster Brown was even more lucrative. He was licensed to promote raisins, musical instruments, a wide range of clothing, and, most importantly, shoes. **K.S.B.**

**BUZ SAWYER** This was Roy Crane's third and final adventure strip. He was hired away from the NEA syndicate, for whom he'd created *Wash Tubbs* and *Captain Easy*, by Hearst's King Features. Having named his first hero after a washtub, he named his new one after a buzz saw. *Buz Sawyer*, daily and Sunday, began in November 1943.

"It was during World War II, so I decided to make Buz a Navy pilot," Crane said once in explaining the origins of the strip. "It promised lots of action, and I also felt that I would be making a contribution to the war effort. Before actually starting the strip, and to ensure authenticity, I did a great deal of research. I've always loved to travel, so I went to many different places in search of information...I even spent some time aboard an aircraft carrier."

Buz was a handsome, clean-cut young man, with none of Easy's world-weary, knocked about look. His sidekick, and also the gunner in the Navy plane he piloted, was an amiable roughneck named Rosco Sweeney. Before the strip was many weeks old, Buz and Sweeney were marooned on a Pacific island. While there was a beautiful girl in a sarong, there were also Japanese soldiers and sudden death. Crane, assisted by Ralph Lane, did some impressive work, depicting authentic planes and weapons as well as lush Pacific scenery.

Like many adventure strips, drawn weeks in advance, *Buz Sawyer* was still fighting World War II after it had ended. Crane rushed out a special strip, which ran on August 16, 1945, to explain, "The current story sequence began before the Jap surrender. In reality, the action takes but a few hours. Its presentation in a strip, tho, requires several days. Can you bear with us while the episode runs its course?"

In the immediate postwar years Crane did some of his best continuities. He had Buz leave the Navy, return to his small-town family home in Texas, and go through the various adjustment problems most GIs were facing.

*Buster Brown*, R.F. Outcault, 1904.

In late autumn of 1945 Buz journeyed to Manhattan to look for a job and also to find out what had become of an old girlfriend. He was hired as a troubleshooter for an international airline, but not before he got entangled with a sexy lady known as the Maharani of Batu, her pet tiger, the fraudulent Count Confetti, and the murder of his former sweetheart. These were all the trappings, updated some, that Crane had had such fun with in the *Tubbs* strips of the 1930s.

There followed adventures all over the globe—Java, Alaska, Latin America, etc. Along the way Crane had Buz break his nose, in order to ugly him up some. Sweeney went along on some of the escapades, but in the late 1940s Buz married his longtime sweetheart Christy Jameson. Sweeney spent most of his time from then on in the Sunday page. In the conservative 1950s Buz returned to the Navy, and the strip lost a good deal of its zest. There was still adventure and intrigue, but not much fun.

Crane had considerable help, notably from Leslie Turner, on the Tubbs and Easy chronicles, and *Buz Sawyer* was likewise a joint effort just about from the start. Lane was his first assistant, followed by Hank Schlensker in January of 1946. Ed Granberry had come aboard in 1944 and took care of most of the actual scripting from then on. Eventually Crane worked chiefly as the supervisor of the feature, with the other two ghosting the daily.

The Sunday page, devoted to separate continuities starring Sweeney, passed from Crane to Clark Haas in the late 1940s. Al Wenzel became the Sunday ghost artist in 1960, and, from 1962 to the end of the page in 1974, he wrote it as well.

After Crane's death in the middle 1970s, Granberry and Schlensker began signing *Buz Sawyer*. Both of them retired in the early 1980s and John Celardo continued the daily, which appeared in but a handful of newspapers, until 1990.

**R.G**

**BYRNE, JOHN** (1950– ) Byrne became a professional comic book artist in the middle 1970s. By the middle 1980s he was among the most popular and successful men in the business. An award winner and a fan favorite, he has specialized in superheroes; he's drawn *Spider-Man, The Hulk, Daredevil, X-Men, The Fantastic Four*, and *Superman*.

The English-born Byrne was raised in Canada. Though his earliest favorite in comic books was Superman, he discovered *The Fantastic Four*, and, as he has said, "After that, my buying habits changed and I started picking up *Spider-Man, The Avengers, Sgt. Fury*." While studying at the Alberta College of Art, he contributed work to school publications and fanzines. He then sold work to Charlton and from there he went to Marvel. Among his first jobs were drawing *Iron Fist, Ghost Rider, Daredevil, Spider-Man*, and *The Avengers*. His style was a combination of Jack Kirby, Gil Kane, and Neal Adams, mixing bravura detail and clarity of storytelling.

It was with *X-Men* that Byrne first solidified his position in comics. He not only drew it, but also contributed to plot and characterization, especially with the popular characters Phoenix and Wolverine. During this same period Byrne briefly worked on *Fantastic Four*, and in 1981 he became artist-writer on the book. Then he came up with *Alpha Flight* and also did *The Hulk*.

Like many another hot Marvel artist, Byrne was eventually hired away by DC. In 1986 he was given the job of revitalizing Superman, and the chief result of that was a six-part miniseries titled *The Man of Steel*. It sold relatively well, garnered considerable publicity, and made Byrne, briefly anyway, into a media celebrity. He recently returned to the Marvel fold and was drawing and writing *Avengers West Coast* and *The She-Hulk*.

**R.G.**

**BYRNES, GENE** See REG'LAR FELLERS.

# C

**CALKINS, RICHARD** See BUCK ROGERS.

**CALLAHAN, JACK** (1889–1954)  A cartoonist who drew in a simple, uncluttered humorous style, Callahan worked for the various Hearst syndicates for roughly a quarter of a century. His most successful decade was the 1920s, when he drew, among other things, *Freddie the Sheik*. Callahan also provided the artwork for the very first crossword puzzles, which began in the Sunday *Fun* magazine of the *New York World* in 1913, and in the 1940s he drew for comic books.

While still with the *World*, in 1916, Callahan drew a syndicated panel. Close in style to the work of John McCutcheon and Clare Briggs, it appeared under several titles, including *Big Moments in Little Lives* and *When You Were A Boy*. By 1918 Hearst's International News Service was distributing Callahan's *Over Here*, which commented on various fads and foibles; though laid out in comic strip format, it consisted of a single panel. One of the recurring characters was Calamity Jane, a thin, nervous and complaining young lady who was to appear in several other Callahan features.

He kept simplifying his style, eventually eliminating all shading and crosshatching and working in just outline and basic black. During the 1920s Callahan produced a number of different strips for King Features, among them *Hattie, The Piffle Family, Clarabelle's Cousin*, and *Freddie*. When Rudolph Valentino starred in *The Sheik* in 1921, the movie put the word "sheik" into the language as a kidding nickname for a romantically-inclined young man. In tune with the times, Callahan modified the title of his strip to *Freddie the Sheik* in the middle 1920s.

Freddie was a vacuous young man with, like most of Callahan's characters, two black dots for eyes. Like many a Jazz Age youth, Freddie spent much of his time pursuing girls, figuring out how to get rich, and avoiding his debts. There was little action and much talk, especially from Freddie and the folks he lived with, who were fond of commenting on his follies.

Callahan's minimalist style and run-of-the-mill wit weren't as popular in the 1930s, and he spent the decade drawing a Sunday page titled *Home Sweet Home*, wherein one of the characters was Calamity Jane. In the 1940s, particularly the World War II and immediate postwar years when many younger artists were away in the service, Callahan found work drawing for comic books. He did humorous fillers, such as *Kafloppos* and *Curly's Cafe*, for various DC titles. He also provided artwork for a few issues of Dell's *Tillie the Toiler*, a comic book based on the King Features strip by Russ Westover.

Callahan died after suffering a heart attack while playing tennis.                                              **R.G.**

**CALVIN AND HOBBES**  An imaginative humor strip that blends elements of Charles Schulz's *Peanuts* and Crockett Johnson's *Barnaby, Calvin and Hobbes* broke records by the speed with which it built a substantial readership. Within a year of its appearance in November 1985, its circulation had passed 400 papers and it was voted the favorite strip in many polls. Its first collection, published early in 1987, remained on the *New York Times* best-seller list for almost a year, and its second, issued in 1988, joined it there at once. Its creator received the National Cartoonists Society award for "Outstanding Cartoonist of the Year" in 1986 and 1989.

Written and drawn by former political cartoonist Bill Watterson, *Calvin and Hobbes* had great difficulty in finding a taker until the Universal Press Syndicate accepted it. They launched it as a daily and Sunday feature on November 7, 1985, with little fanfare and no expectation of the meteoric success it was to have.

Little of Watterson's background in editorial cartooning comes through in this bright and often touching strip. It features Calvin, a manic six-year-old whose inner world is open to unlimited experience. As the valiant spaceman Spiff he conquers hostile planets; as Safari Al he hacks his way through forbidding jungles; as a giant slimy octopus he oozes across the beach, his hideous presence terrorizing the community. Through all of his easy transmogrifications, his steadfast companion is Hobbes, a tiger whom only the rest of the world perceives as stuffed.

Hobbes is perhaps the real hero of the strip: As mature, level-headed, and sympathetic as any tiger in literature, he provides a stabilizing influence on his human chum without ever dampening his exuberence.

When, for example, the bored Calvin complains that they have been fishing for 20 minutes and nothing has happened, Hobbes accommodates him by pushing him in the river.

Watterson's abrupt mid-strip shifts from fantasy to reality, and from one character's viewpoint to another's as Hobbes alternates between dollhood and a highly kinetic personality, are breathtaking. The humor of the strip is one of character rather than of action or situation, and derives as much from the subtle interplay between the real and the imaginary as from the tension between the energetic child and his bewildered parents, teachers, and baby-sitter.

The strip is drawn with simplicity and grace, achieving droll effects with a minimum of detail. The compositions are uncluttered, their economical design subordinating everything to the characters or the frenzied movement, although some of the fantasy scenes are wonderfully atmospheric.

Watterson acknowledges the influence of *Peanuts* and Walt Kelly's *Pogo* in his work; but, although traces of both (the precocity of the *Peanuts* kids, the tenderness and whimsy of *Pogo*) may be seen in *Calvin and Hobbes*, it is very much an original creation. **D.W.**

**CANDY** Much sexier than most of the teenagers to be found on the comic pages until then, the brunette Candy made her strip debut on October 2, 1944, syndicated originally by the *Chicago Times*, and the creation of writer Ed Groggin and artist Harry Sahle (who had worked previously on the highly popular *Archie*). Both of them worked in comic books, which accounted for the pinup aspects of the character, since a great many comic books of those years were aimed at an older GI audience.

*Candy* also showed up in comic books late in 1944. She was featured in, of all magazines, *Police Comics*, where she rubbed shoulders with Plastic Man, the Spirit, and the Human Bomb. She got a magazine of her own in the summer of 1947.

Although sweet and wholesome, Candy was also an aggressive young lady. She saw to it that she got her way and was very adept at managing her blond boyfriend, Ted, and her plump businessman father. She was very much like the energetic girls to be heard on such established radio shows as *A Date With Judy* and *Meet Corliss Archer*. Like all her sisters, Candy was an expert at slang: "But definitely," "I know you're pooched," "All reet," and so on. She doted on jitterbug platters, which her parents, of course, loathed.

Sahle stayed with the strip through 1945, with Bernard Dibble ghosting a couple of sequences. Tom Dorr, who drew very much in the Russel Stamm vein, took over in 1946 and stayed with *Candy* until it ended in the early 1950s. In its final phase, the strip, which had always gone in for humorous continuity, ranging from high school intrigues to haunted house mysteries, became an imitator of the more successful *Penny* in both looks and gag-a-day format. **R.G.**

**CANIFF, MILTON** (1907–1988) For well over a half-century Milton Caniff produced adventure strips. He was one of the best writer-artists ever to work in the genre, and in the 1980s one of the few surviving practitioners of that demanding craft. During a good part of his long career he set the standards against which the competition was measured. He drew two major strips, *Terry and The Pirates* and *Steve Canyon*, and warmed up with *Dickie Dare*.

Milton Arthur Paul Caniff, an only child, was born in Hillsboro, Ohio. From that small midwestern town, where he spent his first 10 years, came several of the influences that shaped his life. His father worked in the print shop of the local newspaper, and Caniff, who went to work in a newspaper art department at 14, thought of himself as basically a newspaperman all his life. The Hillsboro paper was owned by a man who'd been a Sigma Chi at college, and living in town was General Benjamin Runkle, a Civil War veteran known in Sigma Chi annals as one of the seven founders of the fraternity. The Sigma Chi fraternity, which Caniff joined in college, was one of the most important elements in his life for his affiliation helped him attract the attention of Captain Patterson of the *New York Daily News*. Both Pat Ryan of *Terry* and Steve Canyon were Sigma Chis.

Important, too, were the trips his family made each year to California. They would spend their winters in Redlands, a Southern California town about 75 miles inland from Hollywood, and one of the things the young Caniff did while living out West was extra work in some two-reel comedies, which introduced him to acting and to the movies.

When Caniff was 11 the family settled in Dayton, Ohio, the city where the Wright Brothers had had their bicycle shop. The Caniffs lived near McCook Field, where, during the First World War and immediately after, several important aviation firsts took place. As a kid Caniff often sat watching the activities at the field, which began and fed his lifelong interest in aviation.

Caniff had studied with the Landon mail-order cartoon school and had his first cartoon published in the *Dayton Daily News*. As a 14-year-old he had worked as an office boy in the art department of the *Dayton Journal*. He had applied to Billy Ireland of the *Columbus Dispatch* for a job as a cartoonist, and worked for five years in the *Dispatch* art department while attending Ohio State University. He also joined a local stock company and then found he had to choose between art and the stage.

After college he did daily features and a theatrical feature for the *Dispatch*. He later went with the Associated Press, doing feature panels and cartoon strips.

Another young artist who came to cartoonist Ireland was Noel Sickles, whom Caniff remembered in those early years as an unassuming, gangling country boy, of whom he said, "Jesus, could he draw." Caniff and Sickles were friends from then on. Sickles was even, until he gave up college, a pledge in the Sigma Chi house. In the 1920s Caniff "batted around Europe, but I have never been to any of the places I have tried to illustrate in the three commercial strips I have drawn." He graduated from college in 1930 and married his high school sweetheart. His plans for getting rich with his artwork were stimulated by the "arrival of new bride and depression on the scene at same time." As the Depression worsened he and Sickles opened a commercial art studio together in Columbus, but the business didn't exactly prosper. Then came an offer for Caniff from the Associated Press in New York City. Turning the studio over to Sickles, Caniff and his bride headed East. "At one point...I was writing and illustrating a four-line, daily, single-column jingle called *Puffy the Pig*, a three-column panel called *The Gay Thirties*, a six-column strip, and ghosting another daily and Sunday strip at night." Caniff also drew spot illustrations for AP's serialized fiction, political caricatures, and other odds and ends, all of which, except for ghosting *Dumb Dora* for his friend Bill Dwyer, was done on his weekly AP salary.

It was the six-column adventure strip that changed things. Although Caniff had submitted sample strips to the syndicates since college, nothing had thus far sold. The AP offered a blanket feature service with a full page of daily strips available to subscribing clients. When Caniff learned a blank space was coming up in the page, he said, "There's going to be a hole," and, vowing to fill that hole, he spent a weekend doing samples of *Dickie Dare*. The Associated Press bought it and Caniff now had a New York outlet for his work, first the *Post* and then the *Sun*. Meantime, John T. McCutcheon, a Sigma Chi since 1887 and a political cartoonist on the *Chicago Tribune* since 1903, had been touting Caniff to Captain Patterson, as had Mollie Slott, the assistant general manager of the Trib-News syndicate, whose sons were fans of *Dickie Dare*. She brought a batch in for the captain to look at. Patterson had Caniff in for a talk and invited him to try an adventure strip, although he never directly stated he wanted an imitation of *Dickie*. He suggested the locale be China and that the title be *Terry and the Pirates*.

Caniff again shared a studio with Sickles in the middle 1930s, this time in Manhattan. Sickles' influence on his friend was considerable and the look of *Terry* improved greatly. By the early 1940s Caniff's was the strip that many other artists, both in newspapers and comic books, were striving to imitate.

His *Steve Canyon* began in January 1947, two weeks after his last *Terry* had appeared. His new hero was a returning Air Force officer and in the early years of the strip Caniff continued with the sort of movielike adventure he'd done in the 1930s and 1940s. When that sort of thing began to go out of fashion, he added occasional soap opera elements. By the 1980s, with neither continuity strips nor adventure strips any longer popular, *Steve Canyon* was appearing in a relatively small list of papers. The quality of the artwork had slipped quite a bit in the last years, but Caniff remained a first-rate storyteller to the end.                    **R.G.**

**CAPP, AL** (1909–1979) A celebrity-cartoonist for most of his professional life, Capp was the creator of *Li'l Abner*. The strip began in 1934, and the sardonic, pugnacious Capp masterminded it until its end in 1977. During the long lifespan of the satirical hillbilly saga he swung from liberal to conservative politically, earned a great deal of money and publicity, appeared on radio and television and in any other medium that would give him an opportunity to hold forth, carried on some impressive feuds, and gave the outward impression he was having an enormously good time living his life.

He was born Alfred Gerald Caplin in New Haven, Connecticut. "My mother and father had been brought to this country when they were infants," he once said. "Their fathers had found that the great promise of America was true—it was no crime to be a Jew." No crime, but not as advantageous, Capp felt, as being a gentile. He remembered his early years as a period of struggle and lack of enough to eat. "In my real childhood the hunger was painful," he recalled near the end of his life. "In *Li'l Abner* it was hilarious."

When he was nine, he was run over by a trolley car and lost his left leg. The youthful Capp vowed the accident would make no difference, but it obviously did. It curtailed his participation in sports, meant he couldn't dance—things that seemed vitally important in his teenage years. "I looked for other diversions," he said. "I wonder if it wasn't because of the wooden leg, slowing me down, that I had patience to study art." He also had time to read, favoring such humorous novelists as Dickens, Smollett, Mark Twain, and Booth Tarkington.

After dropping out of a couple of art schools, Capp managed to land a job with the Associated Press in New York City. That was in 1932, and he drew a daily panel entitled *Mister Gilfeather*. Gilfeather was a pale imitation of the much more successful Major Hoople of *Our Boarding House*, and young Capp's less than first-rate artwork did little to enhance the feature. He left the job after a few months, agreeing with one of the client editors who'd complained to the AP that the panel was "by far the worst in the country." Some months later he met Ham Fisher and that changed Capp's life for good and all. The panel, meantime, was taken over by Milton Caniff.

The story of how Capp and Fisher met was recounted several times over the years by both men. Initially Capp said he'd been walking along a Manhattan street when an expensive auto pulled up beside him and a prosperous gentleman in the back seat inquired if the portfolio under Capp's arm contained drawings. When Capp replied in the affirmative, Fisher invited him over to his studio to help him finish an overdue *Joe Palooka* Sunday page. Liking the way Capp handled the emergency chore, Fisher hired him as an assistant. Before a bitter and long-lasting feud developed, Capp had said, "I owe most of my success to him, for I learned many tricks of the trade while working alongside him." In later years Capp modified his views. "I regard him as a leper," he said when alluding to his former boss in a 1950 article in *The Atlantic Monthly*, "a veritable goldmine of swinishness." He even implied that Fisher's fancy car, at their initial meeting, had almost run him over.

Be that as it may, it was while working on *Joe Palooka* that Capp first began experimenting with the possibilities of using hillbilly characters in a comic strip. Being Fisher's assistant meant that Capp actually did all the drawing and some of the writing. In 1933 he introduced an uncouth hillbilly boxer named Big Leviticus and his uncouth kin to the strip. The character caught on and Fisher continued to use him after Capp departed. Capp claimed he'd been thinking about some sort of rural characters ever since he'd made a trip to the South some years before. Dreaming of a larger salary and less "swinish" working conditions, Capp began doing samples of a strip of his own, one devoted entirely to rural characters.

Capp initially took his samples of *Li'l Abner* to King Features, but they dragged their feet and kept making suggestions for changes. The impatient Capp took his strip to United Features and they bought it "just as it was." The starting salary was nothing near what King might have offered, but "I was able to do my strip exactly as I wanted to." The first daily appeared in August 1934 and Capp, who'd changed his name from Caplin when the new strip was launched, was on his way to fame and fortune. Although *Li'l Abner* started slowly, it picked up papers throughout the 1930s at an impressive rate. In the 1940s the strip continued to forge ahead toward its eventual peak circulation of 900 newspapers around the world, and Capp found himself being hailed as not only a brilliant artist but also the greatest satirist since Swift, Voltaire, and Mark Twain.

There were *Li'l Abner* comic books, a *Li'l Abner* movie, and lucrative *Li'l Abner* advertising strips.

Capp remained in the limelight for the rest of his life. He was written up in *Life, Time, Newsweek,* and dozens of other magazines, contributed articles to prestigious periodicals such as *The Atlantic Monthly*, wrote a newspaper column of his own, and consulted on the Broadway musical based on his strip. He was frequently interviewed on radio and television, conducted a radio show of his own for a time, and was one of the founding fathers of the cartoon division of the Famous Artists School. In order to follow all these extra activities, Capp had fairly early in the game hired assistants and ghosts to take care of *Li'l Abner*.

By the 1960s Capp had grown increasingly conservative. Many of the targets of his satire were perceived by his younger readers as liberal and therefore above kidding. Capp took to quoting with approval the advice fellow cartoonist Harold Gray had given him: "Buy a farm with a big stone wall around it because they're coming—the bums and the Russians." His strip started losing papers in the 1970s and Capp started losing enthusiasm. "The heart had gone out of me," he admitted, "maybe a year or so before there were any great cancellations." **R.G.**

**CAP STUBBS AND TIPPIE** One of the longest-lived and truest-to-life of the comic strips about boyhood was created and sustained through a 48-year run by a woman, Edwina Dumm, who signed her work with her first name only. Beginning in 1918 and originally titled just *Cap Stubbs*, the strip offered daily gags about a boy and his dog.

Sometimes Edwina told a continuing story for several weeks, without punchlines or cliffhangers. There was just gentle hometown humor about such boyish enthusiasms as playing baseball or make-believe army, swimming, sharing a hoard of candy purchased at the corner grocery store, running a lemonade stand and so on. But mostly there was no story line at all: just a boy being a boy, a dog being a dog and a grandmother being Gran'ma.

Cap was as much a reg'lar feller as any of Gene Byrnes' creations, as inventive at manufacturing excuses, as eager to shun the companionship of the neighborhood girl he secretly admired, as everlastingly energetic and imaginative. Tippie was an authentic dog, Cap's constant companion—tail-wagging, ears cocked, his nose into everything. And Grand'ma—Sara Bailey, who lived with her daughter and son-in-law—was perhaps the most incisively accurate of all Edwina's gallery of portraits. While she was continually astonished at Cap's latest outrage and scolded, nagged, and fussed, she still passed out candy or a slice of fresh-baked pie, one of a series of countless grandmotherly gestures of ill-concealed affection and tenderness.

In the late 1920s Edwina began doing a full-page feature about a frisky, wooly-haired terrier named Sindbad for the humor magazine *Life.* The dog was so lively and cute that her syndicate asked her to replace the shorthaired Tippie with a version of Sindbad. Edwina solved the ticklish assignment cleverly: She had Tippie get lost and then found by a crippled boy, who became so fond of the dog that when Cap at last came to claim his pet, not even he could bear to part them. The solution: Cap got himself a new dog and the fluffier Tippie became so popular that he earned a Sunday page of his own in the mid-1930s.

Edwina's mature drawing style—relaxed and loose penwork, open and airy without being sketchy—was ideal for catching in midflight the energetic antics of boys and dogs. The strip ceased in 1966, and by then Edwina's fond evocation of her own turn-of-the-century tomboy childhood in a small town in Ohio had been stitched securely into the quiltwork of the national memory. **R.C.H.**

**CAPTAIN AMERICA** The prototypical patriotic hero of American comic books was created for Timely Comics by the team of Joe Simon and Jack Kirby in early 1941, on the eve of the United States' entry into World War II.

The cover of *Captain America Comics* number 1 showed the shield-bearing, red-white-and-blue-clad hero hammering the jaw of Adolf Hitler himself, at a time when most American popular culture was studiously avoiding specific mention of the Axis powers, preferring to hint vaguely at "powers of darkness" and "coming troubles." Cap was explicitly a product and agent of the U.S. military: He had been just a 97-pound 4-F weakling until a government scientist injected him with a serum to transform him into a splendidly-muscled superagent, assigned to root out Nazi fifth columnists in our armed forces.

Quickly, however, Cap's action-packed adventures took on the baroque quality of pulp magazine horror, as he and his teen sidekick Bucky battled the likes of the Black Witch, the Ringmaster of Death, Fang ("Arch-Fiend of the Orient"), and their hideously-masked archenemy, a Nazi butcher called the Red Skull. Driven by Jack Kirby's powerful draftmanship and sweeping action-art, the series instantly became an enormous success and the inspiration for dozens of lesser patriotic heroes. But Cap remained America's most powerful piece of wartime comic book propaganda.

In 1942, Simon and Kirby departed Timely Comics, leaving Cap in the generally able hands of such writers and artists as Bill Finger, Otto Binder, Stan Lee, Syd

*Captain America*, Alex Schomburg, ™ & © 1945, Marvel Entertainment Group, Inc. All rights reserved.

Shores, Al Avison, and Vince Alascia. But with the end of World War II, Cap lost his *raison d'être.* His former secret identity as Private Steve Rogers, regular dogface, was replaced by Mr. Rogers the bespectacled high school teacher, while scrappy little Bucky gave way to the sexier Golden Girl. Axis agents and pulp grotesqueries were supplanted by gimmicky criminals such as any superhero might face. But Cap wasn't just any superhero, and he simply didn't work well in the new context. In 1949 the series was canceled.

Four years later Cap's publishers (now known as Atlas Comics) revived him, first in the title *Young Men*, then in his own series again. But times were bad for costumed heroes, and he faded away for another decade.

Jack Kirby had been working again at Marvel (formerly Atlas) Comics for five years when he and editor-writer Stan Lee brought Cap back in 1964 (first as a member of *The Avengers*, then in his own series in *Tales of Suspense*). Rather than try to revamp their 1940s hero for the 1960s, Kirby and Lee chose to explore him explicitly as an anachronism: Having been frozen in an

Arctic iceberg after a plane crash in 1944 (which had killed Bucky), this Cap was a superheroic Rip van Winkle, without loved ones, purpose, or any understanding of the world around him. Although such melancholy and turmoil would have been completely alien to the Cap of the 1940s, it was strangely appropriate and often poignant in the context of the mid-1960s.

*Captain America* became a regular title again in 1968; Kirby left soon after, followed by Lee in 1972, but by then they had established Cap as the thoughtful elder statesman of Marvel heroes. Throughout the 1970s and 1980s he has attracted complex and intelligent scripts, particularly from writers Steve Englehart and Roger Stern, which explore him as a character, a historical phenomenon, and a national symbol. Englehart, with a strong liberal bias, also built a long storyline around the return of the Captain America of the 1950s (trying to "explain" the old Atlas Comics, which didn't fit the new Kirby/Lee biography of the hero), who proved to be a paranoid, jingoistic Red-baiter. The series' art, under Gene Colan, Sal Buscema, John Byrne, Mike Zeck, and others, has also been steady, although lacking Kirby's force (Kirby himself enjoyed a tenure as writer-artist from 1975 to 1977).

During his long life, Cap has also been the subject of a movie serial, a feature film, television cartoons, and other adaptations. **G.J.**

**CAPTAIN EASY**  See WASH TUBBS.

**THE CAPTAIN AND THE KIDS**  This title holds a unique place in the history of newspaper comic strips. Had it not been for a struggle between the Hearst and Pulitzer publishing empires, *The Captain and the Kids* would never have come into existence. Following a series of disputes and lawsuits, Rudolph Dirks, who had created the popular *Katzenjammer Kids*, found himself without the legal right to continue drawing his characters under their original name. The strip went on hiatus for more than a year while the legal tangle wore on. On May 15, 1914, a New York appeals court granted Dirks the right to continue the Katzenjammer cast of characters, so long as they were not represented as such by name. This he proceeded to do for the *New York World*, flagship of the Pulitzer papers.

Carrying no masthead title at first, the Sunday-only feature became *Hans und Fritz* in May 1915. With the entry of the United States into World War I, things German fell into disfavor and the strip changed names once again, becoming *The Captain and the Kids* in the summer of 1918. The Hearst version, continued in the *New York American* under the original title by H.H. Knerr, provided another man's notion of what these characters' adventures might be.

On March 25, 1917, in the Dirks version, the Captain and the Inspector began a race around the world, the Inspector going west and the Captain, with Hans, Fritz, and Mamma in tow, going east. By May 13, the group was in the Sahara, while the Inspector had sprung a leak in the Pacific Ocean. On August 12, the contestants passed each other in the Indian Ocean. The group reached China on September 2 and, following a stop in South America, reached home on December 16. Commandeering a horse from a seafood cart, the Captain raced toward home, arriving at the exact moment as the Inspector, whose plane crashed right in front of the door. Needless to say, the kids tried to sabotage the Captain en route with every prank, explosive, and dirty trick at their command.

In the 1920s Dirks' troops sojourned on Cannibal Island, while over in the Hearst camp, Knerr had his Katzenjammers in the Squee-Jee Islands. Both families had their adventures with the local black royalty, and Long John Silver and his band of pirates popped up from time to time in both versions. In 1928, in *The Captain and the Kids*, the one-legged pirate captured the runaway Hans and Fritz and held them for $10,000 ransom. Despite the Inspector's observation that "Two cents iss too much!" the Captain passed up the opportunity to be rid of the boys. Mamma would never have forgiven him.

For nearly 35 years the two artists battled each other for supremacy. They each had their partisans, yet, oddly enough, most readers, who seldom purchased more than one Sunday paper, probably never even knew there was more than one Katzenjammer family.

Dirks was a man of many interests who needed a break from the weekly regimen now and then. In the early 1920s, Oscar Hitt took over for a while and the masthead included the statement "Directed by R. Dirks." In May 1932, a contract dispute caused Dirks to take an extended leave and the feature was turned over to Bernard Dibble. Dibble, who'd ghosted for Dirks in the late 1920s, stayed with the page for over a year. He also drew the 1930s daily strip for several years. Begun by Dirks upon his return to the syndicate fold, the daily, when assumed by Dibble, became a wild burlesque of adventure continuities—complete with an evil, masked, and tophatted villain known as the Brain—and often sounded very much like a Marx Brothers movie.

Following the end of World War II, John Dirks, the artist's son, began to assist him, gradually taking over the page entirely. Thereafter, it began to stray from the long established pattern, and elements of fantasy and even visitors from outer space were introduced. One 1958 episode includes a reference to the arms race when the poor Captain is tossed by a goat and the boys refer to the ACBM, in this case the Anti-Captain Buttnik

Missile. Rudolph Dirks died in 1968 and the strip was carried on by his son. It ceased to appear in 1979.

That the *Captain and the Kids* and *The Katzenjammer Kids* ran simultaneously for over half a century is ample testament to the longevity of these characters. **J.L.**

**CAPTAIN MARVEL** There have been several comic book heroes doing business as Captain Marvel over the past decades, but the best, and by far the most successful, was a redclad gent who refused to take his profession too seriously. This first Captain Marvel, the joint creation of cartoonist C.C. Beck and editor-writer Bill Parker, came along early in 1940 and within a very few years he was outselling not only Superman but also every other costumed crimefighter, from Amazing Man to the Zebra, who'd followed in the footsteps of the Man of Steel.

Originally the name of Fawcett's first superhero was going to be Captain Thunder. But by the time the first issue of *Whiz Comics* (dated February 1940) hit the stands, the name was Captain Marvel. The captain shared the issue with a batch of other characters that included Spy Smasher, the Golden Arrow, and Ibis the Invincible. In the debut story, which ran to 13 pages, readers were introduced to young Billy Batson. While peddling his papers on a rainy-night street corner, Billy was approached by a mysterious stranger who escorted him to "an ancient underground hall" beneath the city's subway system. There he met a 3,000-year-old wizard who told him he had been using his magical abilities in battling "the forces of evil which every day threaten to extinguish man from the face of the Earth." The old boy is getting a mite weary and is looking for a successor.

The old wizard is Shazam, whose name is an acronym for Solomon, Hercules, Atlas, Zeus, Achilles, and Mercury. By saying the name, Billy, a poor mistreated orphan lad, acquired the abilities of this batch of gods and heroes—wisdom, strength, stamina, power, courage, and speed. He also picked up a snappy red costume and added about 15 or so years to his age. After passing the gauntlet to Billy, the old man was, apparently, squashed by a block of falling granite. The moments of Billy's transition to Captain Marvel, after the magic word has been spoken, were always impressive—accompanied as they were by sound effects, a formidable zigzag of lightning, and great swirling thunder clouds.

The Captain's looks were based on those of Fred MacMurray, one of the most successful comedy leading men of the late 1930s and 1940s. The costume, particularly in its earliest, buttoned tunic phase, was adapted from that of a typical light opera soldier.

There was a nice look to the early adventures in *Whiz Comics*, provided by Beck, who was influenced not by serious illustrators but by such comic strips as *Little Orphan Annie, The Gumps,* and *Barney Google.* The scripts, too, had a tremendous appeal to kids because they were about a kid who could take a shortcut to adulthood when he needed help with a serious problem. Billy became, in a sense, his own tough big brother or ideal father. And all it took was a magic word, not years of growing up and not even the months of exercise Charles Atlas required to turn you from a put-upon weakling into a no-guff-from-anybody muscleman. That Billy was in charge was evidenced by the fact that Cap always said "Shazam!" when his work was done, allowing Billy to become his true self once again.

Captain Marvel was blessed with one of comics' most appealing villains. The equal of the Joker, the Penguin, and Luthor, Sivana was there from the start to plague and bedevil him. And he made more return engagements that just about any other bad guy in the field. The diminutive and hairless mad scientist possessed several qualities that contributed to his being the man you love to hate. He was appealingly nasty and enormously enthusiastic in his villainy. He was eloquent, particularly in his denunciations of the Captain. And, personifying one of the most sacred American ideals, Thadeus

Bodog Sivana didn't know the meaning of defeat. Thwarted issue after issue, seemingly totally destroyed on occasion, he doggedly bounced back. He had a brilliant mind, too, and there were times when you had to admit he was a lot smarter than Cap.

Unlike the vast majority of rather dense comic book bad guys, who never tumbled to the true identities of their superheroic opponents, Sivana realized almost at once—in the third issue of *Whiz*, in fact—that Captain Marvel and Billy Batson were one and the same. He also figured out early on that if he could prevent Billy from uttering the magic word, he wouldn't be bothered by his redclad nemesis any longer.

*The* woman in Captain Marvel's life was Beautia, erstwhile empress of Venus and daughter of the wicked Sivana. A blond of movie star magnitude, she had a beauty that "affects every man who sees her like a powerful drug." Not even Captain Marvel was immune. Despite her genetic code and the fact that she grew up on Venus as ruler of a race of giant frogs, she was basically a nice person. She ceased to be a pawn of her evil dad and at one point she and Captain Marvel even went dancing. But, eventually, being around her caused the Captain to blush and gulp, "My gosh!"— more proof that he was really Billy inside.

Otto Binder, a veteran pulp science fiction author, began writing the Captain Marvel stories during the second year. Almost all the yarns dealing with rocket ships, time travel, parallel worlds, and other SF standards were his, and he also created the talking tiger, Mr. Tawny. The pulps also provided Beck with his first assistant. Pete Costanza had been an illustrator in the pulpwoods before switching to comics. As the demand for Captain Marvel stories increased—the captain was appearing in *Captain Marvel Adventures* and *America's Greatest* in addition to *Whiz* by the early 1940s—Fawcett first went to outsiders and then had Beck set up a shop of his own. Among the outsiders were Jack Kirby, who produced a somewhat slapdash first issue of *Captain Marvel Adventures*. Employed by Beck were Al Fagaly, Chic Stone, Kurt Schaffenberger, Dave Berg, and Marc Swayze.

Captain Marvel proved to be a very salable character. *Whiz Comics* was selling nearly half a million copies a month before its first year was out. By 1943 *Captain Marvel Adventures* was selling about a million copies per issue, and in 1946 the figure approached a million and a half. And that was the year the magazine was coming out every two weeks. Life was not exactly a bed of roses for Cap, though, since in 1941 DC Comics had taken legal action against Fawcett. They claimed that Captain Marvel was so close to their Superman that he infringed on the copyright. The lawsuit was fought throughout the 1940s and into the 1950s. Finally, in the middle 1950s Fawcett gave up and ceased publishing Captain Marvel.

He returned 20 years later, this time under the DC banner. Beck came back, too, for a while and then quit in dissatisfaction over the scripts. For trademark reasons the old, original captain appeared in a magazine titled *Shazam!* That title lasted from 1973 to 1978, with ever diminishing sales. *Shazam!*, this time drawn in a straight musclebound style, returned in a miniseries in 1987.

The reason DC couldn't call their hero by his rightful name was because during his long layoff the title had been usurped by a new Marvel Comics hero. Marvel's Captain Marvel was a warrior-scientist from another planet who came to Earth and set up practice as a superhero. Created by Stan Lee and Gene Colan, he first appeared late in 1967. Not overwhelmingly successful, this Captain Marvel lasted, with several stretches of unemployment, until the middle 1980s. Among his many writers and artists were Roy Thomas, Gil Kane, Wayne Boring, and Jim Starlin.　　　　**R.G.**

**CAPTAIN MARVEL, JR.** An honorary member of one of the most famous families in comic books, the young superhero first appeared as a guest in the Captain Marvel story in *Whiz Comics* #25 (December 1941). After an encounter with the ruthless Captain Nazi that left teenage Freddy Freeman close to death, he was taken by Billy Batson (Captain Marvel's alter ego) to that "forgotten section of the subway" where the spirit of Shazam dwells. Working a variation on the trick he pulled to transform Billy into Captain Marvel, the old wizard arranged for Freddy to become a superhero whenever he said "Captain Marvel!" Unlike Billy, Freddy turned into a super teen, not a super adult, with a blue costume similar to the senior Captain's red version. When not fighting crime he was simply Freddy Freeman, a crippled newsboy.

Junior took over as the star of *Master Comics* with the 23rd issue (February 1942), permanently ending the rivalry between Bulletman and Minute-Man for that spot. His first couple of years in *Master* were quite impressive, thanks mainly to the artwork of Mac Raboy. A careful, realistic artist, Raboy produced an attractive blend of realism and fantasy and drew powerful, poster-like covers.

Captain Marvel, Jr. devoted most of his early years to combating Captain Nazi, both in the U.S.A. and in Germany. Among other frequently seen antagonists were the greenskinned Mr. Macabre and an equally nasty fellow known as Captain Nippon.

A *Captain Marvel, Jr.* monthly was added late in 1942 and lasted until 1953, with Al Carreño the initial artist. The character also appeared regularly in *The Marvel*

*Family*, where his career ended late in 1953. The chief artist of his later years was Bud Thompson, while the prolific Otto Binder provided the majority of the scripts throughout. In 1973 DC revived the character, who stayed around for several years. **R.G.**

**CAPTAIN MIDNIGHT** Originally a radio hero, Captain Midnight branched out in the 1940s into Big Little Books, comic books, and a newspaper strip.

The Captain first took to the air in Chicago in 1939 and by the autumn of 1940 was heard nationally, sponsored by Ovaltine. The radio adventure show—which began with a clock tolling the midnight hour, the sound of an airplane diving, and an announcer intoning the captain's name—was a 15-minute serial heard Monday through Friday. It shared the hour of 5 to 6 P.M. with such other exciting shows as *Jack Armstrong, Tom Mix,* and *Terry and Pirates.*

A flying ace during World War I, Captain Midnight now fronted an organization called the Secret Squadron, made up of pilots who were "hardy, adventuresome fellows who laughed at danger." His private air force, managed for him by a World War I buddy named Major Barry Steel, operated with the sanction of the government in Washington and was initially dedicated to combating spies, subversives, and saboteurs. That such an organization as the Secret Squadron was itself illegal and subversive never seemed to occur to anyone at the time.

The captain had two teenage wards, Chuck Ramsey and Joyce Ryan, who were both members of the SS. Comic relief was provided by Squadron mechanic Ichabod M. Mudd, better known as Ikky. The prime villain on radio was a nasty chap with the nasty name of Ivan Shark. Aided by his equally nasty daughter, Fury, he plagued the Secret Squadron, off and on, for years.

Millions of kids in the early 1940s became devoted followers of Captain Midnight and eagerly joined the Secret Squadron when the chance was offered. (In order to enlist you had to send in a dime and the foil seal from a can of Ovaltine.) The show's popularity made Captain Midnight a likely merchandising property, and in 1941 the Captain, the Secret Squadron, and the Shark family moved into comic books and Big Little Books.

*Captain Midnight and the Secret Squadron* (BLB #1488) was written by Russ Winterbotham and illustrated by Erwin L. Hess, and copyrighted by the Wander Company, makers of Ovaltine. Six- and eight-page comic book stories, drawn by Dan Gormley, were featured in *The Funnies* and then in *Popular Comics.* In the fall of 1942 Fawcett took over the character and launched a magazine that contained nothing but adventures of Midnight and company. It was a big year for the Captain: Colum-

bia Pictures released a 15-chapter Captain Midnight movie serial, and the newspaper strip, daily and Sunday, debuted as well.

The strip was syndicated by Marshall Field's *Chicago Sun,* and the pen name signed to the strip was Jonwan. The chief artist was Erwin L. Hess, sometimes assisted by Henry E. Vallely, and the scriptwriter was Russ Winterbotham. A Midwesterner, Winterbotham had worked as a newspaper reporter from 1931 onward and by the middle 1930s was a frequent contributor to pulp science-fiction magazines as well. He wrote over 50 BLBs for Whitman, many of them illustrated by Hess.

Although Chuck, Joyce, Major Steel, and Ikky all took part in the newspaper doings, Ivan Shark and his daughter were nowhere to be seen. The Captain was out for bigger game, concentrating on fighting the Nazis all across Europe. Wearing a black aviator helmet and spiffy midnight blue uniform with his insignia—a winged clock with its hands pointing at midnight—on the breast, the captain was accepted by Allied military leaders everywhere. None of them had any qualms about working with him and the Secret Squadron, confiding in him, or letting him take part in both combat and intelligence missions.

*The* woman in his life was an enigmatic secret agent named Luna White. Also known as the Moon Woman, because of the strange effect the light of the full moon had on her emotions, she reappeared frequently during the strip's three years of life. Their relationship was a quirky one: At times you were certain she was a Nazi spy, and yet she often saved Midnight's life. He was obviously quite taken with her, but never let himself trust her completely. During the last weeks of the strip, in the spring of 1945, he finally learned that Luna had only been posing as a Nazi and was firmly on the Allied side. Alas, this didn't lead to a romantic union, and the final caption read: "And so these two fighters for freedom, proven friends at last, go their separate ways."

Hess, whose major responsibility was the Sunday page, was worked in a variation of the Caniff style. People were not his strong suit, a fact he compensated for by filling his pages with effective landscapes and imposing scenes of ships, planes, trains, castles, and European cities. He was also able to get coloring that was equal to that of *Terry and the Pirates.*

Captain Midnight was last heard on the radio in 1949. He was seen on television from 1954 to 1958. **R.G.**

**CAPTAIN YANK** Frank Tinsley's strip about "a famous airplane designer and test pilot" began life, daily and Sunday, in the autumn of 1940 under the title *Yankee Doodle.* Its civilian hero was handsome and blond, and readers were told that "mystery veils Yank's secret mission—war against foreign spies and saboteurs who menace America's defences." His first daily adventure pitted Yank against a spy organization, known as the Black Column, that was out to steal the plans for his latest invention, the Bat, "a strange fighting plane, tailless and shaped like an arrowhead." Aiding Yank were Daniel Boone, a pilot and "like his famous ancestor…a dead shot and all-around fighting man," and Capt. Algernon Marmaduke Jeeps, who was black. He was an "A-1 pilot and master mechanic," but that didn't keep him from also serving as Yank's valet. The continuity was deadly serious and filled with breathless dialogue.

Tinsley had been drawing airplanes for quite a few years by the time he entered the comic strip business. A veteran pulp illustrator, he'd had a great deal to do with illustrating the adventures of a daring young pilot-inventor named Bill Barnes. Bill had shown up in the Street & Smith pulp *Bill Barnes, Air Adventurer* early in 1934 and later in its successor, *Air Trails*. When *Yankee Doodle* began, it bore a fairly close resemblance to the Bill Barnes saga.

In June 1942, after America had entered the war, the strip changed its title to *Captain Yank*. The hero was by then a Marine, heading up an elite unit of flying commandos. He had a new gang of sidekicks, including a tough-talking guy named Hacker—"Youse mugs ain't takin' me no place…as long as I got me dukes!"—and a pretty blond nurse named Bonnie. Yank, who was sometimes referred to by his men as Captain Doodle, operated in the Pacific and in the China-Burma-India war zones.

Several other artists ghosted the feature during its run. Lou Fine contributed some Sundays, as did Newton Alfred. Jack Lehti, Mart Bailey, and Henry Kiefer all drew daily sequences. The strip expired a few months after the end of World War II.                           **R.G.**

**CARLSON, GEORGE** (1887–1962) Although best-known for the unique work he did in *Jingle Jangle Comics* in the 1940s, Carlson was a versatile artist. In addition to comic book features, he drew magazine cartoons, book illustrations, and puzzles. For many years he

*The Pie-Face Prince*, George Carlson, © 1948, Famous Funnies Inc.

ghosted the *Reg'lar Fellers* newspaper strip and, in a somewhat more serious vein, he painted the jacket for the original edition of *Gone With the Wind*.

George Leonard Carlson had a long career before getting into comic books. Prior to World War I he was doing gag cartoons plus a color cover now and then for *Judge*. He turned out puzzle, riddle, and alphabet books for publishers like Platt & Munk, and even took a turn illustrating some Uncle Wiggily stories. He did his puzzles for kids' magazines and for a time was an instructor for a mail-order cartoon school. He produced more than one book on how to draw.

Carlson also had a long and anonymous association with Gene Byrnes. He helped out on *Reg'lar Fellers* on several occasions and from the early 1940s to the end of the strip he ghosted it entirely. On a short-lived Sunday topper, titled *Dizzie Lizzie*, he made no attempt to disguise his own style; although it was signed Byrnes, it was unaltered Carlson.

Almost all of his comic book work was done for *Jingle Jangle*. In its 40-some issues it offered funny animals, funny kids, and fantasy, mostly drawn in animated cartoon style. Carlson was responsible for two features: *Jingle Jangle Tales* and *The Pie-Face Prince of Old Pretzleburg*. These blended burlesque, fantasy, and wordplay into a highly individual type of nonsense. Carlson took a streetwise, Broadway approach to fairy tales, quite obviously aware that he was dealing not only with the kids who were buying the comic books but also with the grownups who were going to be cajoled into reading his tales to them.

Among the characters who turned up in his *Jingle Jangle Tales* were Sleepy Yollo the Bedless Norseman, who lived during the days of Real Smorgasbord; Skip Van Wrinkle the High-Hatted Hunter, who "owned a fine blonde one-shot blunderbuss with which he could easily miss any shot"; the Very Horseless Jockey, who became rich from a flavored snowball business. There were all sorts of other unusual props, people, and creatures to be found wandering through Carlson's dynamic and cluttered pages, such as a freshly toasted sandwich board, a steamed-up steam engine, a duckless duck pond, a four-footed yardstick maker, a lovely blond mazurka, and a zigzag zither.

Pretzleburg was similar in appearance and politics to the various light opera settings of the *Tales*. In addition to the pie-faced Prince Dimwitri, there were Princess Panetella Murphy, his true love more or less, the Raging Rajah, billed as the prince's "favorite enemy," and the Wicked Green Witch. A longtime resident of Connecticut, Carlson was no doubt inspired by the way some people mispronounced the name of Greenwich in naming this latter character.

He left comic books when *Jingle Jangle* folded in the late 1940s, returning to children's book illustration.

**R.G.**

**CARLSON, WALLACE**  See THE NEBBS.

**CARREÑO, ALBERT** (1905–1964)  A versatile artist, best known for his work in the 1940s on such comic book heroes as Captain Marvel, Jr., and the Blue Beetle, the Mexico-born Carreño came to this country in the 1920s.

Initially, he was a caricaturist for newspapers and magazines and then for a New York-based motion picture ad service. Changing his style drastically, he entered the comics field in 1935 with a serious cowboy Sunday page called *Ted Strong*, some of whose episodes were reprinted in Dell's *The Comics* later in the decade. By 1940 Carreño had moved directly into comic books, and his style showed the influence of Milton Caniff. For the Fox line he drew the Blue Beetle and Samson, for Fawcett there were Ibis the Invincible, the Phantom Eagle, Golden Arrow, and others. In 1942 he became the chief artist on the new *Captain Marvel, Jr.* monthly, approaching this fantasy material in a somewhat more realistic and less idealized way than the original artist on the feature, Mac Raboy.

Carreño gave up the teenage superhero two years later to draw a plainclothes character for Fawcett's *Master Comics*; Radar was an International Policeman who specialized in foreign intrigue. After World War II he worked for several comic publishers, his longest stint being with *Prize Western* where he drew *Dusty Bellew*. He also ghosted the *Casey Ruggles* daily strip during its last days in the middle 1950s. His comics career ended as it began, with cowboys.

He then returned to commercial art, providing, for example, hundreds of spot drawings for an edition of the *Random House College Dictionary*.  **R.G.**

**CASEY RUGGLES**  A meticulously done adventure strip dealing with the Old West, *Casey Ruggles* began as a Sunday page in May of 1949, with a daily added in September. Casey was an ex-Army sergeant and his initial adventure took him as far West as you can go—to California, in Gold Rush days. In subsequent sequences he tangled with a Black Bart–type highwayman, got mixed up in an Indian uprising, and trekked across the Sierras in the dead of winter, mingling with such real life personages as Kit Carson, Jean Lafitte, Joaquin Murietta, both Mr. Wells and Mr. Fargo, and Millard Fillmore. Casey's was also an era liberally sprinkled with beautiful and fiery women.

The feature was the creation of Warren Tufts, in his middle twenties when it began and a native Californian.

He once explained that his main reason for doing a newspaper strip was "money! As a kid, I had read somewhere that Robert L. Ripley was amassing $365,000 a year from *Believe It Or Not.*" About the sources of his inspiration, he said, "There were storytellers I admired for their special qualities—Twain, Harte, O. Henry, Saroyan—but I undoubtedly absorbed as much from Jimmy Cagney/Wallace Beery/Errol Flynn pics, from dramatic radio, a half dozen or so adventure strips of the day, my own adventuresome kidhood."

His main artistic influences were Alex Raymond and Hal Foster. Blond Casey was pretty much blond Flash Gordon in a Stetson, and in many of the awesome landscape shots one expects to see a broken sword or a dented helmet, left behind when Prince Val and his gang swept through. The stories, structured like slick, big-budget Western movies, moved swiftly through convincing backgrounds.

Tufts stayed with the strip for nearly five years. He said that he put in 80 hours a week on *Casey* and that "it was simply too telling a schedule." He had help from both assistants and ghosts, his most notable employee being Alex Toth. His syndicate, United Features, also brought in ghosts, including Edmond Good on the Sundays (September 1953–January 1954) and Reuben Moreira on both dailies (April 1954–August 1954) and Sundays (September 1954). After Tufts left in the summer of 1954, Al Carreño carried on until the demise of *Casey Ruggles* in October of 1955. **R.G.**

**CATHY** The archetype of the unmarried career woman of the 1970s and 1980s, the titular heroine of *Cathy* originated in a series of self-mocking doodles in letters home with which Cathy Lee Guisewite illustrated her problems of balancing a demanding job and an unrewarding love-life. At her mother's insistence, Guisewite developed these drawings into a comic strip and offered it to Universal Press Syndicate in 1976. The timing was perfect: Universal had been looking for a strip detailing the life of the new breed of working girl for two years and accepted *Cathy* at once. Since its debut on November 22, 1976, the strip has grown steadily in popularity, now running daily and Sunday in more than 500 newspapers. Its artlessly-drawn characters have been featured in 11 successful collections, two television specials, and over 150 spinoff products.

A wry saga of a young woman (Cathy seems to be in her middle twenties) engaged in eternal warfare with bulging thighs, a checkbook she can balance only by changing banks every six months, and a perennially disappointing romantic life, *Cathy* has struck a responsive chord in today's liberated society. The regular characters include Cathy's anxious and anxiety-producing parents, her elusive boyfriend Irving, her insensitive and exploitative boss Mr. Pinkley, and her critical feminist friend Andrea, a combination, the cartoonist reports, of her own conscience and "all those perfect women." The gags in the strip revolve around Cathy's problems with food, love, mother, and career—what Guisewite calls "the four basic guilt groups."

The winner of several awards, including a 1987 Emmy for its first animated television feature, *Cathy* is largely autobiographical, which explains why so much of its painfully humorous insight rings true. With her motto, "Take life one disaster at a time," the indomitable Cathy doggedly survives her failed romances, expanding waistline, and growing workload with endearing courage and faith in her future. As Guisewite has written of her cartoon alter ego, "Cathy can be three months behind on all her work, have millions of phone calls to return, her laundry stacks up, she hasn't written her friends in a year. But she believes with all her heart that she not only will get everything done but that she'll lose 15 pounds by 9:30 that night. That hope is important in her character and, I think, to her readers." **D.W.**

**CAT-MAN** A superhero possessed of nine lives, Cat-Man first appeared in *Crash Comics* #4 (September 1940). The magazine itself crashed after one more issue, but he was reincarnated in *Cat-Man Comics* #1 (May 1941). In both magazines he had the civilian identity of David Merryweather and, like Rudyard Kipling's Mowgli, he was reared in the wild by a maternal tiger, after his family was slaughtered by "jungle wildmen," an experience that endowed him "with all the faculties of the cat family." When he returned to America, "the evils of the world scare[d] his sense of righteousness" and he decided to combat crime. His costume varied but most frequently he wore trunks, tunic, cape, boots, and a cowl topped with pussycat ears. In the earliest days Cat-Man would get killed once a month, then come back to life. Nine lives, though, last only so long, and the device was soon dropped.

Late in 1941 Merryweather, now a lieutenant in the U.S. Army, met a feisty, blond little girl of 11 or so named Katie Conn, who became his costumed partner, the Kitten. Later, perhaps to make this rather odd relationship seem more normal, Katie took to calling him "Uncle David." By the time the magazine folded in the summer of 1946, Kitten had grown into an attractive teenager.

Irwin Hasen drew Cat-Man in *Crash*, and Charles M. Quinlan was the chief artist in *Cat-Man Comics*. **R.G.**

**CAVELLI, DICK** (1923– ) A successful gag-cartoonist whose wry, stylishly drawn humor was a regular feature in such national magazines as the *Saturday*

*Evening Post* and *Collier's* during the 1940s and 1950s, New Yorker Richard Cavelli rose to the more secure status of comic-strip artist with *Morty Meekle* (now entitled *Winthrop*) in 1955. As he describes his beginnings in cartooning, he "fell into a job drawing fossils for the Museum of Natural History" on his discharge from the Army after World War II. "It paid $50 per week and, advancement opportunities for drawers of fossils for museums being what they are, my bride of a few months took to worrying about the future and talked me into enrolling at an art school in New York. I had done lots of cartooning in the past, strictly on an amateur basis, for school publications, Army unit magazines, and the like, but had not seriously considered it as a way of making a living. Although I started at the school with the vague notion of becoming a comic book illustrator, I found myself thrown into a classroom teeming with aspiring gag cartoonists. This seemed like a pretty gay way to make a dollar, so I became one myself."

While attending the School of Visual Arts on the G.I. Bill, Cavelli had such success selling to magazines that by the time he was 33 years old *Writer's Digest* wrote of him that he had "risen to the top faster than any other cartoonist in the business." But although he found freelancing "a nice way to make a living," he could see that "the magazine business was beginning to look shaky" and started to think of doing a strip. When he brought *Morty Meekle* to NEA, they bought it at once.

A somewhat bland daily humor strip about a meek office worker and his girl friend Jill, *Morty Meekle* was in the long-established tradition of victim humor; Morty was the classic figure of humble docility, badgered by his irascible boss E.G. Boomer and bewildered by the world. Among its most attractive characters were a few kids whose observations were sharper than those of any of the adults, and in time such precocious moppets as Winthrop and his hygiene-obsessed pal Spotless McPartland began to take over the strip. Cavelli increasingly shifted the focus of *Morty Meekle* to these articulate youngsters, and on February 27, 1966, the strip formally changed its star and its title and became *Winthrop*.

Drawn with elegant simplicity and featuring a balanced composition and a crisp, economical line, *Winthrop* carries on in the tradition of shrewd commentary from the mouth of babes established by *Peanuts* and *Miss Peach* in the 1950s. Neither mischievous nor sentimentalized, Winthrop and his gang are seldom seen in action; their time is devoted to examining and understanding a world they perceive with the keen eye of innocence. Often ironic but never caustic, *Winthrop* has remained remarkably fresh for almost a quarter of a century. **D.W.**

**CHAFFIN, GLENN** (1897–1978) A wholly accidental participant in the dawn of the adventure strip, Chaffin in 1928 created *Tailspin Tommy*, the first of the grand airplane features. Born May 15, 1897, Chaffin was a Western frontiersman, gold miner, and peripatetic crime reporter who in 1923 became enamored of the movie business and moved to Hollywood. There he quickly established himself as a savvy press agent, studio insider, and sometime screenwriter. His pals included John N. Wheeler, Bell Syndicate chief and groundbreaking comics enthusiast, who asked him in 1926 to take over the writing of a historical Sunday page called *The Pioneers*. After that minor feature folded the following year, Wheeler asked Chaffin to develop a new kind of airplane- adventure strip, unlike anything then in circulation.

He was working in uncharted territory, since there were not yet many fixed adventure strip conventions. Chaffin took the movies as reference and started producing what he called "dramalogues," characterized by cliffhangers and standard sentimental formulas, for what would become *Tailspin Tommy*. He and the strip's artist, Hal Forrest, never got along well, though, and it appears that Forrest forced him out of their partnership in a dispute that was probably over the strip's considerable revenues. Chaffin's last *Tommy* byline appeared in January 1934.

For a time he returned to the Hollywood scene, ghosting the movie gossip column of Jimmy Fidler and churning out fan pieces for *Photoplay*. Soon he was writing another strip, this one for the McClure Syndicate, a minor Western called *Rusty Rollins, Cowboy*, which was drawn by Irwin Shope. In 1940, having married Louis B. Mayer's secretary, he left Hollywood and briefly went home to Corvallis—only to be called by Wheeler once more. This time he succeeded Commander Frank Wead as the scripter of Bell's *Flyin' Jenny* strip. At the same time Wheeler named him a roving war correspondent, and Chaffin spent several very busy years writing both *Jenny* and a column called *Air Rambling* for the North American Newspaper Alliance. After the war he finally got back to his Big Sky country, where he continued to write *Jenny* until it expired in 1946; he also served as Corvallis postmaster and Chamber of Commerce chief for many years. A gentle and modest man, entirely oblivious to comics scholarship, he was astonished to learn in the early 1970s that historians regarded him as an important pioneer or that anyone remembered *Tailspin Tommy*. **J.M.**

**CHARLIE CHAN** A detective noted for his patient gathering of clues and for his aphorisms, Charlie Chan—originally the protagonist of six novels by Earl Derr Biggers—came to the comic sections in 1938. The newspaper strip was by Alfred Andriola—with some help from his friends and assistants—and enjoyed a four-year run, daily and Sunday. At that point in his career Andriola was producing material very much in the Caniff-Sickles style. He had worked as their secretary, and his first assistant, Charles Raab, had also assisted Caniff on *Terry and the Pirates*.

Chan had been around since 1925, when Earl Derr Biggers sold *The House Without A Key* as a serial to *The Saturday Evening Post*. All six Charlie Chan novels are unexceptional, and, had it not been for Warner Oland, Charlie Chan would never have become the valuable property he did. Oland, a Swedish actor who had played Fu Manchu and Al Jolson's father on the screen, was the fourth to portray Chan in the movies. He did his first Chan film in 1931 and brought the character to life in a series that would prove a very successful one for 20th Century-Fox.

Andriola based his comic strip characterization on Oland. Although Warner Oland died the same year the first strips appeared, Andriola continued to think of him as the definitive Charlie. While Andriola had read the Biggers novels, he didn't adapt any of them to comic strip form; his Charlie was the movie Charlie and he borrowed the Number One Son character from the films, drawing him in the early strips to resemble actor Keye Luke. The rest of the characters were his own invention.

Andriola soon found that "an elderly philosophical Oriental detective was not ideal for a story strip...A comic strip needs action." To this end he introduced, early in 1939, a second detective, Kirk Barrow—who from then on would costar with Chan—"a vigorous, attractive American, who can speak softly and forcefully, but still carry a big punch." Son Lee, looking less and less like Keye Luke, appeared chiefly in the Sunday page thereafter. Unlike many of the continuity strips of the time, *Charlie Chan* had a separate story line for the daily and Sunday sequences.

It was also one of the relatively few strips that was allowed to come to a graceful, rather than abrupt, end. In the last panel of the last Sunday page, in May 1942 Charlie and Lee turned to the audience and Charlie waved goodbye. The final caption read: "So Charlie finishes his story to Lee—the last story, for this is the end of the Chan series. And so, for the present at least, many thanks, and good-bye!"

Chan appeared in comic books, off and on, from 1939 to 1966. The Andriola strips were reprinted, first in *Feature Comics*, then in *Big Shot Comics*. In 1948 and 1949 five issues of a Charlie Chan comic book using original material came out. Joe Simon and Jack Kirby provided covers, and Carmine Infantino and Charles Raab did the interior work. The character was revived briefly in the mid-fifties. Later in the decade DC tried six issues

of *The New Adventures of Charlie Chan*. The Chinese detective made his final comic book bow in two Dell issues in the middle sixties.                    **R.G.**

**CHRISTMAN, BERT** (1915–1942) After drawing a strip about a heroic daredevil pilot, *Scorchy Smith*, he went on to become a hero and a daredevil pilot himself. He was killed in battle early in World War II and while the manner of his death has tended to overshadow his accomplishments as an artist in the few histories of the field that mention his name, Christman was an excellent adventure strip artist who accomplished quite a bit in his short life.

Allen B. Christman hailed from Fort Collins, Colorado. Everybody called him Bert and he is remembered as being "a nice quiet kid." In his home town he worked as a department store advertising artist. After graduating from Colorado State with a degree in engineering, he went east to New York in 1936. He got a job in the Associated Press bullpen and when Noel Sickles quit *Scorchy Smith*, the strip was given to the 21-year-old Christman. He and Sickles knew each other, though not well, and they never met again after Sickles left the AP. At first Christman's work on *Scorchy* had a shaky, borrowed look, but he soon developed an effective style of his own, being especially good at depicting the planes and other gadgets so essential to the strip.

Christman guided Scorchy through a Brazilian adventure and then took him stateside for a job as a test pilot. Later Scorchy is in the Orient, a volunteer in a small air force serving a Chinese general. After this prophetic sequence, there were some almost *Lost Horizon*-like doings in the mountains of Tibet before another American adventure. As restless as his hero, Christman stayed with the strip only a year and a half.

He was also involved in the fledgling comic book business. In 1936 he wrote and drew several adventure features for such pioneering titles as *Detective Picture Stories*. He was the first artist to draw *The Sandman*, which began in *Adventure Comics* in the spring of 1939, and *The Three Aces* in *Action Comics*. This latter feature dealt with "three winged soldiers-of-fortune, sick of war and tragedy, who pledge themselves to a new kind of adventure. They came to roam the globe, working for peace and sanity."

Christman, too, believed in a world where soldiers-of-fortune like Scorchy and the Three Aces could do some good. By the middle of 1938 he was in Pensacola training as a Navy flying cadet, and eventually he served in the scouting squadron of the aircraft carrier *Ranger*. The ship became part of the newly formed Atlantic Fleet early in 1941, and when he left it in June of that year to join the American Volunteer Group, it was based in Bermuda. The AVG, which soon came to

*Scorchy Smith*, Bert Christman, 1937.

be known by the more romantic name of the Flying Tigers, was being put together by U.S. Colonel Claire Chennault. Its basic purpose was to help the Chinese defend the Burma Road against the Japanese.

Christman felt that this was a flying job "with real purpose" and he resigned from the service—something the U.S. military allowed the Flying Tiger volunteers to do unimpeded—and joined up. Some historians believe it was Christman who designed the shark-like nose of all the Tigers' P-40s. An eager, if not expert pilot, he kept requesting combat. Though he was slightly wounded early in January of 1942, his enthusiasm never waned. But he wrote to his old AP editor to say, "When 'this' is all over I'm sure I'll be content again to sit at a drawing board and pen my experiences and those of my friends in an authentic aviation comic strip."

On his third combat mission, which took place over Rangoon on January 23, 1942, Christman was shot down. He bailed out and a Japanese plane went after him and machine-gunned him. Christman, 26, was dead before he hit the ground. This was a new world now, with no place in it for the grinning, slightly innocent daredevil pilots he'd drawn.

A drawing showing "how Bert Christman may have died" went out with the AP account of his death. It was by Frank Robbins, his successor on *Scorchy Smith*. **R.G.**

**CICERO'S CAT** An early example of the comic strip spinoff was *Cicero's Cat*, which began in 1933 as an adjunct to Bud Fisher's Sunday *Mutt and Jeff* and grew to become a full-length strip in its own right. It dealt with the pet of Mutt's son Cicero, as *Krazy Kat* began by recounting the activities of the cat of Herriman's Dingbat family. Like her famous predecessor, Cicero's cat Esmeralda could talk, but unlike Herriman's innocent, selfless feline, she employed that skill to gain her own usually discreditable ends, thus making her a prototype for today's self-serving Heathcliff and Garfield.

*Cicero's Cat* was never drawn by Fisher, the creator of its parent strip, but rather by his assistant Al Smith, who was ghosting Fisher's work. Done in the same lively, kinetic style Fisher had established in *Mutt and Jeff*, the often witty and always cynical strip underwent numerous changes in size and status from its inception as a property of H.C. Fisher, Inc., on December 3, 1933, to its demise under the aegis of the Bell Syndicate about 30 years later. Beginning as a single line of panels above the Sunday *Mutt and Jeff*, the feature swelled to a half a page the year after its birth, reducing Fisher's full page by half. Later *Cicero's Cat* shrank to two rows occupying one third of a page, running beneath its progenitor, and when *Mutt and Jeff* was reduced to the same size in the 1940s, the two strips were separated and lost whatever family connection may have remained in their readers' minds.

Although as cunning and resourceful as any of the comic cats that have followed her, Esmeralda never quite shook off her ancillary character, and the strip remains a minor meow in the history of comics. Its place in that history is secure, however, as a pioneer in the graphic depiction of the clever and independent feline.

**D.W.**

**THE CISCO KID** The Robin Hood of the Old West has galloped through every available medium, including movies, radio, and television. He first showed up in comic books in the mid-1940s and in a newspaper strip in the early 1950s.

Although O. Henry is usually credited with creating the character, all that was actually taken from his 1907 short story "The Caballero's Way" was the Cisco Kid name; The movies created the Cisco Kid everyone knows. Believed by many to be no more than an audacious Mexican bandit, Cisco was actually a champion of justice and, in his spare time, a formidable ladies' man. He was a combination of the Lone Ranger and the Saint.

The character appeared at least twice in silent movies, but it was a 1929 talkie, *In Old Arizona*, starring Warner Baxter as the Cisco Kid, that established him. Baxter won an Oscar for his performance and played the character again in *The Cisco Kid* in 1931, a film that introduced Chris-Pin Martin as the caballero's plump sidekick Gordito. In 1939 Baxter returned to play Cisco for the third and final time, then Cesar Romero took over the role. The series was abandoned by 20th Century-Fox in 1941, but in 1945 Monogram revived it with Duncan Renaldo as Cisco and Martin Garralaga as Pancho.

Pancho, a variation of Gordito, seems to have originated on the radio version of *The Cisco Kid*, which initially starred Jackson Beck, and debuted in 1942 over the Mutual network.

The movies continued until 1950. Renaldo was the final screen Cisco, with Leo Carrillo as the definitive Pancho; both of them resurfaced in the next incarnation, a syndicated television show.

Cisco and Pancho first appeared in comic books in 1944, in a one-shot comic book produced by the Bernard Baily shop. The Cisco story, filled with pretty señoritas, was drawn by C.A. Voight. Baily and Voight also worked on a comic strip version but abandoned it when they found that the rights to the character were not available.

Dell introduced an authorized comic book version in 1950, which lasted until 1958. Eventually this Cisco took to dressing like the television Cisco, with an ornately embroidered black caballero outfit. Bob Jenney was among the artists.

King Features introduced a daily newspaper strip in January 1951. The artist was José Luis Salinas, who worked in an impressive illustrational style that was in the tradition of Hal Foster and Alex Raymond. He was a whiz at drawing both horses and pretty women, essential ingredients in the saga. His Cisco and Pancho were based on the Renaldo and Carrillo versions. An Argentinian, Salinas worked out of Buenos Aires and rarely visited the United States. The scripts were by Rod Reed, who'd been an editor-writer for Fawcett's line of comic books. "The Salinas-Reed collaboration may have been one of the longest distance ones ever," he once observed; "it is 5,297 air miles between Buenos Aires and New York City. Another oddity is that, although we worked together smoothly (at least I thought so) for 18 years we never met, conversed on the phone or exchanged correspondence. But my esteem for the artist never flagged and I looked forward each week to seeing a new set of proofs with José's live, vigorous drawings."

The newspaper strip lasted until 1968. The movies and the show are still being seen on television somewhere in the world.

**R.G.**

**CLAIRE VOYANT** Probably one of the only heroines to make her debut while unconscious, Claire was first seen on Monday, May 10, 1943, as one of the two occupants of a drifting lifeboat in the Atlantic, a huddled shape who was "more dead than alive." Rescued and brought aboard a freighter, she had no memory of who she was. Overhearing someone use the word "*clairvoyant*," she adopted it as her name. The feature, written and drawn by Jack Sparling, was originally syndicated by the newspaper *PM*.

"I picked a girl hero here because it has appeal in the papers," Sparling once explained. "I picked a girl with amnesia because we were in the middle of the war and I didn't want to give her any family ties after the war was over." Claire's early adventures took place on the high seas, mixing encounters with Nazi subs and romance with two of the better looking ship's crewmen, Tex and Spike by name. After a spell of Oriental intrigue, Claire returned to the United States at the end of the war. In writing of the strip in *The Comics* (1947), Coulton Waugh observed, "Claire Voyant herself is not too remarkable a character in appearance; it is the group of men, heroic or crooked, who revolve around her which make this strip stand on its handsome feet."

Later continuities involved show business, public relations, and other peacetime pursuits. Claire took less of a part in the action, having been converted into a sort of sexy Mary Worth. The strip, apparently at Sparling's instigation, ceased in 1948.

**R.G.**

**THE CLOCK** The Clock, who has the distinction of being the first masked man created for comic books, made a somewhat scattered debut, showing up on the newsstands simultaneously in the November 1936 issues of both *Funny Pages* and *Funny Picture Stories*. The following month he was also to be found holding forth in *Detective Picture Stories*, and late in 1937 he switched venue to star in the third issue of *Feature Funnies*. He stayed there through 28 subsequent issues, and a couple of his earlier cases were reprinted in *Keen Detective Funnies*. For his final stint the Clock appeared in the first 35 issues of *Crack Comics*.

He was a natty fellow, doing his detecting clad in tuxedo and gray fedora. He covered his face with a black silken mask and, early on, also carried a gold-headed cane. George E. Brenner, who wrote and drew the feature from start to finish, was most likely influenced by the Saint as well as such dapper pulp crime fighters as the Phantom Detective, who was depicted on covers in top hat, tails, and mask. Just as the Saint left behind his card with a haloed stick figure, the Clock left his card with a depiction of a timepiece and the slogan—"The Clock Has Struck." Clearly he called himself the Clock originally solely for the sake of this pun.

In everyday life the Clock was Brian O'Brien, "polished young society man." When he set up shop in *Crack*, he took on a sidekick named Pug Brady, who was his exact double. Pug was phased out after a couple of years, and the Clock's new aide was female this time, a teenage Dead End Kid–type named Butch. Soon after teaming up with her he cut down his mask to domino size.

While never a first-rate feature in either script or art, *The Clock* was the pioneer that paved the way for such later, and more successful, masked detectives as Jack Cole's Midnight and Will Eisner's Spirit. **R.G.**

**COLE, JACK** (1914–1958) Cole succeeded in several areas of cartooning. From the late 1930s through the middle 1950s he was widely and profitably employed in comic books, where his best known creation was *Plastic Man*. After that he became a very popular cartoonist for *Playboy*, and in the last year of his life he drew a syndicated comic strip.

A few months before his suicide Cole provided a short autobiography for the syndicate to use. He said, "Jack Cole was born in 1914 in New Castle, Pa. At 15, he took the Landon School of Cartooning mail correspondence course …1933, graduated from high school. 1934, married Dorothy Mahoney. 1934, got a job at American Can Factory and started mailing out cartoons to magazines. 1935, first sale to *Boy's Life*. 1936, borrowed $500 in small amounts from town merchants and set out with his wife for New York to find cartoon work. 1937–1954, worked for comic magazines. 1954, freelance cartooning …1958, 43 years old, 24 years married."

Despite the fact that he felt that he could cover his years in comic books in a few words, Cole was quite active and successful in the field. He started off working for the Chesler shop, turning out funny filler pages for the most part. By 1940 he was also doing fairly serious superhero material, such as *The Comet* in *Pep Comics* and *Silver Streak* and *Daredevil* in *Silver Streak Comics*. In 1941 he created *Midnight* for *Smash Comics*. This latter hero fought crime wearing a business suit, a fedora, and a mask, looking like a less rumpled version of the Spirit. By this time Cole's layouts were already bold and unconventional, making use of impressive long shots, down shots, and closeups and other approaches that made use of the staging tricks of action movies and animated cartoons. His sense of humor was strong, and Cole never took anything too seriously in his hero strips, not even violence, vast destruction, or death. His humor alternated between broad slapstick and quiet kidding, and there was sometimes a perverse and nasty touch to it.

Plastic Man snapped into view in *Police Comics* #1 (August 1941). Cole seemed to be aware he had created a special character, and in the immodest blurb he wrote for the debut story he said: "From time to time the comic book world welcomes a new sensation!! Such is *Plastic Man!!* The most fantastic man alive!" Though he began as a backup character, within a year Plas had bounced to the star spot in *Police* and remained there throughout the 1940s.

In addition to his adventure material Cole also turned out a considerable quantity of one-page humor fillers in the 1940s. These included *Wun Cloo*, *Dan Tootin*, and *Burp the Twerp*. As the comic book field changed in the 1950s, moving from superheroes to crime and horror, Cole tried to make the transition, doing interesting work in both areas.

He left the field in 1954, having long yearned to get back to his first love in cartooning, drawing gags. He came to the notice of *Playboy* and was soon their most popular artist. His full-page cartoons, often rendered in bright watercolor, became staples of the magazine. At Hugh Hefner's suggestion, he and his wife relocated in the Chicago area, where *Playboy* was then being edited. After settling in to his new home, Cole sold a humor strip titled *Betsy and Me* to the Chicago Sun-Times Syndicate. Just a few months after the strip began running, Cole took his life. **R.G.**

**COLLINS, KREIGH** See KEVIN THE BOLD.

*The Claw*, Jack Cole, © 1940, Your Guide Publications.

**COMIC BOOK MAGAZINE** Given away every week along with the Sunday funnies, the *Comic Book Magazine* was introduced at the end of March 1940 and beat Will Eisner's much livelier *Spirit* weekly into print by a shade over two months. It was put together in the editorial offices of the *Chicago Tribune*, and although the section did appear in a scattering of other newspapers, such as the *Los Angeles Times* and the *Boston Post*, its longest-lived and most hospitable home was the *Tribune.*

The booklet was half-tabloid size, sported a newsprint cover and contained between 16 and 24 pages each week. The earliest issues presented a hodgepodge of features, including reprints of Frank King's long-defunct *Bobby Make-Believe*, Ferd Johnson's *Texas Slim*, and the deceased Gaar Williams' *Mort Green & Wife*. There was also a very clunky, three-page, fumetti-style adaptation of Republic's serial *The Drums of Fu Manchu*. Overall, the book was not the sort of competition to cause Superman and the other new and thriving comic book superheroes any sleepless nights.

Late in June of 1940 new features were introduced: a humorous adventure strip titled *Bucks McKale* by an artist named Sullivan; *Hy Score* by George Merkle, which starred a "secret agent of Army Intelligence"; *Brenda Starr* by Dale Messick. The red-haired girl reporter proved the real hit of the book and by the end of the following year Brenda had been promoted to the comic sections of newspapers all across the country. The reruns of *Texas Slim* had also found some favor, and Johnson, longtime ghost on *Moon Mullins*, commenced producing new pages before 1940 was out.

Although Frank Engli was working as Milton Caniff's assistant and letterer on *Terry and the Pirates* at the time, his contribution was in a decidedly bigfoot style: *Rocky* chronicled the exploits of a Stone Age teenager. Milt Youngren introduced a contemporary and somewhat more serious teenager in his *Lew Loyal*, some four pages long, with Lew and his blond girlfriend Betsy confronting spies and saboteurs. Lew's Uncle Mack happened to be an agent with the United States Secret Bureau, and this further added to the complexities of the lad's life. Each week's installment ended with a code message for readers and they could write to Lew c/o the *Tribune* and get themselves, absolutely free, a red, white, and blue Lew Loyal Patriots badge.

Adventure strips continued to be added. Ed Moore succeeded, late in 1940, in selling them his *Captain Storm*, a nicely done page that included ships, airplanes, and a Latin American revolution. Moore, who'd been an assistant on *Dan Dunn* and *Don Winslow* and was contributing to *Detective* and *Adventure Comics*, took in six different versions of his strip before he finally sold it. The salary was $25 a week. In *Smokey Stover* the *Trib* already had a funny strip about a fireman. They added a serious one about a fireman late in 1940 named *Streamer Kelly* by Jack Ryan. An assistant on *Dick Tracy*, Ryan drew in a style that was somewhat like that of his boss and somewhat like that of Ed Moore. *Streamer Kelly* was an excellent feature.

Early in 1941 Bert Whitman's *Mr. Ex* was added to the comic booklet lineup, which seems only fair, since Whitman may well be the man who inspired the whole project in the first place. A cartoonist since his teens, he was by 1940 heading a shop in Manhattan and putting together comic books for the smaller publishers. Whitman recalls approaching the New York City offices of the Chicago Tribune-New York News Syndicate and offering to produce a weekly comic book for them. Deciding to do it themselves, they did offer him the chance to draw up an idea about a girl reporter. Figuring there were already enough girl reporter strips, Whitman passed. The job was given to Dale Messick.

Whitman eventually sold the *Comic Book Magazine* his *Mr. Ex*. Its hero was originally a mystery-man and a master of disguise. Gradually Whitman loosened up his work, the inking growing bolder and the style more cartoony, while Ex grew younger and took to mixing it up with spies and assorted other villains in locales that ranged from uncharted islands to the high seas. In 1944 Whitman began a daily strip called *Debbie Dean* about a girl reporter for the *New York Post* syndicate.

In the summer of 1942 a contemporary Western was added, *Vesta West*, which starred a cowgirl and her smart horse. Fred Meagher, fresh from drawing the Tom Mix giveaway comic books, drew the page for a spell; then Ray Bailey, who was also assisting on *Terry and the Pirates*, took over. He rendered all the masked marauders and rustlers in his best imitation of the Caniff style.

The comic book supplement expired on April 4, 1943, its end no doubt hastened by the increasing wartime paper shortage. *Brenda Starr* had long since been promoted to the regular comic sections, and *Streamer Kelly* made a similar, though less successful, transition. *Texas Slim* also jumped into the Sunday funnies for a long, if not especially prosperous, career. **R.G.**

**CONAN** Robert E. Howard's wandering barbarian hero began his life in the pulps of the 1930s, faded away after Howard's death in 1936, bounced back with a series of paperbacks beginning in 1968, and appeared as a Marvel comic book in 1970.

Roy Thomas, then Marvel's premiere writer, adapted Howard's sword and sorcery stories with respect and lyricism, mixing in some original stories of his own and adaptations from others who had written in the Howard manner. Barry Smith, a young British artist with a fine sense of design and an elegant line, became a fan favorite with his dreamy Pre-Raphaelite rendering of Conan and his magical world.

Smith seemed to be reaching the peak of his illustrative abilities when he left the series in 1973 to seek painting and illustrating work outside comics. He was replaced by Marvel workhorses John Buscema and Ernie Chua (aka Ernie Chan), who recast Conan in a more standard, hirsute, muscle-bound mold. Although the series then ceased to excite the more discriminating elite of 1970s comic book fans, it remained a solid success and continues to the present under various writers and artists. It has spawned various spin-offs, including *Conan the King* and *Savage Sword of Conan*, and inspired Marvel to adapt a number of other Howard properties, most notably King Kull. The *Conan the Barbarian* movie gave the series a boost in 1982. The sequel to that movie, *Conan the Destroyer*, was written by Roy Thomas and frequent Marvel-writer Gerry Conway.

Because of the framework established by Howard's stories, in which Conan progresses from traveling thief to warrior to king, *Conan* is one of the few long-running comic book series with a clear line of development, a fact that may account for its longevity, despite repetitious handling in recent years. **G.J.**

**CONNIE** As adventure strips go, *Connie* was beautiful but dumb. Frank Godwin was an impressive illustrator, a master draftsman, and a wizard with the pen, but his plots and dialogue never came near to equalling his drawing.

Begun as a Sunday page in 1927, *Connie* initially purveyed flapper and lounge lizard gags in typical pretty-girl–page fashion. When Godwin added a daily strip in 1929, however, strange and drastic changes began to occur. The continuities involved his slim blond heroine with airplanes, kidnappers, south-of-the-border revolutions, African safaris, and lustful sheiks. Connie herself wasn't dumb, but her somewhat aggressive innocence enabled her to walk into trouble with great regularity. Although her early adventures were pretty much parodies of prevailing movie and slick magazine melodramas, as the Thirties got underway Godwin switched to more serious, and more fantastic, stuff. By the middle of the decade, both daily and Sunday, *Connie* was firmly committed to fantasy and science fiction.

As a freelance adventuress, and sometime private investigator, Connie trekked in search of lost cities and tangled with invisible men and crazed scientists bent on world conquest. "Great heavens!" exclaims a character in a typical adventure. "Do you know what these things are? ATOMIC BOMBS! He's preparing to make himself DICTATOR OF THE WORLD!" She also rocketed to the far planets and traveled in time to the far future. "Having arrived in the 30th Century in search of Connie, Jack and Dr. Chrono have been appointed as Connie's assistants in defending the United Nations," explained a 1936 caption, "against the Yellow Invaders who have, in some mysterious manner, caused all the electric power in the city to go dead."

Godwin's Sundays, mixing art nouveau trappings and decor with 1930s pulp fiction plots, are unlike anything done before or since. The lavish sets, fantastic costumes, and rococo dialogue give the impression of a sort of R-rated Oz movie.

The feature continued on into the middle Forties, running in a sparse list of newspapers. It reached a relatively large audience through reprints in the pages of *Famous Funnies*. **R.G.**

**CORY, FANNY** (1877–1972) Her specialty was drawing children and she did that for 60 years for a variety of magazines, newspapers, and books. She also drew a newspaper panel and two comic strips, the most successful of which was *Little Miss Muffet*.

*Connie*, Frank Godwin, © 1938, Ledger Syndicate.

Cory had been a professional children's illustrator for nearly 40 years by the time she got into the comic strip business. She sold her first drawing to *St. Nicholas* magazine in 1896 and her work soon thereafter appeared in *Life*, the *Saturday Evening Post*, and *Scribner's*. By the end of the century she had branched out into children's book illustration. In 1901 she did the pictures for *The Master Key*, the first of several L. Frank Baum books she illustrated. In 1904 Cory, who had spent part of her growing-up years there, returned to Montana, married, and settled on an 1,800-acre ranch near Helena. She continued to illustrate children's books, in a style influenced by Howard Pyle, Arthur Rackham, and Art Nouveau.

In the middle 1920s she and her husband, now with three children ready for college, found they needed something beyond ranching and book illustrating. Cory, whose brother was a political cartoonist, decided to try the newspaper syndicates. She sold a one-column panel, *Sonnysayings*, to the *Philadelphia Ledger* syndicate in 1928. The feature was popular and survived into the 1950s.

In 1934 she did her first newspaper strip, which was also done for the *Ledger* syndicate. It was titled *Babe Bunting*. "Here is HEART INTEREST pitched to its very ultimate," the syndicate announced to prospective buyers. Babe was a curly-haired little tyke, clearly intended to grab the fans of movie moppet Shirley Temple. A seeming orphan, Babe was initially a salty little kid, whose response to patronizing adults was usually "She's just talking through her hat." The following year Cory was hired away by William Randolph Hearst and went over to King Features.

There she drew another little girl adventure strip, this one named *Little Miss Muffet*, inspired by a nursery rhyme and also, most likely, by the Shirley Temple movie of the year before, *Little Miss Marker*. The strip was a moderate success, but Cory never thought much of it. She had no hand in the writing, which she felt was too bland. "There are no gangsters, or divorces or anything like that in her adventures," she told an interviewer in the late 1930s, "so she must be a relief to mothers. But sometimes I think she's too pure." Despite her feelings, Cory stayed with the strip. Living alone on her Montana ranch, she continued with *Miss Muffet* until 1956. When she died, she was five years short of a century old.          **R.G.**

**COUNT SCREWLOOSE**  The count was one of the many certifiable funny paper screwballs created by the inimitable Milt Gross. He first appeared on February 17, 1929, in a Sunday page syndicated by the *New York World*, replacing Gross' earlier *Nize Baby*. The strip's original title was *Count Screwloose of Tooloose*.

The count was ruled by an *idée fixe*, and each and every week the diminutive and cross-eyed fellow would escape from the Nuttycrest Asylum and try his luck in the outside world. Each and every week, too, he encountered such lunacy and hypocrisy outside that he decided to climb back over the wall into the relative sanity of Nuttycrest. Almost every final panel would show Screwloose requesting of his faithful pooch, "Iggy, keep an eye on me!" Iggy was small, loyal, and fond of wearing a Napoleon hat. Like all true naive characters, the count had to remain hopeful. His experiences didn't faze him, since his rigid naivete was part of his problem.

Gross signed on with King Features Syndicate in the autumn of 1930, and the count left the *World* just a few months ahead of the collapse of the paper. A new Sunday page, titled simply *Count Screwloose*, began running in the Hearst papers in March of 1931. For the next several years Gross shifted the elements of his page, sometimes using the count in a topper to *Dave's Delicatessen* and sometimes giving him the star spot. In this new incarnation Screwloose was no longer a resident of the asylum.

By 1934 he and Dave were sharing a Sunday page (sometimes appearing in one another's strips) and had become involved in a long-running burlesque of Foreign Legion adventures. Early in 1935 the page was in the count's name again, and Dave had dropped out. In October of that year King parted company with Gross, but he continued to produce the page for Hearst's *New York Mirror* for the remainder of the 1930s. Count Screwloose acquired a new dog, a spotted wonder named J.R., and Gross himself became a frequent character. But most of the *Mirror* material was ghosted by several others, including Bob Dunn.

J.R., under the name Pete the Pooch, survived into the 1940s and was last seen in the second issue of a comic book called *Milt Gross Funnies* (September 1947). Count Screwloose didn't make an appearance but was credited as the author of a page of gag cartoons.          **R.G.**

**CRAIG, JOHNNY** (1926–  )  Born in Pleasantville, N.Y., but raised in New York City, Craig spent his career in comics almost exclusively at EC (Entertaining Comics). He was with the company, and its predecessor, longer than any other artist, starting with a staff position in 1940 while still in high school. By 1947, he was honing his craft as an artist and writer in such genre titles as *Saddle Justice* and *Crime Patrol*. When publisher Bill Gaines began his trend-setting horror comics, Craig immediately established himself as the lead storyteller and cover artist for *The Vault of Horror*, ultimately taking over as editor of the title for its last six issues in 1954. A slow, meticulous worker, he nonetheless contributed stories to *Crime SuspenStories* during this period, as well as some strikingly designed covers for various EC titles.

Craig eschewed the prevailing EC approach to horror and pursued instead the themes of voodoo, haunted houses, personality transference, and, above all, the psychological aspects of fear. "Fear is inside a person," he has said. "Some people are afraid of some things, some are afraid of other things. But whatever they're afraid of is inside them." Lurking behind Craig's cleanly rendered, apparently illustrational style was a classic cartoonist-storyteller whose art and writing were strongly influenced by Milton Caniff, Will Eisner, and Harvey Kurtzman. Craig's moody, meandering stories were striking in their own right, but he, like the storytellers who influenced him, also searched out ways to advance his work visually and to use purely pictorial means to reveal his characters.

When the horror comics era ended, Craig produced *Extra* for EC, a news reporter adventure title that ran five issues, and also appeared in their short lived Picto-Fiction magazines. Then, when EC folded their comics altogether, he went into advertising, and is currently art director for a firm in Pennsylvania. In the sixties he returned to do some effective horror tales for Warren's *Creepy* and *Eerie* and has occasionally appeared in Marvel and DC comics.                                         **J.B.**

**CRANBERRY BOGGS**  The McNaught Syndicate's attempt to have a *Li'l Abner* of their own, *Cranberry Boggs* first appeared in newspapers on Monday, January 8, 1945. Cranberry was a blond bumpkin built along the lines of Li'l Abner, and he resided in a New England coastal town named Codville (later rechristened Cod Cliffs), "an ancient fishing village totally unscathed by progress or prosperity." A good-hearted and naive young man, whose favorite expressions were "Sufferin' sardines!" and "Gorsh!" he was an orphan who lived with his excessively colorful grandparents, Granny and Cap'n Gramps. He and his bewhiskered grandfather earned a modest living as lobster fisherman. But most of Cranberry's time was taken up with getting entangled with pretty girls, bank robbers, kidnappers, jewel thieves, and assorted crooks and conmen.

Don Dean wrote and drew the strip, which ran daily and Sunday. He'd ghosted *Big Chief Wahoo* in the late 1930s and early 1940s, and his own feature, even though it starred a Li'l Abner type, was usually closer to the *Wahoo* mix of comedy and adventure than it was to the broadly satirical material Capp was vending. After leaving the chief, Dean had put in time in comic books and had drawn another Abner simulacrum, *Pokey Oakey*, for MLJ's *Top-Notch Laugh Comics*. His *Cranberry Boggs* was a nicely drawn effort, but its stories were no more than average. The strip ended with the decade. **R.G.**

**CRANDALL, REED** (1917–1982)  One of the most technically proficient artists ever to work in comic books, Crandall entered the field in 1940. Over the next several decades he drew superheroes, jungle men, science fiction yarns, and horror tales and was the definitive artist on *Blackhawk*.

A Midwesterner, he studied at the Cleveland School of Art during the middle 1930s and was also influenced by such illustrators as Howard Pyle, Joseph Clement Coll, and Henry C. Pitz. After an editorial art job with NEA, Crandall moved East. He hit Manhattan in 1940 and worked first for the Eisner-Iger shop, then directly for the Quality comics line. He drew Stormy Foster and Hercules for *Hit Comics*, the Firebrand for *Police Comics*, Uncle Sam in *National*, and Captain Triumph for *Crack Comics*. For *Smash Comics* he drew the Ray, for *Feature Comics* the diminutive Doll Man. He took over Blackhawk in *Military Comics* in the autumn of 1942. He depicted the daring Blackhawk and the rest of his paramilitary crew in just the right larger-than-life way. He seemed to enjoy drawing the Axis bad guys, the sultry lady spies as well as the required planes, gadgets, and fierce weapons. He was also expert at staging the battle scenes that Blackhawk's life style kept leading him into.

Crandall was busy elsewhere during the 1940s as well. He ghosted Captain America for Simon & Kirby and drew Kaänga in *Jungle Comics*. In the early 1950s he was hired by EC and while the company lasted he drew a wide variety of stories, including crime, war, science fiction, and horror. In the 1960s he worked for *Twilight Zone*, *Classics Illustrated*, and *Treasure Chest*. He was also frequently seen in the black and white horror comics, *Creepy* and *Eerie*. Much of this later stuff was stiff and sterile, having lost the impressive flamboyance of his earlier work. Bothered by ill health and personal problems he did very little comic book work in his final years. At the time of his death he was working in a menial position in a fast food restaurant. **R.G.**

**CRANE, ROY** (1901–1977)  He was one of the earliest cartoonists to turn out an adventure strip, first setting up shop in 1924. A humorous, thoughtful man, Crane perfected a simple, forceful drawing style and a cinematic manner of storytelling that influenced a great many of the artists who followed him. He created three major characters: Wash Tubbs, Captain Easy, and Buz Sawyer.

Royston C. Crane was born in Abilene, Texas, and grew up in Sweetwater, a small town about 40 miles west of Abilene. His father was an attorney and Crane was an only child. "My son says he became interested in art largely because he was a lonesome kid," his father recalled after Crane had started doing *Wash Tubbs*. "Roy had no other brothers or sisters and he had to entertain himself. His mother and I, from the time he was a very small boy, would set him on the floor with picture books and magazines, scratch tablet and pencil and go about our business. By the time he was ten he was drawing comic strips."

When Crane was 14, he signed up for C.N. Landon's mail-order cartooning course. In his high school years Crane worked at odd jobs his father found for him and as a soda jerk in a Sweetwater drugstore, but he kept at his drawing. In 1920, like a good many other cartoonists of the period, Crane went to Chicago to study at the Academy of Fine Arts. Returning to Texas after six months, he worked on a few newspapers, dropped out of several colleges, and then hit the road. He served as a seaman on a freighter and eventually ended up in New York City. Deciding to try for another newspaper job, the young Crane succeeded in getting himself hired on the *New York World* to assist H.T. Webster. He came up with a panel of his own entitled *Music to My Ears* and United Features took it on. Only two papers bought it, meaning that Crane and the syndicate would be splitting the total income of $2 per week. They suggested Crane take it out to Cleveland to another United Press operation, the NEA syndicate, where Landon, his former mail-order mentor, was the art editor. Landon wasn't interested in the ill-fated panel, but he suggested his former pupil try a strip. The result was *Wash Tubbs*.

Crane soon converted the strip from joke-a-day to adventure continuity, which, in the middle 1920s, had very little competition. He introduced the rough, tough Captain Easy to the feature in 1929, and the hawknosed soldier of fortune got a Sunday page of his own in 1933. These full-page Sundays obviously stimulated Crane, and he put some of his best work into them. He was able to stage Easy's adventures much more flamboyantly in the Sunday format, doing much more in the way of backgrounds and action. By the 1930s he was using assistants, including Bill Zaboly and then Leslie Turner. He usually left the daily to the hired help and kept the Sundays for himself.

King Features beckoned in 1943. He created *Buz Sawyer* for the Hearst people and left Tubbs and Easy to Turner. The new strip also mixed action and intrigue with humor and some slapstick. Crane depended more and more on assistants now and within a few years was doing little of the drawing or writing. His most impressive work remains the *Captain Easy* Sunday pages he drew with such enthusiasm and a sense of fun in the 1930s. **R.G.**

**CRIMEBUSTER** Most costumed teenagers in 1940s comic books—Batman's Robin and Captain America's Bucky among them—were merely sidekicks, but Crimebuster worked alone, without benefit of an adult partner. He was, however, sometimes accompanied by a monkey named Squeeks. The youthful hero began his career in *Boy Comics* #3 (April 1942), which was actually the first issue. Charles Biro wrote and drew his early adventures and coedited *Boy Comics* as well, which featured "a boy hero in every strip!!"

Crimebuster, alias Chuck Chandler, "was born out of vengeance!" His parents were "literally slaughtered" by the first-class villain, Iron Jaw, whose name derived from the jagged-toothed device that replaced the lower part of his face. Vicious, heartless, and totally rotten, he bossed "Nazidom's spies and saboteurs in America." With an eye toward vengeance, CB battled him frequently, as well as other bloodthirsty and perverse rascals. After World War II he mellowed and eventually even got rid of his costume. Norman Maurer drew the feature for several years after Biro, as did George Tuska, Joe Kubert, and a host of others. Crimebuster, along with *Boy*, retired early in 1956.

**R.G.**

**CRIME DOES NOT PAY** One of the most successful and influential comic books ever to hit the stands, *Crime Does Not Pay* debuted in 1942, and after the Second World War, when interest in superheroes waned, it gave numerous publishers a new genre to imitate. The bad times that befell the comic book industry in the middle 1950s, caused by increasing criticism, local censorship, and spot boycotting, were triggered in good part by the latter-day imitators of *Crime Does Not Pay*.

Lev Gleason and his soon-to-depart partner, Arthur Bernhard, were the publishers of the magazine, which was the first regularly issued true crime comic. Charles Biro and Bob Wood, both cartoonists, were the editors. Since it replaced the superhero-oriented *Silver Streak Comics*, the first issue was #22 (June 1942). The cover by Biro featured copy, photos of some of the criminals to be found within, and a drawing of a complex brawl in an underworld dive—and proclaimed the book "The First Magazine Of Its Kind!" Among the stories in the first issue were those of Murder, Inc.'s Louis "Lepke" Buchalter and Wild Bill Hickok. For good measure there was also a whodunnit—"Be a detective! Can YOU unravel the riddle?"—and an adventure of a superhero named The War Eagle. The ads for the new magazine make it obvious that it was aiming for an adult as well as a kid audience—"Get 'Crime Does Not Pay'! Show it to Dad, he'll love it!"

Mr. Crime, who acted as the sardonic host-narrator of the first story each month, was added with the third issue. Although most of the stories in *Crime Does Not Pay* were violent, bloody, and sexy, they look mild when compared with some of the postwar competitors.

LUCK WAS WITH ROSATTI'S MOB THAT NIGHT—THE CAR IN FRONT CAREENED INTO A TREE, AND...

From a *Crime Does Not Pay* story
by Fred Guardineer, © 1946,
Magazine House, Inc.

The early artwork was by Creig Flessel, Harry Lucey, Dick Briefer, Norman Maurer, and others. Later artists included George Tuska, Fred Guardineer, Dan Barry, Bob Fujitani, and Fred Kida. Biro drew most of the covers, which provided appropriately tough and nasty packaging.

Gleason had three titles in 1943—*Crime Does Not Pay, Boy*, and *Daredevil*—and a combined circulation of nearly 1,000,000 copies per month, which rose to 1,500,000 in 1945 and to nearly 2,000,000 the following year. Eventually *Crime Does Not Pay* was claiming "More Than 6,000,000 Readers Monthly." Although they were obviously counting on a multiple readership for each copy, the magazine was definitely doing well.

Eventually Gleason branched out, adding *Desperado* (1948–1949) and *Crime and Punishment* (1948–1955). *Crime Does Not Pay* ended with its 147th issue (July 1955). **R.G.**

**CROSBY, PERCY L.** (1891–1964) A creator of oil paintings, water colors, sculpture, poems, fiction, and nonfiction, Crosby made his mark with *Skippy*. The character was a mischievous yet philosophical kid, loosely drawn in a sketchy, effortless manner; at the peak of its popularity the strip ran on the front page of the *New York American*.

Crosby was born in Brooklyn and grew up in Richmond Hill, Long Island. He dropped out of high school to work as an office boy in the art department of the popular *Delineator* magazine, sold an idea to *Life* when he was 16, worked as a newspaper sketch artist at 19, attended Pratt and the Art Students League and began drawing strips for the *New York World*. After doing such titles as *Toddles* and *Beany and the Gang*, he settled in with the McClure Syndicate in 1915 with *The Clancy Kids*. In 1917 he headed overseas to serve in World War I, rising from the rank of second lieutenant to captain and still managing to fill sketchbooks while aboard ship and at the front.

Returning in 1919, he commenced freelancing to *Life* and other markets, drawing *Skippy* in single-page episodes for magazines and moving on to syndication in newspapers. After King Features took over the distribution, the strip quickly spread out into other areas, starting with strip collections.

Books first reprinted the magazine version and then the newspaper strips, and Crosby also wrote his character into illustrated novels. NBC's *Skippy* radio show began in 1931 and Paramount's *Skippy*, starring Jackie Cooper, was also released in 1931. Cooper, then nine, was nominated for an Academy Award, as were the picture, the director, and the scriptwriters. The success of the movie led to an immediate sequel, *Sooky*, that same year, adapted from Crosby's book, *Dear Sooky*.

In a tie-in with the radio show M.C. Gaines published *Skippy's Own Book of Comics* in 1934. The first four-color, single-character comic book of reprints, it was issued as a giveaway with the purchase of Phillip's Tooth Paste.

Crosby drew very rapidly and could usually turn out a year's worth of *Skippy*, daily and Sunday, in less than two months, which gave him time, working out of his 130-acre farm in Virginia, to turn out paintings and watercolors. These were exhibited in New York, London, Paris, and Rome and a few even ended up in the permanent collections of several museums.

He became a crusader as well. He was against communism, Prohibition, gangsters—he allegedly once took out a newspaper ad challenging Al Capone to hand to hand combat—and other evils of the day. He devoted considerable time and money to self-publishing books, pamphlets, and newspaper advertisements, pointing out what was wrong with the nation. There are those who find in these diatribes foreshadowings of Crosby's mental breakdown in the 1940s. At any rate, he gave up *Skippy* in 1945, and his final decade and a half of life was spent in a mental institution.    **B.S.**

**CRUMB, ROBERT** (1932– ) Although he cannot be credited with the earliest contribution to underground comics, no artist is more unanimously acclaimed as their pioneer than Robert Crumb, whose *Zap Comix* (1968) is regarded as the first underground comic book. In fact, Crumb was the first cartoonist of the movement to achieve "mainstream" publication.

Philadelphia-born Crumb never studied art, but got his first job drawing the "Hi-Brow" line of humorous greeting cards for the American Greetings Corp. During his six years with that Cleveland firm, he began contributing to such underground newspapers as *Yarrowstalks* in Philadelphia and the *East Village Other* in New York, and to Harvey Kurtzman's innovative humor magazine *Help!*, which published several of his pieces. Never a member of the counterculture himself, Crumb created a large and diverse body of work during the late 1960s and early 1970s, that to a large extent defined underground comics. He produced a number of solo books produce between 1968 and 1971, including *Zap*, *Big Ass*, *Despair*, *Uneeda*, and *Mr. Natural*, and he contributed to many others.

His subjects—the preoccupations of the rebellious youth of the 1960s—were to become the staples of the genre: sex (Crumb's treatments of it were so explicit they led to a famous censorship trial), drugs, the decay of spiritual values. His pen was merciless. He spared nothing and no one, including himself. Among his most enduring creations were the archetypal "straight" Whiteman; the dumb hippies yearning for spiritual enlightenment (but unwilling to give up their TV), Flakey Foont and Shuman the Human; and the sublimely cynical guru Mr. Natural.

In drawings that spoofed all the cartoonists of the 1930s, Crumb managed to achieve an unmistakable style of his own, which became one of the most pervasive of his period. His collected works, expected to exceed 20 volumes, is now in preparation, a sure sign of his cultural institutionalization.

In the middle 1970s, this eccentric and very private figure dropped from sight almost completely. His Mr. Natural series in the *Village Voice* ended abruptly on November 29, 1976, with the artist appearing in person to say "So long, folks." Crumb thereafter allegedly retired to devote his time to raising chickens in California. The 1980s, however, found him very much back in the field. He launched *Weirdo*, a determinedly underground black and white to which he is a regular contributor, as is his wife Aline Kominsky, who also edits. The year 1987 saw the advent of *Hup*, an infrequent black and white written and drawn entirely by Crumb. (An introductory page claimed that the magazine "wants you to achieve REAL EMOTIONAL MATURITY!") Many of Crumb's best-known characters show up in *Hup*, including Mr. Natural and Crumb himself.    **D.W.**

**CURLEY HARPER**    A Sunday page that began in March 1935 and was devoted almost exclusively to college athletics in its early years, *Curley Harper* detailed the doings of its hero, a clean-cut, dark-haired young man who excelled at every sport imaginable—baseball, football, basketball, crew, hockey, even golf—while attending an idyllic college called Lakespur. (Originally his half-page was titled *Curley Harper at Lakespur*.) The strip ran above *Tim Tyler's Luck* and, like its neighbor, was credited to Lyman Young, but *Curley Harper* was actually the work of Nat Edson, who drew in his own variation of the Alex Raymond style. He'd joined Young the previous year to ghost *Tim Tyler*.

In 1937 Curley abruptly left college, summoned home to help his widowed mother pay off the mortgage, and the title became simply *Curley Harper*. Curley got a job as a reporter on his hometown newspaper and began to lead a life that would have made both the Hardy Boys and Nancy Drew envious, since his newsman duties inevitably involved him with crooks, criminal masterminds, and assorted villains. In 1940 he met a pretty blond named Brynn Brighton who practiced the profession of amateur detective. From then on they were a team, investigating and exploring everything from old dark houses to spy dens. Edson drew the page until its conclusion in 1944.    **R.G.**

# D

**DAN DUNN** The first imitation of *Dick Tracy* and one of the most successful, the strip began on September 25, 1933. *Dan Dunn* was distributed by the Publishers Syndicate and created, if that's the word, by Norman Marsh, who had tried out the character earlier in the year in a one-shot black-and-white comic book titled *Detective Dan*.

Marsh, a man of limited talent but considerable drive, had become a professional cartoonist after having been a Marine, a prizefight promoter, and an agent for the Treasury Department. His Dan Dunn possessed a profile that, except for a squarer chin, was identical to that of Tracy. Dunn's sidekick was a variation on Tracy's Pat Patton, though fatter and dumber and named Irwin Higgs. The plots mixed the hardboiled and the melodramatic.

Also known as Secret Operative 48, Dan didn't limit himself to urban crime. While he might track down a bank robbing gang led by Ma Zinger, he was equally at home battling villainous turbaned masterminds. He also matched wits with Spider Slick, "the brains of a monstrous gang"; Eviloff, a hooded arch-criminal who owned his own island (which he named after himself); and Wu Fang, the quintessential sinister Oriental. The drawing was second-rate at best; yet at the height of its success *Dan Dunn* was appearing in 135 newspapers.

With the help of an assortment of assistants—including Ed Moore and Jack Ryan—Marsh kept the strip going into the Forties. When he heard radio reports of the Japanese attack on Pearl Harbor, he made up his mind to get back into the service. "That afternoon," he said, "I wired the Marine Corps in Washington, and three months later I was on my way to the South Pacific with a commission." Allen Saunders, who took over the writing of the feature, had a different version of Marsh's reason for giving up his detective. "Marsh had had a bitter argument with the syndicate partners," he recalled, "and had stormed out of the office slamming the door so hard he shattered the glass."

Paul Pinson, later a successful advertising artist, was Saunders' first partner. He moved the strip away from its awkward cartoony look and brought it closer to the Caniff school. The next artist brought it all the way there: Alfred Andriola was fresh from a four-year stint of doing *Charlie Chan* when he took over *Dan* in January of 1943.

Andriola would relate his reasons for taking the job many times during his lifetime. "I was approached by Publishers Syndicate to take over their *Dan Dunn* strip," he explained. "I said I was only interested in starting a detective character of my own." Nevertheless, a compromise was reached, and "if I finished their existing contracts with newspapers on *Dunn*, I could concurrently work on my own character." Dan was sent off to War on Sunday, October 3, 1943. The next day *Kerry Drake* began appearing in his slot.                    **R.G.**

**DANNY HALE** King Features began offering funny paper readers a daily dose of American history in 1947. The unlikely professor was Norman Marsh, the hardboiled and somewhat clumsy cartoonist who'd created *Dan Dunn* in the Thirties. Back from the Marines after World War II, Marsh drew *Hunter Keene*, yet another detective strip, for a year. Then he switched to *Danny Hale*, "the story of a clean-cut American boy who was on hand when great American history was being made."

The new daily was initially set in the 1790s, and Danny, clad in buckskins and coonskin cap, was a frontiersman and scout. The early action took place in the wilds of Ohio and had Danny and his grizzled old scout buddy, Bazo, aiding General "Mad Anthony" Wayne in his battles with Tecumseh and the Shawnees. In a few months Danny somehow jumped several years ahead in time to tie up with the Lewis and Clark Expedition, which didn't head westward until 1804.

Despite these and similar lapses, Marsh was evidently enthusiastically dedicated to the feature. While his drawing remained crude, he was obviously taking pains with *Danny Hale*, attempting ambitious battle scenes, awesome landscapes, and authentic detail. There was melodrama aplenty, such as the sequence wherein Danny found his long-lost sister who'd been a prisoner of the Shawnees. But Marsh also loaded the strip with the prosaic, everyday details of frontier life, and the Indians, both hostile and friendly tribes, seemed real. All in all, *Danny Hale* was the best thing Marsh ever did. It was apparently too quiet and educational, though, to be a success and it ended with the Forties. **R.G.**

**DAREDEVIL (I)**  The original Daredevil was born in 1940 in *Silver Streak Comics*, but he graduated to a magazine of his own in 1941 and managed to stay in business for nearly a decade. He fought one of the foulest villains ever to grace the pulpy pages of a comic book, and his costume, while not exactly functional, was among the more striking of the era. And there's something admirable about a hero who went after human fiends, ladykillers, and gigantic Oriental menaces armed only with a boomerang.

He came along in *Silver Streak #6*, slipping into the book without causing much of a stir, but between that issue and the next he became the head man. What transformed Daredevil into a bankable hero were his encounters with "the world's most fantastic criminal"—the Claw. The quintessential sinister Oriental, the Claw loomed into view in the first issue, putting him on the scene several months ahead of the hero. "A monster of miraculous powers who is out to dominate the uni-

*Daredevil*, Charles Biro, © 1941, Comic House Inc.

verse," the Claw had all the vicious attributes of the better known Dr. Fu Manchu, but what gave him an extra edge was the fact that he could grow several stories high at will. Seeing the Claw come swelling up out of a midnight sea right smack in the path of an unsuspecting ocean liner or watching him squeeze a disloyal minion to death in one huge hand while chuckling "Die, swine!" were awesome experiences indeed. In his earliest forays against humanity he was opposed by various business-suited civilians, but he easily upstaged them. What was needed was a hero to match him.

At first glance Daredevil didn't appear to be the man for the job. Drawn by Jack Binder, the initial eight-page exploit was a fairly tame cops and robbers affair, with the big climactic battle occurring in no place more exotic than a lumberyard. The fact that Daredevil was a mute was interesting but not used to any purpose, and about the only striking thing about him was his skintight costume, which was divided from head to toe, bright crimson on the right and midnight blue on the left. The spiked belt around his waist, looking somewhat like a golden dog collar, added just the right unsettling touch. It wasn't practical, but it helped build up the character's sinister image.

Artist-writer Jack Cole was editing the magazine and the next month he audaciously took over the character and treated him as though Daredevil were an old, established hero: His poster-like bright red cover said it all: "DAREDEVIL BATTLES THE CLAW." Cole devoted the first 16 pages of the issue to round one, leading off with a socko splash page that showed the Claw, Daredevil, a sparsely clad young woman about to be burned at the stake, and a half dozen more sinister Asiatics. The story had an equally splashy mix: the war in Europe, Daredevil's lovely girlfriend Tonia, a trip to the Claw's mountain stronghold in Tibet, and a look at the Claw's invasion army heading for America via their own private underground railroad. Cole dropped the notion that the hero was mute and climaxed his yarn with a battle in the streets of Manhattan between the gigantic Claw, the biggest thing to hit town since King Kong, and Daredevil. The Claw's punches toppled skyscrapers while Daredevil gave him a hotfoot with a stick of dynamite.

In the summer of 1941 a second magazine was launched, the first issue titled *Daredevil Battles Hitler*. The pilot issue had all the *Silver Streak* heroes teaming with Daredevil to take turns at giving Hitler and the Nazis trouble. Charles Biro and Bob Wood came in to edit the magazine from #2 on. Biro wrote and drew the hero's adventures and the magazine was called just plain *Daredevil*. In his first story Biro pitted Daredevil against a sexy lady who was actually a reanimated mummy. Unlike many of his do-gooder contemporaries, Daredevil was not above sharing a glass of wine and a warm embrace with a lovely female protagonist of this sort. In subsequent issues he combated a wolf with a human brain, a strangler who committed his crimes in drag, and a nasty group known as the Deadly Dozen.

Initially Biro's Daredevil was akin to Cole's; since he had no superpowers, he had to use his wits and be in tiptop physical shape. As Biro worked with the character over the months Daredevil began to develop a didactic, preachy side, intoning "You look like a smart kid who knows better than to drink." Finally, in issue #13, Daredevil acquired a group he could preach to and feel paternal toward on a fulltime basis, the Little Wise Guys. (He didn't realize that this aggressively likable gang of kids would eventually nudge him right out of his own magazine.)

Daredevil gradually dropped back into an avuncular role as the Wise Guys went on to get involved with street crime, delinquency, and assorted other sociological soap opera topics. The bizarre villains and plots of Daredevil's early years vanished and the more uplifting stories took over. Daredevil finally disappeared for good and all in the winter of 1950. Gradually Biro had farmed out the artwork to Carl Hubbell, Norman Maurer, and Dan Barry, and most of the scriptwriting to Virginia Hubbell. The comic book, still bearing Daredevil's name, continued on until 1956.          **R.G.**

**DAREDEVIL (II)** No relation to the Golden Age Daredevil, this blind, acrobatic superhero with radiation-enhanced hearing and "radar sense" debuted in 1964 as the last of Marvel Comics' first wave of heroes.

Despite writing by Stan Lee and an impressive early lineup of artists (Bill Everett, Joe Orlando, Wally Wood, and John Romita), Daredevil was rarely more than a weak imitation of Spider-Man, grafted to a supporting cast lifted from Iron Man. He got a visual lift in 1966, when Gene Colan began a seven-year tenure as regular penciller, rendering the hero's gymnastic movements with grace and power, and his urban environment with deep-shadowed atmosphere.

Young writer Gerry Conway took over in 1972, followed soon by Steve Gerber; they made Daredevil an interesting character at last, putting him through a tumultuous and convincingly adult love affair with the Black Widow (a Soviet Mati Hari and old Marvel villainess who had defected to become an acrobatic superheroine). After this renaissance, the series fell into less inspired hands, until the arrival of Frank Miller, first as penciller (1979), then also as writer (1981).

Drawing on *film noir* and the early 1970s Batman for inspiration, Miller remade Daredevil into a grim warrior of the night, fighting his way through a horrific, corrupt urban jungle. Abandoning happy endings and easy victories, Miller pitted his hero against an untouchable crime lord called the Kingpin and a conscienceless hired assassin named Elektra (who was also Daredevil's own former lover).

Miller's mastery of action art, dazzling use of storytelling tricks, and frank, often grisly portrayal of violence set the standard for mainstream comic books in the 1980s, and inspired many dark, gritty reworkings of superheroes. He left *Daredevil* in 1983, although he returned in 1986 to write a seven-issue sequence (drawn by David Mazzuchelli) entitled "Born Again," which many consider his finest work.          **G.J.**

**DASH DIXON** Without a doubt the least known science-fiction strip in the history of American comics, *Dash Dixon* came along in the middle 1930s. Although daily in format, it appeared but once a week, in small-town weeklies across the land.

In addition to the major syndicates, there were many small-time outfits in the Thirties and they offered low-cost, and sometimes low quality, material to the smaller newspapers. Among them was the grandly named Lincoln Newspaper Features, Inc., run by a gentleman named H.T. Elmo. A second-rate cartoonist himself, Elmo hired artists and writers who worked cheap. His star employee in the Thirties was young Jack Kirby, who used a variety of names to turn out weekly strips and panels.

The artist on Lincoln's *Dash Dixon* was Larry Antonette, hiding behind the alias Dean Carr. Antonette possessed a highly individual, and slightly goofy, style. After his stint with *Dash* he moved on to comic books, where he drew such heroes as Sub-Zero, Blue Beetle, and the Flame.

The blond Dash shared his adventures with his lady friend, a brunette with the apt name of Dot. These adventures mixed elements of science fiction (disintegrator pistols, metal men) and fantasy (three-headed dragons, giant bats). The copy was breathless stuff, filled with a multitude of exclamation points and question marks: "The Bat-men are attacking!!!!" and "What will happen to Dash?? Will he fall into the vat??"

The strip expired before the decade of the Thirties ended.          **R.G.**

**DAVE'S DELICATESSEN** See GROSS, MILT.

**DAVIS, JACK** (1926– ) A prominent commercial artist whose work has appeared on everything from *Time* covers to postage stamps, Davis first attracted attention drawing for comic books. He was associated with the EC line in the 1950s, working not only for *Mad* but for the war and horror titles as well.

Davis was born in Atlanta, Georgia, and while still in his early teens sent work out to various kid-oriented publications, such as *Tip Top Comics*, that had a page set aside for amateur cartoonists. He contributed to his high school paper and then spent three years in the Navy, where he got a chance to draw for the daily *Navy News*. While attending the University of Georgia on the GI Bill, he contributed to the campus newspaper and also helped to start an off-campus humor magazine, *Bullsheet*—"Not political or anything, but just something with risqué jokes and cartoons." He worked one summer as an inker on Ed Dodd's *Mark Trail* strip.

Heading north, Davis attended the Art Students League, then found a job with the Herald Tribune Syndicate inking Mike Roy's *The Saint* strip. Rejected by several comic book publishers, he finally found work with EC in 1950. He got there just as their new and innovative titles were starting up: *Tales From The Crypt*, *Weird Fantasy*, *Two-Fisted Tales*, and *Vault of Horror*. He contributed to them all, and when *Mad* came along in 1952 Davis became one of the star contributors. He worked out his loose, scratchy style and initially showed himself to be a first-rate caricaturist.

During his early years with EC, working in a more serious manner, Davis drew a great deal of horror stories. One of them, "Foul Play," about a grim baseball game played with various parts of a nasty ball player's body, earned him a mention in Fredric Wertham's *Seduction of the Innocent*. He eventually moved away from that sort of material, concentrating chiefly on humor. He worked with ex-*Mad* editor Harvey Kurtzman on *Trump*, *Humbug*, and *Help!* In addition he illustrated books, record jackets, and even Topps gum cards. He branched out into advertising, movie posters, and covers for *Time*, *TV Guide*, and the like. Davis once explained that many of the art directors who hired him for advertising and illustration jobs had grown up reading *Mad*, which accounted for a lot of his work. He has never given up comic books entirely and can still be found in the pages of *Mad* and some of its few surviving imitators.    **B.S.**

**DAVIS, PHIL** (1906–1964) Another successful imitator of Alex Raymond, Davis drew the *Mandrake the Magician* newspaper strip from its inception in 1934 until his death 30 years later.

He was born in St. Louis and was determined to be an artist from the age of six on. After graduating from high school, Davis got a job as a draftsman in the technical department of the local phone company. He moved on to the art department of the *St. Louis Post-Dispatch* in 1928. After that came various sorts of commercial art until he teamed up with writer Lee Falk, also of St. Louis, to do *Mandrake*. Since both Davis and Falk

were dark-haired gentlemen with mustaches, King Features publicity suggested, at various times, that each was the model for the dapper wizard.

Initially Davis' work on the new adventure strip was, as Coulton Waugh noted in *The Comics*, "very shaky and uneven." Gradually, however, he improved and became very proficient at the illustrative, drybrush style that Alex Raymond was then using on *Flash Gordon* and *Jungle Jim*. Davis' *Mandrake* Sunday pages of the late 1930s were especially impressive, and he did an excellent job of illustrating the flamboyant fantasies Falk was concocting for the tophatted magician and his sidekick Lothar in those years.

During World War II Davis did his bit by serving as an art director at the Curtiss-Wright Aircraft plant in St. Louis. In order to keep up with his strip deadlines, "my wife Martha gave up her career as a fashion artist...to assist me." *Mandrake* never really recovered from Davis' wartime neglect, and in the postwar years, even with both Davis and his wife working on it, the look of the feature steadily deteriorated.

Davis' *Mandrake* has been widely reprinted over the years, here and in Europe. The Sunday pages appeared in *King Comics* from 1936 until 1952, and the dailies showed up in *Magic Comics*, of which Mandrake was the star, from 1939 to 1949. Davis panels also served as illustrations for several *Mandrake* Big Little Books.    **R.G.**

**DEATHLESS DEER** Few strips were ever released amid noisier fanfare and greater expectation than *Deathless Deer*, and few proved to be such monumental disasters so fast. That such a sagacious editor as Capt. Joseph Medill Patterson himself approved its release is clearly a tribute to the formidable nature of his headstrong socialite daughter, Alicia Patterson Guggenheim, who was *Deer*'s creator and scripter.

Deer was a beauteous and extraordinarily cruel Egyptian princess, so despised by her people that an assassin stabbed her to death within mere days of the strip's premiere on November 9, 1942. A quick-thinking priest, though, managed to slip her a life-everlasting potion, and 3,000 years later she awakened when a pair of professors cracked into her sarcophagus. Resurrected in 1940s New York—a much nicer person now, having learned a good lesson—Deer proceeded to embark on an adventure involving gangsters, Middle Eastern brigands, and a lost treasure. The strip's costars were Bruce, "a young engineer," and Deer's faithful pet falcon, Horus, who accompanied her on the immortal journey from the grave.

Alicia Patterson appears to have regarded *Deer* as real literature, regularly citing Bernard Shaw, H. Rider Haggard, and *Sleeping Beauty* as her primary influences. In fact, the strip owed more to *The Mummy* and its various movie sequels. As it happened, the first several weeks of the strip, drawn by the famous fashion illustrator Neysa McMein, were by no means uncharming, and prospective clients were naturally inclined to consider the track record of Patterson's dreadnought Chicago Tribune-New York News Syndicate, which was billing *Deer* as its first major entry since *Terry and the Pirates* eight years earlier. The syndicate even went out on a limb, pitching their record in *Deer's* massive trade promotional campaign, reprinting letters from dubious client-editors, such as: "I have never known you to bring out a dud. I am banking on your judgement."

The full horror set in very fast. Beyond the first several weeks, Alicia Patterson obviously had no story. All intrigues vanished, deathlessness was never brought up again, and the falcon took to uttering comedic asides. The fashionable Neysa McMein, meanwhile, however skillful her covers for the popular slicks, fast began to demonstrate that she had no business drawing comics on deadline. Capt. Patterson unhappily realized all this, and at one point he summoned *Smilin' Jack's* Zack Mosley to repair his daughter's strip. Mosley did what he could, and early *Deer* bears more than a few suggestions of the inimitable Mosley hand.

Within several months it was clear that *Deathless Deer* was a genuine failure, probably one of the worst comic strips ever. The flagships, *New York Daily News* and *Chicago Tribune*, unceremoniously axed it in midstory on June 5, 1943, as did most of the few remaining subscribers. It is believed that another month's worth of already-mailed strips may have run in Mexico and other distant markets.

McMein died in 1949 with her reputation as a portraitist intact. Alicia Patterson, who had founded the Long Island newspaper *Newsday* in 1940, remained as the politically influential publisher of the paper until her death in 1963. None of their authorized biographical materials says a word about *Deathless Deer*.          **J.M.**

**DEBBIE DEAN**   A daily adventure strip written and drawn by Bert Whitman and syndicated by the *New York Post, Debbie Dean* started in January 1944. Debbie, the "heiress to a fabulous fortune," was an attractive brunette who got tired of the debutante life. Deciding she wanted "some honest to goodness excitement," she finagled a job on a large metropolitan newspaper, and before long her aggressive inquisitiveness got her involved with unmasking a sinister cult. After that she exposed a phony countess, uncovered corruption in the boxing game, and tackled some Nazi agents. But eventually the restless deb tired of the newspaper game and switched to a career as a social worker, and the strip,

*Debbie Dean*, Bert Whitman, 1948.

now a bit more sedate, moved closer to the soap opera camp.

Whitman drew in a loose, sketchy style that showed some Caniff influence, but it tightened up during the strip's soap opera phase. *Debbie Dean* ended in 1949. "One big reason that *Debbie Dean* died," Whitman once explained, "was because of cancellations from several large papers. The reason? I used the word 'dope' in a story sequence about narcotics." **R.G.**

**DeBECK, BILLY** (1890–1942)  An exceptional cartoonist, and a good writer as well, DeBeck created some of the most memorable comic strip characters of the 1920s and 1930s, among them Barney Google, Bunky, Snuffy Smith, and the race horse Spark Plug.

Born and raised in Chicago, William Morgan DeBeck studied at that city's Academy of Fine Arts. Among his fellow students were Frank Willard, Ralph B. Fuller, and Frank King. Supposedly DeBeck originally planned to work as a comic artist only until he had earned enough to finance a fine arts career. From 1910 onward he drew for several Midwestern newspapers, including the *Youngstown Telegram*, the *Pittsburgh Gazette-Times*, and the *Chicago Herald*, turning out political cartoons, sports cartoons, and comic strips. According to *Editor & Publisher*, DeBeck was fired from his Pittsburgh job in 1914. Thereafter "he drew his first comic page and took it to New York, but was cold-shouldered everywhere. Unable to make any money at cartooning, he got out a correspondence course at $1 a copy…He sold thousands of the lessons throughout the country before the market was exhausted."

In 1916 he got his job with the *Chicago Herald* and began doing a panel called *Married Life*. The following year William Randolph Hearst tried to hire him away to work for his *Chicago Examiner*. DeBeck declined and stayed put. Shortly after that Hearst bought the *Herald* and merged it with the *Examiner*, and historians of journalism debate as to whether or not Hearst did that

Billy DeBeck, Self Portrait, 1924.

just to get DeBeck to work for him. King Features eventually syndicated *Married Life*, which had changed into a strip. It lasted until 1919, when DeBeck switched to the initially similar *Barney Google*.

DeBeck gradually changed *Barney Google* from a strip about domestic life to a strip about sporting life. He accomplished that by introducing the winning nag Spark Plug in July 1922. From this point he turned away from the simple daily gag format, going instead for comedy continuity. Barney and his horse were national favorites for several years in the 1920s, leading to considerable merchandising and considerable added income to be shared by King Features and DeBeck. In 1927, in the topper to the Sunday page, DeBeck created Bunky, the philosophical, bulb-nosed waif who was Little Orphan Annie and Candide rolled into one. Finally, in 1934, came the shiftless hillbilly Snuffy Smith, who eventually became so popular he nudged the googly-eyed Barney clean out of his strip.

During the 1920s DeBeck also did a panel called *Bughouse Fables*, which was originally credited to Barney Google. Nicely drawn by DeBeck and then Paul Fung, its humor never came near equaling that of the strip.

DeBeck was a first-rate cartoonist and storyteller. He was actually a master of all the things his cartoon school ads had claimed: figure drawing, expression, characterization, layout, staging, perspective. Although he had help over the years—from such assistants as Paul Fung and Fred Lasswell—much of what appeared in the strip was usually his. But his other activities, including his travels around the United States and in Europe and his addiction to golf and bridge, took him away from his drawing board. Deadlines were missed and there were conflicts with editors. (One King Features editor is said to have hauled DeBeck off to a hotel in Atlantic City, taken his pants, and locked him up until a week of new strips was turned out.)

He did very well as a comic strip artist. By the early 1930s his income, as estimated by *Fortune*, was $1,200 a week. In 1935 another magazine mentioned that *Barney Google* "has netted him more than several Rembrandts might bring. He winters in St. Petersburg, Fla., where he has a big house." He also kept a home in Great Neck, Long Island, and a studio apartment on Park Avenue in Manhattan.

DeBeck died of cancer at the age of 52. His characters have continued to appear in the funnies, in comic books, and in television cartoons. But they've never been the same. **R.G.**

**DENNIS THE MENACE**  Hank Ketcham's daily and Sunday comic feature *Dennis the Menace* has presented one of the most consistently popular cartoon views of childhood since it first appeared, on March 12,

1951. Distributed by the Post-Hall Syndicate, it began in 18 newspapers as a daily panel and added a full-length Sunday strip after a year of rapidly increasing circulation established its popularity. *Dennis the Menace* now runs in nearly 800 papers in the United States and in over 100 abroad.

Unlike the prototypes of mischievous children in the comics, the Katzenjammer Kids, Dennis Mitchell is a menace only occasionally and always by accident. Neither malicious nor aggressive, the dynamic five-year-old is a natural force, destructive more to the composure than to the property or person of his staid family and neighbors. His spontaneity and boundless energy exhaust his patient middle-class parents Henry and Alice Mitchell; his tactless remarks and exuberant noisiness exasperate his grumpy neighbor Mr. Wilson; and his flashes of naive insight startle us all; but he is never motivated to mischief. If he shocks others, he is always the last to recognize it. A more open handed or more goodhearted menace would be hard to imagine.

The Mitchell menage created by Ketcham was typical of the cozy nuclear family of the 1950s, when every couple had a five-year-old; and in the nearly four decades since then it has remained essentially unchanged. Indeed, the strip's popularity owes much to its sentimental, somewhat anachronistic spirit. As Steve Jehorek, president of the Field Newspaper Syndicate, observed in 1983, "We all like to remember the good old days, and many other people like it exactly the way Hank's doing it: warm and cuddly and fun."

The widespread popularity of the snub-nosed little dynamo is attested to by the range of exposure the feature enjoys: In addition to the large newspaper circulation attained by its present syndicate, North America, *Dennis the Menace* is regularly collected into book form; it has appeared in its own comic book; was made into a successful live-action television comedy series during the 1960s; and was more recently the basis of an animated television show.

Ketcham continues to draw the daily panels, in an expressive style as simple and wholesome and clean as his characters and setting. The Sunday strips and collateral features are drawn by his assistants Karen Donovan and Ron Ferdinand, and Ketcham has expressed the hope of one day passing the whole enterprise on to them.

Much admired by others in the profession, *Dennis the Menace* has brought Ketcham numerous honors, including the Billy DeBeck Award in 1952 and the Silver T-Square Award in 1978 from the National Cartoonists Society.                                                                 **D.W.**

**DESPERATE DESMOND**   See HERSHFIELD, HARRY.

**DEVLIN, JOHNNY** ( ? –1942) One of several newspaper cartoonists who moved into comic books in the 1930s, Devlin had drawn such strips as *Looy Dot Dope*. From 1937 to 1942 he contributed to magazines like *Feature Funnies*, *Smash Comics*, and *Crack Comics*. During most of that period he was also an assistant to Rube Goldberg.

*Looy Dot Dope* started life in 1926 under the title *The Feitlebaum Family*. It was syndicated by the *New York World* and was the daily version of Milt Gross' *Nize Baby*. Looy was the family's college-age son, alluded to by all and sundry as "dot dope." Gross drew the daily briefly, then Devlin began ghosting it. Eventually the ethnic flavor faded out, and *Looy Dot Dope* became just another gag strip. Subsequently it switched to humorous adventure continuities. A Sunday page was added in the early 1930s. Devlin drew that and a companion feature about a plump mustachioed old gent named Colonel Wowser. Bernard Dibble, who frequently followed in Devlin's footsteps, took over *Looy* in the middle 1930s.

Devlin had gradually modified his style, moving away from the unrestrained Gross approach. As the 1930s progressed he moved closer to reality, also developing a distinctive way of drawing pretty girls. After *Looy Dot Dope* he tried *Honey Dear*, a short-lived humor daily about a newlywed couple. He then began an association with Rube Goldberg, assisting him on *Lala Palooza* and then *Side Show*. Neither of the newspaper features was successful. Devlin helped out, too, when Goldberg drew the Pepsi-Cola Cops ad strips in the early 1940s. And it was through Goldberg that he got into the comic book field.

When comic book titles began to multiply in the mid-1930s, Everett Arnold was one of the those who got into the business. A former printing rep, Arnold formed his own company in 1937 in partnership with the McNaught Syndicate, the Register and Tribune Syndicate, and the Frank J. Markey Syndicate. According to comics historian James Steranko, Arnold "opened an office at 39th and Lexington in New York City. Rube Goldberg, who had just started a new strip called *Lala Palooza*, and his assistant, Johnny Devlin, helped Arnold put together the first few issues of his new comic book, *Feature Funnies*."

In addition to his editorial duties, Devlin drew humor filler pages for *Feature* and the other titles Arnold added to his lineup—*Crack Comics*, *Smash Comics* etc. He did the comic book version of *Lala Palooza*, slimming the lady down considerably for the occasion, and the comic book version of Ed Wheelan's *Big Top*. His own creations included *Molly the Model*, *Dewey Drip*, and *Philpot Veep*, a Sherlock Holmes parody. After Devlin's death, Dibble drew most of these features.                            **R.G.**

**DICKIE DARE** This strip began in 1933 and was Milton Caniff's maiden effort in the adventure strip field—his springboard to *Terry and the Pirates.* Under other artists it went on for over two decades.

Caniff had already been working for the Associated Press in New York City for several months, doing spot illustrations, gag panels, and illustrations for a daily jingle entitled *Puffy the Pig*, when he dreamed up the strip. The AP offered a blanket feature service, with a full page of daily strips available, to subscribing clients. While laboring in the bullpen, Caniff learned there was a blank space coming up in the page of strips. Over a hectic weekend he came up with about a week's samples of *Dickie Dare*.

The AP bought it. The original notion—the first thing that came to mind, according to Caniff—had the 12-year-old Dickie imagining himself into adventures in classic adventure stories. Dickie's imagination first transported him back to medieval England and Sherwood Forest. Decked out in a bowman's outfit, he joined Robin Hood and his Merrie Men. His dog, Wags, tagged along. This first daydream adventure lasted just four weeks, yet Caniff managed to crowd in a good deal of action in the woodlands, castles, and other traditional Robin Hood locales.

Although Caniff's drawing on the strip was bright and attractive, it was done in a cartoony, pen-dominated style that concentrated on illustrating the story rather than simply letting it happen before the reader's eyes. Caniff hadn't yet developed the cinematic approach that would be one of his trademarks. The medium shot and the stationary point of view dominated, and there were few long shots and no closeups.

The second continuity was more ambitious, lasting six weeks. This time Dickie and the faithful Wags joined the marooned Robinson Crusoe, met his man Friday, and tangled with cannibals and mutineers. Caniff stuck with the storybook stuff for the remainder of 1933, moving from Aladdin, to a retelling of the Nativity story, to a move into history with the ill-fated General Custer. Dickie avoided being massacred at the Little Big Horn River by snapping out of his daydream in the nick of time. After that close call he ventured to the court of King Arthur and in April of 1934 began what was to be his final go-round in the past. This time he imagined himself involved with Captain Kidd and the pirates of the Spanish Main.

Meanwhile, in the real world *Dickie Dare* was losing papers, and Caniff figured it must be because his readers already knew the punchlines of the famous stories he was adapting. He decided to create more suspense by making up his own stories and setting them in the present. He introduced a new character, Dan Flynn, "who is as swashbuckling as any of your storybook friends." Flynn is a big, blond pipe-smoking fellow, a vagabond author who travels "around the world writing stories of his adventures." For their initial adventure together, sanctioned by Dickie's parents in hopes it'll make him less of a dreamer, Dan and the boy arrange a passage on a freighter bound for the Mediterranean. The skipper is a shifty-eyed fellow named Turpin, and before too many days at sea our heroes discover he's smuggling guns. Also aboard the ship was a pretty, dark-haired young woman named Kim Sheridan, who explains herself: "I'm supposed to be a sweet little debutante, but the social whirl made me dizzy! So I jumped off the merry-go-round. I like the sea, so I booked a passage on this freighter!" Here, for the first time, are the props and personages for a typical Caniff adventure tale: villains, hardware, and a pretty, intelligent woman. He was also experimenting with his shots, using long shots of the freighter on the stormy sea and closeups of the Sheridan girl.

From the high seas Dickie and company moved to the desert to mix with Arabs and Foreign Legionnaires. The final adventure under Caniff's pen involved Dickie with modern pirates who operate with a sleek submarine and are bossed by a nasty Germanic type named Von Slugg. By the time the sequence began in papers, in mid-September of 1934, Caniff had left the AP and signed with the Chicago Tribune-NY News Syndicate. His last *Dickie Dare* daily, however, didn't appear until December 1st, and by that time *Terry and the Pirates* had been in business for well over a month.

*Dickie Dare*, Coulton Waugh, © 1936, The A.P.

When Caniff departed, he left Dickie in mid-story. Coulton Waugh, who took over, had never met Caniff and had no idea what turn the story was supposed to take. He took a few Caniff originals and some proofs home; he slept little, drank a lot of coffee and continued the submarine story without the apparent missing of a beat. For awhile he stuck fairly close in tone and style to what had gone before. As AP offered him contracts for longer and longer periods, Waugh came to feel the strip was his own. He swung away from the cartoony style, started using brush lines for the figures and trying pen patterns—crosshatching, graded lines and the like—on the backgrounds. He finally arrived at what he felt was a satisfying style.

Waugh identified with the exuberant young Dickie and for most of the run of the feature he let him remain this side of his teens. "Keeping him twelve," he once said, "kept him safe from all the complexities of adolescence." He believed the important thing about Dickie was that he was a "kid trying to adjust to the difficulties of the world with nothing but drive and energy.... I'd been on my own from a very early age, too." While the seafaring under Caniff had been only an interlude in a series of varied adventures, Waugh kept *Dickie Dare* a strip "based on the sea." Almost every story had something to do with the sea, with ships and sailing, and Waugh mingled his own fondness for sailing with ingredients from Robert Louis Stevenson, John Masefield, and other sea adventurers. There were episodes of sailing (Dickie had his own yawl, named the *Dickie Dare*) and episodes of diving for hidden treasure. Nature abounded—there were always plenty of birds and animals, from friendly chimps to vicious lions. Although Waugh's figure work was good, it was at ships and landscapes that he excelled.

In order to try a new strip for the newspaper *PM* and to write a history of comic strips, Waugh quit *Dickie* for a few years in the middle 1940s. The strip stayed in the family, though, since Odin Burvik, who carried it on, was his wife. But *Hank,* his liberal adventure strip about a returning GI, lasted only a few months. After Waugh completed his history, *The Comics,* he took up *Dickie Dare* again. Between Odin and the official return of Waugh, Fran Matera briefly drew the strip.

As the years passed, Waugh ceased to identify as closely with his boy hero. "After a long while I got a little bit fed up with Dickie and his 12-year old reactions." He allowed the lad, with the syndicate's permission, to age a few years and become a naval cadet. *Dickie Dare* ended in October 1957. The last daily showed him sailing away. **R.G.**

**DICK'S ADVENTURES IN DREAMLAND** After a publicity campaign that included special mailings to

schools across the nation, this Sunday page was launched in January 1947 and was devoted, in the words of William Randolph Hearst, to "incorporating American history of a vivid kind in the adventure strips of the comic section." It ran initially as a full page, and there was not a single balloon to be seen, for all of the copy, as in the stately *Prince Valiant*, ran below the illustrations.

Max Trell was the author, a King Features veteran who'd written *Secret Agent X-9* and once ghosted an autobiography for movie moppet Shirley Temple. The artist was Neil O'Keeffe, who, in his middle fifties, had been earning a living as an illustrator since before World War One. He'd illustrated many an issue of the *Adventure* pulp magazine, and later drew the ill-fated *Inspector Wade of Scotland Yard* strip for King. He worked in a loose, drybrush style and turned out a handsome page, though he never gave Hal Foster any serious competition.

The page had been in the works for quite some time before it appeared. Hearst had suggested it to his syndicate in very general terms. "Perhaps a title, *Trained By Fate*, would be general enough," he'd written. "Take Paul Revere and show him as a boy, making as much of his boyhood life as possible, and culminate, of course, with his ride." Editor Ward Greene put forth, cautiously, what he felt was a better way. "There is another way to do it, which is somewhat fantastic, but which I submit for consideration," he wrote back to his boss. "That is to devise a new comic...A 'dream' idea revolving around a boy we might call Dick. Dick, or his equivalent, would go in his dream with Mad Anthony Wayne at the storming of Stony Point or with Decatur at Tripoli." What Greene had done was to swipe the initial premise of Milton Caniff's *Dickie Dare*, right down to the boy's first name. It's possible, too, that he recalled a 1920s Sunday page entitled *Drowsy Dick*, in which the title character dreamed he was taking part in well-known fairy tales.

The Dick of the new Sunday page was an eager, mostly humorless young chap. Being from the future, he tended to lord his knowledge of the past over the historical celebrities he barged in on. Working, for example, as Columbus' cabin boy in the first sequence, he kept saying things like, "We *must* go to Spain! You will get your ships, my captain! I know! I know!" Dick slumbered his way through history, dropping in on the Pilgrims, George Washington, John Paul Jones, and a whole stewpot of others. The page, which kept getting smaller and smaller, ended in the autumn of 1956. **R.G.**

**DICK TRACY** Stripdom's first and always foremost detective thriller, an authentic icon in world literature,

Chester Gould's *Dick Tracy* began its historic run on October 12, 1931 (after a couple of trial Sunday pages that appeared solely in one Detroit newspaper). It was an instant sensation and proceeded to remain in the first rank of comic strip properties for many years. Defined by fast-action storylines, stylized artwork that was both super-realistic and weirdly cartoonish, a roster of villains memorable for their nearly unbearable ghastliness, and an unrelievedly grim Calvinist conscience that informed every move its doomed characters made, *Dick Tracy* has never been less than a fundamental component of 20th-century crime fiction.

Chester Gould (1900–1985) did not invent violence in the comics medium, but he cornered the market early on, and his strip was a dark and perverse and truly vicious thing: There is nothing even close to another citation of a comic strip so full of the batterings, shootings, knifings, drownings, torchings, crushings, gurglings, gaspings, shriekings, pleadings, and bleatings that Gould gleefully flung at his audience as often as he possibly could. Millions of readers loved *Dick Tracy* with all their viscera, and it quickly became the flagship of the Chicago Tribune-New York Daily News syndicate, fast spilling over into other popular media and soon making Gould a wealthy man.

Set in a never-named but often distinctly Midwestern city suggestive of Chicago, in or near which Gould lived for most of his life, the original *Dick Tracy* posited an incorruptible policeman dedicated to the eradication of the period's Prohibition crime gangs, a man much akin to the then-notable Eliot Ness. Plainclothes detective Tracy (Gould's preferred title for his feature had been *Plainclothes Tracy* until overruled by *New York Daily News* boss Capt. Joseph Medill Patterson) had joined the force to avenge the murder of his girl Tess Trueheart's shopkeeper father. In the company of Tess, comic-relief partner Pat Patton, and a street urchin who came to be known as Junior Tracy, he spent much of the 1930s wiping out a collection of torpedoes, goons, and slick gang bosses drawn from the headlines of the period. From its beginning, the strip demonstrated a profound contempt for the lawyers and the politicians with whom the thugs were plainly in collusion; in the history of investigative journalism, *Dick Tracy* is not wholly without its footnote.

Eventually there came a time when the Al Capones were largely done with in the body politic, and, after a gangbusters period of flirting with the day's stock Dillingers, Nelsons and Floyds, *Dick Tracy* went on to invent another form of devil for the righteous to vanquish. These—introduced shortly before World War II and continuing more or less into the late 1950s—were the legendary Grotesques, deformed and disfigured malevolents possessed of visages and tics as repulsive as their rotten criminal souls: the cadaverous Mrs. Pruneface, gaily chatting with her pet rat; the Mole, babbling to himself as he burrowed through the earth; the lock-jawed Laffy, prisoner of his horrible rictus; the Blank, a man who literally had no face; the revoltingly skin-blemished Wormy; the immensely obese Oodles;

*Dick Tracy*, Chester Gould, © 1957, The Chicago Tribune. Reprinted by permission: Tribune Media Services.

the malodorous Flyface, so disgustingly unwashed that insects swarmed around him wherever he walked; Rhodent, a loathsome, rat-like little man who (in one of Gould's many self-referentially parodic moments) asked his blind parents if they thought he was funny-looking.

But *Dick Tracy* was always full of warmth, humor, high spirits, and simple, heartland Christian fellowship as well. The players gathered for toasts on national holidays, celebrated the births of new babes, observed wedding anniversaries, solemnly attended funerals, and regularly fell into prayer when one of their number was somewhere imperiled. Such devotionals also permitted the strip to rejoice in grotesqueries at the other extreme: The smelly hillbilly B.O. Plenty and his hag wife Gravel Gertie were at least as personally awful as any of the criminal miscreants, yet they were honest, good-hearted folk (who, in May 1947, bore a beautiful daughter named Sparkle, an event that drew national press attention and sold millions of dollars worth of Sparkle Plenty dolls). The industrialist Diet Smith—a bilious figure, forever belching and clutching his huge belly as he slurped at the strained babyfood that was his daily sustenance—was the man who gave the strip the famous 2-Way Wrist Radio, the Atom Light, the Teleguard Camera, and the other high-tech scientific astonishments that relentlessly established both Gould and *Dick Tracy* as emblems of a modern world's march toward scientific crimefighting (for which they both won many civic and law enforcement awards). It should not, in truth, be overlooked that Dick Tracy—shovel-chinned, box-nosed, slash-mouthed, often fairly bizarre in his anatomical foreshortenings—has always been one of the Great Grotesques himself.

In the late 1940s, while the strip's manic inventiveness held, the strip was toned down, marked by the promotion of Tracy's longtime, goofy partner Pat Patton to chief of police, the arrival of professional detective Sam Catchem as Patton's successor in the sidekick slot, and Tracy's marriage to, and subsequent domesticity with, the long-patient Tess Trueheart. The 1950s produced some of the mature Chester Gould's best-realized work as the strip became increasingly sleek, with his trademark hard-black spottings becoming design elements unto themselves. The boy Junior Tracy grew into young manhood, and the policewoman Lizz was introduced (in 1955) and came to be a familiar figure in the cadre. Another generation of comic strip entertainment was meanwhile taking its place in the nation's newspapers, themselves only beginning to comprehend the nature of the competitor called television. A few years earlier, Gould's Lolita-like teenage nymphet Popsie and his irredeemably disgusting Flyface might have been among his most popular characters ever, but in 1958

and 1959 they produced loud howls of reader outrage and much unfavorable national publicity. The crowd-pleasing Gould, not unreasonably, felt pressured to move in some other direction. As it happened, the world was at this point entering the space age.

In 1962, the tycoon Diet Smith introduced the Space Coupe, a magnetically-powered interplanetary wonder via which, in short order, the *Dick Tracy* strip relocated itself to the Moon, there to fight space-age crime more or less through the rest of the decade. Gould, to be sure, had always prided himself on keeping his strip on the leading edge of criminology, fanciful or otherwise; in retrospect, perhaps it was no great leap in his mind from the spectroscopes and fingerprint-dusting kits of the 1930s to the wrist radio of the 1940s to, ultimately, the Space Coupe of the 1960s. On the other hand, readership fell off dramatically, and the aging Gould lived to see himself laughed at. The moon proved to be populated with giant escargot and horned humanoids—Junior Tracy married one of the latter, a lass named Moon Maid, daughter of the Governor of the Moon, the both of them as notably Grotesque as the Itchys and Mrs. Prunefaces of a generation earlier. Gould made many public statements earnestly defending his Moon Period as scientifically visionary; apparently he quite truly believed that, as the strip never ceased to declare, the nation that controls magnetism will control the universe. In the wake of the U.S. moon landing of 1969, though, he quickly dropped the space fantasies and returned Dick Tracy to police work on Planet Earth. *Tracy* scholars generally regard the Moon Period as having been, at the very least, lamentable. It is worth noting, meanwhile, that Gould created the wholly earthbound Ugly Christine—arguably his all-time finest villainess—in the very middle of this otherwise baffling digression.

Gould's last years saw him slip discernibly into a querulous dotage fixated upon Supreme Court rulings that he viewed as favoring the hated Criminal Element and shackling the guardians of law and order. Almost precisely as with Al Capp's latter-day *Li'l Abner* Gould's late *Tracy* was perceived as snappish and cranky and, by the standards of the generation, a public embarrassment. When he was retired by his syndicate with the Sunday page of Christmas Day, 1977, it was probably in the strip's better interests. That said, it remains the case that Chester Gould is incontestably a man who will be long honored as a titan in his field and one of the 20th century's great storytellers in any medium.

On December 26, 1977, *Dick Tracy* passed into the collaborative hands of mystery writer Max Allan Collins and longtime Gould assistant Rick Fletcher—and following Fletcher's death in 1983, Dick Locher. Collins, more respectful of the ideal Gould legacy than many another successor might have been, moved quickly to write out some of the unfortunate latter-day baggage. Notably, he killed off Moon Maid and definitively closed out the entire Tracy-in-space tradition, and he has regularly made a point of reprising the strip's grand villains of yore. Meanwhile, cognizant that many of the classic elements have lost their appropriateness in the modern marketplace, he has also endeavored to keep abreast of the times; the Collins Tracy has often run afoul of, for example, computer-literate adversaries. Despite the contemporary syndicate vision that story strips aren't popular, *Dick Tracy* has remained a widely circulated and frequently entertaining property.   **J.M.**

**DINGLEHOOFER UND HIS DOG**   Written and drawn by Harold Knerr as a topper for his *Katzenjammer Kids*, *Dinglehoofer* premiered on May 16, 1926. The gentle and engaging strip featured the adventures of a kindly German-American bachelor and his curious little pup, Adolph. Eight years into the strip, a little orphan boy, "Tadpole" Doogan, literally fell out of a tree and into the life of "Mr. Dinghy." Their subsequent adventures ranged over a wide spectrum, touching subjects as simple as a butterfly and as nefarious as kidnapping.

By 1936, events in far-away Germany affected the American funny pages: It was no longer fashionable for a little dog named "Adolph" to be the focus of amusing antics. The problem was resolved by two of the most poignant episodes ever to grace the pages of the Sunday comics. While on a camping trip, Dinglehoffer and "Taddy" had adopted a tame raccoon. On March 22, 1936, they stopped to visit the farm of one Otto Schmaltz, whose daughter fell in love with Adolph and the raccoon, insisting that they be allowed to stay. Dinglehoofer reluctantly agreed. The following week a basket appeared on Dinglehoofer's doorstep, in which was a foundling dachshund, a most welcome addition to a lonely home. Dinglehoofer, Tad, and "Schnappsy" retired to bed together that night, stars of a strip that would thenceforth be known simply as "Dinglehoofer und His Dog." Adolph was heard from no more.

Knerr continued the charming adventures of the three, and their black housekeeper Lillie, until his death in 1949. The strip survived for several more years in the capable hands of Doc Winner.   **J.L.**

**DINKY DINKERTON, SECRET AGENT 6⅞**   This detective burlesque got going on comics pages in September 1939 and originally carried the byline Jim Wallace. That was a penname of Art Huhta who was also doing a strip called *Mescal Ike* at the time. Within a year or so, however, he was signing his own name.

Dinky was a not too bright master sleuth who wore a Sherlock Holmes deerstalker cap and whose motto was "Crime Don't Pay–Well." He and his partner Sniffy worked on cases ranging from international intrigue to domestic murder, pausing to dabble in horror now and then—as they did in "The Case of Dr. Seek and Mr. Hide." Huhta presented all this in a manner indicating he'd enjoyed such 1930s comedy movies as the Marx Brothers' *Duck Soup* and W.C. Fields' *Million Dollar Legs*. He liked hanging funny signs in the background—All Kinds of Spying Done Cheap, Don't Shoot Till You See The White of the Yegg etc.—pausing to tell old jokes to the readers and generally enjoying himself. He worked in a pleasant cartoon style and was especially good at drawing wicked women, fiendish devices, and crowded lowlife hangouts.

The feature, which also had a Sunday page, was offered by a one-man operation known as the Jones Syndicate. Paul Jones, who'd been a salesman with the McNaught Syndicate, had a difficult time during the World War II years. "One incident that was a blow was when he hit a horse on a highway in Texas," Huhta once recalled, "and demolished the syndicate's one and only car. Traveling by train was out of the question during the war because you could only hit the large towns." Despite these handicaps, *Dinky Dinkerton* held on until 1946.   **R.G.**

**DIRKS, JOHN**   See THE CAPTAIN AND THE KIDS.

**DIRKS, RUDOLPH** (1877–1968)   One of the major figures in the development of newspaper comics, Dirks invented the Katzenjammer Kids in 1897 and drew them for roughly the next half century. Although he remained fond of Hans and Fritz throughout his long lifetime, his major interest was painting.

Born in Germany, Dirks grew up in the Chicago area. His father was a woodcarver and Dirks initially intended to follow that profession: "But one week in the shop settled that. I almost cut off one hand." He decided on cartooning and painting and in the late 1890s followed his older brother Gus, also a cartoonist, to Manhattan: "I decided to go to New York where all the jokes came from." After a variety of jobs, including painting dime novel covers, he went to work for Hearst's *New York Journal*. There, at the age of 20, Dirks created the Katzenjammers. Since comics were brand new, he was among the first to use such devices as the dialogue balloon. In the opinion of historian August Derleth, "the two artists who more than any others were responsible for the popularity of the comics" were Richard Outcault and Dirks.

Dirks took occasional leave from his creation, suspending work during the time he was in the Army

*The Captain and the Kids*, Rudolph Dirks, about 1935.

during the Spanish-American War. He was also on hiatus after his 1912 conflict with William Randolph Hearst, which resulted, after considerable litigation, in Dirks taking his characters but not the Katzenjammer name, over to Pulitzer's *New York World* in 1914. This version of the Hans and Fritz saga eventually came to be called *The Captain and the Kids*. Dirks meantime kept up with his painting and was part of the gritty group known as the Ash Can School.

Dirks' drawing on the Sunday page kept improving. In the 1920s he came to rely increasingly on continuity, mixing fantasy, political satire, and assorted burlesques of popular adventure tales. The feature became more than just a succession of pranks played on Mama, the Captain, and the Inspector by the kids. In 1932 Dirks quit his feature after the general manager of United Features, Monte Bourjaily, refused to give him a raise. Dirks' assistant, Bernard Dibble, started drawing, and signing, *The Captain and the Kids* in May 1932 and stayed with the page until well into 1933. The syndicate then invited Dirks back. He returned to the Sunday and for awhile also drew a newly launched daily version. Dirks soon deserted that to concentrate on the Sunday page and Dibble assumed the daily.

Rudy Dirks had several close friends in the cartooning profession. These included Jimmy Swinnerton and George Herriman, with whom he made trips to the wilds of Arizona, and Cliff Sterrett, a Maine neighbor and frequent golf partner. He took an active part in the drawing and writing of his strip until the late 1940s, and then his son John assumed most of the work. Dirks died in New York City, the place he'd first come to late in the previous century to try his luck. When asked why he never just dumped Hans and Fritz in order to concentrate on his painting, Dirks usually answered, "They gave me my start and I certainly owe them their living."

**R.G.**

**DITKO, STEVE** (1927– ) Although his reputation has slipped some in recent years, Ditko was one of the favorite comic book artists of the 1960s. In that decade he took part in the creation of Captain Atom, Dr. Strange, and the ever popular Spider-Man.

Born in Pennsylvania, Ditko got his art training at the Cartoonists and Illustrators School in New York City. In the early 1950s he started drawing for comic books such as *Strange Suspense Stories, Black Magic*, and *Fantastic Fears*. In 1956 he began doing *Tales of the Mysterious Traveler* for Charlton. By then Ditko had developed a drawing style of his own, based on the work of both Joe Kubert and Jack Kirby. Later in the 1950s he signed on at Marvel to draw for *Amazing Adventures, Journey Into Mystery*, and *Tales of Suspense*. He was still drawing mostly fantasy and horror tales, plus some science fiction.

In 1960 Ditko had produced Captain Atom for Charlton's *Space Adventures*. Then he drew Spider-Man for Marvel, the joint creation of Stan Lee, Kirby and Ditko. Spider-Man initially appeared in *Amazing Fantasy* #15 (September 1962) and graduated to a magazine of his own, *The Amazing Spider-Man*, early the following year. Ditko established the look of all the major characters, including such villains as the Vulture and the Green Goblin, and he drew a very personal version of Manhattan. He also worked on the Hulk and in 1963 added the mystical Dr. Strange to his list of creations.

After a disagreement with Marvel in 1966, Ditko freelanced for a wide range of publishers. For DC he created *Creeper* and *The Hawk and the Dove*. He worked for the Warren black and white horror magazines, and for independent publishers he did the didactic hero he called *Mr. A.* In recent years Ditko returned to the Marvel fold, where he penciled *Rom* and *Indiana Jones*.　**R.G.**

**DIXIE DUGAN**　A showgirl at the start of her career, Dixie had appeared in magazines, novels, a movie, and a Broadway musical before she reached the funny papers. The *Dixie Dugan* strip, written by J.P. McEvoy and drawn by John H. Striebel, began in the late 1920s and lasted until the mid-1960s, by which time Dixie had long since abandoned show business.

McEvoy was a newspaperman, a comic poet, and a playwright, who created Dixie Dugan in a 1928 magazine serial in *Liberty* titled *Show Girl*. It appeared as a hardcover novel that same year and then was made into a movie starring an actress named Alice White. It was a fast-moving, smart-talking sort of story, owing something to the earlier success of Anita Loos' *Gentlemen Prefer Blondes*. McEvoy got his longtime friend Striebel to illustrate the serial. The two had met as teenagers

when both were working on an Indiana newspaper and had collaborated on a Sunday magazine feature called *The Potters*. Striebel was naturally the first choice for artist when the idea of a comic strip was proposed.

The Broadway version of *Show Girl*, produced by Ziegfeld, opened on July 2, 1929. While not an overwhelming success (it closed after 111 performances) the musical brought together an interesting group of talents: Ruby Keeler starred as Dixie, while Eddie Foy Jr. and Jimmy Durante—along with his partners Clayton and Jackson—were also in the cast. Duke Ellington and his orchestra were in the pit and most of the show's music was written by George and Ira Gershwin. The *An American in Paris* ballet was introduced in the show as well as the song *Liza*. As a music historian notes: "In one of the Broadway's most famous incidents, Al Jolson appeared on several nights singing the song from the audience to calm Miss Keeler, who had just become Mrs. Jolson." Other historians have suggested that the self-centered Jolson would've jumped up to sing the song even if his new bride hadn't faltered in her lines.

When the comic strip started late in 1929, it, too, was titled *Show Girl*. Dixie was a dead ringer for show girl-movie actress Louise Brooks, right down to her dark boyish-bobbed hair. A decent kid at heart, the wisecracking Dixie lived with her folks—the plump Ma and the small, balding Pa—and her younger brother. She was good at smart talk, adept at manipulating all sorts and conditions of men, and something of an opportunist. The early continuities dealt with Dixie's life as a chorus girl, her bit parts in movies, her job at a radio station, and other tries at rising in show business. There were all kinds of suitors, too, ranging from nice guys to millionaires to important directors. The strip changed its named to *Dixie Dugan* late in 1929, but many newspapers didn't get around to changing from the old name until into the 1930s.

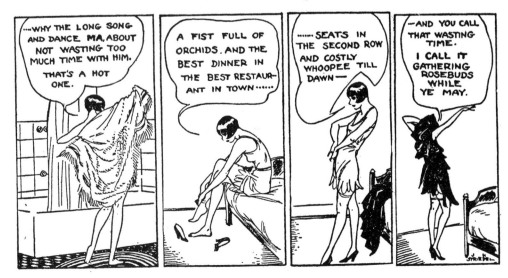

*Dixie Dugan (Showgirl)*, J.H. Striebel, © 1929, The McNaught Syndicate.

As the 1930s progressed, and the Depression worsened, Dixie quit being a show girl and concentrated on earning a living for herself, and sometimes for her parents as well. Usually teamed up with her girlfriend Mickey, who was eventually a blond, she tried such things as running a teashoppe and manufacturing candy. Some of the continuities involved the young women in mystery and intrigue, others in soap opera situations. In the middle 1930s J.P. turned over the writing of the strip to his son Renny, who was a writer and an actor.

A Sunday page was added in the 1930s, concentrating on gags and offering frequent Dixie Dugan paper dolls. For several years Dixie shared the page with her niece Imogene, a little girl who favored a boyish-bob long after Dixie had abandoned it and who was a realistic version of Ernie Bushmiller's Nancy.

Striebel had considerable help with the drawing over the years. Creig Flessel and Al Bare assisted and/or ghosted, as did Edmond Good. The feature ended in the middle 1960s. *Dixie Dugan* did moderately well in comic books, too, being reprinted in *Feature Funnies*, *Big Shot Comics*, and several one-shots of her own.          **R.G.**

**DOC SAVAGE**  He initially branched out into comic books early in 1940. Doc Savage had by then been a highly successful pulp magazine hero for several years and was one of the inspirations for Superman.

Street & Smith, the venerable publishing firm, began planning Doc Savage late in 1932, when they wanted a follow-up to their hit *Shadow* pulp. The basic format they came up with—that of a strong, brilliant hero and his coterie of gifted and whimsical sidekicks—was at least as old as Frank Merriwell, a character S&S had first introduced in the last century. But the new character would have some modern trappings, plus a touch of science fiction. And he would resemble the current movie idol Clark Gable.

When artist Walter Baumhofer was called in to paint the cover for the first issue of *Doc Savage Magazine*, he was handed a description of the character: "A Man of Bronze—known as Doc, who looks very much like Clark Gable. He is so well built that the impression is not of size but of power." Baumhofer ignored that and made Doc look like the model he was using at the moment. In the stories, of course, Doc's full name was Clark Savage.

Back then Doc Savage didn't have his now familiar blond stormtrooper image, which was bestowed decades later by way of the covers gracing the Bantam reprints of the old pulp novels. In his magazine days Doc was simply a clean-cut fellow, handsome in what was then called a "collar ad" way. He didn't dress in

any sort of costume, and sometimes he was even seen in a business suit.

All the pulp magazine novels were credited to the house pen name of Kenneth Robeson, but most of them were written by Lester Dent. When he took on the job in 1933, Dent was in his early thirties and already a prolific writer of pulp fiction. Asked once by a reporter to explain his hero, Dent replied, "He has the clue-following ability of Sherlock Holmes, the muscular tree-swinging ability of Tarzan, the scientific sleuthing of Craig Kennedy and the morals of Jesus Christ."

The first issue of *Doc Savage Magazine* was dated March 1933 and sold for 10 cents. The maiden Doc Savage novel was titled "The Man of Bronze." The novel also introduced Doc's associates, five variously gifted adventurers: Colonel John Renwick (known as Renny), William Harper Littlejohn, Long Tom Roberts, Theodore Marley Brooks (usually called Ham), and Andrew Blodgett Mayfair, aka Monk. Ham was a suave fellow, a lawyer who carried a sword cane, while Monk resembled a gorilla and was a chemical wizard. Ham and Monk squabbled throughout the series and were the most popular of the sidekicks.

Quite obviously Jerry Siegel and Joe Shuster were fans of Doc. Dedicated pulp readers, they were considerably influenced by Dent's character in creating their own superhero. It isn't a coincidence that Superman's name is Clark Kent or that he was originally billed as the Man of Steel.

Doc Savage was first adapted to comic books early in 1940. Apparently nobody at Street & Smith thought he had to be beefed up or decked out in a fancy costume for the new medium. He made his debut, as a backup feature, in the first issue of *Shadow Comics* (March 1940), looking like a typical soldier of fortune in shirt, riding breeches, and boots. The story was adapted from a script used on the short-lived radio show of 1934. Since this initial adventure ran but six pages, there wasn't enough room for Doc's whole crew and he had to make do with only Monk. The stiff, stodgy artwork was by Maurice Gutwirth.

There were two more stories in *Shadow Comics* and then, according to a full-page ad, "the demand for Doc Savage has caused us to issue *his own magazine.*" Doc shared his new magazine with an assortment of other characters, most of them brought over from the pages of the pulps—Cap Fury, the Whisperer, Norgil the Magician, among others. In his own stories Doc worked with a diminished crew. Ham was added early on, and he and Monk were the only two of Doc's "five pals" who were usually on hand.

In the summer of 1941, in an effort to make him more like the other superheroes, Doc Savage was overhauled. In a story drawn by Jack Binder and written by Carl

Formes, Doc's plane crashed in Tibet and he was taken in by a mystical hermit, who informed Doc that he was the chosen one and must put on the Sacred Hood that has the Sacred Ruby mounted on it. As long as Doc wore this he would be known as "The Invincible." Donning the hood, the barechested Doc went forth to fight evil.

*Doc Savage Comics* began as a quarterly and remained one for its first 10 issues. With the January 1943 number it became a monthly and after the 20th (October 1943) it went out of business. Doc returned to *Shadow Comics* with the January 1944 issue, and became a second banana again. This move put an end to his bid for superhero status, and from then on, with few exceptions, he worked in civilian clothes. Usually he wore a sincere business suit, and no one ever again mentioned his magical headgear. Assisted by Monk and Ham, Doc worked as a sort of scientific detective.

The artist who first drew the Doc stories after the drop in status was Al Bare. A succession of lesser artists followed. Doc's looks improved in the postwar years, when Bob Powell and the gang in his shop took over most of the *Shadow Comics* artwork, while the scripts were by Bruce Elliott, a novelist, amateur magician, and bon vivant. Doc ended this phase of his comic book career in the summer of 1949, when Street & Smith canceled all their comic books and all their pulp fiction magazines except *Astounding*.

Doc Savage returned to comic books in a 1966 one-shot published by Gold Key. Marvel tried a color series that began in 1972 and lasted eight issues and a black and white series that began in 1975 and also lasted eight issues. DC took over the character in 1987, first with a miniseries and then as a regularly issued title. **R.G.**

**DOC STRANGE** The first Dr. Strange in comic books—a superhero scientist who used his abilities to fight crime—hung up his shingle early in 1940. During his early months he was known as Dr. Strange and then, probably inspired by Doc Savage, he became Doc Strange. Created by the prolific editor-writer Richard Hughes and drawn initially by Alexander Kostuk, Doc was the star of *Thrilling Comics*.

A scientist with an impressive head of dark, wavy hair, Doc was the inventor of Alosun, "a distillate of sun-atoms endowing its possessor with limitless power." He used Alosun to "gain super-human strength and use it to defeat crime." Doc did his early crimebusting dressed in a business suit, but in *Thrilling* #7 (August 1940) he concocted a new, improved Alosun that gave him even greater powers, including the ability "to soar through the air as if winged," and took to wearing a new outfit. Though nothing to make Superman or Batman envious—boots, blue riding breeches and a red T-shirt—it was an improvement over the suits

and ties. The artist during this transition period was George Mandel.

In 1942 Doc added a boy companion with the unflashy name of Mike. During the World War II years the team concentrated on combating fascist menaces, "destroyers that threaten the entire nation!" Doc Strange was last seen in 1948. **R.G.**

**DR. FATE** Writer Gardner Fox and artist Howard Sherman introduced this intriguing and visually striking mystic hero in DC Comics' *More Fun* in 1940. Although short-lived in his first run (being canceled in late 1943), he has remained in the minds of comic book creators and continues to pop up in varied and interesting forms to the present.

Fox and Sherman's various successors as writer and artist seemed unable to decide what to do with the character. Conflicting origin stories were offered, and his powers and costume changed often. Generally, he had the power to transform matter to energy and vice versa; he derived his powers from an ancient Egyptian named Nabu the Wise (who was also an extraterrestrial); he lived in a stone tower in Salem, Massachusetts, without windows or doors (which he entered and exited simply by passing through the walls); he was secretly archaeologist Kent Nelson; and he wore a gold helmet that covered his entire face and head. He was also a member of DC's *Justice Society of America*.

In 1965, when DC was having luck with revamped Golden Age heroes, Fox and artist Murphy Anderson brought the hero back, and codified his nature, in two issues of *Showcase*. After years of occasional guest appearances, Fate earned a critically-acclaimed backup series in *Flash* in 1982, at the hands of artist-plotter Keith Giffen and writer Marty Pasko. Fate thereafter appeared in several high-profile DC series, including *Crisis on Infinite Earths* (1985) and the new *Justice League* (1986), of which he was a founding member. His early adventures were meanwhile fleshed out in writer Roy Thomas' series set in the 1940s, *All-Star Squadron*. In 1986 he received his own miniseries, another Keith Giffen creation, in which Kent Nelson was killed and Nabu (now cast as a rather sinister figure) fused the souls of two other people to create a new Dr. Fate. An ongoing series followed in 1989; this time the mystic hero took a *female* body, thus generating a bit more attention from the fans. **G.J.**

**DR. MID-NITE** A handicapped comic book hero, the blind Dr. Mid-Nite debuted in *All-American Comics* #25 (April 1941). The character, who had some similarities to the pulp magazine mystery man the Black Bat, was the creation of writer Charles Reizenstein and artist Stan Asch. In addition to his duties in *All-American*, the doctor was also a member of the Justice Society of America and as such could be found in *All Star Comics* from #8 (December 1941–January 1942) onward.

In everyday life he was Charles McNider, M.D. Blinded when mobsters tried to kill one of his patients, Dr. McNider eventually found that he could see in the dark—but not in the light. By fashioning "a strange pair of goggles" with infrared lenses, he was also able to see in the daylight. Rather than resume his medical career, however, McNider donned "this old masquerade costume" of black tights, red tunic, and green cape and cowl to become Dr. Mid-Nite, "avenging figure of darkness." He invented a blackout bomb, which he used to put opponents at a disadvantage. He preferred to work by night, and he often traveled with a pet owl named Hooty.

As McNider he pretended he was still sightless, so that no one would suspect he was actually a nocturnal crimebuster. He practiced in *All-American* until the autumn of 1948 and could be found in *All Star* until it shut down with its 57th issue early in 1951. He returned in the early 1960s when the JSA began to team up now and then with the newer Justice League of America and also turned up occasionally in the 1970s and 1980s. **R.G.**

**DR. OCCULT** Jerry Siegel and Joe Shuster's *Dr. Occult* was the first horror-oriented feature in comic books. Beginning in *New Fun* #6 (October 1935), it was signed with the pen names Legar and Reuths, not quite anagrams of Siegel and Shuster.

Dr. Occult was a ghost detective by trade. Bearing a strong facial resemblance to Siegel and Shuster's Superman who had yet to make his debut, he dressed in the trench coat and snapbrim hat style much favored by movie detectives of the period. His steady girl was named, aptly enough, Rose Psychic. Inspired by the science fiction and weird tale pulps they'd grown up on, Siegel and Shuster filled the feature with some pretty strange stuff.

The doctor's first big case pitted him against the Vampire Master, who had invented something called the Thought Materializer, a complex gadget that could create "monsters of the mind, creatures of the imagination." His career was cut short, however, when one of his creations stabbed him in the heart. In subsequent investigations, each of which stretched through several issues in two- and four-page installments, Occult encountered werewolves, snake gods, spectral killers, and zombies.

One *Dr. Occult* continuity is of particular interest to students of the superhero. The sequence—which comics historian Charles Wooley called "the first true superhero origin"—appeared in *More Fun*, the regular- sized successor to the *New Fun* tabloid, in several late 1936

issues; another installment popped up in *Funny Pages*, a magazine founded by some DC deserters. The story showed Occult journeying to mystic realms, hobnobbing with various magical entities, and then tackling a super villain in an Egyptian tomb to gain possession of "a certain magic belt of miraculous powers." In the second chapter Dr. O was given a magic sword and a costume that included a cape. Flying through misty, vaguely mystical landscapes, he looks a good deal like the then-unpublished Superman. He wasn't a Superman clone, however. (He was already flying before he got the trick suit, and donning it didn't seem to alter him much.) It is obvious, however, that the impatient Siegel and Shuster were fooling around with some elements of their unsold superhero.

In subsequent issues Dr. Occult appeared once again in civilian garb. He retired after *More Fun* #33 (July 1938). But in 1989 DC revived him briefly. **R.G.**

**DR. STRANGE** Created by artist-plotter Steve Ditko and editor-writer Stan Lee as a minor back-up feature for Marvel Comics' *Strange Tales* in 1963, this "Master of the Mystic Arts" won a small but intensely loyal following that has kept him alive to the present.

Arrogant, selfish Stephen Strange was a master surgeon until a car accident caused nerve damage that cost him his amazing dexterity. Down and out, drunk and alone in the Himalayas, he sought out the mystical Ancient One, whom he hoped would cure him; as the Ancient One's pupil, he learned not only the secrets of white magic but also the value of unselfishness. He went on to use his spell-casting powers to defend our universe from such *outré* invaders as Nightmare (who strikes at mortals through their dreams), Baron Mordo (an embittered ex-pupil of the Ancient One), and the dread Dormammu, a mystic tyrant seeking to enslave all the "dimensions" of the cosmos. A freedom-fighter from Dormammu's world, the beautiful Clea, soon became Strange's helper and lover.

The stories were often thin, but they drew an impressive richness and sensual appeal from Ditko's imaginative graphics, conjuring up mind-bending fantasy realms with a blend of highly plastic cartooning, exotic visual quotes, baroque detail, and vaguely psychedelic surrealism. Lee played off these visions with a bizarre verbal whimsy that found the Doctor invoking "the all-seeing eye of Agamotto," "the hoary hosts of Hoggoth," and countless other eldritch forces. Although *Dr. Strange* was never a big hit with superhero readers, it dazzled Marvel's growing number of collegiate and "hippie" readers, including many underground cartoonists, who were convinced that Ditko and Lee were secretly sharing drug-induced hallucinations with them (a notion that no doubt would have shocked the gentlemen themselves).

*Dr. Strange* became a title in its own right in 1968, was canceled in 1970, returned in 1974 and ran well into the 1980s; the Doctor was also a member of the oddball superhero team called *The Defenders* during the 1970s, and pops up frequently in Marvel anthology series and special issues to the present. But by 1966 both Ditko and Lee had left the series, and it has never recaptured its early sense of wonder. Nonetheless, the character has attracted many of the most imaginative artists in comics and inspired them to their finest work, among them Bill Everett, Marie Severin, Gene Colan, Barry Smith, Frank Brunner, Marshall Rogers, Paul Smith, and Mike Mignola. Roy Thomas, Steve Englehart, and Roger Stern have been his principal writers, generally striving for more serious "cosmic" effects than Lee ever did.

**G.J.**

**DODD, ED** (1902– ) The creator of the outdoor adventure strip *Mark Trail* was himself an outdoorsman; that experience provided background material for his popular feature, which began in 1946.

Edward Benton Dodd was born in La Fayette, Georgia. During high school and for several years after, Dodd spent summers at the Pennsylvania camp of Dan Beard, a founder of the Boy Scouts and a well-known wildlife artist and outdoor writer. Dodd once said, "Beard taught me illustration as well as hunting and fishing lore." He also spent a year at Georgia Tech, just long enough to decide not to be an architect. Pursuing his own love of the outdoors, Dodd as a young man ran a dude ranch in Wyoming and was later a guide in Yellowstone Park. He camped and fished throughout the United States.

Eventually he returned to Georgia and took a job as a gym teacher in a Gainesville high school. He dabbled in art, first drawing pictures for calendars, and then experimenting with cartooning, meeting with increasing success. From the middle 1930s to the middle 1940s he drew a newspaper panel titled *Back Home Again*. Filled with nostalgic, homespun humor, it was United Features' answer to J.R. Williams' *Out Our Way*.

Growing restless, Dodd came to feel he needed more training and better contacts. He headed for New York in the early 1940s to study at the Art Students League, but none of his early attempts at comic strips sold. He grew discouraged until he decided to draw what he knew best—the outdoors. The hero of the fledgling strip was initially named Jim Tree, then Mark Trailer and finally Mark Trail.

Dodd took *Trail* to the Hall Syndicate, which bought it and introduced the strip in 1946. It was drawn in Dodd's simple, direct style and showed off his knowl-edge of nature and a wide variety of pen techniques. Although Dodd still shares the credit for *Mark Trail*, the strip is now drawn by his long-time assistant Jack Elrod. Dodd retired in the late 1970s. **W.D.**

**DOLL MAN** One of the very earliest of miniature superheroes, Doll Man stood about eight inches high in his stocking feet. He was the star of *Feature Comics* from #27 (December 1939) through #139 (October 1949) and also appeared in a title of his own from 1941 until late in 1953. Will Eisner created the diminutive crimefighter and wrote the first scripts under the pen name William Erwin Maxwell; Lou Fine was the original artist.

In everyday life Doll Man was a normal-sized young scientist named Darrel Dane. Possibly influenced by the 1936 MGM horror movie *The Devil Doll*, Dane invented a liquid that "will SHRINK a human being to the size of a doll!" For good measure, he also worked out a way to return to his true size. At the end of his initial adventure, and before he'd even devised his tiny red and blue costume, Doll Man pledged himself "to fight crime and evil relentlessly!!" In real life a law enforcement agent or private investigator who was less than a foot high would probably not thrive or even last very long. Someone would more than likely step on him, he might slip through a crack or get flushed down a drain. In comic books, however, Doll Man had a brilliant career that stretched across nearly a decade and a half.

The other regular characters were gray-haired Professor Roberts, a fellow scientist, and his lovely daughter Martha. Martha Roberts was Dane's girlfriend and she admired him greatly. She had another virtue: She wasn't bothered by his shrinking or his doing such things as riding a rat bareback, flying around in a model airplane, or hiding in a crook's pocket.

After Lou Fine departed, such capable artists as Reed Crandall, John Celardo, and John Spranger drew Doll Man's pint-sized escapades. On covers he was depicted by, among others, Gill Fox and Al Bryant. **R.G.**

**DONALD DUCK** A fowl whose long list of character flaws won him almost instant popularity, Donald Duck made his screen debut and his comic strip debut in 1934. From a bit part in a Walt Disney *Silly Symphony* animated cartoon, he quickly climbed to stardom. In addition to movies and newspaper strips, Donald Duck was a major hit in comic books from the middle 1930s onward. Undoubtedly the most gifted artist ever to draw him was Carl Barks.

Donald was first seen in *The Wise Little Hen*, which was released on June 9, 1934. In that animated short he played a lazy loafer and, since he was residing on a houseboat, wore a sailor suit. The most appealing and intriguing thing about him was his voice, supplied by

Clarence Nash. It was said that Walt Disney himself had heard Nash on a local radio station reciting "Mary Had A Little Lamb" and, fascinated by the voice, ordered him to be hired. "Donald's screen personality was largely the creation of animator Dick Lundy," says Leonard Maltin in *Of Mice and Magic*. Lundy used Donald in *The Orphans' Benefit* (released August 11, 1934), wherein the increasingly thwarted duck tries to recite the little lamb poem. It was Lundy who made him a vain show-off with an extremely short temper, a boastful fellow quick to anger.

After appearing in increasingly larger bit parts in Mickey Mouse shorts, Donald costarred in *Donald and Pluto* in 1936 and then, in January of 1937, was the solo star of *Don Donald*. Apparently tired of the sweetness and light and the singing elves of many of the animated cartoons of the period, the public embraced the meanminded, blustering duck.

The *Silly Symphony* Sunday page ran as a topper to *Mickey Mouse*. Donald Duck was first seen there on September 16, 1934, in an adaptation of *The Wise Little Hen*. He was lazy and a mite cunning, and not at all sputtering or short-fused. But he reformed at the end of the continuity in December, observing that "I'm thinkin' that to dodge a job is more work than to do it!" When he returned to the page on August 30, 1936, he was closer to his present self. Donald remained a squatter there until late in 1937. Then, early in 1938, a daily *Donald Duck* strip began, also syndicated by King Features, and by the end of 1939 there was also a regular *Donald Duck* Sunday. Both were written by Bob Karp and drawn by Al Taliaferro. An excellent artist with a lively version of the Disney house style, Taliaferro had been with the studio since 1931. After inking Floyd Gottfredson's *Mickey Mouse*, he graduated to the *Silly Symphonies* Sunday. He was, therefore, the first artist to draw Donald in the funny papers and he remained with the character until his death in 1969.

There was rarely any continuity in the strip, since Karp, and apparently the syndicate, favored a joke-a-day format. Donald's three rascally nephews were regulars, as was his sweetheart Daisy and his lumbering pet St. Bernard, originally named Bolivar. The *Donald Duck* strip still runs, though in a much diminished list of papers. The current creative team consists of Bob Foster and Frank Smith.

Donald also hit the newsstands in 1935 as one of the characters in *Mickey Mouse Magazine*. After a few issues a joke column titled *Wise Quacks* was added and Donald was listed as its editor. In 1940 *Walt Disney's Comics and Stories* replaced the earlier title and *Donald Duck*, in the form of reprints of the Taliaferro strips, was part of the lineup. Carl Barks had gone to work for the Disney studios in the middle 1930s, chiefly as a story man. In

1942 he drew a one-shot original comic book titled *Donald Duck Finds Pirate Gold*. Some of the pages were done by an artist named Jack Hannah and Bob Karp provided the script. As a result of that job, Barks was hired to do a monthly 10-page original Donald story for WDC&S. The first one appeared in #31 (April 1943).

Barks had found his calling at last. He proceeded to turn out a long series of funny, fast-moving duck tales that mixed satire, suspense, fantasy, mystery, and a whole lot more. He turned Donald into one of the great mock heroes, made Huey, Dewey, and Louie into likable and resourceful kids, and he also created Uncle Scrooge. Soon there were full-length comic books about Donald, about Uncle Scrooge and the rest. Barks retired several years ago, but all his work is being reprinted in various forms today. Neither he nor Taliaferro ever got a credit during their active years with *Donald Duck*.

**R.G.**

**DONDI** Yet another comic strip about an orphan, it came along some decades after *Little Orphan Annie*, *Little Annie Rooney*, *Frankie Doodle*, and similar funny paper waif features. The creation of Gus Edson, who wrote it, and Irwin Hasen, who drew it, *Dondi* was syndicated by the Chicago Tribune-New York News outfit. It debuted on September 25, 1955, and lasted for over 30 years.

Edson, a cartoonist as well as a writer, had been producing *The Gumps* since the mid 1930s. That strip was faltering badly by the time he teamed up with Hasen. A comic book veteran who had drawn such costumed heroes as the Green Lantern, the Fox, and Wildcat, Hasen drew in a cinematic style that was strongly influenced by Milton Caniff. Fellow members of the National Cartoonists Society, Edson and Hasen supposedly dreamed up the idea for a strip about a war orphan adopted by a GI while on an NCS tour of Germany. *Dondi* also bore some resemblance to a short-lived strip called *Spunkie*, done in the early 1940s by Edson's onetime assistant Loy Byrnes.

An active and aggressively likable child, all curiosity and enthusiasm, Dondi adjusted very well to the United States, making friends with young and old and mastering the language with only a few trademark foreignisms (such as his perennial exclamation "Goshes!") to remind us of his origin. In the 1960s the strip concentrated increasingly on Dondi, his pals Web and the longhaired Baldy, and his dog Queenie. The adventures of their Explorers Club brought them into contact with a wide range of adults and provided material for a variety of narratives, many with a distinct soap opera tinge.

Edson and Hasen worked together, with some help on backgrounds from Tex Blaisdell, until Edson's death in 1966. Hasen took sole credit for *Dondi* from then on, although most of the scripting and some of the penciling was done by Bob Oksner. Hasen received the NCS award for best story strip in 1961 and 1962. During the 1960s and 1970s the strip ran in over 100 newspapers. With the general decline of the continuity strip, *Dondi* began losing its audience by the end of the 1970s. Its syndicate, by then named Tribune Media Services, canceled it in June 1986. **D.W.**

**DON DIXON** Brooklyn's answer to *Flash Gordon*, the *Don Dixon* Sunday page began on October 20, 1935, with Bob Moore as writer and Carl Pfeufer as artist. The strip was cooked up in the editorial offices of the *Brooklyn Daily Eagle* and distributed by their Watkins Syndicate to a slim list of newspapers that included the *San Francisco Chronicle* and the *Philadelphia Record*.

Although the page fairly soon became a *Flash Gordon* impersonation, Pfeufer made little initial attempt to imitate Alex Raymond's drybrush style, and during the early months Don was an adolescent boy. The continuity began with Don, a teenage buddy, and his mentor Dr. Lugoff—who in spite of his Russian-sounding name was fond of such Germanic exclamations as "Ach!"—arriving in Pharia, the Hidden Empire. There Don became involved in a good deal of political intrigue, as well as sword-and-sorcery adventure. It was in Pharia that Don met the love of his life, the blond Princess Wanda. Before too many months had passed both he and the princess grew into adults. Like Flash, Don was handsome and fair.

Relatively early on Don and the princess strayed from Pharia and for the next several years strived, while undergoing many a picaresque adventure, to get Wanda home again. Among the distractions were the Destroyer, who hung out in the Himalayas with a nasty bunch called the Seven Assassins hatching plans to use his high-tech superweapons to wipe out "this stupid civilization which no longer serves any purpose." Further along Wanda was kidnapped by another mad scientist, Strunski by name, and taken to his stronghold, Robot Island. Don rescued her from Strunski and his giant mechanical men. Don himself was rescued now and then by his father, a gifted superscientist who accompanied his son on some of his adventures.

Moore's writing was not on an especially high level, and both the situations and the dialogue were marked by the clichés of melodrama. Pfeufer, though, was an excellent artist and, while not in Raymond's league, was among the better adventure strip artists of the period.

The page's topper, during most of its lifetime, was *Tad of the Tanbark*. The strip began as a circus life adventure with a teenage boy as hero, but Tad eventually left the tanbark (which is the stuff they spread around in circus

rings) and was off enjoying wilderness encounters in Jungle Jim settings.

*Don Dixon* ended in the summer of 1941, sailing away in the final panel with Princess Wanda, after an encounter with a sorceress. He remarks, "I'm sick of enchanted ladies! It will be good to get back where everything is normal!" **R.G.**

**DON WINSLOW** A hero with a purpose, Don Winslow began life in 1934 in a daily newspaper strip. He soon expanded operations, showing up in a Sunday page, novels, movie serials, a radio show, Big Little Books, and assorted comic books. He'd been created chiefly to interest the youth of America in the United States Navy and to inspire a sufficient number of them to enlist. There is no record as to whether the strip succeeded in that purpose, but the passage of the Selective Service Act in 1940 and the entry of the United States into World War II in 1941 took care of inspiring sufficient young men into the Navy. By that time sufficient people were following Don's adventures just for their entertainment value.

The *Don Winslow of the Navy* strip began in March 1934, from the start mixing entertainment with propaganda. Winslow's creator was Frank V. Martinek, a former Navy Intelligence officer and newspaper reporter, who was a lieutenant commander in the Naval Reserve. He decided to invent Don Winslow when he heard the Navy was having a difficult time recruiting sailors in the Midwest, figuring an adventure strip about a Navy man would give landlocked youths a taste of the sea and, hopefully, push some of them into signing up.

Martinek served as the mastermind of the strip, with two artists, Leon Beroth and Carl Hammond, doing most of the work. As Martinek explained the working setup, he was the producer, Beroth the art director, and Hammond the layout and research man. For some reason Hammond never got a credit, although by the mid 1930s he was writing as well as laying out the feature.

The initial episodes brought not only salt water but also insidious villainy to the readers as Don tangled with the Scorpion, "leader of an international gang of plotters." Martinek was preoccupied with preparedness and with the infiltration of American by foreign agents. Almost all the villains from the 1930s on into the early 1940s were spies and saboteurs of one sort or other. The Scorpion, a sinister, baldheaded fellow, showed up most often, but Winslow was also pitted against the Crocodile, who flew through the air in an immense contraption called the Sky City and killed U.S. sailors in the South Seas by dropping hollow ice cubes full of poison gas on them; Dr. Q, one of the many 1930s villains bent on destroying the Panama Canal; and Dr.

Centaur, who'd invented "the weirdest weapon in the world." There were also the Duchess, Owl-eyes, Dr. Thor, and the Dwarf.

Lt. Commander Winslow was with Naval Intelligence, as Martinek had been during World War I, which gave him considerable mobility; if a continuity started to sag, an order from Washington could rush him into an entirely new adventure. Don was accompanied, almost always, by Lt. Red Pennington, a huge, pudgy fellow almost twice the side of his superior. There was also romance in Don Winslow's life. While he dallied now and then with the various lady spies who frequented the feature, his real love was Mercedes Colby; the daughter of one admiral and the niece of another, she first showed up in the *Don Winslow* panels in 1935 and by 1941 was in the Navy herself as a nurse.

In 1935 a Sunday *Don Winslow* page was added, as well as a companion topper given over to the adventures of *Bos'n Hal, Sea Scout*. Hal, an extremely clean-cut lad, specialized in going on treasure hunts to remote spots.

By the late 1930s Hammond and Beroth took on extra help, and among the new assistants was Ed Moore, who'd been assisting on *Dan Dunn*. Moore joined them in their small offices in Chicago, which he recalled as being "about twenty feet deep and a couple of windows wide." He did backgrounds and lettering on the *Winslow* strip, and penciled the entire *Bos'n Hal* page. Shortly before the start of WW II Moore got a Sunday page of his own and most of the work on *Don Winslow* was turned over to Ken Ernst. After Ernst left Beroth worked with assorted help. Don Winslow served in various war zones, once even working in drag to help his country, but after World War II, his adventures and the strip's circulation grew more modest. When the strip ceased in 1955, neither Hammond nor Beroth were associated with it and the drawing was being done by John Jordan.

Don and Red enjoyed two separate careers in comic books. Their newspaper strip was reprinted as part of the lineup of *Crackajack Funnies*, which started in 1938. During the next two years Dell also published two complete *Don Winslow of the Navy* reprint comic books. After *Crackajack* folded in 1942, the strip moved to *Popular Comics*.

In 1943 Fawcett introduced a Don Winslow monthly using all new material. There were usually four 12-page stories in each issue, and the artwork was by Edd Ashe, Carl Pfeufer, and John Jordan. Though the material was bland and usually didn't go in for the bizarre villainy of the strip, the title did well and hung on until the end of 1948. Fawcett revived it briefly in 1951, and then in 1955 Charlton carried on with three issues. After that Don Winslow sank without a trace. **R.G.**

**DOOM PATROL** Billed as "The World's Strangest Heroes," they were a team of three people who had been given superpowers and transformed physically by strange accidents; rejected as "freaks" by the world at large, they were brought together for training and mutual support by the Chief, a mysterious genius in a wheelchair. In many respects this National (DC) Comics series, launched in *My Greatest Adventure* in 1963, strangely foreshadowed Marvel Comics' *X-Men*, released a few months later (see *X-Men*).

The "freaks" were Elasti-Girl, who could shrink and grow like Alice in Wonderland; Robot Man, a new version of a strange Golden Age hero, with a human brain in a mechanical body; and Negative Man, who went into trances and projected an energy being from his body for periods of up to an hour (if the separation continued any longer, both selves would die). Later they were joined by the telepathic Mento and a teenager named Beast Boy, who could turn himself into various animals.

Written by Arnold Drake, drawn by Bruno Premiani, and edited by Murray Boltinoff, *Doom Patrol* was at first distinguished by its moodiness, oddity, and rather dark humor. Gradually the darkness gave way to the cornball, however, and the oddity became campiness; never a high-selling series, it rambled to an ignoble end in 1968. (The end was distinctive, at least, as the Doom Patrol became the first superheroes actually to die in the pages of their own comic book.)

An unsuccessful revival, with mainly new characters, was attempted in DC's *Showcase* in 1977. A new *Doom Patrol*, with a mixture of new and old characters, began in 1986; when British writer Grant Morrison took over the series in 1989, adding such surreal elements as the Brotherhood of Dada and the Scissormen, it began to generate great excitement among hardcore comic fans. **G.J.**

**DOONESBURY** Garry Trudeau's daily and Sunday comic strip *Doonesbury* grew out of an undergraduate satire feature called *Bull Tales*, first published in 1968 in Yale University's irregularly issued magazine *The Record* and from September 30 of that year in the *Yale Daily News*. An art major in his junior year at Yale, Trudeau early revealed so irreverent a spirit and so keen a wit that the strip quickly began to attract attention extramurally, and on the artist's graduation in 1970 James Andrews of Universal Press Syndicate took it for national distribution. The syndicate changed the title to *Doonesbury* (for the strip's main character, Mike Doonesbury, whose name was a composite of "doone," Yale slang for a simpleton, and "Pillsbury," Trudeau's college roommate) and broadened its field of reference. On October 26, 1970, *Doonesbury* debuted in 28 papers.

The strip quickly acquired a cult following, much of it in the counter culture, as it turned its gentle and literate fire on the national scene. Almost from the beginning the strip was controversial, antagonizing the left and the right alike but also inspiring passionate loyalty in its fans. When *Stars and Stripes* dropped the strip for being "too political," a flood of letters from soldiers and their families forced the paper to reinstate it. Many papers have compromised by running the strip on their editorial pages.

In addition to the touchingly *naif* loser Mike Doonesbury, whose function was often to serve as a sounding board to the TV news and the more assertive characters, the strip soon introduced a large and clearly defined cast of regulars. Among Mike's schoolmates were B.D., a Vietnam vet and staunch Reagan supporter and the quarterback on the school football team; Zonker Harris, "Prince of Inner Space," a free spirit who talks to flowers and devotes his limited energy to the pursuit of the Perfect Tan; and the campus radical, "Megaphone" Mark Slackmeyer, who cost the strip a few papers (including the *Washington Post*) by announcing in mid-trial that John Mitchell was "Guilty, guilty, guilty!!" Off campus, the strip ranged far and deep into the political and cultural arena with Zonker's uncle Duke, former stringer for *Rolling Stone*, whose flexible morality and deep involvement with the pharmaceutical industry at all levels did not prevent him from receiving the positions of governor of Samoa and ambassador to the People's Republic of China; Joanie Caucus, a fortyish defector from marriage and motherhood; Jimmie Thudpucker, retired pop star trying to enjoy his millions meaningfully; and Phred, former Vietcong guerrilla who became Vietnamese ambassador to the United Nations.

Always topical, *Doonesbury* has been a genial and generally liberal voice, though no kinder to knee-jerk liberals than to conservatives, and while it has offended some by its broadside swipes at government officials and its open and sympathetic treatment of such themes as homosexuality, it has continued to grow in both popularity and esteem. In 1975 it was the first comic strip to receive the Pulitzer Prize for editorial cartooning; in 1977 its circulation reached 500, and an animated NBC-TV *Doonesbury* special received an Academy Award nomination and won a Special Jury Prize at the Cannes Film Festival. The subject of a musical comedy in 1983 and now collected in over 50 volumes, it reaches some 900 newspapers worldwide.

Rendered in a spidery, rudimentary style like that of Trudeau's acknowledged inspiration Jules Feiffer (and like Feiffer's cartoons without speech balloons), *Doonesbury* has held its audience as much for the humanity of its humor as for its keenness. Its large *dramatis personae* are fully realized characters whose lives are developed with such sympathy and concern that, when Trudeau took a 20-month leave from January 1983 to September 1984, the strip's absence was widely and deeply felt, and when it returned it found a larger client list than when it had left. Now largely removed from the college scene, the strip has updated its characters and situations, marrying several of the characters off, killing others, sending some to jail and others to Capitol Hill. But the clear-sighted social and political vision of *Doonesbury* has not dimmed, and the strip is felt and feared in high places as much as ever. "The only thing worse than being in it would be not to be in it," admitted former Secretary of State Henry Kissinger, and President Gerald Ford observed, "There are only three major vehicles to keep us informed as to what's going on in Washington; the electronic media, the print media, and *Doonesbury*—not necessarily in that order."  **D.W.**

**DORGAN, TAD** (1877–1929)  He was, during the first three decades of the century, the highest paid sports cartoonist in America. Tad Dorgan was also a knowledgeable sports writer who contributed hundreds of words and phrases to the language, and he drew a half dozen successful comic strips and panels, including *Indoor Sports* and *Silk Hat Harry's Divorce Suit*. And Tad was the man who inspired the song "Yes, We Have No Bananas."

Thomas Aloysius Dorgan was a tall lanky man with sandy hair and a long, lean face. He was born in San Francisco in the Mission District, which was then called South of the Slot. Tad loved sports, particularly boxing and baseball, but when he was still a boy he lost most of the fingers on his right hand in an accident. He learned to write and draw with his left hand and made up his mind he was going to work for a newspaper. Quitting school, he got himself a job as an office boy on the *San Francisco Bulletin*. Tad, who'd made a pen name out of his initials, eventually became the favorite sports cartoonist and reporter in San Francisco. He stayed in the city, as he later explained, "until 'the call of the tame'—money—yelled so loud I had to listen to it." The call had come from William Randolph Hearst and in 1904 Tad went East to work on the *New York Journal*.

As a sports cartoonist and writer Tad covered ball games, prizefights, horse races. He liked the fights best, and both the public and the boxers themselves believed his accounts to be the most accurate available. Tad branched out on the *Journal* and soon became one of the most popular members of the growing comic art department. The most popular feature he ever did was his daily cartoon panel. It appeared in the Teens and Twenties, running under alternating titles, *Indoor Sports* and *Outdoor Sports*. Under neither title did he limit himself to the officially recognized sports. Dorgan did now and then kid such organized activities as baseball, boxing, golf, pool, and poker, but most often he poked fun at more prosaic pastimes, ranging from courtship to commuting to office politics to putting one over on the wife. Tad's favorite target was always the phoney, for which he coined such alternate names as four-flusher, drugstore cowboy, and windbag.

Tad, who wasn't a master draftsman, drew in a simple, direct cartoon style. He was an excellent caricaturist, able to capture the look and attitude not only of current sports celebrities but also of the army of phoneys, flappers, and boobs with which he populated his features.

He tried a variety of strips. One of the oddest, and longest running, boasted a cast of dogs who dressed and acted like humans. It appeared under several titles over the years, running most frequently as *Silk Hat Harry's Divorce Suit*, but also as *Judge Rummy's Court* and *Old Judge Rumhauser.* Dorgan's canines were definitely not for kids, being a carousing, gambling, philandering bunch. In addition to the silkhatted Harry, the cast included his disreputable pal P. McIntire Bunk, the disreputable French poodle Paul Fedinck, the feisty Judge, who was given to such catchphrases as, "Put that boob in the cooler for a week," and a bulldog who smoked a pipe, wore a deerstalker cap, and called himself Curlock Holmes. Sometimes Tad indulged in one-shot gags, but most often he went in for intricate continuities that kidded the sort of scandals being reported elsewhere in the newspaper. His dog strip sometimes stretched across all seven columns of a page, sometimes ran in a four-panel box and shared Tad's space with his *Indoor Sports* panel. Tad's strips and panels almost always appeared on the sports page and not the funny page. Once in a while Harry and the Judge also showed up in a Sunday page.

Another of Tad's sometime dailies was called *Daffydils.* This was considerably stranger than his canine opus, consisting of three hand-lettered columns per day, each of which told a little story that ended in an audacious pun, such as "If a tiger preys does a moccasin?" and "If the water in New York is low is the water in Shanghai?" and "Would a painter put on a heavy coat in hot weather?" Across the bottom of *Daffydils* ran a tiny four-panel strip featuring stickmen. This was obviously a very casual production, done with no penciling and often containing misspellings and typos.

There was also a domestic Sunday page with a cast of humans that Tad drew throughout the 1920s. It was very quiet and bordered on the dull. The title varied and sometimes it was called *Home—That's All* and also *For Better Or Worse.*

Tad seemingly couldn't keep from doodling the small stick-figure men, and a few of them could also be found hanging around his signature in the panel cartoons and strips. Sometimes, in very small print, they'd tell each other jokes: "My girl was pure as the driven snow but she drifted," "I call my sweetie special delivery because she's stuck on something important" etc. More often, they would exclaim some phrase Tad had picked up in his saloon wanderings or made up for no particular reason. "Applesauce," "What—no spinach?" "See what the boys in the backroom will have," "23 skidoo," "Quick, Watson, the needle," and "Yes, we have no bananas" all started that way. Tad also gave nicknames to a large quantity of people, places, and things. He was probably the first to call a Ford a "flivver," a hat a "skimmer," and glasses "cheaters."

To some Tad was "the friend of all actors, turfmen, literary lights, fighters, managers and broken-down sports." To others he seemed "of a misanthropic, antisocial cast." It is certain that the shock of the boyhood accident that crippled his right hand had a deep effect on his personality. One of his editors said, "He either liked you or he despised you. He formed an opinion on first acquaintance. Nothing could make him change his mind." There was a bitterness about Tad at times, and he could be cruel, often violently so. But he did have a great many friends and what he liked to remember about those years were the explorations of Broadway with them. Among his closest friends on the *Journal* were fellow cartoonists Tom McNamara and George Herriman.

In 1920 Tad suffered a serious heart attack while covering the Jack Dempsey-Billy Miske fight in Benton Harbor, Michigan. That was the last fight he attended in person and he spent most of the rest of his life in his home in Great Neck on Long Island. He kept on drawing and writing, however. For reports on the outside world he depended on the radio, the telephone, and helpful stringers. Tad's *Indoor Sports* drawings during that period were often datelined as if done in remote cities—Dublin, Shanghai, San Francisco. Most of his fans thought he was on the move around the world and didn't realize Tad was just having a joke on himself.

In good weather he would go for drives around Long Island or, occasionally, into New York City for a quiet dinner. He went to the movies, but usually only to see Charlie Chaplin or Tom Mix, his favorites. He had cut down his output, explaining that he was getting lazy. Toward the middle of April in 1929 Tad slowed down even more. But he kept drawing and when he died on May 2nd he was still three weeks ahead on his stuff.   **R.G.**

**DOUGLAS, STEPHEN A.** (1907–1967) A cartoonist, writer, and editor, Douglas is something of a forgotten man in the history of comic books, yet he was the editor of *Famous Funnies*, the magazine that launched the comic book industry.

He was born in Brooklyn and by the time he was 12 he was drawing a Sunday page for his hometown paper, the *Brooklyn Eagle*. He studied at New York University and the Pratt Institute, and in 1934 he was hired to work on Eastern Color's new monthly comic book, *Famous Funnies*, serving as editor and production manager. He remained on the job until *Famous* folded in the middle 1950s, editing nearly three dozen other titles for the company over the years. Among the young artists he hired were Alex Toth, Jack Berrill, and Frank Frazetta.

A cartoonist of just average ability, Douglas eventually contributed spot drawings to *Famous Funnies*—usually signed S.A.D.—and drew many of the covers. His covers featured a variety of the newspaper characters reprinted within, including Buck Rogers, Dickie Dare, and Oaky Doaks. He also wrote, creating a number of short-lived superheroes: For *Famous* there was Fearless Flint and for *Heroic Comics* he thought up Rainbow Boy, Man O'Metal, and Music Man.

Douglas was active in the National Cartoonists Society and won several of its awards. **R.G.**

**DRAGO** See HOGARTH, BURNE.

**DRAKE, STAN** (1921– ) Best known as the artist as well as one of the creators of *The Heart of Juliet Jones*, Stan Drake in recent years has added *Blondie* to his credits as one of the most versatile cartoonists in the business. His work on *Juliet Jones*, the realistic romance strip, contrasts vividly with the slapstick adventures of the Bumstead family—providing Drake with the demanding task of going from one style to another in the daily rush to get out two totally different stories.

Born in Brooklyn, Drake began his career at 17, working for pulp magazines, including *Popular Detective* and *Popular Sports*. He also worked in comic books as artist, letterer, and writer, and became friends with fellow cartoonist Bob Lubbers, a friendship that led to Drake's part in the creation of *Juliet Jones*. Drake also studied at the Art Students League in New York. Later, he served in the Pacific during World War II and afterwards went into the advertising field, where eventually he ran a studio of 12 illustrators.

In 1953, looking for a new outlet for his creative talent, Drake followed the advice of Lubbers to try newspaper comics. He joined forces with Elliot Caplin and King Features to create *Juliet Jones*, a successful soap opera strip that's still running. In the late 1970s, following his success in the funnies, he created a new strip for Universal Press Syndicate, *Pop Idols*. It failed to catch on and

died after a few months. But in 1984, after seriously contemplating a career change, Drake got a call from writer Dean Young who was trying to add artistic punch to his late father's enormously popular *Blondie*, asking if he'd draw it while still handling Juliet Jones. Drake jumped at the chance and has been a double-duty cartoonist ever since. **S.L.H.**

**DREAMS OF THE RAREBIT FIEND** See McCAY, WINSOR.

**DUMAS, JERRY** (1930– ) A versatile cartoonist and writer, Detroit-born Gerald Dumas has contributed to every aspect of the comics since joining Mort Walker's team in 1956. He has shared with Walker the writing of *Beetle Bailey* and *Hi and Lois*, drawn by Dik Browne, and has written material for Walker's *Boner's Ark* since it began in 1968. Dumas has also worked on the penciling, inking, and lettering of all three strips over the years.

From 1961 to 1963 Dumas drew and coauthored with Walker the now legendary *Sam's Strip*, a graphic tour de force (or de farce) featuring characters from the entire history of the comics, drawn in their original styles. Since April 18, 1977, he and Walker have done a spinoff of *Sam's Strip* for King Features called *Sam and Silo*, a broad human strip about a rural sheriff and his sidekick.

Other series Dumas has written include *Rabbits Rafferty* (1977–1981), a daily story series illustrated by Mel Crawford and based on Dumas' 1968 children's novel of the same name; *Benchley* (1984–1986), drawn by Mort Drucker, about a Washington bureaucrat; and *McCall of the Wild* (1988– ), drawn by Mel Crawford, about a ten-year-old girl who lives in her own wild imagination. Dumas has also found time to write a memoir of his childhood, *An Afternoon in Waterloo Park*, published by Houghton Mifflin in 1972, and a weekly column for Connecticut newspapers, and to contribute cartoons and spot illustrations to the *New York Times*, the *New Yorker*, and *Connoisseur*.

Dumas draws in the loose, spontaneous style of the "big-foot" cartoonist, but he commands the technical range to adopt any manner his material calls for. **D.W.**

**DUMB DORA** Created by Chic Young in 1925, *Dumb Dora* was later drawn by the gifted Paul Fung and then ghosted for a while in the early 1930s by a youthful Milton Caniff. Dora Bell was a slim brunette and, like many a heroine of Jazz Age films and fiction, was a college coed.

Young's strip reflected the public's growing interest in things collegiate, and it was moderately popular, even though it was drawn by a fellow who'd never been to college. The petite Dora, despite her derogatory nickname, was actually very clever and always got her way. She could, in the charming, scatterbrained manner of so many 1920s ingenues of stage and screen, manipulate just about anyone. Those she'd bested, upon realizing what had befallen them, usually exclaimed, "She's not so dumb!" While Dora dated an assortment of handsome college men, her steadiest beau was a pudgy, well-meaning, redheaded bumbler named Rod Ruckett. Young went in for the simplest of story lines, concentrating on the gags. While never a master draftsman, he drew Dumb Dora fairly well and saw to it she always dressed fashionably.

When Young moved on to *Blondie*, who was originally little more than a peroxide Dora, the *Dumb Dora* strip fell to Paul Fung in the spring of 1930. In addition to greatly improved artwork, the strip now began to go in for more complex plots and somewhat brighter dialogue. It's possible that writer Jack Lait, who had just collaborated with Fung on *Gus and Gussie*, did the scripts on the Dora strip, too.

Fung left the strip in 1932 and Bill Dwyer succeeded him. A very limited artist, Dwyer had sold gag cartoons to magazines like *College Humor*. His friend Milton Caniff, a much better artist, helped him put together the samples that got him the job and ghosted a good deal of the drawing in the early months that Dwyer was signing *Dumb Dora*. During this period Rod was dropped, replaced by a blond lad named Bing. As soon as Caniff graduated to a strip of his own, the look of Dwyer's opus deteriorated. It ended in 1934.

Dora was born again in the early 1940s, when Fung drew her in a series of advertising Sunday pages for Shredded Ralston (now known as Wheat Chex). In this sponsored version Dora was married to Rod and they're the parents of a small red-haired son. These pages rounded off the saga, tied up some loose ends from the 1930s, and served as the final chapter of *Dumb Dora*.                                    R.G.

**DUMM, EDWINA** (1893–1990)  Edwina (she signed only her first name to her life's work) began her long career of incongruities by becoming the nation's first woman political cartoonist at a time when women could not yet vote. She continued on a path of unlikely enterprise when she undertook to do a comic strip about the rambunctious doings of a boy and his dog. How could a woman accurately (and humorously) portray the workings of the juvenile male mind? Well enough, it turned out, to last nearly 50 years at it. The source of her material for a lifetime of drawing *Cap Stubbs and Tippie* was her own fondly recollected childhood as a shy tomboy in Upper Sandusky, Ohio, a small town in which everyone knew everything about every-

body, and all the kids (including Edwina and her brother) played together, trooping jubilantly through streets and yards and across the surrounding countryside in their play. Edwina honed her drawing skill with the Landon School correspondence course but took business courses in high school and worked as a stenographer for a while after graduating.

Around 1915, she went to work as the staff artist for a weekly paper in Columbus, the *Monitor*. When the *Monitor* went to daily publication, she began doing an editorial cartoon every day, becoming the only woman so employed in the nation. She also occasionally did a comic strip called *The Meanderings of Minnie*, about a tomboy and her dog. Edwina knew the big time for a cartoonist was New York, and by the fall of 1917, she had saved enough to stake herself to a year's trial there. She had sent samples of her work to the George Matthew Adams Service and had been encouraged by Adams, who liked her dogs. As soon as she arrived in New York, she went to see Adams; he told her he wanted her to do a strip about a boy and his dog. In six months or so, *Cap Stubbs* (its original name) had the circulation to make her a living. Edwina continued her art education by attending classes at the Art Students League and did a little free-lance illustrating, and in 1928 her work attracted the attention of critic Alexander Woollcott, who asked her to illustrate his book about three dogs, *Two Gentlemen and a Lady*. Those drawings were duly noted by Woollcott's cronies at the humor magazine *Life*, then in one of its final spasms of readjusting its editorial sights in order to survive. Edwina was soon doing a weekly page for *Life* about a frisky, wooly-haired terrier, which a readers' contest christened Sinbad.

Throughout her long life, Edwina drew for magazine articles and books as well as her strip. She also drew *Alec the Great*, a syndicated verse feature about a little dog written by her brother, Robert Dennis Dumm. She never married, maintaining that she had neither the skills nor the interest for it. Cap Stubbs and his grandmother and his dog, kept lively by her vivid memories of a small-town childhood, were both occupation and avocation enough.                                    R.C.H.

**DUNN, BOB** (1908–1989)  The broad, expressive art and genial wit of Bob Dunn were staples of American humor in several media for nearly six decades. A longtime assistant of Milt Gross and Jimmy Hatlo, with whom his work went uncredited for many years, Dunn was to inherit the latter's *They'll Do It Every Time* and *Little Iodine*, both of which he continued to produce until his death in 1989.

Dunn left his home town of Newark, New Jersey, to study at the Art Students League in New York City after

*Knock Knock*, Bob Dunn, © 1936, Whitman Publishing Co.

breaking into the cartoon field with gag cartoons in many national humor magazines. He returned home to take a job in the art department of the *Newark Ledger*, and later worked briefly for International News Service.

His association with Milt Gross began in 1932, and he was soon ghosting Gross' *That's My Pop!*, distributed by King Features Syndicate. In 1939 Dunn became an assistant to Jimmy Hatlo, whose *They'll Do It Every Time* began in 1929 and was syndicated by King in 1936. While poking gentle fun at minor social irritants in his own similar panel feature, *Just the Type* (which featured father-son jokes under the heading "Dunn & Son"), he coauthored *They'll Do It Every Time* for 26 years and Hatlo's collateral Sunday strip *Little Iodine* for 20. When Hatlo died in 1963, both features became his. He signed the daily *They'll Do It Every Time* with Tommy Thompson from January 3, 1965, and with Al Scaduto from July 24, 1967, and shared the credit for the Sunday feature with Scaduto from February 13, 1966. *Little Iodine* first appeared over his and Scaduto's signatures on February 20, 1966; from September 10, 1967, until his death, Dunn signed it with Hy Eisman. He received the National Cartoonists Society's silver plaque for Best Syndicated Panel in 1968 and 1969 and shared it with Scaduto in 1979. He was awarded that organization's

Reuben as Outstanding Cartoonist of the Year for *They'll Do It Every Time* in 1975.

Dunn's contribution to the field of humor extended beyond the confines of the newspaper comics page. Among his published work was a collection of knock-knock jokes (appropriately entitled *Knock Knock*), which sold over a million copies and started the Knock-Knock craze. As a studio cartoonist with NBC-TV he conducted two regular television shows: "Face to Face" (1946–1947) and "Quick on the Draw" (1950). The popularity of these audience-participation shows, in which he drew quick sketches, attested to Dunn's sharp wit, facile hand, and engaging personality.

The enjoyment that Dunn took in his work is evident in his easy, natural line and in the robust humor of his gags. An essentially good-natured cartoonist of the old school, he was very popular in his profession. He served as the fourth president of the National Cartoonists Society from 1965 to 1966 and was for many years that association's unofficial toastmaster-general. **D.W.**

**DWIGGINS, CLARE VICTOR** (1874–1958) He always signed himself "Dwig" and he was already a professional cartoonist before the 19th century ended. His favorite topic was his own boyhood, and he returned to it many times over the years. Dwig drew panels, Sunday pages, and daily comic strips; he also illustrated books, provided artwork for picture postcards, and was the artist selected by the Mark Twain estate to draw the strip based on the Huckleberry Finn and Tom Sawyer characters. In the 1940s Dwig drew for comic books, even managing to revive Huck and Tom one more time.

Dwig was born in Ohio and he said it was his mother who encouraged him to be an artist. "To say that Dwig grew up in Ohio would be misleading," wrote Jay Rath in *Nemo.* "He worked in the winter and spent his summers travelling as a hobo." While on the road Dwig supported himself as an itinerant artist. "A soap box under a tree at the camp meeting," he once recalled. "Name cards, a quarter a dozen. I joined the faculty and taught my art on schoolhouse blackboards." He was hired by the *St. Louis Post Dispatch* in 1897, and by the early years of this century he was in New York City drawing for the *World.* Among his early features were *School Days* and *Ophelia and Her Slate.* Dwig drew in a lively forceful manner that showed the influence of both the Art Nouveau embellishers and of Phil May's spare, pared down sketches of London street urchins. By the start of the second decade of this century he had locked into a highly personal style, one that he never changed over the years.

The Tom Sawyer and Huck Finn feature started appearing in 1918, based as much on Dwig's own Missouri childhood as it was on Twain's novels. He devoted most of the Sunday pages to the endless leisure that small-town kids seemed to have, at least in Dwig's memory. Although there were youthful bullies and sneaks, there were few nasty grown-ups, and the adults' capacity for hypocrisy and for terrorizing children, a staple of Twain, played almost no part in the Dwig version. The daily Tom and Huck panel was also gentle in its humor and its recreation of boyhood. Dwig slipped some of his earlier characters in, too. Ophelia, the cross-eyed little girl whose slate had aphorisms and running comments chalked on it, was frequently to be encountered alongside Becky and Aunt Polly.

Dwig's last major effort was *Nipper,* done for the Ledger syndicate from 1931 to 1937. The theme was again boyhood, but this time in a contemporary setting. Nipper Tucker was a wholesome but adventure-loving lad of about 10, who lived in a small town on a river, a place with plenty of surrounding woods and fields. The humor in the Sunday page grew, as usual, out of the fooling around of kids, out of their squabbles, crushes, and anxieties, and, as before, there were few threatening adults. Nipper's mom, in fact, was a very pretty young woman who was very supportive of his escapades and outlook. She rarely criticized him, finding she could use jokes and kidding to get him to see her side of things. Nipper's best friend was a boy called Ruff Bumps and Ophelia, not a day older than she had been two decades earlier, was one of the gang. The daily strip was much more exciting, involving Nipper and Ruff in shipwrecks, encounters with cannibals, gangsters, and more.

Another of Dwig's inventions was *Footprints on the Sands of Time,* which he was using as early as the late Teens. He would draw a bird's-eye view of a small section of town and indicate with dotted lines and other marks the route taken by a boy named Bill while performing some simple task like going to the store for his mother or starting off for school on a snowy morning. Neither Bill nor any of his friends or relatives ever appeared, only the telltale tracks plus Dwig's annotations: "rolls snowballs…loses dime, meets chum at arboreal clubhouse…discovers sweetheart…discusses the purchasing power of two cents," etc. Dwig used the footprints format in his daily Huckleberry Finn panels, and he later drew it as a bottom strip to the Sunday *Nipper* pages. It was also an occasional part of *Bill's Diary,* the panel he drew in the late 1930s.

The middle 1940s found Dwig drawing in comic books, specifically in two Street & Smith titles. For *Doc Savage Comics* he revived Huckleberry Finn, and when that title folded, he drew more new adventures of Huck and Tom for *Supersnipe Comics.* For this latter title he also did his final comic book work, a kid adventure-fantasy titled *Bobby Crusoe.* Though his stuff looked bolder and blacker, Dwig's basic style was the same as it had been nearly a half century earlier.

Dwig settled in Southern California in the 1940s, associating with other veteran cartoonists such as J.R. Williams and Vic Forsythe. He did some book illustration and after leaving comics for good devoted his time to painting and watercolors. His favorite subject was boyhood scenes. **R.G.**

# E

**EDSON, NAT** (1909– ? ) He ghosted for Lyman Young on the *Tim Tyler's Luck* strip during its most successful years, from the middle 1930s to the middle 1940s. Edson also created and drew its Sunday page topper, *Curly Harper*. Edson's work on these features was printed and reprinted all over the world, but he never got a credit. After leaving *Tim Tyler*, he drew for comic books for over 20 years. Most of his work in that field was anonymous, too.

A handicapped child, Edson spent seven years in hospitals, and that was where he learned to draw. At 18, in 1927, he got himself hired as an office boy at King Features Syndicate and worked himself up to a position in the art department. In the mid-1930s he started drawing *Tim Tyler*. Edson's early work on the strip was close in style to that of his King Features contemporary Alex Raymond, but gradually he developed a look of his own, complete with a personal way of drawing pretty girls. His work was quite good and highly distinctive at this point, and his is the style most closely associated with the heyday of *Tim Tyler's Luck*. The samples of Lyman Young's work reprinted in *Comics and Their Creators*, for instance, are by Edson.

All of Tim's latter African adventures in the Ivory Patrol were done by Edson, as well as Tim's wartime adventures, along with his pal Spud, in the seagoing Coast Patrol. He returned to the character in the late 1940s, drawing several original *Tim Tyler* comic books. In these Tim and Spud were cowboys.

During the war years Edson moonlighted a little in comic books, drawing the *Espionage* feature in *Smash Comics*. After leaving the strip in 1945, he returned to comic books. Late that year he went to work for the nonfiction, news-oriented comic book *Picture News*, the only work he ever signed. Resettling on the West Coast in 1950, Edson began drawing for Western-Dell. He did many of their cowboy and TV titles—among them, *Roy Rogers, Gene Autry, Texas Rangers, Sugarfoot*—and also adaptations of various Disney movies. After an illness in the early 1970s, he cut down on his output and gradually disappeared from the field.                   **R.G.**

**EEK AND MEEK** Originating as a brace of articulate and literate mice, Eek and Meek have held forth on topics timely and timeless since the first appearance of the strip bearing their names on Sunday, September 5, 1965, with the daily strip debuting on the following day. Written and drawn by Howie Schneider and syndicated by NEA, *Eek and Meek* wryly comments on themes ranging from political corruption to personal neurosis. The dominant member of the team, the raffish and disreputable Eek, began as an anarchic little rodent who, not holding a job, went on strike for better unemployment conditions; Meek was his naive and hapless foil who reflected at one point that loneliness wouldn't be so hard to fight if he didn't have to do it all by himself. Meek's love interest is the unattainable Monique, who responds to his hopeful suggestion that she let herself go with, "Okay…I'm going!" The more realistic Eek admits that he too worships the ground Monique walks on but explains that he isn't in love but in real estate.

Although their personalities have remained constant over the years, Eek and Meek have changed in appearance and, finally, in species. Beginning as stick figures ("looking," as the artist describes them, "like cocktail franks with one-line arms and legs"), they acquired thicker limbs during the 1970s, and then, inevitably, clothes. Finally, on February 8, 1982, the metamorphosis became complete, and the characters achieved complete humanity.

As young men (Eek still unshaven and sporting a black derby hat, Meek still wearing a crumpled sweatshirt), the two remain minimally drawn and the strip sparely composed, relying for its humor on its sharply defined characters and its occasionally trenchant reflections on man and society. Collections of the strip have appeared periodically since the first in 1969, and it runs in some 500 newspapers.                   **D.W.**

**EISNER, WILL** (1917– ) Artist, writer, editor, and entrepreneur, Eisner is another of the major figures in the comic book industry. In the business since the middle 1930s, he's an expert on graphic storytelling and he has created such long-lasting characters as Blackhawk, Sheena the Queen of the Jungle, and the Spirit.

Eisner was born in Brooklyn and his first comic book work appeared in 1936 in a short-lived magazine called *Wow*. Forming a partnership with Jerry Iger, *Wow's*

*The Spirit*, Will Eisner, 1949, © 1990, Will Eisner.

editor and a former Hearst cartoonist, Eisner opened one of the first comic book shops. "I was running a shop in which we made comic book features pretty much the way Ford made cars," he once explained. "We made $1.50 a page net profit. I got very rich before I was 22." Among the early laborers in the shop were Bob Kane, Dick Briefer, Mort Meskin, Bob Powell, and Lou Fine. Eventually they mass-produced art and editorial material for the Quality, Fiction House, and Fox lines of comics. Eisner also experimented with several features that could be either newspaper strips or comic book pages. One of the Eisner-Iger clients had him produce pages for an overseas weekly called *Wags*. Among the original features done for it were *Hawks of the Sea*, conceived and drawn by Eisner; *Sheena*, cooked up by Eisner and Iger and drawn by Meskin; and *Peter Pupp*, a funny animal feature by Bob Kane. These were eventually reprinted in America and formed the basis for *Jumbo Comics*.

For the Quality group Eisner drew *Espionage* in *Smash Comics* and dreamed up the tiny superhero Dollman, illustrated by Fine, for *Feature Comics*. After parting with Iger, he edited *National* and *Military* for Everett "Busy" Arnold of Quality. Eisner wrote and drew the early adventures of the superpatriot Uncle Sam in *National* and created Blackhawk and his crew for *Military*. And it was while associated with Arnold that he created *The Spirit*. Eisner's masked man made his debut in 1940 in a weekly 16-page comic book insert that was sold to Sunday papers. "Sartorically the Spirit was miles from the other masked heroes," Jules Feiffer pointed out in

his *The Great Comic Book Heroes*. "He didn't wear tights, just a baggy blue business suit and, for a disguise, a matching blue eye mask." Feiffer felt that Eisner's characters were "identifiable by that look of just having got off the boat. The Spirit reeked of the lower middle class; his nose may have turned up, but we all knew that he was Jewish."

Eisner's work got better as he went along. His stories got trickier and less melodramatic, and his layouts moved further and further away from the traditional. No one has ever equalled him in incorporating the logo into the splash panel and few have come close to capturing the feel, shadows, and grit of urban life.

The insert lasted until 1952, and Eisner, a bit shrewder than his contemporaries, retained ownership to the character. Eisner has been an inspiration to younger artists both for his thoughtful cinematic layout and storytelling techniques and for his business acumen.

After spending many years in the production of comic books for education and advertising purposes, Eisner returned to nonsponsored comics. Although the Spirit material appearing in the current monthly black and white published by Kitchen Sink is reprinted, Eisner still draws his baggypants hero anew on the cover each month. He also did new material for the short-lived *Will Eisner's Quarterly* and has done several graphic novels, including *A Contract With God, A Life Force* etc. **R.G.**

**ELIAS, LEE** (1920– ) After perfecting his own personal version of the Milton Caniff style, Elias used it for

*Beyond Mars*, Lee Elias, © 1952, N.Y. News Co.

both comic books and comic strips. His two most notable comic book characters were the redheaded Firehair and the redheaded Black Cat, both successful 1940s heroines. In the 1950s he drew the impressive *Beyond Mars* Sunday page and then returned to comic books for roughly another quarter of a century.

Born in England, Leopold Elias came to America when he was a child. His family settled in New York City and he studied the violin. Deciding he could make more money as an artist, Elias started studying at Cooper Union and the Art Students League. He broke into comic books in 1943, drawing an assortment of aviation features for Fiction House's *Wings Comics*. Next came *Firehair*, dealing with an attractive and sparsely clad young woman adventuring her way through the Old West for Fiction House's *Rangers Comics*.

He took over *Black Cat* in 1946 and stayed with it until the early 1950s. His sophisticated, lushly inked style was well-suited to the escapades of the bored Hollywood star who was a costumed crimefighter in her spare time. He did well by her in both her identities and drew all the required props—from hoodlums and machine guns to starlets and movie cameras—with ease.

From 1952 to 1955 he collaborated with veteran science fiction author Jack Williamson on *Beyond Mars*, a Sunday page that ran exclusively in the *New York Daily News*. When that ended, he returned to comic books and also found time to devote two years to ghosting *Li'l Abner*. His last comic book work was *The Rook*, a black and white title that ended in 1980. He has been retired since then. **R.G.**

**ELLA CINDERS** Just about everybody loves a Cinderella story, and in 1925 yet another version came along. This one arrived in the form of a newspaper strip with the anagrammatic title of *Ella Cinders*. While not as glamorous as some of her funny-paper contemporaries, the wide-eyed and feisty Ella outlasted many of them and enjoyed a career that spanned over three and a half decades.

The strip was originally the joint effort of writer Bill Conselman and cartoonist Charlie Plumb, both of whom were newspapermen. Since they lived and worked in the Los Angeles area, it was probably inevitable that their particular Cinderella would make her first rise from poverty to wealth in that wonderland known as Hollywood.

When the strip started, first as a daily only, in the spring of 1925, Ella was a slim, freckle-faced girl residing in a small town. Burdened with a mean stepmother and two nasty stepsisters, she spent her days as a "kitchen slavey." Her father had long since fled the wrath of Mrs. Cinders, and her only ally was her kid brother Blackie, her only suitor a not too bright iceman

named Waite Lifter. Conselman, who had dreams of someday conquering Hollywood himself as a screenwriter, was fond of pun names, and most of his dialogue and captions have the glib, wisecracking tone of silent comedy title cards.

In a Roaring Twenties switch on the fairy tale, Ella was transformed not by a magic godmother but by winning a beauty contest in a movie magazine. (It wasn't, by the way, her good looks that clinched the win; the weary editor, in desperation, had picked a photo at random. ) When the triumphant Ella reached Hollywood, she found that the studio that had promised her a job had shut down. After weeks of undaunted struggle, however, she arranged an interview with J. Wallington Whiffle, famous movie magnate and head of Superart Studios. Whiffle turned out to be her long-lost father, Sam Cinders, and Ella found success and got a taste of domestic tranquility. For the next several years the daily continuities—a separate Sunday page was introduced in 1927—were mostly concerned with moviemaking and Hollywood. In fact, an actual *Ella Cinders* movie was made in 1926, with Colleen Moore in the title role.

Plumb drew in a vigorous, correspondence school style. He was also a restless man with a great many other interests and, fairly early in Ella's life Plumb started hiring assistants. The first one was a gifted young man named Hardie Gramatky, who took over the penciling and stuck with it until the early 1930s. He went on to become an animator at the Walt Disney studios and later a successful children's book illustrator—his best known book was *Little Toot*—and gallery watercolorist. Gramatky improved the look of the strip

*Ella Cinders*, Charlie Plumb (and Fred Fox), © 1934, United Features Syndicate Inc. Reprinted by permission, United Features Syndicate, Inc.

considerably, making Ella in particular more attractive, and added movie-style closeups, long shots, and other cinematic effects.

In the early Thirties the daily *Ella Cinders* grew more serious. While Ella herself remained cynical and wisecracking, the storylines moved into the soap opera mode. There were misunderstandings, disappearances, and unrequited love, along with most of the other trappings of the increasingly popular radio serials, as well as several out-and-out action sequences. In the middle of the decade Ella met and eventually married a handsome, mustachioed, and mysterious fellow known as Patches. Not only was he adventure-prone, he also had a tendency to vanish at crucial moments and end up lost in the middle of a South American jungle. The chief daily ghost for most of this period was Fred Fox, who did much of the drawing and at least some of the writing. An effective artist with a passion for crosshatching and sundry other pen techniques, Fox gave the feature an adventure-strip look and further improved Ella's figure.

By the decade's end the strip had changed again, with stories closer to the plots of the mystery-comedy movies of the period. This held true into the Forties as well, with Ella, Patches, and Blackie wisecracking their way through adventures involving gangsters, stolen money, spies, haunted houses, and crackpot inventors. There were also satirical continuities that kidded advertising, show business, and other fads and foibles of the age. Conselman died in 1940, and Plumb took a solo credit from then on. Fox, though, was doing the writing, and from the middle of 1939 on the daily was drawn by Jack W. McGuire.

The Sunday page meantime had been living a life of its own. Throughout the 1930s it avoided melodrama and adventure to concentrate on gags, which most often featured just Ella and Blackie. The writers had a knack for turning public-domain gags and old vaudeville routines into amusing comic pages, now and then converting a well-known dirty joke into a clean gag by modifying the basic situation and sanitizing the language.

The first Sundays were drawn by Plumb and Gramatky. The middle Thirties saw the arrival of a special Sunday ghost in the person of the talented and largely unsung Henry Formhals. A very good cartoonist, Formhals had a special talent for depicting the exploding automobiles, crashing airplanes, and other catastrophes that were often called for. When he left in the late Thirties to take over the ghosting of the daily *Freckles and His Friends*, Fox assumed the drawing of the Sundays. By the early Forties McGuire was drawing both daily and Sunday.

Plumb, perhaps to devote himself full-time to his wanderings, left the feature in the 1950s. Fred Fox got sole credit from then on, although by this time he was only writing. The final artist was Roger Armstrong. Ella, now looking a bit matronly, persisted until 1961.

**R.G.**

**ELLSWORTH, WHITNEY** (1908–1980) Although both a cartoonist and a writer, Ellsworth made his chief contribution to comic books as an editor. He entered the field in its beginnings in the mid 1930s and before moving on served as editorial director for the entire DC line. He also produced the *Superman* television series of the 1950s.

Born in Brooklyn, Ellsworth got his formal cartoon training from a class taught at his hometown YMCA by Ad Carter. He went on to assist Carter on his *Just Kids* newspaper strip. Working in the King Features bullpen in the late 1920s, Ellsworth assisted on such strips as *Dumb Dora* and *Tillie the Toiler*. Next, in the early 1930s, came drawing and writing for various New Jersey newspapers. He drew in a basic cartoon style, adhering to what he'd learned from *Just Kids* in the 1920s, and never changing his style over the years.

He started his association with Major Nicholson late in 1934 and his page, *Little Linda*, a variation of *Little Orphan Annie*, ran in the major's pioneering *New Fun Comics* from the second issue on. He also contributed a kid feature to Nicholson's second title, *New Comics*, and drew the cover for the premier issue. By the middle of 1936 he and fellow cartoonist Vin Sullivan were serving as coeditors for the faltering Nicholson group of original material comic books.

Ellsworth dropped out of comics after Major Nicholson turned DC over to others. After moving to California, he tried his hand at magazine fiction. In 1940, after Sullivan left, Ellsworth was hired again by DC and became editorial director of the ever-growing line of magazines. This meant that he and the editors under him were responsible for such characters as Superman, Batman, the Spectre, Dr. Fate, the Green Arrow etc. During the early 1940s he also wrote some of the continuities for the *Superman* newspaper strip.

When the *Superman* TV show, starring George Reeves, began in 1951, Ellsworth was sent West to act as DC's representative, and in 1953 he became producer and remained such until the last show in 1957. He was responsible for the pilots of "Superboy" and "Superpup," the latter starring midgets in dog costumes. Ellsworth retired from DC in 1970. **R.G.**

**ELMER** A kid comedy strip that survived for 40 years, it was the creation of A.C. Fera. It began as a Sunday page in 1916 under the title *Just Boy*, but when

Doc Winner took over in 1925, the title was changed to *Elmer*.

Fera, about whom little biographical information has survived, drew in an attractive, scratchy version of the Jimmy Swinnerton style. Most of his characters were squat, usually only three or four heads high. Elmer was the only child of Clem and Ella Tuggle and remained about nine or ten for the run of the strip. The Tuggles lived a comfortable, middle-class life in a typical small town, complete with a black maid-cook named Lottie. Like many kids of the second decade of the century, Elmer dressed in short-pants suit and wore a tie. He acquired long pants by the 1930s but never abandoned the neckties.

During Fera's run with *Just Boy*, Elmer was a likable but belligerent and prankish boy. Lottie said of him: "Ah neber see suchy brat!" Discipline was a frequent theme, and Elmer was always trying to work out strategies that would help him escape a thrashing. Both parents whacked him and the woodshed played an important part in the proceedings. For awhile in the late Teens there was a daily *Just Boy*, but for most of the feature's life it was only a Sunday page.

Charles "Doc" Winner inherited it in 1925, and the name became *Elmer*; the tone mellowed as Elmer became less of a brat and the gags moved away from the physical abuse of his person. Winner imitated Fera for several years before shifting over to his more conventional, journeyman cartoon style. Early on Elmer had favored such exclamations as "Gee whiz!" and "Rats!" while with Winner the expletive of choice was "Crim-a-nentlies!"

Winner was a native of Pennsylvania and after working on newspapers in Pittsburgh and Newark, he came to New York in 1918 to join the Hearst organization. He was one of the first to labor in what eventually became the King Features bullpen, and, as such, Winner got to ghost and fill in on several strips before assuming the *Elmer* job. He also drew *Thimble Theatre* after Segar's

death and later took over *The Katzenjammer Kids*. He maintained that much of *Elmer* was based on recollections of his own youth: "And a great many of the stunts they do are ones we either did or tried to do when we were kids." He died in 1956 and *Elmer* came to an end.

**W.D.**

**ELMO**   A satirical strip—a sort of an urban Li'l Abner—Elmo was launched in the optimistic postwar year of 1946. It was written and drawn by noted Chicago political cartoonist Cecil Jensen and distributed, with much initial enthusiasm, by the Register and Tribune Syndicate. Despite the high hopes of all concerned, *Elmo* did not do well, and within a couple of years it was transformed into a rather lackluster kid strip.

Not unexpectedly for a cartoonist who'd spent much of his life in Chicago, Jensen kidded political corruption and big-business greed in his new comic strip. His idiosyncratic sense of humor, however, mixed satire, quirky fantasy, and lowbrow burlesque, and resulted in a highly individual strip that was only now and then as funny as it might have been.

Elmo was a lean, blond young fellow, good-natured and naive. An orphan, he was given a controlling interest in a breakfast food company by a distraught millionaire he saved from suicide. The cereal was Popnut Skrummies, and the head man was a plutocrat named Commodore Bluster. Jensen provided Elmo with an assortment of pretty ladies to get entangled with, among them Sultry LeBair, a stripper at the Goosepimple Burlesque Theater, and Emmaline, Elmo's hometown sweetheart who'd followed him to the big city.

The female who caused his downfall was a pigtailed, wide-eyed little girl named Debbie. She entered the strip in May 1947. By the end of the year she'd elbowed Elmo out of the strip entirely. *Little Debbie* continued for several years, a dull and uninspired gag strip.   **R.G.**

*Elmo*, Cecil Jensen, © The Register Tribune Syndicate (1947).

THE GREAT DOG SHOW IN HOGAN'S ALLEY.

*Yellow Kid,* © 1897.

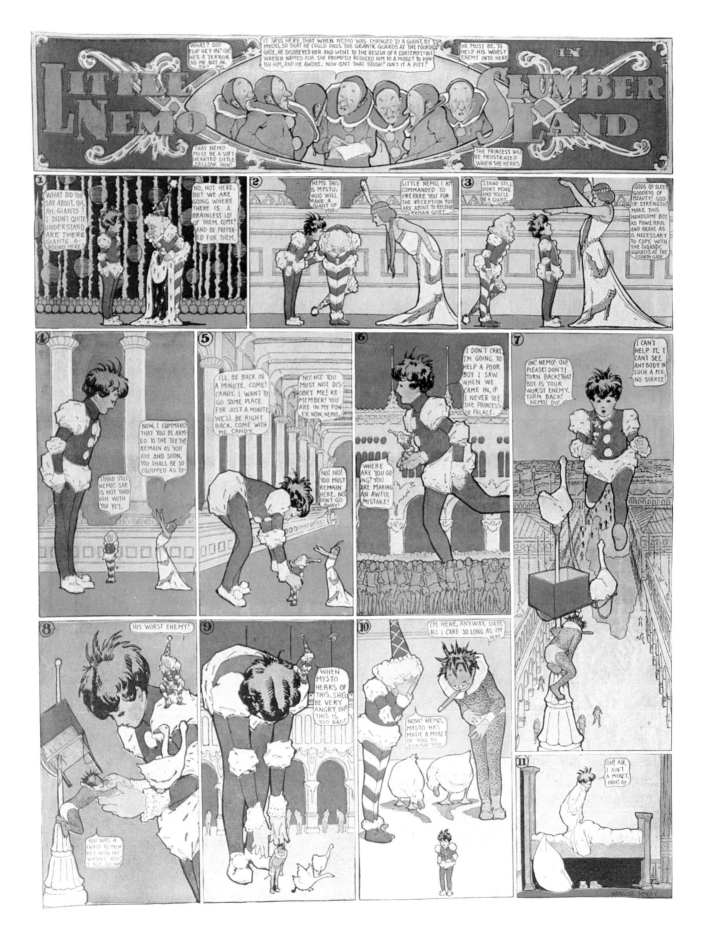

*Little Nemo,* © 1906.

# Piemouth comes to the rescue of the Kin-der-Kids

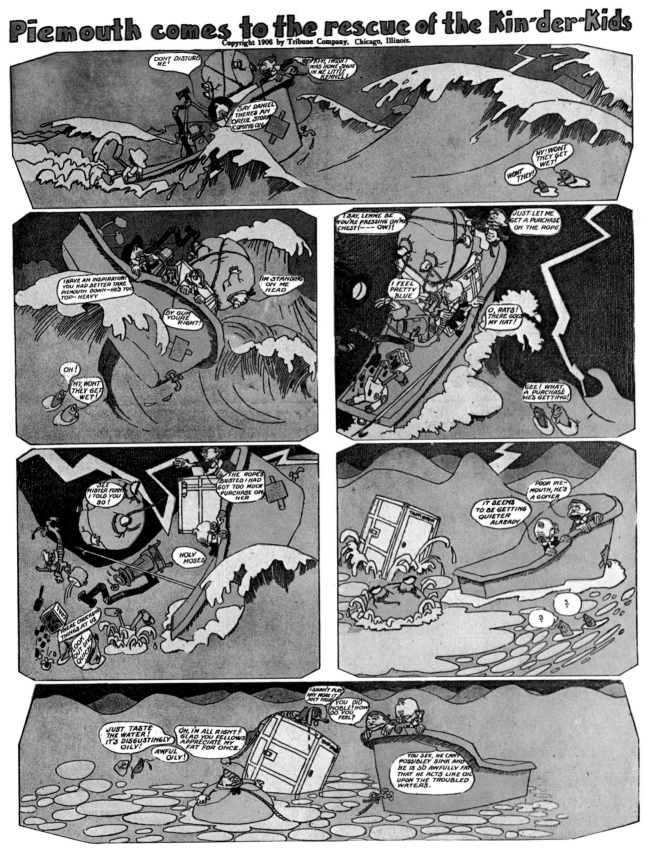

*Kin-der-Kids,* © 1906, Tribune Company.

# THE CAPTAIN AND THE KIDS

Trade Mark 1926, Reg. U. S. Pat. Off.

*By R. Dirks*  *Originator of the Katzenjammer Kids*

*The Captain and the Kids,* © 1926, (N.Y. World) Press Pub. Co.

*Barney Google,* © 1923, King Features Syndicate, Inc.

## Jerry On the Job

*Jerry on the Job*, © 1929, Int'l Feature Service, Inc.

*Nestlé's Nest.*

# ALMOST A BRIDE ~ *By Russell Patterson*

Trade Mark Registration Applied For

**1** PHYLLIS *has had one of those inspirations: wouldn't it be fun—or would it?—to marry the Duke in London? After all, it's the season's peak. A fast phone call to Madame Lucie is put through. Next day, from a swanky assortment of teagowns, lingerie and negligees, Phyl picks Madame Lucie's masterpiece, of glowing satin, chiffon and silver fox. "This is perfection plus," the fiancee exclaims as she descends the stairs in the salon. But, horrors! The Duke, arriving late, treads on her train as he bestows an ogle or two or some of the plenty-prettiest models.*

**2** ZIP! RIP! *Phyl feels the gorgeous gown slipping from her shoulders. She's all cold and bothered, wondering what in fashion's name has happened to her. It doesn't take her long to find out.*

**3** THE DUKE *has certainly panicked the models. It looks as if it were raining mannequins. They flee in all directions as the noble blunderer, all snarled up in the glamorous negligee, bounces down the stairs.*

**4** "THE wedding is off!" *cries Phyllis as she gazes in disdain at her disconsolate boy-friend, draped in the satin tatters. The gown's a worse wreck than the walls of Troy. Once again Phyl's been ALMOST A BRIDE.*

(To Be Continued)

*Almost A Bride,* © 1932, King Features Syndicate, Inc.

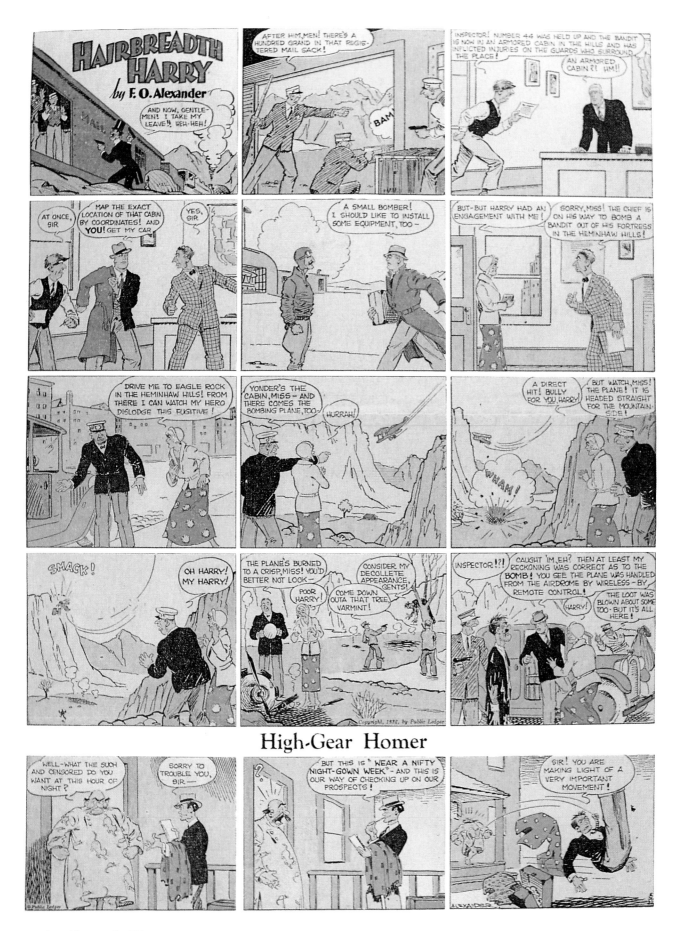

*Hairbreadth Harry,* © 1932.

**ENGLI, FRANK** (1906–1977)  Although he worked as a cartoonist from 1930 onward and drew comic strips and comic book features, Engli's major contribution to the field was as a letterer. He provided the lettering for three of the most influential adventure strips of the century: Milton Caniff's *Terry and the Pirates*, Noel Sickles' *Scorchy Smith*, and Caniff's *Steve Canyon*. These strips were much studied by aspiring cartoonists from the 1930s through the 1960s, and Engli's clear, concise and distinctive lettering was imitated by several generations of comic strip and comic book artists and letterers, many of whom thought they were imitating Caniff and Sickles.

Engli was born in Chicago, made up his mind he was going to be a cartoonist while in high school, and went on to study at the Chicago Academy of Fine Arts. He once said he'd "hitchhiked 10,000 miles around the country before coming to New York." He arrived in time to contribute to Dell's pioneering tabloid comic book, *The Funnies*, in 1930. He next helped Bill Dwyer on the *Dumb Dora* strip and worked at the Fleischer studios animating *Popeye* and *Betty Boop*. He worked as Caniff's assistant on *Terry* from just about the start of the strip in 1934, handling not only the lettering but the coloring of the Sunday page. He took on the lettering of *Scorchy Smith* at about the same time.

For the *Chicago Tribune*'s Sunday *Comic Book Magazine* Engli drew *Rocky, the Stone Age Kid* in the early 1940s. Despite his association with two master comic strip realists, Engli's own drawing style was cartoony and very much in the bigfoot camp. He did a strip called *Looking Back*, which was a recycling of the caveman stuff he'd done in *Rocky*, for Field Enterprises in 1946 and 1947. He also contributed filler pages to some of the Harvey line of comic books.

He assisted on *Steve Canyon* from its inception and stayed with it until his death. He once said that his ambition was "to do a good pantomime strip with *no* lettering."  **R.G.**

**ERNST, KEN** (1918–1985)  He drew the *Mary Worth* strip from 1942 until his death, establishing the slick, sophisticated brush style that most subsequent soap opera strips imitated. Before moving into the realm of romance and anguish, Ernst had drawn some lively adventure features in comic books and in his spare time ghosted the *Don Winslow* newspaper strip.

Born in 1918 in the little mining town of Stanton, Illinois, Kenneth Frederic Ernst grew up on Chicago's West Side. His father ran a delicatessen located just around the corner from the garage where the St. Valentine's Day Massacre took place in 1929. Ernst's father paid for his first art training, a mail-order course in cartooning. By the time he was 12, he had added magic to his interests. "I actually performed for pay in my teens," he once said. "Some cartoons I did for the local magic club magazine caught the eye of a fellow magician who was a commercial artist by profession, and he persuaded me to take up the study of art and cartooning seriously." Ernst went to both the Chicago Art Institute and the Academy of Fine Arts.

Leaving Chicago in 1936 he journeyed to Manhattan, staying for about a year. While there he worked in the art shop run by comic book packager Harry "A" Chesler. His earliest comic book work showed up in *Star Comics* and *Funny Pages*. While in New York, Ernst got to know Milton Caniff and Noel Sickles, and he visited them occasionally at the studio they shared. He soon developed a loose, splashier version of their style. Returning to Chicago, Ernst started to sell material to the Whitman line of comic books—*The Funnies, Super Comics*, and *Crackajack*. For *Super* he drew *Magic Morro*, about a blond Tarzan sort of hero who also happened to be "versed in magic and sorcery." By this time Ernst had fully developed his own style, and features like *Magic Morro*, which he also scripted, read and looked like the sophisticated newspaper adventure strips that Caniff and his disciples were then producing.

Ernst also sold to New York comic books such as *Detective Comics* and *Big Shot Comics*. And he illustrated several of Whitman's Big Little Books, mainly those featuring motion picture cowboys Buck Jones and Tom Mix.

When he married, Ernst decided he needed some extra money, so he took a job ghosting the *Don Winslow of the Navy* newspaper strip. It didn't pay that much and he kept most of his other freelance work. "At one time I spent mornings penciling all the *Winslow* and *Bos'n Hal* art," he once recalled, "afternoons at a Chicago art-agency doing advertising strips, and topped off the day by working all evening on my own comic book creations."

The *Mary Worth* strip had been around, under assorted titles, since the middle 1930s. In 1942 Allen Saunders, who was writing the strip, needed a new artist, and Ernst was suggested by his editor at Whitman. Ernst used the cinematic staging he'd developed in his comic book work, as well as the Caniff-inspired inking. He became an expert on the details of fashion and decor that were essential to the tamer action of a strip that was devoted to romantic tangles rather than action and intrigue. It was his artwork on *Mary Worth*, along with Saunders' slick scripts, that earned the feature an increased list of papers; and throughout the 1940s and 1950s every new soap opera strip that came along tried to look like *Mary Worth*.

Though relying increasingly on assistants, Ernst remained with the strip until his death.  **R.G.**

**ETTA KETT** The eponymous heroine of Paul D. Robinson's homey teenager strip began as an illustration of proper behavior, as her name suggests, but that sententious theme was soon played out, and Etta became indistinguishable from other spirited bobby-soxers in the comics. Distributed by King Features Syndicate from its inception in 1925, the daily and Sunday strips continued until November 3 and 4, 1974.

If Etta stopped representing teen manners, she never exceeded the bounds of middle-class propriety and never troubled her patient parents overmuch. Her life revolved around dances and dates at the Sugar Shack with her amiably simpleminded and eternally ravenous boyfriend Wingey (whose desire to become a doctor prompts Etta's father to remark wryly, as he watches Wingey raid the Kett refrigerator, that he would make a good stomach specialist). Though the strip survived into the sexual revolution, nothing more intense than getting use of the family car ever seemed to preoccupy its characters.

*Etta Kett* faithfully reflected the passing fashions in teen clothes and slang, but its graphic style never changed from the simple conventions of the 1920s. Gracefully drawn by former film animator Robinson, *Etta Kett* maintained its clean line and uncluttered composition, broken by solid patches of black, during its near half-century of wholesome fun. **D.W.**

**EVANS, GEORGE** (1920– ) Best known for his ability to draw airplanes, be they World War I vintage biplanes or current jet fighters, just about as well as any artist in the business. And airplanes have played an important part in much of what Evans has drawn in both comic books and comic strips over the past 40 years and more.

Born in Harwood, Pennsylvania, George Evans had an early fondness for flying that led him to begin illustrating for air adventure pulps at the age of 16. After a period of study with the Scranton Art School and three years in the Air Force, he started with comic books in 1946, working for various Fiction House titles and drawing such features as *Lost World*, *Señorita Rio*, and *Tigerman*. In 1949 he moved on to Fawcett to work on *Captain Video*, *Bob Colt*, and *When Worlds Collide*, while at the same time studying at the Art Students League. In 1952 he became an EC staffer, bringing his meticulous line work to crime stories for *Shock SuspenStories*, science fiction for *Weird Science*, horror for *The Haunt of Fear*, and war for *Frontline Combat*.

His flair for the air made him a key figure when EC replaced its New Trend with New Direction titles. EC editor Al Feldstein recalled, "His work was realistic and controlled, and we would therefore give him the slicker things to do. His work was like his character. George

was a professional. He was a WWI airplane buff, and we did *Aces High* because we knew that George was great at this stuff and would do well."

After EC came much work for Western on *Twilight Zone*, *Classics Illustrated* on *Julius Caesar* and *Lord Jim*, and DC on *Blackhawk*. While drawing for comic books he also turned his talents to the newspaper strip field, beginning in 1960 with behind-the-scenes work on *Terry and the Pirates* for George Wunder. In the early 1980s he took over the *Secret Agent Corrigan* strip for King Features. **B.S.**

**EVERETT, BILL** (1917–1973) A comic book artist who also wrote the majority of his own scripts, Everett's most famous creation was the Sub-Mariner. He entered comics in the late 1930s and during his over three decades in the field he drew numerous other characters, including such aquatic ones as Hydroman, the Fin, and Namora. He was also the first to draw Marvel's Daredevil.

William Blake Everett was both a high school and an art school dropout. He'd worked on cattle ranches in Arizona and Montana, served in the Merchant Marine, and been on the art staffs of newspapers in Boston and Manhattan before getting into the new field of comic books in 1938. His earliest heroes were drawn for the Centaur line and included Skyrocket Steele and the mystical Amazing Man.

He next joined with his former Centaur editor, Lloyd Jacquet, to become art director of the Funnies, Inc. shop. They provided stories and art for such magazines as *Marvel Mystery Comics*, *Blue Bolt*, and *Target Comics*, and it was in *Marvel* that Prince Namor the Sub-Mariner appeared. An antihero in his first years, Namor's vigorous assaults on civilization and his uncommon appearance won him a large and loyal readership. "He was an angry character," Everett once remarked. "He was probably expressing some of my own personality."

Everett had a distinctive way of drawing, a combination of cartooning and illustration. He once listed among his major influences such dissimilar illustrators as Dean Cornwell and Floyd Davis. In addition to the underwater prince, he drew the Patriot, the Chameleon, the Conqueror, Sub-Zero, and Bull's-Eye Bill. He drew occasional covers as well.

In the Army for four years, he came back to comics in 1946, "picking up Sub-Mariner where I'd left off." In the postwar period he drew Namora, Marvel Boy, Namaor, and, in the 1950s, quite a lot of horror material. After the near collapse of the business in the middle 1950s, he found work with greeting card companies. Stan Lee invited him back in 1964 to draw his new hero, Daredevil. Everett, working now in a more conventional style, drew the Hulk, Captain America, Ka-Zar, and a revived Sub-Mariner.                                    **R.G.**

**EVERETT TRUE**   A single-minded and direct character, the bald, middle-aged Everett True was incapable of suffering fools. He couldn't put up with cant, hypocrisy, and rudeness, and he lashed out at them with words or, more often, with his cane, his rolled up umbrella, his feet and fists and just about any other weapon that came to hand. A.D. Condo created him for NEA in 1905, and under assorted titles his strip remained in newspapers until 1927.

Condo's strip, drawn in a simple line style, usually ran in a two-column format with its panels stacked atop each other. It began life under the title *A Chapter From the Career of Everett True*, later became *The Outbursts of Everett True*, and ended its days as simply *Everett True*. Since Everett followed a nothing-but-the-truth policy, he quickly earned a reputation of being meanminded and crusty. But he refused to dissemble, and if he was bored, uncomfortable, hungry, offended, or otherwise out of sorts, he'd say so and usually follow his expression of dissatisfaction with a well-placed blow. He was also opposed to cruelty to animals, and the man who beat a horse or kicked a mutt in his vicinity could expect to be beaten or kicked himself. Just about the only person who ever got the best of him was his wife, always referred to by him as Mrs. True.

*Everett True* was one of NEA's most popular features in the early decades of the century. Condo, who lived in San Francisco, suffered a breakdown in the middle 1920s and his strip ended with the release of January 13, 1927.

In the middle 1980s writer Tony Isabella, working with an assortment of artists that included Gary Dumm and Greg Budgett, revived the character in the pages of the weekly *Comics Buyer's Guide* tabloid. Looking about the same as he had well over a half century earlier, Everett concentrated his scorn on hypocrisy and fatu-

*Everett True*, A.D. Condo, 1918.

ousness in the comic book field. After flourishing in CBG for a time, he moved briefly to the pages of *The Comics Journal*. From there the venerable curmudgeon returned to obscurity.                           **R.G.**

# F

**THE FAMILY CIRCUS** Bil Keane's daily and Sunday look at the domestic scene, *The Family Circus*, is one of the most successful panel features ever created. Distributed by the Register and Tribune Syndicate (now the Cowles Syndicate) to over 1,100 papers, it has been collected into an average of more than one book a year since its debut on February 19, 1960.

Keane (1922– ), a former staff artist with the *Philadelphia Bulletin* and free-lance gag cartoonist, created *Channel Chuckles*, a daily panel about television and its viewers, in 1954 for the Register and Tribune Syndicate. Seeing such free-lance markets as the *Saturday Evening Post, Look,* and *Collier's* disappear, he concluded that syndication was his most promising avenue of endeavor. "Most of the stuff I was selling had to do with family and little children," he recalled in 1980, "so I decided to try another feature dealing with those subjects."

The warm, loving, suburban family whose daily life Keane records is obviously drawn from his own. As his children grew up, he kept notes on 3 x 5 cards of their cute sayings and innocent mischief, providing himself with enough material, he estimated in 1980, "for maybe another 50 years." Keane, his wife Thelma, and their five children have become the panel's Daddy, Mommy ("Thel"), and children Billy, Dolly, Jeffy, and PJ, permanently fixed at seven, five, and three years, and 18 months of age, respectively. Two doting mothers-in-law, a father-in-law, occasional uncles and aunts, a shaggy mutt named Barfy and another named Sam, and Kittycat round out a regular cast. Drawn in a circle instead of the usual square panel, the feature invites us into the frantic but cozy home of a close, rounded family with whom any household can easily identify.

Assisted by Bud Warner, who has done the inking of *The Family Circus* since 1965, Keane employs a firm, clean line and compositions. Keane served as president of the National Cartoonists Society from 1982 to 1983 and won its Best Syndicated Panel plaques in 1967, 1971, 1973, and 1974. In 1982 he received the NCS's Elzie Segar Award and its Reuben as Outstanding Cartoonist of the Year.

*The Family Circus* was the subject of NBC animated cartoon specials in 1978, 1980, and 1981, and its characters have been used on calendars, for porcelain figurines, and in national food advertising. Their universal appeal has made them among the best known families in the popular arts. As *Peanuts*-creator Charles Schulz wrote of them in 1984, "The characters in *The Family Circus* love each other, and because they do, we do."

**D.W.**

**FAMOUS FICTION** Introduced in 1942 by the Bell Syndicate, this half-page was masterminded by *Parents' Magazine* and was intended to provide children something wholesome and educational along with the violence and slapstick of the other Sunday funnies. It often ran as a companion to the equally wholesome and educational *True Comics* half-page. The initial art and continuity were by Chad Grothkopf.

J. Carroll Mansfield had been drawing *Highlights of History* for Bell since the middle 1920s. In the late 1930s he started adding adaptations of classic novels—*Quentin Durward, The Prisoner of Zenda,* among others—under the title *Highlights of Famous Fiction*. His feature faded away in the early 1940s, but the *Famous Fiction* part of the title survived to get stuck on the new Sunday page.

Chad had drawn adventure features for assorted DC comic books, but his specialties were humor and funny animals. The earliest *Famous Fiction* adaptations were *Alice in Wonderland* and *Ali Baba and the Forty Thieves,* both of which allowed him to show off his specialties. When the continuities got more serious, turning to novels like *Under Two Flags*, Chad sought help on the scripts. One writer he recruited was a young fellow named Stan Lee, with whom he had worked at Marvel.

For some reason, after Chad went into the service his name continued to appear on the feature, even though he had nothing more to do with it. Artists didn't stay long with the project. The adaptation of *Robin Hood*, for example, used work by Jack Binder, Harry Anderson, and at least one other. Binder returned to do *Ben Hur* on his own. The page was last seen in 1944. Adapting a large novel to the funny paper format was no easy chore, and *Famous Fiction* offered versions of novels even more truncated than those of its newsstand competitor, *Classic Comics*.

**R.G.**

**FAMOUS FUNNIES**  One of the most influential magazines ever published, *Famous Funnies* was the first four-color, modern format comic book to be offered regularly for sale. After two tryout issues, it reached the newsstands as a monthly title in the spring of 1934. Like its immediate successors, *Famous* was made up chiefly of color reprints of newspaper Sunday pages. Included in the early issues were *Joe Palooka, Mutt & Jeff, Hairbreadth Harry, Dixie Dugan*, and *Buck Rogers*. *Famous Funnies*, with many additions and subtractions to the lineup, lasted until 1955.

The magazine was essentially the invention of Harry I. Wildenberg, sales manager for the Eastern Color Printing Company of Waterbury, Connecticut. One of the things Eastern Color did was print the Sunday funnies for several East Coast papers, and Wildenberg, a former advertising man, got the idea that collections of reprinted newspaper comics would make good advertising premiums. He also discovered that if Sunday pages were reduced, two of them would fit on a standard-sized tabloid page. After some experimenting, Wildenberg and his associates figured out how to use their presses to print 64-page color comic books. With a salesman named M.C. Gaines helping, Wildenberg sold comic books as premiums to such advertisers as Canada Dry, Kinney Shoes, and Proctor & Gamble.

The first *Famous Funnies*, subtitled *A Carnival of Comics*, was issued as a premium. Wildenberg and Gaines next persuaded the Woolworth chain to sell an issue, with a 10 cents price tag. When Woolworth decided against handling any further issues, Wildenberg approached the American News Company and got them to distribute *Famous* to newsstands across America. Within a year the new magazine was netting $30,000 an issue. For nearly its entire run Stephen A. Douglas was editor and production manager.

The success of *Famous Funnies* inspired other publishers to enter the comic book business, and it was followed on the stands by such reprint titles as *Popular Comics, Super Comics, Tip Top Comics*, and *King Comics*. Major Nicholson introduced the first comic book in the new format using original material in 1935. By the late 1930s there was a thriving comic book industry going in America.                                              **R.G.**

**FANTASTIC FOUR**  Launched in 1961, *Fantastic Four* laid the foundation of the Marvel Comics Group and revolutionized the superhero comic book. It originated with three men: Martin Goodman, the publisher of the failing Atlas comics line, who wanted an imitation of DC's *Justice League of America* to exploit the fad for new superheroes; creator-penciller Jack Kirby, who wanted to revitalize such heroes with "a real human dimension"; and editor-scripter Stan Lee, who wanted to "bear down and make something of myself" after 20 years of undistinguished work. They gambled on a new approach to comic books, and won big.

In the first issue, an odd quartet of friends—stuffy scientist Reed Richards, his fiancée Sue Storm, her sparky teenage brother Johnny, and the truculent, self-pitying Ben Grimm—pirated a rocket in a lunatic bid to beat the Reds to the moon, but were belted by cosmic radiation and turned into superpowered freaks: respectively, the elastic Mr. Fantastic, the Invisible Girl, the Human Torch, and the powerful, stone-skinned Thing.

The four promptly dedicated their powers to fighting evil, but there the resemblance to conventional heroes ended. They wore no costumes at first (although they were soon given plain, matching uniforms) and conducted their heroics with an air of secrecy and almost perilous extra-sociality. They argued frequently (particularly Ben Grimm, cursed by his irreversible transformation into the hideous Thing) and often viewed heroism more as a grim destiny than as a blessing. They were alternately adored and feared by the world at large, and suffered some remarkable reverses in their fortunes (including losing their headquarters to Richards' bad investments, thus finding themselves financially indentured to their arch-enemy, the Sub-Mariner). In short, they were far more "realistic" than any superheroes had ever been.

The characters developed over the years, also unlike any earlier comic book heroes, and while they stayed quarrelsome, a familial affection developed to hold them together through eternal emotional turmoil. The Thing found a sense of humor and a Brooklynese voice that made him one of the most endearing heroes in comics, while Sue developed a huge crush on the Sub-Mariner, straining relations greatly until Reed finally swallowed his jealousy, wooed her back, married her (in 1965), and fathered her son (in 1968).

The bad guys were fascinatingly ambivalent and darkly threatening, quite unlike the amusing gimmick-foes of other comics. The Sub-Mariner, revived from the Golden Age, was the noble, bitter monarch of a lost subterranean race, whose enmity toward surface people and the Fantastic Four seemed largely justified; when he recovered his people and much of his emotional equilibrium, he switched from villain to hero. Dr. Doom was a great scientist driven to madness by his hatred of his own deformed face, who often displayed a tragic side and (after becoming tyrant of the Balkan nation of Latveria) a certain kingly nobility.

*Fantastic Four* grew into a significant success, emboldening Lee and his collaborators to create the Hulk, Spider-Man, and other innovative Marvel Comics heroes. The series reached its peak in the mid-1960s, melding Kirby's powerful narrative art, apocalyptic plots, and symbolic, almost mythic inventions with Lee's baroque, witty writing and vivid characterization. In a series of long plots that overlapped and interlinked over a two-year period (another break from comic book customs, which had favored self-contained stories), Kirby and Lee introduced many of Marvel's most enduring characters, including the Black Panther, the Inhumans, and the cosmic duo of the Silver Surfer and Galactus.

The series began to decline in the late 1960s, and with the departures of Kirby (1970) and Lee (1972) it lost its position at the forefront of superhero comics. Periodic attempts to revive the spirit of the Kirby-Lee days (most effectively by writer-artist John Byrne in 1982–1984 and Walter Simonson in 1990) have made it occasionally enjoyable, but it has generally coasted on past inventions for 20 years. Nearly all modern superhero comics, however, have drawn and continue to draw upon the first 80 or so issues of *Fantastic Four* for inspiration and material. **G.J.**

**FARR, JACK** (?–c. 1948) Like several veteran magazine and newspaper cartoonists of the first half of the century, Farr ended his days working for comic books. He'd drawn comic strips and had numerous gag cartoons in humor magazines such as *Judge* and *Life* before entering the comic book field in 1940. Farr tackled every sort of feature in this new market, from funny fillers to detective stories about Nick Carter.

He started his career as a newspaper cartoonist and by the second decade of the century he was drawing comics for the *New York Telegram*. From 1917 to 1920 he did a series of unsuccessful pages—*Mr. Jolt, Chubby*, and others—for the *World*. During the 1920s Farr contributed cartoons to magazines such as *Judge*, where one of his specialties was complicated big-city scenes packed with people, tall buildings, and vehicular traffic. He also drew for *Life* and, in the 1930s, for *Ballyhoo* and *Photoplay*. The burgeoning of the comic book business came at the same time that Farr was slipping down the ladder of success a bit.

Among his earliest employers was Street & Smith, a publisher whose comic books were a haven for aging, down-on-their-luck cartoonists (S&S used newspaper vets such as C.M. Payne, Thornton Fisher, and Dwig). Farr modified his humorous style just a little and initially drew only straight adventure fare. His work appeared in *Shadow Comics*, illustrating the investigations of the master detective Nick Carter, as well as those of a science fiction hero named Iron Munro. For *Army and Navy Comics*, aimed at the growing number of military camps, Farr provided the covers and most of the contents. His main character was a dimwitted recruit named Private Rook.

In 1943 he hooked up with DC. Farr drew several episodes of *Slam Bradley*, the tough private eye created by Jerry Siegel and Joe Shuster, but mostly he concentrated on funny stuff. As a humorist he was not especially subtle, favoring silliness over satire, but he drew with such zest that his work always looked as though it must be funny. Years earlier he'd mastered all the pen and ink patterns and also perfected a highly personal approach to perspective. In addition to funny-looking people, Farr would often throw in vast landscapes or complex urban scenes. Throughout most of the 1940s he provided short humor features for many of the DC titles, including a mock detective named Super-Sleuth McFooey and a mock muscleman named Vitamin Vic.

During his comic book years Farr was an alcoholic, the kind who needed a drink or two to keep his hands from shaking. Yet he was able to turn out an impressive number of pages, almost all of them done in his careful pen and ink style and filled with his meticulous crosshatching. He died of the consequences of his alcoholism in New York's Bellevue Hospital. **R.G.**

**THE FAR SIDE** Gary Larson's daily panel feature *The Far Side* began in 1978 in the *Seattle* (Washington) *Times* as "Nature's Way," but its off beat humor proved too bizarre for the local market and it did not survive its first year there. Picked up by the *San Francisco Chronicle*, it was syndicated by Chronicle Features in 1979, running briefly as *Garyland* ("a skilled young artist draws you through a land of lunacy") and quickly changed to its present name. At the end of its five-year contract, it was taken over by Universal Press Syndicate, which now distributes it daily and Sunday to more than 700 newspapers.

A morbid thread running through Larson's panels links them to the tradition of Charles Addams' *New Yorker* cartoons and the later work of Gahan Wilson—recurrent themes are cannibalism, suicide, and execution—but *The Far Side* is more fantastic than macabre. Much of its humor derives from absurd role-reversals between pet and master: A canary flies away as its master, stuffed into a birdcage, says, "You'll never get away with this"; a dog drives a car with a man leaning out the window. Or the assignment of human characteristics to animals: Cows argue theorems of advanced mathematics, only to switch to "Moo! Moo!" when the farmer comes in the barn; a cow wakes from a nightmare crying, "The golden arches got me!" All creatures great and small are pressed into service: An amoeba pleads as it divides, "No, Elizabeth…Don't go!"; giant prehistoric lizards smoking cigarettes provide "The real reason dinosaurs became extinct."

Larson's expressively simple drawing can transform a man-eating fish into a "shark nerd" by adding a flashy shirt, or a cow into a dowdy suburban housewife by giving her a string of beads and a pair of harlequin glasses. A favorite subject is science and scientists, and he frequently makes fun of academics (professors engage in an eraser fight; paleontologists argue over who gets to ride down a dinosaur skeleton next). The series has been very popular on campuses. A 1985–1986 California Academy of Sciences show of original Larson drawings drew 11,000 visitors in San Francisco and traveled to the Smithsonian Institution in Washington.

Larson's "wonderfully skewed" interpretation of nature has produced several very successful collections; the first three anthologies of *The Far Side* were all on the *New York Times* best-seller list and sold over six million copies by 1987. Larson's characters are merchandised widely on posters, greeting cards, coffee mugs, and sweatshirts. **D.W.**

**FEARLESS FOSDICK** See LI'L ABNER.

**FEIFFER, JULES** (1929– ) The dean of American "intellectual" cartoonists, Jules Ralph Feiffer first introduced his searching graphic vignettes in the *Village Voice* in 1956 and has since grown in stature to become one of the leading social, psychological, and political commentators in the country.

Feiffer was born in the Bronx and attended the Art Students League in 1946 and Pratt Institute from 1947 to 1951. He assisted comic-book cartoonist Will Eisner, ghosting *The Spirit* from 1946 to 1951, and from 1949 to 1951 drew his own cartoon strip, *Clifford*, as a part of the *Spirit* feature, while holding such other art-related jobs as making film slides, designing booklets for an art firm, and writing cartoons for Terrytoons. From 1951 to 1953 he served in a cartoon animation unit of the Army Signal Corps.

Feiffer's trademark cartoons—monologues or dialogues revealing the speakers' psychological or sexual angst in comic-strip form using from six to eight panels—began to appear in the avant-garde New York weekly *The Village Voice* as *Sick, Sick, Sick* in 1956. The relentlessly bleak and painfully acute insight of these features, too negative for many, were exactly on-target for the *Voice* readership and quickly generated a cult. The two-row strip changed its name to *Feiffer* in testimony to the extraordinarily personal voice of its creator, and it was picked up by the *London Observer* in 1958 and syndicated by Robert Hall in 1960. Now distributed by Publishers-Hall to over 100 papers, it has produced published collections every two years since *Sick, Sick, Sick* (McGraw-Hill, 1958). Never paid by the *Voice*, Feiffer earned his first regular money for the strip from Hugh Hefner, who began running it in *Playboy* after the publication of the first collection in 1958.

Feiffer's first recurring character was Bernard Mergandeiler, "a Robert Benchley character launched into the age of Freud." A defeated and hopeless figure, he is described elsewhere by Feiffer as "a young urban liberal given to anxiety attacks, stomachaches, and obsessive confessionals. He either had bad sex or no sex; either way he felt guilty." Later Feiffer created the Dancer, "Bernard's female counterpart, abused and exploited by men no less than he was by women" but eternally hopeful. She dances to the seasons, to the president, to art, to the new year; in 1982 she danced to Reaganomics: "No frills. No excuses. No giveaways. No favors. No money. No job. No government. No thanks."

From the year of his syndication, 1960, Feiffer began addressing himself increasingly to the national scene, pillorying each president as he came along. Kennedy was "The Sundance Kid," Ford was presented with a tin can on his head like Opper's simpleton Happy Hooligan, Carter was "Jimmy the Cloud," and Reagan's administration was "Movie America." In 1986, the strip brought him the Pulitzer Prize for editorial cartooning, an honor his friends Garry Trudeau and three-time Pulitzer winner Paul Conrad thought long overdue.

Feiffer has become as well known for his work in other media as for his cartoons. He has written a novel, short stories, plays, television scripts, and screenplays such as *Carnal Knowledge* (1971). He has contributed essays to magazines such as *Ramparts* and edited a collection of comic-book material, *The Great Comic Book Heroes* (Dial, 1965). His animated cartoon *Munro*, based on one of his cartoon stories, won an Oscar as the best short-subject cartoon in 1961. But it is his sparely drawn, little mini-tales, written with an uncanny ear for the speech, and a penetrating eye into the spirit, of his times that have earned him the status of one of the gurus of his generation. **D.W.**

**FEININGER, LYONEL** See THE KIND-DER-KIDS.

**FELIX THE CAT** The fearless feline was the first animated cartoon character to become the star of a newspaper comic strip. Felix originally appeared on the screen in 1919 and made his funny paper debut four years later. From the early 1940s onward he showed up regularly in comic books as well. Although his movie and comics appearances were credited to Pat Sullivan, Felix was actually the creation of Otto Messmer.

Messmer was working at Sullivan's animation studios in New York at the time he invented the black cat, and thus the ownership of the character was held by his employer. Felix, a loner, was a clever fellow. Film historian Leonard Maltin has cited the two most popular trademarks of the animated series as "Felix's pensive walk, with head down in a thoughtful position and hands clasped behind his back, and his unique gift for turning his tail into any implement necessary at the moment—an oar, a baseball bat, a fishing hook, a telescope."

The cat proved popular, starring in a series of cartoons. In the 1920s merchandising began, with Felix toys, dolls, and timepieces. King Features started syndicating a Sunday page in 1923, adding a daily in 1927. A paper-covered book reprinting a handful of Sunday pages was also published in 1927. The artwork on the strip was taken care of by Messmer. Felix was as clever and inventive at getting out of scrapes in the strip as he was in the movies, and he had the advantage of being able to talk. By the early 1930s the strip was using continuity and Felix enjoyed a wide range of adventures. Messmer was especially fond of sending the cat on expeditions to Africa, Egypt, and assorted desert islands. He also liked to mix Felix up in fairy tale sequences that used giants, ogres, pixies, and princesses.

In 1942 reprints of the strip became one of the features in Dell's *New Funnies*. Dell brought out its initial full book of *Felix* in 1943 and in 1946 started using original material instead of reprints, which was also by Messmer for the most part. Several other publishers brought out the title, which ended in the 1960s. Messmer stopped drawing it in 1955.

An animator named Joe Oriolo bought the rights to the character in the middle 1950s, and eventually produced 260 rather bland cartoons for television. Oriolo's name was signed to the strip from 1955 until its end in 1966, but the actual drawing was done by others.

Felix made a comeback of sorts in 1984. Definitely treated as a second banana, he shared a newspaper strip titled *Betty Boop and Felix*. Offered by King Features, it was a joint effort of Mort Walker's four sons. Most of the time Felix was little more than a house pet of the boop-a-doop heroine. In 1987 the cat exited, though the strip continued until the following year as *Betty Boop and Friends*. Felix' early animated cartoons are available on videocassette and a full-length cartoon is rumored to be in the works. **R.G.**

**FERD'NAND** One of the most enduring of pantomime humor strips, the daily and Sunday *Ferd'nand* was created in 1937 by Danish film animator Henning Dahl Mikkelsen, who signed it "Mik." The strip enjoyed 10 successful years in Europe, its lack of speech enabling it to cross borders without trouble, before United Features Syndicate transported its mute hero to the United States in 1947.

*Ferd'nand's* bland, genial humor revolves around its titular hero, an amiable little fellow with an amiable little wife and son, living in an amiable little town, all singularly free of conflict. Invariably wearing a black

jacket, tie, and white pants, shoes, and vest, and with a conical white hat, Ferd'nand goes about his never-identified business in serene, trouble-free silence. The mystery of what work he goes off to every morning is enhanced by the fact that he carries a lunchbox like a laborer but dresses like an executive—except for his curious headgear, which identifies him with no one except his small son, who wears a miniature replica of it. Cleanly drawn in a simple, balanced style, the strip has for more than half a century maintained a timeless, sunny spirit.

Mikkelsen, who became more interested in real estate than in cartooning after relocating in America, relied heavily on ghosts. From 1955 to 1965, for example, comic book veteran Frank Thomas drew the strip. And in 1970 Mikkelsen hired Al Plastino, comic book and strip veteran, as ghost. Plastino signed his work "Al Mik" and since Mikkelsen's death in 1982 has carried on the strip virtually unchanged. **D.W.**

**FINE, LOU** (1915–1971) An exceptional artist, Fine had at least three distinct careers. He drew comic book superheroes (from the late 1930s to the mid 1940s); he was a prolific producer of Sunday funnies advertising strips (from the mid 1940s to the mid 1950s); and he also drew an assortment of newspaper strips.

Born in New York, Louis Kenneth Fine was stricken with polio in his teens and was left with a crippled left leg. He devoted a good deal of the time he had to spend indoors to studying and drawing, and was especially influenced by such illustrators as J.C. Leyendecker, Dean Cornwell, and Heinrich Kley. The quiet, redheaded Fine studied art at the Grand Central Art School and at Pratt Institute. In 1938 he joined the Will Eisner-Jerry Iger shop, and some of his earliest professional work appeared in the tab-sized *Jumbo Comics*. His first superhero was the Flame, who starred in Fox' *Wonderworld Comics*. Realizing that Fine was an exceptional draftsman, Eisner assigned him to do covers for most of the Fox comics that the shop was packaging, among them *Mystery Men* and *Fantastic*. Fine drew in a confident, heroic style, and even when drawing the requisite costumed heroes, monsters, fiends, engines of destruction, and damsels in distress, he managed to turn out strongly designed covers. Like many good packages, his covers were usually better than the contents within.

He went to work for the Quality line late in 1939 and did impressive work over the next two years on such heroes as Dollman, the Black Condor, Uncle Sam, and the Ray. It was his bravura work of this period that inspired and impressed younger artists such as Gil Kane and Alex Toth. Fine also assisted on the weekly *Spirit* story, and when Eisner went into the Army in the

*Hit Comics* cover, Lou Fine, © 1940, Quality Comics.

spring of 1942, he took over the masked man. Fine underwent a change at this point, turning away from his lyrical fantasy style and adopting a slick, plain-clothes realism, which was highly professional but somewhat dull. When Eisner returned in 1946, Fine gave up comic books and moved into advertising. His new style grew better and livelier, and during the middle 1940s, working in this new vein, Fine also drew a weekly black and white strip, titled *The Thropp Family*, for *Liberty*.

Teamed with Don Komisarow, who served as inker and salesman, Fine proceeded to dominate the field of Sunday comics advertising strips. He had worked initially for the Johnstone & Cushing ad art service before going out on his own. He and his partner provided strips for an impressive list of clients, including Toni Home Permanent, Philip Morris, Pepsi-Cola, General Foods, and RKO Radio Pictures, and Fine drew such characters as Mr. Coffee Nerves, Lucille Ball, and Sam Spade.

He continued with advertising and commercial art for the rest of his career, even though the ad strip field faded by the late 1950s. But he also tried his hand at comic strips. He had drawn a short-lived one, in collaboration with Komisarow, called *Taylor Woe* in 1949. Working with writer Elliot Caplin, Fine drew *Adam Ames*, a soap opera strip, in the late 1950s, and *Peter Scratch*, a tough private eye strip, in the middle 1960s. Despite handsome artwork, none of his strips was especially successful. At the time of his death, Fine was working on samples for a new comic strip.    **R.G.**

**FISHER, BUD** (1884–1954)  He was one of the first to establish that a comic artist could be rich and respectable. Fisher did that by creating *Mutt and Jeff* in 1907 and parlaying it into a multimillion-dollar property.

Harry Conway Fisher was born in Chicago. He quit the University of Chicago after three months and went to California to make history. When he arrived at the *San Francisco Chronicle*, like most early cartoonists, he was assigned to the sports department, where for a few years he did layouts and sports cartoons. Then on November 15, 1907, Fisher made history—he began what would become the first successful daily comic strip. The success of *Mutt and Jeff*, known originally as *A. Mutt*, established the strip form for daily newspaper comics and brought fame and fortune to Fisher.

But his contributions to the medium didn't end with defining its format. To begin with, Fisher had the foresight to copyright the strip in his own name. Further, he had the audacity to go to court to protect his rights. His first legal skirmish took place within months of his strip's debut. William Randolph Hearst had lured the cartoonist over to the *San Francisco Examiner* to draw his feature, but the *Chronicle* kept running the strip, now done by Russ Westover. Fisher sued, but dropped the action when the *Chronicle* stopped publishing their version in June 1908.

Fisher had to take his fight to court in the 1913–1915 period when he left Hearst to join John Wheeler's Bell Syndicate and Hearst continued the strip without him, hiring Ed Mack to do it. In winning his suit, Fisher established a legal precedent: Because of his copyright, the strip and its characters belonged to him and not, as had been customary, to Hearst or the paper that published the strip.

The dapper Fisher was a cocky, scrappy, hard-drinking, carousing denizen of city room and saloon, antagonistic and belligerent. By 1913 the popularity of *Mutt and Jeff* was so great that Wheeler was guaranteeing Fisher $1,000 a week. The widely publicized deal added to Fisher's already considerable fame, and he quickly habituated himself to enjoying both wealth and celebrity. The latter made him welcome in circles normally closed to newspapermen and other such vulgarians, and he relished his position in high society. The first truly famous cartoonist, Fisher worked hard on his public image. He bought a stable of race horses, drove about town in a Rolls Royce, and prowled nightclubs with a beautiful showgirl on each arm.

By the 1920s Fisher was enjoying his social life so much that he left most of the work on the strip to his assistant Ed Mack, whom he had hired after winning the suit against Hearst. The more he moved in society's salons, the less use he had for his erstwhile brethren of the sporting and cartooning worlds, and he regularly snubbed his onetime associates. From 1932 on his latest assistant, Al Smith, produced the strip without much guidance. Fisher's last years were desolate and lonely, spent almost entirely in the huge museum of his Park Avenue apartment, whose ornate rooms he had purchased and moved from historic European houses. Toward the end he seldom left his bedroom, where he slept on a bare mattress and pillows without cases. The rest of his place slipped into shabby decay, its hallways lined with stacks of unopened envelopes from his bank. Like Miss Havisham, Fisher died amid the faded remnants of a once opulent lifestyle as cartooning's first millionaire.    **R.C.H.**

**FISHER, HAM** (1901–1955)  Fisher was first and foremost a promoter. A below-average cartoonist with a knack for storytelling, he created *Joe Palooka* and promoted it into one of the most successful newspaper strips of its time. He firmly believed from the start that his sentimental adventure strip about a clean-cut and innocent boxing champ would bring him fame and fortune. Indeed, it did, and when Fisher took his own life at the age of 54, he left an estate of $2,500,000.

Hammond Edward Fisher was born in Wilkes-Barre, Pennsylvania. After graduating from high school, he worked as a reporter and cartoonist for the local newspaper. While his mother was supportive, his father "had complete contempt for my aesthetic ambitions." Undaunted, Fisher journeyed to New York in 1926 to seek his fortune. He secured a job not as a writer or artist but as an ad salesman for the *New York Daily News*. In 1929 he got himself hired as a salesman for the McNaught Syndicate. While on the road peddling *Dixie Dugan* (then known as *Show Girl*), Fisher also touted a strip of his own, *Joe Palooka*, a sports strip he'd been trying to sell to a syndicate for several years. He managed to persuade nearly two dozen papers to try the ill-drawn strip, and McNaught agreed to give it a try.

Fisher had help on the strip from almost the start. His first regular assistant/ghost was a fellow Wilkes-Barre artist named Phil Boyle. As time went by, Joe got better looking and became less of a rube. The strip began picking up more and more papers. In 1933 Fisher hired Al Capp, laying the groundwork for a feud that would last the rest of Fisher's life. At the time and for a few years afterward both men spoke kindly of each other—at least in the public prints. But gradually the clash of these two oversized egos broke out into the open.

During the period when he drew and helped write *Palooka*, Capp had introduced a hillbilly boxer named Big Leviticus. This bumpkin and his kin proved amusing and popular. In 1934 Capp sold *Li'l Abner* and went into business with a funny hillbilly family of his own, which apparently didn't sit well with Fisher. When Leviticus returned to the Palooka strip, Fisher would add such footnotes as, "The first hillbillies to appear in a comic strip were Big Leviticus and his family. Any resemblance to our original hillbillies is certainly not a coincidence." While this squabble was going on, *Joe Palooka* kept forging ahead and adding papers to its list. Fisher's ghost was now Mo Leff, hired away from Capp. *Joe Palooka* eventually reached a circulation of over 1,000 papers worldwide, and Fisher's income from the strip, comic book reprints, movies, radio shows, and other merchandising was over $250,000 a year.

But the feud went on and Fisher continued to make rude remarks in print. He claimed that he almost literally picked the young Capp up out of the gutter and set him on the path to success: "I was a literate gentleman, and Mr. Capp a wild-haired boy." Capp complained to the National Cartoonists Society, of which they were both members. And he told *Newsweek*, "I regard him as a leper. I feel sorry for him. I shun him." For the April 1950 issue of the *Atlantic Monthly* Capp wrote a piece titled "I Remember Monster." Though never mention-

ing Fisher by name, Capp made it quite clear whom he was talking about. "It was my privilege, as a boy, to be associated with a certain treasure trove of lousiness, who, in the normal course of each day of his life, managed to be, in dazzling succession, every conceivable kind of heel."

Sometime after this attack Fisher became obsessed with the notion that Capp was slipping pornographic material into *Li'l Abner*. Not the gentlest of satirists, Capp had long populated his strip with outhouses, large bosoms, low necklines, lust and lechery and ample double entendres. There were sexual allusions aplenty and a good lot of earthy humor, as might be expected in a comic strip with characters named Moonbeam McSwine and Barney Barnsmell. Building on that, Fisher took to making blowups of certain *Abner* panels, or even of parts of panels, to show not only the verbal sexual references but also to point up the fact that a knot on a tree might resemble a bare breast and the crotch of another tree might resemble a female crotch.

Fisher sent this material out to the news media, and at least one scandal magazine of the day ran an article on the alleged filth in *Li'l Abner. Time* wrote up this latest round in the Fisher-Capp battle in its February 14, 1955, issue. Shortly after that the NCS ousted Fisher, accusing him of altering and tampering with the *Abner* panels in order to strengthen his case. Two days after Christmas that year Fisher was found dead in the Madison Avenue studio he shared with Leff. He'd written two suicide notes, chiefly complaining about ill health, and taken sleeping pills. **R.G.**

**FLANDERS, CHARLES** (1907–1973) One of the most successful imitators of Alex Raymond ever employed by King Features, Flanders followed him on the *Secret Agent X-9* strip late in 1935. He next drew *King of the Royal Mounted* and in 1939 took over *The Lone Ranger*; he remained with the masked man for over 30 years.

After graduating from high school, Flanders worked as a commercial artist in Buffalo while studying art in night school. He migrated to New York City in 1928, working first as an art director in an advertising agency and then with the Macfadden magazines. In the early 1930s Flanders hooked up with King Features Syndicate, going to work in the bullpen and ghosting such features as *Tim Tyler's Luck* and *Bringing Up Father*.

Late in 1934 he crossed paths with Major Malcolm Wheeler-Nicholson, who was about to launch *New Fun Comics*. For the underfunded major Flanders began an adaptation of *Ivanhoe*, handsomely drawn in Sunday-page format and showing the influence of Howard Pyle, and a contemporary adventure page titled *Sandra of the Secret Service*. Flanders also started an adaptation of *Treasure Island* before parting company with the major.

In 1935 he sold a short-lived Sunday page, *Robin Hood*, to King. Impressively drawn in the manner of *Ivanhoe*, it was to be the last thing he'd do in his own style.

By the mid-1930s Alex Raymond's work on *Flash Gordon, Jungle Jim,* and *Secret Agent X-9* was very popular with readers, editors, and the powers at King. Several other artists were apparently encouraged to emulate his approach to figure drawing and brushwork inking, among them Phil Davis on *Mandrake* and Ray Moore on *The Phantom*. When Flanders replaced Raymond on *X-9* in 1935, he, too, was drawing in an approximation of his predecessor's style. He kept the look when he added the Sunday *King of the Royal Mounted* to his chores in 1936. Giving up *X-9* in 1938, Flanders assumed the drawing of the *King* daily as well. Early in 1939, he was assigned to take over *The Lone Ranger* daily and Sunday.

Initially he seemed at home on the range and did a commendable job with the feature well into the 1940s. From then on, due in part to personal problems, his work steadily declined. He took to drawing almost everybody from the back, to save himself the trouble of having to draw faces, and always cut off figures as high as he could. Whole Sunday pages consisted of nothing but the backs of heads and a few scraggly trees in the distance. There were periods when he was unable to do the strip at all, when Tom Gill, who was responsible for the comic book version, usually filled in. Both the strip and Flanders were retired in 1971. **R.G.**

**FLAPPER FANNY** Philosophical and cute, Fanny began life in a one-column panel in 1924, which consisted of a drawing of the dark-haired young flapper with an epigrammatical remark set in type beneath it. The little feature was drawn originally by Ethel Hays and syndicated by NEA.

Hays was born in Billings, Montana, "where one gets plenty of room to breathe." She studied at the School of Art and Design in Los Angeles and the Art Students League in Manhattan. Immediately after World War I she taught drawing in veterans' hospitals in several states. After she took the Landon mail-order cartooning course, C.N. Landon himself got her a job with the *Cleveland Press* art department, which was where *Flapper Fanny* was born.

Hays worked in a style that had some of the black and white simplicity of Russell Patterson and John Held Jr. and some of the fancy frills of the work of Nell Brinkley. With its double entendre title and up-to-the-minute fashions, the panel was aimed at the Jazz Age smart set—or at those, a vaster number, who fancied they were part of it. Each day Fanny, a pretty brunette with her hair cropped in the latest style, appeared and offered a wisecracking observation on life: "When men's

FLAPPER FANNY SAYS:

*If a man wants to see a girl the worst way, he should call in the morning.*

*Flapper Fanny*, Ethel Hays, © 1929, NEA Service, Inc.

clothes are cut along sober lines, they'll leave out the hip pockets," "If a man wants to see a girl in the worst way, he should call in the morning," etc. Often she appeared in her lingerie or negligee and sometimes even lolling in the tub.

Gladys Parker, who drew in a similar style and looked quite a bit like Fanny (as the syndicate was fond of pointing out: "Flapper Fanny—In Person"), took over the feature in the early 1930s. A Sunday page was added, but it was never as innocently racy as the panel. Fanny, who was always chicly dressed, shared Sundays with her kid sister Betty, a blond of about 10.

In the final years of the 1930s, and of the feature, an artist who signed herself simply Sylvia drew *Flapper Fanny*. She worked in a wholesome version of the style, and the panel, enlarged to two columns in width, was devoted to tame gags rather than pithy sayings. **R.G.**

**THE FLASH (I)** The old original Flash came whizzing into view as 1940 started, the star of a brand-new DC magazine entitled *Flash Comics*. He wore a red tunic with a lightning bolt on the chest, blue tights, winged red boots, and a winged tin hat of the sort made famous by Mercury and speedy delivery services. He shared the new book with Hawkman, the Whip, Johnny Thunder, and others. *Flash Comics* was the third title packaged for

Detective Comics, Inc., by M.C. Gaines, publisher, and Sheldon Mayer, editor and boy cartoonist. The chief writer on the magazine was the increasingly productive Gardner Fox, and he was the one who created the Flash. Harry Lampert was the first artist.

The origin story led off the issue and was set at a Midwestern university called Midwestern University. Jay Garrick was a brilliant student and, unlike some of the scruffier jitterbugs of the day, wore a suit and tie on campus. While monitoring an experiment having to do with the "gases emanating from 'hard water,'" he knocked some retorts to the floor and was overcome by the gas. After hovering between life and death for weeks, Garrick rallied. It turned out he'd become "a freak of science" and would be "the fastest thing that ever walked on Earth!!" Instead of rushing out to fight crime, the young man dashed off to the gridiron. Using his newfound speed, he won the game, became a football hero and impressed his girlfriend, Joan Williams. After graduating and taking a job as an assistant professor in New York, Jay decided to become the Flash. His earliest cases found him avoiding the flamboyant villains and cackling mad scientists some of his superhero colleagues specialized in, and favoring instead gangsters, gamblers, and crooked politicians. His speed allowed him to disdain such mundane modes of travel as cars and planes. "At times his speed can touch 1000 MPH," Fox informed readers. His speed also gave him the ability to "disappear from human sight," which he brought off by spinning around very rapidly; this made him an invisible man but apparently didn't result in any dizziness afterwards.

The Flash could toss a hoodlum through a door or wall, "even as a cyclone thrusts straws through trees by the fleetness of its wind velocity." And he could fly at times "just as a glider sails along after getting up speed." Endowed with a sense of humor by his creator, the Flash enjoyed using his gifts to play an occasional prank on a wrongdoer. Once, borrowing a wrench from a garage, he chased after a kidnapper and dismantled the body of his car while it was driving along. His caseload was never a grim one, and his adventures were never completely serious.

Fox continued as scriptwriter, but from the third issue on E.E. Hibbard became the artist. In his thirties when he took over, Hibbard had an effective style that mixed cartoon elements with an inking approach influenced by his idols, Milton Caniff and Noel Sickles.

A few months after his debut, the Flash branched out and started appearing in the newest Gaines-Mayer title, *All Star Comics*. He graduated from that into a magazine of his own, *All-Flash*, which first appeared in May of 1941. Starting in 1943 he was also to be found in *Comic Cavalcade*, a fat 15-cent anthology he shared with the likes of Wonder Woman and Green Lantern.

A great many of the heroes overseen by Mayer lightened up during the Second World War, possibly in an attempt to boost morale. During this humorous period some heroes picked up clowns rather than boy wonders as sidekicks. The Green Lantern, for example, added Doiby Dickles, a blend of such 1940s movie comedians as Lou Costello and William Bendix. The Flash took on a trio of fools, fellows based quite closely on the Three Stooges and eventually dubbed the Three Dimwits. They debuted in *All-Flash* #5, but weren't allowed into *Flash Comics* until #46 (October 1943). Named Winky, Blinky and Noddy, they disrupted the Flash's life for several years and ruined his chances of ever being taken for a serious superhero.

Because of the number of Flash stories appearing, Hibbard didn't always do the artwork. Hal Sharp ghosted a number in the War years, as did an incomparable artist named Louis Ferstadt. A somewhat radical fellow, and trained as a fine artist, Ferstadt's work resembled WPA murals and his splash panels often looked like Picassos.

The Flash became somewhat more serious in the late 1940s. Hibbard left the feature in 1947, and such artists as Lee Elias, Alex Toth, Joe Kubert, and Carmine Infantino took turns slicking up his appearance. He retired in 1949, when *Flash Comics* closed up shop with its 104th issue. Although his name and abilities were passed on, the original Flash has popped up now and then over the years, with these recurrences explained by an increasingly complex mythology.          **R.G.**

**THE FLASH (II)**  The first of National (DC) Comics' canceled Golden Age superheroes to be revived and revamped, the new Flash was developed for a tryout in *Showcase* in 1956 by editor Julius Schwartz, with scripts by Robert Kanigher and John Broome. The pencil art was by Carmine Infantino, who had drawn many Golden Age Flash stories and was then maturing into one of National's most stylish and innovative artists.

The new Flash was distinguished from the old mainly by a sleeker uniform, more amazing speed-powers (traveling through time and between "dimensions," controlling the molecular vibrations of his body), and a more metaphorically appropriate origin: Police scientist Barry Allen is simultaneously struck by lightning and bathed by chemicals. Sales justified three more *Showcase* appearances, then a regular *Flash* comic beginning in 1959. This success encouraged Schwartz to revive other Golden Age heroes, thus launching the "Silver Age" (see ATOM [II], GREEN LANTERN [II], HAWKMAN [II], JUSTICE LEAGUE OF AMERICA).

Broome wrote nearly all the Flash's adventures over the next decade, perfecting a simple but witty style and a deft plot formula that generally involved the Flash saving himself by his wits from some super villain's diabolical trap. (Gardner F. Fox pinch-hit for a few stories, including one in 1961 that showed that DC's Golden Age heroes were still living on a parallel Earth.) Broome created a delightful rogue's gallery for his hero, including Captain Cold, the Mirror Master, Super- Gorilla Grodd, Captain Boomerang, Reverse Flash, and the Weather Wizard, whose names all speak eloquently for their natures and powers, while Infantino brought these stories to life with some of the best-designed and most narratively forceful work of his career. The *Flash* comics of the early- and mid-sixties still stand as superbly crafted children's entertainment.

In the late 1960s, first Infantino and then Broome left the series, which ran rather aimlessly under a succession of writers (including Kanigher, Frank Robbins, Mike Friedrich, and Len Wein) and artists (including Ross Andru and Gil Kane). By the early 1970s it had settled into a pleasant but spiritless routine under writer Cary Bates and penciller Irv Novick. Don Heck replaced Novick briefly and then, in 1981, Infantino returned to join Bates. It wasn't enough to revive the tired character, however, and Flash limped to cancellation in 1985.

The character was killed in DC's *Crisis on Infinite Earths* (1985), replaced by his former sidekick Kid Flash (originally introduced in 1962), whose adventures continue in a new *Flash* series. **G.J.**

**FLASH GORDON** Originally intended as King Features' answer to *Buck Rogers*, it began as a Sunday page early in 1934. Alex Raymond, recruited out of the King bullpen, was the original artist, and Don Moore, a former pulp magazine editor, was the writer.

"World Comes To End" announced a newspaper headline in the first panel of the first Sunday. "Strange New Planet Rushing Toward Earth. Only Miracle Can Save Us, Says Science." In movie fashion readers were then shown shots of the African jungles "as howling blacks await their doom," the Arabian desert where "the Arab…faces Mecca and prays for salvation," and Times Square, where "a seething mass of humanity watches a bulletin board describing the flight of the comet." All was not lost, however, since Dr. Hans Zarkov had been working night and day to perfect "a device with which he hopes to save the world." As fate would have it, an eastbound airliner was struck by a meteor while passing right over Zarkov's house. Among those parachuting from the ill-fated craft were "Flash Gordon, Yale graduate and world-renowned polo player, and Dale Arden, a passenger." What with one thing and another, Flash and Dale end up in Zarkov's

*Flash Gordon*, Alex Raymond, © 1941, King Features Syndicate, Inc. Reprinted with special permission of King Features Syndicate, Inc.

private rocketship on a comet-busting mission. Things go a bit awry and they land on the planet Mongo.

Although Mongo, with its castles and deep forests, had an 1890s Ruritanian feel, the concerns of the 1930s—wars, famines, invasions, dictators—were also to be found there. Ming, the merciless emperor of much of the planet, was an embodiment of the Yellow Peril, and his anti-white bias and purple pronouncements made him a sort of galactic Fu Manchu. The copy, by the uncredited Moore, was plummy stuff and always beautifully stilted. But it was the pictures that seduced readers: Raymond's vast tableaus of lovely women and heroic men in fantasy palaces, scenes of lush, monster-ridden jungles, and all that larger-than-life bravura action, all those adolescent dreams of romance and adventure so patiently given life.

Flash branched out in the spring of 1940 by adding a daily strip, but Raymond, deciding he couldn't handle the extra work, stuck with the Sunday. The task of illustrating the weekday Mongoian adventures fell to his longtime assistant Austin Briggs. Briggs had signed on with Raymond in the middle years of the Depression, when most of the magazines he'd been illustrating for had no work to offer him. He still dreamed of getting back into the slicks, and his lack of enthusiasm shows in the dailies, but even halfhearted Briggs looked better than what many of his adventure strip contemporaries could do. He worked in a looser, more lushly inked version of the style he'd helped Raymond develop.

The scripts were Moore's work, who used the same sort of purple prose and sappy dialogue he turned out on Sunday. A former editor of the pulp magazine *Argosy*, Moore had worked with such stalwarts as A. Merritt, Otis Adelbert Kline, and Edgar Rice Burroughs. In editing Burroughs, Moore demanded "action…action" and advised him "the more fantastic creatures and imaginative scenes [you] can pack in…the better." In his new *Flash Gordon* dailies Moore followed his own advice assiduously. But even Briggs' excellent, if somewhat slapdash, artwork couldn't keep this particular daily version afloat, and it succumbed in 1944.

That same year Raymond entered the Marine Corps, abandoning *Flash Gordon* for good and all, and the Sunday was assumed by Briggs, who stuck with it until the middle of 1948. He never signed his name to his work because "I was ashamed of it." Emanuel "Mac" Raboy took over the page next. Raboy, long an admirer of Raymond's work, was 34 and had spent the past several years drawing for comic books. A meticulous and slow worker, Raboy had drawn *Captain Marvel, Jr., Bulletman, Dr. Voodoo,* and *The Green Lama*. He emphasized the flamboyant, Ruritanian look to the *Flash* page. His early Sundays abound in swashbuckling heroes, beautiful maidens, skulking villains, and highly stylized rockets and weaponry. At long last Moore was given a writing credit, but it didn't inspire him to new

heights: Dale continued to behave and talk like a petulant high school cheerleader and Flash plodded along in his foursquare, humorless way.

There was a science fiction boom in the early 1950s, prompting King to revive the daily. Drawn by Dan Barry, the new version, a very different *Flash Gordon,* began in November of 1951. There was no swashbuckling, no space opera, or light opera, either; the dialogue wasn't stilted and all the gadgets and props looked as though they might actually work. Various writers, among them Harry Harrison, contributed scripts. After years of drawing for comic books, Barry had developed and perfected his own, somewhat earthier version of the Raymond style, and he put it to good use on the strip. Eventually he took to farming out much of the work, and over the years Harvey Kurtzman, Sy Barry, Jack Davis, Frank Frazetta, Al Williamson, and Fred Kida worked on the drawing. Bob Fujintani worked on the strip for many years, finally getting a co-credit. He retired in the late 1980s and was replaced with a new run of assistants and ghosts.

When Raboy died in 1967, Barry and his associates assumed the responsibility for the Sunday page as well. *Flash Gordon* is still running, though in a much smaller list of newspapers than it once did. **W.D/R.G.**

**FLEISCHER, MAX** See BETTY BOOP.

**FLESSEL, CREIG** (1912– ) A professional since the early 1930s, Flessel drew such Golden Age comic book heroes as the Sandman and the Shining Knight, did the *David Crane* soap opera strip in the 1960s, was a prolific advertising artist, and has had cartoons and illustrations in magazines ranging from *Boy's Life* to *Playboy.*

Born in the same Long Island town where he still resides, Flessel studied at the Grand Central Art School in Manhattan. He entered the business in 1934, starting out by selling illustrations to pulp fiction magazines, notably those published by Street & Smith. The following year he broke into comic books and drew for Major Malcolm Wheeler-Nicholson's new line of original material magazines. Flessel, who already had a slick, illustrational style, did *Steve Conrad* in *New Adventure Comics, Pep Morgan* in *More Fun* and also provided a number of covers. He drew both action scenes and quieter stuff—"Kids fishing and so on," he once explained, "Warmed over Norman Rockwell." One of the few artists not owed money by the major, Flessel insisted on working right in the office of the fledgling company, and he saw to it he got paid regularly.

During the next few years Flessel concentrated on branching out, and in addition to his comic book work he assisted John Striebel on the *Dixie Dugan* strip. He took over *Sandman* in *Adventure Comics* and was the first artist to draw *The Shining Knight* in that same book. Not having much faith in comic books as a lifetime occupation, Flessel also moved into advertising. He signed on with the Johnstone & Cushing service and soon became a popular producer of advertising strips. Among his 1940s clients were Ralston cereals, Campbell Soup, and Royal Crown Cola. A friend of Charles Biro, Flessel drew for the *Crime Does Not Pay* comic book that Biro and his partners introduced in 1942. He later worked for a similar comic titled *True Crime*, which earned him a place among the samples Dr. Wertham included in *Seduction of the Innocent*, an important book in the 1950s anti-comic crusade.

Flessel took over *David Crane*, a soap opera newspaper strip about a minister, in 1960 and stayed with it for the remainder of its run. In the 1970s he illustrated a short-lived astrology page for NEA. He has also put in time ghosting such strips as *Li'l Abner* and *Friday Foster*. In the early 1980s he drew a strip about a fellow named Baron Von Furstinbed for *Playboy*. **R.G.**

**FLYIN' JENNY** Although Amelia Earhart flew the Atlantic alone in 1932 and Jacqueline Cochran won the Bendix Trophy in 1938, a girl aviator didn't get to solo in her own comic strip until the autumn of 1939. *Flyin' Jenny*, offering separate continuities daily and Sunday, was by Russell Keaton.

The daily opened with pretty blond Jenny Dare winging over the Starcraft Aviation Factory and impressing everybody with her skills, which included "coming in for a landing—*upside down!*" A feisty, independent young woman, Jenny talked herself into a job as a test pilot for Starcraft. This led to her life being filled with intrigue, sabotage, shipwreck, murder, violence, and romance—the usual components of a fictional pilot's life.

The first Sunday sequence found Jenny, "daring girl pilot," based at the Airdale Airport and getting ready for the Trans-America Trophy Race in which she was flying a plane designed by her handsome friend Rick Davis. Things didn't go smoothly, though, what with gamblers wrecking the plane, competition from a fat, brash pilot named Spinner Martin, and the entry of a mystery woman.

Initially Keaton wrote the scripts himself, then Frank Wead came in to do the writing. A former Navy pilot and author of the scripts for such movies as *Hell Divers* and *Blaze of Noon*, Wead was later the subject of the John Wayne movie *The Wings of Eagles*. During the war Glenn Chaffin, the cocreator of *Tailspin Tommy*, took over the writing.

Keaton worked in an attractive, uncluttered, and slightly cartoony style, though as the strip progressed he swung to a more illustrative approach. While his work was never as realistic as that of Milton Caniff or Noel Sickles, he was nevertheless very good at depicting the airplanes and weaponry the strip required. His Jenny was an attractive character, and, unlike her male contemporaries in the aviation game, she often appeared in her underwear. The Sunday page also included paper dolls—under the title *Jenny's Style Show* —at least once per month.

The daily grew increasingly serious, and soon after the United States entered World War II Jenny began flying missions for Army Intelligence. She teamed up with a plump, dark-haired lady newspaper photographer named Babe Woods, and by 1943 the two were involved in combat missions in Europe. Several fellows, military and civilian, fell in love with Jenny, but she had little time for romance. The chubby Babe fared better, marrying and settling down just as the war came to a close in 1945. For most of the life of the feature Jenny lived a separate life in the Sunday page. She never got to Europe on Sunday, her contribution to the war effort being the organizing of a "bird-girl shuttle command" to fly essential cargo.

Soon after *Flyin' Jenny* got going Marc Swayze joined on as assistant. He left to work in comic books, then

*Flyin' Jenny*, Russell Keaton, © 1945, The Bell Syndicate.

returned to help out on the Sunday page when Keaton became a wartime flying instructor. When Keaton died in February of 1945, Swayze and Chaffin kept the strip going. One of the final stories was concerned with Jenny's attempts to adjust to the civilian world. After cashing in her last war bond, she made the rounds of possible employers. Like her real-life compatriots, she was told, "Sorry, Jenny, pilots are a dime a dozen." Jenny did manage to have a few more adventures in the postwar world, including one that involved hidden Nazi loot and a treasure island. But the feature ended in July 1946. **R.G.**

**FOR BETTER OR FOR WORSE** Lynn Johnston's daily and Sunday feature has been described (by *Garfield*-creator Jim Davis) as "the consummate family strip of the eighties." Bearing little similarity to the traditional domestic humor strip, *For Better or for Worse* is thoroughly contemporary in tone and topic and draws none of its humor from such time-worn comic themes as the henpecked husband, the giddy, extravagant wife, or the mischievous child. The close-knit, well-balanced family of Dr. John Patterson, D.D.S.—wife Elly, children Michael and Elizabeth, and huge, hairy dog Farley—experiences the small conflicts and tensions, triumphs and disasters, of everyday life with affection and reasonable composure. A large readership has taken them to its heart as the ideal family next door.

With a background in film animation and medical illustration ("drawing innards and diagrams," as she describes it), Johnston published three self-illustrated books on bearing and raising children (*David, We're Pregnant* and *Hi Mom! Hi Dad!* in 1977, *Do They Ever Grow Up?* in 1978), and their wit, candor, and gentle irony prompted Universal Press Syndicate to approach the 31-year-old artist to do a comic strip for the young, normal, middle-class household. The result was *For Better or for Worse*, which debuted on September 9, 1979. A realistic series with more compassion than knee-slapping humor, it succeeded from the beginning in evoking the pleasures and pains of domesticity without ever descending into either sentimentality or cynicism. One of Universal's most rapidly growing features, it is now distributed to over 800 newspapers. Collections of the strip have been published annually by Universal's affiliate Andrews, McMeel & Parker since its inception in 1979, and a successful line of greeting cards began in 1988.

Ms. Johnston draws her attractive comic-strip family—based on her real-life, dentist husband, and her two preadolescent children—with a smooth, graceful line as balanced and controlled as the characters it depicts. In its first decade, its people have aged at about the rate of real time. Children (and their parents) have undergone the trauma of the first day in school; women have married, become pregnant, and borne children—all the bittersweet emotions accompanying those events tellingly evoked with sympathy and insight.

Much admired by her colleagues, Ms. Johnston was awarded a Reuben, the annual award for the Outstanding Cartoonist of the Year, by the National Cartoonists Society in 1985, the first woman to be so honored. **D.W.**

**FORREST, HAL** (1892?–1959) The artist best-known for drawing the seminal *Tailspin Tommy* airplane-adventure strip (1928–1942), he scripted it as well after founding writer Glenn Chaffin departed from the enterprise in December 1933. Forrest's penchant for fictionalizing his resumé has clouded some biographical details, but he is believed to have been a Philadelphian, is known to have attended the Chicago Art Institute from 1913 to 1915 and was reported (by himself) to have briefly drawn a strip called *Sid The Sailor*, possibly for the *Chicago Tribune*. After serving with the Army Air Corps, he migrated to California, found employment with several small Los Angeles–area papers, and, in 1926, began to self-syndicate a humorous airplane strip called *Artie The Ace*, which came to the attention of the Bell Syndicate's John N. Wheeler as Wheeler was searching for someone to draw *Tailspin Tommy*. Forrest did in fact become a licensed pilot at some point, and he cultivated a flying-cartoonist persona not unlike that of Zack (*Smilin' Jack*) Mosley, but his later claims to have been a World War eagle and a barnstorming stunt flyer were quite fanciful.

While his scratchy, early *Tommy* work can charitably be termed primitive by most standards, Forrest did succeed in catching the rain-in-the-face exuberance of period aviation and there remains an irresistible open-sky sweetness to much of the pre-1934 feature. Once Chaffin left, however, the now-overburdened Forrest seemed to lose his modest gifts altogether and turned out a truly unlovely strip until early 1936, when, obviously thanks to one or more unsung assistants, Tommy suddenly acquired a slick new appearance and something akin to a second wind. Thereafter Forrest enjoyed great popularity, doing personal appearances for to the model airplane club he created for his boy readers, and signing with a new syndicate (United Features, in June 1939). After basking in fresh promotion, he licensed a series of Tommy movies and became a rich man.

*Tailspin Tommy*'s demise in the spring of 1942, associates recall, broke Forrest financially and spiritually. For a time he feebly attempted to sue Monogram Pictures for canceling production of six more films and at several points he advertised new strips; one, an airplane feature called *Spencer Swift*, evidently came close to seeing print. At the end of his life he was contributing cartoons to the newsletter of his local American Legion post. He died in the Los Angeles Veteran's Hospital on Nov. 22, 1959.                                             **J.M.**

**FORSYTHE, VIC** (1885–1962)  A productive comic strip artist, Forsythe entered the field before World War I. His most successful feature was the long-running *Joe Jinks*, which dealt successively with automobiles, aviation, and boxing. He drew a number of other strips, and for a time shared a studio with Norman Rockwell.

Victor Clyde Forsythe was born in Southern California. Writing, drawing, and sports were among his early interests, and he combined all three when he got a job doing sports cartooning and reporting for a local paper. In the second decade of the century he headed for New York City to work for *The World*. Among his earliest creations were a daily gag strip about boxing titled *The Great White Dope* and a Sunday Western titled *Tenderfoot Tim*. Briefly in 1916 and 1917 he did a daily called *Flicker Films*. This kidded the movies in week-long continuities and was laid out in the two-tier format later used by Ed Wheelan on *Minute Movies*.

*Joe's Car*, a daily, started in 1918; it was a humor strip dealing with Joe Jinks, his domestic life and his obsession with the increasingly popular automobile. Joe was a typical cartoon everyman—vain, petty, argumentative, sentimental, and with the required prominent nose and wispy moustache. Later, in the 1920s, Joe took up flying, and next he met a boxing champ named Dynamite Dunn and became his manager. When a Sunday page was added in 1928, the feature's name was changed to *Joe Jinks*. In the daily Forsythe concentrated on the gritty world of professional boxing, while the Sunday page was a day of rest, covering Joe's home life and problems.

Forsythe left *Joe Jinks*, by then being syndicated by United Features, in 1933. The following year he signed with King Features, initially doing a cowboy strip called *Way Out West*, then switching to a domestic feature, *The Little Woman*, and keeping his Western alive as a Sunday topper. Neither of these efforts succeeded. He went back to *Joe Jinks*, drawing it daily on Sunday from May 1937 into the following year, when he quit comics for good. He also suffered a nervous breakdown at about this time.

Back in Southern California, settled in San Marino, he devoted most of the rest of his life to painting. Years earlier, while living in New Rochelle, New York, he'd met Norman Rockwell. The younger, still struggling Rockwell became a close friend and turned to him frequently for advice. He mentions the cartoonist in his autobiographical writings, saying, "Vic was about the only person I knew who would give me any real criticism." For a time the two shared a studio that had once belonged to Western painter Frederic Remington.

                                             **R.G.**

**FOSTER, HAL** (1892–1982)  Conspicuously talented and greatly influential, Foster drew two of the best-looking adventure strips in comics, *Tarzan* and *Prince Valiant*. He was active in the field from the late 1920s to the early 1970s and during that half-century reached a wide audience and influenced numerous younger artists, including Alex Raymond and Frank Frazetta.

Harold R. Foster was born in Halifax, Nova Scotia. The family moved to Winnipeg when he was still in his teens. An outdoorsman, he went furtrapping as a teenager. After a variety of short-lived jobs, Foster decided to try to make some money with his knack for drawing; he landed a seasonal job illustrating the catalog of the Hudson Bay Company in Winnipeg. By 1921 he had

Hal Foster, Self Portrait, 1972.

made up his mind to go to the United States for formal art training. He spent 14 days bicycling from Winnipeg to Chicago, where he studied at the Art Institute and the Chicago Academy of Fine Arts. During the 1920s he worked chiefly as an advertising illustrator and painted in his spare time.

When one of his ad clients got the notion of turning the Tarzan novels into comic strips, he approached Foster. Foster, whose idols were serious illustrators like Howard Pyle and E.A. Abbey, didn't have a very high opinion of the comics medium: "I thought I was prostituting my art...being a funny page artist." But he soon realized that he and his family could use the money. He illustrated a 10-week daily strip adaptation of *Tarzan of the Apes*, which started on January 7, 1929. Although the new jungle adventure strip was a success, Foster declined to continue with it and returned to commercial art. In 1931, with the Depression in full force, he was persuaded to return to draw the recently launched Sunday *Tarzan*. "I didn't think much of *Tarzan*," he later admitted, "although a lot of people did." The full pages he drew were handsome, achieving a loose, relaxed cinematic quality that owed as much to the movies as it did to Howard Pyle.

Hal Foster's work began to attract increasing attention and to have an effect on the comics field, although, as Coulton Waugh pointed out in *The Comics*, "the man was so good at his particular job that there remained little for subsequent workers to improve on, and very few had the ability to come anywhere near him." Foster attracted the attention of other syndicates as well. "King Features first approached me because William Randolph Hearst liked my *Tarzan* artwork so much," Foster once explained. "They wanted me to do a strip and offered to create one for me. I refused at first, because I wanted to create my own. *Prince Valiant* was the result." Foster had originally called the strip *Derek, Son of Thule*, but King president Joseph Connolly came up with the livelier title.

Foster worked on the new page for two years before showing it to KFS, which launched it in 1937. He kept doing the Tarzan page until then. "The medieval period gave me scope," he admitted. "That's why I picked it. At first I thought of the Crusades, but the theme was too limited. With *Prince Valiant* I have leeway of almost three centuries due to the lack of written records." By blurring the dates of his own Arthurian saga several hundred years from the supposed dates of Arthur's alleged reign, he had better costumes and pageantry to draw on.

While many artists waited at the drawing board for inspiration, Foster traveled widely doing research. "Research has taken me to most of the countries Val has visited to gather authentic material," he once said. He

also read extensively, explaining, "When reading fantasy and about the medieval period, sometimes just a phrase or a word will give me the idea for a plot." He started a page by writing the story in longhand. He drew big—in a 23-inch by 34-inch format. Each intricate Sunday page usually took a full work week.

He often employed an assistant, one of whom was longtime *Superman* artist Wayne Boring. In 1970 he turned the drawing of *Prince Valiant* over to John Cullen Murphy, continuing to write the continuities. He retired officially in 1979.  **W.D.**

**FOX, FONTAINE** (1884–1964)  Fontaine Fox was the creator of the suburban/rural town of Toonerville, whose rickety Trolley has entered the language as a synonym for erratic public transit. For 42 years he celebrated the life of small-town America in a series of widely popular panels and strips.

Born in Louisville, Kentucky, Fox began his career as a reporter and cartoonist for the *Louisville Herald*, and when he went to Indiana University in 1904 he continued the connection with a daily cartoon sent to that paper, for which he received $12 a week. After two years in college he returned to Louisville for a job as a cartoonist and sketch artist with his hometown *Post*. His lively sketches on current events brought him an invitation to work for the *Chicago Post* in 1908, and while there he convinced his reluctant editor to let him compete with Chicago's reigning newspaper artist John T. McCutcheon by doing humorous cartoons of children. His lively small-town scenes with their vividly individualized characters became a regular weekly feature in the *Post* and established the style and setting for which he was to become nationally famous.

In 1913 the Wheeler Syndicate gave Fox a contract that enabled him to move to Greenwich, Connecticut and work from his own home, in which he produced a steady stream of daily panels (and from 1918 a Sunday page) called *Toonerville Folks*. His vigorous, sketchy art and sharp characterizations kept his readership high through several changes of syndication. When he retired the strip in 1955, he, his imaginary town, and the Trolley for which it was chiefly famous, had become a part of American legend.  **D.W.**

**FOX, GARDNER** (1911–1986)  One of the major comic book writers, Fox created a formidable list of heroes that includes the Flash, Hawkman, Sandman, Dr. Fate, Zatara, Starman, and Adam Strange. During his long and prolific career in the field he also wrote countless scripts for characters ranging from Batman and the Green Lantern to Dracula and Dr. Strange and participated in the development of both the Justice

Society and the Justice League. In his spare time he wrote over a hundred paperback novels.

Fox earned a law degree at St. John's, but digressed into writing before he ever practiced as an attorney. He started working for DC in 1937 and the first feature he wrote the script for was *Steve Malone, District Attorney*, for *Detective Comics*, for which he also wrote about an investigator named Speed Saunders. Next came *Zatara* in *Action Comics*, *Sandman* in *Adventure Comics*, and *Dr. Fate* in *More Fun Comics*. A dedicated reader of pulp science fiction, and an especial admirer of H.P. Lovecraft, Fox introduced quite a few standard science fiction and horror gimmicks into his comic book scripts: beings from other planets, eldritch gods, time travel, parallel worlds, lost civilizations, demonic possession, death rays, shapechangers, and more.

When editor Vincent Sullivan left DC to start *Big Shot Comics*, Fox created just about the entire lineup for the launch of the title, including Skyman, the Face, Marvelo the Magician, and Tom Kerry, another fighting DA. He received his first byline in *Flash Comics*, edited by Sheldon Mayer. In addition to inventing the Flash, which he was allowed to sign, he also cooked up Hawkman and an adventurer named Cliff Cornwall. Working with Mayer, Fox developed the Justice Society of America in *All Star Comics*. In this title and in *All-Flash* Fox produced some of the earliest book-length comic book continuities—what would today be called graphic novels—and based all of them on science fiction concepts such as space travel, time travel, and ESP.

Fox remained with Detective Comics, Inc., well into the 1960s, lasting through the Golden Age and the Silver Age, seeing the decline of one era of superheroes and helping usher in the next. After writing cowboy scripts and science fiction, he created *Adam Strange*, about an Earth archaeologist who was regularly teleported to a planet of Alpha Centauri to fight alien invaders, for *Mystery in Space* in 1959. He revived the Justice Society under the new name of the Justice League, wrote scripts for the new Flash, the new Green Lantern, and the recycled Dr. Fate.

In the late 1960s, Fox parted company with DC but continued to write for Marvel, where he worked on *Dr. Strange, Dracula*, and others. Of course, he never got any royalties on the many highly successful heroes he'd created.                                                              **R.G.**

**FOXY GRANDPA** Charles Edward Schultze's attractively drawn and gently amusing strip about a mischievous oldster ran the course from great popularity to virtual oblivion during its brief and intermittent life. If it is almost forgotten today it may yet lay claim to having added a locution to the national vocabulary: A sly old man more than a match for his juniors is still called a foxy grandpa by people who have never heard of the strip.

Schultze (1866–1939), who signed himself with the childhood nickname "Bunny" and drew a staid little bunny-rabbit by his signature for good measure, was born in Kentucky to German immigrant parents who sent him back to their homeland to study. He returned in his teens to a job in the art department of the *Chicago News*, where his clean, tightly-drawn cartoons earned him enough attention to prompt the *New York Herald* to suggest his doing a comic strip for them. Taking a cue from Rudolph Dirks' popular *Katzenjammer Kids*, which had run in the *New York Journal* since 1897, Schultze inverted the theme of roguish children tricking their elders with a Grandpa foxier than the two youngsters who try to outwit him. A refreshing contrast to the malicious and usually successful mischief of Dirks' Hans and Fritz, Grandpa's two would-be tormentors always failed. The genteel old gentleman never initiated the combat but gleefully responded to it with unfailing aplomb and impish ingenuity.

*Foxy Grandpa* first appeared on January 7, 1900, in the *Herald* and moved to the *New York American* on February 16, 1902. It was a great success at once, generating a musical comedy in its first year, and remained a sturdy rival of the Katzies and Outcault's *Buster Brown* (another child-versus-grownup strip, which debuted in the *Herald* three months after Grandpa switched to the *American*) for several years. But the single note on which *Foxy Grandpa* harped did not sustain it; the gentle, genial Bunny lacked the splenetic inventiveness of his more robust rivals, and his readership soon fell off sharply. The strip was dropped by the *American* around 1910 and was picked up by the smaller *New York Press*, which ran it with diminishing regularity until 1918.

The character reappeared in a perhaps more congenial role as the host of a series of animal stories for children, each illustrated with a single panel, around 1923. *Foxy Grandpa's Stories*, as the series was entitled, ran sporadically until near the end of the decade, syndicated by Newspaper Feature Service. But it was already an anachronism and lacked the vitality that a postwar audience had come to demand. The merry old man slipped almost unnoticed from the stage, perhaps leaving behind a faint echo—in Charles Kuhn's spirited 1947 strip *Grandma*. Schultze died in 1939, having worked in his last years with the Chesler comic book shop.                                                              **D.W.**

**FRANK AND ERNEST** A single-panel humorous feature printed in the format of a comic strip, Bob Thaves' *Frank and Ernest* has amused a wide audience with its ingenious and literate gags since 1972. Introduced by Newspaper Enterprise Association as a daily on November 11 of that year, it added a Sunday version on April 1, 1973.

The title characters, like Mutt and Jeff, are respectively tall and short, but the resemblance to the earlier strip ends there. With no clearly defined relationship or identity, the two shabby figures move freely through time, space, and taxonomy, playing an infinite number of roles as vehicles for Thaves' wild wit. Frank, the taller, mustachioed one, delivers most of the lines, but there is no suggestion of subordination in his dumpy sidekick, who seems happy to play straight man.

The humor of *Frank and Ernest* is often based on outrageous puns (Frank as a Western sheriff admonishes an Indian hauling his wigwam through a flower bed, "Sorry, chief, no teepee-towing through the tulips"), but there is an occasional flash of social commentary (Frank, an angel this time, observing the Earth from a cloud, asks God, "You're *sure* you made the ecology idiot-proof?"). The two characters have appeared as animals, plants, insects, and even planets, but they most often exchange their wry observations as tramps sitting on a park bench.

Thaves, a corporate consultant in industrial psychology before he turned to cartooning full time, has won numerous honors for *Frank and Ernest.* In 1983, 1984, and 1986 the National Cartoonists Society gave it the award for Best Syndicated Panel, and in 1985 the Free Press Association voted it the Mencken Award for Best Cartoon. According to *Editor and Publisher* (June 1987), *Frank and Ernest* ranks fifth in readership among American comics, after *Peanuts, Garfield, Blondie,* and *Beetle Bailey.*

Loosely drawn in a broad, cartoony style as freewheeling and anarchic as its humor, *Frank and Ernest* has had a steadily growing audience for its madcap humor and now appears in 1,200 newspapers worldwide.                                **D.W.**

**FRANKENSTEIN**  Mary Shelley's famous monster has made a variety of appearances in comic books over the years. Two of the most successful versions, one humorous and the other dead serious, were written and drawn by Dick Briefer.

Briefer first approached the character, in a more or less sober vein, when he began turning out a series of stories that started in *Prize Comics* #7 (December 1940). In these new adventures he brought the legend up to date, with Dr. Victor Frankenstein and his unruly creation engaged in battles in the contemporary United States. Even though the gigantic monster initially looked a good deal like Boris Karloff's Universal Pictures version, each story stressed its basis in Mary Shelley's classic—and public-domain—novel. In the early escapades the monster was simply vicious, with

*Frankenstein*, Dick Briefer, 1948.

none of the redeeming qualities of the Karloff portrayal. "I am the MONSTER created by Frankenstein," he stated. "As long as he lives, I will make him and the human race SUFFER my revenge!" He issued warnings such as, "At exactly 12 noon I will destroy the business section of Centerville," and, sure enough, at noon he'd do just that, demolishing buildings, men, women, children, buses, cars, and lamp posts.

Early on, Briefer added a costumed hero named Bulldog Denny, crippled in his youth by the creature and nursed to health and hero-hood by Dr. Frankenstein, to combat the heedless monster. Every time Denny defeated the creature, however, it would rise again to cause more bloodshed. Soon, deciding the monster was far and away the more interesting of the two, Briefer dumped Denny. He also accepted the convention of calling the monster by its creator's name, explaining to his readers, "although Frankenstein is the name of the man who created the monster, the name is universally accepted to be that of the ghastly creation."

On his own, Frankenstein continued to have gruesome adventures. He met another eccentric scientist, a fellow who built him a shortlived mate; he visited Hell, played poker with the Devil, and took a part-time job as his emissary; he journeyed to Europe to fight the Nazis. As World War II progressed Briefer became increasingly restless with the feature. Finally he turned *Frankenstein* into a humor piece, parodying all the supernatural elements he'd previously been serious about. The transition was far less jarring than one would assume, since Briefer had always worked in a loose, cartoony style. The funny Frankenstein went on to even greater success than his serious predecessor and in 1945 wound up with a whole comic book of his own, which ran until 1949.

By the early 1950s serious grue was once again popular. Like many a Universal scientist before him, Briefer brought the creature back to life. The new Frankenstein was once more a mean-minded monster dealing in straight horror. This no-fun version lasted until late in 1954; Briefer returned once more to the humorous version sometime in the late 1950s, when he drew up six weeks of samples of a daily *Frankenstein* newspaper strip (which he was unable to sell to a syndicate).

*Classics Illustrated* brought out their version of the Shelley novel in 1945, with artwork by Bob Webb and, once again, a monster who resembled Karloff. Dell toyed with the creature in 1966 and 1967, going so far as to offer three issues of a comic book in which Frankenstein was a sort of superhero. Marvel took its turn in the middle 1970s with 18 issues of *The Monster of Frankenstein*. It seems safe to assume that, as far as comic books are concerned, the monster is not yet dead and gone and will eventually return. **R.G.**

**FRANKIE DOODLE** A boy counterpart of Orphan Annie, Frankie suffered the slings and arrows of nasty grownups in a daily strip by Ben Batsford. Syndicated by United Features, *Frankie Doodle* began in 1934 and petered out by the late 1930s.

Originally the strip was called *The Doodle Family*, but before very long Frankie was out on his own, living the dangerous and adventurous life of a runaway orphan. Batsford had earlier gained waif experience as one of the artists on *Little Annie Rooney*, herself an Orphan Annie surrogate. He put Frankie through all the traditional hurdles and, for good measure, made him "the heir to a great fortune." For a good part of his funny paper career Frankie was plagued by a crooked lawyer named Mr. Shady, who wanted the money for his own evil purposes. Even worse than Mr. Shady was Mrs. Krule, who operated the orphanage from which Frankie repeatedly escaped. Both villains pursued the lad with all the zeal of characters in a Victor Hugo novel.

Unlike either of the Annies, Frankie never owned a dog to confide in, but he did have two epigrammatic Chinese mentors, Ming Low, a cook in Chinatown, and Captain Ku, a Chinese secret agent. Frankie enjoyed the adventures he shared with Captain Ku, though he was often puzzled by his actions and given to exclaiming, "Gosh! These Chinese detectives are MYSTERIOUS!" Batsford alternated orphanage episodes with adventures set in Chinatown, the North Woods, and the Wild West.

Batsford drew in a scratchy style that fell somewhere between cartoon and straight and seemed to suit his somewhat sentimental adventure continuities. Frankie, who remained about nine or ten throughout, was a neatly dressed, curly-haired little chap who almost always wore a bow tie. When the black and white dailies were reprinted as one of the features in United's *Tip Top Comics*, readers learned that Frankie, like Orphan Annie, was a redhead. **R.G.**

**FRAZETTA, FRANK** (1928– ) One of the most famous graduates of comic books, Frazetta's comic career spanned little more than 10 years and his total output was comparatively small. He managed, however, to earn a considerable reputation in the field, mostly with fantasy artwork that foreshadowed what he would later do in posters, illustrations, and cover paintings.

Born in Brooklyn, Frazetta was both a natural artist and a natural athlete. At the age of eight he was enrolled in the Brooklyn Academy of Fine Arts, and while in high school he was offered a baseball contract with the New York Giants. Art prevailed and at 16 Frazetta began assisting John Giunta in Bernard Baily's shop. The gifted and ill-fated Giunta drew in a distinctive and inventive way, and Frazetta's early work shows his influence. His first solo story was for Prize's *Treasure Comics* in 1946. Next Frazetta worked for the Standard outfit, doing small illustrations for text stories in kid titles like *Barnyard*, *Coo Coo*, and *Happy*. He developed his skills on *Louie Lazybones*, a *Li'l Abner* pastiche, *Judy of the Jungle*, and several adventure and funny animal features. The art editor at Standard, Ralph Mayo, is said to have loaned the young artist several original *Tarzan* pages by Hal Foster, and this may account for the changes to be seen in his work by the end of the decade.

He went to work for Magazine Enterprises in 1949, turning out more serious work. It was with such features as *Ghost Rider* and *Dan Brand* that he began to utilize his impressive, Foster-influenced style. In 1952 he produced *Thun'da #1*, the only complete comic book he ever drew; it dealt with a barechested hero in a prehistoric jungle setting. Frazetta moved on to DC, where he drew *The Shining Knight*, *Tomahawk*, and some true crime stories. He also drew some impressive horror and science fiction yarns for EC and drew several Buck Rogers covers for *Famous Funnies*.

He drew a short-lived newspaper strip, about a muscular race car driver named Johnny Comet, in 1952. He next penciled a few months of Flash Gordon dailies for Dan Barry. Next he got a job working for Al Capp on *Li'l Abner*. Capp and Frazetta never agreed as to exactly how long this lasted. Frazetta has said years, but the curmudgeonly Capp insisted it was but a matter of months.

He began doing cover paintings for magazines such as *Eerie* and *Creepy* in the 1960s, and then covers for Ace paperback reprints of Tarzan and other Edgar Rice

*Thunda*, Frank Frazetta, © 1952, Magazine Enterprises.

Burroughs novels. These were followed by covers for Lancer's Conan the Barbarian novels, which established Frazetta as a top sword and sorcery artist and set up a career that continues to this day.          **J.V./R.G.**

**FRECKLES AND HIS FRIENDS**   This long-lived kid strip began on September 20, 1915, and ended on August 28, 1971. In his nearly 60 years of existence, Freckles aged less than 10 years, spending the major part of the feature's life as a teenager.

Merrill Blosser was in his early twenties and "just a greenhorn in the business" when he created *Freckles and his Friends* for the NEA syndicate. The Indiana-born Blosser had taken the C.N. Landon correspondence course in cartooning and studied at the Chicago Academy of Fine Arts, where Billy DeBeck was one of his classmates. After three years of working in the art department of various magazines and newspapers, Frank King introduced him to the NEA comic editor. "Here was the luckiest phase of my life," Blosser recalled years later. "I was hired. Doing little odds and ends in the art line. One day I was asked if I'd like to try doing a kid strip."

Freckles started life as a boy of about seven or eight, living in the pleasant Midwestern town of Shadyside. During the strip's early years Blosser was content to offer nothing more than a joke a day. By the 1920s, however, he'd begun to use continuity. He also changed his style during this decade and moved away from the mail-order school cartoon look to work in a looser style that was strongly influenced by the work of Walter Hoban. In the middle 1920s *Freckles* became somewhat more realistic, and Blosser began alternating adventure continuities with the hometown sequences.

Freckles, most often accompanied by his pal Oscar, would leave the Shadyside schoolroom milieu to ride with cowboys out West, sail to desert islands, fly dangerous missions with daredevil aviators. Blosser stayed in competition with his NEA coworker Roy Crane, producing some attractive adventure episodes, until the middle 1930s. Then Freckles, who'd grown into a teenager, became preoccupied with more important things than adventure, such as high school and girls.

Henry Formhals, who'd been ghosting the *Ella Cinders* Sunday page, took over as ghost on the *Freckles* daily. A new group of costars was added, including

Freckles' girlfriend June and his chubby buddy, Lard. Blosser continued to draw the Sunday *Freckles*, which dealt in separate stories, and eventually went back to concentrating on gags. He left his creation in 1965 and Formhals carried on, finally being allowed to sign it in 1966. **R.G.**

**FREDERICKS, FRED** (1929– ) Fredericks began drawing *Mandrake the Magician*, daily and Sunday, in 1965. Prior to that he had done considerable work in comic books, working on characters ranging from Mister Ed to Daniel Boone.

Harold Fredericks Jr. was born and raised in Atlantic City, New Jersey. In high school he was art editor of the school newspaper, and he became a staff artist on the *Atlantic City Press* before joining the Marine Corps in 1950 for a three-year hitch. While in the service, Fredericks was a staff cartoonist on the *Camp Lejeune Globe*, which "was a lot better than mess duty."

After the service, he studied nights for three years at the School of Visual Arts in Manhattan. During the day, he drew display ads for New Jersey Bell Telephone's *Yellow Pages.* "To assemble a portfolio, there's nothing better," he's said. "You draw everything."

Fredericks did several short-lived history-based features, including *New Jersey Patriots*, a panel about the Revolutionary War, which ran in 14 New Jersey papers in the late 1950s. In 1960 he tried a gag feature, *The Late Late War*, about the Civil War. It survived for only four months. He had more success with a serious cartoon about the Civil War, *Under the Stars and Bars*. It ran in several Southern papers in 1961 and 1962.

From 1960 to 1965 Fredericks also did comic book work. At various times in that period he wrote *Nancy* and *Mighty Mouse* and drew *The Twilight Zone* and *Daniel Boone*. He wrote and drew *Heckle and Jeckle, King Leonardo, Mr. Ed,* and *The Munsters*. As the above titles indicate, he can draw in a variety of styles—from big foot to illustrational.

After the 1965 death of original *Mandrake* artist Phil Davis, King Features asked Fredericks to try out for the job. He submitted samples and "they made the grade. I started in April of that year." He draws the strip in a realistic, romanticized style having said, "I followed the way that Phil did it."

In addition to the magician strip, he's written and illustrated *Rebel*, a popular feature that has run in Scholastic's *Scope* magazine since 1964. And in 1986 Fredericks started inking for Marvel, working on such titles as *The Hulk, Defenders of the Earth,* and *Captain America*. **W.D.**

**FREYSE, BILL** (1898–1969) Best known as the heir to Gene Ahern on the successful strip *Our Boarding House*,

Freyse, who was born in Detroit, began his career drawing cartoons for Ford after graduation from high school. He was an editorial cartoonist for one Detroit paper, then a theatrical caricaturist for another. In 1939 he was working as a commercial artist, when the NEA Syndicate hired him to illustrate the life and times of that champion windbag, Major Hoople. His first daily panel for *Our Boarding House* appeared on September 5, 1939. When he took over the strip he also inherited the Nut Bros., those baggy-pants surrealists whose Sunday page was the topper to Hoople's. Although he tried to follow the style of Ahern, the Major's creator, he was a much slicker cartoonist, and his compositions were consequently surer, his figure work better, and his inking livelier.

The syndicate's policy of having Ahern's successors work anonymously was continued with Freyse, and he was not allowed to sign the feature until after he'd been drawing it for several years. He would stay with the Major until his death in 1969. **R.G.**

**FULLER, R.B.** (1890–1963) He was in his middle forties when he embarked on the major cartoon achievement of his career, the comic strip *Oaky Doaks* in 1935. By then Ralph Briggs Fuller had been one of the most successful magazine cartoonists in the country for close to 25 years.

The Michigan-born Fuller began selling gag cartoons in 1910, initially to *Life* and the *New York World*'s Sunday *Fun* supplement. Eventually he also appeared in *Puck, Judge, Collier's, Liberty, College Humor, Ballyhoo,* and *The New Yorker*. Although his earliest work was not especially expert, he, as *Nemo* magazine has pointed out, "blossomed into an artist of great virtuosity and technical mastery." An expert at pen and ink technique as well as wash drawing, Fuller also painted straight illustrative covers for magazines such as *Adventure*.

Ralph Fuller, Self-Portrait, circa 1920.

His initial newspaper feature appeared in the early 1930s, a short-lived panel starring Elmer Zilch, the mascot of *Ballyhoo*. In 1935 he won the competition for the job of illustrating the Associated Press' new daily *Oaky Doaks*. This mock epic brought out the best in Fuller, and he approached the task not as a former gag cartoonist but as a humorous illustrator, filling the panels with impressive and funny pictures of castles, dragons, brave knights, blackhearted villains, threatened damsels, befuddled monarchs, and his purehearted hero Oaky.

He remained with *Oaky Doaks*, sometimes scripting it, until AP killed it in 1961. Fuller died two years later.

**R.G.**

**FU MANCHU** This creepy little daily strip, every bit as lurid and ghastly as its source texts, premiered in April 1931 by way of John N. Wheeler's often idiosyncratic Bell Syndicate. It was an illustration and text-block treatment of Sax Rohmer's Yellow Peril thrillers, rough comic strip adaptations of the contents of three books, *The Insidious Dr. Fu Manchu* (1913), *The Return of Dr. Fu Manchu* (1916), and *The Hand of Dr. Fu Manchu* (1917). The character had been heard on radio in the late 1920s as a recurring feature on *The Collier Hour*, and the Devil Doctor had come to American movie screens in 1929 in the person of Warner Oland in *The Mysterious Dr. Fu Manchu*, who played him again in 1930 and 1931. The strip was probably a result of the renewed interest in the insidious Oriental.

Artist Leo O'Mealia, who had previously drawn a short-lived *Sherlock Holmes* strip, brought wonderfully evocative atmospherics to Rohmer's mystery tales. His pen and ink style, rococo and painstaking in the manner of illustrators of an earlier era, was well-suited to Rohmer's purple prose, and he was excellent at depicting the mysterious figures, lurking shadows, cringing damsels, and sinister locales essential to the continuities. It always seemed to be three o'clock in the morning during a torrential rain in the strip.

Full of death and torture, and intimations of sexual bondage, *Fu Manchu* stands pretty much alone in newspaper strip history as an exercise in nightmarish fear from beginning to end. This was all very rough stuff by the standards of the day, and the feature, never widely circulated, expired after just two years. In the late Thirties it was reprinted for a while in *Detective Comics*, from #17 (July 1938) through #27 (May 1939). O'Mealia later had a durable career as a *New York Daily News* sports cartoonist.

**J.M.**

**FUNKY WINKERBEAN** A daily and Sunday humor strip that focuses on high school life, Tom Batiuk's *Funky Winkerbean* avoids the clichés of the older teen strips with a decidedly contemporary angle of vision. Deriving its humor from the character of its gallery of only slightly exaggerated high school types, *Funky* never resorts to an ironic or condescending adult's-eye view of teens.

Written and drawn by a former high school teacher, *Funky Winkerbean* began as a weekly panel cartoon drawn for the teen-page of Batiuk's hometown paper in Elyria, Ohio. After a couple of years, Batiuk expanded it to a strip and sold it to Publishers-Hall (later Field, and later yet News America) Syndicate in 1972. It now runs in about 400 papers.

Funky serves as the norm—an average high school student neither hip nor square, "a synthesis," according to his creator, "of about 80% of all students…someone that everybody identifies with." It is against his personality that the more vivid characters reveal themselves in all their droll eccentricity: Crazy Harry, the turned-on nonconformist who plays frozen pizzas on his stereo and wants to spend the summer vacation in his gym locker; Bull Bushka, the star fullback whose IQ is a negative number (he answered every question wrong and his presence lowered the scores of the people on both sides of him); and Les, the wistful loser, whose school career hits its high point when he was a hall monitor during a fire and refused to let the fire department in without a hall pass.

Batiuk's eye for the ridiculous is especially keen when he turns it on his former colleagues, and his shrewdly observed faculty members are memorable: the starry-eyed recent teachers-school graduate, out to apply the latest idealistic pedagogical theory; Mr. Dinkle, the band director whose real talent lies in fund-raising and of whom it is said that he would sell band candy to a diabetic; and the teacher who gives Crazy Harry a "learning contract" in which he agrees to accomplish a certain amount of work within a set amount of time and explains, "If you don't, we send a hit man after you." Among the most original of Batiuk's characters are the talking school computer, which amuses itself by scheduling students' homerooms on the other side of the building from their first-period classes, and the office copier, which reflects that "there must be more to life than just reproduction."

Drawn in a clean, controlled line varied by occasional panels in silhouette, *Funky* has a balanced appearance and achieves its effects with a minimum of graphic detail. A perceptive examination of the teenage condition, it provides a witty and wryly compassionate view of a generation. As Erma Bombeck noted in the foreword to a 1984 collection, Batiuk "is more than just a cartoonist. He chronicles probably one of the most difficult times of our lives."

**D.W.**

**FUNNYMAN** Funnyman was Jerry Siegel and Joe Shuster's attempt to duplicate the success of their own Superman. He first appeared, late in 1947, as a comic book character, and the following autumn, after the comic book had folded, a *Funnyman* newspaper strip was launched. By the fall of 1949 the strip, daily and Sunday, was also gone. All of which proved that the Man of Steel could be a tough act to follow.

Funnyman, who possessed no superpowers whatsoever, was a successful television comedian named Larry Davis, and he looked like a cross between Danny Kaye and Red Skelton. Dressing up in a clownish costume, Davis fought crime as "the Slapstick Sleuth." He often traveled in his rattletrap version of the Batmobile, a car dubbed the Jet Jalopy, but at the time he appeared, interest in costumed heroes was waning and a fellow who kidded them really didn't have much of a chance.

The short-lived comic book was published by Vincent Sullivan, the editor who'd originally bought *Superman* for *Action Comics*, and the strip was syndicated by Bell. A good deal of the artwork in both versions was provided by John Sikela, a longtime *Superman* ghost. **R.G.**

# G

**GAINES, M.C.** (1896–1947)  One of the founding fathers of the comic book industry, Gaines had a hand in the development and launching of *Famous Funnies*, the first regularly issued, modern format comic book. And he was involved in discovering Superman, starting the company that gave the world the Green Lantern and the Flash, issuing comic books based on the Bible, and setting up the company that eventually brought forth *Mad*. Never especially fond of superheroes, his favorite comic remained *Mutt & Jeff*.

Maxwell Charles Gaines had begun his professional life as a salesman during Prohibition, peddling such novelty items as a necktie inscribed with the slogan "We Want Beer." It was while working as a salesman for the Eastern Color printing outfit that he was active in developing and promoting *Famous Funnies*. He went to work for the McClure Syndicate in New York City in the mid-1930s, but he didn't forget what he'd learned at Eastern.

Late in 1935 Dell introduced *Popular Comics* (cover dated February 1936), a reprint title to compete with *Famous*. It was packaged for Dell over at the offices of McClure, whose color presses Gaines was utilizing to cash in on the just starting comic book boom. To edit *Popular* he hired Sheldon Mayer, a teenage cartoonist. The first issue of *Popular* was very much in the *Famous* vein. *Dick Tracy* led off the issue and the other reprints included *Skippy, Tailspin Tommy, Little Orphan Annie*, and *Mutt & Jeff* (who'd also been in *Famous Funnies*). By the time Gaines and Mayer quit putting together *Popular*, sometime toward the end of 1938, it was running fewer reprints and had added a selection of original material.

The second monthly was *The Funnies*. The first issue was dated October 1936, and also was devoted to newspaper strip reprints. The third, and final, magazine produced for Dell had a simple, direct title, too. *The Comics* made its debut with the March 1937 issue and was a hodgepodge of reprints, reruns, and original stuff.

Early in 1938 Gaines, at the urging of the enthusiastic Mayer, had sent Siegel and Shuster's proposed newspaper strip over to DC, which resulted in *Superman* becoming the runaway hit of *Action Comics*. Late that same year Gaines entered into an agreement to produce a series of comic books to be published under the DC colophon. The first titles, edited by Mayer, were *Movie Comics* and *All-American Comics*, and they hit the stands early in 1939. *All-American* used some original features, but was mostly a reprint using such old Gaines favorites as *Skippy, Reg'lar Fellers*, and, of course, *Mutt & Jeff*. *Movie*, which didn't live long, was done in *fumetti* style and made use of real movie stills. Despite being instrumental in the emergence of Superman, Gaines never believed the public would buy more than one costumed superhero. It wasn't until *Flash Comics*, which introduced the Flash and Hawkman, that Mayer was able to persuade him that there was room on the stands for quite a few supermen. Eventually the Green Lantern was added to *All-American's* lineup.

Gaines continued to feel, however, that the comics medium could be used for better things. While still associated with DC, in 1942, he produced *Picture Stories from the Bible*. The seven issues in the series sold several million copies. In 1945, with his *Picture Stories from American History* under way, he ended his association with DC. "Max demanded $500,000, free and clear after taxes," reports Frank Jacobs in *The Mad World of William Gaines*. "He got it, after which he announced his retirement. Two weeks later, he was back in business, happy again to be his own boss." Gaines kept his *Picture Stories* series and formed a new company that he named Educational Comics, Inc. The first two issues of *American History* sold 600,000 copies and Gaines got orders from 800 schools around the nation. He next started a science series. More issues were announced, but Gaines was killed in a boating accident in the summer of 1947. His son, William, took over EC and guided it in other directions.                                                                    **R.G.**

**GAINES, WILLIAM M.** (1922–  )  The publisher of *Mad* and of the EC line of comic books in the 1950s, Gaines is the son of comics pioneer M.C. Gaines.

Born in New York, Gaines grew up with a penchant for puns and practical jokes and a fondness for fantasy radio shows such as *The Witch's Tale*. He flunked out of Brooklyn's Polytechnic Institute during his junior year and joined the Army Air Corps in 1942. After the war, he coedited *Picture Stories from Science* for his father's Educational Comics. He was studying at NYU to become a teacher when he inherited EC in 1947. He gradually transformed a line of funny animal titles into crime, romance, and Western books. In 1950 Gaines launched the "New Trend" line—with EC now standing for Entertaining Comics. These new ECs offered science fiction with *Weird Fantasy* and *Weird Science*, crime with *Crime SuspenStories*, and horror/fantasy with *The Haunt of Fear*, *The Vault of Horror*, and *Tales from the Crypt*. Eventually Gaines added *Frontline Combat*, *Two-Fisted Tales*, *Shock SuspenStories*, *Mad*, *Panic*, and *Piracy*. His SF titles adapted the short stories of Ray Bradbury, initially without Bradbury's knowledge or consent, to comic books.

Gaines assembled a gifted editorial staff—Harvey Kurtzman, Al Feldstein, and Johnny Craig—and hired the more talented artists in the field. Unlike most publishers, he was closely involved in the story material, from devising plot premise springboards to proofreading. The result was a runaway success, widely imitated at the time and very influential for years to come. In 1954 Gaines was caught in the wave of negative publicity generated by investigations into suspected links between comic books and juvenile delinquency, and pressure from parents groups and distributors prompted Gaines to cancel the line. He attempted to rally, first with his "New Direction" comics and then with a group of black-and-white titles. Finally, he concentrated solely on *Mad*, edited by Feldstein after Kurtzman's departure. Gaines turned it into an impressive success, after converting it from a comic book into a black and white magazine, and there have been endless spinoffs and reprints. **B.S.**

**GANG BUSTERS** Initially a radio show, the creation of Phillips H. Lord, and first heard in 1936, *Gang Busters* dealt with the exploits of FBI agents, policemen, and other lawmen and assured listeners that each broadcast was based on "actual police records." Besides its hardboiled content, the show also became famous for the flamboyant opening, which offered the sounds of tommyguns barking, auto tires screeching, and police sirens howling and gave rise to the expression, "Comin' on like Gang Busters."

The show branched out into Big Little Books in 1938, when Whitman published *Gang Busters in Action!*, the first of a series of three illustrated novels based on the show. *Gang Busters* was also one of the earliest true crime comic book features, first appearing in Whitman's *Popular Comics* #38 (April 1939). While not as violent or sexy as later crime comics material, the six-page monthly episodes provided a fast-moving mix of shootouts, car chases, and bloodshed. Many of the stories featured a mustachioed FBI agent named Winston, and dealt not only with bank robbing and kidnapping, but also with protection schemes, extortion, and labor union racketeering. Machine guns and gun molls were common props. Among the artists were Alden McWilliams, Erwin L. Hess, and Jim Chambers. The feature stayed on in *Popular* until the mid-1940s and Whitman reprinted a goodly portion of the stories in a series of *Gang Busters* one-shots.

In 1947, at the height of the popularity of crime comic books, DC began publishing a new *Gang Busters* title, which wasn't nearly as rough and tough as some of the competing magazines. Dan Barry, Nick Cardy, and Frank Frazetta were some of the artists who worked on it. The magazine made it through 67 issues before shutting down late in 1958.

While *Gang Busters* became a television show briefly in 1952, the radio show left the air in 1957. **R.G.**

**GARFIELD** Certainly the most popular cat in the history of the comics, Jim Davis' fat, lazy, sardonic feline Garfield first slouched into public view in 40 newspapers on June 19, 1978. In August 1987, the daily and Sunday comic strip *Garfield* distributed by United Features Syndicate, became the third in cartoon history to

*Garfield* ®, Jim Davis, © 1987, United Features Syndicate, Inc. Reprinted by permission of United Features Syndicate, Inc.

appear in more than 2,000 newspapers. It is translated into seven languages and is published in 22 countries.

Davis, who grew up surrounded by about 25 cats on a farm in Indiana, created *Garfield* after working as an assistant to Tom Ryan on his strip *Tumbleweeds* for nine years. Its phenomenal popularity perhaps owes something to its ambivalent view of its hero. Both cat lovers and cat haters respond to the indolent, self-indulgent Garfield, whose life revolves around naps, lasagna, and his ongoing battle with his rivals Nermal, the world's cutest kitten, and Odie, the world's dumbest dog. Garfield's effortless manipulation of his owner, Jon Arbuckle, strikes a familiar note for anyone who has ever known a cat.

*Garfield* is second only to *Peanuts* in worldwide circulation. Its simple, universal gags and stylishly clean-lined drawings have made it an unprecedented popular success. Of the 28 *Garfield* collections published by Ballantine Books between 1980 and 1987, 25 reached the *New York Times* best-seller list, 11 as number one, and in 1982 seven titles appeared simultaneously, an all-time record. The character appears on more than 3,000 products, marketed in 28 countries, and has generated numerous award-winning television specials. *Garfield* was selected Best Humor Strip in 1982 and 1986 by the National Cartoonists Society.                **D.W.**

**GARY, JIM** (1905– ?)  His major effort as a cartoonist was drawing the *King of the Royal Mounted* newspaper strip, which he took over in 1939 and stayed with until its finish in the middle 1950s. Gary also drew for comic books in the 1930s, specializing in cowboys and detectives.

He was born in Chicago and, according to King Features publicity, lived the kind of early life usually to be found in the book jacket bios of men's adventure novelists. Gary played high school football, hitchhiked to Colorado, worked as a dishwasher, "shipped on a merchant vessel, beginning a career at sea," became a cow-

boy in Arizona, had his appendix out in Australia, took flying lessons, and rode a motorcycle from California to Illinois. He also had a longtime interest in drawing and he became the protegé of licensor/packager Stephen Slesinger. Gary started working for Slesinger in the middle 1930s, drawing several of the features he put together for the Whitman line of comic books. Working in a style that was attractive, but which betrayed his admiration for both Milton Caniff and Alex Raymond, Gary drew G-man features, adventures of cowboys like Tom Mix, and adaptations of Boris Karloff's B-movie Mr. Wong detective series for *Popular Comics* and *Crackajack Funnies.*

In 1939 he became the artist on Slesinger's *King of the Royal Mounted* strip. He also looks to have had a hand now and then in the drawing of *Red Ryder*, another Slesinger product. Gary, his work improved from his comic book days, stayed with the Mountie strip until it ended in 1955. Thereafter he passed into obscurity.
                                                            **R.G.**

**GASOLINE ALLEY**  Fondly cataloged as the strip in which the characters aged, *Gasoline Alley* was created by Frank King in 1918 at the behest of *Chicago Tribune* publisher Robert McCormick, who wanted a feature that would appeal to people learning how to take care of their cars, which, thanks to Henry Ford, were becoming increasingly available to a middle-class public. Set in an alley where men meet to inspect and discuss their vehicular passions, *Gasoline Alley* began on November 24, joining several other panel cartoons (all with similarly departmental headings: "Familiar Fractions," "Pet Peeves," "Science Facts," "Our Movies"), all boxed together on a black-and-white page called "The Rectangle" that King had been doing for several years in the *Sunday Tribune.*

The new panel offered up its mild gags routinely on Sundays until Monday, August 25, 1919, when it began to run daily as well—and with occasional thematic

*Gasoline Alley*, Frank King, © 1940, The Chicago Tribune. Reprinted by permission: Tribune Media Services.

continuity. For a while King focused exclusively on the car talk of his regular cast (Walt, Doc, Avery, and Bill), and then in 1921, Joseph Patterson, McCormick's cousin and partner, decided that the feature would be even more popular if something in it appealed to women. He told King to get a baby into the story fast. Since the cartoon's main character, Walt Wallet, was a bachelor, the baby appeared rather unconventionally—in a basket on Walt's doorstep on Valentine's Day that year. As a direct consequence of this plot development, *Gasoline Alley* evolved its most unique feature.

To King, the aging of his characters was simply common sense: "You have a one-week-old baby, but he can't stay one-week-old forever; he had to grow." And by logical extension, so did everyone else in the strip. With the baby Skeezix preoccupying Walt, the cartoon took on familial overtones and quickly developed a stronger thread of continuity. It also soon assumed comic strip form; it had run in strip form only occasionally until then, appearing most often as a panel cartoon. As a strip, it became thoroughly domestic, its situations those of everyday life in a small town, its humor warm, pleasant, low-keyed, and thoughtful. Walt married Phyliss Blossom in 1926, and the couple had a child, Corky, in 1928; in 1935, Walt found another orphan, a girl this time—Judy. As Skeezix grew up, the strip traced his life: grade school, high school, graduation, his first job (on a newspaper), the Army in World War II. Skeezix became engaged to Nina Clock during the war, they got married, and after the war, Skeezix took a job running the neighborhood gas station. Then they had children—first Chipper, then Clovia—and the cycle of growth, maturation, marriage, and family began anew.

*Gasoline Alley* stayed small-town America throughout King's tenure, and it was wholesome through and through. In 1951, Bill Perry began doing the Sunday page, concentrating on stand-alone gags, and in 1956 Dick Moores began assisting King on the dailies. By 1960, Moores had taken over almost entirely, and King went into semi-retirement until he died in 1969. Moores continued the strip in the same vein King had mined so well, but he paid more attention to characterization—particularly of women—and he varied his compositions more dramatically. Moores' sense of humor, while still wholesome and low-keyed, was somehow warmer, more human, and his comic imagination more inventive than King's. Under Moores' stewardship, two characters outside the Wallet family emerged as the prominent comic figures in the strip; Rufus the handyman and Joel the junkman, who propelled themselves with uncanny regularity into antic predicaments of the wildest sort, were also compelling portraits of loneliness, whose mutual dependency underscored their individual solitude. When Perry retired in 1975, Moores

took on the Sunday page and, soon thereafter, an assistant, Jim Scancarelli, who continued the strip's tradition of generational succession by inheriting *Gasoline Alley* when Moores died in 1986. **R.C.H.**

**GATELY, GEORGE** (1928– ) When popular magazine gag cartoonist John Gallagher introduced his younger brother George Gately Gallagher to the cartoon editor of *The Saturday Evening Post* in the 1950s, she liked his work but declared that the two brothers' styles were so similar that they both couldn't use the same name. The easiest solution was for the younger Gallagher to drop the family name and thus George Gately was born.

While still a Gallagher, Gately attended school in Bergenfield, New Jersey. In 1946 he went to New York to study at the Pratt Institute, and, after graduating, he took a job as a commercial artist with an advertising agency. But as the brother of a highly successful cartoonist and the son of very supportive cartoon lovers, Gately was inevitably drawn to the medium. After a decade in advertising he began selling gag cartoons to major national magazines. In 1964 the Chicago Tribune-New York News Syndicate accepted his gag strip *Hapless Harry*, which featured an engaging loser. Like its hero, however, the strip met with little success and was discontinued after a few years. Gately was by then well established in the free-lance market and continued selling regularly to the *Post*, *Parade*, and other magazines.

The perennial popularity of cartoon cats led him to try another feature in 1971, and he sold his panel series *Heathcliff* to the McNaught Syndicate. A prototype of Jim Davis' *Garfield*, which appeared seven years later, *Heathcliff* features a lovably amoral feline who terrorizes his neighborhood and easily dominates the helpless family that nominally owns him.

Gately's humor tends to be on the conventional side, relying on the classic tradition of pet/master reversal, but a wilder, more inventive imagination emerges in the exaggerated anthropomorphism of the hero and his entourage. And that wilder imagination shows the influence of Gately's older brother. **D.W.**

**GILL, TOM** See THE LONE RANGER.

**THE GIRL COMMANDOS** Something of a rarity in Golden Age comic books, *The Girl Commandos* was a feature about women that was actually drawn by women. When the ladies commenced their career in *Speed Comics* #23 (October 1942), their wartime adventures were depicted by Barbara Hall. (The similarly named Boy Commandos had set up shop over in *Detective Comics* in June of 1942.)

The Girl Commandos developed from one of Hall's earlier strips, *Pat Parker, War Nurse*. Pat had begun life as an army nurse in England, but soon got herself involved fighting espionage and intrigue. In *Speed* #15 (November 1941) she decided, having become too well known, to don a costume and mask as she "continues her heroic battle against the hidden foes that she encounters in the line of duty." The costume was a skimpy outfit with a bare midriff, and the red cross displayed prominently on her mask may well have tipped Pat's hand to some of her hidden foes.

Ever restless, by #23 the dark-haired nurse was calling herself Pat Parker, Girl Commando. In that same issue she decided to organize a group of women who would be "freelance fighters for freedom." Stationed in India, she recruited a fellow British nurse, an American radio operator, a Soviet photographer, and a Chinese patriot. By the next issue Pat, Ellen, Penny, Tanya, and Mei Ling were calling themselves the Girl Commandos and fighting the Japanese in Korea. Since the group got going on the spur of the moment, the girls didn't have uniforms or costumes in their initial adventures. All worked in street clothes, except for Pat who kept her War Nurse outfit.

A few issues later, however, they were all decked out in short-skirted paramilitary outfits, looking a bit like mature Girl Scouts. A feisty and inventive bunch, they battled the Japanese across the China-Burma-India theater and used everything from concealed explosives to cafe dancer disguises in their work. Jill Elgin took over the drawing fairly early on. Pat, formerly a brunette, became a blond, and the "famed and fearless" Girl Commandos took their fight for freedom further afield, showing up in such varied locales as Czechoslovakia, the Sahara Desert, and the Swiss Alps. The group went out of business two issues before *Speed* did, breathing their last in #42 (March 1946).                          **R.G.**

**GODWIN, FRANK** (1889–1959)    A prominent painter, magazine illustrator, and advertising artist, Godwin lent his sophisticated talents to the comics for the last 30 years of his life, contributing to numerous strips in the daily papers. His own creations, *Connie* (1927–1944) and *Rusty Riley* (1948–1959), are among the most highly admired continuity strips in the literature of the comics.

Godwin was the son of an editor for the *Washington* (D.C.) *Star* and began his career in art with his father's paper at the age of 16. A desire both to perfect his work and broaden his range of opportunity drew him to New York City. There he studied at the Art Students League and from his late teens supported himself as a free-lance cartoonist and illustrator. The close companionship and support of the older James Montgomery Flagg, already

an established commercial artist, helped him to enter the market, and he was soon selling to a large variety of periodicals. His advertising art appeared in virtually all the popular magazines of the time, and he was much sought out to illustrate fiction for such magazines as *Collier's, Liberty,* and *Cosmopolitan*. His illustrations for Winston's popular editions of the classics, in the romantic style of Flagg and Charles Dana Gibson, placed him among the most successful book illustrators of the Twenties and Thirties. He also painted in oils, and his murals for the Kings County Hospital in Brooklyn, New York, and the Riverside Yacht Club in Greenwich, Connecticut, are still much admired. He was an active member of the Society of Illustrators for many years, serving for a time as its vice president, and was elected to its Hall of Fame.

In the early 1920s, Godwin became a staff artist with the *Philadelphia Public Ledger*, doing covers for the paper's Sunday magazine section and illustrating its fiction. His *Vignettes of Life*, a series of humorous domestic scenes, began in the *Ledger* in 1924 and was so successful that he was soon much in demand for other assignments with the *Ledger*. He drew *Roy Powers, Eagle Scout* anonymously for a long time, but in 1927 he began his first signed continuity strip, *Connie*, which debuted on November 13 as a Sunday strip and added dailies on May 13, 1929.

*Connie* was an exciting, fast-paced adventure strip, liberally laced with humor, about one of the new, liberated women. Connie Kurridge, a dauntless lass, in the strip's first year bested half a dozen villains as an aviatrix, an interior decorator, a secretary, a travel agent, a private detective, and an ace reporter. The resourceful young lady later served a stint as an astronaut in a prolonged science fiction episode. Never carried in many papers, *Connie* folded in 1944.

In 1948 Godwin launched *Rusty Riley* for King Features, with the dailies, written by Rod Reed, debuting on January 26 and the Sundays, written by Godwin's brother Harold, on June 27. This nostalgic evocation of innocent boyhood called up a period decades earlier, despite the contemporary clothes and automobiles, and romanticized its subject in a way already passé; but it survived, largely because of its handsome art, until a few weeks before Godwin's death on August 5, 1959.

Godwin's elegance of design and meticulous precision of style brought his work to pictorial heights seldom matched in the comics. Never compromising the aesthetic ideals of the illustrator and painter, he employed the same richly textured compositions and painstaking cross-hatching in his comics that he used in book illustration, giving his work a graphic sophistication that virtually disappeared from the comics with his death.                          **D.W.**

**GOLDBERG, RUBE** (1883–1970) One of the most abundantly talented cartoonists in the history of the medium was Rube Goldberg, whose work spanned more than half a century. His strip *Boob McNutt* remains a classic, and Goldberg achieved the rare distinction of adding his name to the American vocabulary for the spoofs of modern technology embodied in his outlandish cartoon inventions.

He was born Reuben Lucius Goldberg in San Francisco, California, and attended the University of California School of Mining. After duly obtaining a degree in engineering in 1904, he worked for six months helping to design the San Francisco sewer system, but gave up that edifying career to pursue a childhood dream of becoming a cartoonist, taking a job with the *San Francisco Chronicle* sweeping out the art department at $8 a week. There he showered his employer with submissions until he finally had a cartoon accepted; he was soon a regular contributor to the sports department. In 1905 he moved on to the *San Francisco Bulletin*, replacing Tad Dorgan as the sports cartoonist when Dorgan left for New York. At the *Bulletin* he often wrote the stories he illustrated when the regular sports reporter was too drunk to send anything in, and he began doing short humorous pieces of his own. In September 1907, he sold a Sunday color feature, *The Look-A-Like Boys*, to the World Color Printing Company comic section.

Encouraged by his success, he decided to tackle the big time and went to New York that same year, taking a job with the *Evening Mail*. Soon his gently ironic whimsy and broad middlebrow slapstick style blossomed into a garland of features: In addition to his sports cartoons, he developed the popular *Foolish Questions* (in which obvious questions are met with sarcastic answers); *Soup and Fish; The Candy Kid; Lunatics I Have Met; I'm the Guy* (whose title was to become a catchphrase and inspire a popular song); *They All Look Good When You're Far Away; The Weekly Meeting of the Tuesday Ladies Club; Mike and Ike, They Look Alike* (a revival of *The Look-A-Like Boys*, also to become a catchphrase); and many others. In the words of Stephen Becker, "He became more than the heart of the art staff; he became the heart of the newspaper." When a new contract was negotiated in 1915, Goldberg (through the mediation of his businessman father) demanded and received a salary of $1,000 a week from the *Mail*.

In May of 1915, he began his second Sunday color feature, *Boob McNutt*, a popular strip about a gentle, lovable boob whose well-meaning efforts at helping others always led to disaster. Later syndicated by Mc-Naught, *Boob McNutt* ran for over 20 years, ending in September 1934.

Goldberg was an astonishingly prolific worker throughout his long career. In addition to a steady stream of cartoons and comic strips, he produced numerous books, from *Foolish Questions* (1909) and *Chasing the Blues* (1912) to *I Made My Bed* (1960) and *Rube Goldberg Versus the Machine Age* (1968), and he wrote hundreds of magazine articles (often self-illustrated) for such publications as *The Saturday Evening Post, Photoplay, American Magazine,* and *Good Housekeeping.* He helped found and wrote part of the cartoon course for the Famous Artists school in Westport Connecticut; cofounded the National Cartoonists Society in 1946, serving as its first president and remaining its honorary one; was the president of the Artists and Writers Club and active in the Society of Illustrators; and traveled for the American Theater Wing to entertain troops during World War II. A genial, outgoing man (he had managed to include in his busy life a second career as a vaudeville comic in 1911), Goldberg was always on call to act as MC or deliver after-dinner speeches for social affairs.

Among the comic strips that Goldberg created, with varying degrees of success, are *Phoney Films, Boobs Abroad,* and *Life's Little Jokes* (with a text in quite skillful doggerel) in the early 1920s, and the daily continuity strip of humorous adventure, *Bobo Baxter* (1927–1928), and the sentimental continuity strip *Doc Wright* (1934–1936), all syndicated by Hearst; the humor strip *Lala Palooza* (1936–1939), distributed by the Frank Markey Syndicate; and *Brad and Dad*, incorporated in his *Rube Goldberg's Sideshow* (1939–1941) for the Register and Tribune Syndicate. His ludicrous "inventions"—diagrams of involved machinery designed to perform simple operations, such as a soup-cooling device requiring a sleeping porcupine, a bag of water, a jack-in-the-box containing a wax figure of a movie magnate, a yes-man, and various weights, pulleys, and strings—appeared in many of his features and were to find a place in our dictionaries.

Goldberg also did notable work as a political cartoonist for the *New York Sun* from the early 1940s until the paper ceased independent publication in 1950. He won the 1948 Pulitzer Prize for his July 22, 1947, cartoon "Peace Today," showing the atomic bomb teetering on the edge of a cliff labeled "World Control."

Goldberg was an active and productive cartoonist until his early eighties, when he turned to humorous sculpture. For his work in that medium he received in 1967 the National Cartoonists Society's highest award as Outstanding Cartoonist of the Year (called the "Reuben" for the trophy he designed). The society that he cofounded also voted him its Gold T-Square in 1955 and a posthumous Gold Key award, representing admission to its Hall of Fame, in 1980. He received the Banshees' Silver Lady in 1959.

An artist of fairly undistinguished graphic style, Goldberg never progressed, during the six decades of

*The Inventions of Professor Lucifer G. Butts, A.K.A. Ruber Goldberg*, ca. 1920s.

his working life, beyond the simple line, exaggerated features, and casual composition that typified the work of most cartoonists during the early decades of this century. It was rather for his fertile comedic imagination, his unflagging inventiveness, and his shrewd perception that he has achieved the status of one of the masters in the field.                                                            **D.W.**

**GORDO**  Gus Arriola's witty and good-natured gag strip featuring a self-indulgent but appealing Mexican debuted in the *New York World-Telegram* on the inauspicious date of November 24, 1941, just 13 days before the United States' entry into World War II. Although immediately popular, the daily strip was suspended in October 1942, when the artist joined the Air Force, but Arriola managed to create a Sunday *Gordo* beginning May 24, 1943. Six months after his discharge from the service, on June 24, 1946, Arriola began the daily strips again.

Distributed by United Features Syndicate, *Gordo* depended for some of its humor on the stereotype of the lazy, womanizing Mexican male and the cynical sharp-tongued women in his life. But the spirit of the strip, as easygoing as its hero, is so genial that few ever took offense. The portly hero (whose name means "fat") drove a decrepit tourist bus called "el Cometa Halley" when he wasn't taking a siesta, ogling the girls, or drinking tequila. His housekeeper, the equally well-padded Widow Gonzáles, provided a counterpoise, with both her ceaseless labor and her earthy realism, to the happy-go-lucky Gordo López.

A striking feature of this long-running strip was the chorus of animals, whose wise and witty observations commented on both the human characters (whom they observed with a keen and often jaundiced eye) and on life in general. Even natural enemies seemed to live and converse harmoniously in Arriola's Peaceable Kingdom: Pancho and Porfirio, the bibulous earthworms, chat comfortably with Popo the rooster; Poosy Gato and the López chihuahua engage in searching philosophical discussions; and the beret-wearing hipster spider Bug Rogers, who spins wildly original webs, gets along with everyone except the hapless flies he traps. A large collection of Sunday animal strips was published in full color in 1989.

Arriola's dialogue is full of puns, and for years his Sunday pages were credited to outrageous noms de plume: A strip about anger was signed "T. Doff," one featuring pain appeared as by "Anne Gwish," and a tale of overindulgence in alcohol bore the byline "Titus Atíck."

*Gordo* was drawn with a graphic elegance that nicely balanced the breezy, lighthearted spirit of its content. Arriola's abundant visual ingenuity gave rise to explosions of pictorial exuberance. His highly imaginative arrangements of line and mass, and his frequent whimsical touches of abstraction or cubism—apparently thrown in just for the fun of it—contributed an often exciting and always pleasing quality to the strip. *Gordo's* stylishness and warmth of tone were remarkably uniform throughout its long life. Arriola received the National Cartoonists Society's silver plaque for Best Humor Strip in 1957 and 1965. The last Sunday *Gordo* appeared on February 24, 1985, and the last daily the next day.                                                            **D.W.**

**GOTTFREDSON, FLOYD** (1907–1986)  N o b o d y ever drew Mickey Mouse better than Gottfredson. For 45 years, from 1930 to 1975, he turned out the daily *Mickey Mouse* newspaper strip. His work was printed and reprinted in newspapers, magazines, and comic books all over the world, but since he was an employee of the Walt Disney organization he was never allowed to sign a single strip. Like his colleague Carl Barks, Gottfredson was for most of his life one of the great unknowns of comics.

Gottfredson was born in one small town in Utah and grew up in another. A childhood hunting accident left him with an injured arm that kept him pretty much housebound for a time, and that was when he became interested in cartooning. Although his Mormon family didn't encourage him, he was allowed to enroll in several correspondence courses, and he availed himself of what both the Landon School and the Federal Schools had to offer. By the late 1920s he was drawing cartoons for trade journals and for the *Salt Lake City Telegram*. His work had a confident, professional look, showing the influence of both his mail-order instructors and of one of his favorite strip artists, Walter Hoban of *Jerry on the Job*. Like all young cartoonists, he'd worked out an impressive signature for himself, one that, as it happened, he was unable to use for the next several decades.

After winning a cartoon contest in 1928, Gottfredson made up his mind to try his luck in Los Angeles. He arrived there with his wife and family just before Christmas of that year. "There were seven major newspapers there," he admitted many years later, "but I couldn't get a job with any of them." He had been a movie projectionist for a time back home in Utah, and he was able to get a job in that profession in Los Angeles. A year later, after the movie theater where he'd been working was torn down, he heard the Disney outfit might be hiring artists. "I rushed home to get my portfolio, went to the studio, and got a job that afternoon. Walt hired me as an inbetweener and possible backup artist for the Mickey Mouse daily newspaper comic strip which was then about to be launched by King Features Syndicate. I went to work the following day—December 19, 1929."

Within a few months he'd taken over on *Mickey Mouse*, and "I continued with the *Mickey* daily strip for 45½ years—until my retirement on October 1, 1975." Soon the strip quit offering a joke a day and went in for continuity, and that was when Gottfredson began to shine. He had a flair for kidding the conventions of action serials, cowboy epics, horror movies, and detective melodramas and still getting a lot of real suspense into his stories. Initially he wrote the strip, too, but later just sat in on the plotting. He said that he had been influenced "by *The Gumps* and Roy Crane's *Wash Tubbs*, the top continuities of the time." His Mickey had many affinities with the diminutive, go-getting Tubbs, and throughout the 1930s the two led adventurous lives filled with both danger and fun.

Gottfredson drew very well, combining the abilities of an animator with those of a strip artist. His human-ized animal characters had life and personality. And like his more serious colleagues in the adventure strip field, he was an expert at depicting the settings and backgrounds—from haunted castles to midnight streets to phantom dirigibles. His work matured and developed throughout he 1930s and 1940s. When King Features decreed that the continuities must be replaced by daily jokes in the middle 1950s, Gottfredson seems to have lost quite a bit of his enthusiasm.

In addition to drawing the daily, he penciled the Sunday page, too, from 1932 until the middle of 1938.

Gottfredson's name had appeared a few times in print over the years he was drawing the strip, usually in fanzines here and in Europe and usually in a list of cartoonists who had possibly worked on the *Mickey Mouse* strip. Then in 1968, two years after Walt Disney's death, the writer Malcolm Willets tracked Gottfredson down at the Disney studios and got permission to do a lengthy interview with him. Though it appeared only in a fanzine called *Vanguard*, the piece was the first to credit Gottfredson publicly for what he'd been doing for so many years, and it finally and definitely identified him for other fans. He never gained anything like celebrity, but he had ceased to be anonymous.

The introduction to a 1974 compilation of his 1934 strips, printed by Western, said, "Two men have been closer to Mickey than any others. First, Walt Disney...The second man is Floyd Gottfredson." In his final years, before he was slowed down by ill health, he appeared as a guest at comics conventions and was interviewed by a variety of comics-oriented magazines and even a few mainstream publications. And whenever the *Mickey Mouse* strips were reprinted, he finally got credit for his work.

**R.G.**

**GOTTO, RAY**  See OZARK IKE.

**GOULD, CHESTER** (1900–1985) When Chester Gould was just a boy he fell under the spell of *Mutt and Jeff* and Sherlock Holmes. In 1931 he created *Dick Tracy*, a strip that became nearly as successful as Bud Fisher's and featured a detective who became nearly as well-known as Conan Doyle's.

Gould was born in Pawnee, Oklahoma, the son of the publisher of a weekly newspaper; Gould later said, "[It] was probably that influence which got me into the frame of mind to become a cartoonist." He migrated to Chicago in 1921 to finish college. Although he majored in business administration, he went from school into drawing for newspapers. The years before he signed his *Dick Tracy* contract, Gould recalled, were a decade of frustrating experiences in just about every Chicago newspaper art department. While he shifted from paper to paper, Gould kept inventing comic strips. Some of them sold, some of them didn't. In 1924 he was doing a topical gag strip called *The Radio Lanes* for the *Chicago American,* and later in the 1920s he drew *Fillum Fables,* syndicated by Hearst.

"It was a burlesque of the movies," Gould once said of *Fillum Fables.* "I cannot claim originality for it. We already had a very capable man doing a strip like that—*Minute Movies* by Ed Wheelan." Gould's movie take-off was one of several imitations—Segar's *Thimble Theatre* was another—that the Hearst syndicate initiated after Wheelan left. Gould's version, like Wheelan's, went in for continued stories that burlesqued current popular types of film: melodramas, Westerns, detective stories. Doing the strip meant Gould had to pay attention to *Minute Movies* and to what was going on in the movie houses. As early as 1927 he was using mock detective continuities.

For *Tracy* he could also turn to real life for inspiration. "Chicago in 1931 was being shot up by gangsters," Gould once said, "and I decided to invent a comic strip character who would always get the best of the assorted hoodlums and mobsters." What was needed, he felt, was a detective who "could hunt these fellows up and shoot 'em down." He added, "So I brought out this guy Tracy and had him go out and get his man at the point of a gun." Besides being tough, impatient, and not much of a civil libertarian, Dick Tracy was totally honest. An honest cop was much needed in places like Chicago and New York, to mention but two cities with less than spotless police departments at the time. Gould's new strip was soon a success in these markets, as well as in other urban areas.

"Gunplay is a part of the strip, and was from the very beginning," Gould once explained. "The law is always armed. Back in 1931 no cartoon had ever shown a detective character fighting it out face to face with crooks via the hot lead route." While gunplay had something to do with the popularity of *Tracy,* it was the increasingly violent and bizarre methods of dispatching crooks and the increasingly grotesque villains that attracted readers and news magazines.

Like several of his Chicago-based colleagues—such as Harold Gray and Frank King—Gould drew his strip in a bold, simple cartoon style and made no attempt to apply a realistic illustrative approach to his tales of death and violence, all of which helped to give an unusual and distinctive look to *Dick Tracy.* Gould, with the help of a succession of assistants—including Dick Moores, Russel Stamm, Jack Ryan, and Rick Fletcher—built his strip into a national institution. He remained a staunch champion of law and order and always responded to criticism that his crooks were too ugly by pointing out that crime was ugly.

Gould remained with the strip until 1977 and then retired. He didn't exactly fade away, but spoke out on at least one occasion when he thought *Dick Tracy* wasn't being carried on properly.                    **R.G.**

**GOULD, WILL**   See RED BARRY.

**GRAFF, MEL** (1907–1975)   He worked as a comic strip artist from the middle 1930s through the late 1960s. A first-rate disciple of Milton Caniff and Noel Sickles, Graff drew *Adventures of Patsy, Secret Agent X-9,* and *Captain Easy.*

Melvin Graff was born in Cleveland and, as a King Features bio once put it, "got his knowledge of the world not from books but from that famous institution, the College of Hard Knocks." He obtained his only art training in high school and from a Landon correspondence cartooning course. After working on the railroad and putting in some time as a hobo, Graff settled down to an art department job in the NEA syndicate's Cleveland offices. Eventually he was transferred to New York, and soon after that he switched over to the Associated Press bullpen, where both Sickles and Caniff were employed.

Initially Graff drew in an angular black and white style that showed the influence of Russell Patterson and Ralph Barton. Gradually, no doubt influenced by his AP coworkers, he developed a style using a much more realistic approach, relying on heavily brushed in shadows, detailed backgrounds, and movie camera angles. His most impressive work was done on *Patsy,* which he started in 1935 and continued until 1940.

King Features noticed him in 1940 and asked him to take over *Secret Agent X-9.* He did a good job during his early years with the G-Man strip, getting some nice effects with the Craftint singletone paper he'd first experimented with on *Patsy.* The strip, however, never did as well as he had expected. By 1945, in a special drawing done for a Sigma Chi salute to Caniff, Graff described himself as "your stalemated old cellmate." Nevertheless, he stayed with *X-9* longer than anyone else thus far. He finally left the strip in March of 1960, claiming he felt that "the cops and robbers theme had grown tiresome." A more important reason was that Graff's drinking problem had grown so serious that he could no longer meet his deadlines.

He got one more chance at a newspaper strip and brought the assignment off well. In 1960 he took over the Sunday *Captain Easy* page from his neighbor in Florida, Leslie Turner. Graff did some nice work on the page, although he never made any attempt to imitate the Turner style. Like Turner and Roy Crane, he was a railroad buff and he came up with some well-done sequences using vintage trains. After leaving *Captain Easy* late in 1969, he went into semiretirement.     **R.G.**

**GRANDMA**   Charles Harris Kuhn had drawn political cartoons for the *Chicago Tribune* for 26 years before he began to do comic features for the Richard Feature Service of Indianapolis. After several fleeting efforts, while still serving as the *Tribune's* editorial cartoonist, he struck the right note in 1947 with *Grandma*, a genial daily and Sunday strip about a hoydenish old lady who led a neighborhood gang of boys.

Kuhn was known for the gentle spirit of his editorial comment, never shrill or caustic, and the same amiable sensibility infused his strip. Drawn in a clean, balanced style with an attractive distribution of line and patches of solid black, it harkened back to an earlier era of pleasant, simple comic strips in both its graphic manner and its content. The jut-jawed, bespectacled heroine, invariably clad in a long black dress with a lace collar, a cameo brooch, and a clean white apron, devotes her full time to cleaning her spotless little house and baking endless cookies for an ever-changing mob of kids. Apparently childless herself despite her name (she is never known, even by her postman and her adult neighbors, by any other name), Grandma is the ideal parent and grandparent to every child in her unidentified little town, defending them when they get in trouble and joyously participating in their innocent mischief.

Kuhn took *Grandma* from Richardson to King Features Syndicate after a year and a half, by which point he was working on it full-time, and King distributed the dailies from June 28, 1948, until its demise on June 23, 1969. A Sunday series, which began with King on November 20, 1969, lasted until the end and included a black and white panel that readers could color in for themselves.

*Grandma's* nostalgic, turn-of-the-century look and spirit kept it popular with both kids and adults until well into the era of sophisticated comic strips, and it is still remembered with affection by those who miss its gentle, good-natured humor.     **D.W.**

**GRAY, HAROLD** (1894–1968)   The creator of *Little Orphan Annie* is regarded as the first strip cartoonist to use the medium as a vehicle for political philosophy, but Gray's gift for narrative and characterization kept the strip popular at a much broader level during its long history and established it as a part of American folk culture that has outlasted its author.

Harold Lincoln Gray was born in the rural town of Kankakee, Illinois, about 50 miles south of Chicago, to a family he proudly traced back to the 17th century in the new world. He graduated with a bachelor of science degree in engineering from Purdue in 1917 and that same year took a job with the art department of the *Chicago Tribune*. In 1920 he became an assistant to Sydney Smith, helping with *The Gumps*, while offering the *Tribune* a series of ideas for strips of his own. After four years of continued rejection, he struck the right chord: Joseph Medill Patterson, who was looking for a new child strip, was sufficiently impressed with Gray's proposed *Little Orphan Otto* to agree to accept it, after submitting its protagonist to a sex change, and on August 5, 1924, the winsome *Little Orphan Annie* made her first appearance in the *New York Daily News*.

Beginning as a heart-tugging tale of a spunky girl's tribulations—Gray once remarked that "in those days she was *East Lynne*, 'Over the Hill to the Poorhouse,' and all the other favorites rolled into one and modernized"—*Little Orphan Annie* soon assumed a clear social and political slant, providing Gray with a forum for his strongly conservative opinions, and his vehement laissez-faire views so offended one liberal paper that an episode was rejected, leading the syndicate to drop the strips from circulation. Gray was to learn to subordinate his message to his always engrossing stories, but he never completely gave up his propagandizing posture, and the strip was often controversial.

Gray devoted the rest of his life to his blank-eyed heroine, though he found time to produce a humorous feature, *Private Lives*, recounting the personal histories of various domestic objects, in 1931 and 1932, and the next year he created a spinoff from *Annie*, an ancillary strip called *Maw Green*, in which that ironic Irishwoman from the parent feature delivered tart observations on life and society. *Maw Green* remained a four-panel companion to *Little Orphan Annie* till Gray's death.

Gray generally worked alone, never employing ghosts, but he used assistants to do his lettering and backgrounds. One of them, his cousin Edwin Leffingwell, developed his own Sunday strip, *Little Joe*, in 1933. Gray is generally credited with contributing to both the authorship and the drawing of this Western-adventure version of *Little Orphan Annie*, at least from 1936 when Ed died and the strip passed into the hands of his brother, Robert, another of Gray's assistants. Gray appears to have left *Little Joe* entirely to Bob Leffingwell sometime in the late 1950s, when its art lost its similarity to that of *Little Orphan Annie*.

Gray's art had little pretension to visual elegance, although it had a powerful, primitive look and a certain dramatic simplicity. "I'm no artist," Gray observed near the end of his life. "I've never gone to any art school. But I know what I want and do the best I can. Bob [Leffingwell] does the dirty work." Nevertheless, his rudimentary style has had its defenders: Coulton Waugh argued that Gray's trademark use of empty ovals for his characters' eyes led the reader to supply the expressions for himself, and thus the meanings are "clearer and more forceful than if the eye details were completely drawn." In any case, it was not his visual style that sustained Gray in a career that was to earn him more than five million dollars, but rather his inspired creation of a heroine whom he described as "tougher than hell, with a heart of gold and a fast left, who can take care of herself because she has to." Long after Gray's fulminations against gasoline rationing, income taxes, the welfare state, and Roosevelt's New Deal have become obscure episodes needing footnotes, his engaging little survivor will remain a vital figure in American folklore.　　　　　　　　　　**D.W.**

**GREEN ARROW** Although one of the few costumed heroes to hang in through the entire "Golden" and "Silver" ages of comic books, National (DC) Comics' modern-day Robin Hood has never been one of its most popular characters. He and his boy sidekick Speedy premiered in *More Fun Comics* in 1941, and headlined there for four years; he then ran for another 18 years as a backup in *Adventure Comics* and *World's Finest Comics*, and has appeared in various venues since then.

Created by editor-writer Mort Weisinger, drawn mainly by George Papp (with a stint by Jack Kirby in the late 1950s), Green Arrow and Speedy battled crooks with an impossible array of gimmicky arrows (net-arrows, flare-arrows, drill-arrows, gas-arrows, and whatever else was needed for the emergency at hand). With an Arrow-Car, Arrow-Plane, and Arrow-Cave, they bore a more-than-accidental resemblance to Batman and Robin, a resemblance reinforced by their secret identities as millionaire playboy Oliver Queen and his orphan ward Roy Harper.

Joining the Justice League of America super-team in 1961, Green Arrow remained a visible but unspectacular hero even after losing his own series in 1963. In 1969 writer Denny O'Neil and artist Neal Adams coincidentally revamped him in separate comics: O'Neil (in *Justice League*) by depriving him of his fortune and making him a defender of the poor; Adams (in the team-up comic *The Brave and the Bold*) by redrawing him as a hip, bearded rebel. When O'Neil and Adams took over *Green Lantern* the next year, they paired the two green heroes in a series of widely-acclaimed, politically relevant comics. They also paired Green Arrow (now separated from Speedy) with the superheroine Black Canary as lover and partner.

Green Arrow continued off and on as Green Lantern's partner and a Justice League member through the 1970s. Although left behind by the "relevance" fad that gave him his new identity, his newly irreverent, argumentative personality won him quite a few loyal fans.

After being dropped from the *Green Lantern* series in 1981 he began to fade away, but in 1987 writer-artist Mike Grell pushed him back to the forefront of DC heroes when his slickly executed, extremely violent and controversial miniseries, *Green Arrow: The Longbow Hunters*, became a huge success in the fan-dominated comic book specialty shop market. An ongoing series followed, with Grell as writer.　　　　　　**G.J.**

**GREENE, VERNON** (1908–1965) A graduate of a mail-order school of art and a professional newspaper sports cartoonist before he was out of his teens, Greene went on to draw two highly different strips: *The Shadow* and *Bringing Up Father.* He also drew advertising strips, ghosted *Polly and Her Pals*, and did a Perry Mason comic book.

Born in Washington state, Greene studied cartooning through the mail with the Federal Schools. By the late 1920s he was doing sports cartoons for an Oregon newspaper. He moved from there to similar jobs in Toledo and then New York City. From 1935 to 1940 he worked on *Polly and Her Pals*, and in 1940 he was picked by writer Walter Gibson to draw the Shadow newspaper strip. Greene was capable of working in several styles and for the adventures of the mysterious foe of crookdom he used an illustrative brush style that combined elements of the styles of both Alex Raymond and Milton Caniff with some more cartoony touches of his own. When the strips were reprinted, in somewhat altered form, in the *Shadow* comic book in the early 1940s, Greene contributed several covers.

After three years in the Air Force, during which he was able to keep up a variety of cartoon work, Greene returned to his profession full time. Among the things he did was a comic book adaptation of Erle Stanley Gardner's *The Case of the Lucky Legs.* At George McManus' death in 1954 Greene was given the job of drawing the daily *Bringing Up Father.* He switched styles again to depict the domestic strife of Jiggs and Maggie, drawing in a lively and creative imitation of the style McManus and his ghosts had established.

Greene was also an enthusiastic comics fan. He collected funny papers and original art and conducted a radio interview series with his fellow cartoonists. He remained with *Bringing Up Father* until his death.　　　　　　　　　　　　　**R.G.**

**THE GREEN HORNET** An influential radio masked man, the Green Hornet inspired at least two successful comic book crimefighters before becoming one himself in 1940. The radio show began on Detroit's WXYZ early in 1936, and by the spring of 1938 it was being heard nationally on the Mutual network.

Created by writer Fran Striker and producer George W. Trendle, the Hornet was a modern, urban version of their Lone Ranger. "With his faithful valet Kato, Britt Reid, daring young publisher, matches wits with the underworld," each broadcast explained, "risking his life that criminals and racketeers within the law may feel its weight by the sting of the Green Hornet!" A humane vigilante, the Hornet used a gas gun on criminals and racketeers, putting them to sleep rather than killing them. He traveled, with Kato at the wheel, in a sleek automobile called the Black Beauty.

The earliest Hornet imitator was the Crimson Avenger, who began his career in *Detective Comics* #20 (October 1938) and was created by artist Jim Chambers. Whereas the Hornet was in reality Britt Reid, wealthy young publisher of the *Daily Sentinel*, the Crimson was Lee Travis, wealthy young publisher of the *Globe Leader*. The only person who knew the Hornet's true identity was Kato, and the Crimson's secret was shared only by his Chinese servant, Wing. Like the Green Hornet, the Crimson Avenger never used a deadly weapon and preferred to put his adversaries to sleep with a blast from his gas gun. He wore a dark blue, slouch hat, a domino mask, and a crimson cape.

Less than a year after the advent of the Crimson Avenger, DC introduced the Sandman in *Adventure Comics* #40 (July 1939). While not a newspaper publisher, wealthy playboy Wes Dodds battled crime in a manner quite similar to that of his two colleagues, and he, too, used a gas gun that put crooks to sleep. A bit more practical than the others, the Sandman wore a gas

mask while on duty. The Green Hornet's influence may also have been automotive: it's possible that Batman's efficient batmobile was inspired by the Hornet's Black Beauty.

The first issue of *Green Hornet Comics* had a cover date of December 1940 and was published by an outfit called Helnit and packaged by Bert Whitman's shop. Whitman had obtained the comic book rights to the character from Trendle, who, anxious to publicize the character, asked no licensing fee. The issues produced by Whitman contained at least a half-dozen short adventures of the Green Hornet plus some filler material; among the artists were Irwin Hasen, Dan Gormley, and Whitman himself. The Helnit Hornet lasted only six issues. Whitman then sold his comic book rights to the Harvey Brothers, later claiming that this was the only money anyone ever made from the Hornet in comics. (During his association with the character, Whitman, collaborating with Frank Robbins, produced a daily *Green Hornet* comic strip, but it seems never to have sold.)

The seventh issue of *Green Hornet Comics* was dated June 1942 and was the first put forth under the Harvey banner. The Hornet, drawn by Arturo Cazeneuve, was reduced to two stories, and the rest of the book was given over to an assortment of other characters—Spirit of '76, the Blonde Bomber, Robin Hood ("Yes! Robin Hood *lives* again!!"), and the Zebra. Covers on the early Harvey issues were by Joe Simon and Jack Kirby.

While never at the top of the sales charts, the Hornet title hung on until the summer of 1949. Artists who drew his adventures included Pierce Rice, Al Avison,

*The Green Lama,*
Mac Raboy, © 1940,
Feature Publications, Inc.

and Jerry Robinson. Alex Schomburg contributed several handsome, and characteristically complex, covers.

The Green Hornet came to television, briefly, in the 1966–67 season, and in 1967 Gold Key tried three issues of a comic book version. The character was revived by an independent publisher in 1989.  **R.G.**

**THE GREEN LAMA**  This mystery man made his debut in a pulp magazine, then graduated to comic books. After two separate comics careers, the second as a flying superhero, he was last heard from as the star of a summer replacement radio show—not bad for a fellow who began life as an imitator of the Shadow.

The Lama was the invention of Kendell Foster Crossen, who was working as an editor for the Munsey pulps at the time. Asked to cook up a Shadow simulacrum to save the faltering *Double Detective* pulpwood magazine, Crossen created Jethro Dumont, alias the Gray Lama. Deciding that gray was too bland a hue, his bosses rechristened him the Green Lama. Under that color, the Lama premiered in a short novel in the April 1940 issue of *Dime Detective*. Crossen used the pen name Richard Foster.

The Munsey folks also had an interest in a faltering comic book, *Prize Comics*, and the Lama showed up there in comics format in issue #7 (December 1940), with early artwork by Mac Raboy. In case readers didn't notice the parallels with the better known Shadow, early captions explained that the Green Lama was "a weird figure of the night! His tireless crusade against crime makes him known in every shadow of the underworld as the greatest scourge of evil the world has yet seen." The Lama wasn't actually that awesome a figure, and he usually looked like a fellow skulking around in a hood and a green bathrobe. Various artists, some gifted and some not, illustrated his crimefighting adventures. Dick Briefer drew the very last one in *Prize*, which ran in #34 (September 1943).

After a year's layoff, the Green Lama returned to the newsstands in his own comic book. The first issue was dated December 1944, and he shared it with such forgotten second bananas as the Boy Champions, Rick Masters, and a mock superhero known as Lt. Hercules. The magazine, which Crossen published, folded in March of 1946 after just eight issues. Once again the artwork was by Mac Raboy, who'd improved considerably since his earlier go-round. The new, improved Lama wore skintight green tights and tunic, an emerald-hued hood, and a flowing cape. He flew through the air now and could perform most of the other feats Raboy's Captain Marvel Jr. did. In all of his incarnations the Lama made use of his Buddhist chant, "Om mani pad-me-hum," before entering into the fray.

CBS brought him briefly to the airwaves in the summer of 1949 with Paul Frees, later one of the most versatile TV commercial voices, as the Lama.  **R.G.**

**GREEN LANTERN (I)**  One of the most popular of the multitude of superheroes who came along in the early 1940s, the Green Lantern was created and developed by artist Mart Nodell and writer Bill Finger with a little help from editor Sheldon Mayer. He made his debut in *All-American Comics* #16 (July 1940), and the initial phase of his crimebusting career lasted until 1951.

In the eight-page origin story readers learned how blond Alan Scott came into possession of a lantern made of a mysterious, glowing green metal. By fashioning a ring from a chunk of the metal and touching it to the lantern once every 24 hours, young Scott acquired an impressive array of powers, including the ability "to streak through the air, to be immune to all metals, to walk through obstacles." The immunity to metal made him bulletproof. He wasn't, however, immune to wood and that meant that a bop on the head with a club or a chair would knock him cold. His costume, which he didn't get around to donning until the last panel of the initial adventure, was a colorful affair. It consisted of a red tunic, green tights, red boots, and a high-collared purple cape. Emblazoned on his chest was a picture of the green lantern that was the source of his supernatural powers.

Mart Nodell, in his middle twenties at the time, had simply walked into the DC offices with an idea for a new character. Mayer was not greatly impressed. "Nodell's drawing was crude," he later said. "What he did have, crude as he was apt to be in his drawing, was an effective first page. He had taken the lead from the *Superman* motif and applied the Aladdin formula to that. I don't know if he included the ring, but he did have the hero with the magical lantern. I didn't want to take it. I thought, what the hell, this is the direction we're already going in, and Nodell didn't seem good enough to handle the feature. And yet he *had* walked in with the idea. I wasn't going to use *Green Lantern* and do it with somebody else. So Bill Finger and I fleshed out the concept…As for Nodell, he made an intense effort to improve."

The greatest improvement in the looks of the new hero was brought about by artist Irwin Hasen, who started ghosting the feature in *All-American* #26 (May 1941). He had a loose, cartoony style, with Caniff touches in his inking and a highly individual way of laying out action. He drew nearly all the GL adventures through *All-American* #51 (July 1943), with some help from inkers such as Chester Kozlak. Hasen did the story in #27 that introduced Green Lantern's unorthodox sidekick, Doiby Dickles. The pudgy cabdriver was tough and excitable—"When a guy smashes me doiby, dat's de last straw!"—and Mayer once said the sidekick was inspired by 1940s movie comedian Lou Costello.

The Green Lantern tales were usually well written, with scripts by Finger and such SF writers as Henry Kuttner and Alfred Bester. The plots mixed mystery, fantasy, and comedy. The postwar GL, with art by Paul Reinman, the returned Hasen, and Alex Toth, went in for combating more colorful villains—such as the villainous jock known as Sportsmaster and the sinister lady called Harlequin—and he eventually replaced Doiby with a wonder dog. He made his last appearance in *All- American* in issue #102 (October 1948).

There was a standard ritual that went along with the recharging of his ring. In the early stories the Green Lantern would recite: "And I shall shed my light over dark evil, for dark things cannot stand the light…the light of…THE GREEN LANTERN!" In 1944 the lines were replaced with the more poetic: "In brightest day…in blackest night, no evil shall escape my sight! Let those who worship evil's might—beware my power, GREEN LANTERN'S LIGHT!"

Popular from the start, the Green Lantern got a magazine of his own in 1941, a title that held on through 38 issues before expiring in 1949. He was also a member in good standing of the Justice Society of America and his initial retirement took place in 1951, when *All Star Comics*—the home of the JSA—ceased publication. He returned to the newsstands in 1963 in the *Justice League of America* comic book, becoming part of the Silver Age superhero revival.                                    **R.G.**

**GREEN LANTERN (II)**   After the auspicious debut of the new Flash in 1956, National (DC) Comics editor Julius Schwartz followed with another revamped Golden Age superhero, Green Lantern, in 1959. In keeping with the science fictional and technological interests of Baby Boom comic book readers, the new hero got his power-ring from an alien, was deputized to guard a "sector of space" by the superhuman Guardians of the Universe, and was in real life Hal Jordan, jet test pilot.

Deftly written by John Broome (and sometimes Gardner F. Fox), sleekly drawn by Gil Kane, the adventures of Green Lantern were among the most varied and entertaining in 1960s comic books. Some were fantastic: The hero teamed up with the alien members of the Green Lantern Corps; fought invaders from the dimension of Qward, where evil is the law; and led an amnesiac double life in the far future. Others centered on Hal Jordan's wacky brothers, his genial Eskimo sidekick Pieface, and his attempts to woo his "lady boss" at the airplane factory, but most involved visually amusing tricks by the power-ring (forming giant scissors, flying fists, and so on). Few comics have made more extensive or more ingenious use of all the devices of the superhero genre.

The series got a shakeup in 1966, when Hal's girlfriend/boss rejected him and he gave up his test-pilot career, rambling around the country doing various odd jobs; this may well have been the first sign of DC responding to the pressure of the innovative, character-oriented, and increasingly popular Marvel Comics Group. At the same time, the art took a quantum leap as Gil Kane began to ink his own pencils and to stretch out in action sequences influenced by Marvel's Jack Kirby.

By 1970, however, both Broome and Kane were gone, and the series was slumping. Writer Denny O'Neil and artist Neal Adams attempted to save it with a startling new direction: They teamed Green Lantern with Green Arrow and made the stories overtly political, pitting Lantern's relative conservatism against Arrow's radicalism in adventures involving slumlords, oppressed Indians, overpopulated planets, drug abuse, and feminist harpies. Although the stories seem rather simplistic and overstated in retrospect, they created a sensation in the comic book industry at the time, culling many awards and rave reviews, and, for the next two years, most DC and Marvel comics at least flirted with "relevance." High praise didn't translate into high sales, though, and *Green Lantern/Green Arrow* died after 13 issues.

Green Lantern's history since then has been one of strained and unsuccessful revivals. He and Green Arrow ran as a backup in *Flash*, then entered their own series, *sans* politics, in 1976. Green Lantern went solo again in the 1980s, went through assorted changes of identity and orientation, and became a part of *The Green Lantern Corps*. A new series alternating the adventures of three different Green Lanterns premiered in 1990.
                                                        **G.J.**

**GROENING, MATT** (1954–  )   The disillusioned spirit of the 1970s produced its inevitable reflection in the comics, and in few cartoonists is that ironic zeitgeist more evident than in the mordant alternative cartoonist Matt Groening, creator of *Life in Hell*.

Born and raised in Portland, Oregon, the son of a cartoonist, Groening (who pronounces his name to rhyme with "raining") evidenced a tendency toward graphic anarchy at least as early as the fourth grade, when he drew monsters for his neighborhood Creature Club, whose motto was "I'm peculiar." He published the first of his distinctively rudimentary cartoons in his school paper at Evergreen State College in Olympia, Washington, from which he graduated in 1977, but the comic strip *Life in Hell* assumed its present form in the Los Angeles magazine *Wet* in 1978, and became a regular weekly feature in the *Los Angeles Reader* the following year. A series of witty and often vehement observations on life as dramatized by a weirdly drawn exophthalmic rabbit named Binky, his even weirder son, the one-eared Bongo, and the apparently human Jeff and Akbar, *Life in Hell* chronicles the collective experience of a frequently unclassifiable cast of sharply drawn types who recapitulate the human lot with a lack of sentimentality that borders on the savage.

*Life in Hell* is divided into the subseries *Love Is Hell*, *Work Is Hell*, *School Is Hell*, and *Childhood Is Hell*, each the subject, and the title, of a successful collection published by Pantheon. The series appears in over 70 newspapers across the country. Groening created a series of animated vignettes, "The Simpsons," which features, as a TV executive described it, "a normal American family in all its beauty and horror," for the Tracey Ullman Show on the Fox Network. It won an Emmy award nomination and appeared as a half-hour series in the fall of 1989. By 1990 the show had become a national craze. **D.W.**

**GROSS, MILT** (1895–1953) One of the true zanies of the cartoon world, Gross created a half-dozen nationally syndicated newspaper strips, including *Count Screwloose* and *Dave's Delicatessen*. He also wrote and illustrated several best-selling books, worked in Hollywood with people such as Charlie Chaplin, produced artwork that appeared in a Bing Crosby-Betty Hutton movie, turned out his own comic book, and once got a fan letter from Calvin Coolidge.

Born in the Bronx in 1895, Gross left high school to take a job as office boy in the art department of Hearst's *New York Evening Journal*. That meant the affable young cartoonist got to rub shoulders with, and sometimes assist, the likes of Tad Dorgan, Gus Mager, Harry Hershfield, Walter Hoban, and Tom McNamara. While still a teenager Gross started selling strips, one to a small syndicate and several to the *Journal* and sister papers. In the early 1920s he switched to the *New York World* where, in addition to drawing strips like *Banana Oil*, he wrote and illustrated his own column for the Sunday edition. It was there that he began fooling around with Jewish dialect. He recounted the adventures of the Feitlebaum family, retold fairy tales and famous poems, even put great moments in history into dialect. The material caught on, and in 1926 Doran published a book collection of the columns under the title *Nize Baby*.

The 1920s were most certainly Gross finest decade, the years when all kinds of people became fascinated with the American language and its colorful variations. These years saw the popularity of Amos and Andy, and the success of the writings of Dashiell Hammett, Ernest Hemingway, and Ring Lardner. When Gross reworked *Hiawatha* and began it

> On de shurrs from Geetchy Goony
> Stoot a tipee wit a weegwom
> Frontage feefty fitt it mashered
> Hopen fireplace—izzy payments…

his Jazz Age audience laughed and was captivated. They were also taken by his cartooning in his columns, books and strips.

Gross was one of the most visually gratifying cartoonists of his day. His drawings are fun to look at and have a lively, restless, sometimes frenzied quality. While not an accomplished draftsman, he possessed a style that was entirely his own and free of swipes, for his characters resembled those of no other artist. It's possible he may have been traumatized early in life by silent movie comedian Ben Turpin, since an unusually high percentage of his characters are crosseyed. Sausage noses were another of Gross' trademarks, so it was probably inevitable that he would eventually do a strip about a delicatessen. Not only the people but also the furniture, buildings, autos, and trees were all distinctly his.

Unfortunately his gags weren't always equal to his artwork, and many strips and pages that are visual delights aren't much fun to read. Gross often comes across as an impatient man, so anxious to get to the drawing that he settles for the first joke that comes to him. He had early discovered the comic possibilities of exposing hypocrites in the tradition of Opper and Goldberg, and he built numerous gags on the notion that

*Count Screwloose*, Milt Gross, Copyright Press Publishing Co. (New York World), 1929.

people don't practice what they preach. That was, in fact, the sole premise of *Banana Oil*, which began as a daily strip and graduated to being a top strip for the *Nize Baby* Sunday page that started in 1927. A husband has a night on the town, for example, and awakens with a monumental hangover, and his wife tells a visitor that, "It was something he *ate* last night," and the family cat observes, "That's a lotta BANANA OIL!!" A couple can barely afford their seaside vacation, but the wife tells a fellow vacationer that her husband "insisted on Europe this year, but I don't like the excitement," while in the background the husband mutters, "Banana oil!!" And so it went. What Gross was using was the basic idée that Jimmy Hatlo later parlayed into the successful *They'll Do It Every Time* panel.

Gross' next feature, *Count Screwloose*, also had an idée fixe, the same one he'd used in *Banana Oil*. The Sunday page replaced *Nize Baby* in February of 1929, and each and every week the diminutive, and crosseyed, Count escaped from the Nuttycrest Asylum to try his luck in the outside world. Each and every week he encountered such lunacy or hypocrisy that he decided to climb back over the wall into the relative sanity of Nuttycrest. Almost every final panel would show Screwloose requesting of his faithful pooch, "Iggy, keep an eye on me!"

Gross switched to King Features in 1930 and drew three alternating daily titles where, again, he relied on the repetition of simple situations. In *I Did It and I'm Glad!* people take revenge on boors and pests; in *Draw Your Own Conclusions* the final panel left the focal character in a dire predicament. *The Meanest Man* was the most bizarre, starring a cloaked and slouch-hatted little villain who did bad deeds—seeing to it that kids who get Lindbergh's autograph have vanishing ink in their pens, giving a hungry dog a rubber sausage that explodes in its face, locking a little henpecked husband in his house so his big wife can lambaste him, and so on. It's hard to tell why such a nasty character, who always won out and never got his comeuppance, appealed to Gross, who was supposedly a gentle and kindhearted man. This triple-threat strip ended in 1931 to be replaced by *Dave's Delicatessen*.

Dave was a likable bumbler, a softie who tried to act tough but always ended up giving hungry people free food, getting taken in by conmen, generally making a fool of himself in front of friends, wife, and community. After a while Gross introduced continuity, usually parodies of the adventure fare of the period: Dave trekked to Africa, joined the Foreign Legion, and tangled with crooks. Early in 1935 Dave drifted away, and Count Screwloose, who'd been sharing the Sunday with him, took over. The daily had already folded.

As the 1930s progressed Gross came up with several new features. There was a daily catchall titled *Grossly Exaggerated* and a new Sunday devoted to *That's My Pop*, and the Count returned in a page of his own. Gross was then living in the Los Angeles area and involved with the movies. Much of the comics work he signed in the last years of the decade was ghosted, usually by the dependable Bob Dunn. During the Second World War Gross turned again to dialect prose, doing a column called *Dear Dollink* for Hearst's Sunday *Pictorial Review*. After the war he showed up in comic books, drawing four pages of comments on the news for *Picture News*, a nonfiction comic book. In the summer of 1947 *Milt Gross Funnies* appeared, written, drawn, and apparently published by Gross. The first issue showcased *That's My Pop!*, his saga of a likable but ne'er-do-well father and his family. The drawing was up to Gross' 1920s standards and the layouts were completely unorthodox. The second issue, which proved to be the last, included a variety of Gross' old characters, including Count Screwloose. His final work appeared in *Giggle Comics* and *Hi-Jinx*.

He'd long suffered with a heart condition and died in 1953 while returning from a Hawaiian vacation with his wife. **R.G.**

**GROTHKOPF, CHAD** (1914– ) An animator by trade, he did considerable comic book cartooning in the 1940s. Signing himself simply Chad, he drew superheroes, soldiers of fortune, and his specialty, funny animals. In the early 1950s he drew the *Howdy Doody* newspaper Sunday page.

Chicago-born, Chad migrated to Hollywood in the middle 1930s. After serving as an art director at Paramount, he moved over to Disney. By 1938 he was in New York working for NBC's television station. Since there were only about 50 TV sets in the area then, Chad's pioneering animated cartoons about Willie the Worm were not seen by a large audience, nor was his salary impressively large. Not surprisingly, he decided to look elsewhere for work.

The comic book business was just starting to blossom when Chad entered it in the late 1930s. Initially he went to work for DC, assigned only serious adventure features like *Radio Squad*, *Three Aces*, *Sandman*, and *Johnny Quick*. This type of material wasn't his favorite, and he drew in a style that owed a considerable amount to Milton Caniff. By the early 1940s he was also drawing for Marvel.

Fortunately Fawcett approached him in 1942, having heard of his animation background, and asked him to create a comic book full of funny animals, which he did. It was called *Funny Animals*, and the leading character was Hoppy the Marvel Bunny, a four-footed version of

Fawcett's most successful hero, Captain Marvel. Also included in the lineup were Billy the Kid, Sherlock the Monk, and Willie the Worm. "Chad worked in an assured animated cartoon style, mixing the cute with the wacky," says *The Great Comic Book Artists*. "His animals were strongly drawn and boldly inked, and his backgrounds were rich with the sort of gingerbread architecture found in the better fairy tale illustrations."

Chad worked as well for the line of comic books published by the *Parents'* magazine company, including *True Comics*. The work led to his drawing a Sunday page called *Famous Fiction*, which adapted such classics as *Ali Baba* and *Alice in Wonderland*. During World War II he served in the Army and on his return he drew again for *Funny Animals*. After that he went into television once more and was associated with the *Howdy Doody Show*. Chad drew the newspaper page about the popular puppet for its entire run, from 1950 to 1953.

After being affiliated with the Famous Artists School's cartoon course, Chad resumed working in animation, a field in which he is still active.  **R.G.**

**GRUELLE, JOHNNY** (1880–1938)  The creator of Raggedy Ann and Raggedy Andy, Gruelle was also a newspaper cartoonist for most of his adult life. He drew two Sunday pages during his career. First came *Mr. Twee Deedle*, which ran from 1910 to 1921, and *Brutus*, which started in 1929 and lasted until his death.

Born in Illinois and reared in Indiana, John Barton Gruelle was the son of a painter father and a writer mother. Despite his father's profession, he insisted on growing up a self-taught artist. Gruelle went to work as a political cartoonist on an Indianapolis weekly in the last year of the 19th century. He next worked on the *Indianapolis Sun*, a daily, and then on the *Star*, another daily. In 1910 he entered a contest run by the *New York Herald*. The paper was seeking a new Sunday page comic, offering a prize of $2,000—a handsome sum in those days. Even though he was ailing at the time, Gruelle was able to rush out samples of a kid's fantasy page he called *Mr. Twee Deedle*. "I wanted to get away from the slapdash style of comics," he said soon after winning. "I have always loved fairy tales and have wanted to illustrate them…I was watching for a chance…and seem to have found it."

Gruelle, like L. Frank Baum, dealt in fairy tales that had a homespun quality, owing as much to his Midwest upbringing as they did to the Brothers Grimm. His page was full of fantasy, impressive drawing and color, and a gentle sort of fantasy. Mr. Twee Deedle was a kid-sized elf who led his child companions through a series of fantasy adventures. Gruelle's first two books were *Mr. Twee Deedle* (1913) and *Mr. Twee Deedle's Further*

*Adventures* (1914), both reprints of his Sunday pages published by Cupples & Leon.

During most of the same years he was drawing his first Sunday page, Gruelle was also contributing a weekly page called *Yapp's Crossing* to *Judge*. He later drew similar bird's-eye views of small-town scenes for *Life* and *College Humor*. In 1918 came the initial Raggedy Ann book, which brought a considerable change in the Gruelle fortunes. During its first 20 years *Raggedy Ann Stories* sold over three million copies.

In the 1920s Gruelle wrote and illustrated over a half-dozen more books about Raggedy Ann and Andy, who came along in 1920. But in 1929 he found time to return to newspaper comics. For the New York Herald-Tribune Syndicate he drew *Brutus*. A quiet and bland Sunday page, it began on November 17, 1929. The feature dealt with the domestic life of Brutus Dudd, who had a dog named Caesar and a cat named Mark Antony. For quite awhile in the 1930s Brutus was out West, residing at the Hot Dog Ranch and indulging in some mild fantasy.

Gruelle and his family had moved to Connecticut soon after he began *Mr. Twee Deedle*. In 1931 they moved again, this time to Miami, Florida. Never in the best of health and bothered by mounting personal problems, Gruelle grew increasingly ill. He was 57 when he died of a heart attack on January 8, 1938. *Brutus* ran seven Sundays beyond that.  **R.G.**

**GUARDINEER, FRED** (1913– )  He started drawing for comic books in 1936 and kept at it for just short of 20 years. Thus Guardineer was active from the dawn of the Golden Age right through to its twilight and he drew every possible sort of character from costumed crimefighter to magician. His style was highly individual, boldly decorative, and there has never been anyone else remotely like him in comics.

Fresh out of college, Guardineer went to work for Harry "A" Chesler's shop, turning out all sorts of features—Western, science fiction, humor, and the like—for such early comic books as *Funny Pages* and *Star Comics*. He moved over to DC in 1938, drawing *Anchors Away* for *Adventure Comics*, *Speed Saunders* for *Detective Comics*, and *Pep Morgan* and *Zatara* for *Action Comics*. Zatara, a Mandrake impersonator invented by writer Gardner Fox, was the first of many magicians that Guardineer would work on. Although he later claimed his favorite genre was the cowboy yarn, he had a definite knack for drawing fantasy and horror material, and his over two years of work on *Zatara* contain some of his most impressive art.

Guardineer drew in a flat, strongly outlined style and treated each panel as part of the overall design of the page. He favored bright, basic colors. The witches, warlocks, monsters, and madmen he drew for features like *Zatara* had individuality, and his damsels in distress were pretty and distinctively dressed.

After leaving DC in 1940, he worked for an assortment of other publishers. He drew a variety of magicians, including Marvelo, Tor, Mr. Mystic, and Merlin, as well as jungle men, masked men, and military men. After the Second World War Guardineer produced a great deal of cops and robbers material for such titles as *Crime Does Not Pay*. From 1952 to 1955 he did *The Durango Kid*, which he later referred to as his "last stand." After that Guardineer quit comics and became a postman in his home town on Long Island, managing as well to do considerable drawing for local newspapers, often on his favorite topics, fishing and hunting. He retired from the postal service in the mid-1970s.

Asked once to sum up his position in comics, Guardineer replied that he didn't know if he'd be ranked with the best, "But I certainly tried."  **R.G.**

**GUISEWITE, CATHY** (1950– )  Since the beginning of her popular comic strip *Cathy* in 1976, Cathy Guisewite has been one of the most successful spokespersons for the young, single career woman. The daughter of an advertising executive who worked his way through college as a stand-up comic, Guisewite was born in Dayton, Ohio, and grew up in Midland, Michigan. After receiving a bachelor of arts degree in English from the University of Michigan in 1972, she followed in her father's footsteps by taking a job as an advertising copywriter in Detroit, and soon rose to the position of vice president of the firm.

Success in her work did not bring a satisfying personal life, however, and during a period when she was, as she reports, "miserable and depressed about [her] love life" Ms. Guisewite began illustrating her letters home with humorous sketches of herself as she coped with overeating, overwork, and the unsuccessful pursuit of a meaningful relationship. In response to what she calls her mother's "constant nagging," she sent some of her drawings to Universal Press Syndicate in 1976. Universal, which had been looking for a strip addressing the problems of the contemporary working woman, offered her a contract at once.

Guisewite kept her job with the advertising agency until the next year, when *Cathy* was well enough established to give her the confidence to turn her attention to it full-time. Although her simple graphic style has changed little since the stick-figures of the mid-1970s, the character has progressed in complexity and confidence. Originally a desperate, helpless victim of both her boss and her boyfriend, Cathy quickly learned to confront the problems of living alone with a candor and

a self-deprecating irony that have captivated a large audience of both sexes.

Guisewite, who has lived in California since 1980, won the Outstanding Communicator of the Year award of the Los Angeles Advertising Women's association in 1982, and her CBS animated special called "Cathy," billed as "TV's first adult animation program," received an Emmy in 1987.  **D.W.**

**THE GUMPS**  One of the first continuity strips in American comics, Sidney Smith's long-running series *The Gumps* chronicled the lives and fortunes of a middle-class family from 1917 to 1959. The strip was conceived by *Chicago Tribune* editor Joseph Medill Patterson, one of the prime influences in early comics, who even gave the strip its name, taken from a word he and his sister, as children, had coined for a blowhard. The head of the cartoon household, Andy Gump, was a braggart whose unmerited self-assurance and excessive optimism inevitably landed him in trouble.

Robert Sidney Smith, who dropped his first name in signing the strip, had created several earlier humorous strips, including a daily gag feature called *Buck Nix*, for the *Chicago Examiner*, in 1908. In 1912 he moved to the *Tribune* to do a Sunday feature named *Old Doc Yak*. Both of these strips dealt with goats so anthropomorphic that it was a small step to *The Gumps* when Patterson asked him to draw the human family that was to make him the highest-paid cartoonist in history, up to then. Andy Gump, his wife Min ("the brains of the family"), and their energetic son Chester made their first appearance in a brief daily series of *Old Doc Yak*, and the new human characters proved so human, and so popular, that on February 12, 1917, they graduated to a strip of their own. *Old Doc Yak* was demoted to a bottom tier of *The Gumps*, where it remained into the 1930s before disappearing altogether. On June 29, 1919, a Sunday *Gumps* feature was added.

*The Gumps* began as a family gag-strip with little daily continuity, employing many of the stock conventions of domestic humor: Andy comes home late and sneaks into the bedroom, Min overspends on clothes, Andy hides liquor in the furnace and pretends to be sweeping the cellar when Min approaches. By the early 1920s, however, the strip was recounting long, complex stories, some humorous, some romantic, but all tightly plotted and suspenseful. Andy ran for Congress in 1922; other characters became involved in sentimental and melodramatic problems of love, crime, business, and sometimes all three. The cast grew to include the Gumps' repulsive maid Tilda, who served up a constant stream of abuse along with her terrible meals, and Andy's Uncle Benjamin (Bim) Gump, an Australian billionaire who controlled his fortune better than he did

his heart. Ching Chow, a minor character in the Sunday strip during the 1920s, became so popular for his potted oriental wisdom that he was given a separate panel in which to issue it—a feature that has outlasted *The Gumps* and still appears.

During the 1920s and 1930s, the failed romances of the susceptible Uncle Bim were a national concern, so enthralling to the public that the Minneapolis Board of Trade shut down one day in 1923 to await the news of whether he had been trapped into marriage with the greedy Widow Zander, and some newspapers carried Bim's narrow escape on the front pages of extra editions. When Mary Gold died in 1929—the first major comic strip character to meet that fate—the *Tribune* had to hire additional staff to handle the volume of incredulous calls and letters it received. The Gumps were a part of American life in many forms during their heyday: Their faces appeared on toys and novelties, fabrics and food packaging. There were Gump games and playing cards and a popular song, and Universal Pictures produced a series of silent films about them from 1923 to 1928. In 1931 Chicago radio station WGN carried *The Gumps*—the first radio show ever made from a

comic strip—and it reappeared, with a new cast including Agnes Moorehead as Min, on CBS in 1934. Numerous successful collections of the strip were reprinted by several publishers.

Drawn in a simple, primitive style, *The Gumps* was to grow more elaborate but never became visually attractive. The characters ranged from the crudely conventional to the positively grotesque; Andy and Bim, two of the most bizarre-looking humans to appear in comics before the undergrounds came along, shared the freakish family trait of being entirely without lower jaws. The strip was often ghosted, and among the artists who drew it for Smith were Chester Gould (no mean hand at grotesques in his own *Dick Tracy*) and Stanley Link, who went on to create *Tiny Tim*. The dialogue—in some of the wittiest and wordiest balloons in the history of the comics—was often supplied by Sol Hess before he went into the comic strip business for himself with *The Nebbs* in 1923.

When Smith died in an automobile accident in 1935, Patterson gave the assignment to Gus Edson, then doing a not-very-successful Sunday strip called *Streaky* and drawing sports cartoons for the *New York Daily*

*News.* In Edson's hands the look of the strip grew no better and the narrative drama declined, along with its readership. From over 300 papers in the 1930s, its circulation fell to fewer than 20 before it was retired on October 17, 1959. **D.W.**

**GUS AND GUSSIE** This comedy continuity daily strip, written by Jack Lait and drawn by Paul Fung, began running in Hearst newspapers in the spring of 1925. It was about two working people, neither blue-collar nor white-collar, who worked on the edges of the smart set world of night clubs and fancy hotels. Eventually Gus and Gussie became part of show business, appearing in cabarets, vaudeville, and the movies.

Lait, who'd become a newspaper man at the turn of the century while still in his teens, had been writing about Gus for well over a decade. "My Gus has starred in every form of expression except grand opera," he explained when King Features launched the strip. "As a daily newspaper serial, as a Sunday-page feature, as a magazine-story hero, in vaudeville, in musical comedy, in the movies, in two books, over the radio, in a popular song, as a lyceum character; and now with a new partner in a comic strip. So far (tapping wood!) Gus has never 'flopped.'" Gus didn't exactly flop as the costar of a daily strip either, but in the five years he worked in this newest medium he never managed to become a top contender.

Like a goodly number of newspaper cartoonists in the Twenties and Thirties, Paul Fung was a graduate of the mail-order Landon School. He worked as a staff artist for the *Seattle Post-Intelligencer*, then drew a short-lived daily titled *The Man from Grand Rapids* for King Features. After that he assisted Billy DeBeck on *Barney Google*. He had one of the liveliest cartoon styles around and, unlike many of his Jazz Age contemporaries, he'd mastered perspective and anatomy. Nobody could draw women better than Fung, in action or, even more difficult, in repose.

When readers first encountered Gus Donnerwetter, he was working as a restaurant busboy. Possessed of a sheepdog haircut, small, brash, and aggressive Gus was hardboiled yet sentimental at the core, full of get-rich-quick schemes and dreams of glory. Even though he mangled the English language—"The mannidger is down on me. It's more than flush an' bleed can stand…An' no he-guy could take it an' detain his manhood."—Gus could talk himself into just about anyplace (or at least give it a try).

Gussie Abadab was a slim brunette, described in the promo copy as "pretty, lovable, and quick-witted," who ran the restaurant check room. Neither a flapper nor a golddigger, she was just an outspoken and self-assured working girl. Gus had an ongoing crush on her, but, although she was fond of him, Gussie kept getting involved with taller and handsomer fellows. These romances never worked out, however, and Gus and Gussie always teamed up again.

The strip was a sort of Roaring Twenties picaresque with the team moving (most often working their way) through a world of night clubs, ocean liners, theaters, and movie lots—wisecracking, hustling, and always

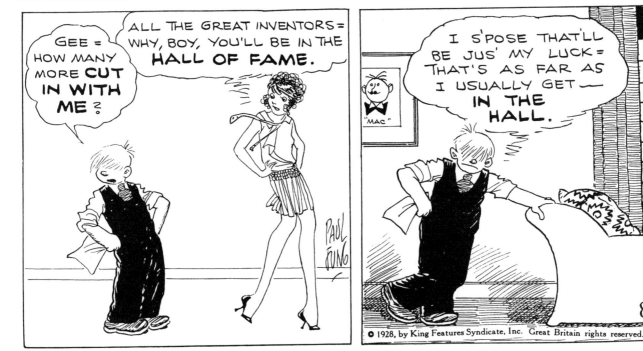

*Gus and Gussie*, Paul Fung, © 1928, by King Features Syndicate, Inc.

having fun. It was relatively sophisticated stuff, using a smart, Broadway approach that more than likely mystified them in the sticks. Early in 1930, while in the midst of a more serious and melodramatic sequence involving crooks and kidnapping, *Gus and Gussie* abruptly folded.

**R.G.**

**GUSTAVSON, PAUL** (1917–1977) Gustavson's career in comic books spanned the entire Golden Age and a bit beyond. Although he could draw in both humorous and straight styles, his most notable work was done on superheroes and costumed crimefighters. From the late 1930s to the late 1940s he drew such characters as the Angel, the Human Bomb, the Arrow, Midnight, Alias the Spider, and Quicksilver.

Born in Finland as Karl Paul Gustafson, he was brought to America by his family in 1921. His first professional cartooning job was as assistant to Frank Owen, a gag cartoonist who also did newspaper strips and panels and who was staunchly of the screwball school. And Gustavson's earliest comic book work was in this vein, consisting of filler pages for *Funny Picture Stories*, *Star Comics*, and the like.

He moved from the Chesler shop to Funnies, Inc., in the late 1930s, gradually shifting over entirely to straight drawing. His earliest costumed hero was the Arrow, and late in 1939 he created the Angle for *Marvel Mystery Comics*. Endowed with more enthusiasm than technical skill, he nonetheless developed a very attractive and effective adventure style. Gustavson went in for inking with a fine brush and loved feathering and shading, with dynamic layouts. His stories—which often involved lovely blond young women being threatened by loathsome monsters—were told in a fast-moving, almost hyperactive way.

Moving to the Quality line he drew a number of heroes, including his own creation, the Human Bomb, a fellow whose barehanded touch could produce impressive explosions. He also inherited Jack Cole's Midnight in *Smash Comics*. After the war, when interest in superheroes waned, Gustavson did humor again and then a good deal of Westerns, crime stories, and romance. He left the field in the late 1950s and was working as a surveyor for the state of New York at the time of his death.

**R.G.**

# H

**HAENIGSEN, HARRY** (1900– ) Reared in the art departments of some of America's great newspapers, Harry Haenigsen was a jack-of-all-trades cartoonist who in the 1940s created *Penny* for the Herald-Tribune Syndicate.

Haenigsen was born in New York City on July 14, 1900, but grew up in New Jersey. As a boy he had two passions—electricity and drawing cartoons. When he was still in high school he sold a cartoon to his home-town newspaper, which was then sued for libel for publishing it. In spite of the suit, the editor continued to buy the youngster's cartoons. After graduation, Haenigsen was given a scholarship to Rutgers University, but a chance meeting with Thornton Fisher, the sports cartoonist for the *New York Evening World*, changed his life. After seeing his work, Fisher advised Haenigsen to study at the Art Students League in New York, adding that as soon as there was an opening on his staff he'd hire him.

While awaiting the coveted job, Haenigsen worked at Bray Studios. In 1919 he joined the *World*, doing a number of drawing chores, including spot art for columns and headlines, illustrations of local events and, because of his electrical knowledge, radio diagrammatics to help readers built their own sets. He even did a strip, *Simeon Batts*, that cashed in on the radio craze. His radio cartoons also found a home at the the *New York Mail*. As he sharpened his talents, the *World*, in 1929, gave him carte blanche for a cartoon that covered the day's news; but two years later the *World* folded and Haenigsen moved to the *American*, where he continued his daily cartoon commentary. By this time he had branched out into magazine illustration; his work graced the pages of *Collier's* and other leading publications. When the *American* went under, Haenigsen worked briefly for Max Fleischer Studios. He was soon back in newspapers as a cartoonist for the *New York Herald Tribune*. He drew *Our Bill*, starting in 1939 and in 1943, on the urging of Helen Reid, the wife of the Trib's president, created *Penny*, the story of a bobbysoxer.

Among the cartoonists who influenced Haenigsen, almost all were newspapermen: Alfred Nee Frueh, the caricaturist of the *World*, Rube Goldberg of the *Mail*, and George Herriman of *Krazy Kat* fame, who worked at the *American*. "Everything I learned," Haenigsen has said, "I learned from newspaper guys." **S.L.H.**

**HAGAR THE HORRIBLE** Dik Browne's daily and Sunday strip about a fun-loving, childlike Viking chief has been among the most popular humor strips in

*Hagar the Horrible*, Dik Browne, 1979.

American comics since its debut. Distributed by King Features Syndicate, it was sold to 136 papers in the United States, Canada, and South America before its first release, on February 4, 1973, and it now runs in 1,550 throughout the world.

Already a highly successful cartoonist collaborating with Mort Walker on the family strip *Hi and Lois* (for which he won the National Cartoonists Society's top award, the Reuben, in 1962, and Best Humor Strip awards in 1959, 1960, and 1972), Browne set out in a totally fresh direction with *Hagar*. The light, delicate line of the cozy domestic strip gave way to a stroke the artist describes as "a lot cruder and bolder," a style fitting "someone as raunchy as Hagar," and the humor followed suit. The gags in *Hagar* draw on the ageless themes of American humor, but freshly adapted to a novel setting. The strip centers on Hagar, a hairy, overweight ninth-century barbarian who works as diligently at his job as any middle-class suburbanite. Although his business happens to be sacking and looting, he still has to face the income tax man every year, his wife Helga nags him to act like a gentleman, and he has to put up with his neighbors' boring stories of their vacation when he should be out pillaging Europe. His son Hamlet embarrasses him by not behaving like a true barbarian, his daughter Honi is in danger of becoming a spinster because she wears armor and carries a sword and helmet like her father, and his simpleminded sidekick Lucky Eddie never understands his orders.

A robust naif, Hagar is a type common to all periods and cultures, a projection of something we all recognize (if a little wistfully) in ourselves. He dreads his yearly bath, eats whatever he can find, and generally lives his life as lustily as he can. It is little wonder that the character has such universal appeal. Indeed, Browne believes that there is a little Viking in everybody.

The vigor and dash of Browne's graphic style and the broad humor of his robust characterization earned him numerous awards in his profession. *Hagar* brought him a second Reuben, along with the Elzie Segar Award for "a unique and outstanding contribution to the profession of cartooning" in its first year, 1973, and the National Cartoonists Society has since voted him its silver plaque for the Best Humor Strip of the Year in 1977, 1984, and 1986. In 1984 the British Cartoonists Society named *Hagar* the Best Non-British International Cartoon, and the Comic Salon of Erlangen, West Germany, gave Browne its first Max and Moritz Preis as the Best Comic-Strip Artist of the year. Collections of *Hagar* strips have appeared in over 20 languages—more than 30 volumes have appeared in English since the first, in 1974—and have sold millions of copies. The strip's daily readership has been estimated at above a hundred million. After his death, Browne's son Chris took over the strip.

**D.W.**

**HAIRBREADTH HARRY** A stalwart mock hero, an early champion of continuity, and a man who was an expert at making hairbreadth rescues, Harry was the creation of C.W. Kahles. Syndicated originally by the *Philadelphia Press*, the first Sunday ran on October 21, 1906.

Kahles got his inspiration for *Hairbreadth Harry* from the swashbuckling exploits of the heroes of 19th-century fiction. Though a burlesque, the page's mixture of fantastic tall tales and dime novel pacing did manage to keep the readers coming back. At first Harry was a boy hero, who dressed in a Rough Rider outfit and roamed

*Hairbreadth Harry*, C.W. Kahles, © 1929, Public Ledger.

the Western wilderness and encountered desperadoes, wild animals, and lots of natural disasters. Saving himself from dire predicaments was his major pastime.

An important development came late in December of 1906, when Kahles started doing continued stories. There had been continuity in strips before, but Kahles was one of the first to use multipart stories and suspense on a regular basis, predating movie serials by several years.

March 3, 1907, marked the debut of Harry's favorite nemesis, Rudolph Rassendale (whose name was inspired by that of Rudolf Rassendyll, the hero of Anthony Hope's popular novel *The Prisoner of Zenda*). Rudy was a typical melodrama villain from the stage, instantly recognizable by his top hat, dress suit, black mustache, and heart to match. On September 22, 1907, Belinda Blinks, destined to be Harry's lifelong love interest, joined the cast. She was originally some years older than he, but Harry aged about 10 years in the next year and caught up with her, proving that love can indeed work miracles. Stealing Belinda from Harry and getting her to the altar became one of Rudolph Rassendale's prime obsessions.

In their travels Harry and Belinda went on wild and woolly adventures around the world, encountering and overcoming evil thugs, black magic, infernal machines and meanminded monsters, most of them put into play by the scheming Rudolph. Kahles moved the strip from a spoof of the tied-to-the-tracks sort of melodrama to sustained science fiction continuities. When the Press syndicate folded on June 27, 1915, *Harry* ended with a hasty wedding to Belinda on a World War I battlefield.

The McClure syndicate brought *Hairbreadth Harry* back on January 16, 1916, and Kahles annulled the marriage of Belinda and Harry. And on May 20, 1923, the Philadelphia Ledger Syndicate added *Harry* to its ranks. The following day a daily strip was added. Here Kahles peaked and his satires of Wall Street, Hollywood, and Prohibition showed both inventiveness and sophistication. There were also fantasy sequences, including an epic trip through time and space in 1924.

At his death Kahles left two months of work, and his final strips appeared at the end of March 1931. The syndicate hired F.O. Alexander as a replacement in April and he carried on admirably in his new job for several years. He maintained the pace and tone and kidded the current forms of melodrama to be found in such mediums as the movies. However, the syndicate began to suffer from poor management, the sales of all the Ledger strips faltered, and in an attempt to bolster *Harry*, some changes were imposed. Harry and Belinda married again, soon produced a son and began to have somewhat more serious adventures. Alexander quit early in 1939.

Ghosts were brought in, including Joe Bowers and Jimmy Thompson. The dailies resorted to completely serious continuity, trying to do in earnest what the strip had been making fun of for decades. Thompson drew them well, but poor strong-jawed Harry simply wasn't suited to playing it straight. The final Sunday appeared on August 13, 1939, and the final daily on January 17, 1940.                                                      **M.J.**

**HAMLIN, VINCENT T.** (1900– ) A fascination with paleontology, acquired while working as a layout man for a Texas oil company, inspired V.T. Hamlin to try his hand at a comic strip set in prehistoric times. *Alley Oop* was the result. He wrote and drew the humorous caveman strip, distributed by Newspaper Enterprise Association, from 1933 to 1971.

Born in Perry, Iowa, Hamlin discovered a talent for cartooning as he illustrated fellow-soldiers' letters home while recovering from poison gas in France during World War I. He studied journalism at the University of Missouri and for a time worked as a reporter, photographer, and cartoonist on newspapers in Iowa and Texas.

From the creation of the stalwart caveman Oop, Hamlin devoted his full time to the denizens of the prehistoric land of Moo and their lively adventures. His gift for graceful layouts, amusing dialogue, and exciting, well-paced narrative made *Alley Oop* popular with all ages, and at its peak it appeared in some 800 papers.

Hamlin relinquished first the drawing and then the writing of the strip to his assistant Dave Graue in the middle 1960s, and retired in 1971. He now lives in Brookville, Florida.                                                      **D.W.**

**THE HANGMAN** One of the grimmer and more violent of the Forties comic book heroes, the Hangman first appeared in *Pep Comics* #17 (July 1941). While not a superhero himself, he was the brother of one.

His name was Robert Dickering, and his brother John had been appearing in *Pep* as the Comet. He decided to take up crimefighting when the Comet was killed by gangsters' bullets. Today, with comic book heroes dropping like flies, the death of one more doesn't have much of an effect, but in 1941 the demise of the Comet was a unique and shocking event for comic book readers.

For his first job, the Hangman went after those responsible for his brother's death. He haunted them with projected images of a gallows, engaged them in hand-to-hand combat, and finally saw to it that the ringleader was executed on the gallows by the state. In the final panel, he looked directly out at the reader and, striking an Uncle-Sam-wants-you pose, warned, "The Comet has died but his spirit lives on...in the Hangman! Beware, criminals, you cannot outrun your own con-science…nor escape the gallows!"

*Hangman* offered a rather steamy blend of violence and sex. There were frequent hangings as well as stab-bings, stranglings, impalings, and brandings, and con-siderable attention was given to cleavage and lingerie. Patriotism wasn't ignored either, and the Hangman frequently battled a vicious, costumed Nazi saboteur called Captain Swastika, whose equally unpleasant sidekick had an icepick in place of his right hand.

The first scripts were credited to one Cliff Campbell, a name that also appeared in pulp fiction magazines, and the initial artist was George Storm. Uncomfortable with Hangman's sort of grue, however, Storm left after four issues. Harry Lucey, a much more realistic artist, followed him and was succeeded by Bob Fujitani. War-ren King also drew the feature. Hangman appeared in eight issues of his own magazine in the early Forties and was last seen in *Pep* #47 (March 1944). He went on the vengeance trial again briefly during MLJ's unsuccessful hero revivals of the middle 1960s and middle 1980s.

R.G.

**HANK**  Coulton Waugh's daily began in the waning days of World War II, on April 30, 1945, but it was clearly a postwar strip. The story started in the Pacific, where Corporal Hank Hannigan is wounded in combat and loses his right leg. Back in the United States, he is rehabilitated at an Army hospital. Syndicated by the liberal newspaper *PM*, replacing *Vic Jordan*, the feature was different from other postwar adventure strips in that it dealt with a character who'd been seriously injured and derived its plots from social and political issues. "This was to be a deliberate attempt," Waugh once said, "to work in the field of social usefulness."

The continuity was well intentioned but somewhat oversimplified, pitting clean-cut Hank and a crusading reporter from the *Daily Liberal* against a fascist group who intended to use a new veterans' organization to spread right-wing propaganda and anti-Semitism. The strip featured action and gunplay, plus a little romance. Waugh worked in a slightly more cartoony style than he'd used on *Dickie Dare*, trying "novel art approaches" that included occasional use of black balloons with white lettering. *Hank* ended on the last day of 1945.

R.G.

**HAP HOPPER**  An adventure strip about a newspa-per reporter, it was masterminded by two nationally known newspaper reporters. *Hap Hopper, Washington Correspondent*, was introduced by United States Fea-tures early in 1940, with artwork by Jack Sparling and scripts edited by Drew Pearson and Robert S. Allen. It lasted, daily and Sunday, until 1947.

Late in 1939 United had announced that a new strip titled *Hap Hazard* would commence early the following year. It was to be the creation of Pearson and Allen, then famous as collaborators on the muckraking *Washington Merry-Go-Round* column. It would be "a humorous con-tinuity strip about a fictional young newspaperman amid the glamour and comedy of the nation's capital, where he meets real, factual individuals whose names make newspaper headlines." The artist would be Spar-ling, former staff cartoonist and political caricaturist for the *Washington Herald*. When a King Features Washing-ton correspondent named Jack Hazard got wind of the venture, he notified the rival syndicate that the strip's title "would be embarrassing" to him. When it debuted on January 29, 1940, the name was *Hap Hopper*.

The actual scriptwriter was William Laas, comics editor at United. Since he envisioned Harold "Hap" Hopper as a sort of journalistic Li'l Abner, his early continuities about the blond, handsome and bespecta-cled newsman presented him as something of a bump-kin, blundering his way around Washington D.C., and muttering, "Gee whiz." As Sparling later pointed out, many feature editors across the country had once been reporters. "Very few cottoned to the idea that there are goofs for reporters. We soon changed this, and the strip began to pick up papers."

Hap became smarter and better looking, though he retained the glasses. Before 1940 was out he'd joined the Army, where he became involved in hunting spies and saboteurs. A year or so later he was again a reporter, but working as such under a special assignment from G-2. His editor was a derby-wearing, cigar-chomping fellow named Rushmore Newes. His hometown sweetheart was a pretty brunette named Holly Woode, who by the middle of 1941 was working in Washington as a re-porter. True to its early promises, *Hap Hopper* did in-clude real newsmakers in its panels. Among them J. Edgar Hoover, Eleanor Roosevelt, Henry Wallace, and Eleanor Patterson, publisher of the *Washington Times-Herald* and ertswhile mother-in-law of Pearson.

In the autumn of 1942 Charles Verral, a prolific pulp fiction writer who was also scripting the *Mandrake the Magician* radio show, was hired to take over the writing. By that time Pearson and Allen had split up and the byline read "Edited by Drew Pearson." Though Verral had never worked on a newspaper, one of the few areas of writing he hadn't tried, he managed to come up with convincing newsroom continuities.

Sparling, never especially content with the low pay on *Hap Hopper*, left in 1943 to draw a strip of his own called *Claire Voyant*. After brief stints by other artists, including Artie Saaf, the regular illustrator of the strip became Al Plastino. In 1947 a private eye with a distinc-tive streak of gray in his dark hair started showing up in the stories. This was Barry Noble, an invention of Verral's. As of May 28, 1947, the strip became *Barry Noble* and Hap was seen no more. Under the new name it lasted until May 14, 1949. **R.G.**

**HAPPY HOOLIGAN** A hobo who persisted in looking on the bright side, Happy Hooligan got into funnies fairly early in the game and remained a regular for over 30 years. Frederick B. Opper first drew him in 1900 and kept him going, with some lapses, until the early 1930s.

Opper began his Hooligan series as a Sunday page for Hearst's *New York Journal* on March 11, 1900. Although it was frequently replaced by other Opper features, it didn't finally end until August 14, 1932. Happy was the perpetual fall guy, the good-hearted failure, the hapless tramp with an old tin can for a hat. Like the later tramp immortalized by Charlie Chaplin, Happy was a generous, kind-hearted soul whose efforts to help other people usually ended in failure. He was, in the words of Opper himself, "a favorite son of misfortune." His buoyant optimism was set in contrast to the gloom of his brother Gloomy Gus, introduced on April 20, 1902, while his simple humility was highlighted by the unfounded pretension of his other brother, Lord Montmorency, who appeared on the scene on February 14, 1904.

As early as December 1908 Happy began to court a young woman named Suzanne, but it wasn't until June 18, 1916, that they were finally married. From then until April 7, 1918, the page was titled *Happy Hooligan's Hon-eymoon*, surely one of the longest honeymoons on record.

Companion features were added to many of the Hearst Sunday pages on January 10, 1926. When *Happy Hooligan* came back after a hiatus, in January of 1927, it was accompanied by one of Opper's earliest series, *And Her Name Was Maud*, which had begun in the *Journal* on May 26, 1901, originally. Throughout the 1920s Opper also drew a daily strip and for periods it was devoted to Happy and his crowd. **K.S.B.**

**HARMAN, FRED** See RED RYDER.

**HAROLD TEEN** One of the first newspaper strips to recognize the teenager as a separate breed, it began in 1919, the work of a 29-year-old cartoonist named Carl Ed (pronounced Eed). *Harold Teen* started off just at the dawn of the Jazz Age and became an acceptable, suitable-for-the-whole-family representation of Flaming Youth. Harold and his gang outlived the Roaring Twenties and remained popular, constantly changing their clothes and their jargon, into the 1940s. The strip itself hung on until 1959.

The 1920s was a very successful decade for the ageless teenager. The Chicago Tribune Syndicate played up the fact that Ed's strip kept continually in tune with the times, or perhaps even a bit ahead of them. In a slangy ad in a 1928 issue of *Editor and Publisher*, for example, they told prospective newspaper clients: "Hot pups! Here's Harold Teen. The sheiks depend on Harold for their styles, their slang, their hobbies. Whatever he favors is popular with the 'jazz' gang." His popularity

*Happy Hooligan*, F. Opper, © 1929, International Feature Service, Inc.

continued throughout the 1930s and into the early 1940s as Harold reflected and influenced the mores and folkways of the swing gang and the jitterbugs.

Underneath the up-to-date wisecracks and fads, Ed's world was an innocent, home-oriented one. Harold, his girlfriend Lillums, his diminutive buddy Shadow, and the rest were basically content with their lives. Their idea of a wild time was to have two Gedunk sundaes at Pop Jenks' Sugar Bowl soda fountain or to cruise around town in a rattletrap jalopy that had flip sayings lettered on its sides. There was no liquor, no drugs, little crime in *Harold Teen*, and only a polite sort of sex.

Ed drew, with the help of various assistants, in a simple, easy-to-digest version of the basic Chicago style. In *The Comics* Coulton Waugh described the drawing as being "without grace...raw and ugly," but he acknowledged that *Harold Teen* "has drugstore truth, and fulfills a function which perhaps cannot be exactly assayed by a non-teenster." Ed kept up with changes in high school styles, drawing his characters in raccoon coats when those were the craze, switching them from knickers to bellbottoms when the time was right. His kids kept up with current slang and insults, too, calling each other squirts, twerps, and drips as changing language patterns dictated.

Early in the Second World War Ed put his young hero into the Navy when a lot of other teenagers were going into the service. Harold survived the war and the strip carried on until the late 1950s, but it was increasingly less popular in the postwar years. **R.G.**

**HART, JOHNNY** (1931– ) A pioneer of the contemporary, hip, freewheeling cartoon, Hart (whose full name is John Lewis Hart) has been a favorite with young adults since he introduced his witty caveman strip *B.C.* in 1958.

Hart's formal study of art never progressed beyond high school classes in his hometown of Endicott, New York. He spent the three years after high school in the Air Force in Korea, doing cartoons for *Stars and Stripes*, and on his release made a serious, if not particularly successful, assault on the cartoon market, living precariously from occasional sales to the *Saturday Evening Post*, *Collier's*, and *Bluebook*. In 1957 he took a job in the art department of Western Electric.

The idea of a gag strip about cave-dwellers was not easy to sell, and five syndicates turned *B.C.* down before the New York Herald Tribune Syndicate took it in February of 1958. It was an immediate success and has remained widely popular.

Feeling that a Stone Age setting limited his range of social satire ("There's no society to deal with in *B.C.*," Hart explained), he evolved an idea for another strip, set in the middle ages. *The Wizard of Id*, drawn by Hart's old friend and mentor Brant Parker, was accepted by Publishers Hall Syndicate (which had taken over *B.C.* when the Herald Tribune Syndicate folded) and debuted on November 9, 1964. (*Wizard* has since moved on the North America Syndicate, and *B.C.* went from Publishers Hall to Field to Creators Syndicate; each now runs in about 400 papers.) Hart shares the scripting of *Wizard* with Jack Caprio and Dick Boland.

The loose, breezy style of his art and the often mordant wit of his gags have earned Hart many honors in the industry: The National Cartoonists Society voted him Outstanding Cartoonist of the Year (1968) and *B.C.* Best Humor Strip (1968 and 1971). In 1967 Hart won the NCS's Reuben award and in 1970 the Yellow Kid award from the International Congress of Comics. Hart has created several *B.C.* television specials and has provided art for TV commercials and NASA decals and posters. His two strips have been collected and published in numerous volumes and have been translated into many languages, including Swedish, Finnish, and Japanese. **D.W.**

**HASEN, IRWIN** (1918– ) Though he is best-known for having drawn the long-running *Dondi* newspaper strip, Hasen was also an important contributor to the comic books of the 1940s. He drew an assortment of heroes, the most notable the original Green Lantern.

Irwin Hanan Hasen was born in New York City and, like many of his colleagues, studied at the National Academy of Design and the Art Students League. "I first worked as a sport cartoonist in the boxing racket," he once said. From that he moved into comic books in the late 1930s and his earliest pages were sports fillers. After that he worked for three different shops—Harry "A" Chesler's, Lloyd Jacquet's Funnies, Inc., and Bert Whitman's. While with Whitman, Hasen drew *Secret Agent Z-2*, *Bob Preston, Explorer*, *Cat-Man*, and the *Green Hornet*.

For MLJ's *Blue Ribbon Comics* he drew a costumed hero named the Fox. In 1940 he did some adventures of a hardboiled private eye named Larry Steele for *Detective Comics*. The next year he started working for Sheldon Mayer at DC's All-American division. He was assigned the *Green Lantern* soon after it began, but didn't sign it until after he'd ghosted several stories. By this time Hasen was drawing very well, somewhat under the influence of Milton Caniff, and had become quite inventive at staging and laying out his pages. While never quite a star of the Golden Age, he was highly admired by many of his contemporaries in the business. During this period he also drew *Wildcat* for *Sensation Comics*.

After serving in the Army, he drew an unsuccessful adaptation of *The Goldbergs* radio show for the New

York Post Syndicate. He then returned to comic books and the Green Lantern. In 1955, collaborating with Gus Edson, he began *Dondi* and remained with it until it ended in the middle 1980s. **R.G.**

**HATLO, JIMMY** (1898–1963) The creator of the popular panel feature *They'll Do It Every Time* and its spinoff strip *Little Iodine*, Jimmy Hatlo was to chronicle the small ironies of social, professional, and domestic life for over a third of a century. A native of Providence, Rhode Island, Hatlo grew up in Los Angeles, where he got his first job in art working as a cartoonist with the *Los Angeles Times*. After five years with the *Times*, he became a salesman of advertising for the growing automobile industry, and, on the basis of his combined experience as a cartoonist and a car expert, he secured the job of automotive editor of the *San Francisco Bulletin*.

Hatlo's devotion to the burgeoning field of automobiles was not great enough to keep him in it, however, and his lighthearted irony was essentially incompatible with the fiercely competitive and aggressive spirit of the industry. In the early 1920s he moved on to the *San Francisco Call* (later to merge with the *Bulletin*) to draw about a subject closer to his heart, sports. His humorous sports series, called *Swineskin Gulch*, was to be a popular feature of the *Call* for several years. When the sports cartoonist Thomas A. ("Tad") Dorgan died in 1929, Hatlo was asked to replace him in the *San Francisco Call-Bulletin* and the *Los Angeles Herald Express*, Hearst's two leading California newspapers.

The result was a regular feature, usually in a split-panel format, revealing the malice, violence, and greed lurking just below the surface of polite social intercourse and gently spoofing the logical inconsistencies of our thought. Drawn in a vigorous, cartoony style, it was an immediate success; Hatlo's perception of the hypocrisy, thoughtlessness, and absurdity of everyday life drew so much fan mail that he began to use ideas suggested by his readers, acknowledging them first with "Thanx" and later with the signature line "Thanx and a hat tip" or "Thanx and a tip of the Hatlo hat" to the suggester. *They'll Do It Every Time* was taken on by Hearst's King Features Syndicate in 1936, and a Sunday version added in 1949. A popular addition to the Sunday feature was *Hatlo's History*, single-panel cartoons giving behind-the-scenes glimpses of historical events, (The Civil War took so long because the Union generals couldn't resist showing off and clowning for Mathew Brady's camera; Caesar's legions have the same trouble with catapults that modern scientists have with rockets.) In 1943, the mischievous child of the suburban family regularly featured in *They'll Do It Every Time* generated a Sunday strip of her own, *Little Iodine*, also distributed by King.

With the diminishing public taste for strips about the pranks of malevolent youngsters, *Little Iodine* has dated badly and has fallen off in circulation, but the wry insights of Hatlo's first and most popular feature, continued until his recent death by his assistant Bob Dunn, have proved a lasting contribution to American humor. *They'll Do It Every Time* earned Hatlo the National Cartoonists Society plaque for best Syndicated Panel in 1957 and 1960 and it has received the plaque three times, in 1968, 1969, and 1979, since his death. **D.W.**

**HAWKMAN (I)** The most successful birdman in early comics, the first Hawkman flapped into view in the premier issue of *Flash Comics* (January 1940). While never quite a full-fledged star during the Golden Age, he did manage to outshine and outlast such avian competitors as the Black Condor, the Owl, and Airman. *Hawkman* was written by Gardner Fox and drawn initially by Dennis Neville, who'd been helping out on *Superman*.

Handsome, blond Carter Hall, described as a "wealthy collector of weapons and research scientist," had invented the Ninth Metal, "which defies the pull of Earth's gravity." Wearing a harness of the stuff and an immense pair of feathery wings he is able to fly.

In the original story readers learned that Hall had lived before in ancient Egypt, where he was known as Prince Khufu. His true love was a lady named Shiera and both of them were murdered in the Temple of Anubis by an evil priest. One day in 1940 the reincarnated Hall bumped into the reincarnated Shiera. Hall took her home with him, and they appeared from thence forward to be cohabiting without benefit of clergy.

The Hawkman's looks improved considerably with the fourth issue, when Sheldon Moldoff, just 20 and already a veteran of several years in the comic book trade, took over illustrating the adventures of the "winged phantom of the night." Like several of his contemporaries, Moldoff was much under the influence of Alex Raymond, and Carter Hall now became a Flash Gordon lookalike. The young artist also admired Hal Foster, Burne Hogarth, and Big Little Book illustrator Henry Vallely, and he was fond of adapting and modifying their panels to his own ends.

Hawkman specialized in villains who were weird and strange; these included a stone man, odd creatures who dwelled beneath the waters of New York harbor, a bodiless hand that committed murders, a golden mummy, an evil giant from another planet, among others. In just about every adventure he followed his policy of "fighting evil of the present with strange weapons of the past." Among these weapons were a quarterstaff, a mace, a war-axe, a bow and arrow, and a sword.

In *Flash Comics* #24 (December 1941), Hawkman had a Hawkwoman costume made up for Shiera, and the two of them attended a costume ball. Moldoff stinted a bit and gave only one shot of the party, a two-shot closeup of the couple dancing. One can't help wondering how the other partygoers managed to dance with those two enormous pairs of wings flapping around the floor. At any rate, Shiera got a chance to tackle some crooks while in costume and liked the idea. Hall, however, was against her becoming a full-time partner, but wasn't able to maintain this sexist attitude, and in the next episode Shiera again donned the outfit and even managed to save him from a tight spot. From the next issue on she was referred to as Hawkgirl and not Hawkwoman.

Although Hawkman was apparently a popular character—he appeared on just about every other cover, alternating with the Flash—he never quite achieved star status during the 1940s. He appeared in *All Star Comics* from the first issue and was a member in good standing of the Justice Society, but he never got such extra perks as a magazine of his own.

In 1944 another youthful artist, the teenaged Joe Kubert, took over the drawing. This was a Kubert who hadn't yet been toughened up by years of service with militant characters like Sgt. Rock, and he did a commendable job with the strange and fantastic people, places, and things the stories required. After the end of World War II, Robert Kanigher assumed the writing, and later in the 1940s Hawkman and Hawkgirl ceased wearing their distinctive feathery masks and switched to more conventional cowls. *Flash Comics* folded in 1949, but the team held on in *All Star* until it, too, collapsed in 1951. **R.G.**

**HAWKMAN (II)** Of editor Julius Schwartz's major revivals of Golden Age heroes for National (DC) Comics, Hawkman had the hardest time getting off the ground: He needed two tryouts in *The Brave and the Bold* (1961 and 1962) and then a backup series in *Mystery in Space* (1963) before finally being given his own title in 1964.

This Hawkman, named Katar Hol (which became "Carter Hall" in his secret identity as a museum curator), was a humanoid visitor from the planet Thanagar, a police detective who journeyed to Earth to study our law enforcement methods. He was aided by his wife, Hawkgirl, by a knowledge-transmitting device called the Absorbascon, and by the panoply of ancient Earth-weapons stored in his museum. All the stories were written by Gardner Fox, with an eye toward charming, archaeologically-influenced mysteries (and occasional

encounters with extraterrestrials); they were drawn at first by Joe Kubert, then by Murphy Anderson in a crisper, less atmospheric style.

Never a high-selling title, *Hawkman* passed in 1967 to editor George Kashdan, and to lesser scripts and art. Schwartz got the character back a year later for a combined *Atom and Hawkman* series, but that perished after a few issues.

Having joined DC's *Justice League of America* in 1964, Hawkman remained a visible but minor hero in the DC pantheon through the 1970s. In the 1980s, emphasis has shifted away from Hawkman's role as an earthbound superhero and toward his involvement with his native race, the Thanagarians; they are portrayed, often sinisterly, as spacefaring warriors in eternal conflict with the denizens of Rann, the adopted planet of spaceman-hero Adam Strange. Writer Tony Isabella and artist Richard Howell produced a popular *Hawkman* mini-series in 1985, in which Hawkman and Hawkwoman (neé Hawkgirl) defended Earth from an insidious invasion by evil Thanagarians. This led to a new regular series in 1986, but it was less well received and ended the following year. In 1989 Timothy Truman wrote and drew the mini-series *Hawkworld*, a dark science-fictional story of Thanagar, which excited new reader interest in the concept and characters. **G.J.**

**HAWKSHAW THE DETECTIVE** The most robust of the Sherlock Holmes burlesquers, the master sleuth enjoyed two separate careers in the funny papers. Created by Gus Mager, Hawkshaw undertook his first series of detecting adventures from 1913 to 1922. Like Holmes, he didn't stay dead but returned in 1931 for a run that lasted until the late 1940s.

A dedicated Holmesian, Mager had previously spoofed the great detective in his daily *Sherlocko the Monk* strip. In 1913, when he began a new Sunday page for the *New York World*, he retained his detective but rechristened him Hawkshaw, a name borrowed from that of the sleuth in Tom Taylor's popular Victorian melodrama *The Ticket-of-Leave Man*. Mager also kept Sherlocko's diminutive associate, Dr. Watso, and renamed him the Colonel.

*Hawkshaw the Detective* offered mock melodramas and burlesque investigations, making fun of the conventions of the detective yarns, not only of the Holmes kind but of the Nick Carter variety as well. There were audacious schemes, outrageous impersonations and disguises, and fiendish plots—all seen through and solved by Hawkshaw. His favorite nemesis was the brilliant though loutish-looking master criminal known as the Professor. Mager kept the page going until 1922, often indulging in continuities that stretched out for several weeks and involved Hawkshaw in the solution of mys-

*Hawkshaw the Detective*, Gus Mager, © 1916, Press Publishing Co.

teries or searching for such rare objects as the Bulbul Ruby.

Mager revived his character late in 1931, this time as a topper to his friend Rudolph Dirks' *The Captain and the Kids* Sunday page. Hawkshaw was unchanged, and his client list again contained such names as Groucho, Henpecko, and Nervo. Watso, who used his original name this time, took credit for authoring the strip and Mager never signed it. When Dirks quit in 1932 over a contract dispute, Mager had to leave too. For the next year or so the syndicate brought in Bernard Dibble to draw the Captain, the kids and Hawkshaw. Dirks was back on the job in 1933 and so was Mager.

The Professor remained the star villain throughout the 1930s. Mager continued to burlesque the traditional detective story, giving each episode a mystery-like title—*The Curious Episode of the Haunted Cell, The Peculiar Affair of the Purloined Parrots, The King Cobra Strikes!*, and so forth—and he kept Hawkshaw on the case until the late 1940s.                                              **R.G.**

**HAYS, ETHEL**   See FLAPPER FANNY.

**HAYWARD, A.E.** (1885–1939)  Chiefly known for his *Somebody's Stenog*, the first of the working-girl strips, Hayward (whose full name was Alfred Earle Hayward) had a wide-ranging career that even extended to fine art. His cartooning began with the *Philadelphia Item* in 1906, where he did caricatures, decorations, and news drawings, even representing the *Item* at the New York

murder trial of Harry Thaw. In February 1909 he switched to the *Philadelphia Evening Bulletin*, where he drew mostly sports and weather spot art.

Hayward's first strip was *Great Caesar's Ghost*, for the New York Herald syndicate, which debuted on December 14, 1913, and was an odd satire on Ancient Rome. Caesar was portrayed as a henpecked, cigar-chomping emperor living amidst fantastic anachronisms. On November 1, 1914, a secondary character named Pinheadus took over the strip, which ended September 12, 1915. Hayward's final *Herald* creation was *Colonel Corn*, a prosaic family series that lasted from October 24, 1915, to November 3, 1918.

On January 13, 1915, he'd joined the *Philadelphia Evening Public Ledger*, launching a topical gag-a-day panel titled *The Padded Cell;* on December 16, 1918, he embarked on *Somebody's Stenog*.

Hayward had a simple yet sophisticated style, somewhat similar to the Postimpressionist school of painting—a marked departure from most other cartoon work of the time. He held a faculty position at the Pennsylvania Academy of Fine Art, teaching caricature from 1924 to 1927. Outside of the cartoon field, he won various awards for his watercolors.          **M.J.**

**HEARST, WILLIAM RANDOLPH** (1863–1951) William Randolph Hearst created the largest newspaper chain in the United States during the first decades of this century; his empire included 18 major newspapers in 12 cities, and nine magazines, including *Good*

*Housekeeping, Cosmopolitan,* and *Harper's Bazaar.* The spectacular promotions and sensational style of the Hearst papers had a revolutionary effect on American journalism.

Born in San Francisco, California, the only child of wealthy, influential parents (his father served for a time in the U.S. Senate), Hearst was a spoiled child who refused to conform. Expelled from Harvard for wild behavior, he assumed control of his father's staid *San Francisco Examiner* in 1887 and restored the failing paper to prosperity by infusing it with his flamboyant personal style. In 1895 he bought the *New York Morning Journal* and successfully competed with the reigning press-lord Joseph Pulitzer in a struggle that was to rock the fourth estate.

Hearst represented New York in Congress from 1903 to 1907, but his aspirations to higher office were consistently frustrated. In 1904 he made a well-backed bid for the Democratic presidential nomination; in 1905 he ran for mayor, and in 1908 for governor, of New York, but was defeated each time. He remained a powerful political force, however, and molded both local and national policy with his wealth and the influence of his newspapers. His papers' sensational (and often exaggerated) coverage of the Cuban revolt of 1895 is widely regarded as having brought about the Spanish-American War.

Although he was to become an arch-conservative in his later years, he never ceased to live a life as flamboyant and extravagant as his journalistic style. Among the many castles he built for himself, his San Simeon, California, mansion alone cost him over $30 million, and his accumulation of artworks, much of it never uncrated, filled many warehouses.

Among Hearst's more positive contributions to American journalism was his important influence on the creation of the comic strip. Observing the immense popularity of the *New York World's Yellow Kid,* the first comic feature to use color, Hearst immediately hired its artist, R.F. Outcault, away from Pulitzer to contribute to his own *American Humorist,* the *Journal's* comic weekly, which advertised in 1896, "Eight pages of polychromatic effulgence that makes the rainbow look like a lead pipe." It was with his creation of the *Katzenjammer Kids* the next year that Hearst had his most significant impact on the genre. Enchanted with the German illustrated narrative series *Max und Moritz,* which he discovered on a trip to Europe, he directed a staff artist, Rudolph Dirks, to adapt it to a sequential cartoon. The debut of the Katzies on December 12, 1897, is considered by many to mark the beginning of the modern comic strip.

Always a lover of the medium he helped to create, he went on to assign Clare Briggs to create *A. Piker Clerk,* one of the first daily continuity strips, for his *Chicago American* in 1904. Thirty years later he was still promot-ing the form. In 1934 he hired Carl Anderson to transform his single-panel feature *Henry,* then appearing weekly in the *Saturday Evening Post,* into the daily strip it remains. Until the end of his life his King Features Syndicate received his close personal attention; the last strip he personally approved, in 1950 at the age of 87, was Mort Walker's *Beetle Bailey.*

William Randolph Hearst's name is still associated with the shrieking typography and sensational news reporting that define "yellow journalism," but the contribution made by comic strips to the gaiety of nations may stand as his most lasting legacy. **D.W.**

**THE HEART OF JULIET JONES** Before television made continuity strips almost as rare as the Dodo bird, *The Heart of Juliet Jones* had become one of the most successful soap operas in the business. Created by Stan Drake and Elliot Caplin in 1953 for King Features, it was carried in 600 newspapers, battling *Mary Worth* for top honors in this genre. Today it struggles on, battling the cramped confines that newspapers now allot to comics—and that test Drake's innovative style and artistic talent.

Juliet Jones is the story of two young, beautiful, and bright daughters of Howard Jones, a widower and retired lumber company executive. Juliet is the eldest (early 30s) and as such is more mature—a confidante to her father, a mother to her younger sister and, of course, the heroine of the strip. The other daughter, Eve, is more impulsive, more emotional than Juliet. After Juliet's ill-fated marriage (her husband, a New York criminal lawyer named Owen Cantrell, winds up getting murdered), Eve is a source of many romantic entanglements. The Jones family lives in the small town of Devon where, for a while, Juliet was mayor.

For Drake, who now draws *Blondie,* the well-crafted strip gave him immediate recognition for his illustrative work when it debuted in March 1953. For Caplin, who wrote the continuity, it provided a showcase for his writing talent and helped pull him out of the shadow of his more famous brother, Al Capp. In fact, it was Caplin who had approached King Features with the idea of a romance strip at a time when it was looking for a competitor to *Mary Worth.* Several years earlier the syndicate had negotiated with Margaret Mitchell, author of *Gone With The Wind,* to write such a strip. But her untimely death had put the idea on hold.

Among the well-known cartoonists who assisted Drake on Juliet Jones over the years were Neal Adams, Tex Blaisdel, Alex Kotsky, and John Cullen Murphy. **S.L.H.**

**HEATH, RUSS** (1926– ) As an artist Heath has always been dedicated to realism, to getting it right. In comics since the 1940s, he has earned a reputation as one of the best illustrators of both Western and war stories. His work has appeared in *Frontline Combat, Our Army At War, Kid Colt Outlaw*, and *Mad*, and he has also assisted on such newspaper strips as *Terry and the Pirates, Flash Gordon*, and *Latigo*. In 1981 he was selected to draw the revived *Lone Ranger* newspaper strip.

Russell Heath Jr. grew up in New Jersey. An only child in a neighborhood where there weren't many other children, he spent a good deal of time drawing. His father, who'd once worked as a cowhand in Arizona, "paid close attention to my drawings and would correct me often when I put the wrong kind of clothing on one of my cowboys." His father also hired an art teacher to tutor him.

Heath sold his first comic book work while still in high school. In 1946 he was hired by Marvel and, while he drew everything from science fiction to humor, his best work was done on Western titles such as *The Arizona Kid, Kid Colt Outlaw*, and *Two-Gun Kid*. He began an association with EC in the early 1950s, working with Harvey Kurtzman on *Frontline Combat* and *Mad*. He helped, too, with the drawing of Kurtzman's *Playboy* feature, *Little Annie Fanny*. Starting in the early 1950s he worked for DC as well and specialized in combat past and present. For DC's *The Brave and the Bold* Heath drew such heroes as the Golden Gladiator and Robin Hood. He began *Sea Devils* in the early 1960s, and later took over *Sgt. Rock* in *Our Army At War*. His war work has earned considerable praise and writer-editor Archie Goodwin has said, "He's brought a new meaning to the word *realism*, maybe even gone beyond it, bringing a sort of super-clarity to combat scenes no film or camera could hope to catch."

After putting in time as an assistant on George Wunder's *Terry*, Dan Barry's *Flash Gordon*, and Stan Lynde's *Latigo*, Heath got a newspaper strip of his own. This was the new *Lone Ranger*, introduced in 1981 to tie in with the ill-fated Lone Ranger movie of that year. The feature, called by one critic "probably the best *drawn* of all the *Lone Ranger* comic strips," expired in 1984. Heath, settled in Southern California, has devoted most of his time in recent years to television animation. But he still does an occasional comic book job, such as inking Mike Kaluta's 1988 Shadow graphic novel. **R.G.**

**HEATHCLIFF** On the comics page since 1973, George Gately's Heathcliff is one of the most unabashedly lowbrow figures in the long Kavalcade of Komic Kats that has frisked down the corridors of the history of American funnies since the time of Krazy. A creature without the least pretension to regality, or even cuteness, Heathcliff maintains a sort of surly truce with his owners, Grandpa and Grandma Nutmeg, but is unmistakably his own cat.

Magazine cartoonist Gately, the younger brother of the equally popular gag cartoonist John Gallagher, created the *Heathcliff* panel for the McNaught Syndicate, which began distributing it on September 3, 1973. The feral feline has been confidently defending his position at the top of the neighborhood's pet—and human—heap ever since. Heathcliff never speaks, even in thought balloons, but there is never any doubt about what is going on in his single mind as he gives the razzberry to the student body of the Dog Obedience School, wrestles the cap and jacket away from the organ-grinder's monkey, or gleefully leads a pack of pursuing hounds into a flea circus. His objectives are clear and simple—food, independence, and the use of the family easy chair. If he has a softer side, apart from a thoroughly macho interest in the dainty pussycat Sonja, it is for his friend and ally the town dogcatcher, with whom he cooperates wholeheartedly and ingeniously. He is also fond of his disreputable Pop, who flaunts his striped convict suit and jeers at his portrait on *Wanted* posters.

Although Gately continues to mastermind the career of his brash creation, much of the drawing in these cleanly done, good-natured cartoons has been undertaken by his brother, John Gallagher, in recent years.

Heathcliff's abilities may strain credulity—it is clearly he, for instance, who has proposed a bill for a municipal scratching post at the town meeting—but his personality never deviates from the profoundly feline, and like Garfield, he appeals to something in both catfanciers and cathaters. **D.W.**

**HEILMAN, DAN** (1924–1965) During his relatively short lifetime Heilman worked on several newspaper strips, but was best-known for drawing the successful soap opera strip *Judge Parker*, which he did from its inception in 1952 until his death.

Born in Cincinnati, Heilman became addicted to drawing at an early age. In his own words, "[I] cut my teeth on cartoon contests," and he was a dedicated contributor to the amateur cartoonist pages in such magazines as *Tip Top Comics* and *The Open Road For Boys* in the 1930s. He also took a correspondence course in cartooning. "My art career, however," he said, "was cut short by World War II." He joined the Army Air Force and spent four and a half years in the service, much of it as part of the crew of a B-29.

When he was a civilian again, Heilman enrolled in the Chicago Academy of Fine Arts. He went from there to a job assisting Roy Crane on *Buz Sawyer*. Next he worked as assistant to Ken Ernst on the influential soaper *Mary Worth*. The first strip he drew on his own was *The American Adventure*, a nonfiction feature that began in 1949 and tried to make history entertaining. His style still owed much to the work of Milton Caniff—at times he even swiped from Caniff. By the time Heilman got the *Judge Parker* job in 1952, his drawing had matured and looked like a variation rather than an imitation of the work of predecessors like Caniff and Ernst. He sometimes experimented with a cartoony approach in the strip, especially when drawing the kids involved, and once commented that *Judge Parker* "happily enables me to do both illustrative and comic styles." **R.G.**

## HELD, JOHN, JR (1889–1958)

The artist whose cartoons, illustrations, and comic strips defined the Jazz Age visually, John Held Jr. (who always signed himself without a comma) commanded one of the most distinctive and identifiable graphic styles of his time. The look of the Roaring Twenties as depicted in his work—the flat-chested, vacant-eyed flappers and their simple-minded, raccoon-coated beaux—became the stereotyped image of the period. As a writer noted in *Vanity Fair* at the beginning of the 1930s, "John Held Jr. had a potent hand in inventing the modern flapper."

Held was born in Salt Lake City, Utah, the son of a stationer and copper-plate engraver who had illustrated an edition of the *Book of Mormon*. At the age of nine John Jr. sold his first woodcut for $9 and began working for his father drawing cartoons for placecards sold in his stationery shop. His only art instruction came from Mahonri Young, Brigham's grandson and a noted sculptor.

His path already clearly set, he left school at 16 for a job as a sports cartoonist with the *Salt Lake City Tribune*, and five years later moved to New York City to follow a career as a commercial artist. During the teens of this century he drew streetcar posters, advertising art for Wanamaker's, seed catalogs, and an endless stream of cartoons and ads for magazines. For his own amusement he began experimenting with linocuts in which he spoofed the melodramatic chapbooks and theater posters of the 19th century.

As the 1920s approached, Held began to develop the characteristic stiff, stylized figures that were to become a symbol of the era. His first recognized "John Held Jr. flapper" appeared in 1920 in *Judge* and was soon a staple in *College Humor*, *Life*, *Vanity Fair*, and *Collier's*. Her high hemline, cloche hat, and capricious manner (like the slicked-down hair, porkpie hat, ukulele, bell-bottom trousers, and unflagging ardor of her Joe College suitors) established themselves as the official portrait of the decade.

Harold Ross, a childhood friend from Salt Lake City, wanted to use Held's work for his new magazine *The*

*Merely Margy*, John Held, Jr., © 1929, King Features Syndicate, Inc.

*New Yorker* in 1925, but considered his flappers too vulgar. He asked him for some of the woodcuts he had done in high school, and Held showed him the linoleum prints he had been experimenting with. Ross liked the broadly ironic nostalgia of their exaggerations of Gay Nineties themes and initiated a long-running and enormously popular series of them under such headings as "The Wages of Sin," "The Way of a Transgressor," and "Just an Old Fashioned Romance."

In 1928 Held created a regular panel feature in his better-known style. *Oh! Margy!* was distributed briefly by United Features Syndicate before Hearst took it over for his King Features and expanded it to a daily and Sunday strip called *Merely Margy* in 1929. With its companion strip *Joe Prep*, recounting the pranks and problems of a bespectacled prep-school nerd, *Merely Margy* captured the fleeting humor of a period already disappearing; the sleek vamp Margy, her devoted but perennially broke swain Arab, and his muscular stooge Bull were by the end of the 1920s something of an anachronism, and with the Stock Market crash in 1929 their humor was doomed. *Merely Margy* lasted, with diminishing popularity, until the early 1930s and faded away with the rest of the genial nonsense of the Jazz Age.

At the peak of his popularity, John Held Jr. was spectacularly successful: His covers were a regular feature of *Vanity Fair*, *Judge*, and *Life*, and every important magazine in the country vied for his work. Editors sent him blank checks with instructions to fill in his own price. For much of the decade, Held was earning over a million dollars a year and kept a home in Miami, a penthouse in the East 60s in New York, and a 163-acre estate in Westport, Connecticut, with its own zoo and golf course.

The end came suddenly for Held. He lost his fortune to the Swedish swindler Ivar Kreuger, the long dress replaced the flapper's mini, and Russell Patterson replaced Held as the iconographer of the era. The syndicates, advertising agencies, and magazines dropped him, and he moved into a furnished apartment over a restaurant on West 46th Street. He tried again with a new girl-strip—*Rah! Rah! Rosalie*, about a cheerleader as frivolous as Margy—but with scant success, and turned to painting and sculpture. By now a relic from the past, he served as artist in residence at Harvard and the University of Georgia, and during the 1930s wrote several novels about the age he had once delineated so successfully as an artist. *Grim Youth* (1930) and *A Bowl of Cherries* (1933) were regarded as slight and dated, and at last Held settled down in Belmar, New Jersey, as a gentleman farmer, making and bottling chili sauce, which he sold at Brooks Brothers in New York.

Held's linoleum prints burlesquing the sentimentality of the 1890s have been reprinted occasionally: a 1931 collection published by Ives Washburn reappeared in 1964 and had a new edition by Dover in 1972. But it is for his elegantly witty depiction of the sheiks and she-bas of the Jazz Age that John Held Jr. has earned a lasting place in both the art and the social history of America.                                              **D.W.**

**HELFANT, ART** (1898–1971)  Drawing in a direct, "no-frills" humorous style that never changed over the years, Helfant was active from the 1920s onward. He drew newspaper strips and gag cartoons and also contributed a great number of filler pages to a wide range of comic books.

Among the newspaper strips he drew in the 1920s were *Educatin' Ollie*, about a bespectacled college boy, and an adaptation of George Ade's then-popular *Fables in Slang*. His last strip was *Ambrose*, which ran briefly in the early 1950s.

Helfant first showed up in comic books in 1929, drawing three features for Dell's pioneering tabloid *The Funnies*. During the 1940s, when quite a few younger artists were in the service, he sold to a number of publishers, including Marvel, DC, Centaur, and Harvey. Among his regular features were *Popsicle Pete, Mighty Midgets, Biff Bannon*, and *Fetlock Groans*. By the early 1950s Helfant was gone from comic books. And after his strip ended he relied on the lesser cartoon markets.

His work was always simple, in a "bare essentials" style, and he was content to draw in the same way through several decades. He was one of several likable second-raters who worked in comics during the Golden Age. *Mad's* Al Jaffee once listed him, perhaps facetiously, as his major influence.                              **R.G.**

**HENRY**  Carl Anderson introduced *Henry* as a single-panel cartoon in the *Saturday Evening Post* on March 19, 1932. The simplicity of both its content and its graphic style won it such popularity that it soon became a regular weekly feature. In his initial appearance, the rotund little boy with a long neck and high-domed, curiously shaped head was seen warming his bald pate against a horse's drooping belly, and the ingenuity with which the lad seized an opportunity to profit from circumstances has characterized *Henry* ever since.

*Henry* continued in the *Post* until 1934. In that year a German magazine reprinted a page of the panels under the title *Henry, der Amerikanischer Lausbub* ("Henry, the American Scamp"). This caught the eye of William Randolph Hearst, who promptly had Anderson signed to use the character in a newspaper strip for his King Features Syndicate. The daily *Henry* began December 17, 1934, and the Sunday page on March 10 of the next year—a month after the cartoonist's 70th birthday. In the first years Henry spoke occasionally, but Anderson eventually silenced him and concentrated on pantomime.

Anderson continued the strip until his health began to fail, relinquishing the dailies to his assistant John Liney and the Sundays to Don Trachte in January 1942. Liney kept on with hardly a perceptible change in style for almost four decades, until his death in 1979. The mantle then fell to Jack Tippit. The latest daily artist is Dick Hodgins, who took over in 1983. Trachte still draws the Sunday *Henry*.                              **D.W.**

**HERKY**  A Sunday page begun by Clyde Lewis for the NEA syndicate in 1935, *Herky* failed to earn a place in comics history for itself or its creator, probably because Lewis was handicapped by being a funnyman and by being a bit ahead of his time with this particular notion.

Herky, short for Hercules, was a superbaby. He could walk and talk, he was smart, and, as his name indicates, he was strong. Indeed, if Ma and Pa Kent had stumbled on the kid something might've been done with him; instead, they and the public had to wait another three years until Jerry Siegel and Joe Shuster introduced a superbaby of their own, treated him much more seriously, and had him quickly grow up into Superman.

Lewis, however, wasn't interested in superheroics and adventure. He simply wanted to have fun with the idea of an articulate baby who didn't have to take any guff from anybody. Readers apparently weren't especially charmed with the diapered little hero, and before too long Herky was converted to an ordinary cute little kid of about six. The page held on for most of the rest of the decade and was still to be seen reprinted in *The Funnies* in the early 1940s.                              **R.G.**

*Herky*, Clyde Lewis, © 1939, NEA Service, Inc. Reprinted by permission of NEA Service, Inc.

**HERRIMAN, GEORGE** (1880–1944) Revered today by comics fans, comics historians, and mainstream art critics, Herriman was never an especially popular cartoonist during his own lifetime. He created the incomparable *Krazy Kat* early in the second decade of the century, drew a dozen or more other strips, and illustrated the archy and mehitabel books. *The Gumps* appeared in nearly 300 papers, *Bringing Up Father* had 500, and *Blondie* well over 1,000 during the years that *Krazy Kat* appeared. The Kat and mouse opus, however, had only 48 papers in this country. It remained in print because William Randolph Hearst was a fan and decreed the strip would run in his papers as long as Herriman wanted to draw it.

George Joseph Herriman was born in New Orleans. Throughout his life he gave out conflicting stories about his parents and his ethnic background, but never mentioned that his birth certificate listed him as "colored." According to the *Dictionary of American Biography*, "the federal census for 1880 designated his parents as 'mulatto.'" In the middle 1880s the family moved to Los Angeles and left the "colored" designation behind, and Herriman usually referred to Los Angeles as his hometown. His father eventually became a baker, and when Herriman dropped out of high school, he worked for a time in the bakery. He was already addicted to drawing, which his father didn't think much of. "Bread the world must have," he once quoted his father as saying, "but art allays neither hunger nor thirst. Nobody ever sees art wagons on the highways, but just look at the bread buses and bun wagons." Ignoring his father, Herriman got himself a job in the engraving department of a Los Angeles newspaper. In 1900 and again in 1902, this time with his brand-new wife, he made trips to New York to assault the cartoon markets. He started selling to *Judge* and *Life*, and he did political and sports cartoons for the *New York News* and the *World*. He was able to find some papers that would let him do comics as well. Among his early pages were *Lariat Pete, Bud Smith*, and *Major Ozone*. These works looked pretty much like all the other comics being done in the first decade of the century.

During those Eastern stays he also worked briefly for Hearst's *New York American*. In 1905 he and his wife and their young daughter returned to Los Angeles, and the next year he was hired by Hearst's *Los Angeles Examiner*. Over the next three or four years Herriman experimented with several new strips, including *Baron Mooch, Mary's Home From College*, and *Gooseberry Sprig*, one of his earliest animal strips. In 1910 he was summoned East once again by Hearst, this time to serve in the Comic Art Department of the *New York Journal*.

Working there when he arrived were some of the best, and most popular, cartoonists that Hearst could buy. These included Tad Dorgan, who was to become one of Herriman's closest friends, Harry Hershfield, Winsor McCay, Gus Mager, and Tom McNamara, who was also to be a lifelong friend. Herriman was a small, dapper man with gray eyes and large feet. He was annoyed by the fact that he had what he considered kinky hair and he kept his hat on almost all the time. Around the art department he was known as Handsome George or the Greek, the latter short for Greek God. Tad also liked to call him Garge, claiming that was the way Herriman pronounced his first name. In those years before World War I the cartooning profession was not considered too honorable, and the *Journal*'s comic artists associated with members of similar outcast fields, chiefly actors and sports people. The saloon that Tad most often

An undated photograph of George Herriman.

frequented was Jack's at Sixth and 43rd, and he frequently talked Herriman into visiting it with him.

*Krazy Kat* was born in the years that Herriman was laboring for the *Journal*. The Kat first appeared in *The Dingbat Family*, a daily strip begun by Herriman in 1910. Soon after a mouse showed up and a reverse cat and mouse game started to take place underfoot in the Dingbat saga. Next Krazy Kat and Ignatz Mouse got a small strip of their own beneath the other one and in 1911 a completely independent strip was introduced. By 1916, when the Sunday page started, the feature had just about achieved its ultimate form. Herriman had developed a distinct style of his own. He drew with a vibrant, scratchy line and a highly personal sense of layout and perspective. Some of his *Krazy Kat* gags tended to be obscure, fey, or downright cryptic, but each strip had a liveliness and spark and was always a joy to behold.

Herriman tried several other strips, all with human casts of characters, while he was working with the Kat. There were *Baron Bean* from 1916 to 1919, *Now Listen, Mabel* (named after his wife) for a brief time in 1919, and *Stumble Inn* from 1922 until 1926. Later on he became associated with another notable cat. He was picked to illustrate Don Marquis' books about mehitabel the cat and archy the cockroach poet. The creators of the two

noted cats never met. Somebody at Doubleday got the idea Herriman would be well-suited for the job, and since Marquis had no objections, he was hired.

Herriman grew restless in New York and in 1922 he and his wife and their two daughters, Barbara and Mabel, moved to Los Angeles. He returned to New York only once, in 1924, when he and McNamara drove there. Just before leaving, Herriman participated in one of the more curious events of the 1922 theatrical season, the Krazy Kat ballet. John Alden Carpenter had become fascinated with the strip and he wrote a seven-minute jazz pantomime; Herriman contributed the story line and the scenery. The backdrops were on rollers and changed every two or three minutes. The ballet was performed at Town Hall in January with Adolph Bolm, dressed up in a black cat suit, in the role of Krazy. With the exception of Deems Taylor, the critics didn't think much of the work.

In the 1920s, before freeways and turnpikes, a cross-country drive was a first-class adventure. Herriman and McNamara stopped at Coconino County, Arizona, on the way and the entire trip took several months. Eventually Herriman and his family settled in a pink stucco, Spanish style house on Maravilla Drive in Hollywood. The desert still fascinated him and he made occasional trips there, taking a drawing board and turning out *Krazy Kat* in a tent. He often traveled with Jimmy Swinnerton, the man who years before had introduced him to the Arizona Navajo country. Herriman admired the Navajo people and hoped to be reincarnated as an Indian.

He loved scottie dogs and there were always a couple of them at the Hollywood house. He tried painting, even painting on garage doors and tabletops, but was never confident about his work. He tried modeling in clay, and, after a visit from Herriman, his friends were likely to find small clay figures perched on mantelpieces or behind table lamps. He had his eccentricities too: He felt lying on his back helped him think, as did dish washing. Even when he was a dinner guest, Herriman would sometimes vanish, to turn up in the kitchen in front of the sink.

In the middle 1930s Herriman's wife died as the result of an auto accident. He lived from then on with his daughter Mabel, whom he called Toodles. In 1938 he spent several weeks in the hospital and was unable to keep drawing the strip. King Features reran old Kat episodes. "The public doesn't know the difference," Herriman told a friend. "Nor care." He died on April 25, 1944. He had penciled a final week of his strip but didn't get around to inking it. **R.G.**

**HERSHFIELD, HARRY** (1885–1974) A raconteur as well as a cartoonist, Hershfield devoted the major part of his nearly 90 years to telling funny stories—in both words and pictures. A professional cartoonist from his teens onward, he drew such early newspaper strips as

*Desperate Desmond*, which began in 1910, and the long-lasting *Abie the Agent*, first seen in 1914. He told jokes on the stage and on the radio, wrote joke books, and served as a toastmaster at innumerable banquets. Hershfield was also one of the few men ever to have his favorite joke included in his obituary in the *New York Times.*

He was born in Cedar Rapids, Iowa, the son of Jewish immigrants. After studying at the Chicago Art Institute, he got himself hired by the *Chicago Daily News* as a sports cartoonist and illustrator in 1899. By 1907 he was drawing for the *San Francisco Chronicle;* in 1909 Hearst summoned him East to work for the *New York Journal.*

Hershfield drew in a vigorous, primitive cartoon style, and was enormously fond of shading, crosshatching, and other basic inking techniques. He occasionally even went in for collages and the kidding of other artists' styles. In 1910 he started *Desperate Desmond*, a humorous continuity strip burlesquing melodramas, dime novels, and fiction weeklies that went in for the hairbreadth rescue and gloating villain sort of material. In addition to the villainous, top-hatted Desmond, the strip featured the stalwart Claude Eclair and the put-upon blond heroine Rosamond. Hershfield's enthusiastic kidding of this sort of cliffhanger hokum did little to sour the public on its conventions, however, and within just a few years such motion picture serials as *The Exploits of Elaine* and *The Perils of Pauline* would be pulling audiences into movie houses by doing the stuff completely straight.

In 1912 Hershfield switched heroes, introducing a new strip called *Dauntless Durham of the U.S.A.* Durham, a handsome, pipe-smoking combination of Sherlock Holmes, Nick Carter, and Frank Merriwell, was the soul of honor, polite to a fault, and able to remain calm whether he was being "surrounded by vicious fish of all species" or finding his wheelchair (where a temporary injury had placed him) suddenly taking part in a six-day bike race. The object of his affection was the beautiful Katrina, and Desmond, as desperate as ever, was once again the resident villain. In 1914 Hershfield abandoned parody for a quieter sort of humor and created *Abie the Agent.* The strip dealt with contemporary Jewish life in a big city, and it continued, with time off for fights and contract squabbles, until 1940.

In 1942 the cartoonist became a national radio star when *Can You Top This?* started its run on the NBC network. The show, which had begun on New York's WOR at the end of 1940, had a panel of three experts vying to tell stories that would get a higher rating on the Laughmeter than those sent in by members of the listening audience. Hershfield specialized in gags with a Yiddish flavor.

As he later recalled it, Hershfield made his first after-dinner speech in 1902. By the 1930s he was speaking at an average of 200 dinners and banquets a year. One estimate had him acting as "toastmaster for 264 banquets over a period of eight months." In *Comic Art in America* (1959), Stephen Becker comments, "It is an article of firm belief in the cartooning field that Hershfield has not had to buy a meal for himself since some time in the early Thirties." He continued with his public joke-telling long after he quit cartooning. He was also a philanthropist and an active member of the National Cartoonists Society.                **R.G**

**HESS, SOL**   See THE NEBBS.

**HICKORY HOLLOW FOLKS**   A dazzling, funny-animal weird fantasy, arguably one of stripdom's great

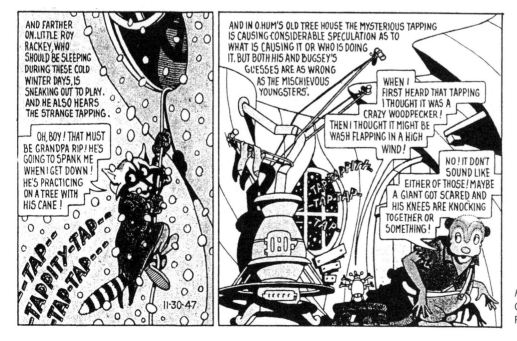

*Hickory Hollow Folks*, Walter Quermann, © 1947, St. Louis Post Dispatch.

lost wonders, *Hickory Hollow Folks* ran for more than three decades in just one paper, the *St. Louis Post-Dispatch*. Originally created by *Post-Dispatch* staff artist Walter Quermann in 1932 as *Toy Talkies*, a tiny tots' story page for the Sunday magazine, the feature jumped to the color comics on May 22, 1938. Quermann's writing was strictly kid stuff, full of morally instructive lessons for the little ones, but his stunning illustration—spectacularly enhanced after September 1946 by the comics' upgrade to rotogravure—merits the recognition of historians. Quermann drew in a detailed and inventive comic style and was meticulous in the Winsor McCay tradition. The strip starred a fretful Ozark Mountains opossum named O. Hum and various sidekick bears, raccoons, squirrels and bugs, who sometimes had homespun storing-up-nuts-for-the-winter adventures down in the hollow but who also went journeying at length into fairy-tale kingdoms, distant universes, and dreamland, much in the tradition of *Felix*. Cumulatively an extraordinary tour de force by an unassuming art department workhorse who appears to have had no larger ambitions in his field, *Hickory Hollow Folks* last appeared on Nov. 6, 1955, a few weeks after its creator's death.          **J.H.**

**HIGHLIGHTS OF HISTORY** The longest running nonfiction comic strip ever done, *Highlights of History* appeared in newspapers for nearly 20 years. Written and drawn by J. Carroll Mansfield, it was distributed by the Bell Syndicate and began in 1924.

Mansfield, a veteran of World War I, had studied at the Art Students League in Manhattan. When *Highlights* started, initially as a daily, on November 17, 1924, he was in his late twenties. A Sunday page was added a few years later. The daily continuities, each of which

lasted several weeks, concentrated on American history. Mansfield did not follow a rigid chronology, but would jump from a sequence about Lincoln to one about the Revolutionary War to one about Daniel Boone. There was considerable copy each day, with considerable information imparted in the captions: "In the dark hour before dawn on the morning of November 7, 1811, the Indians attacked General Harrison's camp near Tippecanoe. The warning shots of the sentries roused the camp…"

A solid artist, Mansfield drew in the tradition of book illustrators, never seeming to be much influenced by the movies or the subsequent developments in adventure strips in the 1930s. His work in the early 1940s looked just about like his work of the middle 1920s, accurate yet a bit on the stodgy side.

The Sunday took up a full page, half devoted to a comic strip continuity and the rest to such features as *Boys and Girls the World Over* and *Would You Believe It?*, offering historical oddities. On Sunday world history was usually the topic, ranging from Hannibal to Cleopatra to the Suez Canal. *Highlights* gave the impression it was well-researched and the pages must have found their way into many a schoolkid's report in the 1930s.

Late in the decade and into the early 1940s Mansfield alternated adaptions of classic novels with his history narratives, daily and Sunday. Among the books he adapted to comic strip format, under the title *Highlights of Famous Fiction* were *Treasure Island*, *The Prisoner of Zenda*, and *Lorna Doone*. The feature ended in 1942.          **R.G.**

**HI AND LOIS** A blend of the wholesome domestic humor of Mort Walker and the clean, crisp art of Dik

*Highlights of History*, J. Carroll Mansfield, © 1938.

Browne, *Hi and Lois* made its first modest appearance in 32 papers as a daily comic strip on October 18, 1954, and, after proving itself by reaching the respectable total of 131, added a Sunday version on October 14, 1956. It now runs in over 1,000 newspapers and in 50 countries.

The idea for this contemporary family strip occurred to Walker after four years of his popular military humor strip *Beetle Bailey* had made him one of the stars of King Features Syndicate. He proposed it to King's comics editor Sylvan Byck, who had admired Dik Browne's kid strip *The Tracy Twins*, which ran from 1950 to 1960 in *Boys' Life*. Walker had been equally impressed by a candy ad Browne had drawn, so he and Byck agreed to ask Browne to draw the strip. Originally a spinoff of Walker's *Beetle Bailey*, featuring Beetle's sister and brother-in-law, *Hi and Lois* developed a life of its own almost at once, and the connection with its parent strip soon disappeared.

Hi and Lois Flagston, the loving suburban couple whose daily experiences the strip recounts, are an updated and more subtly rendered version of Dagwood and Blondie Bumstead, and the series deals with many of the same situations. The Flagstons are a moderately successful family beset with bills and domestic problems but always coping with them. Their rebellious teenage son Chip is at that awkward age that has provided such a rich vein of material to American humor; their eight-year-old twins Dot and Ditto have the combative instincts of all grade school children; and their endearing infant daughter Trixie tries to understand the adult world but, unable to speak, often resorts to one-sided, thought-balloon conversations with a sunbeam.

Much of the appeal of *Hi and Lois* is due to the harmonious character of Browne's economical style and simple format. Unlike the bold stroke with which he renders his robust strip *Hagar the Horrible*, the art of Browne's gentle family strip is kept open and light. "In *Hi and Lois*," the artist explains, "the line is clean and round, and that somehow suits a clean, round, tight, warm family."

*Hi and Lois* is a realistic depiction of the world it affectionately presents and has remained a faithful mirror of changing times through the years. In 1980, for example, Lois took a part-time job selling real estate because, as Walker has explained, "the jokes about cooking, cleaning, and spending money were becoming a bit repetitive" and some women had complained that Lois was "a terrible role-model."

*Hi and Lois* has been widely honored in the comics industry. It received plaques as the Best Humor Strip in 1959, 1960, and 1972 from the National Cartoonists Society, and for *Hi and Lois* that organization awarded Browne its Reuben as the Outstanding Cartoonist of the Year in 1962. Its greatest honor, however, is the affection

it has earned in an audience of many million readers worldwide. Browne's name was signed to the strip long after his death.  **D.W.**

**HIX, JOHN** (1908–1944)  A precocious cartoonist, Hix wrote and drew *Strange As It Seems*, which began in 1928, was the most successful imitation of Ripley's *Believe It Or Not* ever done, and continued for several years after Hix's death.

Hix was born in Alabama, worked as a newsboy, and learned to draw by way of a mail-order cartoon course. He started selling drawings to Southern newspapers while still in his teens. He moved on to a staff job with the *Washington Herald* and sold his *Strange As It Seems* panel to the McClure Syndicate in 1928, when he was just 20. A Sunday page was added in February 1930.

The public's appetite for odd facts and strange news items was especially high in the 1930s, and during that troubled decade *Believe It Or Not, Strange As It Seems*, and several lesser imitations flourished. Hix was a competent illustrator and his was consistently the best of the Ripley simulacra. Each of his daily panels offered three or four items, each accompanied by an illustration or a small spot drawing. For example: Robert Louis Stevenson smoked $450 worth of cigars a year; the chousingha, an Indian antelope, can jump more than twice its height; Marshall O. Cameron is serving time in two states at the same time.

While Hix didn't have the large fact-finding facilities of his rival Ripley, he was still a devoted collector of oddities, and once told an interviewer he had at least 1,000,000 strange facts on hand. Several *Strange As It Seems* movie shorts were produced in the 1930s and a radio show aired on CBS in 1939. Hix, ill for several years, died in Hollywood at the age of 36. His brother Ernest first carried on the writing of the panel, and then Elsie Hix, Ernest's widow, managed *Strange As It Seems*. It faded away in the 1950s.  **R.G.**

**HOBAN, WALTER**  See JERRY ON THE JOB.

**HOEST, WILLIAM** (1926–1988)  A prolific and consistently witty cartoonist for nearly four decades, Bill Hoest was producing no fewer than six successful panel and strip features simultaneously at the end of his productive career. Hoest was born in Newark and grew up in Montclair, New Jersey. He dated his taste for cartooning from the age of three, when his mother kept him quiet with drawing materials, and for two years in the Navy during World War II he drew posters for the USO. Hoest later studied commercial art at Cooper Union in New York City and worked for Norcross Greeting Cards, but by 1951 felt secure enough to go free-lance, designing humorous cards for most of the major companies. The format of a card—an attention-getting "set-up" on the front and a punchline inside—provided a natural transition to gag cartoons and comic strips, and during the 1950s he sold widely to such magazines as the *Saturday Evening Post, Colliers*, and the *Ladies Home Journal*. He also sold a strip, *My Son John*, to the Chicago Tribune-New York News syndicate, but it did not do well and folded after a couple of years.

Noticing the popularity of the bickering-husband-and-wife theme, which he employed frequently in his free-lance cartoons, Hoest created *The Lockhorns*, a daily panel that began on September 9, 1968, with a Sunday version following on April 9, 1972, for King Features Syndicate. In it, Leroy and Loretta Lockhorn trade jibes—he about her cooking and looks, she about his drinking and his roving eye—in over 500 papers, eight languages (including Chinese), and 23 countries.

*Bumper Snickers*, a panel series about cars published by the *National Inquirer*, followed in 1974, and the daily and Sunday strip *Agatha Crumm* began with King on October 24 and 30, 1977. Featuring a feisty old lady who commands a corporate empire, *Agatha Crumm* is distributed to about 150 papers. A weekly trio of gag cartoons, *Laugh Parade*, became a regular feature with *Parade Magazine* in 1980, and was joined the following year by *Howard Huge*, a panel about an enormous, lovable St. Bernard. In 1987 the indefatigable Hoest created the daily and Sunday strip *What a Guy!* for King Features. Its hero, Guy, is a youthful yuppie who echoes the success-oriented adult world (he used to get C's in arithmetic, he admits to a classmate, until he realized that arithmetic could be applied to *money*!). In its first year, *What a Guy!* sold to 125 papers. Hoest regularly produced up to 12 panel cartoons a day, along with six roughs for *Bumper Snickers* and one or two complete strips.

Working in a clean, balanced graphic style, Hoest differentiated his figures for his various markets. "The big nose and foreshortened body of *The Lockhorns*," he pointed out, "are different from all my other cartoons in *Playboy* and the *Ladies Home Journal*."

Hoest published 25 collections of cartoons during his lifetime and left more than two years of work ready for publication at his death. His three King comic features and the *Parade* cartoons are being continued by his assistant John Reiner, under the creative supervision of his widow Bunny, with whom he had conducted Hoest Enterprises for 15 years.

Despite his crowded schedule, Hoest was known for the generosity with which he devoted his time to helping aspiring young cartoonists. In 1987 he was elected president of the National Cartoonists Society, which had given him its awards for Best Syndicated Panel (*The Lockhorns*) in 1975 and 1980 and Best Magazine Gag Cartoons in 1977. **D.W**

**HOFF, SYD** (1912– ) Hoff, a versatile cartoonist, has been gainfully employed at his trade for well over a half century. He came to prominence in the 1930s with his gag cartoons about tenement life for *The New Yorker*. In the 1940s he drew a comic strip called *Tuffy* and later he drew a daily panel called *Laugh It Off*. He has also written and illustrated a great many children's books.

He was born in New York City, dropped out of high school and attended the National Academy of Design. Still in his teens, he sold his first cartoon to *The New Yorker*. Hoff's specialty was depicting lower-middle-class life in the big city; his settings were walkup flats, tenement stoops, park benches, and city streets. He worked in a simple, uncluttered style but got in a lot of telling detail, managing to retain the point of view of a knowing street kid. One recurrent figure in his gags there was a balding, middle-aged man with a walrus mustache who was usually seen roaming the apartment clad in trousers and undershirt.

This familiar paternal figure was transferred to *Tuffy*, becoming the smart, feisty little girl's father. The strip, a daily done for King Features, began in May 1940 and ended with the decade. From 1957 to 1971 Hoff drew his daily panel, *Laugh It Off*, for King Features.

In addition to collections of his cartoons, Hoff has written *The Art of Cartooning* and such perennial kid books as *Danny and the Dinosaur*. **R.G.**

**HOFFMAN, PETE** (1919– ) He became an adventure strip artist in 1945, when he started ghosting *Steve Roper*. After nearly 10 years of ghosting, Hoffman created *Jeff Cobb*, which ran for over two decades.

Hoffman was born in Toledo, Ohio, and "began taking the noble profession seriously while cartooning for the U. of Toledo student newspaper." After serving in the Army during World War II, and emerging as a captain, he went to work for Allen Saunders and Elmer Woggon on the Chief Wahoo-Steve Roper strip. He did all the drawing and proved the most distinctive of the strip's many ghosts. He worked in a fairly realistic yet cartoony style and was very fond of brushing in lots of black shadows.

Steve Roper worked as a roving photojournalist, and when Hoffman invented a hero of his own he made him a newspaper reporter. *Jeff Cobb* first appeared on June 28, 1954, syndicated by General Features. Although Cobb, who eventually came to wear a distinctive eyepatch, resembled Roper, his adventures never had the humor or the pacing that Saunders got into his continuities. Over the years Hoffman's drawing got stiffer, the shadows deeper and his reliance on scrap photos more obvious. After *Jeff Cobb* ended in the middle 1970s, Hoffman shifted into freelance cartooning and commercial art. **R.G.**

**HOGARTH, BURNE** (1911– )  Next to Hal Foster, Hogarth is the best-known artist to have drawn *Tarzan*. Much respected by European critics, he illustrated the Sunday adventures of Edgar Rice Burroughs' jungle lord, with some time off in the middle 1940s, from 1937 to 1950.

Born in Chicago, Hogarth began his professional career in 1926 as an assistant cartoonist with the Associated Editors Syndicate, for whom he drew a panel series titled *Famous Churches of the World*. By 1934 he was working in the King Features bullpen in New York City. The following year the McNaught Syndicate assigned him to take over as artist on the faltering pirate strip *Pieces of Eight*. When Hal Foster left the *Tarzan* page to begin *Prince Valiant*, Hogarth was the one selected to replace him. Hogarth remained with the jungle page initially until 1945, then left to try his luck elsewhere.

He next drew a Sunday page titled *Drago*, about a musclebound gaucho, for the New York Post Syndicate. It survived for less than a year, and Hogarth went back to *Tarzan* and stayed with it until 1950, when he quit for good after a dispute with the syndicate. During this latter period Hogarth had considerable help from such students of his as Al Williamson and Gil Kane. In 1947 and 1948 Hogarth also attempted a humorous Sunday called *Miracle Jones*. The feature, with a hero modeled after Walter Mitty, did not succeed.

Hogarth has also been active as an educator. He taught for the WPA Arts Project from 1933 to 1935 and in 1944 he founded the Academy of Newspaper Art in Manhattan. The Academy offered courses in cartooning and illustration with an emphasis on their journalistic application, and operated until 1946. The following year Hogarth cofounded the Cartoonists and Illustrators School, a more ambitious and diversified establishment that changed its name in 1956 to the School of Visual Arts and was to become an accredited institute and the largest private art school in the world. Hogarth set up the curricula, wrote all the courses, served as vice president and art supervisor, and taught a full schedule until his retirement in 1970. From 1976 to 1979 he taught anatomy at the Parsons School of Design and from 1981 has been an instructor of analytical drawing at the Art Center College of Design in Southern California. Hogarth has written several books for Watson-Guptill, including *Dynamic Anatomy* (1958) and *Dynamic Light and Shade* (1981).

Although *Drago* and *Miracle Jones* had a small circle of fans, it is for *Tarzan* that Hogarth's reputation as one of the better illustrators in comics rests. The dynamic rendering of anatomy that he celebrated in many of his book titles, his dramatic compositions, and the realistic depiction of nature in the page's backgrounds earned him a considerable reputation.

In 1972 he returned to the comic format with a book-length version of *Tarzan of the Apes* for Watson-Guptill. A sequel, *Jungle Tales of Tarzan*, followed in 1976. **D.W.**

**HOLMAN, BILL** (1903–1987)  One of the few comic artists to maintain the broad slapstick tradition into modern times. For nearly 40 years Bill Holman produced a stream of madcap gags about a group of firemen in *Smokey Stover*.

Holman, who once described himself as "always inclined to humor and acting silly," was born in Nappanee, Indiana. Although he never finished high school, he took the Landon correspondence course in cartooning while still in his home town, and when his family moved to Chicago in 1919 took night courses at the Academy of Fine Arts there. In 1920 he got a job as copy boy at the *Chicago Tribune* for $6 a week and had the chance to work around such cartoonists as Harold Gray (later to create *Little Orphan Annie*), Carl Ed (who did *Harold Teen*), E.C. Segar (creator of Popeye), Frank King (of *Gasoline Alley*), and Sidney Smith (of *The Gumps*).

Intimidated by the size of the *Tribune*, Holman moved to Cleveland for a job with Newspaper Enterprise Associates, which syndicated his first strip, *Billville Birds*, a daily animal feature, in 1922. He roomed for a while with Chic Young, who was later to produce *Blondie*, and shared an office with cartoonists like Gene Ahern of *Our Boarding House*, Jim Williams of *Out Our Way*, Edgar Martin of *Boots and Her Buddies*, and Merrill Blosser of *Freckles and Her Friends*.

Holman spent three years with NEA and in 1923 went to New York, where he did a child-strip called *G. Whizz Jr.* for the *Herald-Tribune* and began free-lancing to such magazines as *Redbook*, *Collier's*, *Saturday Evening Post*, *Life*, and *Judge* in the United States, and others in England. A frequent setting for his cartoons was firehouses, for no particular reason except that, as he explained it, he thought firemen were funny—"running around in a red wagon with sirens and bells." In 1934 he learned that the *Daily News* was looking for a Sunday strip and that its publisher Joseph Patterson specifically wanted a fireman character. With a big file of fireman gags already to his credit and thinking it was "a good gimmick to hang things on," Holman submitted a page and Patterson signed him up. On March 10, 1935, *Smokey Stover* made its first appearance.

The popular cartoonist Gaar Williams died a month later, and Holman added most of his papers to his already growing list. Soon the zany wordplay of *Smokey* became a national fad, and "Foo" clubs, named for the nonsense- syllable wit with which Holman randomly studded his panels, sprang up all over America. The broad buffoonery of the gags, drawn in a style no less goofy, struck a note of antic silliness that had all but disappeared from American comics, and Holman sustained it well into modern times. Holman continued *Smokey Stover*, along with a daily panel called *Nuts and Jolts*, until he retired in 1973. For a time he also did a bottom tier called *Spooky*, about the firehouse cat, which was later absorbed into the main strip.

Bill Holman was president of the National Cartoonists Society from 1961 to 1963. A genial man who enjoyed practical jokes and was described by his colleagues as "a naturally funny guy," he willingly gave chalk talks to entertain at army camps and drew booklets for local fire-safety campaigns. If his visual and verbal clowning seemed dated at the end, it remained one of the last sources of robust burlesque humor in the comics pages. **D.W.**

**HOMER HOOPEE** A daily strip that represented the Associated Press' attempt to provide its clients with a low-budget version of *The Gumps, Homer Hoopee* debuted in 1930 and was written and drawn by Fred Locher. Although Homer had a bit more chin, he was a mustachioed would-be go-getter very much in the Andy Gump mold. (He also resembled Cicero Sapp, the title character in the strip Locher had done in the 1920s.) And like Andy, Homer was much given to soliloquizing about his plans and predicaments.

He had an attractive wife named Helen, who was intermittently supportive, although his hefty mother-in-law held him in low esteem (her favorite terms for him included "hyena" and "eel"). Assorted other kin popped in and out. While Locher now and then indulged in domestic situations, he favored melodramatic continuities. In a typical year Homer might start a detective agency, go to Hollywood, get shipwrecked, suffer from amnesia, and find buried treasure.

Locher was a dedicated minimalist, drawing in a terse, cartoony style, concentrating on people and using few props and mostly blank walls and open skies for backgrounds. When he died in 1943, at the age of 56, the AP turned the strip over to Rand Taylor. It ended as the 1950s began. **R.G.**

**HOPALONG CASSIDY** Western writer Clarence E. Mulford's hard-bitten limping cowboy, considerably modified and spruced up, first appeared in comic books in 1942. The Hopalong Cassidy comic strip began in 1949. In these graphic adaptations Hoppy looked just like William Boyd, the silver-haired actor who'd been portraying him on the screen since 1935.

Illinois-born, Mulford started writing while holding down a civil service job in New York. In the early years of the century he sold a series of cowboy stories to a travel monthly called *Outing Magazine*. The stories dealt with the men of the Bar 20 Ranch and their trail boss, Hopalong Cassidy. Even though he'd never seen the West, Mulford's Bar 20 tales are not romantic and exaggerated but played-down and realistic. His hero was a rough, tobacco-chewing redhead with nothing fancy about him. The first Hopalong novel, *Bar-20*, was published in 1907.

Paramount brought the character to the screen in 1935 in *Hopalong Cassidy*, the first of nearly 70 Hoppy movies and the start of one of the most successful B-Western series ever. (The final one was released in 1948.) William Boyd was in his late thirties when he took on the role, a veteran of 16 years in motion pictures. He played the Mulford hero, as one cinema historian has pointed out, as an "idealistic and gentlemanly Western hero." Boyd dressed against tradition, wearing the black clothes and black Stetson usually associated with Western movie badmen. His horse, though, was snow-white and named Topper.

In the waning days of the movie series Boyd took a gamble and bought the rights to the Hopalong films. He started licensing them to television stations and by 1948, with TV stations burgeoning, the silver-haired cowboy was being seen all across the country. A half-hour series, with Boyd back in the saddle as Hoppy, debuted on NBC in June 1949. Hopalong Cassidy became a superstar and Boyd, thanks to all the subsequent merchandising, became a millionaire. "In public, Boyd wore a ten-gallon hat and cowboy boots all the time," reports David Zinman in *Saturday Afternoon at the Bijou*. "On tours, he added his famous black Hoppy outfit, and never smoked while he wore it. Crowds flocked to see him wherever he went. In 1950...*Time* magazine did a cover story on him."

The merchandising of Hoppy had actually begun long before the television craze. Comic books preceded toys and premiums. Fawcett was the first publisher to use Hoppy, adding him as a backup feature in *Master Comics* #33 (December 1942). Up until then Buck Jones—real-life cowboy and a licensed character—had been the resident cowpoke in the magazine, which starred Captain Marvel Jr. and Bulletman. In real life, movie Westerner Jones had died earlier in the year, which didn't, by the way, prevent the character from returning to comics in a book of his own during the Western boom of the 1950s.

The stories in *Master* were simple and straight-forward, taking place in a movie-like Old West and running six or seven pages. Early artists included Ralph Carlson and Harry Parkhurst. While in the movies Hopalong most often worked with two sidekicks—an active, two-fisted younger one and a crusty cantankerous older one—in comic books he usually made do with just one, a grizzled, mustachioed old coot name of Mesquite Jenkins, who said "ain't" a lot and studiously dropped his G's.

A *Hopalong Cassidy* one-shot appeared in 1943, and in 1946 Fawcett began issuing the title on a regular basis. Hoppy was also one of the Western heroes in *Western Hero*, which began in 1948. The quick success of the television show in 1949 inspired yet another magazine. "*Hopalong Cassidy* did so well after TV," Fawcett editor Will Lieberson has said, "that we brought out a second book, calling it *Bill Boyd*." In that one Boyd wore a different outfit and even rode a horse of a different color. After Fawcett retired from the comics field, DC picked up *Hopalong Cassidy* and published it from 1954 to 1959. Gil Kane was one of the regular artists.

The Hopalong newspaper strip, started in 1949, was produced out of Boyd's Los Angeles offices and Dan Spiegle was the artist picked by the actor himself to draw it. According to Spiegle, Boyd selected him because he liked the way he drew horses: "It didn't matter how I drew him—I'd learn how through practice—as he considered horses the most important in a Western strip." Spiegle drew the feature, daily and Sunday, until it ended in 1955. **R.G.**

**HOP HARRIGAN** The clean-cut, blond young aviator Hop Harrigan was created by artist-writer Jon L. Blummer and made his debut in *All-American Comics* #1 (April 1939). During the 1940s Hop also flew his way through a newspaper strip, a radio show, and a movie serial.

The youthful flyer shared the early issues of *All-American* with a variety of other features, new and old—*Red, White and Blue, Scribbly, Mutt & Jeff, Bobby Thatcher, Reg'lar Fellers*, among them. After running away from home, or rather flying away in a biplane he'd rebuilt, Hop gets a job with an airfield run by an avuncular fellow named Prop Wash. He's also befriended by a pudgy, redheaded mechanic named Ikky Tinker. (Ikky eventually changed his name to Tank, probably to avoid being confused with Captain Midnight's mechanic Ikky Mudd.) A love interest was added in the person of a spoiled rich girl named Gerry; initially, Hop wasn't much taken with her: "You and your mush!—Make me sick!" Eventually Hop outgrew this phase and accepted Gerry as his steady girl.

In *All-American* #17 (August 1940) Hop Harrigan's All-American Flying Club was launched. For just 10 cents you got "a beautifully engraved membership card…a beautiful golden winged emblem…opportunity to enter many contests for prizes and free trips." The club flourished throughout World War II, adding an American Observation Corps for junior plane spotters in 1942; membership cost an additional 10 cents. If AOC recruits also wanted the book *How You Can Defend Your Home*, "in which over fifty American, British, and enemy planes are authentically illustrated and described!" the cost was yet another dime.

Hop and his friends had adventures similar to those enjoyed by other fictional aviators of the period, including tangling with kidnappers, spies, saboteurs, and plane highjackers, and the flying of serum to Alaska. *All-American* added the Green Lantern to its lineup in #16 (July 1940), and soon thereafter came the Atom, Dr. Mid-Nite, and Sargon the Sorcerer. For a few months in 1941 Hop was stricken with costumed-crimefighter fever and went around in a strange helmet and a pair of what he called soaring wings, all the while calling himself the Guardian Angel. Soon tiring of that, Hop became a cadet in 1942 in what was then called the Army Air Force, seeing action in the Pacific and in Europe. After the war he returned to civil aviation and carried on as a daredevil pilot.

A daily newspaper strip appeared in May 1942, also produced by Blummer, but this version of *Hop Harrigan* lasted less than a year. The *Hop Harrigan* radio show began in the summer of 1942; 15 minutes long, it was heard every weekday during the 5 P.M. to 6 P.M. children's hour—a time period it shared with such kilowatt heroes as Jack Armstrong, Captain Midnight, and Tom Mix. Hop and Tank took to the air against both the Nazis and the Japanese. The show opened with the announcer enthusiastically announcing, "Presenting Hop Harrigan, America's Ace of the Airways!" a line Blummer had started using in the comic books the year before. Columbia Pictures released a 15-chapter *Hop Harrigan* movie serial in 1946, with an actor named William Bakewell, who looked to be approaching middle age, portraying the usually youthful Hop.

Hop was grounded in 1948 and left both comic books and radio. **R.G.**

**HOWARD THE DUCK** In 1973 writer Steve Gerber transformed Marvel Comics' horror series, *Man-Thing*, into a work of funny, absurdist fantasy; in the course of doing so, he created a smart-mouthed, cigar-chomping duck from another dimension named Howard. The audacity of the concept, along with Gerber's sly, witty handling of the character, thrilled Marvel's older and more intelligent readers and made Howard one of the most talked-about comic book characters of the 1970s.

*Howard the Duck* earned a comic of its own in late 1975, becoming a fan sensation with its parodies of Marvel and other comics. It ran for 31 issues, with attractive art by Frank Brunner and Gene Colan, and briefly spawned a large-format black-and-white companion magazine, intended for adult readers.

When Gerber left Marvel in 1978, he sought to take Howard with him, but Marvel claimed ownership of the character. The ensuing legal battle shook the comic book industry and helped force changes in the relations between publishers and creators, which have led to greater opportunities for the latter to own their own creations. It also contributed to the growth of "independent" comics publishers in the 1980s, when Gerber teamed up with Jack Kirby and Eclipse Comics in 1982 to produce *Destroyer Duck*, a blistering satire of the comic book industry that helped pay Gerber's legal bills. Gerber finally won ownership of Howard, and was able to license the character himself to LucasFilms, who produced the ill-fated *Howard the Duck* movie in 1986.

**G.J.**

**HUBERT** The short, potbellied little Everyman who figures in Dick Wingert's perennial *Hubert* began his career in 1942, as an Army private first class stationed in England, when PFC Wingert was assigned to the London office of the Army newspaper *Stars and Stripes*. He remained in uniform, in a single-panel format, for three and a half years, never advancing in rank, even when his creator made sergeant. He accepted his lowly lot patiently and adapted with ease to the daily frustrations of army life. With George Baker's *Sad Sack* and Bill Mauldin's *Willie and Joe*, he became a symbol, a type with whom every GI could identify. When *Stars and Stripes* sent Wingert to France after the Normandy invasion to see life near the front lines, Hubert accompanied his creator, becoming a somewhat cruder figure, in keeping with his setting, but never losing his essentially good-natured irony.

In 1945 Wingert carried Hubert with him, out of uniform and into the domestic arena. Syndicated by King Features as a daily panel on December 3, 1945 (with Sundays following on February 3 of the following year), *Hubert* underwent the process of fission that Hearst imposed on many of the panel features he took on. In the decades that followed it has remained a full-blown strip, in some 100 papers worldwide—one of the few World War II army strips successfully to survive the transition to civilian life. "Hubert as a civilian is not as shaggy looking as he was in the army," Wingert notes, "but he still operates on the same level of inefficiency." The occasional earthiness of the soldier has given way to the bland resignation of the suburbanite, and his tough sergeant has been replaced by a no

less tough mother-in-law, but the spirit of the strip remains essentially unchanged. "Hubert was just a poor clunk…caught in a war he didn't understand," Wingert has written. "He was frustrated, baffled, and bewildered at every turn by the army life—the same as he is today."

Wingert's graphic style, too, has remained much the same. The bulbous-nosed blob Hubert, his pretty wife Trudy and daughter Elli, his formidable mother-in-law, pompous boss Dexter L. Baxter, and clumsy, affectionate giant of a sheepdog Freddy—all are drawn with the same broad, loose, slapdash stroke that characterized the strip in the early 1940s.

Wingert has in recent years added the wry humor of the "senior citizen" to his strip with the introduction of the sardonic retired couple Rita and Al, but if the focus of the strip shifts occasionally, its basic nature does not. An indomitable survivor of a simpler era in comics, *Hubert* maintains a hearty, cheerfully brash character, which the passage of time has done nothing to subdue.

**D.W.**

**HUCKLEBERRY FINN** Mark Twain's character inspired both newspaper strips and comic books, but none of the adaptations came anywhere near to capturing the flavor, strength or satirical outlook of the *Huckleberry Finn* novel.

The earliest newspaper version began in 1918 as a Sunday page written and drawn by Clare Victor Dwiggins, who always signed himself Dwig. Twain had died eight years earlier, and the feature was sanctioned and supervised by the executors of his estate. Dwig, who devoted most of his long professional career to humorously recapturing the joys and sorrows of boyhood, looked back on youth in a much gentler way than Twain. While his page, titled *Tom Sawyer and Huck Finn*,

*Tom Sawyer and Huck Finn*, Dwig, 1924.

was nicely drawn in his quirky, homespun style, it took a much more serene view of barefoot kid life in a Missouri river town. In tone the page was closer to Twain's earlier and blander *The Adventures of Tom Sawyer*.

The page changed its title to *The School Days of Tom Sawyer and Huck Finn* in the mid-1920s and by the late 1920s was simply *School Days*, without any of the Twain characters except Tom on view. It ended before the next decade commenced. Earlier there had also been a short-lived daily strip. As Richard Marschall points out in *Nemo* magazine, Dwig used not only Twain's characters but also several of his own: Ophelia, the kid with the slate upon which she scribbled comments on the actions and events of the page; Pip Gint, the town bully; and J. Filliken Wilburfloos, the perennial sissy. "Aunt Polly was present in Dwig's version, and so was Becky Thatcher," says Marschall, "but one character was conspicuous by its absence: the river. Substituted, frequently, were the swimming and fishing-holes, but the majesty and more profound implications of the river—as a locale and as a device—were missing."

Dwig returned to the Twain characters again in 1940, drawing a *Huckleberry Finn* strip for the Ledger Syndicate. Unsuccessful, it was gone by 1942. He then sold it as a backup feature to an unlikely market—*Doc Savage Comics*. On at least one cover Doc and Huck appeared together. When Doc's magazine folded, Huckleberry Finn moved over to *Supersnipe Comics* where he remained until 1946. These latterday adventures were a long way from life on the banks of the Mississippi and involved Huck and Tom in fantastic encounters with strange flying machines, pirates, and cannibals.

*Classic Comics* (later *Classics Illustrated*) put forth a bland, poorly drawn, comic book version of *Huckleberry Finn* in the spring of 1944. Their adaptation of the Tom Sawyer novel appeared in 1948. In 1960 Gold Key issued a comic book based on the *Huckleberry Finn* movie of that year.                                    **R.G.**

**HUHTA, ART**  See DINKY DINKERTON, SECRET AGENT 6⅞.

**THE HULK**  Hard on the heels of *Fantastic Four*, Jack Kirby and Stan Lee created *The Hulk* as the second Marvel superhero comic book in early 1962. Its hero (or antihero) was the powerful, green, savage alter ego of Dr. Bruce Banner, belted by gamma rays while trying to save a teenager from a bomb test. That teenager, Rick Jones, became Banner's companion, helping him keep his brutal Hulk-self under control, while helping the Hulk survive the attacks of the U.S. military, which feared and misunderstood him.

Kirby and Lee disagree as to which of them created the Hulk, but both acknowledge a debt to Stevenson's *Dr. Jekyll and Mr. Hyde*. Unlike the walking id of that Victorian parable, however, the Hulk was portrayed sympathetically, as a personification of natural man trapped in a world of technology and civilization that frustrates and baffles him. Though quickly enraged and wantonly destructive, he could also be guileless, childlike, and touchingly loyal. It was a powerful concept, especially as executed by Kirby's monumental art and Lee's effectively bombastic scripting.

Unfortunately, the two creators didn't seem to know quite what to do with the character: In some issues he was angry but eloquent, while in others, he was simply crude, with a blue-collar speech pattern and a hatred for Commies. Even later he would succumb to a Johnny Weissmuller protoverbalism. Sometimes Banner could control his transformations, other times not. And the plots seemed to miss the point, setting him less often against the forces of civilization than against aliens and supercriminals.

The Hulk lasted only six issues in his own comic, but built up enough fans to encourage a return in 1965, sharing *Tales to Astonish* with Giant-Man and then the Submariner. The following year the Hulk's secret identity was revealed to the world, he separated from Rick Jones, and he finally found an identity as a wandering, persecuted brute who wants only peace but can find no shelter. Further, it was established that Banner becomes the Hulk when he is enraged, which strengthened the metaphor. He received his own series in 1968. Written by Gary Friedrich and others, drawn attractively by Marie Severin and Herb Trimpe, *The Incredible Hulk* chugged dependably along through the 1970s. It was given a boost in 1978–1982 by a prime-time CBS-TV adaptation.

Since the end of the TV series, the Hulk has been given a series of creative facelifts: turning gray, combining Banner's mind with the Hulk's body, being accepted as a good guy, and so on. Such changes have made for a livelier series, but at the cost of the strong (if limited) original concept.                                    **G.J.**

**THE HUMAN TORCH**  Despite his name, he wasn't human: The Torch, created by Carl Burgos, was a "synthetic man—an exact replica of a human being." For an android he did very well, and, even though his adventures were neither the best written nor the best drawn of the Golden Age, he was just about the most popular and successful character Marvel had in the 1940s. Only Captain America and Sub-Mariner offered any real competition.

The Human Torch's origin story is not one of the most coherent in the annals of superheroes, but the basic facts can be gleaned from the first issue of *Marvel Comics* (November 1939). It seems Professor Horton has been working at creating a synthetic human, and he holds a press conference to announce that, although he's more or less succeeded, he has some trepidations. "I call him THE HUMAN TORCH," Horton explains as he unveils a large, airtight glass cylinder that contains his blond, red-suited creation. "Something went wrong with my figuring somewhere—every time the robot…contacts oxygen in the air, he bursts into flame!" Sure enough, as Horton allows air into the glass cage, the Torch catches fire. Rather than tell the white-haired scientist that he should've expected somebody he dubbed the Human Torch to burst into flame now and then, the reporters shout things like, "Destroy that man!"

Although Horton does try to incapacitate his android by burying him in cement, that doesn't work, and before long "the HUMAN TORCH is on the loose again!" The Torch gets mixed up, appropriately enough, with a gang of arsonists and cleans up their dirty racket. By the end of the first yarn he's learned to melt iron bars, throw fireballs, and turn his flame on and off at will. When the old professor suggests that they might be able to make a fortune, the now altruistic Torch informs him, "No, Horton, I'll be free and no one will ever use me for selfish gain—or crime!"

What Burgos jumbled together in this account were bits from the horror movies of the 1930s—most notably *Frankenstein* and *The Invisible Man*—plus stuff from the pulp magazines. Only a scattering of true comic book supermen had come into being at this early date, and the props and mythology had to be borrowed not only from other comic books but from outside sources as well. The early Human Torch behaves like both a Universal monster movie character and a pulp magazine do-gooder. What Burgos had stumbled on was a basic idea that had a tremendous appeal to kids, most of whom go through a phase where they're touched with a little pyromania. They play with matches, yearn after fireworks, and attempt to concoct fiery explosives with chemistry sets. The Human Torch was a hero who could play with fire and get away with it, and the notion was so strong that Burgos' admittedly less than masterful drawing couldn't smother it.

As the Torch's career progressed he toyed with the idea of having a civilian identity. For a while, calling himself Jim Hammond, he took a job as a uniformed cop. His true identity sometimes got him in trouble with his fellow officers and even put him in the awkward position of being told to go arrest himself. On one such occasion the Torch "burned down a block of old tenement houses infested with the black plague." Unaware of the plague, the police label him an arsonist.

In the first issue of the *Human Torch* quarterly (Fall 1940) he acquired a boy sidekick. While "winging his way across the country with his flame on…the Torch is attracted by the gay colored tents of a traveling circus below…and as he nears the ground, panic breaks out as Toro, the fire-eating boy, suddenly topples from his stand with his body ablaze!" The Torch intervenes, helps the lad get his flame under control and out, and realizes that here's the perfect companion for him. Quite probably he was also aware that Dick Grayson, the original Robin, had a circus background, too.

Interestingly enough, there was no explanation as to what was burning when Toro flamed on. Was his flesh going up in flames? Did some kind of gas come from his pores and burn? The impossibility of producing fire without burning something didn't bother either the readers or the writers, and nobody ever worried about the possibility of Toro or the Torch himself ending up someday as a pile of ashes.

The Human Torch and Toro did some impressive work in their early adventures together in both *Marvel Mystery* and *The Human Torch*. Each story was like a fireworks display, with the team tossing fireballs, building bridges of flame, burning through solid walls. The most impressive villain they combated was a large, nasty chap whose face made it obvious why he was nicknamed the Parrot. A taunting fellow, much like the Joker, he liked to send the Torch announcements of his upcoming crimes. Sometimes a real parrot was used to deliver the message. In *Marvel* #24 his intended target was the Cosmopolitan Opera House, and readers got to see the Torch, flame off, attending the gala opening night decked out in tuxedo and homburg.

When Burgos entered the service in 1942, the Torch was passed on to other hands. Edd Ashe was his immediate replacement as artist, and eventually a wide range of others filled in. The Torch and Toro remained hot in the 1940s, showing up in such books as *All Winners, All Select, Mystic,* and *Daring.*

In the spring of 1949 *Marvel* and *The Human Torch* quietly folded and the Torch and Toro were extinguished. They came back briefly in the 1950s and then, in that particular team form, were gone forever.

In 1961, Marvel Comics created a new version of the Human Torch—this one actually a human teenager named Johnny Storm—as a member of the Fantastic Four. From 1962 to 1965, this new Torch ran in his own series in *Strange Tales*, joined for his last two years by the Thing, also from the Fantastic Four.

The original Human Torch returned to battle the new version in *Fantastic Four Annual* #4 (1966), as the dupe of the villain Quasimodo, and was destroyed. Later Marvel's writers revealed that the body of the original Torch had been converted into an android called the Vision, a member of the Avengers. The old original flamed again in a 1990 miniseries.          **R.G/G.J.**

# I

**IGER, JERRY** (1910– ) Cartoonist, writer, and entrepreneur, Iger entered the comic book industry when it was just beginning in the middle 1930s. The shop he formed with Will Eisner in 1937 created and packaged such magazines as *Jumbo Comics, Planet Comics, Hit Comics,* and *Wonderworld Comics* and invented such characters as Sheena, the Blue Beetle, Wonder Man, Wonder Boy, and the Flame. On his own in the 1940s, Iger continued as a packager and put together numerous comic book titles and features, as well as many issues of *Classics Illustrated.*

Born in New York City and raised in Oklahoma, Samuel Maxwell Iger returned to Manhattan in his teens and got a job in the art department of Hearst's *New York American.* As a cartoonist, he entered comic books in the middle 1930s by contributing one-page fillers about his kid characters Bobby and Peewee to the pioneering *Famous Funnies.* He drew in a simple cartoon style and eventually put most of his time into editing, writing, and selling. In 1936 he put together a short-lived comic book *Wow! What A Comic!*, a mixture of reprints and original material. Among his contributors were Bob Kane, Dick Briefer, and Eisner.

The following year Iger and Eisner teamed up and hired a staff of artists and writers to produce complete comic books for Fox, Fiction House, and Quality. Besides acting as a supersalesman for the shop, Iger invented characters and wrote scripts. Two of his favorite pen names were Jerry Maxwell and S.M. Regi. Among the second banana characters he created were Shark Brodie, Firebrand, Shorty Shortcake, Neon, and the Strange Twins.

During the 1940s Iger's shop provided material for several publishers, and he also served as feature editor for the Fiction House line—*Jumbo, Jungle, Planet, Wings,* and the like. In the middle 1940s he added *Classics Illustrated* to his client list, which accounts for noted Good Girl Art artists such as Matt Baker and Bob Webb, who were also Iger's employees, drawing adaptations of famous novels like *Lorna Doone* and *Frankenstein.*

Iger also ran various small newspaper syndicates, the most successful being Phoenix Features, which offered his own *Bobby,* Baker's *Flamingo,* and, from 1953 to 1954, the comic strip version of Mickey Spillane's *Mike Ham-*mer. After leaving the comic book field in the late 1950s, Iger continued on with commercial art and promotion.
**R.G.**

**INGELS, GRAHAM** (1915– ) Much to his chagrin, Ingels is best remembered for his gruesome artwork in the EC horror comics of the 1950s. He sometimes used the pen name "Ghastly," an appropriate description for the stories he drew in *The Haunt of Fear, The Vault of Horror,* and *Tales From the Crypt.* As EC publisher William Gaines once put it, "Ingels was Mr. Horror himself."

Born in Cincinnati, Ingels spent part of his childhood in Georgia, the inspiration, perhaps, for his Southern Gothic EC horror tales. By the time he was in his early teens, Ingels was living in the New York area. After a series of odd jobs he set forth as a free-lancer and moved from commercial art into illustration. In the early 1940s he joined the Fiction House publishing outfit, drawing for their pulps (among them, *Planet Stories, Jungle Stories, Wings*) and their comic books (*Planet Comics, Jumbo Comics,* and the like). The year 1947 found him serving as art director-editor for publisher Ned Pines, scripting and drawing for such comic book titles as *Startling Comics* and *Thrilling Comics.* He was hired by Gaines a year later. Ingels' gnarled, atmospheric style, with its roots in the drybrush strokes and rich blacks common to pulp illustration, was soon identified with the tales told by EC's Old Witch narrator.

Although Ingels later drifted from comics into employment as a painting instructor, his EC horror work became legendary and has been reprinted several times over the intervening years. Eventually it even received a mention in one of Stephen King's stories: "*Tales From The Crypt,* you remember that? Christ! They had a guy named Graham Ingels; he could draw every god-awful thing in the world—and some out of it." Despite such accolades, Ingels long ago turned his back on the past and will have nothing to do with fans or interviewers interested in his Ghastly career.
**B.S.**

**INSPECTOR WADE** In 1935 King Features seemingly revived the dead when they added a daily detective strip entitled *Inspector Wade* to their list and credited the writing to Edgar Wallace. A highly successful and extremely prolific mystery novelist, Wallace had died three years earlier. The actual author of the new Scotland Yard feature was Sheldon Stark and the artist Lyman Anderson.

As Anderson once recalled, King had contracted to convert several Wallace novels into comic strip form. The inspector became the hero simply because he happened to be the leading character in the first book Stark was given to adapt, *The India Rubber Men*, published originally in 1929. Stark's comic section version was a very free adaptation; little of Inspector Wade's humor and flippancy, or much of his astuteness, survived and almost nothing of the English waterfront lowlife Wallace had detailed. It took Stark about 10 weeks to use up a novel; once finished he'd set about translating the next one into panels and balloons. Anderson, who later did some impressive illustrations for *The Saturday Evening Post* and *Cosmopolitan*, was still earning his living as a pulp illustrator in the 1930s. His artwork had a spare drybrush look and was too bland to be very compelling.

His Wade was a handsome fellow with two odd gray waves at the front of his otherwise dark head of hair. The inspector's Watson was a sturdy mustachioed chap named Donavan, who apparently also had something to do with Scotland Yard. Nowhere near as observant as Wade, Donavan went in for remarks like:"You're daffy, Wade—*I* didn't hear a *thing*!" The rather tame continuities mixed detection with action and often ended with Wade confronting the criminal and reeling off a bill of particulars: "Hamon, you're under arrest for the murder of Slone—and the murder of Bill Morlake in Morocco four years ago!"

When Anderson graduated to the slicks in 1938, Neil O'Keeffe took over the drawing. O'Keeffe had put in several years illustrating for pulp fiction magazines such as *Adventure*. His work—blacker, livelier and better composed—improved the appearance but not the circulation. *Inspector Wade* succumbed in May of 1941.

**R.G.**

**INVISIBLE SCARLET O'NEIL** An unconventional lady crimefighter, Scarlet O'Neil first materialized in the funny papers in 1940, roughly a year after Clark Gable had told Scarlett O'Hara he didn't give a damn. Owing something to both the movies and the burgeoning comic books, the strip was the work of Russell Stamm and was syndicated initially by the *Chicago Times*.

Invisible people had been fairly popular in motion pictures during the 1930s. *The Invisible Man* had started the fad in 1933, and the notion soon spread into B-movies and serials. *Topper*, released in 1937, offered a variation and had Cary Grant and Constance Bennett as ghosts who could turn from visible to invisible and back

again at will. In 1940 Universal struck twice, with *The Invisible Man Returns* and *The Invisible Woman*. This latter film, starring Virginia Bruce as the unseen lady, came out at about the same time as Stamm's new strip. The Shadow, who'd done much to popularize invisibility by way of his radio show, entered both comic books and newspaper strips early in 1940.

The increasingly popular comic books used a good deal of fantasy material. Stamm and his syndicate were obviously aware of the increasing competition from that area, and the promotional copy described Invisible Scarlet as "America's new superheroine."

Stamm, born and raised in Chicago, had gone to work for Chester Gould while still in his teens. After some five years with Gould he succeeded in selling his own strip. When he started the new feature, his lettering was the same as that used on the Gould feature and his backgrounds were nearly identical. It was as though he were using the *Dick Tracy* sets after the hard-boiled detective got through with them. Stamm's people, though, had more of a cartoony, bigfoot appearance. Scarlet herself, like the ideal screen woman of the 1940s, had long hair and broad shoulders.

She came by her phenomenal power because she was curious. "My father was a scientist," she explained in the first day's episode, "and one evening a few years ago I was in his laboratory when..." What she did was stick her finger in front of a "weird-looking ray." This particular weird-looking ray turned anybody who stuck his or her finger in front of it invisible, clothes and all. Fortunately for Scarlet, she eventually discovered "a highly sensitive nerve in my left wrist." When she pressed it, she became visible again. The wrist switch worked both ways, giving her the ability to materialize or disappear at will. An invisible heroine might have been an opportunity to save on drawing for some, but not Stamm. He drew Scarlet even when she was not supposed to be seen, making her seem more transparent than invisible.

Stamm had a sentimental side and once he left the tough guy climate of *Dick Tracy* he displayed it. His early continuities involved helping kids with broken arms, saving blind boys from the machinations of their greedy guardians, and reuniting circus freaks with their long-lost mothers. The daily *Invisible Scarlet O'Neil* started on June 3, 1940, and the Sunday came along on January 5, 1941. In the early days Stamm kept two separate stories going.

The strip got somewhat tougher as it progressed. In 1944 Stamm went into the service, and *Scarlet* continued with ghost artists. When he came back in 1946, his style was considerably altered, being scratchier and less cartoony, and the tone of the stories changed, too. By the early 1950s, when the strip was called just plain *Scarlet*

*O'Neil*, there was no more invisibility, and Stamm was making fun of the adventure and detective genres. In 1950 he'd brought in a new character in the person of an excessively virtuous and handsome Texan named Stainless Steel. The circulation started to climb, and as of January 1955 the strip changed its name to *Stainless Steel*. Stamm had been assisted for several years by an artist named Emery Clarke, and just before Scarlet was dumped, Clarke began to share the credit on the strip.

Stamm started to get national publicity, including a writeup in *Time*. He explained his dauntless hero's growing popularity by saying, "His saving grace is that he isn't deadly serious like most heroes. He's got a sense of humor." Despite the publicity and the increased number of papers, Stamm managed to keep the strip going only until 1956. Giving up newspaper work, he opened Russell Stamm Productions, where he created and produced television commercials. **R.G.**

**IRON MAN** Created by Stan Lee for Marvel Comics' *Tales of Suspense* in 1963, Iron Man was secretly munitions manufacturer Tony Stark; while inspecting his weaponry in Vietnam, Stark stepped on a communist landmine, had his heart severely injured by shrapnel, and was captured by fiendish Reds. While pretending to develop a superweapon for the enemy, he devised a set of superpowered armor for himself (which not only enabled him to fly and fire "repulsor rays," but also kept his damaged heart beating). He escaped—to fight crime and the communist menace in America.

In the early days, *Iron Man* was an odd mélange of political realism, shrill anti-communist jingoism, and fanciful superheroics (Iron Man's archenemy was the Mandarin, a Fu Manchu clone in communist clothing). As the years passed, emotional subplots came to dominate the series, particularly those involving Tony Stark's secret tragedy (trapped in the iron chest-plate that keeps him alive). Iron Man was also a charter member of *The Avengers* (and more recently of its spin-off group, *West Coast Avengers*), and became heavily involved with Marvel's resident super-espionage group, S.H.I.E.L.D.

Stan Lee wrote most of the stories until 1968, when Archie Goodwin replaced him to good effect; that same year, *Iron Man* earned a comic book of its own. Don Heck drew most of the stories from 1963 to 1966, when he was replaced by the bold, atmospheric art of Gene Colan. Goodwin and Colan were both gone by the end of the 1960s, however, and Iron Man limped through the 1970s under lesser hands. His fortunes have risen in the 1980s, especially under writer David Michelinie and artists John Romita Jr. and Bob Layton.

Stark's role as a munitions maker seems to have made the writers of the 1970s and 1980s uncomfortable, which may explain why they've repeatedly put him through the emotional ringer. In 1979 Industries was taken from him by S.H.I.E.L.D., and in 1981 he suffered a devastating battle with alcoholism in a highly-publicized series of stories by Michelinie. He was replaced for a time by another man wearing the Iron Man armor, before piecing his life back together in recent issues. **G.J.**

# J

**JACK ARMSTRONG** During the 1930s and 1940s one of the most famous All-American boys in the land was a clean-cut, clean-living lad named Jack Armstrong. He began his adventurous career on radio in 1933, starting as an all-around jock hero at Hudson High. Soon, however, accompanied by his pals Billy and Betty Fairfield and their Uncle Jim, Jack was playing perennial hooky and trekking to the four corners of the globe.

The Jack Armstrong shows, broadcast every weekday afternoon and sponsored by Wheaties, were especially wild and woolly from 1935 to 1940. During these years Talbot Mundy, whose novels about Tros of Samothrace and Jimgrim had been highlights of the pulp magazine *Adventure*, wrote the scripts, tossing the same sort of African and Indian mysticism and intrigue into the radio show that he used in his magazine yarns and novels. (In fact, one radio adventure had Jack and his gang hunting for the same elephants' graveyard that another crew of Mundy adventurers had sought in his 1919 novel, *The Ivory Trail*.)

In 1937 Whitman turned the radio serial into a Big Little Book entitled *Jack Armstrong and the Ivory Treasure*. The impressive Henry Vallely illustrated this small, fat novel, and his Jack was a stalwart fellow in riding breeches, possessed of a matinee idol profile. A second BLB followed in 1939.

Finally, in the spring of 1947, the Register and Tribune Syndicate launched a Jack Armstrong newspaper strip. It was drawn by Bob Schoenke, an artist of modest attainments whose Jack was nowhere near as dashing and heroic as Vallely's and looked more like the sort of youth who'd spend much of his time on the bench. The continuities were sedate, moderately technological, and a far cry from the radio days of Talbot Mundy. Uncle Jim didn't appear, having been replaced, as he was on radio, by a graying scientific detective named Vic Hardy. The strip, daily and Sunday, limped along until 1949.

A Jack Armstrong comic book was introduced by *Parents'* late in 1947. Like their *True Comics* it was on the dull side. Thirteen issues appeared before the magazine folded in the summer of 1949.

Even had the strip and the comic book been better done, they probably wouldn't have caught on. Jack's popularity had already started to slip soon after the end of World War II, and in August of 1947 the radio show, formerly aired five times a week, was demoted to a twice-weekly half-hour offering; it ran until June of 1951.

**R.G.**

**THE JACKSON TWINS** Jan and Jill, a pair of identically cute teenage girls, remained youthful throughout the nearly 30-year run of their strip. *The Jackson Twins*, written and drawn by Dick Brooks and syndicated by McNaught, began in 1950 and ended in 1979.

The twins had first appeared during the postwar 1940s in *Elmer Squee*, the Sunday page Brooks did for King Features. Elmer worked as a bellhop at a resort hotel, and the girls, relatives of his, showed up now and then as visitors. Under new names they became the Jacksons. Elmer had first appeared in a service panel Brooks turned out while serving in the Navy during World War II.

The strip, a daily and Sunday feature, started on November 27, 1950. Jan and Jill lived in Gardentown, a pleasant spot that looked pretty much like the towns where Archie Andrews, Henry Aldrich, Corliss Archer, and all the other clean-cut teens of comics, movies, radio, and the newcomer television dwelled. They had a plump, balding businessman father, an understanding mother, a kid brother named Junior, and a wide circle of friends and beaus. Brooks, who drew in a simple style that was more cartoony than it was illustrative, went in for simple, light continuities of the sort that could be found on most radio and television situation comedies.

As the years went by and teenagers in the real world started protesting, coping with drugs and becoming more openly engaged in the events of the day, Brooks tried to reflect this in his strip. "Some of these themes, however, were not universally popular," Hedges Macdonald pointed out in *Strip Scene*. "Brooks once bemoaned the difficulty of trying to be contemporary while still pleasing the total readership...The use of a single word such as 'tranquilizer' would lose the strip a newspaper. And, as the '70's progressed, it lost a great many."

Brooks had considerable help with the strip, although he almost always drew the twins himself. Ed Moore was his assistant for many years, as was Warren Sattler, who took on the job in 1964. The final *Jackson Twins* strip, showing the girls looking as young as ever, ran on March 24, 1979. **R.G.**

**JAFFEE, ALLAN** (1921–  ) A much respected zany, Jaffee has been drawing funny pictures professionally for almost 50 years. Starting in comic books in the early 1940s, he eventually became one of *Mad*'s most popular contributors. He did a newspaper panel titled *Tall Tales* from the late 1950s to the middle 1960s, has worked widely in advertising, and early in his career invented a character named Ziggy Pig.

Jaffee was born in Savannah, Georgia, and grew up in a small town in Lithuania. When he and his parents returned to America in the early 1930s, they settled in the New York City area, where he attended Manhattan's High School of Music and Art. He sold his first feature, a two-page monthly humor filler called *Inferior Man*, to *Military Comics* in 1941. Jaffee also sold material to Marvel. For *Krazy Komics* he drew *Ziggy Pig and Silly Seal*; for *Joker Comics* there was *Squat Car Squad*.

After serving in the Army Air Corps during World War II, Jaffee returned to comic books. Working again for Marvel he drew such titles as *Super Rabbit* and *Patsy Walker*. In 1955, when Harvey Kurtzman changed *Mad* from a comic book to a magazine format, Jaffee joined the staff. He later said that "giving up lucrative income to go with barely started *Mad*" was the positive turning point of his career.

Jaffee moved into newspaper syndication in 1958 with *Tall Tales*, a long, thin pantomime panel that survived until 1965. The panel and his frequent appearances in *Mad* attracted the attention of advertising agencies, and he began working regularly for a wide range of accounts. He's also done a very successful series of *Mad* paperback originals, including his *Snappy Answers to Stupid Questions* titles.

Once asked by the National Cartoonists Society to state his life's goal, Jaffee replied, "To become a vital force reshaping the social, intellectual, and political destiny of mankind with a view toward bringing peace, prosperity, and a higher degree of understanding between people regardless of race, color, or creed throughout the world and elsewhere." **R.G.**

**JANE ARDEN** For most of her comic strip life Jane Arden worked as a newspaper reporter. The feature, created and written by Monte Barrett, began in the late 1920s and lasted for 40 years.

A newspaper man himself, Barrett "worked his way up from cub reporter to managing editor." *Jane Arden*, a daily at first, began in November of 1928. Frank Ellis, possessor of a flat, wispy style, was the original artist. Jane wasn't yet in the newspaper game, most of her intrigues being romantic ones. Eventually, however, she became a newspaper woman.

A Sunday page was added in the early 1930s, with a separate story line and a separate artist, Jack W. McGuire. A conspicuously better, and more forceful, cartoonist than Ellis, he did a capable job of illustrating the various adventures Jane's investigative reporting assignments involved her in. She posed, for instance, as a circus performer, a movie actress, and even as the princess of a small European country while in pursuit of her stories. It was McGuire who introduced paper doll cutouts to the Sunday page in a weekly sidepanel titled *Jane Arden's Wardrobe*. There was also a topper called *Lena Pry*, about a busybody spinster; now and then a Lena paper doll would appear.

By 1935 Russell Ross was drawing both the daily and the Sunday. Jane became somewhat more realistic during Ross' long run with the strip, eventually abandoning Ruritanian intrigues for somewhat grittier big city crimes and conspiracies. Ross had previously drawn *Flying To Fame* (sometimes known as *Slim and Tubby*), and it was through his efforts that Tubby eventually found employment on Jane's newspaper.

Barrett died in 1949 and Ross left the strip a few years later. Jim Seed drew *Jane Arden* next and Walt Graham provided scripts. For the next several years Jane, though still gainfully employed as a newsperson, came to resemble a typical soap opera heroine. After Seed, William Hargis drew the strip, and in 1964 Bob Schoenke took over. He eventually introduced a cowboy hero from an earlier strip of his into the feature and shifted the locale to the Old West of the 19th Century, with Jane working on a frontier town paper. The strip was called *Laredo and Jane* in its final years and ended in 1968. **R.G.**

**JASPER JOOKS** A daily strip that strove to imitate Al Capp and the Dogpatch style, *Jasper* was launched in late April of 1948 by the New York Post Syndicate. It was the work of Jess "Baldy" Benton, who'd been around long enough to have contributed to *Captain Billy's Whiz-Bang*. He'd also worked on Fawcett comic books and as a newspaper political cartoonist. On his comic strip Benton labored mightily not only to draw like Capp but to think like him as well. He got down the look of *Li'l Abner* pretty well—bowlegged rustics, overflowing bosoms, gnarled trees, popeyed silhouettes, and so on—but the Capp humor, that patented blend of curmudgeonly social comment and stag party kneeslappers, eluded him.

*Jasper Jooks*, Baldy Beaton, © 1946, N.Y. Post Corp.

The strip was set in Appleknock Territory, a remote New England area where everything remained as it had been in Colonial times. Jasper was a big, blond Abner in tricorn hat, innocent—"Ding bust it…I'm *still* th' most un- kissed boy in th' New World!"—well-meaning and reluctantly brave. His true love was Ellabella Chugg, a bosomy brunette who was most impatient with his shyness. Among the other characters were a sorceress known as Witch One, a bearded little genius named Homer Sapiens, and Thomas Cyclops, a private eye. Yet another example of a strip that looked better than it read, *Jasper Jooks* made it to 1949 and expired.

**R.G.**

**JENSEN, CECIL** (1902–1976)  A longtime political cartoonist, Jensen also dabbled in comic strips, among them the satirical, eccentric, and unsuccessful *Elmo* of the middle 1940s and its blander, longer lasting successor *Little Debbie*.

Born in Ogden, Utah, Cecil Leon Jensen began his journalism career as a newsboy on his hometown paper. In 1920, having worked his way up to circulation manager, Jensen headed for Chicago to study at the Academy of Fine Arts. After holding down jobs as the editorial cartoonist on the *Salt Lake Telegram* and the *Los Angeles News*, he settled with the *Chicago Daily News*. He remained associated with the *News*, a sheet that supported the Democratic Party, for the rest of his life.

Although Jensen managed to sell a couple of comic strips in the 1920s, including one called *Syncopating Sue* to his own paper's syndicate, he never came up with a hit. In the early 1940s he introduced an occasional character called Colonel McCosmic to his editorials, a broad caricature of the militantly conservative Colonel McCormick who published the rival *Chicago Tribune*. The cartoons about McCosmic earned considerable notoriety and got Jensen a spread in *Life* in 1942.

Jensen tried a strip again in 1946. *Elmo* was a mixture of burlesque, slapstick, satire, and Jensen's rather bleak view of society. He drew it in a simplified version of the scratchy, crowquill pen style he used in his politicals; the Register & Tribune Syndicate launched it, with much enthusiasm and publicity (*Elmo* even got a writeup in *Newsweek*). The strip was often funny and original, but too quirky and inconsistent to grab the same audience that supported strips like *Li'l Abner*. It faltered fairly soon and by 1949 was being called *Little Debbie*. A cute little girl who'd been Elmo's pal, Debbie elbowed him out into the cold and starred in the strip until its demise.

Jensen had once thought that doing a strip would allow him to escape the editorial page, but he was never able to do that completely, for he continued doing political cartoons for the rest of his days. By the middle 1970s he was living in the Ozark Mountains and calling himself semiretired, just "doing a few a week to keep from getting senile."

**R.G.**

**JERRY ON THE JOB**  One of the few comic strip characters who made a comeback, Jerry Flannigan was first seen late in 1913 in Hearst's *New York Journal* and soon thereafter in Hearst newspapers across the country. Walter Hoban, who wrote and drew *Jerry on the Job*, was in his early twenties when the strip began. His diminutive blond hero was an office boy, a job Hoban had held a few years earlier in the art department of his hometown paper, the *Philadelphia North American*.

Jerry remained on the office job, where he worked for a Mr. Fipp, until 1915. During that year he tried out a variety of other occupations, working as a messenger

*Jerry on the Job*, Walter Hoban, © 1923, International Feature Service, Inc.

boy, and in a clothing store, a pet shop, and a grocery. Finally in December of 1915 he was hired by a railroad as a ticket agent, conductor, and all around handyman. As the feature evolved Hoban's drawing improved and his strips became increasingly ambitious. He was a champion of the take, and many a strip ended with one of the characters reacting to the punchline by falling over. He also developed an interest in props and backgrounds, even growing more and more fascinated with the signs on the walls. At first most of his signs were fairly straight, but then he began to indulge in puns and wisecracks, such as "Do not strike matches on the ceiling," "Our exits are the only way out," "Round trip tickets save a lot of walking," and the like. This practice, obviously contagious, eventually spread to the work of Bill Holman, Gene Ahern, and George Swanson.

In the spring of 1916 Jerry left the railroad to go jobhunting once again. The strip then went on leave while Hoban was in the service during World War I. When Jerry returned to business, and Hoban returned from the Army, he settled into a job with the railroad again, working for a crotchety gentleman named Mr. Givney for most of what was to be his finest decade—the 1920s. The suburban railroad station where he worked, which chiefly served travelers who wanted to get to the town of New Monia, was frequented by a wide range of eccentric commuters, cunning bums and deadbeats, and out and out loons. A boy of all work, Jerry not only sold tickets, but also handled baggage, swept out the station, waited tables in the station cafe, and served in his spare time as Givney's office boy.

Hoban indulged in simple continuities from time to time. The strip's gags weren't hilarious but what appealed was its small hero (who, contrary to all accepted rules of drawing, was just two heads high), his casual, slangy approach to life, and the screwball decor he functioned in. Hoban developed a distinctive, and today unacceptable, way of drawing blacks, introducing a pair of Jerry-sized lads called the Blotts. Eventually their Uncle Tom inherited a taxi and went into business as Uncle Tom's Cab. Jerry drove the hack on occasion.

The strip, which added a Sunday page in 1921, began to fade in the early 1930s. By 1932 Jerry was appearing only in a topper to Hoban's *Rainbow Duffy* Sunday. And then he dropped out entirely.

But he was destined to rise again. In the late 1930s Jerry started showing up in comic sections, this time in a series of strips advertising Grape-Nuts. These were signed by Hoban, but some were ghosted by King Features veteran Bob Naylor. Hoban died in 1939, but Naylor remained fascinated with Jerry. In the early 1940s he drew variations of the character in one-page humor fillers for assorted DC comic books. Then in 1946 he persuaded King to revive *Jerry on the Job* as a daily strip. Naylor did a pretty good job of imitating Hoban's drawing style, but he never captured his quirky approach to humor. And the 1940s just weren't the 1920s. Jerry was gone again by 1949. **R.G.**

**JET SCOTT** This adventure strip began in September of 1953 and offered science fiction in a contemporary setting. Advance ads emphasized the fact its hero "was not a ray-blasting space ranger but a scientific investigator for the Pentagon." A lean, dark man, Jet Scott worked for a little-known branch of the Pentagon called the Office of Scientifact and specialized in cases involving such up-to-the-minute topics as sonic weapons, the illegal dumping of toxic chemical waste, and the bootleg use of plutonium. Syndicated by the *New York Herald Tribune*, the strip was the joint effort of writer Sheldon Stark and artist Jerry Robinson.

Stark had worked in the comic book field in the middle 1930s, written the *Inspector Wade* strip, and in the 1940s scripted the *Straight Arrow* radio show. Robinson was a comic book veteran, and after working on *Batman* and other Golden Age features, he teamed up with the gifted Mort Meskin to do some memorable work in the late 1940s—on such features as *The Black Terror, Johnny Quick,* and *The Vigilante.*

His drawing on *Jet Scott* was somewhat in the Meskin tradition and was quite impressive. The strip, which ran daily and Sunday, was relatively sophisticated, and the slim, stylish women who inhabited its panels had such provocative names as Tawney, Feather, Topaz, and Safron. Like many another Pentagon employee, Jet didn't limit himself to homeground adventures, but journeyed to exotic locales such as Saudi Arabia and the South Seas, all of which Robinson depicted in his best cinematic fashion.

Despite its looks and "the best of expert knowledge and experience," the strip never reached a large list of newspapers. Efforts to lighten it by doing continuities kidding show business and advertising didn't help. *Jet Scott* folded in 1955, just short of its second birthday.             **R.G.**

**JIM HARDY** Few newspaper readers of the late 1930s or early 1940s, got a chance to follow *Jim Hardy* on their comic pages, since Dick Moores' somewhat folksy adventure strip ran in only a handful of papers. Comic book enthusiasts, however, eventually found reprints every month in *Tip Top Comics*. And it was in this magazine, which Moores' feature shared with better-knowns like *Tarzan, Li'l Abner,* and *Nancy,* that it gained its major audience. There were also several one-shot reprint comic books. The strip, a daily only, ran from 1936 to 1942, and Moores' characters were last seen in a comic book in 1947.

Moores had been Chester Gould's assistant, doing backgrounds and lettering on *Dick Tracy* throughout the early 1930s. He sent out samples of about 30 different stripes of his own before United Features got interested in his *Jim Hardy.* Initially Jim was an ex-convict trying to make his way in the world. However, when the syndicate sent its salesmen out with proofs of this version, not a single newspaper bought the strip.

"We changed him to 'a man against the world,'" Moores once explained. This time United salesmen managed to sell Jim to three papers. "It was launched in June of 1936, with a total billing of $27," Moores explained. "We went into the red on it to about $4,000 by September, 1936...I started doing it for $25, I had been getting $75 a week. It ran until October, 1942, when I quit to go to work for Walt Disney. I was getting $50 a week by then."

The main problem with *Jim Hardy* was that Moores was somewhat too original. He was a much better artist than some of the others who tried to imitate Gould, but he lacked the singlemindedness to do a one-for-one imitation of the successful Tracy property. He drew in a personal, gentler version of the Chicago Style, that bold, flat poster-like approach favored by Gould, Harold Gray, Sydney Smith, and others. Despite the fact that he wasn't earning much on his strip, he obviously lingered over it, taking the time to put in a variety of patiently inked pen patterns and drawing detailed long shots of city streets and country landscapes. There were all sorts of other small touches that were his alone.

After drifting from job to job, Jim Hardy settled on the profession of newspaper reporter. In that incarnation he went after racketeers, corrupt politicians, and the like. Nevertheless, he couldn't seem to get himself to act enough like Dick Tracy, remaining basically small-town at heart. Moores' continuities, mixing sentiment with adventure, didn't offer the kind of wacky, slam-bang action that made readers take Dick Tracy to their hearts. Moores was a good storyteller, but he never quite found the right blend of the hardboiled and the homespun that he seemed to be trying for. *Jim Hardy,* however, remains one of the most attractive failures in the history of comic strips.

Eventually Jim wandered out of the strip entirely, relinquishing his place to a lanky cowboy character named Windy. As caretaker of a racehorse named Paddles, Windy had to keep various villains from making trouble for them. In the final months of its life the strip changed its name to *Windy & Paddles.* "Mainly because," said Moores, "we were struggling and the ship was about to sink." The ship sank anyway.             **R.G.**

**JOE JINKS** Joe always had his enthusiasms: first automobiles, then airplanes, and, for the greater part of his career, the prizefight racket. His newspaper strip, cre-

*Jim Hardy*, Dick Moores, © 1938, United Features Syndicate, Inc. Reprinted by permission of United Features Syndicate, Inc.

ated by Vic Forsythe, began in 1918 under the title *Joe's Car*. In 1928 it became *Joe Jinks,* and by that time he was managing a heavyweight boxer. He hung around the funny papers for another twenty-odd years.

Joe was small and balding, with the sort of scraggly mustache much favored by newspaper strip husbands of the era. When Forsythe began his strip, which was syndicated originally by the *New York World*, it concentrated on Joe, his wife Blanche, and Joe's enthusiasm for cars and the open road. In the 1920s Joe eventually branched out into flying and other outdoor sports. Finally, in the late 1920s the nervous, cigar-chomping Joe became the manager of a boxer named Dynamite Dunn. Dunn won the World's Heavyweight crown, turning *Joe's Car* into a strip about the fight game. And beating Ham Fisher and *Joe Palooka* to the punch by a few years.

In August 1928 the title became *Joe Jinks*. A Sunday page was added on December 9, 1928, concentrating on Joe's domestic life and having nothing to do with fisticuffs. Several boxers besides Dynamite figured in the daily continuities over the years, among them Pete Humus, a big palooka; Pepito Diablo, a Latin bombast expert; and Elmer Deacon, a country bumpkin. At various times the excitable, belligerent Joe would have a falling out with Dynamite and take up the management of another pugilist. Like the more successful latecomer, *Joe Palooka*, Forsythe's strip often gave over a week or two to a nearly blow by blow account of an important fight.

When Forsythe was lured away to King Features in the early 1930s, Pete Llanuza, a sports cartoonist and caricaturist for the *World-Telegram*, took over the strip. He kept Dynamite handsome and square-jawed, but drew everybody else in a broad cartoon style. He stayed with *Joe Jinks* until November 1936 and was let go because the syndicate—United Features by this time—wanted a more serious looking strip. From out of the United bullpen came Mo Leff. A very good artist, Leff had drawn a kid fantasy Sunday page called *Peter Pat* and was then doing a good deal of the drawing on Al Capp's *Li'l Abner*. He improved the looks of the Jinks strip, got all the muscles right, made the women prettier, spruced up the staging. He had some help, mostly in the scripting, from his brother Sam. He left the strip in May 1937 and by the end of the year was ghosting *Joe Palooka*.

It's unusual for an artist to return to a strip he's walked out on, yet that's what happened next. Forsythe, all his King ventures having flopped, came home to *Joe Jinks*. His return engagement didn't last long and, because of illness, he was gone from the strip by early 1938. The next artist was Harry Homan, a longtime political cartoonist who'd also done the short-lived Sunday *Billy Make Believe* for United. He drew in a fairly

cartoony style and focused initially on Dynamite rather than Joe. Homan's first continuity had to do with the boxer's adventures while marooned on a tropical island and had nothing to do with the fight game. At about this same time the Sunday page, still dealing with Joe's home life, was taken over by Henry Formhals.

Homan died in 1939 and a succession of artists followed on the daily, some sticking with the job only a matter of weeks. These included George Storm, Al Kostuk, Morris Weiss, and Al Leiderman. Finally in 1944 Sam Leff began signing the strip. Basically a writer and an inker, Sam had persuaded his talented brother Mo to do most of the drawing. Fairly soon after he took over, Leff introduced a new boxer for Joe to manage. This was a big, blond, clean-cut lad named Curly Kayoe, a very definite Joe Palooka surrogate. For the next several years, unbeknownst to the public, Mo Leff was actually drawing both *Joe Palooka* and its chief imitator as well. The title was changed to *Curly Kayoe* in December 1945.

Early in 1947 Joe learned that his wife was suffering from "a very rare malady," one that would require her to go live in "a rather desolate area out west." Knowing his place was with her, Joe retired as Curly's manager and left the daily. The Sunday page, still titled *Joe Jinks* and with Blanche's health unimpaired, held on for a few more years.

In June 1961 there was another title change, this time to *Davy Jones*. Davy, who'd been gradually easing the champ out of the feature for several months, went in for seagoing adventures. Alden McWilliams drew the new feature until 1968, bringing it firmly into the realistic Alex Raymond camp. Wayne Boring, late of *Superman*, drew *Davy Jones* until it sank without a trace in 1971.

R.G.

**JOE PALOOKA** The feature was not, as its creator Ham Fisher liked to boast, "the world's greatest comic strip." *Joe Palooka* was, however, the most successful sports strip ever done. It began in 1930 and for a good part of the next half-century appeared in an impressively large list of newspapers.

*Joe Palooka* made its debut in April of 1930 in less than two dozen papers. But it kept growing and by the late 1930s was appearing in several hundred. Joe's rise was helped by his winning the World's Heavyweight Championship in 1931, and Fisher's hiring ghost artists who were significantly better than he was.

The basic cast was small. There was Palooka, whom Fisher had originally intended to call Joe the Dumbbell, and Knobby Walsh, the small, nervous, one-time haberdasher who became the fighter's manager and enjoyed the benefits of the championship with him. While Fisher certainly identified with his boxer hero, it is quite obvious that the argumentative, often unhappy Knobby was closer to a self-portrait. In 1932 Ann Howe, a pretty blond society girl whose father was a cheese tycoon, took on the role of Joe's sweetheart, and a while later a black named Smokey became Joe's valet, second, and close friend. Joe's large and loving family also came to figure in the stories.

Initially Joe was a true rube, naive and not especially bright. After winning the title from Jack McSwat, though, he grew both smarter and better looking, although at heart he always remained an innocent and was as clean-cut as a platoon of Boy Scouts. He moved through life as a kind of Candide with muscles, accompanied by Knobby or in some sequences by Smokey. While Fisher gave Smokey the vocabulary and the looks of a stereotyped movie black man of the 1930s, he was always treated as Joe's equal and Joe made it clear that they were friends rather than prizefighter and servant.

Boxing was a popular sport in the 1930s, and a great many people, as Fisher indicated in the frequent fight scenes, listened in over the radio. At the time Palooka first won the heavyweight crown in the strip, Max Schmeling was the heavyweight champ in real life. Fisher apparently had a sincere interest in prizefighting, and publicity photos of him at various bouts and gyms were frequent in the 1930s and 1940s. Although there have been very few successful strips with a sports background, Fisher's creation worked because *Joe Palooka* also offered, in addition to realistically staged boxing matches, adventure in exotic places, romance and pretty women, sentiment, and Joe's rather aggressive integrity. In 1940. before the United States entered World War II, Fisher put his hero into the Army, which generated considerable publicity, helped recruiting efforts, and provided the strip with a great many new story possibilities.

In spite of a king-sized ego, Fisher was aware that he was, at best, a second-rate artist. Despite a tendency for hearts and flowers, he was an adequate writer. He began hiring ghost artists fairly early on; Phil Boyle, whom he'd known in his hometown of Wilkes Barre, Pennsylvania, was the first. In 1933 he added Al Capp to his staff. After Capp went off to do his own *Li'l Abner* in 1934, Boyle came back to do most of the drawing again. Later in the 1930s he hired Mo Leff, a gifted artist and a member of the United Features bullpen who had been drawing *Joe Jinks*, another boxing strip, and who also did a good deal of the artwork on *Li'l Abner*. He drew *Joe Palooka* for the next two decades, continuing it after Fisher's death in 1955. Legend has it that Fisher made a point of always drawing the heads of Joe and Knobby himself.

Leff continued with the strip throughout the 1950s, and an artist named Joe Certa also did some work on it during that period. After a falling out with the Fisher estate, Leff took his leave, to be replaced by Tony DiPreta, who stayed with the strip until the end. From the early 1960s into the early 1970s Morris Weiss, who'd been a longtime friend of Fisher and had written and drawn *Joe Jinks* in the middle 1940s, wrote the continuities.

Fisher had added new characters over the years, such as the fat, good-natured Humphrey and the maudlin mute newsboy named Little Max, who had tended to upstage Joe. In its last years *Joe Palooka* became a very quiet and bland strip, and the champ abandoned the ring for much tamer venues. The strip went down for the count in 1984.                                      **R.G.**

**JOHN CARTER OF MARS**   Author Edgar Rice Burroughs' first hero, though never as popular as his Tarzan, was an Earthman who traveled to Mars—known as Barsoom to the locals—and partook of a string of swashbuckling adventures. He initially appeared in *All-Story* in 1912. The six-part monthly serial was issued in book form as *A Princess of Mars* in 1917, the first in a series of novels. In addition, he had several comic book incarnations and also appeared in a short-lived newspaper Sunday page.

Early in the 1930s Burroughs had begun trying to interest newspaper syndicates in a strip about the heroic swordsman of Barsoom, and in 1933 he'd had J. Allen St. John, illustrator of many of the Tarzan and Mars novels, draw up a batch of samples. Nobody was interested. Finally in 1941 the persistent Burroughs at last persuaded United Features, distributors of the *Tarzan* strip, to give a John Carter Sunday page a try. This version, written and drawn by Burroughs' son, John Coleman Burroughs, arrived just as America was entering World War II.

The author's son had warmed up for the job by drawing John Carter in his earliest comic book appearance, in Dell's *The Funnies* #30 (April 1939), in which the Barsoomian doings were presented in four- and eight-page continued episodes, based on the novels. The initial artist was Jim Gary, but after a few issues John Coleman Burroughs took over. *John Carter of Mars* ran until #56 (June 1941) and was replaced by *Captain Midnight*.

The younger Burroughs' work was better on the Sunday page, and John Carter was handsomer and a bit more Tarzan-like. Burroughs' whole extravagantly wacky version of life on Mars was transferred to the comics page, with no attempt to simplify things for newspaper readers unaccustomed to science fiction. This was the pure stuff of SF, with the lovely heroine named Dejah Thoris and not Dale Arden, with four-armed green warriors, woolas, calots, and even "the giant chicken men of Mars." A failure that ended early in 1943, it gave funny paper followers a taste of what real pulp magazine science fiction was like.

John Carter didn't return to comic books until 1952, two years after Edgar Rice Burroughs' death. Dell tried a comic book, again adapting the novels, with Jesse Marsh, longtime *Tarzan* comic book artist, doing the drawing. The book lasted for three issues, all of which were reprinted in 1964.

In 1972 DC tried Carter in *Weird Worlds*, with Murphy Anderson the initial artist. The hero held on for seven issues. Marvel took a turn in 1977 with *John Carter, Warlord of Mars*, on which Gil Kane led off as artist. The book lasted, in various formats, for a little over two years.

No one has ventured to Barsoom in comic books since then. **R.G.**

**JOHNNY HAZARD** This handsome adventure strip by Frank Robbins made its debut on June 5, 1944, one day before D day.

Late in 1943 King Features got in touch with Robbins, asking him if he'd like to take over *Secret Agent X-9*. Even though he was making only $125 a week drawing and writing *Scorchy Smith* for the Associated Press, he turned the offer down. What Robbins wanted to draw was a new strip of his own. "Several months later I brought in some examples of *Johnny Hazard*," he once explained. "We signed a contract and then began a long period of experimentation to get the characters set." Despite all the conferences, Johnny Hazard was pretty much Scorchy Smith under a new name—but that wasn't bad.

Robbins had made *Scorchy Smith* his own during his five-year stint, and his tough, wisecracking hero was closer to the street-smart characters played in the movies by John Garfield than he was to Charles Lindbergh, the original inspiration for Scorchy. Johnny Hazard in his early days was not long and lean, like a Caniff hero, but average in height and a bit on the chunky side—almost a working stiff, a proletarian type. "Johnny Hazard started off as an Air Force flying officer," Robbins said. "I had him escaping from a Nazi prison camp, stealing a bomber from a field and taking off amid gunfire." Things kept right on moving after that, especially when a blond and feisty lady combat photographer entered. Her name was Brandy, and she and Johnny started off disliking each other in a way that could only lead to romance.

The strip invaded China a few months later and, possibly at the suggestion of the syndicate, set up shop in *Terry and the Pirates* territory. Quite obviously what King Features was hoping for was their own version of Caniff's impressively successful strip. And Robbins looked to be the man to do it. He staged his action like the movies, and he had a lushly inked style, rich in black. He could draw anything that this sort of sophisticated contemporary adventure strip called for, and his dialogue, while not up to Caniff's, was good.

"After the war, I decided not to keep him in the service," Robbins said. "In the postwar years Hazard became a freelance, roaming the world. I had done a lot of reading of fiction. Adventure stories, science fiction…and apparently I had a feeling for the dramatic." What Robbins began turning out in those years immediately after the war were comic strip versions of the sort of adventure films being made at the time. It was a transitional period, where cynicism and hope mixed. Servicemen were becoming civilians again, many of them anxious not to get back into prewar ruts, and movie plots reflected that anxiety.

On the screen Alan Ladd, Dick Powell, and others appeared in movies about freelancing adventurers in odd corners of the world. Johnny moved around a lot, too, encountering crafty hustlers like Sidepocket Sam, sultry villainesses like Lady Mist, and flamboyant masterminds like Captain Gore. It was all fast-moving and enjoyable.

*Johnny Hazard* kept separate continuities going daily and Sunday, a device that allowed Robbins to put his hero in two exotic locales at once and have him mingle with at least two different exotic ladies. Over the years there were dozens of the latter—Velvet, Fern Frost, Sabina, Paradise, Kitty Hawke, and Baroness Flame among them. Haz' looks changed as the decades passed: He got leaner and taller and eventually he started to gray at the temples.

Although the strip fared better than most of the adventure strips launched during the postwar boom, it finally succumbed in August of 1977. On the last day of the final daily sequence, which involved the return of Baroness Flame, Johnny observed, "Guess the day of the he-man is finally *over!*" To which Robbins added—"And so an era passes…" **R.G.**

**JOHNNY THUNDER** DC's earliest mock superhero, Johnny Thunder got involved with thunderbolts at just about the same time Billy Batson (aka Captain Marvel) did. The consequences were even less serious. He debuted in *Flash Comics* #1 (January 1940) and was ousted from his own feature late in 1947 by a costumed lady crimefighter calling herself the Black Canary. His name was borrowed by a DC cowboy character from 1948 to the early 1960s and briefly by a lady adventurer in 1985.

His career got started under the name Johnny Thunderbolt (for the first few issues, the title of his adventures). John B. Wentworth, who also wrote more serious features such as *The Whip* and *Red, White and Blue*, provided the scripts, and Stan Aschmeier, under the pen name Stan Josephs, drew the pictures. They gave Johnny an origin that equaled that of any sobersided superman. Kidnapped as a small child, Johnny was taken to far-off Badhinisia, "thousands of miles away from the Bronx." There, for complex mystical reasons, he was endowed with the power of Cei-U, "which sounds in the American language like say-you." He eventually got home to the Bronx, unaware as he grew to manhood that whenever he uttered, "Say you," he gained for one hour the magic power to make his wishes reality. It took him quite some time, however, to figure this out, even though a huge zigzag of lightning struck every time he uttered the magical phrase. The grownup Johnny was a good-looking blond fellow, well-meaning but failure-prone, the sort of likable bumbler Danny Kaye would play in several 1940s movie comedies.

Wentworth seems to have been influenced in equal parts by pulp adventure stories and zany radio shows like *Vic and Sade*, and he clearly had a good deal of fun with Johnny's wishes. If our hero says, "Well, blow me down," somebody does; when he threatens to knock somebody into the middle of next week, that's exactly what happens, and everyone in the strip has to wait around until next week before they can continue with the story.

For a while Johnny worked as a G-Man and then decided to become "a mysterious avenger of righteousness like in the comic books." He even went so far as to fashion a costume, but he still had no control over his own abilities, and the superhero phase of his career didn't last long.

Finally, in *Flash* #11 (November 1940) the thunderbolt was depicted as a sort of humanoid figure, a guardian angel who popped in to carry out Johnny's wishes and get him out of the latest jam. It took Wentworth several issues to realize the potential of the new character. By mid-1941, however, the Thunderbolt was a full-fledged sidekick, making snide remarks and behaving like a sort of electrical Jeeves. And in *Flash* #20 (August 1941) Johnny at last realized the source of his power—"Those words Say You! When I say 'em, the bolt comes around!" Strangely enough, this new insight didn't change his life much, and he continued to be an amiable nitwit whose life wasn't much improved by the eventual adoption of a bratty orphan he called Peachy Pet.

During the war Johnny served in the Navy. In the postwar period, with new writers and artists, he became more serious. After he met the Black Canary his days were numbered, and with *Flash* #91 (January 1948) he retired. During his earlier heyday Johnny Thunder was also to be seen in *All Star Comics* and was a member of the otherwise serious Justice Society of America.			**R.G.**

**JOHNSON, CROCKETT** (1906–1975) Best known for his sophisticated fantasy strip *Barnaby*, Johnson enjoyed three separate careers in art from the 1930s till his death in 1975.

Born David Johnson Leisk in New York City, he studied art and typography at Cooper Union and worked as a magazine art director, freelancing advertising art and gag cartoons during the 1930s. From 1938 to 1940, *Collier's* carried his untitled feature, popularly called "The Little Man with the Eyes," depicting a man reacting to events only by minute changes in the expression of his eyes.

This economy of line also characterized the creation that was to make him famous, *Barnaby*, which first appeared in the highbrow newspaper *P.M.* on April 20, 1942. A strip of acerbic whimsy drawn with minimalist simplicity, *Barnaby* recounted the adventures of an engagingly realistic little boy and his inept, orotund fairy godfather, whose well-intentioned magic never worked out quite right. Witty and literate, it became the darling of intellectuals, and the collections published in 1942 and 1943 drew rapturous responses from leading artists and writers. It was distributed by the Chicago Sun (and later the Bell) Syndicate, but although it appeared in many forms—two hardcover books, a quarterly magazine, an animated film, a stage play, a radio series, a TV special, and a popular song—it never had a large audience, claiming a maximum of 52 U.S. papers and 12 overseas. Johnson found the strain of writing and drawing it too great and turned the strip over to a ghost team in 1946, acting as story consultant till he returned to write and draw the last episode and put it to sleep in 1952. He allowed it to be revived briefly in the 1960s, but had nothing to do with the drawing.

Johnson turned to his third and most lucrative career—writing and illustrating children's books—in the 1950s. His seven books about Harold, a Barnaby-clone who draws his own world with a purple crayon, were to become classics. In his last years he devoted himself to serious paintings of geometric abstractions, some of which have been acquired and displayed by General Electric and the Hall of Mathematics of the Smithsonian Institution in Washington. Johnson died of cancer in 1975.			**D.W.**

**JOHNSON, FERD** (1905–   ) A pioneer in the comic strip field, Ferd Johnson has been associated with *Moon Mullins* since 1923, two months after its debut, and has created several of his own strips during his nearly 80 years in cartooning.

Johnson was born in Spring Creek, Pennsylvania, to parents who supported his early taste for drawing by sending for the Landon correspondence course. When he justified his early promise by winning a competition in the *Erie Dispatch- Herald* at the age of 12, his father helped him pursue his career by subscribing to the Federal course. Johnson was the art editor of his high school, and after graduating in 1923 attended the Chicago Academy of Fine Arts. During that time his work caught the eye of Frank Willard, then teaching a course there while developing *Moon Mullins* for the *Chicago Tribune*. Willard invited the 17-year-old Johnson to visit the paper, and Johnson became such a regular guest that Willard hired him to color the Sunday strip and help with backgrounds and lettering. The $15 a week he got from Willard was supplemented by an additional $16 from the *Tribune* for coloring *Winnie Winkle* and *The Gumps*, at $8 each.

Johnson recalled years later that although he had almost no formal instruction in cartooning, he had had "the greatest teachers in the world" at the *Tribune;* among the people he worked with during those early years were Gaar Williams, Carl Ed (creator of *Harold Teen*), Frank King (of *Gasoline Alley*), Harold Gray (of *Little Orphan Annie*), Chester Gould (of *Dick Tracy*), Martin Branner (of *Winnie Winkle*), Sydney Smith (of *The Gumps*), Carey Orr, and John T. McCutcheon.

Johnson was kept to coloring, lettering, inking, and doing backgrounds on *Moon Mullins* for about 10 years before Willard let him work on characters, but in 1925 the *Tribune* invited him to do his own strip as well. *Texas Slim*, a broadly humorous Western series, began its Sunday run on August 30 and ran until early 1928. It was revived as an ancillary to Johnson's short-lived domestic comedy strip *Lovey Dovey* in 1932, ending when that strip ended after a few months, and reappeared as a half-page on March 31, 1940, under the title *Texas Slim and Dirty Dalton*. In its final form it lasted until 1958. *Texas Slim* was a lively feature about a cowboy-naif in Chicago, a sort of slapstick *Midnight Cowboy*, but in its later avatar its setting frequently shifted to the West, and the character of Dirty Dalton, Slim's musta-

chioed ranch-boss and antagonist, achieved equal status as a full partner in the strip and the title.

Johnson had been contributing gags to *Moon Mullins* since about 1943 ("when Willard became 50 years old," as Johnson recalls, "[and] said he'd had it, he couldn't think any more"), and, as Willard's health failed, assumed more of the duties of the strip. When Willard died in early 1958, Johnson took the strip over completely and began signing it. The added work load forced him to drop *Texas Slim*, which, he reports, "didn't amount to a hill of beans—maybe $200 a week."

In Johnson's hands, *Moon Mullins* became a tidier, crisper strip with a clean, firm line and simpler, less detailed compositions. Johnson kept the original six characters who define the strip and has added a few more to update it. His son Tom joined him as an assistant in 1958 and now does the Sunday page alone, but Ferd Johnson continues to write and draw the dailies with unflagging zest. **D.W.**

**JOHNSON, LYNN**   See FOR BETTER OR FOR WORSE.

**JOHN WEST**   Written and drawn by John J. Olson, the *John West* Sunday page began in April 1946. It dealt with the adventures of a young man in a small seaport town and was one of several features added to the Sunday comic section of the *Chicago Tribune* after the end of World War II (among the others were Richard M. Fletcher's *Surgeon Stone* and Art Huhta's *Wild Rose*).

Olson, who was to spend several decades as assistant and ghost on *Brenda Starr*, was an Indiana boy who had worked in the steel mills before attending art school in Chicago. He had been Ed Moore's assistant and then done a bit of comic book work on his own in the early 1940s. His *John West* started off as a sort of folksy small-town adventure strip, drawn in Olson's attractive variation of Moore's uncluttered style, but gradually both the artwork and the continuity changed. Olson began

*John West*, John J. Olson, © 1949, The Chicago Tribune.

drawing in a more illustrative style and experimenting with more sophisticated layouts, while his blond hero went from gawky youth to husky adult. There were some especially impressive sequences in which West went to sea with a marine salvage crew.

By 1949 another influence was in evidence: Olson had obviously fallen under the spell of Rockwell Kent's *Moby Dick* illustrations, and he turned out a handsome, modern day whaling sequence. He had also become intrigued by the increasingly popular young motion picture actor Robert Mitchum, and West came to look more and more like the sleepy-eyed movie maverick. Olson once said he felt the change in his hero's looks hadn't been wise. By the time readers began noticing the resemblance, Mitchum was getting in the headlines for his then unorthodox offscreen activities, and Olson believed that may have hastened the demise of the strip. By 1950 it was gone. **R.G.**

**JUMBO COMICS** One of the tabloid-sized magazines issued in the days before readers, distributors, and publishers had all agreed on the only acceptable size and shape for a comic book, *Jumbo* was Fiction House's earliest comic. The first issue was cover-dated September 1938, and it introduced Sheena the Queen of the Jungle to America.

*Jumbo Comics* recycled material created by the Eisner-Iger shop for an overseas tabloid called *Wags*. Mort Meskin drew *Sheena*, Jack Kirby provided *The Count of Monte Cristo*, and Eisner himself did *Hawks of the Seas*. By the fourth issue Lou Fine had replaced Kirby. All the material was in black and white, but printed on colored paper of various pale shades to liven things up. *Jumbo* #9 was a transition issue, and with #10 *Jumbo's* jumbo days were over, for the unwieldy tabloid size had proved unpopular with readers, possibly because the magazine wasn't always displayed with the other comic books.

The tab hadn't been popular in the past either. *The Funnies*, Dell's pioneering effort at a regularly issued original material comic, had appeared late in 1929, also in the tabloid format. It offered 16 pages and appeared weekly for the 36 issues of its life. Major Nicholson's *New Fun* came along in 1935 and tried tab-size for six issues; it then became *More Fun* and by #9 had shrunk down to the common size.

Undaunted, Fawcett experimented with the format in 1940 with *Master Comics*. The first three issues offered 48 pages, measuring 10¼ by 14 inches, and sold for 15 cents, while the next three dropped to 32 pages and 10 cents. With its seventh issue, *Master* became the same size as all the other comics on the stands, and its initial star, Masterman, "World's Greatest Hero," was replaced by Bulletman. **R.G.**

**JUNGLE JIM** Drawn by Alex Raymond, *Jungle Jim* began in January 1934 as a topper to his *Flash Gordon* Sunday page. It was syndicated by King Features and helped them to compete on a single page with both *Buck Rogers* and *Tarzan*.

It seems likely that several movies of the early 1930s served as at least part of the inspiration for the feature. In 1931 MGM released *Trader Horn*, an adventure film based on the less than veracious autobiography of an African explorer and trader. The following year came *Tarzan the Ape Man*, introducing Johnny Weismuller as Edgar Rice Burroughs' jungle lord. Also shown in 1932 was *Bring 'Em Back Alive*, a documentary about big game hunter Frank Buck's daring exploits in the Malayan jungles.

*Jungle Jim*, Paul Norris, © 1948, King Features Syndicate, Inc. Reprinted with special permission of King Features Syndicate, Inc.

Jungle Jim Bradley, whose usual outfit in his early years included pith helmet, riding breeches and holster, worked mostly in the Orient, in the jungles of places like Sumatra, Borneo, Malaya, and on many of the thousands of islands of the South Seas. He was aided by a sidekick named Kolu, who was initially his servant and called Jim "massah" and "tuan." Like Jim, the turbaned and barechested Kolu was an expert on jungle lore and tracking.

During his second year in business, Jungle Jim encountered Lilli deVrille, a femme fatale who reformed and became both "one of the best secret agents in China" and Jim's closest ladyfriend. Also inspired by the movies, Lil owed her looks to the type of shady lady Myrna Loy had been portraying on the screen in the early 1930s. Most of her original personality came directly from Shanghai Lily, the character played by Marlene Dietrich in the 1932 *Shanghai Express.*

Jim was wide-ranging in his talents and fairly soon he was being recruited for espionage assignments by the American government. "Your fame as a hunter and trapper is exceeded only by your reputation as a sort of jungle detective," the U.S. consul in Shanghai told him when assigning him a job as "a crusader for right against wrong."

*Jungle Jim* was written by Don Moore, the former pulp magazine editor who also scripted *Flash Gordon.* His copy, which usually appeared beneath the illustrations, did not exactly sing, and much of the prose seemed better suited to silent movie title cards. His sleazy villains addressed women captives with such lines as "I'm going to crush you 'till you grovel at my feet." And the captive women pleaded, "Oh, please—I beg of you—I implore you—Give me back my baby!—You couldn't be so cruel!" What saved the strip was the artwork.

Raymond had learned to depict jungle action while ghosting *Tim Tyler's Luck.* Ambitious to become an illustrator eventually, Raymond was strongly influenced by such slick magazine illustrators as Matt Clark. He became especially good at the dry brush technique then favored by many pulp magazine illustrators. At its best *Jungle Jim* was a handsomely done visual equivalent of a good, rousing pulp adventure yarn.

The size of the *Jungle Jim* topper fluctuated and by the late 1930s it was occupying a single tier, looking like a king-size daily. The continuities became somewhat more sophisticated as the feature grew smaller. The masked villains and tormented ladies gave way to slightly more subtle characters. Jim, now doing even more work for the U.S. government, was just as likely to appear in slacks and a tweedy sport jacket as he was to show up in sun helmet and jodphurs. Once America entered the Second World War, Jim became a captain in the Army. He operated pretty much as before, still aided by the loyal Kolu, fighting the Japanese instead of river pirates, slavers, and other freelance scoundrels.

Eventually Jim, in civvies, was assigned to work with the FBI. Just as Terry never ran out of pirates of various sorts, Jim had always found plenty of jungle in which to ply his trade. By 1944, however, he'd left the foliage behind and was to be found in such urban settings as Washington, D.C. Before he left the strip in the spring of that year, Raymond did some very impressive work. If Jim had donned a pair of glasses the strips could've served as tryouts for *Rip Kirby.* Lil and Jim parted for a while, because she'd enlisted in the Marines. Raymond became a Marine, too, and left the drawing board for the next two years.

After his departure Austin Briggs, his one-time assistant and the artist on the daily *Flash Gordon,* assumed the drawing of the *Flash Gordon* Sunday page. Since Briggs intended eventually to get back into magazine illustration, he never signed his work from this period. That fact, and a lack of visual acuity on the part of some historians, has led to Briggs' being credited with taking over *Jungle Jim* as well. He didn't, however, and after a few weeks of work turned out by the King bullpen, an artist named John Mayo took over. He was only moderately gifted.

In 1948 yet another artist was given the job and Jim entered the final phase of his career. Paul Norris, originally a protégé of Milton Caniff, had worked in comic books in the early Forties, cocreating Aquaman and drawing Sandman. He'd drawn the *Vic Jordan* newspaper strip before entering the service and after the war got a job in the King Features bullpen, ghosting the *Secret Agent X-9* strip and working on comic book versions of *Flash Gordon* and *Perry Mason.* He drew in a style that was an effective variation of Caniff's, and he improved the look of *Jungle Jim* considerably.

Jim, who'd long since ceased to be a neighbor of Flash's, was restored in 1949 to a two-tier Sunday strip again. Don Moore was, at long last, given credit for the writing. Once the Second World War had ended Jungle Jim had gone back into the woods. He spent the rest of his years exploring the jungle, contending with stubborn old scientists, headstrong heiresses, and traitorous guides. The strip, after a two decade trek, ended in the middle 1950s. **R.G.**

**JUSTICE LEAGUE OF AMERICA** In early 1960, with interest in superheroes growing again among comic book readers, National (DC) Comics editor Julius Schwartz launched a new version of the Justice Society of America. The members this time around were Superman, Batman, Flash, Green Lantern, Wonder Woman, Aquaman, and the Martian Manhunter; Green Arrow, the Atom, and Hawkman had joined by 1964. The writer was Gardner F. Fox (who had written the old JSA), the artist Mike Sekowsky.

The stories were unwieldy at first, as Fox attempted to use all his heroes in every adventure, but as he shifted to using just four or five heroes in each episode he turned in some of the cleverest and best-crafted plots of the Silver Age; this group-within-the-group strategy continues to be the standard approach to large hero-teams. Among the JLA's adventures were a series of annual team-ups with the Justice Society (and other Golden Age DC heroes), who lived on a parallel world, Earth-2. Earth-3, populated by villains, and then still more alternate Earths, were added later. (Such cross-overs in *JLA* and other series became increasingly numerous and confusing over the years, until DC felt compelled to press all the Earths into one in its *Crisis on Infinite Earths* maxi-series in 1984–1985).

In 1968, Fox left the series. He attributed his dismissal to his involvement in a push to win health insurance and other benefits for comic book writers and artists; Schwartz attributes it to the falling quality of Fox's work. He was replaced by young Denny O'Neil, who put some Marvel-style complexity into the heroes and gave the stories a more serious tone, even dabbling in political relevance. After him, in the 1970s, nearly every one of DC's writers zipped through *JLA's* pages, all working in more or less the same vein. Sekowsky left soon after Fox, replaced by the dependable but unremarkable Dick Dillin.

Sales on the once-popular title slowly declined until desperate measures were needed; in 1984 writer Gerry Conway and artist Paris Cullens scrapped nearly all the old heroes in favor of the likes of a super-breakdancer named Vibe and a lubricious animal-woman called Vixen. The measures didn't work, and the venerable series was soon canceled.

In 1987 it was replaced by *Justice League* (then *Justice League International*), starring Batman, Martian Manhunter, Green Lantern, Black Canary, Mr. Miracle, Captain Marvel (the old Fawcett hero), and Blue Beetle (an old Charlton hero newly acquired by DC). Plotted by Keith Giffen (one of DC's more popular artists) and scripted by J.M. DeMatteis, it took a campy, smart-alecky look at superheroes that readers found refreshing in the self-consciously grim world of mainstream 1980s comics. With clean, attractive art by Kevin Maguire, *Justice League* quickly became DC's best-selling title. A companion series, *Justice League Europe*, was added in 1989.

As a meeting-point for popular DC heroes, the JLA provides an interesting microcosm of DC history, from the light fun of the early 1960s to the revampings inspired by Marvel Comics, through the aimlessness of the 1970s to a fairly sophisticated, innovative twist on superhero clichés in the 1980s.       **G.J.**

**THE JUSTICE SOCIETY OF AMERICA**   The Justice Society was the very first superhero team in comics. It held its first meeting in *All Star* #3, which hit the stands late in 1940, although each of the individual members already led separate lives in various other DC comics titles, here they teamed up to tackle a specific criminal threat.

The *All Star* hero group was created by editor Sheldon Mayer and writer Gardner Fox. The idea that these assorted superheroes were chums and got together at their clubhouse had a special appeal to many young readers, and the magazine, which had begun as a quarterly, stepped up to bimonthly immediately after the launch of the JSA.

The founding members of the society included the Flash, the Spectre, Hawkman, Sandman, the Green Lantern, and Hour-Man; Superman and Batman were honorary members, apparently supportive but too busy to attend meetings regularly. The makeup of the group fluctuated as some characters went on to stardom and others waned in popularity. During the 11 years it was initially in existence the Justice Society had such names as Johnny Thunder, Dr. Mid-Nite, Wildcat, Starman, the Black Canary, and Wonder Woman on its roster. Wonder Woman also served as club secretary.

The JSA was "for America and democracy" and its members were avowed "foes of crime...enemies of evil." Since the organization was formed when America was on the brink of World War II, it fought subversion and sabotage as well as organized crime. The society's meeting room was spartan, consisting of a large blank-walled room and a round table. The JSA gathered there at the beginning of each issue to find out about the latest threat, be it a group of foreign saboteurs, the problem of starvation in Europe, or such master villains as the Brain Wave, Degaton or the Psycho-Pirate. Each member had a separate chapter in which to deal with one aspect of the problem, and at the book's end everybody gathered again at headquarters to tie up the loose ends. In early issues, though Fox scripted the whole book, the individual artists associated with the characters drew the chapters: Sheldon Moldoff did Hawkman, Bernard Baily the Spectre, Howard Sherman Dr. Fate, and so on.

In its 14th issue (December 1942) *All Star* announced the formation of the Junior Justice Society of America: "thousands of you all over the country asked for it, so here it is." The Jr. JSA was one of the classier comic book clubs of the Forties and seemed well worth the 15 cents initiation fee. Among the items sent out in the membership kit were a letter from Wonder Woman, a silver-plated metal JJSA badge (later replaced by a fabric sew-on emblem), a decoder with 13 different codes, and a patriotic four-page comic book story titled *Minute Man*. The four-color membership certificate had a somewhat more liberal tone than those of most of the other clubs and committed each member to a pledge to "help keep our country united in the face of enemy attempts to make us think we Americans are all different, because we are rich or poor; employer or worker; native or foreign-born; Gentile or Jew; Protestant or Catholic."

While several other publishers tried the notion of putting their most popular characters together in one anthology book—Marvel's *All Winners*, Fox' *Big 3*, etc.—the team idea itself wasn't immediately emulated. Not until 1946 did Marvel give it a try with its short-lived All Winners Squad, consisting of such as Captain America, Sub-Mariner, the Human Torch, and Miss America. *All Star* reached 57 issues before shutting down early in 1951, and the original JSA disbanded at that time. In later years, of course, the superhero team was to become a staple of the field, and even the Justice Society itself would make several comebacks. **R.G.**

**JUST KIDS** A gag strip that began in the early 1920s, *Just Kids* was offered by King Features and was a very close imitation of *Reg'lar Fellers*. It was done by Ad Carter, a jovial cartoonist who never learned to draw very well.

Arthur Daniels Carter (1894–1957) grew up in Baltimore. He dropped out of school, came to the New York area, and, after becoming a protégé of cartoonist Clare Briggs, got a job as a reporter on a Brooklyn newspaper. He first tried kid characters in the Teens, doing a short-lived strip titled *Our Friend Mush*, which mixed humor and boys adventure continuity, somewhat in the manner of Tom McNamara's *Us Boys*. In 1922 King took on *Just Kids*, which brought back Mush Stebbins from Carter's earlier strip and added his best pals Fatso Dolan and Pat Chan. In its early years the strip tried mightily—hampered only by Carter's limitations as writer and artist—to impersonate Gene Byrnes' successful *Reg'lar Fellers.*

Carter sedulously aped the other man, imitating even the houses with sharply slanting roofs that were a regular part of the *Reg'lar Fellers* backgrounds and the stylized lampposts that dotted the streets. His kids, like Byrnes', were continually in motion and leaving clouds of dust in their wake. Some readers of both strips must have gotten the impression that Mush Stebbins and Jimmy Dugan lived in the same small town and wondered why the two lads never bumped into each other. An apparently original touch of Carter's, though, was the eccentrics frequently glimpsed in the streets as the kids went rushing by—the mustachioed street cleaner who sang snatches of popular songs that often commented on the action of the day, the bewhiskered old gent who went rollerskating along carrying his baby grandson and exchanging bits of old vaudeville routines with the baby, and the like.

In the early 1930s, when adventure strips were blossoming, Carter returned to continuity. An early story, running for 12 weeks, had Mush and the gang befriending a circus bear and then running off with the circus. Subsequent continuities took them to a succession of exotic locales and involved them with crooks, madmen, and other villains.

The Sunday page continued to offer gags, pausing frequently for a sentimental page in which Mush expressed his deep love for his Mom. The topper for the Sunday was titled, for most of its life, *Nicodemus O'Malley and His Whale Palsy Walsy*. An odd, quiet fantasy, it dealt with a kid who traveled around the world on the back of his pet whale.

*Just Kids* ended in the middle 1950s. During its last days it was called *Mush Stebbins and His Sister*.

**W.D./R.G**

# K

**KAÄNGA** The hardiest Tarzan impersonator in Golden Age comic books, Kaänga was the king of his particular patch of jungle from 1940 until 1954. He debuted in Fiction House's *Jungle Comics* #1 (January 1940) and was a product of the Eisner-Iger shop. (Fiction House also published *Jumbo Comics*, where Sheena reigned as queen of the jungle.)

The blond Kaänga strongly resembled the blond Ki-Gor, who hung out in Fiction House's pulp fiction magazine *Jungle Stories*, which had begun in 1939. In Kaänga's origin story, drawn by Alex Blum, readers learned that he had been raised in the wilds by a friendly native tribe after his explorer father had been killed by an unfriendly native tribe. When full-grown he meets a young lady named Ann, who's visiting his domain with her explorer father. Ann teaches the noble savage to speak English and in tutoring her primitive man, she makes use of a grammatically correct version of Johnny Weismuller's famous movie-Tarzan line: "You Kaänga, I Ann." She remains in the jungle with him, becomes his mate and adapts as well as Tarzan's Jane, wearing costumes of nondescript animal skin at first but eventually switching to the more traditional leopard skin. (From the beginning Kaänga had appeared in leopard skin shorts on the magazine's covers, drawn initially by the formidable Lou Fine.)

The jungleman and his mate enjoyed adventures similar to those of their motion picture, pulp magazine, and comic strip counterparts, including encounters with evil white hunters, slavers, rampaging tribes, sinister witch doctors, lost civilizations, and meanminded jungle goddesses. This standardized fare was tarted up with story titles that were usually more exciting than the yarns that followed: *Terror Raid of the Congo Caesar, Scaly Guardians of Massacre Pool, Blood Raiders of the Tree-Trail*, and the like.

Undoubtedly one of the major appeals of the saga was the many sparsely clad women to be found among the foliage. Titles like *Jungle* appealed especially to adolescent boys and, during World War II, to a large serviceman audience. Kaänga's Ann rarely wore more than a leopard-spotted two-piece bathing suit and the majority of the other female denizens of the jungle didn't overdress either.

No matter who scripted the stories the pen name signed was usually Frank Riddell. A succession of uncredited artists, most of them quite capable, drew the feature, including George Tuska, Dan Zolnerowich, John Celardo, Reed Crandell, Reuben Moreira, and Maurice Whitman. Two of them, Moreira and Celardo went on to draw the *Tarzan* newspaper strip. It was said that Crandell was actually one of the artists United Features wanted for the *Tarzan* job, after seeing his uncredited work on *Kaänga*. But by the time they got around to contacting Fiction House and asking who was drawing the feature, Reuben Moreira had taken over. And that's how he got the job.

The final issue of *Jungle* was #163 and it hit the stands early in the summer of 1954. The jungle lord also appeared in 20 issues of his own quarterly from 1949 to 1954. He made a modest comeback in 1988, when the Blackthorne company tried a *Jungle Comics* revival.

**R.G.**

**KAHLES, CHARLES WILLIAM** (1878–1931) The creator of *Hairbreadth Harry*, Kahles was among the founding fathers of the American comic strip. He worked on over 20 strips in his lifetime, often doing several at once.

After education at Pratt Institute in Manhattan and Brooklyn Art School, he went to work in the 1890s as a news artist for papers that included the *New York World*, the *New York Recorder*, and *Grit*. From 1901 to 1905 Kahles found an outlet for his work with several syndicates.

Most of Kahles' earliest efforts were for Joseph Pulitzer's Press Publishing Company, for which he produced *The Butt-ins, The Terrible Twins*, and *Clarence the Cop*, a strip about a bumbling, catastrophe-prone flatfoot. At the *Philadelphia North American* Kahles invented the Jekyll-and-Hyde character Pretending Percy as well as *Sandy Highflyer*, the first aviation strip. *Sandy* premiered on May 25, 1902, over a year and a half before the Wright Brothers' first flight. Most of its episodes usually ended with a crash, but on occasion Sandy would round up air pirates or visit outer space.

For the *Philadelphia Press* Kahles created *The Merry Nobles Three, They Never Can Agree*, which featured visiting noblemen from England, France, and Germany who, as the title suggests, argued a great deal, usually about their countries' products and characteristics. In October 1906 came *Hairbreadth Harry*, Kahles' magnum opus.

For the next 24 years he dedicated most of his efforts to Harry but occasionally undertook other tasks. These included ghosting *Slim Jim* for World Color Printing in 1915 and their *Kelly Kids* series a few years later. He also contributed cartoons to *Life* and *Judge*. His death at middle age was attributed in part to overwork.     **M.J.**

**KANE, BOB** (1916–  )  He began drawing for comic books in the middle 1930s and did a variety of features, both serious and humorous, but Kane will always be best known for cocreating *Batman* in 1939.

Born in the Bronx, he studied at the Art Students League and Cooper Union. Kane began his professional career in 1936, drawing a funny feature for a short-lived comic book titled *Wow!* The editor was Jerry Iger and when the Eisner-Iger shop was formed the following year, the 21-year-old Kane was invited to join. He drew gag cartoons, under such titles as *Jest Laffs*, and a comedy-adventure strip called *Peter Pupp* for *Jumbo Comics*. In the Pupp feature, which was inspired by Floyd Gottfredson's *Mickey Mouse* newspaper strip, Kane first dealt with elements he'd be handling more seriously in *Batman*. Pete was a daring little fellow, and a typical four-page sequence had him going up in a fighter plane to combat a giant robot controlled by a satanic villain with one eye in the middle of his forehead. Kane also assisted Iger on *Bobby*, a kid filler page that ran in *Famous Funnies*.

His first sales to DC were also humorous, one- and two-page fillers. There were *Professor Doolittle*, a pantomime effort for *Adventure Comics*, *Ginger Snap*, about a wise little girl, for *More Fun*, and *Oscar the Gumshoe* for *Detective*. Kane also began trying his hand at more serious fare. In his entry in Jerry Bails' *Who's Who of American Comic Books* Kane listed the artists who had a major influence on him as Alex Raymond, Billy DeBeck, and Milton Caniff. His first serious feature, *Rusty and his Pals*, showed the Caniff influence. It started in *Adventure* in 1938 and dealt with three boys, Rusty, Specs, and Tubby, and their Pat Ryan-type mentor, Steve Carter. Like Caniff's Terry, Rusty and company tangled with pirates and sinister Orientals. Kane's drawing was cartoony on the early episodes, but he grew a bit more serious as *Rusty* progressed, even emulating Caniff's style of inking.

The scripts on his first adventurous ventures were provided by Kane's Bronx neighbor Bill Finger. Two years older than Kane and working as a shoe salesman, Finger was a dedicated reader of pulp fiction and a movie fan. After the two met at a party, they decided to collaborate. They also produced *Clip Carson*, which dealt with a soldier of fortune, for *Action Comics*. And for *Detective Comics*, starting in the spring of 1939, there was *Batman*.

Kane's early work on Batman had a distinctive look that fit the melodramatic nighttime in the big city stories he and Finger liked to tell. As his old high school chum, Will Eisner, had done, though on a smaller scale, Kane set up a shop of his own early on to meet the increasing demand for Batman and Robin material. Finger was the chief writer and youthful Jerry Robinson the chief assistant artist. Others who worked on the art over the years were George Roussos, Charlie Paris, Jack Burnley, Lew Schwartz, and Sheldon Moldoff.

Kane left comics in the late 1960s, about the same time that the *Batman* television show left the air. He has also been involved with TV animation—*Courageous Cat, Cool McCool*, etc.—and has dabbled in gallery painting of the pop art sort. He was associated with the phenomenally successful 1989 *Batman* movie in a public relations capacity.     **R.G.**

**KANE, GIL** (1926–  )  Kane first attracted fan attention in 1960 when he started drawing the new improved Green Lantern. A much admired and much copied comic book artist, he has been in the business since the early 1940s. In addition to the Green Lantern, he's drawn most of the major comic book heroes, including Batman, Superman, Conan, and Spider-Man.

He was born as Eli Katz in Latvia. "I was brought up in New York City," he's said. "I grew up feeding my imagination on the inspired work produced by my personal gods of that time—Hal Foster, Alex Raymond, and Milton Caniff." By his middle teens he was working in the comic book field, free-lancing and also working for the art shops of Jack Binder and then Bernard Baily. In 1947 editor Sheldon Mayer hired him to draw *Wildcat* in *Sensation Comics*. He went on to draw such cowboy creations as *Johnny Thunder, Hopalong Cassidy*, and *The Trigger Twins* for DC. He also participated in the revival of superheroes in the 1960s, drawing Green Lantern, the Atom, and the like. He next did a number of features for Tower's short-lived *Thunder Agents* titles. Kane had by this time at last worked out a style he was satisfied with and could build on. "Everything that had to do with understanding how things worked and what they looked like underneath" became something he became fascinated with. "And that for me became a point of view. I worked out of that attitude and I think it's made me what I am today."

Branching out, Kane moved to Marvel in the 1970s, drawing Spider-Man, Warlock, Conan, Kazar. He was also their top cover artist. In the early 1980s he was back again with DC, drawing the Superman annuals, *Sword of the Atom*, and quite a few covers. He also drew the *Star Hawks* newspaper strip, which started its four-year run in 1977 and during part of that time he did the *Tarzan* Sunday page as well.

In the middle 1980s he moved to Southern California and continued doing work for DC off and on. He got into television animation, designing the characters for the most recent *Superman* Saturday morning show. Kane still draws occasional comic books and late in 1989 DC began to publish his four-part miniseries adapting Wagner's *Ring* into graphic novel format.          **R.G.**

**THE KATZENJAMMER KIDS** Originated by Rudolph Dirks, this historically important strip premiered on Sunday, December 12, 1897. It featured the everyday affairs of a German-American Mamma and her incorrigible twin sons, Hans and Fritz. The concept is a direct descendant of similar characters, *Max und Moritz*, who enjoyed widespread popularity in 19th-century Germany. Literally "the howling of cats," *katzenjammer* is colloquial German for a hangover.

In the words of their creator, himself of German birth, "Rudolph Block, comics editor of the *New York Journal*, asked me to draw a strip emulating the work of Wilhelm Busch, whose drawings of children had been popular for more than 40 years. I submitted a number of sketches from which emerged the two kids which Editor Block christened the Katzenjammer Kids." The resulting innovative feature is widely regarded as the first true comic strip. While the point can be argued, there is little doubt that the format and conventions introduced or developed by Dirks with *The Katzenjammer Kids* set a pattern that has continued to influence its successors to this day.

Hans and Fritz took the practical joke, as well as downright meanness, and raised it to an art. Tranquility was their nemesis, and they delighted in putting it to rout. No trick or prank, however outrageous, escaped their scheming genius. With the appearance of that old seadog, the Captain, on August 31, 1902, Dirks began assembling the cast of players that would transform the strip from one of simple household violence into an adventure series that would usher its modest German-American characters around the world. The Captain, who was neither Mamma's husband nor the father of Hans and Fritz, became the central figure and the chief target of the terrible twins' trickery.

Many of the Captain's old seafaring pals, particularly the rogue, Long John Silver, and his companions, the Herring Boys, would figure into future plots and serve as a persistent point of tension between Mamma's desire for domesticity and the Captain's wanderlust. Who could blame him, when hardly a week went by without a firecracker under the seat cushion or a water hose in the face of a distinguished visitor? In truth, the Captain was something of a hero. No other character in all of fiction endured such an avalanche of indignity.

The other major cast member, "der Inspector," first appeared on January 15, 1905. He is not an inspector in the normal sense but, rather, an officer of the school system. A sidekick who shared in the loafing and playing of pinochle, the Inspector became a kind of Hans to the Captain's Fritz. They were gentlemen who shared a world view, a duo who would react to the shenanigans of the day with empathy for each other. Indeed, they occasionally conspired to seek revenge on little Hans and Fritz. Yet, just as Hans and Fritz could occasionally turn on each other, so, too, did the Captain and the Inspector. At such times the Captain became a "fat stuff" and the Inspector a "shrimper." They also share another curious characteristic—neither is ever addressed by name.

In 1913, at a time when the *Journal*'s owner, William Randolph Hearst, was engaged in a pitched battle with the rival *New York World*, Dirks and Hearst had a falling out. When the smoke cleared, Harold Knerr became the new artist on *The Katzenjammer Kids*, and his brilliant stewardship would last for 35 years. Dirks, meantime, took his characters but not his title elsewhere.

In response to the First World War and resulting anti-German emotions, the title was changed to *The Shenanigan Kids* in June 1918; the family's origin was changed to Holland and the boy's names became Mike and Aleck. It would be nearly two years before it became acceptable to be German again, and the strip reverted to *The Katzenjammer Kids* in April 1920. A daily version entitled *The Katzies* began running on June 4, 1917. It lasted for several years, first by uncredited artists, later from the pen of Oscar Hitt, a onetime Dirks assistant. Knerr, by the way, didn't agree with Dirks as to the Kids' first names. In the Dirks' version the blond twin was Fritz and the dark-haired one was Hans; Knerr, for some reason, reversed that.

It's a popular misconception that the adventures of the Katzenjammer family took place exclusively in some jungle location that may or may not have been in Africa. To the contrary, their adventures, at least in the early years, were not nearly so mono-dimensional. Between 1915 and 1935, Knerr escorted his troops to many exotic locations: They visited the Grand Canyon (1915), sojourned in Panama a bare three years after the opening of the canal (1916), operated a circus in Peru (1917–1918), visited the Amazon (1925–1926), and even pursued adventures in the frozen Arctic (1919–1931). (The episode of October 5, 1930, discloses Hans and Fritz were enrolled in North Pole District School No. 1.) Many adventures at sea were interspersed. Indeed, during the entire first 20 years of Knerr's duty only a little over two years of the family's adventures took place in the Squee-Jee Islands of Africa.

In addition to their travels, the family engaged in a number of business enterprises. In 1920, the Captain began operating the Katzenjammer Moving Picture Studio, and in 1923 he ran the Katzenjammer Department Store. Following the reappearance of Long John Silver in 1924, the family left the "compartment store" business to set sail once more, this time in search of gold in Mexico. Hans and Fritz put "the compass on the bum" and they never reached their destination.

It was not until 1936, when meanminded little Rollo Rhubarb, his teacher Miss Twiddle, and her niece Lena were introduced, that the strip took up permanent residence in the Squee-Jee Islands. Miss Twiddle filled the role of righteous indignation, and Lena was mostly an astonished bystander or, early on, the object of one of the boys' affections. Her oft-declared "He brought it on himself, Miss Twiddle!" entered the vernacular. The beleaguered Captain had suffered too long to maintain any sense of surprise at the boys' outrageous antics— "Alvays it iss like diss"—and poor gullible Mamma was oblivious to the mayhem all around. Thus, the comic came full circle, abandoning world travel and returning to a somewhat repetitive pattern of domestic mischief.

After the death of Knerr, the Katzenjammer Kids passed into the hands of Doc Winner, Joe Musial, and several others. Though severely restricted, and with limited exposure, it continues to this day, written and drawn by Hy Eisman, more than 90 years after its creation stirred a revolution in the world of popular entertainment.  **J.L.**

**KEANE, BIL**  See THE FAMILY CIRCUS.

**KEATON, RUSSELL** (1910–1945)  In his short lifetime Keaton drew three major features: *Buck Rogers*, *Skyroads*, and *Flyin' Jenny*. He became a professional cartoonist while still in his teens, and his work was seen in newspapers from 1929 until his death in 1945.

Keaton—his nickname was Buster—left his hometown of Corinth, Mississippi, in the late 1920s and came to Chicago to study art. Fresh out of school he was hired by Dick Calkins, as was another young cartoonist named Zack Mosley. The two young men did most of the drawing on the *Skyroads* aviation adventure strip that Calkins was signing his name to, and Keaton alone did all the drawing on the *Buck Rogers* Sunday page Calkins was taking credit for. Keaton seems to have been a natural-born artist, and his work on the *Buck Rogers* Sundays in the early 1930s was considerably better than anything his employer could do. Without doubt Keaton's Sunday pages contributed a good deal

to the initial success of *Buck Rogers*. After leaving the feature, he took over *Skyroads* and was allowed to sign it.

Like several other strip artists of the Chicago area, he had developed a style that was an attractive blend of the cartoony and the illustrative. And his handling of air adventure material was an effective alternative to the more realistic approach of the gifted Noel Sickles.

Keaton finally got a strip of his own when *Flyin' Jenny* began late in 1939. His interest in planes had by this time gone beyond the drawing board, and when his lady aviator made her debut Keaton was only a few hours of flying time away from getting his own pilot's license.

When he sold *Jenny* to the Bell Syndicate he was living again in Corinth. Early in 1945 he entered the hospital for what was expected to be a short stay. But Keaton turned out to have a very rapidly progressing cancer. He died on February 13, 1945, at the age of 35.  **R.G.**

**KELLY, WALT** (1913–1973)  A cartoonist and humorist of considerable talent, Kelly created *Pogo*. He used his own personal version of the Okefenokee Swamp as a slapstick wonderland and populated it with a wild array of talking, and often wisecracking, animals. He also drew for comic books, worked in animation for Disney, and served for a time as a political cartoonist.

Walter Crawford Kelly was born in Philadelphia and moved to Bridgeport, Connecticut, in 1915 along with, as he put it, "father, mother, sister and sixteen teeth, all his own." The desire to be an artist hit him in childhood and, while in high school, he drew not only for the school paper and yearbook but for the local newspaper as well. One of the things he drew for the paper was a biographical comic strip about P.T. Barnum, a flamboyant character he remained fond of all his life. In the middle 1930s young Kelly sold a bit of work to the fledgling comic books. For Major Nicholson's *New Comics* he did a few centerspreads, based on such works as *Gulliver's Travels*. *Funny Pages* ran two examples of *Can-*

Walt Kelly, Self Portrait, 1961.

*nonball Jones*, about a fellow who was trying to get back to nature. Not particularly amusing or well-done, these were probably samples of an unsold comic strip.

He next headed for Southern California, where he got a job working, as he said, "for Walt Disney while that worthy and 1500 other worthies turned out *Snow White, Fantasia, Dumbo* and *The Reluctant Dragon*. At a showing of the last he quietly disappeared and next showed up on the Mojave Desert trudging East." Kelly, who'd been criticized by some of the 1,500 worthies for crossing the picket line during the Disney studio strike of 1941, may also have felt that working conditions would be more healthful elsewhere. In Manhattan he found work with Western Publishing, who were producing the comic books that carried the Dell imprint. Editor Oskar Lebeck hired him to write and draw a large number of stories for *Animal Comics, Our Gang, Fairy Tale Parade, Raggedy Ann & Andy*, and *Santa Claus Funnies*, magazines primarily aimed at very young readers. Kept out of the service by health problems, Kelly also illustrated a series of books for the Foreign Language Unit of the Army—books designed to provide soldiers in foreign countries with sufficient language skills to communicate.

While some of Kelly's work for kids was cute and gently amusing, he also turned out a more hard-boiled brand of stuff, sort of roughhouse Disney. One such feature was *Seaman Sy Wheeler*, which ran in *Camp Comics* and offered raucous humor and even had its characters dressing up in drag now and then. Kelly also let loose in *Pat, Patsy and Pete*, a screwball saga that starred a pair of real kids, a talking penguin, and a short-tempered pirate named Percy. It appeared in *Looney Tunes*, where he drew six episodes in 1943. Moving away from what his predecessors had done, Kelly turned the feature into a series of slapstick comedies. Percy was a violent yet lovable rascal with a distinctive speech pattern: "Blow me down! It's November an' time for me annual bath!" In the yarn about Percy's bath Kelly managed to include crabs in the bathwater, nudity, collapsing chimneys, sundry other mock violence, and a few digs at Christmas and Santa Claus. At one point sweet little Patsy took off after Percy with a blunderbuss loaded with small cannonballs, crying, "Some dirty ol' geezer is tryin' to steal our chimney!" Chimneys fascinated Kelly and he used them, and their collapsing, more than once.

It was in the pages of *Animal Comics* in 1942 that Kelly first introduced Pogo, Albert the Alligator, and the other swamp characters that would bring him fame and fortune. In 1948 he was hired to draw political cartoons for the *New York Star*, a new and liberal paper. Kelly drew his first version of *Pogo* as a newspaper strip for the ill-fated and short-lived *Star*. In 1949 *Pogo* began national syndication.

Kelly served as president of the National Cartoonists Society and often appeared in public promotions of Pogo and cartooning in general. He even sang on the recording of *Songs of the Pogo*. A hard drinker and a great fan of saloon life, Kelly died of the complications of diabetes. **M.T./R.G.**

**KEN STUART** He was an outdoor hero of an aquatic bent, and he first sailed into view in the autumn of 1947. *Ken Stuart*, a daily strip, was written and drawn by Frank Borth and distributed by the Frank Jay Markey Syndicate, pretty much a one- man operation.

Borth, born in 1918, had worked in comic books in the early 1940s, first out of the Jacquet shop and then on his own, drawing such features as *Captain Battle, Spider Widow*, and *Phantom Lady*. Markey, an executive with the McNaught Syndicate, had also distributed several noble failures in the late 1930s and early 1940s through his own small subsidiary operation, including Rube Goldberg's *Lala Palooza*, Ed Wheelan's *Big Top*, and Boody Rogers' *Sparky Watts*.

Ken Stuart was based in Montauk Point, New York, "a narrow finger of land pointing the way to the open sea and adventure!" He operated a charter boat, a two-masted schooner called the *Barracuda*. He and his crew dealt with buried treasure, pirates, leftover Nazis, an assortment of lovely ladies, and a lost city in the jungle.

Borth had spent his first summer out of the service in Montauk, which had revived an earlier interest in boating and sailing and started him thinking that they would be good topic for an adventure strip. He was, he once explained, "following the lead of Milton Caniff," and hoping for that kind of success.

Markey was the syndicate's only salesman, and he was able to place *Ken Stuart* in several papers up and down the East Coast. "But we couldn't get the damn thing inland," Borth once said. During 1950, when he and the syndicate realized it had reached its peak, they decided to end it. Borth felt, "I spent too much time on the art and not enough on the story…The pen is mightier than the sword, but I forgot that the pen was used to write with first, then draw." Despite his dissatisfaction, *Ken Stuart* was a well-drawn and attractive adventure strip, one that might have, with a larger syndicate, done as well as *Mark Trail*. **R.G.**

**KENT, JACK** (1920–1985) With no formal training in art, Jack Kent began to sell gag cartoons to such national magazines as *Collier's* at the age of 15. He was born in Burlington, Iowa, but his family moved frequently when he was young, and he spent his adolescence in Chicago. After a stint in the Army from 1941 to 1945, he worked as a moderately successful free-lance artist, and dreamed of creating a comic strip like that of his hero

*King Aroo*, Jack Kent, © 1952.

George Herriman's *Krazy Kat*. At the age of 30, in November 1950, he succeeded in selling the McClure Syndicate his *King Aroo*.

This daily and Sunday strip, with its sensitive and literate whimsy, was to establish Kent's reputation as one of the most sophisticated cartoonists in the literature. Sweet-tempered but never sentimental, it recounted the adventures of the diminutive and not very regal King of Myopia and his improbable associates. Its witty wordplay and absurd stories had a limited appeal (its largest circulation was reported to be no more than 100 papers), but it inspired fierce personal loyalty among its fans, and when McClure finally canceled it, the *San Francisco Chronicle* maintained it alone until the paper's editor created Golden Gate Features to syndicate it. But the devotion of its select audience was not enough, and *King Aroo* was dropped in November 1965, after a 15-year reign that established it as a small, recherché classic among comics. A collection was published in 1952 by Doubleday.

Once more Kent returned to free-lance cartooning, selling advertising art and gag cartoons to a wide range of magazines ("from *Humpty Dumpty* to *Playboy*," the artist recalled) and greeting card designs to Hallmark. It was not until 1968, three years after the demise of his strip, that Kent found the métier that was to reach a wide public and grant him his first taste of financial security. In that year he published his first self-illustrated children's book, *Just Only John*, which won an award from the Chicago Graphics Association and sold 400,000 copies. For the remaining 16 years of his life, Kent produced books for young readers and pre-readers. In all, he wrote and illustrated 39 and illustrated 22 by others. Many of his books received awards (*Jack Kent's Happy-Ever-After Book* was named Outstanding Picture Book of the Year by the *New York Times* in 1976, and the Texas Institute of Letters honored Kent twice, consecutively, in 1983 and 1984); his books were selected frequently by book clubs and several were re-corded. Translations of Kent's books have been published in 15 languages.

Kent's loose, graceful art, as droll and imaginative as his characters and stories, remained remarkably constant throughout his career, retaining the same flowing line and expressive features from his early cartoons through the years of *King Aroo* to his children's-book illustrations. Perfectly fitted in spirit to his texts, whether comic strip or fable, his cheerfully slapdash style contributed to a harmonious whole that places Jack Kent among the best-loved cartoonists in American history. **D.W.**

**KERRY DRAKE** The *Kerry Drake* strip, daily and Sunday, was one of *Dick Tracy's* most formidable rivals for most of its four-decade run. It started in 1943 and ended in 1983, and during much of that time Alfred Andriola took sole credit for the feature.

In the initial sequences, Kerry Drake's occupation is somewhat vague, but promotional material described him as "a keen-witted, cotton-topped private investigator who is attached to the staff of the district attorney." He operated out of his own office and had a pretty secretary, Sandy Burns, and a redheaded office boy known as Firetop. Eventually Drake lost his private status and worked directly for the DA, and after the murder in the early 1950s of Sandy—by then his fiancée—Drake became a police detective. Gradually the strip moved closer to soap opera: Drake married in 1958, became the father of quadruplets in 1967, and along the way discovered he had a detective brother named Lefty. The personal problems of the silver-haired detective and his kith and kin became as important as the nabbing of criminals. "Now my characters look and act," said Andriola of these changes, "much more like everyday people."

Andriola told about the birth of the strip many times during his lifetime. "I was approached by Publishers Syndicate to take over their *Dan Dunn* strip," he once explained. "I said I was only interested in starting a detective character of my own." A compromise was reached and "if I finished their existing contracts on newspapers with *Dunn*, I could concurrently work on my own character." Dan was sent off to war on Sunday, October 3, 1943, and the next day *Kerry Drake* began appearing in his slot. Andriola said he enjoyed doing both the detective strips, but favored *Kerry Drake*, "who, after all, was my creation."

Allen Saunders, longtime scriptwriter on *Mary Worth* and *Steve Roper*, gave a different account of the conception and birth of the silver-haired sleuth. "Eventually, to avoid possible steps by [Norman] Marsh to recover his abandoned property [*Dunn*], it was decided to substitute in client papers an entirely new strip, *Kerry Drake*. In 1943 this step was taken, with the loss of very few papers. As an artist partner I was teamed with Alfred Andriola, a Greenwich Village resident." Saunders did not find the relationship especially pleasant. "Andriola demanded credit for the writing as well as the art work and in all publicity identified himself as the sole creator of *Drake*. We differed often on plots and dialogue, exchanging argumentative letters or wrangling over the phone."

Despite a less than harmonious team, the strip was a first-rate one in its early years. The Andriola version of the Caniff style, achieved with the help of a variety of assistants and ghosts, was attractive and made the new strip look considerably more sophisticated than any of its older cops and robbers competitors. Saunders' continuities, using villains that now and then must have made Chester Gould a shade envious—Fingers, No Face, Dr. Zero, Bottleneck, Stitches, Mother Whistler—were good. Saunders also knew how to build suspense just about as well as anybody in the business.

Among the artists who drew the strip over the years were Fran Matera and Jerry Robinson. In October of 1955 Sururi Gumen went to work for Andriola, penciling and inking *Kerry Drake*, and, except for time out to ghost Andriola's *It's Me, Dilly!*, Gumen drew the *Drake* strip for the rest of its life. In the early years of Gumen's employment Andriola took care of coloring the Sunday page and inked all heads and hands. From late 1975 onward Gumen did everything in the drawing department, and early in 1976, after threatening to quit, he was allowed to sign his work along with Andriola.

When Andriola died in 1983, his syndicate decided to end the strip.                                                        **R.G.**

**KETCHAM, HANK** (1920– )  The creator of *Dennis the Menace* was born in Seattle, Washington, and attended the University of Washington there in 1938, but his education in art began with a job in film animation the next year. He worked in Hollywood at Walter Lantz

Productions of Universal Studios for a time, and later moved to Walt Disney Productions, contributing to *Pinocchio* and *Fantasia.*

The son and grandson of naval officers, Henry King Ketcham joined the navy in 1941 and for the next four years was chief photographic specialist of the United States Naval Reserve in Washington, D.C. At the same time, he wrote and drew a comic strip named *Half Hitch* about a hapless little sailor—a sort of naval Sad Sack—for the camp newspaper.

For three years after the war, Ketcham free-lanced gag cartoons and advertising art from his home in Westport, Connecticut, making the rounds in New York City with his sketches. In 1948 he moved to California, where he developed the idea of the panel series *Dennis the Menace*, based on his four-year-old son Dennis. Donald Hall, who had just started the Post-Hall Syndicate and was looking for new material, saw his roughs in October 1950 and offered him a contract. In March of the next year, the feature debuted in 18 papers, and the towheaded whirlwind of energy was on his way to becoming an American institution and a part of the national vocabulary. The innocently mischievous Dennis Mitchell and his bewildered family earned Ketcham the first Billy DeBeck Award (later renamed the Reuben) as Outstanding Cartoonist of the Year from the National Cartoonists Society in 1952 and the Silver T-Square Award in 1978.

Ketcham's first wife Alice, the model for Dennis' cartoon mother Alice Mitchell, died in 1958, and Ketcham remarried and moved to Switzerland. He remained in Geneva for the next 18 years, continuing (with the help of "a great memory and a Sears Roebuck catalog" for reference) to draw his warm, affectionate vignettes of a cozy middle-American family and their energetic child. During that time he also wrote a humorous travel book about a trip he had taken to Russia (*I Wanna Go Home*, McGraw-Hill, 1959), and from 1970 to 1975 he brought back *Half Hitch* as a daily and Sunday feature, drawn by Dick Hodgins and distributed by King Features Syndicate. In 1970, Ketcham married for a third time, and eight years later returned with his wife to California so their two young children could attend American schools.

After more than a third of a century, the indefatigable little mischief maker continues to occupy much of Ketcham's time, and the artist admits to having wearied of the daily demands the feature makes on him. Two assistants now draw the Sunday strip and take care of the numerous books Dennis generates, and Ketcham has expressed the hope of one day turning the whole industry he has created over to them. "As a matter of fact," he reported in 1986, "I've been getting more grumpy as the years tick by and often yearn for freedom. Time to travel, to write, to golf, to develop other properties, to goof off." **D.W.**

## KEVIN THE BOLD

One of the relatively few historical adventure strips, *Kevin the Bold* started on October 11, 1950; a Sunday page, it was drawn by Kreigh Collins and syndicated by NEA. While no match for *Prince Valiant*, it lasted for close to 20 years.

*Kevin* had developed out of Collins' earlier Sunday page, a contemporary adventure feature titled *Mitzi McCoy*. Kevin was a handsome fellow and an Irish ancestor of Mitzi's, who, when first encountered, was employed as a shepherd late in the 15th century. Over the next few years he worked his way up the social ladder and was eventually hobnobbing with King Henry VIII and serving him as a sort of early 16th century James Bond.

An experienced magazine illustrator, Collins turned out an attractive page: All the villains were properly costumed, the wenches were appropriately saucy, the princesses disdainful, and all the other personages and props just right for this sort of swashbuckling saga. Since Collins was interested in ships and sailing, many of Kevin's boldest adventures took place at sea.

In the final years of the feature, the scripts were provided by NEA stalwart Russ Winterbotham. By 1969 *Kevin the Bold* was gone, replaced by yet another Collins page, a modern-day seafaring strip called *Up Anchor*. **R.G.**

## THE KIN-DER-KIDS

When the *Chicago Tribune* undertook, in 1906, to raise the tone of its Sunday comic section, its editor James Keeley called on 35-year-old Lyonel Feininger to contribute a strip that might rival the already celebrated *Katzenjammer Kids*, begun nine years before in Hearst's *New York Journal*. The result was *The Kin-der-Kids*, whose redundant name (*kinder* is the German word for "kids") clearly echoed Rudolph Dirks' title, but whose kids were nothing at all like the formidable Hans and Fritz, or, indeed, like anyone else before or since.

Feininger, who was born in New York but educated in Germany, was beginning to make his mark as a serious painter and illustrator in Europe when the offer came, but he accepted it with gusto and carried it out with a manic imagination for which nothing in his more ambitious work would prepare us. The *Tribune* proudly introduced the Sunday feature as by "Feininger the Famous German Artist" on April 29, 1906.

At the center of the strip's cast were the grotesque Kin-der-Kids themselves: the pompous Daniel Webster, who wore an undertaker's crêpe-ribboned hat and was always engrossed in a book; Strenuous Teddy, who could break chains with his biceps and whose knowl-

edge of jiu-jitsu enabled him to best whole teams of strong men; and the gluttonous Pie-Mouth, who ate so continuously that at one point he became a perfect sphere and had to be rolled like a ball. Accompanying them were an emaciated dachshund named Sherlock Bones and an Oriental wind-up toy, the "Clockwork Waterbaby," named Japanski.

There was little coherence in the story of *The Kin-der-Kids*, but a tenuous thread of continuity linked its 31, rather self-consciously fanciful weekly installments. Putting to sea in a bathtub, the Kids are pursued by Aunt Jim-Jam, a sepulchral lady whose elongated face and weird triangular body might give anyone the jim-jams and whose only goal in life appeared to be to dose everyone with castor oil. Their episodic adventures take them to England, where everyone speaks Feininger's notion of Cockney, and they are captured by broadly caricatured Russians who add "-off," "-ovich," or "-ski" to most of their words.

As surreal in look as in content, *The Kin-der-Kids* was clearly the work of an original and highly inventive artist. The sense of design, which Feininger was to display as an abstractionist and influential instructor at Germany's Bauhaus School, is as clearly present in the strip, and in his later strip *Wee Willie Winkie's World*, as in the paintings now hanging in major museums around the world. The story, such as it was, made little sense, but the bizarre graphic style could not fail to fascinate the *Tribune's* readers, and it was due to a financial, rather than to an aesthetic, disagreement between the artist and the newspaper that it was discontinued, after less than seven months, on November 18, 1906. *The Kin-der-Kids* remains one of the most interesting experiments in the early days of the new medium and was reprinted in its skimpy entirety by Dover Press in 1980. **D.W.**

## KING, FRANK

(1883–1969) Best-known as the creator of *Gasoline Alley*, the man who would be the first to make comic strip characters age was born in Cashton, Wisconsin, and grew up in nearby Tomah. After high school, King spent four years on newspapers in Minneapolis and then studied for two years at the Chicago Academy of Fine Arts while working Saturdays at the *Chicago American*. Following a short stint at an advertising agency, he joined the art department at the *Chicago Examiner* for three years.

In 1909, King deserted to the *Chicago Tribune* for a better salary, and in 1911, he started doing a daily cartoon feature called *Motorcycle Mike* and a Sunday color comics page, *Bobby Make Believe*. Later King filled in briefly for John T. McCutcheon when the *Tribune's* celebrated front-page editorial cartoonist went to Europe to reconnoiter the outbreak of war there. In addition to his Sunday color strip, King was doing a black-and-white Sunday feature—a miscellaneous collection of topical cartoons grouped together in the embrace of a single large panel called "The Rectangle." There, on November 24, 1918, King introduced a new cartoon department about automobiles. "Cars had character in those days," King said once, "and there was plenty to discuss." And plenty of interest in the subject and King's treatment of it: In eight months, *Gasoline Alley* had outgrown "The Rectangle" and was a daily feature all by itself, and King had found his life's work.

King's graphic style was not particularly distinguished—pedestrian linework embellished with routine cross-hatching and shading—but it was thoroughly competent and perfectly suited to the unpretentious, homey, everyday preoccupations of the strip. In the daily strips, King seemed quite content to watch his characters grow older and explore the everyday concerns of small-town America. But on the Sunday pages in the Thirties, his graphic imagination bubbled to the top, and he produced some of the most inventive strips in the history of cartooning. Once Walt and Skeezix strolled through a countryside of modern German expressionism; another time, they walked through a woodcut autumn. And once King drew a full-page bird's-eye view of the Wallet neighborhood, and then, by imposing the usual grid of panel borders on the scene, he created 12 independent vignettes. The result was a portrait of backyard society in double-exposure. Overall, the page showed us the geography of the neighborhood while the characters in actions and words in each panel enacted the life of that neighborhood.

But King made his mark in comic strip history not with such rare, spectacular displays but through the more mundane device of aging his characters, which is a shorthand way of referring to the life he breathed into them, life that seemed real to readers and built a devoted readership that followed the strip even after King died—no small accomplishment.                R.C.H.

**KING AROO** An engaging blend of childlike fantasy and literate wordplay, *King Aroo* ascended the throne in November 1950, and immediately captured the hearts of a small but devoted public. The McClure Syndicate distributed the daily and Sunday strip for a time, but never to more than 100 papers, and finally dropped it. So great was the loyalty it inspired, however, that one paper, the *San Francisco Chronicle*, sustained it alone and even established a syndicate for it. But to no avail; in 1965 the King tearfully abdicated.

Written and drawn by gag-cartoonist, and later successful children's book writer, Jack Kent, *King Aroo* was one of the rare "intellectual" strips that appealed as much to children, who loved its absurd stories and endearing characters, as to adults, who relished its verbal ingenuity, literate allusions, and often astonishingly subtle perceptions. *King Aroo* was imbued with a tender and playful spirit, its humor springing only from its creator's gentle love of nonsense. Frequently the action is propelled by wordplay: The literal interpretation of a phrase will send the characters off on mad tangents. The line between art and reality is straddled and crossed so often that the distinction disappears, as when a character trips on one of the "perspective lines" (they are in the strip, another explains, "to give the illusion of depth") and becomes so entangled in it he has to be cut loose.

The modest monarch of Myopia enjoys the complete devotion and most cordial companionship of his subjects, human, animal, and unspecified. His circle includes Prof. Yorgle, the top-hatted resident scholar who is a man except for an interlude when he accidentally becomes a seal; Yupyop, the King's advisor-cum-housekeeper-cum-guardian; Mr. Pennipost, a kangaroo plausibly employed as the national mailman since he has a built-in pouch; the court poet Dipody Distich, who seems to be more or less a duck; and the forgetful Mr. Elephant, who can never remember what he is. The problems of Myopia don't go very deep. Wanda Witch, who pitches her spells rather than casting them, often misses her target since her arm is rusty, and Drexel Dragon needs a furnace repairman when his fire goes out; but no one suffers much, or for long, in this enchanted nonsense land.

Gracefully drawn with loose, flowing strokes, *King Aroo*'s squashy little characters are perfectly adapted to the merry, warmhearted whimsy of its text. It was very much in keeping with the spirit of its fifteen-year run that the artist signed the last panel, on June 14, 1965, "With all my love, Jack Kent."                D.W.

**KING OF THE ROYAL MOUNTED** Although technically a "Northern" rather than a Western, the strip nonetheless had most of the trappings of cowboy adventure—including blazing six-guns, galloping outlaws, and a hero on horseback. *King of the Royal Mounted* began in February of 1935, with artwork by Allen Dean and continuity attributed to best-selling Western novelist Zane Grey. Originally a Sunday only, a daily was added in March of the following year.

Stephen Slesinger, a pioneering comic strip packager, had been contemplating a strip about the Royal Canadian Mounted Police for quite a while before he sold *King* to King Features. He'd approached other writers to lend their names, among them the then popular outdoor adventure author Rex Beach. He was finally able to interest Grey, whose son Romer had a hand in the actual writing of the new feature.

It's possible that one of Slesinger's sources of inspiration was a Canadian newspaper strip titled *Men of the Mounted,* written by Ted McCall, drawn by Harry Hall, and syndicated from the *Toronto Telegram.* A daily, it ran from February 13, 1933, to February 16, 1935 and featured a different hero for each story sequence, one of whom was a Corporal King. Whitman Publishing, with whom Slesinger had had a long affiliation, reprinted *Men of the Mounted* in this country in a 1934 Big Little Book, and King Feature's King, also a corporal in his first months, began his career the day after the Canadian strip ended.

Allen Dean, who drew in a passable version of the drybrush style then popular in pulp magazine illustration, worked directly for Slesinger. Unfortunately, his staging was unimaginative, and his work had a monotonous sameness. He could never master the strip's greatest drawing challenge, King's low-crown, widebrim hat, and he gave up the Sunday page in 1936 and the whole job early in 1938. Charles Flanders, who was working right there in the King Features bullpen, took over, doing an attractive job until he switched horsemen and assumed *The Lone Ranger.* Jim Gary became the artist in April 1939, working in a style that was somewhere between that of Alex Raymond and Milton Caniff.

Although Sergeant King was as dedicated as any RCM policeman when it came to getting his man, some of the men he got during the Jim Gary years were a cut above the villainous trappers and crazed Indians most fictional Mounties went after. King chased a deranged doctor who dressed up in a winged suit and called himself the Black Bat, a tonsured inventor who prowled the coastal waters of British Columbia in a mysterious submarine, a homicidal acrobat, a hooded terror, and a lady Robin Hood. In the majority of his cases he was accompanied by a boy called Kid. The feature ended in March 1955.                                                **R.G.**

**KIRBY, JACK** (1917–  )  Next to Superman, Kirby is probably the most important figure in the history of comic books. In the business from the late 1930s, he changed the look of comic books and gave them a vocabulary of their own. He discovered that he was telling stories in a medium that was different than newspaper strips. He broke up pages in new ways, for example, introducing innovative splash panels that stretched across two pages. And he made sure they moved, since he felt he was competing with the movies. During his long career he took part in creating such characters as Captain America, Spider-Man, the Fantastic Four, the Boy Commandos, the Young Allies, the Hulk, Sgt. Fury, and the Silver Surfer.

He was born Jacob Kurtzberg on New York's Lower East Side. It was a tough area to grow up in, and Kirby, a lifelong movie fan, has described his neighborhood as "Edward G. Robinson territory." He read a lot; the novels of H.G. Wells and Edgar Rice Burroughs were among his favorites. Kirby was drawing from childhood and "I drew my first cartoons for the weekly newsletter of…a club for the underprivileged." In 1935 he was hired by the Fleischer animation studios, then located on Broadway in New York City, and worked as an in-betweener on the *Popeye* cartoons. "The pay was steady, the work was lousy," he's said. "You sat at a table surrounded by rows and rows of other tables, 300 people. I thought of my father's garment shop. And I thought of Chester Gould breaking the mold with *Dick Tracy,* and my idol, my art school, Milton Caniff with *Terry and the Pirates.* I got impatient."

By 1937 his impatience had taken him to a shoestring syndicate called Lincoln Features, run by a third rate cartoonist named H.T. Elmo. This outfit supplied strips and panels to several hundred small-town weekly newspapers. Kirby drew political cartoons, true fact panels, and almost a half-dozen comic strips. Some were drawn in an imitation Alex Raymond fashion, others in a rough version of the later Kirby style. Among them were the adventure strips *Detective Riley, Cyclone Burke,* and *The Black Buccaneer* and the humor strips *Socko the Seadog* and *Abdul Jones.* They were drawn in daily strip format, even though they ran only once a week. To a couple of the features he signed the name Jack Curtiss.

He used the name Jack Curtiss, and two other pen names, when he broke into comic books. His first work appeared in *Jumbo Comics,* originally a tabloid-size publication, in the summer of 1938. Kirby did *The Count of Monte Cristo, The Diary of Dr. Hayward,* and *Wilton of the West.* At just about the same time, for another low budget syndicate, he drew a strip titled *The Lone Rider,* a fairly close imitation of the radio hero the Lone Ranger, using the name Lance Kirby. And in 1940 he combined two of his earlier aliases and was Jack Kirby from then on.

From the late 1930s on Kirby concentrated on comic books, since the pay was better. He drew one more comic strip in 1940, though, doing a *Blue Beetle* daily for several months. BB was a leading character in the Fox line of comic books. Though his earliest comic book work was done alone, Kirby's best-known features of the 1940s were done in collaboration with Joe Simon. They first worked together, with Kirby penciling and Simon inking, on the superhero Blue Bolt. They next teamed on Marvel Boy, Captain America, the Young

Allies (which they invented but didn't draw), the Boy Commandos, the Newsboy Legion, Sandman, and Manhunter. Their work in the decade, especially on Captain America, established a style that many subsequent Marvel artists have followed. There was a freshness and energy to Kirby's pencils. His characters moved—sometimes clean out of the panels—and when they exchanged punches the reader practically felt them. Kirby's fight scenes combined the violent with the lyrical, a mixing of wrestling and ballet that worked.

After World War II, Simon and Kirby turned to true crime comic books and Westerns, and they also came up with the first love comic book, *Young Romance*. In the 1950s Kirby went out on his own. Working with editor-writer Stan Lee he came up with the Fantastic Four, Thor, the Hulk, and the Avengers. The blend of explosive fantasy and operatic heroics established by Kirby and Lee was the foundation of Marvel's vastly increased popularity and sales from the 1960s onward.

When Kirby left Marvel in the early 1970s, he went back over to DC to draw and write his Fourth World series. This was a complicated undertaking and included such titles as *The New Gods* and *Forever People* and made use of Kirby's bravura drawing and his personal punchy cosmology. In more recent years he's worked in animation, drawn for independent publishers on such titles as *Captain Victory* and *Destroyer Duck*. For a brief time he returned yet again to DC for one more try at his Fourth World series.                **R.G.**

**KNERR, HAROLD H.** (1882–1949) A quiet, reserved cartoonist, Knerr plotted wild and destructive mischief for over 30 years. He began drawing the Hearst version of *The Katzenjammer Kids* in 1914 and remained on the job for the rest of his life.

The son of a German physician, Knerr studied art for two years in Philadelphia and got his start as a newspaper cartoonist just after the turn of the century. "My first newspaper work was drawing pictures of gravestones atop the oldest graves in a local cemetery for the *Philadelphia Record*," he once said. "These were paid for at the fee of three dollars each." Knerr moved from tombstones to comics and between 1903 and 1914 he drew several Sunday page features for the *Philadelphia Inquirer* and the *Ledger*. These included *Mr. George and Wife, Scary William, Zoo-Illogical Snapshots,* and *Die Fineheimer Twins*, the latter being a close imitation of Rudolph Dirks' Katzenjammers.

When William Randolph Hearst won his legal battle against Dirks over ownership of the Katzenjammers, he turned to Knerr on the assumption that a man who could ape the Hans and Fritz page could also draw the real thing. Starting on November 29, 1914, Knerr be-

came one of the most successful stepfathers ever to adopt another man's creation.

In his youth Knerr had fallen in love with aviation. As he once recalled, "We young chaps in Philadelphia had some of the first gliders in the country. They were…attached by ropes to automobiles. We would swing into them, using our bodies to balance the planes, and fly like kites when the automobiles speeded up." Aeronautics became a familiar theme in stories as Knerr led the Katzenjammer family through many fantastic adventures, from the tropics to the arctic. He also had an interest in things mechanical, filling his pages with all sorts of infernal machines and engines of destruction.

As an artist he was a master of the cartoony style. His drawings were soft and round, a characteristic that gave them a special warmth and appeal. His funny animals were particularly noteworthy, and in 1926 he added *Mr. Dinglehoofer and his Dog* as a topper to the Kid page.

Knerr never married and spent his last years in a hotel apartment in New York City. He died there alone of a heart attack.                **J.L.**

**KNIGHT, CLAYTON**   See ACE DRUMMOND.

**KNIGHT, TACK** (1895–1976) Though seldom mentioned in histories of comics, Tack Knight had a varied and influential career. He ghosted *Reg'lar Fellers* during its most popular years in the 1920s, drew newspaper strips of his own, contributed to one of the earliest comic books and authored a book on cartooning that stayed in print for several decades.

Born Benjamin Thackston Knight in North Carolina, he picked up the Tack nickname as a kid. When he was 14 he sold his first cartoon to a local paper. He "drifted to San Francisco in 1913" and, after studying art there for a year, got a job doing sports cartoons for the *Oakland Tribune* across the Bay. He next worked in animation in San Francisco and Los Angeles and during World War I served in the Navy.

In 1923, without that many credits but with considerable audacity, he issued an instruction book titled *Tack's Cartoon Tips*. Selling originally for 50 cents, the small, straightforward instruction book went into seven printings over the years and, according to Bob Dunn, helped him and such fellow artists as Vernon Greene and Hank Ketcham learn cartooning in their youths.

The next year Knight heard that cartoonist Gene Byrnes, vacationing in nearby Carmel, was in need of an assistant. Using his cartoon book as a portfolio, he got the job and spent most of the rest of the decade ghosting *Reg'lar Fellers*. The looks of the kid strip improved considerably during those years, most of which Knight spent in the New York City area. When *The Funnies*, Dell's original material, tabloid-size comic book started late in 1928, he was one of the contributors. He drew two kid features, *My Big Brudder* and *Peaches.* Late in 1929 he had a meeting with Captain Patterson of the Chicago Tribune-New York News Syndicate. The captain wanted a Gene Byrnes sort of strip, and Knight obliged with *Little Folks.*

The strip, daily and Sunday, began in 1930. It was nearly a dead ringer for *Reg'lar Fellers*, except that there were three girl regulars in the gang, a higher percentage of females than could be seen in the rival strip. The public, though, was apparently not in the mood for yet another gang of comic kids in those early years of the Depression, and *Little Folks* ended in 1933. Knight retained ownership of the characters and, living again in California, used them in advertising strips for several West Coast accounts.

During the remainder of the 1930s Knight returned to animation, working for both Walt Disney and the Fleischer brothers. In the early days of television he did a cartoon show for a San Francisco station. He settled into semi-retirement while in his late fifties. For the rest of his long life he was active in the National Cartoonists Society and local cartoonists groups.    **R.G.**

**KOTZKY, ALEX** (1923– )  A professional cartoonist since his teens, Kotzky has worked in comic books, comic strips, and commercial art. He has drawn such comic book heroes as Plastic Man, Sandman, Johnny Quick, and Blackhawk, and worked on the Spirit, too. Since 1961, he has drawn the *Apartment 3-G* soap opera strip.

Born in Manhattan, he attended the High School of Music & Art and spent some time at the Art Students League in 1941. His first comic book work, done while still in school, was in collaboration with Chad Grothkopf on several DC features—*Three Aces, Johnny Quick, Sandman*, among them. He next assisted Will Eisner on his weekly *Spirit* insert and drew a variety of features, including *Blackhawk* and *Espionage*, for the Quality line of comic books. He did covers for them, too. At that point Kotzky was drawing in a straight, heroic style somewhat akin to the bravura approach of Lou Fine.

In the fall of 1943, "I was invited to vacation with the U.S. Army." Returning to civilian life early in 1946, Kotzky again drew for Quality. He had a lighter style now and his main job was drawing Plastic Man. He also worked with Jack Cole, an influence on his drawing at the time, on some true crime comic books.

As the comic book business started to falter in the early 1950s, Kotzky moved into advertising and joined the staff of Johnstone & Cushing, who specialized in newspaper ad strips. Among those he drew was *Duke Handy*, which starred a two-fisted, redheaded hero who

smoked Phillip Morris cigarettes. Allen Saunders, who wrote *Mary Worth* and *Steve Roper*, provided the scripts. Kotzky did some ghosting of newspaper strips in the 1950s, too, notably on *Steve Canyon.*

His work came to the attention of Publishers Syndicate, possibly by way of Saunders, and he was asked to draw Nick Dallis' newest soaper, *Apartment 3-G.* The strip debuted on May 8, 1961, and Kotzky has remained close to his drawing board ever since. "My ambition," he once said, "is to find a quicker way to draw my strip and take a 3 day vacation." He draws in a much slicker style now, but his work has a personal look and his staging is highly effective.    **R.G.**

**KRAZY KAT**  In the first panel of the strip an open-faced, potbellied cat was sitting in the middle of the desert. The cat said, "I got no figga, no face, no fortune. Nor purse, poise or position." In the next panel the cat was still sitting on the same log but the desert background had shifted. "And yet. He's true by me. Why should I complain?" A scratchy and dissolute mouse appeared now behind the cat to let fly with a large brick. As the brick hit the cat with a pow, the cat exclaimed, "L'il dollink." In the final scene a large, authoritarian bulldog policeman dragged the mouse off to jail. "Is there anybody," asked the love-stunned cat, gazing fondly at the departing mouse, "in this woil more constint than him?" And the cop replied, "There sure is." That was one day in the lives of the ambiguous trio who starred in *Krazy Kat*, and for over 30 years Krazy, Ignatz Mouse, and Officer Pupp concerned themselves with brick throwing. The creator of the Kat was George Herriman, who, by switching the usual cat and mouse relationship and adding a brickbat, produced a complex and cockeyed allegory of love.

*Krazy Kat* was born during the years that Herriman worked for the *New York Journal.* The Kat first appeared in *The Dingbat Family*, which started in June 1910. Eventually a mouse showed up, and a reverse cat and mouse game began to take place underfoot in the Dingbat saga. Krazy and Ignatz were soon appearing in a small, separate strip under the Dingbats. The early encounters between the two were fairly simple, and at that time Krazy didn't enjoy the brick at all. Gradually Ignatz and Krazy took to holding conversations, and a Mutt and Jeff relationship developed. Herriman tried out a *Krazy Kat and I. Mouse* strip briefly in 1912 and in October of 1913 launched a completely independent *Krazy Kat* daily.

The family lasted until January of 1916, and in April of that year a *Krazy Kat* Sunday page was begun. By that time Herriman had relocated Krazy, Ignatz, and the rest of his cast in Coconino, and the feature has just about achieved its ultimate form. There is a real Coconino

*Krazy Kat*, George Herriman, © 1928, King Features Syndicate, Inc. Reprinted with special permission of King Features Syndicate, Inc.

County in Arizona; it's Navajo country and the home of the Grand Canyon, the Painted Desert, and Monument Valley. John Ford looked at the same landscape and was inspired to make John Wayne movies there. Herriman filled his strip with rocks and mesas, cactus, joshua trees, but he also threw in fireplugs, lampposts, and other urban props. His Coconino was always in flux, his backgrounds shifting from panel to panel. In this restless atmosphere lived Krazy, Ignatz, and Officer Pupp. Other inhabitants were Mock Duck, Walter Cephus Austridge, Mrs. Kwakk Wakk, Don Kiyote and Sancho Pansy, Gooseberry Sprig the Duck Duke, Mrs. Ignatz Mouse and the Mouse boys, Milton, Marshall, and Irving, and Kollin Kelly the brick dealer.

The lives of the three main characters revolved around the brick. Ignatz lived to throw it, Krazy loved to get hit by it, and Officer Pupp was dedicated to stopping the brick. The singleminded Ignatz haunted Kelly's brick yard, and if bricks were absolutely unobtainable, he creased the Kat's bean with cobblestones, snowballs, boards, watermelons, bathtubs, and grandfather clocks. A master tactician, he was capable of setting up elaborate plans so that he could get at Krazy with a brick. He'd wait all day up in a tree or climb a mountain. Krazy always interpreted the brick as a token of love and affection. On being hit by a brick, Krazy would exclaim, "Oy, a message of love," or, "L'il ainjill, no matta where I'm at his love will find me out."

Krazy was an optimist and, like all cats, curious. He often sang a song that began, "There is a heppy land, fur fur away." Herriman reacted to Krazy the same way many people do to cats, and he was never sure what sex it was. Krazy was sometimes a female, sometimes male, and there were even strips where Krazy starts out she and ends up he.

Officer Pupp began life as a free-lance civilian bulldog. After a time he was put on the police force, and he eventually became Coconino County's entire law and order force. In his early days he sometimes revealed his dog nature openly—when under pressure he would drop to all fours and run. He overcame this at last and took to walking only on his hind legs and radiating a kind of paunchy dignity. Pupp loved Krazy and was in awe of her eccentricities. Though his love was unrequited, he spent most of his time around Krazy, his excuse being that he was protecting her from Ignatz. Officer Pupp's obsession didn't interfere with his police duties, since Ignatz was just about the only criminal in Coconino.

Next to the brickbat Herriman's most frequent prop was the one he called the bundle. On the Enchanted Mesa lived Joe Stork, and his preoccupation was the delivering of bundles. He favored dropping a bundle down a chimney. Though Herriman labeled the stork the "purveyor of progeny to prince and proletariat," the higher class citizens went to great lengths to avoid the bundle. They hid in storm cellars, kicked the stork off their roofs, or simply attempted to outrun him.

A distinctive feature of the strip was the language. Herriman developed as a creator at a time when there was considerable preoccupation with the American language and its variations. In *Krazy Kat* he made use of slang, Yiddish, Victorian rhetoric, Elizabethan stage dialogue, and his own whims. The most complex mixture was in the speech of Krazy himself, where there were traces of Dickens, the Bronx, Shakespeare, the Deep South, and George Herriman. "Like a flet-iron my heart is warm again for 'Ignatz Mice,' l'il ainjil," remarked Krazy after Ignatz had dumped a hod of hot bricks on him. In explaining Ignatz' soul Krazy said, "And so, 'Offissa Pupp,' you & me gotta be werra watchful, & wigilint around the unlimitless etha, and from roaming around unfeathered, & loosely, y'understand?"

Officer Pupp had originally spoken like a stock Irish cop, but several years in the hot Coconino sun caused him to develop a style of speech that mixed flowery phrases with slang. Pupp was capable of flights like "I have long had much to tell that dear 'Kat'—words my too timid lips could not utter," And also, "Better git y'self over to the clink." Ignatz spoke a similar mixture, a blend of stage villain and Bowery lowlife. Such as "I realize the error of my ways, and so, contrite and humble, I promise to toss no more 'bricks' at that Krazy Kat's dome."

The Kat had some champions in its day. In 1924, for instance, Gilbert Seldes gave it a whole chapter in *The Seven Lively Arts*, calling it one of the highest achievements of American popular art and ranking Herriman with Chaplin. None of its partisans over the years agreed on what the strip was about exactly. Some found it a parable of love, others a symbolic presentation of the conflict between the individual and society. A case can even be made for interpreting Ignatz' brick throwing and Krazy's reaction to it as a charade of the sex act.

Newspaper readers were often mystified as to what Krazy was up to. The strip was never appreciated by the majority of newspaper readers, and compared to many of the other strips syndicated by Hearst's King Features it was never much of a success. When Herriman died in 1944, Krazy Kat was allowed to end. While this has sometimes been interpreted as a gesture that recognized the artist's unique genius, it was actually because King didn't think the strip was worth continuing. **R.G.**

**KRIGSTEIN, BERNARD** (1919–1990) Krigstein's earliest comic book work, influenced by Simon and Kirby, was for *Prize Comics*. In the late Forties and early Fifties he worked for many comics outfits, producing, particularly at Hillman, some fine illustration. However, Krigstein's stature as a comics artist is chiefly measured by his brief tenure at EC in 1954–1955, where he did fewer than 50 stories for their crime, horror, and science fiction comics, and for *Valor* and other "New Direction" titles.

Inspired by the atmosphere of artistic freedom fostered by publisher William Gaines and the above average scripts, Krigstein brought new and visually striking techniques to comics story telling. He adapted his style to the story that he was telling: twisted expressionistic figures and distorted shadows for "You, Murderer," about an evil hypnotist; a clean, contemporary, angular look for murder in suburbia in "More Blessed to Give…"; shadowy, sketchy images for Johnny Craig's "Pipe Dream," set in a Chinese opium den; the influence of classic Oriental prints for Ray Bradbury's parable of ancient China, "The Flying Machine"; formal caricature for a story in *Mad*. Chafing at the prelettered boards that EC gave its artists, Krigstein began to draw two and more pictures where one was intended. When editor Feldstein gave him a story about a New York subway rider whose past as a concentration camp commandant is revealed by a chance recognition, Krigstein was so impressed that he asked permission to expand the story by two pages. He cut up the lettering and completely redesigned the story, climaxing it with a practically wordless page breaking down into 11 panels the character's fall under the wheels of the subway. This most famous page from "Master Race," his best known story (which has been frequently reprinted), has given Krigstein the reputation of being excessively concerned with depicting the breakdown of small moments of time; in fact, his use of this technique was infrequent. Unlike countless other comics artists, who have thought of comics as movies on paper, Krigstein sought his inspiration in illustration and fine art. "The panel has to exist by itself, otherwise the integrity of the art is in jeopardy," he said. "Only when the artist realizes that a single panel is a work of art that exists as a statement that can live by itself can all the panels live together."

After the demise of EC, Krigstein continued briefly in comics at Atlas, where he did a few extreme experiments in breakdown; one four-page story had 73 panels. He then switched to commercial illustration, appearing in prestige markets like *Harpers* and *American Heritage*. Ultimately, he found the commercial art field frustrating and switched to teaching painting at New York's High School of Art and Design. After retiring he continued to paint prolifically until his death. **J.B.**

**KUBERT, JOE** (1926– ) A professional since his early teens, Kubert has been in the comic book business for over 50 years. During that time he has drawn everything from superheroes to cowboys to horror tales; among the many characters he's drawn are *Hawkman*,

*The Vigilante, Sgt. Rock, The Black Cat, Tor*, and *Tarzan*. He's worked on comic strips, is the coinventor of the 3-D comic book and the founder of his own art school.

He was born in Brooklyn and attended the High School of Music and Art in New York City. In 1939 he started working as a sort of apprentice at the art shop run by Harry "A" Chesler. At 16 he was drawing for *Smash Comics, Speed Comics*, and *Police Comics*. He also inked the work of Jack Kirby, Lou Fine, and Mort Meskin, a task that contributed to his own education. Coming to the notice of editor Sheldon Mayer in 1944, he was given Hawkman to draw for *Flash Comics*. During his first stay with DC Kubert drew the Flash, Dr. Fate, the Vigilante, and Sargon the Sorcerer. His drawing style in the 1940s had a highly individual look. While his figure work wasn't yet perfect, his staging and depiction of action were impressive and he had a feel for fantasy.

In the Army in the early 1950s, he returned to comics and free-lanced for a wide range of publishers. In the middle 1950s, working with his longtime friend and associate Norman Maurer, he worked out the process that led to the 3-D comic book. During its brief boom he contributed to *Mighty Mouse, Tor*, and other three-dimensional titles.

He returned to DC in the 1960s, remaining there ever since. He did Hawkman once again and then moved into more realistic areas with the World War II hero Sgt. Rock in *Our Army At War* and the World War I German aviator Enemy Ace in *Star-Spangled War Stories*. When DC took over Tarzan in 1972, Kubert was the first man to draw it. In recent years he has concentrated more on editing and on running the Joe Kubert School of Cartoon and Graphic Art, Inc., in New Jersey. He still does some impressive covers for DC and an occasional story. Two of his sons are also in the comic book business.

In 1966 Kubert entered the newspaper strip field with *Tales of the Green Beret*. A great many people weren't in the mood for a strip about the Vietnam war at that point in history and, sensing the thing wouldn't last, Kubert left it after a year. Briefly in 1981 he and some of his pupils drew the *Winnie Winkle* strip. **R.G.**

**KUDZU** An amiable gag strip with flashes of both poignance and cutting social satire, Doug Marlette's *Kudzu* began syndication by Tribune Media Services as a daily on June 15, and as a Sunday strip on June 21, 1981. Its hapless title character, named for the rank weed spreading uncontrollably throughout the South, is a wistful adolescent trying to grow up in Bypass, North Carolina. Blending something of Al Capp's rural Candide, *L'il Abner*, and Garry Trudeau's perceptive loser, *Doonesbury, Kudzu* endures all the pain and humiliation of adolescence with a wry grace that is both touching and very funny.

Doug Marlette, the Pulitzer-prizewinning editorial cartoonist of *New York Newsday*, admits that the strip is autobiographical. "I knew what it was like to grow up in small Southern towns," he reports. "I knew what it was like to be an unsuccessful adolescent." His engaging hero, Kudzu Dubose, is recognizable to anyone who has suffered the same experience, and surrounding him is an ironic chorus of equally recognizable types: his possessive Mama, who always remembers her phlebitis just before he introduces the subject of leaving home; his dream girl Verandah, who sends him printed rejection slips in response to his passionate poems; Uncle Dub, "the Grand Old Man of Good Ol' Boys"; Kudzu's parakeet Doris, who endures an uncontrollable passion for chocolate; his black chum Maurice, whose clear vision balances Kudzu's starry-eyed dreams; Nasal T. Lardbottom III, world-class wimp, who holds a black-and-blue belt in wimp fu, the ancient Oriental art of giving up; and the sanctimonious and ambitious town preacher, a televangelist with presidential aspirations, Rev. Will B. Dunn.

Drawn in a clean, simple style with a minimum of clutter and with invariably pleasing compositions, *Kudzu* captures the spirit of adolescence and of rural life without condescension or sentimentality, and often addresses larger social issues with the same biting wit Marlette shows in his political cartoons.

In 1988, Marlette transferred the distribution of *Kudzu*, along with that of his editorial cartoons, to Creators Syndicate. The strip runs in over 150 newspapers around the world and has been collected into several volumes, four of them dealing with the popular character of the preacher Will B. Dunn. *Kudzu* is being considered for a live-action television series and is beginning to be merchandised on several other fronts. **D.W.**

**KUHN, CHARLES** (1892–1989) Already noted as a political cartoonist, Charles Kuhn reached a new and wider audience with the syndicated humor strip *Grandma* which he originated in 1947 and wrote and drew for the 22 years of its run. Kuhn was born in the small midwestern town of Prairie City, Illinois, and began placing drawings in newspapers and magazines while still a boy, (He claims that his first sale, for 50 cents, came at the age of 12 and determined him to become a cartoonist and a millionaire.) In 1913 he attended the Chicago Academy of Fine Arts, where he studied cartooning with Frank King, creator of *Gasoline Alley*.

Kuhn drew cartoons in Chicago and secured a full-time job as editorial cartoonist with the *Rocky Mountain News* in Denver around 1920. When noted cartoonist Gaar Williams left his post at the *Indianapolis News* to join the *Chicago Tribune*, two years later, he proposed

Kuhn as his replacement, and Kuhn held the job of editorial cartoonist with the *News* for the next 26 years. A skilled artist with pen and ink whose graceful, neatly detailed drawings were expressive without being grotesque, he presented balanced comments on the local, national, and world scene with wry but good-natured wit.

Never limited to the editorial cartoon as a medium, Kuhn drew humorous panels from the beginning of his career, and during his long professional life produced many different comic features. While with the *Indianapolis News* he tried several strips, and in 1947 sold *Grandma*—a robust humor series featuring a waggish and vigorous old woman and a gang of little boys she palled around with—to the Richardson Feature Service of Indianapolis. Initially he signed the strip with the pen name Harris.

*Grandma* was the first of Kuhn's non-editorial efforts in art to meet with any real popular success, and he began to devote more of his time to it. "As she began to roll," he reported. "I left editorial cartooning for the comic strips and have never been sorry." *Grandma* remained with Richardson until King Features Syndicate took it over, distributing the daily strip from June 28, 1948, and adding a Sunday feature on November 20, 1949. In 1964 Kuhn moved to Florida "to catch up on fishing and loafing," and retired *Grandma* in 1969.  **R.G.**

**KURTZMAN, HARVEY** (1924– ) A topseeded humorist for many years, Kurtzman has functioned as a cartoonist, writer, and editor. His many creations include *Mad*, *Help!*, *Frontline Combat*, and *Little Annie Fanny*.

Kurtzman was born in New York and was working in comic books before he was out of his teens. He drew such second banana superheroes as Magno and Lash Lightning and did humor fillers for magazines like *Police Comics.* None of it was drawn in the bold, quirky style now associated with him. In 1945, after leaving the service, he formed an art studio with his old friend Will Elder and a third partner named Charlie Stern. Kurtzman began working in his distinctive humorous style at that period. He did a series of one-pagers titled *Hey Look!*, which ran in assorted Marvel titles. Drawn in a loose, thick-outlined way, the pages were wild and violent. Working in a similar style, Kurtzman did *Silver Linings* for the *New York Herald Tribune.* Drawn in daily strip format, it nevertheless ran in color in Sunday comic sections.

In 1950 he took a job with William Gaines' EC company, which eventually resulted in his editing and drawing for *Frontline Combat* and *Two-Fisted Tales.* Everything in these basically antiwar war comics was thoroughly researched, and Kurtzman's own stories had a grim, stark look that was anything but gung ho. He thought up *Mad* in 1952 and convinced Gaines to add it to the EC lineup. *Mad*, a sort of a graphic version of a college humor magazine, was a hit almost from the beginning and is still flourishing. Kurtzman left it soon after it turned from comic book to magazine format in 1955. He next edited and contributed to *Trump, Humbug*, and *Help!* While all were admirable humor magazines, none repeated *Mad*'s success. He also began drawing and writing, with considerable help from friends like Elder and Russ Heath, *Little Annie Fanny* for *Playboy*, which started in the early 1960s and lasted until the middle 1980s. More recently he edited a humor magazine called *Nuts!*, which appeared briefly in paperback format, and also contributed some ideas to *Mad.*  **R.G.**

# L

**LANCE** See TUFTS, WARREN.

**LARSON, GARY** (1950– ) A unique angle of vision, described by *People* magazine as "the inner workings of his eerily unconventional mind," has made Gary Larson one of the most distinctive cartoonists of the 1980s. His panel feature *The Far Side* has a slant unmistakably its own.

Born in Tacoma, Washington, Larson studied communications at Washington State University with no very clear professional goals, and it was on an impulse in the late 1970s that he sketched six animal cartoons unlike any he had ever seen before and offered them to the nature magazine *Pacific Search*. To his amazement, they were all purchased, and the $90 he was paid encouraged him to repeat the experiment. Despite the bizarre nature of his cartoons, he succeeded in selling the *Seattle Times* a weekly panel series called *Nature's Way* in 1978, but it was canceled within the year after complaints about the "unnatural selection of the subject matter."

Larson began selling his material to the *San Francisco Chronicle* just as his *Times* deal fell through, and in 1979 he signed a five-year contract with Chronicle Features to syndicate a daily panel as *Gary Land*, a name soon changed to *The Far Side*. Since 1984 it has been distributed by Universal Press Syndicate, and by 1988 was appearing in over 700 papers.

Larson's style is deceptively crude, conveying much with a few simple lines. His ingenious wit, featuring infinite variations on the theme of human and animal roles being exchanged, has been described as macabre, zany, weird, whimsical, fiendish, twisted, odd, and "the stuff of a demented imagination."          **D.W.**

**LASSWELL, FRED** See BARNEY GOOGLE.

**LAZARUS, MEL** (1927– ) The creator of the popular humor strips *Miss Peach* and *Momma*, Brooklyn-born Melvin Lazarus began his career in art as a free-lance magazine cartoonist immediately after finishing high school, in 1945. During the next decade he contributed to many national magazines and created two regular panel series, *Wee Women* and *L'il One*, which adum-

brated his later work by employing the device that was to establish his national reputation, the use of precocious children as vehicles for ironic commentary on the adult world. For a time Lazarus worked for Al Capp, copying his *L'il Abner* characters for comic books, games, greeting cards, and other merchandise, and from 1949 to 1954 he served as art director and comics editor for Toby Press.

A 1964 novel, *The Boss Is Crazy, Too*, grew out of his experience with Toby. Lazarus has also written three plays, a juvenile novel, two books of humorous pieces, and another adult novel, as well as the scripts for several television specials based on his strip Miss Peach.

With the launching of *Miss Peach* by the *New York Herald-Tribune* in 1957, Lazarus (who signs the strip "Mell") achieved immediate success. This unconventional strip, drawn in a single long panel, was clearly influenced by *Peanuts* and, like it, deals with a group of articulate schoolchildren given to analysis of their world.

In 1966, Lazarus collaborated with Jack Richard on *Pauline McPeril* for Field Newspaper Syndicate, which had taken *Miss Peach*. A spoof of cliffhanging adventure strips, *Pauline McPeril* (which derived its name from the motion picture serial *Perils of Pauline*) was not well received and lasted only until 1969. Lazarus, who signed the strip "Fulton," perhaps because he considered it a folly, accounts for the failure of the strip by admitting, "I really didn't know how to write continuity," but the explanation lies at least as much in the general unfamiliarity of the public with the genre it parodied.

The year after *Pauline McPeril* folded, Lazarus again hit upon a successful formula with a strip that was to become his most popular creation. *Momma*, signed Mell like *Miss Peach*, began with Field in 1970. Its shrewd and witty exploration of the relationship between a possessive and self-pitying mother and her three grown children has earned Lazarus the grudging admiration even of some mothers and a wide audience among their suffering progeny. In 1988, Lazarus took both of his strips to Creators Syndicate.

Simply and almost grotesquely drawn with a deliberate disregard of scale, Lazarus' popular strips have been much honored in the industry. The National Cartoonists Society voted him awards for the Best Humor Strip in 1973 and 1979 and named him Best Cartoonist in All Categories in 1982. **D.W.**

**LEE, STAN** (1922– ) Writer, editor, and eventually publisher of Marvel Comics, Lee is best-known as one of the architects of the modern comic book. In 1961 he cocreated and wrote *The Fantastic Four*, the prototype of the "superheroes with problems" theme, which still prevails. He institutionalized the artist and writer credits, letter pages, and continuity of story lines that define the contemporary comic book.

Born Stanley Lieber, Lee entered the comics field in 1939 as an assistant editor and copywriter for Marvel, then known as Timely Comics, Inc. He was hired by publisher Martin Goodman, a cousin-in-law of his, and reported to editors Joe Simon and Jack Kirby until they left Timely in 1942. Lee then became editor and chief writer. During the 1940s, he wrote stories for most of the Timely characters—such as Captain America, Sub-Mariner, the Human Torch—as well as creating new ones to fill the expanding market for comics. By 1947 he had helped turn Timely into one of the half-dozen top companies in the business.

Lee set up a bullpen of artists, writers, inkers, and letterers and kept them at work in the Timely offices from 1947 to 1951. By channeling their output to crime, Western, romance, or horror, depending on the current craze, Lee's editorial skills took precedence over his writing.

When the company changed its name to Atlas Comics in 1951, Lee disbanded his in-house shop, further expanded production, and took up scripting again. Titles like *Menace* were under his personal supervision and displayed a quality of writing a notch above the norm. By 1952, Lee was running the largest comic book company, in terms of sales, in the world; it was 50% larger than second-place Dell and twice as big as third-place DC.

Hard times forced Lee and Goodman to retrench in 1958. Lee again became the sole writer and developed an approach to drawing comics that is still known as the Marvel method. Lee would have a plotting session with an artist, throw out the idea for a story, kick it around with the artist. Then the artist would go draw it, and when it was finished, Lee would script it.

In the early 1960s, collaborating with Jack Kirby, Steve Ditko, and other artists, Lee had a hand in creating *The Fantastic Four, The Incredible Hulk, The Mighty Thor, The Amazing Spider-Man, Ant Man, Iron Man, The X-Men, Daredevil, Sgt. Fury and His Howling Commandos*, and others for the newly christened Marvel Comics company. He pioneered a brand of irreverent humor and adolescent pathos that quickly caught on with fans. The common thread—that these characters, though noble and superheroic, were human and had foibles—appealed to an audience that for the first time seemed to stay on and grow with the comics. Lee became a popular speaker on college campuses and even lectured at Carnegie Hall in 1972. He won fan awards as Best Editor and Best Writer throughout the 1960s.

Lee moved up to the publisher's desk in 1972 and by 1978 was spending most of his time at Marvel Productions, a film studio based in California. Today he lives in Southern California, supervising the merchandising and adapting to television and movies of the Marvel stable of characters. **J.V.**

**LEHTI, JOHN** (1912– ) A professional artist since the 1930s, Lehti has worked on both comic books and comic strips, drawing everything from the Crimson Avenger in *Detective Comics* to a newspaper Sunday page based on the Bible.

Born in Brooklyn, Lehti studied at several schools, including the Art Students League and the Grand Central Art School. In the middle 1930s he did illustrations for pulp magazines, and in 1939 he started working for DC. "The price in comics in those days was five bucks a page," he once explained, "and you wrote the story, too, and lettered it—the works. I started working for Vince Sullivan and then continued with Whit Ellsworth. *O'Malley of the Red Coat Patrol* (in *More Fun*) was the first thing I did. Although after the first month or so I was doing *O'Malley, Steve Conrad* (in *Adventure*), *Cotton Carver* (in *Adventure*) and the *Crimson Avenger* (in *Detective*). I wrote them, too—did everything." Lehti, who signed himself Jack Lehti in those days, put a great deal of effort into his early work and showed the strong influence of his mentor: "I was influenced by Alex Raymond. Well, I was a good friend of Alex. He gave me a lot of tips."

Next came four years of service in the Army. "Fought in Italy, France, Holland," he's said. "Got wounded, got the Bronze Star. Didn't do much artwork in the service. I killed people is what I did." Back home again, he worked as art director for *Picture News*, a monthly comic book, lasting just 10 issues, which attempted to present current events and nonfiction material in comic book format. Next came *Tommy of the Big Top*, a daily strip that ran from 1946 to 1950. King Features, always partial to artists who worked in the Raymond style, bought it. "While I was working with *Picture News*…I had an idea for a circus strip. I did, oh, about two weeks of it and went to King Features on a Friday. And on Monday they called me up and said they wanted to do it."

Much more successful than *Tommy* was *Tales from the Great Book*, a Sunday page that began in 1954 and lasted until 1972. After that Lehti did a bit more comic book work. Most recently he drew a Bible panel that he and a partner syndicated.                                    **R.G.**

**LEONARD, LANK** (1896–1960) The creator of the comic strip *Mickey Finn*, Portchester, New York-born Frank E. Leonard once wrote that he had always wanted to be a cartoonist and had worked to that end since his early childhood. Encouraged by Clare Briggs and *Chicago Tribune* editorial cartoonist Carey Orr, he took an art course from the W.L. Evans Correspondence School and later studied at night at the Academy of Fine Arts in Chicago and the Art Students League in New York City.

Leonard found his way into the cartoon world in 1925 with a job as an inker, for $11 a week, with Bray Productions, an animation studio. He worked for Bray until 1927, when he took over Wood Cowan's sports cartoon feature with the George Matthew Adams Service, drawing on his experience as a professional basketball player and sporting goods salesman. He maintained this feature for nine years, supplementing his work for the Adams syndicate with sports cartoons for *Ring Magazine*, the *Weekly Baseball Guide, Sporting News*, and the *New York Sun*.

Leonard effectively abandoned the sports arena in 1936 when he sold the McNaught Syndicate his strip *Mickey Finn*, a warm and humorous continuity series on the life of a city policeman. Although sports continued to surface from time to time as Mickey came into contact with boxers and baseball players, the focus of the strip was the personal life of young Patrolman Finn and his family.

Leonard's plain, workmanlike art never aspired to any graphic sophistication, but it was as honest, simple and pleasing as his hero. Avoiding cluttered backgrounds, the artist maintained a delicate balance between detail—kept to a minimum necessary for the story and the composition—and blank space, the well-arranged elements in each panel propelling the story without distracting the reader. Over the years Leonard's style became firmer and more assured, but it never lost its attractive simplicity.

The wholesome sentiment and well-paced narrative of *Mickey Finn* earned it the affection and loyalty of a large public; at its peak, the strip was appearing in over 300 newspapers. Leonard devoted his energies to his creation for over 30 years and turned it over to an assistant when he retired to Florida in 1968.    **D.W.**

**LEWIS, CLYDE** (1911–1976) A cartoonist with a distinctive bigfoot style, Lewis worked on several features in his long career. He drew Sunday pages such as *Herky*, daily panels such as *Hold Everything* and *Private Buck*.

One of his earliest professional jobs was assisting on *Alley Oop*.

Lewis, born in a small town in Iowa, grew up in Des Moines. After attending the American Academy of Art in Chicago, he eventually returned to Des Moines. In 1933 he was hired by the *Register and Tribune* as the second banana editorial cartoonist, the top man at the time being J.N. "Ding" Darling. Next Lewis moved to Cleveland to assist V.T. Hamlin on his new NEA strip, *Alley Oop*. He sold his own feature, *Herky*, to NEA in 1935. Originally a comedy Sunday page about a superbaby, it soon toned down to a more routine kid feature. By 1937 Lewis was also doing a daily gag panel titled *Hold Everything*. Late in 1939 he was carried off in one of Hearst's periodic raids and ended up doing a new panel, this one titled *Snickeroos*, for King Features.

That became *Private Buck* at just about the time America entered World War II. Buck, a small, dark-haired, and round fellow, was continually at odds with the Army. After the war the title became *The Private Life of Buck*. Buck also shared a new Sunday page, *Fatso*, with a fat friend of his. Lewis left syndication in the 1950s, returning to newspaper work. For many years he drew political cartoons for the *Sacramento Union* in California. At the end of his life he was again settled in a small town in Iowa and getting by as a free-lancer.    **R.G.**

**LICHTY, GEORGE** (1905–1983) One of the most successful of the gag panel cartoonists who worked in newspapers, he was the creator of *Grin and Bear It*. He was born in Chicago as George Maurice Lichtenstein but used the pen name Lichty for nearly all of his professional life.

The sale of his first drawing to *Judge* for $20 at the age of 16 encouraged Lichty to make a career of cartooning. He attended the Chicago Art Institute in 1924 but, as one account has it, was ejected for putting his gag captions under the Rembrandts and El Grecos on its walls. He moved on to the University of Michigan, edited the *Gargoyle*, the campus humor magazine, and won an Essex sports car as first prize in a college humor competition (third prize that year went to Milton Caniff of the Ohio State *Sundial*). After graduating in 1929, Lichty took a job with a former classmate's newly begun newspaper, the *Chicago Times*, doing spot and sports cartoons and also working as a photo retoucher. In 1930 Lichty tried his hand at a comic strip entitled *Sammy Squirt*, about an employee of a soda fountain. Sammy squirted his last soda after less than a year, and in 1932 Lichty created the series that was to occupy him for the next several decades—*Grin and Bear It*.

Begun as a Sunday panel feature in March 1932, it added a daily panel several months later. Both were syndicated by United Features from 1934 to 1940, and then Lichty went over to Field Enterprises. He drew his cartoons in a wildly loose, free style, working over his penciled sketches with brush and ink. Although his humor was never too caustic, no one was safe from his barbs. Subjects of his perceptive humor included the young, the old, the space program, the "Eternal Revenue Service," politics (Senator Snort complains of the difficult job of talking about everything without making his position clear on anything), the generation gap (a child asserts, "I reject all your establishment values starting with spinach!"), big business (Octopus Industries promotes someone to Vice President in Charge of Taking the Blame for Price-Fixing), psychiatry ("You must face reality, Mr. Sneedby," explains Dr. Sigmund Couch. "You ARE insignificant.") the automotive industry, Washington, Moscow, and Hanoi—all came in for equal mockery at Lichty's hands.

A consistent favorite with his colleagues, he was the first recipient of the National Cartoonists Society silver plaque for Best Syndicated Panel, in 1956. He went on to receive the award three more times, in 1959, 1962, and 1964. He moved to Northern California in the 1940s and for many years drew his feature in the midst of the noise and frenzy of the *San Francisco Chronicle*'s busy newsroom. During the last years that his name was associated with *Grin and Bear It* he had little to do with it. Fred Wagner drew the daily and Rick Yager ghosted the Sunday. Lichty officially retired in 1974, possibly to devote more time to his hobby of appreciating and playing brass band music. **D.W.**

**LI'L ABNER**   In the summer of 1934, a few days short of his 25th birthday, Alfred Gerald Caplin became Al Capp. As Caplin he'd been a struggling art student, an unsuccessful cartoonist in the Associated Press bullpen, and an underpaid ghost on the top-selling *Joe Palooka* comic strip. As Capp he would become rich and famous with the strip he had assumed his new identity to write, *Li'l Abner*. Syndicated by United Features, the fledgling comic strip made its debut in August of 1934, in a slim list of just eight papers around the country. It began to catch on, however, and by the end of the decade it was outselling all the other United strips—including *Tarzan, The Captain and the Kids, Ella Cinders*, and *Nancy*—and appearing in nearly 400 newspapers.

Capp came up with the idea for his hillbilly strip after a brief spell in the AP offices and a longer spell ghosting *Joe Palooka* for Ham Fisher, a gentleman he later described as a "veritable goldmine of swinishness." Capp's interest in the rustic was shared by quite a few people in America in the 1930s. The "Lum and Abner" radio show had taken to the air nationally back in 1931, bringing the comedy adventures of a pair of hick Arkansas shopkeepers to a wide audience, while in 1933 "The National Barndance," a radio show that offered country music and hillbilly humor, made its debut. That same year *Tobacco Road*, the hit play based on Erskine Caldwell's novel, caused a sensation on Broadway. And in July of 1934 Billy DeBeck took his Barney Google into the hillbilly country where he would eventually encounter the formidable Snuffy Smith. Abner made his debut at an auspicious time.

*Li'l Abner*, Al Capp, © 1938, Capp Enterprises, Inc. All rights reserved.

For his initial story Capp turned to a classic comedic theme, that of the country boy in the big city. After introducing the benighted rural community of Dogpatch, along with Abner Yokum, his Mammy and Pappy, and the lovely—though nowhere near as fleshy as later years—Daisy Mae, Capp had his handsome hero journey to far off Manhattan to visit a rich relative. Most of the early humor derived from this innocent-abroad setup. It's possible that Capp didn't originally realize the fun that was to be had right around home in Dogpatch. Eventually he began to explore its possibilities, especially in the new Sunday page that started in 1935, and to utilize all of Dogpatch's potential for commenting upon the greed, stupidity, and outright "swinishness" of humanity in general.

Capp was also fascinated with the movies, and his continuities in the 1930s occupied themselves with both parodies and imitations of current motion pictures. Although he was already christening characters with names like Cecil Cesspool, Basil Bassoon, and Herkimer Haggle, Capp was still capable of producing a sentimental yarn, one that would conclude with a teardrop showing at the corner of his bucolic hero's eye.

Capp alternated the more serious episodes with lighter ones, such as the recurrent recounting of one or another deep-dyed villain's attempts to capture and eat the Yokums' beloved pig, Salomey. In was late in the 1930s that he invented Sadie Hawkins Day. The annual event, in which the single ladies of Dogpatch get to pursue eligible (such as they are) bachelors, was a freewheeling parallel to one of the strip's major themes—Daisy Mae's dogged pursuit of the obtuse Abner. Gradually Capp introduced his continuing cast: Hairless Joe, Lonesome Polecat, Marryin' Sam, and, in a strip within a strip, the indestructible detective, Fearless Fosdick.

During the Second World War there was a swing to broader, more raucous comedy in America. *Li'l Abner* changed in the 1940s, too, as Capp switched to more obvious, low-down continuities, and perfected that blend of the satirical and the scatological that made him a sort of outhouse Voltaire. The voluptuous women remained the same, or possibly became even more so, but everybody else got cartoonier and, usually, uglier. It was in this decade that Capp introduced some of his most memorable characters and stories. In the Forties Abner first wandered into snowbound Lower Slobbovia, "where the favorite dish of the natives is raw polar bear and vice versa." Capp took to kidding contemporary fads and personalities, lampooning everyone and everything from Frank Sinatra to zoot suits. And he introduced the Schmoo and used it to cast doubts on the American dream. The Fifties might have been another decade of smooth sailing for the strip if Capp hadn't committed the tactical error of allowing

Abner and Daisy Mae, at long last, to wed. Something went out of the strip with the wedding, and the domesticated Abner was not the man he had been before the fateful day when Marryin' Sam tied the knot.

In its last days, in the 1970s, *Li'l Abner* was in decline. Circulation continued to drop from the 900 newspaper high to the 300 it would end with. One contributing factor was that Capp had grown increasingly conservative and cantankerous. Younger readers, who had no recollection of the happier days of the Thirties and Forties, found little to admire in his broad kidding of the politicians and political stances they held sacred. Older readers, many of whom had assumed Capp a liberal, didn't much care for Abner anymore either. "My politics didn't change," Capp maintained to the end. "I had always been for those who were despised, disgraced, and denounced by other people." In 1977 he made up his mind to let the strip die and he closed up shop, saying, "It's been an exhilarating forty-three years." He died two years later.

Capp had always had considerable help in turning out *Li'l Abner*. His first assistant, who joined him soon after the strip began, was the gifted Mo Leff. Capp rarely mentioned him after his departure, possibly because Leff quit Capp's employ to go to work for Ham Fisher. Andy Amato and Harvey Curtis followed Leff and worked with Capp for just about the rest of the life of the strip. Walter Johnson assisted Capp for many years, and a number of others among them Frank Frazetta, Lee Elias, Bob Lubbers, and Stan Drake, put in time. Eventually Capp did almost no drawing, concentrating instead on the scripts.  R.G.

**LINK, STANLEY** (1894–1957) Link ghosted *The Gumps* during its most successful decade, from the middle 1920s to the middle 1930s. On his own, in the early 1930s, he created the *Tiny Tim* fantasy strip, and he also drew the popular *Ching Chow* panel.

He was born in Chicago, and from 1914 to 1916 he attended that city's Academy of Fine Arts, after which he took a job drawing animated cartoons for a local studio. During the last year of World War I Link joined the Navy, where one of his fellow sailors was a humorous chap who later became Jack Benny. After his discharge he returned to Chicago to work as a free-lance artist and cartoonist.

Link worked on the *Chicago Daily News* for two years, and then in the mid-1920s he became Sidney Smith's assistant, which actually meant that he did just about all the drawing on Smith's increasingly popular strip. He was a considerably better artist than his boss, and his ghosting improved the look of *The Gumps* greatly, especially in those Sunday sequences devoted to the globetrotting adventures of little Chester Gump and his aphoristic Chinese companion Ching Chow. Link stayed with the feature until Smith's death in 1935. There have been several explanations put forth as to why Link was not given the job of carrying on *The Gumps*. The most plausible is that the syndicate was not willing to continue to pay him as well as Smith had. Therefore they hired Gus Edson, a lesser cartoonist but one who'd work more cheaply. Although Link officially ended his affiliation with the Gump clan soon after Smith died, he seems to have returned to ghost some sequences for Edson later in the 1930s.

Link's *Tiny Tim* Sunday page began in the early 1930s. It was an appealing blend of humor, fantasy, and adventure, and featured a lad who by means of a magic amulet could reduce his size to a few inches high. Tim was thus able to engage in thrilling and dangerous activities unseen—a fantasy common to most children. In the feature's later years Link would sometimes forgo fantasy and involve a full-size Tim in melodramas that probably made both Chester Gump and Little Orphan Annie envious. *Tiny Tim* ended with Link's death.

Ching Chow graduated to a panel of his own in the mid-1930s. *Ching Chow* provided a daily dose of fortune cookie wisdom, delivered by a caricatured mandarin shown in a seemingly endless variety of ludicrous poses. Each bit of philosophy was prefaced by such oriental-sounding formulae as "Who can deny...," "It is truly written...," or "It is wisely said..." The feature has survived, in other hands, and remains a popular one.

In the late 1940s Link added a daily family strip, aptly titled *The Dailys*, to his chores. Syndicated by the *Chicago Tribune*, it dealt in continuities similar to those found in *The Gumps* a decade or so earlier and boasted a cast of unlikable, self-serving, and meanminded characters. It faded away in the early 1950s. **D.W.**

**LITTLE ANNIE FANNY**  See KURTZMAN, HARVEY.

**LITTLE ANNIE ROONEY**  The most successful imitation of *Little Orphan Annie*, the strip was introduced in 1927 by King Features.

The first artist to draw *Little Annie Rooney* signed himself Verd. His name was Ed Verdier, and he worked in a simple, uncluttered cartoon style. Annie was a feisty kid in those days, much better looking than Harold Gray's waif but close to her in her wisecracking approach to life's pitfalls. In the opening sequence she is living with her old Uncle Bob, and a crooked lawyer named Scringe is trying to do her out of her grandfather's fortune. By 1930 Annie Rooney had wandered a lot, had even put in some time working with a circus, and was being looked after by Aunt Aggie and Uncle Paddy, an overwhelmingly good-hearted pair.

Annie switched artists almost as frequently as surrogate parents, and she began the Thirties being rendered by Ben Batsford, whose work was more nervous and noodled than Verd's. Batsford's Annie was still a spunky kid—"That's a lotta carrot oil!" being a favorite expression.

She next fell into the hands of Brandon Walsh and Darrell McClure. The plots and dialogue were by Walsh, who'd earlier been employed to fashion predicaments for the Gump family, especially little Chester. According to King Features publicity some years later, Walsh began writing the strip in 1928. If this is true, something must have happened to him when Darrell McClure joined him, because in the early 1930s Annie lost all of her spunk and feistiness at that point. Her attitudes and speech patterns altered radically: "Gee, Zero, I got the wim-wams awful bad. I keep tryin' to pretend I ain't scared of Mrs. Meany, but I know I am. An' I kin tell by the way Uncle George looks that he is worrying 'bout something, too...If I ain't here Uncle George kin help that nice prince who saved his life an' I kin go someplace where Mrs. Meany can't find me—I kin tell Uncle George I'm gonna stay with Mrs. Cleanly at the laundry." Zero was Annie's bedraggled mutt, surely the most long-suffering animal in comics. He had to listen to all Annie's monologues as she talked to him night and day, sometimes across entire Sunday pages. "Don't worry, Zero—it ain't snowing very hard. This is a big city—an' I'll betcha I get a job someplace—besides, we have over sixty cents, so we don't have to be hungry!"

When she wasn't being aggressively optimistic or suffering from recurrent bouts of the wim-wams, Little Annie Rooney was in a euphoric state of happiness, exclaiming "Gloryoksy!" She was on the run for most of her career, eluding "heartless, cruel Mrs. Meany," her legal guardian. The continuities were a paranoid's dream, for no matter how well Annie did or how prominent were her temporary parents, Mrs. Meany would always track her down. "I'd do anything to get my hands on that little brat!" she often declared.

McClure had drawn several other things for King prior to *Annie*, including *Hard-Hearted Hicky* and *Vanilla and the Villains*. Both were parodies of the hapless orphan-mustachioed villain melodramatics that Walsh took so seriously in the Annie Rooney story, so McClure adopted a much more realistic style for the new venture.

Early in 1934 Nicholas Afonsky was lured away from his job ghosting the more sober *Minute Movies* scenarios, and his soulful style was turned loose on *Little Annie Rooney* on Sundays. McClure was never happy about giving Annie up every seventh day to another artist, even though King attempted to pacify him by letting him try a new Sunday page of his own (the short-lived

*Donnie*, about a seagoing orphan lad). Afonsky kept the Sunday *Annie* until his death in 1943.

During his early tenure the little girl rarely appeared, and the adventures were concerned with a sweetfaced, wandering friend of hers named Joey. Joey's mentor was an epigrammatic Chinese named Ming Foo, who spouted the same fortune cookie philosophy as Ching Chow, the epigrammatic Chinese Walsh had invented for *The Gumps* Sunday pages. Since the Oriental didn't have a dog, it was little Joey who had to endure all his aphorisms. In 1935 Ming Foo moved upstairs into a Sunday half-page of his own, which lasted through the decade.

Walsh died in 1954, and McClure carried on alone. *Little Annie Rooney* survived until the middle 1960s.

**R.G.**

**LITTLE IODINE** The fearless little redhead with the curly ponytail earned her own color Sunday page in 1943. Prior to that she'd appeared frequently as a character in creator Jimmy Hatlo's panel *They'll Do It Every Time*.

"I tried to make her the embodiment of all the brats I knew," Hatlo once explained. "I tried to make her naughty as hell—and still likeable." It's probable that Hatlo was also inspired by Baby Snooks, the popular brat character that funny girl Fanny Brice had first impersonated on Broadway and had brought to radio in the middle 1930s.

The strip's humor was broad, with lots of action and momentum building to the gag payoff, and the style of the art was traditional big foot. While Iodine often caused trouble and turmoil, she had a knack for dispensing a jokey sort of wisdom at just the right moment. Serving as foils and counterpoints for the energetic kid were her timid father, Henry Tremblechin, and his pompous and rotund boss, Mr. Bigdome. Her mother was usually an innocent bystander.

A Californian, Jimmy Hatlo had started out as an artist in the advertising department on a San Francisco newspaper. He later directed his pen to cartooning and eventually created *They'll Do It Every Time*. The instantly popular panel came to the attention of William Randolph Hearst, and in 1936 Hearst's King Features Syndicate picked the feature up and began distributing it worldwide. In time it became one of the most widely syndicated panels, appearing in over 800 newspapers.

Hatlo was assisted for many years by cartoonist-writer Bob Dunn, who took over both features after Hatlo's death in 1963. Working with Dunn were Al Scaduto and Hy Eisman. Scaduto, who has drawn *They'll Do It Every Time* for many years, also drew *Little Iodine* in the middle 1960s. Eisman became the artist on

the Iodine page in 1967 and remained with it until it was discontinued in 1986.

The brat also appeared in a series of Dell comic books from 1949 until 1962. Early issues offered reprints, then switched to original material, most of it provided by Scaduto.

**W.D.**

**LITTLE JIMMY** Of all the strips Jimmy Swinnerton drew in his long career, this was his favorite. He first drew the tiny tyke early in the century and last drew him over 50 years later.

The feature began life in 1904 as a Sunday page called simply *Jimmy*. Jimmy was a very small, wide-eyed boy who was destined, because of his overwhelming fascination with all and sundry aspects of the world around him, to cause considerable havoc and frustration for the adults in his life. His parents continually sent him on errands that he rarely completed for he was always sidetracked. To a child everything is of equal importance, and to Jimmy watching an old black man singing on a street corner was of equal value to getting his father's mud-splattered overcoat to the cleaners, and following a man posting circus signs around town was equal to fetching a pound of butter from the grocer. His parents didn't share his outlook, and many of the pages ended with Jimmy, innocent of any willful wrongdoing, either getting an enthusiastic spanking from his father or on the brink of receiving one. Comics historian and essayist Donald Phelps has commented on "the hesitant, quirky, harassed rhythm" of Swinnerton's strip, a rhythm based on "interruptions, postponements, distractions—the tilting of formality."

A daily strip was added in 1920, under the revised title *Little Jimmy*. In addition to Jimmy and his friend Pinkie, Jimmy's bulldog Beans became a featured player. Swinnerton alternated gags with continuities, moving from the parlor to a desert island, from the city to the wilderness. By the late 1920s, both daily and Sunday, *Little Jimmy* was set permanently in the Arizona desert country that Swinnerton loved. He added Navajo Indians to the cast, including versions of those who appeared in his *Canyon Kiddies* page in *Good Housekeeping*. Jimmy was an observer as much as he was an adventurer and he was still getting sidetracked, but the thrashings had long since ended. Swinnerton abandoned him in the early 1940s, on orders from King Features, to do a straight Western adventure strip called *Rocky Mason*. He was relieved when that ended in the middle of the decade, and he was allowed to pick up *Little Jimmy* again. He continued with the feature, which had become a Sunday only in the late 1930s, until 1958. Though he was in his eighties by then, Swinnerton would have liked to continue, but an injury to his hand prevented him from drawing any longer. **W.D./R.G.**

**LITTLE JOE** An exciting Sunday adventure strip originated by Ed Leffingwell on August 1, 1933, *Little Joe* starred a 13-year-old redhead living on a contemporary Western ranch. Its violent action, humorous dialogue, clearly defined characters, and even more clearly defined moral confrontations, kept it on the Chicago Tribune-New York News Syndicate's lists for over three decades.

When he conceived *Little Joe*, Leffingwell was an assistant to his cousin Harold Gray, lettering and doing backgrounds for *Little Orphan Annie*, and both the tone and the look of the Western strip were later to become so similar to those of Gray's feature that it is generally supposed that the better-known cartoonist contributed materially to its development. Though less sententious and sentimental than *Little Orphan Annie*, Leffingwell's strip had much the same theme—a resourceful child's survival in a generally corrupt and hostile adult world—and a similar world view.

Joe Oak, the youthful protagonist of *Little Joe*, is the son of a rancher murdered before the strip begins. He lives with his mother and an aged gunslinger named Utah who runs the Oak ranch and initiates Joe into the Code, and the survival skills, of the West. A wholesome lad, neither improbably heroic nor cloyingly sweet, Joe likes adventure and enters into it with a whole heart but with sound, realistic instincts. His world is fraught with peril: Desperados kidnap him, scheming city slickers try to cheat him, wild animals stalk him, but he emerges triumphant because of a combination of moral straightness, physical courage, the loyal support of his loving Maw, the wisdom and ingenuity of Utah, and the unfailing support of the sagacious Indians who recognize and respect the principles the little boy represents. Like *Little Orphan Annie*, the strip relates a series of moral confrontations, but they are lightened with the humor of Utah's salty Western speech and the frequent injection of pure slapstick, and animated by breathless action. Among the recurring characters who add to the fun is a cynical Mexican charlatan identified as Ze General, a friend to Utah and Joe who repeatedly saves their lives by extralegal means (since he is bound by no laws) but never fails to cheat them if he thinks he has anything to gain by it. For many years this colorful character had a sidebar feature—a masculine, Mexican version of *Little Orphan Annie*'s *Maw Green* called *Ze General* —of his own.

*Little Joe*'s plots ranged in subject from frontier justice to international espionage, with Utah and Joe capturing enemy spies during World War II, and in its last years became a gag strip with little weekly continuity. It was seldom as openly preachy as *Little Orphan Annie*, but the moral tone was always high during its days as a story strip, and a note of political conservatism was often sounded. The New Deal and labor unions came in for frequent, if oblique, criticism, and the traditional American values of independence, justice, and self-sufficiency were praised by example if not always openly by precept.

Ed Leffingwell died following an appendectomy on October 10, 1936, and the strip was officially taken over by his brother Robert, who signed only the family name, though much of its composition was presumably contributed by Gray after its creator's death. Robert Leffingwell shared his brother's job as an assistant on *Little Orphan Annie* and remained with it until Gray's death in 1968. The art of *Little Joe* was simple but expressive, and the Western backgrounds were both accurate and often striking. The characters seem to reflect Gray's hand most clearly from the late '30s to the 1950s. *Little Joe* lasted until the late 1960s with a diminishing readership; it appeared frequently in Dell's *Popular Comics* and *Super Comics* and in the four-color series during the late 1930s and early 1940s but has seldom been reprinted since. Nevertheless, it remains a respected example of the Western adventure genre and one of the most attractive of the early child strips.    **D.W.**

**THE LITTLE KING** Otto Soglow's diminutive monarch was born in the pages of *The New Yorker* in 1931. The Little King, who appeared at regular intervals in the magazine, eventually caught the eye of William Randolph Hearst, who hired Soglow. Hearst's King Features Syndicate introduced *The Little King* Sunday page in September 1934.

On the little side himself, Soglow used a minimalist style to diagram the doings in the Little King's kingdom, his palace and environs. The page was almost pantomime. The king, whom Soglow never got around to naming, didn't speak, but now and then the queen or one of his minions or ministers would utter enough words to set up a gag or establish a premise. Many of the gags grew out of the fact that the king usually behaved like an independent, everyday citizen rather than a monarch. He paused to leave a note for the milkman before fleeing from the palace when it was under siege, he washed the dirty dishes in the palace swimming pool when the royal dishwasher quit, and the like.

Soglow used his page to kid not only royalty but also civilization in general. In describing the pintsized ruler, art critic Thomas Craven said, "He is a sophisticated character and his sleights, schemes and attitude are not only modern but urban."

The king was among the many King Features characters whose strips were reprinted in *King Comics*, which first hit the newsstands in 1936. He also served as the comic book's mascot, his likeness appearing next to the title on each cover.

In its early years the page had *Sentinel Louie*, also a semi-pantomime strip, as its accompanying topper. While *The Little King* was never one of the syndicate's big hits, it held on for over 40 years and ended only with Soglow's death in 1975.                          **R.G.**

**LITTLE LULU**  One of the most successful mischievous cartoon kids, Little Lulu first appeared in a panel by Marjorie Henderson Buell that appeared in 1935 in *The Saturday Evening Post*. Lulu eventually branched out into animated cartoons, comic books, advertisements, and a comic strip.

Patterning the character after herself when she was a child, the cartoonist, who signed herself Marge, created a little girl with corkscrew curls who constantly played imaginative pranks. Lulu's first appearance showed her as a flower girl who was tossing banana peels in a wedding procession—with bridesmaids and bride tumbling behind her. The otherwise wordless panel was captioned "LITTLE LULU." It appeared in the February 23, 1935, issue of the *Post*, where Marge's panel replaced Carl Anderson's *Henry*.

Lulu spent 10 years in the magazine, starred in 26 animated cartoons, was spokesperson for Kleenex for 16 years, had her panel cartoons collected in several books, and was licensed for a number of products. She debuted in comic books in Dell's four-color #74 in 1945.

Dell tried 10 issues in the four-color series, and then, its sales judged good enough to support a run of its own, a regular *Marge's Little Lulu* magazine began, with its first issue dated January-February 1948.

Marge maintained creative control, but the comic books were written and drawn by John Stanley, who initially followed the basics of the panel cartoons and fleshed out the concepts to suit the format of comic books. He visited Marge soon after the comic book began, but later worked on his own. Stanley eventually did roughs (plots, layout, penciling, and scripting), which were then turned over to others for finishing.

The first comic book established Lulu, Tubby, and Alvin (the nasty little kid Lulu often took care of). Lulu's last name was Moppet from the third special number on, but Tubby Tompkins' last name was originally Trimble. In the panel Tubby had been named Joe.

Recurring themes also became part of the series. Tubby belonged to a gang of boys who played in a clubhouse with "No Girls Allowed" printed across its front. They had a tradition of "Mumday" on which boys were not permitted to speak to girls—including mothers—on pain of expulsion. Lulu was assigned to take care of Alvin and kept him under control by telling him stories featuring "a beautiful girl"—who looked like Lulu. In #39 That Awful Witch Hazel was introduced and eventually she and even her niece Itch became mainstays of a series of ongoing fantasies.

Other themes included Mr. McNabbem, the truant officer (who always mistakenly assumed Lulu was playing hookey); Gloria (a beautiful, shallow snob); Wilbur Van Snobbe (a handsome, shallow snob); the tough West Side Gang; Tubby's toot-agonizing violin playing; and the attempts to avoid taking nasty-tasting Tiny Tots' Tonic. Tubby eventually became so popular that he was given a separate title of his own.

In *Little Lulu* #49 appeared the only full credits ever printed. After acknowledging that the characters were created by Marge, the staff writers and illustrators were listed as John Stanley, Gordon Rose, Irving Tripp, and Al Owens. The comic books continued, though Stanley eventually severed his connection, until the 1980s.

A *Little Lulu* newspaper strip was syndicated by the Chicago Tribune-New York News organization from June 1950 until May 1969. Among the artists who drew it was Roger Armstrong.                    **M.C.T.**

**LITTLE MARY MIXUP**  It took Mary several decades to grow up, and in her nearly 40 years on the comic pages she managed to mature only from childhood to her teens. The creation of R.M. Brinkerhoff, *Little Mary Mixup* began in the pages of the *New York World* in 1917. The paper syndicated it originally, and after the collapse of the *World* in the early 1930s, United Features took over. Initially a strip about a cute, clever, and sometimes prankish little girl, it gradually changed into a more serious continuity feature about an aggressively adventuresome teenager.

Mary's most successful decade was probably the 1930s, when the strip, daily and Sunday, ran in over a hundred newspapers and was reprinted in United's *Tip Top Comics* and *Comics on Parade*. There were two one-shots devoted entirely to *Little Mary Mixup* as well. In addition, Bob Brinkerhoff contributed a column on how to draw comics to early issues of *Tip Top*.

Brinkerhoff's father had been one of the founders of the *Toledo Post*, and the young man went to work as a newspaper cartoonist as soon as he was free of high school. He worked in a loose, scratchy style that was closer to illustration than it was to cartooning.

In his Sunday pages, which eventually included a topper called *All in the Family*, Brinkerhoff concentrated on gags, usually fairly gentle ones, built on the various mixups Mary brought about, on her frustrations, and her conflicts with her little brother Snooker. The dailies, by the 1930s, were given to melodrama and had plucky auburn-haired Mary hunting treasure, being kidnapped, chasing crooks, and generally behaving in the manner established by Little Orphan Annie and Little Annie Rooney.

Never quite at the top of United's list, and no rival for *Tarzan* or *Li'l Abner*, the strip ran most often in smaller circulation newspapers. It managed, looking very wispy at the end, to survive until the middle 1950s.

Brinkerhoff was residing in Minneapolis when he died early in 1958.                                    **R.G.**

**LITTLE NEMO IN SLUMBERLAND**   W i n s o r McCay's classic fantasy strip, unequivocally described by his biographer John Canemaker as "the most beautiful comic strip ever drawn," made its first appearance in James Gordon Bennett's *New York Herald* on Sunday, October 15, 1905. A work of grace and imagination, it has remained the highest expression of comic-strip art and perhaps the medium's greatest claim to serious attention as an art form.

For nearly 12 years, in over 600 full Sunday color pages, Nemo enjoyed weekly visits to a Slumberland wrought in wondrous color and fantastic design. The series began with a messenger from King Morpheus summoning Nemo from his bed to visit the kingdom. The lad mounts Somnus, "a little spotted night horse" brought to convey him there, and rides into the night sky, where he encounters among the stars the fantastic shapes of other animals—a kangaroo bearing a monkey, a pig ridden by a rabbit, a lion mounted by a frog—who race him until he falls off his horse, tumbles through the air, and lands on the floor beside his bed.

In each installment Nemo penetrates deeper into the land of dreams, frustrated at the end of the strip by some new mischance that wakes him. In the early episodes, one of his parents or grandparents usually explains his dream as caused by the little boy's eating before going to bed. (His nocturnal diet included, from week to week, raisin cake, peanuts, huckleberry pie, raw onions and ice cream, turkey dressing, doughnuts, sardines, candy, and mince pie.)

McCay reported in a 1907 newspaper interview that *Little Nemo* was "an idea [he] got from" his strip *Dreams of a Rarebit Fiend*, which began earlier the same year in Bennett's other New York newspaper, the *Evening Telegram*. The rarebit fiend's dreams were always nightmares—painful distortions of everyday reality—brought on by his incurable habit of eating the toasted-cheese confection at bedtime; McCay deliberately chose to vary the formula with a less frightening feature "to please the little folk." Nemo (originally a generic little boy whose name is Latin for "no one" but who later takes on a well-defined and endearing personality of his own) was modeled on McCay's young son Robert, then nine years old.

On March 4, 1906, Nemo finally succeeds in passing the last gate of Slumberland, after braving fearful perils, but his meeting with King Morpheus (and his daughter, the Princess, whom he has been summoned to play with) is once again thwarted, this time by Flip, the first of the denizens of Slumberland to appear regularly. Flip, "a bad and brazen brat," is an ugly dwarf of Nemo's size, identified later as "an outcast relative of the Dawn people, arch enemies of Slumberland and its people." Wearing a top hat labeled "Wake Up" and chewing a long cigar, he represents the reality principle, and his function throughout the strip is to keep Nemo from the Princess by shocking him back into wakefulness. In time, Flip becomes more of a friend than a rival, but his cynical and mischievous nature inevitably lead the good little boy into trouble, and Flip is always regarded as an enemy by the citizens of the idyllic kingdom of Slumberland.

Other regular characters include Impy, a youthful cannibal (taken over from McCay's first Sunday feature, *A Tale of the Jungle Imps*, which ran in the *Cincinnati Enquirer* from January to November, 1903); Dr. Pill, a physician referred to as "the wise guy of Slumberland"; the Professor; and of course King Morpheus and his delectable daughter, the Princess.

*Little Nemo in Slumberland* was a huge success from the beginning and generated books, a Victor Herbert musical comedy in 1908, films (beginning with McCay's own pioneering animated version in 1911), and such merchandising artifacts as greeting cards and note paper. The strip ran in the *Herald* until April 23, 1911, when McCay was lured by an offer of more money to the Hearst papers, where it ran from April 30, 1911, to July 26, 1914, as *In the Land of Wonderful Dreams*. McCay renewed his contract with Bennett in 1924 and drew the strip for the *Herald* again until 1927, before awakening his little boy for the last time. In 1947, 13 years after McCay's death, the artist's son, the original Nemo, resurrected the strip briefly, organizing the McCay Feature Syndicate to reprint old installments. The Richardson Feature Syndicate distributed the exhumed *Little Nemo* from March 2, 1947, but it ran only a short time. The wonderful world of Slumberland had no place in postwar America.

The spectacular visual effects of *Nemo*—the elegantly sinuous Art-Nouveau line, the dazzling perspective, the ingenious trick angles and grotesque distortions of scale—have earned the strip the highest place in comic-strip art. It has been rhapsodically described as "the supreme all-time masterpiece of the comic strip considered as a graphic art" and credited with anticipating both surrealism and cinematic storytelling technique. In 1966 McCay's work was exhibited in New York's

Metropolitan Museum of Art, and it has often been reprinted.

By turns droll and terrifying, *Nemo* displayed a singular sensitivity to dream psychology, illustrating many of the points made by Sigmund Freud in his *Interpretation of Dreams* just five years before. Such is the timeless universality of its imagery that it has lost none of its visual and emotional impact at the end of the century whose beginning saw its first appearance. Perhaps no strip in the brief history of the medium has a more certain claim to immortality than Winsor McCay's brilliant, visionary *Little Nemo in Slumberland*.     **D.W.**

**LITTLE ORPHAN ANNIE** The most famous and most successful waif in comics, Annie began her funny paper life on August 5, 1924. Destined to become famous for her pluck and her blank eyeballs, she was the creation of Harold Gray, who wrote and illustrated her conservative picaresque for the next four decades and more.

Gray had just put in five years assisting on *The Gumps*, and it was at Sidney Smith's side that he learned all he needed to know about how to fashion a successful newspaper strip. It's also probable that Captain Patterson of the Trib- News syndicate contributed to the creation, since he was a firm believer in the movies as a barometer of mass public taste. The *Orphan Annie* strip began as a composite of the most successful Mary Pickford films: There was the tough little orphan lass taken into the palatial home, her back-talking and joke-playing and her slangy honesty, and there was the gruff millionaire who becomes her mentor and protector. And that squiggly mass of hair Gray endowed Annie with was an attempt to imitate the Mary Pickford curls so many millions of people were in love with.

At the end of the strip's second month Gray introduced the character who would shape the philosophy of independence initially embodied in Annie into a political stance. Annie was adopted out of a grimly Dickensian orphanage by Oliver "Daddy" Warbucks, a millionaire industrialist and the epitome of Gray's idea of the self-made man who achieves success through hard work and canny capitalism. But Annie didn't tarry long with Daddy, since Gray realized he could get more suspense out of separating them. When Warbucks went off on a business trip, Annie was driven from the house. Accompanied by a pet dog named Sandy, whom she'd acquired in January 1925, she went forth into the world. Sandy, who had to listen to Annie's uplifting monologues over the years, always responded with a resigned "Arf."

Annie finally finds refuge with a poor yet kindly farmer and his wife, but she is no burden to them. Through purposeful enterprise and her own ingenuity, the 11-year-old waif is able to contribute to the couple's welfare and happiness. After a few months, though, Daddy Warbucks finds her again and takes her and her dog back to live in splendid comfort with him. Thus Gray inaugurated the cycle of separation and hardship, rescue and reunion that animated Annie's adventures throughout the strip's run.

The strip reached the height of its popularity during the Depression, when it addressed and assuaged the greatest fear of the period. Annie's adventures proved again and again that the traditional American ethic of hard work was not bankrupt and that capitalism could still work. And as Gray's exemplar, Warbucks could scarcely espouse self-reliance and free enterprise during the Roosevelt years without at the same time attacking FDR's policies. The New Deal, after all, tended to encourage people to look to the government for help rather than exhorting them to help themselves. And so *Little Orphan Annie* became unabashedly and unrelentingly political, and Gray used his strip to heckle Roosevelt and the Democrats.

Throughout the 1930s Annie drifted from place to place, into Daddy's care and out of it, spending much of her time with ordinary folks and reviving by precept and example their faith in the values of hard work and economy. Sometimes the villainy she faced in greedy landlords and corrupt politicians would be too much to be overcome by such simple virtue, and then Daddy Warbucks would show up to rescue her and everyone else.

In the 1930s Gray introduced another element into the harsh reality of his rendition of the Depression—the element of fantasy. On February 3, 1935, a giant, turbaned Indian, eight (perhaps nine) feet tall, showed up as Warbucks' new right-hand man. Punjab was that paragon, a kindly man of enormous strength and vast intelligence, who could also supply an appropriate punishment for those unsavory villains who were too unspeakable for ordinary legal disciplining. Throwing a blanket over them, Punjab muttered an incantation and banished them from this world. Two years later, on February 21, Gray gave Warbucks another memorable assistant, a black-garbed, hooded-eyed agent of vengeance much more single-minded in purpose than Punjab—the Asp.

Gray's drawing ability seemed too crude for rendering either his reality or his fantasy convincingly, but his artwork actually cast a spell that enhanced his stories. Filling his drawings with solid blacks, heavy shadows, and darkly shaded nooks and crannies, Gray created a threatening and sinister world. And in that world his people stood around rigidly, posturing woodenly, as if inhibited, restrained in their movements—perhaps because they were nearly paralyzed with fear.

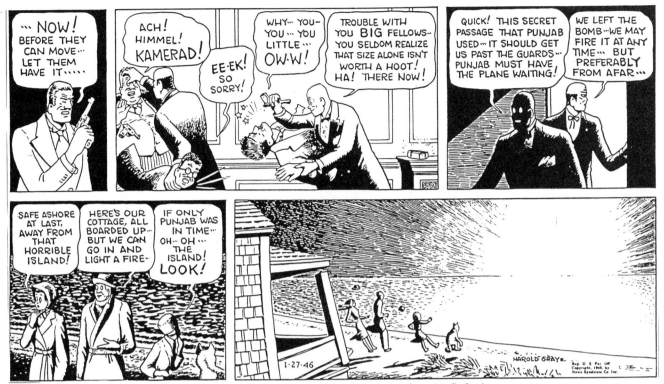

*Little Orphan Annie*, Harold Gray, © 1948, News Syndicate Inc. Reprinted by permission: Tribune Media Services.

For 44 years Gray wrote homey sermons for Annie to deliver while keeping her hands busy baking pies or sweeping out the store or doing laundry—activities she habitually indulged in while she preached. Gray, though a rigid conservative, was as much against social pretension, religious intolerance, moral hypocrisy, abuse of power, and censorship of the press as he was for self-reliance and free enterprise. So personal a vision did the strip embody that when Gray died in 1968, *Little Orphan Annie* almost ended as well, for Gray's longtime assistant, his cousin Robert Leffingwell, proved unequal to the task of continuing it. A succession of artist-writer teams—first Henri Arnold and Henry Raduta, then Tex Blaisdell and Elliott Caplin, then David Lettick, writing and drawing—did no better. Finally, on April 22, 1974, in an unprecedented move, the syndicate began reissuing Gray's *Little Orphan Annie* from the middle 1930s.

After the Broadway musical *Annie* opened in April 1977 and became a hit, with Hollywood planning a big budget movie, it was decided to try to revive the strip, and, by the autumn of 1979, Leonard Starr had been interested in the project. Abandoning the realistic illustrative style he'd used for 22 years on his own *On Stage*, Starr recreated the strip in a much crisper interpretation of the Gray style. Starr's version, titled simply *Annie*, began running December 9, 1979. Over the years he has successfully sustained his rendition of Gray's character,

recapturing the excitement of her early adventures and the flavor of the strip's visuals without hazarding Gray's politics.

**R.C.H.**

**THE LITTLE PEOPLE** See SCOTT, WALT.

**LONDON, BOBBY** (1950– ) He first attracted attention as an underground cartoonist in the late 1960s. His best-known creation, *Dirty Duck*, went from underground to *Playboy*. Since early in 1986 he's been drawing the respectable *Popeye* daily strip for King Features.

A native of New York City, London went to Adelphi University. He started selling cartoons to underground—that is, counterculture—publications in the late 1960s. After moving to the West Coast, he sold *Dirty Duck* to the *Los Angeles Free Press* in 1971. *The National Lampoon* introduced the disreputable fowl to slick paper in 1972, and in 1977 he moved up to the pages of *Playboy*, where he remained until 1987.

While drawing the duck for these various outlets, London also contributed to underground comic books. His work showed up in such comix as *Dopin' Dan*, *San Francisco Comic Book*, and *Merton of the Movement*, which he also edited. He also drew for *Air Pirates Funnies*, the underground that utilized Mickey Mouse and prompted the Walt Disney organization to go to court.

London draws in a scratchy, anachronistic big foot style, taking a 1920s approach to cartooning and filtering it through a 1980s sensibility. He admits that the cartoonists who influenced him most in his youth were E.C. Segar, Billy DeBeck, Bud Fisher, Al Capp, and Walt Kelly. Later in life he discovered *Krazy Kat* and became quite adept at imitating Herriman when the mood struck him. He was so good, in fact, that one of his *Dirty Duck* pages was mistaken for the real thing by the editors of an encyclopedia on comics and appears therein as an example of *Krazy Kat*.

In February of 1986 he took over the daily *Popeye* newspaper strip. He's updated it some, allowing Popeye to show concern for at least some of what's going on in the real world. London has also brought back continuity, something that was long banished in favor of a gag a day, and he's reactivated some of the characters—such as Castor Oyl—whom he was fond of when he discovered the strip as a kid.              **R.G.**

**THE LONE RANGER**  The daring and resourceful masked rider of the plains first led his fight for law and order in the early Western United States over the radio. He started there in the early 1930s, and before the decade was over he and his faithful Indian companion Tonto had moved into novels, pulps, Big Little Books, movies, comic books and newspaper funnies.

Since the Lone Ranger was created by committee, there is some disagreement as to who contributed what to his birth. He was first heard on radio station WXYZ in Detroit, and among those involved were the station owner George W. Trendle, the station dramatic director James Jewell, and Buffalo-based script writer Fran Striker. Trendle wanted shows for a Michigan network, and a cowboy series seemed like a good idea. It was decided that the program would be called *The Lone Ranger* and that it would involve a masked man and his Indian sidekick (initially Tonto was going to be "a halfbreed"). Masked avengers on horseback were nothing new and had flourished in dime novels, pulp fiction magazines, and movies, but the version that WXYZ started offering early in 1933, was one that quickly caught the fancy of a great many kids. Fairly soon the Lone Ranger, Tonto, and Silver were heard all across America, sponsored by 17 different bread companies.

Considerable merchandising followed, but since no one quite agreed on what the unseen radio hero looked like there were several different images of the masked man to be found appearing on toys and promotion pieces. In some he wore chaps, in others he didn't; in some he wore a high-crown Stetson, in others the crown was flat. Tonto's appearance varied, too. The first Big Little Book devoted to the character, *The Lone Ranger and His Horse Silver*, was published in 1935. The story was based on scripts for two of the radio shows, and the illustrations were by Hal Arbo. His masked man looked

like the one in publicity photos provided by WXYZ, wearing a flat-crowned hat and a leather vest.

Seven more BLBs followed in the 1930s, some credited to Striker and some to Buck Wilson (a pen name for the prolific Gaylord DuBois), and, again, the Lone Ranger's appearance varied from book to book. Five further titles were issued in the 1940s, including *The Lone Ranger on the Barbary Coast* and *The Lone Ranger and the Secret Weapon*. These were all illustrated by Whitman's star artist, Henry Vallely, whose Lone Ranger and Tonto looked like the movie serial and newspaper strip versions. The final Big Little Book devoted to the masked rider appeared in 1968.

Republic Pictures released its 15-chapter Lone Ranger movie serial in 1938. The appearance of the masked man in this chapter-play set the look of the character for years to come. The white hat, string-front shirt, and dark neckerchief were picked up by the comic strip and spread from there. The only difference was the mask, which covered his whole face in the serial. Republic's Tonto, with headband and fringed buckskin suit, influenced all subsequent Tontos.

King Features introduced the Lone Ranger comic strip on Sunday, September 11, 1938. "You've seen him on the screen, you've heard him on the radio," the promotion ads announced, "NOW see him in the funnies!" The initial artist was Ed Kressy, and the continuities, based on previous radio scripts, were done by his wife. Kressy worked in a loose cartoony style and he had trouble getting the Lone Ranger's eyes to look right behind the mask. There was almost immediate dissatisfaction with his work, and complaints came in even from Trendle and Striker. Within a few months Kressy left the feature. His name continued to appear, but the actual artist was Jon L. Blummer, who was much better suited to the Western adventure strip. For some reason he did not stay with it long, a year later he went into comic books, where he created *Hop Harrigan*.

Charles Flanders, a reliable member of the King Features bullpen and one of the syndicate's best Alex Raymond imitators, took over the drawing of the strip in January 1939. The Lone Ranger became more virile-looking, a better match for the impression conveyed by the radio voice. The stories were pretty much like those of the radio show, simple white-hat versus black-hat stuff, but with more pretty women around. The scripts were now credited to Fran Striker.

Flanders peaked on the strip in the middle 1940s. The strip was written in its last years by Paul S. Newman and ended in September 1971.

The Lone Ranger entered comic books in 1939, initially in an original material one-shot drawn by Vallely and used as a premium to promote Lone Ranger Ice Cream Cones. That same year the McKay company issued a black and white comic reprinting the Kressy dailies. Soon thereafter the strip became one of the reprints in *Magic Comics* and *King Comics*. McKay also published four issues of *Future Comics* in 1940, which offered more *Lone Ranger* reprints along with translations of an Italian comic strip titled *Saturn Against the Earth.*

Dell began a Lone Ranger reprint series in the middle 1940s, converting it to a regular bimonthly early in 1948, which reprinted Flanders' material through the 37th issue. After that Tom Gill and his staff drew original adventures of the masked man. The *Lone Ranger* television show began, on ABC, in September 1949. Such was the Lone Ranger's popularity in the 1950s that Dell also brought forth a comic book devoted to his sidekick and another dealing with his horse. The complete title of this latter magazine was *The Lone Ranger's Famous Horse Hi-Yo Silver*, and there were 36 issues in all between 1951 and 1960. The official title of the faithful Indian's comic was *The Lone Ranger's Companion Tonto*. From 1951 to 1959 33 issues appeared.

The masked man returned to the comic sections, a smattering of them anyway, on September 13, 1981. Betting that the big budget *The Legend of the Lone Ranger* would be a movie box office hit, the *New York Times'* Special Features syndicate initiated a new strip. It was handsomely drawn by comic book veteran Russ Heath, scripted by another comic book veteran Cary Bates. The fact that the movie turned out to be one of the great turkeys of the cinema didn't help the feature's fortunes. "The strip at its best never had more than 60 papers," Heath has said, "and not many of the more important ones either." The Lone Ranger and Tonto rode out of the funnies for good on Sunday, April 1, 1984.

In all his graphic manifestations over the years the Lone Ranger remained the same basic good guy he was when he started out at WXYZ in the relatively innocent Thirties. He never drank, smoked, or cursed and he never killed anyone. Being an expert gunman, he favored shooting the weapon out of an outlaw's grasp. "Ow! My hand!" was the inevitable response of the outlaw on such occasions.                    **R.G.**

**LONG SAM**  The strip was created by Al Capp, the man responsible for *Li'l Abner*, and ran from 1954 to 1962. Drawn by Bob Lubbers, *Long Sam* dealt with a pretty young woman who was, like Abner, a rural type possessed of an invulnerable innocence and a considerable attractiveness to the opposite sex. Her encounters with city slickers and urban eccentrics formed the basis for the humorous, sometimes satirical, continuities.

Capp, who took credit for writing the strip, had initially tried out the notion of a distaff Abner in the *Li'l Abner* strip itself. That was in October 1938, when he introduced a character known as Strange Gal—"a child of the southern jungle who has never seen any other place but the Great Swamp, who has never seen any other human being but her mammy, now at rest back in the Great Swamp." The sequence, in which Strange Gal leaves her home to venture into Dogpatch and points beyond, lasted only about two months. But obviously it stuck in Capp's mind.

*Long Sam* was built on a very similar premise and starred a young woman who was raised in rustic isolation by her mother, kept innocent of any knowledge of the world in general and men in particular. When she finally ventured outside her valley her picaresque adventures—most of them involving all sorts and conditions of men—began. In the *Long Sam* version the mother remained alive, with Sam returning to her isolated cabin now and then. Capp, fond of the *Candide*

*Long Sam*, Bob Lubbers, © 1959, United Features Syndicate, Inc. Reprinted by permission of United Features Syndicate.

approach, worked variations on the innocence abroad situation in both *Li'l Abner* and *Long Sam.*

Lubbers, a comic book veteran who had been recruited off the *Tarzan* strip, did an impressive job of drawing the strip, daily and Sunday. "Lubbers' art was always exciting," Richard Marschall has said in *The World Encyclopedia of Comics,* "supple, full of motion, with a command of composition and anatomy." His dark-haired, long-legged Sam was among the most attractive ladies in the funnies.

Eventually the writing of *Long Sam* was turned over to Capp's prolific brother, Elliot Caplin, who was also handling the continuity for such strips as *Abbie an' Slats* and *The Heart of Juliet Jones.* For the strip's final years Lubbers took over the scripting. The strip last appeared in December 1962. Lubbers continued to work with Al Capp, ghosting *Li'l Abner* for many years.     **S.L.H.**

**LOOY DOT DOPE**   See DEVLIN, JOHNNY.

**LUBBERS, BOB** (1922– )  Some artists are very fast, some are very good. Relatively few manage to be both and Lubbers is one of them. A prolific and very proficient cartoonist, specializing in the depiction of pretty women, he had a long career in comic books and comic strips; among the many characters he drew were Long Sam, Firehair, Captain Wings, Secret Agent X9, Li'l Abner, and Tarzan.

He was born on Long Island and studied at the Art Students League in New York City. One of his classmates was Stan Drake, and in 1940 the two of them decided to make some extra money in the burgeoning comic book field. They both found work with the Centaur company. Lubbers' first effort was *Reef Kincaid,* about a world-roaming adventurer who encountered lost cities, wild men, and lovely ladies. It appeared in *Amazing Man Comics.*

Throughout the 1940s, with time out for service in the Air Force, Lubbers remained very active in comic books. He drew the Masked Marvel, the Arrow, Captain Wings, Senorita Rio, Camilla, and Firehair, the last three for various Fiction House titles. Fiction House was a champion of what collectors now call Good Girl Art, and Lubbers was one of the most accomplished practitioners in the genre. For good measure he also did an excellent job of drawing the airplanes, weapons, jungle foliage, Wild West frontier towns, and rotten villains appropriate to the various stories.

Lubbers moved into newspaper comics in 1950, when United Features hired him to draw *Tarzan,* daily and Sunday. He did some of his best work thus far on the jungle man's adventures, filling the panels with graceful people, flora and fauna. In 1954, chiefly because of the attractive women he drew, he was asked by Al Capp

to do the artwork on Capp's new *Long Sam.* A distaff Li'l Abner, the attractive young lady had a career that lasted until 1962. Not satisfied with just one strip, especially from a financial standpoint, Lubbers also drew *Secret Agent X-9* from 1960 to 1967. In the 1950s and 1960s he also put in short stretches ghosting *The Saint, Big Ben Bolt,* and his longtime friend Stan Drake's *The Heart of Juliet Jones.* His final strip, begun in 1968 for NEA, was the short-lived *Robin Malone.*

Next, in 1970, he went back to work for Capp, penciling *Li'l Abner.* He remained with the strip until close to its final days in the late 1970s. After some comic book work, Lubbers went into advertising, where he has stayed.     **R.G.**

**LYNDE, STAN** (1931– )  One of the last contributors to the already declining tradition of the Western comic strip was Stan Lynde, whose *Rick O'Shay* and, later, *Latigo* were among its most distinguished exemplars.

The authenticity of Lynde's work was assured by his personal background, which, like his strips, was set squarely in the American West. He was born near Billings, Montana, and went to school on a Crow Indian reservation in Lodge Grass. After graduating from the local high school in a class of nine, he attended the University of Montana, where he majored in journalism and took a minor in art.

Lynde got his first heady taste of the cartoonist's life during a stint in the Navy from 1951 to 1955. Stationed on Guam, he did a daily humor strip called *Ty Foon* for the *Marianas Mariner,* the camp newspaper there.

Lynde spent a summer on his family ranch in Lodge Grass after his discharge, and then worked on the weekly Colorado Springs newspaper *Week End* as a reporter. With the $30 he was able to save up on that job, he made a break for New York in 1956. There he spent a couple of years working for the *Wall Street Journal,* beginning as a typist and working his way up to a reporter. In his spare time, he sold occasional cartoons to "all too occasional buyers" and attended night classes at the School of Visual Arts.

The comic strip he developed at that time, *Rick O'Shay,* was not greeted with much enthusiasm when he offered it around, and Lynde was about to give up when the Chicago Tribune-New York Daily News Syndicate accepted it in 1958. A humorous Western strip that reflected Lynde's intimate knowledge of the area, *Rick O'Shay* ran nearly 20 years, but by the early 1970s the artist had become increasingly dissatisfied with the promotion it was getting by the Tribune-News Syndicate and found himself "not only operating at a loss but incurring increasing debts." He decided to discontinue the strip in 1977. A loyal audience responded with regret and the San Diego ComiCon awarded Lynch an Inkpot Award ("for getting out of the business?" he wondered), but negotiations with the syndicate proved fruitless and Rick tethered his mount for good.

In the spring of 1978, the Field Newspaper Syndicate approached Lynde to do a new Western strip, and on June 25, 1979, *Latigo* made its appearance. Set in the post-Civil War West, *Latigo* was a dramatic adventure series, more serious than *Rick O'Shay* but no less stylishly drawn, which focused, as Lynde explained, on "the less spectacular 'common' people—the homesteader, the miner, the underpaid frontier horseman, the American Indian." *Latigo* was well received but never reached a large audience and it folded in 1982. Russ Heath helped with the drawing.

Lynde never lost touch with his Western origins and returned to Montana in 1962. There he bought a 160-acre ranch near his father's at Lodge Grass, where he now raises black angus cattle (which he brands RIK in memory of the strip that paid for them) and devotes his spare time to serious Western painting.          **D.W.**

# M

**McBRIDE, CLIFFORD** (1901–1951) An excellent artist, McBride is best-known as the creator of the huge, clumsy dog Napoleon.

Born in Minneapolis, Minnesota, McBride grew up in Southern California, where he earned the distinction of being the only boy ever to flunk the art course at Pasadena High. While still in high school, however, he succeeded in entering the professional art market with the sale of a political cartoon to the *Los Angeles Times*, and after college, in 1923, he went to work with the *Times* drawing humorous pantomime strips. The next year the *Chicago Tribune* hired him away to illustrate fiction, but after a year in Chicago he returned to California with a contract from the McNaught Syndicate to produce more of the pantomime strips he had been doing for the *Times*.

McBride's syndicated strips were moderately successful, and one recurrent character, who first appeared in the late 1920s, caught the popular fancy enough to acquire an identity and a name of his own. In time the rotund Uncle Elby, based on McBride's uncle Henry Elba Eastman, was joined by a dog, a gigantic, bumbling creature named Napoleon, who disrupted his would-be master's existence with every sweeping wag of his long, irrepressible tail. The beautifully balanced team—the fat man, all stasis and order, and the lean dog, all motion and chaos—assumed the central roles in the ever-changing show and moved on to become stars of their own feature. In June 1932 the LaFave syndicate began distributing *Napoleon*.

Essentially a pantomime strip, it was drawn with a vigor and spontaneity that concealed the refinement of its detail and the extraordinary graphic elegance of its composition. In his engaging duo McBride created two of the most precisely conceived and gracefully portrayed figures in the literature of man and dog. He continued drawing *Napoleon* until his death.      **D.W.**

**McCAY, WINSOR** (1869 [or 1871]–1934) Regarded by many as the first great master of both the comic strip and the animated cartoon, Winsor McCay is best known for his strip *Little Nemo in Slumberland*, whose visual elegance and thematic originality set a high-watermark never surpassed in the medium. Born Winsor Zenic McCay in Spring Lake, Michigan, he studied art only briefly in 1888 at Ypsilanti Normal College before his family moved to Chicago. Unable to afford further art instruction, the young McCay found work painting signs and illustrating for theatrical productions and traveling circuses, an exposure to fantasy illustration that was to prepare him for his later career in the comics. In 1889 he went to Cincinnati with a carnival, for which he created posters, and became a full-time employee of the Vine Street Dime Museum, drawing freaks so dramatically that the *Cincinnati Times Star* hired him as a staff artist in 1897. Here he illustrated the news, sports events, criminal trials, and occasional advertisements and fiction, and drew political cartoons. The next year he transferred to the *Commercial Gazette* and in 1893 moved on to the *Enquirer*.

In January 1903, McCay created his first Sunday color page, a 43-panel sequence illustrating a verse text by *Enquirer* Sunday editor George Randolph Chester, called *A Tale of the Jungle Imps*. Patterned after Kipling's *Just So Stories*, which had appeared the year before, each Sunday installment recounted how some animal got its most striking feature, as observed by mischievous little black natives, the Jungle Imps of the title. The feature ran through November of that year.

During this period McCay was also selling work to several national magazines, such as *Life*, and publisher James Gordon Bennett invited him to come to New York and work for him in 1903. He became an illustrator, at a much increased salary, on Bennett's *New York Evening Telegram* and soon began doing comic strips for his morning *Herald*. McCay worked for Bennett's papers for the next eight years, during which time he created an astonishing flood of strips, among them *Pilgrim's Progress* ("by Mr. Bunion"), *Poor Jake, Day Dreams*, and, most important as a foreshadowing of what was to come, *Dreams of a Rarebit Fiend*, all signed "Silas" because his contract with Bennett did not permit him to use his real name until 1905. Over his own signature he drew *Dreams of a Lobster Fiend, It Was Only a Dream, Midsummer Day Dreams, Autumn Day Dreams, Oh! My Poor Nerves, Mr. Bosh. The Faithful Employee, Little Sammy Sneeze, Hungry Henrietta*, and many others. Most were fantastic rather than satiric: Sammy Sneeze

*Dream Days*, Winsor McCay.

(1904) destroyed buildings with his volcanic sneezes, Hungry Henrietta (1905) was a bulimic infant who could consume anything, and the strips about dreams—the theme that was to become McCay's trademark—depicted weird and often disquieting sleep visions.

*Dreams of a Rarebit Fiend* dealt with dreams in a particularly frightening way, including such oneiric elements as deformity, cannibalism, dismemberment, and death. It was nonetheless popular enough to prompt Frederick A. Stokes to publish a collection in 1905 (the same year Stokes brought out a volume of *Little Sammy Sneeze*), and Edwin S. Porter produced a live film of it in 1906.

The *Rarebit Fiend* was an adult feature, but it inspired McCay to attempt the same idea "to please the little folk," and in 1905 he created his masterpiece, *Little Nemo in Slumberland*. Modeled on his son Robert, Nemo had a weekly adventure in the land of dreams, a gorgeous setting quite unlike the grim contemporary world of the Rarebit Fiend's nightmares. At the end of many episodes Nemo falls out of bed, and one or the other of his parents diagnoses his trouble as resulting from overindulgence in rich (and often improbable) food, ranging from peanuts to raw onions with ice cream.

McCay is credited with the single-handed invention of film animation, and if this is something of an exaggeration it is sure that he did more than anyone else not only to popularize the medium but also to widen its range of possibilities. From 1908 until 1911 he created 4,000 drawings, each hand-colored on its 35mm frame, for his first effort. He toured on the vaudeville circuit with his animated version of *Little Nemo* in 1911 and met with so much successes that he created another, *The Story of a Mosquito*, in 1912. Unlike *Nemo*, this film had a plot, of sorts: A mosquito overeats (again the perils of gluttony) and explodes. In 1914 McCay released his third and most successful animated film, *Gertie, the Trained Dinosaur*, a film that remains endearing today. He produced at least seven more films, most notably *The Sinking of the Lusitania*, with 25,000 frames, the first of such length, in 1917, and toured with them all, giving lectures and demonstrations as part of his act.

McCay left Bennett for William Randolph Hearst in 1911 and continued *Little Nemo* in the Hearst papers under the title of *In the Land of Wonderful Dreams* until 1914. Hearst kept him busy doing editorial cartoons, however, and his career as a comic-strip artist drew to a close. In 1924 he went back to the *Herald* (by then the *Herald-Tribune*) and revived Nemo for three years before returning to Hearst to draw more editorial cartoons for Arthur Brisbane's conservative editorials. Along with these political statements he drew large Sunday illustrations of moral ideas, meticulously executed but not very imaginative preachments on such subjects as the value of hard work and education and the danger of drugs and alcohol.

The graphic sophistication of McCay's best work, influenced by book illustration and the then current Art Nouveau style, is unparalleled in American comics. An innovator from the beginning, he opened up new horizons to the strip-artist, exploring different formats and compositions for the first time. His extraordinary draftsmanship and complex, unflagging imagination have remained an inspiration and a source of ever-renewed pleasure through the years. **D.W.**

**McCLURE, DARRELL**   See LITTLE ANNIE ROONEY.

**McCOY, WILSON** (1902–1961)   One of several artists to draw the *Phantom* comic strip, McCoy devoted the final 20 years of his life to the Ghost Who Walks. Born in Missouri, he had taught art, worked in advertising, and free-lanced before he began ghosting the *Phantom* dailies in 1941.

Ray Moore was the artist taking credit for the daily work and drawing the Sunday page. Like many another King Features cartoonist of the period, Moore drew in his version of the realistic, drybrush style perfected by King's favorite, Alex Raymond. McCoy, however, favored a simpler, much more cartoony, diagrammatic approach. He was, therefore, one of the least successful ghosts in comics history. But his stark, shorthand style gave the strip a distinctive, if not exactly appropriate, look. When Moore retired for health reasons in 1947, McCoy was allowed to take credit for his own work. **R.G.**

**McEVOY, J.P.**   See DIXIE DUGAN.

**McGILL, RAY** (1892–1963)   Like the majority of cartoonists, McGill never garnered much fame. He was, nonetheless, a productive artist with a recognizable style of his own, and during his many years in the profession he drew for both comic strips and comic books. His best-known feature was *Blondie*, which he never got to sign.

He began his long association with Hearst in the 1920s. For the *New York Journal* he drew a daily strip that commented on events in and around Manhattan; it featured a reporter named Brodie Betts, who resembled a pint-sized W.C. Fields. There was also *Gerald Greenback*, a short-lived syndicated strip in the *Desperate Desmond* vein.

It was in the early 1930s that McGill first worked as assistant to Chic Young on *Blondie*. He next held a similar job with Lank Leonard on *Mickey Finn*. He eventually became a member of the King Features bullpen, and when the syndicate started producing and packaging a line of comic books—including *King Comics*, and *Ace Comics*—McGill drew many filler pages for them, all of which were always signed by his boss, Joe Musial. When the comic book boom really hit later in the decade, McGill turned out feature pages for a great number of titles. He drew such features as *Marco Polo Jones*, *Oliver Drab*, and *Hayfoot Henry* for such magazines as *Thrilling Comics*, *Big Shot Comics*, and *Action Comics*.

McGill drew all of his pages in a style that was unabashedly of the 1920s; it was simple and direct, though embellished with the various pen shadings favored by such longtime colleagues as Billy DeBeck and Paul Fung. In the early 1940s he drew a newspaper strip called *The Funny Money Man*. An invention of Allen Funt, during his pre-*Candid Camera* days, the short-lived daily dealt in puzzles plus prizes that were supplied by subscribing papers.

McGill returned to work for Chic Young in the 1940s, eventually moving to Florida when Young did. He helped to draw both *Blondie* and its Sunday topper *Colonel Potterby and the Duchess*. He was still associated with Young at the time of his death.    **R.G.**

## McGOVERN, STAN   See SILLY MILLY.

## MACHAMER, JEFFERSON (1900–1960)  His specialties as a cartoonist are best summed up in the title of the Sunday page he drew throughout the 1930s—*Gags and Gals*.

Born in Nebraska, Machamer began his professional career drawing for the *Kansas City Star*. He came East in the 1920s and became a weekly contributor to the popular humor magazine *Judge*, where, in addition to *Gags and Gals*, drawn in a scratchy, uninhibited variation of the Russell Patterson style, Machamer also provided comment on Broadway doings and smart-set night life.

In the spring of 1928 he began *Petty Patty*, about a bright, liberated flapper. It was syndicated by King Features and, like much of Machamer's work, looked much better than it read. King advertised it to the trade as "the smartest new feature of the year," but *Patty* didn't survive the decade.

His *Gags and Gals* page started in the *New York Mirror* in the early 1930s and was picked up for national distribution by King Features in 1935. The gags featured Machamer's favorite subjects—long-legged, pretty girls, predatory males, and old boys in tuxedos. He himself—portrayed as a short, rounded, mustachioed loser—starred in a strip that ran across the bottom of his page.

*Hollywood Husband*, a family strip about a fellow whose wife becomes a movie star, came and went in 1940. Machamer did mostly magazine gags and adver-

tising illustrations from then on. In the last years of his life he also ran an art school in Santa Monica.    **R.G.**

## MACK, STANLEY (1936–  )  An award-winning art director and children's book author, illustrator, and designer, Stan Mack is best known for two weekly cartoon strips: *Real Life Funnies*, carried regularly in *The Village Voice* since 1974, and *Out-Takes*, a feature in *Adweek* since 1981. Both are remarkable in taking all their dialogue verbatim from real conversations Mack has overheard.

New York-born Mack grew up in Rhode Island, at whose School of Design he studied art before becoming an editorial art director for the *New York Herald-Tribune*. During the 1960s he worked with the *New York Times* and created more than a dozen children's books. In the early 1970s he went free-lance, contributing to the *Times, Esquire*, and the *Evergreen Review* and creating *Mule's Diner*, a series of bizarre narrative strips running irregularly in the *National Lampoon* from 1972 to 1974.

But it is his *Real Life Funnies* and *Out-Takes* (whose setting is the special world of the media) that have established Mack as one of the keenest observers of changing contemporary folkways. *Real Life Funnies* was collected into a volume by Putnam in 1979 and *Out-Takes* by Overlook in 1984. Although both found only a small, specialized audience, Mack's incisive draftsmanship and sure ear for the absurdities of informal speech make these ongoing strips a valuable contribution to the documentation of our culture.    **D.W.**

## McMANUS, GEORGE (1884–1954)  A fun-loving and gregarious man, who came to resemble his most successful creation, McManus tried all sorts of comic strips before he discovered the right one. Once he came up with Jiggs and Maggie and *Bringing Up Father* in 21913, he settled down to become a millionaire cartoonist.

Born in St. Louis, McManus was working as an office boy in the art department of the *St. Louis Republic* by the time he was 15, and soon he was doing the sort of graphic reportage expected of newspaper artists before photographs could be reproduced—drawing hangings and the scenes of murders, suicides, and assorted disasters. Early in the 20th century, acting on a bootblack's tip, McManus bet $100 on a horse running at 30-to-1 odds. When he won, he staked himself to a try at Manhattan. He got himself hired by the *New York World* in 1905. (One advantage of the job was that his work was reprinted in Joseph Pulitzer's other paper, the *St. Louis Post-Dispatch*, which was McManus' hometown newspaper.)

He drew a variety of short-lived comics—*Snoozer, The Merry Marcelline, Ready Money Ladies, Cheerful Charlie, Let George Do It*—before he hit his stride with *The New-*

*lyweds.* With that strip McManus attracted the attention of Pulitzer's chief rival in the circulation wars, William Randolph Hearst. As was his wont, Hearst lured the young cartoonist to his *New York American* stable in 1912, where McManus launched an imitation of his domestic comedy strip and called it *Their Only Child.* He also drew *Rosie's Beau* before finding his forte in 1913 with *Bringing Up Father*, a gag strip that pitted the unaffected lowbrow desires of Jiggs against Maggie's vaulting social pretensions in an epic of husband and wife strife that would outlast its creator.

Apart from his ability to play seemingly infinite variations on his strip's central theme, McManus had an inventive graphic imagination, which he displayed in some of the most elegant penmanship in cartooning. His line was fine and delicate, and, once his style matured, *Bringing Up Father* was distinguished by copious decorative detail in rococo backgrounds and ornate props—the filigree of a city skyline, the graceful curlicues in the design of a stair-railing or in the pattern of Maggie's dress—and by the judicious and telling placement of solid blacks. His tricks with silhouette were also striking.

McManus, one of the highest paid cartoonists in the country, had moved to Southern California early on. He settled in Beverly Hills to live a life that rivaled that of the movie stars, many of whom he hobnobbed with. After his death King Features took over the production of his strip.               **R.C.H.**

**McNAMARA, TOM** (1886–1964)  He was a versatile man who drew several newspaper strips, worked in comic books, wrote and directed films, and is credited by some etymologists with coining the word "movies." McNamara's *Us Boys* was a popular Hearst newspaper strip in the second and third decades of the century; he also created the *Our Gang* series in Hollywood, and worked as an artist and editor for the pioneering *New Fun* comic book.

McNamara was born and raised in San Francisco. By 1906, the year of the Great Earthquake, he was working as a reporter-photographer-artist for the *Chronicle.* He next moved on to Nevada to try his hand at prospecting and in 1908 was to be found back in the newspaper business and working on the *Salt Lake Herald.* Late that same year he teamed up with fellow cartoonist Myer Marcus to enter vaudeville. Billed as Mack and Marcus they toured the Orpheum Circuit doing an act that involved drawing cartoons on a large sketch pad with charcoal. A contemporary review described the turn as "an exhibition of rapid and skillful picture-drawing and cartooning, with just a dash of humor to brighten it."

After touring the country and appearing in London and Paris, the act broke up. McNamara stayed in France for a while, drawing for the Paris edition of the *New York Herald* and also teaching rollerskating at a local rink. The second decade of the century found him in Manhattan, working in the Comic Art Department of Hearst's *Journal.* Among his coworkers were Tad Dorgan, George Herriman, Harry Hershfield, and Cliff Sterrett. His kid strip began in 1912, and featured a gang of city kids that included Shrimp Flynn, a fat boy named Skinny Shaner, and a born leader called Eaglebeak Spruder. It was entitled *Us Boys* (a title his editor stuck on it) as a daily and *On Our Block* on Sunday.

McNamara was not an exceptional cartoonist and drew about as well as the boys he was depicting in his strip. He was inventive, though, and had a sense of humor. He didn't go in for conventional gags, preferring to get his humor out of the street-life situations his kids experienced. Fairly early he introduced continuity, using such familiar boys book situations as being marooned on a tropic island. According to some experts it was in *Us Boys* that the word "movies" was first used, spoken by Shrimp Flynn.

Like several other syndicated cartoonists, McNamara moved to Southern California in the early 1920s. He got into the motion picture business soon after. In 1922 he went to work for Hal Roach and developed the *Our Gang* series of short comedies. He wrote and directed most of the early entries, the ones with the original gang members such as Sunshine Sammy, Mickey Daniels, and Farina. More of a realist than Roach, McNamara never much liked the idea of the gang dog having a black circle painted around one eye. In the middle 1920s he signed on with Mary Pickford. A press release listed his chores as "'gag' man, helping to frame comic situations. He is also titling the picture. He directs the taking of the 'still' and publicity pictures, and also directs when two cameras are shooting on different sets." He worked on three films with Pickford, including *Little Annie Rooney* and *Sparrows.* During all this studio activity, he continued to write and draw his strip. *Us Boys* lasted until early 1929.

He had one more crack at a syndicated feature. In May of 1929 he began drawing a Sunday page called *Teddy, Jack and Mary* for the *Chicago Tribune.* Another kid strip, this was about the unfortunate inmates of a rundown boarding school and combined elements of both the *Our Gang* comedies and the Pickford films he had worked on. The *Trib* also launched Tack Knight's *Little Folks* at about the same time, eventually asking readers to pick their favorite of the two. McNamara lost and his page was dropped.

In 1932 he cowrote the script for RKO's *Little Orphan Annie*, which starred Mitzi Green as the curly-topped waif and Edgar Kennedy as Daddy Warbucks. McNamara had lost a good deal of money in the Crash of

1929, and his personal problems mounted in the 1930s. He was back in New York by the middle of the decade, working as art editor on Major Nicholson's original-material comic book, *New Fun*. He drew a kid page called *After School* with a topper called *My Grandpa*, the latter drawn in a deliberately boyish style and attributed to Lefty Peters. It recounted tall tales Lefty's grandfather had told him and managed to burlesque the sort of material to be found in the magazine's more serious fare. This was McNamara's best feature, and he revived it, under the title *Grandpa Peters*, as a filler for assorted DC titles in the early 1940s. He worked for comic books until the late 1940s. For several years beyond that McNamara also wrote gags for his friend Sterrett's Sunday *Polly and Her Pals* page.

He eventually returned to San Francisco and, using a Masonic pension, took a room in a hotel in a run-down section of town. A newspaper story in the *Chronicle* in 1960 described him as living in "a mean little room in a shabby Tenderloin hotel, a room cluttered with fading clippings and photographs," and went on to describe him as feeble and nearly blind.

Still spry and feisty and given to hiking all over the city of his birth, McNamara wrote a letter to the paper complaining that the piece on him "gave the impression to several of my associates that I've turned into a sort of beatnik type." He held on to his room, and his independence, until the final months of his life.　**R.G.**

**MacNELLY, JEFF** (1947–　)　The youngest person ever to win the Pulitzer Prize for political cartooning and one of the few to win it three times, Jeff MacNelly has also achieved a notable success as a comic-strip artist with *Shoe*, a broadly ironic humor strip about journalism. Born Jeffrey Kenneth MacNelly in New York, he is the son of a magazine executive who later turned to painting portraits. He grew up on Long Island and attended Phillips Academy and the University of North Carolina, where he contributed cartoons to both the college *Daily Tarheel* and the *Chapel Hill Weekly*, a community paper that, despite its name, appeared twice a week. In 1969 he left school to work full-time for the *Weekly*, but, unable to live on $120 a week, he began looking for a more substantial affiliation. In December 1970, he began to draw for the *Richmond* (Va.) *News Leader* and in 1972 received his first Pulitzer Prize.

Both of MacNelly's careers have flourished from their beginnings. His political cartoons—shrewd, wildly funny commentaries with a tendency to the conservative—have earned him an impressive collection of awards: Pulitzers in 1972, 1978, and 1985, the George Polk Award, the National Cartoonists Society's silver plaque for Best Editorial Cartoon in 1977, and its highest award, the Reuben, for his editorial cartoons in 1978.

His cartoons are distributed to over 400 papers. The comic strip *Shoe*, which began in 1977, won the NCS's Reuben in 1979 and is distributed to over 1,000 papers by Tribune Media Services. Both his editorial cartoons and his strip are regularly collected into books.

MacNelly retired from the *News Leader* in June 1981, intending to devote himself to leisure and watercolor painting, but found that he missed political cartooning and returned on March 7, 1982, to draw three cartoons a week for the *Chicago Tribune*.

An innovative cartoonist with a highly distinctive graphic style, MacNelly alternates areas of rich detail with sparse, clear spaces and employs an expressive, broadly cartoony line. He has been so influential on younger cartoonists that a whole class has been labeled "MacNelly clones," but he declines either credit or blame for that, observing, "Well, they can call me a Mauldin or an Oliphant clone." Whatever the influences MacNelly's cartoons reveal—whether the acerbity of Bill Mauldin or the leavening humor of Pat Oliphant—there is no doubt that he has evolved something that is uniquely his.　**D.W.**

**McWILLIAMS, ALDEN** (1916–　)　McWilliams is a cartoonist with a special affinity for drawing planes, ships, guns, and the other mechanical props and paraphernalia of war and adventure. He started contributing to comic books in the mid-1930s and has also drawn 2such newspaper strips as *Twin Earths* and *Dateline: Danger*.

A native of Greenwich, Connecticut, he studied at what is now the Parsons Institute in Manhattan. His first professional work was illustration for pulp fiction magazines, and in the mid-1930s he started drawing for the Whitman-Dell line of comic books, including *Crackajack Funnies*, *Popular Comics*, and *The Funnies*. McWilliams started before there were any superheroes on the scene and he never did get around to drawing one. Instead, he concentrated on daring aviators and realistic detectives such as those to be found in *Gang Busters*. He has said that his major artistic influence was Alex Raymond, and he drew in a bolder, hard-boiled version of the Raymond style. McWilliams worked for a variety of publishers over the years, his meticulous work showing up in *Military Comics*, *Crack Comics*, *Crime Does Not Pay*, *Airboy*, and the like. In more recent times he has drawn *Star Trek* and *Buck Rogers*.

He has also been associated with several newspaper strips. In the 1930s he put in a stint assisting on *Tim Tyler's Luck*. He drew *Twin Earths*, the science fiction strip written by Oskar Lebeck, from 1952 to 1963, *Davy Jones* from 1961 to 1968, and *Dateline: Danger* from 1968 to 1972. He assisted on *Rip Kirby* and *On Stage* and was one of several artists to ghost *Dan Flagg*.　**R.G.**

**MAD** A comic book that became a magazine, *Mad* debuted in 1952 and is still thriving. Invented by Harvey Kurtzman and published by William Gaines, it has provided sophomoric satire for several generations of adolescents, made artists like Jack Davis, Don Martin, and Allan Jaffee rich and famous, and promoted Alfred E. Neuman into a national hero. It has also inspired, over the years, dozens of imitations, from *Panic* and *Sick* to *Cracked* and *Plop!*

Kurtzman was already working for Gaines' EC company, editing the straight war titles *Two-Fisted Tales* and *Frontline Combat,* when *Mad* was launched. "I've heard twenty stories about who was responsible for *Mad's* creation," he once said. "As I remember it, I became desperate to do a quick comic book. I wasn't making money with the war books...So I somehow convinced Gaines that I should do something else that was easier. He said, 'Go ahead.' Now I'd always been doing satire in school, in the streets; it was my kind of clowning...The format would make fun of comic books as they were at that particular period." Gaines pretty much agrees with the Kurtzman version of history. "Our official reason for publishing *Mad* was [that] we were tired of horror, weary of science fiction, we wanted to do a *comic* comic book," he's said. "That was not true; it was just publicity. It was so Kurtzman would get a 50 percent raise."

The first issue of *Mad*, with a cover by Kurtzman, appeared in the autumn of 1952. Among the contributing artists, all recruited from the EC regulars, were Jack Davis, Wally Wood, and Bill Elder. Soon moving away from stories that were just funny, Kurtzman and his crew began kidding not only comic books but television and movies as well—with *Dragged Net, The Lone Stranger, Manduck the Magician,* and the like. As Gaines has recalled, "*Mad* lost money for three issues." Then came a parody of *Superman* drawn by Wood. "*Superduperman* was in issue #4. *Mad* then became popular." So popular that other publishers stepped in with imitations. Gaines even imitated *Mad* with *Panic,* started in 1954 and edited by Al Feldstein.

The 1950s was a somewhat inhibited decade, and Kurtzman's irreverent and fairly broad kidding of the mass media and current celebrities served as an oasis for high school and college students. In 1955, to avoid having the title sink because of increased criticism and boycotting of comic books, Gaines converted it to a 25¢ black and white magazine. The 24th issue, the first in the new format, was dated July 1955. Alfred E. Neuman, whose face was adapted from a face on an old novelty postcard, had first appeared a few issues earlier. He now became *Mad's* official mascot. Norman Mingo, a veteran commercial artist and illustrator, painted him in a series of covers for the next several years.

Kurtzman left *Mad* after the 28th issue and Feldstein replaced him as editor. Several new artists came along in the next few years. Among them Mort Drucker, George Woodbridge, Bob Clarke, Don Martin, and Sergio Aragones. *Mad's* targets have remained pretty much the same, and any kid who watches television and goes to the movies will have no trouble knowing what's being spoofed. The sales have risen and fallen, but as the 1990s began seemed to be on the rise again.

R.G.

**MAGER, GUS** (1878–1956) A newspaper cartoonist for much of the first half of the century, Mager drew both humor strips and straight adventure strips; *Hawkshaw the Detective,* which was his most famous feature, had two incarnations. In addition, he was a painter and also contributed to the naming of the Marx Brothers.

Charles Augustus Mager was born in Newark, New Jersey, and lived there all his life. He was apparently a self-taught artist, and, according to comics historian Bill Blackbeard, "German humor magazines featuring the cartoon art of Wilhelm Busch, Karl Arnold and other continental giants of the time influenced his developing graphic style as a boy." After selling cartoons to magazines while in his teens, Mager went to work for Hearst's two New York dailies, the *Journal* and the *American,* around the turn of the century. He had an affinity for drawing animals and by 1904 was doing a strip about assorted monkeys for the *Journal.* These humanized creatures were called monks, and the strip ran under such alternating titles as *Knocko, the Monk, Tightwaddo, the Monk, Groucho, the Monk.* The monks gradually changed into real humans, or near approximations, and when *Sherlocko the Monk* started in 1910, the master detective, his companion Dr. Watso, and all his perplexed clients were roughly human in appearance.

A Conan Doyle buff, Mager stuck with Sherlocko for the next few years and gave each daily an appropriately Holmesian title, such as "The Mystery of the Unpainted Flagpole" or "The Curious Episode of the Vanished Biscuits." When he went to work for the *New York World* in 1913, he took his detective with him, changing his name to Hawkshaw in the process and using him in a Sunday page. This second version of the sleuth lasted until 1922.

Although he had a highly distinctive style of his own, one that stood out in what the *New York Times* referred to in his obituary as the "bulb nose era" of cartooning, Mager also possessed a talent for aping the styles of others. He showed this in the early 1920s with *Main Street,* an unsuccessful page that owed much of its look to the work of George McManus, and from the late 1920s to the early 1930s he drew *Oliver's Adventures,* a straight boy adventurer daily that was closely modeled on the approach of George Storm.

Mager revived *Hawkshaw* in 1931, when his detective started appearing in the topper to his longtime friend Rudolph Dirks' Sunday *Captain and the Kids* page. Since Mager was already employed by another syndicate doing the Oliver strip, he worked directly for Dirks with *Hawkshaw* and signed it Watso. Ironically, in the early 1930s, the work that Mager signed his own name to was drawn in a blatant imitation of someone else, and the work done in his own style was signed with a pen name.

An unusual situation arose in 1932 when Dirks, in a disagreement over money, quit United Features. Mager, as a side effect, lost his job, too, and Bernard Dibble was brought in by the syndicate to draw both features. When Dirks went back to work in 1933, Mager did too, and he remained with the detective until the strip ended in the late 1940s. But he never signed his own name to it.

Like Dirks, Mager had painted throughout his life, and his canvases were in the permanent collections of several museums, including the Whitney Museum of American Art in Manhattan. **R.G.**

## MAIN STREET  See MAGER, GUS.

**MALE CALL**  Quite probably the most widely circulated comic strip of all time, Milton Caniff's wartime *Male Call* appeared in an estimated 3,000 service newspapers around the world. It started late in 1942 and lasted until early in 1946. For most of the strip's run the leading lady was a sexy but chaste brunette named Miss Lace.

Originally, after Caniff had volunteered to donate a once-a-week daily-format strip to the Camp Newspaper Service, he had drawn a somewhat more adult version of his *Terry and the Pirates*. Neither Terry nor any of the pirates were to be seen in this GI version, which concentrated on the wisecracking, worldly blond known as Burma. Though drawn in Caniff's usual real-

*Male Call*, Milton Caniff, 1943.

istic style, the strip had no continuity and aimed instead at delivering a gag each time around. Burma lived in China and fraternized with enlisted men, and an occasional officer, and her encounters with lecherous servicemen provided the basis for the humor. The situations were usually politely risque, involving cleavage, double entendres, and, mostly, frustration. The first of these special *Terry* strips ran on October 11, 1942.

Fairly soon Caniff's syndicate decided that two separate versions of his strip wasn't a good idea. Rather than give up the GI strip, Caniff simply came up with a new leading lady. "I wanted a short, sexy name…I gave her black hair. I viewed her as innocent but sexy as hell." He also concluded that "she might be playing poker with you, but she won't necessarily be going to bed with you." The key word with Lace was *maybe* and she remained unattainable for the life of the feature. The Camp Newspaper people came up with the new title, *Male Call*, and the first one—following a two-week gap after the departure of Burma—ran on January 24, 1943. Though Lace initially showed up in the same part of China that her blond predecessor had lived in, the strip soon became less specific as to locale. Miss Lace might show up anywhere, and sometimes *Male Call* ignored her to concentrate on a gag situation taking place in another combat zone.

Caniff kept the strip going for several months after the end of the war, not concluding it until March 3, 1946. Now and then in its final year he'd allowed some fairly bitter comments to slip in, especially when dealing with civilian attitudes toward returning servicemen. "I also did *Male Call* strips about wounded GIs, including amputees and blind men." In the final strip Lace just disappeared, leaving behind a note that promised, "I'll be there if you ever need me again." Caniff did draw her again over the years, usually in special drawings for veterans organizations. "But for the most part," he said, "Miss Lace and *Male Call* went back into the inkwell after the World War. The strip is frozen in time. It served its purpose, and I did not revive it for the Korean or Vietnam Wars." **R.G.**

**MANDRAKE THE MAGICIAN**  Written by Lee Falk and drawn by Phil Davis, *Mandrake* first appeared in 1934, but Falk recalls having created the idea of the magician-crimefighter in 1924, when he was 19 and still an undergraduate at the University of Illinois. He offered the two weeks of it that he had drawn to King Features Syndicate on a visit to New York, some years later and, as he reported in 1975, "To my amazement, they bought the strip!" Since he had a poor opinion of his own drawing, he looked up fellow Missourian Davis, then a commercial artist working in St. Louis, and persuaded him to illustrate the script.

*Mandrake the Magician* debuted as a daily on June 11, 1934, and was so popular from the first that King added a Sunday version, also drawn by Davis, on February 3 of the next year. The strip was an irresistible combination of stylish art, well-paced plotting, and terse, witty dialogue. Its hero, the single-named Mandrake (whose name Falk has explained as deriving from the root used in medieval pharmaceuticals, with its magical associations lending a supernatural tone to the character) is a suave magician garbed in the traditional stage-magician costume of opera hat, Spanish cape, and tails. Originally possessed of genuine magical powers, he soon came to rely merely on his quick wit, his moral superiority, and his uncanny skill as a hypnotist to right the wrongs he encounters around the world.

With all his natural gifts, Mandrake does not have to work alone. The dapper gentleman-adventurer is frequently accompanied by Lothar, the first major black character in an adventure strip. Lothar, whose fez, leopard-skin tunic, and quaint pidgin-English mark him as an African, was in fact no less a personage in his home continent than the prince of the Federated Tribes but had abdicated his throne to take service with the dashing Mandrake. Beginning as a sort of bodyguard-valet, he was in time to work his way up to a companion. With the public's increased sensitivity to racial slurs in the comics he has lost his dialect, but he remains the muscleman of the team and has retained his simple, droll humor.

Mandrake is too charming, and too good-looking, to be untouched by romance, and is frequently the object of the amorous attentions of the ladies he saves. He remains faithful, though, to his voluptuous girlfriend Narda, the former princess of Cockaigne. Another recurring character is "The Cobra," a persistent villain who was in the first Mandrake story. Mandrake's teacher back at magic-school in the mountains of Tibet, The Cobra (whose real name is Luciphor), later turns his supernatural powers to evil, although he inevitably eludes Mandrake's efforts at destroying him.

Mandrake's settings are infinitely varied; he has saved orphans from scheming villains in small towns, foiled unscrupulous Hollywood movie producers, and reformed muggers in New York's Central Park. He has traveled to outer space and worked with the poor in the inner city. "Perhaps one reason these strips have had a long life," Falk observed in 1975, "is that I've kept them fresh with my own current interests."

Davis continued drawing *Mandrake* until his death in 1964, when comic book artist Fred Fredericks took over. Fredericks has been signing the strip with Falk since June 1965.

The strip's continued appeal lies in part in the consistently high level of visual elegance maintained by both

*Mandrake the Magician*, Phil Davis, © 1949, King Features Syndicate, Inc.

Davis and Fredericks, and in Falk's ingenious narrative and amusing special effects. Mandrake always triumphs through trickery—cunning disguises, slight-of-hand, hypnotism—but he is a shrewd detective who knows whom to trick and when, and his illusions are both graphically striking and droll. With a quick gesture of the hand he renders himself or others invisible, turns people into animals, bends guns to direct their bullets at the villains shooting at him, and makes inanimate objects talk and accuse the guilty. He plays on the superstition and cowardice of the criminal, and he does it all with such elan and wit that even the malefactors he thwarts are impressed. Falk's plots are scripted with drama and suspense, and with enough pure fun to keep them from becoming melodramatic or sententious.

Despite the decline in public taste for continuity strips over the years, *Mandrake* has held its audience and has been particularly popular in Europe. After more than 50 years, King Features Syndicate still distributes the strip to over 200 papers. It appears in eight languages and is published on six continents. **D.W.**

**MANEELY, JOE** (1926–1958) Although he was active in comic books for only 10 years, Maneely produced an impressively large amount of work and all of it drawn in his strong distinctive style. He worked primarily for Marvel, in the years from 1948 to 1958, drawing stories in just about every category—from horror to humor. He also turned out hundreds of first-rate covers.

Maneely was born in Pennsylvania, studied at the Hussian School of Art in Philadelphia and worked on that city's *Daily News*. His first comic book work was done for Street & Smith and appeared in such titles as *Shadow Comics* and *Super Magician*. He began working for Marvel in 1948, eventually settling in the New York area and becoming a star member of their bullpen. Among the many characters he drew were Sub-Mariner, Kid Colt, Combat Kelly, the Ringo Kid, Gunhawk, Speed Carter–Spaceman, the Black Knight, and Dippy Duck. Maneely also worked on Marvel's war, true crime, horror, humor, and romance books and provided over 500 covers. "His design sense was strong," says *The Great Comic Book Artists*, "his figure work good, and he'd developed a distinctive style of inking—one utilizing a considerable bit of quirky feathering."

He also had time to draw for DC, Hillman, Charlton, and several other publishers and to team up with Stan Lee on a short-lived Sunday page titled *Mrs. Lyons' Cubs*. He died in an accidental fall from a Long Island Railroad train car.                    **R.G.**

**MARCOUX, GEORGE** (1896–1946) After a moderately successful career in newspaper strips, Marcoux, who had a fairly realistic humor style and specialized in drawing kids, moved into comic books and was the cocreator of Supersnipe.

Marcoux had worked as an assistant to Percy Crosby on *Skippy* before launching a kid strip of his own in the middle 1930s; *Toddy*, which ran daily and Sunday, featured a boy who was more down-to-earth and less philosophical than Crosby's tyke. His strip was not a winner, and by 1940 Marcoux was working for the Street & Smith line of comic books.

Initially he drew straight adventure stories featuring such characters as Nick Carter, the Avenger, and an assortment of plucky Horatio Alger Jr. boy heroes. He finally had a hit when he teamed up with writer Ed Gruskin in 1942 to produce *Supersnipe*. Koppy McFad, who was in reality the union-suited hero, was a slightly older version of Toddy, and the feature kidded not only costumed crimefighters but the youths who thrived on their comic book exploits.

Marcoux died of a heart attack in 1946 at the age of 50.                    **R.G.**

**MARK TRAIL** A clean-cut, outdoorsy strip by Ed Dodd, *Mark Trail* began in April of 1946. Its hero was a long, lanky fellow, one of several returning GIs who were showing up on comics pages at the time, and his traveling companion was a loyal St. Bernard named Andy. A folksy fellow, Mark is enamored of nature and the great outdoors: "Gosh, Andy, what a country…It makes you want to take off your hat and whisper like you do in church!" He is a sort of Jimmy Stewart of the funnies, much given to such expressions as, "Holy jumpin' catfish!" An outdoor photographer and woodsman, he joins forces with "kindly Dr. Tom Davis, who is striving to prevent the extinction of our animals and forests. With him is his daughter, Cherry, an outdoor girl." The Davises own Lost Forest, "a wild game refuge and outdoor paradise." The viper in this Eden is one Barton McBlane, "who wants the Lost Forest because he's secretly learned of immense gold deposits in its streams."

Mark's first adventure introduces him to landgrabbers, grizzly bears, lumberjacks, forest fires, and a romance with Cherry Davis. Next he's hired by *Woods & Wildlife* magazine to protect the beavers in Sundance River County from big time poachers, and take pictures of it all. Hardly have Mark and Andy set foot aboard the river steamer that's to carry them to their destination when "a small boat manned with a murderous looking crew puts out from the shore." And so it goes, year in and year out, with the first ecology-minded adventure strip hero.

Dodd was in his early forties when he began doing *Mark Trail*. A protégé of no less an outdoor artist than Dan Beard, Dodd led an early life as a rancher and woodland guide. In the 1930s he signed on with United Features to draw a daily panel: *Back Home Again* was a folksy, homespun effort, obviously inspired by J.R. Williams' long-popular *Out Our Way*. His *Mark Trail*, in its first years anyway, was nicely done. Dodd enjoyed depicting animals and forests, all of which he rendered in his patient pen style. The Sunday page never went in for continuity, offering instead an endless series of rather pious nature lectures. For many years Jack Elrod, a long-time assistant, has shared a credit on the feature.                    **R.G.**

**MARLETTE, DOUG** (1949– ) Doug Marlette had already established himself as a highly successful political cartoonist when he created the popular daily and Sunday humor strip *Kudzu* in 1981, and he has gone on to achieve new successes in both areas of his career since.

Born in Greensboro, North Carolina, and raised in Laurel, Mississippi, and Sanford, Florida, Marlette did his first professional work while in high school. Although the comics were his first love, "political cartoons came," as he explains, "during [his] turbulent adolescence, which corresponded with the turbulent sixties."

He worked his way through community college in the art department of the Orlando (Fla.) *Sentinel* and drew three cartoons a week for *The Flambeau*, the student newspaper at Florida State University, where he majored in philosophy and minored in art. In 1972, after graduating, he became the editorial cartoonist for the *Charlotte (N.C.) Observer*. In 1987 he moved on to the *Atlanta Constitution*, and in 1989 to *New York Newsday*.

Marlette's editorial cartoons were syndicated by King Features Syndicate in 1975, and *Kudzu* started in 1981 with Tribune Media Services, but the cartoonist brought both features over to the newly founded Creators Syndicate in 1988. His political cartoons, now syndicated to over 125 papers worldwide, have earned him numerous honors. In 1980–1981 he was the first, and so far remains the only, cartoonist to receive a Neiman Fellowship at Harvard University. He won the National Headliners Award in 1983 and 1988, the Robert F. Kennedy Memorial Award and the Sigma Delta Chi award in 1985, the First Amendment Award and first place in the John Fischetti Competition in 1986, and the Pulitzer Prize in 1988.

The bare, minimal style Marlette employs in his trenchant political cartoons carries over into his genial comic strip. *Kudzu*, the saga of an adolescent hayseed who dreams of growing hair on his chest, getting a date with the local belle, and escaping his hometown of Bypass, North Carolina, is a blend of sympathetic humor and shrewd social commentary, and has seen a steady increase in readership.　　**D.W.**

**MARSH, JESSE** (1907–1966)　The first—and some feel the best—artist to draw original Tarzan stories for comic books, Marsh began depicting Edgar Rice Burroughs' jungle lord in 1947, when Dell published a successful one-shot titled *Tarzan and the Devil Ogre*. A subsequent one-shot also proved successful, and late that year a *Tarzan* monthly began; Marsh stayed with the King of the Apes until 1965.

He was an unusual choice to do Tarzan, since his style was in the Caniff-Sickles camp and the apeman was usually drawn by disciples of the Hal Foster school; nevertheless, he produced an excellent version. Marsh became an expert on the peoples, flora, and fauna of Africa and gave a look of authenticity to the most improbable of the jungle man's adventures. His work was much admired by many of his colleagues, most especially Alex Toth and Russ Manning.

Marsh, who lived in the Los Angeles area, had worked for the Disney studio from 1939 through 1948 as a story man on such features as *Fantasia*, *Pinocchio*, and *Melody Time*. He first drew for comic books in 1946, debuting on Dell's Gene Autry title. He turned out an enormous amount of comic book pages for the Dell-Whitman offices in Southern California. Besides Tarzan and Gene Autry, he worked on Daniel Boone, Roy Rogers, Davy Crockett, John Carter of Mars, and Annie Oakley, among others.

A prolific artist, he also drew the newspaper Sunday page *Walt Disney's Treasury of Classic Tales*, from its inception in 1952 into the 1960s. Among the Disney movie adaptations that Marsh illustrated were *Robin Hood*, *Rob Roy*, and *The Swiss Family Robinson*.

When he retired in 1965, it was his intention to devote the rest of his life to painting. He died the following year.　　**R.G.**

**MARSTON, WILLIAM MOULTON**　See WON-DER WOMAN.

**MARTIN, EDGAR**　See BOOTS AND HER BUDDIES.

**MARY MARVEL**　The first teenage superheroine in comic books and a member of an illustrious family, Mary made her debut late in 1942 and stayed in business until 1954. (She would be revived some two decades later.) Mary initially appeared in *Captain Marvel Adventures* #18 (December 1942), where it was revealed that she was the long-lost sister of Billy Batson (better known as Captain Marvel). And, like the Captain, she became Mary Marvel, superteenager, simply by saying "Shazam!" She had her own separate but equal version of the famous acronym, which in Mary's case stood for Selena, Hippolyta, Ariadne, Zephyrus, Aurora, and Minerva.

Mary Marvel took over as the leading character in *Wow Comics* in the ninth issue (January 1943), nudging Mr. Scarlet out of the star spot. She had a magazine of her own from 1945 to 1948 and was a regular in *The Marvel Family*. When DC revived her brother in 1973, she also returned to comics for a few years.

Otto Binder provided a goodly portion of the Golden Age scripts, and Marc Swayze was the first artist to draw her. Jack Binder illustrated her adventures for most of her original career.　　**R.G.**

**MARY WORTH**　The most influential of the soap opera strips that blossomed in the 1940s, *Mary Worth* had actually begun in the 1930s under a different name. During the amiable busybody's most successful years she was looked after by writer Allen Saunders and artist Ken Ernst.

In October of 1934 Publishers Syndicate introduced *Apple Mary*. It did fairly well, picking up 96 client papers in its first six months. Although it owed something to the increasingly popular radio soap operas, more important to the strip's creation was a Frank Capra movie released in 1933. The film was called *Lady For a Day* and was based on a Damon Runyon short story. Featuring May Robson as a colorful street peddler named Apple Annie, the picture was Capra's first big hit.

The *Apple Mary* strip was most certainly inspired by the movie. It was the work of Martha Orr, as the syndicate put it, a "comely artist, only 26 years old." Miss Orr was also the niece of *Chicago Tribune* political cartoonist Carey Orr, which may have had as much influence on the syndicate editors as her comeliness. Her drawing was competent though on the bland side, and her continuities were similar to what Oxydol, Rinso, and Ivory were offering over the airwaves. Plump, lovable, gray-haired Mary struggled against an assortment of skinflints and conmen as she sold her apples on the street and saw to it that her crippled little nephew Denny got a fair shake in life. Things went on like that until 1939, when Martha Orr quit to concentrate on her real-life family life.

Her assistant, a young woman named Dale Conner Ulrey, took over the drawing, and the writing was turned over to Allen Saunders, who was already scripting the successful *Big Chief Wahoo* for the syndicate. When he took over *Apple Mary*, he made the strip considerably slicker and changed the title to *Mary Worth's Family*. Mary, who was no longer hawking apples on the corner, ceased to be a major focal character and became instead "a linking character, who provides continuity by tirelessly meeting very interesting people." Many of these interesting people were rich and glamorous—movie actresses, playboys, industrialists, and the like.

Saunders had realized that, as the Depression finally gave way to a growing economy, readers were more interested in the lifestyles of the rich and famous than they were in tenement life among the poor. Mary became much more mobile, dispensing her wisdom and advice to a wide range of middle- and upper-class lovelorn, becoming a peripatetic Miss Lonelyhearts. Under the pen name Dale Allen, Saunders and Ulrey remained a team for three years. Then the artist, teaming with her writer husband, left to try a strip of her own, *Hugh Striver.*

The next artist was Ken Ernst, a longtime disciple of Milton Caniff and Noel Sickles. A while after he began his job the strip shortened its title to just plain *Mary Worth.* His slick brush style increased the appeal of the strip, as did Saunders' somewhat more sophisticated continuities. "For soap opera suffering," said Saunders about the changes he and his partner wrought, "we decided to substitute romantic novelettes about glossy girls in more glamorous professions." Ernst's girls were certainly glossy, but the stories were still soap opera. What Saunders was doing was bringing them into line with the less naive stuff offered by radio soap operas and women's movies in the middle 1940s. He got inspiration, too, from the mass media concerns of the day, building stories around advertising, show business, fashion, and other fields that the public believed were exciting. In the postwar years, he also dealt with contemporary problems, such as returning GIs, and housing shortages. By the end of World War II *Mary Worth* was on its way to becoming a top-selling strip, and the postwar years saw more strips trying to get into the act, among them *Cynthia, Rex Morgan, M.D.,* and others.

*Mary Worth* continues to appear, though in a smaller number of newspapers. John Saunders writes it currently, and Ernst's longtime ghost Bill Ziegler supervises the drawing.                                    **R.G.**

**MAULDIN, BILL** (1921– ) The best-known cartoonist-illustrator of World War II, the creator of the archetypal foot soldiers Willie and Joe, Bill Mauldin became nationally famous with his syndicated series *Up Front.* Mauldin's humorous and poignant depictions of the unromantic face of war were to become emblematic of their period of American history, and his subsequent career as an editorial cartoonist has sustained his early reputation.

William Henry Mauldin was born in Mountain Park, New Mexico, and began doing posters for stores and filling stations at the age of 13. He went to high school in Phoenix, where he worked on the school newspaper and was encouraged by a teacher to go on to art school. With $500 borrowed from his grandparents, he paid a year's tuition at the Chicago Academy of Fine Arts and studied under Pulitzer-prizewinning political cartoonist Vaughan Shoemaker.

Although actively free-lancing—"I managed to send out ten cartoon roughs every day to the magazines," he recalls—he couldn't quite support himself in those late-Depression years, and in 1940 he joined the National Guard. About a week later his unit was the first called up, and he became a part of the regular Army. At once Mauldin began placing his work in his division newspaper, and when he was transferred from a truck unit to a rifle company of the infantry he created the two eloquently taciturn cartoon figures who came to symbolize the Common Man at war. A sardonic voice for the enlisted man, his sketches of Willie and Joe kidded the brass in a tone more mischievous than really seditious, and, though they drew trouble from the upper echelons, they proved too popular with the rank and file to suppress. When he moved from the *45th Division News* to *Stars and Stripes* in 1944, Mauldin was already a national figure. Distributed by United Features Syndicate in the United States, he received a Pulitzer in 1945.

Mauldin came out of the Army at the war's end with a contract for $150 a week from United and continued his feature as *Willie and Joe*, dealing with his characters' return to civilian life. Although he published a best-selling collection as *Up Front* in 1945 and another, called *Back Home*, in 1947, his panel was losing papers. Willie and Joe were no longer spokesmen anyone wanted to hear from, and papers were unsure where to put them. As Maudlin himself put it, "So I set two records in a very short time. I rolled up more papers than anyone had and I think I lost more than anyone had." So Mauldin quit when his contract ran out in 1949. He took a job with the short-lived *New York Star*, working with Walt Kelly, and when the *Star* set in 1949 began what he called "a ten-year sabbatical," writing books, acting in movies (including *The Red Badge of Courage*), and flying a plane. For a lark he even ran for Congress, an experience that gave him insight he could never otherwise have acquired into the political process.

After a year filling in without pay for the ailing Herblock at the Hall Syndicate, Mauldin accepted the position of Daniel Fitzpatrick at the *St. Louis Post-Dispatch* in 1958, and four years later switched to the *Chicago Sun-Times*, where he has remained since.

Willie and Joe have long since been retired, and Mauldin has emerged as a shrewd and incisive social and political commentator. A powerful voice in defense of civil rights and the environment, he has for more than a quarter of a century maintained a consistently clear-headed liberal stance. Syndicated to more than 200 papers, his forceful crayon renderings combine the wry humor of his now-classic wartime illustrations with a mordant and thoroughly contemporary indignation.

In addition to the Pulitzer Prize that he won in 1945— at the age of 24, he was the youngest ever to receive that honor—he received another Pulitzer in 1959. That same year the National Cartoonists Society voted him its Silver T-Square and a plaque for the Best Political Cartoon of the year. In 1961 he received the NCS's top award, the Reuben, and he took the Sigma Delta Chi Award in 1969 and 1972. **D.W.**

**MAURER, NORMAN** (1926–1986) He had one of the most varied careers of any cartoonist. While still in his teens Maurer began drawing for comic books, working on such 1940s heroes as Crimebuster and the original Daredevil. He also contributed to the innovative *Crime Does Not Pay*, and he later had a hand in the invention of the first 3-D comic books. Eventually Maurer went into movie production, being responsible for, among other things, several epics starring the Three Stooges.

The Brooklyn-born Maurer attended the High School of Music and Art in Manhattan. It was there he met his lifelong friend and colleague, artist Joe Kubert. Both of them began drawing for comic books in their teenage years. Maurer became a protégé of Charles Biro and did his earliest work for the magazines coedited by the artist-writer—*Boy Comics* and *Daredevil*. Eventually Maurer, whose style was influenced by that of Biro and of Milton Caniff, was drawing the star heroes of both magazines, Crimebuster and Daredevil. He also drew for the early issues of the semi-true *Crime Does Not Pay*, Biro's bloodiest, most violent, and most successful title.

After serving in the Navy, Maurer relocated to the Los Angeles area and married the daughter of Moe Howard, head Stooge of the Three Stooges movie comedy team. Maurer returned to working for Biro, doing it by mail now. In 1953 he headed East briefly, getting together with Kubert to turn out comic books for the St. John company. One of the things they produced was the very first 3-D comic book. "The 3-D effect was put together by Norman Maurer, his brother Lenny, and myself," Kubert has recalled. "I had been in the Army in 1950 and 1951 and while in Germany I had come across some magazines with photos in 3-D. I thought it would be terrific to use the effect in comic books...Norm, Lenny and myself sat down and we finally came up with a procedure to produce 3-D comic books and eventually gave it to St. John." The initial book was *Mighty Mouse*, which sold a million copies. Kubert's *Tor*, a caveman adventure, and Maurer's *Three Stooges* followed. "By the tenth or eleventh 3-D book," said Kubert, "the sales were down to about 19%, so we had to stop publication."

Maurer did some work for Marvel, then left comic books. Back in Hollywood he worked as a producer/director-writer. He was involved with such movies as *Angry Red Planet* (1959), *The Three Stooges Meet Hercules* (1961), *The Three Stooges in Orbit* (1962), and *The Outlaws Is Coming* (1965). He went on to produce animated Stooge shows for Saturday morning television. In the early 1970s he returned briefly to comic books and did some jobs for DC's *Our Army at War*, which Kubert was editing. By the middle 1970s he was out of comics for good and back in television. **R.G.**

**MAUS** When Art Spiegelman's extended comic strip *Maus: A Survivor's Tale* was collected into a bound volume and published by Pantheon in September 1986, it was the literary bombshell of the year. Using the old comic strip convention of animal characters, the author retold the story of his parents, survivors of the Nazi Holocaust. Though some readers might have been shocked by the depiction of genocide in a traditionally frivolous medium, the book had a profound impact on three separate audiences: comics buffs, who saw it as giving a new dimension to the medium; the Jewish community, who recognized in it a profoundly sensitive account of the most moving historical event of the century; and the general public, who were deeply affected by its gripping narrative.

*Maus* originated in 1972 as a three-page graphic spread in the ephemeral underground comic book *Funny Aminals* [sic]. Seeking "a story worth telling," Spiegelman chose that of his parents, who had escaped from a concentration camp in Poland, adopting the metaphor of the helpless mouse for the Jews, the powerful cat for the Nazis. The story of his parents and his own complex and ambivalent relationship with them was expanded and presented in numbers two through eight of *Raw*, the annual magazine of avant-garde graphics (which Spiegelman still produces with his wife, Francoise Mouly) from 1980 to 1986. Spiegelman is now working on a sequel.

The stark simplicity of *Maus'* imagery greatly enhances the book's dramatic effect. Surprisingly, almost no one has accused Spiegelman of trivializing his material. The winner of awards in many countries and a nominee for the National Book Critics Award for biography, *Maus* has been translated into over a dozen languages.

*Maus: A Survivor's Tale* tells the story of the author's parents through their incarceration in a concentration camp. Spiegelman plans a second volume, to be called *Maus, Part Two: From Mauschwitz to the Catskills and Beyond*, which will complete their story. **D.W.**

**MAXIMO** A superhero who appeared only in a series of Big Little Books in the early 1940s, Maximo represented the Whitman Publishing Company's attempt to extend the comic book craze into a new medium. The first book, *Maximo the Amazing Superman*, appeared in 1940 with a text by Russ Winterbotham and 200-some illustrations by Henry Vallely.

Maximo Miller was a handsome, blond young man who was not only "athletically built" but "gifted with a superbrain." In the course of the book, with the help of Professor Arvid and his lovely daughter, Maximo learned how to tap the full power of his extraordinary brain, and was soon able to lift all sorts of objects, including automobiles, simply by willing them to rise. He could also levitate himself and fly.

Winterbotham, a veteran pulp magazine science fiction writer, was attempting to create a superhero who was almost plausible, whose abilities grew out of extrapolation about current speculations on the latent powers of the mind. Unfortunately, the appeal of Maximo's many comic book colleagues was not to logic and reason but to the daydreaming side of the mind.

Maximo did his superhero work in everyday clothes—riding pants, boots, and a paramilitary jacket.

It was a practical outfit for his sort of business, but not especially flamboyant. He starred in two more BLBs in 1941, then was heard from no more. **R.G.**

**MAXON, REX** (1892–1973) Despite the fact that Edgar Rice Burroughs never liked his work, Maxon drew the *Tarzan* strip, based on Burroughs' fictional jungle lord, for 18 years, with one hiatus in the late 1930s. After leaving the feature for good in 1947, he moved on to comic books and worked for them for almost the rest of his life.

Born in Nebraska and raised in St. Louis, Rex Hayden Maxon got his first art job with the *St. Louis Republic*. "I went to New York and did feature drawings for *The Evening World, The Evening Mail*, and *The Globe*," he said, "but dropped it to draw *Tarzan*." Maxon was the first artist to draw the strip after Hal Foster, and his initial daily appeared on June 17, 1929. Foster was indeed a hard act to follow, but Maxon still seems an odd choice since he lacked his predecessor's skill in figure drawing, composition, and several other abilities essential for the drawing of a jungle adventure strip. Burroughs, who had no control over who drew the strip, disliked Maxon's approach and complained frequently to the syndicate, even suggesting that Maxon be given photos of animals so he could learn to draw them correctly. Maxon, however, was kept on, possibly because he put up with the small salary.

When a Sunday page was added in March of 1931, Maxon drew that, too, and again Burroughs wasn't especially pleased with his work (and didn't much care for the story line either). Foster was persuaded to return and took over the Sunday in its 29th week, while Maxon continued with the daily until he asked for a raise, was turned down, and quit. In 1937 and 1938 William Juhré did the daily, but Maxon returned in 1938 and remained with *Tarzan* until 1947, writing the strip as well during the World War II years. (In one of his sequences he had Tarzan meet Hitler.)

Maxon's work improved some over the years, especially after he took to imitating magazine illustrator John Clymer. But he lacked the bravura approach, evidenced in the work of Hal Foster and Burne Hogarth, that most readers demanded.

He managed to stay on in the jungle with his comic book work. His major assignment for Dell was *Turok, Son of Stone*, which dealt with an Indian brave in the prehistoric world. Under the pen name R. Hayden he drew a black-and-white feature, *K-Bar Kate*, for the *Six-Gun Western* pulp. During many of his years with *Tarzan*, Maxon had also moonlighted as a pulp illustrator, working exclusively for the magazines published by the venturesome Frank Armer—*Spicy Detective, Private De-*

*tective, Speed Western*, and so on. He continued to draw for comic books until 1971, two years before his death.

**R.G.**

**MAYER, SHELDON** (1917– ) Basically a cartoonist, Mayer got into the comic book business shortly after it started in the middle 1930s. He soon became an editor and a writer as well and by the early 1940s was the most important editor in the field. As a cartoonist he drew such comic book features as *Scribbly* and *Sugar & Spike* and ghosted the *Bobby Thatcher* newspaper strip. As an editor he had a hand in the creation of such superheroes as the Flash, Hawkman, and the Green Lantern. He was also instrumental in getting DC to buy *Superman* in 1938.

Mayer was born in New York, in a far from genteel neighborhood. "East Harlem…was a rough, tough neighborhood in those days," he's said. "Kids began to think about what they were going to do for a living from the day they were born, because everybody wanted to get out of there as soon as possible." Cartooning was the means of escape young Mayer chose. He began haunting newspapers and syndicates from the time he was 14. The first comic book work he did appeared in 1935 in Major Nicholson's *New Fun* and *New Comics;* and the following year he went to work for M.C. Gaines on *The Funnies, Popular Comics*, and eventually *The Comics*. These were 64-page monthly compilations of newspaper strip reprints that Gaines was producing to cash in on the just commencing comic book boom. Listed as Dell publications, all the magazines were put together in the offices of the McClure Syndicate, whose color presses Gaines was using. Mayer's *Scribbly* was created for *The Funnies*. A fairly autobiographical feature about a boy cartoonist, it was laid out like a Sunday page so that Mayer's upstart creation could rub shoulders undetected with the real Sunday funnies being reprinted.

In the spring of 1937 George Storm quit producing his *Bobby Thatcher* strip, which was being syndicated by McClure. Mayer was just 20 when the job of ghosting the strip fell to him, but a few weeks later the strip was allowed to end.

One of the strips that was submitted to McClure was *Superman*. Mayer was impressed by Siegel and Shuster's submission, so much so that he persuaded Gaines to send it over to DC when he heard they were looking for a new character to use in *Action Comics*. The Man of Steel turned out to be an even bigger hit than Mayer had anticipated.

Late in 1939 Gaines agreed to produce a line of comic books for DC, and took Mayer with him as editor. The Gaines-Mayer titles included *All-American Comics*, where the original Green Lantern made his debut; *Flash Comics*, which of featured the Flash and Hawkman; *All Star Comics*, the home of the Justice Society; *Sensation Comics*, where Wonder Woman (a character Mayer never much cared for) was the star. He also drew *Scribbly* for *All-American*.

Mayer abandoned his boy cartoonist in the middle 1940s to concentrate on editing. He did some drawing for *Funny Stuff*, turning out the fifth issue of the funny animal title entirely on his own. After stepping down as a DC editor, he drew all sorts of funny animal strips. In 1956 came his other major creation, *Sugar & Spike*. It wasn't like most other kid comics in that its two toddlers weren't even able to talk yet, or so the unimaginative adults around them thought. In those panels without adults, Sugar and Spike spoke English while those within earshot of grownups showed nothing but gibberish! All of this helped them get through the wild and fantastic adventures Mayer concocted for them. There were nearly 100 issues of the *Sugar & Spike* title.

Over the past few years, after some time off because of eye trouble, Mayer has been drawing again. He produced new *Sugar & Spike* material for overseas markets and drew new covers for some digest reprints of the adventures in this country. **R.G.**

**MERRIE CHASE** A sitcom sort of continuity strip about a pretty blond policewoman, *Merrie Chase* started in July 1949, written by Renny McEvoy, actor and longtime scriptwriter on *Dixie Dugan*. The strip's first artist was Carl Hubbell, who'd worked in comic books throughout the 1940s. After a few months, however, he was replaced by Paul Reinman, also from comic books.

The strip tried for that same mixture of comedy, adventure, and pretty girls that had worked for *Dixie Dugan*, but the stories never quite succeeded, and Reinman's art was well intended but second-rate. In September 1950 Merrie left the police force to become a private eye. That didn't help much, and the strip ended a few months later. **R.G.**

**MESKIN, MORT** (1916– ) He worked in comic books for nearly 30 years and was considered by many of his peers to be one of the best artists in the business. Entering the field in 1938, Meskin was the first to draw *Sheena*, and he went on to turn out impressively executed adventures of superheroes, cowboys, detectives, soldiers of fortune, lovelorn ladies, and ghostbreakers.

Although he was never a favorite with the fans, fellow artists and comics historians have always regarded Meskin highly. Steranko in his *History of the Comics*, for example, lauds Meskin's "genuine vitality and crackle" and points out that he "experimented, developed a new set of comic book tricks, and deplored the use of 'stock shots.'"

*Golden Lad*, Mort Meskin, 1946.

Born in Brooklyn, Meskin studied at the Pratt Institute and the Art Students League. The newspaper artists who influenced him the most were Alex Raymond and Milton Caniff, and he was also a great admirer of pulp illustrators Herbert Morton Stoops and Edd Cartier. The imaginative, impressionistic illustrations Cartier did in *The Shadow* pulp especially impressed Meskin.

After a brief stay with the Eisner-Iger shop, where he drew the jungle queen, he moved to MLJ (now Archie Comics, Inc.) and drew a variety of features, including the mustachioed superhero the Wizard, for such titles as *Pep Comics* and *Zip Comics.* His best work was in the early and mid-1940s for DC, where he drew impressive adventures of the Vigilante, Johnny Quick, Starman, and Wildcat. His splash panels rivaled anything Jack Kirby ever cooked up, and Meskin's layout, staging, and figure work gave life to scripts that were often rather lame. Later, sometimes teamed with Jerry Robinson, Meskin worked for several other publishers and

drew Golden Lad, the Black Terror, and the Fighting Yank. When heroes declined in the late 1940s, he switched to romance, horror, true crime, and Western.

A shy, reticent man, Meskin eventually tired of the comic book business. In the mid-1960s he took a job as an art director for a major New York City advertising agency and remained there until his recent retirement.

**R.G.**

**MESSICK, DALE** See BRENDA STARR.

**MESSMER, OTTO** (1892–1983) Versatile and virtually unknown to the public during most of his active years as a cartoonist, Messmer was the creator of Felix the Cat. He drew him first in 1919, for Felix' debut as an animated movie cartoon character, and later drew him for his appearances in the funny papers and in comic books.

Messmer grew up in Fort Lee, New Jersey, which was a motion picture production center in the early decades of this century. He studied commercial art at night school and worked days painting scenery at the Universal studios. He became fascinated with animated cartoons and set up his own animation stand. In 1916 he went to work for an animator named Pat Sullivan. The following year Messmer did a series of authorized animated cartoons for Sullivan using the Charlie Chaplin tramp character. After World War I service in the Signal Corps, he returned to Sullivan's small studio.

"In 1919 I created a character which Paramount named 'Felix the Cat,'" Messmer once explained. "I used the style of Charlie Chaplin and kept him alone in his antics, unhampered by supporting characters. Being a loner, he could roam to various locations, without being limited to any fixed place." Since he was employed by Sullivan, Messmer's Felix was the property of his boss, and Sullivan's name appeared on the cartoons.

The feisty black cat was an immediate hit. Dozens of Felix cartoons followed, and in the 1920s he became an important merchandising property, which resulted in, among other things, a newspaper strip. Messmer had a hand in that from the early 1920s to the early 1950s, drawing it in an amiable, slightly cute animation style. Pat Sullivan's name was the one signed to the strip.

Felix broke into comic books in 1927 when a publisher named McLoughlin Brothers reprinted some Sunday pages in an odd-size 24-page format. Fifteen years later the peripatetic feline showed up as one of the characters in Dell's *New Funnies*. Dell published their first comic book devoted entirely to Felix in 1943. After a few more one-shots reprinting old newspaper strips, Dell launched a regular *Felix the Cat* title, which used original material, a good deal of which was produced by Messmer. Toby Press took over the title in 1951, then it passed to Harvey in 1955. Messmer quit drawing the feature at that point.

After Sullivan's death in 1933, Messmer free-lanced for other studios but had nothing to do with the movie phase of his cat's career. He also worked for an outfit called Douglas Leigh that did the immense animated electric signs that lit up Times Square in Manhattan. Briefly in the 1940s Messmer was an animator with the Famous Studios. He retired in the early 1970s, and in the last years of his life was finally given credit, by critics and historians, for having invented one of the most enduring cartoon characters of the century.   **R.G.**

**MICKEY FINN**   Patrolman Michael Aloysius Finn, as Irish as Paddy's pig and as honest as the day is long, was the hero of one of the few comic strips ever to portray a city policeman in a manner neither sentimental nor sensational. Created by sports cartoonist Lank Leonard for the McNaught Syndicate, *Mickey Finn* began as a daily continuity strip on April 6, 1936, with

a Sunday version starting on the 12th of the following month.

For over three decades Leonard maintained the cheerful, slow-paced saga of Mickey, his sweet widowed mother, and his genial but fatuous Uncle Phil. The daily recounted the police adventures of the good-natured Mickey, who was to reach the rank of detective, and Phil, whose childish, boastful, bibulous nature frequently made him the comic relief. Phil was to become a sheriff and an alderman, but he remained more a victim than a hero. Most of the Sunday episodes centered on his misadventures at his club, the Goat Hill Lodge of the Ancient Order of American Grenadiers, whose members frequently made him the butt of their jokes.

For many years the Sunday had a topper called *Nippie: He's Often Wrong*, about a willful little boy who insisted on doing things his own way and was *always* wrong. The cautionary note it struck, though seldom very funny, was consistent with the moral tone of the feature strip it accompanied, wherein evil, or folly, were always duly punished. In fact, there was probably more violence in *Nippie*, whose hero was always falling out of trees he had been warned not to climb or being bitten by dogs he had been told not to tease, than in *Mickey Finn*, which usually included nothing more threatening than the inevitable black eye after one of Uncle Phil's brawls or the peaceful arrest of a crook.

*Mickey Finn* was competently drawn, and its plain design and stereotyped figures fitted with the simple characterizations and plots. During its heyday it was carried in as many as 300 papers. Morris Weiss started as Leonard's assistant and sometime ghost during the feature's first year; from 1952 to 1958, when Weiss was occupied elsewhere, Mart Bailey worked with Leonard. A comic book veteran, Bailey had drawn the Finn characters on the covers of several comic book reprints of the strip.

When Lank Leonard retired in 1968, Weiss succeeded him and carried on without a break, maintaining the style and tone effectively while updating the stories. The Sunday *Mickey Finn* ended on December 21, 1975, and the daily followed it into oblivion on July 31 of the next year, three months after its 30th birthday.   **D.W.**

**MICKEY MOUSE**   The celebrated rodent was born in a Walt Disney animated cartoon in 1928. He quickly won public favor and grew to be one of the most widely merchandised characters of the century. The *Mickey Mouse* newspaper strip began in 1930, and comic books followed a year later.

Mickey Mouse was created by Disney and developed by animator Ub Iwerks. The first cartoon the struggling Disney Southern California studio turned out with him was a silent titled *Plane Crazy*, the second was *Gallopin' Gaucho*. Initially, however, Disney was unable to find a distributor for either one. Then came *Steamboat Willie* with its hastily added soundtrack; it took advantage of the sound craze ushered in by *The Jazz Singer* and became a hit. The two earlier mouse cartoons, with new sound tracks, were released next. In 1928 and 1929 Disney and his crew turned out another dozen Mickey animated shorts.

The year after Mickey's screen debut King Features became interested in doing a newspaper strip based on him. They'd had fair success with a *Felix the Cat* strip started a few years earlier and apparently felt there was room in the funny papers for another popular animated cartoon character. The *Mickey Mouse* daily started on January 13, 1930, followed by a Sunday page on January 10, 1932.

The beginning strips used a gag-a-day format and Disney himself wrote the copy. Iwerks penciled the first four weeks, and then Win Smith, who'd been his inker, took over the drawing. Smith had a falling out with Disney in the spring of 1930 and walked out. He was replaced by young Floyd Gottfredson, who remained on the strip for the next 45 years.

Gottfredson was the ideal man for the job. He drew well, doing an excellent job not only on the optimistic go-getter Mickey, but on all the other animal characters as well. He could also draw the complex backgrounds the continuities called for. The strip soon changed from daily jokes to continued narratives, and Gottfredson was good, too, at working out the mock adventure continuities that were a staple for over two decades. He took care of the scripting himself for the first few years and, even after writers were brought in, always took part in the plotting.

Throughout the 1930s and 1940s Mickey led an adventurous life as Gottfredson and his collaborators starred him in lively spoofs of every kind of action movie of the day. The plucky mouse went up against mad scientists, ghosts, Western bandits, air pirates, and racketeers. He searched for lost treasure, impersonated royalty, served a stretch in the Foreign Legion, dwelled with cavemen, and visited the far future. Minnie Mouse costarred in many of the stories, and Mickey's usual sidekick was Goofy. The most frequent villain was Peg-Leg Pete. The huge, rotten-hearted tomcat first plagued Mickey in a 1930 continuity and was last seen in a 1952 sequence. As of early October 1955 *Mickey Mouse* became a joke-a-day strip and its great days ended. "When he was in a corner, he was a feisty little guy, who could fight his way out—pretty scrappy and so on. He remained pretty much that way throughout the continuities," Gottfredson once said. "But when we stopped the continuities and got into the gag-a-day business…he became just a straight man."

Over the years Gottfredson collaborated with an assortment of writers and inkers. Among the scripters were Ted Osborne (from 1933 to 1938), Merril deMaris (1938 to 1942), and Bill Walsh (1943 to 1955). Inkers included Al Taliaferro, Ted Thwaites, Dick Moores, and Bill Wright. After Gottfredson's retirement in 1975, the drawing of the daily was taken over by Roman Arambula. Gottfredson had relinquished the Sunday page back in 1938 and it was capably carried on by Manuel Gonzales for the next 40-plus years. Among the more recent Sunday artists are Bill Wright, Tony Strobl, and Daan Jippes.

In 1931 the David McKay company published a 52-page black and white, cardboard-covered book of daily strip reprints. McKay followed with annual reprint books for the next three years, the 1933 edition featuring color reprints of Sunday pages. *Mickey Mouse Magazine*, containing stories, games, puzzles, and comics, began in 1933. Initially it was used as a premium given away by various dairies. A newsstand version, published by Whitman in collaboration with Disney, appeared in 1935. The title was changed to *Walt Disney's Comics and Stories* in 1940, with the contents switching almost entirely to reprints of such strips as *Mickey Mouse* and *Donald Duck*.

Gottfredson's Mickey strips were recycled for several years. Next came adaptations of some of the strip continuities by other hands. Finally in the middle 1950s Paul Murry began drawing new Mickey Mouse stories for *WDC&S*. In these Mickey was teamed with Goofy and enjoyed farflung adventures similar to those he'd encountered in the newspaper strip. The comic book shut down in 1984 but was revived by Gladstone in 1986. Mickey appeared again, but in reprints of earlier stuff.

Mickey got a four-color comic book all his own in 1941, and it has continued, with a two-year hiatus in the middle 1980s, to this day. Initially it dealt in reprints, but soon switched to original material. The Disney outfit took over in 1990, publishing the title themselves.

**R.G.**

**MIKE AND IKE**  See GOLDBERG, RUBE.

**MILLS, TARPE**  See MISS FURY.

**MINUTE MOVIES**  Written and drawn by Ed Wheelan, *Minute Movies* began in the early 1920s and lasted until the middle 1930s. Wheelan revived it again in the early 1940s, this time as a backup feature in *Flash Comics*. Later in his life he claimed he was a pioneer of the serious adventure strip. In its early years, though,

*Minute Movies* burlesqued and satirized the sort of adventure fare to be found upon the silver screen. He did use continuity earlier than many of his comic strip colleagues and was taking a week or two to tell each story while they were still concentrating on getting across a joke each day.

Wheelan had gone to work for Hearst's *New York American* in the middle of the second decade of the century. After he was there for a while he began to do a strip that ran across the top of one of the sports pages—"It had no name but burlesqued various films and stars of the silent era." This evolved into larger strip he called *Midget Movies*, the first of which appeared on April 8, 1918. It was a one-day parody of a travelogue. The next two days were given over to a two-part continuity titled *The Heart of a Vampire.* His strips were all takeoffs of current films, making it difficult to award him the title of inventor of the serious adventure strip, since he obviously wasn't taking any of it seriously.

Wheelan quit the Hearst outfit at the end of the decade. Signing up with the George Mathew Adams syndicate, he began drawing his strip under the new title *Minute Movies* in 1921. Gradually he introduced a regular cast of characters. They'd appear in various kinds of films, playing all sorts of roles. The first regular was Dick Dare, a pretty boy in the Hairbreadth Harry mold. The epics, now running a week at least, were always directed by Art Hokum. Among the other regulars on the Wheelan lot were the sweet and innocent Hazel Dearie, the somewhat livelier Lotta Talent, the sinister Ralph McSneer, "a composite of Lew Cody, Stuart Holmes, Lon Chaney, etc.," Blanche Rouge, "inspired by Theda Bara," and the resident Valentino named Paul Vogue. There was also a fat comic named Fuller Phun and a skinny comic named Archibald Clubb (a reference to the fact that he frequently played a cop). Eventually Wheelan also added a child star named Herbert Honey, a wonder dog named Dynamo, a mutt dog named Patches, and Milo, the Marvel Monk of the Movies.

Using the motion pictures as a takeoff point, Wheelan put his company of actors into every kind of story. Thus he was working in several of the categories adventure strips would use, from Western and detective to aviation and sports. He utilized long shots, closeups, and other camera-inspired setups. As the 1920s progressed his continuities grew longer, taking up three to four weeks. In between he ran mock newsreels, animated cartoons, and travelogues. He also frequently gave biographical information about his stars, kidding gossip columns but at the same time giving some life to the characters: "Dick Dare, popular leading man with 'Minute Movies,' having fallen in love plans to disregard his signed contract with the Wheelan forces," or "The new cafeteria recently opened on the Wheelan Lot proves very popular with the stars," or "During the hot weather Hazel Dearie decided to bob her hair."

In the serials themselves Dick Dare was inevitably the hero, appearing as Hal Fracas, Robert Rich, Bob Manley, Basil Spongecake, Emery Stone, and similar dashing types. Blonde Hazel Dearie was always a heroine, starring in such vehicles as *The Hazards of Hazel*, in which she portrayed Hazel Knutt, "the cleverest lady-detective in all the East." Ralph McSneer, as might be expected, was rarely a good guy and showed up in such parts as Cyril Sinister, Sherwood Skamp, James Hound, Li Low, Sam Malice, and the Spider.

By the late 1920s Wheelan, perhaps sensing that adventure strips were on the horizon, turned somewhat serious. He had Art Hokum address the readers directly to tell them that "our serials have changed. They have become longer and we have stopped trying to make them funny, in an endeavor to make them thrilling and interesting." The stories did become serious, and sometimes sentimental, and Wheelan also began to adapt classics. His productions of *Ivanhoe, Treasure Island,* and other worthy properties won him favor among school teachers, but they changed the strip into something Wheelan once would have made fun of himself. As all clowns are supposed to yearn to do, he even did *Hamlet.* Dick Dare was Hamlet, Hazel Dearie was Ophelia, Ralph McSneer was Claudius.

Wheelan's dailies had always been two-tiers, allowing him to fit in more dialogue and pictures. In the middle 1930s, as his list of papers began to shrink despite the serious continuities, he changed *Minute Movies* to a single-tier strip and dropped most of the cinema touches, such as the iris shots. He went back to humor, giving Fuller Phun and Archibald Clubb more time on screen. He even used them as Padlock Homes and Dr. Watsis, characters he'd return to later in comic books. Nothing helped and by 1936 *Minute Movies* was gone.

He brought back his characters in six- and eight-page stories in *Flash Comics* in the early 1940s, putting Dick Dare, Hazel Dearie and the rest in the odd position of sharing a magazine with such heroes as the Flash, Hawkman, and the Whip. Phun and Clubb, who had initially played the characters Fat and Slat in the newspaper strip in the late 1920s, recreated the roles in *Flash Comics* and then went on to do them in a comic book of their own. They were the last of the *Minute Movies* characters to appear anywhere. **R.G.**

**MISS CAIRO JONES** Readers of the *Miss Cairo Jones* Sunday page got to know the blond heroine fairly well right from the start. She made her debut on the last Sunday of July 1945, and before the initial page was over

*Miss Cairo Jones*, Bob Oksner, 1945.

she'd stripped down to little more than her lacy lingerie. By the end of the second Sunday, still clad only in her undies, she was being pursued by a nasty fellow brandishing a sword cane. For the next several months that was the story of her life—skimpy attire and one peril after another. As drawn by Bob Oksner, the blond Cairo was one of the most attractive lady adventurers of the Forties. Oddly enough, however, she had begun life as a man.

While Oksner was drawing for comic books, he was struck with the urge to try a newspaper strip. What he had in mind was an adventure strip with a tough foreign correspondent as the hero. Christening his leading man Cairo Jones, he took his samples to John Wheeler, head of the Bell Syndicate. Although Wheeler was impressed by Oksner's work, he felt that what the public really wanted was another pretty girl adventure strip. *Miss Fury* was doing well for his syndicate, so Wheeler borrowed the "Miss" and stuck it in front of *Cairo Jones*. Oksner transformed his character into a sexy, long-legged blond, and Wheeler bought the strip for the Associated Newspapers syndicate, a subsidiary of Bell.

When the strip began, the writing was by Jerry Albert, a comic book editor and scripter. In the new version there was still a tough newspaper man, named Steve Racy, who was trying to track down and expose a notorious Nazi war criminal to whom Cairo had apparently been married. Originally she'd felt the stories about his evil activities were press distortions, but eventually she saw the light. Teaming up with the newsman, she helped him track down her alleged husband (it later transpires that they were never really married) and contributed to his downfall and demise.

Cairo kept moving around, getting embroiled in other postwar intrigues around the globe, dodging bullets, knives, and attempted beatings. No matter how serious the danger, however, she always managed to look terrific, and readers go to see her in everything from a slinky evening gown to the shower. She returned stateside in time to save Steve from being framed for murder and then decided to settle down with a nine-to-five job as a secretary.

Before the strip was a year old, Albert had dropped out and left the writing to Oksner, who converted it into a lighter, more satirical feature. The switch to the new type of continuity coincided with the addition of a daily strip in July of 1946. A working girl now, Cairo settled down to American locales and adventures that allowed Oksner to kid big business, advertising, and Hollywood. *Miss Cairo Jones* ended in the spring of 1947. At the height of its success it had been seen in just over a hundred papers.                                                    **R.G.**

**MISS FURY** A Sunday page that brought the action and violence of comic books to the funny papers, along with some of the props and attitudes of bondage literature, *Miss Fury* was written and drawn by Tarpé Mills, a lady who had been working in comic books since 1938. It began its run on April 6, 1941.

Originally the title was *Black Fury* but that soon was changed to the less ominous and more feminine *Miss Fury*. Jack Wheeler's Bell Syndicate distributed the page, which was no doubt intended to cash in on the growing national interest in comic book superheroes and masked avengers. Superman himself had added a newspaper strip to his media list in 1939, and Will Eisner's weekly *The Spirit* comic book had begun appearing in newspapers in 1940. Mills' heroine was as tough as any crimefighter in comic books, and she wore a striking costume, too.

In civilian life Miss Fury was a lovely, bored socialite, the female equivalent of Batman's alter ego, Bruce Wayne. When she donned her black leopard-skin costume, which had once been "worn by a witch-doctor in Africa," she became a very formidable crimefighting vigilante. She didn't have any superpowers, but was plenty dangerous without them. In her first month of Sundays, Miss Fury, after surviving an auto crash, claws a detective across the cheek, steps on his gun hand, kicks him in the face, and then sees to it that a thug nearly goes smashing through the windshield of a car. Mills seems also to have been influenced by some under-the-counter publications. There were quite a few of the traditional bondage elements in the feature—whips, branding irons, spike-heel shoes, men beating women, women tearing each other's clothes off, and the frequent display of all sorts of frilly lingerie. For good measure she added an assortment of handsome, sometimes ruthless, men for Marla to become entangled with.

During the Second World War years Miss Fury was continuously involved with espionage and intrigue, dealing with beautiful blond spies, handsome and dashing secret agents, and sadistic villains. A standout in this latter category was baldheaded, monocled Bruno Beitz, a Nazi spy of the worst sort, who slapped women around, carried a sword cane, loved to use a branding iron on human flesh, and once tried to assassinate an enemy by taping a bomb to a cat. In the postwar period *Miss Fury* grew a bit tamer. It ended finally in 1952, never having run in a very large list of newspapers. Marvel reprinted the strip in eight issues of *Miss Fury Comics* between 1942 and 1946.          **R.G.**

**MISS PEACH**  A droll strip about the doings of a gang of improbably bright children whose private clubs, squads, and committees virtually control their school, *Miss Peach* is described by its creator Mel Lazarus (who signs it "Mell") as his "personal palliative for the incurable disease of Growing Up." The strip debuted on February 4, 1957, in the *New York Herald Tribune* and was later distributed by Field Newspaper Syndicate until Lazarus transferred it, along with *Momma*, to Creators Syndicate in 1988. It now runs in over 200 papers.

Drawn in the usual comic strip format but in a single panel, *Miss Peach* deals with an engagingly verbal and astonishingly analytical group of moppets who seem to command their own world unencumbered by parents and unhampered by the bewildered teachers in nominal charge of them. Students of the Kelly School, a supremely progressive institution named in honor of Walt Kelly, the creator of the comic strip *Pogo*, they are seldom seen in a normal classroom situation but devote their time and abundant energies to a kind of complex interaction, which serves as a social and political microcosm of adult society. They form endless committees: the Mutual Self-Improvement Society ("to help each other see our weak points") functions by screaming "Ira, you're a ninny," "Walter, you're a wretch," and the like at each other; the Joint Committee to Straighten Everything Out drives the aptly named principal, Mr.

Grimmis, to "leave a little early today" out of his office window.

The membership of this fantastic crew is made up of clearly differentiated types: the enterprising bully Marcia, who dominates by sheer force of her personality, along with a pair of formidable fists; the gluttonous Ira, whose fear of everything qualifies him as "a free-lance coward"; the serenely stupid Arthur, whose contribution to the class' gardening project is a highly successful weed patch, since "weeds are human, like any other plant." When Marcia wins Ira in a raffle, she undertakes a 15-year project to turn him into a simpering, witless hulk of a man—"in short, a perfect husband."

Over this menagerie presides the unflappable young teacher Miss Peach, an oasis of sweetness and calm in the chaos of the children's world, and, in general, a real peach. Along with her colleague, the sprightly octogenarian Miss Crystal, she adds an element of sanity that keeps the strip in balance.

The strip is drawn in the same elemental style as *Momma*, and its distortions (the children seem about six inches high and are all head) seem quite in keeping with the antic spirit of the script. It was a success with sophisticated readers from its beginning. It has been collected into several volumes and been presented in animated television specials, and has helped earn Lazarus three awards (two as Best Humor Strip Cartoonist, in 1973 and 1979, and one as Best Cartoonist in All Categories, in 1982) from the National Cartoonists Society.    **D.W.**

**MITZI McCOY**  A Sunday-only adventure strip, debuting on November 7, 1948, *Mitzi McCoy* was nicely drawn by Kreigh Collins, who'd been an illustrator for such magazines as *Blue Book*. Mitzi was a pretty blond heiress, who was fiercely independent but inclined to get into trouble and need a man to help her out. Within less than two years she was ousted completely from her own page, replaced by a swashbuckling male ancestor.

In the initial sequence, after learning that the man she's on the brink of marrying is a fortune hunter, Mitzi takes off in her personal seaplane to be alone. She crashes, and Tim Graham, a handsome dark-haired reporter from her hometown newspaper, sets out to find her in the Canadian wilds. Tim, and his crusty old editor on *The Clarion*, stay on as regulars, along with the editor's Irish wolfhound. After she's rescued, Mitzi proceeds to get tangled up with a succession of crooks and swindlers, including an art thief named Swyndal.

Collins drew well; beautiful women and boats were his specialties. Not long after beginning the strip, he began to evidence an interest in the past. In the summer of 1949 he devoted a couple of Sundays to a history of the Irish wolfhound; that Christmas season there was a Nativity sequence. Finally, on September 24, 1950, he had the editor begin to tell a young fellow the story of Mitzi's ancestors. Beginning in Ireland in 1497, it involved a "beautiful and headstrong" young woman, a dashing shepherd who was "arrogant as a baron," an Irish wolfhound, and Barbary pirates. The arrogant shepherd was named Kevin the Bold, and before too long the page was in his name.  **R.G.**

**MIX, TOM** (1880–1940)  He was the most popular and successful movie cowboy of the silent screen, and he had a career as a comic book hero that began in 1938 and continued long after he was dead. Fictional adventures of Tom Mix could also be heard on the radio, sponsored by Ralston cereals, from 1933 to 1950. Ralston also used the hawknosed cowboy in comics-format ads in the Sunday funnies in the 1930s and the 1940s.

Mix entered the movies in 1910, making one- and two-reel Westerns; by 1917 he began starring in feature films for Fox. He outdrew all the competition and by the mid-1920s was earning $17,000 a week. His specialty was straightforward action, with some humor tossed in, including a horse named Tony.

In the middle 1930s he retired from the screen, having made relatively few talkies; he was last seen in the 1935 serial *The Miracle Rider*. He devoted much of his time in the decade to circus and Wild West show appearances, and as a result, never stopped being a fairly valuable merchandising property.

A series of Tom Mix Big Little Books was started by Whitman in 1934 and lasted until 1940. The first was *Terror Trail*, adapted from one of his movies and illustrated with stills from it. Several more followed, among them *Tom Mix and the Hoard of Montezuma*, and *Tom Mix and His Circus on the Barbary Coast*. These were original novels, illustrated by Henry Vallely, Hal Arbo and Jim Gary.

Tom Mix made his comic book debut in Whitman's *Crackajack Funnies* #1 (June 1938), which offered a combination of original material and strip reprints. The heroic cowpoke appeared in a four-page episode each issue and dealt with such serialized problems as the Fence War in Painted Valley and the Kidnappers of Cholla Wash. Artists included Jim Chambers and Jim Gary.

Mix dropped out of *Crackajack* in the magazine's second year. In 1940, the year the real Mix was killed in an auto accident, Ralston introduced a *Tom Mix* comic book as a premium. Promoted on the daily radio show and designated the "official publication of the Tom Mix Ralston Straight Shooters," it could be obtained only by sending in two box tops from either Ralston Whole Wheat Cereal or Instant Ralston. The Ralston Straight Shooters was the clean-living club that listeners to the show could join, and all the various premiums given away over the years tied in with the organization.

The magazine ran to 12 issues before being stopped in 1942. Episodes in each issue were based on the Mix radio program. After America entered the war the cowboy became more militant, and the title of the giveaway was changed to *Tom Mix Commandos Comics*. Each issue was 32 pages, half the size of a normal comic of the day, and the artwork was by Fred Meagher. Struck by a wave of nostalgia in 1983, Ralston gave away a tiny new Tom Mix comic book with boxes of Instant Ralston. Script was by Jim Harmon, art by Alex Toth.

When cowboys became popular in the postwar 1940s, Tom Mix was resurrected for a newsstand comic book by Fawcett. *Tom Mix Western* started in 1947 and lasted until the spring of 1953. Tom had the whole magazine to himself, and the stories were drawn mostly by Carl Pfeufer. Tom Mix as a fictional character still pops up once in a while, most recently in Blake Edwards' movie *Sunset*.  **R.G.**

**MOMAND, POP** (1886–1987)  The strip he drew is virtually forgotten, but its title has become a part of the American language. Just before World War I, Momand created *Keeping Up With the Joneses*, a domestic comedy strip about an aspiring middle-class family. The phrase "Keeping up with the Joneses" soon passed into everyday usage and is still found in most dictionaries.

Arthur R. Momand, whose nickname Pop was inevitable, was born in San Diego and educated in Manhattan. He started working as a newspaper artist in 1907, doing sketches for the *New York World*. His *Keeping Up With the Joneses*, which began in 1916, looked originally quite a bit like *Bringing Up Father*, though it was less rowdy and lowbrow. The central characters were the members of the McGinis family, Aloysius and Clarice and their daughter Julie. Pa was a small bald fellow with white whiskers and, like many an early comic strip father, looked to be well along in middle age. Ma was younger and twice his size. Daughter was a pretty, college-age lass.

Momand dealt in simple gags, but managed to get in frequent allusions to the Jones family: "Remember how you've always wanted me to join a swell club like Mr. Jones, m'dear?" or "Wait'll the Joneses see that, Julie!" The Joneses, like Herriman's Family Upstairs, were never actually seen. Rounding out the cast was a large black maid named Belladonna.

In the early years of the strip, Momand also drew a small companion daily called *Cat Tales*. Despite its title, the strip dealt with a wide range of creatures and included a family of bugs.

As the years passed the McGinises became less involved with acquiring material goods and maintaining social status. The gags became more general, and Momand took to drawing in a style that was a simplified version of that of his friend Billy DeBeck. A longtime topper to the Sunday page was *Holly of Hollywood*, about a pretty blond young woman who never quite managed to land a job in the movies. Cupples & Leon issued two books of daily reprints, in 1920 and 1921, and the 1930s Sunday pages were reprinted in the first few years of *Famous Funnies*.

After giving up his feature in the middle 1940s, Momand devoted himself to portrait painting. He lived to be 101 years old.                                                    **R.G.**

**MOMMA** Introduced by Field Newspaper Syndicate on October 26, 1970, the daily and Sunday strip *Momma* maintains a remarkable level of variety and wit with a single topic: the nagging of a manipulative, interfering mother. Written and drawn by Mel Lazarus (who created *Miss Peach* 13 years earlier and signs both "Mell"), the strip succeeds in avoiding the twin dangers of pathos and cruelty in ringing seemingly endless changes on the theme of an aging parent's efforts at remaining a part of her children's lives. The struggle of Sonya Hobbs, who comes up to her children's waists, to control their lives meets with no success whatsoever, but she manages to keep them all in a state of permanent guilt.

Admittedly autobiographical, *Momma* is based on Lazarus' filial experience. The strip was, he has stated, "the result of my own growing interest in my mother's psychology—now that I'm out of her grasp."

Momma is the eternal martyr: Scraping the food from her plate onto that of her surfeited son who pleads that he is stuffed, she fantasizes a gravestone reading "Here Lies Momma/She Starved Herself for Her Children."

Her brood remains unchanged despite all her well-intentioned pressure. Thomas, at 42 a successful and happily-married man, endures her constant jibes at his wife's housekeeping and cooking; the 22-year-old swinger Francis continues to avoid getting a job, dressing properly, or doing his laundry; and the romantic 18-year-old Marylou goes on dating the wrong men. Indeed, much of the humor of the strip derives from the justice of Momma's complaints. She is a pain in the neck, but the "nag du jour" she serves with the gigantic meals she stuffs into her children is often well deserved.

Drawn in a spare style with no backgrounds and the barest minimum of detail, *Momma* shares with *Miss Peach* the Picasso-like idiosyncrasy of including both eyes in its facial profiles, but if its art is rudimentary, its script is often highly sophisticated. The cutting wit and keen insight of the strip have kept it consistently popular among adults since its inception. Running it over 400

papers, it has been distributed by Creators Syndicate since Lazarus brought it and *Miss Peach* to them in 1988.
                                                                        **D.W.**

**MONTANA, BOB** (1920–1975) Although he was best known as the creator of *Archie*, one of the most popular teenage characters in America, Montana drew a wide range of other comic book features, including adventure and superheroics, in addition to comedy.

Born in Stockton, California, he traveled all across the country in his youth; his family was in vaudeville and Montana "did rope tricks in Pop's Western act." He managed to study art in Arizona, Boston, and Manhattan, and at the beginning of the 1940s he got a job assisting comic book artist Bob Wood, then started turning out features of his own.

Montana worked in a realistic-cartoony style and was fond of such pen techniques as crosshatching, which he could adapt to straight adventure or screwball humor. For the MLJ titles he drew *Danny in Wonderland*, *The Fox*, *Inspector Bentley*, and others, and for Victor Fox's line of comic books he drew such forgettable features as *Lu-Nar* and *Spark Stevens*. He also produced a number of well designed covers for MLJ during the early years of World War II, and depicted the likes of the Shield, Steel Sterling, and the Black Hood fighting drooling Japanese and snarling Nazis on covers for *Pep*, *Zip*, *Top-Notch*, and *Jackpot*.

Archie himself showed up late in 1941, at just about the same time in both *Pep* and *Jackpot*. The trouble-prone redheaded teenager rapidly caught on, edging out the Shield as leading man in *Pep* and adding a book of his own, whose first issue was drawn by Montana, in 1942. At the same time Montana was also contributing to *Crime Does Not Pay*.

He went into the Army soon after, spending four years in the Signal Corps and working on training films with William Saroyan and fellow cartoonists Sam Cobean and Charles Addams. After the service Montana started the *Archie* newspaper strip, daily and Sunday. He didn't own the character, however, and a crew of other artists and writers were producing the many Archie comic books that had sprung up. Montana, his style gradually losing much of its early snap, stayed with the strip until his death.                              **R.G.**

**MOON MULLINS** Unquestionably the biggest boor in the funnies, Moonshine Mullins barged into print in the early 1920s. The creation of Frank Willard, who shared his hero's interest in the roughneck aspects of life, *Moon Mullins* became a very successful strip and at the height of its popularity ran in over 250 newspapers around the country. A bit politer and more sedate, it still appears today and is signed by Ferd Johnson, who

"—'AND LITTLE WILLIE RABBIT RAN JUST AS FAST AS HIS LITTLE FEET COULD SCAMPER— BECAUSE RIGHT BEHIND HIM HE SAW A PAIR OF BIG POP-EYES AND A BIG MOUTH WITH GLEAMING YELLOW TEETH, AND A LONG SHARP NOSE AND WHO DO YOU SUPPOSE IT WAS—"

EMMY SCHMALTZ!

I'LL SMACK YOUR SASSY FACE!

*Moon Mullins*, Frank Willard, © 1929, Chicago Tribune. Reprinted by permission: Tribune Media Services.

started off as Willard's assistant when the strip was only a few weeks old.

Initially the feature was intended as the Chicago Tribune-New York News Syndicate's version of King Features' increasingly successful *Barney Google.* Willard, the friend and former assistant of Billy DeBeck, could draw like Barney's creator and had an equally good working knowledge of lowlife. *Moon Mullins* commenced in June 1923, a little less than a year after DeBeck had introduced the racehorse Spark Plug to his *Barney Google* and begun his strip on its impressive climb in circulation.

Willard's Moon was much taller than Barney, but like him he wore a derby and smoked a cigar. Unlike Barney, Moon had no sentimental side and was incapable of being snubbed or slighted by his betters. Moon could push his way into a mansion or a beer joint with equal ease, completely oblivious to what sort of impression his brash and ill-founded self-confidence was making. He was insulting, ill-mannered, and generally offensive to all decent folk. Readers of the funnies loved him and Willard's strip thrived.

The roughneck cartoonist started off with a continuity set in the boxing world and then shifted to a circus background. It was on the sawdust that Moon first encountered the love of his life, Little Egypt (named after a real dancer of an earlier era). In the strip's second year Moon moved permanently into a boarding house run by a scrawny, vain spinster named Emmy Schmaltz, and from then on that became the base of operations for the strip. Other members of the cast followed: the pompous Lord Plushbottom, who married Emmy eventually; Kayo, Moon's small kid brother who slept in a bureau drawer; Uncle Willie, fat and even lazier than Moon; Mamie, maid, cook, and Willie's wife, whom Emmy first encountered in the local hoosegow.

Using this basic cast, and dozens of others from highlife and lowlife, Willard and Johnson constructed an intricate, long-running picaresque that mixed mystery, adventure and burlesque.

Johnson was already doing much of *Moon Mullins* by the time Willard died in 1958. He started to sign the strip after that, and in recent years his son Tom shares the credit. The strip now concentrates on a joke a day.

**R.G.**

**MOORE, RAY**  See THE PHANTOM.

**MOORES, DICK** (1909–1986)  A distinctive artist and an inventive writer, Moores did the unsuccessful *Jim Hardy* strip from the middle 1930s to the early 1940s.

He officially took over the very successful *Gasoline Alley* in 1960 and remained with it until his death. Back in the early 1930s, before he got a strip of his own, he assisted Chester Gould on *Dick Tracy*. In the 1940s and 1950s, before he signed on with Frank King, Moores worked on several Disney strips, including *Mickey Mouse*. At one point he also ghosted some of Virgil Partch's gag cartoons.

Richard Arnold Moores was a long, lean man, well over six feet tall. He was born in Lincoln, Nebraska, "when bread was 5¢ a loaf," grew up in Omaha and graduated from high school in Fort Wayne, Indiana. He worked with his father in the family wholesale radio business, managed a movie theater, and eventually saved enough money to go to Chicago and enroll in the Academy of Fine Arts. While in Chicago he became friends with a fellow cartoonist named Bob York. Moores, according to his own account, was kicked out of art school and eventually found himself "broke and jobless." That was in the early 1930s, after the Depression had hit. York, who was by that time working as assistant on *Harold Teen*, told Moores that Chester Gould needed someone to help him out. "So I went to my basement room, shared with three other broke and jobless, and sat up all night lettering," Moores once explained. "I took it in the next morning and Chester hired me. Not because the lettering was any good, but because there was so much of it."

Gould paid him $5 a week. Moores joined up at just about the start of *Dick Tracy*'s run, and he stayed on for five years. "I did the lettering and backgrounds on the daily and Sunday and colored the Sunday prints. I never inked a figure." The characteristic *Tracy* style of lettering, carried on by subsequent assistants, seems to have been Moores' invention.

While working for Gould, Moores devoted his nights to turning out samples of strips of his own, about 30 different ones. Finally he succeeded with *Jim Hardy*, which United Features launched in 1936. The strip was never a hit, but Moores stuck with it until 1942. By that time he and his wife were living in Southern California, and he was able to get a job with the Walt Disney studios. He was assigned to the comic strip department and worked on a variety of features—all anonymously, of course. "My first job was inking the *Mickey* strip for Floyd Gottfredson," he once said. "I had never seen such meticulously drawn, beautiful pencil work. And here I was going to have to take my clumsy pen and go over those beautiful lines. That was about as scary a thing as I ever had to do."

During his 14 years at the Disney factory, Moores put in stretches drawing and/or inking *Scamp*, *Brer Rabbit*, and Sunday adaptations of such films as *Alice in Wonderland*. In those same years he also did considerable comic book work on sundry animated characters, including Mickey Mouse, Bugs Bunny, Porky Pig, and Donald Duck.

He was next offered an assistant job by Frank King, an old associate from his Chicago days, and he went to Florida to work on the daily *Gasoline Alley* in 1956. By 1960, when he was allowed to share the credit with King, he was writing and drawing the strip. When King died in 1969, Moores continued the feature, one of the very few cartoonists who took over a popular strip and kept it at a level of quality equal to that of the creator. Gradually he had swung over to his own style of drawing, an updated version of that cartoony illustrative style he'd first used on *Jim Hardy*, with a strong sense of design and a fondness for a variety of shading techniques. The years with Disney had improved his figure drawing and his depiction of animals. While continuing with most of the *Gasoline Alley* regulars, he added several of his own and moved into storylines that were folksier and humor that was a bit broader than King's. In 1975, when Bill Perry retired from doing the Sunday page, Moores took on that job, too.

He won a Reuben award from the National Cartoonists Society in 1974, along with many other awards. In writing what was to be his final autobiographical entry for the NCS albums a few years ago, he concluded with the words: "I've just read this over and I wouldn't change a line!"                                                    **R.G.**

**MOOSE** Bob Weber's daily and Sunday humor strip *Moose* (sometimes known by its hero's full name *Moose Miller*) began at the suggestion of King Features Syndicate comics editor Sylvan Byck. Weber, a successful magazine gag-cartoonist who had also contributed material to *Laff-a-Day* and the comic strip *Barney Google and Snuffy Smith*, put together a strip in the classic slapstick tradition, featuring the lazy, greedy, simple-minded, but essentially likable slob Moose Miller, his equally goofy-looking wife Molly, and various male and female children, as needed by the daily gag. Drawn in a broadly exaggerated style, the characters usually sport feet longer than their torsos and noses like Genoa salamis.

The strip is set in no particular place, time, or class. Moose seems sometimes to occupy a comfortably middle-class suburban home and at other times to live in a ramshackle shanty. He wears nondescript clothes, usually a white T-shirt and black pants, and always, indoors or out, an unidentifiable, squashed-down hat. He seems to hold no job but has no apparent financial problems. Indeed, no one in *Moose* has any real problems. The worst of it seems to be that Moose's stomach not only growls but howls at the moon ("It thought the moon was a pizza," Moose explains) and that his adolescent son is turned down for a goodnight kiss on a date. A cheerful domestic strip, *Moose* contains no pain or tension in its genial, easy-going humor.

King Features Syndicate introduced the daily *Moose* on Monday, September 20, 1965, and the Sunday version six days later. A modest success from the beginning, it now runs in about 200 papers. **D.W.**

**MOREIRA, RUBEN** (c. 1922– ) An adventure artist in the Alex Raymond vein, Moreira drew for both comic books and comic strips. His best-known newspaper work was on the *Tarzan* Sunday page in the middle 1940s. He was active in comic books from the early 1940s to the early 1960s, drawing for such publishers as DC, Fiction House, and Marvel.

Born in Latin America, Moreira immigrated to the United States and settled in the New York City area. After studying at Cooper Union and Pratt Institute, he entered the comic book field in 1942. Moreira's first work was done for the Quality line, where he drew *Espionage* in *Smash Comics*, *G-2* in *National Comics*, and covers for *Crack Comics*. He moved next to Fiction House, drawing a variety of features, most notably *Kaänga* in *Jungle Comics*. Moreira also illustrated such Fiction House pulps as *Planet Stories* and *Jungle Stories*. All his early work was signed with the pen name "Rubimor."

In 1945 he moved to a new jungle, when United Features hired him to replace the departing Burne Hogarth on the Sunday *Tarzan*. Moreira did a passable job, but was not in the same league with such predecessors as Hal Foster, or even Hogarth. In 1947 he returned to comic books, drawing again for Fiction House. His work improved considerably over the next few years, and he began an association with DC in 1949 that was to last for well over a decade.

Although he had done some superhero material over the years, he now concentrated mostly on features that were a bit closer to reality. He drew crime stories for *Gang Busters*, along with Western material and an occasional science fiction title like *Rip Hunter, Time Master*. In addition, he also got briefly back into newspaper strips when United hired him to ghost *Casey Ruggles* in 1954. He drew the daily from April 4 through August 28 as well as two Sunday pages in September.

Moreira's work showed up in Marvel and ACG titles in the late 1950s. He left DC and comic books in 1962, returning to South America. **J.V.**

**MOSLEY, ZACK** (1906– ) Mosley was not the first to create an adventure strip about flying, but his *Smilin' Jack* was one of the most popular, and the longest-lived example of the genre in American comics. Mosley (whose full name is Zack Terrell Mosley) kept the strip in the air from a 1933 takeoff until 1973.

His love for airplanes goes back to his childhood in Hickory, Oklahoma, where he was born the year before that Indian Territory became a state. The sight of a plane that crashed there when he was seven years old so seized his imagination that he never lost his fascination, and when an Army "Jenny" landed nearby four years later, he began the habit of sketching planes that was to continue throughout his professional life. At the age of 20 he took his savings and enrolled at the Chicago Academy of Fine Arts. Three years there and at the Art Institute of Chicago prepared him to get a job, along with his roommate Russell Keaton, assisting cartoonist Dick Calkins with *Buck Rogers* and *Skyroads*, the pioneer aviation strip. In time, he and Keaton came to do most of the drawing of *Skyroads*, and Mosley began to write some of the episodes.

Mosley's early style was somewhat crude, but his lively imagination (and his friendship with popular cartoonist Walter Berndt) enabled him to sell Joseph Medill Patterson, an aviation buff and owner of the Chicago Tribune-New York News Syndicate, his own strip in 1933. The Sunday feature *On the Wing*, a comedy–adventure strip about three terrified student pilots, left the runway on October 1; 14 Sundays later, on December 31, Patterson ordered the named changed, and as *Smilin' Jack* it was to remain aloft (with dailies added three years later) for the next four decades.

Mosley's expertise on matters aeronautical derived from first-hand experience in the field. Along with fellow-cartoonist Keaton (who had taken over *Skyroads* and was to create his own aviation strip, and so had an equal reason for knowing the subject), he had taken flying lessons since 1932, and was licensed to fly in 1936. He was very active in aviation throughout the 1930s and '40s: A founder of the Civil Air Patrol in 1941, he flew over 300 anti-sub patrols during World War II, and as wing public relations officer for Florida he held the rank of colonel and won the United States Air Medal. In 1976 he was inducted into the United States Air Force Hall of Honor. He cheerfully lent his talents to illustrating aviation material and designed many squadron insignia for units of all branches of the armed services. He has owned nine planes and flown over a million miles.

Mosley went into what he calls "semi-retirement" with the grounding of *Smilin' Jack* in 1973, but he still does some advertising work from his home in Stuart, Florida, along with organizing and publishing collections of old *Smilin' Jack* material. He has issued two books with episodes from the 1930s and '40s, *Hot Rock Glide* (1979) and *De-Icers Galore* (1980), as well as his memoirs, *Brave Coward Zack* (1976). **D.W.**

**THE MOUNTAIN BOYS** One of the several hillbilly comic strips that blossomed in the 1930s, *The*

*Mountain Boys* was the work of magazine cartoonist Paul Webb, who'd introduced the characters in a series of gag cartoons in *Esquire* in 1934. The panels quickly became popular and, along with E. Simms Campbell's harem gags and the Petty Girl pinups, were trademarks of the magazine in the Thirties. *The Mountain Boys* branched out into a strip in 1935 and was syndicated by Esquire Features, Inc.

Webb relied on all the accepted clichés about poor mountain folk. They were lazy, dumb, and none too sanitary, and the boys themselves—three identical brothers named Willy, Luke, and Jake—were lean lads with long black beards who wore floppy, high-crown hats, jeans, T-shirts, vests, and no shoes. They were often seen lounging in front of the ramshackle cabin they shared with Granmaw and Granpappy. Webb alternated between jokes and continuities. Some of his continued narratives were quite simple—a sequence built around the boys thinking about going into Gullytown to pick up a keg of nails at the general store, for example. (This took several days to unfold.)

The strip was gone by decade's end.    **R.G.**

**MR. AND MRS.** The squabbling married couple was already a cliché in American humor when the popular cartoonist Clare Briggs created a Sunday page to exploit the national taste for family quarrels. *Mr. and Mrs.* debuted on April 14, 1919, and focused so unwaveringly on that single subject that its survival for more than 40 years is somewhat remarkable.

Joe and Vi Green argue over an infinite range of trifles; *everything* about each irritates the other, and both are unrestrained in their criticism. Neither bullies the other; they are perfectly matched, and indeed their reciprocal acrimony seems to be the only basis for their relationship. Joe was bald, mustachioed, bespectacled and nearly chinless, resembling many another henpecked husband of the funnies, while Vi was thin and plain. In its early years *Mr. and Mrs.* seldom extended beyond the two antagonists, except for their mysteriously begotten child Roscoe. His sole function was to intone the recurring coda "Mama love Papa?" or "Papa love Mama?" at the end of each fall. He eventually vanished from the scene.

Briggs died on January 3, 1930, and his last signed page ran on January 26, but the Herald-Tribune Syndicate brought in a team to keep the feature going. Arthur Folwell, erstwhile *Herald-Trib* drama critic and longtime friend of Briggs, took over the scripting for many years. Frank Fogarty, who also drew a page called *Clarence*, was one of those who illustrated the Sunday. Ellison Hoover, a magazine cartoonist, came in to draw a daily version, Kin Platt, a comic book veteran, drew the feature, daily and Sunday, from 1947 until its end in 1963.

*Mr. and Mrs.* remained steadfastly dull until the very last.    **D.W.**

**MR. BREGER**   See BREGER, DAVE.

**MR. NATURAL**   See CRUMB, ROBERT.

**MR. TWEEDEEDLE**   See GRUELLE, JOHNNY.

**MURPHY, JIMMY** (1892–1965)  A self-taught artist, Murphy worked as political cartoonist for over a decade before finding his true calling. Then in 1918 he created *Toots and Casper*, a domestic strip mixing comedy and continuity, which lasted for nearly 40 years.

James Edward Murphy Jr. was born in Chicago and grew up in Omaha. While still in high school he started selling political cartoons to the newspapers in town. Restless, he left home in 1910 and for the next eight years drew political cartoons for papers in Spokane, Portland, and San Francisco. Hearst summoned him to New York in the summer of 1918 to draw for the *Journal* and the *American*, and late that same year Murphy decided to try his hand at a comic strip.

Murphy's first daily, drawn for the *American*, was *Doc Attaboy* and featured a middle-aged medic who thought more about his big fees than he did about his patients. This one didn't last long, breathing its last early in December 1918. In the middle of that month *Toots and Casper* commenced. During its early weeks a character named Bachelor Bill, who was a dead ringer for the departed Doc, appeared as the then-pintsized Casper's best friend. From the start, Murphy presented Toots as a pretty and up-to-date young woman, and many of the gags were built around her experiments with the latest fashions, with smoking and the other daring activities that the liberated women of the new postwar world

Jimmy Murphy, Self Portrait, 1925.

were exploring. Casper wasn't initially the focus of the strip, and it took several months for him to grow in stature, lose a few years and became something more than just the traditional long-suffering hubby. Once the couple had a child, things picked up. By the middle 1920s, when Murphy was relying on continuity and suspense along with gags, *Toots and Casper* was appearing in a sizable list of papers around the country.

His early strips, signed J.E. Murphy, had been crudely drawn and awkwardly staged, but gradually, obviously watching and learning from such Hearst colleagues as George Herriman and Billy DeBeck, Murphy improved and arrived at a lively cartoon style of his own. By then he was signing himself Jimmy Murphy.

He was one of many cartoonists of the time who migrated to California. He lived in Beverly Hills for many years and listed his hobbies as motoring and golf. The good life in sun-filled California was not without its distractions, and Murphy was in continual trouble with his syndicate in Manhattan over deadlines. His records from the 1930s, for example, show that he was almost always sending his work off several days late, having to rush it eastward by air express.

In his later years Murphy became quite ill and the strip was ghosted—sometimes old art was reused with new dialogue added. *Toots and Casper* ended in the middle 1950s, and Murphy died less than a decade later.
**R.G.**

**MURPHY, JOHN CULLEN** (1919– ) The creator of *Big Ben Bolt* and the longtime artist of *Prince Valiant* came to strip-cartooning after establishing himself as a magazine and newspaper illustrator, and he brought a stylishness of draftsmanship and composition.

John Cullen Murphy was born in New York City and raised in Chicago, where he attended the Art Institute at the age of nine. In 1930, he attended the Grand Central Art School, the Phoenix Art Institute, and the Art Students League and came to know magazine artist Norman Rockwell, who was a neighbor and used the frecklefaced youngster as a model.

By the age of 17, Murphy was already selling sports cartoons, and it was as a seasoned professional who had painted covers for such magazines as *Liberty* that he joined the Army in 1940. As an aide-de-camp in the South Pacific, he painted portraits of military personnel, including General Douglas MacArthur, and did war scenes for the *Chicago Tribune*. Murphy returned to civilian life in 1946 to work in film promotion and soon began selling cover and interior illustrations to *Esquire, Holiday, Collier's, Look,* and *Sports*. When Elliot Caplin of King Features Syndicate approached him to draw the boxing strip *Big Ben Bolt* in 1949, Murphy was already a well-known sports illustrator.

Murphy drew, or oversaw the drawing of, *Big Ben Bolt* for over a quarter of a century from its inception in 1950 till its last appearance in 1978, although the strip was ghosted by various other artists over the years and carried the name of Murphy's assistant Gray Morrow for its last eight months. In 1970, the 78-year-old Hal Foster asked him to assist with his much-honored *Prince Valiant*, and when Foster retired to Florida the next year, Murphy effectively inherited the strip, which he began signing on May 23, 1971.

Murphy's sense of design and control of his medium have earned him wide honors in the profession. He has won the National Cartoonists Society's silver plaque for the Best Story Strip of the year six times—for both *Big Ben Bolt* and *Prince Valiant* in 1971 and for *Prince Valiant* alone in 1974, 1976, 1978, 1984, and 1987—and won the Elzie Segar Award for "a unique and outstanding contribution to the profession of cartooning" in 1983. Murphy continues to draw *Prince Valiant*, now written by his son Cullen, with undiminished verve—despite the painful reduction in size in most newspapers that still carry this heroic survivor of the great days of the adventure strip.
**D.W.**

**MURRAY, FEG**  See SEEIN' STARS.

**MURRY, PAUL** (1911– )  Because he drew mostly Walt Disney characters throughout his long career, the majority of Murry's comic book and comic strip work was done anonymously or had the Disney name signed to it. He's worked in animation, drawn newspaper strips and magazine cartoons, and from 1950 on was the artist responsible for the majority of Mickey Mouse's comic book appearances.

He was born in Missouri, grew up on a farm, and remained there until he was in his twenties. From the late 1930s into the early 1940s, after trying out for the job by mail, he worked as an animator in Disney's Southern California studios. Among the features he had a hand in were *Fantasia, Saludos Amigos,* and *Dumbo*. Eventually he moved over to the comic strip department. During the World War II years Murry drew separate Sunday pages based on the *Three Caballeros* characters Jose Carioca, the natty Brazilian parrot, and Panchito, the feisty Mexican rooster.

He also penciled the *Uncle Remus* Sunday page for a time and in 1946 entered comic books by drawing the first issue of Dell's *Uncle Remus*. Murry left Disney in the late 1940s, relocated in Oregon, and divided his time between lumberjacking and free-lancing gag cartoons to such magazines as *Gags*.

When Murry returned to California, he went to work for Western, who produced and printed the Disney comic books. In the early 1950s, with longtime animator

Dick Huemer as writer, he drew a comic strip called *Buck O'Rue*. It was a broad burlesque of the cowboy genre, and lasted but two years. He first drew the noted rodent in 1950 and by 1954 was doing the regular Mickey Mouse story in each and every issue of *Walt Disney's Comics & Stories*. These were humorous adventure yarns, usually continued from issue to issue, and they gave Murry the opportunity to draw Mickey and his sidekick Goofy in a variety of locations. He stayed with Mickey until Western gave up the Disney titles in 1984. **R.G.**

## MUSIAL, JOE (1905–1977)

A journeyman cartoonist, Musial had a long and active career. He is probably best-known for having drawn *The Katzenjammer Kids* for over 20 years. Associated with the King Features Syndicate from the early 1930s onward, he ghosted a wide range of popular strips and also had a hand in putting together such reprint titles as *King Comics*, *Magic Comics*, and *Ace Comics*.

He was born in Yonkers, New York, and studied at the Pratt Institute. After assisting Billy DeBeck, Musial became a member of the King bullpen. While there, according to his own account, he ghosted—usually for short periods—such strips as *Pete the Tramp*, *Elmer*, *Blondie*, and *Secret Agent X-9*.

In 1936 King Features entered into an agreement with the David McKay Company that eventually resulted in *King Comics*, *Ace Comics*, *Magic Comics*, *Future Comics*, and others. All of them reprinted King newspaper strips—*Flash Gordon*, *Popeye*, *Mandrake*, and more. Musial was in charge of packaging the titles and he also drew many of the covers and provided original filler material. For *Ace Comics* there was *Teddy and Sitting Bull*, a page about a kid and his dog, and for *Magic* there was *Jan and Aloysius*, dealing with a little girl and her parrot. Oddly enough Musial, who was a longtime ghost artist himself, got other cartoonists to ghost his features for him, initially Ray McGill, then Bob Dunn. In the late 1930s Musial also produced a book titled *Popeye's How to Draw Cartoons* for McKay. It sold for 50 cents and in the ads Musial was described as "Popeye's creator" and "the man who draws Popeye." In the period between E.C. Segar's death and the signing on of Bill Zaboly as regular *Thimble Theatre* artist, Musial was apparently one of the ghosts, and he and his publisher decided to take advantage of the credit.

The death of Billy DeBeck in the early 1940s provided him another opportunity. He filled in on both *Barney Google* and *Bunky* until Fred Lasswell took over. Though he never signed his name to either strip, he did initial them J.M.

In 1956, at the death of Doc Winner, Musial was given *The Katzenjammer Kids* page. He didn't do an especially impressive job, and comics historian Maurice Horn has gone so far as to label him "the man most responsible for the mindless emasculation" of the venerable feature. Musial stayed with the Kids until his death. **R.G.**

## MUTT AND JEFF

A long-running team, the tall Mutt and the short Jeff met in the first decade of the century and remained together until the early 1980s. Bud Fisher created them, and his pioneering strip, originally devoted to Mutt alone, was among the very first regular dailies.

*Mutt and Jeff* actually helped establish the daily format of the medium. Clare Briggs at the *Chicago Examiner* had strung his comic pictures together in a single file across a daily newspaper page a couple of years before Fisher's A. Mutt debuted in the *San Francisco Chronicle* on November 15, 1907, but Briggs' *A. Piker Clerk* ran sporadically and didn't last long. Fisher's strip, which turned into *Mutt and Jeff*, ran regularly, eventually six days every week, and so it attracted a steady following and survived. Its popularity inspired imitation, making a permanent fixture of the strip form for daily newspaper comics.

Since Fisher was a sports cartoonist on the *Chronicle*, his Augustus Mutt was a compulsive horse-player, and the strip focused on his daily quest for the right horse to bet on and for the wherewithal to place the wager. Though Mutt usually lost, readers of the strip initially took his tips seriously. The feature graduated from racetrack touting to comedy when the tall and gangling Mutt acquired his diminutive sidekick. Mutt first encountered Jeff among the inmates of an insane asylum he dropped in on in late March of 1908, and when he took him away with him, the historic team was born. Jeff at the time was suffering under the delusion that he was former heavyweight champ James J. Jeffries, from whom his name derives. By then the strip was appearing in Hearst newspapers and well on its way to national distribution, for with the arrival of little Jeff the strip assumed a human dimension that made it endure.

Mutt remained the scheming conniver that he had been as a horseplayer, and his role in the strip continued to be coming up with ways to make a buck, while Jeff's seeming mental limitations made him the perfect innocent and the ideal foil for Mutt. The strip's comedy soon took its classic form with Mutt's avaricious aspirations always frustrated by Jeff's benign and well-intentioned ignorance. Often deploying gentle Jeff as a shill in a succession of careers and enterprises together, Mutt sometimes conceived plans that had the incidental effect of victimizing the little fellow, but Jeff invariably wound up on top anyway, victorious over whatever traps and pitfalls may have lain in his path. In working out his little dramas, which also included such regulars as Mutt's initially shrewish wife, his son Cicero, and the teams' pals Gus Geevum and Sir Sidney, Fisher often resorted to borrowing jokes from various sources, including burlesque, vaudeville, and Broadway. The strip in its early decades was raucous and rowdy and, now and then, a bit racist.

After World War I Fisher left more and more of the work of the strip to assistants. One of the earliest was Ken Kling, who went on to draw several unsuccessful imitations of his boss' work, until he came up with a racing-tip strip called *Joe and Asbestos* that ran from the middle 1920s to the late 1960s. Ed Mack carried the load on *Mutt & Jeff* throughout the 1920s and drew the sequences about Mutt's campaign for the presidency of the United States in 1928. Al Smith guided the strip from 1932 until 1980, signing his name only after Fisher died in 1954. Smith was a much better cartoonist than Fisher, Kling, or Mack, and he improved the look of the strip greatly. He also created the Sunday topper, *Cicero's Cat*, that began in 1933.

Smith came to emphasize hearth and home, toning down Mrs. Mutt and moving away from sports and gambling. His successor George Breisacher gave the venerable strip a new look by using brush and a bolder, more flexible line. *Mutt and Jeff* ended in 1982.  **R.C.H.**

**MYERS, RUSSELL** (1938–  ) A cartoonist who says his prolonged efforts at entering the profession qualified him as "probably one of the world's most accomplished failures," Russell Myers broke his pattern of rejection in 1970 with *Broom-Hilda*, a gag strip about a love-starved witch.

Born in Pittsburgh, Kansas, Myers specialized in commercial art at the University of Tulsa, Oklahoma. Immediately after graduating in 1960 he got a job with Hallmark in Kansas City, and for the next 10 years wrote and illustrated greeting cards by day and tried to interest syndicates in a series of comic strips in his spare time. He claims to have gotten a strip's drawing, submission, and rejection down to a one-day experience. Since the creation of *Broom-Hilda*, Myers has devoted his full time to the writing and drawing of the successful strip, which is distributed to more than 300 papers by Tribune Media Services. As the strip adheres to no time frame and contains no topical references, Myers has

been in the rare position of being able to keep as much as a year ahead of his deadline from the beginning.

Myers draws the adventures of the engagingly repulsive Broom-Hilda and her bizarre friends in a loose, free style as brash and broad as his characters and gags, maintaining a nice balance of slapstick and fantasy.

In 1985, Myers created *Perky & Beanz*, a daily and Sunday gag strip about the generation gap between a perky little girl and her full-of-beans grandfather. *Perky & Beanz* was distributed by Tribune Media Services until its demise in 1987.  **D.W.**

**MYRA NORTH, SPECIAL NURSE** An adventure strip that had very little to do with the day-to-day routines of the medical profession, *Myra North* began as a daily in February 1936, with a Sunday added four months later. Charles Coll, a veteran newspaper artist, drew *Myra North*, and Ray Thompson wrote it. Thompson was also a cartoonist, of the bigfoot school; his major creation was Pud and the gang of kids who appeared in 1940s bubblegum comics and ads for Fleer's Dubble Bubble.

Myra's caseload was special indeed, and she was forever running into master criminals, fiends, and international spies. A simple house call would inevitably lead to assault by a crazed ape, an invisible man, or worse. Even some of her coworkers were not to be trusted. Dr. Duval, for instance, was conducting sinister experiments with Myra's sweetheart, Jack Lane, and the aforementioned ape. And there was Dr. Zero, who had unlocked the secret of invisibility and intended to use it for evil purposes and to satisfy his "colossal greed for gold."

Pretty blond Myra didn't limit herself to hospital work or even private patients: She scoured the world for new locations in which to get into trouble. She posed as a cigarette girl in the Purple Slipper and got mixed up in murder, was hired out as a nanny to the most famous child actress in the world, donned a Red Cross uniform in a nameless war-torn European country, and was forced to be a lab technician in the underground Asian stronghold of the beautiful Ming Sin, where "that ambitious lady herself is plotting one of the most amazing offenses the world has ever seen!"

The daily ended in 1939; the Sunday held on until 1941.  **R.G.**

# N

**NANCY** One of the most popular kids in comics, the fuzzy-headed little Nancy was first seen in the funny papers early in the 1930s, when her creator, Ernie Bushmiller, casually introduced her into *Fritzi Ritz*. Nancy proceeded to take over and within five years the name of the strip was changed to hers.

When Nancy initially showed up in her Aunt Fritzi's household in 1933, she was much thinner than she would be in a few years, but she already had her trademark hairdo and bow. At that period Bushmiller was using continuity as well as gags, and Nancy accompanied her aunt out to California while Fritzi pursued a movie career in Hollywood. She didn't appear every day and was very much a supporting player. Bushmiller used the new niece only now and then in 1934, still building the stories and most of the jokes around Fritzi. In the spring of the following year, however, he did a sequence about Nancy's running away from home and ending up at an Indian reservation.

By 1937 Nancy was putting on weight and appearing in an increasing number of strips without her aunt. In January of 1938 Sluggo Smith entered the strip, saving Nancy from a bully and commencing a friendship/romance that has lasted for over a half-century. That same year the *Fritzi Ritz* daily changed its name to *Nancy*. On Sunday Bushmiller had been doing *Fritzi Ritz* and *Phil Fumble*. The Sunday *Fritzi* continued but *Nancy* replaced

the other half-page, and the redheaded Phil became Fritzi's steady beau. *Nancy* proved to be an extremely popular strip and reached a circulation of several hundred newspapers by the early 1940s.

Eventually Bushmiller abandoned continuity altogether. He was an expert at constructing gags and even after the artwork grew tired and repetitive, there was usually a good gag every day. In the final years of his association with *Nancy* Bushmiller left all the drawing to Will Johnson. After his death in the early 1980s, several artists took turns carrying on. Since 1983 Jerry Scott has drawn and written the strip. **R.G.**

**NAPOLEON** Clifford McBride's great hound originated in his unnamed Sunday pantomime page distributed by the McNaught Syndicate during the late 1920s. The large, lumbering beast and his eternally discommoded master/victim Uncle Elby captivated the public and earned themselves a strip of their own. *Napoleon*, syndicated by LaFave Newspaper Features, debuted on June 6, 1932, in just seven newspapers. A Sunday version was added on March 12 of the following year.

A gigantic dog of undetermined breed (he's been identified as an Irish wolfhound, a caricature of McBride's own St. Bernard, and a mongrel), Napoleon was an undisciplined and undisciplinable creature whose slightest impulse created chaos in the prim life of his owner. In the nature of dog-human relationships there is little dialogue, so most of the strip's humor was conveyed by pantomime, as portly Uncle Elby's efforts at maintaining order in his tidy bachelor life were perennially defeated. Napoleon's motives were always innocent, and often noble; but the irrepressible force behind them inevitably resulted in Uncle Elby's embarrassment, arrest, or financial loss, with something always broken or buried or dug up along the way.

Drawn with a wonderfully fluid, clean line and great expressiveness, Napoleon's facial expressions somehow seemed remarkably plausible, his pride, fear, alarm, woe and satisfaction uncanny but never wholly uncanine. McBride worked in the meticulously detailed style of the 1920s magazine illustrator but nevertheless rendered his clumsy behemoth of a dog and his fat man with the kinetic liveliness of the cartoonist. McBride's

*Nancy*, Ernie Bushmiller, © 1941, United Features Syndicate. Reprinted by permission United Features Syndicate.

*Napoleon*, Clifford McBride.

gag ideas never equaled his impressive drawing, and his humor was, at best, quiet.

Several collections of *Napoleon* were published during its nearly three-decade run, and a Hollywood film was based on it, using live actors, in 1941. After McBride's death in 1951, the strip was continued with much of its original verve by Roger Armstrong until its end in 1961.
**D.W.**

**THE NEBBS** It was, not surprisingly, the most successful of the family strips that imitated *The Gumps.* Sol Hess, who created and wrote *The Nebbs*, had written *The Gumps* for several years before deciding he wanted a strip of his own. Wally Carlson, who drew it, had been in animation, and one of the properties he had adapted to the screen was *The Gumps*. The new strip began in the spring of 1923, distributed by the Bell Syndicate, and lasted for the next three decades.

The Nebb family—whose name derived from the Yiddish term for a sap or born loser, *nebich*—was headed by Rudy Nebb. Like Andy Gump, he was middle-aged, balding, and possessed of a large nose and a scraggly mustache. He had more of a chin, though, and was better drawn. His wife Fanny was plump and amiable and knew exactly how to manipulate the often blustering Rudy. They had two children, a teenage daughter, and a son of about 10 who was known as Junior.

The Nebbs lived a comfortable middle-class life, and Rudy supported them by working as a businessman. Hess' continuities dealt with Rudy's get-rich-quick schemes, with domestic crises, and with an occasional mystery. While Rudy Nebb had a somewhat abrasive personality, he was given to wisecracking, and he could be counted on to run if confronted with physical danger.

As with *The Gumps*, there were separate continuities for the Sunday page. A good many of these involved Junior Nebb, a dark-haired version of Chester Gump, in adventures and intrigues aimed at the kid audience that was assumed to be following the weekend funnies. Junior was a brave, likable lad who did such things as travel with a circus as "the world's youngest trick rider and exponent of the lariat," and visit a ranch in the West where he bested a gang of outlaws led by Black Holt and subsequently discovered a lost gold mine.

*The Nebbs*, though syndicated by the rival Bell organization, was a great favorite of William Randolph Hearst. It appeared in all the Hearst papers and at its peak had a circulation of 500 newspapers. When Hess died late in 1941, his daughter Betsy Baer with her husband Stanley took over the scripting of the feature. Since the Baers had just begun a family strip of their own, *The Toodles*, for another syndicate, they didn't sign *The Nebbs*; it continued with a credit that read simply "by Hess." Wally Carlson, with considerable help from Art Huhta, stayed on as artist. In the middle 1950s the Baers decided to merge the two strips, something rarely done in comics. They first sent the little Toodles twins to visit the Nebbs, who turned out to be relatives. Then the Nebb clan moved in as neighbors of the Toodles and *The Nebbs* as a separate strip ended. Wally Carlson's job was also over at that point. Eventually the Nebbs faded out of the other strip and were seen no more. **R.G.**

**NED BRANT** While very few sports strips have succeeded—even fewer when devoted to college athletics—*Ned Brant* was an exception and, while not a major hit, it managed to last for nearly 20 years. Begun in 1929, it was drawn by B.W. Depew, and the writing was credited to the famous football coach Bob Zuppke.

Zuppke, who coached the University of Illinois team from 1913 to 1941, was at the height of his fame in the 1920s, due in great part to the playing of such stars as Red Grange. It seems unlikely that he actually wrote the continuity; in any case, Zuppke definitely didn't think enough of the strip to list it among his credits in *Who's Who*.

Originally titled *Ned Brant at Carter*, the strip was wholesome and sentimental, with a hero as honest and forthright as such dime novel jocks as Frank Merriwell. Devoted to his widowed, ailing mother, blond, good-looking Ned had been reluctant to leave home to attend

Carter University. Once there, though, he excelled at every sport they had to offer, including football, baseball, basketball, and hockey. While there was a bit of kidding between Ned and his chums, and a little romance with the coeds, *Ned Brant* concentrated chiefly on sports. An entire week of continuity might be devoted to a crucial play against a rival football team. Often the entire lineup of an opposing outfit was listed, and a good deal of technical material showed up in the strip. Depew drew in a dependable, somewhat dull, illustrative style, but always got the plays and equipment of the various sports right.

Ned finally left college around the end of the 1930s, and worked as a reporter for the Carterville newspaper. During World War II he served in the Navy, seeing action in the Pacific. In the postwar years he returned again to Carter for another stint as a college athlete. Zuppke's name was dropped in the early 1940s, and Ted Ashby was listed as writer. Since the style of the writing didn't change and the fondness for punning names for characters—e.g., a rich man named Mr. Wallet—was continued it's possible Ashby was the scripter all along.

*Ned Brant* ended in 1948. Depew and Ashby tried another college strip, *Dick Ember*, but it was short-lived.

**R.G.**

**THE NEWLYWEDS** See McMANUS, GEORGE.

**NEW MUTANTS** Writer Chris Claremont and artist Bob McLeod created this spin-off from Marvel Comics' extremely popular *X-Men* in late 1982. Much like the early issues of *X-Men*, *New Mutants* told of an international group of adolescent "mutants" (in Marvel terminology, those born with superpowers as opposed to those who have acquired them) who have been persecuted in their homelands and are brought together for training and protection by the telepathic Professor X.

The series prospered from the beginning, thanks to its place in the X-Men's extended family, to attractive art by McLeod and Sal Buscema, and to Claremont's affectionate development of his naive, troubled characters, which struck a chord in many young readers. *New Mutants* was briefly a "fan sensation" in 1984 and 1985, due to the brash, design-conscious, quasi-abstract art of Bill Sienkiewicz. Since then it has attracted little critical attention but continues to be a reliable seller. **G.J.**

**NICKEL COMICS** One of the lowest priced comic books ever published, *Nickel Comics* appeared eight times during the spring and summer of 1940. It was put out by Fawcett Publications, offered 32 full-color pages—half the amount of the average comic book of the period—and sold for just 5 cents—half the price of

the average comic book. *Nickel* appeared every other week rather than monthly, and, if it caught on, Fawcett intended to step it up to weekly publication.

The designated star of the experimental comic was Bulletman, a costumed, flying crimefighter who wore a bullet-shaped metal helmet. Sharing the early issues were *The Jungle Twins*, which borrowed from both *Jungle Jim* and *Tarzan*, and a magician strip titled *Warlock the Wizard*. Later features included *The Red Gaucho* and *Captain Venture*. When *Nickel* folded, Bulletman and some of his colleagues relocated to *Master Comics*.

*Nickel Comics* was nowhere near as good a package as Fawcett's *Whiz Comics*, but magazines of far less quality succeeded in those early bandwagon years. It's not certain whether reader antipathy to the skinny comic book or dealer dissatisfaction with the seemingly slimmer profits doomed the *Nickel* experiment. Fawcett's initial announcement to magazine distributors admitted that "we surmise there will be some agitation against *Nickel Comics*," and went on to point out that a weekly five-center was potentially more profitable than a 10-cent monthly. "Further, if we felt for one minute that a 5¢ comic would contribute to the detriment of the comic field," explained circulation manager Roscoe Fawcett, "we should be fools to jeopardize the profitable one million monthly circulation we now maintain on the comic publications we distribute."

Dell had tried its own *Nickel Comics* in 1938, a strange hybrid that consisted of 64 pages of black-and-white material and measured just 7½ inches by 5½ inches. A mix of British strip reprints, new material, puzzles, and text, it lasted for only one issue. **R.G.**

**NICK FURY, AGENT OF S.H.I.E.L.D.** Marvel Comics' superscientific spy series began in *Strange Adventures* in 1965, written by Stan Lee and drawn by Jack Kirby. It starred the hero of Marvel's war comic, *Sgt. Fury*, now middle-aged and wearing an eye-patch, as director of the top-secret government agency S.H.I.E.L.D. (Supreme Headquarters, International Espionage Law-enforcement Division). It strongly resembled the James Bond movies and TV's *Man from U.N.C.L.E.* with its explosive action, mind-boggling weaponry, hidden headquarters, and villainous secret armies intent on conquering the world. But where Bond and his ilk were suave, Fury was hard-bitten and crusty.

In 1967 an innovative young advertising artist named Jim Steranko took over writing and drawing the series. He gave it the glitz and hipness of the Bond movies, making Fury more a jaded man of the world than a snarling platoon sergeant: He now drove fancy sports cars and engaged in an affair with a seductive woman agent that was more clearly sexual and adult than anything comic book readers had seen since pre-Comics

Code days. Steranko brought a campy, faintly cynical edge to his stories, arming Fury with absurd super-devices (bearing names like Pseudo-Elliptoid Wrist Tracer) and surrounding him with vain, buffoonish fellow agents. Enemies included an ultra-scientific oriental menace called the Yellow Claw and Fury's evil brother, Scorpio.

Often Steranko's stories were little more than excuses for his flashy art, an explosion of commercial op-art effects and visual quotes from surrealism and psychedelia, draped over a streamlined version of Kirby's action style. His work stunned astute comic book fans, bored with the status quo and not used to seeing comics reflecting art trends outside the medium. Almost overnight, Steranko made *Nick Fury* a fan sensation and helped push comics toward greater sophistication.

In 1968 Marvel made *Nick Fury* a title unto itself, thus doubling Steranko's workload and quickly driving him off the series. Barely a year later, it was canceled.

Nick Fury has appeared frequently in Marvel Comics in the 1970s and 1980s (thanks to an immortality formula that keeps him perpetually in vigorous middle age). In the changing political climate of the 1970s he often played an ambivalent role, embodying blind patriotism and militarism, especially in a long tenure as Tony Stark's opponent in *Iron Man*. Recently he has been presented more heroically and become a popular character in guest appearances and special projects, such as the glossy miniseries *Nick Fury vs. S.H.I.E.L.D.*

**G.J.**

**NIZE BABY** See GROSS, MILT.

**NORDLING, KLAUS** (1915–1986) One of the more active comic book artists and writers of the 1940s, Nordling drew the definitive version of *Lady Luck*. He entered the field in 1939 and left it in 1950, and during the little more than a decade that he worked in comics he drew a wide assortment of characters, from superheroes to detectives to daredevil aviators. What differentiated him from many of his contemporaries was the strong sense of humor that showed in everything he did.

Nordling had no formal art training; he just started drawing when he was a kid. He was born in Finland, came to America as a child, and settled in Brooklyn with his parents. After doing some magazine illustration and trying a weekly comic strip about Baron Munchausen, he was hired by the Eisner–Iger shop. The first thing he worked on, which he hated, was a humorous adventure feature about a little fellow named Shorty Shortcake that ran in Fox's *Wonderland Comics*. Next came a string of more or less serious adventure stuff for other Fox comic books—*Spark Stevens*, *Lt. Drake*, etc. He went on

to produce a batch of features for such Fiction House magazines as *Fight Comics* and *Wings Comics*.

Nordling possessed a lively, cartoony style, and his adventure stories had inventive layouts and considerable humor. In the early 1940s, soon after he became a contributor to the Quality line, he was allowed to concentrate on lighter, more humorous stories. His major creation for Quality was Pen Miller, a cartoonist-detective whose not quite serious cases first appeared in *National Comics* and then in *Crack Comics*. The blond, pipe-smoking sleuth looked a good deal like Nordling did at the time, but he always maintained the stories weren't autobiographical—"I never had adventures like that."

*Lady Luck* was a backup feature in Eisner's weekly *Spirit* section and dealt with a pretty blonde socialite who donned a green dress, green hat, and green veil to fight crime and chicanery. When the current artist was drafted in 1942, Eisner invited Nordling to take over. Nordling drew it every week for the next four years, producing over 200 four-page episodes. He converted *Lady Luck* into a screwball mystery-comedy series, always mixing satire and burlesque with his crimes and clues. Starting in 1943 the feature was reprinted in *Smash Comics* every month. The magazine became *Lady Luck* with #86 (December 1949), and Nordling returned to draw and write new stories for the five issues the new title lasted.

While associated with Eisner, Nordling also worked on *The Spirit*. "I wrote quite a few stories," he once recalled. "I actually penciled some. And I even, if I

*Bob and Swab*, Klaus Nordling, © 1948, Quality Comics.

remember rightly, was forced into inking one." He took over *The Barker* in *National Comics* in 1944 and remained with it throughout the rest of the decade. He left regular comic books in 1950.

For the next several years Nordling worked with Eisner on educational and advertising comics. He continued to do commercial comics and cartooning for the rest of his life. In addition to drawing, he had a lifelong interest in acting and was much involved with little theater. **R.G.**

**NOWLAN, PHILIP**  See BUCK ROGERS.

# O

**OAKY DOAKS** No doubt the Associated Press was thinking about the success of NEA's *Alley Oop* when it launched the *Oaky Doaks* daily strip in 1935. Here, too, was a strip that took place in the past—in this case the period when knighthood was in flower—and starred a strong hero who had somewhat more heart than brains. Comics editor Bill McCleery came up with the initial idea and wrote the continuity in the early years. The artist picked to do the drawing was Ralph Briggs Fuller, and the result was a comic strip that was better looking and considerably funnier than its probable source of inspiration.

R.B. Fuller had already been a professional cartoonist for some 25 years, a frequent contributor of gag cartoons to such weekly humor magazines as *Judge* and *Life*. He had also painted covers for pulp fiction magazines such as *Adventure* and had tried his hand at an unsuccessful newspaper panel based on *Ballyhoo* magazine's mascot, Elmer Zilch. Fuller had an impressive pen and ink style and could draw anything the strip called for, including gloomy castles, lovely damsels in distress, armored knights, fiery dragons, and galloping steeds.

The dark-haired, lanky Oaky Doaks was a simple farm boy who yearned to become a knight. He fashioned himself a suit of armor, making it out of a tin shed roof, and borrowed his father's plow horse for his mount. The animal's name was Nellie, and she served Oaky faithfully for the entire long run of the strip. Soon after riding off in search of adventure, Oaky encoun-

tered the local monarch, and the two teamed up for a series of picaresque adventures that pitted them against amazons, pirates, blackguards, and sorceresses. Plump, bespectacled King Cedric was a lazy bumbling sort, much more interested in pretty blondes and mealtimes than in ruling the land. Oaky was pure of heart, a bit naive, stubborn, brave, attractive to just about every beautiful woman they encountered, and ruled by the motto "No day without a good deed," which appeared in Pig Latin on his coat of arms.

A typical sequence ran in 1936, an election year. King Cedric was nominated for the presidency of Maple Island. A beautiful blond young woman named Constance Considine persuaded Oaky—who could be persuaded by beautiful blonds on occasion—to persuade Cedric to allow her to run for vice president on his ticket. The campaign got rolling and, thanks to Oaky, all the posters and billboards featured pictures of Constance and not the king. The campaign manager of his rival, Sir Cadwell Morgan, suggested a whole chorus of lovely vice presidents. But they finally decided to stage an amateur contest to pick Cadwell's running mate. After a campaign that stretched across several months and involved Oaky in a romance with Constance, a kidnapping, and a battle with a giant, King Cedric and the blonde won.

Oaky and Cedric parted for good and all in the summer of 1940, when the king stayed behind to woo the woman he loved and Oaky rode on to the kingdom of

*Oaky Doaks*, R.B. Fuller, © 1937, The A.P.

277

New Topia. That was another election year, and Okay again got involved in political doings. He ended up running for mayor against a charming young lady named Gracie Giddings who appeared on all her posters in a bathing suit. Arrested on a fake charge, Okay carried on much of his campaign from a jail cell.

In the summer of 1941 Oaky arrived in Camelot, and readers became aware for the first time that he was a contemporary of Prince Valiant. After a few years amidst King Arthur, Merlin, Morgana Le Fey, and the Round Table crowd, Oaky traveled on to the kingdom of Uncertainia, where he encountered King Corny and, more importantly, his daughter, the trouble-prone Princess Pomona. For the remainder of his newspaper days Oaky was based in Uncertainia. By the time the strip ended late in 1961, he and Pomona were married and the parents of an infant son.

AP didn't get around to offering Sunday pages on any of its features until late in 1941. The earliest years of *Oaky Doaks* Sundays were drawn by Bill Dyer; Fuller took over in February 1944. Continuity was used, but the stories remained separate from what was going on weekdays. *Oaky Doaks* was one of the funnies reprinted in *Famous Funnies*, where it could be found from the middle 1930s to the middle 1950s. Oaky frequently appeared on the covers, usually drawn by Steve Douglas. There was also a one-shot devoted entirely to Oaky in 1942, which included the sequence chronicling King Cedric's memorable presidential run.  **R.G.**

**O'KEEFFE, NEIL** (1893– ? )  A self-taught artist, O'Keeffe had a long and varied career before he undertook the *Dick's Adventures in Dreamland* Sunday page, his best-known feature, in 1947.

He went to work for the art department on the *St. Louis Post-Dispatch* in 1913, moved on to the *Chicago Tribune* the next year, and by the early 1920s was in Manhattan working on the *World*, where he took a turn drawing the *Metropolitan Movies* panel.

O'Keeffe branched out into magazine illustration in the 1920s, doing a great deal of work for the top fiction pulp, *Adventure*. There he developed the ability to draw figures in action in well-wrought contemporary and historical settings, and a forceful drybrush style, which he utilized when he moved into newspaper strips. He also contributed to such slicks as *Collier's* and the *American Magazine*.

He took over King Features' *Inspector Wade of Scotland Yard* daily in 1938 and saw it to its demise in May 1941. Briefly in the mid-1940s he worked as art director of Hearst's *American Weekly* Sunday supplement. After *Dick's Adventures* ceased in 1956, he returned to illustration.  **R.G.**

**OKSNER, BOB** (1916– )  An artist who has drawn pretty women, in both comic books and newspaper strips, for over half a century, Oksner has depicted Supergirl, Miss Cairo Jones, and Lucille Ball, among others.

He entered comic books in 1939 by way of the Funnies, Inc., shop. Oksner had originally intended to be a lawyer, but shifted to art and from NYU to the Art Students League. He was working for an MA at Columbia and planning to become an art teacher when he started drawing comics. His first feature was *Terry Vance*, about a teenager known as the School Boy Sleuth, for *Marvel Mystery Comics*.

In 1943 he shifted to a shop run by B.W. Sangor, which was supplying art to such comic books as *Real Life*, *Thrilling*, *Startling*, and *Mystery*. Oksner drew a wide variety of material for these titles, and during that period his style changed, becoming looser and more inventive. He also developed a personal, easily recognizable way of drawing women. In 1945 he drew his first newspaper strip, *Miss Cairo Jones*, which starred a pretty blond young woman who managed to get mixed up in mystery and intrigue in several choice locations around the globe.

When his strip ended in 1947, Oksner returned to comic books and worked for DC, doing adventure features (*Hawkman* and *The Ghost Patrol*) and funny features (*Leave It To Binky* and *Miss Beverly Hills*). During the middle 1950s, using the pen name Bob Lawrence, he drew the *I Love Lucy* newspaper strip. After that came more comic books, based on Bob Hope, Jerry Lewis, and the *Dobie Gillis* television show. All were populated with the distinctive Oksner women.

He wrote, and sometimes drew, Irwin Hasen's *Dondi* strip from 1967 until its finish in the early 1980s. He tried one more strip of his own, a pretty girl thing called *Soozi* that was briefly seen in 1967 and 1968. Until recently he was again at DC, where one of his best-known features was *Supergirl*.  **R.G.**

**OLD DOC YAK**  See SMITH, SIDNEY.

**OLIVER'S ADVENTURES**  While this daily made its 1927 debut a few weeks before *Bobby Thatcher*, it still looks like a blatant imitation of George Storm's strip, probably because both features were inspired by the earlier *Phil Hardy*. *Oliver's Adventures* was the McNaught Syndicate's entry in the adventure field, and the work of Gus Mager. A veteran bigfoot cartoonist and the creator of *Sherlocko* and *Hawkshaw*, Mager seems an unlikely choice to handle a strip fraught with bloodcurdling action and hairbreadth escapes, which may account for his abandoning both his drawing style and his sense of humor and aping Storm so diligently.

Oliver, a loner who owed his name to Dickens' better-known orphan, had some pretty hair-raising adventures. Teaming up with aviators, detectives, and tycoons, he devoted a good part of his time to mixing it up with South American revolutionaries, crazed lumberjacks, wild jungle animals, escaped killers, and the like. Since Mager had a real interest in the outdoors and wildlife, he managed to slip in a good deal of authentic flora and fauna into the strip, but it was otherwise a standard boy-adventurer feature.

Mager was still under contract to do the Oliver strip when his old friend Rudolph Dirks invited him to revive *Hawkshaw the Detective* as a topper to the *Captain and the Kids* Sunday. Mager agreed, but didn't use his name; he signed the pages, which utilized his old bulb-nosed style and his knack for parodying melodramatic conventions, simply Watso. For the next several years he alternated between detective parodies on Sunday and fairly straight adventure on weekdays, sometimes kidding in *Hawkshaw* the things he was taking seriously in *Oliver's Adventures*. The plucky Oliver hung on through 1934, although the strip's name in its final days was *Oliver and His Dog*. **R.G.**

**OLSEN, JOHN J.** See JOHN WEST.

**O'MEALIA, LEO** (1884–1960)  Best known in newspaper comics as the illustrator of the Bell Syndicate's bizarre, early 1930s *Fu Manchu* daily strip, O'Mealia was a longtime newspaper artist, an early figure in comic books, and a working-press sports cartoonist.

Born in 1884, according to certain accounts in Rochester, New York, he worked variously for *The Times* and *The Herald* in that city before going to New York in the early 1920s, at the urging of his mentor Tad Dorgan, where he joined the staff of Hearst's *Journal*. He had in 1912, meanwhile, begun the family-comedy strip *Wedlocked*, which was distributed by the Associated Newspapers syndicate until its demise in 1929.

In 1930 he drew the short-lived *Sherlock Holmes* strip. *Fu Manchu* followed, and it folded in April 1933. By the middle 1930s O'Mealia had moved into the fledgling comic book industry. He had two styles, straight adventure and slapstick, and he did both types of features for such early DC tiles as *More Fun* and *New Adventure*. One of his most impressive works was *Barry O'Neill*, which covered familiar Fu Manchu ground as daredevil Barry battled a vigorously recurrent Oriental mastermind named Fang Gow. O'Mealia provided several covers for early issues of *Action Comics*, before it was realized that Superman on the front would increase sales. In the middle 1930s he also drew advertising strips for the Sunday funnies. But by 1940 he was out of the comic book field.

Leo O'Mealia, Self Portrait, circa 1950.

In 1943 he joined the sports department of the *New York Daily News*. His popular cartoon panel for the sports page had its finest hour in October 1955, when the Brooklyn Dodgers won the World Series, and the newspaper devoted its entire front page to O'Mealia's famous "Who's A Bum!" drawing. He died in May 1960. **J.M.**

**O'NEAL, FRANK**  See SHORT RIBS.

**ON STAGE**  Leonard Starr's stylish *Mary Perkins On Stage* (usually known simply as *On Stage*) was one of the most maturely written and elegantly drawn continuity strips in American comics. Starr, with a successful career in both comic books and commercial art behind him, offered it along with six other strip proposals to several syndicates before the Chicago Tribune-New York News Syndicate (now Tribune Media Services) agreed to take it on. The strip opened on February 10, 1957, and did not bring down its final curtain until 1979.

Often dismissed as a soap opera (its thematic similarity to the popular daytime radio serial "Backstage Wife," which ran on NBC from 1936 to 1959, is obvious), *On Stage* transcended the conventions of the sentimental romance and the tearjerker, incorporating elements of high comedy and often gripping adventure and suspense. It was written with considerable polish and presented the glamour of the Broadway theater world with neither sensationalism nor cynicism as it recounted the saga of Mary Perkins, a small-town ingenue making her way in the Big City and passing, like Pippa, undefiled by its various pitfalls. Surrounded by sexually liberated colleagues usually no better than they should be and sometimes not even as good, the uncorrupted Mary sails through to Broadway stardom and marriage to a handsome, successful photographer without losing either her ideals or her virtue—no mean feat when sustained over a period of 22 years.

The heightened realism of Starr's illustrational style nicely complements the narrative flow of the stories, creating an atmosphere at once elegant and tense, like the life of their heroine. Although readership began to fall off toward the end of the strip's long run, as it declined for all continuity strips in the 1970s, *On Stage* was always much admired by the artist's colleagues and faithfully followed by its loyal, if diminishing, body of fans. It was voted the Best Story Strip of the Year by the National Cartoonists Society in 1960, and remains one of the most memorably written and drawn strips of its type in the literature.                                    **D.W.**

**OPPER, FREDERICK BURR** (1857–1937) Best known for his comic strips *Happy Hooligan, And Her Name Was Maud!*, and *Alphonse and Gaston*, Frederick Burr Opper had a distinguished career as a political cartoonist and book illustrator before creating the strips on which his fame now rests.

Opper was born in Madison, Ohio, and began his career in art early, dropping out of school at the age of 14 to work as a staff artist with the *Madison Gazette*. His success as a free-lance contributor to national magazines led him to move in 1877 to New York City, where he began working with the humor magazine *Wild Oats*. From 1878 to 1881 he was a staff artist for *Leslie's Magazine*, and then moved up to a job with *Puck*, the leading satirical magazine of the time, as political and gag cartoonist. Opper remained with *Puck*, drawing trenchant editorial panels and creating several popular humorous features such as *The Streets of New York* and *The Age of Handbooks*, until 1899. During that time he continued to publish humorous material in many other magazines, and several collections of his satirical art appeared. An evidence of his growing reputation in the field was his selection to illustrate the books of such noted humorists as Bill Nye, and later Finley Peter Dunne (*Mr. Dooley*), Eugene Field, and Mark Twain.

In May of 1899, Opper joined William Randolph Hearst's team and began drawing political cartoons that were among the most influential of their time. He lambasted President McKinley and his big-business backers and attained a reputation for acerbic wit that rivaled that of Thomas Nast. Increasingly, however, he turned his talents to the emerging medium of the comic strip. March 1900 saw the debut of his most famous feature, *Happy Hooligan*, a gag strip about a touching and ludicrous Irish hobo whose well-meaning efforts always landed him in trouble. A prototype of the eternal loser, which was to become so fertile a source of graphic humor in America (and suggested as a possible influence on Charlie Chaplin's later, lovable tramp), Happy stayed enormously popular. A 31st-birthday celebration for the strip, given the year before it ceased in 1932, was attended by Herbert Hoover, Calvin Coolidge, and Al Smith.

In the same year *Happy Hooligan* appeared, Opper created *Our Antediluvian Ancestors*, a strip featuring a cave-dwelling family, which ran until 1903. In 1902 *Alphonse and Gaston* appeared, a series about two Frenchmen whose excessive courtesy was to make the strip's title a national catchphrase, and two years later Opper initiated *And Her Name Was Maud!*, dealing with a recalcitrant mule. Later strips include *Howson Lott*, a satire of suburban home-ownership (1905); *Mr. Dubb*, another born-loser feature (1919); *On the Farm*, satirizing life in the country (1921); and *Mr. Dough and Mr. Dubb*, an effort at revitalizing his earlier strip *Mr. Dubb* (1925). Most of these strips were short-lived, although *Maud*, which ended in the teens of this century, was revived from 1926 to 1932, and many of the characters visited other strips even after their own had been canceled.

*Happy Hooligan, Maud, Alphonse and Gaston*, and *Our Antediluvian Ancestors* all had collections issued by Stokes during the first decade of Opper's long tenure with Hearst, and *Happy* has been widely reprinted since. Regarded as "the Dean of American Cartoonists," Opper submitted to Hearst's forced-retirement policy at the age of 75 against his will and died five years later.
                                                            **D.W.**

**ORLANDO, JOE** (1927–  ) Currently the creative director of DC Comics, Orlando has had a long career as a comic book artist, and he was one of the contributors to the much-praised EC line of innovative comic books in the 1950s.

He was born in Italy and came to the United States with his family two years later. After attending the High School of Industrial Arts in New York, he served with the military Police among the occupation forces in Europe and then returned in 1947 to study under John Groth at the Art Students League. He entered comics in 1948, doing work for *Catholic Comics* and *Treasure Chest*. Then he met Wally Wood. "When Wally put his brush to my drawing, I was always amazed at the wonderful results," he's said. "Wally was fascinated with how fast I could pencil. I was knocked out by his ability to make

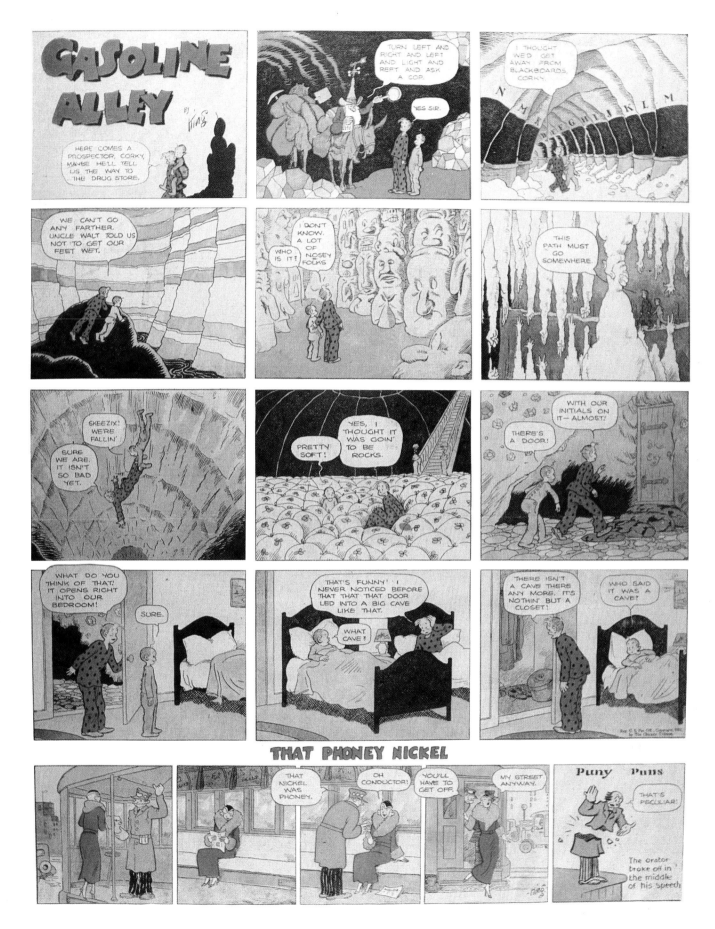

*Gasoline Alley*, © 1933, The Chicago Tribune. Reprinted by permission: Tribune Media Services.

*Captain Easy*, © 1934, NEA Service, Inc. Reprinted by permission of NEA Service, Inc.

*Connie*, © 1938, Ledger Syndicate.

*Skull Valley*, © 1938, Chicago Tribune—N.Y. News Syndicate.

*Terry and the Pirates*, © 1939, Chicago Tribune—N.Y. News Syndicate. Reprinted by permission: Tribune Media Services.

*Mr. Coffee Nerves*, © 1936, G.F. Corp.

*Marvel Mystery Comics*™., © 1941, Marvel Entertainment Group Inc. All rights reserved.

*Whiz Comics*, © 1940, Fawcett Publications.

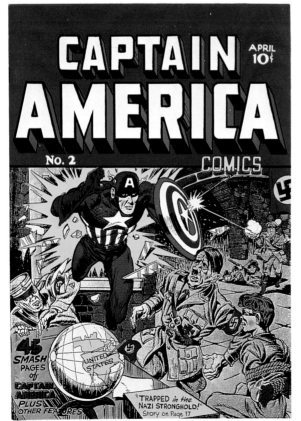

*Captain America*™, © 1940, Marvel Entertainment Group, Inc. All rights reserved.

*Captain Marvel Jr.*, © 1942, Fawcett Publications.

*Flyin' Jenny*, © 1943, The Bell Syndicate, Inc.

*Don Winslow*, © The Bell Syndicate, Inc.

*Dickie Dare*, © 1944, Associated Press.

my scribbles look good. We ended up renting a studio in a building that was later torn down to make room for Lincoln Center."

They shared the studio with Harry Harrison, and the trio began producing material for such publishers as Fox, Fawcett, Ziff-Davis, Avon, and EC. In 1950 things fell apart at the Columbus Avenue studio when Fox collapsed, owing the young artists nearly $6,000. Disillusioned, Orlando abandoned his art career and went to work in a Long Island stockroom. But he soon returned to assist Wood and then went on in 1951 to draw his own stories for EC. Working in a style similar to Wood's, he specialized in horror, science fiction, and humor. Fellow artist Roy Krenkel once recalled, "Joe was another workhorse. He was a deadline lover's fool. He would make a deadline if they had to get him back from the grave." After EC, Orlando contributed to Atlas titles such as *Mystic* and *Astonishing*, to *Classics Illustrated*, *Mad*, and *Creepy* before joining DC as an editor in 1966. In addition to his executive duties at DC, Orlando has returned to the drawing board in recent years, with contributions to such titles as *Secret Origins*.  **B.S.**

*Our Boarding House*, Gene Ahern, © 1931, NEA Service, Inc. Reprinted by permission NEA Service, Inc.

**OUR BOARDING HOUSE**  The undisputed champion windbag of the funny papers is Major Hoople. It was in *Our Boarding House*, created by Gene Ahern, that he held forth. The panel started on September 16, 1921, but the major, late as usual, didn't make his first appearance until January of the following year. Once established, he hung on for nearly 60 years, loafing, scheming, harumphing, and never doing an honest day's work.

The boarding house, with its component of snide and bickering residents, was owned and operated by Major Hoople's large, formidable wife Martha. She put up with him, but not with any of his schemes, and she was frequently laying down the law to him. She offered a "no" that was, as she put it, "as final as a cobra's bite!" Among the long-term tenants were Buster, Mack, and Clyde, assorted bachelors, and also young Alvin, the Hooples' nephew. Everybody saw through the major, but Alvin could often be persuaded to sit still for one of his tall tales. Donald Phelps, writing in *Nemo* magazine, suggests that the household needed Hoople and his flights of fancy "because they realize his nonsense is basic to their lives."

Ahern's daily panel was laid out like a single panel from a comic strip, with well-packed dialogue balloons, and sounded like a play—or radio show—that was part realistic and part screwball fantasy. The major was one of the great talkers, punctuating his discourses with "Egad!," "Fap!," or "Hrummf—hakkaff!" As Bill Blackbeard has pointed out in *The World Encyclopedia of Comics*, "Hoople was a Fieldsian figure before W.C. Fields himself had developed...his classic conman character."

Though Ahern switched to King Features to draw the very similar *Room and Board* in the middle 1930s, his fez-wearing braggart continued on. At first Wood Cowan was given the job of writing and drawing the panel, but the NEA syndicate grew unhappy with his artwork. He was kept on as writer and Bill Zaboly was brought in to take over the drawing. Zaboly eventually followed Ahern to King Features, and in September of 1939 Bill Freyse became the *Our Boarding House* artist, daily and Sunday. A writer named Bill Braucher provided the scripts from 1939 until his death in 1958. After Freyse's death in the late 1960s, several artists and writers worked on the feature. Les Carroll, an assistant on *Boots and Her Buddies*, drew the major's adventures in the final years and Tom McCormick wrote them. Major Hoople retired after the release of March 29, 1981.

**R.G.**

**OUTCAULT, RICHARD F.** (1863–1928)  One of the earliest newspaper comic artists, Outcault created two of the field's important characters, introducing the Yellow Kid in 1895 and Buster Brown in 1902. He pioneered not only in the developing of the Sunday funnies but also in the merchandising of comics characters.

Richard Felton Outcault was born in Lancaster, Ohio, and educated at McMicken College in Cincinnati. On the basis of his drawing ability he was hired by Thomas Edison and was later engaged to do technical drawings for *Electrical World* magazine in New York. On the side he sold cartoons to *Truth, Judge,* and *Life*.

His free-lance work led him to a contract with Pulitzer's *New York World*, where his work began to appear as early as September 1894. Included among these early panels were several that depicted life in the mainly Irish slums of Manhattan, and out of these came the *Hogan's Alley* series, which introduced the Yellow Kid.

When William Randolph Hearst decided to start his Sunday Comic Supplement in competition with Pulitzer, he raided the latter's staff. Outcault was one of those hired away, and his work appeared in the first issue of Hearst's *The American Humorist*, on October 18, 1896, and his *Alley* series, under the new title, *The Yellow Kid*, began the following Sunday.

In 1898 Outcault returned to the *World* and over the next three years drew four new series, including *Kelly's Kindergarten/Kelly Kids* and *Gallus Coon*. In 1898 he also turned out two short series for the Philadelphia *Inquirer*, called *The Country School* and *The Barnyard Club*. By early 1900 Outcault was contributing to the *New York Herald*, whose publisher James Gordon Bennett was also active in the newspaper comics competition. Here Outcault tried three series before achieving success with *Buster Brown*, which began on May 4, 1902.

Restless, Outcault again responded to an offer from Hearst in January 1906 and took Buster and crew to the Hearst newspapers. The page lasted at least until December 11, 1921. More a humorous illustrator than a cartoonist, his work never lost its 19th-century magazine illustration look and by the third decade of the 20th century it appeared quite old-fashioned.

Outcault grew tired not only of Buster Brown but also of comic art in general. He left the field in the early 1920s to found an advertising agency. **K.S.B.**

**OUT OUR WAY** A daily panel by J.R. Williams, *Out Our Way* shifted from the past to the present as it commented in its quietly humorous way on small-town life, factory work, the cowboy's lot, and the joys and sorrows of childhood. It began in 1922, distributed to a large number of newspapers by the NEA syndicate.

Williams had a series of favorite topics and locales, which he covered under such recurrent titles as *Born Thirty Years Too Soon, Why Mothers Get Gray,* and *Heroes Are Made–Not Born*. He also reported frequently on factory and machine shop doings, cowboy and ranch life, and the misadventures of an unkempt, ill-fated younger brother known as the Worry Wart.

He drew in a homespun style, giving the impression he had taught himself to draw by studying the panels of Tad and Clare Briggs. He added something of his own, though, a kind of amused sympathy for his char-

acters; Williams was especially good at catching the attitudes of defeat, frustration, and restless yearning. A nostalgia for vanished times pervaded much of his best work, and he never tired of returning to the scenes of his own youth, retaining a special pride in his cowboy drawings, which he based on his memories of his own days as a cowhand and more recent experiences as a ranch owner. Williams believed that the movie notion of what a cowboy was didn't ring true at all.

A Sunday page was added in the early 1920s, and although Williams' name was signed to it, he never had anything to do with it. Presented in strip form, the page dealt with a family named the Willits, who were loosely adapted from some of the characters in the daily panel. Various artists, including Neg Cochran, ghosted the page, which never caught the flavor of Williams' daily stuff.

Williams died in 1957, but the feature continued for another 20 years. Included among the artists who carried it on were Cochran, Paul Gringle, and Walt Wetterberg. **R.G.**

**OVERGARD, WILLIAM** (1926–1990) One of several protégés of Milton Caniff, Overgard drew the *Steve Roper* newspaper strip from 1954 to 1982. He also worked in comic books, ghosted *Steve Canyon*, wrote *Kerry Drake*, and created a strip of his own about a talking chimp.

As a boy growing up in Southern California, Overgard discovered *Terry and the Pirates* and was prompted to send a fan letter to Caniff. That, as Overgard put it, "began a correspondence which lasted through high school and two years in the Navy, and was the only formal training in the cartooning field I was to have." In 1948 Overgard moved East and succeeded in getting hired to draw comic book features for Lev Gleason's company. Working in his loose, bold version of the Caniff style, he drew the boy hero Crimebuster in *Boy Comics* and the Little Wise Guys in *Daredevil*. Displaying an affinity for the props and locales of the Old West, he also drew the adventures of a masked cowboy called Black Diamond in the comic book of that name.

Overgard next moved to Dell, where he drew a variety of things, including at least one issue of an original-material *Steve Canyon* comic book. About this same time he also worked as assistant to Caniff on the strip itself. In later years he stepped in now and then to ghost the strip when Caniff was ailing.

He was hired to draw *Steve Roper* in 1954. Although the adventure strip had been ghosted for many years, Elmer Woggon's name had continued to appear as that of artist. Woggon gave up that practice at this point, and Overgard was allowed to sign his own name. He stayed with the strip, daily and Sunday, for nearly three decades, taking a hand in the writing and creating Roper's hardbitten partner Mike Nomad. He quit in 1982 to develop *Rudy*, which began in January 1983. A quirky humor strip about a talking chimp making his way in the world of show business, it had many dedicated admirers but failed to last for more than a few years.

Overgard was also a writer, with several thriller novels to his credit and several television scripts, among them scripts for such animated television shows as *Thundercats*. When his partner on the *Steve Roper* strip, Allen Saunders, gave up the writing of *Kerry Drake* in the early 1970s, Overgard took over that job and kept at it for several years. **R.G.**

**OZARK IKE** A newspaper strip that combined elements of *Li'l Abner* and *Joe Palooka*, it was written and drawn by Ray Gotto, produced by Stephen Slesinger, and distributed by King Features. *Ozark Ike* began in 1945 and dealt with the exploits of a dumb but honest hillbilly ballplayer named Ike McBatt.

The Tennessee-born Gotto had been a high school athlete, later working as sports and editorial cartoonist for the *Nashville Banner*. He came up with the idea for *Ozark Ike* while serving in the Navy and stationed in Washington, D.C. After he'd drawn up five sample weeks, packager-agent-entrepreneur Slesinger sold the sports-oriented strip to King Features. Gotto drew in a bold, stiff cartoon style, favoring all sorts of patiently rendered pen patterns. He used considerable humor in his continuities.

In addition to Ike, the strip offered Dinah Fatfield, a Daisy Mae surrogate who wore tight, striped sweaters and was built along the lines of the pinup girls to be found in magazines like *Esquire*. Though her family and Ike's were forever feuding, the two of them, much like Romeo and Juliet, carried on a romance. Unlike Abner, Ike didn't run from girls.

The strip alternated between broad hillbilly continuities and more serious sports sequences, swinging from feuding to big league baseball. In addition to baseball, *Ozark Ike* also dealt with, depending on the season, football and basketball. According to writer and comics historian Max Allan Collins, "Gotto could spin a sports yarn like nobody in comics, with the possible exception of Ham Fisher."

Gotto spun his yarns until 1954 when he quit. "My agent [Slesinger] died in 1953," he's explained. "This left the strip's rights tied up in his estate. So, after years of frustration...I decided to back out and move on." Gotto came back the following year with *Cotton Woods*, a slightly more serious baseball strip done for a smaller syndicate. *Ozark Ike* went on until 1959, drawn by Bill Lignante and at least one other artist. The Sunday page in its final years was attributed to Ed Strops, which is "sports" spelled backwards. **R.G.**

# P

**PANHANDLE PETE**   See McMANUS, GEORGE.

**PARKER, BRANT** (1920– )  The creator of *Crock* and artist for *The Wizard of Id*, Brant Parker was a technical artist with no comic strip experience when Johnny Hart approached him in 1963 to draw *The Wizard*, but within the next decade he became one of the most admired cartoonists in the country. Parker grew up around art (his mother was a fashion illustrator who worked at home) and was doing "weird doodles" at the age of three. After high school he studied illustration at the Otis Art Institute in his home town of Los Angeles for nearly two years and worked his way up from a job as copy boy to the art department of the *Los Angeles Herald Express*. From there he went on to the *Los Angeles Daily News*, where his creative spirit qualified him to perform such less than inspiring work as retouching maps.

Parker attended the animation school at Walt Disney Productions, where he worked on short features for a couple of years in the mid-1940s, and then moved to New York state and a job as staff artist and political cartoonist with *The Binghamton Press*. After a stint in the navy, Parker took a job with IBM in Endicott, New York, where he met Hart, whose *B.C.* was already an established success, and accepted the offer to collaborate on his new strip. *The Wizard of Id* began publication in 1964. Its wide popularity over the next quarter-century owes much to Parker's casual-seeming, expressive art.

In 1975, Parker created his own strip, *Crock*, which he produces in collaboration with artist Bill Rechin and writer Don Wilder. Distributed by North America Syndicate, *Crock* recounts the dismal adventures of a troop of Foreign Legionnaires under the iron command of Vermin P. Crock, who, according to his creators, "could have taught Atilla how to Hun."

Parker's art has earned him numerous awards from his colleagues. *The Wizard of Id* brought him National Cartoonists Society plaques for Best Humor Strip in 1971, 1976, 1980, 1982, and 1983, and the Reuben as Outstanding Cartoonist of the Year in 1984. In 1986 Parker received the NCS's Elzie Segar Award for "a unique and outstanding contribution to the profession of cartooning."                                   **D.W.**

**PARKER, GLADYS** (1910–1966)  An autobiographical cartoonist, Parker modeled her character Mopsy after herself. *Mopsy*, which was initially a daily panel, ran from 1939 to 1965. The slight, dark-haired Parker started working as a professional artist while still in her teens, and she drew several other newspaper features. She also wrote a newspaper column and even took a turn ghosting the *Flyin' Jenny* adventure strip during World War II.

Gladys Parker was born in Tonawanda, New York, and was once voted the prettiest child in her hometown. She moved to Manhattan in 1927, hoping for a career in fashion design. "My first job," she once explained, "was to design striptease dresses for burlesque queens." She moved up, slightly, when she became a staff cartoonist for the *New York Graphic*, an energetically sleazy daily tabloid.

Next came a strip called *Gay and Her Gang* for United Features in 1928 and 1929. She moved next to NEA, taking over Ethel Hays' *Flapper Fanny* panel and also drawing *Femininities*, a panel combining fashion tips and a touch of humor. "I wrote my own gags for *Flapper Fanny*," she once confessed. "They were all puns. After thinking up six puns a week for seven years, I knew what the guy meant when he said a pun was the lowest form of humor." During her stay with the feature NEA sent out publicity photos of "the petite artist herself in a modish outfit" and referred to her as "'Flapper Fanny' in person."

In her drawing Parker avoided the frills and cuteness of some of the earlier women cartoonists—such as Nell Brinkley and Grace Drayton—and worked in a style that was simple, streamlined, and decorative, a variation of the black-and- white Jazz Age style developed by Russell Patterson in the 1920s.

She began *Mopsy* in 1939 for John Wheeler's Associated Newspapers syndicate. A Sunday page was added in 1945, and in 1949 *Newsweek* was able to report that "*Mopsy* appears in some 300 papers in addition to comic books, and probably earns her real-life double something more than $50,000 a year." Although married to cartoonist Stookie Allen, Parker kept her feathercut funnypaper counterpart single. A smartly dressed working woman, Mopsy wasn't as bright as her creator either, and Parker usually described her as dumb to interviewers, adding that "people like dumb characters best—it flatters their own intelligence." The gags in *Mopsy* were built around men, clothes, money, and jobs.

During World War II Parker found time to do a *Betty G.I.* panel for service newspapers and to fill in as a ghost occasionally for the ailing Russell Keaton on *Flyin' Jenny*. This latter assignment was Wheeler's idea and never sat well with Glenn Chaffin who wrote the strip. Parker could draw Jenny but she never mastered the airplanes and the weapons the aviation strip called for.

In her last years she lived alone in Hollywood with her cat and added an advice column called *Dear Guys and Gals* to her list of chores. **R.G.**

**PATTERSON, JOSEPH MEDILL** (1879–1946)  Born to wealth and influence, Patterson was associated with two major newspapers, the *Chicago Tribune* and the *New York Daily News*. He believed, as an editor and publisher, in getting involved with every aspect of the business, and he had a hand in the creation and development of such comic strips as *The Gumps, Little Orphan Annie, Dick Tracy*, and *Terry and the Pirates*.

When he and his cousin, Robert McCormick, came to share the family throne of the *Chicago Tribune* upon the death of Patterson's father in 1910, Joe Patterson brought with him the variegated experiences of an active youth. He had interrupted his schooling at Yale in the summer of 1900 to cover the Boxer Rebellion as a reporter for the *Chicago American*. After graduation in 1901, he worked briefly as a reporter for his father's paper and then entered Chicago politics with a reformer's zeal. When neither the Republican nor the Democratic party yielded results, he scandalized his family by becoming a socialist in 1906 and announcing that he would henceforth earn his own living. He became a dairy farmer and a writer, producing socialist tracts, novels, and plays (three of which were produced on Broadway).

By 1910, however, Patterson had become disillusioned with politics as a means of achieving reform, and he was ready for his journalistic patrimony. To the variety of his experiences Patterson soon added that of military service in World War I. He enlisted as a buck private, but by the time his unit was sent to France he had worked up the ranks to captain, a title he would invoke the rest of his life.

He started America's first successful tabloid, the *New York Daily News*, on June 26, 1919, and in four years it moved from last place among New York's 18 daily newspapers to first in the nation with a average daily circulation of over 600,000. Believing that people wanted more romance and adventure than their ordinary lives afforded them, Patterson produced an outrageous, tearjerking, glamorous sheet showcasing sex and scandal, pictures and contests. As he had in Chicago, he concentrated on improving his features, especially the comics.

As editor of the *Chicago Trib* he'd imagined a strip about people with whom his readers of the lower-middle-class could identify. Patterson harkened back to his novelist days and invoked the social realism of Dreiser to invent, with the help of Sidney Smith, *The Gumps*. Started in 1917, the strip became so popular it virtually established the Chicago Tribune Syndicate, which was set up to sell the feature to out of town papers that were clamoring for it.

In 1920 at the *Daily News* he went looking for a cartoonist to do a strip about a working girl. Martin Branner's *Winnie Winkle* proved so successful that it yielded the *News'* nickname—"the working girl's paper." Sensing that the lower class was being neglected, Captain Patterson found Frank Willard to do that paean to lowlifers, *Moon Mullins*, and supplied Moonshine's first name. And in 1934, to give his comics the flavor of exotic adventure, Patterson commandeered Milton Caniff from the Associated Press to do an adventure strip about a kid and his mentor and a long-legged line of sexy women in the Orient.

Not all of the *News'* successful strips were invented by Patterson. Part of his gift was the ability to recognize the potential of a new strip and bring that potential out. Feeling that Frank King's *Gasoline Alley* lacked appeal for women, he told King to get a baby into the strip fast—ignoring the fact that the principal character was a bachelor. When Harold Gray brought in a strip about an orphan boy named Little Orphan Otto, Patterson suggested an important change: "Put a skirt on him and we'll call it Little Orphan Annie." He gave Chester Gould's submission, *Plainclothes Tracy*, a new first name, christened Tess Trueheart, and plotted Dick Tracy's first adventure.

The captain's suggestions came in person and by memo, phonecall, and wire. He telegraphed Zack Mosley to change the name of his faltering airplane strip, *On the Wing*, to *Smilin' Jack*, thereby providing readers with a protagonist with whom they could identify. Not all of Patterson's strips became popular; *A Strain on the Family Tie, Streaky, White Boy*, and *Little Folks* didn't last long. And *Sweeney and Son, Little Joe*, and *Texas Slim*, while long-running and reasonably successful, were not big sellers. But in nurturing to success such hits as *The Gumps, Gasoline Alley, Little Orphan Annie, Dick Tracy*, and *Terry and the Pirates*, Patterson established his reputation as comic strip artist without peer—even if he couldn't draw a stroke. **R.C.H.**

**PATTERSON, RUSSELL** (1894–1977)  He usually listed himself as a designer, decorator, cartoonist, and

Russell Patterson, Self Portrait.

illustrator. Patterson, who both depicted and influenced the look of the Jazz Age, often later admitted that he "was greatly responsible for the flapper and collegiate eras." At one time the Patterson Girl was as well known, and as representative of her time, as had been the Gibson Girl. He drew newspaper strips at various points in his career and had an influence on many cartoonists, ranging from Milton Caniff to Gladys Parker.

Patterson was born in Omaha, but, because his father was an attorney with the Canadian Pacific railroad, he grew up and was educated in Newfoundland, Toronto, and Montreal. He studied architecture for a year, then got a job with the *Montreal Standard* as an artist. Moving to the French language *La Patrie*, he drew his first comic strip, *Pierre et Pierrette*. He moved next to Chicago, attending both the Art Institute and the Academy of Fine Arts. Next, in 1920, Patterson embarked for Paris, where he studied art, painted, drew, and lived the expatriate life. Back in America by the middle of the decade, he began to get work as a magazine illustrator.

Although he sometimes used color, it was as a black and white illustrator that he excelled. Patterson had developed a very distinctive way of drawing women. The Patterson girl was pretty, sophisticated, and sexy; she was long-legged and slim. Patterson once maintained that he was asked to leave a Chicago art class because he drew the models not as they were but as he felt they ought to look. "The models are too big and fat," he told the instructor.

Patterson worked then in a fine pen line and was an expert at composition and at spotting his blacks. His was, in a way, a warmer, livelier version of what Beardsley had been doing at the end of the 19th century. The Patterson approach caught on, especially with the flappers and collegians he was depicting in most of his drawings. His pictures graced the pages of such magazines as *Life, Redbook, Cosmopolitan*, and *College Humor*. By 1926 he was earning $100,000 a year.

William Randolph Hearst, who owned *Cosmopolitan*, next hired him to do newspaper illustrations. From the late 1920s to the early 1930s Patterson drew several Sunday-page miniseries for King Features. Appearing in the magazine sections and not the funnies, each lasted six weeks and offered a mixture of adventure and romance. Full of the patented Patterson women, in various states of dress and undress, the pages were imaginatively laid out and boldly colored. All the copy was set in type and appeared in boxes without balloons. The writing, apparently by Patterson, was flippant and very much of the time. A 1932 continuity, titled *Almost A Bride*, ended with: "Phyllis' long-drawn suspense is all mopped up now. She and Harry have decided that two hearts in waltz time can beat just as cheaply as one. So they're off on a cruise, all lit up with the honeymoon."

The 1930s proved a very good decade for him. In addition to his illustration work, he was also gainfully employed in Hollywood, where he designed sets and costumes and contributed to the Art Deco look of the cinema. Abandoning the typical Patterson Girl, he even designed the wardrobe for Shirley Temple in *Baby Take a Bow*. Patterson, a very dapper man who somewhat resembled matinee idol John Barrymore, also appeared on the silver screen himself in *Artists and Models* in 1937. His success continued in the 1940s as he designed hotel lobbies and railroad cars and the WAC uniform.

United Features brought Patterson back to the Sunday funny papers in the 1950s. His *Mamie* was about a pretty young model who was obviously a direct descendant of his 1920s flappers. His line was much thicker now, and he used a brush much more lavishly. Like many illustrators, he was not an especially strong gag writer, and the humor of the page never equaled the drawing. *Mamie*, which occupied a third of a page in most of the papers carrying it, ended in the middle 1950s.

Patterson lived long enough to be forgotten in his own lifetime, along with other celebrities of the Roaring Twenties. In the last years of his life, the ailing artist was the subject of a few newspaper articles that referred to him as an "old artist" who'd seen better days.  **R.G.**

**PAYNE, CHARLES M.** (1873–1964)  A professional cartoonist since late in the 19th century, he began drawing his *S'Matter, Pop?* in 1910 and kept it going until 1940. In the 1940s, somewhat down on his luck, Payne worked in comic books. Among the features he drew were *Supersnipe* and *Abbott and Costello.*

Payne was born in Pennsylvania and grew up on his grandmother's farm. At 17 he was on his own in Pittsburgh, already convinced he was going to become rich and famous as a cartoonist. The *Pittsburgh Post* hired young Charlie in 1896 to do illustrations and political cartoons. Early in the 20th century he started drawing Sunday pages, some of them—such as *Bear Creek Folks*—dealing with funny animals. In 1910 he introduced the strip that became *S'Matter, Pop?* Done in Payne's loose, folksy style, the strip devoted its long life to simple domestic gags, with emphasis on the kids Willyum and Desperate Ambrose. A popular strip, daily and Sunday, it lasted until 1940, although by the time it finally expired *S'Matter, Pop?* was looking quite dated.

In 1941 Payne found work with the Street & Smith line of comic books. Besides humor fillers, he tried his hand at straight adventure features, too. For *Doc Savage Comics* he came up with *Astron, Crocodile Queen,* a fantasy about a strange, mystical blond young woman who was "garbed in a peplos, the dress of the girls of ancient Greece," lived in the jungle, wielded a spear, and could command a nasty herd of huge crocodiles. An American pilot named Hard Luck Cassidy teams up with her after crashing in her patch of foliage. Together they combat a range of evils, including a wizened old sorceress who commands a troupe of murderous gorillas. Payne obviously enjoyed himself on this and drew it in a bold, broody brush style. *Astron* ended along with the magazine in 1943.

For S&S's *Air Ace* comic book Payne drew many nonfiction stories. He was especially good at explaining how planes and other gadgets worked. In most issues of *Supersnipe Comics* the young would-be superhero would have a fantastic daydream, and most of these stories-within-the-stories were illustrated by Payne. One of his last jobs was the first issue of the Abbott and Costello comic book. He drew that entire 1948 number, an adaptation of the team's comedy movie of the previous year, *The Wistful Widow of Wagon Gap.*

Payne lived on in a Manhattan apartment, eventually not far from the poverty level. He died as the result of a mugging.                                    **R.G.**

**PEANUTS** It began quietly in 1950. Drawn in a disarmingly simple style but with richly delineated kid characters that readers could identify with, it went on to become one of the most widely read and commercially successful strips of all time. *Peanuts* has made its creator Charles Schulz, who has always identified with his main character, the likable loser Charlie Brown, just about the richest cartoonist in the world.

The daily and Sunday *Peanuts,* distributed by United Features, has evolved from largely a gag-a-day strip to more of an amusing character study, a humorous slice of child life. It's a wry exploration of childhood's trials and tribulations, which young readers are living through and adult fans remember. Despite Charlie Brown's constant bad luck, the strip usually carries an upbeat message. But Schulz has always remained honest in his view of childhood and has been able to make humor out of situations that are often traumatic, or at the least embarrassing, to the hapless Charlie Brown.

A funnies fan from childhood, Schulz began selling magazine cartoons in the late 1940s. He went on to convince the *St. Paul Pioneer Press* to run his panel *Li'l Folks,* which lasted two years and was the forerunner of *Peanuts.* After trying *Peanuts* with several syndicates, Schulz sold it to United Features. "There was an attempt to make a few changes when we were first starting," Schulz has said. "My original submission was a panel feature…and then they discovered that I would rather draw a strip."

*Peanuts* was originally marketed as a space-saver—a small, one-tier, four-panel strip. But as its popularity grew, so did *Peanuts'* physical size, and its positioning on the comics page improved dramatically.

The drawing is remarkably plain and simple. "I learned a long time ago that I was going to have to struggle for attention on the comic page when I had the smallest amount of space and others were using black borders and all sorts of dramatic heavy areas to gain attention," Schulz has explained. "One of the best ways, of course, to counteract this was simply to use a little more white space." Amid the white space the cast of characters stands out strikingly: Charlie Brown, the sensitive, luckless one; Lucy, the overbearing yet endearing loudmouth and fussbudget; Linus, the blanket-dependent philosopher; Snoopy, probably the most human of them all; the red-haired girl whom Charlie Brown yearns for.

*Peanuts* currently appears in over 2,000 newspapers worldwide. It has generated numerous books, with combined sales of 300 million copies, has inspired four feature films, 40 animated television specials and countless toys and products and advertising campaigns using the images of Schulz' characters. In 1987 Schulz was inducted into the Cartoonist Hall of Fame, and his work has twice received the National Cartoonists Society Reuben Award.                              **W.D.**

**PEKAR, HARVEY** (1939– ) A true American original, the self-taught "new wave" comic book author Harvey Pekar almost singlehandedly brought a new dimension to the genre with the low-keyed, realistic, autobiographical stories in his own comic book series *American Splendor*. Described by critic Donald Phelps (in *The Comics Journal*, April 1985) as "one of the most encouraging and deeply engaging phenomena to appear in American comic-books," *American Splendor* has become a cult classic, increasingly embraced by the mainstream.

Pekar was born in Cleveland, Ohio, and had little early contact with the world of comics. He spent three semesters at Western Reserve University before dropping out to work at various menial jobs, spending most of the 1960s as a microfilmer and photocopier, a janitor, an elevator operator, and an office clerk. In 1966 he took a job as a file clerk for a Cleveland hospital and still derives his principal income from it.

From 1960, Pekar contributed articles on jazz, popular culture, and social and political issues to such periodicals as *Jazz Review, Downbeat, Evergreen Review*, and the *Cleveland Plain Dealer*. He met fellow jazz-fan Robert Crumb in 1962 and wrote about his work in underground comics in the *Journal of Popular Culture* in 1970 and again in *Funnyworld* in 1971, and the next year Crumb illustrated a one-page story of Pekar's for *People's Comics*. Pekar began to write for several underground comics during the next few years, making appearances in *Bizarre Sex* in 1975 and in *Flaming Baloney, Flamed-Out Funnies, Snarf*, and *Comix Book* in 1976. But it was with his self-printed, self-distributed *American Splendor*, of which he wrote the entire text, that Pekar first made a reputation beyond the private world of comics fandom. Published annually since 1976 and reprinted as a trade paperback in two large omnibus volumes, *American Splendor: The Life and Times of Harvey Pekar* and *More American Splendor: From Off the Streets of Cleveland Comes...* (Doubleday-Dolphin, 1986 and 1987), it has carried him to such heights of celebrity as guest appearances on the David Letterman television show.

Illustrated most notably by Crumb, Pekar's stories have also been graphically realized by Gerry Shamray and the team of Greg Budgett (penciller) and Gary Dumm (inker), who draw his stories with a gritty naturalism like that of Crumb's, and by Sue Cavey, who works in an elegant, detailed style. Cranky, sullen, self-centered (he acknowledges his admiration for Dostoevski's *Notes from the Underground*), and unromantic, Pekar's slice-of-life vignettes have little plot or narrative development, but his sensitive ear for American demotic speech lends them an urgent vitality and authenticity.

Pekar volubly rejects the idealized art and fantastic or sensational stories of traditional comics, rendering his commonplace anecdotes of failed love, occupational dissatisfaction, and social anomie with unsparing can-

dor. "I want to write literature that pushes people into their lives," he has stated, "rather than helping people to escape from them." **D.W.**

**PENNY** In 1943, when the Herald Tribune Syndicate was searching for a new comic strip, Helen Reid, the wife of the president and editor of the *New York Herald Tribune*, made it clear that she wanted it to feature a girl. Veteran cartoonist Harry Haenigsen, who was already drawing *Our Bill* for the *Trib*, was given the task of creating the strip. Haenigsen hesitated at first, making up his mind whether he wanted to do a strip about a girl. When he decided that he did, he went with a bobbysoxer—a relatively new social phenomenon. He named his teenager Penny because he wanted a middle-class name that also carried an air of stuffiness, and Penelope, of which Penny is a derivative, sounded stuffy enough for him.

Her full name was Penelope Mildred Pringle, and her life was filled with the trials and tribulations of growing up in 1940s America. She was often found in acrobatic sprawl on the couch in her loafers and white socks, rolled up jeans, and her father's white dress shirt hanging almost to her knees. Glued to her ear was a telephone, and out of her mouth spilled teenage slang that struck adults of the day as a foreign tongue. Her father was Roger Pringle, a pipe smoker with a fancy for Scandinavian sweaters, while Penny's mother, Mae, was often mystified by her only child. Other characters included Aunt Ellen, Penny's best friend Judy, a basketball player named Steeple who was so tall his head never fit inside a panel, and a rotating assortment of other boyfriends.

As for the story line, Haenigsen looked for the moral behind the joke, hoping to say something meaningful about the relationships between generations. The strip's slang, while an honest representation of how teenagers talked, was in many cases made up on the spot by Haenigsen to fit the dialogue. For 15 years, Howard Boughner, who also wrote for Ernie Bushmiller, helped with the writing. In the 1960s, a car accident severely injured Haenigsen, and he was forced to have *Penny* ghosted by Bill Hoest. For Hoest, it was a big break. The *Trib* gave him a lot of freedom, even allowing him to create some new characters of his own. After Hoest left to start *My Son John*, Haenigsen called it quits to his career and to *Penny*. The strip was last seen in 1970. **S.L.H.**

**PETER, H.G.** ( ? –1958) A veteran newspaper and magazine artist, Harry G. Peter found fame relatively late in life by way of comic books. That happened toward the end of 1941, when he was given the job of drawing the first major superheroine, Wonder Woman.

Peter, a native of Northern California, was already working as a staff artist on a San Francisco newspaper when the big earthquake hit the city in 1906. By the 1910s he was contributing to such magazines as *Judge*. He worked in a bold pen and ink style, favoring the scratchy, energetic inking seen in the work of European artists like Heinrich Kley.

His style never substantially changed over the years, except to get bolder and even more liberal in the use of black. He entered comic books in 1940, having resettled in Staten Island. He first drew for the short-lived *Hyper Mystery Comics*. In 1941 he teamed up with editor Steve Douglas to draw an unusual hero known as Man O' Metal—"Whenever he contacts heat or electricity, he becomes a being of super-HEAT, capable of burning his way through the most resisting steel barriers."—for *Heroic Comics*. Next, again teamed with Douglas, Peter drew another unusual hero, this one named Fearless Flint, for *Famous Funnies*.

Later that same year, at the request of the feature's creator William Moulton Marston, he was given the job of drawing *Wonder Woman*. Marston had cooked up a heady mix of female superheroics, Germanic symbolism, Greek mythology, bondage and submission fantasies, World War II propaganda, and a touch of lesbianism, and he felt Peter was the ideal man to turn it all into pictures for he especially liked the way the artist drew women. Sheldon Mayer, who edited the magazines the starspangled heroine appeared in—*Sensation Comics, Wonder Woman, Comic Cavalcade*—devoted considerable effort to keeping Marston's steamy fantasies within the bounds of what could then be done in a kids' comic book, but he admired Peter's work and thought he was a very effective illustrator.

Certainly nobody else in the comics of the 1940s was drawing in Peter's slightly decadent turn-of-the-century manner. To meet the artwork demands of the increasingly popular new character, Peter set up a shop in Manhattan. Several women were hired to assist on *Wonder Woman*, though he did all the basic drawing and much of the inking. He was also responsible for the newspaper strip that ran briefly in the middle 1940s. Peter stayed with the feature until the late 1950s and was then abruptly fired. He died soon after that. **R.G.**

**PETER PAT** This handsomely drawn, short-lived kid fantasy page by Mo Leff began on Sunday, June 3, 1934, and expired at the end of July the following year. Leff, who got to sign this one, later went on to ghost *Li'l Abner* and then *Joe Palooka*.

Peter Pat, always called just plain Pat in the copy, was a plucky dark-haired lad of nine or ten. While standing on a mountain top one day he was lifted aloft by a winged warrior and carried off to the fantasy locale of Pagoland. There he encountered belligerent midgets, a monstrous giant, a two-headed dragon, political conspirators, and a little princess named Judy.

The story was told in captions, without dialogue balloons, as in *Tarzan* and *Flash Gordon*. And like those other pages, *Peter Pat* was much more fun to look at than it was to read. **R.G.**

**PETER RABBIT** This rabbit gentleman was no relation to Beatrix Potter's well-known creation; he was an entirely different fellow who appeared in a Sunday page that ran from 1920 to 1956. Syndicated by the *New York Herald Tribune*, *Peter Rabbit* was drawn for the better part of its life by Harrison Cady.

Cady, a first-rate pen and ink artist, had been illustrating books and magazine stories for most of the century, and one of his specialties was animals—particularly animals who dressed as humans and walked upright. The Peter Rabbit character figured as part of the cast of the Green Meadows stories by Thornton W. Burgess that had appeared in magazines and books, which Cady had illustrated. Burgess' bunny could talk and was fond of wearing jackets and waistcoats. He resided, however, in "the dear Old Briar-patch" with his wife and usually made the sound "liperty-liperty-lip" whenever he hurried anyplace. Cady's Peter Rabbit lived in the suburban town of Carrotville and in addition to Mrs. Rabbit had twin bunny sons. Portly and well-dressed, he was more of a white-collar rabbit than he had been in his Green Meadows days.

While essentially a page for children, *Peter Rabbit* built most of its humor around the kidding of middle-class domestic and social life. Peter, amiable but monumentally accident prone, was continually getting into trouble with his neighbors and/or the community in general. Nothing he planned ever went quite right, be it a picnic or a parade, and when he wasn't cleaning up after the messes he got himself into or being presented with bills for damages, he was trying to placate the outraged citizens his prankish offspring had managed to devastate. There was more slapstick than satire, and one of Cady's models must certainly have been The *Katzenjammer Kids*.

Though he modified his style for the newspapers, forgoing the intricate crosshatching and shading of his illustrations, Cady managed to pack his pages with animals, insects, and plenty of action. Almost every week's episode ended with a chase and these could involve anything from snarling bears to an outraged platoon of bugs. The residents of Carrotville and the neighboring communities of Possum Hollow, Hickory Ridge, and Bugville were almost universally short-tempered and excitable. When an arrow shot by Peter accidentally knocked off somebody's top hat or his runaway car demolished a row of houses, all and sundry would howl with rage, jump up and down, wave their arms and perspire profusely. Probably no one before or since was better at depicting an indignant suburban ladybug than was Cady.

Cady turned out over 1,400 *Peter Rabbit* Sunday pages before retiring with the release of July 25, 1948. Anyone who'd followed the feature since 1920 would no doubt have had a surfeit of whimsy, but since Cady was aiming at a kid audience, most readers probably didn't stick with the page for more than a few years. He was replaced by Vincent Fago, a former Fleischer studios animator and a contributor to many funny animal comic books of the 1940s. Fago was not an especially inspired cartoonist, and the strip took a great leap backward with his advent. It managed, nonetheless, to hang on until March 11, 1956.                                    **R.G.**

**PETER SCRATCH**  This newspaper strip about a tough private eye who lived with his mother ran from 1965 to 1967. Syndicated by the Long Island newspaper *Newsday*, the daily and Sunday feature was drawn by Lou Fine and written by Elliot Caplin, who typically allowed the artist to take sole credit.

Scratch, a big rough-hewn op with a broken nose and a short temper, narrated his cases himself in a not-quite-convincing tough guy manner: "Characters who'll do anything for a laugh call me 'Pete the Itch.' They do it once—never again." Private eyes had had a cycle of popularity on television in the late 1950s and early 1960s, and *Peter Scratch* may have been an attempt, although belated, to duplicate the popularity of *Peter Gunn* and *Richard Diamond* on the comics page.

Lou Fine, working in the slick illustrative style he'd developed after leaving comic books for advertising, did an impressive job of storyboarding the strip (which was ghosted by Neal Adams for several weeks in 1966). But *Peter Scratch* never caught on, in spite of the impressive artwork and later attempts to turn its hero into a James Bond type.                                    **R.G.**

**PFEUFER, CARL** (1910–1980)  A versatile and productive artist, Pfeufer worked on newspaper strips and in comic books. He started doing strips in the mid-1930s, moved into comic books in the early 1940s, and had another go at strips in the 1950s. His first newspaper feature was a credible imitation of *Flash Gordon* called *Don Dixon*, and in comic books he drew everything from *Sub-Mariner* to *Tom Mix*.

Pfeufer was born in Mexico City and came to New York with his family at the age of seven. After attending Cooper Union art school, he moved into magazine illustration in the early 1930s. Next he joined the art staff of the *Brooklyn Eagle*, drawing three newspaper strips for them: *Don Dixon and the Hidden Empire*, *Tad of the Tan-*

*Carl Pfeufer, 1947.*

bark, and *Gordon Fife*. "His style was roughly similar to that of Alex Raymond, but looser and more casual," says *The Great Comic Book Artists*. "His figure work and composition were always excellent."

After a period of pulp magazine illustrating for *Argosy*, *Dime Detective*, and the like, he broke into comic books. Pfeufer's first big job was drawing the aquatic adventures of the Sub-Mariner in *Marvel Mystery Comics*. By the middle 1940s he was working for the Fawcett line, drawing costumed heroes like Commando Yank and Mr. Scarlet as well as Navy hero Don Winslow. After the war cowboys became popular in comic books and he drew the wild west adventures of such celluloid heroes as Tom Mix, Ken Maynard, and Hopalong Cassidy.

He took over *The Bantam Prince* Sunday page for its last year in the early 1950s and did more comic book work along with book illustration. He was living in Texas and doing painting and watercolors at the time of his death.                                    **R.G.**

**THE PHANTOM** One of the first of the costumed vigilantes—a prototype of the caped superheroes—was the mysterious protagonist of Lee Falk's adventure strip *The Phantom*, created two years after the successful debut of Falk's *Mandrake the Magician* and destined to find an even larger audience. Drawn at first by Ray Moore, *The Phantom* began as a daily on February 17, 1936, and added a Sunday feature with a separate story on May 28, 1939; it was distributed, like *Mandrake*, by King Features Syndicate.

Growing out of Falk's boyhood taste for mythology, the Phantom was conceived as a legendary figure on the order of King Arthur, Roland, and El Cid, along with such fictitious characters as Edgar Rice Burroughs' Tarzan. A man of mystery who always worked alone and whose face no one ever saw, he was known as The Ghost Who Walks and was believed to be immortal.

Unlike the superheroes who emerged later in the comics, the Phantom had no special powers, lacking even Mandrake's skills in illusion. What gave him an edge over the evildoers, besides a quick draw with a pistol and a good right hook, was his legend and the awe it inspired in the villains he confronted. That legend, recounted in a four-panel summary of its origin before each new episode, establishes the romantic and heroic context in which the stories are developed.

The secret of the seemingly immortal Phantom is that the present Ghost Who Walks is in fact the 21st holder of that title in a line that extends back over 400 years to the son of a seaman who had served as cabin boy to Christopher Columbus. Washed up on a remote Bengal shore after seeing his parents killed and his ship scuttled by pirates, he swore an oath on the skull of his father's murderer "to devote [his] life to the destruction of all forms of piracy, greed and cruelty," and the eldest son of each succeeding generation carried the tradition on. People seeing masked men dressed in the same skin-tight purple jumpsuit and striped shorts through the centuries thought them the same man, and so, as Falk explains, "the legend grew!" Befriended by the pygmies, the first Phantom established a reign from his home—a skull-shaped cave in the Deep Woods—and became the Keeper of the Peace, settling disputes in the jungle. His successors have maintained the same pygmy court (the only people in on his secret) and domicile but have ranged through the world righting wrongs. When his mission takes the current Phantom to the cities of Europe or the United States, he wears an overcoat with the collar turned up and travels as Mr. Walker, always alone except for his faithful wolf, Devil. Later, as a citizen of the United States, he established the Jungle Patrol to assist him, but his true identity remained a secret known only to the pygmies.

Since the Phantom must pass his hereditary duties on to his first-born son, the incumbent had a girl friend, Diana Palmer, an Olympic gold-medalist diver, explorer, pilot, athlete, and paramedic, whom he pursued for some four decades before the impatience of the public finally impelled their marriage during the 1980s and assured a 22nd Phantom. A contented homemaker in the skull cave, she shares his adventures with the aplomb of the various spirited wives of previous Phantoms.

Ray Moore, originally the assistant to Phil Davis, the artist for *Mandrake*, was *The Phantom*'s first artist, and when he went into the Air Force the assignment fell to Wilson McCoy, and later to Bill Lignante. Since 1963 *The Phantom* has been drawn by Seymour Barry. Its exotic settings—the Ghost Who Walks is frequently called on to uncover and punish evil in the jungles of Africa and the remote cities of Asia—are depicted with a sinuous, flowing line, which captures the kinetic action of the story and holds the eye as the narrative holds the mind.

The tightly plotted stories of *The Phantom* weave their spell in part by their romantic settings and their well-developed characters, blending epic adventure with touching romance, leavened with the wisecracking humor of their hero; but much of the appeal derives from the atmosphere of mystery that surrounds the Ghost Who Walks. Falk was awarded the Silver T-Square of the National Cartoonists Society in 1986 and has been honored throughout the world for his creation. Described by its syndicate as "the most widely read super hero comic on earth today" on the occasion of its 50th anniversary, *The Phantom* is distributed to nearly 600 newspapers in some 40 countries, and translated into 15 languages. It was made into a motion picture serial in 1943 and has appeared in numerous comic books as well as a long series of paperback novelizations published by Avon. In September 1986, the Phantom, along with Falk's earlier characters Mandrake and Lothar, joined Flash Gordon in an animated series of television adventures, *Defenders of the Earth*, extending his range of service to justice beyond the galaxy. **D.W.**

**PHANTOM LADY** Since the world stubbornly remains a fundamentally sexist place, Phantom Lady is better-known for her figure and scanty costume than for her intelligence and abilities as a crimefighter. First seen in comic books in 1941, she has reappeared several times since. In 1954 she was even criticized in Fredric Wertham's *Seduction of the Innocent* and cited as a probable cause of juvenile delinquency.

In the initial phase of her career, which began with her debut in *Police Comics* #1 (August 1941), she was relatively demure. The only female character in a magazine that housed the likes of Plastic Man and the Human Bomb, she usually occupied six pages toward

*Phantom Lady*, Matt Baker, © 1947, Fox Feature Syndicate.

own magazine and also as part of the lineup in *All Top Comics*. This revived Phantom Lady wore an even skimpier costume and had a noticeably larger bosom. She had also developed a marked fondness for being tied up and chained, and she frequently appeared in these states, especially on covers. As drawn by Matt Baker, she bore a strong resemblance to the noted cheesecake model of the day, Betty Page. This was Phantom Lady's most successful phase, the one that earned her the most attention. Despite that, both magazines featuring her folded early in 1949.

The Fox version was the one that found its way into Dr. Wertham's files for his anti-comics crusade. Matt Baker's bondage cover for *Phantom Lady* #17 (April 1948) was reprinted in *Seduction of the Innocent* in 1954, along with the psychiatrist's contention that such drawings mixed sexual stimulation and sadism in an unhealthy and potentially dangerous way.

Publisher Bob Farrell brought back the character in 1955. That time around, wearing a more modest and conservative costume, she lasted for only four issues. Present ownership of Phantom Lady is not clear-cut, and she's been revived sporadically by both DC and Americomics in recent years. **R.G.**

**PHIL HARDY** Most of the early adventure strips, which got going in the middle 1920s, featured boys rather than men as protagonists, and most were a mixture of the pluck-and-luck success stories favored by Horatio Alger and his dime novel imitators and the more contemporary thrills and perils offered in action movies and serials. The earliest was *Phil Hardy*, a daily written by Jay Jerome Williams under the pen name Edwin Alger and drawn by George Storm, which started in November of 1925.

"This is the story of Phil Hardy's climb to fame and fortune," announced the first strip, also pointing out that Phil, "a bright boy of fifteen," was the sole support of his widowed mother. The story got off to a quiet, small-town start, but before a month had passed Phil had been shanghaied and found himself bound for Cape Town, South Africa, aboard the steamer *Black Castle*. From then on the strip was full of action, including murder on the high seas and intrigue ashore. Although Storm drew in a cartoony style, he had broken away from the traditional comic approach: His inking was bolder, his layouts much more varied.

Before Storm quit the strip, in the fall of 1926, it had changed its name to *Bound to Win*. Under this new title, and with a new young hero named Ben Webster and a succession of unexceptional artists, it continued in business for more than a decade. The enterprising Williams kept Phil alive in a series of novels for Grosset &

the back of the book. The stories, set in Washington, D.C., and its environs, were drawn by Arthur Peddy. "The society columns record the activities of Sandra Knight, debutante daughter of Senator Henry Knight," explained a caption. "No one suspects that frivolous Sandra is also the Phantom Lady, whose battles against spies and public enemies constantly make headlines." The notion of a deb who doubled as a crimefighter was also to be found in *Lady Luck*, which had debuted a year earlier.

In the Peddy version Sandra was a slender, dark-haired young woman, and her costume consisted of a yellow one-piece bathing suit, yellow boots, and a green cape. Though she never wore a mask, she was never recognized. Phantom Lady had no superpowers, and her only weapon was a black flashlight that could surround crooks and spies in blackness and render them temporarily blind. When Frank Borth took over the feature in 1943, he filled out Sandra's figure, redesigned the costume, and plunged the neckline. Phantom Lady left *Police* after the 22nd issue (October 1943).

In 1947 the enterprising publisher, Victor S. Fox, somehow acquired the character, launching her in her

Dunlap, wherein his strip was described as "a daily inspirational picture for boys and girls."  **R.G.**

## PLASTIC MAN

The red-suited rubber man began his career, modestly, in the middle of the first issue of *Police Comics* (August 1941). A creation of Jack Cole, he had just six pages in which to introduce himself, go through the obligatory origin routine, and establish himself with the reader. He did a pretty good job of it, and by issue #5 he was also getting the covers of the magazine. By #9 Plas had ousted a dull hero named Firebrand from the leadoff spot and had nine pages to work in. Less than six months after that, poor Firebrand had departed the magazine entirely and Cole's flexible hero had 13 pages.

Cole, who'd originally wanted to do gag cartoons, never developed a completely serious style. When doing adventure material he still conveyed a feeling of fun and he exaggerated both the figures and the action. He did have a good sense of what the fast-growing new comic book business was all about, and, like his former colleague, Charles Biro, he knew how to package his work and how to communicate directly. Out of the 11 features in the first issue of *Police*, his is the only one with its own blurb. Right there on the splash panel Cole proclaimed, "From time to time the comic world welcomes a new sensation. Such is PLASTIC MAN!! The most fantastic man alive! Vermin of the underworld shudder at the mention of his name! And yet he was once one of them!! Now, read of how this incredible character came to be!"

Cole had a fondness for making heroes out of reformed crooks, and in this case it was Eel O'Brien, "the toughest gangster afoot...wanted by the police in eight states," who went straight and became Plastic Man. While taking part in a safecracking job at a chemical works, acid had spilled on Eel. Left to fend for himself by his gang, he wandered out of the city, "through swamps, then up a mountain side." He passed out and awakened to find he'd been taken in and cared for by a kindly monk who ran a peaceful mountain retreat. The monk's faith caused Eel to reform on the spot, and shortly after his reformation he realized that the acid bath had given him the ability to stretch his body into all sorts of shapes. "What a powerful weapon this could be...AGAINST CRIME!"

Within a year or so Cole grew tired of the dual-identity device and Plas was just Plas from then on—when he wasn't being a chair, a snake, an umbrella stand, a beautiful actress, a lap dog, or a throw rug, that is. In issue #13 Woozy Winks, who looked something like movie comedian Lou Costello, came along. After using his gift of invulnerability to commit a few crimes, Woozy reformed, too, and joined Plastic Man as his sidekick. Their subsequent adventures mixed crime, violence, fantasy, and satire. Plastic Man, with several others beside Cole rendering his adventures, remained the star of *Police* until issue #102 (October 1950).

A separate *Plastic Man* comic book ran from 1943 to 1956. DC eventually took over the character and attempted, with the help of various artist and writer teams, to revive him in the middle 1960s, the middle 1970s, and, most recently, in 1988. Plas also had a fairly successful fling, though greatly altered, as a TV cartoon character. So far, though, no one has shown Jack Cole any real competition.  **R.G.**

## PLUMB, CHARLIE

(1900–1982) The cocreator of the long-running *Ella Cinders* newspaper strip, Plumb actually did very little of the drawing he signed his name to over the years. For most of the time that he was associated with the wisecracking modern Cinderella story, he was more a straw boss than a cartoonist.

Born in New Mexico, Plumb grew up in Missouri and studied journalism at the University of Missouri. He got most of his art training by mail, through a Federal Schools correspondence course in cartooning. After working as a staff cartoonist for a Chicago-based magazine called *The Drover's Journal*, Plumb went on to draw cartoons that were syndicated to Midwest newspapers. Moving to Southern California in the mid-1920s, he got a job in the art department of the *Los Angeles Times*. "His fellow artists on the paper were wracking their brains for comic strip ideas. Charlie did, too," explained a later syndicate publicity release. "He got one, then met Bill Conselman. Result—*Ella Cinders*." Conselman, who'd been a reporter, was then an editor on the *Times*.

*Ella Cinders* started, initially as a daily, in 1925. Plumb drew it in a simple, direct cartoon style, using the tricks he'd picked up from his Federal course. Fairly soon, though, he began using assistants and then ghosts, who included Hardie Gramatky, Fred Fox, Henry Formhals, and Jack McGuire. Thus freed from the drawing board, Plumb devoted a good deal of his time to travel in the warmer parts of the world. United Features publicity liked to play up his peripatetic nature, claiming "a good part of Ella's life was drawn on a South Seas island." By the early 1940s Plumb was residing, as he described it, "in a bougainvillea-smothered house in Mexico." He said he'd crossed the border to escape being hounded by fans who were continually stopping him on the street and begging for autographs and sketches. Some of his coworkers maintained that Plumb was holed up in Mexico chiefly to avoid creditors and alimony lawyers.

Eventually Plumb left *Ella Cinders* and returned to the United States, ending up quietly in the Northwest.  **R.G.**

**POGO** One of the brightest, and funniest, newspaper strips to emerge in the post-World War II period was *Pogo*. The work of Walt Kelly, it began national syndication in 1949. The patient, rational possum who was its star had first appeared in comic books a few years earlier.

The newspaper strip had begun as a local feature in the liberal and short-lived *New York Star* on October 4, 1948, the work of a 35-year-old staff artist and political cartoonist. Born in Philadelphia and raised in Bridgeport, Connecticut, Kelly was a veteran Hollywood animator, having helped turn out *Snow White, Fantasia, Pinocchio, Dumbo,* and *The Reluctant Dragon.* He had also worked in comic books, including *Fairy Tale Parade, Raggedy Ann & Andy, Our Gang, Santa Clause Funnies,* and *Walt Disney's Comics & Stories.*

Kelly was a contradictory man. In his work he could be gentle and whimsical, while in real life he was often quite the opposite. An expert at drawing lovable animals, pixies, and princesses, he was also an enthusiastic participant in the Manhattan saloon life of the 1940s.

The feature wherein he was able to indulge both his cute and his rowdy modes began in *Animal Comics* in 1942. Although the original star of the magazine was the venerable rabbit gentleman Uncle Wiggily, Kelly's upstart Pogo and associates fairly soon pushed him into a second-rank position. Initially Pogo was merely a "spear carrier," hampered by the fact he looked "just like a possum. As time went on, this condition was remedied and Pogo took on a lead role." The feature appeared under a number of titles in its early days—e.g., "Bumbazine and the Singing Alligator," "Albert and the Noah Count Ark,"—before settling down as *Albert and Pogo.*

Bumbazine was a small black boy who shared the swamp setting with the animal characters and, somewhat like Christopher Robin, was able to talk to them. As the feature progressed, Bumbazine and the other swamp denizens abandoned conventional speech for a sort of patois that was part Deep South, part *Li'l Abner:* "Man! Ah di'n't know yo' was a edge-you-cated owl."—"Oh, sho! Ah comes from a long line of smart-headed owls." By the time Pogo reached his cute, non-scraggly state, Bumbazine had departed. The first comic book of nothing but Pogo came along in the spring of 1946, and by 1949 a Pogo Possum comic book, costarring the cigar-smoking Albert the Alligator, was being issued on a fairly regular basis. The *Star* folded in January of 1949, and in May of that year the *Pogo* strip had been revived and was being syndicated nationally.

Kelly's training at the Disney studios out West and his stretch with Whitman-Dell comic books served him well. He filled the strip with some of the best-drawn and most individual animal characters ever seen by man—the turtle Churchy LaFemme, Howland Owl, Porky Pine, and Albert, who combined all the best qualities of Major Hoople, P.T. Barnum, and a conman.

The strip offered satire, smart dialogue, and broad comedy situations, and the result was something that was amusing to look at and amusing to read. Kelly couldn't always control his bawdy leanings, and old burlesque routines, including characters dressing up in drag, would frequently show up. At times he'd even slip in the punchline of a well-known dirty joke. In the early years of the strip Kelly was having fun and not taking *Pogo* too seriously.

When the grimmer 1950s came along, the years of Eisenhower, Nixon, and the vile Senator Joe McCarthy, Kelly grew increasingly concerned with political satire. His audience had blossomed as the strip picked up newspapers, and Simon & Schuster began reprinting *Pogo* in paperback form. Kelly, who'd put in time as a political cartoonist, decided to use his strip to speak out against the less-than-liberal things that were happening in America. He managed to be, initially, both courageous and funny, and his insidious bobcat, Simple J. Malarky, quite probably helped topple the senator from Wisconsin. As the years passed, however, Kelly's political stuff seemed to grow increasingly heavy-handed, or perhaps it was simply that targets like Spiro Agnew and Lyndon Johnson were too much like sitting ducks. Editors now and then dropped Kelly's most outspoken *Pogo* dailies, and for them he now and then prepared extra dailies—always featuring two innocuous bunny rabbits.

By the time Kelly died in 1973, at the relatively early age of 60, *Pogo* had lost much of its fire, its fun, and quite a bit of its audience. The strip carried on, managed by his heirs, until July 1975. In 1989 a new version started running. Titled *Walt Kelly's Pogo,* it was written by Larry Doyle and drawn by Neal Sternecky. Well-intentioned, it has served to prove that genius rarely strikes twice in the same place—or in the same swamp. **R.G.**

**POLLY AND HER PALS** One of the first strips to present a woman as title character, Cliff Sterrett's masterpiece debuted December 4, 1912. At first called *Positive Polly,* the strip seemed to be about what was called at the time a new woman. Polly was a young miss of considerable self-possession who was attending college and otherwise making a place for herself in the world. But as Sterrett came to focus on Polly and her suitors and her father's reactions to them, the strip acquired a larger subject and was rechristened accordingly.

Even the title *Polly and Her Pals,* however, didn't embrace Sterrett's real concerns. As his cast grew to include numerous relatives, it became increasingly apparent that the strip was actually about Polly's father,

*Polly and Her Pals*, Cliff Sterrett, © 1934, King Features Syndicate, Inc. Reprinted with special permission of King Features Syndicate, Inc.

the irascible Sam Perkins, and the fools he had to suffer. Through the years Paw would be plagued by his wife, Susie; Aunt Maggie, an old maid who moved in on them; Cousin Carrie, a snob, and her spoiled brat daughter Gertrude, whom her mother called Angel; Paw's nephew, Ashur Url Perkins, a graduate student with no discernible vices; a Chinese valet named Neewah; and the household pet, Kitty.

In the face of this competition, Polly eventually faded into the background. But in the early days of the strip, she attracted considerable attention for daring to display her sex. At the beach, for instance, her bathing costume showed her leg, inspiring readers to complain at Sterrett's licentiousness. And in Polly's facial profile—bulging brow, tiny nose, pouting mouth—Sterrett established a convention for depicting a pretty girl's face that was widely adapted by other cartoonists.

But very little else about Sterrett's way of drawing could be so readily imitated. His graphic style was easily the most distinctive thing about the strip, and it was unique on the comics pages. As Sterrett's style reached its maturity in the middle 1920s, *Polly* became a spectacular symphony of line design in black and white, in daily strips, and in color on Sundays. Its earmark was the interplay of patterned line and geometric shape. Checks, stripes, black solids, quilty patchworks, and surrealistic details were juxtaposed in panels peopled with creatures whose anatomy was thoroughly abstract, wholly geometric: Heads were simple spheres; bodies and limbs were tubular shapes. This abstraction of the human form permitted wildly unrealistic but effectively comic expressiveness in both face and figure, and Sterrett exploited the possibilities with playful exuberance. Undoubtedly inspired by dis-

ciples of Futurism in the Cubist movement, such as Fernand Leger, Sterrett's Sunday pages in particular were unparalleled in their comic distortions of reality.

Although the strip ended each installment with a punchline, it also frequently had thematic continuity, concentrating for a week or two on the same situations for related gags. In the 1930s, for example, Paw and the entire Perkins menage went to the country and tried to run a farm, installing livestock at the rate of one species at a time, with jokes about hens for a few days, then cows, horses, ducks, and so on.

Suffering from arthritis from the middle 1930s onward, Sterrett surrendered the art on the daily to assistants, keeping the Sunday page for himself. Among those who ghosted the daily were Vernon Greene and Paul Fung. In the feature's last years it became a Sunday only and Sterrett drew it, frequently using gags supplied by his onetime *New York Journal* associate Tom McNamara. Growing increasingly tired, and watching both his list of papers and his salary diminish, Sterrett retired in 1958 and ended *Polly*. He died six years later.

**R.C.H.**

**PORKY PIG**   A multimedia star, the pantsless Porky made his comic book debut in 1941 in *Looney Tunes and Merrie Melodies*, and got a title of his own the following year, remaining a newsstand regular until the middle 1980s.

The stuttering pig was first seen in *I Haven't Got a Hat*, a Warner Brothers animated cartoon released in 1935. Porky was an obese kid in that one, and it took a couple of years for the more mature, more appealing Porky—and the Mel Blanc voice—to emerge. Friz Freleng was in charge of the first Porky cartoon, and other animator/directors who worked with him included Tex Avery, Bob Clampett, and Frank Tashlin. Altogether, from 1935 to 1988 Porky appeared in over 150 cartoons, including a cameo in *Who Framed Roger Rabbit?*

The *Looney Tunes* comic book also offered stories about Bugs Bunny, Elmer Fudd, and Sniffles the mouse (teamed in comic books with a blond little girl named Mary Jane). In the earliest issues Porky Pig occupied the star position at the front of the book, but soon the increasingly popular Bugs usurped the top spot.

Porky led a somewhat more adventurous life in the early comic books, but usually avoided the impressive physical disasters and complex pratfalls that routinely befell him on the screen. Frequently accompanied by his ladyfriend Petunia, he explored haunted houses, hunted for buried treasure, became involved with bank robbers, and frequented all sorts of other action-packed locales. Never an astute detective or a daring adventurer, Porky always managed to muddle through and win. Among the first artists to draw the feature were Chase Craig and Roger Armstrong. The renowned duck artist, Carl Barks, drew him once, in a 1944 four-color comic titled *Porky of the Mounties*, in which Bugs and Petunia costarred.

Porky's first solo comic book, *Secret of the Haunted House*, was also in Dell's four-color series and appeared in 1942. Porky Pig eventually had a regular title of his own, which didn't end until 1984. In later years Porky's comic book adventures were quieter and more domestic than in earlier years. It's possible that DC, long a part of the Warner empire, will eventually return America's foremost pig to comic books. **R.G.**

**POSEN, AL** (1895–1960)  The creator of such popular comic series as *Them Days Are Gone Forever*, *Jinglets*, *Rhymin' Time*, and the long-running Sunday humor page *Sweeney & Son* never studied art but produced some of America's best loved cartoons for nearly four decades.

New York-born Al Posen began drawing for the public in *Stars and Stripes* while serving in the infantry during World War I, with little thought of a career in the field. After the war he went to China and Siam with a mining syndicate, and returned to find a job with a film advertising agency, where his show business associations brought him into contact with the Marx Brothers, then a popular vaudeville team. He produced their first film, a two-reeler recording their vaudeville act, but theater managers were unenthusiastic, and he was never able to sell it.

In 1922, Posen found his feet in cartooning with *Them Days Are Gone Forever*, a wistful panel series recalling the good old days, each panel with a three-line verse ending with the title refrain. Catching the prevailing postwar mood of nostalgia, *Them Days* was an immediate hit, and it was clipped from newspapers and pinned on bulletin boards all over the country. He also drew a romantic humor strip called *Ella and Her Fella* for the *Detroit Mirror*, but it did not last long, and he continued trying to market other cartoon ideas during the 1920s.

Posen found the affiliation he had been looking for in 1927 when the Chicago Tribune Syndicate accepted the Sunday strip feature *Jinglets*, built on slight, humorous anecdotes recounted in four rhyming words, each illustrated by a cartoon panel. Seven years later, still carried by what was then the Chicago Tribune-New York News Syndicate, *Jinglets* became the topper to the full-length Sunday strip on which Posen's reputation rests, *Sweeney & Son*. One of the warmest and most engaging depictions of family life in the history of comics, the weekly frolics of Pa Sweeney and his young son amused a large reading public for 27 years, until it was retired with Posen's death in 1960.

Always ready for a lark, Sweeney—appropriately the proprietor of a toyshop—is forever playing hooky at the swimming hole or the sandlot with Sonny and Me-Too, the younger child the Sweeneys have adopted (so named because he always chimes in with those words to anyone else's remarks). Quite properly adored by his children and his retarded shop assistant Pushface, the endearing Sweeney *père* blackens his own eye with a jack-in-the-box, gives toys freely to everyone, and constantly gets in harmless trouble, to his level-headed wife's occasional embarrassment and annoyance.

A productive artist whose simple linear style and unsophisticated humor were popular at all levels of public taste, Posen found time to do illustrated advertising continuities while maintaining *Jinglets* and *Sweeney & Son* during the 1930s and 1940s, and still worked to broaden his output. On January 17, 1949, he returned to his first source of cartoon success with a third feature, *Rhymin' Time*—an illustrated jingle set to the tune of "Turkey in the Straw" and ending with the phrase that the cartoonist had added to the national vocabulary more than a quarter of a century before, "Them days are gone forever." Distributed by the Tribune-News Syndicate, it was as whimsically rueful as its predecessor, but it covered a larger range of themes, occasionally including political commentary.

Posen was personally very popular, both within and outside of his profession. A charter member of the National Cartoonists Society, he was from 1954 the chairman of its overseas shows, directing programs for U.S. servicemen around the world, and always responded to calls to entertain at orphanages and hospitals. The N.C.S. voted Posen its Silver T-Square award for "outstanding service or contribution to the Society or the Profession" in 1956. **D.W.**

**POWELL, BOB** (1917?–1967) His bold layouts and distinctive, fluid style were evident in comic books for several decades, starting in the late 1930s. Bob Powell was an expert at staging action, handling every kind of adventure story from superhero to cowboy, although his realistic approach to drawing was always leavened with some cartoon exaggeration. There was usually humor in his work, and Powell developed a way of drawing women that was completely his own.

S. Robert Powell, who had begun life as Stanley Pulowski, joined the Eisner-Iger shop in the late 1930s and then worked for Eisner alone in the early 1940s. He produced features for comic books published by Fox, Quality, Temerson, and Fiction House. Powell's most successful feature in those early years was *Sheena*, drawn for *Jumbo Comics*, although he also wrote and drew *Mr. Mystic* for Eisner's weekly *Spirit* section.

He went over to Harvey publications next and did some impressive work on *The Spirit of '76*, and such attractive ladies as Black Cat and the Blonde Bomber in the 1940s. As *The Great Comic Book Artists* points out, his women at the time "were usually wide-shouldered, longhaired, longlegged and fullchested, borrowing attributes from such 1940s movie goddesses as Rita Hayworth, Betty Grable and Jane Russell." *The Man in Black* was introduced in 1945, after Powell came back from the service, and he put the *film noir* approaches learned during his Eisner days to good use in these shadowy tales of mystery and fantasy.

With a recognizable and saleable style, Powell set up a shop of his own in 1947. With Howard Nostrand and others assisting him, he was soon providing material for Magazine Enterprises, Hillman, Fawcett, Harvey, Atlas, and Street & Smith. For the latter's *Shadow Comics* he did the title character as well as Doc Savage and Nick Carter. His shop was so prolific that Powell had features running concurrently in a half-dozen comics as well as one story (at least) in each of Harvey's horror, war, and romance titles.

When Harvey switched to reprints in 1954, Powell did a bit more work for Magazine Enterprises and Atlas and then dropped out of the field for a time. His primary comics outlet from 1959 to 1961 was the Prize outfit, where he drew mystery and romance stories. From 1961 until his death, he was art director for *Sick* magazine, during which years he also produced commercial art. His final appearance in comics was for Marvel's *Daredevil* in 1965. **J.V.**

**POWERHOUSE PEPPER** A very unorthodox 1940s comic book superhero, Powerhouse Pepper was totally bald and usually combated evil wearing a striped turtleneck sweater, baggy trousers, and heavy work shoes rather than a costume. Powerhouse, who debuted in Marvel's *Joker Comics* #1 (April 1942), was the creation of the certifiably zany Basil Wolverton, and his adventures kidded all that the more soberminded supermen held dear. Wolverton refused to take violence, evil, crime, or even the American way of life seriously.

Although *Powerhouse Pepper* owed a bit to such newspaper strips as *Salesman Sam* and *Smokey Stover* and to movies like Olsen & Johnson's *Hellzapoppin*, it was 99% pure Wolverton, lowbrow and high class at the same time, wacky, inventive, and audacious. Before Powerhouse was many issues old, Wolverton had given way to his compulsive fascination with alliteration, and he could no longer even sign his name straight, favoring instead such bylines as Basil Baboonbrain Wolverton or Basil Weirdwit Wolverton.

He was equally fond of internal rhyme, and his dialogue, as well as the numerous signs and posters that cluttered almost every inch of wall (and often floor and ceiling) space in the strip, were full of them. "Zounds! Your snappers are as sound as a hound's," observes one of the physicians giving Powerhouse his Army physical in a typical episode—the three medical chaps involved are Dr. Ash Gash, Dr. Bill Drill, and Dr. Jack Hack. Our hero is finally rejected because of his head. "You're out, sprout, because it's helpless to hang a helmet on a head like yours! It's too lean, if you know what I mean! See? A helmet teeters over your cheaters, and there's no way to clap a strap under your map!" "Fap!" responds the crestfallen Powerhouse. "I must look like a sap!" This particular yarn ends with a visit to a restaurant named simply Crude Food, wherein are offered such delights as blue blackbirds broiled in brown bovine butter and buzz bugs basted in bilgewater.

All in all, Wolverton produced nearly 500 pages about Powerhouse over the next six years, sending him to just about every spot on Earth and also to some heretofore unknown planets. The hairless hero held forth in *Joker*, *Gay Comics*—not to be confused with the more recent *Gay Comix*—*Tessie the Typist*, *Millie the Model*, and in five issues of his own magazine. For some reason there was a five-year lapse between issue #1 and issue #2. "I was never able to make a lot of sense of their [Marvel's] publishing policies," Wolverton once said. "To even matters, though, they were never able to make much sense out of what they bought from me." **R.G.**

**PRINCE VALIANT** Created by Harold Foster in the mid-1930s, *Prince Valiant* chronicles the adventures of a royal family in the "days of King Arthur," focusing mostly on Prince Valiant, son of the exiled King of Thule and a Knight of the Round Table. In later years, the focus turns to Valiant's own son, Prince Arn. *Prince Valiant* is considered one of the top adventure strips of all time, on a par with *Flash Gordon* and *Steve Canyon* as well as *Tarzan*—a strip in which Foster had more than a passing interest.

Before he started *Prince Valiant*, Foster spent nearly eight years on *Tarzan*, getting that great strip off the ground and, in the process, sharpening an artistic style influenced by illustrator Howard Pyle. Although *Tarzan* provided an ample showcase for Foster's considerable talent, it left little room for the kind of creativity he longed for in a strip. By creating his own story, Foster, who started out drawing mail-order catalogs, felt total artistic freedom would be his—from concept to continuity to illustration. But when he presented his idea of a medieval adventure strip to United Features, Tarzan's syndicate, it was turned down. Undaunted, he made the same pitch to rival King Features and won over its president, Joe Connolly. As Foster saw it, his hero was to be named Prince Arn, but Connolly successfully argued for the catchier moniker, Prince Valiant.

On February 13, 1937, the Sunday-only strip made its premiere. Readers of the Sunday funnies were treated to a dazzling opening as a band of frantic fugitives, led by the King of Thule, commandeer a fishing vessel and sail to England. Shipwrecked at the mouth of the Thames River, the fugitives—young Prince Valiant among them—battle their way inland, seeking a new home. Their fearlessness earns the respect of the half-savage Britons who grudgingly allow them to live in peace on an island "far out in the great fens." It is in the fens where Prince Valiant grows to manhood, learning to hunt and fish and to be a warrior, even befriending Horrit the Witch. She tells his fortune—a life in which he will meet knights in shining armor, take part in bloody battles and come face-to-face with King Arthur.

Those opening sequences resemble, in style, Foster's work on *Tarzan;* the same uniformly boxed pages—three panels across and four down, with an occasional double panel thrown in for variety's sake, and the narrative free of the typical speech balloon. At the beginning of each strip he added in a "Synopsis" to let readers know what had happened the previous week, which in time, was changed to "Our Story." But it wasn't until the 15th Sunday that Foster finally broke away from the seemingly caged-in format of *Tarzan* and turned *Prince Valiant* into the epic he envisioned, with panoramic panels of artistic splendor in the grand style of Howard

Pyle. From then on, his story picks up in excitement, both narratively and visually. The young warrior saves the life of Sir Gawain, travels to Camelot with the handsome, dark-haired knight and meets King Arthur. As a "wandering squire" to Gawain, he departs on his first quest. He next falls in love with the beautiful Maid Ilene of Branwyn, only to find out that she is betrothed to Prince Arn (obviously not Prince Valiant's son, but the son of King Ord). The princes battle for Ilene's hand, but are forced into an uneasy truce when she is kidnapped by pirates and they must rush to her rescue. As a sign of good faith, Prince Arn gives Prince Valiant the "Singing Sword," forged by Flamberge of "Excalibur" fame. Their rivalry ends tragically when Ilene perishes in a shipwreck.

The adventure continues, of course. Prince Valiant earns his knighthood, courts Princess Aleta, the Queen of the Misty Isles, raises a family and names his firstborn Prince Arn. He battles Saxon invaders and explores a new world—America. (In fact, Foster was praised for his honest treatment of the American Indian.) But as Prince Valiant grows into middle age, Prince Arn begins to take on more of a leading role.

In the meantime, as Foster got on in years, he suffered from arthritis, and so in 1970 he began a search for an assistant with the ability to eventually take over *Prince Valiant*. Several good comic artists auditioned for the coveted job, including Wally Wood. But the nod went to John Cullen Murphy, noted for his outstanding work on *Big Ben Bolt*. The men got along well and to make the transition as smooth as possible, they'd alternate drawing pages—Foster would do a page one week, Murphy a page the next week and so on. Murphy finally took on the entire illustration in 1971. Foster continued to write the narrative for a number of years before Murphy added that to his chores. Eventually, Murphy's son, Cullen Murphy, a well-known magazine editor, became the strip's author.

Although *Prince Valiant* is not the grandiose strip it once was—thanks mostly to space constraints in today's newspapers—it is as popular now as it was in the halcyon days of Hal Foster. And Murphy, who in his youth had as a mentor Norman Rockwell, wants to keep on illustrating *Prince Valiant* until the day he dies.

**S.L.H.**

# Q

**QUINCY** Deliberately patterned on the model of Morrie Turner's *Wee Pals* (1965) and Brumsic Brandon's *Luther* (1968), Ted Shearer's *Quincy* joined the ranks of racially-mixed kid strips on June 17, 1970, under the aegis of King Features Syndicate. Like its predecessors, it dealt genially with racial issues, preferring to deliver its warmhearted message obliquely, with references to the problems of poverty and ghetto life.

Shearer was born in Jamaica, British West Indies, but came to the United States at an early age. He studied at the Art Students League and Pratt Institute while working as a busboy and later a waiter, and sold his first cartoon at the age of 16. It was as an art director with Batten Barton, Durstine, and Osborne, where he won five art director's awards, that he first conceived of the comic strip that was to enable him to retire from advertising after 15 years' service to it.

Quincy, the title figure of Shearer's strip, is a bright nine-year-old street kid whose playmates are much less self-conscious about their own racial integration, or aware of the problems in the larger society, than the children in *Wee Pals*, the prototype of the genre, whose characters are preoccupied with the issue of equality.

Quincy and his small brother Li'l Bo, his sexy girlfriend Viola, and his white pals, seldom refer to race.

Like the gangs in *Skippy, Tiger,* and other pre-integration strips, Quincy and his buddies are natural, not particularly precocious children, neither mischievous nor sentimentally virtuous. They explore their environment and accept their problems with the serenity and resignation of little stoics, securely at peace in their slum. The benevolent Granny Dixon, one of the few adults in the strip, exudes affection and support and provides a positive role model of discipline, love, and fatalism.

Gracefully drawn, the realistic treatment of squalor in the crumbling tenements and cracked sidewalks of the backgrounds in *Quincy* is presented without rancor. Shearer rendered his characters sympathetically, without irony or indignation, and the social and economic problems that afflict them were cheerfully endured in an atmosphere of fellowship and fun. The strip had a modest success and generated one paperback reprint (*Quincy*, Bantam Books, 1972) before being laid to rest in 1986. **D.W.**

# R

**RAAB, CHARLES** (ca. 1912–ca. 1952) A friend and disciple of Milton Caniff, Raab drew both newspaper strips and comic books in his version of the Caniff style. His major credit was for the *Adventures of Patsy* strip, which he drew in the early 1940s.

Born in Ohio, Raab attended Stivers High School in Dayton, the same school Caniff had gone to a few years earlier, where they apparently had the same art teacher. Raab later studied at the Dayton Art Institute. In the mid-1930s he headed eastward, working first as assistant to Caniff on *Terry and the Pirates* and then as the first assistant to Alfred Andriola on *Charlie Chan.*

In June 1940 Raab took over the *Patsy* strip. After the first few weeks, when the strip looked as though Caniff may have helped out, Raab's own style was in evidence—a bolder, cruder, less assured version of his mentor's. By the end of 1940 the appearance of the strip had improved, largely because Noel Sickles was doing much of the drawing for Raab.

After leaving *Patsy* late in 1942, Raab tried unsuccessfully to sell a strip of his own. He eventually moved into comic books and in 1948 was drawing Charlie Chan again, this time in a short-lived comic book version. The following year he drew some original adventures for the *Johnny Hazard* comic book. By that time Raab was heavily into swiping and quite a few panels were copied from Sickles' *Scorchy Smith*. In 1950 Raab illustrated a kind of graphic novel, a 132-page black and white digest-size comic book featuring a private eye yarn titled *The Case of the Winking Buddha.* After drawing some true crime stories for various publishers, including DC, Raab dropped out of the field. He had a drinking problem and, according to those who knew him, he spent his last days on Skid Row. **R.G.**

**RABOY, MAC** (1916–1967) An impressive artist, as well as one of the slowest, Raboy drew adventure features for comic books throughout the 1940s and then graduated to newspaper funnies. In comic books he was the definitive artist on Captain Marvel Jr., and in the comic sections he drew the *Flash Gordon* Sunday page for nearly 20 years.

Emanuel "Mac" Raboy was born in Manhattan and learned to draw in free Work Projects Administration classes. After a job with an art service, he signed on with the Chesler shop, which led to his early work in *Silver Streak Comics, Prize Comics*, and Fawcett's *Whiz Comics.* Raboy was an admirer of the work of Alex Raymond, but after only a few years in comics he developed a very effective, straight illustrational style of his own. He had a flair for fantasy and larger-than-life adventure, and he came to draw pages that were equal to those of his idol.

Eventually Raboy went to work directly for Fawcett, drawing *Bulletman, Dr. Voodoo*, and *Zoro*—a modern-day mystery man not to be confused with the swordsman who had two Rs in his name. When the Captain Marvel Jr. character was introduced in 1941, Raboy was picked to be the chief artist, drawing the monthly adventure of the boy superhero that led off each issue of *Master Comics* and most of the covers for the *Captain Marvel Jr.* monthly. His covers show a strong design sense and are among the most striking of the 1940s. His interior stories were striking as well, displaying a mastery of figure drawing and a good sense of fantasy. His major flaw was his slow, meticulous pace as an artist and, as time went on, he was forced to resort to pasteups and the help of other artists to meet his commitments.

After leaving Fawcett in 1944, Raboy teamed up with editor-writer Ken Crossen to draw the lead feature in his *Green Lama* comic book and also provide the covers. He'd drawn the character a few years earlier in *Prize*, and Raboy's work, what there was of it, was outstanding. But he never seemed able to finish an entire story, and a typical *Green Lama* episode would start off with some handsome Raboy pages and finish with pages by artists such as Harry Anderson.

In 1948 Raboy was offered the *Flash Gordon* Sunday page, when Austin Briggs decided not to continue with it. His early years on the page contained work that equalled anything he'd done in comic books, but gradually he settled into a comfortable rut and did drawing that was competent but dull. He stayed with the page for the remainder of his life. **R.G.**

**RADIO PATROL** The first adventure strip to star uniformed cops, *Radio Patrol* made its national debut in April 1934. A Sunday page was added in November of that year. The feature, eventually retitled *Sergeant Pat of Radio Patrol*, lasted until December 1950.

The strip had begun in Boston in August 1933, under the title *Pinkerton, Jr.*, in Hearst's *Daily Record*. The managing editor had come up with the basic idea and assigned it to Eddie Sullivan, his night city editor, and Charlie Schmidt, who'd been in the art department since the days of World War I. The editor gave the pair 48 hours to come up with a new strip, and they turned in a feature built around the crimefighting activities of young Pinky Pinkerton; his Irish setter, Irish; Sergeant Pat and Stuttering Sam, partners in patrol car 11; and Molly, a plainclothes policewoman. According to subsequent King Features publicity, "two months after its initial appearance in the *Boston Record*, readers voted *Radio Patrol* winner in the paper's popularity contest over nine other strips with national reputations!" That sort of reader reaction impressed King feature editor Joseph Connolly, and he added the strip to the syndicate's list.

The *Radio Patrol* crew usually dealt with smaller crimes than their detective strip contemporaries. Even so, there was a good deal of action and excitement, and in the Thirties the very idea of a radio car was enthralling. Writer Sullivan did have a fondness for involving his protagonists with a mad scientist now and then, but more frequently he had them going after pickpockets, shoplifters, bank robbers, car thieves, and hijackers. On one occasion car 11 even got a radio call to "go to Pier Thirty One…thieves pilfering lobsters from fish loft."

The redheaded and handsome Sergeant Pat shared the star role with several of the other characters. Pinky, aided by his highly intelligent dog, frequently solved cases on his own. So did Sam, who in the best sidekick tradition was fat. Even more than *Dick Tracy*, the strip dealt with relatively accurate police procedures. It never managed, though, to affect the national newspaper audience the way it hit those Boston readers in 1933 and apparently never made its creators rich. Sullivan was finally able to give up his newspaper job, but Schmidt stayed in the *Record* art department for the rest of his life. King Features releases mentioned Schmidt's workhorse nature: "His life in a nutshell has been thus: wake up, go to work in the offices of the Hearst papers in Boston, work all day, come home, eat dinner—and then start to work on his action-packed adventure strip." For a strip drawn in his spare time, *Radio Patrol* wasn't bad, and Schmidt's moderately old-fashioned style neatly fit the day-to-day crimes that Sergeant Pat and the gang dealt with.                         **R.G.**

**RAGGEDY ANN** The best-known rag doll in the world, she was created by writer-artist Johnny Gruelle in his illustrated book *Raggedy Ann Stories* published in 1918. Her companion came along two years later in *Raggedy Andy Stories*. The two of them entered comic books in 1942 and were to be found on newsstands, off and on, for the next 30-some years, but Gruelle, who died in 1938, had nothing to do with this phase of his characters' careers.

In the series of books, which stretched to well over a dozen, Gruelle dealt in fairly gentle fantasy. He continually emphasized how kindly and goodhearted Raggedy Ann and Andy were, a judgment all the other characters in the stories, even the villains, concurred with. In Gruelle's world, dolls, humans, animals, and assorted other creatures fraternized, all of which was carried over into the comic book adventures.

They began in Dell's *New Funnies* #65 (July 1942), a title the rag dolls shared with Andy Panda, the Brownies, Billy and Bonny Bee, and Felix the Cat. The artist on the eight- and 10-page adventures was George Kerr, a longtime children's book illustrator and newspaper artist and, during this period, a drinking companion of Walt Kelly. *New Funnies* was also, briefly, the home of *Mr Tweedeedle*, drawn by his son, Justin Gruelle. This fantasy feature was based on the Sunday page Gruelle had drawn from 1910 to 1921 and was drawn in the comic book by Justin.

The first comic book devoted entirely to Raggedy Ann and Andy appeared in 1942, as part of Dell's four-color series, and over the next three years three more issues followed. Then in 1946 a regular monthly began. Edited by Oskar Lebeck, each issue opened with a 14-page Ann and Andy adventure done by Kerr. Among the other features that appeared in the magazine over its three-plus-years run were *Eggbert Elephant* by Dan Noonan, *Animal Mother Goose* by Kelly, and *The Hair-raising Adventures of Peterkin Pottle* by John Stanley. This last was about a kid with Walter Mitty tendencies, and it took over the leading spot in the magazine during its final days. After ceasing to have a monthly of their own, Raggedy Ann and Andy appeared in occasional one-shots. They were last seen in comic books in 1971.
                                             **R.G.**

**RAYMOND, ALEX** (1909–1956)  Noted for his illustrative style. Raymond rose from the bullpen at King Features Syndicate to become one of the most celebrated cartoonists of the 1930s, 1940s, and 1950s. In a career that spanned a quarter-century, Raymond was responsible for four influential strips: *Secret Agent X-9*, *Flash Gordon*, *Jungle Jim*, and the cerebral *Rip Kirby*.

Alexander Gillespie Raymond was raised in the affluent suburb of New Rochelle, New York, the son of a civil engineer. If he showed any sign of following in his father's footsteps it was a closely guarded secret. In fact, he credits his father for having "a vision to see beyond his own business, to realize that art could be a worthwhile career, too"; he claimed the elder Raymond's office walls were tattooed with his artwork. But when, or even why, Raymond decided on a career as a cartoonist can only be surmised. It is known, however, that his family lived near Russ Westover, of *Tillie the Toiler* fame, and it's possible that on visits to the Westover home, Raymond became fascinated by his neighbor's work and wanted to be a cartoonist, too.

In any case, when his father died, Raymond was still leaning toward sports, having entered Iona Prep School in New Rochelle on a football and baseball scholarship. He is said to have been offered an athletic scholarship to Notre Dame University as well. But, as the eldest of five children, he was forced to be the family's breadwinner and took a job on Wall Street as an order clerk while still a teenager. The Great Crash of 1929 sent him scurrying elsewhere to earn a dollar, and he wound up, as he described it, a solicitor for a mortgage broker. He also enrolled in the Grand Central School of Art and was soon calling on his old neighbor, Russ Westover, for advice.

Westover apparently recognized Raymond's talent and used him as an assistant on *Tillie the Toiler*. He then landed Raymond a job in the bullpen at King Features in 1930, where he did some toiling of his own at $20 a week, assisting the Young brothers, Lyman and Chic, on *Tim Tyler's Luck* and *Blondie*, while also continuing to work on *Tillie*.

For the next four years—about the time it takes to earn a college degree—Raymond got as good an education in the field of cartooning as could be found anywhere. Under the management of Joe Connolly, its president, King Features was one of the premier syndicates in the country. While Raymond was going to "school" in the KFS bullpen, Connolly was a whirling dervish of ideas, looking for anything to capture the lucrative newspaper market—detective stories, jungle stories, science fiction, mystery. He hired Dashiell Hammett, the famous author of *The Maltese Falcon*, to write *Secret Agent X-9*, a new strip based on the hard-boiled detective characters Hammett had created for pulp magazines. He also hungered for a strip to go head-to-head against *Buck Rogers*, and another to counter *Tarzan*. A major beneficiary of all these ambitions was the former clerk from Wall Street.

In late 1933 and early 1934, Raymond, then barely 23 years old, emerged from the bullpen to win the illustrating chores of *Secret Agent X-9* as well as *Flash Gordon* and *Jungle Jim*. All three debuted in 1934.

In the beginning, Raymond's style was stiff, almost amateurish in contrast to his later work. However, he quickly developed into one of the leading cartoon artists of his day, a fitting rival to Hal Foster to whom he was often compared. But three strips proved too much—even with the assistance of the able Austin Briggs—and so Raymond stopped work on *Secret Agent X-9*.

During World War II, Raymond relinquished *Flash Gordon* and *Jungle Jim* to Briggs and enlisted in the Marine Corps where he served aboard an aircraft carrier as combat artist and public information officer. In 1946, with the war behind him, he expected to resume *Flash Gordon*, but to his surprise, King Features had other plans—a detective strip to compete against *Dick Tracy*. As an enticement, KFS offered him ownership of the new strip, which turned out to be *Rip Kirby*. Kirby was a private investigator with intellect, a retired Marine officer (like Raymond) who wore glasses, smoked a pipe and (as Raymond did) loved classical music and golf and drove sports cars. Devoting nearly all his energies to the strip, Raymond turned *Rip Kirby* into a tour de force.

In 1956, Raymond drove a sports car into a tree in Westport, Connecticut, killing himself and cutting short a brilliant career. He was a month shy of his 47th birthday.　　　　　　　　　　　　　　　　　　**S.L.H.**

**RAYMOND, JIM**　See BLONDIE.

**RED BARRY**　It began in March of 1934, one of several tough cop strips that flourished during the Depression. *Red Barry* was written and drawn by erstwhile sports cartoonist Will Gould. Its redheaded protagonist was a grim, humorless undercover man who often posed as a crook in order to bring real crooks to justice. Gould's continuities, mixing hard-boiled pulp fiction elements with movie hokum, and his nervous, energetic drawing made for a highly individual feature.

Initially King Features Syndicate was enthusiastic and described *Red Barry* in trade ads as "a two-fisted hero in a detective-adventure strip that crackles with hair-trigger action, authentic atmosphere and thrilling plots." Red, who worked for a large metropolitan police force, had a kid pal known as Ouchy Mugouchy, and the most frequently seen female character was a blond newspaperwoman named Mississippi. The early stories tried to be as violent as anything in *Dick Tracy*, but, according to Will Gould, Hearst himself protested, and the strip was toned down.

Gould's continuing interest in golf and night clubs led to missed deadlines and increasing trouble with the syndicate. He hired an assistant, Walter Frehm, but then ended up taking him along to the golf course and night spots. Finally, in the late 1930s, after a disagreement over subsidiary rights, Gould quit, by which time Red wasn't appearing in the strip at all: Red had gone away to recuperate. Ouchy and two of his contemporaries, known as the Terrific Three, had been solving modest crimes in Red's place. **R.G.**

**THE RED KNIGHT** The only serious superhero created directly for newspapers, the Red Knight debuted in a daily strip in the spring of 1940. He had an array of powers that many a comic book counterpart would have envied, including incredible strength and speed, the ability to control men's minds, and a talent for invisibility. Although he couldn't fly, he was an impressive leaper.

The strip was distributed by the Register and Tribune Syndicate, and they clearly intended to compete with Superman and the other costumed crimefighters who'd come along in his wake. Their ads made clear the sort of audience the strip would pull in: "Mystery! Action! Adventure! Suspense! Made for 'the kids' who have zoomed the sale of comic magazines featuring just this type of thriller!" To entice an even larger audience, they also promised "just the right number of beautiful blondes and gorgeous brunets!"

Unlike most of his colleagues, the Red Knight had no civilian identity. He became a superhero when a Dr. Van Lear charged him up with Plus Power. His first exploits were on the small potatoes side, including such chores as rescuing "a crowd menaced by a madman's pistol" and stopping a "runaway bus piloted by a crazed driver"—admirable acts, yet not quite in the same league with Captain Marvel or the Human Torch. One of the strip's flaws, indeed, was its conservatism; it was anxious to cash in on the superhero craze but fearful of being too fantastic or violent. The Knight would often travel to the scene of a crime in a taxi, and once, when anxious to get to a Nazi sub lurking off the coast, he hopped into a rowboat. None of his exploits were as flamboyant as those of his newsstand counterparts. He went in for stopping masked gangland masterminds, powermad dictators, and the like. Once, in a moment of rare abandon, he did wrestle a gorilla.

The spring of 1943 found him flying to Japan with Van Lear on an important mission. Their plane was forced down near Mt. Fuji and, cut off from recharging his powers, he eventually became an ordinary mortal.

By June a caption was referring to him as "our hero, formerly the Red Knight," and shortly thereafter our hero assumed the less colorful name of Alan Knight. Late in September, as Knight and a Japanese girl were escaping in a fishing boat, the strip came to a sudden halt. A crudely lettered balloon, pasted over the original one, tied up the loose ends.

*The Red Knight* was written by John J. Welch and drawn by Jack McGuire. Welch had been writing strips for the R&T syndicate throughout the Thirties. McGuire, a high school art teacher in Texas, had spent the previous decade moonlighting as a comic strip artist. He drew the *Jane Arden* Sunday page and *Bullet Benton*, and from the late 1930s through the middle 1940s he also ghosted *Ella Cinders*. His drawing was forceful and possessed of a sloppy charm and could have fit into the eclectic comic books of the period. **R.G.**

**RED RYDER** Fred Harman's red-haired cowboy first rode into view on Sunday, November 6, 1938. "The restless urge of a wandering cowboy brings Red Ryder down the slopes of the Shokandes into Devil's Hole," explained a caption, "in the broken country of the Southwest." On that first Sunday Red acquired Little Beaver, a freshly orphaned Navajo kid, and stumbled across a stagecoach holdup. Within the next two weeks, after scaring off the outlaws, he met up with Beth Wilder, who would be *the* woman in his life, and first encountered Ace Hanlon, the ruthless gambler and scoundrel who'd also play an important longtime role.

Red was actually Bronc Peeler, Harman's earlier comic strip cowpoke, under a new name; Little Beaver, under the same name, had been Bronc's sidekick. But this time around, aided by agent-merchandising entrepreneur Stephen Slesinger, the redheaded Harman's redheaded hero became an impressive success. It was Slesinger who advised the artist to convert the unsuccessful Peeler into Red Ryder. And Slesinger sold the new version to NEA. Within 10 years *Red Ryder* was appearing in an estimated 750 newspapers around the world and had been seen in serials and movies and heard on a radio show. There were also comic books, Big Little Books, and novels. Red even replaced Buck

*The Red Knight*, Jack W. McGuire, 1940.

Jones as the spokesman for the Daisy BB gun company. And for good measure Slesinger sold reprints of the *Bronc Peeler* strip to *Popular Comics*.

Harman's feature, which added a daily in March 1939, was set initially in Colorado in, as *Collier's* pointed out in 1948, "that section…in which Fred Harman grew up and still lives—Pagosa Springs, Archuleta County, in the Blanco Basin of the San Juan Mountains." The strip took place during the post-Civil War era so popular in just about all movie Westerns, although eventually Harman moved far enough forward in time to allow his characters to have telephones. Harman knew what he was drawing, and *Red Ryder* had an authentic, gritty look; but he had also spent some time in Hollywood, and his continuities favored many elements found only in the B-movie West. Little Beaver in particular was the worst kind of cinema Injun and spoke soundstage patois: "Me sneakum away to trailum," "You betchum!" and so on. Early in the strip Red's ranch-owning aunt, the hefty Duchess, was introduced, and she always added an element of humor to the adventures—sometimes a bit too much.

While publicity stressed that Harman was "a perfectionist temperamentally incapable of working with a helper," *Red Ryder* was actually written and drawn by divers hands over the years. Among the ghost artists were Jim Gary, John Wade Hampton, Edmond Good, and Bob MacLeod. After Harman left the strip in the early 1960s, MacLeod carried on until the end in December 1964.                                                         **R.G.**

**RED SONJA**  A very capable young woman, Red Sonja was first seen in a *Conan* comic book late in 1972. She eventually went on, billed as a "She-devil with a Sword," to star in a regular comic book title of her own, a series of paperback novels, and a movie. Roy Thomas was the chief writer of her comic book adventures, while the artists included Barry Windsor-Smith and Frank Thorne.

Sonja was a byproduct of the barbarian boom of the 1970s, an increased interest among comic book fans in the swords and sorcery genre, which had been encouraged mainly by Marvel's *Conan the Barbarian*. Masterminded by Thomas, drawn by Smith, and loosely adapted from Robert E. Howard's 1930s pulp magazine stories, the barechested swordsman had hit the stands in 1970. He proved a hit and in #23 of *Conan*, which came out toward the end of 1972, Thomas borrowed a character named Red Sonja from another Howard pulpwood tale and transplanted her into the mythical Hyborean age. He changed her name slightly and let her loose in that mythical era when swords and sorcery were in flower and violence and bloodshed much in evidence.

*Red Sonja*, Frank Thorne, ™ & © 1977, Marvel Entertainment Group Inc.

Much more conservatively attired than she would later be, Sonja still proved a formidable second banana in the two issues she guested in. She returned in 1974 for a single appearance in *The Savage Sword of Conan*. Then, starting early in 1975 and with Howard Chaykin as artist, she cut a swath through two issues of Marvel's black and white *Kull and the Barbarians*. Later that same year Sonja starred in *Marvel Feature*. From the second issue on Frank Thorne was the artist. By this time her figure had filled out, her bright orange hair was a flowing mane, and she wore a sort of chainmail bikini. Inspired by the character, Thorne did some of his most impressive and ambitious work to date. While never at the top of Marvel's list in terms of sales, the she-devil managed to garner considerable publicity during Thorne's run with her.

Finally, late in 1976, a comic titled *Red Sonja* was issued. It lasted, with lapses, until 1986. Thorne had long since departed; eventually Thomas left, too. By the middle 1980s Tom DeFalco was scripting and Mary

Wilshire was penciling. The 1985 motion picture, starring Brigitte Nielsen, inspired two issues of *Red Sonja: The Movie*. But the film was not able to keep the character from fading away the next year.     **R.G.**

**REG'LAR FELLERS**  It began as a panel in the middle of the second decade of the century, and by the early 1920s *Reg'lar Fellers* was a regular strip, complete with Sunday page. The feature was created by Gene Byrnes (1889–1974), a former shoemaker and bug spray salesman who became quite wealthy from the feature. Byrnes, a graduate of the Landon correspondence school of cartooning, realized early on that he was a limited artist at best, and he proceeded to hire a series of talented ghosts to do most of the drawing for him.

During most of its early life, which commenced around 1917, the *Reg'lar Fellers* panel ran as part of Byrnes' larger *It's a Great Life If You Don't Weaken* daily, which originated in the *New York Telegram*. In 1919 he branched out with a Sunday page in the *New York Herald* titled *Wide Awake Willie*. Willie and Jimmie Dugan, the central kid in *Reg'lar Fellers*, were identical, down to the checkered cap and short pants. Late in 1920, after *Reg'lar Fellers* was running daily in strip form, the Sunday page changed its name to *Reg'lar Fellers*, too. The feature did so well that by the early 1920s Byrnes was earning the then handsome salary of $25,000 a year. Byrnes owned *Reg'lar Fellers*, and it was distributed by various syndicates over the years.

*Reg'lar Fellers*, Gene Byrnes, © 1927, N.Y. Tribune, Inc.

Although the kid characters in the strip talked like New York street urchins—using such locutions as boithday, my toin, I dunno—they actually lived in a quiet suburban town that contained both streets and shops as well as fields, lots, and wooded areas. Jimmie was the star, and his was usually the only home life depicted in the strip. His closest buddy and confidant was Puddinhead Duffy, a fat kid in beanie and striped shirt, and his best girl was Aggie Riley. Later on, Puddinhead's brother Pinhead, a miniature replica of his older sibling (but without a beanie), entered the strip. It wasn't until 1930 that Jimmie acquired a full-time dog, and not until 1932 did the mutt, a sort of bulldog with a black circle around his left eye, get named Bullseye.

*Reg'lar Fellers* delivered a gag a day, but they weren't joke book gags, because Byrnes and his crew built the humor around the lives of children of about 10 or so. Jimmie, Puddinhead, and the rest were plagued by school, sometimes perplexed by parents, anxious about what they were going to be when they grew up, continually hungry (especially for candy, ice cream, cake, and pie), now and then interested in girls, and willing to speculate on anything from the nature of the universe to the relative speeds of various types of motorcycles. They rarely, unless sick, sat still, and most of the strips were like story boards for a movie about hyperactivity. Jimmie and Puddinhead carried on conversations, arguments, and debates while running, jumping, hopping, playing leap frog, climbing fences, roller skating, and playing ball. They and their pals always moved so swiftly through the strip that they churned up clouds of dust.

Byrnes started hiring assistants early in the life of his strip. His chief ghost in the 1920s was Tack Knight, who left him at the end of the decade to start a similar strip called *Little Folks* for the *Chicago Trib*'s syndicate. After him came magazine cartoonist Burr Inwood. Another unheralded artist on *Reg'lar Fellers* was George Carlson, an illustrator and comic book artist. Carlson looks to have had a hand in the strip for most of its life, and in its final years he did most of the drawing. All in all, the strip was always lively, well-written, and well-drawn. It ended in 1949.

*Reg'lar Fellers* was reprinted in two black and white books in the 1920s by the Cupples & Leon company. In the 1930s the Sunday pages were among those reprinted in *Popular Comics*. Later they showed up in early issues of *All-American Comics*. *Reg'lar Fellers Heroic Comics* came along in 1940, offering a mix of strip reprints and superheroes such as Hydroman. The comic book introduced a club called Reg'lar Fellers of America; all a kid had to do to join was read the magazine. Byrnes and the fellers ended their association with *Heroic* after the 15th issue.                                                    **R.G.**

## THE REUBEN AWARD
An internationally recognized journalism award presented annually by the National Cartoonists Society to the "Outstanding Cartoonist of the Year," the Reuben was originally called the Billy DeBeck Award, from 1946 to 1953; it was renamed "The Reuben" the following year after NCS cofounder and longtime honorary president, Rube Goldberg. Bill Crawford created the statuette, using one of Goldberg's irreverent pieces of sculpture as a model.

The winner of the Reuben is selected by secret ballot, and only regular members of the NCS are allowed to vote. The recipient need not be a member of the organization. (It has gone five times to non-NCS members.) To present the award, a special ceremony is held each spring in various cities around the world.

In the profession, the Reuben is considered the highest honor a cartoonist can receive. However, the National Cartoonists Society has other awards it bestows, namely: Category Awards in the areas of advertising, animation, comic books, editorial cartoons, humor strips, illustration, magazine gag cartoons, special features, sports cartoons, story strips, and syndicated panels. In addition, there is also the Silver T-Square, presented to persons who have made a significant contribution to the society; the Elzie Segar Award, presented to persons who have made significant contributions to the profession; and the Gold Key Award, for those inducted into the National Cartoonists Society Hall of Fame. There is also a Gold T-Square, the only recipient being Rube Goldberg in 1955, commemorating his 50th year in cartooning.

The past winners of the Reuben Award are:

1946  MILTON CANIFF, Steve Canyon
1947  AL CAPP, *Li'l Abner*
1948  CHIC YOUNG, *Blondie*
1949  ALEX RAYMOND, *Rip Kirby*
1950  ROY CRANE, *Buz Sawyer*
1951  WALT KELLY, *Pogo*
1952  HANK KETCHAM, *Dennis the Menace*
1953  MORT WALKER, *Beetle Bailey*
1954  WILLARD MULLIN (Sport Cartoons)
1955  CHARLES SCHULZ, *Peanuts*
1956  HERBLOCK (Editorial Cartoons)
1957  HAL FOSTER, *Prince Valiant*
1958  FRANK KING, *Gasoline Alley*
1959  CHESTER GOULD, *Dick Tracy*
1960  RONALD SEARLE (Cartoon Illustrations)
1961  BILL MAULDIN (Editorial Cartoons)
1962  DIK BROWNE, *Hi and Lois*
1963  FRED LASSWELL, *Barney Google and Snuffy Smith*
1964  CHARLES SCHULZ, *Peanuts*

1965  LEONARD STARR, *On Stage*
1966  OTTO SOGLOW, *The Little King*
1967  RUBE GOLDBERG, *Humor in Sculpture*
1968  JOHNNY HART, *B.C.*, and *The Wizard of Id* PAT OLIPHANT (Editorial Cartoons) (tied vote)
1969  WALTER BERNDT, *Smitty*
1970  ALFRED ANDRIOLA, *Kerry Drake*
1971  MILTON CANIFF, *Steve Canyon*
1972  PAT OLIPHANT (Editorial Cartoons)
1973  DIK BROWNE, *Hagar the Horrible*
1974  DICK MOORES, *Gasoline Alley*
1975  BOB DUNN, *They'll Do It Every Time*
1976  ERNIE BUSHMILLER, *Nancy*
1977  CHESTER GOULD, *Dick Tracy*
1978  JEFF MACNELLY (Editorial Cartoons)
1979  JEFF MACNELLY, *Shoe*
1980  CHARLES SAXON, *The New Yorker*
1981  MELL LAZARUS, *Miss Peach*
1982  BIL KEANE, *The Family Circus*
1983  ARNOLD ROTH (Humorous Illustration)
1984  BRANT PARKER, *The Wizard of Id*
1985  LYNN B. JOHNSTON, *For Better or For Worse*
1986  BILL WATTERSON, *Calvin and Hobbes*
1987  MORT DRUCKER, *Mad Magazine*
1988  BILL WATTERSON, *Calvin and Hobbes*
1989  JIM DAVIS, *Garfield*                                      **J.R.**

## REX MORGAN, M.D.
A product of the postwar boom in soap opera strips, *Rex Morgan, M.D.* was introduced by Publishers Syndicate in the spring of 1948. The author was a doctor named Nicholas Dallis, a practicing psychiatrist. The artwork was handled by Marvin Bradley, who drew the characters, and Frank Edginton, who had the less exciting chore of providing the backgrounds. Bradley, who worked in a variation of the Caniff style, had been Ken Ernst's assistant on *Mary Worth*. Unlike many of the strips begun in imitation of *Mary Worth*, this one is still among the living.

Dr. Morgan is handsome, dark-haired, and unmarried. He arrived in the town of Glenbrook to take over the practice of a deceased medic, and he'd hardly had time to hang up his diploma before he was tangled up with a spoiled and reckless heiress, the cute freckle-faced kid she'd run down with her fast convertible, her rich doting father, and his lovely dark-haired nurse June Gale. From then on the doctor mixed medical problems with romance, murder, and the other staples of soap opera. Since doctors still made housecalls back when the strip started, Dr. Morgan had considerable mobility and was always walking into something interesting.

Bradley did a slick, enthusiastic job in the early years, and the strip was a good-looking companion to *Mary Worth*. The good doctor was usually more actively involved in what was going on than Mrs. Worth. The strip has had a variety of assistants and ghosts over the years.

These include Alex Kotzky and Andre LeBlanc. After Bradley's death in the middle 1980s, Tony DiPreta became the artist.

Dr. Morgan managed to earn a place in comic book history by way of the Harvey company's tastefully titled 1950s reprint *Teen-Age Dope Slaves*, which used a strip sequence dealing with teens and drugs. "This is nothing but another variety of crime comic of a particularly deplorable character," noted Dr. Fredric Wertham in *Seduction of the Innocent* (1954). The magazine is listed as being worth as much as $400 in the *Official Overstreet Comic Book Price Guide*.      **R.G.**

**RICK O'SHAY**  One of the last comic strips about the American frontier, Stan Lynde's *Rick O'Shay* was distributed by the Chicago Tribune-N.Y. News Syndicate from its debut in 1958 until its demise in 1981. It managed for over two decades to make broad fun of the clichés of Western fiction while sustaining an exciting and plausible story line within those same conventions. And, though it seldom ran in more than 100 papers, it had a loyal audience.

Originally intended as a spoof on contemporary dude-ranching and set in modern times, *Rick O'Shay* began as a Sunday page on April 27, 1958. A daily was added the following month. It regressed in 1964 to the usual period of the genre, the post-Civil War years. Placed in the fictitious small town of Conniption, which was based on Lynde's home town of Lodge Grass, Montana, it recounted the fussin' and fightin' of an assorted band of frontier types, all given such heavyhanded punning names that it was never possible to take the action very seriously.

The mayor of Conniption was a gambler named Deuces Wilde, and its marshal was Rick O'Shay, an amiable youth whose function was essentially to react to the others. The tough gunslinger who was to become the real hero of the strip was Hipshot Percussion. Rick's voluptuous girlfriend was the barroom chanteuse Gaye Abandon, and the town physician was Basil Metabolism, M.D. Other characters rejoiced in such names as Manual Labor and Sudden DeMise. The strip ranged from slapstick in its self-contained Sunday stories to well-plotted continuous adventure in its dailies.

Drawn in a style that was a blend of the illustrational and the cartoony, the strip was much admired for its fidelity to its material, rendering the costumes and scenery of its time and place both accurately and elegantly.

Lynde quit in 1977 after a financial disagreement with the syndicate. Marion Dern was brought in to write *Rick O'Shay*, and Alfredo Alcala, a comic book veteran, became the artist. A few months later the very realistic Alcala was replaced by Mel Keefer, who'd drawn several unsuccessful strips over the years. The strip lasted until 1981.      **D.W.**

**RIP KIRBY**  A daily private eye strip drawn initially by Alex Raymond, *Rip Kirby* began in 1946. Syndicated by King Features, it continues to this day.

Rip Kirby set up shop as a private detective on March 4, 1946. On the cerebral side, he was closer to Ellery Queen than he was to Sam Spade: He was an intellectual—readers realized that right off, since Rip wore glasses—and definitely upper class. He lived in a posh Manhattan apartment, complete with grand piano and British valet. He was a golfer and had a blond ladyfriend

*Rip Kirby*, Alex Raymond, © 1948, King Features Syndicate, Inc. Reprinted with special permission of King Features Syndicate, Inc.

who was pretty enough and slender enough to be hired as a fashion model before the strip was two weeks old.

Raymond (just out of the Marine Corps, as was Rip Kirby) took sole credit for the strip, although he actually did little of the writing. The original notion came from King Features editor Ward Greene, author of several mystery novels, and Fred Dickenson was signed on as scriptwriter fairly early. Raymond's style had changed considerably since he'd abandoned *Flash Gordon* in the spring of 1944; he no longer went in for heroic tableaus and melodramatic action, and *Rip Kirby* was much more relaxed and realistic. Raymond seemed intent on proving he could draw people in natural poses and settings and was capable of indicating character and attitude a great deal more subtly than he had in the days of Ming the Merciless.

The strip was impressively well drawn in its first years. Raymond had long wanted to be a magazine illustrator, and in *Rip Kirby* he demonstrated he could compete with the best of them. The continuities were never quite as good as the pictures that went with them, being modest reworkings, for the most part, of the kind of plots to be found in the B-movies of a decade or so earlier. There were always interesting characters, however: Honey Dorian, Rip's blond girlfriend; Desmond, his Jeeves-like man; the loathsome villain known as the Mangler; Pagan Lee, the gunmoll with a heart of gold.

Raymond was killed in 1956, while test-driving the car of his colleague Stan Drake, and John Prentice, another veteran of World War II, was picked to take over the strip. A magazine illustrator with extensive comic book experience, Prentice drew in a style similar to Raymond's, a fact due partly to his magazine background and partly to the influence of Raymond's earlier work on *Secret Agent X-9* and *Flash Gordon*. Prentice, with some help over the years from such artists as Alden McWilliams and Al Williamson, has kept the strip going. Since Dickenson's death in the middle 1980s, Prentice has also written the continuity. **S.L.H.**

**RIPLEY, ROBERT L.** See BELIEVE IT OR NOT.

**RITT, WILLIAM** (1901–1972) Creator of *Brick Bradford* and writer of that feature's legendary early yarns, Bill Ritt was otherwise a prolific columnist and staff editor at Central Press Association, King Features' Cleveland branch office. Born in Evansville, Indiana, Ritt had been a sportswriter for both *The Post* and *The Times* in that city and had briefly worked for United Press in New York before landing at King's midwest shop, where he added scriptwriting to his daily duties. He wrote many gags for Paul Robinson's *Etta Kett* and Wally Bishop's *Muggs McGinnis* (later *Muggs and Skeeter*); he probably wrote the *Frank Merriwell* feature (1931–1934) officially credited to Burt L. Standish; he bylined the *Merriwell* spinoff strip *Chip Collins' Adventures* (1934–1935) for part of its run; and he wrote in its entirety the short-lived 1935 baseball feature *Gabby*, drawn by Joe King. Ritt's enduring masterwork, *Brick Bradford*, premiered on August 21, 1933, and for the next dozen years—influenced by Verne and Burroughs and Merritt and his own library of arcane archaeologia—Ritt invented some of the most ambitious fantasy-adventure romances that the comics have ever known. Several of them are certainly the longest on record, continuing for years, literally.

In the late 1940s Ritt wearied of *Bradford* and surrendered it to artist-collaborator Clarence Gray (the daily strip in October 1948, the Sunday page in June 1949). Thereafter his stripwork was limited to the Central Press annual Christmas strip *Eski* (1951–1959), drawn by Alfred J. Buescher. He continued to write numerous daily sports and general-interest columns for the boilerplate Cleveland service until King Features closed the office in 1971, whereafter he retired and, on September 23, 1972, died. **J.M.**

**ROBBINS, FRANK** (1917– ) During his long career in cartooning, Robbins drew two successful adventure strips, *Scorchy Smith* and *Johnny Hazard*. He also did magazine illustration, considerable comic strip advertising, and, briefly, he even drew *Batman*.

Born in Boston, Robbins was something of a prodigy and was helping earn the family living from his early teen years. Though he yearned to be a serious painter like his friend and contemporary Jack Levine, from the time his family relocated in Manhattan in the early 1930s, he had to concentrate on the more commercial aspects of art. He worked on the murals for the Radio City Music Hall, drew promotion pieces for RKO Pictures, and even put in time in Bert Whitman's comic book shop. In 1939 he was hired by the Associated Press to take over the *Scorchy Smith* strip. He was the first artist to do the *Scorchy* Sunday page, which started in 1942.

Although he has sometimes been characterized simply as a disciple of the Sickles-Caniff school, Robbins was never actually that. He arrived at his highly individual, impressionistic style by his own route, guided by his own sensibilities as much as by any desire to emulate others.

Early in 1944 King Features contacted him, which resulted in his creating a new adventure strip, *Johnny Hazard*. In its first years the new strip was a virtual twin of *Scorchy Smith*. Robbins had a very strong design sense, and his wartime black and white strips are impressive.

At about the same time he'd been doing *Scorchy Smith*, Robbins also drew *Lightnin' and the Lone Rider*, a thinly syndicated cowboy strip. This poor man's Lone Ranger had originally been drawn by Jack Kirby.

In the early and middle 1940s Robbins, who always worked rapidly, started doing magazine illustrations and advertising strips. He drew pictures for *Life* and ad strips in soap opera style for such products as Dr. Lyons' Tooth Powder.

By the early 1970s *Johnny Hazard* was not producing the income it once had, and Robbins turned to comic books as a new sideline. He began writing for DC on such features as the *Flash, Superboy*, and *Batman*, then drew both *Batman* and *The Shadow*. His style was looser now and he went in for a very bold, choppy inking and a great deal of black. The style of his *Batman* stories that appeared in *Detective Comics* in 1971 caused many of the more traditionally minded readers to write letters of protest. Robbins worked briefly for Marvel in the middle 1970s, on *Captain America, The Invaders*, and *Ghost Rider*.

*Johnny Hazard* was retired in 1977, and in the summer of 1978 Robbins moved to Mexico. Giving up comics for good, he has devoted himself full time to painting.

R.G.

## ROBINSON, JERRY (1922– )

Although he is probably best-known for the work he did on *Batman* in the early 1940s, Robinson has had a varied career in cartooning and is still active. In addition to comic books, he has drawn newspaper strips, political cartoons, and book illustrations, as well as written several books, including a history of comic strips.

Robinson got into comics in 1939, through a chance meeting with Bob Kane. He became his first assistant on the just-started *Batman* and was present at the creation of Robin the Boy Wonder (whom he named) and the Joker. He learned on the job, and by the early 1940s Robinson was penciling and inking complete stories. His major artistic influence was his gifted comic book colleague Mort Meskin, with whom he shared a studio; as a result, his drawing moved away from Kane's slightly cartoony look and closer to realistic illustration. In 1942 and 1943 Robinson did a handsome series of covers for *Detective Comics* and the *Batman* comic book. "He'd developed a personalized way of drawing figures, one that mixed the heroic with a slight fantasy element," comments *The Great Comic Book Artists*, "and his staging was both inventive and effective. Most of all, Robinson gave the impression he was enjoying himself."

In the middle 1940s Robinson left *Batman*. "I wanted to do more of my own stories and characters," he has said, "and I felt that I needed to do something new." He began drawing *The Green Hornet*, created a short-lived superhero named Atoman, and then teamed with Meskin to produce some striking stories for such heroes as the Black Terror, the Fighting Yank, Johnny Quick, and the Vigilante. Usually Meskin penciled, while Robinson inked. By the 1950s Robinson was drawing crime, horror, and war for Stan Lee at Marvel and tamer stuff such as *Lassie* for Western.

Robinson drew his first newspaper strip in 1953: *Jet Scott* offered science fiction adventure in a contemporary setting and was nicely done. Syndicated by the *New York Herald Tribune*, it lasted just two years. By the early 1960s he began to turn away from comic books and adventure. He started doing a syndicated humor panel called *Still Life* and also drew a Sunday page titled *Flubbs & Fluffs* for the *New York Daily News*. In the 1970s he started *Life with Robinson*, a one-panel comic strip offering political comment and satire. The strip is still going, and the syndicated Robinson formed to market it now "represents cartoonists from 40 countries." Among the books he's written the most notable is *The Comics: An Illustrated History of Comic Strip Art*, which was published in 1974.

R.G.

## ROCKY MASON, GOVERNMENT MARSHAL

A serious Sunday page by one of the pioneers of funny comics, *Rocky Mason* got its start on August 24, 1941. Written and drawn by Jimmy Swinnerton, the cowboy feature supplanted his long-running *Little Jimmy*.

Possibly at the urging of King Features, Swinnerton apparently wanted to try a straight adventure strip, but he drew *Rocky Mason* in pretty much the same style he'd been using since late in the 19th century. A contemporary Western, it took place in the dry, sun-drenched Arizona country that Swinnerton loved and had been drawing and painting for decades. Rocky Mason was a lanky blond lawman along the lines of Gary Cooper and Randolph Scott.

The page looked authentic, since Swinnerton knew his locales and was familiar with the ways of both the cowboys and the Indians. But his continuities tended to slip in a good deal of hokum and to rely on the tried and true conventions of Saturday matinee movies: The villains were all 100% blackhearted and sometimes even went around hooded like serial heavies.

*Rocky Mason* was put out to pasture in 1945 and *Little Jimmy* returned.

R.G.

## ROGERS, BOODY (1904– )

Rogers first drew for comic books in the late 1920s, before there was even a comic book industry in America. He went on to ghost *Smilin' Jack* and to create *Sparky Watts*, the foremost mock superman in both newspaper strips and comic books.

*Sparky Watts*, Boody Rogers, 1941.

Gordon Rogers was born in the Oklahoma Territory and reared in Texas. "I first thought of being a cartoonist as soon as I was big enough to hold a pencil," he once recalled. His art work first saw print in his high school yearbook. "Then I was art editor of the University of Arizona *Kitty Kat*—and *College Humor*, a mag in New York, reran some of my cartoons and paid a buck per column inch. To pad the fee I drew a guy sitting on top of a cliff trying to hit a cuspidor in the canyon below. It was two columns wide and six inches deep. Damned if they didn't pick it up and send me $12."

In the late 1920s he moved to Chicago to study at the Academy of Fine Arts, where he first met Zack Mosley. They were both protégés of the *Chicago Trib*'s Carey Orr and became close friends, scuffling and rooming together. "I went to New York in 1928. My first art work was tracing my feet on cardboard and cutting them out and placing them in my shoes to plug the holes," he's said. "I started selling a few cartoons to *Life, Judge, Collier's, Film Fun*, and anyone who would buy."

Though he wasn't aware of it at the time, he was a comic book pioneer. He worked on both George Delacorte's *The Funnies* in 1929 and Major Nicholson's *New Comics* in the middle 1930s. For the relatively short-lived Dell tabloid Rogers drew *Deadwood Gulch, Rock Age Roy*, and *Sancho and the Don*. For Nicholson he did similar things. During the late 1920s and early and middle 1930s he also did a complete comic book of *Deadwood Gulch* (a cardboard-covered black and white in the then familiar Cupples & Leon format), ghosted

Frank Beck's *Gas Buggies* strip, lettered *Dumb Dora* (this while sharing a room with the strip's artist Bill Dwyer), did the coloring of the *Winnie Winkle* Sunday pages, drew strips for a one-shot pulp fiction magazine called *Boy's Adventures*, and "anything to make ham and eggs."

In 1936 the Chicago Tribune-New York News Syndicate added a daily *Smilin' Jack* to go with the Sunday. Zack Mosley summoned his old friend to come to Long Island and help out. Rogers was associated with the aviation strip during its best years, the years during which Jack first encountered the likes of Downwind, Fat Stuff, and the Head, first grew his Gable-like mustache, and began his interrupted marches to the altar with the lovely ladies Mosley always called de-icers.

While with Mosley, Rogers was visited with the urge to draw a strip of his own. He'd tried *Possum Holler* in the middle 1930s, a hillbilly feature that included Treetop Timmons, a fellow who was so tall his head never appeared in the panels. The McClure Syndicate had shown interest in that one, but had absolutely no luck in selling it. Rogers did better with his next try, wherein he took a comedy approach to the notion of a superhero. He sold *Sparky Watts* to the Frank Jay Markey Syndicate and the daily began its run on April 29, 1940, in approximately 40 papers.

Sparky was working his way through college by selling magazine subscriptions door-to-store when exposure to a cosmic ray machine turned him into the strongest man on Earth. During his subsequent newspaper career he sabotaged Nazi submarines by tying knots in their periscopes, defeated a fishfaced master villain known as the Shark, singlehandedly laid an oil pipeline from Texas to New York, discovered the only way he could shave his super beard was with a blowtorch, kidnapped Hitler right out of Germany (or so he thought), shrank down to the size of a speck when his cosmic ray charge wore off, played professional baseball (after overcoming his tendency to throw the ball so high it came down with ice on it), and joined the Air Corps and then had to explain why he wouldn't be needing a plane. Unlike all the other super guys, Sparky never took off his mild-mannered glasses when he was doing good deeds. He had no costume either, preferring to work and fight evil wearing slacks, sweater, and a tie, although once he did dress up like a chicken as part of a subchasing escapade.

Rogers was drafted soon after America entered World War II, and the strip ended in the spring of 1942. Back in 1941, however, *Big Shot Comics* (owned in part by Markey) had begun reprinting the strips in four- and six-page chunks. After the war, Rogers resumed drawing Sparky's adventures, turning out 27 new six-page episodes for *Big Shot* and six original-material issues of Sparky's own magazine. The hero's postwar career was even more flamboyant than the one he'd had in the newspapers, involving him with Amazons, giant bugs, reanimated mummies, crazed inventors, and nuclear holocaust. Rogers took none of these problems seriously. The final issue of *Big Shot* came out in the summer of 1949. Sparky was left in the middle of an adventure, trying to get a lady to the altar.

The 10th and final issue of *Sparky Watts* also hit the stands in 1949, but Boody Rogers wasn't quite through with comic books because a year earlier he'd started doing *Babe*. The beautiful blond, also known as the Darling of the Hills, had most of her adventures in a world that mixed the hillbilly elements of *Possum Holler* and the fantasy of Sparky. Babe was also a crackerjack baseball player. Her magazine expired in the spring of 1950. In the next to the last issue Sparky Watts, accompanied by some of his associates, made a final appearance in a crowd scene. Rogers left comic books in 1950.

For some years he ran an art supply store in Phoenix, Arizona, claiming he made more money that way than he ever did as a cartoonist. Retired now, he lives in Texas. In 1984 he wrote and published his autobiography, *Homeless Bound*.  **R.G.**

**ROGERS, ROY** (1912–  ) A very merchandisable movie cowboy, he was born as Leonard Slye far from the Wild West, in Cincinnati, Ohio. Rogers reached California in the late 1920s and by the middle 1930s was part of the Sons of the Pioneers singing group. He went on to star in a long series of very successful Republic westerns, more than earning the title of King of the Cowboys. He was a comic book hero from the middle 1940s to the early 1960s, and also appeared in Big Little Books and in a newspaper strip.

There were 10 Roy Rogers Big Little Books published between 1942 and 1950. The first was *Roy Rogers, Robinhood of the Range*, written by Ed Gruskin and illustrated by the ubiquitous Erwin Hess. Dell published the first issue of *Roy Rogers Comics* in 1944, the same year the radio show began on the Mutual network. Albert Micale was among the earliest comic book artists, followed by such as Jesse Marsh, Russ Manning, and Alex Toth. Like his movies, Roy's comic book adventures were wholesome, homespun, and full of action. The title lasted until 1961.

Both the singing cowboy's horse and his wife also had comic books. Seventeen issues of *Roy Rogers' Trigger* were published by Dell from 1951 to 1955. That same year, 1951, *The Roy Rogers Show* began running on NBC television. Dale Evans, Rogers' frequent movie costar—and his wife from 1947 onward—debuted in her own DC comic book in 1948 and it lasted until 1952. This was drawn chiefly by J.N. McArdle, who'd previously drawn newspaper strips and illustrations for such pulps as *Spicy Detective*. Dell issued *Queen of the West, Dale Evans* from 1953 to 1959. Manning and Toth both contributed.

The Roy Rogers newspaper strip, daily and Sunday, started on December 2, 1949. It was signed Al McKimson, which was a pen name for the two McKimson brothers, Tom and Chuck. They were both art directors at Western Publishing, the outfit that packaged and printed the Dell comic books, and they also packaged the cowboy strip. Several artists drew it; the one who held the job longest was Mike Arens. King Features was the syndicate and the strip lasted until 1961.  **R.G.**

**ROMANCE COMICS** At least until recently, the great forgotten comic book genre was romance. In terms of sheer volume, however, it was the major category in the Fifties, outperforming crime, Western, and science fiction, and beating out horror three-to-one. Approximately 3,750 issues of romance comics were published from the genre's inception through 1959, according to romance comics expert Michelle Nolan, and at the height of the phenomenon there were nearly 150 titles being published simultaneously.

The Overstreet *Price Guide* cites Hillman's *My Date* #1, dated July 1947, with art by Jack Kirby, as the first romance comic, but *My Date* was basically a teenage humor comic. The show really began with *Young Romance* #1, produced by Joe Simon and Jack Kirby two months later. Simon and Kirby were so sure that *Young*

*Romance* would succeed that they took the highly unusual step of producing an entire issue on speculation. After looking for financing outside the industry, they finally took the book to Crestwood/Prize, where they evidently obtained a profit sharing arrangement. By early 1949 other publishers had discovered that *Young Romance* was a smash hit, and an explosion occurred, with everyone scrambling to get in on the bonanza. Victor Fox alone brought out over 20 titles with virtually indistinguishable red and yellow logos heralding *My Life, My Private Life, My Secret Life, My Secret Affair, My Love Life, My Love Affair, My Love Secret, My Love Story, My Story,* and so on.

No one really knows who was reading comics in the Fifties, but it's clear that most of the readers of romance comics were female. "The theory," according to Irwin Stein, a romance comics editor in 1950, "was that kids liked to read about people who were just a few years older. So, since your readership generally stopped about 12 or 14, you wrote about high school kids." But many romance comics creators obviously thought (probably correctly) that their readers were older than that, since they dealt with marital, workplace, and other adult problems. And contrary to popular belief, sex was sometimes dealt with quite frankly.

A small army of artists and writers was required to turn out this material (and, indeed, the flood of comics in general that appeared between 1949 and 1953), so naturally the quality of the material varied. Scripts were, for the most part, produced by the same men who wrote in other genres for the same publishers, and they were free to recycle the romantic clichés of the previous 30 years of movies, pulps, confession magazines, and romantic novels, not to mention the work of their contemporaries in comics published the previous month. However, unlike horror, science fiction, and Westerns, the subject matter was within the personal experience of the writers, and these men (and some women who wrote primarily for the romance genre) also had the opportunity, if they chose, to write solid, original stories about a broad range of human relationships. In Fifties romance comics, the simple boy-girl romance shared space with stories that focused on job and career, and on relationships between generations, siblings, classes of society, and so on. Simon and Kirby set the standard, encouraging variety and creativity in their writers.

The variety that characterized comics in general also derived from the nature of the business. Comics of the era were often published by small companies, some of which were one-man operations. No market surveys were conducted in this nickel-and-dime business, and none were needed when comics were expected to sell well from their first issue. Consequently publishers gave their writers latitude simply through lack of interest, or set a style according to their personal taste.

Victor Fox, for example, published melodramatic epics of sleaze about gals with drunken dads who eloped with grease-monkeys, or who worked in shirt factories and had to fight off the owner's advances, with titles like "He Knew My Weakness," "I Am Damaged Goods," or the incredible 11-page "I Was Crazy For Clothes," in which the heroine's obsession nearly leads to her incarceration for her boyfriend's death. Art for Fox was provided by young Wally Wood, Al Feldstein, Jack Kamen, Ken Battefield, Chuck Miller, and various other guys just out of art school who weren't too worried about whether they'd be paid.

Rae Herman, editor and publisher of *Love Diary* and *Love Journal* at Orbit, was the very opposite of Victor Fox. Her two titles always displayed excellent production values and contained well written stories and outstanding art by such illustrators as John Buscema, Mort Leav, Mort Lawrence, and the unjustly neglected Harry Anderson. Herman cared about her readers, and in each story she made sure her writers implored them to work hard, be considerate, listen to their elders, not be a pinchpenny, not be a spendthrift, stay away from playboys, watch their appearance, lose weight, overcome their shyness, avoid pickups, and so on. Otherwise they'd *suffer* and feel *guilty* for the rest of their lives. In her advice column written under the name Ray Mann, she asked, "Can you know the sordid misery of those girls who went wrong in the mistaken belief that they had to 'live for the moment?' OF COURSE IT'S NOT EASY TO WAIT! You'll find that the fruits of marriage will seem much more desirable than the unripened fruits you pick today. Living is a complicated business…and it must be conducted like one."

Publisher Archer St. John cared about quality, too, but that's where his resemblance to Rae Herman ended. In titles like *Teen-Age Temptations* and *True Love Pictorial,* writer Dana Dutch and artist Matt Baker were producing bright, understated naturalistic tales in which the girls made all kinds of mistakes, learned to do better next time, and hardly ever *suffered* no matter what. While other companies gave their heroines two choices only—homebody high-school sweetheart or dashing wicked playboy—St. John heroines often had three or more suitors, and the final choice might fit neither stereotype. In a most entertaining and totally undidactic way, St. John readers learned to think and make choices for themselves, to recognize romance's pitfalls but not to be terrorized by them.

The Ziff-Davis stories were competently done, though dull. In *Cinderella Love* and other titles, they usually expressed a single theme, making explicit the message that in any romance or marriage the girl should subordinate her interests and desires to those of her partner.

Quality comics, in the early issues of *Flaming Love, Forbidden Love, Heart Throbs,* and other titles, interpreted the term "romance" rather more loosely, with exotic locales and corny tales of adventure bearing titles like "Siren of the Tropics" and "Swamp Flame." The heroines were spies, circus performers, or reporters kidnapped by sheiks in foreign lands. Exotic art for these exotic tales was provided by Paul Gustavson, Reed Crandall, pin-up artist Bill Ward, and others.

At Star comics, editor Leonard Cole began his romantic "teenager" series with *School-Day Romances,* starring heroines like Ginger Snapp ("some cookie") who could beat the guys on the playing field and in the locker room. He soon changed the title to *Popular Teenagers,* broadened his line, and switched to reprints from Fox comics plus earnest tales written and drawn by "primitive" Jay Disbrow. Cole did all the Star covers, in a style that betrayed his cigarbox–design beginnings.

Standard comics produced many above-average stories about realistic problems of love and marriage, illustrated by Nick Cardy, Vince Colletta, and Alex Toth, doing some of the best work of his career. Artful, Ajax, and Superior bought their material by the yard from S.M. "Jerry" Iger's shop, which produced repetitive, artless fluff that nevertheless had a certain visual charm. Avon featured painted covers, some recycled from their paperback line. And Lev Gleason Publications, as with their trend-setting crime books, concentrated on solidly written stories (mixing typeset captions with hand-lettered balloons so that more text could be used); the art, however, was usually static and unattractive, despite a roster of talented artists.

Then there were specialty titles. Western romances, such as *Cowboy Love, Range Romances,* and *Flaming Western Romances,* flourished in 1949 and 1950. Fawcett brought out three issues of *Love Mystery,* a prototype of the "gothic romance" paperbacks of the Seventies, with longer than usual stories and art by George Evans, a formula that should have worked but didn't. Fawcett also published three issues of *Negro Romance.* After the Korean War broke out, another sub-genre appeared, which included *True War Romances* and *G.I. War Brides.* The problems of newlyweds spawned another series of specialty titles such as *Bride's Romances* and *My Secret Marriage.* Advice specialists were featured in *Mr. Anthony's Love Clinic* and *Dr. Anthony King, Hollywood Love Doctor.* And speaking of Hollywood, romances of the stars and hopefuls were covered in titles like *Hollywood Diary,* and Pix Parade's *Youthful Romances* featured a different singer or band-leader (Tony Martin, Tex Beneke, Tony Bennett) in each lead story. There were even two 3-D love comics, from Mikeross.

Most of these companies had strong house styles. But there were other organizations that published interesting romance comics, some in much greater volume and/or with higher quality than those detailed. Virtually every one of the 40 or so comics outfits operating in the Fifties published romance titles.

When the horror comics were killed off by the censors at the end of 1954, many publishers fell by the wayside, and the number of romance comics dropped drastically along with those of other genres. The verve and variety of the stories was curtailed even more sharply. Covers featuring a closeup of a girl's tear-stained, tortured face with a plaintive thought balloon, a cliché almost unknown during the heyday of romance comics, were adopted by Quality under Al Grenet's editorship (and often drawn by him) and by DC (which later bought out the Quality line). In the late Fifties and the Sixties DC romance comics dominated the shrunken field. Their *Girls' Love Stories,* for example, which had started in 1949, ran 180 issues before it expired in 1971. DC had always adhered to rigid formulas, and the formulas became more restrictive as time passed. "One of their rules was that every story had to have some kind of exciting climax or crisis of a physical nature, a fire, you know, or a rescue of some kind," commented one writer who worked for them in the Fifties. "They paid very well, but they were namby-pamby books. I wrote my best stuff for Simon and Kirby because I knew they would go for it more; I could use humor, character. They were the kind of people who would break the rules." In the later years DC and their chief competitors, Marvel and Charlton, ran only slight, repetitive fantasies. Romance became a form fit only for parody, as Bill Griffith so ably proved with his *Young Lust* burlesques of covers featuring the tear-stained face. A lead article on the death of romance comics in the *Washington Post Magazine* in 1977 could state with absolute truth, "There was nothing portrayed in romance comics that had anything to do with real life—or real romance." It was a sad end for a fascinating comics genre.          **J.B.**

**ROOM AND BOARD**  In an effort to make certain that their proposed imitation of the very popular *Our Boarding House* panel would be a hit, Hearst's King Features hired Gene Ahern himself away from the rival NEA syndicate to draw *Room and Board.* The new feature, consisting of a daily panel and a Sunday page, began in 1936 and lasted until 1953. But it failed ever to come anywhere near Ahern's original feature in either circulation or revenue.

The title was taken over from a failed and unrelated King panel that Sals Bostwick had done a few years earlier. The inhabitants of Ahern's latest rooming establishment he borrowed, modifying them slightly, from his *Our Boarding House.* The longtime star of Ahern's earlier work was Major Hoople, an ingratiating braggart much given to procrastination, laziness, and sloth. Heading up the cast of *Room and Board* was Judge Puffle, yet another version of the harrumphing windbag. Initially the judge was somewhat different in appearance from the Major, having a smaller nose and a different sort of mustache and wearing a beret instead of a disreputable fez. After a few years, however, he became a dead ringer for Ahern's original windbag—except for the beret. He was, like Hoople, a champion producer of mouth noises and mutters—e.g., um, awp, drat. And he never ran out of tall tales—"Um...Duncan...did I ever tell you about 'Old Oscar,' a giant tree in Montana?"

In the daily, laid out like a single-strip panel, Ahern went in for continuity of sorts, usually involving some prank worked up by the boarders to deflate the judge or detailing, at a leisurely pace, one of the judge's get-rich-quick schemes.

Sharing the Sunday page was the topper *The Squirrel Cage.* Another of Ahern's nonsense epics in the vein of *The Nut Bros.*, it introduced a little bearded hitchhiker who never tired of asking the question, "Nov shmoz ka pop?" **R.G.**

**ROSS, RUSSELL**   See JANE ARDEN.

**ROY POWERS, EAGLE SCOUT**   Touted as the "official story of the Boy Scouts of America," this daily strip was launched in the spring of 1937 by the Ledger Syndicate of Philadelphia. The first daily introduced Roy as "17 years old and a leader of boys," and explained that the new feature was going to provide "the thrilling adventure story of Roy Powers and the Beaver Patrol. Produced with the official consent and cooperation of the Boy Scouts of America."

*Roy Powers* was credited to Paul Powell, but was actually the handiwork of writer Paul Roberts and a succession of Ledger staff artists. During his several years as an Eagle Scout, Roy's adventures were illuminated by Kemp Starrett, Frank Godwin, Jimmy Thompson, and Charles Coll. The longest term of service was put in by Godwin, who took over early in 1938, but who, since he was also drawing *Connie* at the time, never signed his name to the Boy Scout strip. Godwin nevertheless did some very impressive work on it.

Roy was a tall, handsome lad, in the Charles Dana Gibson hero tradition, who had the requisite fat friend—this one named Chunky. Never hindered by obligations to school or family, Roy Powers and Chunky roamed the world the whole year round. They hunted lions in Africa and tackled crazed inventors and airline highjackers closer to home. This was very much a boy's strip, probably intended for kids a few years younger than Roy. While there was a good deal of action and camaraderie, there were practically no girls—which must have been a disappointment to Godwin whose specialty, after horses, was certainly pretty women.

The strip, which never had a large list of papers, came to an end in the early 1940s. *Roy Powers* was reprinted, at the rate of four or five pages of dailies per issue, in the *Famous Funnies* comic book from #38 (September 1937) through #115 (February 1944).   **R.G.**

**RUSTY RILEY**   Frank Godwin's final comic strip, it was introduced by King Features in 1948 and lasted for over a decade. *Rusty Riley* dealt with the adventures of a redheaded adolescent boy caught up in the world of horse racing and horse raising. Godwin, who'd previously done *Connie* and *Roy Powers*, drew with his usual illustrational verve, and Rod Reed, a comic book veteran, provided the scripts, although Godwin spent considerable time developing the feature before Reed became involved, submitting at least two earlier versions to the syndicate.

Undoubtedly one of the most gifted pen and ink artists ever to work in comics, Godwin could draw anything and was especially good with animals. *Rusty Riley*, a daily and Sunday feature, began in January 1948. Rusty was another of the long line of plucky orphans who served as central figures in strips, movies, and dime novels for most of the century. His favorite expressions were "Gee whiz!" and "Golly!" and his burning ambition was to be a jockey.

The early continuities involved him with the world of horsebreeding and racing, allowing him to meet rich ne'er-do-wells who scorned him, crooks who tried to corrupt him, and a few decent folks who befriended him. Godwin illustrated all this in masterful fashion, like someone providing real gold settings for dime store gems. In later years the strip moved away from horses fairly often to involve its innocent hero in a wider range of activities, all of them guaranteed to put him in jeopardy.

*Rusty Riley* was appearing in over 150 newspapers when it ended in 1959, the year Godwin died of a heart attack at his home in New Hope, Pennsylvania. **W.D.**

# S

**THE SAD SACK**  The quintessential born loser, Sad Sack started out during World War II. He first appeared in a raunchy pantomime strip that soldier George Baker drew for *Yank*, the servicemen's weekly magazine. He moved into a civilian Sunday page in the postwar years, and then became the somewhat unlikely star of a whole string of kids' comic books.

For a character whose name derived from the popular Army slang expression "a sad sack of shit," his later career is somewhat surprising. In his initial incarnation Sad Sack was the personification of the hapless draftee, and the pages that Baker drew showed his unhappy encounters with the brass, fellow soldiers, prostitutes, and other perils and perplexities of wartime service life. Popular with GIs from the start, the *Sad Sack* strips were reprinted for the civilian population in both newspapers and books.

In 1946 the Bell Syndicate introduced a *Sad Sack* Sunday page. Baker and his hero were both civilians now, and the humor was toned down considerably. There was a bitterness in the strip, too, and the civilian world that Sad Sack wandered silently through was full of crooks, conmen, and conniving women. The page faltered and faded away after a few years.

The Harvey company brought out its first *Sad Sack* comic book in the summer of 1949. Originally Sad Sack was a civilian, but in the spring of 1951 he reinlisted in the service. "Back in the Army," proclaimed the cover. The return to uniform gave the character a significant boost, and he became a bestseller—not with servicemen but with preteen and early teenage boys. The new stories were not pantomime, and Baker had little to do with them. He did, however, draw the covers.

The original title lasted until 1982 and inspired a number of others, including *Sad Sack and Sarge, Sad Sack Laugh Special*, and *Sad Sack's Army Life*. For a while there was even a female counterpart named Sadie Sack. The chief artist on the Sad Sack comic books from 1953 onward was the unsung Fred Rhoads, an ex-Marine who'd drawn for the *Leatherneck* magazine during the Second World War.                                        **R.G.**

**SAGENDORF, BUD** (1915–  )  He started his association with Popeye in the early 1930s, when he became assistant to E.C. Segar on *Thimble Theatre*. Sagendorf has been involved with the spinach-eating sailor, off and on, ever since. He officially took over the newspaper strip, daily and Sunday, in 1958, and he still produces the Sunday page.

Forrest C. Sagendorf was born in Wenatchee, Washington, and grew up in Southern California. "At the age of seven, I started wanting to be a cartoonist...I decided at a very early age that it was easier to learn to draw than to learn to spell," he once said. He was encouraged in his drawing by his mother and his older sister, who happened to work in the stationery store where Segar bought his art supplies. The sister introduced her younger brother to the cartoonist. "He invited me up to his house to talk cartooning," Sagendorf has recalled. "When I went to see him I was wearing my leather jacket with Popeye on the back and he was amazed that I could get 25 cents apiece, in the depths of the Depression, for drawing this."

Soon after, Segar was taking a trip East and asked the young Sagendorf to help out for three weeks. The assignment soon became full-time. Segar was an outdoorsman, and the two often came up with gags for the strip while out fishing or hunting.

After Segar's death in 1938, King Features Syndicate brought Sagendorf to New York. They gave him a job in the bullpen, but considered him too young to assume the responsibility of *Thimble Theatre*. That assignment went first to Doc Winner and then to Bela Zaboly. Sagendorf helped out with the newspaper strip now and then, but didn't become the full-time artist (and writer) until 1958. Starting in 1946, though, he drew the original-material *Popeye* comic books for Dell and was allowed to sign them. His association with comic books had begun several years earlier, when he helped put together strip reprint titles, among them *King Comics*, and *Ace Comics*. He also drew a few fillers for early funny books.

His style is obviously derived from Segar's, although Sagendorf now draws larger heads and uses more closeups than his mentor did, because of the shrinking format. He always works with a hard-tip pen, unlike many of today's artists who prefer a felt-tip.

Early in 1986 Sagendorf turned over the daily strip to Bobby London, although he continues to draw the Sunday. In addition, he's illustrated several children's books and invented toys and games, including Popeye Golf. A railroading buff, he also drew a short-lived strip called *Spur Line* in the middle 1950s. **W.D.**

**THE SAINT** Simon Templar, the Robin Hood of modern crime, first came along in 1928 in Leslie Charteris' novel *Meet the Tiger*. In the 1930s and 1940s the enterprising Charteris managed to have his character translated into several other media, including movies, radio, and comic books. *The Saint* began as a daily strip in September of 1948, adding a Sunday page the next year.

The continuities on the newspaper strip were written by Charteris himself. The first artist was Mike Roy, a comic book graduate who had ghosted the *Sub-Mariner* and done quite a bit of true crime work in a style that was reminiscent of Dan Barry's. The quality of his work fluctuated, being somewhat dependent on his inkers. The best period on *The Saint* occurred when Jack Davis served in that capacity.

The first week of the strip showed Templar and his lowbrow sidekick, Hoppy Uniatz, rescuing a little girl from kidnappers. This segued into a sequence about a fat villain named Jolly Joe who was running a protection racket with nightclub showgirls. The girls who didn't cooperate got acid in the face. At story's end Jolly Joe was shot with his own acid gun, after the Saint rigged it to backfire. Charteris varied his continuities, using spoiled heiresses who were being victimized by hoodlums, searches for pirate gold, stolen chemical-biological weapons, foreign intrigues in mythical kingdoms, and so on.

When Mike Roy departed the strip in 1951, John Spranger stepped in. He modified his style for the new job, moving away from the Eisner influence he'd shown on *Bodyguard*. Later on in the Fifties he gave the Saint, who'd first appeared as a clean-shaven chap, a rather satanic Vandyke beard. Spranger stayed on until 1959, and then, following a few weeks of ghosting by Bob Lubbers, the strip was turned over to Doug Wildey. Gil Kane had been picked to carry on after Wildey, but the Herald Tribune Syndicate decided the strip's diminishing list of papers didn't make it worth continuing, and it folded in the early 1960s.

The Saint's career in comic books was somewhat shorter, beginning in 1939 with the character's appearance in DC's short-lived *Movie Comics*. In the second issue, along with adaptations of *Stagecoach* and other films, readers were treated to a wretched *fumetti* version of *The Saint Strikes Back*, using stills from the George Sanders B-movie and badly lettered balloons.

The Saint made his true comic book debut, in real comics format, in 1942 in *Silver Streak Comics* #18. "At last! At great expense, the publishers of *Silver Streak* bring you the most sensational find in the history of comics!" proclaimed a blurb accompanying the first story. Readers were further informed that "Simon Templar, better known as the Saint—the Twentieth Century's gayest buccaneer, the modern Robin Hood—hero of a thousand adventures, is now fighting his own war against the Nazis." Hoppy was along, as well as Patricia Holm, Templar's longtime ladyfriend—described here as his "lovely, reckless, resourceful assistant."

Charteris got a credit in letters over half an inch high and seems actually to have written the scripts. Art was by Edd Ashe Jr. Simon Templar and company added a touch of class and a bit of sophistication to what had been chiefly a hangout for superheroes. But the magazine closed down with its 21st issue.

Avon brought out a Saint comic book in 1947. This used original stories in the early numbers and then switched to strip reprints. Jack Kamen provided the cover for the first issue. Rather sporadically issued, it got through but a dozen issues before folding in 1952. **R.G.**

**SALESMAN SAM** A pioneering screwball strip with a Jazz Age go-getter as its central character, *Salesman Sam* began on September 26, 1921. George Swanson, who always signed his work Swan, was the original perpetrator. The strip was syndicated by NEA, who also employed Gene Ahern and, briefly, Bill Holman, and who seemed to have a fondness for the sort of slapstick lunacy purveyed in Swan's strip. (The preferred spelling of the title, by the way, was with dollar signs in place of the S's—$alesman $am.)

Sam Howdy was a lean, bespectacled young man, full of the self-confidence and vim that was a hallmark of the Roaring Twenties salesman. Unfortunately, he wasn't too bright, and his lack of intelligence brought more trouble than triumph into his life. The feature, which added a Sunday page late in 1922, went in for the joke-a-day format most of the time. But Swan wasn't content simply with telling old jokes. No doubt influenced by the one- and two-reel comedies of the silver screen, he enjoyed showing his characters walking through brick walls, falling through plate glass windows, disappearing down manholes, and getting bopped with an assortment of heavy objects. Sam, and his eventual boss J. Guzzlem, did reaction takes that put any and all silent comedy actors to shame. They flew out of their shoes, executed backward somersaults, fell flat amid clouds of dust and debris. The decor of the strip was also very busy. Guzzlem ran a general store, and Sam was his chief salesman, which allowed for a wide variety of silly signs to be posted on walls and

counters, and all sorts of products to be dropped, broken, and fallen into.

Swanson was lured away from NEA in 1927 and started producing a similar strip called *High Pressure Pete*. C.D. Small, a sometime magazine cartoonist, succeeded him and drew Sam in a very close imitation of his predecessor. The reaction takes grew, if possible, even more exuberant, and the clutter of funny signs increased: "Assorted golf and meat balls," "Assorted marbles and jelly beans," "Apples 50¢ a bushel—don't peck at 'em." In addition to the gags, there were occasional continuity sequences, with Sam playing on a local amateur baseball team or going on an expedition to a remote spot. The strip ended in September of 1936.

**R.G.**

**SALLY THE SLEUTH**   Sally, a blond lady detective noted chiefly for doing her best work while clad only in her lingerie or less, first appeared in a two-page comics-format filler in the steamy pages of the *Spicy Detective* pulp magazine in 1934, where she remained until the magazine ended in 1942. She then carried on for a while in its successor, *Speed Detective*. From 1950 to 1953 Sally returned as one of the stars of a comic book entitled *Crime Smashers*. The artist throughout was Adolphe Barreaux, who drew in a simple, effective cartoony style and always signed his real name to the strip.

*Spicy Detective's* first issue was dated April 1934, and *Sally the Sleuth* began there in the second number. The pulp fiction magazine, published by some of the same people who would later offer Superman and Batman to the world, featured hard-boiled and moderately risqué private eye yarns. Dan Turner, Hollywood Detective, was the pulpwood's star gumshoe, while comics format Sally was sort of a plainclothes cop who worked for a fellow known as the Chief. "Her plain clothes," as *The*

*Dime Detectives* points out, "didn't stay on her long, since Sally lost most of her outer garments in just about every investigation. Villains never ran out of plausible-sounding reasons for ordering her to 'take off those clothes—or I'll tear them off!' Her standard working outfit, therefore, was usually bra and panties. One spy case ends with her holding up her underwear to an FBI agent who's asked for the whereabouts of the missing formula. Sally explains, 'You'll find it written in invisible ink on the trimming of my panties.' She also got tied up a lot." Because Sally's cases were presented in comic book format, she can be considered a pioneer of sorts. The first regular, original-material comic books—*New Fun* and *New Comics*—didn't get going until 1935, the year after her debut.

Civic pressures eventually forced *Spicy Detective* to tone down and then to become *Speed Detective* with the

January 1943 issue. "After four or five issues, Sally the Sleuth was discontinued," pulp historian Robert Sampson has written, "her fascination evidently smothered by clothing." In 1950 Sally's old publisher put out *Crime Smashers*, and she was back in business, this time in a real comic book. Fully clothed but as tough and audacious as ever, Sally still worked for the Chief, who was now the "head of a private investigation bureau." When the magazine ended in 1953, Sally retired. She was brought back in 1988, when the Eternity Comics company reprinted a sampling of her early pulp adventures in their *Spicy Tales* comic book. **R.G.**

**SAM'S STRIP** A comic strip addressed specifically to the comics buff, *Sam's Strip* demonstrated that the genre had reached a level of maturity where it could examine and spoof itself. Drawn by Jerry Dumas and written by Dumas and Mort Walker, it was perhaps too rarefied to command a large popular audience, and King Features Syndicate, which distributed it from its inception in October 1961, never sold it to more than 60 papers. They brought it to an end in June 1963, when its circulation had fallen to 48.

The strip featured Sam, a goofy-looking figure who, with an unnamed assistant, owned and operated the strip itself as a territory. It was peopled with characters from other strips, classic and current, all skillfully drawn in the styles of their original artists. Pogo and Happy Hooligan, Popeye and Krazy Kat, Snuffy Smith and the Yellow Kid, all mingled freely, discussed the formulae and conventions of the medium, and reminisced about its golden age. The existential premise—that it is possible simultaneously to be a comic strip and to be *about* being a comic strip—was unique to *Sam's*, and it was perhaps inevitable that it would prove too recondite for the general public. Dumas recalled an educated friend demanding an explanation of how Blondie could appear in his strip and be in her own at the same time.

In 1977 Dumas and Walker resurrected Sam and his pal (now named Silo) as a pair of small-town Keystone Kops, but *Sam and Silo* is not *Sam's Strip*. That highly sophisticated inside joke belongs to the ages. **D.W.**

**THE SANDMAN** One of the earliest costumed crimefighters in comic books, the Sandman began his career in *Adventure Comics* #40 (July 1939). He was a mystery man in the tradition of the Shadow, the Spider, and the Green Hornet: By day he was millionaire playboy Wesley Dodds, but by night he donned green business suit, slouch hat, gas mask, and cape. He used a gas gun of his own invention to put crooks and criminal masterminds to sleep—hence his name. Unlike some of his colleagues, Dodds didn't pretend to be a milksop when out of costume, and he enjoyed his wealth, driving a fast car and frequenting night clubs and ritzy social affairs. He was usually in the company of lovely brunette Dian Belmont, who knew his identity but never tipped off her father, the district attorney.

Writer Gardner Fox and artist Bert Christman shared the Larry Dean pen name attached to the earliest stories, and Ogden Whitney, Creig Flessel, and Chad Grothkopf drew the Sandman through his first two years. During this period he was pretty much a pulp magazine avenger in comic book form. But in the autumn of 1941, after a convivial evening meeting, DC editor Whit Ellsworth and Chad decided the character ought to look more like Superman and Batman, and *Adventure* #69 (December 1941) showed the new improved Sandman, complete with yellow tunic and tights, purple trunks, cowl, and cape and a sidekick named Sandy the Golden Boy. Paul Norris drew the next two episodes, and then Joe Simon and Jack Kirby took over, giving him the same slambang action treatment they'd developed for Captain America, using lively layouts and fantasy plots that usually dealt with dreams and nightmares. Sandman, who'd taken a backseat to such latterday *Adventure* heroes as Hourman and Starman, became the leading man again, and he remained so until he and Sandy retired in 1946.

Over the years DC has both reprinted and revived him, in both gas mask and golden tights modes. He seems to be defunct once again, but perhaps he only sleeps. **R.G.**

**SANSONE, LEONARD** (1917–1956) The most successful feature Sansone ever drew was *The Wolf*, the popular panel about the lusty, lupine soldier that appeared in nearly 1,600 service newspapers during World War II. Before entering the Army Sansone drew for an assortment of comic books, and after returning to civilian life he did a newspaper panel and a comic strip.

Born in New England, Sansone studied for four years at the Massachusetts School of Art in Boston. There he met Ben Flinton and Bill O'Connor, and in the late 1930s the three came to New York looking for work as artists. Initially things didn't go well for them. "We were literally kept from starving by some kind soul in an all night hamburger joint," Sansone once recalled, "who was very generous in giving us the burgers on credit until we got going." Finally FOS, as they signed themselves, were hired by the Funnies, Inc., shop and their work started appearing in *Mystic Comics* and *Blue Bolt*. Sansone, who was the inker in the group, also did some solo drawing for *Thrilling Comics* and *Startling Comics*. All of this was adventure stuff. Without Sansone, Flinton and O'Connor created the original Atom for DC.

A month after the Pearl Harbor attack, Sansone was in the Army. While stationed at Fort Belvoir in Virginia he started drawing his Wolf panel for the camp magazine. It was soon picked up by the Camp Newspaper Service, and Sergeant Sansone got stationed in Manhattan. He carried his hero into civilian life after the war, but the panel wasn't a hit. It eventually turned into a kid comic strip titled *Willie*, which Sansone was still doing at the time of his death. **R.G.**

**SAUNDERS, ALLEN** (1899–1986) He was one of the most accomplished writers in the comic strip field, scripting *Mary Worth*, *Steve Roper*, and *Kerry Drake*. Saunders had also written *Big Chief Wahoo*, and *Dan Dunn*, and earlier in his career he had been a reporter, drama critic, pulp fiction writer, and cartoonist. The soap opera strip, a genre that flourished for several decades, was largely his invention.

Born in Indiana, Saunders was interested from boyhood in both writing and drawing. He took a Landon mail-order course in cartooning in his youth and later journeyed to Chicago to study at the Academy of Fine Arts. After graduating from Wabash College in his home state, he took a job there as a teacher of French. On the side he sold cartoons and pulp magazine stories. It was in 1927 that Saunders entered journalism, joining the *Toledo News-Bee* as a reporter-cartoonist. A meeting with Elmer Woggon, artist for a rival Toledo newspaper, eventually led to their creating *Big Chief Wahoo* in 1936. Saunders wrote it, Woggon drew it. The strip caught on, especially after the addition of the heroic Steve Roper.

In the late 1930s Publishers Syndicate, for whom he was doing *Wahoo*, asked Saunders to take over as writer on *Apple Mary*. He accepted, even though he felt "soap opera just wasn't my field." After he had been on the job for a while, it occurred to him that "no strip was making a serious effort to offer the sort of fiction dealing with the emotional problems of average people, stories that might interest a reader of the day's magazines for women." By renovating the feature, making it slicker and more sophisticated, Saunders succeeded in reaching a larger audience, the same audience that was buying *The Ladies' Home Journal* and *Cosmopolitan* and weeping over the latest Bette Davis or Joan Crawford movie at the neighborhood cinema. He'd already learned how to make readers come back the next day on *Big Chief Wahoo*; now Saunders found he could also do it not with adventure cliffhangers but with romantic tangles and emotional dilemmas. The strip, drawn by Dale Conner Ulrey and then Ken Ernst, became *Mary Worth's Family* and then just plain *Mary Worth*. A bestseller among strips, it inspired several imitators.

Some of them, such as *Rex Morgan, M.D.* and *Judge Parker*, Saunders had a hand in developing.

During the 1940s he also wrote the final years of the *Dan Dunn* detective opus and then created its successor, *Kerry Drake*. Artist Alfred Andriola, as specified in the contract he insisted on, took sole credit for the new detective strip. This rankled Saunders over the years, and he and the self-promoting little artist never became close chums.

Saunders retired officially in 1979, "bowing under the weight of some minor, but annoying, infirmities and growing pressure from the syndicate." His son, John Saunders, who'd been helping out with the scripts for several years, took over completely. Saunders, not especially elated at the prospect of no longer writing for a living, observed, "Retirement years are, I suspect, golden only for those who have long established hobbies such as tending gardens or carving wooden whistles." **R.G.**

**SCADUTO, AL** (1928– ) The long-time assistant to Bob Dunn, Scaduto assumed the total production of *They'll Do It Every Time*, daily and Sunday, after Dunn's death in January 1989. The two had been teamed for 41 years.

Scaduto draws in the classic bigfoot style. "I was influenced primarily by Jimmy Hatlo, Bob Dunn and the old greats—*Krazy Kat, Barney Google, Bringing Up Father*," he has said. His first important artistic influence was his father, who drew as a hobby and encouraged his son's drawing.

Alvaro Frank Scaduto was born in the Bronx, and attended high school at the School of Industrial Art in Manhattan where he majored in cartooning. He also took courses at the Art Students League. After graduating from high school in 1946, with an award in cartooning, Scaduto went right into a job in the comic art department at King Features Syndicate. "I worked in the bullpen," he's recalled. He did promotional art for the King comics, filled in when needed on various strips, and did corrections, mostly spelling; as he put it, "Cartoonists aren't the best spellers."

In 1948 cartoonist Bob Dunn invited Scaduto to assist him on the *They'll Do It Every Time* panel. Scaduto also drew the comic book versions of *Little Iodine* for 14 years and did the Sunday Iodine page for many years. After Jimmy Hatlo's death in 1963, Dunn continued writing *They'll Do It Every Time*, which was based on ideas submitted by readers. Scaduto drew the panel from Dunn's roughs. Since 1989 Scaduto has written and drawn the feature.

He and Dunn were honored in 1979, when their panel was picked by the National Cartoonist Society as that year's best panel. In his free-lance work Scaduto has illustrated children's books, designed greeting cards, toys, and toy packaging; he has also drawn cartoons and illustrations for advertising. He's had a lifelong interest in opera, and his studio is crowded with his record collection.                                    **W.D.**

**SCHMIDT, CHARLIE**   See RADIO PATROL.

**SCHOMBURG, ALEX** (1905– )   When it comes to the drawing of comic book covers, Schomburg is the undisputed champ. Throughout the 1940s, working for Marvel and several other publishers, he produced some of the liveliest and most imaginative covers ever to grace funny books. He was a master of controlled clutter, the Hieronymus Bosch of comics. His flamboyant cover drawings were packed with dozens of figures, weapons, infernal machines, and enough action for a dozen or more of his competitors' efforts.

Born in Puerto Rico, he came to the United States when he was seven. He was interested in art from childhood, as were several other members of his family, and in the early 1920s he and three of his brothers opened a commercial art shop in New York City. Later in the decade Schomburg worked for an art service specializing in movie promotion art. It was there he mastered the airbrush, one of the trademarks of many of his comic book covers of the late 1940s. By the 1930s he was doing magazine covers for several houses and interior illustrations for such pulp fiction magazines as *Thrilling Detective* and *Startling Stories*. As the 1940s commenced, he branched out and started doing comic book covers. Among his earliest clients were Timely (which is what Marvel was calling itself then) and Standard Magazines.

His most memorable efforts were for Timely in the years just before and during World War II. Schomburg became an expert at depicting the Human Torch, Sub-Mariner, and Captain America, singly or as a team, in the most complicated and improbable situations. His spectacular and intricate covers appeared on *Human Torch, All Winners, Young Allies, Marvel Mystery Comics,* and *USA Comics*, among others.

There was usually no single center of attention on one of his bright, ambitious covers. They were more like three-ring circuses, with Sub-Mariner pulling down a bridge and causing Nazi troops and tanks to go plummeting into a ravine in one corner, the Human Torch saving Bucky from being fed to a blast furnace in another, and Cap parachuting down and blasting away at a dozen or so hooded Japanese with a tripod machine gun. His covers were for browsing over, loaded as they were with bizarre weapons, fiendish engines, and unsettling perils about to befall Toro, Bucky, helpless females, and brave soldiers, sailors, and marines. With his

bravura style, and meticulous patience, Schomburg always managed to convince readers that all the action and noise he'd jammed into a cover might actually be occurring in that single frozen second of time.

For magazines like *Thrilling Comics, America's Best Comics*, and *Green Hornet Comics* he illustrated equally complex situations involving such heroes as the Black Terror, Pyroman, Doc Strange, the Commando Cubs, and the Fighting Yank. He never worked directly inside a publishing office. "I had my own small studio over on Eighth Avenue and Forty-fourth Street," he once explained. "I seldom submitted pencil roughs. They bought sight unseen, just as long as the Japs showed their ugly teeth and glasses and the Nazis looked like bums." It took him about a week to do a cover, and the pay rate was usually $40 each. After World War II he used the pen name Xela on most of his Standard covers. Many of these were simple and uncluttered, more posterlike, and done in airbrush technique. On these he rendered such characters as Princess Pantha, Jann of the Jungle, and Brick Bradford.

Schomburg left comics in the early 1950s, returning to illustration work for such science fiction magazines as *Amazing Stories* and, later, *Isaac Asimov's*. He has also done a series of paintings recreating some of his memorable wartime covers in all their intricacy.   **R.G.**

**SCHULTZE, CARL EDWARD**   See FOXY GRANDPA.

**SCHULZ, CHARLES** (1922– )   The artist and writer of *Peanuts* became one of the richest men in America by using his childhood insecurities and failures as material for his comic strip. Charlie Brown, the strip's likable loser, shares more than a first name with his creator and was inspired by Schulz' bittersweet memories of his Midwestern boyhood.

Charles Monroe Schulz was born in Minneapolis. His father, like Charlie Brown's, was a barber. Schulz' parents nicknamed him Sparky, after the racehorse Spark Plug in one of his favorite newspaper strips, *Barney Google*. He read the funnies avidly, copying all the characters he was fond of, especially those in Segar's *Thimble Theatre* and Percy Crosby's *Skippy*.

Schulz skipped two grades in school, but still had to struggle with his studies. He wasn't very good at sports, felt he was awkward, had a bad complexion, and was shy with girls. Schulz still has painful memories of having his cartoons rejected by the high school yearbook.

While still in school he started taking the Art Instruction Schools correspondence course in cartooning. During World War II he served in the Army and was sent to Europe. On his return he got a job with his old correspondence school and stayed there five years. He also became a letterer for *Topix*, a religious comic book. In his spare time the determined Schulz sent gag cartoons to magazines, collecting a large quantity of rejection slips before he succeeded in selling a cartoon to *The Saturday Evening Post* in 1948.

That same year he started drawing a feature titled *Li'l Folks* for the *St. Paul Pioneer Press*. It ran for two years, and in 1950, after repeated "mailbox rejections" of the sort that Snoopy the budding author still suffers, he sold *Peanuts* to United Features. It has gone on to become the most widely read comic strip in the world, appearing daily in some 2,200 papers. It has inspired animated cartoons, a Broadway show, innumerable toys, and reprint books that have sold over 300 million copies. In addition, Schulz and his syndicate, who split all profits, have licensed the use of the Peanuts gang to a multitude of advertisers over the years.

*Forbes*, the business magazine, has estimated that Schulz is one of the 10 richest entertainers in the country, with an income in 1987–1988 of $62 million. In 1987 he was inducted into the Cartoonist Hall of Fame, and he has twice won the National Cartoonists Society Reuben Award. He has lived in Northern California for many years and draws *Peanuts* from his studio in Santa Rosa. **W.D.**

**SCORCHY SMITH** A very influential adventure strip, *Scorchy Smith* began modestly in 1930, one of the Associated Press' initial batch of low-budget daily strips. It was about aviation and was drawn by an assortment of artists during its 30 years in the air, among them some of the best illustrative cartoonists, including Frank Robbins and Noel Sickles.

It started in the spring of 1930, in the days before the airplane was taken for granted as just another means of transportation, even before most of the world had heard much about fighter planes and bombers. Back 60 years ago there was an enormous interest in aviation, triggered in good part by the exploits of daredevil flyers like Charles A. Lindbergh. People were eager to follow the topic in newspapers and magazines and in all the entertainment media.

*Scorchy Smith* was created by John Terry, a former animator and political cartoonist, and the brother of animator Paul Terry. Despite the clumsy quality of the strip, it attracted readers and client papers. By the end of 1933, when Terry was forced away from the drawing board by tuberculosis, the strip was AP's top seller. Not wishing to tamper with it, the feature editor looked around the art department for somebody to ghost the strip until Terry recuperated. He picked Noel Sickles, then in his middle twenties, who was doing political cartoons and general art in the bullpen. At the time he accepted the assignment, Sickles, who'd gotten his AP

berth through his longtime friend Milton Caniff, didn't have a very high opinion of the hero he'd been handed or of John Terry's work. "It was the worst drawing I had ever seen by anybody," he once said.

Gritting his teeth, the young Sickles imitated his predecessor as best he could and signed John Terry to the strips. The very first one ran in some 200 papers across the country on Monday, December 4, 1933. Actually it wasn't a very good job of ghosting, since Sickles was so much better an artist that even his attempted impersonation was a vast improvement. Terry was never able to come back to the feature and at his death in 1934, Sickles was allowed to sign his own name, but cautioned not to change the overall look of the strip too swiftly. "Within the next six months," he has said, "I had to decide how I wanted to do it." His decision turned the newspaper strip field upside down.

What he began to develop was the impressionistic, lushly black style that his friend Caniff later adapted for *Terry and the Pirates*. By the early 1940s, the impact of the style was such that half the straight strips in the country were trying to imitate it.

All of Sickles' work of those years shows an excitement and a love of drawing. He was able to draw anything—a New York street scene, stretches of jungle, a beautifully staged aerial dogfight that stretched across a week. He was a master at conveying attitude, and he possessed a very good sense of time and place. He could suggest the intense light and heat of a desert noon, the shadows of a jungle twilight, the feel of a big city in the early morning. He brought to the strip a kind of 1930s lyricism, a combined affection for the pastoral and the mechanical.

Scorchy Smith himself had begun as a lanky lad, very much in the Lindbergh mold. Sickles never much liked him, and he turned him into a more mature fellow and less of a mooncalf. He added several characters of his own; one of the most notable was Himmelstoss, a German ex-World War I flyer who was briefly a villain before becoming Scorchy's friend and sidekick. An admirer of Von Richthofen, Sickles saw Heinie Himmelstoss as a man who might have been a friend of the Red Baron. In the autumn of 1935 he introduced his version of the Jean Harlow-Carole Lombard brassy blonde; her name was Mickey, and Scorchy and Heinie met her while adventuring in Canada. She was tough enough to hold her own with the timber pirates, gold diggers, and crazed Arabs that she and her pals ran into while journeying around the globe. A year later Mickey and Himmelstoss decided to get married and they dropped out of the strip forever, while Scorchy flew on alone to yet another South American adventure.

That Brazilian plantation sequence would be Sickles' last. He was growing tired of the strip and of the Associated Press. He was, as always, putting in 12-hour days at the drawing board and his salary was far too low. Since he had some money saved, he decided to quit. At the end of 1936 his name no longer appeared on the strip.

His replacement was from the AP bullpen, a young man named Bert Christman. He and Sickles knew each other, though not well, and they never met again after Sickles left AP. At first Christman's work on *Scorchy* had a shaky, borrowed look, but he soon developed an effective style of his own, marked by his skill at depicting the planes and other gadgets so essential to the strip. Christman stayed with the strip only a year and a half. *Scorchy Smith* then spent a prosaic 10 months with Howell Dodd, another staffer. Dodd, who later became a successful magazine illustrator, didn't want to do the strip at all, and he absolutely refused to write it. During his hitch the scripts were provided by comics editor Frank Reilly.

Fortunately another exploitable young man came along in the person of 22-year-old Frank Robbins. Through a free-lance scriptwriter named Bob Farrell, Robbins learned AP was looking for someone to keep the faltering Scorchy aloft. With Farrell's help on the writing, he prepared a week's samples. The samples impressed the Associated Press, as did, no doubt, the fact that he was young and would work cheap. Robbins got the job, and his first daily appeared on May 22, 1939. Farrell stayed on as writer for eight months, and thereafter Robbins took over the entire production.

During his first months Robbins seemed a bit unsure of himself, especially in the important area of depicting airplanes. By the time Scorchy got into the Air Force in 1942 Robbins had everything under control and was drawing in a highly individual, impressionistic style of his own. In *The Comics* Coulton Waugh said of one of the wartime sequences: "Robbins' Russia has a formidable reality; it creates the sense of deep snows, it is full of bitter, bloody struggle."

Early in 1944 King Features lured Robbins away. In its early years his *Johnny Hazard* was a virtual twin of *Scorchy Smith*, and it's easy to see that Scorchy would have had a better time had Robbins stuck with him. From 1944 a succession of other artists worked on the strip. Some, such as Edmond Good and George Tuska, were good; others, like Rodlow Willard, unsuited. And some, particularly Milt Morris who saw *Scorchy Smith* to its final resting place, were terrible. When the strip folded in 1960, its great days were long behind it.

**R.G.**

**SCOTT, WALT** (1894–1970) A cartoonist with a definite gift for whimsy and fantasy, Scott did his best work on *The Little People*, a Sunday page that ran from 1952 until his death. In the 1940s, in a more serious vein, he drew the *Captain Easy* Sunday page and ghosted the lesser-known *Biff Baker*. Scott also worked as an animator for the Disney studios and once even drew a newspaper strip based on the life of Christ.

Born in Sandusky, Ohio, Scott became a printer's devil after graduating from high school. In his spare time he studied art, and in 1916 he moved to Cleveland in search of a career. After working in engraving houses and for ad agencies, he got a job in the art department of the Cleveland *Press* and then moved to the *Plain Dealer* for a 13-year stay. During these years some of Scott's work got syndicated, including an Easter season series of strips about the life of Jesus.

The NEA syndicate was also in Cleveland, and Scott went to work for them in the middle 1930s. Then, when "California called in the form of Walt Disney," Scott relocated in the West for five years and worked as an animator. When Roy Crane left NEA for King Features in 1943, Scott returned to Cleveland and NEA to draw the Sunday *Captain Easy*. He'd developed a cartoony style of drawing adventure, going in for odd angles and bold inking. His Easy didn't look like Crane's nor like the fellow Leslie Turner was drawing in the daily *Wash Tubbs* strip. Scott stayed with the Captain until August 1952. During the war years he drew the *Biff Baker* Sunday page as well, assuming the Henry Lee pen name from Hank Schlensker when the latter went into the Air Force.

His Little People first appeared in 1951 in an NEA Christmas strip. Tiny elfin folk, they lived in a magical woodland. The Sunday page started in 1952, while Scott was still drawing *Easy*, and brought out facets of his talent that hadn't been evident in his more serious work. There was a knack for drawing fantasy creatures, an ability to do impressive landscapes and a gift for humor and gentleness. The year after the page began, Dell started issuing an occasional *Little People* one-shot in their four-color series. Ten of these were done from 1953 to 1959, most using original material drawn by Scott and two devoted to Christmas stories.

**R.G.**

**SCRIBBLY** The boy cartoonist, who began his career before a single superhero had trod a funny book page, survived longer than many of those who came in the wake of Superman. *Scribbly*, created by Sheldon Mayer when he was 19 and still a boy cartoonist himself, began in the second issue of *The Funnies* (dated November 1936). Along with *Popular Comics* and the later book *The Comics*, the magazine was essentially a 64-page compilation of newspaper strip reprints produced by M.C. Gaines and edited by Mayer for Dell.

"Scribbly was a thing I dreamed up during my lunch hour one day in a noisy cafeteria," Mayer has said. "I followed the old rule of writing only what you know about. What was more natural than writing about the adventures of a boy cartoonist?" The feature was drawn in a style that was appealing, exuberant, and, yes, scribbly. The story, as it unfolded in the bright, crowded pages of *The Funnies*, dealt with Scribbly Jibbet, who was young, diminutive, bespectacled, and possessed of a head of hair like an untidy haystack. He was intent on breaking free of the bonds put upon him by home, school, and contemporaries, and entering the charmed world of newspaper cartooning. Mayer has maintained that the strip was a blend of autobiography and fantasy and that some of the elements that seemed most true were the most unreal. His pages mixed lower-middle-class apartment life with wacky excursions into the worlds of newspaper publishing, radio, and even Hollywood.

Scribbly stopped appearing in *The Funnies* early in 1939, and by that time Mayer was occupied elsewhere. He and Gaines had started another string of comic books, the first of which was *All-American*, and Scribbly found a home there. The early Scribbly pages were still laid out like newspaper Sundays. In *All-American* #3 Scribbly met for the first time the warm-hearted and rowdy Hunkel family, presided over by the warm-hearted and rowdy Ma Hunkel. (There really was a Ma Hunkel, and in real life Mayer had a room in her house, which he used as a studio.) His entrance into this menage was by way of Huey Hunkel, a boy of his own age who wanted to be a writer. Through the efforts of the Hunkel clan Scribbly again got a newspaper job, this time as the boy cartoonist on the *Daily Dispatch*.

In the real world, meanwhile, Mayer the editor was knee-deep in supermen—Green Lantern, the Flash, Hawkman, and others. He needed a place to comment on some of the sillier aspects of the super life, and what better place than his own *Scribbly*? Thus the Red Tornado was born. Anticipating Wonder Woman, that monumental creation of William Moulton Marston, possibly even influencing it, Mayer chose a woman to be his costumed avenger, remaking the formidable Ma Hunkel into the even more formidable Red Tornado. Actually the people in the strip never knew the true sex of the Tornado. They only knew that this bulky figure in the red flannels, bedroom slippers, cape, and inverted stew pot could be counted on to tackle all sorts of criminals from the biggest to the smallest.

Ma Hunkel first donned the stewpot in *All-American* #20 (November 1940), a mere four issues after Alan Scott had his momentous run-in with a magic lamp and became the Green Lantern. What inspired her to embark on her caped crusade was the kidnapping of Scribbly's little brother and her own small daughter, Sisty. The police seemed unable to get the kids back,

and, after Scribbly and Huey told Ma about the Green Lantern, she decided to take a hand.

By issue #23 Scribbly was sharing billing with the Tornado, and in #24 Sisty and his brother Dinky joined the act as the Cyclone Kids. A few more issues and the Red Tornado's name had swollen to twice the size of the boy cartoonist's in the title. Mayer was obviously enjoying himself with all this, kidding the dual-identity mystique and showing how someone would fare in the real world as a masked marvel. Ma Hunkel's celebrity was such that on one occasion, in *All Star* #3, she sat in with the prestigious and sobersided Justice Society of America. "I'm tellin' ya," the Red Tornado complains to the Flash, Hour Man, and the Sandman, "I've never been the same since I started battlin' crime in this crazy costume!!" Ma Hunkel continued to slip into the crazy costume for the rest of Scribbly's stay in *All-American*. And right up until the last appearance in #59 (July 1944) Scrib never quite tumbled to the fact that Ma and the kids were actually the crimestopping trio.

Scribbly came back to life once more, during the late 1940s. Superheroes were falling by the wayside, while funny animals and zany teenagers were in vogue. Mayer was much more enthusiastic about his new teenage creation, *Leave It to Binky*, done in collaboration with Bob Oksner, but he was persuaded to revive his boy cartoonist, this time in a bimonthly all his own. Once more Scrib, still wearing the sincere black suit and badly knotted tie of a Depression youth, was at the drawing board and working on a newspaper. But Mayer's heart didn't seem to be in it, and sales apparently were not impressive. Scribbly retired for good and all before the Fifties had much progressed. **R.G.**

**THE SEA HOUND** One of the least successful adventure strips ever offered by King Features Syndicate, *The Sea Hound* began in 1944 and ended in 1945. It was based on a kid's radio serial that first surfaced in 1942 and sank forever in 1948.

All the major radio characters showed up in the daily newspaper strip. The hero was handsome, stalwart Captain Silver—"few seem to know many facts about him, though his exploits and his great accomplishments and heroism are known to seafaring men everywhere." Silver commanded the Sea Hound, a ketch that sailed the seven seas in search of adventure. Also on board were Jerry, a teenager; Tex, a former cowpoke; and Kukai, who was billed as a "Chinese philosopher...the capain's oldest and most trusted friend and counselor." Rounding out the cast was Silver's clever police dog Fletcha. Linguists will note the similarity of the dog's name to the Spanish and Portuguese word for "arrow," *flecha*.

The artist on the short-lived feature was Jon L. Blummer. He had worked, very briefly, on the *Lone Ranger* strip in the late 1930s. Moving into the burgeoning comic book field, he created his best-known feature, *Hop Harrigan*, for *All-American Comics*. A dependable artist, Blummer had a lively though somewhat old-fashioned style. The continuities, credited to Fran Striker (cocreator of the Lone Ranger), were fairly simple, dealing with storms at sea, buried treasure, Nazi spies, and damsels in distress. One of the things the radio show stressed was understanding "the people of other countries," especially those of Latin America. The strip followed a similar policy, making use of South American locales. And it was the only adventure strip of the Forties to have a heroine with a name like Marie Lopez. **R.G.**

**SECRET AGENT X-9** One of America's best-known undercover men, X-9 made his newspaper debut in January of 1934. The strip was drawn by Alex Raymond and written by Dashiell Hammett. Under its original title, and the more recent one of *Secret Agent Corrigan*, the strip has continued in business for well over a half-century.

By the early 1930s Hammett was garnering considerable slick paper attention. A former Pinkerton detective, he had started writing for the pulp fiction magazines in the early 1920s. He did most of his work for *Black Mask*, and it was in that pulp that *The Maltese Falcon*—the work that introduced Sam Spade—*The Glass Key*, and his series of stories and novels about the Continental Op first appeared. His last novel, *The Thin Man*, was featured in *Redbook* in 1933. The hardcover version came out in January 1934, simultaneously with the advent of the X-9 strip.

Hammett biographer William F. Nolan has said, "Hammett combined the Op and Sam Spade in the character of X-9. He was cool, efficient, quick with a gun or a wisecrack and, like the Op, was a man without a name." Not only that, but during the first few weeks of the new strip it was even difficult to tell who X-9 was a secret agent for. Although he talks and acts like a pulp private eye when he is on a case, X-9 lives in a fashionable apartment and has a Filipino valet. When readers first met him he was lounging in his apartment wearing a silk smoking jacket. The opening continuity involved him in protecting a millionaire. There were lurking hoods, an unfaithful wife, a crooked lawyer, crooked servants, and a virginal blond niece, along with some tough dialogue: "So you think this mug that Powers called is a dick, huh? O.K., we'll take care of him."

Hammett was mixing bits and pieces of several of his old pulp stories and tossing in a little of *The Thin Man*. The police didn't seem to have any idea what sort of secret agent X-9 was either. Eventually, after Hammett had left the strip and G-men had become nationally popular, it was revealed that X-9 was with the FBI.

Alexander Gillespie Raymond started the X-9 strip just two weeks after his *Flash Gordon* Sunday page had made its first appearance. His X-9 is a handsome and lithe fellow, in the Flash Gordon mode; and many of his thugs and gunmen even give the impression they're actually male models dressed up for a costume party. His drawing never quite matched the gritty, side-of-the-mouth dialogue of the continuities.

There have been rumors in recent years that Hammett may have farmed out the writing of the strip to one or more of his less well-off *Black Mask* contemporaries. By 1935 he was off the strip. According to a magazine account at the time, Hammett was fired "when he lagged behind schedule with ideas that lacked the power of his printed work." Raymond kept on with the strip for a while, using scripts provided by Leslie Charteris, creator of the Saint. In the autumn of 1935 Raymond left, too.

As of the strip dated November 18, 1935, Charles Flanders became the artist. The hero remained the same tall, handsome fellow he had been under Raymond. He went in for double-breasted suits and trenchcoats, and he still struck fashion model poses. While the Charteris continuities were a shade lighter than those of Hammett, there was little of the devil-may-care attitude and bright dialogue to be found in the Saint stories and novels. Charteris devoted only a few months to the strip, and after his departure the author credit went to "Robert Storm."

Tired of the shifting personnel of the strip, the syndicated editors decided that at least one thing would remain constant, so they made up a writer's name to attach to *Secret Agent X-9*. The person who did most of the scripting under the Storm byline was Max Trell, a former newsman and movie scriptwriter. He'd been working as a writer, off and on, since the 1920s and had even ghosted two autobiographies for little Shirley Temple. In the 1940s he'd get a credit on the *Dick's Adventures* Sunday page.

During the Flanders-Storm period the strip finally came out and admitted that X-9 was with the FBI. His chief became a dead ringer for J. Edgar Hoover, and more sophisticated crime-fighting and detecting techniques started showing up in the stories. X-9 now relied on fingerprints and use of the FBI's lab and record facilities.

Nicholas Afonsky took over the drawing in April 1938; he was doing the *Little Annie Rooney* Sunday page at this time, and his version of X-9 had a hammy, tearjerker look. He was gone after seven months. Austin Briggs, who'd been working as Alex Raymond's assistant, next drew the strip. His X-9 was a bit less heroic in stature and more inclined to let his suits get rumpled. The continuities swung from the prosaic to the highly improbable: X-9 had to deal with a spy ring, with a lady who highjacked helium and sold it to foreign dirigibles, and with a villain named Dr. Stix who planned to sabotage the Panama Canal. Despite the wild events, the tone of the strip became less melodramatic, and there was somewhat more emphasis on character. In 1940 Briggs was assigned the new *Flash Gordon* daily and Mel Graff replaced him.

Graff felt that Trell "was doing a shoddy job on the story," and he eventually persuaded the syndicate to allow him to take over the writing. "You were supposed to love him because he wore a badge and carried a gun. He never fell in love," Graff explained in the middle 1940s. "I'm changing all that…Also, I've finally given the guy a name. After all, an agent who's supposed to be secret doesn't have everybody yelling 'X-9' at him. And so he will be known as Phil Corrigan from hence on." Under Graff the strip swung away from the Raymond look and closer to the Caniff-Sickles camp. X-9's love life did improve, to the point where he finally married and fathered a child. The lady Phil Corrigan eventually married first appeared in the strip late in 1944; her name was Wilda Dorray, and she was, appropriately enough, a mystery novelist.

Graff got rid of much of the hokum and the ignorance about police procedures that had built up, making the strip more realistic, dealing with the kind of cases the FBI might actually handle, and involving his characters' problems with the story. He also had a fondness for downbeat plots, ones that mixed romance and sleaziness, the same kind of stories found in the movies of the 1940s that critics now call *film noir*. He stayed with the strip until 1960. He later explained that he left because "the cops and robbers theme had grown tiresome." But it's likely King Features suggested he retire. For many years personal problems had been affecting his work and causing him to miss deadlines.

X-9's appearance had changed, briefly, in November of 1942. For seven weeks he somewhat resembled Jay Garrick, better known to comic book readers of the day as the Flash. E.E. Hibbard, who'd been drawing the adventures of the Fastest Man Alive since 1940, came in to ghost a sequence of Graff's strip. Another artist who worked on X-9, also secretly, was Paul Norris. He first did that in 1943, and from 1946 on, after getting out of the Army, "I would do two ten-week continuities a year…until Bob Lubbers took over the strip."

Lubbers, who was already drawing *Long Sam* for another syndicate, took over *Secret Agent X-9* in 1960, under the pen name Bob Lewis. His X-9 was a handsomer fellow who went in for sportcoats and slacks rather than sincere business suits. When Lubbers quit in 1967, Al Williamson took over. A longtime admirer of Raymond, Williamson drew in his own version of his idol's style. Teaming with Archie Goodwin as writer, he took over with the daily that ran on January 20, 1967. Espionage and government spying had changed considerably since X-9's initial advent back in the 1930s, and the strip, under the new title *Secret Agent Corrigan*, took that into account. Goodwin has said that he was more influenced by James Bond than by what his predecessors had done. Foreign locales became a regular thing, the weaponry grew ever more complex, and many of the villains were, to say the least, larger than life.

*Corrigan* was not one of the top money-makers, and that was one reason Williamson and Goodwin gave the strip up in the early 1980s. George Evans, veteran of EC comics and all-around excellent illustrator, took over the drawing and writing. His Corrigan is a variation of Williamson's, though a bit more hard-bitten and worldweary. **R.G.**

**SEEIN' STARS** A cartoon panel devoted to facts and gossip about motion pictures and movie stars, *Seein' Stars* began in 1933 and lasted until the early 1950s. It was syndicated by King Features, written and drawn by Frederic "Feg" Murray.

The 1930s was one of Hollywood's most successful decades and movie fans seemingly couldn't get enough information about and pictures of their favorite actors and actresses of the silver screen. Movie magazines, such as *Photoplay*, *Motion Picture*, and *Screenland*, flourished and every major newspaper ran one of the syndicated gossip columns conducted by the likes of Hedda Hopper, Louella Parsons, and Jimmy Fiddler. These Hollywood reporters also broadcast avidly followed radio shows.

Feg Murray provided a graphic version of a Hollywood gossip column. Making use of studio publicity handouts and photos, he drew a daily panel that mixed facts and hype. He'd been a sports cartoonist for United Features, and he used the then common sports cartoon format (also adapted by Ripley for *Believe It Or Not*) of one large portrait and two or three spot drawings. On a typical day readers might get: a handsome ink and crayon portrait of Shirley Temple, "The most photographed person in the world today! She has her picture taken (exclusive of motion pictures) 10,000 times a year!"; a drawing of a two-headed turkey with the notation that it had been "raised on Richard Dix's ranch near Hollywood"; a drawing of Ginger Rogers wearing shorts, with the news that she was "an honorary admiral in the Texas navy"; a drawing of an envelope with a rebus for an address and the notation that "Sonia Henie received the above letter."

JUST AFTER MAKING A SCENE FOR "THE GRACIE ALLEN MURDER CASE," IN WHICH THEY LIGHT 3 SMOKES ON A MATCH, (A VERY BAD THING TO DO ACCORDING TO THE SUPER-STITIOUS), A SELTZER BOTTLE EXPLODED IN THE FACES OF GRACIE ALLEN, WARREN WILLIAM AND BILL DEMAREST.

RITA WAS BORN IN PARIS AND RAN AWAY FROM HOME WHEN SHE WAS 13

RITA LA ROY, WHO PLAYS A CIRCUS RIDER IN "FIXER DUGAN," HAS BEEN AN EQUESTRIENNE SINCE SHE WAS 4 MONTHS OLD .. (AT THAT AGE HER MOTHER FIRST LIFTED HER UP IN THE SADDLE FOR HER FIRST RIDE).

BASIL RATHBONE HAD TO LEARN THE RUDIMENTS OF VIOLIN PLAYING FOR HIS ROLE AS "SHERLOCK HOLMES" IN "THE HOUND OF THE BASKERVILLES ... (HE NEARLY DROVE HIS WIFE CRAZY PRACTICING AT HOME).

*Seein Stars*, Feg Murray, © 1939, King Features Syndicate, Inc.

Murray almost always included his mascot, a tiny semi-cherub named Feggo, in his panel. Feggo would make punning remarks or ask trivia questions of the readers. A highly competent artist, Murray was especially good at converting publicity photos into drawings. From the middle 1930s on artist Arthur Beeman assisted him, drawing most of the small cartoon spots that accompanied the larger portraits.

*Seein' Stars* started as a daily panel on October 31, 1933. On September 11, 1938, a Sunday half-page was added. Murray used all sorts of recurring departments, including those that chronicled the stars' most embarrassing moments, their earliest jobs, their hobbies. Several similar panels were launched in the 1930s, including *Screen Oddities*. Murray's feature ended in the early 1950s, a period when Hollywood wasn't considered especially romantic or glamorous.　　**R.G.**

**SEGAR, E.C.** (1894–1938)　A cartoonist of only modest ability but a humorist and fantasist of considerable talent, Segar created one of the century's most memorable characters—the self-assured sailor Popeye. The squinty-eyed seadog made his debut in *Thimble Theatre* in 1929, and Segar drew him until his death less than a decade later.

Born and raised in the Mississippi river town of Chester, Illinois, Elzie Crisler Segar began his varied apprenticeship in the entertainment industry at the age of 12, working in the Chester Opera House, which offered both movies and live performances. He drew ads for slide projection and posters, played a drum to accompany the movies, changed the reels, and sometimes, when the show was over, recreated the performances outside on the sidewalk in chalk. He took an 18-month W.L. Evans correspondence course in cartooning and, as soon as he was certified as a cartoonist in the spring of 1916, he took off for Chicago where he found a cartooning job on the *Chicago Herald*.

On March 12, 1916, his first comic strip work appeared in the Sunday funnies when he took over a pen and ink incarnation of the country's most popular movie comedian, called *Charlie Chaplin's Comic Capers*. His drawing made a crude attempt at realistic, albeit comic, rendering, and when the strip perished a year later, Segar continued in the same style. In April of 1917 he started *Barry the Boob*, a strip about a nutty soldier in the European War. When the *Herald* was absorbed by Hearst the next year, Segar went to the *Chicago American*. On June 1, 1918, he deployed a simple, big-foot cartooning style to do *Looping the Loop*, a vertical daily strip that made comic commentary on movies, plays, exhibitions, and other newsy doings in downtown Chicago.

Late in 1919 Segar was sent to Hearst's *New York Journal*, presumably to do a vertical feature that would replace the motion picture parody strip *Midget Movies*, which the defecting Ed Wheelan would shortly resurrect as *Minute Movies* for the George Matthew Adams Service. Hearst christened Segar's version *Thimble Theatre*, and it began on December 19, 1919. Initially it starred Olive Oyl and her family, notably Castor, her enterprising, and short, brother. Throughout the 1920s Segar also drew a daily that had various titles but always featured a hapless commuter named Sappo. In 1929 Segar introduced a bit player named Popeye, and almost overnight he had a hit strip on his hands.

With a character congenial to his genius, Segar converted his undistinguished but adequate comic strip into a classic, a masterpiece of the art form. He went in for complex continuities, throwing in fantasy, science fiction, political satire, and anything else that struck his fancy. By March 1931 *Thimble Theatre* was carrying the subhead "starring Popeye." The antithesis of the invincible sailor, J. Wellington Wimpy, appeared shortly thereafter, and a host of brilliantly obsessive comic characters began to pour from Segar's inventive brain. Sadly, Segar's graphic genius was to illuminate the comics scene for only a few years. In late 1937 he was diagnosed with leukemia, and by the next autumn he was dead. Ill for much of 1938, he worked only at intervals. His last daily strip appeared in August, his last Sunday on October 9.　　**R.C.H.**

**SERGEANT STONY CRAIG**　The Marine Corps' answer to *Don Winslow of the Navy*, the strip began as a daily in September 1937, with a Sunday page added in June 1940. The creators were two career Marines, writer Sergeant Frank H. Rentfrow and artist Lt. Don Dickson, and both were on the staff of the Marine magazine *The Leatherneck* at the time.

The main characters besides Stony, who had been a leatherneck since World War I, included Jed Fink, a hillbilly Marine, and Slugger Wise, a broken-nosed tough-guy Marine. Dickson, one of whose "proudest boasts is that he is an expert rifle shot," worked in a simpleminded outline style, and his Stony Craig looked something like a schoolboy's copy of Captain Easy. Since it was still peacetime, Stony and his Marines limited their combat to situations other than battle. They might be ordered to Alaska on "a secret and dangerous mission" or become embroiled in the political problems of the tiny European country of Littenburg.

After nearly three years, and even though the strip still had less than 50 client papers, the Bell Syndicate added a Sunday page. The topper was titled *Daredevils of Destiny*. Subtitled "True Stories of Gallant Men," it was much more openly gung ho about the Marines than *Stony Craig*, and to avoid charges that they had any other motive than providing entertainment, Rentfrow and Dickson always made it perfectly clear, in syndicate press releases and interviews, "that the strip contains no propaganda for the Marine Corps."

At the close of 1940 Dickson was recalled to active duty. Rentfrow continued to write the feature, using an assortment of artists. Gerard Bouchard, even less of a talent than Dickson, drew the strip until early in 1945 and then was "ordered by physicians to less confining occupations." Eventually Stony and the gang got overseas and by the end of 1944 were in the Pacific fighting the Japanese. Bill Draut, a Marine veteran who had seen combat in the South Pacific, came aboard next as artist, drawing in a hurried, sloppy version of the Caniff style, which gave the strip a more realistic look. Draut moved on to comic books in June 1946, and Lin Streeter, whose work was more cartoony, took over for the last months. *Sergeant Stony Craig* ended on December 16, 1946, when Stony retired from the Corps and Rentfrow bid his readers farewell.                                   **R.G.**

## SGT. FURY AND HIS HOWLING COMMANDOS

The ads called it "The war mag for people who hate war mags." Launched by Marvel Comics in 1963, the "Howlers" were artist Jack Kirby and writer-editor Stan Lee's answer to World War II platoons like DC's Sgt. Rock and Easy Company—elite soldiers who rarely endured the grit and grime of infantry war, but went howling jubilantly into rambunctious action, pulling off missions that all others dismissed as impossible.

They were a flamboyantly colorful crew: Nick Fury, cigar-chomping, tough-as-nails super-sergeant; Dum Dum Dugan, big and strong but slow in the head; "Pinky" Pinkerton, English dandy who wore a tam o'shanter and carried an umbrella into combat; Gabriel Jones, jovial black jazz musician; Dino Manelli, a handsome cabaret singer based on Dean Martin; and the hootin', howlin' Kentucky boy, "Reb" Ralston. Another Howler, a young Ivy Leaguer named Junior, was killed in the fourth issue for a dose of "Marvel realism." In the same spirit, Fury's refined English girlfriend was killed several issues later.

Kirby and Lee got the series off to a fun, if cliché-ridden, start; they dropped it quickly, however, passing the art chores to Dick Ayers, the writing to Roy Thomas and then Gary Friedrich. The new crew tried to take it in a more sober direction, especially as America's Vietnam experience forced popular culture to take a different look at warfare. At the same time, they tried to keep it in line with other Marvel comics, by way of the archvillain Baron von Strucker and tie-ins to the history of the Marvel superhero universe. It was an uneasy mix,

and was far weaker in story and art than DC's competing war comics. An attempted spin-off, *Captain Savage and His Leatherneck Raiders*, did poorly. With *Sgt. Fury's* discontinuation in the early 1970s, Marvel essentially gave up on war comics until it tackled a more recent war in *The 'Nam* in 1986.                              **G.J.**

**SGT. ROCK** "When the goin' gets so rugged that only a *rock* could stand…he stands!" Created by writer-editor Robert Kanigher for the *Our Army at War* series in 1959, Sgt. Frank Rock and his Easy Company were the first continuing characters of National (DC) Comics' line of war comic books.

Initially an idealization of the tireless, silent heroism of the U.S. Army's platoon leaders in World War II, Rock became increasingly humanized in Kanigher's sensitive stories. By the late 1960s, he had come to represent the weary, boot-slogging fatalism with which real soldiers (and not comic book characters) generally view war. The rest of Easy Company was a well-developed supporting crew, including Jackie Johnson, perhaps the first respectfully-created black character in comic book history.

Although launched in a story drawn by Ross Andru and Mike Esposito, Rock's principal artist was Joe Kubert, whose powerful compositions, expressive characters, and lush inks set the standard for DC's war line. In 1968, Kubert took over as editor of *Our Army* (along with *G.I. Combat, Our Fighting Forces*, and *Star Spangled War Stories*), freeing Kanigher for full-time writing. The result was a group of thoughtful and extremely well-crafted comics bearing the motto, "Make War No More," of which *Our Army* was the most consistently compelling.

In addition to Kanigher and Kubert, others who have contributed to the DC war titles over the years were John Severin, Mort Drucker, Alex Toth, Frank Robbins, Neal Adams, Sam Glanzman, Archie Goodwin, Bob Haney, Russ Heath, and many more.

Changes in the comic book business and American attitudes have made it difficult for war comics to survive. DC's war line shrank in the 1970s and early 1980s until only *Sgt. Rock* (as *Our Army* had been rechristened in 1977) survived. In 1988 it was quietly canceled. **G.J.**

**THE SHADOW** The mysterious Shadow began his crimebusting career in his own Street & Smith pulp fiction magazine in 1931, entered his invisible man phase in 1937 on his radio show, and first showed up in comic books and comic strips in 1940.

This latter-day Shadow had a long, rather complex gestation period. In the summer of 1930, to promote the sales of their *Detective Story* magazine, Street & Smith went on the air with a radio show called *The Detective*

*Story Magazine Hour.* Initially an actor simply read a story from the magazine, but soon it was felt the narrator ought to be called something mysterious, and the whole production needed beefing up. The name that was eventually agreed on was the Shadow, and gradually the program went in for more production, stories were dramatized, and the narrator took to talking in a hollow voice while he assured listeners that "The Shadow knows." The Shadow became a modest celebrity in his own right, and Street & Smith found they had, almost by accident, a new and popular character. The publishers decided to turn him into a hero with a magazine of his own.

To help on the project they hired Walter B. Gibson, friend of—and ghostwriter for—such magicians as Houdini, Blackstone, and Thurston; he wrote the Shadow under the pen name Maxwell Grant. The first issue was dated April 1931.

The Shadow of the pulps never appeared before the reader undisguised. A grim avenger out to destroy crooks and evildoers and live up to his reputation as gangdom's foe, he hung out in dark and shadowy places and behaved as a first-class mystery man, but never, not once, did he exhibit the slightest tendency to become invisible.

Eventually the pulp Shadow picked up an assortment of alter egos. His best-known alias was millionaire man about town Lamont Cranston, but he also took to appearing as Fritz, janitor at police headquarters. Toward the end of the 1930s pulp magazine readers learned that the Shadow was actually a noted aviator named Kent Allard. By this time most people thought he was actually Lamont Cranston. At least one of the writers who filled in on the magazine series also believed that, and the writers of the radio show had long since accepted the fact.

A new version of the Shadow had taken to the air in the autumn of 1937. This Shadow was in reality Lamont Cranston, and he fought against not only crooks but also madmen, crazed scientists, werewolves, and all sorts of other horror tale threats. More importantly, he was "a seemingly supernatural nemesis" with the ability to become invisible at will. Cranston, in an apparent effort to humanize him, was given a lovely companion in the person of Margo Lane. Besides sharing the knowledge that the playboy was in reality the Shadow, Margo had an exceptional affinity for getting into not only trouble but also dire peril week after week. The first actor to portray the new, improved Shadow was a 22-year-old stage veteran named Orson Welles; the original Margo was Agnes Moorehead.

The first issues of *Shadow Comics*, which started early in 1940, offered yet another variation: a Shadow who was indeed Lamont Cranston and had a lady companion named Margo Lane, but had absolutely no talent for invisibility. With the ninth issue (March 1941) the Shadow newspaper strip, which had also commenced in 1940, began to be recycled in the comic book. Eventually the strip Shadow picked up the trick of becoming invisible, and when those sequences were reprinted, later in 1941, the comic book Shadow was finally invisible.

The first artist to draw the comic book Shadow was Vernon Greene, who also did the short-lived strip. Greene entered the service in 1942, and among the other artists who illustrated the feature in the comic book were Jon L. Blummer, Al Bare, Jack Binder, William A. Smith, and Charles Coll. After World War II Bob Powell took over, upgrading the look of the feature and converting Margo into a much sexier young woman. *Shadow Comics* ended in the summer of 1949 with its 101st issue. The radio show proved healthier, lasting until December 1954.

The Shadow has returned to comic books several times since, usually in his visible crimefighting mode. There were short-lived revivals in the mid-1960s and in the mid-1970s, and he returned once more in the mid-1980s. Among the artists who have rendered his return engagements are Mike Kaluta, Frank Robbins, and Bill Sienkewicz. No comic book Shadow has yet equaled the success of the pulp or radio version. **R.G.**

**SHEENA** The first and foremost jungle girl of the comic books, Sheena combined the prowess of Tarzan with the sex appeal of Jane. A product of the Eisner-Iger shop, the blond Queen of the Jungle debuted in 1938 in an overseas tabloid called *Wags* and later appeared in a tab-size comic book named *Jumbo* in this country. She shared the magazine with pirates, detectives, and funny animals, but by the time *Jumbo* shrank to standard size with its ninth issue she was indisputably its star. The original artist was Mort Meskin, and scripts were credited to W. Morgan Thomas, one of the many dashing pen names concocted by Will Eisner.

Sheena was a white goddess who ruled just about all of Africa, sharing her adventures with Bob Reynolds, a handsome dark-haired explorer. Almost from the start she and her consort took turns rescuing each other from a host of perils, which included slave traders, Nazi invaders, blackhearted white hunters, renegade tribes, and a variety of gigantic birds and beasts. On the covers the stories were given intriguing titles like "Viper Gods of the Vengeance Veld" and "Victims of the Super-Ape."

Sheena appeared in all 167 issues of *Jumbo*, as well as in 18 issues of her own magazine, whose last issue appeared in the spring of 1953. She had a sporadic career in other media: A Sheena television show, starring the striking six-foot Irish McCalla, was syndicated in 1955, and in 1984 a motion picture, with Tanya Roberts as the jungle queen, came and went. Marvel produced a two-issue adaptation of the film, and the following year Blackthorne reprinted *3-D Sheena, Jungle Queen*, originally seen in 1953.

Among the other artists who depicted her adventures amidst the flora and often hostile fauna were Bob Powell and Bob Webb. On *Jumbo*'s exuberant covers she was also portrayed by Eisner, Dan Zolnerowich, and Artie Saaf. **R.G.**

**SHERLOCK HOLMES** The best-known fictional detective in the world has been adapted to both comic books and newspaper strips several times. Thus far, however, Sir Arthur Conan Doyle's sleuth has never been notably successful in a graphic format.

In 1930 the Bell Syndicate offered a daily *Sherlock Homes* strip, drawn by Leo O'Mealia, who had a patient, detailed, old-fashioned style. The copy, adapted from such Doyle stories as *Silver Blaze* and *The Musgrave Ritual*, was set in type and ran beneath the illustrations, without talk balloons. The strip, which never achieved a large list of newspapers, ended in 1932. Holmes and Watson were absent from the comic sections for over two decades, not returning until March 1, 1954.

This time the *New York Herald Tribune*, syndicated a daily and Sunday version. Edith Meiser, who had written a Sherlock Holmes radio show in the 1930s, provided the scripts, and Frank Giacoia was listed as the artist. Holmes was younger and handsomer than he had been in the O'Mealia strip, while Watson was older and stodgier. Obviously the 1940s series of movies starring Basil Rathbone and Nigel Bruce had influenced the look of the two characters. While Giacoia, who was essentially an inker with considerable comic book experience, signed the strip, he didn't actually draw it. The chief penciller was Mike Sekowsky, another comic book veteran. This *Sherlock Holmes* was more dramatically staged, more concerned with Victorian atmosphere, and more given to action and movement. Dialogue balloons were used, and each daily tried to end on a note of suspense. Some Doyle material was adapted, but Meisner fashioned new adventures as well. Professor Moriarty put in an appearance once, trying to wipe out Edinburgh with the black plague. The strip ceased in 1956.

Although Holmes was frequently parodied and burlesqued in comic books—in such 1930s and 1940s features as *Hemlock Shomes*, *Padlock Homes*, and the like—he has never appeared much himself. *Classic Comics* included an adaptation of *The Sign of Four* in #21 (July 1944) and then issued *The Adventures of Sherlock Holmes* as #33 (January 1947). Charlton put out two issues of a Holmes title in 1955, Dell did two, in 1961 and 1962.

These latter issues looked very much like the strip, not surprisingly, since Sekowsky and Giacoia provided the artwork.

DC tried a single issue of Sherlock Holmes in 1975; Marvel attempted two in the late 1970s. In the 1980s several independent publishers issued Holmes comic books, with Eternity Comics reprinting the 1954–1956 and the 1930–1932 newspaper strips in a monthly series. **R.G.**

**THE SHIELD** The first superpatriot in comic books, the Shield beat Captain America into print by over a year. His star-spangled costume, adapted from the American flag, set the style for what the well-dressed ultra-patriotic superhero should wear. The United States didn't officially enter World War II until December of 1941, but as war jitters increased during the tense two years before, well over a dozen superpatriotic heroes and heroines showed up in comic books, all of them fighting spies, saboteurs, and would-be invaders.

Created by writer Harry Shorten and artist Irv Novick, the Shield debuted in *Pep Comics* #1 (January 1940), a magazine he shared with such characters as the Comet, Bentley of Scotland Yard, and Kayo Ward. The following January he acquired a partner in the person of Dusty the Boy Detective. In his heroic mode the Shield was billed as the G-Man Extraordinary, while in civilian life he was an ordinary G-man. His avowed purpose was to "shield the U.S. government from all enemies."

The team of the Shield and Dusty devoted their first months together to combating a cloaked, pointy-eared master-criminal and super-saboteur named the Vulture, who had green skin and was fond of plunging daggers into his victims. After the onset of World War II, the exploits grew bloodier and more violent; the bloodthirsty Axis villains included the Strangler, the Fang, and, worst of all, the Hun. The team hung on until *Pep* #65 (January 1948).

The Shield had several reincarnations over the years—in the late 1950s, in the camp-happy middle 1960s, and in the middle 1980s. But by the autumn of 1985 he was once again unemployed. **R.G.**

**SHOE** A streak of madcap humor has run through Jeff MacNelly's editorial cartoons from the beginning, so it came as no surprise to the public when he added a daily and Sunday humor strip to his already impressive list of accomplishments. Distributed by Tribune Media Services, *Shoe* was hatched in September 1977, and now flies to over 1,000 newspapers.

Shoe details the experiences of a group of birds who run a newspaper, projecting the problems not only of their business but also of a broad spectrum of familiar humanity through its ornithological metaphor. The nominal hero is P. (presumably for Purple) Martin Shoemaker, the rumpled editor of the *Treetops Tattler Tribune*, the disorder of whose habits, garb, and schedule is more human than avian. He struggles with his diet, computer, and income tax like any biped. Surrounding him is a flock of sharply-drawn fowl wittily representing various human types. It includes Perfessor Cosmo Fishhawk, an absentminded political analyst; Loon, a nearsighted reporter and part-time skywriter; and Skyler, the Perfessor's neurotic nephew, who adds the special problems of a nervous adolescent to the general existential malaise.

Drawn with the same ingenious grotesquerie as MacNelly's editorial cartoons and with much of the bite, *Shoe* has generally resisted the temptation to comment on the national scene, although it makes trenchant observations on the social, professional, and economic condition of man (or bird). "*Shoe* has never been a political thing," MacNelly explained in 1982. "It can't be topical because of the lead time." Nevertheless, MacNelly puts in an occasional political dig by means of such characters as Senator Battson D. Belfry, an obese leaker of information whom the *Tattler* offers to identify as "a large, whale-shaped source." Most of the humor of *Shoe*, however, draws on familiar sources: Shoe overeats; the food at the local diner, Roz's Roost, is terrible and Roz herself is merciless; Skyler fakes his school papers, begins noticing girls, and suffers the humiliations of little league baseball and the terrors of 6th grade football. Usually genial, the wit of *Shoe* has an edge that elevates it to the level of commentary.

Admired by other cartoonists as much for his impressive graphic style as for his penetrating wit, MacNelly has been widely honored for both his editorial cartoons and his comic strip. *Shoe* brought him the National Cartoonists Society's Reuben award as Cartoonist of the Year in 1979 and has been reprinted in several popular collections.                                                    **D.W.**

**SHORT RIBS** A daily and Sunday gag strip that drew its humor from a limitless range of setting, situation, and character, *Short Ribs* was created by Frank O'Neal for Newspaper Enterprise Association on November 17, 1958, and added a Sunday strip on June 14 of the following year. Although there was little repetition in the random selection of place, time, and performer, recurring characters did appear, including a vaguely medieval king and his court, two bewildered extraterrestrials, a couple of Soviet commissars, and a Western-frontier sheriff. "The fact that *Short Ribs* is not locked into a strong central character gives it flexibility," noted Frank Hill, O'Neal's assistant, who took over the strip on O'Neal's retirement in 1973. "Having the

characters in a different time frame than the readers allows people to laugh at themselves painlessly." Hill stuck closely to O'Neal's original graphic style and content, but kept it up to date with references to women's lib, college athletics, and political corruption when those topics were in the news.

The simple gags with which the strip ribbed the public were mildly satirical but never biting. They often depended on chronological incongruities, with characters in distant historical eras observing modern phenomena. Its art was equally basic, with minimal backgrounds and little detail or shading.

*Short Ribs* was an imaginative and unconventional strip, which commanded a loyal, though never a very large, audience. In the 1960s several collections of the strip were published by Gold Medal Originals. NEA cancelled the strip on May 2, 1982.            **D.W.**

**SHUSTER, JOE** (1914–  ) The most important cartoonist in the history of comic books, Shuster was the cocreator of *Superman*. The Man of Steel and the dozens of superheroes who followed in his wake revolutionized the comic book business and turned it into a multimillion-dollar industry. While Superman became one of the most successful and salable characters in the world, Shuster didn't do as well.

He was born in Toronto and moved to Cleveland with his parents when he was 10. He worked at a variety of jobs while going to school, including selling newspapers and helping out in a sign painting shop. He managed to win a scholarship to the Cleveland School of Art and also attended night classes at another local art school. He met fellow science fiction enthusiast Jerry Siegel at Cleveland's Glenville High School. By the early 1930s the two were working on comic strips together. *Superman* was conceived in 1934 but took several years to sell. Meanwhile, with Siegel providing the scripts, Shuster began drawing for comic books.

He started selling when only a few titles were being published. He drew two features for *More Fun Comics*—originally titled *New Fun*—in 1935, both of which look to be unsold Sunday pages. They were *Henri Duval*, about a dashing French swordsman, and *Dr. Occult*, starring a trench-coated ghostbuster. Next came *Federal Men*, *Radio Squad*, *Spy* and *Slam Bradley*. Of this latter feature, a private eye opus, Shuster has said, "We turned it out with no restrictions, complete freedom to do what we wanted. The only problem was we had a deadline. We had to work very fast, so Jerry suggested that we save time by putting less than six panels on a page: four panels or three panels, and sometimes two panels. I think one day we just had one panel a page. The kids loved it because it was spectacular. I could do so much more. Later on, the editors stopped us from

*Dr. Mystic*, Joe Shuster, © 1936, Comics Magazine Co., Inc.

doing that. They said the kids were not getting their money's worth."

What Shuster did was change the format of the comic book. Almost all his colleagues in those early days were trying to make their pages look like newspaper strips and Sunday pages. Shuster had understood that a comic book page was not a newspaper page. He broke his up in new and interesting ways, was one of the first to us a full-page splash panel. These big panels were often like posters advertising the story to follow. The newspaper artist who had the most influence on the young Shuster was Roy Crane, who was also breaking away from conventional layouts in his impressive *Captain Easy* Sunday pages. Crane was living and working in Cleveland at the time, but he and Shuster never met.

In 1938 the two partners finally sold *Superman* to DC's *Action Comics*. The first superhero proved almost immediately popular, which in turn created more demand for Superman artwork—for the new *Superman* magazine and for titles like *World's Finest*. A comic strip, daily and Sunday, was also added in 1939. Shuster, who was already suffering from vision problems, hired several more assistants to help meet the deadlines. In addition to Wayne Boring and Paul Cassidy, there were Leo Nowack, Dennis Neville, and John Sikela. A great deal of the work Shuster signed his name to in the 1940s was drawn by others.

Siegel and Shuster had sold all rights to their creation, and in 1947, after unsuccessfully taking DC to court in an attempt to get a larger share of the profits, they lost the job of turning out the adventures of Superman. Siegel was able to continue writing for comic books, but Shuster, after working briefly on their unsuccessful *Funnyman*, did almost no drawing for the rest of his life. In November 1975 the *New York Times* reported that he

was destitute and legally blind. Soon after, a settlement from DC provided him with a modest income for life. He moved to Southern California.                **R.G.**

**SICKLES, NOEL** (1910–1982) Although he was active in the field for only a relatively few years, Sickles was one of the most influential comic strip artists of the century. His work on *Scorchy Smith* in the middle 1930s had an important influence not only on his longtime friend Milton Caniff, but also on Alex Toth, Frank Robbins, Ken Ernst, Lee Elias, Mel Graff, and sundry others who fell under the spell of his impressive black and white style. Sickles also ghosted several sequences of *Terry and the Pirates*, and from the 1940s onward was a major magazine illustrator and commercial artist.

Noel Douglas Sickles was born in Chillicothe, Ohio, and from childhood on he wanted to be a cartoonist. Not a fine artist or an illustrator, but "just a newspaper cartoonist." To reach his goal he chiefly taught himself. One of the places he studied was at the local library, "the only thing available in a small town." He pored over the work of the old masters and the Impressionists, but he was equally fascinated by the work of magazine cartoonists—ranging from Charles Dana Gibson to the contributors to German magazines like *Jugend* and *Simplicissimus*. He tried to get a look at as wide a range of drawing as he could. "I was hungry for it," he once said, "hungry to learn." Sickles wasn't interested just in technique, but in subtler things. He felt that Gibson, for example, was "a master of attitude." Gibson understood people and what they did, "but he also dramatized that in such a subtle way that you never even noticed it."

In his early teens he began to hitchhike to Columbus to visit Billy Ireland, veteran cartoonist on the *Dispatch*. Milton Caniff, a couple of years older than Sickles, was

*Scorchy Smith*, Noel Sickles, © 1936, The A.P.

making similar pilgrimages, and it was in the Dispatch offices that they first met. Sickles, like a good many others, had taken the Landon cartoon course, which resulted in his working for six months as a mail-order instructor in the offices of the Cleveland-based correspondence school. He next did political cartoons for local newspapers. He and Caniff eventually teamed up and ran an art service. Some months after Caniff went East to work for the Associated Press in the early 1930s, Sickles, whom Caniff had been touting, also got a job in AP's Manhattan art department.

Sickles took over *Scorchy Smith* late in 1933, and during his three-year stay with the aviation adventure strip he developed the style that was to spread far and wide. It was an impressionistic, lushly black style that mixed elements of illustration with movie techniques. His first major disciple was Caniff, with whom he shared a studio. "Not until Noel Sickles…worked out a means of delivering illustration quality pictures on a seven-day basis was I able to buck some of the chains of my working schedule while dramatically improving the overall value of *Terry and the Pirates*," Caniff once said. "I shall always be grateful that Noel allowed me to pick his brain those formative years."

By the middle of 1936 Sickles was growing tired of *Scorchy* and of the AP. He was still putting in 12 hours or more a day at the drawing board, though his salary had risen only from $42.50 a week to $125. It was the Associated Press' policy not to tell any artist how many papers his feature had, nor were salaries based, as at the larger syndicates, on circulation. Sickles had been checking through all the out-of-town newspapers that came through the AP offices, and he'd determined *Scorchy Smith* was running in nearly 250 of them, earning

AP something like $2,500 each week. He'd been thinking lately of moving into magazine illustration, and since he had some money saved, he decided to quit. By the end of 1936 his name was no longer appearing on the strip.

He'd already been lending Caniff a hand on *Terry and the Pirates* and had even designed the distinctive Sunday logo. And he and Caniff, using the pen name Paul Arthur (Caniff's two middle names reversed), had done considerable work on advertising strips in the middle 1930s. Their most successful was a handsome series of Sunday pages extolling Postum and dealing with the villanous Mr. Coffee Nerves. Usually Sickles penciled and Caniff inked. After leaving *Scorchy*, Sickles was a frequent houseguest at the Caniffs' new home in New City, New York. During the late 1930s and early 1940s he ghosted several *Terry* sequences, including one set in and around the then exotic city of Hanoi.

In the early 1940s the obliging Sickles also helped Charles Raab on *Adventures of Patsy*, ghosting many weeks of the adventure strip. By the 1940s he was well-established as an illustrator, and his highly individual work—both in black and white and in color—was appearing in such prestigious and well-paying markets as *The Saturday Evening Post* and *Life*. He also did a great deal of advertising illustration. In 1946, when Caniff was getting ready to launch *Steve Canyon*, he asked his old friend to design the logo for his new strip, too.

For many years Sickles had not talked about *Scorchy Smith* or even thought much about it. The fan attention he started getting in the 1970s, although moderate, got him to discuss the aviation strip again and to take a look at the old strips. Some of them he felt were only "fair," but "some of it is excellent." In explaining what he'd been up to with *Scorchy*, he said, "I had no pretense of being a writer or a novelist, coming out with a story. What I felt was that if people read this from day to day, that I would draw it as they read it. And the hell with a complicated story. I was making an adventure, practically a Tom Mix Western…It's pure entertainment, pure action, from one darn thing to another and always visually interesting." Sickles had returned to adventure in his last years and was working on paintings of Western scenes at the time of his death in Tucson, Arizona.

R.G.

**SIEGEL, JERRY** (1914– ) He was the writer who cocreated one of the most famous fictional characters in the 20th century. His Superman was first seen in *Action Comics* in 1938, but helping to bring him into the world proved to be a mixed blessing. For many years, treated somewhat like a surrogate parent, he wasn't allowed to have anything to do with his brainchild. And only a very small portion of the enormous profits reaped by the Man of Steel ever found their way to his creators.

Jerome Siegel was born in Cleveland, Ohio, the son of parents who ran a small men's clothing store. School work didn't come easy for Siegel, and in his spare time he worked as a delivery boy for a printing plant. A shy, nearsighted boy of the Clark Kent sort, he found escape in reading. His favorite form of literature was science fiction, and he was a dedicated fan of such pulps as *Amazing Stories*. Siegel first got into print in *Cosmic Stories*, a fanzine he published in his early teens. It was in the late 1920s, when he'd finally graduated into high school, that he met fellow SF fan Joe Shuster.

By 1931, with Siegel writing and Shuster drawing, they were collaborating on comic strips. They created *Superman* in 1934 and, according to Siegel, they "thought we had invented a surefire, super action hit, and that the overjoyed comics industry would turn cartwheels and come rushing to our doorstep." The feature syndicates, however, weren't interested. While waiting for success to strike, Siegel and Shuster turned to other things. The comic book came along in 1934, and by 1935 the Cleveland duo was selling material in the new field.

Although *Famous Funnies*, the earliest regularly issued newsstand comic book, consisted mostly of reprints of newspaper strips, it did run a few pages of original material each month. Siegel and Shuster submitted several ideas to the fledgling title. "I remember," Siegel has said, "they returned the package unopened and among the stuff we submitted was *Superman*." The team fared better with Major Malcolm Wheeler-Nicholson, the enterprising and underfunded publisher who founded the company that would eventually become DC. Their first work appeared in the sixth issue of the major's tabloid-sized *New Fun*. There was one page of *Henri Duval*, a swashbuckling French swordsman no doubt inspired by the team's boyhood movie idol Douglas Fairbanks Sr., and one about *Dr. Occult*, a ghost detective.

Next came *Radio Squad* for the same magazine, *Federal Men* for *Adventure Comics*, *Spy* and *Slam Bradley* for *Detective Comics*. Finally in 1938 the team succeeded in selling *Superman* to DC's new *Action Comics*. They were paid $130, $10 a page, for the first story. At the same time they signed away all rights and agreed to work exclusively for DC for the next 10 years. By its third year on the stands *Action* was selling nearly 1,000,000 copies a month, and the *Superman* magazine, begun in 1939, soon climbed to a circulation of 1,250,000 copies per issue. By the early 1940s Siegel and Shuster were splitting about $150,000 a year.

The Superman property, by way of the newspaper strip that had started in 1939, the radio show, the ani-

mated cartoons, and assorted merchandising, was bringing DC over $15,000,000 in the 1940s. In 1947 Siegel and Shuster, feeling they weren't getting anywhere near a fair share of these profits, went to court. They lost their suit and had to give up Superman entirely. Their names were removed from the feature and, at the age of 33, they were both out of work.

In collaboration with other artists Siegel had created several other characters in the early 1940s. The most successful was the Spectre, drawn by Bernard Baily and first seen in *More Fun Comics* #52 (February 1940). He also invented the Star Spangled Kid and Robotman. In his years away from DC he wrote for nearly a dozen other publishers. Late in 1947, working with Shuster and longtime *Superman* ghost John Sikela, he created *Funnyman* for Vincent Sullivan's Magazine Enterprises. The mock superhero didn't succeed in comic books nor in the concurrent newspaper strip. In the 1950s Siegel wrote *Joe Yank, G.I. Joe, Kid Cowboy*, and *Nature Boy* as well as a lot of horror and romance scripts, and also worked as editor for the unsuccessful Ziff-Davis line of comic books. Finally in 1959 he was hired again at DC, writing scripts again for his hero and also for *Legion of Super-Heroes* and *Adam Strange*. In the seven years he was there, he was never allowed to sign any of his work.

In the middle 1960s he did scripts for the Archie outfit's ill-fated revival of such 1940s superheroes as Steel Sterling, the Shield, and the Black Hood. Next came scripts for the Phantom and Mandrake comic books. Siegel's final writing in the field was done for Marvel in the early 1970s on *X-Men, Human Torch*, and *Kazar*.

In 1975, by then working for the state of California as a clerk-typist, he began a campaign to try to get some sort of settlement from the owners of Superman. He and Shuster had tried several legal moves over the years to no avail. Since the first Christopher Reeve *Superman* movie was in the offing, it was a favorable time for Siegel to go public. He sent out letters to comic book artists and writers, to fanzines, to just about anybody he thought would pay attention. Quite a few people took up the cause of Siegel and Shuster, and eventually the management of DC agreed to pay the two an annual stipend. The initial amount was said to be $25,000 a year for each partner. "There is no legal obligation," a DC spokesman explained, "but I sure feel there is a moral obligation."

Siegel has lived a bit more comfortably since then. His name and Shuster's now appear on every *Superman* story—"Created by Jerry Siegel and Joe Shuster."

R.G.

**SILLY MILLY** A highly personal blend of news commentary, screwball humor, and what's been called aggressive childishness, Stan MacGovern's *Silly Milly* had its beginnings in the late 1930s. It lasted a few years beyond a decade and was syndicated to a select list of newspapers.

MacGovern, who drew in a simple decorative style that had affinities to both the work of Milt Gross and the energetic scrawls of kindergarten kids, had been turning out strips and cartoons since the 1920s. When the Silly Milly opus started up in the *New York Post* in June of 1938, it was titled *Extra Extra.* Each day MacGovern would take a minor news item—"Just lying down gives you as much energy as sleeping" or "Shortages force the use of makeshift N.Y.C. police cars"—and build a strip around it, showing the more ridiculous and slapstick possibilities in each situation, a tradition among newspaper cartoonists around the country, including Harry Haenigsen, Will Johnstone, and Francis Dahl. MacGovern's version of commenting on the news of the day was somewhat more raucous than that of his colleagues and more given to rowdy burlesque.

His strip was eventually rechristened *Silly Milly*, but retained its topical format. Milly was an uninhibited young lady with a head shaped like a small watermelon resting on its side, huge eyes, and not much of a nose. Her black hair was abundant and resembled the mane on a merry-go-round horse. Among her favorite comments were "Har! Har!" and "Yuk yuk yuk!"

In his book *The Comics* (1947), Coulton Waugh had nothing but praise for the strip, lauding "the lively gagging, the bold, decorative" drawing. Despite its critical acclaim, *Silly Milly* was never especially popular and ended its life in the early 1950s.          **R.G.**

**SILVER SURFER**  This silver-coated, alien rider of the currents of space was created by Jack Kirby in 1965 for Marvel Comics' *Fantastic Four.* He appeared as the herald of the planet-devouring Galactus, assigned to warn the people of Earth of their impending doom; he sensed nobility in the earthlings, however, and defied Galactus, saving the Earth. As punishment, Galactus cursed him to be trapped forever within Earth's atmosphere, making the Surfer the noblest and most tragic of Marvel's heroes.

Stan Lee, editor and scripter of *Fantastic Four*, was immediately enamored of the character and gave him an agonized, moralizing, sometimes pompous but often poetic style of speech that meshed well with the pure, statue-like nobility Kirby had given him. When not lamenting his own lost freedom, the Surfer loudly bemoaned the follies and passions that trap mankind in barbarism; as a pacifist often forced to fight by an uncomprehending world, he was an explicit study in moral agony.

The more intellectually ambitious of Marvel's fans seized on the Surfer, and he became a regular guest in *Fantastic Four.* During the mid- and late-1960s, when comics became a brief craze among college kids and the pop-culture intelligentsia, the Surfer was among the most talked-about characters in the field, an odd mélange of heavyhanded philosophizing, high camp, and sheer comic book verve.

In 1968, Lee launched the hero in his own comic book, but rather than working with Kirby he gave the art chores to John Buscema. After a few strong issues, marked by elegant Lee writing and powerful Buscema art, *Silver Surfer* seemed to lose its momentum and purpose; the agony of this hypersensitive prisoner of Earth didn't seem to lend itself to a continuing series. It was canceled in 1970, after 18 issues.

Many fans continued to demand the Surfer's return during the 1970s, but they had to be content with his stint in the team comic *The Defenders* and his various guest appearances. It was said that Stan Lee, who graduated from editor to publisher of Marvel Comics in 1972, refused to let anyone else write the character. Lee and Kirby finally teamed up for a *Silver Surfer* "graphic novel" in 1978 (published by Simon and Schuster), but the result was disappointing to creators and readers alike.

In 1986 the Surfer was given a new series, written by Steve Englehart and drawn by Marshall Rogers, which

*Silly Milly*, Stan MacGovern, © 1945, N.Y. Post.

tied together many of Marvel's "cosmic" characters and elements. In 1988, Stan Lee teamed up with the French comic book artist Moebius (Jean Giraud) for a miniseries. Neither has generated any of the magic or excitement of the Surfer's first several stories, emphasizing that he was very much the product of a unique moment in American popular culture. **G.J.**

**SIMON, JOE** (1915– )  One of the major creative figures in comic books, Simon has worked as an artist, writer, and editor. He entered the field in 1940 and created, singly or in collaboration with Jack Kirby, such characters as the Blue Bolt, Captain America, the Young Allies, and the Boy Commandos. He also invented the romance comic.

Joseph H. Simon was born in Rochester, New York, and attended Syracuse University. By 1937 he was a sports cartoonist for the *Syracuse Journal*, and by 1940 he was in New York City involved in the growing comic book industry. He did free-lance jobs for the Funnies, Inc., shop, creating such characters as the Blue Bolt, and he also became an editor at the Fox line of comic books. It was there that Simon met Jack Kirby: "Kirby was a *very* good artist. I recognized that as soon as I saw him work. I think I was the first one to really discover his talents." The two decided to team up and the first joint venture was *Blue Bolt*. Kirby joined with the second episode. "I'd letter the stuff," Simon has said, "and Jack would complete the pencils. Then I would ink it. If we were in a jam, Jack would pitch in with his shading."

Early in 1941, inspired by the nation's impending entry into World War II, Simon and Kirby came up with their most successful character. Captain America, done for Marvel, was a hit. "We didn't want to go to war, but we felt very intense about what was going on in Europe," Simon once explained. "Captain America didn't want to fight, but he knew that the Nazis had to be stopped and he was prepared to do his best to stop them." The impressive sales of the superpatriot caught the attention of DC, and they made the team an offer. Moving over there at an increase in pay, Simon and Kirby created *The Boy Commandos* and *The Newsboy Legion*. They also revitalized *The Sandman* and *Manhunter*. Kirby's dynamic layouts and Simon's bold inking, coupled with fast-moving stories that included fantasy and humor, made their stuff stand out in the comic books of the early and middle 1940s.

Simon served in the Coast Guard during part of the Second World War. While in the service, he drew a few Sunday sequences of the *True Comics* strip. In the immediate postwar years he and Kirby teamed again, first producing action stuff for Harvey—*Stuntman, The Boy Explorers*, and the like. Finding that costumed heroes and boy adventurers weren't as popular as they had

been, the partners turned to crime and produced *Justice Traps The Guilty* and *Headline Comics*. They also introduced *Young Romance*, the first out-and-out love story comic. While he was in the Coast Guard Simon had noticed that "there were so many adults, the officers and the men, reading kid comic books." He figured adults would go for comic books aimed at a somewhat more mature audience. That proved to be the case. *Young Romance* debuted in 1947, billed as "Designed For The More ADULT Readers Of COMICS" and very quickly climbed to a monthly circulation of 1,000,000.

Simon and Kirby operated a shop and turned out many other titles, including *Police Trap* and a Western costumed hero known as *Bullseye*, before breaking up in the middle 1950s. On his own Simon continued in comics, creating such characters as Brother Power the Geek and Prez for DC in the 1960s and 1970s. He also edited and drew for *Sick*, the *Mad* simulacrum, in the late 1960s and early 1970s. He has since then moved into other areas of publishing and commercial art. **R.G.**

**SKIPPY**  A highly popular kid strip, and one that critics have lauded for both its intelligence and its artwork, *Skippy* was the creation of Percy L. Crosby. It ran from the early 1920s to the middle 1940s, making Crosby rich and inspiring movies, a radio show, and other merchandising.

Skippy was born as the star of a full-page feature in the old *Life*, which announced his advent on March 15, 1923. In 1925 Crosby, who held the copyright on the character, syndicated *Skippy* as a daily comic strip. Beginning June 23, it was first distributed by Johnson Features and then by the Central Press Association. King Features launched a Sunday page on October 7, 1926, and took over the distributing of the daily on April 1, 1929.

Even sitting down, Skippy Skinner seemed charged with motion. Crosby's sketchy, unlabored line had a ferocious energy, the vitality born of pen tearing breakneck across paper, and Crosby's subjects were imbued with that energy even if drawn in repose. And Crosby's distinctive style was as much a part of his nine-year-old protagonist's character as the daily gags that gave him personality. Strangely, Skippy's anachronistic costume belied his character. Attired always in an English schoolboy's gown (a smock-like jacket), high Eton collar with flaring bow-ribbon tie, and short pants, Skippy should have been a well-behaved momma's boy. Only his shapeless hat, tilted rakishly over his eyes and his down-at-the-ankle socks betrayed him as a boy's boy, rowdy and roguish and just a trifle quarrelsome, who swaggered into view with hands jammed deep into his pockets.

*Skippy* was a kid strip of extraordinary authenticity. In addition to pursuing all the usual kid activities, Skippy and a pal often simply sat for hours on the curbstone, talking the perfect logic but impractical sense of juvenile philosophy, arguing and bickering about the monumental trifles of youth. More significantly, they were sometimes puzzled and unhappy and lonely—like real kids. And the setting of the strip evoked the unexpressed horrors of the very young. *Skippy's* small-town landscape is often nearly barren, its horizon line perpetually unblemished by houses or trees, a desert as bleak and comfortless as the world can sometimes seem to a child.

The strip proved very popular and by the middle 1930s Crosby's income was said to equal that of Franklin Roosevelt. The first motion picture, with Jackie Cooper in the title role, was released in 1931, and a radio show also started that year. By the early 1940s Crosby was already suffering from the problems that would eventually place him in a mental institution. He stuck with the strip, doing an increasingly hurried and sketchy job, until 1945. *Skippy* ended on December 8 of that year. **R.C.H.**

**SKYROADS** One of the several early aviation strips inspired by the increased public interest in planes and pilots in the late 1920s, *Skyroads* was written by Lt. Lester J. Maitland and drawn by Dick Calkins. It managed to stay in the air for well over a decade.

A daily only, it was syndicated by the John F. Dille Co. and started in 1929. Both the author and the artist were aviators. In June of 1927 Maitland and a fellow Army lieutenant had made the first flight from California to Hawaii, a 2,400-mile nonstop hop in a Fokker trimotor. Calkins had been a pilot and flight instructor with the Army Air Service toward the end of World War I. The strip concerned itself initially with Ace Ames and Buster Evans, who "find themselves the owners of a new biplane" and form a business called Skyroads, Unlimited. "Some crate," observes Ace of their new craft. The early continuities involved the two heroes with smugglers, a lost race of the Amazon, and similar problems.

Unlike most adventure strips, *Skyroads* never settled on one hero or team of heroes; instead, it gave room to an assortment of daredevil pilots over the years. In the late 1920s there were Ace and Buster; by the early 1930s, after Maitland's name had been dropped from the credits, a youthful aviator named Hurricane Hawk took over as star. Typical of the villains Hurricane tangled with were a gang of Asian bandits and their hooded leader, the Crimson Skull. The Skull was a first- rate pilot himself and a sinister Oriental as well. At other times Hurricane concentrated on his flying, planning things like "a super atmosphere flight which might revolutionize aviation." Later on in the decade, Speed McCloud was the head man, and in the feature's final years a new group of good guys, with a mature ace named Clipper Williams, a boy flyer named Tommy, and a skyful of others known as the Flying Legion, were in charge.

Calkins, who was also signing *Buck Rogers*, had help on the strip. The two young men he had working for him in the early 1930s, at very small wages, were Russell Keaton and Zack Mosley. Close inspection of the early dailies will show them sneaking their names into panels now and then, usually on the sides of boats or planes. Mosley moved on to *Smilin' Jack* in 1934; Keaton, a much better artist than his boss, took over the drawing of *Skyroads* in the early 1930s and was soon getting a credit.

Keaton took off with an aviation strip of his own, *Flyin' Jenny*, in the late 1930s. The final artist to draw *Skyroads* was Leonard Dworkins. Using the pen name Leon Gordon, he did the strip until its end in 1942. **R.G.**

**SLIM JIM** A spindly, peripatetic hobo, Jim first appeared in a Sunday page that began in the autumn of 1910. Drawn initially by George Frink, he spent just about all his funny paper life being pursued by the three members of the constabulary of the small town of Grassville. Known as the Force, they chased the wily but basically warmhearted Jim across the length and breadth of the United States, across Europe, Asia, and several fantasy kingdoms. Seen mostly in rural newspapers, *Slim Jim* survived until 1937.

Frink had drawn a similar character, Circus Solly, for the *Chicago Daily News* from 1904 onward. Skinny, acrobatic, and an extremely artful dodger, Solly was also a hobo on the run from the somewhat clumsy minions of the law. His escapades foreshadowed not only those of Slim Jim but also those of many a silent movie comedian being pursued by clusters of bumbling cops.

After converting Solly to Jim, Frink drew the new version for only a few months, and Raymond Crawford Ewer took over in January 1911. An ambitious and inventive artist, Ewer filled his pages with handsomely rendered and inventive scenes of the pursuits and inevitable chaos and confusion that followed. "During this period," comics historian Richard Marschall has said, "*Slim Jim* achieved first rank status as a comic strip of memorable imagery and invention."

Ewer left the job late in 1914. The next permanent artist was Stanley Armstrong, who illustrated the endless chase of the fugitive beanpole for the remainder of the strip's days. **R.G.**

**SMILIN' JACK** One of the first and most enduring aviation-based adventure strips, *Smilin' Jack* began as a

Sunday page called *On the Wing* on October 1, 1933, and added a daily strip on June 15, 1936. It was created for the Chicago Tribune- New York News Syndicate by flying-enthusiast Zack Mosley, who had earned his professional wings assisting Dick Calkins on his similar strip *Skyroads* from 1929.

Beginning as a humorous series about nervous flying students (exactly the situation in which Mosley, who had begun flying lessons in 1932, found himself), *On the Wing* had only modest success for its fourteen-week trial flight, but when the syndicate ordered its name changed to *Smilin' Jack*, it began to assume the lively narrative form it was to maintain for the next 40 years. Mack Martin, the scared student-pilot, became Jack, grew a snappy little mustache, and acquired a suave smile that four decades of harrowing adventure were never completely to wipe off his handsome face.

Jack became a commercial pilot whose delivery of goods and passengers carried him to the most remote places and called for an astonishing range of talents. Forever entangled with bizarre crooks and spies, the unflappable Jack prevailed through a combination of resourcefulness, skill, and luck. He bested the Head, whose drooping eyelids were the epitome of the sinister; the Claw, whose prosthetic hook dealt death; and Toemain the Terrible, who raised piranhas with an appetite for human flesh.

Mosley's talent for extraordinary characters extended to the good guys as well; Jack's friends included such memorable figures as his Polynesian pal Fatstuff, who kept popping his shirt buttons into the open mouths of hungry chickens, and the sexually hyperactive Downwind Jaxon, whose face was so handsome that we were never permitted to see more than a one-quarter profile. Jack was never without appropriate female companionship, either: "Hellcat" Cindy, the Incindiary Blonde; the tempestuous Gale; and an endless succession of anonymous sexpots, the famous "li'l de-icers" who were so hot they de-iced the airplanes' wings, kept the strip balanced.

Always suspenseful even when they stretched the limits of credibility, Jack's adventures were fast-paced, and the occasional romantic interlude (women could no more resist his smilin' face than they could Downwind's averted one) was never long enough to interrupt the slam-bang action.

Unlike all but a few continuity strips, *Smilin' Jack* had genuine development. Kids grew up, adults got old, some even died. Jack married, not once but twice, and sired a son. His improbably-named offspring "Jungle Jolly" progressed from an infant to a toddler to a clean-cut young man, as dashing as the now graying hero, and with a boyish smile all his own.

Always personally active in aviation, Mosley kept *Smilin' Jack* both current and accurate. However fantastic his plots may have been, the technical details of his aircraft drawings were flawless, and two generations of American youth got an education in aeronautics from them. Otherwise, the graphic style of the strip tended to a simplicity that many regarded as awkward, though it never seemed to cost it any readers. Among Mosley's assistants were Gordon "Boody" Rogers and Ward Albertson.

*Smilin' Jack* was widely reprinted in comic books by Dell, which also brought out numerous volumes through the 1940s. In addition, the strip was the basis of a thirteen-episode movie serial produced by Universal in 1943.

As the romance of aviation and the public taste for adventure comics declined, *Smilin' Jack* was felt to have flown its course, and the venerable strip was brought in for a landing on April 1, 1973.          **D.W.**

**SMITH, SIDNEY** (1877–1935) He drew *The Gumps* from 1917 to 1935, and throughout the Twenties and early Thirties no list of the highest paid cartoonists in the country was complete without his name. Robert Sidney Smith was born in Bloomington, Illinois, the son of a successful dentist. More interested in athletics than academic topics, Smith never got around to completing high school. At 18 he was drawing cartoons for his hometown paper, and shortly thereafter he became an itinerant "chalk talk" artist, going on to hold art department jobs on newspapers in Indiana, Pennsylvania, and Ohio.

The *Chicago Examiner* hired him in 1908 as a sports cartoonist. He'd earlier developed a humanized goat character and used him in a new incarnation as *Buck Nix*. (When Smith was hired away by the *Chicago Tribune*, the well dressed goat became *Old Doc Yak*.) The Nix saga, which unfolded in a daily strip, had eventually become a mock melodrama, utilizing continuity— "What will tomorrow bring?" Yak starred in a Sunday page for most of his career, but also dabbled in melodrama and suspense. *The Gumps* began early in 1917, moving into a slot where a short-lived *Old Doc Yak* daily had been running. According to the final goat daily, Doc had headed elsewhere in his car, "going 50 mi. an hour."

Smith's drawing style had a scratchy, self-taught look and was full of echoes of the work of Bud Fisher, Clare Briggs, and Tad Dorgan. Throughout his career he continued to draw like a fairly gifted high school boy. It wasn't the artwork that sold *The Gumps*, but the continuities, and by the early 1920s, it had become one of the most popular strips in America.

The Twenties was the decade when comic strip artists—the most successful and widely followed ones—

were first treated as celebrities, and Smith was one of the most prominent; his swift rise to fame, and his ever-increasing salary, were often written about in national magazines. In fact, the *Trib* itself used Smith's salary increases for publicity purposes; an ad in a 1922 Sunday edition, for example, was headlined: *Creator of Gumps signs a Million Dollar Tribune Contract and rides off in this car.* The car was a Rolls-Royce, and the contract guaranteed him $100,000 a year for the next decade. According to the paper, "it is the highest salary paid by any newspaper to a cartoonist." Smith's fondness for fast cars was another common subject for the publicists. "His chief aim in life for years was to go somewhere else as rapidly as possible," commented *Collier's* magazine in 1924. "No one ever yet has built an automobile fast enough for him."

Smith was also a pioneer at assembling a team to turn out the work he signed his name to. He had help on the story lines from Captain Patterson, script assistance from Sol Hess and Blair Walliser; Harold Gray was an early art assistant and Stanley Link did a majority of the drawing from the early 1920s onward. Smith admitted to having help, but maintained he always drew the heads of his characters.

Dedicated to physical fitness, Smith was a long-distance runner and an amateur boxer. He also had, as one magazine reported, "an elaborate wardrobe and loves to play the role of a Beau Brummel," usually wearing his suits a size too small to show off "his football player's build and physique." He owned a spacious estate near Chicago, a townhouse, and a 2,200-acre farm, where he erected a six-foot bronze statue of Andy Gump atop a six-foot pedestal.

On Saturday, October 19, 1935, Smith signed a new, three-year contract at the *Tribune*'s offices, which upped his guarantee to $150,000 a year. He and some friends then did some celebrating. At 3:45 A.M. the next morning, while Smith was driving alone back to his farm, he had a head-on collision. "Mr. Smith's small sedan was whirled around, hurtled off the road and into a telephone pole," reported *Editor & Publisher*. "Mr. Smith was killed instantly in the impact, suffering a crushed skull." He was 58 years old. **R.G.**

**SMITTY** Walter Berndt had spent some five years as an office boy at the *New York Journal* before he began to draw on that experience for a comic strip. After leaving the *Journal* in 1920 and spending an unrewarding year with the Bell Syndicate, he developed a strip based on his humble employment in the *Journal*'s office. Emboldened by the popularity of Walter C. Hoban's humorous strip *Jerry on the Job*, which had flourished since 1913 in the *Journal* and other Hearst papers, Berndt sold *Bill the Office Boy* to the *New York World* in 1922. Temperamental differences led to his separation from that paper within a couple of weeks—his boss wouldn't tolerate his independent spirit—and he sent a sample of the strip to publisher Joseph M. Patterson at the *Chicago Tribune*. Patterson wired back at once, "Very interesting—meet me Monday morning *Daily News*—change the heads—they're too big" and bought the strip for the *New York News*. The only thing he was not satisfied with (once the heads had been reduced) was the title, which he considered too long. Picking up a telephone book and flipping through it at random, he hit on the name Smith and said, "There we are—good name—'Smitty!'"

The modest daily exploits of Augustus Smith—universally known, even by his parents, as Smitty—began on November 27, 1922, in the *New York Daily News*, and a Sunday strip followed on February 25 of the next year. Smitty began as a lively, ingenious 13-year-old, unfailingly dressed in black shorts and sporting a cap and a bow tie. His loving Ma and Pa, his devoted four-year-old brother Herby, and his benevolent boss Mr. Bailey complete as attractive a cast as any in comics; there isn't a mean bone in any of their bodies, and it was not surprising that America took the genial strip to its heart for over half a century.

Over the years the titular hero of *Smitty* matured somewhat, reaching what appeared to be his early 20s. His kidding of the steno Ginnie stopped when he married her in the late 1950s, though his sly tricks to get around the always complaisant Mr. Bailey never did. Herby outgrew his lisp and his pinafore but never seemed to pass the age of about eight, and remained as engaging as ever. In 1930 his popularity reached such a height that Berndt created an ancillary strip for him, and the four-panel *Herby* ran with the Sunday *Smitty* till the end of its career.

Drawn in a fresh, simple style, *Smitty* was a bright, energetic strip that made little demand on the attention or the sophistication of the reader. The Sunday strip always contained a complete humorous anecdote, but the dailies relied increasingly on continuity: Smitty becomes involved in and extricates himself from office problems; in 1929 the enterprising lad, an ardent baseball fan, gets to know Babe Ruth (drawn very much from life) and becomes something of an entrepreneur; he loses his youthful heart to a variety of little girls from time to time before the great romance of his life results in his happy marriage to Ginnie; and in a more fanciful spirit, the droll little Professor Atom tries, in the science-conscious 1940s, to divert the Gulf Stream to make palm trees grow on Broadway. There were also frequent outdoor adventures over the years, usually stemming from camping trips with his boss.

The Chicago Tribune-New York News Syndicate distributed *Smitty* and its companion strip *Herby* to about

100 papers through most of its long life. Berndt received the National Cartoonists Society's highest honor as the Outstanding Cartoonist of the Year for it in 1969, and sustained it for another five years. The eternal office boy, as high-spirited and youthful as ever, sharpened his last pencil and ran his last errand in 1974, when his creator laid the 52-year-old strip to rest. **D.W.**

**SMOKEY STOVER** One of the longest-lived of the good-natured slapstick strips in American comics, Bill Holman's Sunday feature *Smokey Stover* was a fountain of screwball humor for almost four decades. Distributed by the Chicago Tribune-New York Daily News Syndicate from March 10, 1935, until its creator's retirement in 1973, it dealt with the antics of its fireman hero, his wife Cookie and son Earl, and his firechief Cash U. Nutt. The firehouse also supported a dog with a glove on its tail, various mice carrying signs with puns on them, and a cat named Spooky who sported a perpetually bandaged tail. For a time Spooky had a bottom strip of his own before joining the team above.

The gags of *Smokey Stover* were of the broadest sort: Smokey hides in a pile of leaves to avoid the job of raking, only to be set on fire when the Chief burns them; the two firemen drive through the city park and stop for a soda on their way to a fire at the Tax Bureau; Cookie commandeers Smokey's funnel for an "adorable" new hat. But the real zest of the strip was in the widely anarchic graphic and verbal touches with which Holman peppered it. Signs everywhere read "Foo" (which he claimed to have seen on a Chinese figurine and had translated as "good luck"), "1506 Nix Nix" (derived from a personal prank involving a warning to girls to avoid a bachelor's hotel room with that number), and the eternal mystery "Notary Sojac" (which Holman explained as his phonetic rendering of the Gaelic "Nodlaig Soghach," meaning Merry Christmas). Pictures on the walls held figures that stuck out beyond the frames, often with punning titles: An insect with a rifle is labeled "Bug Private"; an actor in Richmond is called "Virginia Ham"; and, Holman's personal favorite, two pairs of colorful women's undergarments are entitled "Rose's are Red and Violet's are Blue." The firehouse car, called the Foomobile, rode on two wheels and so intrigued the public that a manufacturer in Indiana actually produced one that worked. "Foo" swept the country, finding its way into popular songs and generating over 500 "Foo Clubs."

From the middle 1940s, Holman ran a daily panel called *Nuts and Jolts*, harking back to his days as a free-lance gag cartoonist, but it was the foolish firefighters that most captured the popular fancy. Drawn in a slam-bang style cluttered with wacky details and following no logic but that of the artist's own mad sense

of humor, *Smokey Stover* was a lively and inventive strip that survived long after the end of the simpler, cheerier era that gave it birth. **D.W.**

**SOGLOW, OTTO**   See THE LITTLE KING.

**SOMEBODY'S STENOG**   The first office girl strip began in A.E. Hayward's *Padded Cell* panel in the *Philadelphia Evening Public Ledger* and ran there from November 10 to December 18, 1916, as *Somebody's Stenographer*. Two years later, on December 16, 1918, it returned as a strip, distributed by the Ledger Syndicate, under the abbreviated title *Somebody's Stenog*. A Sunday page was added on April 30, 1922.

The heroine was Cam O'Flage, tall blond secretary to Sam Smithers, long-suffering head of a nut and bolt company. Other characters included the boss' son Reggie, a rich playboy who was a bit too dim-witted to be taken seriously by Cam; Kitty Scratch, a rival stenographer; Venus, a spinster secretary; Mary Doodle, a plump little coworker who was Cam's best friend and was given to exclaiming, "Holy Buckwheat!"

Although many of the strip's gags and continuities were based on office life, the characters also went on outside adventures, including a lark in Atlantic City in which Cam won the Miss America crown and another in Paris where a giant nut from the Smithers company pulled down the Eiffel Tower.

Hayward drew most of the Sunday pages but fell ill in 1933, and from April of that year the daily was ghosted by such artists as Ray Thompson. After Hayward's death in 1939, Sam Nichols drew *Somebody's Stenog* until it bowed on May 10, 1941.

Although the strip inspired a genre, it was never as popular as such imitators as *Tillie the Toiler* and *Winnie Winkle*. **M.J.**

**SPACE CADET**   See TOM CORBETT, SPACE CADET.

**SPACEHAWK**   Also known as "the lone wolf of the void," he was the major serious comic book creation of the certifiably zany Basil Wolverton. All told, Spacehawk appeared in 30 issues of *Target Comics*, from the June 1940 to the December 1942 issue, gracing the cover solo but once. Initially his exploits took him to the far reaches of the universe, but later he shifted to wartime Earth exclusively.

Spacehawk wore a bulky green spacesuit and, while his interplanetary adventures somewhat paralleled those of pulp magazine and newspaper strip heroes of the day, nobody else had encounters quite like his. He met the oddest aliens, prowled the most peculiar planets, and experienced some of the most cockeyed incidents of any of the planet-hopping do-gooders. On

Mars he prevented a sore loser, green political candidate from smashing a moon into the planet, on Saturn he casually admitted to being 800 years old, and once on Uranus he transplanted the brain of a dying friend into the gigantic body of a warty green hornosaur.

**R.G.**

**SPARKY WATTS** See ROGERS, BOODY.

**SPARLING, JACK** (1916– ) A fast and capable artist, Sparling has drawn more syndicated newspaper strips than almost anyone else in the business, as well as managing to produce a prodigious amount of comic book work over the past half-century.

When asked some years ago to provide autobiographical information for a National Cartoonists Society album, Sparling responded with, "I was born several centuries ago at a drawing board." Actually he was born in 1916 in New Orleans, and by the middle 1930s he was working as an editorial and sports cartoonist for the *New Orleans Item.* Early in 1940, after having relocated in Washington, D.C., Sparling began drawing *Hap Hopper.* He left that in 1943 to launch *Claire Voyant*, which survived until 1948. In the 1950s came two short-lived creations, *Mr. Rumbles* and *Sam Hill.* Early in the next decade he came up with a soap opera strip titled *Honor Eden*, announcing at the time that he was ready to "bid farewell to the losers club," since his new strip looked to be a winner. Alas, that didn't prove to be the case.

During the same years he was doing the strips that he signed his name to, Sparling also anonymously drew several sequences of the *True Comics* newspaper strip and ghosted stretches of Don Sherwood's *Dan Flagg.* In addition, he became a prolific contributor to comic books, first entering the field in 1943. He did considerable nonfiction material for *True Comics* and drew Nyoka the jungle girl for Fawcett. Over the years Sparling worked for Harvey, Dell, ACG, DC, Charlton, Marvel, and sundry other comic book publishers. His feature credits include *Challengers of the Unknown, Bomba, Doc Savage, X-Men, Iron Man, Mission Impossible, John Wayne*, and *Robin Hood.*

Of necessity some of his comic book work had a hurried, slapdash look. But at his best Sparling had an attractive, realistic brush style and was fond of odd and unusual angle shots. **R.G.**

**THE SPECTRE** It took about a year for comic book publishers to realize the importance of the advent of Superman. From then on superheroes began to proliferate and comic book titles to multiply. Early in 1940 DC got around to introducing a superhero to the pages of *More Fun Comics*, their oldest title. The new feature was somewhat unusual and one of the relatively few in which the hero began his career by dying. The Spectre made his debut in *More Fun* #52 (February 1940), written by Superman's cocreator Jerry Siegel and drawn by Bernard Baily. He was, as his name implied, an honest to goodness ghost.

In the first installment of the Spectre's two-issue origin story, tough redheaded cop Jim Corrigan was knocked off in the classic gangland fashion by being tossed into the river in a barrel of cement. His spirit flew heavenward, and a great light, presumably God, gave him a pep talk: "Your mission on Earth is unfinished…You shall remain earthbound battling crime on your world, with supernatural powers, until all vestiges of it are gone!!" Saddled with what was obviously a long- term job, Corrigan plummeted back home. In some mystical fashion his spirit was able to go around looking like his late body, down to sincere suit and tie. Corrigan decided he ought to have a distinctive costume in which to fight crime, and readers saw him sewing one up on his sewing machine. Donning a green cloak, turning his skin dead white and somehow making the pupils of his eyes disappear, he became the Spectre.

In his earliest escapades Corrigan had to transform himself into the Spectre, although in later stories the Spectre functioned as a sort of astral projection, leaving the hard-boiled cop's body to go off and battle injustice. The early Spectre had some impressive abilities: He could, for example, will his size to "increase to tremendous proportions." While in this mode he could do such stunts as pick up a speeding automobile filled with hoodlums, lift it into the air, and crush it. When the occupants pleaded for mercy, he coldly replied, "Why? Cold-blooded killers deserve but one fate!" He could also shrink down to teenie-weenie size, which was handy for traveling through telephone wires and tracing calls to their source. He was a first-class hypnotist as well and could make tiny skulls appear on his eyeballs while putting a reluctant subject into a trance. He could fly, vanish in a puff of smoke, and, since he was already dead, he couldn't be killed. His venue was the town of Cliffland, a city no doubt based on Siegel's native Cleveland.

At first the Spectre used his mystical powers on rather prosaic criminals. Fairly soon, however, he took to tackling wilder foes, including ghosts, little green alien invaders, and huge, ravenous purple monsters as tall as office buildings—as tall as Cleveland office buildings, anyway.

The Spectre's popularity started to wane toward the end of 1941. Adding a humorous sidekick in the person of bucktoothed, bespectacled Percival Popp the Super Cop didn't help much. Other *More Fun* heroes—Dr.

Fate, Johnny Quick, Aquaman, and the Green Arrow—nudged him out of the star position. Relegated to the back of the book, now turned out by Baily alone, the Spectre retired after *More Fun* #101 (January–February 1945). DC has brought him back several times in the years since, in the late 1960s and again in the late 1980s. Artists have included Neal Adams, Murphy Anderson, Jim Aparo, and Gene Colan. **R.G.**

**SPEED SPAULDING** An unusual, fairly grim and eventually unsuccessful science fiction strip, it began a little less than two years before the United States entered World War II. Drawn by Marvin Bradley, it was based on the novel *When Worlds Collide* by Edwin Balmer and Philip Wylie.

The new feature began appearing early in 1940, daily and Sunday; in most client papers, the strips were numbered, not dated, and *Speed* commenced at different times in different cities. The John F. Dille Co., which was responsible for *Buck Rogers*, syndicated *Speed Spaulding*. The novel it was based on, plotted by Balmer and written by Wylie, first appeared as a serial in *Bluebook* magazine in 1932. The hardcover went on sale the following year and sold very well. Though the strip was credited to Balmer and Wylie, it seems unlikely they had much to do with the scripting.

Unfortunately, the book's basic notion of a runaway planet on a collision course with Earth had already been borrowed by *Flash Gordon* and a string of others, and wasn't quite as fresh as it once had been. It is sometimes true that a public worrying about approaching disaster—in this case involvement in the war—will rush to be entertained by fictions about an even greater disaster, and probably Dille was operating on this assumption. *Speed Spaulding* dealt not with invasion or war, but with the impending total destruction of Earth. "Extry! Extry!" shouted a newsboy in an early daily. "Earth to be destroyed by planet from outer space…Get your paper here—AND KISS THE WORLD GOODBYE!"

Speed, who didn't appear in the novel or its sequel, was the hero of this saga of the waning days of the planet. Professor Bronson, the first man to become aware of two spheres hurtling toward Earth—modestly dubbed Bronson Alpha and Bronson Beta—was transferred from the novel, though not without having his name changed to Bronton (the spheres, too, were renamed). The continuity moved from Speed and a group of scientists and their efforts to build spacecraft for an escape from the doomed Earth, to scenes of the chaos and crime caused by worldwide panic. When it becomes clear there won't be enough time to construct sufficient ships, the scientists must decide who will go aboard their single escape ship.

A glum, pessimistic strip with only brief flashes of humor, it was nicely illustrated in a creditable variation of the Caniff-Sickles style, but it apparently proved too downbeat for a public suffering from war jitters and ended after little more than a year.

No comic strip ever concluded in a more impressive way than *Speed Spaulding*. Speed and his selected friends clambered aboard their spaceship hours before Alpha was due to strike Earth. They blasted off, using atomic engines. In the final panel of the final strip the world blew up. **R.G.**

**SPIDER-MAN** In mid-1962, while he and Jack Kirby were redefining superheroes with *Fantastic Four* and *The Hulk*, Marvel Comics' editor-scripter Stan Lee teamed with artist-plotter Steve Ditko to go a step further. In the last issue of a dying science fiction anthology, *Amazing Adult Fantasy*, they tried out a new character—insecure high school egghead Peter Parker, who gains strength, agility, wall-crawling ability, and an intuition for danger when he's bitten by a radioactive spider. Reader response was encouraging, and *The Amazing Spider-Man* premiered in early 1963, eventually becoming Marvel's most popular series.

Where the Kirby cocreations were epic in scope and impact, *Spider-Man* was intimate and sensitive. Advertised as "the hero who could be you," Peter Parker was a fragile kid trapped in an adolescent soap opera of unrequited crushes, peer rejection, and oppressive family obligations, who found that becoming a superhero only made everything worse. Like a real teenager, Parker swung wildly from hubris to self-hatred, from callousness to nobility. (His first desire, upon gaining his powers, is to become a celebrity on the Ed Sullivan Show; only after his selfishness leads to the death of his beloved Uncle Ben does he vow to hunt down criminals.)

Ditko and Lee created a gallery of colorful villains (the mysterious Green Goblin, the tragic Lizard, the implacable Kraven the Hunter) and turned in the best-plotted and best-scripted of all early Marvel stories; Ditko's finely detailed, observant, cartoonish art was perhaps the most charming in the superhero genre. But still the greatest appeal of the series was usually its emotional content. Earlier Marvel comics had already shown heroes as fallible and morally ambivalent, but it was *Spider-Man* that first tried to connect superheroes to the readers' daily life and show what a superbeing might be like in the real world. These have both become prime concerns of modern superhero comics.

Ditko's departure from Marvel in 1966 came as a shock to veteran "Spidey" fans, but it was under new penciller John Romita that the series reached its peak popularity. Lee and Romita told the now college-age

Parker's adventures in a loose, snazzy, more "adult" manner that largely determined the Marvel "house style" for years to come (Romita, in fact, would later become Marvel's art director). In the 1970s, Spider-Man's success engendered two additional series, *Marvel Team-Up* (now replaced by *Web of Spider-Man*) and *Peter Parker, the Spectacular Spider-Man*.

Although the developments of his life are now mainly reworkings of familiar situations, such as the frail health of Peter's Aunt May, who has been on the verge of death since 1963, Spider-Man has remained one of the livelier of Marvel's long-running heroes, perhaps because of the strength of his personality and supporting cast. Numerous writers (Gerry Conway, Marv Wolfman, Roger Stern, Peter David and others) and artists (Gil Kane, Ross Andru, Todd McFarlane and many more) have served the web-spinner.  **G.J.**

**SPIEGELMAN, ART** (1948– ) A die-hard survivor of the already fading comics underground, Art Spiegelman might have joined the roster of those who toiled for that noble experiment and were forgotten if he had not created *Maus*. The book-length graphic memoir, published by a mainstream trade press in 1986, not only catapulted him to fame but, to a large extent, also revitalized the medium itself, and Spiegelman was credited with single-handedly justifying the comic strip as a serious creative medium.

Born in Stockholm, Sweden, to Jewish immigrants who had fled the Holocaust, Spiegelman studied art in high school in New York City and later in college in Binghamton, and during the 1960s and 1970s was deeply committed to the idea of social revolution. He contributed widely to many of the underground publications and created several of his own. His work, intensely personal and often atypical, even within the ill-defined framework of the underground, ranged from sophisticated and literate satire to searing psychological self-revelation. To support himself, he has illustrated books, drawn for newspapers and magazines including the *New York Times* and *Playboy*, and, since he was in high school, created bubblegum cards and novelty packaging for candy. Since 1979 he has taught a course in the aesthetics of the comics at New York's School of Visual Arts.

In 1980 Spiegelman and his wife Françoise Mouly founded *Raw*, an avant-garde comics annual, to revive the faltering spirit of the underground press. It was in *Raw* that *Maus* was first serialized, and when it appeared as a book Spiegelman became a celebrity. He continues to produce *Raw* in New York and is working on a sequel to *Maus*.  **D.W.**

**THE SPIRIT** A somewhat unconventional masked man, the Spirit has been a comic book hero for more than half a century. He was created by Will Eisner in 1940 to star in a weekly 16-page comic book that was distributed with the Sunday funnies; although the weekly halted in 1952, the Spirit's adventures are still being reprinted in this country and around the world.

The Spirit was actually Denny Colt, criminologist and private detective, who was apparently murdered by a villain named Dr. Cobra. As it happened, Colt wasn't really dead, but he decided to let Central City go on believing that he was, so that he could fight crime more unconventionally as a masked avenger. Those who shared his secret were crusty Police Commissioner Dolan, his pretty blond daughter Ellen, and Ebony White, a young black man who served as the Spirit's sidekick. Settled in a roomy, furnished crypt in the Wildwood Cemetery, Colt went forth to fight crime. These are the basics of many another comic book feature—as well as many a movie serial—but in Eisner's hands the result wasn't at all conventional.

*The Spirit* weekly owed its existence to the advent of Superman and the burgeoning of the comic book business in the late 1930s. The impressive sales of the flamboyant kind of adventure fantasy offered by the upstart comic books caused some newspapers and syndicates to fear that the sales of Sunday papers, which were bought by many chiefly for the colored funnies, would be hurt. As a result, the *Chicago Tribune* added a special Sunday *Comic Book Magazine* in the spring of 1940, and a few months later the Register & Tribune Syndicate started offering *The Spirit* to newspapers around the nation. As backup features readers got *Lady Luck* and *Mr. Mystic*.

Eisner refused to draw a superhero for the new venture, so he compromised on a masked man. His Spirit wore a blue business suit, often the worse for wear after his assorted encounters with the underworld, a fedora, and a cloth mask which covered the upper half of his face. In the very first appearance of the character Eisner forgot to draw the mask at all, so the Spirit didn't show up wearing it until the second week. Eisner was a great reader of short stories, and an enthusiastic movie fan. He began trying to emulate his favorite writers, O. Henry and Ambrose Bierce, while experimenting increasingly with movie approaches to layout. Radio also influenced him, and he came to use sound effects and narration in his *Spirit* stories. His experiments extended to the splash page of his weekly story as well. The logo changed drastically each time; one week the name might appear on the front of a newspaper floating along a gutter, the next his hero would be leaning against gigantic stone letters spelling out The Spirit.

Eisner had a sense of humor, which meant he never took his leading character seriously. "I could never figure out why any crimefighter could go out and fight crime," he's confessed. "Why the hell a guy should run around with a mask and fight crime was beyond me. Except that I, and there again it was part of my background, had this kind of mystical thinking, in which I've always felt that people do the things they have to do...The Spirit had all the middle class motivations...Of course, the big thing, the big problem each week was to figure out an acceptable reason why he should get involved in this in the first place." In his stories Eisner used super villains, sultry sirens, and the other essentials of comic books, but he also took an interest in more earthy details: civic corruption, life on the underside of a large city, the problems of the mean streets and the crowded tenements. Even when muckraking Eisner was not completely serious, he managed to throw in humor and, fairly often, fantasy.

In October 1941 a daily newspaper strip was added. Eisner had help from a variety of artists over the years, including Alex Kotzky, Lou Fine, Jack Cole, John Spranger, and Jules Feiffer. The strip lasted only until 1944, but the weekly went on until 1952. *Police Comics*, the home of Jack Cole's Plastic Man, began reprinting *The Spirit* in 1942, and a comic book devoted just to him started up in 1944. Since then there have been several other reprint series, and currently Kitchen Sink Enterprises publishes a black and white that reprints four stories per issue. Because Eisner was a bit shrewder than many of his contemporaries, he owns his character, and the income from all reprints is his. **R.G.**

**SPRANGER, JOHN** (1922– ) During his fewer than 20 years as a cartoonist Spranger produced a good deal of work in both comic books and newspaper comic sections; between the years 1942 and 1959 he drew such characters as Plastic Man, Spy Smasher, Doll Man, The Spirit, Ben Friday, and The Saint.

Going to work on the production line at the Jack Binder shop in 1942, he was involved in the drawing of Blackstone, Captain Midnight, Bulletman, Spy Smasher, Mary Marvel, and a number of others. He next worked for the Quality line, and in 1945, soon after Will Eisner returned from the Army, he was also hired to help out on the weekly *Spirit* magazine. His style became, of necessity, strongly influenced by that of Eisner. Spranger remained with him throughout 1946. At Quality he carried on a variety of chores, most notably doing a creditable job of filling in for Jack Cole on Plastic Man.

In the spring of 1948 he became part of the New York Herald Tribune Syndicate's plan to add adventure strips to its list. With Lawrence Lariar as writer, he began drawing a Sunday page called *Bodyguard*. The strip eventually changed its name to *Ben Friday* and then to *The Bantam Prince*, adding a daily along the way. Spranger's early work was very forceful, combining what he had learned about inking and layout from Eisner with a somewhat more sophisticated drawing and storytelling style of his own. His Sunday pages were distinctive and strong and must have unsettled some of the more sedate *Herald Trib* readers who had grown accustomed to the dependable blandness of *Peter Rabbit*, *The Timid Soul*, and *Mr. and Mrs.*

He was reassigned in 1951 and promoted to the ongoing Saint strip. He modified his style again, moving to a slicker, less black approach. Influenced by what Alex Raymond was then doing on *Rip Kirby*, Spranger paid more attention to fashion and decor, and he seemed to be trying for a politer, slick magazine look.

He left the strip abruptly in 1959 and at the same time left comics for good. **R.G.**

**SPY SMASHER** He debuted in the first issue of *Whiz Comics* early in 1940, when many people in America were starting to worry about spies and fifth columnists; after Captain Marvel, he was the most popular and successful character in the magazine. Spy Smasher, in reality wealthy sportsman Alan Armstrong, lived up to his name and specialized in combating spies, saboteurs and would-be invaders. His fiancée Eve was the daughter of Admiral Colby, head of Naval Intelligence, a relationship that kept Alan up to date on Axis activities. He had no superpowers, and when he wanted to fly, he had to hop into his gyrosub—"a super craft which travels as fast as light on the ground, in the air and underwater." Initially his costume and goggled helmet were brown, but later on he switched to a tighter-fitting green ensemble.

Recurrent villains included America Smasher, a mean-minded Nazi dwarf, and the master spy known as the Mask. It was the Mask who used the Brain-o-graph on Spy Smasher, converting him into a rampaging traitor for several issues in 1941. (It took coworker Captain Marvel to set him straight.)

Spy Smasher got his own magazine in 1941, and the following year Republic released a movie serial. The character didn't fare well in the postwar world, however, and in 1947 he traded in his uniform for a trench coat and became a private eye, changing his name to Crimesmasher and installing Eve as his secretary. A few months later he left comics.

His appearance fluctuated considerably, since a great many different artists drew his adventures over the years. Among them were C.C. Beck, Charles Sultan, and Emil Gershwin. A disciple of Alex Raymond, Gershwin gave the feature its most formal, realistic look. **R.G.**

**STAMATY, MARK ALAN** (1947– ) One of the most innovative of contemporary cartoonists, Mark Alan Stamaty defies easy classification, producing neither conventional political cartoons nor anything like the usual continuity strip, and fitting neatly into neither the mainstream nor the underground. His bizarre, late 1970s social satire *MacDoodle Street*, and his current political series *Washingtoon*, have established Stamaty in a unique position among cartoonist-commentators.

Born in Brooklyn, New York, Stamaty was the son of two cartoonists: Stanley Stamaty, an illustrator and gag cartoonist who published regularly in the *Saturday Evening Post*, *Look*, and *Colliers*, and Clara Gee Kastner, whose teen-panels included *Sitter Sue* and *Ginnie*. Stamaty studied art at Cooper Union and had gallery exhibitions of his etchings, winning an award from the State Museum of New Jersey in 1970. In 1971 he illustrated a children's book written by a classmate. Two years later he wrote and illustrated one of his own, *Who Needs Donuts?*, and won a gold medal from the Society of Illustrators for it. Three other juveniles followed, and from 1977 to 1981 Stamaty was a member of the faculty of Parsons School of Design, teaching the writing and illustrating of children's books.

It was in the fall of 1977, however, that Stamaty initiated the wild Greenwich Village comic strip satire that was to create his cult following. *MacDoodle Street* (named for the Village's MacDougal Street) details the events of a naive poet's confrontation with Life in the Big City, its panels surrounded by a frieze of grotesque figures, human, animal, and mixed, commenting vividly on the action within. *MacDoodle Street* ran weekly in the *Village Voice* until September 1979, and a collection was published in 1981.

From April 1980 to April 1981, Stamaty produced his most personal, and most hermetic, strip, *Carrttoooonnn*, also for the *Voice*. In this essentially serious "stream-of-consciousness strip," as he describes it, Stamaty experimented with art and allowed his drawing to loosen into a freer line.

Stamaty's involvement with the political scene began when the *Washington Post* called him in January 1981, requesting something for its op-ed page. The result was *Washingtoon*, which has appeared every Wednesday since October 27, 1981, in the *Village Voice* and been reprinted the following Monday, since November 1, 1981, in the *Post*. Originally self-syndicated, it is now distributed to about 35 papers by the Washington Post Writers Group. A keen parody of life in our capital, it recounts the adventures of Bob Forehead, senator and would-be talk-show host (two roles he finds indistinguishable), and reveals his complex relations with a firm that manufactures bombs that kill only people without credit cards. Stamaty's broad lampoon of rightist rhetoric is irresistibly witty, and although, as the artist admits, some find its extreme liberal orientation excessive and its deliberately grotesque graphic style "too unusual," *Washingtoon* has built an ardent and widely distributed audience, and collections of the strip have been published in 1983 and 1986.

Stamaty has done, and occasionally still does, covers for the *New Republic* and illustrations for *Esquire*, *New York*, the *New York Times*, and *Harpers*. But his principal activity now is *Washingtoon*, which has a growing readership and has been described as "one of the most fully realized and sustained satires of political America to make it into the mainstream." **D.W.**

**STAMM, RUSSELL** (1915–1969) Yet another exponent of the Chicago style of cartooning, Stamm created the *Invisible Scarlet O'Neil* newspaper strip in 1940. Prior to that he had worked with Chester Gould, providing the backgrounds against which Dick Tracy's violent confrontations with crookdom took place.

Born in Chicago, Stamm got most of his training at the Academy of Fine Arts there. Interested in drawing since childhood, he had also taken the Landon mail-order course. In 1934 he got a job in the art department of the *Chicago Tribune*, and after assisting for short spells on *Tiny Tim* and *The Gumps*, he began a five-year stint helping out on *Dick Tracy*.

Stamm left Gould's employ in 1940 when he sold his strip about a young lady with a talent for turning invisible at will to Marshall Field's Chicago Times Syndicate. But initially he worked in a style that had many affinities with that of his former boss. Both artists took a flat, cartoony approach to illustrating their fairly serious, often hard-boiled continuities. Like other Chicago-based cartoonists—such as Zack Mosley and Harold Gray—they didn't feel that adventure strips required the realistic approach favored by such artists as Milton Caniff and Alex Raymond.

In addition to his strip, Stamm illustrated some Big Little Books in the early 1940s. There were two Dick Tracy originals and one titled *Gangbusters Smash Through*. When he entered the service in 1944, the strip was ghosted for a time. He returned to *Scarlet* full time after the war and stayed with it until the end when, as he put it, "she became completely invisible." He then left comics for good and formed Russ Stamm Productions, creating and producing animated television commercials for a number of national clients. **R.G.**

**STANLEY, JOHN** (1914– ) A comic book artist and writer who never courted fame, Stanley was responsible for the *Little Lulu* comic books from their beginning in the middle 1940s to the early 1960s. Anonymous during his active years in the field, he's gained some recognition in recent years. In 1981 the *Smithsonian Book of Comic Book Comics* reprinted over 40 pages of his work, and more recently Another Rainbow, the same company that reprints the Carl Barks duck material, set out to reprint all his *Little Lulu* issues in handsome hardcover volumes.

A native New Yorker, Stanley attended the New York School of Art on a scholarship. He went from there into animation at the Fleischer studios in Manhattan. Next he began contributing to *The Mickey Mouse Magazine*, and in the early 1940s he went to work for Oskar Lebeck in the New York offices of the Dell-Western outfit. Lebeck, whom he'd met on the Mickey venture, was also an artist-writer, and it seems likely that his simple, deliberately childlike drawing style influenced Stanley's own approach.

He was assigned the *Little Lulu* comic book when it started in 1945. "Oskar handed me the assignment but I'm sure it was due to no special form of brilliance that he thought I'd lend it...I just happened to be available at the time."

Although a capable cartoonist, it was as a writer and idea man that he excelled on *Lulu*. What he provided, after drawing and scripting the first couple of issues was what amounted to rough storyboards for others to work from. Stanley, so to speak, drew his scripts and others took care of the finished art. Stanley stayed with the character until the early 1960s, masterminding about 175 issues of the magazine. He inherited Lulu's boyfriend from the original gag cartoons of Marge Henderson Buell, but invented most all the other characters. He changed Lulu from a lovable brat to a basically nice kid who was smarter than just about anybody around, especially her boy associates.

It was his inventive stories, running from simple tales of school life to satirical fantasies, that won child readers and kept many of them fans for the rest of their lives.

Stanley wrote and drew several other comic book titles, including *Nancy*, *O.G. Whiz*, and *Choo Choo Charlie*. In a few issues of *Raggedy Ann and Andy* he drew and scripted *Peterkin Pottle*, a feature about a kid with Walter Mitty tendencies. He left comics entirely in the late 1960s and went into commercial art. **R.G.**

**STARR, LEONARD** (1925– ) Few professional cartoonists have survived the decline of the continuity strip as successfully as Leonard Starr, whose *Mary Perkins On Stage* (and later the resuscitated and updated version of *Little Orphan Annie*) have been among the most consistently popular narrative strips in the field.

Manhattan-born Starr went to the High School of Music and Art (where his early exposure to the world of the theater was to provide him with valuable material for *On Stage*) and spent a year at the Pratt Institute, but never felt he got much from either. Nervous about being able to make a living as an artist, he specialized in "art education" so he could be sure of a job teaching, but while still a student at Pratt he got a job at Funnies, Inc., doing backgrounds for comic books. He soon advanced to both penciling and inking with "every publisher in the business except Quality Comics," he reports, "which may be a comment on the level of work [he] was doing." At last he became so dissatisfied with his "rather haphazard" training that he went to the Art Students League, in New York City, to study under Frank Reilly.

As his work grew more polished, he became a successful advertising artist, but never lost his love of the comics and doggedly submitted strip ideas to the syndicates. His personal favorite was one about a medical missionary, but it was rejected by everyone. Finally, after King Features turned down seven of his efforts, the Chicago Tribune-N.Y. News Syndicate took a chance on a strip about the glamorous New York theater world, and in February of 1957 the curtain went up on *Mary Perkins On Stage* (more often known simply as *On Stage*), which he wrote and drew until it was discontinued in 1979. In that year, he accepted a call from his syndicate to take over the perennial adventure strip *Little Orphan Annie*. The strip, renamed *Annie* "to make it seem less dated and to reflect the highly successful Broadway musical," as Starr explains, continues to be popular, one of the few survivors of its genre. In 1980 Starr collaborated with Stan Drake to write another adventure strip called *Kelly Green*, about the widow of a murdered policeman, for the French publisher Dargaud, but the venture was short-lived. He has also written television scripts since the early 1970s and in 1984 developed and wrote the animated show "Thundercats."

Starr's art is consistently slick and graceful, adapted to the readership of each of his series. Reflecting the artist's lifelong admiration for cartoonists Alex Raymond and Milt Caniff, *On Stage* utilized a photographic realism to deliver the sophisticated dialogue of its elegant characters—the beautiful people of the theater—in a visual package no less sophisticated. The cinematic compositions and dramatic lighting effects of *Kelly Green* were perfectly suited to the sensational plots. *Annie* is done in a simpler, less detailed style, as befits the younger audience for which it is intended.

Among the most skillful writers in the comics, Starr has always worked alone on his scripts. His tightly plotted and well-paced narratives have brought him the National Cartoonists Society's Best Story Strip award twice—in 1960 for *On Stage* and in 1980 for *Annie*—and he received that organization's Reuben award as the Outstanding Cartoonist of the Year in 1965. **D.W.**

**STARRETT, KEMP** (1890–1952) Although he got a credit on the *Vignettes of Life* Sunday page that he drew from 1939 to 1952, much of Starrett's other comic strip and comic book work appeared anonymously.

Prior to drawing comics, he had worked as a successful illustrator for such magazines as *Cosmopolitan* and *The Saturday Evening Post* and was a gag cartoonist for *The New Yorker* and *Life*. Starrett joined the Philadelphia Ledger Syndicate in the middle 1930s and was the first artist to draw the *Roy Powers, Eagle Scout* strip, the chief artist on *War On Crime* and a fill-in on *Babe Bunting*. An excellent artist of the illustrational school, he drew in a scratchy, realistic style. In fact, he was good enough to have his unsigned work confused by some comics historians with that of his very gifted Ledger colleague Frank Godwin. When J. Norman Lynd switched to King Features in 1939, Starrett took over the *Vignettes of Life* Sunday and was allowed to sign it.

In the early 1940s he branched out into comic books, drawing the fictional adventures of real life magician Blackstone in Street & Smith's *Super Magician Comics*, although he never signed the feature or any other of his comic book work. He later drew the adventures of Nigel Elliman, the magician who replaced Blackstone. He was one of the few comic book artists of the period to apply the principles of solid 1930s magazine illustration to comic book pages. The result was sedate, well-mannered work that seemed a bit quiet for such a usually flamboyant medium.

Whether by choice or by chance, Starrett never achieved fame or great recognition. His lack of recognition was perhaps exemplified by his obituary in *The New York Times* which ran to only a few lines and misspelled his name throughout. **R.G.**

**STEEL STERLING** An early comic book superhero, the blond Steel Sterling made his debut roughly a year and a half after the advent of the original Man of Steel. Drawn by Charles Biro and written initially by editor Abner Sundell, he first appeared in *Zip Comics* #1 (February 1940) and soon became one of the MLJ publishing company's most popular characters. He began appearing in a second title, *Jackpot Comics*, in 1941.

Steel's origin was a painful one, since he acquired his powers by diving into a "tank of molten steel and fiery chemicals!" Fortunately, as his unorthodox scientific researches had led him to believe, that risky bath gave him "all the attributes of this sturdiest of metals!!" His associates included Dora Cummings, pretty dark-haired daughter of a famous scientist; Clancy, a fat red-haired cop; and Alec Looney, a skinny and inept detective. Among the frequent villains were the Black Knight, who always dressed in brown, and the Rattler, a fellow who sported a snake suit.

Biro dropped the feature in 1941, and Carl Hubbell took over. Irv Novick followed and while his Steel Sterling was the best-drawn of the three, it lacked the flamboyance of Biro's lumpier version. Steel originally retired in 1944, but came back to work briefly in the mid-1960s and again in the mid-1980s. **R.G.**

**STERANKO, JAMES** (1938– ) Cartoonist, illustrator, writer, publisher, and magician, Steranko produced some of the most interesting and provocative comic book pages of the late 1960s while he was drawing Marvel's *Nick Fury*. And while he has long since moved on to other creative areas, his influence is still felt.

He was born in Pennsylvania and still lives there. Before breaking into comics in 1966 Steranko had worked as a carnival pitchman, escape artist, magician, guitar player, photographer, and advertising art director. During the superhero boom of the middle 1960s Steranko, still in advertising, developed several new characters and sold them to the Harvey company. Although he designed the heroes and wrote the scripts, he did none of the actual drawing. His *Spyman* survived for just three issues, and none of his others did any better. By the end of 1966 he was working for Marvel, inking Jack Kirby's *Nick Fury, Agent of S.H.I.E.L.D.* Soon he assumed both the writing and drawing of the belligerent, one-eyed superspy's adventures.

"Everything from films, from radio, pulps, business, everything I could possibly apply from my background, including the magic I've done, the gigs I've played—everything goes into every comic story," Steranko once explained. "Nick Fury became Steranko." He blended the Marvel house style, as personified at the time in the work of Kirby, with the storytelling techniques of Will Eisner and Bernard Krigstein, adding the flash of op art posters and the glitz of Madison Avenue layouts. Fans and readers responded and Steranko's work of those years certainly paved the way for much of the innovative and experimental work that's been done in comic books since.

By 1969 he'd quit doing comic book pages. In the early 1970s he drew covers for such titles as *Fantastic Four* and *Doc Savage*. After abandoning Nick Fury, Steranko founded his own publishing company, Supergraphics. He published two well-researched volumes of his never-completed history of comic books and continues to publish the magazine *Prevue*, which is dedicated mostly to current action motion pictures. He's undertaken a wide range of art jobs over the years, including posters, book jackets, paperback covers, the graphic novel *Chandler*, and illustrations for his own magazine. Steranko still occasionally does a comic book cover. One of his recent ones was for the debut issue of the returning *Green Hornet* title. **R.G.**

**STERRETT, CLIFF** See POLLY AND HER PALS.

**STEVE CANYON** Milton Caniff's third and final adventure strip began in 1947 and lasted for over 40 years. Such was his reputation from *Terry and the Pirates*, that the new strip was sold to many newspapers around the country even before an editor had seen a sample. In its early years *Steve Canyon* lived up to expectations and was the model of what a first-rate adventure strip should be. It had appealing characters, beautiful women, exotic locations, bright dialogue, compelling plots, and impeccable staging. As time passed, however, and the public taste changed, *Steve Canyon* grew increasingly less popular, and by the 1980s it was appearing in only a handful of papers. When it ended, the adventure strip pretty much ended, too.

*Steve Canyon*, which began on Monday, January 13, 1947, fit the postwar adventure pattern. It was about a returning Air Force officer, his shift from the service to civilian life, and the possibilities for adventure, romance, and profit in the new world that was coming into being after a devastating war. Significantly, Canyon called the shoestring air service he was trying to launch Horizons Unlimited.

At that point there was nobody who could handle that sort of material as well. After 12 years with *Terry*, Caniff was an expert at slicing his movie-like continuities into daily episodes, and he knew all about the planes and the weapons. Equally important was his feeling for character, his awareness that every actor, even the bit players, was important. In fact, he may have been too inventive in the first weeks of the strip and introduced more interesting characters than it could hold. Besides the lean, lanky Canyon, there was his secretary Feeta Feeta, Copper Calhoun—the Dragon Lady of Wall Street—and her various goons and toadies, plus Canyon's own crew of veterans. After the advent a few months later of Happy Easter, the quintessential old coot, most of the crew faded into the background. The first continuity took place in South America, far away from postwar Europe and Asia, where the scenery was better and undamaged, although before too long Caniff did return to the Orient, even providing Canyon with a Terry-like sidekick in the person of Reed Kimberly.

The world, however, was changing, and it wasn't possible to recapture the feel and excitement of Terry Lee and Pat Ryan adventuring across the China of the 1930s. The politics were trickier, less clear-cut. By the time the Eisenhower years arrived, the free-lance adventurer was no longer as popular as he'd once been, and horizons didn't seem so unlimited. Sensing this, Caniff put his hero back in the service and then varied his foreign intrigues with domestic dramas that came close to being soap opera. He gave Canyon a teenage ward named Poteet Canyon to intrude into his life now and then, and in 1970, after a courtship that had begun in Asia and lasted for 18 years, Canyon at last married Summer Smith.

A military hero, even one whose adventures were written and drawn by a former Roosevelt supporter, was not going to be universally popular in the 1960s—especially with younger readers. By the late 1960s something started to happen that had never happened before—Caniff began to lose papers. "During the Vietnam War, he underestimated momentarily the extent of the anti-war sentiment in the country," comics historian R.C. Harvey has commented. "When readers protested the hawkish tone of the strip, Caniff quickly regrouped, taking Canyon out of uniform to serve the Air Force as a special agent in mufti. But the strip's circulation was irreparably damaged; it never again approached the number of papers it had enjoyed at its peak."

Caniff had had a variety of helpers on the strip over the years. Frank Engli, longtime letterer on *Terry*, continued in that job on *Steve Canyon* until the middle 1970s. The distinctive logo was designed by Noel Sickles, who'd also designed the one used on *Terry*. Among the assistants—and occasional ghosts—were William Overgard, Ray Bailey, and Alex Kotzky. In 1953 Caniff hired Richard Rockwell to assist, and for the strip's final years Rockwell did all the penciling. It seems odd that Caniff, whose specialty had been laying out his stories cinematically, would turn over the responsibility of calling the shots to an assistant. Yet he did, doing only the inking. By the early 1980s *Steve Canyon* was a sad, pathetic shadow of what it had once been. It continued to lose papers, and after Caniff's death it was allowed to end. The final strip appeared on June 5, 1988. **R.G.**

**STEVE ROPER** The adventurous photographer and investigative reporter was first seen in Allen Saunders and Elmer Woggon's *Big Chief Wahoo* in 1940. Gradually he upstaged the little Indian, and the strip changed its name to *Chief Wahoo and Steve Roper* and to *Steve Roper and Wahoo*. Finally in 1947 the title became simply *Steve Roper* and the Chief was seen no more.

By the time the blond, pipe-smoking Roper took over, he was working on the *Life*-like news magazine *Spotlight*. Saunders, who was also scripting *Mary Worth* and *Kerry Drake*, blended soap opera and detective story elements in the strip. Roper specialized in investigating criminals, racketeers, conmen, and bunco artists, managing at the same time to find romance with a succession of attractive women. Saunders often managed to build suspense over the solution of a mystery and the outcome of a love affair at the same time.

Woggon had long since stepped aside as artist on the strip and, when Roper went solo in 1947, the ghost artist was Pete Hoffman. In 1954 William Overgard became the artist. A disciple and former assistant of Milton Caniff, Overgard was given co-credit with Saunders. Overgard came to do most of the writing as well and introduced a new character in the person of Mike Nomad. Originally invented for an unsold strip of Overgard's, Nomad was rough-edged, a lot tougher and nastier than Roper. He had affinities with the tough private eye Mike Hammer and the equally tough biker portrayed by Marlon Brando in *The Wild One.*

Eventually Nomad did to Roper what the reporter had done to the Indian. The strip changed its name yet again, this time to *Steve Roper & Mike Nomad.* The prematurely gray, crewcut Nomad took over much of the action, while Roper, now an editor, sat it out on the sidelines. When Overgard left in the middle 1980s, artist Fran Matera replaced him. John Saunders is the writer.

**R.G.**

**STORM, GEORGE** (1893–1976) A restless and somewhat elusive man, Storm seems never to have courted fame. When he died, his obituary didn't make the wire services, and the notice that ran in his hometown paper in Oklahoma failed to mention most of his cartooning credits. Yet during a professional career that began before the First World War and continued for over a half-century, he racked up an impressive list of achievements.

Storm drew *Phil Hardy,* one of the first adventure strips, in the middle 1920s. Next he created *Bobby Thatcher,* which was by the early 1930s one of the most popular strips in the country. Entering the fast-growing comic book business in the late 1930s, he worked for most of the major houses. Impressively versatile, he turned out everything from costumed superheroes to funny animals and was the first artist to draw the avenging Hangman for MLJ and one of the first to do Bugs Bunny for Dell. The early 1940s found him taking over *Adventures of Patsy,* after a brief stint ghosting the *Joe Jinks* daily strip, and also creating *Buzzy* for DC. This teenage comic book character competed successfully with *Archie* for several years.

George Storm was born in a small town in Arkansas and grew up in a small town in Oklahoma. By the time he was in his early teens he was working for an Oklahoma weekly, but as a copy boy and not a cartoonist. He was employed for a while as a file clerk on the ST. L & SF Railway. "On the face of official reports concerning the annihilation of cows began to appear my sketches of Bossy hurtling over the telegraph wires and irate farmers and claim agents in the background," Storm later confessed. "The result was inevitable; art

and commerce clashed." Out of a job, young Storm migrated to Chicago. After a few months of art instruction, "I began to make the rounds of the Chicago papers applying for a job. I was one of 500 with that ambition. John T. McCutcheon continued to hold his job against the field. Then followed two years of more or less precarious freelancing among trade publications, with intervals of employment in other fields."

Eventually Storm got a job as a reporter, at a salary of $8 per week, on the *Chicago Herald.* When that paper folded, he found work on other papers in the area. By 1919 he had headed West, working as a reporter for both the *Los Angeles Examiner* and the *San Francisco Chronicle.* "But the ambition to become a cartoonist remained with me and I aspired to become an editor and run my own cartoons on page one…The editor of the *San Francisco Daily News* recognized the strategy and gave me a job as a cartoonist in self-defense."

After five years of drawing local cartoons for the *News,* the restless Storm journeyed East to work for the *New York Mirror.* He had by this time done a variety of cartoon work for newspapers, one of his specialties being panel cartoons offering bird's-eye views crowded with dozens of characters at various local sites. For the *Mirror,* again imitating a format often used by his idol McCutcheon, he did a series of such panels under the title *Little Old New York in Pictures.* In 1925 Storm encountered newspaperman and author Jay Jerome Williams. The result was *Phil Hardy.*

Storm had a style entirely his own and it is next to impossible to find predecessors or, for that matter, latter-day disciples. His drawing was quirky, full of energy, and he often suggested more than he showed. Even when handling fairly serious features, Storm was clearly a cartoonist and not an illustrator. His anatomy was a bit off, but his people all move and have life.

Sometime in the late 1940s he went home again to Enid, Oklahoma, and remained there for the rest of his life. He worked at advertising, gag cartooning, and illustrating. He also attempted at least one more newspaper strip, but it didn't sell, and his last nationally seen work appeared in the early 1950s in the less than prestigious humor digest called *Charley Jones' Laugh Book.*

**R.G.**

**STRANGE AS IT SEEMS**   See HIX, JOHN.

**STRIEBEL, JOHN H.**   See DIXIE DUGAN.

**SUB-MARINER**   Marvel's longest-running and, at times, least amiable superhero, Sub-Mariner debuted in 1939. Also known as Prince Namor, he has continued to appear in comic books, with occasional lapses, ever since.

He began his comic career not as a superhero but as a super villain. Originally he had a temperament that combined all the best features of Fu Manchu, King Kong, and the Frankenstein monster. Although he reformed a couple of times during his first years in business, he backslid, too, and his angry rampages provided some of the liveliest moments in Golden Age comics. While Prince Namor didn't at that time speak in the Shakespearean cadences of some of his later incarnations, he did possess the attitudes and outlook of the revengeful protagonist of an Elizabethan tragedy.

The creation of artist-writer Bill Everett, Sub-Mariner emerged in the spring of 1939 in a short-lived and minimally circulated comic entitled *Motion Picture Funnies Weekly*. Since the artwork therein was printed in black and white, Everett worked on Craftint paper. While this allowed him to add some handsome halftone effects, it made for a somewhat muddy look when the origin story was reprinted, with four additional pages, in full color in the first issue of *Marvel Comics* in the fall of 1939. The new magazine, which changed its name to the snappier *Marvel Mystery Comics* with the second issue, was also the home of such characters as the Human Torch and the Angel.

Appropriately enough, the Sub-Mariner was first seen underwater at the bottom of the sea, living with his people in an undersea kingdom. At this early point in the history the kingdom wasn't yet identified as Atlantis. Readers learned that the prince had been born as the result of a misalliance between his underwater mother and an explorer named Leonard McKenzie. Misinterpreting a new ocean expedition, his mom told him it

was time to begin an all out attack on "the land of the white people!" She also reminded him that he is the only one of them "who can live on land and in water, and who can fly in the air...you have the strength of a thousand earth-men." Inspired, the Sub-Mariner headed for civilization and revenge.

In the second issue the prince arrived in New York City and commenced his one-man rampage. He destroyed a powerhouse, clashed with and killed several policemen, and tried to kidnap a wealthy young woman. Gradually, however, over the next few months he mellowed. An important influence on Sub-Mariner was Betty Dean, a pretty Manhattan policewoman. She was able to prevail on him to use his powers to "help stop this terrible war." For a while Namor concentrated on wiping out Nazis, sometimes with the aid of warriors from his undersea hometown.

Miffed again when the authorities tried to electrocute him for his earlier crimes, Sub-Mariner went on another binge of violence. At one point the Human Torch joined in the fight against him. The battle stretched across two issues and ended only when Betty Dean got the boys to make up. By *Marvel* #17 (March 1941) Prince Namor was nearly a nice guy, and he and the Torch teamed up to halt an attempted Nazi invasion of the United States. For the next several months after that a rather subdued Sub-Mariner returned again to Manhattan. He resumed his friendship with Betty and devoted himself to such jobs as solving an airliner mystery and rounding up a gang of spies. Everett entered the service shortly after America entered the Second World War, and by the spring of 1942 he had left his feature.

By that time the Sub-Mariner, one of Marvel's most popular characters, had branched out considerably. He was the backup feature in the Human Torch comic book that was introduced in 1940. In the following year he got a magazine of his own—"40 Thrilling Pages of Sub-Mariner! 20 Pages of the Angel." Everett provided most of the early artwork, getting help from such assistants as Sam Gilman, George Mandel, and Mike Roy. In many of these adventures the prince could be heard uttering his favorite exclamation, "Sufferin' shad!"

Unlike some superheroes—notably Superman and Batman—the Sub-Mariner took an active part in the war, fighting both the Japanese and the Germans with vigor and earning himself the title of "the Axis' greatest enemy." Quite a few artists drew the character while Everett was away, among them Carl Pfeufer, Jimmy Thompson, and Lee Elias.

After the War Bill Everett came back to resume his old job. His aquatic hero hung on until 1949, aided from 1947 by a handsome blond lady named Namora, a cousin of his. In 1953 there was a brief flutter of interest in superheroes again, and Sub-Mariner returned in a comic book titled *Young Men*. The following year his own title was revived. The world situation had changed a bit, and on most of the covers the prince was to be seen bashing Russians and such scourges as Commie Frogmen. This particular resurrection didn't take and in 1955 he retired once again.

When the Silver Age began the prince surfaced once more. Initially he popped up in *Fantastic Four* #4 (May 1962), wandering the Bowery and not aware of who he was. After assorted appearances in other Marvel titles, he settled into a regular berth in *Tales to Astonish*. Then in 1968 a new *Sub-Mariner* title started. By this time Namor was clearly established as a prince of Atlantis. John Buscema was the first artist, followed by such as Marie Severin, Gene Colan, and George Tuska. Namor went through various phases, sometimes reverting to his old vengeful days and spouting phrases like "Imperious Rex!" Everett picked him up again in 1972 and 1973. In 1974 Sub-Mariner took another leave.

He was back in a miniseries in 1984 and again in 1988, and in 1989 in a 12-part limited series with art by Rich Buckler. He resurfaced again in 1990, written and drawn by John Byrne.                              **R.G.**

**SUPERGIRL** Superman's teenage cousin Kara, the last survivor of Argo City, which in turn was the last surviving portion of the destroyed planet Krypton, first appeared in *Action Comics* in 1959, the creation of National (DC) Comics editor Mort Weisinger and writer Otto Binder. She had her own backup series in *Action* for the next 10 years, drawn mainly by Jim Mooney and written by various Weisinger free-lancers, especially Leo Dorfman.

She figured prominently in other Superman stories as well: for three years as Superman's "secret weapon," her existence concealed from the world; thereafter as his occasional partner in heroism, and an affectionate link to his lost past.

Supergirl possessed the same powers and vulnerabilities as her cousin, but her adventures were specifically slanted toward young girls. A glance at her two regular animal friends is revealing: There was Streaky, a cat who gains superpowers and engages in cute but dangerous high-jinks when he sniffs kryptonite; and Comet, a glorious, white winged stallion who is in truth a beautiful young man transformed by an ancient curse. Her early adventures revolved around her secret identity as orphan Linda Lee and her life at Midvale Orphanage. In 1961 she was adopted by a couple named Danvers, and her stories took on a suburban quality, like Superboy's with an extra dose of melodrama.

In 1969 Supergirl took over *Adventure Comics*, and was soon after allowed to grow into adulthood by new editor-writer-artist Mike Sekowsky. Sekowsky's tenure was short, however, and a constantly changing roster of writers and artists followed him, making Supergirl one of the least interesting of DC's characters. She had her own *Supergirl* title twice, in 1972–1974 and 1982–1984, but neither did well. In 1985 she was killed in DC's *Crisis on Infinite Earths* maxiseries.                    **G.J.**

**SUPERKATT** This dedicated costumed crimefighter strove to be completely serious about his profession, but since he was the leading character in a comic book titled *Giggle Comics* he never succeeded.

Written by the prolific Richard Hughes and drawn by former animator Dan Gordon, the *Superkatt* made its debut in *Giggle* #9 (June 1944). He coexisted in a world with human beings, but was able to talk—a fact that didn't seem to surprise anyone. Superkatt's costume consisted of a blue baby bonnet and a diaper, filched off a clothes line by a helpful mouse who was trying to bolster the cat's self-esteem. Most of his adventures read like storyboards for the raucous 1940s animated cartoons made famous by Tex Avery.

Gordon provided all the standard props, including a fat black maid named Petunia, while the costumed cat went up against rats, dogs, and other wrongdoers. His best friend, though, was also a dog—a dedicated if less than brilliant hound named Humphrey. Since Superkatt hadn't a smidgen of real superpowers, he had to rely on his pluck and cunning and a great deal of behind-the-scenes help from Humphrey. He was an appealing fellow, and he soon became the star of the magazine, appearing on each and every cover for several years. He was last seen late in 1950, and *Giggle Comics* went on without him until 1955.       **R.G.**

**SUPERMAN** The very first comic book hero, and the most influential, he made his debut in the spring of 1938 in the initial issue of DC's *Action Comics*. *Superman* was the creation of two young men from Cleveland, writer Jerry Siegel and artist Joe Shuster, who'd spent the past few years trying to persuade newspaper syndicate editors and comic book editors that their hero in the red and blue costume was worth publishing. They finally succeeded and the Man of Steel became one of the biggest moneymakers of the century. His creators didn't fare as well.

The first comic book story, made up chiefly of cut up and rearranged panels from the unsold newspaper version, offered a one-page introduction and then commenced in the middle of the narrative. The new hero managed to tackle several problems. Racing against time, he prevented an innocent woman from dying in the electric chair, taught a wifebeater a lesson, saved the already trouble-prone Lois Lane from being kidnapped by gangsters, and then whizzed off to Washington,

D.C., to investigate corruption in the Senate. Clark Kent was on hand, just beginning his reporting career and mild-mannered to a fault. He's already having difficulties with Lois, whom he asks, "Why is it you always avoid me at the office?"

As a pioneer, Superman had the field of superheroism entirely to himself. He didn't function in a fantastic comic book universe peopled with dozens of other superheroes, super villains and other bizarre creatures; instead, his venue was an approximation of the United States of the late 1930s, a nation recovering from a grim Depression and on the verge of entering another world war. Siegel and Shuster were fascinated by thoughts of what a man with superpowers might accomplish in the real, everyday world that they knew. So even though Superman now and then battled a mad scientist or a runaway plague in his first few years, he concentrated on helping widows, orphans, and working stiffs and seeing to it that crooks, warmongers, and corrupt politicians got their comeuppance. The early Man of Steel was basically a do-gooder, "a savior of the helpless and oppressed," and a fellow who was engaged in a "never-ceasing war on injustice."

He wasn't anywhere near as super at the beginning as he later came to be. Superman was fast as the devil and could outrun a streamlined train; he could lift tremendous weights—he was especially fond of lifting automobiles over his head—and bullets bounced off him. He couldn't fly, though, and got through the air by making enormous leaps of up to an eighth of a mile. It also took him a while to become completely invulnerable; in fact, early in his career he could be knocked unconscious by such things as exploding shells. He was slow to realize that he had X-ray vision.

The public, mostly Depression-reared kids who wanted the most they could get for their dimes, recognized Superman as something special almost from the moment they saw him lift the first hoodlum-filled car over his head. Although the sales of the first three issues of *Action* were not especially impressive, the fourth issue really took off. The sales soon climbed to 500,000 copies a month, and by 1941 the magazine was selling close to a million copies each month. While Superman was appearing in *Action*, he began to appear simultaneously in a separate *Superman* magazine. Launched in 1939, the new DC title reached a circulation of 1,250,000 by 1940.

Continuing to branch out, Superman got a newspaper strip of his own in 1939, and there the first detailed account of his origins appeared. Therein the destruction of the planet Krypton was first shown and the baby Superman was seen being rocketed, like a streamlined Moses, off to Earth in a ship of his scientist-father's invention. *Action* #1 had covered all that in one caption, merely stating, "As a distant planet was destroyed by old age, a scientist hastily devised a space-ship, launching it toward Earth." For the funny papers, though, two full weeks were devoted to Superman's folks and all the dire events leading up to his emigration.

To meet the demand for an ever increasing amount of material, Siegel and Shuster expanded the Cleveland shop they'd first set up in 1938. Wayne Boring and Paul Cassidy had been the first recruits and now Leo Nowak, Dennis Neville, and John Sikela were added.

Some of the best-known lines associated with Superman originated not in the comics but on the radio show, which began broadcasting nationally over the Mutual Network in early 1940. There were three 15-minute episodes each week. They aired Monday, Wednesday, and Friday, sometime between five and six in the afternoon, which in those days was the children's hour. It was on the radio show, broadcast out of New York, that such memorable phrases as "Up, up, and away!" and "This looks like a job for…*Superman!*" were first heard. The former was always followed by a great rush of wind, indicating that Superman had just leapt from a rooftop or out a window. The Man of Steel's first irrefutable flying, as opposed to impressive hopping, took place on the radio program.

The show's opening was built around an unforgettable introductory narration: "Faster than a speeding bullet! More powerful than a locomotive! Able to leap tall buildings at a single bound. Look! Up in the sky! It's a bird! It's a plane! It's…Superman!"

Superman's conquest of the media continued. In 1941, he reached the movie screen, starring in the first of a series of 17 animated cartoons. Released by Paramount Pictures, they were produced by Max Fleischer and his brother Dave. Their studio was also responsible for Betty Boop and Popeye, but the Superman epics were nothing like them. Brightly colored and imaginatively designed, they were done in a broad-shouldered, angular style, and looked something like 1930s WPA murals come to life. The emphasis was on action, with Superman tackling Nazi agents, mad scientists, Japanese spies, revitalized mummies, and erupting volcanoes. He managed as well to rescue Lois from some terrible fate each time out. It was in these cartoon shorts that Clark Kent was first seen ducking into a phone booth to strip to his superhero outfit, something he hadn't practiced in the comic books or elsewhere up to that time.

Superman's importance had been noticed fairly early in the business community. In 1942, *Business Week* reported that kids were spending an estimated $15 million a year on comic books. "Superman has shown the way in a new field of publishing," the magazine declared. As the years passed and the property continued to pile up bigger and bigger profits, Siegel and Shuster grew less and less happy. In 1947, with a joint annual income of $46,000, they went to court—seeking to regain the rights to their characters, to cancel their newspaper contracts, to recover the $5 million they maintained Superman should have brought them since his debut. There was also a dispute over the new Superboy character, launched by DC in 1945 without their authorization.

They fared none too well. While the court ruled that the publisher had acted illegally so far as Superboy was concerned, it also found that DC did indeed own Superman outright. The partners were paid off for Superboy, in a settlement rumored to be around $50,000, but they were fired.

Superman was untroubled by the departure of his creators. Cliffhanger serials appeared in 1948 and 1950, and in 1953 George Reeves brought the character to television. The comic books kept rolling along, too, with all sorts of new gimmicks being added. The fellow responsible for many of the innovations and modifications in the Superman saga was DC editor Mort Weisinger. He introduced the Phantom Zone, where old evildoers from Krypton had been banished, and the "what-if?" concept that permitted stories that were explained away at the end as never having happened—such as the one wherein Superman married Lois Lane. Weisinger it was who cooked up red Kryptonite—the usual stuff, fragments of Superman's home planet, was green—and it caused the Man of Steel even more trouble than regular Kryptonite did. Exposed to it, he'd grow to gigantic size, shrink down to kewpie doll proportions, turn into a dragon, become twins. Weisinger even came up with Superman's canine pal, Krypto the Super Dog.

The series of big budget movies that commenced in the late 1970s, with Christopher Reeve, did much to revive the Man of Steel's fortunes. Merchandising flourished, resulting even in Superman Peanut Butter. And during that period the new management of DC reached an agreement with Siegel and Shuster, instituting an annual pension for each. In the summer of 1986, amid much publicity, John Byrne was hired away from Marvel to revitalize the character. Byrne felt it was time to return to basics, getting rid of "all the debris that has accumulated over the years," and his Superman was meant to be closer to the original one of the 1930s. The Superman of today, though, is a more complex one than the young man who arrived here from Krypton over a half century ago. He's burlier of build and more concerned with cosmic conspiracies and monumental villains than he is with widows and orphans. He has, like many another hero before him, lost some of his innocence. **R.G.**

**SUPERSNIPE** This strip about Koppy McFad of Yapburg, billed as the Boy with the Most Comic Books in America, debuted in 1942. When Koppy first appeared in public, a majority of those comic books were devoted to superheroes. And it was Koppy's ambition to be a hero, too, so he fashioned a costume, using his grandfather's red flannels and his father's lodge cape. Unable to fly, Supersnipe traveled to the scene of his adventures on foot or on his bicycle.

By 1942 dozens of more or less serious superheroes were to be found on the newsstand and the category was so well established that it could be kidded and parodied, which such characters as Stuporman, Powerhouse Pepper, and Sparky Watts did in their individual ways. *Supersnipe* was somewhat gentler in its kidding of the whole idea of costumed heroes as well as boyhood yearnings toward adventure and daring deeds. Kid readers were not offended at the mild razzing, and the character was a fair success.

Ed Gruskin did the writing, newspaper veteran George Marcoux the drawing. Frequently Koppy would have dream sequence adventures wherein he was a true, full-grown superman. These interludes were drawn by another newspaper vet, C.M. Payne. Supersnipe auditioned in various Street & Smith comic books—including *Shadow Comics* and *Doc Savage Comics* —before settling into his own magazine in the autumn of 1942. The bimonthly lasted until the summer of 1949. **R.G.**

**SWINNERTON, JIMMY** (1875–1974) A pioneer comic artist, Swinnerton is most often credited in histories of the funnies for things he never did. He never drew anything titled *Little Bears and Tigers*, and the feature he *did* draw about bears was not the first newspaper strip. In fact, it wasn't a comic strip at all. A talented artist, Swinnerton did, however, contribute significantly to the development of comics in the more than 60 years he worked as a cartoonist. His most successful strip was *Little Jimmy*, and he's the one who introduced his friend George Herriman to the Arizona desert that became the permanent locale for *Krazy Kat*. Swinnerton, too, put the desert country to good use in his own work.

James Guilford Swinnerton was born in Eureka, California, where his father was a judge, the publisher of a weekly paper, and a staunch Republican. Swinnerton studied at the California Art School in San Francisco and went to work for the *Examiner*, the first of William Randolph Hearst's newspapers, in 1892. In 1887, after he had asked his father for it several times, Hearst was allowed to take over the faltering little daily, and most of the tricks that became Hearst trademarks were first tried out on the *Examiner*. As a boy Hearst had become interested in German humor magazines and while at Harvard had worked on the *Lampoon*. For his new paper he wanted drawings and funny pictures, which is where Swinnerton came in.

At first he was only a part-time comic artist, and it wasn't until he got back to New York several years later that he was allowed to do comics full time. Because there was still no practical way to use photographs in a newspaper in 1892, all pictorial reporting was done by sketch artists. These artists—Swinnerton included—covered parades, crimes, trials, sports, and whatever else turned up. Swinnerton even had to go out to sketch high school field days. Once, to cover a hotel fire down the coast in Monterey, Hearst hired a train and shipped a whole carload of reporters and artists down.

*The Little Bears*, one of the earliest comic art features in an American newspaper, started out as spot drawings to decorate the weather reports, inspired by the bear on the California state flag. His little bears multiplied and began to show up throughout the paper and to be used in promotion stunts. In the middle 1890s Swinnerton also started turning out large quantities of drawings of his very small little kids, whom he liked to call tykes. Often the bears and the tykes would get together in parades that stretched across the bottom of a page. They were sometimes referred to editorially as *Little Bears and Tykes*, but they never appeared in an actual comic strip.

Impressed by the public response to his work, Swinnerton asked for a raise of $2.50 a week, but the editors didn't feel he was worth the extra money, so he quit and headed for New York City, where Hearst had bought the *New York Journal* in 1895. Hearst was involved in circulation wars with Pulitzer's *New York World* and most of the many other local dailies, and one of the results of the battles with Pulitzer was the Sunday comic section. Cartoonists were bought back and forth—for a time *The Yellow Kid* ran in both the *Journal* and the *World*. Finally, Hearst got out a color comics section.

Swinnerton's little bears had always been favorites of Hearst. For the *Journal*, however, Hearst suggested they be transformed into tigers. Tammany Hall, symbolized by the tiger as conceived by Thomas Nast, was a popu-

lar target then, and the little tigers found a ready audience. Gradually the tigers developed from a pantomime strip into a Sunday page complete with dialogue balloons; this version, titled *Mr. Jack* from 1903 on, dealt with a domesticated tiger who had an office job, a wife, and quite a few lady friends.

During this early trial period, when color comics were expensive and there was some doubt that they would ever catch on enough to turn a profit, Swinnerton continued to do sports cartoons on the side. In 1904 he turned again to tykes and introduced Little Jimmy, a very small boy who shared his first name. Originally titled just *Jimmy*, the feature began life as a Sunday page. With some lapses, and a hiatus or two, Swinnerton drew the feature until 1958. A daily was added in 1920, at which time the name was changed to *Little Jimmy*. Swinnerton drew in a simple, uncluttered style, using very little shading and favoring long shots to close-ups.

When comics began to pay off, the *Journal* decided to let Swinnerton draw them to the exclusion of everything else, which meant the paper needed a new sports cartoonist. Asked to recommend a replacement, Swinnerton said, "There's a fellow named Dorgan out in San Francisco, calls himself Tad. But if you're going to get him, you'd better send for his friend, Hype Igoe." The paper sent for the pair, and both became successful sports cartoonists and reporters. Swinnerton once estimated he had helped over three dozen artists get started, ranging from illustrators such as Harold Von Schmidt to newspaper cartoonists such as Darrel McClure and Robert Ripley.

In the first decade of the century doctors advised Swinnerton that his days were numbered. Resigned, he moved to Arizona to await the end. He kept right on waiting, but he didn't die; instead he fell in love with the desert country. He used the scenery in *Canyon Kiddies*, a handsome color page he drew for Hearst's *Good Housekeeping* from the early 1920s to the middle 1940s. He didn't relocate the diminutive Jimmy to Navajo country until the late 1920s. The Canyon Kiddies also became frequenters of the strip. Swinnerton started painting desert landscapes, too, and remained a painter even after he was no longer able to cartoon. **R.G.**

# T

**TAILSPIN TOMMY** The first and most exuberant of the great airplane strips that enjoyed massive popularity in those innocent pre-World War II years when speed racers and globe girdlers were the nation's foremost romantic heroes, *Tailspin Tommy* premiered as a daily strip on May 21, 1928, not quite a year after Lindbergh flew the Atlantic (a Sunday page was introduced on Oct. 20, 1929). Young Tommy Tompkins was considerably less a soldier of fortune than most of the revolution-settling aviators who followed him in the funny papers; always a responsible and level-headed lad, he worked mostly as a mail pilot in the American Southwest, though sometimes he chased rumrunners in Canada for the Treasury Department and flew relief missions to flood districts on the Gulf Coast. He did turn up a lost civilization from time to time, and occasionally he fell into the clutches of cackling scientists who had invented death rays, but for the most part his adventures owed more to the *National Geographic* and the day's headlines than to the pulps. Primitively drawn by Hal Forrest—"a hair-raising thing to look at," scowled Coulton Waugh in *The Comics*—the early *Tommy* was nonetheless possessed of a lovely windblown joyfulness that perfectly reflected the noisy triumph of the air machine, and the strip was a huge reader favorite through the early 1930s.

But founding scripter Glenn Chaffin departed in January 1934, and with him went the feature's prime. Forrest soloed dismally for several years (devoting, it would appear, his greater energies to *Four Aces*, the intriguing Sunday companion strip he had launched to supplant Chaffin's *Progress Of Flight* topper—which took over more and more of the *Tommy* page as time went on). In the spring of 1936 an unheralded assistant took over much of *Tommy* proper and slicked it up notably—the later *Tommy*, in fact, became a strikingly handsome enterprise—but by now *Smilin' Jack* had definitively established itself as the leader in the field, and by decade's end the tanks were running dry for the secondary airplane strips in general. *Tommy* jumped from the Bell Syndicate to United Features in June 1939 and lost a lot of visibility despite substantial promotion; Monogram Pictures, which had made several *Tommy* programmers, busted out of a contract to make several more; the alarmed Forrest sent *Tommy* to Europe and tried to restage it as a modern clouds-of-war strip. But its day had simply passed. By the summer of 1942 the old flivver had disappeared, leaving the sky to another generation. **J.M.**

**TALES FROM THE GREAT BOOK** See LEHTI, JOHN.

**TALIAFERRO, AL** See DONALD DUCK.

**TARZAN** The most famous fictional wildman in the world, Tarzan was created by Edgar Rice Burroughs and originally appeared in the October 1912 issue of the pulp fiction magazine *All-Story*. That first novel, owing quite a bit to the works of Rudyard Kipling and H. Rider Haggard, was titled *Tarzan of the Apes* and proved to be an immediate success. The hardcover edition followed in 1914, and a silent movie version in 1917. Over the years Burroughs wrote nearly two dozen books about his jungle lord. Tarzan branched out into both newspaper comics and comic books in the late 1920s.

In 1928 an advertising man named Joseph H. Neebe formed Famous Books and Plays, Inc., to sell a strip adaptation of *Tarzan of the Apes*. His adaptation was sober-looking, with no rowdy balloons or sound effects, and the Burroughs prose set in little blocks of type beneath the illustrations. The first choice for artist was J. Allen St. John, the veteran illustrator who had painted covers and interior illustrations for several of the hardcover Tarzan novels. But he and Neebe couldn't come to terms, mainly because St. John had little faith in a comic page version of the Lord of the Jungle. Neebe next went to a fellow advertising man, Hal Foster. "Joe Neebe had the idea of putting famous books and plays into newspaper comic strips," Foster once recalled. "I'd done a lot of work for him as he was with an advertising agency I did work for, and he thought of me when he got his idea. He wanted to raise the tone of comics and Tarzan was the first."

Unable to sell the proposed strip, Neebe had to turn to the Metropolitan Newspaper Service (later United Features) for help, and they managed to place *Tarzan of the Apes* in "a small but important list of newspapers."

The first strip of the adaptation, which consisted of 60 dailies, appeared on January 7, 1929. The reaction to Foster's impressive drawing was favorable, but he had returned to servicing his ad accounts and wanted nothing more to do with the apeman. Fortunately there was another ex-advertising man handy, doing artwork right there in the Metropolitan bullpen. It was Rex Maxon, 37 and well-intentioned, although no match for Foster as an artist; from the 11th week on, the jungle habitat became his. The next adaptation was of *The Return of Tarzan*.

A Sunday page was added in March of 1931, and at first Maxon drew that as well. But the extra work supposedly became too much for him and he stepped aside. (There was also the fact that Burroughs disliked Maxon's work and was writing notes of complaint to the syndicate, even including tips on how to draw animals!) Foster was approached again and he agreed to draw the Sunday. A page meant a full page in the early 1930s, and so Foster had a good deal of space to work with. His pages were full of action, and there were long shots and close-ups. A major influence was obviously the movies and, like most good movie makers, Foster was interested in the props and sets as well as in the characters and the action. When, early in 1933, he followed Tarzan into a lost civilization based on that of ancient Egypt, Foster had everything under control. The backgrounds and the staging were so expert that the reader could simply accept them and then sit back and enjoy the narrative and all its magnificent hokum.

Foster's exceptional work came to the attention of William Randolph Hearst's King Features, and in 1937 he was lured away from the jungle to begin his own *Prince Valiant*, at better pay. Burne Hogarth, yet another artist with an advertising background, who had studied with J. Allen St. John in Chicago and worked on other newspaper strips, took over the *Tarzan* Sunday in May 1937. Initially Hogarth kept close, as best he could, to the Foster look, but gradually his own style took over, with a new, muscular look. He also created a very personal version of the jungle, and his twisted, gnarled trees and swirling foliage became a trademark. He stuck with the page initially until the middle 1940s.

Meanwhile, all through the 1930s and into the 1940s, Rex Maxon had been laboring away on the daily. For a short time in the middle 1930s, after an unsuccessful attempt to get a raise, Maxon walked off the feature. William Juhre pinch-hit until Maxon was hired back. The copy, which eventually came to be lettered inside the panels with the pictures, was provided by Donald Garden until the World War II years. From then until he left it in August of 1947, Maxon wrote the strip himself.

Hogarth left the Sunday page in the middle 1940s and was replaced by Ruben Moreira, who used the pen name Rubimor. Hogarth, after trying an unsuccessful page about a muscular South American youth named Drago, returned to the apeman. His enthusiasm had waned, however, and he got his students at the New York School of Visual Arts to pencil for him. He quit for good in 1950.

A parade of artists followed Maxon on the daily, all of them comic book alumni. Dan Barry was the first (his earliest dailies were signed Hogarth, but Hogarth had nothing to do with them), followed by such as Paul Reinman, Nick Cardy, Bob Lubbers, John Celardo, and Russ Manning. In 1950, with the advent of Lubbers, the same artist became responsible for both the daily and the Sunday. After Celardo's 15-year stint, Edgar Rice Burroughs, Inc., brought in Manning, who had been drawing the comic book version. The salary connected with the job still wasn't enough, causing Manning to give up the daily. ERB, Inc., began the practice of reprinting old dailies.

The Sunday page has continued to offer original material. Gil Kane (with scripts by Archie Goodwin) followed Manning. Then came Mike Grell and most recently Gray Morrow. *Tarzan* currently appears in a very small number of newspapers in this country.

Tarzan's career in comic books began the same year as his newspaper strip. In 1929 Grosset & Dunlap reprinted the dailies in a hardcover black and white collection that sold for 50 cents. The book was issued again in 1934, with the price lowered to 25 cents for that Depression year. The ape man was first seen in full color in *Tip Top Comics* #1 (April 1936), wherein several of the Foster Sundays were reprinted along with samples of just about every other United Features feature. United added *Comics on Parade* to its list of comic books in 1938, and recycled *Tarzan* dailies by Foster and then Maxon could now be seen in full color. Dell reprinted the initial *Tarzan of the Apes* dailies in a black and white comic book in 1939, with some additional art by Henry Vallely thrown in. In 1940 United issued a *Tarzan* one-shot that reprinted Foster's impressive Egyptian sequence in color. In 1941 came United's *Sparkler Comics*, with Hogarth's Sundays among the reprinted features. Hogarth also contributed several original drawings for covers.

It wasn't until 1947 that an original Tarzan comic book showed up, Dell's *Tarzan and the Devil Ogre*, with art by Jesse Marsh, which was followed later in the year by *Tarzan and the Tohr*. The success of these led to a monthly comic book in 1948, with Marsh providing the majority of the drawing. Other artists included Manning and Doug Wildey.

Edgar Rice Burroughs, Inc., ended its relationship with Dell/Gold Key in 1972, next licensing the jungleman to DC. The DC version was nicely drawn by Joe Kubert and followed the Hal Foster approach, but never became a successful title. Marvel took a turn next, picking up the character in 1977 and putting in John Buscema as the chief artist. Marvel gave up within two years, but returned to the jungle in 1984 for a two-issue adaptation of the latest Tarzan movie.

Both Dell/Gold Key and DC did a companion book devoted to Tarzan's son, Korak. Artists included Russ Manning, Warren Tufts, and Frank Thorne. Charlton, under the misapprehension that the character had moved into public domain, attempted an unauthorized *Jungle Tales of Tarzan* in 1964–1965. The art was by Sam Glanzman, and there were four issues before the title was halted.                                              **R.G.**

**TED TOWERS** One of several jungle strips that began in the 1930s, *Ted Towers, Animal Master* was a Sunday page introduced by King Features late in 1934. It was billed as being written by Frank "Bring 'Em Back Alive" Buck, who had already turned his animal-gathering exploits into profitable books and movies. A likeness of Buck, complete with pith helmet, graced the title panel.

Franklyn Howard Buck (1884–1950) led a life as interesting and exciting as that of any comic strip hero, especially in the version of it he created for public consumption. A Texas boy, Buck left school before reaching the eighth grade, and by the time he married a Chicago drama critic and one-time light opera star who was nearly 30 years older than he was, he'd been a carnival worker, a cowpoke, and a hobo. He was employed as a bellboy at the time of his marriage in 1901.

Encouraged and pushed by his influential wife, Buck flirted with various aspects of show business; afterwards, he moved on to other things. He started dealing in the importing of tropical birds just before World War I, and a few years later, based in Singapore, he was selling wild animals to zoos and circuses. "Only infrequently did Buck actually participate in the capture of his specimens," points out *The Dictionary of American Biography.* "His more usual method was to purchase them from dealers in Singapore, Calcutta or other major centers." A whiz at capturing publicity, Buck turned himself into a daring and humane big game hunter in the eyes of the public, "parlaying what had been a colorful but hardly remarkable career into a reputation of national proportions." He created, with considerable help, a series of books about himself and his exploits. The first, and most successful, appeared in 1930 and was called *Bring 'Em Back Alive.* Movies and public

appearances followed. By 1934 he was just the sort of dashing celebrity King Features could use to front a new adventure strip, at a time when they also hired Dashiell Hammett to write a detective strip and Eddie Rickenbacker to sign his name to an aviation strip.

Ted Towers was a handsome young man who also wore a pith helmet. In the Sunday page he did all the adventurous things Buck wanted the public to think he did. Ted, usually in the company of his ladyfriend Catherine Custer, captured tigers and elephants, defied nasty savages and crazed tiger-men cultists, guided movie companies on location, and took time now and then to hunt for lost treasures. Roaming the same turf as Frank Buck, Ted did his hunting and adventuring in Singapore, Siam, Calcutta, and even wilder spots. King Features' Jungle Jim also operated in this part of the world, and it's a wonder he and Ted never bumped into each other on some woodland trail.

Joe King was the first artist on the page, followed by Paul Frehm, Glenn Cravath, and Ed Stevenson. The identity of the actual scriptwriter remains unknown. The feature folded in 1939.                                  **R.G.**

**TEENAGE MUTANT NINJA TURTLES** The most successful funny animal group of the waning years of the 20th century, TMNT began humbly in the spring of 1984. Created by writer Kevin Eastman and artist Peter Laird, the four battling humanoid reptiles—Raphael, Leonardo, Michaelangelo, and Donatello—made their debut in a black and white comic book that cost their creators $1200 to self-publish. The initial print run was 3,000 copies.

Something in the title appealed to the comics fans who came across the ad for the new book. It seemed to combine some of the major preoccupations of the more serious comic books of the time. Mutants were, especially at Marvel, a staple of the 1980s, and titles like *The New Mutants,* begun in 1983, were very popular. Ninjas were hot, too, and as *The Comics Buyer's Guide* has pointed out, Frank Miller in particular had been making use of "the world of ninjas and samurais and Japanese combat" in *Daredevil* and then in *Ronin.* Since the time seemed right for a spoof of all this, readers decided to give the sewer-bred and street-wise young turtle warriors a try. The first issue of *Teenage Mutant Ninja Turtles* caught on and an additional 15,000 copies followed a month after the magazine was launched. Soon another 36,000 copies were run off.

The mock adventures of the turtles and their interactions with the world of humans proved popular with teenage and college-age readers. But more importantly, the characters eventually became popular with children. TMNT branched out into television cartoons, toys, and an impressive amount of merchandising to become one of the top licensing properties in the country. The live-action movie in the spring of 1990 was a box office hit. "If we had been asked five years ago," Laird said just prior to the film's opening, "to pick the most unlikely thing that would happen, it would have been to think that Jim Henson's studio would be designing outfits for the Turtles." Asked to comment on the burgeoning success of the Turtles, he replied, "It has been such an amazing trip thus far." **R.G.**

**THE TEENIE WEENIES** A strange, intensely imagined children's page, it amused and fascinated generation after generation of kids for nearly 60 years. *The Teenie Weenies* was created by William Donahey and drawn by him for all of its long life.

The characters, who owed a bit to Palmer Cox' earlier Brownies, ranged in height from 2.5 inches to 3 inches and were proportioned like children, though most of them were adults. With few exceptions they looked very much alike and were distinguished by their costumes. Most of them didn't have names and were known simply as General, Dunce, Old Soldier, Indian, Cowboy, Chinaman, Grandpa, Lady of Fashion. They lived in their own village behind a rosebush at what appeared to be the edge of someone's backyard. Everything else in the Teenie Weenie world was normal-sized, meaning they could convert discarded articles like hats, shoes, and cartons into dwellings, roof them with playing cards, make several meals out of a single strawberry, and go bareback riding on mice.

Donahey, who'd been doing a Mother Goose page for the *Cleveland Plain Dealer*, was hired by Captain Joseph M. Patterson to draw a kid page for the Sunday *Chicago Tribune*. Reviving a notion he'd first had as a child, when he used to turn flatheaded screws into toy people by painting them and dressing them up, Donahey came up with the idea for *The Teenie Weenies*. It first appeared in the *Trib* on June 14, 1914. In 1923 the page, which consisted of one large and intricate panel and an accompanying block of copy, went into syndication and picked up some 30 newspapers around the country.

Each big panel featured a patiently and meticulously drawn scene of some Teenie Weenie activity, ranging from building a house to swimming in a fish bowl to having a squirrel family over for dinner. Their society was rural and basically agricultural, and they worked more than they played. Donahey never tired of depicting them amid found objects from the real world—hatboxes, hairbrushes, teacups, penknives, and so on—and quite obviously had as much fun playing with his tiny people as he had when he was young. After briefly trying a multipanel format, complete with dialogue balloons, in the middle 1930s, he returned to a one-panel format. There was also at that period, briefly, a daily strip.

A simple feature, one that was gentle most of the time, *The Teenie Weenies* was last seen on February 2, 1970. Donahey had retired a few weeks earlier, and the final page ran on the day after his death. **R.G.**

**TERRY AND THE PIRATES** The *Terry and the Pirates* comic strip officially ended in February of 1973. There are those, however, who feel it died quite a few years earlier—at the end of 1946, to be exact, when Milton Caniff gave it up for the greener pastures of *Steve Canyon*. Caniff had begun *Terry* in 1934 and wrote and drew it for the next dozen years.

"Introducing *Terry and the Pirates*," announced the first panel of the very first daily in October 1934. "Terry is a wide awake American boy whose grandfather left him a map of an abandoned mine in China." Accompanying the youthful Terry through his adventures will be Pat Ryan, "two-fisted adventurer," the Chinese guide George Webster Confucius, "better known as Connie," plus pretty Dale Scott and her crusty father, who bore the name Ol' Pop. In order to live up to the new strip's name, Caniff included in the cast a gang of Chinese river pirates headed by Poppy Joe, "a half-caste who has learned of the treasure." The early weeks of the strip, as Terry and Pat arrived in China and ventured up river in quest of the hidden treasure, had a wide-open cartoony appearance and a wide-eyed boys' adventure novel plot. There were few hints of what *Terry* would look and sound like in another year or so.

During the first year in the Orient, Caniff had separate continuities going in his Sunday page. In the initial Sunday adventure Pat and Terry sailed along the China coast in a steamer that was "laden with rich cargo." The steamer was captured by pirates who were led not by a man but, as Terry exclaimed, "Luvva Pete! We're captured by a WOMAN!" It was the Dragon Lady, making her debut on December 16, 1934. Besides speaking movie Chinese, the Dragon Lady was noticeably slim, and gradually both her diction and her figure improved. After the Dragon Lady, Caniff brought in a Sunday villain straight out of the silent serials, a fellow in a black robe and death head mask who called himself the Skull. About that point, Caniff must have had to make some sort of decision as to whether he would keep Terry a "luvva Pete" kid or allow him to grow up.

He was sharing a Manhattan studio with Noel Sickles, and the things Sickles was accomplishing with his *Scorchy Smith* strip began to stimulate Caniff. Adapting his friend's impressionistic style Caniff changed the look of his own strip and "dramatically improved the all-over value of *Terry*." When looking over the dailies and Sundays of 1935 and onward, it's obvious, that,

*Terry and the Pirates*, Milton Caniff, © 1937 Chicago Tribune - N.Y. News Syndicate, Inc. Reprinted by permission: Tribune Media Services.

besides giving advice and inspiration, Sickles was now and then doing some of the penciling and inking. Caniff used the pen less and less, switching to the brush and the liberal use of black ink. He gave much more attention to the staging of his events and, like Sickles, made use of motion picture approaches. Caniff also used the movies for inspiration when it came to more adult story lines.

Actors, too, were important. The huge, mute Big Stoop was a caricature of the Karloff monster; the Dragon Lady could have been played by the Marlene Dietrich of the von Sternberg epics; and Sandhurst, the recurrent weakling villain, was based on Charles Laughton. Burma, who came along in 1936, was Caniff's version of the wise, brassy blond that Jean Harlow and Carole Lombard were famous for portraying, although she also owed something to the Joan Crawford version of *Rain*. In that 1932 film, Sadie Thompson spends a good many of her rainy afternoons in her room listening to the *St. Louis Blues* on her windup phonograph. This song was also Burma's favorite, always heard before the blond reappeared. Asked once if he remembered seeing the movie, Caniff answered, "I stole the whole character from Sadie Thompson."

He had a good deal of fun in the middle 1930s living up to the pirate part of his strip's title, working every sort of pirate into his stories, from the suave, seagoing Captain Judas to the blustering land pirate and smuggler Captain Blaze. Burma herself, as a result of having been Judas' mistress, was wanted for piracy by the British police in Hong Kong, which kept her moving in and out of the strip.

By having Terry go through adolescence and into manhood, Caniff provided himself with a wider range of possibilities. Terry's first big romance was with his teenage contemporary April Kane. He later had a crush on Burma and eventually romanced the formidable Dragon Lady. Caniff used sexual motivations more than any of his contemporaries, and because the comics, like the movies of the time, couldn't be too explicit, he made circumspection a virtue and built up tension by suggestion rather than showing. Along the way he dealt with some unusual types, among them the lesbian Sanjak, whose interest in the young April Kane was used to move a story sequence, and the nymphomaniac Cheery Blaze, whose failure with Pat Ryan prompted her to betray him.

His dedication to authenticity got Caniff into the war against Japan several years ahead of anyone else in the United States. The China he was portraying in *Terry* was much closer to the real China of the late 1930s than it had been when little knickered Terry had first arrived with his treasure map. In the real China, they had been fighting a Japanese invasion army since 1937, and by

1939 there were one million Japanese troops in China. Caniff started mentioning the invaders in the spring of 1938 and from the end of 1939 onward the stories were almost all concerned with the invaders. Although Caniff did some of his most ambitious work during World War II, there are critics and historians who contend that something went out of *Terry* in the early 1940s. Terry Lee moved from boyhood to manhood in those years, and the strip became somewhat grimmer and less melodramatic. During the war, while Caniff showed a certain respect for most of the officers he depicted, his real sympathy was with the enlisted men, the "dogfaces."

The wartime action of the strip was limited to the China-Burma-India theater, which still gave Caniff quite a bit of territory to cover. He separated his two protagonists, putting Pat Ryan into the Navy as a lieutenant and letting Terry join the Air Force. The continuities shifted from Pat's adventures to Terry's, and part of the fascination in following the strip was seeing the ingenious ways Caniff contrived to have their paths cross. It was in the war years that he introduced some of his most successful and memorable characters. Air Force Colonel Flip Corkin, based on Caniff's longtime friend Colonel Phil Cochran, became Terry's new mentor. One of the best remembered characters didn't pop up until 1944. His real name was Charles C. Charles and he hailed from Boston; small, freckled, redheaded, wisecracking, brash, and vocally lecherous, everybody called him Hotshot Charlie, and he and Terry, even though they sometimes competed for the same girl, became fast friends.

By war's end Caniff already knew he was going to give up his characters. Terry, though still connected with the Air Force, posed as a mercenary pilot and flew for a shoestring airline called Air Cathay, with Hotshot as his copilot. Like the final chapter of a Victorian picaresque, the last months of *Terry* brought back all sorts of scattered characters; the Dragon Lady, Burma, Captain Blaze, and nurse Jane Allen all showed up once again. The final Sunday showed Terry saying goodbye to Jane at a snow-covered airfield. She started for her plane, ran back to him, there was a clinch, and then she was on the plane and flying away into the fading day. Terry turned toward his waiting jeep, passing a New Year's party poster that read, "Ring out the old, ring in the new."

George Wunder, like Caniff a graduate of the Associated Press art department, took over the writing and drawing of *Terry* at the very end of 1946. He continued the strip, with the help of assistants such as George Evans and Frank Springer, until it was canceled in 1973.

**R.G.**

**TEXAS SLIM AND DIRTY DALTON** See JOHNSON, FERD.

**THEY'LL DO IT EVERY TIME** When *San Francisco Call-Bulletin* staff artist Jimmy Hatlo became the sports cartoonist in 1929, he also created an enduring feature that added a catchphrase to the American vocabulary with *They'll Do It Every Time*. First appearing on February 5, 1929, as a local feature, it was structured in a panel format, often in two parts, with the first depicting a common situation and the second its surprising and revealing outcome: A neighborhood swarms with noisy kids until a mother needs someone to run an errand; a woman yearns for heat during the winter, and for cold in summer; a shabby customer is loftily ignored by an arrogant car salesman, then buys the most expensive car on the lot, for cash, from the cub of the sales force. Never mordant, Hatlo's tart and obvious observations on the dishonesty, shallowness and illogic of the daily scene became popular, and Hearst's King Features Syndicate began to distribute the daily feature nationally on May 4, 1936. A Sunday version, comprising a collection of panels, was added on May 8, 1949.

From its first year, Hatlo received letters of praise and suggestions for future panels. His use of readers' ideas, acknowledged with "Thanx and a tip of the Hatlo hat to—," became a frequent footnote. *They'll Do It Every Time* has never had regular dramatis personae, but several characters have appeared often enough to receive their own names. The usual victim of others' cunning, domination, or chicanery is a weak-willed suburbanite named Henry Tremblechin, who is henpecked by his boss, badgered by his wife, and easily manipulated by his daughter Iodine. The latter, described by her creator as "the embodiment of all the brats I knew," became so popular that she was made the star of a feature of her own. *Little Iodine* began appearing as a Sunday on July 4, 1943.

On Hatlo's death in 1963, *They'll Do It Every Time* was officially taken over by his longtime ghost Bob Dunn, who had worked with him anonymously since 1939. The dailies were signed by Dunn and his assistant Tommy Thompson from January 3, 1965, and by Dunn and Al Scaduto from February 13, 1966. Through all the feature's changes of staff, it has continued to be a favorite with the public. When Dunn died in 1989, it was appearing in 250 papers worldwide. Scaduto carries it on.

**D.W.**

**THIMBLE THEATRE** E.C. Segar's strip began modestly in 1919, but its most famous character didn't step before the footlights in *Thimble Theatre* until the enterprise was in its second decade. In 1929 Popeye did a walk-on and proceeded to steal the show for good and all.

*Thimble Theatre*, E.C. Segar, circa 1935.

When the curtain first went up on December 19, 1919, the show went on without the one-eyed sailor. The strip was supposed to parody movies and stage plays, and its cast consisted of actors who would take parts in lampoon productions: Willy Wormwood, a mustache-twirling villain akin to Desperate Desmond; the pure and innocent Olive Oyl; her boyfriend, Harold Hamgravy. After a few short weeks of daily or weekly productions along the intended line, Segar abandoned the original plan in order to focus on the actors and their real life adventures. He introduced Olive's pint-sized brother Castor, whose get-rich-quick schemes motivated the action for the next 10 years. By often pausing to dwell for days on some minor wrinkle in the unfolding plot, Segar stretched his continuities out for months.

One of his devices for prolonging the action and creating burlesque cliffhangers was to introduce wildly eccentric characters into his stories. Popeye was one of these. In early 1929, Castor had to go on a voyage, and he went looking for a crew to sail his ship. On January 17, he found Popeye, who turned out to be all the crew he needed. The sailor had a prickly personality and a perfectly logical sense of justice: Rather than redress a wrong with words and sweet reasonableness, he simply walloped it on the nose. The scrawny, scrappy Popeye soon turned out to be indestructible and well as invincible. Segar rendered him with bulging forearms—watermelons that were attached to his body with pipe cleaners. This ploy defied anatomy, but it succeeded remarkably in suggesting pugilistic power.

Popeye's direct approach to correcting injustice made him the hit of the strip overnight, and by March 1931 his name was on the marquee—*Thimble Theatre Starring Popeye.* The popularity of the strip increased greatly after his arrival and in the 1930s Popeye was one of King Features' most widely merchandised characters, bringing in millions of dollars in licensing revenue. In July 1933, Popeye appeared in the first of many Max Fleischer animated cartoons. Spinach as the source of strength was emphasized in the films. Segar had originated the notion in the strip, but he didn't dwell much on it until the films proved to be very popular.

On March 31, 1931, Segar introduced another of his one-note characters, one of those obsessive personalities whose fixations he was able to parlay into a comic refrain of indefinite length—J. Wellington Wimpy, the perfect antithesis of heroism. Wimpy was a craven coward, a traitorous friend to Popeye, a shiftless moocher whose placid determinism was as elemental as Popeye's basic goodness. Segar etched Wimpy's shallow character in a series of unforgettable one-liners: "I'll gladly pay you Tuesday for a hamburger today" and "Let's you and him fight." Segar was able to construct remarkably complex comic plots, with similarly inspired, one-trait characters: the evil and ruthless Sea Hag (the last witch on Earth), her monstrous minions Alice the Goon and Toar, Popeye's completely uncivilized father Poopdeck Pappy, his adopted child Swee'pea, the belligerent cafe owner Roughhouse, the kindly Eugene the Jeep—to name but a few.

After his death in 1938, the genius went out of the strip, but it was continued with professional competence by Segar's successors. Tom Sims wrote it until the early 1950s. Doc Winner was the first artist after Segar, but was soon replaced by Bill Zaboly. Ralph Stein signed on in the 1950s, chiefly as a writer, but his hand can be noted in the drawing as well. In 1958 Bud Sagendorf, who had first assisted on the strip when he was a teenager in the early 1930s, finally inherited the strip. He wrote and drew *Thimble Theatre,* daily and Sunday, until early in 1986, when the daily became the responsibility of Bobby London. **R.C.H.**

**THOMPSON, RAY** (1905–1982) A cartoonist and writer, Thompson drew humorous features and wrote serious ones. He created and scripted *Myra North* in the 1930s, and in the 1940s and 1950s he drew one of the most widely circulated comic strips of all time. Starring a kid gang led by a fat boy named Pud, Thompson's tiny feature was wrapped around every chunk of Fleer's Dubble Bubble gum.

Thompson was born in Pennsylvania and educated at Temple University and Tyler Art School. In the 1930s he did considerable work for the Philadelphia-based Ledger Syndicate, serving as ghost artist on the *Somebody's Stenog* strip in the middle 1930s and scripting both *Connie* and *Roy Powers* for Frank Godwin. Teaming with artist Charles Coll, he wrote *Myra North, Special Nurse* for NEA from 1936 to 1941. He sold a panel called *Homer (the Invisible)* to the Herald-Tribune Syndicate in the middle 1940s, which featured a prankish and rather meanminded ghost.

Over the years he drew thousands of pieces of advertising art for numerous clients, but his best-remembered series was the Dubble Bubble strips he did for Fleer's. Featuring the beanie-wearing Pud and his kid associates, these were printed on the wax paper inner wrapper of the penny squares of bubble gum. Thompson drew over 700 different strips in his simple, direct cartoon style for this series, and in each and every one told an old joke. His Fleer's kids also appeared in ad strips that ran in newspapers and comic books in the 1940s and 1950s. Many a middle-aged adult harbors fond memories of those strips, and Robert Crumb went so far as to adopt Pud and use him now and then in his work. **M.J.**

**THOR** In 1962 *Journey into Mystery* began featuring the adventures of Thor, becoming the first of several Marvel horror comic books to turn to superheroes following *Fantastic Four's* success. The series' odd premise was that lame Dr. Don Blake finds an ancient hammer and is transformed into the Norse god of thunder; by tapping the hammer (which masquerades as a cane when necessary) he can switch back and forth between godhood and mortal frailty.

Although created by artist Jack Kirby and writer Stan Lee, Thor was turned over to lesser talents for most of his first year. Even after Lee and Kirby settled in for keeps, they seemed unsure what to do with their hero until about 1965, when they began jettisoning standard superhero/villain battles in favor of "epic-length" interlocking stories, well-grounded in Norse mythology (with a good dose of Greek myth and high-faluting science fiction as well).

Kirby, who had always been a master of action-art and powerful composition, now brought a monumental quality to his work that seemed to breathe a bit of real godhood into his characters. Lee forged a pseudo-Elizabethan dialogue style, equal parts literary pretension and high camp, that set his deities charmingly apart from normal folk ("Verily," Thor tended to cry, "I say thee nay!"). Between them they created an impressive pantheon of quasi-mythic figures unlike anything ever seen in comics: the swashbuckling Warriors Three (Hogunn the Grim, fun-loving Fandral, and the fat, Falstaffian Volstagg); the self-made scientific god called the High Evolutionary; and their own versions of stern

Odin, scheming Loki, and the brawling, wenching, boozing Hercules.

Like most Marvel series, *Thor* (as it became when it absorbed *Journey into Mystery* in 1966) began to run out of gas in the late 1960s. Kirby left Marvel in 1970, Lee stopped writing comics to become Marvel's publisher in 1972, and Thor trundled along at a workmanlike level through the 1970s, mainly under writer Roy Thomas and artist John Buscema.

A new spark was added in 1983, when writer-artist Walt Simonson took over the series and for a few years restored to it much of the verve, violence, and epic quality of the Kirby-Lee days—while adding a few bold strokes of his own, such as eliminating Thor's Don Blake self and apparently killing Odin. **G.J.**

**THORNE, FRANK** (1930– ) A highly distinctive illustrative cartoonist, Thorne has worked on both comic strips and comic books. He finally attracted the attention of a large number of comics fans in the mid-1970s when he began drawing Marvel's *Red Sonja*. The encounter with the sword-wielding barbarian girl had a profound effect on Thorne, changing the way he drew and the entire course of his career. He even grew a beard!

Born in the same New Jersey town where he still lives, Thorne's boyhood ambitions were to be a cartoonist and a magician. By his teen years he was emphasizing the drawing, and he entered the Art Career School in Manhattan. He once explained that a major goal of his throughout his career was to "find my own style." Initially he imitated the much-imitated Alex Raymond. After some magazine illustration jobs and a strip on local history for a New Jersey newspaper, he was hired, at the age of 22, to take over the *Perry Mason* newspaper strip. King Features, the home of Raymond, was syndicating it. "Working in Alex's style pleased King Features, but bothered me," Thorne has said. "I struggled for years to move away from the Raymond look."

After the *Perry Mason* strip, Thorne moved over to Dell-Western and drew comic book versions of such King properties as *Flash Gordon* and *Jungle Jim*. In 1956 he took over *Dr. Guy Bennett*, a second-string soap opera strip. During that period he started to develop a distinctive style of his own, drawing more realistically and experimenting with layouts. Thorne's next comic book work, on such titles as *Twilight Zone, Mighty Samson*, and *Boris Karloff*, showed the progress he had made. In 1968, when he signed on with DC, Thorne had a fully developed style of his own. He drew *Enemy Ace, Korak*, and *Tomahawk*.

Then, in the mid-1970s, he was hired by Marvel to do *Red Sonja*. Billed as a "She-devil With a Sword," the scantily clad red-haired barbarian had been created back in the 1930s in one of Robert E. Howard's pulp stories about Conan. Thorne was inspired by the assignment. "Call it midlife crisis. Call it Faustian," he's said. "Something clicked between Sonja and me, it threw the doors open." He did his most ambitious work to date and also revealed a hitherto dormant ability to draw very effective, sensuous women. From then on, even after leaving the She-devil, Thorne concentrated on drawing pretty women. He produced strips for *The National Lampoon* and *Playboy*, and created a barbarian lady of his own, Ghita of Alizarr, and drew two X-rated black and white albums about her. Most recently he's done a four-issue miniseries in full color about a diminutive green lady named Ribit. **R.G.**

**TIGER** Bud Blake's daily and Sunday humor strip *Tiger* details the activities and speculations of a gang of kids delicately poised between the farcical simplemindedness of an earlier generation of slapstick strips about children and the improbable sophistication of such strips as *Peanuts* and *Miss Peach*, striking a nice balance between the goofy and the shrewd.

King Features Syndicate had distributed Blake's daily panel *Ever Happen to You?* for over a decade when he sold them *Tiger* in 1965. The daily strip debuted on May 3, with the Sunday following six days later. Its cast is a gang of natural, not particularly bright children trying to figure the world out and often observing it with the oblique, accidental wisdom of youth. Its members are not very clearly differentiated, but include some identifiable types: Tiger and his kid brother Punkinhead serve as the norm; their dull-witted and esurient pal Hugo holds down one end of the intellectual scale and the bespectacled, polysyllabic Julian the other; Suzie and Bonnie represent the girl's eye view; and Tiger's irresistibly sloppy spotted dog Stripe is the convenient, patient victim.

Admired more for its art than for its wit, which is not notably innovative or penetrating but always engaging, *Tiger* is expressively drawn in a distinctive and deceptively simple style, with an economical and often elegant distribution of line and black areas. Among the most attractively executed humor strips in the field, it is syndicated to about 400 papers in 19 countries. The National Cartoonists Society voted it the Best Humor Strip of the Year in 1970 and 1978, and several volumes of the strip have been published. **D.W.**

**TILLIE THE TOILER** A year after the type of the attractive working girl was established in the comics with Martin Branner's Chicago Tribune-N.Y. Daily News strip *Winnie Winkle the Breadwinner*, Russ Westover sold the similarly-titled *Tillie the Toiler* to King Features Syndicate. *Tillie the Toiler* began as a daily feature on January 3, 1921, and added a Sunday page on October 10 of the following year.

Tillie Jones was a secretary, stenographer, occasional model, and all-around girl-Friday in the fashion business of J. Simpkins. Her toil was never either onerous or very glamorous, but her life had its share of excitement, mostly of a romantic nature, away from her desk. Comely but not voluptuous, after the fashion of comic strip flappers of the period, she was somewhat more of a gold digger than Boots or Winnie, but she remained essentially chaste. Winnie Winkle was a breadwinner from the beginning and has survived as a successful business woman; Boots settled down as a sober middle-class matron and homemaker; but Tillie toiled for more modest and immediate ends, and although she sometimes dreamed of a career and was always on the lookout for a rich husband, she was generally contented with survival and an occasional good time. There was nothing defiantly "liberated" about Tillie; she wore her luxurious black hair bobbed and her hemline high, but her self-sufficiency was dictated rather by the need to make a living than by any rebellious spirit of independence.

Tillie lost her fickle heart repeatedly—partly from greed and partly from incurable naiveté—to a series of dashing young sports in flashy roadsters, but she recovered just as easily. Although she quit her job from time to time to pursue livelier prospects, she always returned to her typewriter and steno pad, where she belonged. Throughout her many amatory escapades, Tillie had a single, pathetically constant swain whom she kept dangling: Clarence MacDougall—the eternally hopeful shrimp "Mac" who worked with and often covered for her—remained humbly faithful and tenaciously suppliant for the nearly four decades of her comic strip career.

Graphically, Tillie was the stock type of 1920s sexpot, complete with lissome body, pert button-nose, and bee-stung lips; her various quarries were similarly conventionalized handsome young men, indistinguishable except for the patterns of their vests, ties, and convertibles. Only Mac, with his huge, bulbous nose and open, goofy face, seems capable of any real expression. If Tillie was unvaried in personality and facial expression, she was, however, sensitive to the subtlest nuances of change in clothing style, and whatever her never-very-clearly stated fortunes, she always managed to dress fashionably. Probably she got a discount from Mr. Simpson.

Tillie became more responsible during World War II. The Women's Auxiliary Army Corps was set up in the summer of 1942, and among the earliest volunteers was Tillie the Toiler. She said goodbye to the office job she'd held since the early 1920s, gave away many of her clothes and shoes—"They'll all be out of style by the time I get out of the service."—and donned a uniform. Her long-suffering boyfriend Mac joined the Army soon after, remaining a private throughout his military career.

Westover employed various assistants over the years, including Joe Musial and Alex Raymond, and in 1951 Bob Gustafson took over most of the duties of the strip. With its creator's retirement in 1954, *Tillie the Toiler*, by then much modernized in look and tone, passed officially into Gustafson's hands and bore his signature from October 4th of that year until King Features discontinued the daily strip on March 9, and the Sundays on March 15, 1959. In the final episode, Tillie's heart surrenders at last to Mac's 38-year siege, and she consents to become his wife.

Somewhat rudimentary in execution at the hands of Westover (though it was to perk up considerably under his successors) and repetitious in story line, *Tillie the Toiler* remained a popular strip throughout and beyond its period. It generated several published collections and a movie during the 1920s and another film in the 1940s. **D.W.**

**THE TIMID SOUL** One of the relatively few cartoon characters who has earned a place in most dictionaries, Caspar Milquetoast's last name gave the English language a word. A "milquetoast" is now defined as "a man who is easily dominated or intimidated," and Caspar certainly lived up to that definition in his nearly 30 years in the funnies. He first appeared in 1924 in H.T. Webster's daily panel. The panel had different titles on different days—*Bridge, How to Torture Your Husband, Life's Darkest Moment,* and the like—and on the days that Caspar Milquetoast appeared it was titled *The Timid Soul.*

Webster built hundreds of gags around his character's timidity. Milquetoast was fearful not only of being embarrassed, but also of giving offense to anyone in any way. He would lie rather than get into an argument with his barber, deny his name if he overheard someone laughing at it, and give up his plans for the evening if he got a bulky piece of junk mail that told him to "Read every word of this!" What Webster was doing was kidding the very proper suburban readers who followed him in the *New York World* and, via syndication, around the country. Neither he nor they tired of the game, and *The Timid Soul* flourished for decades.

In 1931, when Webster signed on with the *New York Herald Tribune*, a *Timid Soul* Sunday page was added and offered more, and lengthier, variations on the theme. A good deal of the drawing on the Sunday Milquetoast page was done by Herb Roth. An excellent cartoonist and illustrator and a colleague of Webster's on the *World*, Roth started assisting him in 1923. He continued drawing the daily panels, including *The Timid Soul*, from the time of Webster's death in 1952 until his own death late in 1953.                    **R.G.**

**TIM TYLER'S LUCK**   It's one of the longest running adventure strips, begun in the summer of 1928 and still appearing in a handful of newspapers around the world today. The ostensible creator of *Tim Tyler's Luck* was Lyman Young, who signed his name to the strip up until his death in 1984; but for most of its long life Young employed a succession of talented ghosts. Among them were Alex Raymond, Charles Flanders, and Nat Edson.

When the strip began, initially as a daily, Tim was on the brink of his teens and a plucky orphan trying to make his way in the world. Several other plucky orphans preceded Tim into the funnies, most notably Little Orphan Annie and Little Annie Rooney. King Features apparently couldn't get enough of them, syndicating not only the Rooney strip but the Tim Tyler one as well. After meeting an older lad named Spud at an orphanage, Tim teamed up with him, and they set off on a series of adventures that continue to this day.

By 1930 the blond Tim and the dark-haired Spud were working at the local airport, even learning to fly. They next took to traveling around the world, finding adventure and intrigue in every country, real and fictitious, that they passed through. In 1932 they arrived in Africa, for what turned out to be a stay of several years. This was the Africa of the movies, packed with jungles, wild animals, blackhearted white hunters, savages, white goddesses, and evil witch doctors. Tim and Spud, after nearly two years of jungle excitement, joined the Ivory Patrol, a paramilitary outfit that policed a goodly stretch of Africa and wore snappy uniforms.

They aged some after joining up, eventually coming to look like boys in their late teens. In 1940, with rumors of war in the air, they returned to America and joined the Coast Patrol, who dressed and behaved pretty much like the real Coast Guard. Tim and Spud now divided their time between seagoing activities and landlocked encounters with spies and saboteurs. At the end of World War II they tried various world-roving careers and in the mid-1950s returned to the jungle, where they remain.

A *Tim Tyler's Luck* Sunday page was added in 1931 and lasted until 1972. From the mid-1930s to the mid-1940s *Curly Harper* ran as a companion feature to the Sunday.

Young, who was an extremely limited cartoonist of the bigfoot school, started hiring ghosts early on. In the early 1930s the young Alex Raymond drew the feature; then Charles Flanders and later Burne Hogarth took brief turns. Nat Edson assumed the job in the middle 1930s and did all the drawing for almost a decade. After

him came Clark Haas, who went on to ghost the *Buz Sawyer* Sunday page. He was followed on *Tim Tyler* by Tom Massey. An artist of modest talent, Massey was eventually allowed to sign the strip along with Lyman Young. Today only the name of Young's son, Bob, appears.

*Tim Tyler's Luck* was reprinted in the 1930s and 1940s in *Ace Comics*. From 1948 to 1950 eight issues of an original-material comic book were published; in these Tim and Spud were cowboys. Nat Edson returned to do the drawing.                    **R.G.**

**TINY TIM**   When it started on July 23, 1933, *Tiny Tim* was a pleasant, mildly humorous fantasy about two orphan children, Tim and his sister Dotty, who were only two inches tall. Running only on Sundays, it derived its humor chiefly from Tim's ingenuity in adapting the accoutrements of the "normal sized" world to his own special needs. Thus, two pencils became stilts, a turtle was commandeered as a raft, and a puppy was harnessed to a tiny cart to serve as a pony. The protagonists' minute size quickly proved more of a hindrance than a useful novelty in developing gags and stories, so by October they'd grown to eight inches, and by the end of the year they'd lost their homeless status, having been adopted by a kindly farmer and his wife. But the possibilities here too were soon exhausted.

Created by Stanley Link, *Tiny Tim* was drawn in the scratchy, hayey style of *The Gumps*, on which Link was then assisting Sidney Smith. But the patched and threadbare look (and Link's own storytelling penchant) was better suited to the tear-jerking melodramas of Smith's strip than to the fairy-tale cuteness of Link's. Before too long, Link changed his approach and began telling heart-rending stories in which Tim's happiness was continually threatened by a parade of greedy, slavering landlords or selfish foster parents or crazed scientists. The stage was set by the loss of Tim's sister and, assisted by a gypsy's magic, his assuming of the size of a normal boy. Then, Sunday after Sunday, Link plunged the kid into one harrowing predicament after another, ending each weekly installment with trumpeting cliffhangers of overwrought suspense. Finally, on April 13, 1941, Link introduced the element that would make his orphan kid's adventures distinctly different from all others. On that day, the old gypsy woman reappears and gives Tim a magic amulet inscribed with the words, "Nemesis of All Evil." Reciting the words aloud, Tim shrinks to his former two-inch stature; repeating the incantation, he resumes "normal" size.

For most of the remainder of the strip's run, Tim uses his amulet to good advantage in his unrelenting struggle against the evil tyrants with which Link infested his world. Pursued by thugs, the normal-sized Tim dashes around a corner, and then, clutching his amulet and repeating the words on it, he shrinks to his diminutive dimension and hides in a tin can. Once to help a crippled boy win prize money for an operation, Tim took the controls of a model airplane, piloting it to victory in a model airplane race. Too eccentric to survive the death of its creator, *Tiny Tim* ceased on March 2, 1958.

**R.C.H.**

**TOM CORBETT, SPACE CADET** Tom, who lived in the middle of the 24th century, was originally seen on a kids' television serial that began in 1950, but in 1951 he branched out into a comic strip. The following year his interplanetary adventures began in a comic book of their own.

Seen three times a week, and starring the ever-youthful Frankie Thomas Jr., the television show dealt with the adventures of Tom, Roger Manning and Astro the Venusian lad at the Earth-based Space Academy and assorted other locations in the universe. It was one of the earliest science fiction shows on the new medium, generating merchandise such as toys, costumes, and lunch boxes.

The strip, syndicated by Field Enterprises, began on Sunday, September 9, 1951. Ads for the new feature proclaimed, "A Thrilling, Educational Adventure Strip Based on Authentic, Scientific Fact!" Written by Paul S. Newman, it was drawn by Ray Bailey in his bold, black version of the Milton Caniff style. Caniff, Bailey's one-time boss, was doing *Steve Canyon* for Field and was probably instrumental in getting him the job. Appearing daily and Sunday, *Tom Corbett, Space Cadet* began life with an impressive list of papers that included the *New York Herald Tribune*, the *St. Louis Post Dispatch*, and the *San Francisco Chronicle*.

The initial Sunday page caption set the stage: "In the year 2351 A.D., Earth, Mars and Venus are united to form the Great Solar Alliance...Here, at Space Academy, USA, the Space Cadets train to defend the liberties of the planets." Readers then met the stalwart Tom, the less than bright Astro, and the sneaky Roger as they reported to Captain Strong. Also on view were such future marvels as slidewalks, study-spools, and very short skirts on the women, though the captain smoked a 20th-century pipe. After some weeks at the Academy the three cadets "board the rocket cruiser Polaris to blast off on a secret mission." The first mission involved invaders of Venus Space Station J, and most of the rest of the adventures were standard space opera stuff. These included encounters with Sultra, a female space pirate built along the lines of the Dragon Lady. For the first few months the Sunday pages were one-shot sequences having nothing to do with the daily continuity: They dealt with cadet life at the academy and at the

Luna Station and Venusport and usually imparted a bit of scientific knowledge. The strip ended in September 1953.

Dell began a series of Space Cadet comic books in 1952, using original material, not strip reprints. Alden McWilliams drew the early issues, followed by Frank Thorne. After publishing their 11th issue in 1954, Dell abandoned Tom and his bunch. The next year the Prize outfit tried two issues of a Tom Corbett comic, with artwork by Mort Meskin. After that the graphic career of the Space Cadets came to an end for several decades. The characters returned to comic books in 1989.   **R.G.**

**THE TOODLES** A family continuity strip that told its adventure and soap opera stories with a touch of humor, it was written by Betsy and Stanley Baer and drawn by Rod Ruth. *The Toodle Family*—later known as *The Toodles*—began in the early 1940s and lasted until the early 1960s.

*The Toodles* started on the same day as its home newspaper, the *Chicago Sun*, in December 1941. Eventually it ran in nearly 300 papers across the country. Mrs. Baer was probably ideally suited to the writing of continuity, since she was the daughter of Sol Hess. Hess, originally a jeweler by trade, had written *The Gumps* almost from the start and then created a family strip of his own, *The Nebbs*, in 1923. Betsy Baer has said that her father "was really the reason we started the cartoon." She and her husband, who was in the wholesale grocery business, were both comics fans. Hess "said one night, 'If you know so much about cartoons, why don't you do one yourself?'" Deciding that was a good idea, the Baers came up with *The Toodles*.

It was a more modern and sophisticated family than the one Hess had been writing about: The father in their strip was the head of a large manufacturing plant, and he and his wife had two college-age offspring, boy and girl, and a set of preschool twins, boy and girl. Mrs. Baer had two children of her own, a boy and a girl, but she'd always wanted twins and realized the only way she could have them was by way of the comic strip. "I wrote all the dialogue," she's explained, "and my husband got the ideas for the stories."

The artist the Baers picked to draw the strip was Rod Ruth, who was working in advertising at the time and moonlighting as an illustrator for such Chicago-based pulp fiction magazines as *Amazing Stories*. He had a very effective, individual style and was especially good at drawing the children and young people who were essential to the strip. Ruth was also good at rendering both the slambang action sequences and the lighter domestic comedy ones. *The Toodles* was a strip that mixed everyday family problems with large amounts of adventure and comedy, plus frequent touches of soap opera.

Ruth left the strip in its final years to return to illustrating. The drawing was carried on by Pete Winter. *The Toodles* continued until the 1960s. **R.G.**

**TOONERVILLE FOLKS** A series of panels and strips chronicling the life and idiosyncratic populace of a small American town in the early years of this century, *Toonerville Folks* was the product of the abundant imagination of Fontaine Fox. The community crystallized in a regular weekly panel Fox did for the *Chicago Post* from 1908, and assumed its distinctive character and name with daily syndication by the Wheeler Syndicate in 1913. In 1918, Fox added a Sunday page.

The endearing Folks of Toonerville ranged from the poor to the middle class, and none was without a sharply defined character. Mickey (Himself) McGuire, the town bully of the younger set who terrorizes all the sissies on both sides of the track, uses a hornet's nest as a punching bag, while the Powerful Katrinka, an Amazonian domestic whose strength "is almost entirely physical," swelters in an extra jacket because she was told to put on two coats when she painted the barn. Aunt Eppie Hogg, The Fattest Woman in Three Countries, has to use an opened drop-leaf table as an umbrella. Other memorable inhabitants of Toonerville include Little Woo-Woo Wortle, Who Has Never Been Spanked; Grandma, The Demon Chaperone, who foils all the town's courting couples; Uncle "Chew" Wilson, a Two-Quid Man; Pinckney Wortle, The World's Laziest White Man; The Terrible Tempered Mr. Bang, whose rages made him a national byword; and the malicious punster "Snake-Tongue" Tompkins. But the character that was to fix itself most firmly in the American consciousness and vocabulary was the Toonerville Trolley That Meets All Trains, surely the most ramshackle vehicle in comics history. It was to become a national institution. During the 1940s, in deference to the spirit of progress, it was replaced briefly by a bus (driven by the same nameless Skipper), but it soon returned to its twisty tracks. In many papers, the strip went by the name *The Toonerville Trolley.*

*Toonerville Folks* was taken over by the Bell Syndicate in 1920 and later switched to the McNaught Syndicate. At the height of its popularity in the 1920s and 1930s, it ran in about 300 papers.

Drawn in a fresh, energetic style from an elevated angle, as though seen from a balcony, the sprightly series has been collected in numerous volumes, and several short films starring Mickey Rooney as Mickey (Himself) McGuire were made in the 1920s. The Toonerville Trolley met its last train when Fox retired on February 9, 1955. **D.W.**

**TOOTS AND CASPER** A long-running domestic humor strip written and drawn by Jimmy Murphy, *Toots and Casper* began in 1918 and lasted until the middle 1950s. In the course of its lengthy life the strip went from daily gags about marriage and child rearing to breathless continuities offering mystery, melodrama and romance. For good measure Murphy threw in dog races and an occasional murder.

When *Toots and Casper* began in the *New York American* and other Hearst newspapers in December of 1918, it was an awkwardly drawn daily that dealt in rather quiet jokes. Casper Hawkins was initially a very small fellow with a bald head, a bulb nose, and a minute mustache. Toots was young and pretty, as pretty as Murphy could get her at that point. The very first gag had to do with Casper's jealousy, a theme that Murphy (whose wife was the model for Toots) would return to frequently over the years. This version of the strip lasted until February of 1919, then went on hiatus. Upon its return in May, Casper was younger, taller, smaller of nose, and less bald; Murphy's drawing had improved considerably and even Toots was better looking now. At about that time King Features began advertising the strip as a bright new feature about newlyweds, emphasizing that "Toots is the magnet that attracts all eyes."

A Sunday page was added in July 1920, and in November of that year Toots and Casper became the proud parents of a baby boy they nicknamed Buttercup. Murphy now built his gags around the baby and the doting, indulgent parents. Since Buttercup was a hit, he remained a baby for the next two decades and more. He didn't grow any, and then only into a six-year-old, until the early 1940s.

As the 1920s progressed Murphy, or his editors, may have fallen under the spell of the strips of some of his colleagues—notably Sidney Smith's *The Gumps* and Billy DeBeck's *Barney Google*. He introduced neighbors, such as Colonel Hoofer and his wife, and rich relatives, such as Uncle Everett, and a dog named Spare-Ribs. He went from daily gags to continued stories, involving his characters with the neighbors, the relatives, and assorted villains and their stooges. Murphy also had Casper enter Spare-Ribs now and then in a dog race that, like the horse races that Google's Spark Plug ran in, took several days to unfold. There were stories about crime, about the hunt for a lost love, about Casper's jealousy, about the quest for a missing valuable. Since Murphy wanted to involve his readers as much as possible, he frequently addressed them directly: "The door slowly opens! The detectives breathlessly await their prey! It's a tense moment! Watch closely!"—"Tomorrow's newspaper will announce the winner."—or "Casper is still trying to think up a good campaign slogan! Mail in your suggestions to him."

*Toots and Casper* remained a popular strip throughout the 1930s and into the 1940s. It began to slip thereafter, possibly affected by the competition from the slicker, more sophisticated, and not at all humorous new soap opera strips in the *Mary Worth* mode. Ghosted by others, often using recycled art, the strip hung on until the middle 1950s.                                    **R.G.**

**TOTH, ALEX** (1928– )  An innovative and independent cartoonist, Toth has been drawing for comic books since the middle 1940s. Impatient as well, he hasn't stuck with one style or approach and has continued to experiment. After doing impressive work on such heroes as Green Lantern and the Atom in the late 1940s, he moved on to war, romance, true crime, and horror and also put in time drawing adaptations of such television shows as *Sea Hunt* and *Zorro*. Though no longer a fan favorite, he remains, as many a fanzine has pointed out over the years, an artist's artist.

Born in New York City, Alexander Toth was an only child with a good deal of time on his hands. "I began to doodle at the age of three," he once confessed, "but couldn't sell a thing until I was fifteen." While at the High School of Industrial Arts, he began selling two- and three-page stories to *Heroic Comics* and in 1947 was hired by Sheldon Mayer to work for the All-American division of DC.

Superheroes were still going strong and Toth drew several, including Green Lantern, Dr. Mid-nite, and the Atom. He was very much influenced by the adventure strip work of Frank Robbins, Milton Caniff, and espe-cially Noel Sickles, a lifelong idol. "What I gained from Noel," he said, "was an appreciation for economy, clar-ity, line, mass, pattern, perspective, dramatic moment, subtlety, light source and drop shadow mechanics, neg-ative and positive silhouette values, shapes and the overlapping of same, tension." Toth's work, while it showed the influences of the artists he admired, was very strong, and he got a lot of work from DC.

He worked for a variety of publishers in the 1950s, changing his style several times and always trying for greater simplicity. He drew romance comics, devising a clean, cinematic style that other artists picked up and went on using for years after he'd abandoned it. He did some exceptional work for an issue of *Crime and Punish-ment*, using doubletone paper to get his depth effects. He ghosted the *Casey Ruggles* strip, served a hitch in the military and then settled in Southern California. From the middle 1950s into the 1960s Toth worked almost exclusively for Western-Dell, drawing *Zorro, 77 Sunset Strip, Rio Bravo, The FBI Story, The Real McCoys*, and others. He continued to experiment and was one of the first comic book artists to use a Rapidograph pen and the now fairly common markers.

He also became interested in animation, doing his first work in that area in the early 1960s. He was in and out of animation for many years, mostly as a character design man for studios such as Hanna-Barbera. He contributed to the Warren black and white comic books, drawing *Bravo For Adventure* originally for *The Rook* magazine. Set in the 1930s, *Bravo* allowed him to draw the sort of props and people, especially airplanes, that

*The Crushed Gardenia*, Alex Toth, © 1953, Standard Comics.

have always been favorites of his. Toth's done a little work for European publishers, plus some covers and an occasional one-shot story for American independents. But in the late 1980s he led a very quiet life and drew infrequently.

**R.G.**

**TRUDEAU, GARRY** (1948– ) The creator of the trenchant topical satire strip *Doonesbury* was born Garretson Beekman Trudeau in New York City and grew up in the fashionable upstate resort area of Saranac Lake. As a student in St. Paul's School in New Hampshire, which he entered in 1960, he was president of the Art Association, coedited the yearbook, won the senior class art prize, and drew murals for a local hospital, and when he went on to Yale in 1966, he continued to pursue his artistic inclinations. He created a comic strip his first year there—"a Feifferesque embarrassment," according to *Time* magazine, about the social failures of a Yale freshman—but he made no efforts to publish it because he recognized its graphic defects. In his junior year, he tried again with *Bull Tales*, satirizing not only the social problems of freshmen but the entire range of campus life. The strip appeared that year in the Yale newspaper and proved so popular that it was noticed by James Andrews, then in the process of creating Universal Press Syndicate with John McMeel. When Trudeau graduated with an M.A. in art and architecture in 1970, Andrews persuaded him to bring *Bull Tales* to the new syndicate, and, cleaned up for the general market and renamed for its principal character, it appeared in 28 newspapers as *Doonesbury* in 1970.

Quickly outgrowing its academic setting, *Doonesbury* made Trudeau the most prominent cartoonist-commentator on the political scene during the 1970s, bringing him the 1975 Pulitzer Prize—the first ever awarded for a comic strip—and 13 honorary degrees, one from his alma mater. In 1977 he received an Academy Award for his animated show "A Doonesbury Special," presented on NBC-TV. He accompanied the press corps on President Ford's trip to China that same year and became a frequent contributor to such liberal publications as *Harper's*, *The New Republic*, and *Rolling Stone*.

Trudeau has steadfastly refused to license his characters for advertising or merchandising and, with all the attention his often controversial strip brings him, rejects the lure of personal publicity, explaining, "I don't like celebrification. Everything I have to share I share in the strip." The tremendous success of that strip, appearing in nearly 900 newspapers and publicly quoted by every president since Richard M. Nixon, has made him probably the most influential comic strip artist in history.

**D.W.**

**TRUE COMICS** Both a comic book and a newspaper strip, *True Comics* began as a magazine early in 1941, launched by *Parents' Magazine* as an antidote to the ever increasing number of wild and woolly comic books to be found on newsstands across the land. *Parents'* assured concerned mothers that while *True Comics* might look just like another comic book, it was actually "attractive, interesting, and worthwhile" and that the big "difference is in the subject matter, which deals with past and present history." The first issue, despite its mild-mannered appearance, sold out a first printing of 300,000 in less than two weeks and went back to press for more. The contents has been prepared by Funnies, Inc., the same shop that had previously cooked up the somewhat more flamboyant *Marvel Mystery Comics* and *Target Comics*.

The year after the magazine's debut, the Bell Syndicate introduced a *True Comics* comic strip, daily and Sunday. Elliot Caplin, editorial director of the comic book by that time, was in charge of the production of the strip. The newspaper version concentrated mostly on World War II events and personalities, offering continuities on subjects ranging from the Flying Tigers to "pretty Adeline Gray, courageous young parachute tester."

*Parents'* seemed to consider comics as simply another product and they rarely gave credit to writers or artist. An assortment of cartoonists took turns drawing segments of the strip, including Jack Sparling, Ed Smalle, and Joe Simon. Simon, who drew some propaganda pages while serving in the Coast Guard, once said that working on these true stories was one of the things that inspired him to invent the true romance comic book after the war.

By the time Simon was back in civvies the *True* strip had ended. The comic book, however, lasted until 1950 and inspired several imitations.

**R.G.**

**TUFTS, WARREN** (1925–1982) Although he had a relatively short comic strip career, Tufts left an indelible mark in the field by creating *Casey Ruggles* and then *Lance*, two of the best Westerns ever produced and the only ones done in the ambitious illustrational manner of Alex Raymond and Hal Foster. The strips, well-researched and written for adult audiences, each followed the adventures of cavalrymen in mid-19th-century America. Tufts' portrayal of the hard life of the pioneer, as well as his devotion to detail, won him acclaim. But his effort to maintain what he felt was artistic integrity led to deadline problems, conflicts with his first syndicate, and the eventual demise of both features.

Born in Fresno, California, he was in the same high school class as Western movie director Sam Peckinpah (*Ride the High Country*, *The Wild Bunch*, etc.). Tufts was, from the start, someone who strove to do things his way; his contrariness first showed itself in school when he and his art teacher got into a disagreement that led to his banishment from class. But, characteristically, Tufts didn't let that stifle his creativity; he just found another outlet. As a Boy Scout he took part in a short-lived radio program, and when that show went off the air, he stayed with radio as announcer, producer, and scriptwriter while still a high school student.

His introduction to comics probably came during his stint in the U.S. Navy during World War II where, as part of his duties, he wrote and illustrated a survival cartoon. A few years after the war, in 1949, he created *Casey Ruggles*. The strip itself lasted six years, but a dispute with United Features prompted Tufts to leave his creation in 1954. Later that year he formed Warren Tufts Enterprises, a new syndicate whose entire staff consisted of Tufts, his father, and his brother. Its first venture was *The Lone Spaceman*, a humorous science fiction strip that Tufts drew in an Al Capp style. Not especially successful, it folded in the spring of the following year.

A couple months thereafter Tufts returned to the Old West and began syndicating *Lance*, which began as a Sunday page, an impressively drawn and colored production. Eventually a daily was added. *Lance*, which Tufts once said took him at least 100 hours a week to do, was concluded in 1960.

After abandoning the strip Tufts worked briefly as an actor in Peckinpah's 1960 television series *The Westerner*, and "off and on for several seasons I performed odd tasks for Hanna-Barbera...voice-over work for animation series and records, storyboards, etc." He also drew for comic books from the late 1950s to the late 1960s, handling such titles as *Rifleman, Zorro, Korak*, and *Wagon Train.* He never cared much for this aspect of cartooning, claiming that for him "comic books were strictly a bread-and-butter activity."

He spent his last years in the field of aeronautical engineering. He founded Tufts Aircraft where he could design and fly his own planes. On July 6, 1982, he was killed in the fiery crash of one of those experimental planes.                **S.L.H.**

**TURNER, LESLIE** (1899–1988) Roy Crane was a very hard act to follow, but Turner succeeded him as artist-writer on *Wash Tubbs* (later known as *Captain Easy*) and came close to equaling his work. He signed the strip from 1943 until early in 1970 and was undoubtedly the best strip successor in the long history of comics.

Turner once described his life and career this way: "When Crane left in 1943, I inherited the strip...This chore has left little time for anything eventful." He had been Crane's assistant and frequent ghost for several

*Captain Easy*, Leslie Turner, © 1953, NEA Service, Inc. Reprinted by permission NEA Service, Inc.

years before the strip officially passed into his hands. "In 1937 I pinch-hit for Roy Crane on *Wash Tubbs* while he frolicked in Europe," he explained. "Stayed on to assist till he left for greener pastures." Turner was born in Cisco, Texas, "in time to see the last week of the nineteenth century." He grew up in Wichita Falls, almost completed four years at Southern Methodist University, and spent part of a term at the Chicago Academy of Fine Arts. It was in Chicago at the Academy that he first met his fellow Texan, Crane. Like Crane he suffered from wanderlust in his youth and devoted his summers to riding the rods. That fondness for trains stayed with him and, even though he no longer traveled under them, he often built Tubbs and Easy adventures around trains.

His first professional job after drifting out of college was in a Dallas engraving plant, but at the same time he was sending in cartoons to *Judge* and selling a few. After marrying in 1923, he and his new wife headed East. In New York Turner abandoned cartooning for illustration. He became a friend and protégé of then prominent illustrator Henry Raleigh, and began doing work for *Redbook, Ladies' Home Journal*, and *The Saturday Evening Post.* In the late 1920s he and his wife and daughters moved to Colorado, and he tried raising sheep. Turner stuck it out for three years, "drawing with one hand while rearing a herd of ungrateful sheep with the other." Finally, after another and less successful period of free-lancing in New York, he accepted an invitation from Crane to come to Cleveland and help out on *Wash Tubbs.*

At first Turner couldn't get the hang of his friend's style, but gradually he simplified his work and by the late 1930s was ghosting just about all the dailies. Many of the handsome Craftint dailies reprinted in histories to illustrate Crane's mastery of the doubletone shading technique are actually ones drawn by Turner. Turner officially took over the strip in 1943, when Crane went to King Features to do *Buz Sawyer*. An excellent figure and action man, Turner was equally good at backgrounds. His continuities were among the most convincingly placed in comics. He could convey the look and feel of any location—a rundown English pub, a bleak stretch of Southwest desert, a brooding Victorian mansion. Turner also had a great eye for clutter, particularly lower-class clutter.

For nearly a decade Turner was responsible only for the daily strip. Crane was originally replaced on the *Captain Easy* Sunday by Walt Scott, but Turner took it over in 1952. The extra burden apparently buoyed him up, at least for a while, and the first two years contain some of his finest work. He exuberantly filled the pages with sweeping desert scenes, idyllic shots of the New England seacoast, panoramas of English country estates and stately homes. It abounded with vintage automobiles, ocean liners, jets, and, of course, trains.

Turner stuck with the Sunday page throughout the 1950s, alternating moderately bloodcurdling adventures with broader farces. After suffering a heart attack he had to give up the Sunday. Mel Graff began ghosting it early in 1960, though Turner occasionally returned to draw a page or two. Turner retired late in 1969, a few weeks before his 70th birthday. The last of his dailies ran in January of 1970.                R.G.

**TURNER, MORRIE** (1923– )   One of the first black cartoonists to use race relations as a major theme for humor in a nationally syndicated strip, Morrie Turner, creator of *Wee Pals*, grew up in an ethnically mixed neighborhood in Oakland, California. Self-taught in art except for a correspondence-school course in cartooning, Turner was writing and illustrating his own weekly *Neighborhood Nooz* (sold on street corners for 5 cents) while still in grade school and drew for his high school newspaper. During World War II Turner served in the Army Air Force and contributed to *Stars and Stripes*.

In 1947, Turner made his first free-lance sale, to *Baker's Helper*, for $5, and went on to sell to *Better Homes & Gardens*, *True*, *Argosy*, and *Negro Digest*. In 1963, he was the first black to join the Northern California Cartoonists and Gag Writers, and that same year developed his first comic strip, *Dinky Fellas*, a carbon copy of *Peanuts*, which was taken by the weekly *Berkeley* (California) *Post* and later by the *Chicago Defender*. The next year, with the encouragement of cartoonist Charles Schulz and comedian Dick Gregory, he integrated the all-black *Dinky Fellas* and sold it as *Wee Pals* to the Lew Little Syndicate.

Active in education, Turner was a delegate to the White House Conference on Children in 1960 and has received many national awards for his work, including the Brotherhood Award of the National Council of Christians and Jews in 1968 and the B'nai B'rith Anti-Defamation League Humanitarian Award in 1969. He has taught a course in cartooning at Laney Community College since 1970 and has been artist-in-residence at the University of Portland. His expressively drawn characters have been used to illustrate many community publications, public-service television spots, and animated cartoons.                D.W.

**TUSKA, GEORGE** (1916– )   A professional cartoonist for over 50 years, Tuska has turned out an enormous amount of work for comic books and also drawn several newspaper strips. Among the many characters he has done are Captain Marvel, Nyoka, Sub-Mariner, Captain America, Superman, Uncle Sam, Scorchy Smith, and Buck Rogers.

Tuska did his first comic book work in 1939 while an employee of the Eisner-Iger shop. Tuska had an assured style from the start, one that combined illustrational and cartoon elements; chief among the things he drew best were pretty girls and boats. Plenty of both were depicted in such comics as *Jungle*, *Planet*, *Wings*, *Mystery Men*, and *Wonderworld*. In the early 1940s Tuska switched to the Chesler shop. Fast and dependable, he drew the original Captain Marvel, Golden Arrow, El Carim, Uncle Sam, and dozens of others.

In 1946 he started drawing for *Crime Does Not Pay*, and his work became more realistic. He was very successful at depicting the gangsters, gunmolls, machine guns, and getaway cars the true crime tales required. During those same postwar years he also drew superheroes such as the Black Terror and Doc Strange. In the 1960s and 1970s he drew just about every major Marvel hero from the Avengers to the X-Men and found time to work for DC as well on *Challengers of the Unknown*, *Superboy* and *Superman*.

Tuska's first newspaper strip was *Scorchy Smith*, which he wrote and drew from 1954 to 1959. He next drew the venerable *Buck Rogers* from 1959 to 1965, and in the 1970s he penciled the *World's Greatest Superheroes* strip.

In recent years he has worked mostly as a penciller in comic books.                R.G.

**TUTHILL, HARRY J.** (1886–1957)   For nearly 30 years, roughly from the end of World War I to the end of World War II, Tuthill wrote and drew *The Bungle Family*. The strip was a slightly cockeyed family saga that dealt with the woes of middle-class urban life in a way that was snide, cynical, and very funny. George

Bungle, the head of the household, was impractical, conceited, belligerent, and a perennial fall guy. Tuthill, as witty as his strip, liked to assure interviewers that his comic strip was autobiographical.

Born in Chicago, Tuthill wandered considerably while growing to manhood, working for a dairy and then clerking in a drugstore before joining a traveling medicine show and then a carnival. All that time he was also drawing and sketching in whatever spare time he had. "I hate to say that I studied nights," he once said. "It sounds trite and is apt to discourage the boys who are studying nights with the hope of being President some day. 'Look at Tuthill,' they'll say to their fathers, 'he studied nights—and see what happened to him.' However, the truth must out even though it sounds as if I have been reading Alger books. I did study nights." He claimed he got all his formal art training during a single week in night school.

That proved sufficient to get him a job as an editorial cartoonist with the *St. Louis Post-Dispatch.* Tuthill next drew for the *St. Louis Star* and then moved eastward for a job with the *New York Evening Mail.* He tried an assortment of features for them. "At one time I was making three comic strips," he said. "They were based on various ideas of mine. Two of them didn't survive. The third underwent various changes until it became George Bungle."

Originally the Bungle opus ran under the title *Home, Sweet Home,* but by the mid-1920s, when the McNaught Syndicate was distributing it, the name was *The Bungle Family.* Tuthill had returned to Missouri by then and settled in the town of Ferguson, 12 miles out of St. Louis. A *Kansas City Star* reporter who visited him in 1927 described Tuthill's home as "a big, brown frame house on Elizabeth Street, with an enameled clock in his hallway, a monkey that has a cough in his basement, and three roadsters that have no resale value in his barn." Tuthill had his studio in a small outbuilding next to the barn. He had kept the habit of drawing at night and was to be found out in the studio most evenings.

Tuthill drew in a raw, scratchy style that was admirably suited to the content of his strip. He was especially proud of his street scenes, which included a wide variety of urban types in the background—quite often bickering couples. He was a master at writing dialogue and felt his copy was as important as the pictures because for him, a comic strip was "similar to a play. The characters have much to say in a limited space. It should be funny and it must smack of the colloquial."

His strip was one of the most popular of the 1920s and 1930s, and it had a large list of client papers. *The Bungles* even ran in some Hearst newspapers, where it was the only strip unassociated with Hearst's own King Features. A 1933 article on funny papers in *Fortune* estimated Tuthill's income at about $1,400 a week—not a bad take for that grim Depression year. Tuthill retired the strip in 1945. He was still living in St. Louis when he died 12 years later.                                          **R.G.**

# U

**ULREY, DALE CONNER** See MARY WORTH.

**UNCLE WIGGILY** Once one of the best-known rabbits in the nation, Uncle Wiggily was the creation of writer Howard R. Garis, and he originally appeared in a bedtime story column that began running in newspapers in 1910. Over the next half-century the clever rabbit gentleman multiplied his outlets, showing up in the funny papers, Big Little Books and comic books. Among the artists who illustrated his woodland adventures were Walt Kelly, Lang Campbell, and George Carlson.

Uncle Wiggily Longears, who lived in a hollow tree bungalow in Animal Land, was an elderly fellow. Dapper, he wore a tailcoat and topper, using one wooden crutch because of his rheumatism. He was looked after by a kindly muskrat housekeeper named Nurse Jane Fuzzy Wuzzy, had such friends as Uncle Butter, and had pranks played on him by the likes of Bully and Bawly, the froggie boys. "Uncle Wiggily and his friends crammed all the early 1900s funfilled happenings into their lives, "observed Martin McCaw in *Strip Scene*, "corn roasts and marshmallow roasts, sleigh rides and hay rides, quilting parties, cider making and taffy pulling."

Life, however, was not always tranquil in Uncle Wiggily's neck of the woods, and an unsavory assortment of villains frequently attempted to catch him. The object of their quest was the souse in his ears. Since Garis never supplied any details or definitions for his kid readers, the precise nature of "souse" is open to argument. Souse meat, including the ears, feet, and nose of pigs is used to make head cheese, and apparently Uncle Wiggily's pursuers had a similar recipe they were anxious to try. Dedicated to chasing the rabbit gentleman, singly, in pairs, and now and then in teams, were the Fuzzy Fox, the Woozie Woolf, Bob Cat, the Skillery Skallery Alligator, the Blue Nosed Baboon, the Scudlemagoon, the Boozap, the Pipsisewah, and the Skeezicks. These last two, who resembled a rhino and a very tall, thin crow, were the most persistent and frequently seen of sousehunters. Needless to say, Uncle Wiggily, using cunning and an occasional bit of physi-cal violence, never got caught and always outwitted the lot of them.

Garis had been a reporter for the *Newark Evening News* before embarking on a career as a prolific producer of children's books. After turning out fiction about Tom Swift and the Motor Boys for the Stratemeyer shop, he began doing an assortment of series of his own. His wife Lillian equalled him in output on cheap children's stories. On January 30, 1910, Garis' first Uncle Wiggily column appeared in the *Evening News*. Syndicated by McClure, the six times a week series of bedtime stories appeared all across the country. In 1919 a Sunday page, mixing drawings and text, was added. The artist was a gifted lady who signed herself Lang Campbell. Over three dozen of the Uncle Wiggily story books that were published over the next decades were adaptations from the Sunday page, which lasted throughout the 1920s. There was also, in the middle 1920s, a daily strip drawn by Hubert Main and others. In the late 1940s a short-lived Sunday page appeared, credited to Garis and drawn by Francis Kirn. The rabbit gentleman had married in the Sunday page in 1925, but in later incarnations was once again a bachelor looked after by the loyal Nurse Jane.

Dell adapted Wiggily to comic books early in 1942, adding him to the lineup of *Animal Comics* with the second issue. While several artists drew him inside, Walt Kelly depicted the top-hatted bunny on the front covers and in pantomime strips on the back covers. Kelly's *Pogo* was also in *Animal*, and eventually the possum and his pals shoved the elderly rabbit from the star spot. Although George Carlson was working in comic books at the time, he never drew Wiggily in that medium and limited himself to book illustrations. Uncle Wiggily was last seen in comic books in a one-shot in 1954, but held on in his daily bedtime story until Garis' death in the early 1960s.                **R.G.**

**UP FRONT** See MAULDIN, BILL.

**US BOYS** See McNAMARA, TOM.

# V

**VAN BUREN, RAEBURN** (1891–1987) When Al Capp created *Abbie an' Slats* in 1937, he turned to a balding, middle-aged magazine illustrator with an eye for beautiful women and a flair for the comic to handle the artwork. Nearly 50 years old, Van Buren was entering the twilight of a successful career, and Capp was forced to use his considerable persuasive powers to convince him to make the change. Capp reasoned that radio was killing off magazines and the best bet for an illustrator was in the funny papers. Buying that argument, Van Buren made the switch and stayed with the strip until its demise in 1971.

Born in Pueblo, Colorado, Van Buren was raised in Kansas City, Missouri, which, at the turn of the century, was a wild and woolly cow town, whose citizens longed for a better life. Bill Nelson of *The Kansas City Star* believed his newspaper could single-handedly turn KC into the jewel of the Midwest and hired only the best editors. One was Harry Wood, who ran the art department from 1892 to 1943, and created one of America's first comic strips when he introduced *The Intellectual Pup* in 1907—two years before Van Buren became one of his pupils as a sketch artist. This was the only training Van Buren ever received.

In 1913, after selling gag drawings to the old *Life* magazine, Van Buren went to New York. When World War I broke out, he enlisted with the 107th New York Regiment of the 27th Infantry Division and went on to serve as art editor of its magazine, *Gas Attack*. After the war, his work had matured, and *The Saturday Evening Post* wanted him as a regular contributor. By the time Capp put in his call from Dogpatch, Van Buren's illustrations were appearing regularly in *The Post*.

Quickly adapting his illustrative style to the comic strip, he won critical acclaim. Comics historian Coulton Waugh noted his "absorbing realism, mysterious overtone, subtle humor." In *Comic Art in America*, Stephen Becker described his "sense of pure fantasy" as "the best since Winsor McCay's." In 1979 Van Buren was elected to the National Cartoonist Society Hall of Fame.

When he retired his strip, after 34 years of hunching over the same drawing table in the same cramped garage studio where he had illustrated more than a thousand magazine stories, Van Buren was in his 80th year. He died two weeks shy of his 97th birthday. **S.L.H.**

**VANILLA AND THE VILLAINS** See HERSHFIELD, HARRY.

**VIC FLINT** A tough, hard-boiled private eye, Vic Flint introduced himself on Sunday, January 6, 1946. Like many a novelistic private eye, including all the creations of Raymond Chandler and most of Dashiell Hammett's, Flint narrated his cases in the first person. The initial daily began: "The whole thing started late one afternoon. I was sitting in my office reading the papers about a killing. And then my door opened."

Flint was a good-looking blond guy who went in for herringbone suits and snapbrim hats and who almost always had a cigarette between his lips. He was fond of wisecracks, got along with the cops, but didn't take any guff from them. His world was a somewhat watered down version of the period's typical *film noir* setting, complete with cigar-chomping cops, oily gangsters, blond showgirls, crooked politicians, glittery nightclubs, and dark alleys.

The writing on *Vic Flint* was credited to one Michael O'Malley, actually a pen name for NEA syndicate feature editor Ernest "East" Lynn. The strip's artist was Ralph Lane, a former gag cartoonist who'd spent his last few years assisting Roy Crane on *Buz Sawyer*. His style was a bit more realistic than Crane's, and he liked to do detailed long shots that established the strip's various locales. In the autumn of 1950, he was rather abruptly relieved of his duties, disappearing in the midst of the Sunday page for October 8th, with the final panel provided by Dean Miller, his successor.

Miller was a man of lesser talent who had previously drawn a Sunday page entitled *Mighty O'Malley* for the *Chicago Tribune*. After Miller left, Art Sansom took a turn. The daily concluded in January of 1956, while the Sunday limped along, changing its name in 1965 to *The Good Guys* and turning intentionally humorous. Russ Winterbotham, using his J. Harvey Bond alias, became scriptwriter. The strip's final artist was John Lane, who was Ralph Lane's son. The feature finally went to its rest in March 1967. **R.G.**

**VIC JORDAN**   Although the strip began on December 1, 1941, the Monday before the attack on Pearl Harbor, it was very much involved with World War II from the start. Syndicated by the liberal New York newspaper *PM*, the strip was drawn by comic book alumnus Elmer Wexler and written by Kermit Jaediker and Charles Zerner under the pseudonym "Paine" (after Tom Paine).

The early sequences were set in Paris during the summer of 1940. Jordan, a handsome, glib fellow, was the publicity man for an American musical show playing in the Nazi-occupied city. As a stunt he had one of the young ladies in the show do an impersonation of Hitler—"This should put Adrienne on page one from New York to Frisco." It did more than that, and before long Jordan was on the run from the Gestapo.

Aided by a blond young lady who was both a dancer and a British secret agent, he teamed up with Marty O'Brien, "ex-heavyweight champion of Rhode Island," and started working with the underground. Jordan led a band of freedom fighters in midnight assaults on munitions plants, rail links, U-boat bases, and the various impregnable redoubts occupied by a recurrent nemesis known as the Noose.

The real war was having an effect on the staff of the feature before too long. Wexler entered the Marines in 1942, and Paul Norris, also with a background in comic books and a protégé of Milton Caniff, took over as artist. Vic roamed Europe during Norris' tenure, a sort of free-lance saboteur, even fighting the Nazis on their home ground in Germany, under the guise of a Gestapo officer. The strip mixed realistic violence and acts of guerilla warfare with melodrama and romance.

It lasted until April of 1945, when the war was just about over in Europe. Norris had entered the service in 1943 and was followed on the strip first by David Moneypenny and later by Bernard Baily.   **R.G./J.M.**

**THE VIGILANTE**   An urban cowboy, the Vigilante fought crime in the big city, not on the prairie and rode a motorcycle, not a horse. He first appeared in *Action Comics* #42 (November 1941) and was created by two Morts, editor-writer Mort Weisinger and artist Mort Meskin, which probably accounts for the pen name, Mort Morton Jr., used on the early stories.

Unlike most costumed crimefighters, the Vigilante was a celebrity in his civilian identity as well. Greg Sanders was known to radio listeners from coast to coast as the Prairie Troubadour, a guitar-pickin' cowboy crooner. Sanders tried to behave in a mild-mannered way, causing many of his fans to believe he was "just a drugstore cowboy." But in truth he was born in Wyoming, the grandson of an "Indian fighter and stalwart frontiersman…the son of a fearless county sheriff." After his father was killed by stagecoach bandits, Greg vowed to carry on the family tradition, but in a manner less hampered by rules and red-tape.

He became the Vigilante, "nemesis of all crime from border to border!" His costume was simply a cowboy outfit—including spotless white sombrero—with a crimson bandana masking the lower part of his face. Pretty much the standard outlaw getup, but in this case used in the cause of justice. The Vigilante carried six-guns, but favored using his lariat and his wits to catch crooks. In *Action* #45 he added a sidekick, an Oriental teenager known as Stuff, the Chinatown Kid.

Among the recurring villains were the Dummy, a mean-minded midget who disguised himself as a ventriloquist's dummy in order to commit assorted clever and nasty crimes, and the Rainbow Man, who used color—in the form of colored lights, bright paints, and the like—to bring off capers that were nearly as audacious and eccentric as those of the Joker and Lex Luthor. As Ethan Roberts pointed out in *Comic World*, almost every story involved Vig and Stuff having to use their wits and whatever props were at hand to escape from the trap set for them by that month's criminal. "The trap sequences probably made the readers of the day, who spent their Saturdays at the movies with serials and the invariable cliffhanger chapter endings, comfortable," Roberts observes. "Mort Weisinger may even have patterned his writing on the serials."

Meskin was one of the most gifted artists of the period. He took an illustrator's approach, but was also an

*Vic Jordan*, Elmer Wexler, © 1941, The Newspaper PM, Inc.

expert at staging action and moving his narrative from panel to panel. He did some impressive two-page splash panels and was one of the first to use that layout approach in comic books. He penciled every story up to *Action* #101 (October 1946). Meskin returned a year and a half later, with Jerry Robinson as inker, to draw another batch of Vigilante adventures. Later artists included Joe Kubert, Bob Lubbers, and Dan Barry.

The first phase of Vig's career ended with *Action* #198 (November 1954). He returned in the 1970s, appearing sporadically in *Justice League of America, Adventure,* and *World's Finest.* DC revived the name but not the character in 1983 with a Vigilante who was a very different, and much more violent, big city avenger. This new Vigilante expired early in 1988.          **R.G.**

**VOIGHT, CHARLES A.** (1887–1947) Voight was responsible for two long-running features, the daily strip *Petey* (also known as *Petey Dink*) and the Sunday page *Betty*. After leaving newspaper funnies in 1943, he devoted the final years of his life to drawing anonymously for comic books.

The Brooklyn-born Voight was a school dropout, a self-taught artist, and a filler of odd-jobs. "At fourteen I was forced to give up all this and go to work as a comic

artist on the staff of the *New York Evening World*," he once said, "eventually becoming sports cartoonist for that paper."

He had a vigorous, sketchy style and was an expert at drawing both pretty women and impressive landscapes. His chief handicap was a sense of humor that allowed him too often to settle for the obvious.

After the *World* he moved on to the *Boston Traveler*, where in 1908 he first drew *Petey Dink;* later he worked on newspapers in Chicago and Manhattan. He began drawing *Betty* in 1920. For the next two decades he also did magazine illustration, and beginning in the 1930s he took on considerable advertising work, in both magazines and newspapers. One of his last efforts in this area was a daily strip-format series for Hostess Cupcakes, featuring a character named Toofer A. Nickel.

Voight did all his comic book work for the shop run by Bernard Baily. His *Boom Boom Branigan,* a straight adventure feature about a prizefighter, and *Sir Prize,* which featured humor in the *Oaky Doaks* mode, appeared in *Prize Comics.* He drew a superhero named *Atomic Man* for *Headline Comics* and a variety of other material for low-budget publishers. Baily himself pub-

*Petey*, C.A. Voight, 1919.

lished one issue of *The Cisco Kid* in 1944, with Voight doing a handsome job on the Robin Hood of the Old West. Unfortunately, a confusion over the rights to the character killed the magazine, as well as the proposed newspaper strip Voight was supposed to do.

He never modified his style for comic books (nor his distinctive brand of pretty women), and his pages were as enthusiastically inked and imaginatively laid out as his newspaper pages. All in all, Voight brought a touch of class to the medium, though he never felt compelled to sign his work.                                    **R.G.**

# W

**WALKER, MORT** (1923– ) One of the most prolific cartoonists working today, and one of the most widely read, Mort Walker is the creator of the perennially popular *Beetle Bailey*. Over the years he's also managed to contribute to and sometimes draw over a half-dozen other strips, including *Hi and Lois* and *Boner's Ark*.

Born in El Dorado, Kansas, and raised in Kansas City, Missouri, Addison Morton Walker was dedicated to cartooning from his early childhood. At 15 he was already doing a strip for a Kansas City paper and working as a staff cartoonist for an industrial publication. At 17 he went to work for Hallmark Cards, and at the University of Missouri, where he studied humanities, Walker edited the campus humor magazine.

The sale of a cartoon to the *Saturday Evening Post* emboldened him to try his luck in New York after graduation, and from 1948 to 1950 he worked as an editor for Dell on the magazine *1000 Jokes*. Seeing the business from the editor's position provided an education, which he quickly put to use. While at Dell he produced such a stream of cartoons for other magazines that in 1949 he was named the topselling gag cartoonist in the country.

Walker wanted something more secure than the life of a free lance, however, so in 1950 he developed a character he'd frequently used in gag cartoons—a feckless college student named Spider—into a comic strip and offered it to King Features. The syndicate took it at once, altering the hero's name to Beetle, and *Beetle Bailey* was born. It was the first of many strips Walker was to create and, after a change of setting from campus to army camp, the most successful.

Since then Walker has generated a wide assortment of comic creations, all but one for King Features. In 1954 he joined with artist Dik Browne to write the family strip *Hi and Lois*. From 1957 to 1972 he authored the saga of a testy landlady, *Mrs. Fitz's Flats*, drawn by Frank Roberge, and from 1961 to 1963 he collaborated with Jerry Dumas, who did the drawing, on the ingenious *Sam's Strip*. In 1968 came *Boner's Ark*, which he signed with his little-known first name, and which Frank Johnson took over several years ago. He and Dumas revived *Sam's Strip* in a less esoteric form as *Sam and Silo* in 1977, and in 1982 Walker created *The Evermores*, a historical strip drawn by Johnny Sajem that ran until 1986. In 1987, again signing himself Addison, he came up with a kid strip about a lovable city urchin and his bedraggled dog. Titled *Gamin and Patches* and distributed by United Features, it proved to be his least successful venture and lasted a little more than a year.

Still working in the timeless minimal cartoon style of his early magazine days, Walker maintains an open, uncluttered look that perfectly matches the unchallenging, middlebrow humor of his gags. Never an innovative artist, he remains a fellow of infinite jest.    **D.W.**

**WAR ON CRIME** Capitalizing on the popularity of gangbuster material in general and J. Edgar Hoover's ripsnorting Federal Bureau Of Investigation in particular, Philadelphia's tiny Ledger Syndicate, on May 18, 1936, launched *War on Crime*, a fast-moving semidocumentary daily drawn from Bureau files and starring actual, notorious public enemies recently killed by the fearless G-men. It was written by *Washington Star* crime reporter Rex Collier, an enthusiastic Bureau drumbeater who had won the Director's favor, and luridly drawn for most of its run by Kemp Starrett in a trademark Ledger drybrush style derived from James Montgomery Flagg and Frank Godwin (the latter was long misidentified as the strip's illustrator). *War on Crime* enjoyed vigorous life for a time and was a reprint staple in *Famous Funnies*; but once John Dillinger, Baby Face Nelson, Pretty Boy Floyd, and the other premium-grade bandits had been used up, Collier increasingly had to resort to such distinctly lesser figures as Two-Gun Brunette, and the feature gradually ran out of firepower. Drawn in its last few months by Jimmy Thompson, *War on Crime* concluded on Jan. 22, 1938.    **J.M.**

**WASH TUBBS** An early and influential adventure strip, it always mixed humor with its action. Drawn and written by Roy Crane, *Wash Tubbs* set the pattern for many strips to follow and introduced Wash's memorable pal and partner, the formidable Captain Easy.

Originally titled *Washington Tubbs II*, Crane's strip began running early in 1924. It was originally supposed to be a gag feature about the funny things that happened to a small-town grocery clerk. Crane, then in his middle twenties, soon grew restless. His sense of humor wasn't the sort that could turn out six gags each week, and, besides, he had a fondness for action and intrigue. Working at the NEA syndicate offices in unromantic Cleveland, Crane dreamed of faraway places. "I wanted to be a hell of a long way off," he once explained. "About the furthest I could think of was the South Seas." Since he couldn't go himself, he sent the diminutive Wash. Abandoning the jokes, he began a continuity that got his hero involved with a treasure hunt that eventually led him to a tropic isle.

Over the next two years Wash, an optimistic go-getter, got involved in both foreign and domestic adventure. In the fall of 1926 he was marooned again, which led to his meeting Gozy Gallup. Gozy was a slick, mustached young man who shared Wash's interest in quick riches and dimpled girls. But he wasn't much good in a fight. After the two did a stint with a circus and then tangled with Mexican bandits, they embarked on another treasure hunt, where they met Bull Dawson.

Dawson, a thick-necked and low-browed sea captain, was the prince of rotten guys. He picked on people smaller than he, especially Wash, and when he punched them a "Bam!" was heard. Neither Wash nor Gozy was a match for the likes of Dawson, and since it was obvious the bully would eventually come back to plague poor Wash, a tougher sidekick was needed. Crane introduced Captain Easy in the spring of 1929. Crane's brother-in-law had long been urging him to come up with such a character, and so "I used him as a model."

In December of 1928 Wash had journeyed to the tiny European kingdom of Kandelabra and, what with one thing and another, he got locked up in an ancient for-

*Wash Tubbs*, Roy Crane, © 1930, NEA Service, Inc. Reprinted by permission NEA Service, Inc.

tress known as the Black Castle. Then on May 6, 1929, Wash meets the hooknosed, uncouth Easy, and the captain helps him escape. Easy was hard-boiled, tough, cynical, and could fight his way out of any sort of trouble, and, since he's exactly the sort of partner Wash needs, the two team up. Easy had been posing as a captain of artillery while doing intelligence work in Kandelabra, and that's where the captain part of his name came from. The new team has a wide variety of adventures all around the globe, including encounters with Bull Dawson.

In the summer of 1933 Captain Easy made his debut in the Sunday funnies, starring in a full page of his own. It was called *Captain Easy, Soldier of Fortune*, and Wash didn't set foot in it for several years. The opening sequence had Easy soldiering as a pilot in the Chinese air corps. The time Crane began devoting to the Sundays meant he had to take on extra help, and, after a few assistants, he hired his old friend Les Turner to help out in 1937. Turner pretty much took over the daily strip. He had the task of handling the increasingly serious continuities that came up as Easy went to work for the FBI, and Wash eventually settled down to domestic life, married to the lovely blonde daughter of blustering tycoon J.P. McKee.

When Crane left for King Features in 1943, Turner started signing the dailies. He stuck with Wash and Easy for another quarter of a century, retiring late in 1969, a few weeks before his 70th birthday; he turned the strip, which had been called *Captain Easy* since 1949, over to his longtime assistant Bill Crooks. *Captain Easy* continued to appear until 1988. In his last years he was a more sedate fellow and worked as a private eye, a different man than the Easy of old who, when asked his occupation, had replied, "Beachcomber, boxer, cook, aviator, seaman, explorer, soldier of artillery, infantry and cavalry, suh."

**R.G.**

**WATTERSON, BILL** (1958– ) The creator of *Calvin and Hobbes*, a humor strip whose immediate popularity brought it to the top of the polls within months of its 1985 debut, Watterson did not find it easy to break into comics.

Devoted to the field since he was a child, Watterson created cartoons for his high school paper before he left his discouragingly-named home town of Chagrin Falls, Ohio, and continued with a weekly political cartoon at Kenyon College, where he majored in political science. After graduating, he took a job as editorial cartoonist with the *Cincinnati Post*. Perhaps, as he later reflected, because he lacked the killer instinct on political issues his career in the field was brief. He was fired in a few months and couldn't find another job.

Turning back to his earlier love, comics, Watterson began trying to develop a salable strip. An outer-space parody was returned with appalling speed by five syndicates, and various other ideas he thought topical met with little more encouragement. Finally, after five weary years of rejection, a syndicate suggested he create a strip around two minor characters in one he had submitted. The result was *Calvin and Hobbes*, a winsome series about a hyperactive boy and a stuffed tiger who is alive to him and more than his verbal match. Several syndicates, including the one that proposed it, turned *Calvin and Hobbes* down before Universal took it in November 1985.

Watterson's clean, expressive lines and warm perception of childhood made the strip an immediate success. He was awarded the National Cartoonists Society's Reuben award as "Outstanding Cartoonist of the Year" in 1986 and 1989. **D.W.**

## WAUGH, COULTON (1896–1973)

He considered himself a painter first and last and took the job of drawing *Dickie Dare* in 1934 to help finance his painting. He stayed with the strip, except for a sabbatical or two, until it ended in October 1957. Waugh also drew a liberal and experimental strip called *Hank* in the months just after the end of World War II. He wrote *The Comics*, published in 1947; despite some factual errors, it is still the best overall history of comic strips. And, of course, he never stopped painting.

He was the son of the noted marine painter Frederick Waugh, and he, too, was fascinated with ships and the sea. Waugh had been on the staff of the *New York World*, where some of his fellow artists were Milt Gross and Ernie Bushmiller. "I did caricatures for them and special pages for the metropolitan section," he once explained. "All sorts of humorous and historical subjects." Looking for work in 1934, he happened to drop by the Associated Press just about the time Milton Caniff was leaving them and *Dickie Dare* to begin *Terry and the Pirates*. The fact that Dickie was aboard a destroyer and the villain was down in a submarine when Caniff went away gave the strip a distinct marine flavor, which is probably the reason Waugh got the job.

He wrote and drew the strip, for the first six months or so sticking fairly close in tone and style to what had gone before. As AP offered him contracts for longer and longer periods, Waugh came to feel the strip was his own and not Caniff's any longer. He swung away from the stiff, cartoony look, using brush lines for the figures and trying pen patterns—crosshatching and the like— on the backgrounds. He eventually arrived at what he felt was a "satisfying style."

In order to try his new strip, *Hank*, and to write his history of comics, Waugh took some time off from *Dickie*

*Dare* in the mid-1940s. But the strip stayed in the family, since Odin Burvik, who carried on, was his wife. Between Odin and the return of Coulton Waugh, an artist named Fran Matera briefly drew the strip. After completing *The Comics*, Waugh was "at loose ends…and I got in touch with AP." He was invited to resume doing *Dickie Dare*.

In the 1960s, with some help from his wife, he drew a panel for kids called *Junior Editors*. As he'd promised himself, he continued painting and had several one-man shows. His book, *How to Paint With a Knife*, was one of Watson-Guptill's more successful titles. At the time of his death he was at work on another book. **R.G.**

## WEBER, BOB (1934– )

The prolific cartoonist who produces the daily and Sunday strip *Moose* aspired to be a cartoonist from the time he was in grammar school. Born and educated in Baltimore, Maryland, while still in high school, he wrote a letter to Bob Grams, the editorial cartoonist of the *Baltimore News-American*, asking for advice. With Grams' encouragement and a national scholarship prize to give him confidence, he took evening and Sunday classes at the Maryland Institute of Art.

In 1953 he went to New York to study at the School of Visual Arts and began selling gag-cartoons to national magazines. When illness forced him to return to Baltimore, he took a job there as a technical illustrator, but found it very unsatisfying. At last, undeterred in his determination to become a cartoonist, he made it back to the New York area in 1959—which he calls "the big turning point in my life"—and found himself living near Orlando Busino, a cartoonist to whom he attributes much of his own success.

Weber continued selling gag-cartoons, contributing to *Laff-a-Day*, and writing material for such comic strips as *Barney Google* and *Snuffy Smith*. After a time he moved to Connecticut to work with cartoonist Dick Cavelli on Cavelli's strip *Winthrop*.

An experienced and familiar figure in the cartoon world, Weber was well known for his fertile imagination and his broadly exaggerated cartooning style. In 1965, Sylvan Byck, the comics editor of King Features Syndicate, suggested that he start a new humor strip. The result was *Moose*, a broad, old-fashioned domestic humor strip, which now appears in over 200 papers. Weber's son Bob Jr. has followed in his father's footsteps; since March 1987, he has produced the Sunday half-page *Comics for Kids*, which runs in about 240 papers. **D.W.**

## WEBSTER, H.T. (1885–1953)

One of the shrewdest observers of American life in the first half of the present century, Harold Tucker Webster wrote and drew nearly a dozen cartoon panel series whose mellow blend of compassionate insight and biting irony earned him the designation "the Mark Twain of American cartoonists." Such creations as *The Timid Soul*, featuring that prototype of the antihero, Caspar Milquetoast, amused and embarrassed a wide audience for over four decades and have remained lasting parts of American popular culture.

Webster was born in the small rural town of Parkersburg, West Virginia, and grew up in the even smaller Tomahawk, Wisconsin, of which George Ade wrote that it was once on the map in pencil until "some fresh drummer rubbed it out." At the age of 17, after an encouraging sale of a drawing to the magazine *Recreation*, Webster made the break to Chicago, where he studied in the Frank Holmes School of Illustration until it closed, 20 days after he enrolled. With those academic credentials (and a correspondence course in art he had taken in his teens) behind him, he got a job with the *Denver Republican*, which he held briefly before going on to the *Denver Post*. There he drew sports cartoons for $15 a week, a sum he later called "more than I was worth." He left the *Post* after two months, as he recollected, "just in time to avoid being fired," and returned to Chicago in 1905.

By now a seasoned professional, he managed to stay afloat as a free-lance, selling illustrations to such papers as the *Chicago Daily News*, and finally found regular work doing political cartoons for the *Chicago Inter-Ocean* at $30 a week. These attracted enough attention to land him a job at the *Cincinnati Post* in 1908, at a salary more than twice what he was making in Chicago and at $70 a week he was able to save up enough to take a world trip in 1911. He hoped to be able to finance the yearlong trip with illustrated travel sketches; while the trip didn't quite pay for itself that way, his dispatches brought him to the attention of the *New York Tribune*, where he was to find an audience for the kind of work that at last made him both rich and famous.

The many series that Webster produced regularly for the *Tribune* from about 1912—with an interlude at the *N.Y. World* from 1924 till just before it folded in 1931—were among the best-loved examples of the form in American literature. His vignettes of childhood—*Our Boyhood Thrills*, which became *The Thrill That Comes Once in a Lifetime*, and *Little Tragedies of Childhood*, which was renamed *Life's Darkest Moments*—lasted until after Webster's death more than 40 years later and were collected into several books. Others, such as *Poker Portraits, Bridge, How to Torture Your Wife/Husband, Dogs, And Nothing Can Be Done About It, The Boy Who Made Good*, and *Events Leading Up to the Tragedy*, all captured the little frustrations and pleasures of everyday life with warmth and often with keen irony. Webster soon took

his place as a chronicler of life's modest triumphs and tragedies alongside his older *Tribune* colleague Clare Briggs, whom he outlived by 23 years and whose mantle he inherited.

Perhaps Webster's most popular and enduring series was *The Timid Soul*. Its cowardly titular hero Caspar Milquetoast was to achieve lexical immortality, his name a common noun in most dictionaries. He appeared in books, movies, radio, and vaudeville, tipping waiters for unwanted services, rushing past "No Loitering" signs, and apologizing to barbers for the length of his hair.

Webster was usually identified with Briggs as a genial nostalgist, but his work often had a bite that the older cartoonist's lacked. Although he most frequently dealt with the amusing trifles of childhood, some of *Life's Darkest Moments* had a poignance that cut to the bone. A one-legged boy watching his friends play ice hockey, or a 58-year-old job seeker rejected by an arrogant young punk because "the firm took on an old man of 40 last year and lost money on him," are among the many images that strike a deeper note and give Webster's work a resonance seldom equaled in American cartooning.                                            **D.W.**

**WEE PALS** A daily and Sunday humor strip featuring a companionable gang of racially diverse moppets, Morrie Turner's *Wee Pals* has carried a benevolent message of social harmony since its inception in 1964. Developed from his all-black *Dinky Fellas*, which ran in two black papers in 1963, it added kids of many races, nationalities, and personality types who have continued ever since to exchange their diverse views and eat their ice-cream cones together in perfect amity. Nipper is black, George is Oriental, Rocky is an American Indian, Paul a Mexican-American, Jerry is Jewish, and, for complete balance, Oliver is a white intellectual and Connie a militant white feminist. When Nipper calls for Black Power, George for Yellow Power, Rocky for Red Power, and Paul for Brown Power, Jerry joins in with a demand for Bagel Power, and the whole gang compromises by naming themselves the Rainbow Power Club. As Oliver observes, "The manufacturers of flesh-colored bandaids would go broke in this neighborhood!"

First syndicated by the Lew Little Syndicate, *Wee Pals* went over to the Register and Tribune Syndicate in 1969 and then to King Features on May 8, 1972. It switched to North America Syndicate on July 2, 1977, and returned to King when King acquired North America in 1987. During its wanderings, it has remained stable at from 75 to 100 newspapers.

Drawn in a simple, controlled style with an attractive balance of white space and shaded areas, the strip maintains an easygoing, good-natured tone that prevents it from becoming sententious, and its positive message has won it numerous humanitarian awards from educational and religious organizations. The characters of *Wee Pals* have appeared in many public service features, have been used to illustrate civic projects, and have been featured in a series of 17 animated television shows. Several volumes of the collected strip have been published by Signet.                                         **D.W.**

**WEE WILLIE WINKIE'S WORLD** Perhaps the most important "serious" artist to lend his talents to the comics was Lyonel Feininger, who was to become a significant figure in art in the 1920s. In 1906, however, he was not above doing illustrations and cartoons for German publications and was happy to accept William Randolph Hearst's invitation to try his hand at a comic strip. In that year he created two for Hearst's *Chicago Tribune, The Kin-der-Kids* in April and *Wee Willie Winkie's World* four months later.

The earlier strip prepared the public for the grotesque graphic style and weird fantasy of the German-trained artist, and both were signed "Your uncle Feininger." *Wee Willie Winkie's World* first appeared on August 19, 1906, and ran for 23 Sundays before personal conflicts with the *Tribune* led the artist to discontinue it on January 20, 1907, nine weeks after he terminated *The Kin-der-Kids.*

The name of the titular hero derives from that of a nursery rhyme personification of sleep, and Feininger's Wee Willie lives in a world no less dreamlike than that of Winsor McCay's Little Nemo, whose debut had taken place 10 months before. With little narrative structure and no continuity from strip to strip, WWWW takes its wee hero through a series of bizarre and often frightening adventures in which familiar objects change their forms in order to play with or menace him.

Wildly innovative in design and imaginative in content, *Wee Willie Winkie's World* was as sophisticated in its way as the expressionistic canvases Feininger was producing at the time, and foreshadowed the cubism he was later to employ in his gallery work. Its dark whimsy was never coy or cute; like the German folk tales that inspired it, the strip held elements of beauty and terror, which have given it a lasting place in the literature of the comics.                                            **D.W.**

**WERTHAM, FREDRIC** (1895–1981) A respected psychiatrist and author, Dr. Wertham was a key figure in the anti-comic book crusade that blossomed in the middle 1950s. In the late 1940s he had become concerned about the possible effects on children of the violence and sex to be found in an increasing number of postwar comic books. He began writing articles and making speeches, following in 1954 with *Seduction of the Innocent.* It was a book that proved to be very influential.

The German-born Wertham studied medicine and psychiatry at universities in London, Munich, Vienna, and Paris. He came to America in the early 1920s to work in the psychiatric clinic at Johns Hopkins Hospital, becoming a citizen in 1927. He relocated in New York City in the 1930s, teaching at NYU and also holding various positions on the psychiatric staff at Bellevue Hospital. Dr. Wertham is credited with setting up the first facility to provide all convicted felons with a psychiatric evaluation. In the middle 1940s he helped establish a psychiatric clinic in Harlem for "low-income people in general and Negroes in particular."

One of his lifelong interests was violent crime, a percentage of which he believed could be prevented if psychiatry and the law worked together. From the 1940s on he reached a wide audience with such bestselling books as *Dark Legend* and *The Show of Violence.* Working with children over the years, Wertham grew interested in the comic books he found them reading. Sampling these led him to conclude that comics "overstimulate the children's fantasy in the direction of violence and cheap sexiness." Wertham's conclusions got attention from the press as well as in national magazines like *Collier's* and the *Saturday Review of Literature.* He charged that comic books undermined morals, glorified violence, and "were sexually aggressive in an abnormal way." The doctor concluded that comic book reading "was a distinct influencing factor in the case of every single delinquent or disturbed child we studied."

Comic books had definitely changed in the years immediately after the end of World War II. The titles of many publishers, inspired by the huge GI audiences of the war years, grew even more adult. When superheroes began to fade in popularity, new genres replaced them. True crime and horror flourished, providing a great deal of tasteless gore and gratuitous sex. While most of the larger houses avoided flagrant displays of bad taste, their lesser competitors based whole lines on just such an approach. While there was considerable dubious material to be found on the newsstands of the period, the dedicated Dr. Wertham and his followers were never able to prove satisfactorily that trash can cause delinquency, mental illness, or even purse snatching. Several of his colleagues disagreed with him in print, but that didn't halt the crusade.

The attacks on comic books went on, including: the banning of magazines considered objectionable by various newsdealers and civic officials across the country; threats of legal action against newsstands by police departments; and the setting up of citizens' committees to rate and control comics. By 1954 the feeling was running strong against funny books. In that year

Wertham's book-length indictment, *Seduction of the Innocent*, was published; the Senate Subcommittee on the Judiciary held hearings in Manhattan on comic books; and the self-regulating Comics Code Authority was established by comic book publishers. All the attention and criticism caused serious damage to the industry. When many comic books never left the distribution warehouses, many publishers went broke. Even those who'd never gone in for sex and violence suffered sales losses. Of course, television was establishing itself in America during these same years, and comics would have felt the competition even without the moral crusades.

A well-intended book, *Seduction of the Innocent* was lacking in specific details and was vague even as to the sources of the worst examples. Wertham failed to establish comic books as a causative factor in juvenile crime and really proved only that he was deeply concerned about children. That many of the crime and horror comics of the period were deplorable and tasteless is certainly so, but that they were the direct cause of crimes of violence is questionable. In the middle 1970s in an interview with Jay Maeder, then a reporter on the *Miami Herald*, Wertham said, "I never spoke of comic books. I only spoke of crime comic books. That is important because there are of course good comic books, but a crime is a crime." He explained that "in psychological life, it isn't so that you can say one factor has a clear causal effect on anything…I never said, and I don't think so, that a child reads a comic book and then goes out and beats up his sister or commits a holdup." In 1954, however, a great many of the readers of *Seduction of the Innocent* concluded that that was exactly what he was saying.  **R.G.**

**WESTOVER, RUSS** (1886–1966) The creator of *Tillie the Toiler*, Russell Channing Westover, was born in Los Angeles and attended the Mark Hopkins Institute of Art in San Francisco, where he got his first newspaper job as a sports cartoonist for the *San Francisco Bulletin* at the age of 18. He moved on during the next few years to the *Oakland Herald* and back to San Francisco, where he held positions successively with the *Globe*, the *Chronicle*, and the *Post*. For the *Post* he covered the famous Jeffries-Johnson heavyweight fight, and did his first comic strip, a baseball series called *Daffy Dan*.

When the merger of the *Post* with the *Call* in 1913 cost him his job, he headed East and soon found work at the *New York Herald*. For them he did a daily strip called *Fat Chance*. When the *New York Herald* merged with the *Tribune*, Westover found himself once more unemployed, and he returned to the life of the free-lance. In 1920 he sold King Features Syndicate on *Tillie the Toiler*, which debuted on January 3 of the next year.

*Tillie the Toiler* was a success from the first, taking its place among such popular flapper strips as *Polly and Her Pals* (another KFS property) and the just-begun *Winnie Winkle*, distributed by the Tribune-News Syndicate. It dealt with the newly emerging class of the working girl, and it showed its svelte heroine in the short skirts of the time. Timely and modestly titillating, though it never even bordered on impropriety, *Tillie the Toiler* had a distinctive voice and look. A little harder and more cynical than *Polly* or *Winnie*, it was drawn in a seemingly casual, spontaneous style, which included stereotyped flappers and gallants along with broadly caricatural cartoon figures.

In 1922 a Sunday *Tillie* joined the daily strip, and four years later Westover created a topper, *The Van Swaggers*, to accompany it. This weekly domestic feature ran until his retirement in 1954.

Westover employed numerous assistants to help with the art and the scripting of *Tillie the Toiler*—Joe Musial and Alex Raymond among them—and on his retirement relinquished the strip to Bob Gustafson, who had been writing and drawing the strip for some years and began to sign it on October 4, 1954. The strip lasted another five years, and its creator outlived it by seven.  **D.W.**

**WEXLER, ELMER** (1918– ) His entire career as a cartoonist covered just a few years in the 1940s. During the early part of the decade, Wexler worked in comic books and drew several superheroes. He then did the *Vic Jordan* newspaper strip. After World War II, he tried another comic strip before moving on to illustration and commercial art.

Wexler was born in Bridgeport, Connecticut, and graduated from the Pratt Institute in Manhattan in 1938. He entered comic books in 1940, drawing a minor hero named Hercules for *Blue Ribbon Comics* and a magician named Zambini, the Miracle Man, for *Zip Comics*. A relatively young artist, Wexler had a slick illustrative style, though the influence of both Alex Raymond and Milton Caniff showed some. For *Exciting Comics* he drew the superhero known as the Black Terror, for *Startling Comics* a patriotic superhero called the Fighting Yank.

The next year Wexler was picked to draw *Vic Jordan*, an adventure strip about an American who helps out the French underground. It was syndicated by *PM*, the liberal New York newspaper. Wexler left the strip to enlist in the Marine Corps in April 1942. He served as a combat artist in the South Pacific. After the war, he tried a strip about a private eye, *Jon Jason*, for *PM*, which didn't last. Wexler subsequently moved into illustration and advertising.  **R.G.**

**WHEELAN, ED** (1888–1966)  His chief contribution to comics was *Minute Movies*. Wheelan drew it first as a daily newspaper strip, kidding the casts and conventions of contemporary motion pictures, from the early 1920s to the middle 1930s. From the late 1930s to the middle 1940s, fallen somewhat on hard times, he drew *Minute Movies* as one of the features in *Flash Comics*. Over the years he did several other newspaper strips, worked for a variety of other comic books, and carried on a feud with William Randolph Hearst.

Edgar Stow Wheelan graduated from Cornell in 1911. He worked on a Brooklyn newspaper before heading westward for a job on Hearst's *San Francisco Examiner*. He was doing editorial cartoons and filler art there, when Hearst summoned him East again to work on the *New York American*. "Hearst had heard I could draw just like Tad," Wheelan once said. "What he really had in mind was to *scare* Tad into a ten-year contract, which he did by threatening to put *me* in *his* place...It was a typical Hearst 'dirty trick.'" Wheelan began drawing comic strips for the *American*, the most successful of which was *Old Man Experience*. In 1918 he started doing a strip that ran across the top of the sports page—"it had no name but burlesqued various films and stars of the silent era." This evolved into a larger strip called *Midget Movies*. Wheelan drew in a very eclectic and personal version of the big-foot style, and some of his early burlesques ran two or three days.

Wheelan quit the paper at the end of the decade. When alluding to his reasons in later years he was vague about specifics, but he implied his reason involved more of Hearst's dirty tricks. Signing up with George Mathew Adams' syndicate, he began doing his strip under the new title of *Minute Movies* in 1921. Wheelan kept on kidding the hokum and sentimentality of films and gradually introduced his cast of regulars, among them: the handsome and daring Dick Dare, the virginal Hazel Dearie, the wicked Ralph McSneer. The epics, usually running a week at least, were directed by Art Hokum. By the middle 1920s *Minute Movies* was among the most successful strips.

As comic strips grew more serious in the 1930s, Wheelan introduced longer continuities and also started adapting such classics as *Ivanhoe* and *Hamlet*. All his stories grew serious as the Depression progressed, putting him in the position of trying to do seriously the sort of hokum and melodrama he'd once made fun of. The strip started losing papers and by the middle 1930s was gone.

He tried a new strip, *Big Top*, for a small syndicate. Though it was an entertaining feature, allowing Wheelan to indulge his lifelong interest in the circus, it didn't make it. Wheelan was never able to sell another newspaper feature, and for the rest of his life he believed that Hearst had blacklisted him. Fortunately for him, the comic book business was blossoming in the late 1930s. At the end of 1939 *Flash Comics* was launched. The magazine offered such heroes as the Flash, Hawkman, the Whip, and Johnny Thunder. Young editor Sheldon Mayer, a longtime fan of Wheelan's, hired him to draw an eight-page feature. Wheelan's first original material for comic books was quite a bit like *Minute Movies*; although there were no iris shots and no continuing cast, *Flash Picture Novels* could otherwise have passed for a funny book adaption of his old strip.

To make certain everyone knew who Wheelan was, Mayer lettered in blurbs at the end of the stories, describing him as "the famous creator of 'Minute Movies!'" Finally, in *Flash* #12 (December 1940) Wheelan, giving in to "popular demand," brought back *Minute Movies*. Since there'd never been a Sunday page, this was the first time his stock company appeared in color. All in all he produced 43 new Minute Movies for the comic book. As he'd done with the newspaper strip, he alternated melodramas with burlesques. In *Flash Comics* #38 (December 1942) his actors Fuller Phun and Archibald Clubb were teamed in a one-pager plugging War Bonds and Stamps. This was the first time they were cast as Fat and Slat, roles that would outlive the feature.

The other major achievement of the Forties was *The Adventures of Padlock Homes*. Done for the Harvey Brothers, it began in *Champ Comics* in the spring of 1942, and moved over to *Speed Comics* in 1943. More than a burlesque of Sir Arthur Conan Doyle's celebrated sleuth, it was also a parody of detective melodramas, movie serials, and just about everything else that caught Wheelan's fancy.

The first complete Fat and Slat book was issued in 1944, with the official title *Ed Wheelan's Joke Book Featuring Fat and Slat*. The magazine was a compendium of one-pagers in which the team did their best to perpetrate some of the most venerable and corniest jokes known to man. When M.C. Gaines terminated his association with DC to start his EC line, he hired Wheelan to draw him a Fat and Slat quarterly. This lasted for four issues in 1947 and 1948.

Wheelan's final comic book work was mostly fillers and four-pagers drawn for DC. Usually unsigned, they included *Foney Fairy Tales* and *Watt the Question Man*. He left the field in the early 1950s. Wheelan eventually retired to Florida and in the years before his death devoted a good deal of his time to doing a series of clown paintings.                    **R.G.**

**WHEELER-NICHOLSON, MALCOLM** (1890–1968)  Major Nicholson was an Army cavalry officer, a pulp fiction writer, and, most importantly, a comic book publisher. Late in 1934 he founded, on slightly less than a shoestring, the company that became Detective Comics, Inc. DC went on to introduce Superman, Batman, and several other lucrative heroes and heroines. The major, who was forced to give up his company in 1937 for financial reasons, went on to obscurity, and, in the best military tradition, just faded away.

According to one autobiographical account, which may have benefited from Major Nicholson's undisputed ability as a writer of fiction, he "was born in the South, raised on a western ranch, worked for a while as a cub reporter, became a second lieutenant of cavalry in the regular army, chased bandits on the Mexican border, fought fevers and played polo in the Philippines, led a battalion of infantry against the Bolsheviki in Siberia, helped straighten out the affairs of the army in France, commanded the headquarters cavalry of the American force in the Rhine, and left the army as a major equipped with a select assortment of racing and polo cups, a sabre, and a busted typewriter." Taking up that battered typewriter, Nicholson, who had already written professionally on military topics, began a career as a fiction writer. He soon started selling to many of the popular pulps, notably *Adventure* and *Argosy*, and he specialized in tales of military action around the world and historical adventure and swordplay.

Sometime in the fall of 1934 the major decided to publish comic books, and he founded National Allied Periodicals, Inc. He didn't intend, however, to reprint newspaper strips but to introduce original material. His initial title was *New Fun*, a tabloid-size comic book whose first issue had a cover date of February 1935. He followed that late in the same year with a conventional-sized comic book titled *New Comics*. Though the two magazines didn't exactly thrive, they managed to stay in business (with *New Fun* becoming *More Fun*). They offered a mix of humor and adventure features, laid out like newspaper Sunday pages for the most part and offering one-and two-page snippets of continued stories. For his staff the enterprising major recruited art students, old-timers down on their luck, and any other artist or writer he could con and cajole into working for paltry fees that were often never paid. His fellow pioneers included Lyman Anderson, Charles Flanders, Vincent Sullivan, Whit Ellsworth, Creig Flessel, Tom McNamara, Sheldon Mayer, Jerry Siegel, and Joe Shuster.

What Major Nicholson had created, partly by chance, was the first line of original material comic books in the modern format. Due to his efforts, and those of a few others, the American comic book industry was founded. Unfortunately, he never got himself out of debt, and in order to launch his third title, *Detective Comics*, he had to take one of his creditors, printer and distributor Harry Donenfeld, on as a partner. He was

eased out of Detective Comics, Inc., in 1938, before his fourth title, *Action Comics*, ever appeared. He returned to writing and gradually dropped from sight. In 1985 DC commemorated their 50th anniversary with a booklet entitled *Fifty Who Made DC Great*. They included the Major.
**R.G.**

**WHITE BOY**  The best drawn and least successful Western strip of the 1930s was Garrett Price's *White Boy*. This Sunday page began in the autumn of 1933, distributed by the Chicago Tribune-New York News Syndicate. It ceased to be, after two title changes and one change of venue, in the summer of 1936.

Prince, once employed in the *Trib* art department, recalled that it was the syndicate that came to him with the idea of doing a strip. "I was hampered by authentic knowledge of the West," Price explained. "My folks (Papa was a doctor) left Kansas when I was a year old. Until I was nineteen we lived in Wyoming, Oklahoma and South Dakota—mostly in Wyoming." Originally set in the past, the page dealt with an adolescent boy who was captured by the Sioux and then rescued by a rival tribe. White Boy is befriended by an Indian girl named Starlight and by two young braves, Chickadee and Woodchuck. The pages were drawn in a gentle style, quite different in appearance from what Price was doing as a regular and favored contributor to *The New Yorker*. "A style at once decorative, tender, and with a true feeling for the open air," is how Coulton Waugh described it in *The Comics*. "The stories had an imaginative, dreamy character."

Price was continually experimenting, breaking up the page into all sorts of patterns. Sometimes he used the conventional 12-panel layout, but more often tried things like using one huge panel bordered by two or three long thin ones. His rendering grew bolder, poster-like. His color, alternating harsh basic reds with subdued autumnal pastels, was unlike anything being done on the comic pages.

Unfortunately the feature did not collect a sizable audience. In 1935 it moved to the present, to a place known as Skull Valley, and the title was changed to *White Boy in Skull Valley* and eventually to just *Skull Valley*. The dreamy stories and Indian folktales gave way to galloping outlaws and masked heroes. In spite of the new story material, Price was incapable of doing a conventional job. His melodramatic pages, rich with thick black and villainous greens and yellows, still stood out from more more conventional fare such as *The Gumps* and *Winnie Winkle*.

In 1936 the page was dropped. "Captain Joe Patterson thought the story was not carrying over from week to week," Price once recalled. "It was suggested that I make it a daily, too. As it was, even once a week was getting to be a grind, the episodes harder and harder to think up. Things at the *New Yorker* were picking up, the Depression was easing. Still, I made one last try. For new material I looked for a new field, went to Mexico." But when he returned, rather than continue with *Skull Valley* at all, Price decided to quit to concentrate on magazine cartooning and illustration, areas much closer to his heart. Price, a small, modest man was content to let his Sunday page remain unsung and unremembered. "If there is anything I wish to be remembered for," he said, "it is not for being an unsuccessful comic strip artist."

R.G.

**WHITMAN, BERT** (1908– )  During his long career as an artist Whitman has managed to work in several areas, including comic books, newspaper strips, and political cartoons.

He was born in New York City and got his first art job in the mid-1920s with the *Los Angeles Times*. He drew for Major Nicholson's pioneering comic books in the mid-1930s while continuing to work for various newspapers. In 1940, with the funnybook business booming, Whitman set up a shop in Manhattan to produce stories and art for publishers, employing, among others, Jack Kirby, George Storm, and Frank Robbins. He packaged several short-lived comic books, including *Crash Comics*, *Whirlwind Comics*, and *Green Hornet Comics*. The Hornet title was taken over by the Harvey Brothers, and Cat-Man, one of the superheroes from *Crash*, lived out several more of his nine lives in a later comic book of his own.

By that time Whitman was working for the Fawcett comic books. During the early years of World War II he drew a variety of second bananas, both heroic and humorous—*The Phantom Eagle, Companions 3, Balbo the Boy Magician, Little Sneezer*. He had developed a bold, brash style, mixing exaggerated cartoon elements with the forceful inking techniques favored by artists like Robbins; his work stood out.

For the *Comic Book Magazine* produced by the *Chicago Tribune* in the early 1940s Whitman drew an adventure page titled *Mr. Ex*. For several weeks in September and October of 1943 he ghosted the *Scorchy Smith* newspaper strip for his friend Robbins. Then in 1944 his own *Debbie Dean* daily strip started. He also scripted Irv Novick's soaper strip *Cynthia*.

After the demise of *Debbie Dean* in the late 1940s, Whitman returned to editorial cartooning. He spent many years with the *Stockton Record* and the *Phoenix Gazette*, winning an impressive number of awards. Though he has retired from the daily grind, he is still turning out political cartoons on a less frequent basis.

R.G.

**WILDEY, DOUG**  See SAINT, THE.

**WILLARD, FRANK** (1893–1958)  A leading depicter of lowlife, Willard created *Moon Mullins* in the early 1920s. A pugnacious, aggressive, and hard-drinking cartoonist, he hired an assistant in the early days of the strip and turned an increasing amount of the work over to him so that he could concentrate on his social life and his addiction to golf.

The son of a dentist, Willard was born in a small Illinois town—"a nice quiet place where if somebody rang a curfew bell at 9 P.M. everybody would holler because it woke them up." After being tossed out of or dropping out of several schools and working in a mental institution and at county fairs, he ended up in Chicago as the result of a family move in 1909. Willard attended the Academy of Fine Arts in 1913 and the following year found a brief association with the *Chicago Tribune* as a cartoonist. Later in 1914 he moved to the *Chicago Herald*, where he drew a kid page titled *Tom, Dick and Harry* and another page called *Mrs. Pippin's Husband*. Among the other upcoming cartoonists on the *Herald* staff were E.C. Segar and Billy DeBeck.

In the spring of 1917, the United States entered World War I, and in October of the same year, Willard went into the Army, where, as he put it, "[I] Was a pretty punk soldier, had a pretty good time. Our outfit built roads and did no fighting." He served overseas in France, not getting sent home until the summer of 1919.

Willard's former associate, Billy DeBeck, was now residing in New York and drawing *Barney Google*. Although DeBeck was married, he invited the unemployed Willard to move in. Willard worked on the *Barney Google* strip, modifying his style to match DeBeck's. In 1920, through DeBeck's influence, he got a job in the King Features bullpen and did just "about everything but carry water for the elephants." He drew an unsuccessful strip called *The Outta Luck Club* and substituted for cartoonist Jean Knott on his poker panel *Penny Ante*. He was calling himself Dok Willard in those days, a nickname apparently derived from his dentist father's original aspirations for his son.

In 1923 Willard learned that Captain Patterson of the Chicago Tribune-New York News Syndicate was looking for a roughneck, lowlife strip; in other words, Patterson was anxious to get an imitation of the increasingly successful *Barney Google*. Willard, who'd ghosted his friend's strip, seemed like the logical man for the job, and *Moon Mullins* got going, first as a daily, on June 19, 1923.

Just a few weeks later Willard hired a young cartoonist named Ferd Johnson to assist him. Willard gradually turned much of the work on the strip over to Johnson so that he might concentrate on his social life and his golf game. The two moved around a lot. "We'd go to Florida and follow the golf guys all the way to Maine," Johnson has recalled. Florida served as a home base for a while, and later Los Angeles, and the restless Willard worked out of hotel rooms from North Carolina to Maine to Wisconsin and, one summer, Mexico.

Bothered by increasing ill health, he had little to do with *Moon Mullins* in the last years of his life. He died in Los Angeles.  **R.G.**

**WILLARD, RODLOW** (1911– ? )  A journeyman cartoonist, Willard worked in several categories from the 1930s through the 1950s. He did gag cartoons, newspaper strips, and comic books, handling such characters as Scorchy Smith, King of the Royal Mounted, and Sam Spade.

A graduate of the University of California at Berkeley, where he had been on the student humor magazine, Willard started selling cartoons to magazines like *Collier's* and *College Humor* in the early 1930s. Moving to Manhattan, he served as an assistant art editor on *College Humor* and moved on to similar positions with other publications.

In the early 1940s he put in a hitch ghosting the *King of the Royal Mounted* strip. Willard's adventure strip style retained many cartoony elements, but it also incorporated the lushly inked, impressionistic approach of artists such as Frank Robbins. In the spring of 1946 Willard took over *Scorchy Smith*, which Robbins had drawn earlier in the decade. His Associated Press colleague Coulton Waugh said in *The Comics* that "his *Scorchy* has a lighter line than his predecessors'; it has spirit and action, and best of all, he shows a tendency to allow poor old Scorch to smile occasionally, a feat which still seems a strain after all these dour years."

Willard never quite came close enough to his predecessors to be considered a member of the school that included Robbins, Noel Sickles, and Bert Christman. And during his eight years with the strip (which he also wrote) he grew increasingly sloppy and hurried.

During the mid-1940s he also contributed to comic books, drawing such features as *Tiger Man* for the Fiction House line. In 1946 he drew McKay's comic book adaption of *The Maltese Falcon*, the novel that had introduced private eye Sam Spade to the world. This book is listed at well over $200 in price guides, but that's only because Dashiell Hammett completists want it.

After *Scorchy Smith* Willard took a position as an advertising agency art director. He tried several other comic strips, but without much success.  **R.G.**

**WILLIAMS, J.R.**  See OUT OUR WAY.

**WINGERT, DICK** (1919– )  Richard C. Wingert was an army private when he created his cartoon character Hubert in 1942, and for almost half a century since then he has continued writing and drawing his hapless little hero.

Wingert was born in Cedar Rapids, Iowa, and attended the John Herron Art School in Indianapolis on a scholarship. Soon after he graduated in 1940, with what he describes as "vague ideas of doing some kind of illustration work," he joined the National Guard. In 1941 he was inducted into the army and sent to Camp Claiborne, Louisiana, and from there with the 34th Infantry to Ireland. By the time the United States entered World War II, Wingert was a regular contributor to the newly revived army paper *Stars and Stripes*, printed weekly by the *Belfast Telegraph*, and was soon assigned as a staff cartoonist to its London office. During his three and a half years there, his panel feature *Hubert*, about a dumpy GI stationed in England, assumed a clear and consistent identity. Wingert drew cartoons regularly for *Boy's Life* during this period, but it was *Hubert* that established his reputation, and when he met publisher William Randolph Hearst in France during the war he received an offer of syndication for it.

Hubert left the army with his creator in 1945, and as a middle-class suburban husband and father began appearing for Hearst's King Features Syndicate in 1945. The single panel was expanded to a strip, and Wingert added a Sunday feature in 1946. The strip now appears in about 100 newspapers in 13 countries.

Wingert published his first collection of Hubert cartoons in London in 1944, and another, featuring Hubert on the Continent, appeared in 1955. The cartoonist traveled all over the world with the USO, giving cartoon shows for servicemen, before he settled down in Westport, Connecticut, to chronicle the ongoing domestic conflicts of Hubert. He recently relocated in the Midwest.  **D.W.**

**WINNIE WINKLE**  One of the first independent, liberated women of the comics, the titular heroine of *Winnie Winkle* was to become a prototype of the working girl heroine in the medium, serving as a model for characters from Tillie the Toiler to the present day Cathy. *Winnie Winkle the Breadwinner*, as it was originally entitled, was created by Martin Branner, who was already producing two Sunday strips, *Looie the Lawyer*, for the Bell Syndicate, and *Pete and Pinto* for the *New York Sun* and *New York Herald*, when the New York News-Chicago Tribune Syndicate hired him. *Winnie Winkle* made its debut on September 20, 1920, with a Sunday version following two years later.

*Winnie Winkle* was a gag strip at first, but Branner soon switched to a continuity format, featuring a likable and believable family. Its mainstay, Winnie, was a levelheaded, resourceful young stenographer for the Bibbs Pin Co. Her salary supported her devoted, indolent father (appropriately named Rip), her amply padded Ma, and her mischievous brother Perry. In the early years, the daily strip recounted the events of a working girl's life with reasonable fidelity: Winnie deftly sidestepped the mashers who pursued her, humored her hypochondriacal boss Mr. Bibbs, and tactfully managed her shiftless and occasionally bibulous father. The Sunday page, however, reverted to the gag format and centered on the pranks of Winnie's brother Perry and his chums, the Rinkydinks. A final recruit, the flapeared, pin-headed Denny Dimwit, joined the club in the early 1940s and came to dominate the Sunday feature with his moron-joke humor until the 1950s. In June 1954, the continuity of the daily strip absorbed the Sunday series, and the Rinkydinks, Denny included, passed into the background.

Winnie has undergone many changes in her seven decades. She was married to a handsome engineer named Will Wright in 1937, and for a time her marital problems with her horseplayer husband gave the strip a note of real pathos. Will mercifully enlisted in the Army in 1941 and soon disappeared from the strip, leaving his wife expecting a child. Over the years Winnie's daughter Wendy has grown into an attractive and spirited young woman, but the years have robbed Winnie of none of her own appeal, and she still stirs hope in the men in her life. Now a successful fashion designer, she continues to make her own way and to protect both her heart and her business interest.

Branner employed several assistants over the years to help with the art and the story, including Jack Berrill and Max van Bibber. When he suffered a stroke in 1962, the strip was taken over by van Bibber, who had worked for him since 1938. The droll, caricature style of Branner, whose demure, blond Winnie, a stylized 1920s beauty, contrasted with the exaggerated grotesques who surrounded her, gave way in van Bibber's hands to a graceful, moderately realistic look. Pa's weirdly shaped head became conventionally round and Winnie's chastely flat chest swelled to sensual fullness. With the help of writer Jean Sparber, van Bibber updated the story until his retirement in January 1980. Joe Kubert and some of the students at his New Jersey school of cartooning next took over the production of the strip, but stayed with it only a few months. Frank Bolle, a comic book veteran with several previous newspaper strips to his credit, has continued Winnie Winkle since then and moved it even closer in style and tone to realistic continuities—in 1986, for example, Wendy was arrested for murder and Winnie got involved with narcotics dealers.

With the decline of popular taste for continuity strips, Winnie Winkle's share of the comics market has declined, but it remains a sturdy survivor, adapting to the interests and looks of its times. One of the notable features has been the sartorial elegance of its characters; as befits a fashion designer, Winnie herself is always dressed in the latest styles.

**D.W.**

## WINTERBOTHAM, RUSS (1904–1971)

A fast and dependable writer, Winterbotham produced copy for newspaper strips, comic books, Big Little Books, pulp fiction magazines, and paperback novels. Among the syndicated strips he wrote were *Red Ryder, Captain Midnight,* and *Kevin the Bold.*

Kansas-born, Winterbotham worked as a newspaper reporter in the Midwest throughout the 1930s. During those same years he began selling stories to such pulps as *Astounding.* In the late 1930s he linked up with the Whitman outift, writing for comic books like *Crackajack Funnies* and doing Big Little Books as well. Winterbotham continued writing BLBs into the 1940s, producing 60-some small, fat novels about Gene Autry, Maximo the Amazing Superman, Smilin' Jack, Captain Midnight, and the like. His first newspaper strip, begun in 1942, was *Captain Midnight.* The next year he took a job with the NEA syndicate in Cleveland, initially as a book editor.

He remained with NEA until retiring in 1969. During his stay Winterbotham scripted *Red Ryder* from 1943 to 1955 and *Kevin the Bold* from 1964 to 1968. He also wrote the *Captain Easy* Sunday page from 1943 to 1946, the period when Walt Scott was drawing it, and he created *Chris Welkin, Planeteer* in 1951. Under his own name and as J. Harvery Bond, he wrote paperbacks in the mystery and science fiction categories.

**R.G.**

## THE WIZARD OF ID

Johnny Hart's comic strip *B.C.* had run for five years before the thematic limitations of its prehistoric setting led him to seek an outlet for a wider range of topics in 1963. The result was a collaboration with artist Brant Parker, then working as a technical illustrator for IBM, on a humor strip set in the imaginary medieval kingdom of Id. *The Wizard of Id* joined Hart's *B.C.* at Publishers-Hall Syndicate on November 9, 1964, and later transferred to North America, which now distributes it to more than 1,000 papers around the world. Written by Hart, with the help of the team that contributes to *B.C.,* Jack Caprio and Dick Boland, *The Wizard of Id* is drawn by Parker in a similarly loose, slapdash style of broad caricature befitting its less-than-subtle humor. Like its cave-man predecessor, *The Wizard of Id* makes no effort at staying within its time frame; it ranges freely across contemporary social, political, and personal issues for subject material, parodying everything from women's lib, income taxes, and campaign speeches to such staples of humor as domineering wives, pettifogging lawyers, and crabgrass.

Under the reign of a diminutive despot (his face a sketchy version of that of the king in the traditional design of playing cards), the bleak kingdom of Id suffers from every economic and social problem of our or any other time. The characters are stock types, pushed to extremes that border on black humor: His Majesty of Id, described by his creators as "a tyrant's tyrant," who grants a protestor's request to be a picket with the order "Nail him to a fence"; the bibulous court jester Bung, who juggles one ball because he sees six; the cowardly knight Rodney, who slays dragons by running them to death; the perennial prisoner Spook; and the Wonderful Wizard himself, who sees clearly through the king even if he can never get his spells straight.

Ranging from crude slapstick to cutting satire, the wit of *The Wizard of Id* has been described as being "in the mainstream of today's off-beat, irreverent topical humor that has wide appeal for college audiences." Its keen commentary and dashing art, which conceal a tight discipline under a surface of breezy insouciance, have earned it the National Cartoonists Society's top award, the Reuben (1984), and it has won that society's plaque for the best humor strip of the year five times (1971, 1976, 1980, 1982, and 1983). More than 20 collections of the strip have been published since the first in 1964.

**D.W.**

**WOGGON, ELMER** See BIG CHIEF WAHOO.

**THE WOLF** A popular GI panel during World War II, it eventually ran in nearly 3,000 service newspapers. In 1945 *The Wolf* made an uneasy, and ultimately unsuccessful, transition to civilian life when United Features syndicated the postwar version of Leonard Sansone's panel about the lusty fellow with the lupine head. But the Wolf in civvies never made the hit he had while in an Army uniform.

Sansone, born and schooled in Massachusetts, got into the comic book business in 1940. Based in Manhattan, he turned out adventure features for *Blue Bolt*, *Mystic Comics*, *Startling Comics*, and others. After he was drafted early in 1942, he started his Wolf panel for the Fort Belvoir camp paper. It was picked up by the Camp Newspaper Service—which also syndicated Milton Caniff's *Male Call*—and Sansone spent the war in New York City drawing, in *Life's* phrase, his "wolf in GI clothing."

"Wolf" was a popular term for an aggressive amorist in the early Forties, and the appreciative wolf whistle was frequently heard throughout the land. Tex Avery used a similar, though considerably more exuberant,

character in several of his wartime animated cartoons—commencing with *Red Hot Riding Hood* in 1943. He and Sansone may both have been inspired by the shaggy makeup worn by Lon Chaney Jr. in the 1941 horror movie *The Wolf Man*.

The Wolf was rarely seen in actual pursuit of a woman, and much of the humor derived from the fact that only the reader saw his shaggy head and was aware of his true character and intentions. In one typical panel his pretty dinner date is admonishing him, "Food—food—food! Is that all you ever think of?" In another, a young lady seeking shelter from the rain is about to duck into an alcove where the Wolf is already stationed. "Ah," she sighs, "safe at last!" In his introduction to a 1945 collection of Sansone's cartoons, Caniff said, "Every soldier thinks himself a pretty hot deal, capable of endless conquests."—which is why the Wolf was easy to identify with. And Sansone was a talented cartoonist, especially good at depicting attractive young women, another reason the panel was popular with servicemen.

The postwar Wolf was just as enthusiastic and single-minded about girls, but he had to be considerably more subdued in civilian newspapers. By 1947 he'd lost his head and become a blond crew-cutted fellow named Wally. Wally eventually turned into *Willie* and starred a little kid by that name. The panel then became a strip, which Sansone drew—without much evident enthusiasm—until 1956.

**R.G.**

**WOLVERTON, BASIL** (1909–1979) Over the years the comic book field had provided a haven for some eccentric and highly individual artists. Standing out even among these was Basil Wolverton, a true nonpareil. He first showed up in comic books in the late 1930s and was last seen there in the middle 1970s. Along the way he created Spacehawk, a more or less serious science fiction hero, and Powerhouse Pepper, a far from serious superhero. Wolverton also drew everything from movie star caricatures to apocalyptic religious illustrations.

The self-styled "producer of preposterous pictures of the peculiar people who prowl this perplexing planet" was born in the Pacific Northwest and remained there most of his life. He sold his first cartoon at the age of 11 and broke into comic books in 1938, more or less by chance. He'd been aiming at newspaper syndication. "On a trip to New York I'd left samples with United Features Syndicate," he once explained. "In 1937, Monte Bourjaily, former manager of United, formed his own newspaper syndicate, called Globe, planning to pick his cartoon features by first establishing them through his own comic book, *Circus Comics*. He asked me to contribute." Wolverton complied with *Disk Eyes the Detective,* a humor strip, and *Spacehawk,* his first serious feature. *Circus* died after three issues and the proposed syndicate with it.

Wolverton's next comic book venture was *Space Patrol,* which commenced in the December 1939 issue of *Amazing Mystery Funnies.* Although the plots were pulpy, the Wolverton artwork made a great leap forward. Here he began depicting the intricate alien landscapes that came to characterize his highly individual version of the universe. The magnum science fiction opus of his career was *Spacehawk.* The feature began in the June 1940 issue of *Target Comics* and ran for 30 issues before expiring in December of 1942.

Among Wolverton's other major achievements was the creation of the only baldheaded superhero in comics. It was for the Marvel group that he concocted, in the spring of 1942, the formidable Powerhouse Pepper, who first showed up on the newsstands in *Joker Comics* #1. All in all Wolverton produced nearly 500 pages about Powerhouse over the next seven years. From 1938 to the end of the 1940s he also drew over 300 pages of such funny filler features as *Leanbean Green, Bingbang Buster and His Horse Hedy, Flap Flipflop the Flying Flash, The Culture Corner* (conducted by Dr. Croucher K. Cronk, Q.O.C., short for Queer Old Coot), *Inspector Hector the Crime Detector, Mystic Moot and his Magic Snoot* (a parody of Ibis the Invincible that appeared in the magician's own magazine), and *Scoop Scuttle.* Scoop was a reporter on the *Daily Dally* and nearly made it into the comic sections. United Features signed Wolverton to do a *Scoop Scuttle* daily in 1944. According to Wolverton, nothing happened because "there was a newsprint cutback because of the war…Scoop was scuttled."

In 1946 Wolverton suddenly gained national fame. Not because of his comic book work, but because he won the contest to depict Lena the Hyena. The fabulously ugly Lena of Lower Slobbovia was one of Al Capp's teaser characters, alluded to but never seen in his *Li'l Abner* strip. Wolverton submitted seven entries in all and the one that finally graced an *Abner* daily was selected by a jury made up of Salvador Dali, Boris Karloff, and Frank Sinatra. "The $525 award was relatively small for a contest of such magnitude," Wolverton once commented. "But for the next year or two, after *Life* publicized the event with its cover shot of Lena, there was much caricature work to be done. Among the buyers were a national radio network, the movie studios and several advertising agencies. At long last I was able to afford an eraser for each hand."

There wasn't much market for his type of humor in the 1950s, though he did contribute to *Mad.* He also did some deadly serious science fiction for comic books such as *Marvel Tales* and *Weird Tales of the Future.* The work that Wolverton did from then on is not his best. He increased the ugly content, drawing people who looked even more like animated intestines, private parts, and malignant growths. This is particularly notable in the work he did for DC's *Plop* comic book in the middle 1970s. In his last years he drew some serious illustrations based on the Bible for a religious magazine called *Plain Truth.* In recent years quite a bit of his comic book work, from *Spacehawk* to the random SF tales, has been reprinted by various independent publishers.

**R.G.**

*Spacehawk,* Basil Wolverton, © 1941, Funnies, Inc.

**WONDER BOY** The first kid superhero to appear in comic books, Wonder Boy began his career in *National Comics* #1 (July 1940). A product of the Eisner-Iger shop, the *Wonder Boy* feature was a backup to the magazine's leading character, Uncle Sam, and also had to share the limelight with such heroes and heroines as Merlin, Sally O'Neil, and Pen Miller.

The spring and summer of 1940 saw the advent of several boy wonders. First came Robin to team up with Batman in *Detective Comics* #38 (April 1940), then Dick Cole, Wonder Boy, in *Blue Bolt* #1 (July 1940). While Robin wore a costume and Dick Cole was a crackerjack athlete, neither was a superhero; Wonder Boy was. Wearing red tights and a blue tunic with a golden star emblazoned on its chest, he arrived on Earth via space-ship "from the vacuous depths of outer space…From a strange planet of another universe."

Wonder Boy was "half-pint in size but a full-grown tornado in power and action." Polite and helpful, he had a Boy Scout's zeal for doing good deeds. Though he possessed a variety of superpowers, including incredible strength and invulnerability to any weapon, he usually limited himself to fairly prosaic crimes and criminals—tackling landgrabbers, crooked officials, petty crooks, and the like. And since he was a boy, he often arrived on the scene on his bicycle rather than by flying through the air like many of his adult competitors.

Wonder Boy remained in business, always as a backup feature, through *National* #26 (November 1942). He returned in four issues of *Bomber Comics* in 1944 and 1945 and, briefly, in a couple of other titles in 1955. The writing was credited to Jerry Maxwell, a pen name for Jerry Iger, and among the artists who illustrated his rather tame adventures were Nick Cardy and Klaus Nordling. **R.G.**

**THE WONDERLAND OF OZ** The only daily strip based on the characters of L. Frank Baum, *The Wonderland of Oz* was syndicated to a small number of newspapers in 1932 and 1933. The continuities, adapted from several of Baum's Oz books, were illustrated by an artist named Walt Spouse.

The strips were distributed by the C.C. Winningham Co. of Detroit, not one of the major syndicates. They were numbered rather than dated, apparently running on different dates in different papers, usually from the spring of 1932 to the autumn of 1933. According to the *Baum Bugle* there were 443 daily episodes in all. No balloons were used; the copy ran in blocks beneath the drawings. The initial sequence, which lasted for three months, was based on *The Land of Oz*, the second novel in the series. This particular book didn't contain Dorothy, but did utilize such Oz residents as Jack Pumpkinhead, the Scarecrow, H.M. Woggle-Bug, and

the Gump. Dorothy showed up in some of the later adventures, which included adaptations of *Ozma of Oz* and *Tik-Tok of Oz*. Spouse's drawings were a mite stiff, though he took a more cartoony approach than was used by John R. Neil in illustrating the novels.

*The Wonderland of Oz* was not a hit, and no other Oz daily was ever attempted. Some of the strips were reprinted, usually in two- to four-page excerpts, in *The Funnies* comic book from 1938 to 1940. **R.G.**

**WONDER MAN** The first superhero to go into competition with Superman, Wonder Man came along in the spring of 1939, stayed in business for just one month, and was the joint creation of publisher Victor S. Fox and artist-writer Will Eisner. When Fox decided to start his own comic book line, he approached the Will Eisner-Jerry Iger shop with an idea for a comic book that would star a character to be called Wonder Man.

The new hero was to have a red costume, and the rest of the "specifications were almost identical to Superman." Eisner said, "We knew it was very much like Superman, that it was imitative, but we had no idea of its legal implications." Eisner wrote and drew Wonder Man's first—and only, as it turned out—adventure and signed it "Willis." The 14-page story appeared in *Wonder Comics* #1 (May 1939), a little less than one year after the advent of the Man of Steel.

Unlike Superman, Wonder Man was blond and didn't hail from another planet. He picked up his many impressive abilities—which included leaping over tall buildings in a single bound, catching shells in his bare hands, smashing through solid walls, and so on—in Tibet. In everyday life he was Fred Carson, "a timid radio engineer and inventor." When trouble struck, he "removes his outer garments and becomes the Wonder Man, mightiest human on Earth."

Harry Donenfeld, the head man at DC, felt this was too close to Superman's method of operation. "He hit Fox real hard," according to Eisner, "and right away." Detective Comics, Inc., sued Fox for infringement of copyright, though the case didn't get to court—the Federal District Court in New York City—until 1940. At that time the judge ruled in favor of DC, though Wonder Man was long gone by then, since Fox had never risked a second appearance. **R.G.**

**WONDER WOMAN** Created in 1941 by psychologist William Moulton Marston (under the pseudonym Charles Moulton), this superstrong Amazon princess would prove to be the most popular of all comic book superheroines and, along with Superman and Batman, one of National (DC) Comics' most enduring characters.

Her origin, in *All Star* and *Sensation Comics*, is set on Paradise Island, a lost world of heroic, immortal women ruled by the wise and courageous Queen Hippolyte, guided by the goddesses Aphrodite and Athena. When the goddesses see mankind threatened by world war, they arrange for U.S. Army officer Steve Trevor to crash-land on the island; one Amazon, they say, must journey with Trevor back to the world of men, "to help fight the forces of hate and oppression." Hippolyte's daughter Diana, who has fallen in love with Trevor, wins the right to accompany him by her prowess in combat. As Wonder Woman she battles Axis agents with an invisible "robot plane," a golden lasso that controls the will of whomever it ensnares, bullet-deflecting bracelets, and a gang of adolescent sidekicks called the Holliday Girls (led by chubby Etta Candy). She also assumes the identity of plain Diana Prince in order to remain secretly near the man she loves, Steve Trevor.

Wonder Woman earned her own comic book quickly, in the summer of 1942. Her gallery of foes expanded to include criminals, wicked gods and supernatural powers, and a number of colorful arch-villainnesses, including the suboceanic Queen Clea, Queen Flamina of the sun, and the catty Cheetah. Her adventures came to life through the naive, dreamlike art of Harry G. Peter.

Dr. Marston's stories showed a sly but imaginative use of psychological themes, especially those dealing with domination and subservience. Chains, manacles, and other fetishistic paraphernalia abounded. Wonder Woman could only be subdued if her "bracelets of submission" were chained together by a man. Some of her villains tyrannized their loved ones: The "psychopathic madman" Dr. Psycho hypnotized his fiancée to make her an agent of his plan to enslave all women; Hypnota the Great, a woman posing as a man, mentally enslaved her sister Serva. Such elements, and more, caused Dr. Fredric Wertham to call *Wonder Woman*, "one of the most harmful" comic books in his *Seduction of the Innocent*.

Yet Marston also played with some noble philosophic themes, especially the conflict between "the cruel despotism of masculine aggressiveness" and the humane ways of women. Wonder Woman told women to "Think! And free yourselves!" Her most fiendish foe, Gestapo agent Paula von Gunther, eventually spent time on Reform Island, rejected "the Hitler principle that women must remain men's slaves," and became Wonder Woman's close friend. The Amazon became a strong role model for young female readers, and stood as a symbol for some of those readers as they matured into adult feminists; in 1972 *Ms.* magazine compiled a book-length *Wonder Woman* collection with an introduction by Gloria Steinem.

Marston died in 1947, and a few years later the series lost Peter as well. Under editor-writer Robert Kanigher and artists Ross Andru and Mike Esposito, Wonder Woman cruised through the 1950s and 1960s with directionless stories and little trace of her former depth or oddity. In 1968, writer-artist Mike Sekowsky took over the series, and tried to battle slipping sales by transforming the Amazon into a hip, karate-chopping, nonsuperheroine, wearing a mod jumpsuit and aided by an old Chinese mystic named I Ching. This led to an overt "women's lib" phase in the early 1970s, punctuated by a couple of pedantic scripts by science fiction writer Samuel R. Delany.

Wonder Woman returned to her old costume and powers in 1973, but it wasn't enough to keep her from slumping deeper into dull stories and poor sales. Various efforts were made to rejuvenate her in the 1980s, most notably 1986's *The Legend of Wonder Woman* by prominent female cartoonist Trina Robbins and writer Kurt Busiek—a fond tribute to the early Marston-Peter adventures. In 1987 George Perez, one of DC Comics' artistic stars of the '80s, overhauled the character in a new series, emphasizing the mythological pageantry of Paradise Island.

G.J.

**WOOD, HARRY** (1870–1943)  Harry Wood's importance to American comics is twofold. First, as art editor of *The Kansas City Star* from 1892 until his death in 1943, he trained a number of cartoonists and illustrators, including Ralph Barton, C.D. Batchelor, Burris Jenkins Jr., Robert Lambdin, Jefferson Machamer, Garrett Price, and Raeburn Van Buren. (Even Mort Walker, who did not work at the *Star* but was an avid reader, came under Wood's influence.) Second, in 1907 Wood introduced to the *Star's* readers "The Intellectual Pup," one of America's first comic strips—and an inspiration to his talented staff. (In fact, whenever Van Buren drew a dog in his own strip, *Abbie an' Slats*, it was always the "Pup.")

A shy, uneducated railroad clerk, Wood was picked to run the *Star's* art department in 1890. In those days, even though newspapers were turning to halftones to illustrate articles, the *Star* stayed with pen-and-ink sketches—a policy that demanded a large art department and placed a lot of responsibility on Wood. To relieve that pressure, Wood created "The Intellectual Pup." The adventures of this curious canine soon made the strip, which was never syndicated, the *Star's* most popular feature.

It was Wood's talent as a teacher, however, that earned him a place in the comic world. As *Star* alumnus Daniel MacMorris wrote, Wood was "patient with his score of artists. He got the work out, met the deadline, no matter what were the pressures and frustrations. Not only was he a fine teacher of newspaper art, but a fatherly adviser to us all."

S.L.H.

**WOOD, WALLY** (1927–1981) He had roughly one good decade as an artist, the 1950s, during which Wood did some outstanding work for the EC titles, ghosted *The Spirit*, collaborated with Jack Kirby on a newspaper strip, turned out Topps gum cards, and did illustrations for *Galaxy* and other science fiction magazines. After that it was a slow, painful slide downhill.

Born in Minnesota, Wood was mostly self-taught. He came to New York and got work in comic books in 1947, and by 1949 he was working for EC. Columnist Pete Hamill has said, "The drawing was wonderful. Wood had learned much from the men who came before him…But Wood had taken these influences, mixed them up, and made something of his own."

It was in the EC science fiction titles, *Weird Fantasy* and *Weird Science*, that Wood did some of his best work. He had a way of drawing gadgets, technical hardware, space gear, and spacecraft that dozens of other cartoonists later aped. The impressive Wood technical clutter became one of his trademarks. For *Mad* he worked in a more cartoony style, one that suggested Walt Kelly was an influence. Wood stayed with the magazine when it moved from comic book to black and white format and also went on to produce material for *Panic, Trump, Humbug,* and *Plop*.

In the 1950s he also ghosted Eisner's *The Spirit* during an impressive space travel sequence, worked with Jack Kirby on an unsuccessful SF newspaper strip called *Sky Masters*, did illustrations for magazines like *Galaxy*, and comic book work for Marvel, Harvey, Charlton, and DC. He turned out advertising art for several accounts and found time to draw a series of gum cards for Topps.

Wood had unfortunately developed a life-style that wasn't especially healthful. He alternated periods of heavy drinking with around-the-clock sessions at the drawing board. His work in the 1960s showed a decline, but he kept busy drawing the Avengers and Daredevil for Marvel, and he created and drew *T.H.U.N.D.E.R. Agents* for the unsuccessful Tower line of comic books. By the 1970s much of his work had a slapdash, shaky quality. He worked as an inker for DC, and for military-oriented publications he drew *Sally Forth*, a weak imitation of *Little Annie Fanny*. "Looking at those late drawings," Hamill said, "you knew something was terribly wrong."

In his last years Wood was hit with kidney disease. He took whatever work he could get, including stories for a pornographic comic book. In 1981, after resettling in Southern California, his health grew worse. In November of that year Wood took his life. **R.G.**

**WORTMAN, DENYS** (1887–1958) An illustrator more than a cartoonist, Wortman drew the *Everyday Movies* panel for nearly three decades. He dealt in a fairly realistic, gritty sort of humor and his best known characters were a couple of tramps named Mopey Dick and the Duke.

The discovery of a stack of old issues of *Puck* in a trashcan in his hometown of Saugerties-on-the-Hudson, New York, set the nine-year-old Denys Wortman on a path toward a career in art. "I loved everything in them," he reported more than half a century later, "but outstanding and above all others were those early drawings of tramps by F. Opper that I thought to be the funniest and most beautifully drawn pictures I had ever seen, and the jolliest and most human and delightful characters I had ever met." Those tramps were to be the inspiration for Wortman's own immortal Mopey Dick and the Duke, in cartoon history two of the most eloquent voices from society's underside.

Against his conservative family's wishes he dropped out of Rutgers and went to the New York School of Fine and Applied Arts, "a vigorous and lusty place, " as he recalled, "[which] was considered radical because it assumed that the proper way to learn to draw pictures was to draw pictures." Wortman sold his pictures freelance during his twenties, living at the edge of poverty in New York and learning "by first-hand experience how [the tramps he was later to draw] have always been able to survive with almost no visible means of monetary support." Although he supported himself precariously with "High Art," he was relieved to find a job as an illustrator with the *New York Tribune*, and later with the *World*, doing "exactly what I wanted most to do…report[ing]…the life around me in a great city."

He remained with the *World*, through its mergers with the *Telegram* and the *Sun*, from 1924 to 1954, depicting "the vast and rich and diversified life" of New York City. Originally he illustrated news articles, but soon took over *Metropolitan Movies*, a regular *World* cartoon feature begun in 1913, from Pulitzer prize–winning editorial cartoonist Rollin Kirby. Distributed nationally by United Features Syndicate as *Everyday Movies* but continuing in Wortman's home paper as *Metropolitan Movies*, the daily panel ranged across social and economic boundaries. Among the recurring features within the daily panel were *Mrs. Rumpel's Rooming House, Dolly and Dolores, In and Out of the Red With Sam,* and, of course, *Mopey Dick and the Duke*.

The artist's heart remained with his beloved tramps, whose oblique view of life provides a witty and sometimes touching commentary on three decades of American social history. Mopey Dick and the Duke, his two happy, well-adjusted bums, sail serenely through the Depression (when they were happy not to have to worry about getting jobs) and World War II (when they had enough ration stamps but no money) and into the prosperous 1950s (when their hobo camp became

Shantyville-by-the-Mer). "Begotten in a trash barrel [and] growing up in the Ash Can School of Art," as Wortman described his creations, these richly human portrayals of humble urban life can stand with the work of John Sloan and other American realists of the period. With neither sentimentality nor social outrage, Wortman lovingly documented how the common man looked and talked and acted.

Wortman's dynamic, free-flowing renditions of New York's teeming beaches and parks and shantytowns, in grease-pencil and ink, earned him many honors. He served as president of the Society of Illustrators in 1936 and 1937 and was elected to the National Academy. A collection of his tramp drawings, *Mopey Dick and the Duke: Their Life and Times*, was published by Fairchild Publications in 1952. **D.W.**

**WRIGHT, LARRY** (1940– ) Political cartoonist for the *Detroit News* and creator of the comic strip *Wright Angles*, Larry Wright began his career in art in Okinawa where, after his discharge from the Army, he worked as news editor and political cartoonist for the *Okinawa Morning Star* and drew a strip called *Uncle Milton* from 1961 to 1965.

Wright was born in Youngstown, Ohio, and went to school in Detroit, to which he returned in 1965. There he got a job with the *Detroit Free Press*, to which he brought a resurrected *Uncle Milton* in 1967. In August of the next year he introduced a new feature called *Needlescope* in the *Scope*, and that same year took it over to the *Free Press*, where he was working as a copyreader. A six- to eight-panel weekly with no recurring characters, it gradually assumed the form it now has as *Wright Angles*, taking on a regular cast of characters in 1974. Wright carried it with him when he moved to the *Detroit News* in 1976 as a full-time editorial and strip-cartoonist, and in August sold it to United Feature Syndicate, which now distributes it to about 100 papers.

A mordant family strip featuring the Kanes and their cynical cat Motley, it reflects some of the acerbity Wright employs in his editorial cartooning, although it rarely makes topical references. Cleanly drawn with a precise and elegant line, it has a special appeal for cat fans with the sharply ironic depiction of the calculating and self-serving Motley, by all accounts its most popular character.

In 1980 Wright created the blander and more loosely-drawn panel feature *Kit 'n' Carlyle* about a working girl and her kitten. With little of the bit of *Wright Angles*, *Kit 'n' Carlyle* has a wider appeal and is distributed by Newspaper Enterprise Association to some 400 papers.

Wright has published a collection (*Kit 'n' Carlyle*, 1983) and an unrelated volume of caricatures, *Celebrity Cats* (1983). For his shrewd and caustic editorial cartoons he won the National Cartoonists Society's Best Editorial Cartoon plaque in 1980. **D.W.**

**WUNDER, GEORGE** (1912–1987) Wunder has earned a place in comic strip history chiefly as the artist who attempted the near impossible task of succeeding Milton Caniff on *Terry and the Pirates*. He took over the popular adventure strip at the end of 1946 and stayed with it until its finish early in 1973. He thus drew *Terry* for twice as many years as its creator, but never came near to equaling him. Probably no one could have matched Caniff's performance.

A native of Manhattan, Wunder grew up in Kingston, New York. He got most of his art training through a correspondence school course and in 1936 was hired by the art department of the Associated Press in New York City. Noel Sickles was still drawing *Scorchy Smith* for AP when the 24-year-old Wunder went to work, and Bert Christman who would take over *Scorchy* later in the year, was in the bullpen already. Wunder did photo retouching, drew sports cartoons and spot illustrations, but he was never given the opportunity to draw any of the AP strips or panels, though he did try to sell strips of his own to various syndicates. Wunder's work of those years was distinctive and appeared to be in no way influenced by the style of either Sickles or Caniff.

Wunder was in the Army from late 1942 until early 1946. After he left the service, he heard rumors that Caniff was giving up *Terry*. He submitted samples—as did quite a few other artists—and was chosen for the job of successor. At first he stuck close to the style Caniff had developed and also made an effort to write in the wisecracking, movie dialogue fashion of his predecessor; gradually, though, Wunder's own style emerged. It was almost a parody of Caniff's, with wrinkles in everything, and enough shadows in an average daily to black out a small town. Wunder also apparently had some sort of fixation about ears and everyone in his *Terry*, male or female, had huge ears.

Wunder maintained most of the earlier characters—Terry, Pat Ryan, Hotshot Charlie, the Dragon Lady, etc.—but for some reason he never used Burma. Despite the changes wrought by Wunder, *Terry and the Pirates* remained a successful strip in terms of sales. By the 1970s its increasingly pro-military outlook made it unpopular with a sufficiently large part of the newspaper reading public, and after it ended in 1973 the ailing Wunder went into semi-retirement. **R.G.**

# X

**X-MEN** Billed as "The Strangest Super-Heroes of All," this Marvel Comics team was launched by artist Jack Kirby and editor-writer Stan Lee in 1963. The members were teenage "mutants," possessed of odd powers since birth, and thus shunned by an uncomprehending world: The guilt-ridden Cyclops fired destructive beams from his eyes; the intellectual Beast was physically deformed but highly agile; Iceman could turn his body to ice; the Angel could fly; and the shy Marvel Girl was a telekinetic.

They were brought together by the paraplegic Professor X, a mutant with great mental powers, who sought to teach them to control their powers, give them a sense of worth and comradeship, and use them to defeat "evil mutants" who try to use their powers to conquer normal mankind. (In most of these respects the X-Men bore a remarkable and still-unexplained similarity to the Doom Patrol, a team launched almost simultaneously by DC Comics.)

The series got off to a lively start, but both Kirby and Lee left it within 20 issues. Under writers Roy Thomas, Gary Friedrich, and Arnold Drake, and artists Werner Roth, Jim Steranko, Barry Smith, Neal Adams, Jack Sparling, Don Heck, and several others, *X-Men* had some lively moments but many dull ones; although it built up a small core of loyal fans, poor sales led to its cancellation in 1970.

A series of reprints of early issues slowly built up reader interest, and in 1975 artist Dave Cockrum and writer Len Wein (succeeded almost immediately by Chris Claremont) introduced the new X-Men. Cyclops and Professor X remained to lead a multi-national band of newcomers: the naive Russian strong-man, Colossus; the deformed but cheerful German teleporter, Nightcrawler; the moody Storm, who controlled the weather; and the ferocious Wolverine, with "adamantium claws" and a killer instinct, who would become a fan favorite. Claremont developed these mutants and their relationships in a complex, lively way that helped make *X-Men* the best-selling comic book of its time.

He and Cockrum soon brought back Marvel Girl in a more powerful and more emotionally troubled form, Phoenix. In some ambitious stories she died and came back to life, then saved the universe, meanwhile enduring romantic troubles with Cyclops. With Marvel Girl and Storm, Claremont found a flair for developing agonized, bigger-than-life heroines, which won *X-Men* a far larger female following than was usual for superhero comics.

*X-Men* became a sensation among comic book fans when John Byrne took over as artist in 1977, with his attractive style and clear, bouncy storytelling. The "Dark Phoenix" storyline that he and Claremont unfolded in 1980—in which Phoenix is intoxicated by her new powers, destroys a whole planet, and submits to death as punishment—set the standard for 1980s superhero comics.

Byrne left the next year, opening the door to a long string of artists. Claremont continues as writer, weaving dark and complicated storylines, adding countless mutants to the X-Men's extended family. Although the series has lost much of its earlier charm, it commands a large and loyal following. Marvel has built upon its success with many other mutant comics, including *Alpha Flight*, *New Mutants*, *X-Factor*, *X-Calibre*, and several miniseries. **G.J.**

# Y

**YATES, BILL** (1921– ) Bill Yates is a versatile comic artist who has served the cartoon profession as a gag- and strip-artist, author, and editor in his long and productive career. Born in Samson, Alabama, as Floyd Buford Yates, he studied cartooning with a correspondence school before attending the University of Texas, where he majored in journalism and edited the school's humor magazine, the *Texas Ranger*. When he left school in 1950, he was already a seasoned professional with enough cartoon sales behind him to step into his friend Mort Walker's post as a humor editor with Dell Publications in New York.

Yates has illustrated books, done advertising art, written and drawn comic books, penciled strips, and written gags for other artists, and for years produced two editorial cartoons a week for the Brooks Community Newspapers in Connecticut—all while ranking among the top sellers of gag cartoons to the major national markets. But it is probably for his daily comic strip *Prof. Phumble* that Yates is best known to the general public. Launched by King Features Syndicate on May 9, 1960, *Prof. Phumble* was an amiably goofy gag-strip about the classic absentminded professor and inept homeowner whose wife cringes when he heads for the cellar to fix a leaking pipe. Beginning in a home laboratory, Prof. Phumble graduated to a chair in physics at Hoohaw U. when the space program began to fill the headlines, and he phumbled through a variety of academic, scientific, and domestic crises until his retirement on June 17, 1980. Now an emeritus, he shows up in occasional reprints in local newspapers.

During and after Phumble's long tenure, Yates contributed to many other strips. He worked with Jimmy Hatlo on his *Little Iodine;* from 1972 to 1975 he collaborated with Jim Berry on *Benjy* for N.E.A.; he recently took over the authorship of Gordon Bess' *Redeye*, drawn by Mel Casson; and since 1985 he has written and drawn *Small Society*, which he cosigns with its creator Morrie Brickman. When Sylvan Byck retired as comics editor of King Features Syndicate in 1978, Yates assumed that post, which he held until his own retirement late in 1988.

For nearly four decades, Bill Yates' assured graphic line, balanced compositions, and broad, genial humor have virtually defined the American gag cartoon and strip. His official retirement from a regular desk job seems likely to free him to produce more of the good-natured fun with which his name is associated in the history of American cartooning.

D.W.

**THE YELLOW KID** In the opinion of many comics historians *The Yellow Kid* was the first successful newspaper comic series. On May 5, 1895, a large cartoon panel by Richard F. Outcault appeared in Pulitzer's *New York World*, entitled "At the Circus in Hogan's Alley." Included in the cast was a bald, oriental-looking urchin in a night shirt, who became known as the Yellow Kid because of the color of his perennial garment.

Outcault had been doing one-panel cartoons about juvenile life in the predominantly Irish New York City slums for some months before the first appearance of the Kid. A panel with Mickey and Chimmie appeared in the *World* as early as September 23, 1894, and one with a prototype of the Kid was reprinted in the *World* on February 17, 1895, from an earlier magazine appearance.

Outcault, who drew in a stiff, formal 19th-century cartoon style, used some basically unpleasant ingredients for his panel—tenements, slum life, poverty, the casual cruelty and violent humor of big city street kids. Pain of one kind or another was the basis for much of his humor, and his satire was about as subtle as a brick cracking a head. Initially there was no dialogue but simply a caption. Soon the Kid started to communicate with his readers by way of comments scrawled on his soiled night shirt—e.g., "Gee, dis beats de carpet, wich is hard to beat." After a time the single panel gave way to a series of panels, and *The Yellow Kid* took to looking like many of the Sunday pages to come. Dialogue balloons were added, too, but the humor remained lowbrow and rough.

Outcault continued his *Hogan's Alley* series for the *World* until the autumn of 1896 when he was persuaded to move to William Randolph Hearst's *New York Journal* to draw a new version for the *Journal's* new Comic Supplement section. George Luks, who'd already done at least one Yellow Kid page before Outcault's departure, took over the *World* version on a regular basis as of October 11, 1896, and kept it going until December 5, 1897.

When Outcault switched allegiance to Hearst and the *Journal*, he left the *Hogan's Alley* name behind. Some of his early pages used the title *McFadden's Row of Flats*, but *The Yellow Kid* soon became the standard title. His initial Hearst page appeared on October 18, 1896, and his last on February 6, 1898. **K.S.B.**

**YOUNG, CHIC** (1901–1973) He had something of a knack for drawing pretty girls, and from the early 1920s on had been drawing comic strips about them, but it wasn't until he put an apron on one of his paper dolls that he was able to parlay this ability into a personal fortune, an empire, and then a dynasty. That all began in 1930 when Young created *Blondie*.

Murat Bernard Young grew up in St. Louis, but after graduating from high school, he returned to his native Chicago where he worked as a stenographer while attending night classes at the Art Institute. Late in 1921 he heard that the Newspaper Enterprises Association (NEA) was looking for someone to draw a comic strip about a pretty girl, so he went to Cleveland, and *The Affairs of Jane* was the result. By the time it ended six months later, Young was already on his way to New York. On July 15, 1922, he started another strip about a flapper, this one titled *Beautiful Bab*, for the Bell Syndicate. This entry ran only four months, but with it Young attracted the attention of King Features, who offered him a job in their art department.

At King in 1924 he created *Dumb Dora*, about a pretty brunette who "wasn't as dumb as she looked." *Dora* proved popular enough to last longer than its forerunners, prompting Young in the spring of 1930 to ask for more money and ownership of his creation. The final result was yet another pretty girl strip, *Blondie*, which debuted on September 8, 1930. By this time Young's style had reached its maturity, and it was neat and tidy with no loose ends.

At first Blondie was just another flighty sheba, a leftover from the Roaring Twenties, with a flock of beaux. Eventually, though, she fell in love with one of them and, when she married Dagwood Bumstead in 1933, the strip became a domestic comedy. And with the birth the next year of Baby Dumpling, the nation—and a vast number of papers—really took the Bumstead family to its bosom.

A man with an excellent gag sense, Young saw to it that nothing got in the way of getting each day's joke across. Yet he provided enough domestic details—especially in the area of Blondie's attractive but sensible wardrobe—to make the growing Bumstead family seem real to his ever increasing readership. Young was a shrewd packager of his strip, seeing to it that the various assistants and ghosts he hired stuck to the uncluttered, minimalist style he'd perfected. Among the many helpers he had over the years were Alex Raymond, Ray McGill, and Jim Raymond.

*Blondie* kept on picking up more and more papers, and the characters were aggressively merchandised. Before the end of the 1930s they began to invade other media. In 1938 the first of 28 movies starring Arthur Lake and Penny Singleton was produced; next came a radio show and then a television series. Young was a very wealthy man when he died in March of 1973. His son Dean inherited *Blondie*, and he and a succession of artists have sustained his father's efficient formula for the strip. **R.C.H.**

**YOUNG, LYMAN** (1893–1984) A cartoonist and the brother of Chic Young, he signed his name to the *Tim Tyler's Luck* strip for several decades. The feature began in 1928 as one more saga of a put-upon orphan and was drawn in a simple cartoony style. In the early 1930s, probably at the syndicate's suggestion, it was changed to a serious adventure strip. Since Lyman Young was an artist of very limited ability, he couldn't draw well enough for this new phase of his boy hero's career, and he was forced to hire a ghost. He never did draw the strip again after that, although he continued to take the credit.

Born in Chicago, he attended the Art Institute there, drove an ambulance in France during World War I, and then returned to Chicago to go into commercial art. He broke into comics when he took over a strip called *The Kelly Kids* in 1924. Eventually following his younger brother, Chic, to New York, he signed on with King Features and began *The Kid Sister*, a daily strip, in 1927. Young drew this in a plain, no-frills cartoon style that was fairly close to that of his brother.

*Tim Tyler's Luck*, originally in the Horatio Alger Jr. vein, started in the summer of 1928. It became preoccupied with aviation a year or so later and then in the early 1930s turned toward straight adventure. At that point Young hired Alex Raymond, who'd been assisting Chic, to ghost his strip. Raymond changed the look of the feature drastically, and the subsequent ghosts of the 1930s and 1940s kept it in the same illustrational camp.

Young supervised the strip, devoting his leisure time to golf and fishing. He was residing near Santa Barbara when he died. *Tim Tyler's Luck* survived him and continues to appear in a few newspapers. **R.G.**

**THE YOUNG ALLIES** A combination of Our Gang, the Dead End Kids, and an underage Justice Society, the Young Allies first teamed up in the summer of 1941. The comic book was published by Timely/Marvel and listed Joe Simon as art editor and Jack Kirby as art director. The two had created Captain America for Timely a few months earlier, and they apparently created this bunch as well, the first of many kid gangs they had a hand in. The Young Allies, however, were not the first such group in comic books, having been preceded, for example, by the Kid Patrol, which had debuted in *National Comics* a year earlier.

Neither Kirby nor Simon had anything to do with the actual drawing of the 56-page adventure. One of their assistants on Captain America, Charles Nicholas (who had also drawn *The Kid Patrol*), did most of the artwork. There was some crossover between strips: Cap's sidekick, Bucky, was a prominent member of the group, as was the Human Torch's inflammable buddy, Toro. The other four Allies were regular fellows: Jeff, Knuckles, Tubby, and Whitewash. A black youth in a junior-size zoot suit, Whitewash not only played the harmonica but also had a passion for watermelon.

In its first outing the gang managed to get mixed up with spies, Nazis, counterspies, and the insidious Red Skull, who was also Captain America's favorite foe. At the end of the book, the Torch and Cap showed up to help the Young Allies out. The final panel asked: "Do you want to see more of the Young Allies?"

The answer must have been in the affirmative, since the feisty Axis-bashing bunch stayed in business for the next six years. They were in 20 issues of their own, and they also showed up in *Kid Komics, Amazing Comics, Mystic,* and *Marvel Mystery* after the war. Both Otto Binder and Stan Lee provided scripts. Alex Schomburg was the most impressive depictor of the group, but he limited himself to covers.

R.G.

# Z

**ZABOLY, BILL** (1910–1985) He took over the *Thimble Theatre* strip in 1939, drawing it for nearly two decades. Before Zaboly began illustrating the adventures of Popeye, he had been an assistant and a ghost and worked on such characters as Wash Tubbs, Captain Easy, and Major Hoople.

Born in Cleveland, Bela "Bill" Zaboly attended high school there and drew for the school paper. He went straight from school to the art department of the NEA syndicate, which was located in his hometown. Zaboly began as an office boy and worked his way up to a staff position as a cartoonist. From 1932 he assisted Roy Crane on *Wash Tubbs*, helping to draw Wash, Captain Easy, Bull Dawson, and a wide assortment of pretty girls. During these same years he started a feature of his own for NEA, a Sunday topper titled *Otto Honk*, drawn very much in the Crane manner. Otto was a blond, moon-faced young man who was not especially bright. The Sunday strip followed him through a series of moderately funny adventures in such roles as a college football player, a movie stuntman, a private detective. Zaboly abandoned him in March 1936.

After Gene Ahern went over to King Features Syndicate in the mid-1930s to draw *Room and Board*, a close imitation of his NEA panel *Our Boarding House*, the job of illustrating the life and times of Major Hoople eventually fell to Zaboly. He was quite good at it, and the feature didn't suffer because of Ahern's departure.

In the late 1930s Zaboly himself was hired away from NEA by King Features, allegedly to get him off the still highly successful *Our Boarding House*. After a short while in the King offices in Manhattan, he was made the Popeye artist. When Popeye's creator E.C. Segar wrote and drew *Thimble Theatre*, it was a highly personal mix of slapstick, burlesque, satire, and fantasy, all of it done in Segar's simple, crude, but attractive style. He died in 1938 and proved to be inimitable. Doc Winner, a long-time resident of the King bullpen, drew the strip for a while and then in 1939 Zaboly was given his crack at it.

Zaboly did a commendable job of drawing *Thimble Theatre*, and technically he was a much better artist than Segar, but the scripts by Tom Sims were strange, eccentric, and never especially funny. The Popeye strip, therefore, lost a good deal of its appeal. During Zaboly's later years with it the syndicate brought in Ralph Stein to help with the scripts and with the drawing. Zaboly was let go in 1958, replaced by Segar's former assistant Bud Sagendorf.

Eventually Zaboly returned to Cleveland. He worked again for NEA, doing spot drawings, and he attempted to start a small feature syndicate of his own. He met with diminishing success and spent his final days troubled with illness and financial problems.      **R.G.**

**ZIGGY** Tom Wilson's daily and Sunday panel *Ziggy*, starring "America's Most Winning Loser," originated as a comic strip in 1966, but Wilson never succeeded in placing it with a syndicate. An employee of American Greetings Corporation, he turned to his own company and, in 1968, published a collection of panels, entitled *When You're Not Around*, illustrating the awkward and uncomfortable situations his hapless hero gets into. The volume was an unexpected sensation. The all-time-best-seller on American Greetings' list, it was to sell some two million copies, in various editions, during its five-year history and to call into being one of the most successful syndicated features in the country. The editor of Universal Press Syndicate liked the book so much he asked Wilson to do a regular panel feature based on it. In June 1971, *Ziggy* made its newspaper debut, and a Sunday version, sometimes in strip form, began appearing soon afterward.

Wilson has deliberately sought "reader involvement" in his work, and from the beginning his engaging little creation—a charter subscriber to *Losers Monthly* who is a victim equally of natural mishap and of his own ineptitude—struck a responsive chord in the public heart. *Ziggy* is drawn in so rudimentary a style as to have no specific class or character. "[He's] of no particular race or color," the artist has noted, "he has almost no clothing…so that practically everybody can identify with him, or at least they won't be locked out." With a single name (appropriately beginning with "Z") and a single unidentifiable garment, Ziggy is a universal type—Man reduced to the lowest common denominator, the eternal victim we all sometimes feel ourselves to be. Doorknobs come off in his hand, he gets a traffic ticket in a carnival bumper-car (number 13, of course), a blind man picks his pocket as Ziggy puts a coin in his cup. His humility and resignation are cosmic; every time there's an eclipse, he admits, he thinks it's his fault. Ziggy is, as his creator expresses it, "a million broken shoelaces."

Ziggy began, in Wilson's original, unsold strip, as an elevator operator (with more downs than ups, naturally), but he was to lose all distinguishing demographic characteristics. He shops and watches television and talks with his dog and parakeet, but otherwise engages in little social interaction. The only phone calls he receives are wrong numbers, for which he is sometimes asked to accept the charges. But few failures have been such commercial successes. Wilson, who now holds the resounding title of vice president in charge of inter-divisional exploration of alternate solutions (neatly ab-breviated IDEAS) with American Greetings, has published numerous collections of his panels with Andrews and McMeel, an affiliate of Universal Press Syndicate, which distributes the feature. *Ziggy* runs daily and Sunday in over 400 newspapers, and the shapeless figure is one of the world's most popular licensed cartoon characters, appearing on some 13 million greeting cards a year, as well as on stationery, coffee mugs, clothes, calendars, and innumerable gift items. In 1982, Ziggy debuted as an animated-film star in "The Thief Who Never Grew Up," which received an Emmy for Best Animated Special. Amorphous in appearance and nature, he is as popular abroad as he is at home. The character is seen, in its many media, in 19 countries, and his wry, self-deprecating remarks are translated into 10 foreign languages.                              **D.W.**

# INDEX

Bold numbers denote main entry, italic numbers denote illustrations.